History of Medieval India

Published by :
Lotus Press Publishers & Distributors

History of Medieval India

J.L. Mehta
M.A., Ph.D.
Sarita Mehta
M.A., Ph.D.

4735/22, Prakash Deep Building
Ansari Road, Darya Ganj,
New Delhi - 110002

Lotus Press : Publishers & Distributors
Unit No. 220, 2nd Floor, 4735/22, Prakash Deep Building,
Ansari Road, Darya Ganj, New Delhi- 110002
Ph.: 41325510, 98118-38000
• E-mail : lotuspress1984@gmail.com
www.lotuspress.co.in

History of Medieval India

First Edition 2026
ISBN: 978-81-8382-305-0

Printed & Published by : **Lotus Press Publishers & Distributors,** New Delhi-02

Dedicated
To
My Beloved & Wife
Mrs. Swaran Lata Mehta
In the Diamond Jubilee Year 2013
of Our Blissful Conjugal Lives

PREFACE

This is the second volume of our study on the history of India, the first volume of which was brought out by the Lotus Press, Publishers & Distributors five years ago; it gives a comprehensive, analytical and critical account of the political and military history of the medieval period. It makes a modest attempt to reconstruct and preserve for the posterity a concise and objective national history of our country during the period under review by making liberal use of the Persian and Arabic literary sources, particularly, as left by the contemporary Muslim historians and chroniclers. It has been repeatedly emphasised by us in our earlier publications that the ancient Indians took little interest in recording the political, social and other material developments of their times in proper sequence as their sages and scholars preoccupied themselves primarily with the moral, spiritual and higher values of human attainments and did not bother much about the mundane affairs of this materialistic world. The credit for introducing the art of historiography, as it is understood today, was brought to India by the Muslims, and the Indian historiography is essentially an Islamic heritage. It were the Muslim *ulema* and chroniclers who showed a keen sense of history and wrote detailed accounts of the day-to-day happenings and political upheavals. The Muslim generals and rulers employed chroniclers, diarists and court historians to maintain profuse records of their military exploits, conquests of new lands and subjugation of the new peoples in their bid to transform the *Dar-ul-Harb* of this world into *Dar-ul-Islam* by the conversion of 'infidels' to the Islamic faith. Their primary object in doing so was, of course, the glory of Isam; but even otherwise, they were men of this world who valued their material possessions and strove hard to multiply their worldly gains; this instinct helped them in keeping track of the events, past and present. Some of the great Muslim warriors and rulers, like Amir Timur, Babar and Jahangir, even wrote personally or with the assistance of their scribes, autobiographical memoirs to pass on to the next generations. Accordingly, historiography flourished in all of its forms under the patronage of the Muslim rulers of medieval India; and the age produced a number of professional historians, chroniclers and men of letters who have bequeathed to us a rich treasure of historical literature.

The establishment of the British rule in India and the foundation of the Asiatic Society of Bengal in 1784 gave birth to the Oriental or Indological studies, some of whose scholars started a vigorous collection and translation of these invaluable documets from Persian and Arabic into English and other languages for the benefit of the modern researchers. We have made use of their English translations. We do not pretend to be a*u fait* on each and every aspect of the national and regional history of this period which covers more than six hundred years. Needless to say, we have leaned heavily on the original researches done by numerous other historians and are under heavy obligations to all of them. With due regard to the considered opinions of modern historiographers of medieval India, historical facts have, nevertheless, been reorganised and reinterpreted by us wherever deemed necessary. Some of the more important of these contemporary and modern works which have been utilised judicially and quoted in the reconstruction of this narrative have been introduced in the first chapter of this study, entitled, 'Sources of Medieval Indian History', and listed in the Select Bibliography, towards the end of the book.

My grateful thanks are due to Sarvshri A.J. Sehgal and Saurabh Sehgal, the Proprietors of the Lotus Press, Publishers & Distributors, New Delhi, who have taken keen interest in this voluminous publication and brought it out in an impressive hard-bound volume in which it is being placed in the hands of the readers. I am pleased to extend my thanks and good wishes to my assistant, Shri Bharat Sharma--an experienced computer typist and thorough gentleman, for having computerized the manuscript of this book, and feel highly obliged to the brilliant and painstaking Editors, including Ms. Rakhi of the Lotus Press, who have made their own contribution in the processing and printing of this beautiful book.

In conclusion, I express with immense happiness and satisfaction my sincere gratitude and obligations towards my sweetheart and wife, Swaran Lata Mehta, but for whose constant inspiration and moral support, this study could never have been undertaken and successfully accomplished. I am overwhelmed with may feelings of intense love and personal attachment to my life-partner while dedicating this book to her in the Diamond Jubilee year of our blissfull conjugal lives.

Panchkula (Haryana)
India: 134109

J.L. Mehta

TABLE OF CONTENTS

INTRODUCTION

The Fading Glory of Ancient Kanauj

The thirteenth century marks the beginning of the Turkish rule in India. It ended the Rajput period of ancient Indian history and set in the medieval age. It is generally held that the imperial line of ancient Indian rulers had come to an end towards the middle of the seventh century. Harsha Vardhana, the last great imperial ruler of northern and central India, with his capital at Kanauj in the Ganga valley, died in 647 A.D., while his imperial rival in the south, Pulakesin II of the Chalukya dynasty of Maharashtra, had breathed his last five years earlier. With their deaths started the scramble for power among their erstwhile feudatories and provincial governors, and political disintegration of the country was the natural consequence. Just like Delhi of today, Kanauj was then renowned as the imperial capital of India, and all the claimants to the imperial power tried their best to take control of it. Yasovarman (c. 700-770), a military stalwart of the Ganga valley, who established himself at Kanauj, did make an abortive attempt to bring about the political unification of northern India but lost his life at the hands of his adversaries. It was followed by a triangular contest for the conquest of Kanauj and the establishment of supremacy in the country between the Gurjara-Pratiharas of Malwa, the Palas of Bengal and the Rashtrakutas of the Deccan. In consequence, Nagabhatta (725-40 A.D.) of the Gurjara-Pratihara clan of the Rajputs occupied Kanauj and revived its imperial glory for a short while. The last ruler of this dynasty, named Rajyapal, suffered a defeat at the hands of Mahmud of Ghazni and acknowledged his suzerainty in 1018-19, but was put to death by the Rajput rulers of Gwalior and Kalinjar soon thereafter for having made his cowardly submission to the Muslim invader.

The Rajputs

The period from the death of Harsha to the establishment of the Muslim rule at Delhi, viz., from 650 to 1200 A.D., is usually known as the Rajput period of Indian history. It marks the transition from the ancient to the medieval age. This period saw, apart from the above-mentioned contenders for imperial power, the rise and fall of numerous other regional states and principalities of feudal character. By the end of the eleventh century, the Rajput dynasties had come to control the whole of northern and northwestern and central India. The Rajputs constituted but a fraction of the Indian society but they imparted their name to the period because of their predominance in the political and socio-cultural fields of the whole country. The Rajputs were great warriors and warfare was their main occupation. Their chivalrous spirit, undaunted courage and love for freedom gave them such respect and prestige in the Indian society that even the traditional Hindu ruling chiefs of southern and central India also 'felt the need to forge their own genealogies in order to be addressed as the Rajputs'. The Rajputs formed, in fact, the 'Sword-arm of Hindustan'.

The historians differ about the origin of the Rajputs. There are prevalent a number of theories about their origin. Some clans of the Rajputs or the *Rajputras,* viz., 'the ruling elite', rightly traced their descent from the ancient Suryavanshi (Solar) and Chandravanshi (Lunar) dynasties of the Vedic age but most of them were of mixed origin. Several reigning families of the Rajputs were descended from the foreign invading tribes from central Asia, like the Sakas, the Kushanas, the Huns and the Gurjaras, etc., who had made their settlements in northern and northwestern India and embraced Hinduism. The ruling dynasties of the four premier clans of the Agnikula Rajputs, i.e. Parmaras, Pratiharas, Chauhans and Chalukyas, were definitely foreign immigrants; they seem to have been admitted into the Hindu fold through formal conversion and purification by the Brahman priests, and are said to have emerged out of 'the *havan-kund* of sacred fire' at Mount Abu. The Rajputs were staunch Hindus, who took pride in styling themselves as 'the protectors of Brahmins and cows'. They built magnificent temples for their deities, like Vishnu, Shiva, Ganesha and Durga, many of which stand as the marvellous architectural monuments in different parts of India even today. The Rajput women were usually educated and enjoyed great respect in the society. There was no *purdah* system among them, and the popular practice of *swayamvara* (*swayambara*) gave them some freedom of choice of their life partners. Polygamy was in vogue, albeit the widow remarriage was not encouraged. The evils of child marriage and infanticide were prevalent. Rajput women were known for their courage and bravery besides chastity to their husbands. They took active part in public life and sometimes fought battles, shoulder to shoulder with their men folk, against the foe. The practices of *sati* and *jauhar,* prevalent among the Rajput ladies of the upper classes, particularly, bespeak highly of their undaunted courage and fortitude that stand unparalleled in the history of the world civilization. The martial qualities of the Rajputs were badly marred by some serious defects, however. Their hot temper, love for personal freedom, vanity and mutual jealousies made them quarrelsome and defiant of authority. They indulged in clannish feuds and neutralized their strength and resources in incessant warfare. It hampered the growth of national unity among them, and they could not establish a strong central authority or national government. Because of these inherent defects, besides their poor weaponry and defective methods of warfare, the Rajputs miserably failed to take a united stand against the Muslim invaders and were beaten by them one by one.

The Rise of Islam

Islam originated in Arabia in the beginning of the seventh century A.D. Its founder, the Prophet Muhammad, was born of a poor family of the Qureshi tribe of Arabs at Mecca in c.570 A.D. A posthumous child of his father Abdullah, Muhammad also lost his mother, Amina, by death in his infancy, and was brought up to be a handsome young man of personality and character. Muhammad took up to trade for a living and traversed the whole of Arabian Peninsula. He worked for a rich Qureshi widow, named Khadija, whom he later married at the age of twenty-five; he was younger than his wife by about 15 years.

Muhammad spent much of his time in isolated retirement and meditation. The barren and sandy desert land of Arabia was inhabited by poor and backward people. They were divided into small tribes, which fought with one another, thus making their lives still more miserable. The Arabs were idol-worshippers. They suffered from numerous superstitions and social evils. They practised many primitive customs, and were nicknamed as *Baddus* or 'ignorant and foolhardy' persons. Muhammad was much perturbed to see the wretched plight of his people and wanted to improve their lot. Khadija proved a very dedicated wife to Muhammad. She took off all of his financial and household worries, and allowed him to spend his time as he pleased. Accordingly, Muhammad, very often, retired to Mount Hira, in the vicinity of Mecca, and spent long hours in prayers and meditation. At the age of forty, he had a 'vision of truth' and declared himself the prophet of a new religion, called Islam. It was a monotheistic faith, the tenets of which are contained in the holy Quran. Muhammad proclaimed that there is no God but Allah, and that he is His Prophet. He condemned idolatry and prescribed five tenets of Islam for the pious conduct of their lives by his followers, called Muslims. These tenets, which form the five basic 'pillars of Islam', called upon the

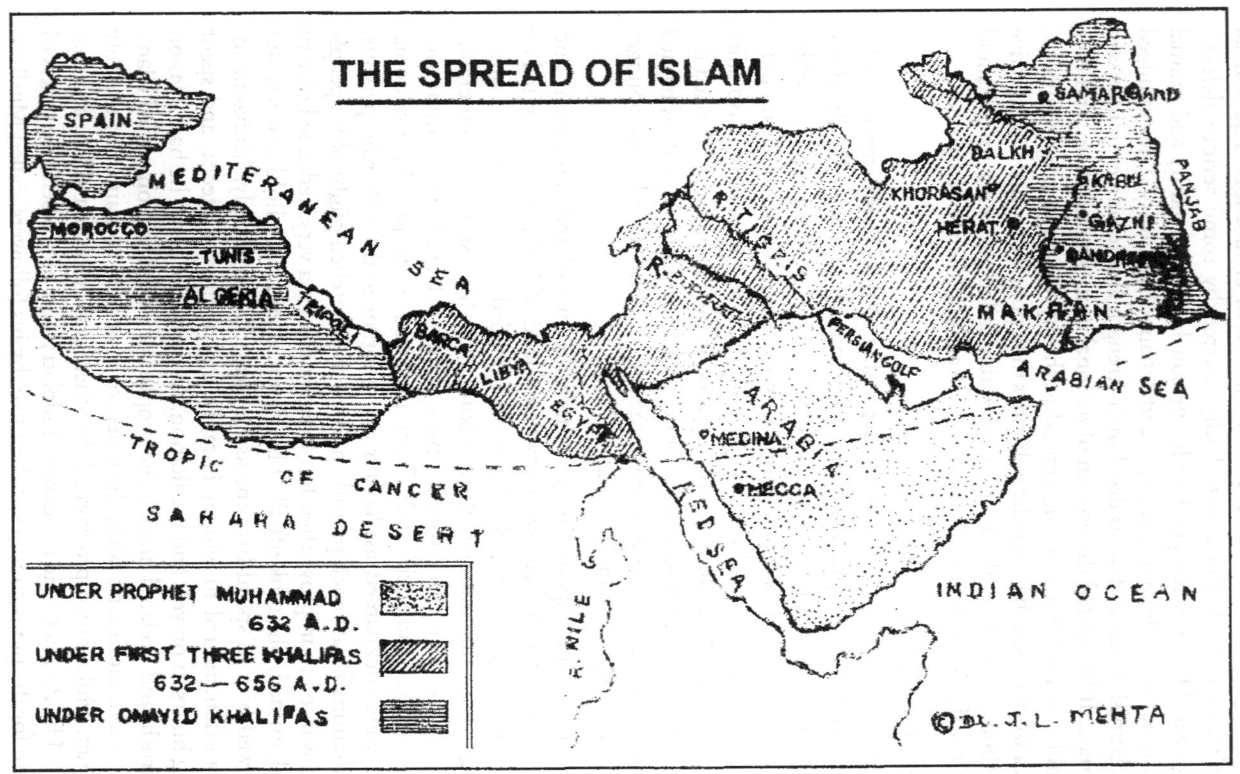
THE SPREAD OF ISLAM
SPAIN
MEDITERANEAN SEA
MOROCCO
TUNIS
ALGERIA
TRIPOLI
BARCA
LIBYA
EGYPT
R. TIGRIS
PERSIAN GOLF
ARABIA
MEDINA
MECCA
RED SEA
R. NILE
SAMARQAND
BALKH
KHORASAN
HERAT
KABUL
GAZNI
PANJAB
MAKRAN
ARABIAN SEA
INDIAN OCEAN
TROPIC OF CANCER
SAHARA DESERT
UNDER PROPHET MUHAMMAD 632 A.D.
UNDER FIRST THREE KHALIFAS 632 — 656 A.D.
UNDER OMAYID KHALIFAS
© Dr. J.L. MEHTA

Muslims (1) to have faith in God (Allah) and the Prophethood of Muhammad; (2) to offer prayers to Allah five times every day, after proper ablution, wherever they were, and in the mosque on Friday afternoons; (3) to fast daily from dawn to dusk in the month of holy Ramzan; (4) to give a part of their earnings in charity to the poor and the needy as their religious duty, and (5) to perform Hajj or pilgrimage to Mecca at least once in their lifetime.

The Prophet Muhammad vigorously preached the gospel of Islam to eradicate the socio-religious evils and improve the miserable condition of his countrymen. Some inhabitants of Mecca readily believed in him but most of them turned against him so much so that he had to leave Mecca for Medina with a handful of his followers for reasons of security. This incident, which took place on 22 July 622, is known as *Hijarat* or 'departure', and the Islamic era, called Hijri, starts from this date. Nevertheless, Muhammad was firmly convinced of the righteousness of his cause and did not discard his efforts towards the propagation of his newly founded religion. The number of his followers increased rapidly, and with their help, he reoccupied Mecca by force of arms in 630 A.D. Muhammad died two years later and was buried at Medina, but, before his death, his followers had established their domination over the entire country of Arabia, and almost all the Arabs had embraced Islam.

Spread of Islam

The Arabs selected Abu Bakr of the Qureshi tribe as their leader after the death of Prophet Muhammad. He assumed the title of Khalifa as spiritual and temporal head of the Muslims but, while doing so, made it clear that he was a Khalifa or religious representative of the Prophet and not that of God that Muhammad was. Under the leadership of the first four Pious Khalifas (632-61 A.D.), i.e. Abu Bakr, Umar, Usman and Ali, Islam made rapid strides and the Arab arms spread in all directions. The Arabs overran the countries of Syria, Mesopotamia, Egypt and Iran, besides large territories of central Asia, and enforced their religion on the vanquished peoples. The first three Khalifas ruled from Medina but the rapid expansion of the Muslim empire necessitated the change of its headquarters to Al-Kufa under Ali, the fourth Pious Khalifa. A large segment of the Arab leadership disputed Ali's succession to the *Khilafat*, and, as a result, he became a victim to the dagger of an assassin on 25 January 661. Thereafter, the supreme authority of the Arab empire passed into the hands of the Umayyid Khalifas of Damascus (661-750 A.D.). The Abbasids, who also happened to be Arabs, in turn, overthrew them. They made Baghdad as

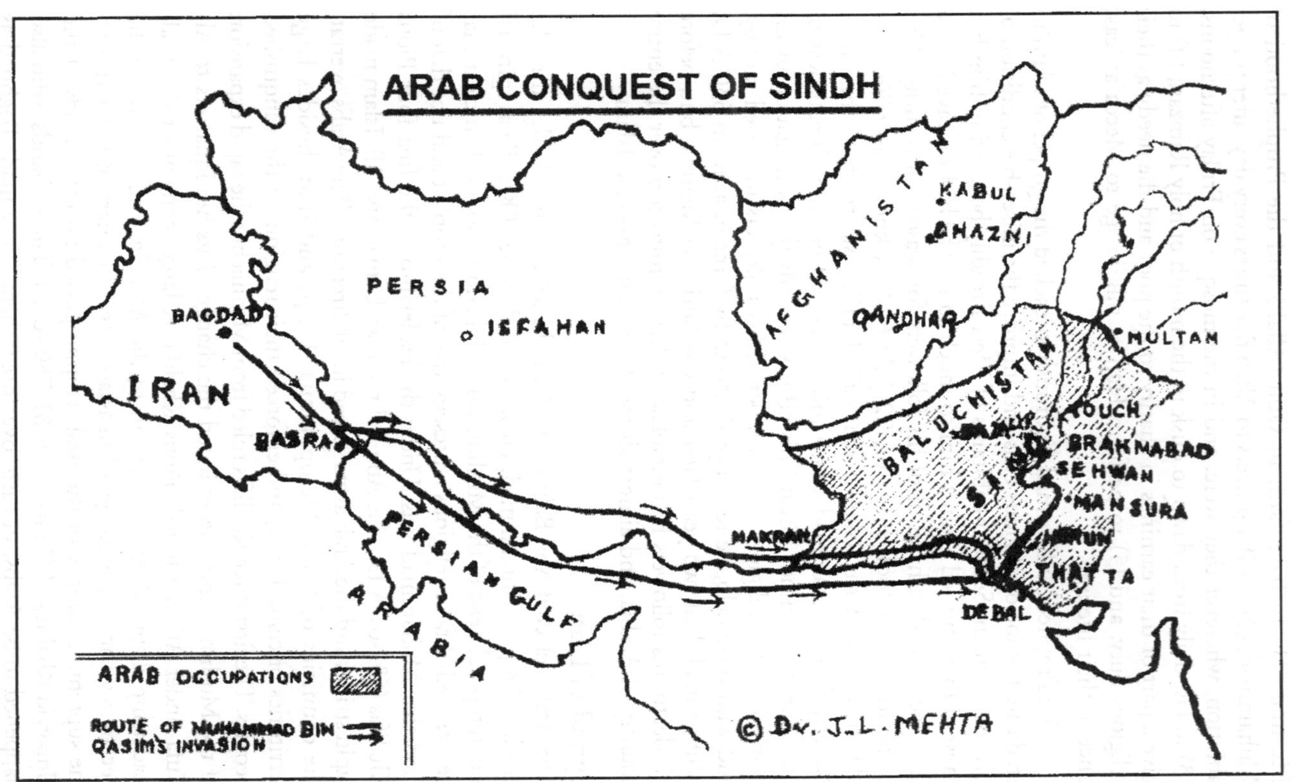
ARAB CONQUEST OF SINDH
PERSIA
ISFAHAN
IRAN
BAGDAD
BASRA
PERSIAN GULF
ARABIA
AFGHANISTAN
KABUL
GHAZNI
QANDHAR
BALUCHISTAN
MAKRAN
DEBAL
THATTA
MANSURA
SEHWAN
BRAKNABAD
MULTAN
ARAB OCCUPATIONS
ROUTE OF MUHAMMAD BIN QASIM'S INVASION
© Dr. J.L. MEHTA

their capital and continued to expand the frontiers of their imperial possessions for another three hundred years until the Seljuk Turks conquered Baghdad in 1258 A.D. and brought the Arab domination of the Muslim world to an end.

India and the Arabs

After conversion to Islam, the Arabs cast their covetous eyes on the rich seaports and borderlands of western India. Khalifa Umar (634-44 A.D.) dispatched two naval expeditions, one to Tana (Thana) and the other to Barwar (Broach) with aggressive designs but they were not fruitful. The third expedition, which was directed against Debal, the seaport of Sindh at the mouth of the Indus, in 643 A.D., also proved abortive. The Arabs then started encroachments by land, and the outlying Hindu kingdoms of Kabul, Zabul and Sindh felt the first shock of their invasions. After the conquest of Northern Africa and Iran, they strengthened their naval bases in the Arabian Peninsula, and commenced their naval activities with equally great zeal and determination. Before long, they succeeded in laying their hands at many places along the eastern coast of Africa, and established their naval supremacy in the Arabian Sea. They, thereby, acquired the monopoly as 'carriers of the Asian part of the Indian trade with Europe' all the same. However, the European part of the Indian trade with the West continued to remain in the hands of the Italians as before. The Arabs enjoyed this monopoly for many centuries until the discovery of the Cape route to India in 1498 by the Portuguese.

The lower Indus valley, including Sindh and Mekran (Baluchistan), comprised an independent Hindu kingdom. In the opening years of the eighth century, its Brahmin ruler, named Dahir, who had ascended the throne in c.708 A.D., faced the Arab invasion and perished with family in the armed struggle. Al-Hajaj, the Arab governor of Basra (Iraq), sent two military expeditions against Sindh at the bidding of his master Walid I, the Umayyid Khalifa of Damascus, but the Arabs were beaten back with heavy losses by Dahir. Incensed at these reverses, Hajaj dispatched his youthful nephew and son-in-law, Muhammad bin Qasim, at the head of a large army in 711 A.D. Passing through Mekran, which had been conquered by the Arabs earlier, Qasim overran the seaport of Debal and confronted the main army of Dahir at the battlefield of Rawar on the Indus. Dahir fell fighting after two days of bloody battle, but his widowed queen, Ranibai, refused to surrender the fort of Rawar. She fought the invaders to the bitter end, and having exhausted all the resources in men and material, tasted death by performing *jauhar* along with numerous other besieged ladies. The Arabs took about eight months to occupy

Brahmanabad, the capital of Sindh, and other major towns as they met with tough resistance from the local populace wherever they went. Qasim also overran Multan and its region of southwestern Punjab in 713 A.D., but his promising young career was cut short by his sudden recall by the Khalifa. He was put to death on the orders of the Khalifa on the charge of moral turpitude. The Arab conquest of Sindh made no permanent impact on the history of India. The Indian princes successfully foiled all the subsequent attempts of the Arab governors of Sindh – now known as the province of Mansura, after its newly built headquarters, and Multan to extend their possessions and penetrate into the heart of the country.

Modern Afghanistan was a part of ancient India, and the people now known as Afghans belonged to the pale of Indo-Aryan civilization. In the eighth century, it was divided into two Hindu kingdoms of Kabul and Zabul. The northern state, called Kabul, was ruled by a Buddhist dynasty; its capital and the river, on the banks of which it was situated, also bore the same name. Lalliya, a Brahman minister of the last Buddhist ruler Lagaturman, deposed his master and laid the foundation of Hindushahi dynasty in c.865 A.D. The Rajputs of the Bhatti clan then ruled Zabul, the southern region of modern Afghanistan. The Arabs started inroads into these states under the leadership of Yakub ibn Lais, the founder of the Saffarid dynasty. He conquered Seistan, Herat and Zabul during 867-70. The fort of Kabul was wrested by him from Lalliya in 870-71, though the main valley of Kabul continued to be held by the Hindushahis. Their dominions stretched from the river Chenab in Punjab to the Hindukush. The Hindushahi rulers acted as a bulwark against the Arab and Turkish onslaughts on their western borders for a long time. Yakub subjugated the Arab provinces of Mansura (Sindh) and Multan in 871 A.D., and is also credited with the foundation of Ghazni as a fortified town; Alptagin was the first Turkish general who conquered Ghazni from the last Arab chief, Abu Bakr Lawik, in c.962 A.D. The central authority of the Abbasid Khalifas of Baghdad became successively weak and started disintegration towards the end of the ninth century. Gradually, most of the outlying provincial governors threw off the imperial yoke and setup their independent Muslim states. One such small principality that came into existence in c. 962 was that of Ghazni. It was founded by Alptagin, a slave officer of the Samanid *amirs* of Bukhara. Alptagin died in 969 A.D., and after a protracted wrangle over the succession between three of his Turkish slave officers, Sabuktagin ultimately ascended the throne of Ghazni in 976 A.D., and laid the foundation of what is known to history as the Yamini or Ghaznavid dynasty. He extended his dominions by the conquest of the bulk of Afghanistan and some territories of eastern Iran during the twenty years of his rule. Besides, he befriended the Samanid ruler by assisting him in the suppression of a revolt in Khurasan in c.994 A.D., and in return, secured the governorship of Khurasan for his son, Mahmud, from his patron. All through this period, the Turks used to carry out depredations—called the 'holy wars', into Lamghan, the border region of the Hindushahi kingdom, which comprised the valleys of Kabul and Jalalabad. Hard-pressed, Jaipal, the ruling Hindushahi king, challenged Sabuktagin for an open fight in 986-87 but was defeated twice and taken prisoner by the victorious Turks. He secured his release by surrendering about half of his dominions, including Lamghan and the northwest frontier up to the banks of the Indus. Thereafter, Jaipal removed his capital to the east of the Khyber Pass at Udabhandapur or Waihand on the western bank of the Indus in about 995 A.D; it was situated near Attock on the ancient highway from Peshawar to Lahore. Sabuktagin is credited with the mass conversion of the Afghans of the Kabul valley to Islam.

The Invasions of Mahmud of Ghazni (998-1030 A.D.)

Sabuktagin died in 998 A.D. and was succeeded by his eldest son, Abdul Qasim Mahmud, as the Amir of Kabul at the age of twenty-seven. He secured recognition from Al Qadir Billah, the Abbasid Khalifa of Baghdad, as the ruler of Afghanistan and Khurasan. Mahmud assumed the title of 'Sultan', and at the time of his investiture by the Khalifa's representative, took a vow that he would wage *jihad* (holy war) against the *kafirs* (infidels) by organizing annual expeditions into India –'the land of the idolaters'. He led as many as 17 invasions on India under his personal command during 1000-1027 and carried fire and sword wherever he went. The frequency of his invasions throws light on the ambition, determination and fanatic zeal of the invader. He usually left Ghazni in September-October, after the end of the Indian rainy season, and carried out bloody carnage, accompanied by destruction and plunder in India during winter which was not as cold as in Afghanistan. He retraced his steps towards Afghanistan in March-April, before the commencement of the next rainy season, heavily laden with booty, including gold, silver, precious stones, horses, elephants and every type of valuable household goods and Indian manufactures, besides hundreds and thousands of men and women as slaves that his marauders could lay their hands on. Many of the Indian captives used to die of starvation and exhaustion en route to Ghazni.

Mahmud started his Indian invasions in 1000-01 A.D., when he crossed the Khyber Pass with his troops for the first time. He occupied some hill forts and territories of the Hindushahis and returned after stationing a strong contingent on the Indian side of the Khyber. In his second expedition, Mahmud crossed the Khyber with 15,000 state cavalry and thousands of *ghazis,* viz., the Muslim unpaid volunteers and plunder-seeking adventurers. Jaipal encountered him with a large army near Peshawar on 27 November 1001. He was defeated at the hands of the Turks for the third time, and was again taken prisoner with many of his generals and kinsmen. His son, Anandpal, who was left behind to hold charge of the state of Waihand, had to pay a heavy ransom to secure the release of his father and others. Unable to bear this disgrace, Jaipal burnt himself to dearth on the self-lit funeral pyre and was succeeded on the throne of Waihand by Anandpal. Peshawar fell into the hand of Mahmud. This victory encouraged him to make inroads into the interior of the country with unabated zeal and fury. During 1002-6, Mahmud took possession of Seistan and Baluchistan, and subjugated Fateh Daud – the Karmatia ruler of Multan. In his sixth expedition (1008-9), he launched a full-fledged attack on the Hindushahiya chief. A pitched battle was fought on the banks of the Indus, in which Anandpal's army overwhelmed the Turks but, in the thickest of the battle, the wounded elephant of Anandpal fled the field, carrying the master along with him. It spread panic among the Hindu fighters, who, mistaking it as a signal for flight disengaged, and fled pell-mell, thus leaving the victory into the hands of the Turks by default. The victorious Turks moved swiftly to take possession of Waihand and other major towns of the region, while Mahmud himself made a surprise attack on the famous Hindu temple of Nagarkot (mod. Kangra) which alone yielded him '7,00,000 minted gold coins, 700 *maunds* of gold and silver ingots and jewellery, and 20 *maunds* of pearls and rubies'. Anandpal retired into the northern hills with his family. He setup his headquarters at Nandana in the Salt Range to carry on the struggle against the Turkish aggressors. The Hindushahiya chief died in c.1012 and was followed by his son Trilochanpal as successor. Nandana was also attacked and captured by Mahmud in 1013-14, but Trilochanpal escaped to the mountains.

In 1015-16, Mahmud made an unsuccessful bid to conquer the valley of Kashmir but his army lost the way in the hills; being caught in heavy snowfall and the freezing temperature, and returned to Ghazni in shambles. Taking advantage of Mahmud's discomfiture, Trilochanpal and his son Bhimpal returned to Punjab and established themselves at Lahore to checkmate the advance of the Turks. Hence, Mahmud had to fight yet another battle against Trilochanpal to wrest the stronghold of Lahore from his hands in 1021-22. Trilochanpal escaped alive from Lahore but was assassinated by one of his own treacherous followers. His son, Bhimpal, assumed the insignia of royalty but died a fugitive in 1026 A.D., and, with his death, came to an end the Hindushahiya dynasty of Kabul and Punjab. Mahmud appointed a Turkish governor to rule at Lahore and annexed the whole of Punjab from Lahore to Multan to his Ghaznavid Empire as a matter of expediency. It protected the Turkish lines of communications with Ghazni and facilitated the movement of his armies into the heart of India for loot and plunder.

The Nagarkot exploit had provided a clue to the centuries-old accumulated wealth of India in the holy shrines of the Hindus. It sharpened Mahmud's avarice and encouraged him to strike at other famous temples and flourishing towns, with a still greater ferocity. Accordingly, he targeted the holy towns of Thanesar and Mathura in his subsequent campaigns, which he undertook in the most secretive and unpredictable fashion like highway robberies. In 1018-19, Mahmud sacked Kanauj and destroyed the Gurjara-Pratihara kingdom while the Rajput chiefs of Gwalior and Kalinjar were humbled by him in 1022-23.

The most sensational invasion of Mahmud of Ghazni, which established his reputation as the 'idol-breaker' (*Butshikan*) throughout the Muslim world, was directed against the Hindu temple of Somnath, situated on the seacoast of Kathiawar in Gujarat. He left Ghazni at the head of 80,000 crusaders for Multan in October 1025. From there, he made a detour towards Ajmer and after crossing the most hazardous and waterless desert of Rajputana, reached his target in mid-January 1026. The battle of Somnath lasted three days and claimed the lives of about 50,000 defenders of the temple and volunteers, who had rushed from far and wide to fight the invaders. The victory was followed by pillage and general massacre of the populace. After sacking the temple, it was razed to the ground and set on fire, while loot and plunder of the town, accompanied by all sorts of brutalities and vandalism of the marauders, continued for about two weeks before Mahmud ordered the return march of his forces by the western route, passing through Gujarat and Sindh, to evade the Rajput chiefs, who were by that time ready to block his passage. The immense wealth of Somnath, carried by Mahmud to Ghazni defies all description; the value of his spoils in modern currency would come to billions and trillions of rupees. The last two expeditions of Mahmud were directed against the Jats, in the lower valley of Indus, and some other rebels of Punjab respectively. He died in 1030 A.D. after a brief illness at the age of fifty-nine. Mahmud was one of the greatest military generals of the world and a religious fanatic but he was neither an empire-builder nor a missionary of Islam; conversion of infidels was not his primary object. Of course, he exploited the name of his religion and raised the cry of *jihad* against the *kafirs* to muster recruits from the Muslim countries as *ghazis*. His attacks on Hindu temples served both the purposes – the acquisition of wealth and fame as idol-breaker. In fact, the insatiable greed and other base elements of mundane desires spurred him and his camp-followers to launch repeated attacks on India wherein they committed such deeds of vandalism and avarice that put the civilized world to shame. Mahmud is said to have been a patron of art and letters, and was known as 'just and upright ruler' to his own Muslim subjects of Ghazni, albeit he and his camp-followers behaved as greedy, aggressive and blood-thirsty monsters towards the Indians and earned the title of *mlechchas* from them. The annexation of Punjab to his dominions by Mahmud was a measure of necessity. But it facilitated the drainage of Indian wealth and destruction of the political and socio-economic fabric of the country. The Arabs and the Ghaznavids prepared the ground for the final conflict, to be followed two centuries later, that administered a deathblow to the Rajput polity and led to the establishment of the Muslim rule at Delhi. It constitutes the core of the subject matter of this book.

❑ ❑

1

SOURCES OF MEDIEVAL INDIAN HISTORY

The people of ancient India took little interest in writing the secular history of their times. Their sages and scholars cared more for religious, spiritual and philosophical studies, and seldom bothered to record the political, social and other material developments of their country in proper sequence. No wonder, it was in keeping with the intensely religious and spiritual background of the ancient Indian civilization and culture. The credit for introducing the art of historiography, as it is understood today, was brought to India by its Muslim conquerors. It has, therefore, correctly been said that 'the Indian historiography is an Islamic heritage'. Unlike Hinduism, Islam is a missionary faith. From the very inception of this religion, the Muslim leaders are known to have waged wars of aggression against 'the infidel lands' for the glory of Islam. Their rulers 'employed chroniclers, diarists and court historians' to maintain the detailed records of their victories, in their bid to transform this world into *dar-ul-Islam;* and some of the great Muslim warriors, like Amir Timur and Babar, even wrote autobiographical memoirs, to pass on to the next generations. Accordingly, the discipline of history and historiography formed an important subject of study in the Muslim system of education. Their scholars had a keen sense of history. Unlike the ancient Hindu saints and scholars, they were not indifferent towards the mundane affairs of this materialistic world. They took note of the political and military developments, and recorded the achievements of their leaders, who conquered foreign lands and the peoples for the expansion of their empires and propagation of Islam. They were essentially 'men of this world' who highly valued their material assets and were ever eager 'to multiply their worldly gains'. Accordingly, the Muslim scholars of medieval India wrote in Arabic and Persian languages and produced a lot of historical literature which helps us in the reconstruction of a fairly accurate account of the conquest of India by the 'armies of Islam'. Some of the important contemporary writers and their books and chronicles, which form the primary sources of medieval Indian history, are as follows:

1. *Chachnama*

This is the earliest known book which gives detailed account of the conquest of Sindh by the Arabs in the beginning of the eighth century. It is said to have been written in Arabic by *Qazi* Ismail, a camp-follower of Muhammad bin Qasim, who was appointed the first *qazi* (judge) of Alor after its conquest by the Arabs. It was translated into Persian by Muhammad Ali bin Hamid bin Abu Bakr Kufi, under the patronage of Nasiruddin Qabacha—a Turkish slave officer of Muhammad Ghori, who had been entrusted the governorship of Multan and Uchh by his master. The book was titled as *Chachnama* after the name of the founder of the Hindu ruling dynasty of Sindh, whose son and successor, king Dahir, fought against the Arab invaders to protect the independence of his state and perished in the war with the whole of his family. It was first translated and edited into English from Persian by U.M. Daudpota, but now its fresh English translation by Mirza Kalichbeg Fredunbeg is also available. For extracts, see *The History of India as Told by its Own Historians: The Muhammadan Period* (hereinafter abbreviated as E&D.) by H.M. Elliot & John Dowson, 8 Vols; Trubner Company, London, 1867-77. (vol. i, pp. 131-211).

2. *Tarikh-i-Yamini* of Utbi

Utbi was a famous Muslim scholar and historian of the eleventh century; his full name was Abu Nasr Muhammad ibn Muhammad al-Jabbar ul'Utbi. He was attached to the court of Mahmud of Ghazni, and wrote a comprehensive history of the military conquests and achievements of Sabuktagin and sultan Mahmud up to the year 1020 A.D. He lived at Ghazni and never visited India. He did not know nor tried to learn any of the Indian languages, and was also ignorant of the Indian topography; therefore, he makes many mistakes in describing the military campaigns of Mahmud but otherwise, his book, variously entitled, *Tarikh-i-Yamini* or *Kitab-ul-Yamini* forms a beautiful piece of historical literature in Arabic. It was translated into Persian by Abul

Sharaf Jarbazkani in 1205-6, and from Persian into English by James Reynolds in 1858. (For extracts, see E&D.ii, pp. 14-52).

3. Alberuni's *Tarikh-ul-Hind*

Alberuni was the first great Muslim theologian, philosopher and Indologist of his age. He belonged to the Persian stock and was born in 973 A.D. at Khiva (Khwarizm). When Mahmud of Ghazni conquered Khiva, Alberuni was brought to Ghazni as one of the captives. When the sultan came to know of his intellectual attainments and fame as *munujjim* – viz., 'astrologer-cum-astronomer', well-versed in many languages, he was released from prison immediately, but, having been uprooted from his native land, he declined to lead a settled life at Ghazni and became a wanderer. In 1018-19, he came to India along with Mahmud's army of invasion and stayed back in the Ganga valley for many a year. He felt disgusted to see the wanton destruction of the towns and temples of the Indians and the barbarous treatment meted out to the men, women and children by the Muslim soldiers in the name of Islam. Alberuni travelled extensively in various parts of the country, accepted the hospitality of the Indian public and studied Sanskrit language from the Brahmin scholars and saints to acquire first-hand knowledge of the Hindu religion and philosophy. In his advanced age, he returned to Ghazni, with a rich treasure-trove of the Indian scriptures and books, on the basis of which he wrote the classic account of India and its people in Arabic, captioned, *Tarikh-ul-Hind*; its full Arabic title reads: *Tahqiq (or Tahrir) mali-li Hind min-maqala-fi-l-aql ao mar-dhula*. Later on, it was translated into Persian. During the British rule in India, it was translated from Persian into English and edited by Edward C. Sachau under the title, *Alberuni's India*: '*An Account of the Religion, Philosophy, Literature, Geography, Astronomy, Customs, Laws and Astrology of India about 1030 A.D.*' in two volumes. (Extracts, E&D., II, PP. 1-13). Alberuni's treatise forms an authentic source of information about the socio-religious condition of the period and 'gives a dispassionate account' of the virtues as well as weaknesses of the Indian character which made them suffer at the hands of the Muslim invaders.

4. *Tarikh-i-Baihaqi*

Tarikh-i-Baihaqi or *Mujalladad-i-Baihaqi* is a ten-volume comprehensive history of the Ghaznavid dynasty up to the year 1059 A.D. Its author, Abul Fazl Baihaqi (c. 996-1077) was an official of sultan Masud, the son and successor of Mahmud of Ghazni. Each of its volumes carried a specific caption, like *Tarikh-us-Sabuktagin*, *Taj-ul-Futuh* (history of sultan Mahmud of Ghazni), and *Tarikh-i-Masudi*, etc. The first five volumes of this study seem to have been lost to the posterity, while volumes 7, 8, 9 and parts of volumes 6 and 10 were edited and published in *Bibliotheca Indica* under the supervision of Major W.N. Lees and his Indian staff. Though written in detail, the contents of its text, except those of the history of sultan Masud, the patron of the author, are not very reliable. Baihaqi was said to be a knowledgeable person with keen interest in historiography, and he was, probably, commissioned to write this account at the behest of his master. He was, therefore, in a hurry; and, for want of time, 'scribbled the material; in colloquial Persian, which contains broken sentences, grammatical mistakes and obscure words'. (Extracts, E&D. ii, pp. 14-52).

5. *Taj-ul-Ma'sir* of Hasan Nizami

Hasan Nizami belonged to an aristocratic Muslim family of Khurasan. He came to India during Muhammad Ghori's invasions on the country, and settled down here permanently. He took up service under Qutubuddin Aibek when the latter became the viceroy of Muhammad Ghori's newly conquered territories in northern India, with his headquarters at Lahore. After the death of Aibek, Hasan Nizami shifted to Delhi and served under Iltutmish also. His history of the nascent Muslim state in India, titled, *Taj-ul-Ma'sir*- 'the Crown of Exploits', gives a detailed account of Muhammad Ghori's grim struggle against Prithvi Raj (III) Chauhan, and the conquest of Delhi and Ajmer by him and his brilliant military generals and successors in India, including Qutubuddin Aibek and Iltutmish, from 1191-92 to 1228. (Extracts, E&D. ii, pp. 204-243).

6. *Tabaqat-i-Nasiri* of Minhaj-us-Siraj

Minhaj-us-Siraj was related to the ruling dynasty of sultan Mahmud of Ghazni from his mother's side. His father was attached to Muhammad Ghori's army of invasion as *qazi* and spiritual guide of the sultan. Minhaj-us-Siraj himself also rose to be a distinguished scholar of Islamic theology and jurisprudence and acted as the chief *qazi* (chief justice) of Delhi during the reign of Iltutmish and Nasiruddin Mahmud respectively. He was an accomplished historian who wrote a comprehensive history of the Muslim world in 23 volumes, titled, *Tabaqat-i-Nasiri*, after the name of his royal patron. It gives the most authentic account of the foundation of the sultanate of Delhi. The author begins with the Indian invasions of Muhammad Ghori and covers the narrative up to the year 1260 A.D. As Minhaj-us-Siraj had himself played an active role in the political upheavals of his time, he possessed first-hand knowledge of many important events, and gives an accurate account of the military exploits and conquests of the sultans in proper chronological order. The relevant portions of the *Tabakat-i Nasiri*, dealing with Indian history (books 11 and 17 to 22) were printed in the *Bibliotheca Indica* under the superintendence of Major W.N. Lees in a separate volume in 1863-64. (Extracts, E&D. ii, pp. 259-383).

7. *Khazainul Futuh* and other Works of Amir Khusrau

Amir Khusrau was by far the most celebrated scholar, poet and writer of the sultanate period. He rose into prominence in 1325 and adorned the courts of all the sultans of Delhi from Balban to Ghiasuddin Tughluq as the poet laureate. Amir Khusrau was not a professional historian but he is known to have produced some prose chronicles as well as poetic compositions on historical themes, including *Qiranus Sa'adain, Miftahul Futuh, Khazainul Futuh, Dewal Rani Khizr Khani, Nuh Sipihr* and *Tughluq Nama.*

Khazainul Futuh, which has been translated into English by M. Habib under the title, *The Campaigns of Alauddin Khalji* (Madras, 1931) gives an historical account, in prose, of the military conquests and other achievements of Alauddin Khilji. Among other things, it gives a detailed account of Mongol invasions on India and the stern measures adopted by Alauddin Khilji to checkmate them. Amir Khusrau was, in fact, 'the most prominent representative of the Indo-Muslim culture' of early medieval India, and his profuse writings comprise 'a treasure-house of knowledge and information regarding the life and conditions of the people of Hindustan for full four decades when the sultanate of Delhi was at the apex of its glory'. (Extracts, E&D. iii, pp. 67-92).

8. *Tarikh-i-Firoze Shahi* of Ziauddin Barani

Ziauddin Barani belonged to a rich family of Turkish immigrants to India; his immediate ancestors held high offices of state under Balban and Alauddin Khilji. He was born at Baran (modern Bulandshahr) in Uttar Pradesh in 1285 and was brought up in the best traditions of the Turkish nobility at Delhi. Barani joined the royal service under Muhammad Bin Tughluq and enjoyed patronage of the sultan for 17 long years. He was a personal friend and associate of Amir Khusrau and is regarded as the greatest of all the contemporary historians of the sultanate period. He compiled a critical and analytical history of the establishment and progress of the Muslim rule in India from 1259 to 1355; it was titled as *Tarikh-i-Firoze Shahi*, after the name of sultan Firoze Tughluq. It was edited by S.A. Khan (Bib. Indica, Calcutta, 1860), and translated into English by Muhammad Habib of Aligarh. (Extracts, E&D. iii, pp. 93-368). In the concluding years of his life, Barani fell a victim to the jealousy and intrigues of his colleagues. He was dismissed from the court; and his properties and assets having been confiscated, he died a broken-hearted man. In our opinion,

> 'Barani's account is not descriptive but analytical and critical; he does not bother about the details; instead, he takes up the political and administrative issues as a compact whole, and through a manner of scientific presentation, reveals the characteristics of the period to which they belong. Even his minor comments on the characters and cryptic references to the events throw a flood of light on the working of the minds of the rulers, and prides and prejudices of the age. In spite of his subjective approach, which involved his religious outlook, class consciousness, aristocratic complexion and his subsequent personal discomfiture, Barani reveals the true historian in him, and those who understand his personal shortcomings can evaluate and appreciate his work much better'.(*Advanced Study in the History of Medieval India*; Sterling Publishers, i, 15th ed. 2010, pp. 13-14).

Barani had written yet another book, titled *Fatawa-i-Jahandari*, in which he elaborated, in historical perspective, the traditional Islamic theory of kingship and the exotic political institutions as they underwent radical changes in India at the hands of the sultans of Delhi.

9. *Futuh-us-Salatin* of Khwaja Abubakr

Khwaja Abubakr wrote this book in 1349 during the reign of Alauddin Hasan Gangu, the founder of the Bahmani kingdom. It gives a detailed account of the Muslim rule in India from the beginning of Mahmud Ghazni's invasions to the rule of Muhammad bin Tughluq; it was edited and published by Agha Mahdi Husain in 1938.

10. *Tarikh-i-Firoze Shahi* of Shams-i-Siraj Afif

Born in c.1350 A.D., Shams-i-Siraj belonged to Abohar in the Punjab, the native town of Firoze Tughluq's maternal grandparents; Afif's ancestors were close associates of the Tughluq ruling dynasty. Shams-i-Siraj rose to be a great scholar of repute, who was held in the highest esteem by the Tughluq monarchs although he never held any official assignment under them. He wrote three books on the life-history, conquests and administrative achievements of all the three major sultans, Ghiasuddin Tughluq, Muhammad bin Tughluq and Firoze Tughluq respectively, of which only the one book on Firoze Tughluq has survived the vagaries of time. Like Barani, Shams-i-Siraj Afif was also an accomplished historian, and he devotes this book exclusively to the career and political-cum-administrative achievements of sultan Firoze Tughluq. According to Elliot, it 'gives us altogether a better view of the internal condition of India under a Muhammadan sovereign than is presented to us in any other work, except the *Ain-i-Akbari*.'—(E&D. II, p. 270). Recently, the English translation of the book, done by the late Dr. R.C. Jauhri was brought out by Sundeep Prakashan, New Delhi, under the title –*Medieval India in Transition.*

11. *Futuhat-i-Firozeshahi* of Firoze Tughluq

Sultan Firoze Tughluq was a devout Muslim and a great philanthropist. He has left behind a unique literary contribution in the form of a small brochure of 32 pages only, entitled, *Futuhat-i-Firozeshahi,* which implies the chronicle of his 'victories' or achievements. Elliot and Dowson (Volume iii, pp. 374-88), who give the complete translation of this treatise, 'with the exception of a few lines in the preface laudatory of the Prophet', observe that 'it exhibits the humane and generous spirit of the sultan in a very pleasing unostentatious light, recording his earnest endeavours to discharge the duties of his station with clemency, and to act up to the teaching of his religion with reverence and earnestness'. It makes a brief reference to his military campaigns most of which did not produce the desired results. Nevertheless, Firoze Tughluq 'does not attempt to hide the truth or give a clever explanation of their failure' but, instead, portrays his true mindset in handling his state affairs. Being an orthodox Muslim, he publicly declared the sultanate of Delhi as 'an Islamic state' and adopted religious bigotry as a state policy. In fact, he suffered from an inferiority complex that he was born of a Hindu mother; therefore, in his bid to secure the support of the powerful Sunni nobles and the *ulema,* and to establish his credentials as the ruler of the 'Muslim state', he went out of the way to demonstrate his contempt for the Hindu infidels, and all those who did not conform to the true tenets of Islam; persecution of the Hindus, Shias and the heretics was its natural corollary. He records in his memoirs with pride that

> 'I encouraged my infidel subjects to embrace the religion of the Prophet, and I proclaimed that everyone who repeated the creed and became a Musalman should be exempt from the *Jaziya*'.

It has now been ascertained that, originally, this document, entitled *Futuhat-i-Firozeshahi*, was inscribed by him on a dome of the Friday mosque of Firozabad, on the pattern of Ashoka's inscriptions, It was addressed to the Muslim congregation. Firoze Tughluq seems to have been fascinated by Ashoka's pillar inscriptions, two of which were brought by him from Topra and Meerut and reinstalled at Delhi out of curiosity.

12. *Tuzuk-i-Timuri* or *Malfuzat-i-Timuri* of Amir Timur

After Mahmud of Ghazni and Muhammad Ghori, Amir Timur was the third greatest Turkish ruler of Central Asia who invaded India and sacked Delhi in 1398-99. He has left a detailed account of this venture in the form of autobiographical memoirs like Firoze Tughluq. Entitled variously as *Malfuzat-i-Timuri* or *Tuzak-i-Timuri*, it has been found by the modern researchers as a 'genuine' and the most authentic piece of autobiographical literature of great historical importance. Written originally in Chaghtai Turki, it was translated into Persian by Abú Tálib Husaini during the reign of Shah Jahan. The book was not written by Timur himself. Instead, during his campaign, he had taken in his train a number of diarists and chroniclers, who maintained detailed records of his activities and progress of the expedition, and, thereafter, prepared the narrative under his personal direction and supervision. The language of the book is simple, and it describes the events in plain and straightforward manner. The crude and unpleasant facts relating to Timur's barbaric and inhuman actions, under the impulse of his greediness and religious fanaticism, are narrated without any attempt to hide the objectives of the blood-thirsty warrior, and they are explained in the first person. It was translated from Persian into English by Major Stewart (Oriental Translation Fund, London, 1830). In the treatment of the subject, we have quoted profusely from it (E&D. iii, pp. 389-477) so that the readers may visualise the real motives of the invader and form their own opinion.

13. *Zafarnama* of Maulana Yazdi

The exploits of Amir Timur form the subject-matter of yet another contemporary work, entitled *Zafarnama* or 'Book of Victory'. It was written by Maulana Sharafuddin Ali Yazdi, a courtier of his ruling house, about thirty years after his death; he wrote this book under the patronage of Timur's grandson Ibrahim. In his preface, Yazdi details all the available sources, including *Tuzuk-i-Timuri*, from which his work was drawn, and the auspices under which it was written. *Zafarnama*, in fact, is nearly a reproduction of *Tuzuk-i-Timuri* (E&D. iii, pp. 478-522) but with the difference that the author, being a great scholar and prolific writer, produces a fine piece of historical literature by the use of highly polished language and ornate style of writing. Besides, Yazdi attempts 'to hide, behind his literary style, the naked and brute force of Timur's actions'.

14. *Tarikh-i-Mubarak Shahi* of Yahya bin Ahmad Sirhindi

Sir Jadunath Sarkar writes that of all the historians of the sultanate period, Yahiya bin Ahmad Sirhindi was the only Shia Muslim. All the other writers belonged to the Sunni sect of the Muslims; hence his is the only work that is free from religious bias and orthodoxy. Moreover, *Tarikh-i-Mubarak Shahi* of Yahya is the only contemporary source of our information on the history of the short-lived Sayyid dynasty of Delhi, which lasted from 1414 to 1451, and produced only four sultans. The author tells us nothing about himself nor refers to any office of profit held by him in the court of the sultans although the book was written with the specific object of recording the achievements of his royal patron, sultan Mubarak Shah Sayyid (1421-34). Edited by M. Hidayat Husain (*Bib. Indica*, 1931), the book proceeds with a brief description of the invasions of Muhammad Ghori and the conquest of northern India by the Turks and then details the political and military achievements of the Sayyid rulers but ends abruptly in 1434-35 when sultan Sayyid Muhammad was on the throne. Yahya consulted most of the contemporary works for compiling the earlier portion of his book but his account of the Sayyids was based on his personal knowledge and authentic information. Yahya bin Ahmad Sirhindi, 'like a typical medieval Indian writer, visualizes the divine will in shaping the fortunes of Islam in India and ends the account of each monarch with the phrase —*God alone knows the truth*'. Elliot declares him to be 'a careful and apparently an honest chronicler'. (For extracts, see E&D. iv, pp. 6-88).

15. *Futuhus Salatin* of Khwaja Abdullah Malik Isami

Khwaja Abdullah Malik Isami belonged to an aristocratic family of the Tazik Turks who had migrated to India in the very beginning of the Muslim rule in Delhi. Born in c.1311 A.D., Isami was an accomplished scholar and poet of sorts. He wrote the book, entitled, *Futuhus Salatin* in 1349-50 which deals exclusively with the rise of the Muslim power in India and the development of the sultanate from the time of Muhammad Ghori to the reign of Muhammad bin Tughluq. He was hardly 16 years old when he had to migrate along with his parents to the newly established imperial capital of Daulatabad under the orders of Muhammad Tughluq. He had to suffer great hardships because of this forced migration, and remained an eternal bachelor. He settled down permanently in the Deccan and was extended royal patronage in his old age by Alauddin Hasan, the founder of the Bahmani kingdom. Isami wrote this book to secure the goodwill of his patron and hence gives an exaggerated account of his political and military achievements while his narrative of Muhammad Tughluq, on the other hand, paints his character as the 'wisest fool' of the Islamic world. Apart from the personal prejudices of the author, even otherwise, the author makes a selective use of the historical material then available, and his text suffers from many factual mistakes and omission of important events. Of course, he is the only contemporary author who records the events belonging to the closing years (1259-66) of sultan Nasiruddin Mahmud's reign, which did not find mention in the books of Minhaj-us-Siraj and Barani. The book was edited and published first by Agha Mahdi Husain (Agra, 1938), and then by A.S. Usha (Madras, 1950).

16. *Waqiat-i-Mushtaqi* of Sheikh Rizkullah Mushtaqi

Sheikh Rizkullah Mushtaqi was born at Delhi in 1492 A.D. He lived like a Sufi *darvesh* (recluse) and the Afghan nobles held him in the highest esteem. He witnessed the rise and fall of the Lodhi dynasty at Delhi and its ultimate replacement by the Mughal rule. Because of his close contacts with the Muslim courtiers and bureaucracy of the capital, Mushtaqi was a well-informed person who used to maintain a chronicle of political events which became known as the *Waqiat-i-Mushtaqi*. He enjoyed a long life and breathed his last in the year 1581 A.D. His chronicle contains an authentic and first-hand account of many important historical events and developments belonging to the reigns of the Lodhi sultans, Babar, Humayun, Sher Shah as well as the early phase of Akbar' rule. (For extracts, see, E&D. iv, pp. 534-556).

17. *Tarikh-i-Salatin-i-Afghana* of Ahmad Yadgar

Ahmad Yadgar was an old servant of the Sher Shah's parental family. He wrote a history of the Suri dynasty during the time of Sher Shah's successors. Titled as the *Tarikh-i-Salatin-i-Afghana* or *Tarikh-i-Shahi*, it records an authentic history of the Lodhi and Sur (Suri) dynasties of the Afghans in India which is based on almost all the contemporary sources then available on the subject. It gives a refreshing material on the final phase of the struggle carried on by the Afghan nobles against Babar and Humayun for the recovery of their political ascendancy in the country. It was edited by M. Hidayat Husain (*Bib. Indica*, Calcutta, 1939; for its extracts see E & D. vol. v, pp. 1-66)

18. *Tarikh-i-Sindh* of Mir Ma'asum

Mir Ma'asum wrote this book in about 1600 during the reign of Akbar. Also referred to as the *Tarikh-i-Ma'sumi*, it is based upon the original contents of the *Chachnama*, but it provides a lot of fresh material about the conquests of Muhammad bin Qasim and the administrative setup of the Arabs from the contemporary Arabic and Persian sources. (For extracts see, E&D. i, pp. 212-252).

19. *Rauzat-us-Safa* of Mir Khwand

Mir Khwand or Mirkhond was an Arab writer whose parents had migrated to Herat, then the capital of Khurasan. Born in 1433, he enjoyed the patronage of Ali Shir, the minister of Khurasan ruler, and wrote the history of Central Asia under the title, *Rauzat-us-Safa*, viz., 'the Garden of Purity', in two volumes. Divided into seven parts, the book records the comprehensive history of the career and achievements of Changez Khan, Amir Timur and their descendants. According to the author, he had made use of 19 Arabic and 22 Persian contemporary sources for the reconstruction of his narrative. His book is a valuable piece of historical literature which forms the basis of many other literary works of the central Asian chroniclers. It was translated into English by E. Rehatsek and published in London in 1891-93 (Oriental Translation Fund, New Series); (For extracts see E&D. IV, pp.127-40).

20. *Babarnama*

Babar, the founder of the Mughal Empire in India, was a man of literary taste and invariably resorted to self-examination and self-appraisal in the course of wanderings from place to place. He maintained a diary in which he used to record the important events of his daily life. His memoirs, variously titled as *Tuzuk-i-Baburi, Waqiat-i-Baburi* or simply *Babarnama* forms one of the most authentic original sources of our information about his career and achievements, besides the history of his times. Originally written in Turki, the mother tongue of Babar, it was translated into Persian during the reign of Akbar, and now its translations are available in many languages of the world. Three valuable translations of the book in English, now available, are those of Leyden and Erskine (Longman, London, 1826), L. King (revised version, 1922) and Mrs. A.S. Beveridge (2 vols; London, 1922). Babar probably started writing his diary in the twelfth year of his life, and the earlier part of it was written during his time of leisure from memory. Even otherwise, it is not a complete record of his whole life, and shows long gaps, particularly, from 1509-19, 1520-26 and September 1529 onwards. Babar's style of writing is very simple, straightforward and truthful; at times, he becomes emotional in his expression and his narrative is frequently interspersed with his poetic couplets to show the intensity of his feelings. *Babarnama,* as memoirs, ranks with the Confessions of St. Augustine, and Rousseau, and the autobiographies of Gibbon and Newton.

21. *Humayun-nama* of Gulbadan Begum

An interesting book, titled *Humayun-nama* was written by his sister, Gulbadan Begum. The princess was only eight years old at the time of Babar's death, and she was brought under the protection and care of the emperor Humayun. She was a highly educated and accomplished lady who was held in the highest esteem by members of the royal household. Her book makes a welcome diversion from the exclusively political and military activities of Humayun's reign, and instead gives a more elaborate treatment to the Mughal *harem* and socio-cultural activities of Mughal nobility and the princely order. Gulbadan's recollections of Babar are very brief but she gives a refreshing account of Humayun's household and provides us with a rare material regarding his conflict with his brother Kamran; she records the fratricidal struggle between his brothers with a sense of disgust and grief.

22. *Khulasat-ul-Akhbar* and other works of Khwand Amir

Khwand Amir or Khondamir was a maternal grandson of Mir Khwand or Mirkhond, the renowned author of *Rauzat-us-Safa*. His original name was Ghiasuddin. Born in Herat in 1475, he grew up to be a great scholar of Persian and Arabic and held the charge of Prince Ali Shir's personal library. His first standard work on the history of the Muslim world was titled *Khulasat-ul-Akhbar.* (For extracts, see *E&D*, IV, pp. 141-47). It spread his reputation as a professional historian. Soon afterwards, he received appointment as the chief *qazi* and *sadr*, in charge of the ecclesiastical affair, at Khurasan during the reign of Sultan Buduiz Zaman, the last descendant of Amír Timur. In 1507-8, Khurasan was conquered by the Uzbeks and Khondamir migrated to Afghanistan.

Unmindful of the political upheavals, he continued his literary activities and produced a number of books pertaining to the history and culture of Islam. After the establishment of the Mughal rule in India, he migrated to Delhi and was extended patronage by Babar. He accompanied Babar's camp in the course of his Indian campaigns and completed valuable treatise, entitled, *Habibus Siyar*, somewhere on the banks of the Ganga in 1528. Divided into three volumes, it gives a comprehensive account of the rule of the sultans of Delhi (excluding the Tughluqs). Chapter four of the third volume of this study is devoted exclusively to the military exploits of Babar. After the death of Babar, Khondamir was attached to the court of Humayun also for some time, and for him he produced yet another book, entitled, *Humayun Nama* or *Qanun-i-Humayuni*. It describes the early career of Humayun and the administrative innovations introduced by him soon after his accession to the throne. It was edited by M. Hidayat Husain (*Bib. Indica*, Calcutta, 1940) and translated into English by Beni Parshad (Calcutta, 1940).

23. *Tazkirat-ul-Waqiat* by Jauhar Aftabchi

Jauhar Aftabchi was a domestic servant of Humayun who stood by his master in all the vicissitudes of life and lived to see the restoration of the Mughals under Akbar. He was not a scholar but, having been intimately connected to the royal family, wrote his reminiscences at the bidding of Akbar, obviously, to assist Abul Fazl in the preparation of *Akbarnama.* His book variously titled as *Tarikh-i-Humayuni, Tarikh-i-Jawarshahi or Tazkirat-ul-Waqiat,* is not a scholarly work but it throws a flood of light on the character and personality of Humayun and the early childhood of Akbar. As a faithful and trustworthy servant of the Mughal household, Jauhar throws many interesting sidelights on the personal life and activities of Humayun and other members of the royal *harem*. It was translated into English by Major Charles Stewart (Oriental Translation Fund, London, 1832). (For extracts, see *E&D*, V, pp. 136-49).

24. *Tarikh-i-Rashidi* of Mirza Haider Dughlat

Mirza Haider was a cousin of Babar. Born in 1499, Haider lost his father in his childhood and was brought up by Babar with great affection and care. He faithfully remained attached to the Mughal family for long as a trustworthy friend and camp-follower of Humayun. Haider fought as a commander of Humayun in the battle of Kanauj in 1540, and after his flight from Agra and Delhi, retired towards Kashmir with some of his troops. He carved out a small estate for himself and lived as a petty chieftain there, till his assassination at the hands of the local rebels in 1551. Mirza Haider was a scholar of sorts and a well-informed person. His book, entitled *Tarikh-i-Rashidi* is the second most important primary source of our information, after *Babarnama*, about the establishment of the Mughal ruler in India under Babar. The book is divided into two parts; its first part gives a brief but scholarly account of the rise of the Mughal power in Central Asia since the days of Amir Timur, including the account of Babar and Humayun up to 1541, while the second part is reserved for his personal biography and reminiscences. Mirza Haider made full use of Babar's memoirs in the compilation of his book. It was translated into English and edited by N. Elias and E. Denison Ross under the title, *A History of the Moghuls of Central Asia*; Being the *Tarikh-i-Rashidi* of Mirza Muhammad Haider Dughlat; (London, 1895). The Indian reprint of the book by Academica Asiatica (Patna, 1973) is also available.

25. *Tarikh-i-Sher Shahi* of Abbas Khan Sarwani

Abbas Khan Sarwani was a distant Afghan kinsman of Sher Shah Suri. He started his career as a soldier, and, later on, took up service under Akbar. He was a man of no distinction but had some literary taste and came to the notice of Akbar as a writer when he was holding a petty *mansab* of 500 *zat* and *swar* rank. At the persuasion of Abul Fazl, probably, he agreed to write whatever he knew of Sher Shah Suri and his times. His book, though titled as *Tarikh-i-Sher Shahi*, is, in fact not an historical narrative but a sort of autobiography of the author, in which the various characters are made to speak for themselves. (For extracts, see, *E&D*, IV, pp. 301-433). Therein, Abbas takes pains to describe the achievements of Sher Shah Suri and his successors as he knew on the basis of his personal experience, or heard from the other men of knowledge and wisdom. The book is deficient of dates and of little literary merit, but its author possessed first- hand knowledge of the character and administrative achievements of Sher Shah which he has attempted to portray faithfully through the pages of this book. The book is divided into three parts; its first part deals with the history of Sher Shah's rise to power; the second part describes the important events of Islam Shah's reign, and the third part gives biographical sketches of the descendants of Islam Shah and their fratricidal wars, which created a near anarchy and facilitated the return to power of the Mughals.

Similarly, some other contemporary works of historical importance, which throw light on the history of the Suri dynasty of the Afghans, include *Makhzan-i-Afghani* of Niamutullah Afghani, *Tarikh-i-Daudi* of Abdullah and *Daulat-i-Shershahi* of Hasan Ali Khan.

26. *Akbarnama and Ain-i-Akbari* of Abul Fazl

Akbar was destined to transform the Mughal kingdom into a mighty all-India power. His period of rule abounded in the availability of numerous historical works and rich treasure of official documents and records. It was he who introduced the practice of appointing official historians to record the history and growth of the empire as it unfolded with the passage of time. Accordingly, Abul Fazl, the prime minister and court historian of Akbar, took seven years, from 1589-96, to write *Akbarnama,* which forms the most comprehensive account of the foundation of the Mughal rule in India and its development; it was based on the extensive use of all the contemporary source material then available. Thereafter, he continued to update it from year to year till his death in 1602. *Akbarnama* consists of three volumes; its first volume narrates the history of his predecessors, including Babar and Humayun; the second book deals with the military exploits and achievements of Akbar in chronological order, while the third book, with the sub-title *Ain-i-Akbari*, gives the most analytical and elaborate treatment to the administration, the concept of Mughal monarchy, political and legal institutions and the state policy of the imperial Mughals. All the three volumes of *Akbarnama* were translated into English and edited by H. Beveridge (*Bib. Indica*, Calcutta, 1897-1909); whereas, the exclusive translation of the third volume of *Akbarnama*, under the title, *Ain-i-Akbari,* has been split up further into three volumes and translated into English and edited by F. Gladwin with the title, *Ayeen Akbery of Abul Fazl* (3 vols; Calcutta, 1783-86). 'After Kautilya's *Arthashastra,* the *Ain-i-Akbari* is the second greatest work of historical significance, produced by an Indian, the like of which is hard to find even in the annals of European historical literature'. Of course, though factually correct and authentic, the author had definitely produced this three-volume monumental work in the spirit of eulogizing his master, and, therefore, he always refrains from presenting the dark side of his character and questionable actions. Abul Fazl was the most prominent bureaucrat, courtier and personal friend of the monarch; as a consequence, the description of career and achievements of Akbar can never be complete without reference to the contributions made by Abul Fazl towards the success of the Mughal crown.

27. *Tabakat-i-Akbari* of Nizamuddin Ahmad

Khwaja Nizamuddin Ahmad, the author of *Tabakat-i-Akbari,* was a *bakshi* (the paymaster) under Akbar. As a sober and serious historiographer, he compiled a history of the Muslim rule in India from the beginning of Mahmud's invasions to the year 1593 on the basis of numerous chronicles and books of history then available on the subject. Like Abul Fazl's *Akbarnama,* his composition is also a monumental work, consisting of three volumes. The first volume gives a critical and analytical account of the Sultanate period, the second volume describes the history of the Mughal Empire from Babar to 1593, and the third volume deals with the local and regional kingdoms of India. *Tabakat-i-Akbari* of Nizamuddin Ahmad is one of the most objective and reliable contemporary sources on the political history of medieval India. Its Persian text was edited and published by B. De and Muhammad Hidayat Husain (ASB, *Bib. Indica*, Calcutta, 3 vols; 1913-40), and translated into English by B. De and B. Prasad (*Bib. Indica*, 1927-40).

28. *Muntakhab-ut-Tawarikh* of Badaoni

Mulla Abdul Qadir, the author of *Muntakhab-ut-Tawarikh*, was born at Badaun in mod. Uttar Pradesh in 1542. A great scholar and political thinker, Badaoni enjoyed the patronage of Akbar, though being an orthodox Sunni Muslim by faith, he did not like his master's religious views and the liberal state policy based on secular principles. As a result, Akbar also became lukewarm towards him and he stopped attending the court altogether. Nevertheless, he continued to write the history of his times. Badaoni's book, though strongly critical of Akbar's policies, is much more detailed than that of Nizamuddin; it contains a lot of original material which is not found in any other contemporary work on Akbar's regime. The book was kept concealed by the family of Badaoni for a long time, and its existence became known to the public during the concluding years of Jahangir's reign. Badaoni's book is a comprehensive history of the Muslim rule in India from the Ghaznavids to the fortieth year of Akbar's reign. The scholars of the Asiatic Society of Bengal edited and published its Persian text in three volumes (*Bib. Indica*, Calcutta, 1861-69) and each of these volumes was subsequently translated and edited into English by different scholars: volume i, by George S.A. Ranking (Calcutta, 1898); volume ii, by Lowe and further annotated by Ambashthya (Calcutta, 1898), and volume iii, by T.W. Haig (Calcutta, 1925).

29. *Tarikh-i-Firishta*

Tarikh-i-Firishta is one of the most popular books on the history of medieval India by a contemporary historian. Completed in 1612 during the reign of Jahangir, his monumental work, entitled the *Gulshan-i-Ibrahimi* or simply *Tarikh-i-Firishta* is a compact history of the Muslim rule in India up to the accession of Jahangir. Besides consulting extensive literary sources on the subject, available during Akbar's reign, Firishta also made critical and analytical use of the writings of Abul Fazl and Nizamuddin Ahmad to reconstruct a more objective history of the times. Needless to say, the art of historiography had reached the pinnacle of its glory during the age of Akbar. *Tarikh-i-Firishta* was translated into English and edited by John Briggs under the title, *History of the Rise of the Mahommedan Power in India Till the Year 1612* (4 vols; London, 1829).

30. *Tuzuk-i-Jahangiri*

In the likeness of Babar, Jahangir had also started writing his memoirs soon after his accession to the throne. He wrote his autobiography in his own hand for the first 17 years of his reign and thereafter entrusted the work to Muhammad Khan, who continued to write on behalf of the emperor for the next two years. Its text was edited by Sayyid Ahmad Khan (Aligarh, 1864) and translated into English by Rodgers and Henry Beveridge in two volumes (Royal Asiatic Society, London, 1904-14). It forms the most compact and comprehensive account of the earlier part of Jahangir's rule and carries a few glimpses of his early career too. Sometimes, the emperor becomes very frank and vivid in recording the activities of his private life and court, but usually he is reserved and rather secretive about his personal weaknesses and shortcomings. Though held in great esteem like *Babarnama* by his successors, *Tuzuk-i-Jahangiri* stands no comparison with the former.

31. *Padshahnama*

Shah Jahan's reign saw the emergence of many historiographers and chroniclers who wrote elaborate accounts of his glorious age under the popular title of *Padshahnama* or *Badshahnama*. The earliest work, bearing this title was prepared by Muhammad Amin Qazwini, who was appointed the royal historian by Shah Jahan. Following the tradition set by Abul Fazl, Muhammad Amin wrote the detailed political and military developments of Shah Jahan's reign, during the first ten years. The book was written by him in a simple and graceful style in Persian. It included a very romantic and interesting account of the early life and education of Prince Khurram, later styled as Shah Jahan. Qazwini was thereafter replaced by Abdul Hamid Lahauri, the most celebrated historian of Shah Jahan's reign. He compiled afresh the history of all the first twenty years of his reign up to 1648 in two volumes; of which the first volume attempted to rewrite and polish the write-up of Qazwini in more sophisticated language and style. 'Just like the *Akbarnama* of Abul Fazl, the *Padshahnama* of Abdul Hamid Lahauri was acclaimed as the best historiographical production of the day; it ranks among the first-rate authorities on the history of the Mughal period.' The Persian text of the two-volume study of Abdul Hamid Lahauri was edited and published by the Asiatic Society of Bengal (*Bib. Indica*, Calcutta, 1866-72) (For extracts, see *E&D*, VII, pp. 5-72).

Abdul Hamid was unable to continue the work because of his advanced age and physical disabilities; therefore, Muhammad Waris, one of his brilliant students, was deputed by Shah Jahan to continue his assignment as the state historian. Hamid died in 1654. Waris was originally expected to pick up the thread of the story from where Abdul Hamid had left; but, just like his teacher, he also dedicated himself to the task of re-writing the whole account of Shah Jahan's reign, incorporating the earlier *Padshahnamas* of Qazwini and Abdul Hamid respectively. It gave birth to yet another three-volume study, with the same title of the *Padshahnama*. He continued this work till the dethronement of Shah Jahan by Aurangzeb in 1658. 'As regards the history of the last ten years of Shah Jahan's reign, Waris, like his predecessors—Amin Qazwini and Abdul Hamid Lahauri, has made a very valuable and original contribution to the enrichment of medieval Indian historical literature; one of its special features is a detailed and picturesque account of the magnificent buildings of Shah Jahan.'

32. *Shahjahan-nama* of Muhammad Saddiq

Muhammad Saddiq, the author of *Shahjahan-nama or Tarikh-i-Shahjahani* was *waqia-navis* (news-writer) in the court of Shah Jahan; and he had participated in the battle of Samugarh as a soldier also. As a lot of court documents were available with him, he reconstructed a very authentic and most reliable account of the reign of his master in the simple and straightforward style; it constitutes by far the most valuable history of the period after the *Padshahnama* of Waris'. (*E&D*, VII, p. 133).

33. *Alamgirnama*

Aurangzeb also got the history of the first ten years of his reign prepared by the state historian, Mirza Muhammad Qazim; it was entitled *Alamgirnama*. The book was prepared to order and was revised by the emperor himself. 'Written in verbose and tedious style, it is full of gross flattery and suppression of all incidents discreditable to Aurangzeb'. Its Persian text was edited and published by Khadim Husain and Abdul Hai (ASB, *Bib. Indica*, Calcutta, 1865-73). Thereafter, he adopted the policy of Islamic fundamentalism and religious intolerance towards his non-Muslim subjects, which induced him to reverse the liberal and more transparent state policy of his predecessors. As a result, he not only abolished the office of the royal historian but, in the twenty-first year of his reign, he prohibited all the chroniclers and writers of his regime not to write the history of his times.

34. *Muntakhab-ul-Lubab* of Khafi Khan

In spite of Aurangzeb's prohibitory orders, Muhammad Hashim *alias* Khafi (secretive) Khan, continued to record the day-to-day political and military developments of his reign secretly. His strenuous efforts to maintain the historical traditions of the time led to the emergence of a most objective and monumental work, entitled *Muntakhab-ul-Lubab*; it covers the history of the imperial Mughals from Babar to the fourteenth year of the reign of Muhammad Shah *Rangila* (1719-48). It was brought to light long after the death of Aurangzeb, and its author earned the title of Khafi Khan humorously from Muhammad Shah for having concealed his invaluable work for so long. Its Persian text was published by the Asiatic Society of Bengal in 1869 (*Bib. Indica*,

Calcutta). In the words of Jadunath Sarkar, the *Muntakhab-ul-Lubab* of Khafi Khan 'is professedly an abridgement of more original works up to the middle of Aurangzeb's reign. Thereafter, he writes from personal knowledge...He took care to consult many of the surviving actors of the earlier scenes and to verify his information by diligent inquiry. His reflective style, description of the condition of society, and characteristic anecdotes save his work from the dry formality of the court annals, and he is specially informing with regard to the Deccan affairs'.– (*History of Aurangzeb*; 5 vols; ii, Calcutta, 1912, pp. 303-04).

The Travelogues

***Kitab-ur-Rehla* of Ibn Batuta:** Ibn Batuta was an Arab traveller and adventurer from Morocco. Born in c.1304, he received education in Islamic theology and jurisprudence and left his home at the age of 21 to become a free-lance observer to wander about in the vast Muslim world. In the course of his wanderings, he made it to Sindh in 1333, from where he shifted to Delhi after some time. Muhammad bin Tughluq, the Sultan of Delhi, was impressed by the scholarship and wisdom of youthful Ibn Batuta and readily offered him the post of chief *qazi* of Delhi. He held this exalted office for about eight years, when he was dismissed and thrown behind the bars on charges of corruption and dishonesty. After having suffered imprisonment for more than a decade, Ibn Batuta was pardoned by the sultan on humanitarian grounds, and sent to China at the head of a diplomatic mission in 1342. To his misfortune, Ibn Batuta's party met with a shipwreck, and his mission proved abortive. Thereafter, he bade goodbye to Delhi and started on his wanderings once again. After passing through the Maldives and Sri Lanka, he paid a pilgrimage to Mecca before his return to Morocco in 1349. Ibn Batuta received a warm reception from the king and people of his country and died at the ripe old age of 73 as a reputed Muslim saint, scholar and philosopher. His travelogue in Arabic, entitled *Kitab-ur-Rehla* that he wrote in the concluding years of his life, contains substantial material on the life and conditions of the people of Hindustan although his characterization of Muhammad bin Tughluq is highly biased because of the personal grudge that he bore against him. *Kitab-ur-Rehla* was translated into English by A. Mahdi Husain with the title, *The Rehla of Ibn Battuta* (Baroda, 1953). (For extracts, see, *E&D,* III, pp. 585-612).

Matlaus Sa'dain wa Majma-ul-Bahrain of Abdur Razzak

Abdur Razzak, the reputed author of *Matlaus Sa'dain wa Majma-ul-*

Bahrain was a Persian scholar, who was born at Herat in 1413 A.D. He held the post of *qazi* of Samarqand during the reign of Sultan Shah Rukh of Khurasan, a descendant of Amir Timur. He enjoyed the patronage of the sultans of Khurasan till his death in 1482. Abdur Razzak was sent as an ambassador by his master to the court of Vijayanagar; and he remained in the Deccan for about two years in 1442-43. On his return to Persia, he wrote a comprehensive history of Central Asia in two volumes which contains substantial material about the kingdom of Vijayanagar, besides Amir Timur, who had invaded India and sacked Delhi in 1398-99. For relevant extracts on India, see R.H. Major's *India in the Fifteenth /Century: Being a Collection of Narratives of Voyages to India;* (Hakluyt Society, London, 1857). Its Indian reprint by Deep Publications, Delhi, 1974, is also available. A few European travellers also visited India during the early medieval period, who recorded valuable information about India and its people in their chronicles; they included among others, Marco Polo, Nicolo Conti, Duarte Barbosa and Domingos Paes.

Marco Polo –'the father of modern Geography', was a native of Venice in Italy. He belonged to the family of sailors. In his early life, he went on his wanderings on the sea along with his father in 1271, and, passing through many countries, landed in China where he entered into service in the court of Kublai Khan and remained there for about 17 years before returning to his homeland. On his way back, Marco Polo visited Andaman & Nicobar Islands in 1294-95, and sailed along the eastern and western seacoasts of India to acquaint himself with the life and conditions of its people. His travelogue makes profuse references to the flourishing Indian harbours, brisk maritime trade, dress, food habits, manners and social customs of the people of the Deccan peninsula. H. Yule and H. Cordier brought out the English transaltion of his travelogue with notes under the title, *Travels of Marco Polo* in two volumes (London, 1903 & 1920).

Yet another Italian traveller, Nicolo Conti visited south India in similar conditions. He had migrated to Damascus in his youth and settled down there as a trader. The spirit of adventure and exploration prompted him to visit the countries of the East, including India, Sri Lanka, Sumatra, Java and China. He returned to his motherland after about twenty-five years of wanderings in c. 1444. 'While in Cairo, he fell into the hands of some Arab fanatics, lost his wife and two children, and was compelled to renounce Christianity in order to save his life.'

It is said that when he returned to Italy, he pleaded for his reconversion to Christianity from Pope Eugene IV. The Pope granted his request but asked him to record his 'true adventures in the far-off lands as a penance'. His narrative was recorded by the Pope's secretary in Latin which is called the travelogue of Nicolo Conti. The original version of his narrative has been lost to the posterity but its Portuguese and Italian translations are available. It was translated into English with notes by J. Winter Jones in R. H. Major's *India in the Fifteenth Century* (*op. cit*; pp. 1-99). Nicolo Conti had sailed along the coast of Malabar and visited the interior of the Deccan in c. 1420, and his travelogue gives a very refreshing account of the city and royal court of the Vijayanagar Empire.

Duarte Barbosa was a Portuguese official in Cochin for about fifteen years in c.1500-16. His description of south India, particularly, the Vijayanagar Empire, is of great geographical and political significance. His narrative was translated into English by L. Dames in two volumes, under the title, *The Book of Duarte Barbosa* (Hakluyt Society, London, 1918 & 1921). Similarly, the travelogue of another Portuguese traveller, Domingos Paes, who visited Vijayanagar Empire in c. 1500-02, also throws interesting sidelights on the socio-political history of south India in the beginning of the sixteenth century. Fairly detailed accounts of Domingos Paes and Duarte Barbosa are available in K.A.N. Sastri's *Foreign Notices of South India* (Madras, 1939).

The Records of European Traders, Travellers and Missionaries

With the discovery of Cape Route to India by Vasco de Gama in 1498, the European traders, including the Portuguese, English, French, Dutch and others, established their commercial establishments and factories all along the seacoast of India. They wrote chronicles and maintained their business records and diaries which form invaluable sources of economic, social and even political history of medieval India. Most of these records are now edited and published by the official as well as non-official agencies which help us in the reconstruction of history of the times. The European travellers, official emissaries and Christian missionaries, who flooded the Indian subcontinent and enjoyed liberal patronage of the Great Mughals, have left very valuable descriptions of their observations and experiences in India in the form of diaries, travelogues, letters and other documents, sent by them to their friends, relations and officials in their homes; they provide us with the abundance of literary sources which also supplement the Persian and Arabic sources.

Indigenous Literature

The indigenous literature in Sanskrit, Hindi and other regional languages, having a bearing on the history of medieval India, is scanty but not altogether conspicuous by its absence. To mention but a few of them, *Prithviraja Raso* of Chand Bardai, the royal bard of the well-known Prithvi Raj Chauhan III, narrates the exploits of his master in a popular epic composition. *Prithviraja Vijaya,* written by Jayanka in about 1194-1200 is also a reliable source of history of the Chauhan rulers of Delhi and Ajmer. Kalhana Pundit was the pioneer historian of Kashmir, who wrote the history of Kashmir, entitled *Rajatarangini*, from the earliest times to 1148-49, in verse; and his disciples, Jyotsnakara *alias* Jonaraja and others continued the narrative under the same title up to the year 1596. It is a unique contribution in the field of indigenous historiography by the Kashmiri scholars. R. Sewell was the first European historian who prepared a monumental work on the history of Vijayanagar Empire, under the title- *A Forgotten Empire*, by making use of the indigenous sources in Telugu and Sanskrit languages. The library of the Punjab University, Chandigarh, possesses a rare document in Sanskrit, entitled *Survadesha Vritant Samgrah*, which gives an account of Amir Timur's invasion on India. It was written by Mahesh Thakur sometime during the reign of Akbar. Written in simple language in the style of a story-teller, the author dispassionately explains the horrors of the sack of Delhi by foreign army of invasion in the midst of the wretched political condition and anarchy.

Archaeological Sources

The Muslim rulers of Delhi, especially the great Mughals have left behind numerous public buildings, forts and rare monuments, like the Red Fort of Delhi and the Taj Mahal of Agra, adorned with inscriptions and other antiquities of invaluable historical significance for the reconstruction of, particularly, the socio-cultural history of medieval India. These sources are used mostly as supplements to the rich literary evidence. Of the archaeological sources, numismatic evidence was used extensively by Edward Thomas to produce the history of the Sultanate period in the most authentic chronological order, under the title, *Chronicle of the Pathan Kings of Delhi*. The researches done by John Marshall, Percy Brown, Burgess, Fergusson, Havell, Cousins and many other authorities in the fields of art and architecture have enriched the historical literature on the medieval Indian history in the modern times.

❑ ❑

2

INDIA ON THE EVE OF MUHAMMAD GHORI'S INVASIONS

Separation of Afghanistan from India (c. 1158)

India remained free from foreign invasions for about one century and a half after the death of Mahmud of Ghazni. He had annexed Punjab to his empire, and his successors held it under their control till 1186. The empire of Ghazni disintegrated under the weak successors of Mahmud. The town of Ghazni itself fell into the hands of the Ghuzz (or Ghizz) Turks in c. 1158, and Khusrau Shah, a descendant of Mahmud, fled to Lahore to save his life. The enemies of the Ghaznavids took possession of all the Afghan territories up to the Khyber Pass, and the entire region of erstwhile Kabul and Zabul, now known as Afghanistan, was cut off from the main land of India forever. Khusrau Shah was thus reduced to the position of a local chieftain of Punjab, with Lahore as its capital. As regards Ghazni, it was, in turn, wrested from the hands of the Ghuzz Turks in 1173 by the Ghurids who established their own dominance in Afghanistan.

The Rise of Ghurids in Afghanistan

Shihabuddin Muhammad, styled Muizzuddin, the sultan of Ghazni, is better known in the history of India as Muhammad Ghori. He invaded India in the last quarter of the twelfth century, and is credited with the foundation of the Muslim rule at Delhi. He belonged to a ruling house of Ghur or Ghor – a small principality, situated in the mountainous region of Afghanistan between Ghazni and Herat. It was founded by a Tajik Turk of the Persian descent. The chiefs of Ghur were feudatories of Ghazni, but taking advantage of the weakness of Mahmud's successors, they became their political rivals. In the course of protracted struggle between them, Alauddin Hussein of Ghur plundered the town of Ghazni and set it on fire, thereby earning the nickname of *Jahansoz* –'the world-burner'. In the long-run, it was Ghiyasuddin of Ghur – a nephew of Alauddin Jahansoz, who brought Ghazni under his permanent control by expelling the Ghuzz Turks from there in 1173; the victorious army of Ghur was commanded by the younger brother of Ghiyasuddin, named Shihabuddin Muhammad. Ghiyasuddin preferred to stay back at Ghur, however, and allowed Shihabuddin to rule at Ghazni, and carry on his military exploits as he liked. Accordingly, Shihabuddin alias Muhammad Ghori became virtually an independent ruler of Ghazni though he continued to offer his nominal allegiance to his brother at Ghur. He assumed the title of Muizzuddin after the conquest of Khurasan in 1201. Ghiasuddin died in the year following, and Muhammad Ghori ascended the throne of Ghur by brushing side the claim of his nephew – a son of his deceased brother. He, however, continued to reside at Ghazni, which was converted into a huge army camp for the organization of military campaigns to India.

The Muslim States of Northwestern India

Mahmud of Ghazni had conquered the northwestern provinces of Sindh and Multan and annexed them to his Ghaznavid Empire. After the conquest of Lahore, he had placed these provinces under the overall supervision and control of the Ghaznavid governor of Lahore. Soon after the death of Mahmud, Multan rose in revolt under the leadership of a Karmatia prince of the erstwhile ruling dynasty of the Arabs, and regained its independence. Similarly, the indigenous tribesmen of Sindh, who had embraced Islam, and were called the Sumras, also raised their standard of revolt against the Ghaznavids and established themselves as independent rulers of Sindh; Debal was their capital. Northwestern India thus came to consist of three sovereign Muslim states on the eve of Muhammad Ghori's invasions, viz., Lahore, Multan and Sindh. After the fury of the barbarous and anti-Hindu campaigns of Mahmud of Ghazni was over, the Indian populace and the Rajput chiefs gradually adopted a conciliatory attitude towards them. The Indians, by and large, recognized these Muslim rulers as the Indianised regional powers. Accordingly, they became a part and parcel of the Indian feudal polity and began to be treated at par with the other Indian chiefs. Similarly, the Muslim immigrants to India and the Hindu converts to Islam, within the jurisdiction of the Rajput states, were shown consideration and allowed to follow their newly adopted religion without any feelings of ill-will or discrimination by the Rajput rulers and the Hindu public, in general. Likewise, the Muslim rulers of these states, having been completely cut off from the rest of the Muslim world, and heavily outnumbered by the Hindu subjects of their states, thought it prudent to adopt a liberal attitude towards them for their survival.The Ghaznavids of Lahore usually maintained an aggressive posture against their Hindu neighbours and, finding them off their guard, did not hesitate in carrying out plundering raids into their territories. Nevertheless, in the absence of any rigid or inviolate dividing lines between the various feudal states, territorial rivalries and border disputes between them were a common affair throughout the country, and such conflicts, which periodically led to mini wars between the Muslim states and their neighbouring Rajput chiefs should not always be interpreted as the Hindu-Muslim confrontation nor construed to imply that the newly emerging Indo-Muslim society was torn asunder by the virus of religious intolerance and communalism.

The Rajput States of Delhi, Ajmer and Kanauj

Mahmud of Ghazni had given a deathblow to the imperial glory of Kanauj in 1018-19 A.D., when he inflicted a crushing defeat on its last Gurjara-Pratihara king, named Rajyapal. The latter acknowledged the nominal suzerainty of Mahmud but it proved fatal for him. The Chandella Raja Ganda of Kalinjar and the ruler of Gwalior made a frontal attack on Kanauj soon after the return of Mahmud to Ghazni and put Rajyapal to death for having shown cowardice in the face of the invader. Thereafter, Kanauj became a bone of contention between the various warring clans of Rajputs for its possession, and was engulfed in bloodshed and political anarchy for many a year until a Rashtrakuta prince, Chandra, took control of it and restored law and order there in 1027 A.D. His successors ruled over Kanauj for four generations. Gopala, the last Rashtrakuta king, was weakened by his defeat at the hands of the Ghaznavid ruler of Lahore in 1089-90, and lost Kanauj to a new clan of the Rajputs, called Gahadavalas. Their leader, Chandra Deva, assumed the insignia of royalty and laid the foundation of the Gahadavala dynasty of Kanauj in 1090 A.D. He extended his sway in the Ganga valley, from Varanasi to the borders of Delhi, within a decade, and claimed himself to be the overlord of Aryavrata (northern India). The rulers of this dynasty were always at daggers drawn with the neighbouring chiefs of Delhi and Ajmer in their bid to establish their hegemony in northern India.

The modern town of Delhi came into existence after the sack of

Kanauj and ravage of the Ganga valley by Mahmud of Ghazni in 1018-19; it was founded by Bilandeo, a chief of the Tomar (or Tumar) clan of the Rajputs, near the ruins of the ancient city of Indraprastha of the Mahabharata period. The Tomar Rajputs originally belonged to the Ganga valley. Mahmud's army of invasion had destroyed their hearths and homes but the uprooted Rajputs undauntedly selected their new abode along the Yamuna, on the very route of the Turkish invaders, to challenge them if they reappeared in the region again. Bilandeo claimed his descent from the Pandavas, and, after the establishment of his sovereignty, assumed the title of Anang Paul. His kingdom included within its domain the region of Hariyana, which now comprises the modern union territory of Delhi and the Gurgaon district of the state of Haryana.

The kingdom of Ajmer was ruled over by the Chahamanas or Chauhan Rajputs, who claimed to be Suryavanshi Kshatriyas. The Chauhans were, in fact, the most widely spread and powerful clan of the Rajputs in northwestern and central India. They were divided into several offshoots or branches, each with a formidable kingdom of its own. The ruling dynasty of the Chauhans of Ajmer hailed from Sakambhari or modern Sambhar, in Jaipur (Rajasthan), where their earliest known progenitor Vasudeva had set up a small principality in the seventh century. The town of Ajmer (Ajayameru) was founded by one of his successors, named Ajayadeva in c. 1093 A.D. Ajmer grew into a powerful and huge kingdom in the twelfth century, and its rulers played a great role in checkmating the inroads of Muslim arms from Sindh, Lahore and Ghazni. The Chauhan ruler, Vigrahraja IV alias Bisaldeva (c.1153-63), conquered Delhi from the Tomars. However, instead of annexing it to his kingdom, he allowed it to retain its separate entity under the suzerainty of Ajmer, so as to act as a buffer state between the Chauhan dominions and the Ghaznavids of Lahore.

The last Tomar ruler, Anang Paul II, had two daughters but no male issue. He had already married off his first daughter to Vijaya Chandra (1154-70), the fourth successor of the Gahadavala dynasty at Kanauj, to buy peace with his mighty neighbour. From this wedlock was born Jaya Chandra (Jai Chand), who became the king of Kanauj after the death of his father in 1170 A.D. Meanwhile, after acknowledging the overlordship of Ajmer, Anang Paul II had offered the hand of his second daughter to Prince Somesvara, a nephew of Vigrahraja IV. The latter's death was followed by a couple of short-lived rulers, leading ultimately, to the succession of Somesvara as the king of Ajmer in 1169 A.D. He ruled for about eight years and, after his demise, was succeeded by his seventeen years old son from his Tomar wife, styled as Prithvi Raj III. Being a minor, he was placed under a council of regency, but, within a year, Prithvi Raj took the reins of government in his own hands, and proved a very capable and popular ruler. He was the celebrated Prithvi Raj Chauhan who gallantly fought against Muhammad Ghori for the defence of northern India and perished in the struggle at the second Battle of Tarain in 1192 A.D. Prithvi Raj inherited the kingdom of Delhi by nomination from Anang Paul II in 1182 A.D., which aroused the jealousy of his cousin, Jai Chand of Kanauj, who, being much older in age than Prithvi Raj, felt deprived of his maternal grandfather's bounty. Obviously, it tilted the balance of power in favour of the Chauhans of Ajmer, and created a bad blood between the two royal contestants for imperial power of northern India. To add insult to the injury, Prithvi Raj is said to have carried off Jai Chand's beautiful daughter, Sanyogita (Sanyukta) from the *swayambara* with the tacit willingness of the damsel, of course. However, it made Jai Chand a sworn enemy of Prithvi Raj although the latter had now become his son-in-law. The mutual rivalry between them proved very harmful for themselves as well as the country. As a shortsighted and foolhardy person, Jai Chand stood aloof when Prithvi Raj confronted the foreign armies of invasion under Muhammad Ghori; and, as a consequence, both of them were annihilated one by one by their common foe, leading to the establishment of the Turkish rule in India.

Other Regional States

The central and western India was dotted with a conglomeration of big and small Rajput kingdoms, set up on clannish affiliations. Apart from Kanauj, the Gurjara-Pratiharas had carved out a few other independent principalities in Rajputana and Malwa. The Parmars of Dhar (Ujjain) started as feudatories of Gurjara-Pratiharas but asserted their sovereignty before long. Their most famous ruler, Raja Bhoj, was a contemporary of Mahmud of Ghazni, who marshalled his troops to intercept the invader on his return march from Somnath temple, albeit the latter got wind of it and rushed back through a different route, passing through the Rann of Kutch and the Sindh desert, to reach Ghazni in 1026 A.D. On the eve of Muhammad Ghori's invasions, the Parmars were still there but as the feudatories of the Chalukyas of Anhilwara (Gujarat) who were witness to the sack of Somnath temple by Mahmud. The Chalukya rulers remained constantly engaged in internecine warfare with their neighbours, including the Parmars of Malwa, Guhilots of Chittor, and Chauhans of Ajmer. At the time of Muhammad Ghori's invasions, Mool Raj II was at the helm of affairs in Gujarat. Similarly, the ruling dynasty of Chandela Raja Ganda of Bundelkhand, who had fought Mahmud of Ghazni, also survived itself in the intervening century and a half. The Chandelles were the lords of Mahoba, Kalinjar, Khajuraho and Jhansi, and they displayed imperial pretensions. They humbled the Parmars of Malwa but suffered reverses at the hands of Gahadavalas of Kanauj and Chauhans of Ajmer. The Kachchwaha rulers of Gwalior were the feudatories of the Chandelles of Kalinjar but the position of the Guhilots or Guhila Rajputs of Mewar was different. Bappa Rawal founded a small state of Mewar, with its capital at Chittor, and his successors, styled *ranas,* were highly self-respecting and self-contented rulers, who neither expanded their territories at the cost of others nor tolerated encroachments of their state by others at any cost. Of all the Rajput dynasties of the period, it were the Guhila Rajputs of Mewar alone who zealously safeguarded their sovereignty against all the external foes until the middle of the sixteenth century.

In eastern India, Bengal, Bihar and Orissa comprised the central domain of the Mauryan and Gupta empires in the remote past. Gopala is credited with the foundation of the Pala dynasty of northern Bengal in the ninth century. His successors gradually extended their sway over the entire region of Bengal, Bihar and Orissa. The Palas maintained their existence, with varying degrees of fortunes, till the last quarter of the twelfth century. Meanwhile, the eleventh century saw the rise of Sena dynasty at Nadiya (or Nudia) in eastern Bengal whose sovereigns hailed from the south. Vijaya Sena (1097-1159) wrested big slices of the Bengal territories from the Palas and also fought against the rulers of Mithila (northern Bihar) and Kamrupa (Assam) for territorial aggrandizement. Being situated far away from the northwestern frontier of India, Bengal escaped the fury of the Turkish invaders under Mahmud of Ghazni; it was Lakshman Sena, the last ruler of the Sena dynasty, who was ousted from Nadiya by Muhammad bin Bakhtiyar Khilji, a Turkish officer of Qutubuddin Aibek, in 1202 A.D.

The Brahmaputra valley of Assam, called Kamrupa (Kamrup), was under the rule of Brahmans since ages; they were feudatories of the imperial Guptas. King Bhaskarvarman of Kamrup, with his capital at Durjaya (mod. Gauhati), acknowledged the suzerainty of Harsha Vardhana but his successors asserted their independence. In the eleventh century, yet another formidable kingdom rose in the lower valley of Brahmaputra, with its capital at Srihatta (mod. Sylhet). Its rulers remained free from the Muslim intervention till the beginning of the fourteenth century. On the northern periphery, the valley of Nepal formed a part of the Mauryan and Gupta empires, and the history of its independent existence, under a local dynasty, can be traced back to the fifth century. Raghudeva, a Rajput chief, laid the foundation of Thakuri dynasty in Nepal in 879 A.D; he commemorated this event by starting a Nepali era. Similarly, the northernmost Himalayan valley of Kashmir was a part of the Mauryan and Kushana empires but, thereafter, the Kashmiri Brahmins, who constituted the bulk of the population, established their rule in the valley. In spite of the dynastic changes, the Brahmins retained their sovereignty over Kashmir till the fourteenth century. Because of its isolation from the plains, Kashmir did not play any role in the political upheavals of the times.

❑ ❑

3

INVASIONS OF MUHAMMAD GHORI (1173-1205 A.D.)

The Arab invasions were confined to the conquest of Sindh and Multan. Mahmud of Ghazni trampled the whole of northern India under his feet, but he annexed only the Punjab, including Lahore and Multan to his Ghaznavid Empire, as a matter of expediency to protect the lines of communication and to facilitate the movement of his troops into the heart of India for loot and plunder. He was not an imperialist by instinct and did not attempt to establish his political dominance in the country. After the death of Mahmud, India remained free from foreign invasions for about a century and a half until another Turkish general, Muhammad Ghori replaced the Ghaznavid dynasty in Afghanistan and recommenced the onslaughts on India. As mentioned in the preceding chapter, Ghazni was conquered by the Ghuzz Turks in 1173 A.D. under the command of Shihabuddin Muhammad, better known to the Indian history as Muhammad Ghori. He received appointment as the viceroy of Ghazni by his elder brother, Ghiyasuddin, the ruler of Ghur, and was allowed to administer his territories as he pleased. He became the sovereign ruler of Ghazni after the death of Ghiyasuddin in 1201 A.D. After consolidating his position at Ghazni, Muhammad Ghori started invasions on India in 1175 A.D.

Objectives of his Invasions: Muhammad Ghori was not a very brilliant military general of world-wide fame like Mahmud of Ghazni, but unlike the latter, he was a great imperialist who started his invasions with the solemn determination of establishing the Muslim rule in India. This was his primary objective. Loot and plunder and the expansion of Islam or his zeal to glorify his name for his military exploits may be said to be the secondary objects of Muhammad Ghori. An interesting feature of his invasions of India is worth mentioning. Unlike Mahmud of Ghazni, he refrained from using the premier Khyber Pass of the northwestern frontier mountains as the route for attacking India; instead, he selected the Gomal Pass, situated to the west of Dera Ismail Khan, which, in his movements between India and Ghazni, was found to be safer and shorter route. Moreover, after their ouster from Afghanistan, the Ghaznavid power was confined to Punjab, with its capital at Lahore, and the Khyber Pass, on their northwest frontier was strongly defended by them. It was but natural that Muhammad Ghori would like to avoid direct clash with the Ghaznavids of Lahore all at once. 'His plan seemed to be to penetrate into Sindh and Gujarat and from there into central India, thus encircling the Ghaznavid dominions, and, subsequently compelling the latter to acknowledge his suzerainty'.

Conquest of Multan and Uchh

As per the new route adopted for the invasions of India, the Arab kingdom of Multan and its adjoining region, called Uchh, were the first to fall on the way of Muhammad Ghori. Accordingly, first of all, he invaded Multan in 1175 A.D. Taken by surprise, its Arab chief of the Karmatia community acknowledged Muhammad Ghori's suzerainty after a brief skirmish. Thereafter, he marched upon the Uchh territories which were held by the Bhatti Rajputs. Their only stronghold, the fortress of Uchh, was put under siege by the army of invasion and stubbornly held out by the besieged garrison for many days. Hard-pressed, the Rajput chief opened negotiations for a settlement. According to Firishta, the wicked queen of the Bhatti chief, having been won over by the secret agents of Muhammad Ghori, treacherously opened the gates of their fortress to allow the entrance of the Turkish army and got her husband killed at the hands of the invaders. We are told that Muhammad Ghori had promised to marry the beautiful daughter of the deceased Rajput chief and to make her his chief queen but he never fulfilled his promise.

Invasion of Gujarat

Using Multan as a springboard, Muhammad Ghori invaded Anhilwara, the capital of Gujarat, in 1178 but his attack was repulsed with heavy losses by its Chalukya king Bhimdeva II. Thereafter, Muhammad Ghori did not dare to attack Gujarat again.

Subjugation of Punjab

The Gujarat debacle compelled Muhammad Ghori to revise his plan of action. He diverted his attention towards Punjab for the conquest of which he made the concerted bid. In 1179, he pushed through the Khyber Pass with full force, and, after annihilating its Ghaznavid defenders, took possession of Peshawar. Like Mahmud, Muhammad Ghori now heavily garrisoned Peshawar and converted it into a base camp for further penetration into India. In 1181, he overran Sialkot, and forced Khusrau Malik, the Ghaznavid ruler of Lahore, to make peace with him by ceding the conquered territories to the Ghurid chief. Khusrau had to send his minor son as a hostage to the invader to ensure the implementation of the terms of the treaty. It gave the Ghaznavid ruler a temporary respite from his Ghurid antagonist.

Submission of Sindh

Muhammad Ghori utilized this opportunity to invade Debal, the seaport of Sindh, in the year following. Taken unawares, the Sumra chief of Sindh hastened to offer his submission on the payment of a hefty tribute. The invaders celebrated their victory by laying their hands on the undefended cargoes of the anchored ships and godowns of the traders, and returned to Ghazni, heavily laden with booty.

The Annexation of Punjab

In the winter of 1185, Muhammad Ghori made the third and final assault on Lahore with determination to annihilate the Ghaznavid power for ever. He led his army of invasion through the Khyber Pass, and assisted by the Khokhars of the Salt Range, marched on Sialkot which had been put under siege by Khusrau Malik, alias Khusrau Shah, as a pre-emptive move. On the approach of Muhammad Ghori's armies, he raised the siege and retired into the fort of Lahore. The invaders promptly laid siege to the metropolis which was heavily garrisoned and gallantly defended by the Ghaznavid ruler. Finding his instant victory in doubt, Muhammad Ghori resorted to a stratagem for a negotiated settlement. Khusrau Malik fell into his trap, and as he came out of the fort for a dialogue, he was taken captive by Muhammad Ghori, and the besieged garrison was called upon to lay down arms. Thus it was that the leaderless Ghaznavid army surrendered without a fight and Muhammad Ghori took possession of the stronghold. The whole of Punjab was declared annexed to the Ghurid Empire and Khusrau Malik was sent in chains to Ghor to join the company of his son in the prison. Both of them were put to death in 1192 A.D. Most of the Ghaznavid soldiers, who willingly offered their services to him, were absorbed in the imperial army by Muhammad Ghori; they proved very helpful to him in the foundation of the Muslim rule in India.

Encounter with Prithvi Raj Chauhan

The annexation of the Ghaznavid state of Lahore made Muhammad Ghori the master of the whole of northwestern India and the Punjab, besides Sindh, and pushed the frontiers of his empire to the borders of the Rajput states. Powerful and brave, the mighty Rajputs were ever ready to lay down their lives for freedom and honour but lack of political foresight and internecine warfare between themselves had completely blurred their national vision. Leaving behind the bitter memories of the ravages of Mahmud of Ghazni and his Turkish marauders, they seemed to have reconciled themselves to the existence of the hostile Muslim chieftainships in their neighbourhood. Accordingly, none of them took serious notice of the political and military upheaval that took place in the Punjab and no attempt was made to challenge the authority of Muhammad Ghori at Lahore. As a shrewd military general, Muhammad Ghori also did not display hostile intentions against his Rajput neighbours all at once. Keeping in mind his long-range political and religious objectives to establish the Muslim rule in India, his confrontation with the Rajputs was inevitable. But he exhibited great patience and fortitude in his dealings with them. After the occupation of Lahore, he brought it under an effective civil and military control and gradually converted it into a strong base of operations against them.

Taking advantage of the disunity among the Rajput chiefs of northern India, Muhammad Ghori decided to strike against them one by one. He looked upon Delhi and Ajmer with covetous eyes, but he made thorough preparations for three years before challenging Prithvi Raj (III) Chauhan. In 1189, Muhammad Ghori made a surprise attack on Bathinda (Tabarhind) and compelled its besieged garrison to surrender before the arrival of reinforcements from Delhi. He posted there only 1,200 picked horsemen, with 'adequate munitions of war', under the charge of a seasoned general, Malik Ziauddin, with special instructions to hold on against the Rajputs at least 'for eight months' until his return from Ghazni with a fresh army.

Prithvi Raj Chauhan had taken no notice of the rise of the Ghurid power in Ghazni. He did not adopt suitable measures to defend his dominions even when Multan and Lahore fell into the hands of Muhammad Ghori. As usual, he retained Ajmer as his seat of governance even after 1182, when he inherited the Tumar kingdom of Delhi from his maternal grandfather. He put Delhi under the charge of his younger brother, Govind Rai, as its governor, and took no steps to strengthen its border outposts along the Muslim territories of the Punjab. In his shortsightedness, Prithvi Raj did not realize the strategic importance of Delhi, situated in the proximity of Lahore, which posed a direct threat to the safety of his dominions. It is a sad commentary on the mismanagement of his state affairs that Prithvi Raj came to know of Muhammad Ghori's intrusion into his dominions and the fall of Bathinda through an official deputation sent by Govind Rai from Delhi. Thereafter, he marched on Bathinda with a huge army to chastise the invaders, and Govind Rai and some other chiefs joined him on the way to Bathinda. Before they could reach there, the fort had been taken over by the Muslims, and its Rajput garrison totally annihilated. Not only this; even Muhammad Ghori had also made a safe exit from the Rajput territories and was on his way to Ghazni to fetch more troops. Much of the valuable time was wasted by the Rajputs in evolving the strategy to tackle the Turkish menace. Meanwhile, the rumours spread that Muhammad Ghori was planning to invade Delhi. It was only then that the gravity of the situation dawned on Prithvi Raj Chauhan that Delhi was in danger, and he started making hectic preparations for its defence.

First Battle of Tarain (1191 A.D.): The rumours were found to be correct. Muhammad Ghori had, in fact, mustered well-equipped combat troops from Lahore and Ghazni to challenge Prithvi Raj within the Rajput dominions. He encountered the Rajputs at Tarain, modern Taraori near Karnal, in early 1191. A pitched battle was fought in which Muhammad Ghori was defeated and fled the field for his dear life. According to Minhaj-us-Siraj, in the thickest of the battle 'Govind Rai threw a javelin at Muhammad Ghori and severely wounded his arm. The sultan turned round his charger's head and retreated. Due to the agony of the wound, he was unable to remain steady on horseback and was about to fall on the ground when a lion-hearted warrior recognized him; (he) sprang up (on the horse) behind the sultan, and, supporting him in his arms, urged the horse with his voice and brought him out of the field of battle'. Firishta gives a different account of the episode, however. He writes that the wounded sultan lay unconscious in the battlefield among the dead and the dying soldiers, and was picked up by his slaves at night. 'During the night, they carried him on their shoulders by turns. Next morning, they reached their camp and placed him in a litter'. The Rajput fighters were too tired to give a hot chase to the fleeing Turks can at night.

The triumphant Rajputs now marched on Bathinda and put it under siege. The besieged Turkish garrison held out stubbornly against heavy odds for no less than thirteen months before laying down arms. That only twelve hundred determined Turkish fighters, besieged in the Rajput stronghold should be able to hold on against thousands of the Rajput warriors for more than a year does not speak highly of the Rajput military machine and the war strategies, especially when we remember that the Turks had conquered this very fort from the hands of its Rajput defenders in a single sweep a short while ago.

Second Battle of Tarain (1192 A.D.): Muhammad Ghori, though seriously wounded, had escaped alive from the battlefield, and took a long time to regain health. But he took his lieutenants to task for the debacle of Tarain; some of them were beheaded for showing cowardice and others languished behind bars for a whole year until they lamented and sought an opportunity to give a better account of themselves in the future contests against the foe to wipe out the stigma of the previous defeat. According to Firishta, Muhammad Ghori was 'so overwhelmed with a sense of grief and humiliation that he would neither eat nor drink. He did not go to his wife and did not change the clothes that he wore next to his skin. Day and night he spent in preparation to fight Prithvi Raj Chauhan. Then after a year's preparation, all at once, he took the road to Hindustan'. He brought 1,20,000 combat troops from Ghazni to Lahore, where, his army was further strengthened by the addition of contingents from the Punjab. While ordering the march of his forces towards Delhi, Muhammad Ghori sent an emissary, named Ruknuddin Hamzah, to Ajmer with a proposal to Prithvi Raj 'to embrace Islam and acknowledge his supremacy in order to avoid the dreadful consequences of the war'. The Rajput chief turned down the proposal with the contempt it deserved, and met his foe on the same battleground of Tarain with his army, which, according to the Muslim chroniclers, numbered 3,00,000 horse, 3,000 elephants and a large infantry.

Muhammad Ghori employed clever tactics to defeat the Rajputs. His four divisions of 13,000 mounted archers engaged the Rajputs from all the four sides, including their rear. They had special instructions not to come very close to the foe but to exhaust the Rajput patience and energy by scattered engagements, and make an orderly retreat if pressed hard on any front. The reserves were kept by him at a distance of several kilometres from the scene of action. He did not give an opportunity to the Rajputs to gauge his real strength. When the Rajputs were nonplussed and disorganized by the day-long skirmishes and tactics of the over-fleeing Turkish archers, Muhammad Ghori thrust the reserves into the battlefield and made a clean sweep of it. The entire Rajput army was destroyed; Govind Rai fell fighting while Prithvi Raj was seriously wounded and fled the field but was caught and beheaded immediately or soon thereafter.

The fall of Prithvi Raj Chauhan proved disastrous for all the Rajputs of northern India. Thousands of the valiant fighters were killed at Tarain, and the vanguard of Rajput defenses in the northwestern India was annihilated. It exposed the incorrigible weaknesses of their military and political setup and emboldened the Turkish invaders to penetrate deep into the Ganga valley.

Conquest of Delhi: Muhammad Ghori's victory over Prithvi Raj Chauhan did not lead to the conquest of Delhi and Ajmer all at once. Both of these cities were defended stubbornly by those who escaped alive from the battlefield of Tarain. Muhammad Ghori, therefore, deputed his most capable Turkish slave officer Qutubuddin Aibek to take charge of his army of occupation to establish their control over the territories of the vanquished, and himself returned to Ghazni. Aibek setup his head-quarters at Indraprastha near Delhi and exerted his military-cum-diplomatic pressure over the Rajput defenders of the metropolis to acknowledge the overlordship of Muhammad Ghori. He extended support to Govind Raja, a young and inexperienced son of Prithvi Raj Chauhan, to succeed him on the throne of Ajmer, and, at the same time, created dissensions among the Rajputs by advancing the claims of a scion of the old Tumar dynasty over Delhi. Govind Raja was formally placed on the throne of Ajmer under the suzerainty of the Turkish regime. Nevertheless, Qutubuddin Aibek was keen to take possession of Delhi which was as yet held desperately by its Rajput defenders. He cut off Delhi from Ajmer by taking possession of the highway between the two cities and then laid siege to the fort of Delhi in 1193 A.D. Hard-pressed, the besieged Rajputs vacated the fort after a few months and escaped through the Turkish lines by making a sudden assault; about half of them laying down their lives in their bid to attain freedom. Qutubuddin entered Delhi in triumph and read the *Khutba* in the name of Muhammad Ghori. The Turks became the masters of Delhi in 1193, but, after the death of Muhammad Ghori, Qutubuddin installed himself as the king of India in 1206 with his capital at Lahore. It was Iltutmish who transferred his capital from Lahore to Delhi in 1211 A.D.

Conquests in the Ganga Valley: The conquest of Delhi boosted the morale of Qutubuddin Aibek, and he chalked out an ambitious plan to penetrate into the Ganga Doab in stages. As a first step towards this direction, he took possession of Meerath (Modern Meerut), which belonged to the Gahadavalas of Kanauj, in a sudden assault before the year 1193 was out. Thereafter, he led an attack on Baran (Bulandshahr) but failed to conquer it and put its fort under siege. The besieged garrison offered stubborn resistance for many days and compelled Qutubuddin to raise the siege as he could not afford to absent himself from Delhi for a long time.

The failure of Qutubuddin to conquer the fort of Baran had a salutary effect on his rash calculations to speed up the programme of his aggressive warfare. Muhammad Ghori recalled him to Ghazni for his instructions and advice. It may be mentioned here that Muhammad Ghori had three daughters and no male issue. All of his daughters had been given in marriage to three of his most capable and trustworthy Turkish slave officers, Qutubuddin Aibek being one of them. He, therefore, treated his sons-in-law as partners in the scheme of his imperial pursuits. Accordingly, Aibek stayed in Ghazni as the most important member of the Ghurid family for about six months, and then returned to Delhi in early 1194 after receiving special instructions from his master and father-in-law regarding their future line of approach. Muhammad Ghori furnished Qutubuddin with the best of the armaments, and put under his charge a large number of fresh troops and promising young officers, who intended to migrate to India to seek fortunes and to settle down there permanently. Muhammad Ghori had, in fact, prepared Qutubuddin to take independent charge of his Indian dominions after his death.

The Fall of Jai Chand of Kanauj

On his return from Ghazni, Qutubuddin launched a massive military campaign for the conquest of the Ganga valley. The towns of Baran (Bulandshahr) and Koil (Aligarh) were conquered by him in 1194 A.D. before the arrival of Muhammad Ghori with a well-equipped force of 50,000 horsemen. Qutubuddin, with his contingent, made a junction with his master and the combined armies marched towards Varanasi (Benaras). Jai Chand, the Gahadavala chief of Kanauj, intercepted them at a place, called Chandwar, on the Yamuna between Etawa and Kanauj. A bloody battle ensued in which the Rajputs had an upper hand all through the day. Then what happened was the same sordid story of 'the king and his elephant' which finds repetition throughout the ancient Indian history. Jai Chand, seated on a mighty elephant, led the attack. Towards the evening, a chance arrow struck him in the eye and he collapsed. This was a signal for the fighters to disperse, thus converting their sure victory into a decisive defeat. Barani styles Jai Chand of Kanauj as 'The Rai of Benares', and explains the battle scene thus:

'The Rai of Benares, who prided himself on the number of his forces and war elephants, seated on a lofty *howdah*, received a deadly wound from an arrow, and fell from his exalted seat to earth. His head was carried on the point of a spear to the commander, and his body was thrown to the dust of contempt'. (*Tarikh-i-Firoze Shahi*; E&D, ii, Aligarh reprint, p. 221)

A large number of the Rajput soldiers, who fled the field, took shelter in the stronghold of Kanauj. Harish Chandra, son of Jai Chand, declared him the Raja of Kanauj and made appropriate arrangements for the defence of the capital. Jai Chand's death broke the backbone of the Gahadavala resistance but it was not possible for the Turks to lay their hands on the whole of the Ganga valley. Muhammad Ghori, therefore, was not eager to march on Kanauj all at once. Instead, he made a dash for Varanasi, where the imperial treasury of the Gahadavalas was situated. All the villages and towns which fell on the way of the victors were plundered. Varanasi and Asni were also thoroughly sacked and the royal treasures appropriated by Muhammad Ghori. He setup strong military contingents there and himself returned to Ghazni with a compact body of his personal guards and 1,400 camels, laden with booty, primarily gold and silver. Qutubuddin was left behind at Delhi with the advice to carry on his plan of conquests and extension of his possessions slowly and steadily. Those of Muhammad Ghori's soldiers, who expressed the desire to stay back at Delhi and serve under Qutubuddin, were permitted to do so; it further strengthened the armed might of Qutubuddin.

The Conquests of Qutubuddin

Qutubuddin Aibek had to face many revolts and uprisings in the newly conquered territories and he was constantly on his horseback to restore law and order. It goes to his credit that he not only strengthened his hold over the conquered lands and the alien subjects but also extended the boundaries of his possessions by further conquests. His greatest military achievements during his period of viceroyalty of Lahore, from 1195 to 1205, were the conquests of Ajmer, Kanauj, Kalinjar and Gwalior.

Varanasi and its adjoining territories were wrested by the Gahadavalas of Kanauj from the hands of the Turks. Hari Raja, a brother of Prithvi Raj (III) Chauhan, wrested the control of Ajmer from the hands of his nephew Govind Rai, and declared his sovereignty. He sent an army for the recovery of Delhi also but Qutubuddin Aibek intercepted it within the jurisdiction of Ajmer itself and put it to route. Thereafter, Qutubuddin made a frontal attack on Ajmer and conquered it after a very bloody struggle that lasted many days. The defenders of the fort fought to the bitter end; and the handful of those, who were left behind, sacrificed their lives by performing *Jauhar* along with their commander Hari Raja. The conquest of Ajmer by Qutubuddin Aibek, in fact, marked the final victory of the Turks over the dominions of Prithvi Raj Chauhan. He appointed a Turkish governor at Ajmer with a strong military force and with full powers to crush all resistance to the Turkish rule by the natives with an iron hand. The people of Ajmer and Delhi did not reconcile themselves to the loss of their national independence. Therefore, during the next few years, Qutubuddin had to fight hard against the disgruntled public and the sporadic uprisings of the Hindu youth, whose ranks were supplemented by the volunteer freedom-fighters from different parts of Rajputana, Malwa and even Gujarat. That is why he needed constant support from Ghazni to consolidate his hold over the nascent Turkish state.

Muhammad Ghori brought a fresh army from Ghazni in 1195-96 to reinforce his Indian garrisons. It was placed at the disposal of Qutubuddin. Now Muhammad Ghori did not need to take personal command of the Turkish armies in India and left everything to the discretion of Aibek to manage the things as he pleased. Accordingly, it was Qutubuddin who conquered Bayana in 1196 A.D., and put it under the charge of a Turkish commander. Gwalior was invested by Qutubuddin but its Rajput chief, Sulakshana Paul, held out against the invaders for a long time, and, ultimately, got rid of them by offering a nominal submission. Nevertheless, Qutubuddin was determined to bring Gwalior under his direct sway. Therefore, soon after raising the siege of Gwalior, he deputed his Turkish governor of Bayana to resume hostilities against the Rajputs of Gwalior at his level. The latter was successful in this enterprise though at the cost of hundreds of the Turkish lives; Gwalior had become a part of the Turkish dominions before the end of 1200 A.D.

Raja Bhima II of Anhilwara (Gujarat) was known to be the staunch enemy of the Turks. He had not taken kindly to the fall of Prithvi Raj Chauhan and Jai Chand, and the volunteers from Gujarat had made their presence felt as associates of the Rajput rebels of Ajmer. Therefore, after the conquest of Ajmer, Qutubuddin Aibek retaliated by invading Anhilwara in 1296-97. It is said that, on the approach of the Muslim forces, Bhima II retired to some distant stronghold as a strategy, and left the defence of his capital Anhilwara in the hands of his trusted military generals. One of them, Rai Karan, assisted by Dharavarsa Parmara of Abu, intercepted the Turks at the foot of the Abu hills but Qutubuddin, having been taken by surprise, 'feigned fright and resorted to shock tactics' to give the impression that he was trying to avoid the open confrontation. It made the Rajputs to take the contest very lightly, leading to the disruption of their fighting lines. When the confusion prevailed in the Rajput camp, the Turks pounced upon them with full fury and slaughtered 15,000 of their solders in the battle and took another 20,000 as captives. The Turks mercilessly sacked the town of Anhilwara, desecrated and demolished its temples and carried out bloody carnage for many days until all resistance to the aggressors ceased. Flushed with victory, Qutubuddin posted a Turkish noble there to consolidate his hold in Gujarat and returned to Lahore, laden with untold booty. Shortly after the return of Qutubuddin from Gujarat, Bhima II came out of his hiding and waged a relentless war against the Turkish forces of occupation until the whole of Gujarat was liberated from the Muslim yoke by him. After Muhammad Ghori's debacle of 1178 A.D., it was the second time that the Turks had to turn their tails from Gujarat with a bloody nose. It was probably because of the determined fights put up by the rulers and people of Gujarat to hold the Turks at bay that it remained immune from the Muslim attacks during the next century. Nevertheless, Qutubuddin launched repeated military campaigns for loot and plunder into Central India to weaken and demoralize the Indian chiefs. He carried fire and sword into the Chauhan states and compelled them to surrender all the important footholds in the neighbourhood of Ajmer. In despair, they migrated further south and set up new states of Kota, Bundi and Sirohi.

Qutubuddin Aibek conquered Badaun from a Rashtrakuta prince in 1997-98 and appointed Iltutmish, one of his slave officers, to be its first Muslim governor. In 1198-99, he inflicted a crushing defeat on the Gahadavalas and wrested Kanauj from their hands; the town of Benaras was also re-conquered. In 1202-03, Aibek invaded Bundelkhand. Its Chandella ruler Parmardi Deva was besieged in Kalinjar for many months. Out of frustration, he became ready to submit to the Turks, but his minister Ajayadeva put him to death out of indignation, and resumed the leadership of the Chandella freedom-fighters to continue the struggle against the Muslims. The besieged garrison held out against the aggressors for quite sometime until their water supply was cut-off by the enemy, and they were constrained to vacate the fort on the promise of safe conduct by the besiegers. After the occupation of Kalinjar, the Turks acquired control of Khajuraho and Mahoba also. The defeat of the Chandellas established the domination of the Turks in Central India.

Penetration of Muslim Arms in Bihar and Bengal: The credit for the introduction of the Muslim arms goes to Ikhtiyaruddin Muhammad bin Bakhtiyar Khilji, a brilliant young officer of Qutubuddin Aibek. After the conquest of Kanauj, he was granted an estate in the Ganga valley along the western borders of Bihar, with the predominantly Buddhist population. On his own initiative, he started plundering raids into Bihar and, within four or five years, conquered a substantial part of it. Like all other enterprising Turkish officers, he enjoyed full support from Qutubuddin for the extension of the Muslim dominions at the cost of the neighbouring Hindu states. He wantonly ransacked the Hindu habitats and destroyed their temples and Buddhist monasteries, including those of Nalanda, and put thousands of the peace-loving and unarmed Bhikshus to the sword. Many of them fled to Nepal and Tibet to save their lives.

In 1202-03 A.D., Bakhtiyar Khilji marched on Nadia (Nudia or Navadwipa), the capital of Lakshmana Sena of Bengal. The latter fled the capital without a fight. Minhajus-us Siraj writes that

> 'Muhammad Bakhtiyar...suddenly appeared before the city of Nudia with only eighteen horsemen, the remainder of his army was left to follow. He did not molest any man, but went on peacefully and without ostentation, so that no one could suspect who he was. The people rather thought he was a merchant, who had brought horses for sale. In this manner, he reached the Rai Lakhmaniya's palace when he drew his sword and commenced the attack. At this time, the Rai was at his dinner... all of a sudden, a cry was raised at the gate of his palace and in the city. Before he had ascertained what had occurred, Muhammad Bakhtiyar had rushed into the palace and put a number of men to the sword. The Rai fled barefooted by the rear of the palace, and his whole treasure, and all his wives, maidservants, attendants and women fell into the hand of the invader'. (*Tabaqat-i-Nasiri*; E&D. ii, pp. 305-6)

Lakshmana Sena lost northern Bengal at the hands of the Muslims but he and his successors continued to rule over east Bengal and probably south Bengal also for another half a century. He died in 1206 A.D., but he had given up the ancestral Buddhist faith and become a devout Vaishnavite before his death. Meanwhile, the Turks had taken possession of the districts of Malda, Dinajpur, Murshidabad and Birbhum. Bakhtiyar Khilji could not retain his hold over Nadia for long and made Lakhnawati or Lakhnauti as his capital. Having become over-confident of the Turkish arms, he invaded the Brahmaputra valley with 10,000 horsemen. The Assamese tribesmen surrounded them from all sides and destroyed the whole of the Muslim army; the Khilji chief returned to Lakhnauti with hardly a hundred Turkish survivors. Terribly shaken by the grief, he fell ill and was done to death by one of his soldiers in 1206.

The Concluding Years of Muhammad Ghori (1203-06)

Ghiyasuddin, the elder brother of Muhammad Ghori, died in 1203 A.D., and the latter acquired an independent status as a ruler. He assumed the title of Muizzuddin. The last two years of his reign were full of troubles and misfortunes. He suffered a defeat at the hands of the Shah of Khwarizm in 1205, and soon thereafter, he received the news of a revolt by the Khokhars in central Punjab. Hard-pressed, Qutubuddin Aibek appealed to Muhammad Ghori for help. The latter came to Punjab, crushed the revolt, and helped Aibek in restoring law and order. On his return journey to Ghazni, Muhammad Ghori was encamped at Dhamyak, in district Jhelum, on the Indus when a party of the Khokhar desperados stealthily entered his tent and assassinated him on March 15, 1206. His dead body was carried to Ghazni and buried there. As he had no male issue to inherit his empire, he was succeeded on the throne of Ghazni by his slave officer Tajuddin Yaldoz, to whom he had given his first daughter in marriage. The Indian possessions of Muhammad Ghori were untagged by Qutubuddin Aibek from the apron-strings of Ghazni, and he setup as an independent ruler with his capital at Lahore. He thus laid the foundation of the first independent Turkish kingdom in India whose boundaries extended from the northwestern frontier to Bihar and Bengal in the east. The Rajput domination of northern India came to end for ever, and with it passed out the last pageant of the ancient Indian history.

Muhammad Ghori – An Evaluation

Muhammad Ghori was the real founder of the Muslim rule in India. He was not a great military general like Mahmud of Ghazni but a farsighted politician and a man of vision. He made a correct estimate of the decadent political structure of India and made up his mind to bring it under the Muslim rule. Mahmud of Ghazni had thoroughly exposed the hollowness of the Indian polity and showed the way to the later Muslim invaders. Muhammad Ghori fully benefited from the spade-work that had been done by his predecessor to pave the ground for the transplantation of Islam in the rich and fertile land of the infidels. He was an empire-builder who visualized the establishment of a Turkish empire in India by all means. He made it the mission of his life and was lucky enough to see its fulfilment during his very lifetime. For the achievement of this objective, Muhammad Ghori refrained from concentrating all the powers of the state into his own hands as an autocratic and self-willed feudal lord; instead, he diversified the military functions and resources among his capable and trustworthy slave officers and gave them complete freedom to chalk out their schemes of action for the attainment of their common goal. The foundation of the Muslim rule in India was, in fact, the outcome of the corporate activity of Muhammad Ghori and his brilliant military officers. He richly rewarded those who won laurels and reprimanded the incapable officers who were quickly replaced by the more enterprising youthful upstarts. Mahmud of Ghazni had struck at the very roots of the obsolete and outdated political organisation based on regional and feudal principles and shaken its foundations; and, as its logical finale, Muhammad Ghori demolished it with determination and steadfastness. He was an empire-builder par excellence.

The Causes of Defeat of the Rajputs

Arnold J. Toynbee, while analyzing the circumstances leading to the fall of the great civilizations, expresses the view that no 'foreign invasion' had ever been the cause of their collapse; 'it simply gave the coup d'grace'. The decadent Indian polity, distorted by the inherent political defects of regional, feudal and parochial elements, the defunct military organization, the stagnant Indian society and economic imbalance between its various segments, in fact, carried the seeds of decay of the pre-Muslim Indian society and its Rajput leadership. It was plagued further by the self-destructive tendencies, like the neglect of a sound political-cum-military infrastructure for collective self-defence, the general lack of feeling of over-all national consciousness, mutual rivalries and internecine warfare between the premier ruling houses, who were supposed to undertake collective responsibility for the protection of their people and defence of national freedom. He elaborates his thesis with reference to the downfall of the ancient Indian civilization and culture, as a result of the collapse of Rajput polity at the hands of the Turks, by the observations that

> 'The criminal intent of...the Turks may have been fully as heinous as is commonly alleged, but there is reason to doubt the effectiveness of their criminal action; for there is reason to believe that the alien body social into which they plunged their sword was the body of a suicide, whose life-blood was already ebbing away through a self-inflicted wound'.

As inferred by Toynbee,

> 'about the middle of the twelfth century of the Christian era, the Hindu powers...had fallen into an internecine warfare with one another....If this fatal division of the house of Hinduism against itself, that made it possible for the Turkish highwaymen to force an entry.....if in the twelfth century, the Rajputs had not turned their swords suicidally (*sic.*) upon themselves, the Hindu world might have continued, without any undue drain upon its energies, to keep the Turks at bay and to work out its own destinies under its own control. And thus the ***verdict*** proves, on appeal, to be ***suicide instead of assassination***...' (*The Study of History*; iv, pp. 71 & 98-100)

No wonder, the Rajputs stood a very poor chance of survival in the struggle against the Turkish invaders. R C Majumdar, the doyen of Indian history, who spent the whole of his life in the scientific study and research on the subject, arrived at almost similar conclusions regarding 'the real causes that lay behind the political catastrophe that overwhelmed India at the hands of the Muslim invaders'. He writes that

> History had no meaning for the Hindu kings who presided over the destinies of this woe-stricken land. The repeated warnings of the past went unheeded. The onslaught began with the Arab conquest of Sindh in the eighth century when the Hindus got a foretaste of what might happen in the future'.

But they failed to set their house in order in spite of the golden opportunities, provided by the long intervals, which separated the next two major holocausts, wrought by Mahmud of Ghazni and Muhammad Ghori respectively. It is really amazing that Prithvi Raj

Chauhan had not adopted any protective measures, after his victory in the first battle of Tarain, to strengthen the defence of Delhi against the invader, who had escaped alive in the first encounter. Majumdar also finds no evidence to show that the great king Lakshmana Sena of Bengal 'bestirred himself early enough to stop the marauding excursions of Bakhtiyar Khilji in Bihar and Bengal'. He is constrained to conclude that

> 'No realistic adjustment, no far-sighted approach to the problem, which had stared them in the face for centuries and threatened their very existence, no improvement in outlook, no elevation of political vision from their petty jealousies and parochial ideals, and consequently no preparation for a concerted defence, commensurate with the extent of the danger – these were the conspicuous traits of the Hindu rulers and their priestly conscience-keepers of the twelfth and thirteenth centuries'.

Majumdar continues the argument that

> 'National consciousness, love of country, and pride of freedom were smothered under the weight of a mass of rituals and social conventions, a petty-minded vanity, and narrow selfishness. Add to this the no infrequent cases of treason and treachery on the part of ministers and other officials, and we shall have a fairly complete picture'.

It is really shocking to note that

> 'At a time, when the country was threatened with a grave peril, the rulers of the land devoted the best part of their energies in mutual fighting. The enormous wealth of the country was spent in building and enriching the temples which they proved unable to protect, whereas the most appropriate use for these resources should have been to organize a common defence against the invaders, backed by a national effort. On the contrary, it was the very fabulous wealth of these defenseless temples and sacred towns which invited the foreigners and contributed greatly to consequent disaster'. (*The History and Culture of the Indian People*; v, BVB, pp. 124-28)

It is also universally recognized that the Indians had to pay heavily not only for their faults but also for their virtues of character. The Rajputs did not resort to treachery in warfare; they were generous and merciful to their enemies. A Rajput would seldom attack his foe when the latter was without adequate armament, injured or fallen on the ground; he would rather give him a fair chance to settle the scores between the parties. A Rajput knew how to fight and die a chivalrous death whereas the sole object of a Muslim soldier was to win by hook or by crook. The doctrine of *Ahhimsa or* non-violence had made the Indians, in general, and the Buddhists among them, in particular, humane and peace-loving to a fault. They displayed non-aggressive, rather non-defensive attitude even in the face of the unscrupulous invaders and thus fell an easy prey to their aggression. The eleventh and twelfth centuries presented the last phase of the declining ancient Indian civilization and culture, during which Toynbee's formula of *Beat-Rally-Rout* played its full circle. Throughout this period, the uncreative political leadership of the Rajputs faced a recurring challenge which it repeatedly failed to meet. At the first holocaust, i.e. during the invasions of Mahmud of Ghazni, the Rajput polity of northern India suffered a serious setback from which it never fully recovered; and at the next crisis, wrought by Muhammad Ghori's invasions, it 'went to pieces irretrievably'. The breakdown of their political and military structure was followed quickly by the disintegration and decay of ancient Indian civilization. Toynbee describes this outcome as due to the 'nemesis of creativity'. To use his phraseology, the Rajput 'leadership had lost its claim to the mimesis of the society at large'; 'nevertheless, it insisted on imposing its will on the society'. It marked 'the most fateful occurrence' in the life-history of the Indian civilization because the Rajputs represented merely 'the dominant minority' who had ceased to be creative in their outlook, were 'hardened into some self-stultifying idolatry – the 'worship of the ghost of the defunct polity'. They crumbled down to the dust before the Turkish invaders owing to their 'sin of pride'.

The Defunct Military Organisation

The military system of the Rajputs was out of date and old-fashioned. There was no dearth of military talent or fighting skill in the country but the Rajput princes exhibited utter lack of imagination in the matter of military organisation. An average Rajput soldier took pride in displaying his muscle-power and personal fighting skills but their leaders failed to harness them into a compact and well-disciplined army on the basis of uniform methods of training and provision of better armaments. The Rajput armies suffered from lack of unitary command; the soldiers were led by their own feudal chiefs who sometimes did not cooperate or coordinate their efforts with one another. The pride, prejudice and the inflated ego of Rajput forbade obedience to a leader belonging to another clan or region. At many critical moments when concentrated and unified action was needed in a battlefield for the attainment of success, the Rajput commanders pursued their individualistic plans and whims and thus neutralized the advantages that they possessed over their enemies. The Rajput chiefs did not keep themselves abreast of the latest developments in war strategy that had been taking place in other countries, nor did they make any contribution towards the development of its techniques. The Hindu soldiers fought mainly with swords and spears while the Muslims were excellent archers; the former fought mostly on foot while the latter used efficient cavalry.

The excessive dependence upon the war elephants and their use in the advance guards proved disastrous for the Rajputs. The beasts fled in terror when attacked fiercely by the Turkish cavalry force, and trampled their own armies under their feet. Mahmud of Ghazni was fascinated by the sight of mighty elephants. He secured no less than 2500 of the trained war elephants from India and made a much better use of the beasts on the war fronts in Central Asia.

Last but not the least, the deep-rooted evil of caste system among the Hindus restricted military duties to a particular caste; and the great mass of the people were rendered psychologically unfit for military service. They did not take interest in the political-cum-military upheavals that shook the country to its very base. Every time the Rajputs did their best to check the advance of the invaders but, unsupported by the national will and the people at large, they failed to hold out for long against the incessant attacks of the Turks. Even the mightiest of the mighty chiefs collapsed after a couple of military debacles, and very often a single battle or the sudden death of the Rajput leader was enough to signal instant fall of the ruling dynasty and annihilation of the whole kingdom.

The Causes of Success of the Turks

On the other hand, the Muslim invaders displayed superiority over their Indian adversaries in many respects. They possessed better military organisation, discipline and coherence. They invariably followed one leader and fully realized the value of unity of command. Their leaders were well-acquainted with the latest techniques of warfare, and they took keen interest in updating their knowledge in this respect. The Turkish invaders were fine archers who depended primarily on the use of efficient and well-disciplined cavalry against the Rajput infantry. They made intelligent use of the strategies; they resorted to sham fights, laid ambuscades, made sudden attacks, kept armies in reserve and employed all means, fair or foul, to win the war. They were aware that they had to fight in a foreign land; therefore, if defeated, they might not be able to return alive to their country.

The Turkish invaders were full of religious zeal; they stood to spread Islam by force of arms. They were made to believe by their clergy that if successful in the *Jihad* (Holy War), this world would lie at their feet; otherwise, they would attain martyrdom in their death and go straight to paradise (*Jannat*). Thus the invaders fought for a cause while the Rajputs had nothing better than clan or class interests to defend.

The love for loot and plunder was, of course, a great material incentive to the Turkish invaders to fight stubbornly. They justly distributed the spoils among themselves and their leader on set principles. They received promotions and reward from their leaders for excellent performance in the war. Naturally, every Muslim soldier, who took part in the expeditions, had his personal career and fortune at stake. No high office, not even that of the sultan or supreme commander of the forces was beyond the reach of a really capable soldier. They produced, even from the ranks of their slaves, highly capable men like Qutubuddin Aibek and Bakhtiyar Khilji, but for whose contributions, Muhammad Ghori might not have been able to conquer the whole of northern India during his lifetime. Attracted by the fabulous wealth of India and the love of adventure, thousands of the Muslim youth from Central Asia swelled the ranks of the Turkish armies as *Ghazis*, who usually brought with them their own horses and weapons of war; on the other hand, the military resources of the Rajput chiefs were confined to their own principalities, whose dimensions were sometimes not greater than those of a modern Indian district. The Turkish commanders could afford to exercise qualitative control over the selection of their soldiers whereas the Rajput princes had to be content with the addition to their numbers alone. Above all, the Muslim victories in other parts of the world boosted their morale and invigorated their efforts to push through against heavy odds to ensure the victory of Islam in the land of the idolaters; they had a perennial source of the manpower from Central Asian Islamic countries in the role of adventurers, freebooters, prospective immigrants and the *ghazis* or religious fanatics. The medieval age set in with the foundation of the Muslim rule in northern India during the first quarter of the thirteenth century.

❑ ❑

4

FOUNDATION OF THE MUSLIM RULE IN NORTHERN INDIA (1206-90)

The Slave Dynasty

The conquest of Lahore and Delhi encouraged Muhammad Ghori to lay the foundation of the Muslim rule in India. He annexed the conquered territories to his Ghaznavid empire. He appointed Qutubuddin Aibek, one of his slave officers, as the viceroy of his Indian possessions and authorized him to carry on the banner of Islam all through the Ganga valley and interior of India as far as possible. As mentioned earlier, Muhammad Ghori was assassinated by one of the Indian rebels of the Khokhar community in northwestern India on March 15, 1206. He had three daughters but no male issue; therefore, his vast dominions were inherited by his three brilliant Turkish slave officers, each one of whom had been married to one of his daughters, and had made a positive contribution towards the extension of his empire and the fulfilment of his imperial objectives. Muhammad Ghori had once observed that his slave generals were just like his sons 'who would inherit his name, fame and the fortunes of his empire'. In his heart of hearts, he had clearly envisaged that his vast Asian empire should be parcelled out among his slave generals, and that, he had deliberately earmarked the respective spheres of influence of each one of them under their distinct commands. As a consequence, after his death, while his nephew sat on the ancestral throne of Ghor, Tajuddin Yaldoz—one of his slave generals, to whom Muhammad Ghori had given his first daughter in marriage, succeeded him on the throne of Ghazni, while Nasiruddin Qabacha became the sovereign ruler of Sindh and Qutubuddin Aibek setup as the independent ruler of his Indian possessions, with his headquarters at Lahore. During the period of his viceroyalty of Lahore, from 1195 to 1205, Qutubuddin had considerably extended the boundaries of his imperial charge by the conquest of Ajmer, Kanauj, Kalinjar and Gwalior, and the Muslim arms had penetrated as far as Bihar and Bengal in the east. Therefore, at the time of his accession, Qutubuddin Aibek had under his control fairly vast possessions of northern and northwestern territories to claim himself as the sovereign Muslim ruler of Hindustan, viz., 'the land of the Hindus'.

The ruling house founded by Qutubuddin Aibek became known as the Slave Dynasty (Mamluk dynasty of the Arabic nomenclature). It ruled northern India from 1206 to 1290, and, in fact, comprised the ruling families of as many as three slave generals—Qutubuddin Aibek, Iltutmish and Balban respectively. All told, it produced nine rulers. As a result, before the thirteenth century was out, the Muslim rule in northern India had been fairly extended and well consolidated. It was Iltutmish who shifted his capital from Lahore to Delhi in 1211 A.D. and laid the foundation of what is known to history as the Sultanate of Delhi.

SECTION 1: QUTBI DYNASTY—THE FIRST RULING HOUSE OF SLAVES (1206-11)

Qutubuddin Aibek

Qutubuddin Aibek was the first Muslim ruler of northern India who untagged himself from the imperial yoke of Ghazni. He was a Turk of the Aibek tribe. When Turkistan was overrun by the 'armies of Islam', he was taken prisoner along with thousands of the other men, women and children, and sold out to a Qazi (judicial officer) of Nishapur in Persia. His kind-hearted master provided facilities for his education in Islamic theology, horse-riding and swordsmanship in the company of his sons. After the death of the Qazi, his sons sold off Qutubuddin to a merchant, who took him to Ghazni, where he was purchased by Muhammad Ghori. He caught the fancy of his imperial master because of his academic and martial qualities and, before long, Qutubuddin rose to the position of *amir-i-akhur* or 'master of the royal stables'. Thereafter, the rise of Qutubuddin as a trustworthy military general of Muhammad Ghori was almost spectacular. He held charge of Ghazni's vast army of Hindustan, and played a leading role in the Indian conquests of Muhammad Ghori. He was married to a daughter of the sultan. After the fall of Prithvi Raj Chauhan and conquest of Delhi and Ajmer, Qutubuddin received appointment as the viceroy of Muhammad Ghori's Indian possessions. He recruited a huge standing army, primarily of the foreign Turkish and Afghan soldiery, and with great competence and determination, considerably expanded his master's possessions in India, the detailed account of which has already been given in the preceding chapter.

Qutubuddin as Independent Ruler: Muhammad Ghori could not name his successor because of his sudden death. Ghiasuddin Mahmud, his nephew and the legal successor was not a very enterprising person, however; and was fully contented with his rule over the ancestral principality of Ghor (Ghor). Therefore, Muhammad Ghori's vast empire was parcelled out among his Ghurid nobles and slave generals. After the death of his master, Qutubuddin Aibek defied the authority of Tajuddin Yaldoz, one of his fellow slave officers, who held control of Ghazni, and setup as independent ruler with his headquarters at Lahore on June 24, 1206, three months after the death of Muhammad Ghori, and thus forestalled the claims of Yaldoz to assert his imperial domination over him. Qutubuddin commenced his reign with the modest titles of *malik* and *sipahasalar*, which had been conferred upon him by Muhammad Ghori. He did not get the *khutba* read nor struck coins in his name to avoid the jealousy of his political rivals, particularly because he was technically still a slave of Muhammad Ghori and had not been granted formal manumission by his master.

Qutubuddin Aibek was fully aware of the strategic importance of the metropolis of Delhi, the imperial capital of the Kaurvas and Pandvas in the pre-historic times of the Mahabharata, and its pivotal position in the latest Rajput amphitheatre of northern India, albeit he stayed put at Lahore to safeguard his nascent state from the sudden attack of Yaldoz from Ghazni or encroachments of Nasiruddin Qabacha from Sindh, both of whom had declared their sovereignty in their respective areas. To the good fortune of Qutubuddin, Tajuddin proved to be a weak ruler and failed to stabilize his position as the sovereign ruler of Ghazni. Meanwhile, the political situation in Central Asia underwent rapid changes. Early in 1208, the Khwarizm Shah invaded Afghanistan and wrested the town of Ghazni from the hands of Tajuddin. The latter was badly mauled and sought refuge in the Punjab to the great chagrin of Qutubuddin Aibek. He could not tolerate the intrusion of an unwelcome guest. Without a moment's loss, Qutubuddin Aibek mustered a strong army and fell upon the intruder like a hawk and drove him out of the Punjab in a couple of months. Flushed with victory, Qutubuddin Aibek triumphantly marched upon Ghazni in 1208-09, apparently 'at the invitation of its people', and took possession of the town. It was there that Ghiasuddin Mahmud, the nephew and legal successor of Muhammad Ghori, sent him the formal deed of manumission from Ghor and conferred the title of *Sultan* upon him.

Qutubuddin Aibek's Ghazni adventure proved very short-lived, however. It so happened that the Khwarizm Shah had to vacate Afghanistan soon afterwards to confront the rising tide of the Mongols in Central Asia. Taking advantage of the changed circumstances, Tajuddin Yaldoz, backed by a powerful section of the Afghan nobility, made his appearance at Ghazni once again, and Qutubuddin Aibek had to beg a hasty retreat from there. He safely retreated into his Indian territories with his army quite intact and felt great relief in entering Lahore which had escaped the challenge from the neighbouring Rajput chiefs during his period of absence. Thereafter, he never thought of interfering into the political complexities of Afghanistan and concentrated his whole-hearted attention in consolidating his hold over whatever Indian possessions he had.

Qutubuddin Aibek's period of rule as independent Muslim chieftain of Lahore lasted about four years from 1206-10. During this period, he did not make fresh conquests nor attempted to engage neighbouring Rajput chiefs into unprovoked warfare. At this precarious stage, Qutubuddin aspired to hold on to his master's dominions and his primary aim as sovereign ruler was to establish the separate entity of his infant Muslim state in northern India whose existence depended upon its military strength and the stabilization of its specific political frontiers. With the object of achieving this aim, in the first instance, he sought to establish friendly relations with the rival Turkish nobles and slave officers of Muhammad Ghori, who held important political-cum-military assignments under him, and strove to bring them firmly under his control by hook or by crook. For strengthening his position, Qutubuddin Aibek, like his master Muhammad Ghori, also made matrimonial alliances, as a political strategy, with the prominent Turkish chiefs and Muslim military generals of his times. He was very happy to marry the daughter of his once arch-rival, Tajuddin Yaldoz, and, on his part, did not hesitate in giving his own sister in marriage to Nasiruddin Qabacha of Sindh. At the same time, following in the footprints of Muhammad Ghori, he created a new class of his own capable and loyal camp-followers and military officers, who became known as the 'Qutbi slaves' in contradistinction to the 'Ghurid slaves' to which category he himself belonged. To cement his bondage of attachment and fidelity with the most capable and trustworthy of his 'Qutbi slaves', Qutubuddin Aibek, was immensely pleased to give his own grown-up daughter in marriage to Iltutmish. At the same time, he avoided clash with the vanquished Rajput chiefs who were eager to recover their lost territories or to overthrow the Turkish yoke. Accordingly, during his short period of independent rule, Qutubuddin had to face continuous resistance from many a Rajput chief and the sporadic uprisings of the volunteer freedom-fighters among the indigenous peasantry and the exasperated urban Indian youth, who stood aghast at the sudden collapse of the Rajput states and the loss of their national and religious independence. As a consequence, Qutubuddin remained constantly engaged with the problem of preserving his nascent Muslim state in the midst of his foes and the hostile Indian populace. Soon after his accession to the throne, the Chandela Rajputs reoccupied Kalinjar and the Pratihars re-conquered Gwalior from the hands of the Turks. Likewise, Harish Chandra, the Gahadavalla chief regained some of his lost territories in the Badaun region but Qutubuddin could do pretty little about it. In fact, large tracts of thickly-populated lands in the heart of the Turkish dominions were still held by the Hindu chieftains whom Qutubuddin Aibek failed to bring under his effective control. His task was only half-done when, in 1210, he met with an accidental fall from his horse while playing *chaugan* (medieval polo) and succumbed to his injuries soon thereafter. He was buried at Lahore.

On the sudden death of Qutubuddin Aibek, the *amirs* of his court at Lahore placed on the throne an inexperienced and nondescript youth, named Aram Shah, purported to be the son of the deceased sultan, apparently to keep the Turkish army under control and to ensure law and order in the state. Aram Shah does not seem to be the real son of Qutubuddin Aibek as Minhaj-us-Siraj refers to only his three daughters and no son, if any. Probably, Aram Shah belonged to the ruling family of Aibek but, otherwise, he had no standing among the Turkish nobility to whom the hereditary succession of an unworthy son of their worthy sire was not acceptable. Aram Shah proved an incompetent ruler and failed to win the confidence of army and the people. The Rajputs of Gwalior and Ranthambhor took the opportunity to throw off the yoke of Turkish overlordship while Ali Mardan, the governor of Bengal, set up as independent ruler at Lakhnauti; and the whole state was engulfed in confusion and anarchy. Above all, the Ghurid chiefs, Tajuddin Yaldoz and Nasiruddin Qabacha, refused to accept Aram Shah as the sovereign ruler of the Turkish dominions in India and prepared to march on Lahore and Delhi. Alarmed by the impending danger of civil war between the rival Turkish factions, some of the Qutbi nobles rose to the occasion and sent distress call to Malik Shamsuddin Iltutmish, who held charge of Badaun as its governor, to assume their leadership and save the nascent Muslim state from disintegration. Iltutmish promptly responded to their appeal and called upon Aram Shah to abdicate. On the refusal of the latter to do so, he was defeated in the plain of Jud near Delhi, and deposed by Iltutmish in 1211; the reign of Aram Shah lasted about eight months. Accordingly, Iltutmish was not the usurper but the consensual candidate of the Turkish nobility to become their king.

An Estimate of Qutubuddin Aibek: Qutubuddin Aibek was a seasoned warrior and a great military general. He acted as the right-hand man of Muhammad Ghori in his military campaigns and made a substantial contribution towards the establishment of the Turkish rule in India. The hero of many a victory, he seldom lost a battle. Hasan Nizami, a native of Nishapur, who came to India along with the armies of Muhammad Ghori and took up service under Qutubuddin Aibek, wrote the first historical work, entitled, *Tajul Ma'asir* – 'the Crown of Exploits', pertaining to the establishment of Muslim rule in northern India; he credits much of Muhammad Ghori's success in India to the untiring and devoted services of Qutubuddin Aibek. According to him, Muhammad Ghori 'supplied the motive power' while Aibek 'organized the expeditions and executed the plans' of his master.

Qutubuddin was not a brilliant administrator, however. He setup what may be termed as the police state with the help of a strong military power. He recruited a huge army of foreign Turkish and Afghan mercenaries and crusaders of Islam (*ghazis*) to fight against the infidels (*kafirs*), and heavily garrisoned his capital and other important towns to suppress revolts and establish law and order in his dominions. Civil administration was left in the hands of village panchayats and other local agencies of the pre-Muslim era. He granted partial civil liberties to his Hindu subjects, now addressed as the *zimmis* in return for the payment of *jaziya.* Wars between the Indians and the invaders were, obviously, full of blood-shed on both sides, but there is ample evidence to show that every Turkish victory was usually followed by the forcible conversion of the prisoners of war besides enslavement of thousands of unarmed civilians, including men, women and children, demolition of Hindu temples and construction of mosques on their ruins etc., to strike awe and terror in the hearts of the vanquished. Qutubuddin Aibek rendered great services to the cause of Islam in India. In the words of Hasan Nizami, 'by his orders, the precepts of Islam received great promulgation and the sun of righteousness cast its shadow on the countries of Hind from the heavens of God's assistance'.

Qutubuddin Aibek showed some taste for architecture by building two magnificent mosques, one at Delhi and the other at Ajmer. He laid the foundation of the first of the so-called 'seven cities' of medieval Delhi by constructing buildings in the vicinity of the old Rajput fort, called *Quila-i-Rai Pithaura*. He also started the construction of a tower of victory, called the Qutub Minar in 1199 A.D.—the tallest stone tower in India, after the name of Khwaja Qutubuddin Bakhtiyar Kaki, a famous Sufi saint of his times; it was completed by Iltutmish. The first and the oldest mosque of Delhi, namely the *Qubbat al-Islam* or *Quwwat al-Islam* was constructed by Qutubuddin Aibek 'in H. 587 (1192 A.D.) after demolishing the temple, built by Prithvi Raj, and leaving certain parts of the temple (outside the mosque proper); and when he returned from Ghazni in H.592 (1197-98 A.D.), he started building, under orders from Shihabuddin (Muhammad) Ghori, a huge mosque of inimitable red stones, and certain (other) parts of the temple were (also) included in the mosque'. Thereafter, when Iltutmish became the king, he extended the mosque by the construction, on both sides of it, edifices of white stones, and by completing the construction of the Qutub Minar, situated on the third side of it. According to another contemporary version, the materials of 27 idol temples, on each of which 2,000,000 *Delhiwals* (a gold coin of high denomination, prevalent in the Rajput era) had been spent, were used in the construction of the above mosque.

SECTION 2: SHAMSI OR THE FIRST ILBARI DYNASTY (1211-66)

Shamsuddin Iltutmish (1211-36)

Early Career and Accession: Shamsuddin Iltutmish or Altamish, who deposed Aram Shah and took the reins of the Turkish government, was a slave officer and son-in-law of Qutubuddin Aibek. He belonged to a respectable family of the Ilbari Turks. It is said that, being a very handsome and intelligent boy, he excited the jealousy of his half-brothers, who, after the death of their polygamous father, deceitfully passed him on to a slave-trader. After passing through many hands as a slave, he was brought to Delhi and purchased by Qutubuddin Aibek for a hundred thousand *jitals* (equivalent to 2,000 silver *tankas*).

The Turkish rule brought in its train to India the evil system of slave-trade which had become a legally-organized and flourishing profession throughout the Muslim world. In the words of K A Nizami, 'some enterprising slave-merchants carefully picked up a few of the most promising young Turkish slaves and trained them not for menial work...but for the service of the kings and governors. These selected slaves were generally brought up with the sons of their master; but spending money on their education was an investment that paid itself many times over...They had to be taught all subjects necessary for government...what the kings and high officers wanted were Turkish slaves to whom proper military and academic instruction had been given, and who could be appointed to a responsible office after a few years of probation'. (*Comp. HI*; v, pp. 196-97). Iltutmish belonged to this category of gifted slaves who had been specially educated and trained as administrator and warrior. That is why he quickly rose to become the *amir-i-shikar* and son-in-law of Qutubuddin Aibek before long. He received appointments as the governor of the *iqtas* of Gwalior and Badaun (Bulandshahr) in quick succession during the viceroyalty of Qutubuddin Aibek. Iltutmish was the most trustworthy of Qutubuddin's lieutenants; he had been granted formal manumission by his master before the latter assumed his sovereignty in 1206. Therefore, Iltutmish seems to have been fully groomed to become the rightful successor of Qutubuddin Aibek. He was governor of Badaun at the time of the death of Qutubuddin Aibek and showed no pretensions to challenge the authority of Aram Shah, royal nominee to the throne, until he was invited by the Turkish nobility of Delhi to proceed against him in the interests of the state. He, therefore, came forward as the saviour of the newly established Muslim kingdom and took the reins of government in his hands without much bloodshed. Iltutmish had no hereditary claim to the Turkish crown but he was not a usurper. His claim to royalty was, obviously, based on his competence and popular support of the Turkish military officers and the army. The recognition of this principle of *survival of the fittest* went a long way in the rapid expansion and strengthening of the Muslim rule in India.

Transfer of Capital to Delhi: Iltutmish fully realized the political and strategic importance of Delhi in preference to Lahore as the headquarters of the Turkish dominions in India and, instantaneously, shifted his capital there. He was, in fact, the real founder of the Sultanate of Delhi so-called. He proved a very capable and strong ruler and enjoyed a long reign of 46 years from 1211 to 1260. He gave a tentative shape to the geographical dimensions of the state, protected it from external dangers and internal forces of disruption, and laid the rudiments of Muslim civil administration in India. Hereafter, Delhi became the hub of all political and military activities of the Muslim rule and came to occupy premier position as the imperial capital of Hindustan. It continued to enjoy this privileged status throughout the medieval period.

Establishment of the Islamic State: The Turks had brought with them a theocratic concept of state according to which the sultanate of Delhi was declared 'an Islamic state'. Accordingly, Iltutmish was expected to enforce the Islamic law (*shariat*) and administer his dominions in a way to transform the *dar-ul-harb*, viz., "land of the infidels' into *dar-ul-Islam*. Iltutmish professed allegiance to the Khalifa of Baghdad and duly received investiture from him, whether he had made a special request to him or obtained it voluntarily from the latter is not known. The Khalifa conferred the title of *Sultan-i-Azam* (great sultan) 'in possession of all the lands and sea which he had conquered' on him. Iltutmish was, in fact, a sovereign ruler who depended solely on his military strength to sustain himself, but the sultans of Delhi, with a few exceptions, usually felt pride in securing this recognition and 'fastening the fiction of Khilafat on the sultanate of Delhi' because 'being foreign adventurers, who were called upon to rule over vast territories of the country, inhabited primarily by the Hindus, they thought it politically expedient to maintain formal contacts with the Islamic world beyond the Khyber so as to produce a psychic of fear among the Hindus by alluding to the potential source of their strength' *(Advanced Study, i , p. 294)*. They were conferred additional titles such as *nasir-i-amir-ul-momnin* – 'assistant of the leader of the faithful' and *yamin-ul-khalifa*, viz., 'the right-hand man of the Khalifa' etc. Iltutmish was the first sultan of Delhi who struck gold and silver coins in his name, describing himself as the 'lieutenant of the Khalifa'.

Difficulties of Iltutmish: Iltutmish ascended the throne at Delhi without much difficulty but his accession did not go unchallenged. During the short reign of Aram Shah, some of the provincial governors had raised their standards of revolt. Ali Mardan Khalji of Bihar and Bengal had cut off all connections with Lahore and Delhi and tended to behave as independent ruler. Most of the Turkish nobles, under the employ of Qutubuddin Aibek, submitted to Iltutmish but some of them, who had rushed forward from different places near Delhi, and who felt jealous of Iltutmish – 'one of their equal rising to the position of the sultan', were not willing to recognize him as their master without measuring their swords with him. Therefore, immediately after defeating Aram Shah in a skirmish at Jud, Iltutmish fell upon the army camp of the doubting Thomases and completely annihilated them. In the words of Khwaja Nizamuddin Ahmad, 'as the lamp of his greatness had been illuminated by the light of divine help, the attempts made by his foolish enemies to extinguish it had no other effect than their own discomfiture; they all became food for the merciless sword, and the field of his empire was cleared of the thorns and weeds of their existence'. (*Tabqat-i-Akbari*, vol. i, Eng. Trs. by Brajendra Nath De, p. 64).

Iltutmish had to face persistent hostility of his Ghurid rivals, Tajuddin Yaldoz of Ghazni and Nasiruddin Qabacha of Sindh who had bluntly refused to acknowledges Aram Shah as the rightful successor of Qutubuddin Aibek. They watched with concern the change of guards at Delhi, and apparently felt reconciled to the accession of Iltutmish but with a grain of salt. Nevertheless, they were his arch enemies and left no stone unturned to dislodge him from power until they were crushed and liquidated at the hands of Iltutmish. The impending contest of Iltutmish with his Turkish rivals was soon intermingled and eclipsed by the more dangerous onslaught of Changez Khan and his Mongol hordes from Central Asia against whom Iltutmish had to fight a life and death struggle to safeguard his nascent Turkish state in India. Above all, the setup of 'an Islamic state' in the midst of the hostile population of the *kafirs* or infidels, either condemned as *kabil-i-gardan zadni* (worthy of being put to the sword) in case of their refusal to convert to Islam, or to acknowledge their humiliating status as *zimmis*, viz., the second-class citizens of the state on payment of the exorbitant toll tax or *jaziya*, was really an uphill task. Nevertheless, Iltutmish proved himself equal to the task and faced all these difficulties with courage and determination.

Important Events of his Reign

The End of Tajuddin Yaldoz: Tajuddin Yaldoz was by far the most formidable and treacherous rival of Iltutmish. Having been entrusted the charge of Ghazni, the imperial capital of Muhammad Ghori, he rightly or wrongly considered himself to be the rightful successor of his master; it was this factor which made him the eternal foe of all the incumbents of viceroyalty of Muhammad Ghori's Indian possessions. He had refused to acknowledge the accession of Aram Shah and was vigorously preparing to march on Lahore but Iltutmish forestalled him by taking possession of Delhi. Chastened by the news about the subsequent defeat and deposition of Aram Shah at the hands of the latter, Tajuddin called off his proposed attack on Lahore, changed the tone of his diplomatic gestures and tried to assert his political dominance over Iltutmish by sending the robes of honour and royal canopy in the style of his overlord at the time of his coronation at Delhi. As a shrewd politician, Iltutmish pocketed the insult by assuming complete silence over this incident for the time being but always remained apprehensive about the protection of the northern frontiers of his kingdom. To the misfortune of Tajuddin, he was himself defeated by Alauddin Muhammad, the Khwarizm Shah, before long and retreated towards the Punjab. He preferred his claim to the throne of Delhi on the pretension of being the senior most Ghurid officer and, in 1215, marched upon Delhi with a threatening posture. Tajuddin was defeated by Iltutmish in the battlefield of Tarain (Taraori) and taken prisoner. He was kept in confinement in the fortress of Badaun and put to death soon thereafter. It eliminated the most serious contender to the throne of Delhi and liberated it from the imperial domination of Ghazni. Nevertheless, in spite of his strenuous military deployments and vigilance, Iltutmish's hold on the western Punjab was not very effective.

Protracted struggle against Nasiruddin Qabacha: The Ghurid general Nasiruddin Qabacha, the governor of Sindh, was the second most formidable political rival of Iltutmish. His importance as the equally serious contender to the throne of Delhi, within India, can be gauged from the fact that he had been given not one but two daughters in marriage, in succession, by Qutubuddin Aibek, though Iltutmish was his eldest son-in-law. He had conquered the region of Multan and Uchh and was allowed to retain these territories also as his charge. On the death of Aibek, he not only refused to acknowledge Aram Shah as his rightful successor but also overran some other territories of southwestern Punjab. When Tajuddin Yaldoz entered Punjab in 1214-15, Qabacha fought an indecisive battle with him also, and took possession of Lahore after the fall of Tajuddin, thus posing a real challenge to the sovereignty of Iltutmish. His encroachments in the Punjab squeezed the northern borders of Delhi kingdom to as far as Sialkot only'. Therefore, it left no alternative with Iltutmish but to declare war against him immediately after defeating Tajuddin. On the advancement of troops from Delhi, Qabacha vacated Lahore and retreated towards Multan but Iltutmish gave him a hot chase and inflicted a crushing defeat on him at Mansura, on the banks of the Chenab. Iltutmish did nor think it prudent to rush head-on into the un-traversed and well-defended territories of his adversary and returned to Delhi to tackle more pressing problems of the state. It provided a breather to Nasiruddin who continued to rule over his possessions uninterrupted for about another decade. During this period, his reputation as one of the sovereign Muslim chiefs of Hindustan, soared high when 'many of the great men of Khurasan, Ghur and Ghazni, after being overthrown by Changez Khan, entered his service, and he conferred favours and gifts over every one of them'. (*Tabkat-i-Akbari*, i, p. 48).

In 1227, Iltutmish redirected his attention towards Nasiruddin Qabacha and surprised him by launching a sudden attack on the border post of Uchh. The siege of Uchh, which was directed by Iltutmish under his personal supervision, lasted two months and 25 days before it was vacated by the besieged garrison after heavy losses. It obliged Nasiruddin to take the field in person against the army of Delhi. He took a stand against Iltutmish at the stronghold of Bhakkar which was very heavily defended. After a prolonged siege, when the fall of Bhakkar became imminent, Qabacha, realizing the gravity of the situation, made overtures for peace and sent his son, Masud Behram, as his emissary for this purpose. Instead of negotiating a settlement, Iltutmish highhandedly imprisoned his son and demanded unconditional surrender of Qabacha. Completely unnerved by the aggressive posture of Iltutmish, Qabacha lost heart and, in his bid to flee from Bhakkar, was drowned in the river Sindh while crossing it. The fall of Nasiruddin Qabacha marked the end of Sindh's isolation from Delhi. The Sumra chief of Debal hastened to acknowledge the suzerainty of Iltutmish and the provinces of Multan and Uchh were declared annexed to the sultanate of Delhi. The conquest of Sindh yet remained incomplete but Iltutmish returned to Delhi in triumph after deputing his Vazir, Muhammad Junaidi and certain other commanders to complete the task.

The Mongol Menace

About this time, the Mongol menace had assumed alarming proportions in Central Asia. The two most barbaric and ferocious nomadic races of the Turks and the Mongols once formed a part of the Tatar or Tartar tribes who inhabited the vast steppes of northern Asia. With the passage of time and the global climatic changes, they gradually descended down into the plains of Central Asia, preceded by the Turks and the Mongols following close upon their heels. They were 'the people, who, in the first half of the thirteenth century, shook the foundations of every kingdom from China to the Adriatic Sea in their campaigns'. (*Encyclopaedia of Islam*, London, 1913, p. 856). The Turks were, obviously, the first to come into contact and deadly confrontation with the Arabic crusaders of Islam after their conversion to the new faith by the Prophet Muhammad (c.570-632 A.D.). Their hearths and homes were vandalized by the Arabs, thousands of them being killed in the holocaust, and the rest being enslaved and forcibly converted to Islam. It swelled the armies of Islam to spread their aggressive campaigns in the far-off lands, including India, now under the leadership of their Turkish slave officers.

The Mongols came into prominence with the emergence of Changez Khan (c. 1162-1227)—'the empire-builder', when they acquired the status of a ruling tribe among the Tatars. He and his followers were not Muslims but professed, what is called the *shamanist* faith—a varied form of Buddhism, which had spread in Central Asia since long. The word Mongol was changed into Moghul or Mughal when they came into contact with the Persian culture and entered the fold of Islam much later. They made their appearance on the northwestern borders of India in 1220-21 during the reign of Iltutmish. It so happened that Alauddin Muhammad, the ruler of Khwarizm – 'the greatest Muslim monarch of the age', after his defeat at the hands of Changez Khan, fled towards the Caspian Sea while his eldest son, Jalaluddin Mankbarni, retreated into Afghanistan. The latter was followed by Changez Khan in hot chase. Hard-pressed, Mankbarni passed through the Khyber to enter the Indus valley and asked for help from Iltutmish to fight against the Mongols. Setting aside the religious considerations, Iltutmish threw the emissary of Mankbarni into prison and refused to oblige the intruder with the plea that the climate of India would not be suitable for him, and, at the same time, he mustered his troops and prepared to fight against the fugitive

Muslim chief. In disappointment, Alauddin Mankbarni turned towards Sindh to take on Nasiruddin Qabacha to the great relief of Iltutmish. He thus saved the newly established Turkish kingdom of Delhi from the fury of the Mongols who retraced their steps towards Central Asia without venturing into the Indian territories. Because of the tough resistance put up by Nasiruddin Qabacha, Mankbarni failed to establish his foothold in Sindh also, and, ultimately, retreated towards Iran through the desert of Mekran. Iltutmish was so much scared of the Mongols that he neither tried to conquer the western Punjab nor launched any military expedition against Qabacha until after the death of Changez Khan in 1227.

Reconquest of Bihar and Bengal: After the death of Qutubuddin Aibek, Ali Mardan, the governor of Bihar and Bengal, had stopped paying tribute to Delhi and setup as independent ruler at Lakhnauti with the title of sultan Alauddin Khalji. Two years later, he was assassinated by some of his rebellious officers because of his tyrannical rule, but his son and successor, Hisamuddin Iwaz, who ascended the throne of Lakhnauti with the title of Ghiyasuddin, proved a capable ruler. He got the Khutba read and coins struck in his name to assert his sovereignty, and also succeeded in extracting tribute from the neighbouring Hindu chieftains of Jajnagar, Tirhut, Vanga and Kamarupa. The setup of two rival Turkish monarchies in northern India was too much for Iltutmish to bear with; therefore, after the fear of Mongol invasion receded, he dispatched a military expedition for the recovery of Bihar and Bengal. In 1225-26, he took the field personally against Iwaz and wrested south Bihar from his hands, while Iwaz offered his nominal submission to Iltutmish without a fight on the promise of paying war indemnity and annual tribute. Iltutmish appointed Malik Alauddin Jani as the governor of Bihar and returned to Delhi. Nevertheless, as soon as the sultan turned his back, Ghiyasuddin reasserted his independence and reoccupied south Bihar. It necessitated the dispatch of a second expedition to Lakhnauti, which was led by the eldest son of Iltutmish, named Nasiruddin Mahmud. Prince Nasiruddin was successful in re-conquering both the provinces of Bihar and Bengal from the hands of the rebellious chief; Iwaz was defeated and killed in the battlefield and Lakhnauti was taken possession of by the royal forces. Elated to hear of this grand victory, Iltutmish was pleased to appoint the victorious crown prince as the viceroy of Bihar and Bengal. To the great shock of the sultan, however, prince Nasiruddin died a premature death in harness, throwing Bihar and Bengal into turmoil once again. Iltutmish had, therefore, to send fresh reinforcements to supplement the battered royal army, now commanded by his trustworthy officer, Malik Alauddin Jani, the ex-governor of south Bihar. He suppressed the rebellious elements and successfully restored law and order in Bengal and Bihar. Jani received appointment as the governor of Bengal as a reward for his services, but, in order to maintain firm control over the eastern territories, Iltutmish separated Bihar from Bengal permanently and appointed a separate governor to take charge of the latter.

Confrontation with the Rajputs

The Hindus of northern and central India were not reconciled with the loss of their sovereignty and religious freedom at the hands of the foreign armies of aggression. The Muslim historians of the medieval period record that the Turkish victories were almost invariably accompanied by the wanton pillage of the towns and villages, desecration of temples, destruction of public property and cultural institutions, and general massacre of the civilian population. The combatants who submitted and laid down their arms were beheaded or converted to Islam on pain of death. The system of slavery having become a legalized institution in the Muslim countries, the victorious Turks took pride in capturing large numbers of the unarmed men and women as booty, to be enslaved for personal service or for sale like cattle in the foreign markets. After the establishment of the Turkish rule, the Hindu subjects were declared as *zimmis* and granted partial civil liberties on the condition of paying *jaziya.* The vanquished Rajput chiefs, who offered submission under duress, were made to pay annual tribute or *jaziya* on behalf of their Hindu population collectively. The indigenous inhabitants of the land and their leaders were induced to embrace Islam to liberate themselves from the payment of *jaziya* and other handicaps and indignities to which they were submitted by the Muslim state.

Obviously, none of the vanquished Rajput chiefs was a willing partner of the foreign Turkish rule, and the Sultanate of Delhi was never popular with the Hindus of the country; they all formed a disgruntled lot, ever eager to take up arms against it at the first opportunity. Some of the Rajput chiefs had thrown off the Turkish yoke and recovered many of the important towns and territories lost to the Turks immediately after the death of Muhammad Ghori. Qutubuddin Aibek avoided direct confrontation with them and suffered the loss of many historic towns like Varanasi, Kanauj, Kalinjar and Gwalior. Kalinjar was lost to the Chandellas. The *iqta* of Gwalior, which included the towns of Narwar, Gwalior and Jhansi, where Iltutmish had held his first assignment as its governor under Qutubuddin Aibek, was re-conquered by the Pariharas and remained under their sway at least from 1220 to 1233. The weak rule of Aram Shah further encouraged the Hindus to organize armed resistance against the sultanate of Delhi, leading to the emergence of many independent Hindu principalities within and close to the borders of the Turkish dominions. During the first 15 years of his reign, Iltutmish was unable to take any action against them because of his deadly conflict with his Turkish rivals, besides the Mongols, and his preoccupation with the protection and defense of northwestern borders of his state. It was only after the fall of his arch enemy Tajuddin Yaldoz, and retreat of the Mongols and elimination of danger from across the Hindu Kush that he directed his attention towards the Rajputs and launched a full-fledged campaign them. The uprisings of the Rajputs and an account of their confrontation with Iltutmish and his successors about this time are in order.

Unfinished Struggle for the Subjugation of Ranthambhor: Like Ajmer, the historic fort of Ranthambhor, situated in the erstwhile Jaipur state in Madhya Pradesh, was founded by yet another offshoot of the Chauhans (Chahamanas) of Sakambhari (Sambhar). Variously spelt by the Muslim historians as Rantambor, Rintambor or Runtamboor, the name of Ranthambhor is identified by Cole Brooke with the Sanskrit epithet *rana-sthama-bhramara*, viz., 'the bee of the pillar of war'. According to Minhaj-us-Siraj, the author of *Tabqat-i-Nasiri*, 'it was celebrated in all parts of Hindustan, for its great strength and security', while the Rajput annals describe that this 'invincible fort was invaded by the enemies more than 70 times, but none of them was able to take it'. The Chauhans of Ranthambhor were also related to the ruling house of Ajmer. Towards the close of the thirteenth century, Ranthambhor was ruled by Govindraja Chauhan who was a feudatory of Ajmer. As narrated earlier, after the fall of Prithvi Raj (III) Chauhan, Qutubuddin Aibek, the lieutenant of Muhammad Ghori in India, intended to install Govindraja or Govind Rai (not to be confused with his namesake, the chief of Ranthambhor), a minor son of Prithvi Raj, as his puppet nominee on the vacant throne of Ajmer, but Hari Rai alias Hariraja, a brother of the fallen hero, who had escaped alive from the debacle of Tarain, took possession of Ajmer and prepared for the defence of the Chauhan capital against the Turks. Brushing aside the claim of his nephew, Hariraja formally installed himself on the throne and declared his sovereignty with the consensus of the prominent Chauhan stalwarts. It was after the occupation of Delhi that Aibek made a frontal attack on Ajmer and wrested the stronghold from the Rajputs in 1294 after a prolonged siege, which was accompanied by a lot of bloodbath and huge loss of life on both sides. The besieged garrison perished in the struggle, and the handful of survivors, including their chief Hariraja, performed *Jauhar* by burning themselves on the funeral pyre to save them from the humiliation of defeat and captivity at the hands of the foe. Recapitulation of this incident here is necessitated to bring home the fact that it was the family of the deceased Hariraja and some other members of the royalty, who were helped to escape from the fort by its defenders before the dreadful finale. The fugitives took shelter in the fort of Ranthambhor where they were accorded cordial reception and protection by its reigning chief Govindraja.

After the capture of Ajmer, it was declared annexed to the Turkish dominions by Qutubuddin Aibek. He appointed a Turkish governor at Ajmer, and with it the kingdom of Prithvi Raj Chauhan came to an end. As Ranthambhor had been a tributary of Prithvi Raj, when the Turkish army prepared to march on it from Ajmer, Govindraja, having realized the fate of the heavily out-numbered Rajput defenders of Ajmer, and finding him too weak to take a determined stand against the Turks, exercised discretion as the better part of valour and, instead of facing complete peril, hastened to acknowledge the nominal suzerainty of Delhi. Nevertheless, after a couple of years, Valanadeva or Balhana of the Muslim chroniclers – the son and successor of Govindraja, defied the Turkish authority and stopped payment of annual tribute to Delhi sometime after 1215. About that time, Iltutmish failed to take any action against the rebellious Rajput chief because of his preoccupations, and Ranthambhor enjoyed freedom for about a decade during the reigns of Balhana and his son Prahladana. Of course, the existence of a hostile Rajput power at Ranthambhor, so close to the Turkish borders, constantly rankled in the eyes of Iltutmish. Therefore, when he decided to launch his military campaigns against the Rajputs in 1226, Ranthambhor was the first to attract his attention. The fort was conquered by him after a protracted siege which lasted quite a few months.

Minhaj-us-Siraj states that Iltutmish laid his hands on the fort of Mandur or Mandawar, probably Mandsor, the headquarters of the Paramaras in Malwa, in the year following and conquered it.

Ranthambhor remained beyond the pale of the Turkish rule during the remaining part of the reign of Iltutmish, but immediately after his death, there was an uprising in the state and the rebels, who comprised the discontented peasantry of the region and were commanded by Vagbhata, the younger son of Balhana, laid siege to the fort. Sultana Raziyya (1236-40) sent reinforcements from Delhi under the command of Malik Qutubuddin Hasan Ghuri to suppress the uprising. He defeated the besiegers and compelled them to raise the siege of the fort for a short while but failed to break their resistance. Nevertheless, he succeeded in securing the liberation of some of the besieged Turkish troops, and after, demolishing the defences of the fort, returned to Delhi.

Vagbhata took possession of Ranthambhor, rebuilt its defences and restored the sovereignty of his family. Gradually, he retrieved most of the lost territories of his predecessors and extended the boundaries of his state by defeating the neighbouring Rajput chiefs of Malwa and Gujarat. He ruled over Ranthambhor for twelve years and proved a successful and popular king. So was his son and successor, Jaitrasimha, who enjoyed a fairly long reign. Both of them have been described as 'the greatest Rais of Hindustan' by Minhaj-us-Siraj. They built many forts and setup military posts all along the Turkish borders to ward off the Muslim invasions. Ulugh Khan (later sultan Balban), commander-in-chief of the sultans, invaded Ranthambhor in 1248 and 1253 respectively, during the reigns of Iltutmish's successors but failed to conquer it, and 'had to rest content only by securing some spoils'. In 1259, Jaitrasimha was discomforted by the Turkish army of invasion, dispatched by Sultan Nasiruddin Mahmud (1246-65), in a surprise attack, but he soon reassembled his forces and pushed them out of his dominions. In 1283, on his death, Jaitrasimha was succeeded by his son Hammir, who was also a formidable sovereign ruler. Ranthambhor maintained its independence in the teeth of opposition from the sultans of Delhi, till the end of the thirteenth century, and it was left to Alauddin Khalji to conquer it in 1301.

Subjugation of Jalor (1229): To pick up the threads of the story from Iltutmish again, after the conquest of Ranthambhor, Iltutmish assaulted the Chauhan stronghold of Jalor sometime in 1228-29. It was then ruled by Udayasimha or Udai Singh, the grandson of Kirtipala —a scion of the ruling family of Nadol, who had laid the foundation of this town in 1178. The rulers of Jalor were known to have put up a continuous fight against *Turushkas* or the Turkish invaders ever since the occupation of Delhi by them; the Rajputs had defeated and repulsed their attacks more than once. Hasan Nizami tells us that, after the fall of Rantambor and Mandur, the Turkish nobles 'represented to His Majesty that the inhabitants of the fort of Jalewar (Jalor) had determined to revenge the blood, which had been shed', and that, 'once or twice, mention of the evil deeds and improprieties of the people was made before the sublime throne. Shamsuddin, accordingly, assembled a large army and headed by a number of the pillars of the state, such as..., valiant men and skilful archers, who could in a dark night, hit with their arrows the mirror on the forehead of an elephant', and marched on Jalor. After a number of bloody skirmishes, Udai Singh retired into the fort and prepared for defence. The Turkish siege of the fort lasted many days and Udai Singh put up a stout resistance, but was, ultimately, obliged to acknowledge the suzerainty of the sultan on the presentation of barely 200 horses and 200 elephants as a tribute.

Partial success of the Turkish arms on other war fronts: The bloody carnage of Iltutmish against the Rajputs bore little fruit. According to the researches of A.B.M. Habibullah, 'the extent of the revival of Hindu Powers and the difficulties facing the Delhi troops were heavily underlined by the inconclusive results of Iltutmish's operations in Rajputana'. He writes that

> 'Opening the campaign in A.D. 1226, he (Iltutmish) took Ranthambhor and Mandawar, and humbled Jalor, but was repulsed with heavy losses by the Guhilots from Nagda. Rajput records speak also of his failure in an attack on the Chaulukyas of Gujarat. A similar expedition, conducted by one of his officers against the Chauhans of Bundi, also ended in failure. While he recaptured Bayana and Tahangarh, and widened the Ajmer base by garrisoning the neighbouring positions of Lawah, Kasili and Sambhar, his success proved temporary, for it failed to arrest the Chauhan revival'. (*History and Culture of the Indian People*, BVB, v, p.134)

The military campaigns of Iltutmish 'on the southern front' elsewhere also did not produce more decisive results. He recaptured the fort of Gwalior after a year-long siege in 1231-32 from the Parihara chief, Mangal Deo, under very dramatic circumstances; having lost most of their fighters and run out of their food stuff and ammunition, the Rajputs secretly evacuated the fort one dark night to the great surprise of the besiegers. It took some time before the Turks realized the situation and entered the deserted fort. Iltutmish heavily garrisoned the fort under the command of Malik Rashiduddin as its governor but the power of the Rajputs could not be broken and they continued to hold the whole of the countryside of Gwalior state as far as Jhansi under their firm control. A big slice of the Jodhpur state, including the fort of Nagaur, was overrun and annexed to the sultanate but Turkish attack on Nagada, the capital of Guhilots, proved a failure; and Iltutmish suffered a defeat at the hands of Rana Kshetra Singh. The Turks were repulsed with heavy losses by the Chaulukyas of Gujarat as well. Iltutmish did not lose heart, however, and led yet another expedition into Malwa under his personal command in 1234-35, in which he plundered the towns of Bhilsa (Vidisha) and Ujjain. He desecrated and demolished the Mahakal temple of Ujjain, and carried on wanton destruction in the countryside before returning to Delhi, over-laden with booty. But, "a seemingly successful raid into Malwa in 1234-35 similarly gave Iltutmish more plunder and righteous satisfaction than political or military advantage, for the Paramaras remained in undisturbed possession of the country for the rest of the century." (Habibullah—*Foundation of the Muslim Rule in India*; p.103)

Likewise, the Turkish operations south of the river Yamuna also proved abortive. Malik Tayasai, who led an expedition through Central India against the Chandellas, was 'provided a foretaste' of a new rising power of the Rajputs around Narwar; who made a surprise attack and inflicted a defeat on the royal army during its return march to Delhi. It was 'by great exertion that Tayasai was able to extricate his forces and reach Gwalior', the nearest Turkish post. The hero of this Rajput exploit was Rana Chahara Deva of Jajapella (Yajvapalla) dynasty, which was destined to supplant the Pariharas in Narwar and Gwalior sometime after 1247.

Military Campaigns in the Ganga Valley: The mention of Badaun, Kanauj and Varanasi among the conquests of Iltutmish by Minhaj-us-Siraj in *Tabakat-i-Nasiri*, though these towns had been conquered earlier by Qutubuddin Aibek during his viceroyalty of Muhammad Ghori, makes us believe that all these territories of the Ganga valley had overthrown the Turkish rule after the death of Ghori, either during the rule of Aibek or soon thereafter. Nothing is heard about the erstwhile imperial Gahadavalla line of Kanauj but, probably, there was a revival of the Rashtrakuta ruling family, represented by Lakhanpala. A

Mahasamanta of the Rashtrakuta line, named Bharahadeva, is known to have been ruling somewhere in the country of the Kanyakubjadesa (Kanauj) in the beginning of the thirteenth century. Large tracts of land, north of the Ganga, in modern Uttar Pradesh, were still dotted with a number of autonomous Hindu states and estates. Not far from Badaun, there flourished an independent state of the Rajputs in Katehar (Rohilkhand), who had driven out the Muslim forces of occupation from there and cut off all contacts with Delhi; Ahichhatra (mod. Anola) was their headquarters. Katehar (Rohilkhand), with its capital Ahichhatra, was conquered by Iltutmish after a long siege and numerous battles in which more than two *lakhs* of the Muslim soldiers are said to have been killed. Together, these Rajput chiefs barred the uninterrupted extension of the Turkish arms in northern and central India much beyond the rule of Iltutmish and Balban.

Iltutmish deputed his eldest son Nasiruddin Mahmud to undertake military expeditions to suppress the refractory Hindu chieftains in the Ganga valley. In the words of Minhaj-us-Siraj, the crown prince 'was an intelligent, learned and wise prince, and was possessed of exceeding bravery, courage, generosity and benevolence. The first charge that the sultan had confided to him was that of Hansi. Sometime in 623 H (1226 A.D.), Oudh was entrusted to him. In that country, the prince exhibited many estimable qualities. He fought several battles, and, by his boldness and bravery, he made his name famous in the annals of Hindustan. He overthrew and sent to hell the accursed Bartuh, under whose hands and sword more than one hundred and twenty thousand Musalmans had received martyrdom. He overthrew the rebel infidels of Oudh and brought a body of them into submission'. (*Tabakat-i-Nasiri* in E&D. ii, p. 325). According to a Jain source, Bartuh was probably Bharata Pala of the Chauhan family, who had their capital at Chhandavada or Chandwar on the river Yamuna, near mod. Firozabad, in the district of Agra. (BVB, pp.349-50).

Inclusive struggle to subjugate the Khokhars: The Khokhars in central Punjab, though defeated and formally subjugated by Muhammad Ghori, were not reconciled themselves to the loss of their freedom at the hands of the foreign invaders. It resulted, ultimately, in the assassination of Muhammad Ghori at the hands of a Khokhar rebel when he was encamped at Dhamyak, in March 1206, in the course of his last military campaign to India in his bid to restore law and order in the northwest frontier. Qutubuddin Aibek failed to crush the Khokhars, nor could Iltutmish take any effective measures to bring them under control. In 1235, Iltutmish, himself led a military expedition against the Khokhars; the town of Baniyan, which constituted the nucleus of their power in the Salt Range, was conquered by him, but the Khokhars showed no signs of appeasement. Totally exhausted by continuous warfare, Iltutmish fell ill, returned to Delhi and died in his sick-bed in April 1236. He was buried in a magnificent tomb that he had got built for himself in Delhi.

An Estimate of Iltutmish

Shamsuddin Iltutmish was the real founder of the Sultanate of Delhi. Though not a brilliant administrator, he was a capable ruler who restored law and order within the territories under his direct control. He established a military dictatorship like that of Qutubuddin Aibek but with the difference that all the reins of government were concentrated in his own hands. Iltutmish laid the foundation of an absolute monarchy of the Turks in northern India. He made all the key appointments of central ministers and regional military governors himself; the *wazir* (prime minister), *sadar-i-jahan* (head of the ecclesiastical affairs) and the chief *qazi* (justice of peace) held office during his pleasure, and were responsible to him directly. He did not permit the Turkish nobility to interfere in the state affairs beyond certain limits. The disaffected and insubordinate Ghurid or Qutbi officers were gradually downgraded or eliminated.

Iltutmish created an entirely new class of the Muslim bureaucracy which comprised his personal Turkish slave officers, called the Shamsi slaves; at one stage, they were headed by as many as forty top-ranking officers of the state, which earned them the nickname of the *Chalisa, Chihalgani* or *Chehalgan*, viz., 'the Forty'. They held charge of the various *iqtas* or regions into which the kingdom was divided and wielded great influence at the royal court. Iltutmish was a sovereign ruler; he set up an Islamic state in northern India to legitimatize which he secured a letter of investiture from the Abbasid Khalifa Al-Mustansir Billah of Baghdad in February 1229; the latter bestowed the titles of 'the Sultan of Hindustan' and 'the deputy of the leader of the faithful' (*nasir amir-ul-momnin*) upon Iltutmish. Great significance has been attached to this incident by the contemporary historians. Minhajus Siraj narrates it as follows:

'When His majesty (Iltutmish) returned from that fort (Uchh), the compiler (Minhaj-us-Siraj) also came to Delhi... with the victorious army of that invincible king, and reached the city in the month of Ramazan AH 625 (August 1228). At this time, messengers bringing splendid robes from the seat of the Khilafat reached the frontiers of Nagore, and on Monday, the 2nd of the Rabiulawwal AH 626, they arrived at the capital, and the city was adorned by their presence. The king and his chief nobles and his sons and other nobility and servants were all honoured with robes sent from the metropolis of Islam'...(*Tabaqat-i-Nasiri;* p. 322).

Hasan Nizami adds to this information in the following words:

'...a dress of honour was received from the Imam Mustansir Billah by the sultan (Iltutmish), accompanied by a diploma, confirming him in the kingdom of Hindustan, with the title of the Great Sultan. He received the diploma with deep respect and appointed the following day, namely the 23rd Rabiulawwal, 626 H (February 1229 AD), for a general assembly, in which the *Farman* was read out in the presence of the king, the princes and nobles. It declared that he was confirmed in the possession of `the land and sea which he had conquered'. Robes were bestowed upon the ambassadors, the chiefs, the nobles, in honour of the event, and great joy prevailed upon the occasion throughout the capital. (*Tajul Ma'asir;* E & D; ii, Aligarh reprint, p. 243).

The acknowledgement of his allegiance to the Khalifa by Iltutmish accorded a legal recognition and religious sanction to the Sultanate of Delhi as an Islamic state with a separate entity, quite independent of Ghazni. It also strengthened the position of Iltutmish as the king and ensured the succession of his children to the throne. All those of the Turkish nobility who had hitherto dubbed him as usurper to the throne and cast aspersions on his rule were silenced. Iltutmish thus became the first legal sovereign of the Indian Turks in the comity of the Muslim states of Central Asia. The investiture ceremony of Iltutmish was celebrated in Delhi with great pomp and show.

Iltutmish introduced a purely Arabic currency of gold and silver. He adopted silver *tanka* as his standard coin; it weighed 175 grams and proved to be the precursor of the later rupee which is still prevalent as the standard coin of modern Indian currency. Iltutmish inscribed on his coins in Arabic—'The Mighty Sultan, Sun of the Empire and the Faith, Conquest-laden Iltutmish' besides the title *`nasir amir ul momnin'*. The silver coins on which these titles appeared were new to the traditional Indian currency.

Iltutmish was an orthodox *Sunni* Muslim and devoted to the faith but he was not a fanatic like Mahmud of Ghazni. He persecuted the *Ismaili Shias* of Delhi and his treatment towards the Hindus was equally harsh but not cruel. He had desecrated the magnificent Hindu temples at Bhilsa and Ujjain but he did not resort to idol-breaking just to satisfy the whims of his fanatic co-religionists. He adopted a policy of moderation to win the cooperation of Hindus in running the administration. He encouraged the Muslims to make settlements in the Hindu habitats, particularly, in the mountainous and forest regions so as to exert pressure over the Hindus and discourage them from harbouring rebellious feelings towards the Sultanate.

Iltutmish was a patron of Islamic art and learning. Because of the Mongol upheavals in central Asia, hundreds of Muslim theologians, scholars and artists fled their hearths and homes and sought shelter in Delhi; Amir Khusrau's father was one of them. Iltutmish extended liberal patronage to them and enriched the cultural life of the ruling elite. He completed the construction of Qutub Minar and enjoyed his association with the *Sufi* saints of the day.

Iltutmish was undoubtedly one of the great rulers of India. Sir Wolseley Haig assigns him the first place among the rulers of the Slave dynasty. In our opinion, he was 'a man of courage and foresight who unified the Turkish leadership under one central authority and saved the infant sultanate of Delhi from disintegration. He protected it from the fury of the Mongols and gave a legal and independent status to it in the comity of the Islamic states. He was an empire-builder who strove to accomplish the unfinished task of Qutubuddin Aibek in laying the foundations of the Delhi Sultanate'. (*Advanced Study,* i, p.98).

Successors of Iltutmish: *Chalisa* - 'The Kingmakers'

There was no fixed law of succession in the Islamic polity. Occupation of the throne depended on the general law of nature, i.e. 'the survival of the fittest'. It was, perhaps, the single major factor which had led to the rapid expansion of the Muslim arms in the various parts of the world because it afforded ample opportunities to the ambitious and capable military generals to carve out vast empires for themselves. The same aggressive principle facilitated the rapid spread of Turkish arms in northern India under the leadership of Muhammad Ghori and his brilliant slave officers.

It was no mean achievement for Iltutmish - the ex-slave of Qutubuddin Aibek, who himself started his career as the slave officer of Muhammad Ghori, and thus rightly called 'the Slave of the Slave', to have become the Sultan of Delhi. Of course, it was primarily because of the loyalty and unstinted support of his own slave officers, called the *Chalisa* or 'the Forty', that Iltutmish felt himself secure on the throne and thought of ensuring the succession of his children, thus making the monarchy an hereditary institution. This was perhaps too much to expect from his ex-slaves who constituted the real power behind the throne. Their loyalty to the person of Iltutmish had been unquestioned but they considered themselves 'the partners in the state enterprise which was the outcome of their collective contribution'. They, therefore, refused to accept the principle of hereditary monarchy in preference to that of selection on merit—the very principle on which Iltutmish had once acquired the throne for himself. Accordingly, after the death of Iltutmish, most of the Shamsi slave officers did not cooperate with his successors whole-heartedly. The court intrigues, conspiracies and defiance of authority were the natural consequences. It led to frequent revolts of the disaffected nobility, depositions and murders in cold blood in quick succession in which the Shamsi nobles or the Chalisa played the role of king-makers. This process continued until one of their leaders, Ghiasuddin Balban himself ascended the throne in 1266. Therefore, very often the period from 1236 to 1266 is called the era of 'the rule of the Forty' in the history of the Sultanate of Delhi. Because of their state politics and manipulations, as many as five children of Iltutmish sat on the throne of Delhi and had their varied spells of rule during this period; they were:

1. Ruknuddin Firoze,
2. Razia Begam,
3. Behram Shah,
4. Alauddin Masudshah, and
5. Nasiruddin Mahmud.

1. Ruknuddin Firoze (April-November 1236)

Iltutmish had many children from a number of his legally married wives and concubines. Nasiruddin Mahmud, his eldest son and the most accomplished of his children, had died a premature death during the very lifetime of his father. Iltutmish did not hold a high opinion of his second son Ruknuddin Firoze because of his ease-loving habits and indulgence in sensual pleasures. That is why he had nominated his daughter to be his successor to the throne. Nevertheless, after the death of Iltutmish, the Shamsi nobles placed Ruknuddin Firoze on the throne. Being an incapable ruler, Ruknuddin failed to win the confidence of his mentors, some of whom happened to be powerful governors of various *iqtas* (provinces). He was deposed and put behind the bars by the king-makers after about seven months, and was probably put to death some time later on the orders of Razia Sultan.

2. Razia Sultan (1236-40)

Razia Begam succeeded her half-brother Ruknuddin as the Sultan of Delhi. She was an educated lady of courage and political acumen. Born of the chief queen of Iltutmish, she had been brought up by the sultan like a son and imparted education and training in statecraft. She was also taught horse-riding, shooting and swordsmanship. 'Free from all inhibitions, Razia used to attend the court of her father like other princes and had acquired sufficient experience in statecraft in her youth. She, in fact, possessed all the qualities befitting an administrator and ruler; that is why Iltutmish, unmindful of the Islamic traditions, and ridicule of the orthodox *ulama*, nominated her to succeed him to the throne after his death'. Nevertheless, the haughty and proud Turkish nobility, who hated to be ruled by a female, had brushed aside Razia's claim in preference to that of her incompetent and worthless half-brother, Ruknuddin, who was placed on the throne as their puppet ruler.

Razia's dramatic rise to power: Razia's accession to the throne took place under very dramatic circumstances. Ruknuddin had proved to be a very weak and imbecile ruler. He could neither establish his position as independent ruler nor could win the confidence of his masters- 'the Chalisa'. As a result, administration suffered and there was wide-spread anarchy. Taking advantage of the confusion that prevailed in the state, Saifuddin Hasan Qarlugh of Ghazni took possession of the lower Indus valley region, including Sindh. Alarmed by this lurking danger beyond the Indian borders, the four governors of Lahore, Multan, Hansi and Badaun—the all-powerful Shamsi nobles or 'the Chalisa', joined their hands together to take possession of Delhi. Nizamul Mulk Junaidi, the *wazir* of Ruknuddin Firoze, also joined hands with the rebels. Ruknuddin, in the face of wide-scale desertions from the royal army, was incited by the conspirators to challenge the rebels before they reached Delhi. Completely confused and nervous, the sultan moved out of the capital half-heartedly, and that proved his ruin. Taking advantage of the discontent among the populace of Delhi, Razia picked up courage to face the audience to stop the public wrath turning against the whole ruling family of Iltutmish. At the time of Friday prayers, she suddenly appeared in the Jama Masjid, adorned in red clothes, and aroused the 'pious congregation in her favour through a forceful speech'. She appealed for her protection from the persecution of Shah Turkan, called upon the audience to exercise their sovereign right to remove a worthless king like Ruknuddin Firoze and reminded them of their illustrious father's will to nominate her as his successor on merit. In her youthful frenzy, Razia held out a promise to the people of Delhi that she would voluntarily abdicate the throne and be prepared to face any penalty imposed by them, including even death, if she failed to perform her functions as ruler according to their expectations. The Her speech had a magic effect on the mob which attacked the handful of royal guards, posted at the gates of the Red Fort, made their forced entry into the royal apartments in connivance with the conspirators, and put Shah Turkan to death. Razia was instantly declared as the Sultan of Delhi by 'the military junta of Delhi' amidst the excited populace of the capital. It was, in fact, a political revolution, the like of which had perhaps never been witnessed by Delhi. On hearing of these developments, Ruknuddin Firoze hastened to Delhi to save his tottering crown but was captured and thrown behind the bars by the rebels. Khutba was read and coins struck in the name of Razia as the sultan of Delhi to complete the revolution.

Fizzling out of the Opposition to Razia's Accession: Razia thus ascended the throne of Delhi by the popular choice of the people of Delhi. In view of her public popularity, the Shamsi nobles did not dare to challenge her accession all at once. As a class, the Muslim theologians were not willing at all to give their assent to her assumption of royal powers but, faced with public excitement and her popularity among the masses, the *ulama* of Delhi were for the time being hypnotized. Once on the throne, Razia gave a good account of herself as a capable ruler and shrewd politician. The four rebel provincial governors, who had encamped their forces in the neighbourhood of Delhi, were yet undecided regarding their future course of action. Razia had but only a few thousands of the soldiers and meager resources at her command but she made move out of the Red Fort with a show of force and wide publicity on the beating of the drums and trumpets to boost the morale of his soldiers and people at large. Working on the principle of 'divide and rule', she initiated secret parleys with two of the junior rebel governors, Malik Izzuddin Muhammad Salari and Malik Izzuddin Kabir Khan Ayaz, to her side, and then launched a vigorous propaganda that the other rebels, including their ring-leaders, would soon be brought to Delhi without a fight. Thereby she aroused the suspicions of the disaffected nobles against each other. It unnerved all the rebellious leaders, who hurriedly decamped and retreated from the capital to their respective provinces. At the same time, Razia's ranks swelled by thousands of fighters and she despatched picked contingents in pursuit of each of them. Junaidi, the ex-*wazir* of Ruknuddin also died a fugitive in the Sirmur hills. Razia's prestige soared high, and all the provincial governors hastened to offer their submission with profuse promises of unflinching loyalty to her, thus acknowledging her as the sultan in name as well as in fact.

Razia as a Ruler: Razia Sultan rapidly strengthened her position as sovereign independent ruler without obligation to or dependence upon the all-powerful Shamsi nobles for the time being. She bluntly refused to fall under their dominating influence. She richly rewarded those who had stood by her at this critical juncture and gave rapid promotions to her favourites. Khwaja Muhazzabuddin, the ex-*naib wazir* of Ruknuddin Firoze, was promoted as *wazir* or prime minister of the Sultanate. With the object of breaking the monopoly of power, hitherto held by the *Chalisa*, she began to offer high offices of the state to capable and trustworthy non-Turk Muslim officers as well. She reshuffled many provincial governors from one place to the other and deputed new officers to take charge of the more important *iqtas* (provinces).

Razia attained popularity as ruler by adopting stringent measures to restore law and order in her dominions. The erring officers were taken to task and the inefficient and dishonest officers among them were promptly downgraded or dismissed. Within a couple of months she had mustered a strong and loyal army at her command and earned reputation as the most worthy successor of her illustrious father, Shamsuddin Iltutmish. In the royal capital of Delhi, therefore, she won public acclaim as the ideal ruler of her subjects where none could dare to defy her commands or think of doing her any harm. She thus gave a unique and raring twist to the otherwise stereotype and fundamentalist Islamic polity. 'Kind-hearted, liberal in religious outlook, and unconventional in her social habits, she was far ahead of her times in her mental make-up'.

It was, however, a misfortune that she was a woman, and 'the orthodox Muslim society, particularly, the fanatic *mullas* of those days, did not like that she should deviate from the traditional social norms, set by the Muslim ruling elite of the country. The proud Turkish nobles thought it beneath their dignity to be governed by a woman, especially the one who did not allow them to have a say in the state affairs'. Therefore, it was not surprising that the orthodox *mullas* and some of the disaffected Shamsi nobles started a 'whispering campaign against her just to malign her in the eyes of the public' on frivolous and non-political issues. Having failed to beat Razia on the administrative and military fronts, they launched a secret campaign of character assassination against Razia. They spread wild rumours casting aspersions on her personal character, including the one about her illicit sexual relations with her Abyssinian slave officer, named Jalaluddin Yakut, whom she had promoted as the *amir-i-akhur* or 'master of the royal stables'. By such underhand means, the conspirators attempted to tarnish her image as the ideal ruler of 'an Islamic State' that the Sultanate of Delhi had been made out by them. Obviously, 'Razia's only weakness seemed to be her sex and even the best of her talents and virtues were insufficient to save her from that solitary weakness'.

The fall of Razia: Razia Sultan, while following an independent course of action unmindful of the hurtful feelings of the mighty Shamsi nobles or 'the Chalisa' was fully conscious of the impending danger to the exercise of her authority. She did apprehend trouble at their hands sooner or later and attempted to take all precautions against the fall-out of her state policy. She, therefore, made all security arrangements for her personal safety in the royal household as well as in the court. Nevertheless, out of the capital and in the courts of her powerful provincial governors, particularly, it was not always possible for her to keep a vigilant eye, through her secret agents, upon the clandestine activities of the trouble-shooters. In spite of her best efforts, however, there emerged a traitor under her very nose in the royal court. He was one of her cabinet ministers, called Ikhtiyaruddin Aeitigin—'the lord chamberlain', who became the ringleader of the conspirators at the capital. In 1238, Razia received the feedback from her agents at Gwalior about the rebellious intentions of its governor, Ziauddin Junaidi, a kinsman of the ex-*wazir* and rebellious noble of Ruknuddin Firoze. He was summoned to the court, and having been found guilty of disloyalty, was put to death. It spread panic among 'the *Chalisa*' on the grounds that Razia Sultan was vindictive and had started 'political murders' of the reputed military generals 'on mere suspicion'. It triggered off an instant wave of revolts in various parts of the kingdom. Kabir Khan Ayaz, who held the dual charge as the governor of Lahore and Multan, was the first to raise his standard of revolt on the ground that Razia Sultan was guilty of moral turpitude because of her alleged intimacy with Yakut 'which was derogatory to the pride of the Turkish race'. Razia at once marched upon Lahore with the best of her troops and thundered at the gates of Lahore in no time. Taken utterly by surprise, Ayaz hurriedly arranged his army in battle array to give a battle to the royal forces. Badly mauled in action, he fled from the field towards Multan and sought apologies from the enraged sovereign. The latter pardoned the rebel for his misdemeanor but gave him back the governorship of Multan only, the *Iqta* of Lahore being taken out of his control.

Razia had hardly reached the capital after her triumphant expedition to Lahore when she received the news about the revolt of Altunia, the governor of Bathinda or Bhatinda. Accordingly, she felt constrained to leave for Bhatinda with her troops but was defeated and taken prisoner by Altunia. Yakut also fell into the hands of the conspirators and was done to death. On hearing of her discomfiture at the hands of Altunia, the conspirators in Delhi at once placed Razia's younger brother and the third son of Iltutmish, Behram Shah on the throne as their puppet ruler and prepared to block the return of Razia to the capital for ever. As referred to earlier, stunned by the sudden change of fortunes, Razia sought her freedom by agreeing to marry Altunia, and their combined forced marched upon Delhi in their bid to re-install Razia on the throne. Their passage to Delhi was blocked by the rebellious nobles at Kaithal where they duo were defeated in a pitched battle, and taken prisoners on October 13, 1240; the very next day, Razia and Altunia were both beheaded. It marked the equally dramatic end of Razia Sultan. "The people of Delhi, inspite of their love for Razia, could do nothing against the selfish Turkish nobles because there was none to lead the public movement; the people's voice was drowned under the clatter of arms'. (*Advanced Study*, i, p.104).

An Evaluation: Razia Sultan was by far the ablest of all the five successors of Iltutmish. As a person of character and capabilities, she was 'better than a man'. Razia's installation 'as the sultan was based on the popular support of the people of Delhi; such an unqualified support was never enjoyed by any other sultan of Delhi. Given the opportunity, she would have proved to be a very capable ruler like her illustrious father. Unfortunately, her career was cut short by non-cooperation of the self-seeking Shamsi nobles and the hostility of the orthodox *mullas* who failed to see the virtues in her as the sovereign. She failed to play the second fiddle to them; this was the main reason why they turned against her. Her sex was, of course, the next important factor which brought about her fall... Had she got a reasonable time to rule the state she might have generated new socio-political forces for the better and healthier growth and development of the Turkish polity, in particular, and the Indo-Muslim society, in general'. (*Ibid*; p. 105).

Irrespective of what the modern historians may write about the merits or demerits of Razia Begam as the sovereign sultan of Delhi, the Islamic fundamentalists and the haughty Turkish nobility of the mid-thirteenth century India could never gloss over the 'pious' injunctions of the Prophet Muhammad that 'a virtuous woman is the most precious thing in the world'; but 'the people who make a woman their ruler will not find salvation'.

3. Bahram Shah (1240-42)

Muizuddin Bahram Shah was placed on the throne by the Turkish conspirators on the clear understanding that he would act as the nominal ruler of the state, and accord complete freedom of action to the Shamsi nobles to exercise full powers of the state. He also agreed to nominate their leader as his deputy or viceroy, called the *Naib-i-Mulk* or *Naib-i-Mamlikat*. Accordingly, Ikhtiyaruddin Aeitigin, the ringleader of the conspirators at Delhi, now assumed the authority as *Naib-i-Mulk*. Muhazzabuddin continued to act as the *wazir* of the empire but now he was required to take orders from the *Naib-i-Mulk*. It led to the establishment of complete supremacy of the Turkish nobility at Delhi. Before long, Aeitigin, the *Naib-i-Mulk* married a sister of Bahram Shah and made himself more important than the sultan himself; he usurped even some of the royal prerogatives of the crown as well.

As a reaction to the excesses of the Turkish nobility in the royal *harem*, a body of the lower cadre of the royal guards developed sympathies for the hapless sultan. With their connivance, Bahram Shah got Aeitigin murdered but another powerful Shamsi noble, Badruddin Sunqar—the *Amir-i-Hajib*, lost no time in usurping all powers of the crown, thus making Bahram Shah as a virtual prisoner in his hands. Muhazzabuddin, the *wazir*, who felt jealous of the sudden rise to power of Badruddin Sunqar, now came to the rescue of the sultan, and helped him in liquidating Sunqar through a 'clever diplomacy'. It made the other Shamsi nobles conscious of the power of mischief of the otherwise weak and imbecile sultan, and the military officers of the royal army at the capital were alerted not to fall into his trap to further his evil designs, if any. About this time the Mongols, under their leader, called Tair or Tahir, had invaded India. They were repulsed from Multan by its governor Kabir Khan but they turned their direction towards Lahore. A royal army was despatched by Bahram Shah from Delhi under the command of his *wazir* Muhazzabuddin to defend Lahore. On the onward march, however, the crafty *wazir* took some of the commanding officers into his confidence to say that 'the sultan had sent secret orders for their arrest and execution' during the campaign. It enraged the commanders who immediately ordered the return march of their troops to Delhi with a vow to wreak their vengeance against Bahram Shah. It is said that the faithful followers of the ruling house of Iltutmish and much-bewildered 'citizens of Delhi fought desperately' to protect the sultan but 'they were no match for regular troops', and the metropolis was taken possession of by the royal forces after a day's resistance; Bahram Shah was captured and beheaded the next day. This development took place sometime in May 1242.

Meanwhile, Malik Qarqash, the Turkish governor of Lahore, had suffered a defeat at the hands of the Mongols in December 1241 and fled from the town to save his dear life. Lahore fell into the hands of the Mongol marauders and was thoroughly sacked. To the good fortune of the people and the Sultanate of Delhi, the Mongols retired from India after the plunder of Lahore.

4. Alauddin Masudshah (1242-46)

It is said that immediately after the murder of Bahram Shah, one of the more ambitious slave officers among the *Chalisa,* named Izzuddin Kishlu Khan declared himself the sultan but, fearful of the public wrath, majority of his colleagues did not approve of his name, and instead, nominated Alauddin Masudshah, son of Ruknuddin Firoze and a grandson of Iltutmish, as the next sultan. As usual, the ruling *junta* of the *Chalisa* wielded all powers of the state while Alauddin held the reins of government as puppet ruler for the next four years. Qutubuddin Hasan Ghori acted as the *Naib-i-Mulk* while Muhazzabuddin continued as *wazir* for some time before being replaced by others. This period saw the spectacular rise to power of Ghiasuddin Balban, one of 'the Forty' slaves, then holding the governorship of Badaun. During the reign of Masudshah, he shifted to the royal court in his capacity as *amir-i-hajib* or 'the lord chamberlain'. Balban gave one of his daughters in marriage to the young sultan to gain greater influence in the ruling house of Iltutmish.

Masudshah's period of rule saw the rapid disintegration of the sultanate. Having been deprived of opportunities to receive education and training befitting a prince, he lacked the qualities of a ruler and freely indulged in sensuous pleasures, leaving all responsibilities of the state to his ministers. Taking advantage of the centre's weakening hold over the provinces, Tamar Khan, the governor of Bengal, annexed Bihar and stopped paying tribute to Delhi. Similarly, Kabir Khan Ayaz, the governor of Multan and Uchh, having been left to fend for himself against the Mongols, also cut off his relations with Delhi. The Khokhars in the Salt Range defied the centre's authority and many Hindu chieftains of the Ganga valley also took up arms against the Turkish rule. Finding him completely unfit to hold the exalted office of the sultan even in the ceremonial capacity, the Shamsi nobles deposed him in June 1246; he was kept in confinement where he died after some time. The choice of the king-makers now fell on yet another grandson of Iltutmish, named Nasiruddin Mahmud, who was destined to enjoy a peaceful reign for twenty years..

5. Nasiruddin Mahmud (1246-66)

Early Career and Accession: Nasiruddin Mahmud, who succeeded Alauddin Masudshah on the throne of Delhi, was the posthumous child of prince Nasiruddin, the eldest son of Iltutmish, who had died a premature death during the very lifetime of his father. Because of his intense filial attachment to the child, Iltutmish brought him up under his personal care and protection by making special arrangements for the comfortable stay of his widowed daughter-in-law. He gave him the same name and titles of his deceased son and fondly used to address him as *ibn* or son. According to some, Nasiruddin Mahmud might have been formally adopted as his son by Iltutmish. Nasiruddin Mahmud was made nominal governor of Baraich while yet a boy; obviously, administration of his charge must have been carried on by some of the most trusted officers of the state on behalf of the minor prince. He grew up to be an educated and religious-minded person of very gentle and pious nature and was least interested in the material pursuits of life or the state affairs.

Nasiruddin Mahmud was only seventeen, when the Shamsi nobles decided to install him on the throne. The prince had no illusions about the new role that the power-hungry nobles intended him to play. He, therefore, adopted an attitude of complete self-surrender to the ruling *junta* and willingly played the puppet in their hands. 'It would be more appropriate to say that Nasiruddin was the constitutional chief executive of the Turkish oligarchy. That is why he became acceptable to all the nobles who were left free to settle between themselves all matters of state politics. He kept himself aloof from all administrative problems and did not take any step without the prior consent of the ruling *junta*. To his good fortune, equilibrium was established amidst the nobles in the matter of distribution of loaves and fishes which ensured peace in the state. Had the Turkish nobles failed to arrive at a compromise among them, and had they split themselves into rival factions, on any issue whatsoever, Nasiruddin might have been put to death like a sacrificial lamb any moment. It was, therefore, also due to his good luck that he enjoyed a peaceful and undisturbed reign for twenty long years and died a natural death'. Isami makes a very interesting observation about the conduct of Nasiruddin Mahmud as the sultan of Delhi; according to him, the sultan 'expressed no opinion without the permission of the Shamsi nobles. He would not move his hands or feet except at their order. He would neither drink water nor go to sleep except with their knowledge'. Nasiruddin was devoted to his faith and lived a virtuous life; he had never more than four living wives and no concubines. Isami makes us believe that the sultan did not take a penny from the state treasury to meet his personal expenditure; instead, being a good calligraphist, he used to prepare copies of the Holy Quran from the sale proceeds of which he made his living. Be as it may, Isami is the only contemporary writer to have made mention of this aspect of the sultan's life. (*Futuhus Salatin*, pp. 150-51.). In our opinion, the all-powerful Shamsi nobles might have exploited this characteristic of Nasiruddin Mahmud to make a fad of it by bidding very highly for the copies of the Quran, written by their puppet sultan, to provide enough and to spare for the royal family.

Selection of his Prime Minister: It is said that because of his very humble and cooperative nature, Nasiruddin Mahmud was given the choice to nominate any one of the king-makers as his *wazir*; he expressed the desire to have Ghiasuddin Balban, then 'the lord chamberlain', to be his prime minister, and his wish was promptly granted by the ruling *junta* of Delhi. Balban took charge of the *wizarat* with the title of Ulugh Khan. Earlier, he had developed very cordial relations with the members of royalty as an elder through the marriage of one of his daughters to sultan Alauddin Masudshah; the latter proved to be a worthless fellow and was done away with by the ruling *junta* but Balban, inspite of being the father-in-law of the deposed sultan, had kept his cool and maintained warm relationships with the members of the royal household. That is why he had earned reputation in the royal palace as the most civilized and sober of all the Shamsi nobles. Balban, therefore, lost no time in winning the love and confidence of his humble and shy new sultan by an equally tender and dignified conduct towards him. At an appropriate occasion in 1249, Balban readily offered the hand of his second daughter in marriage to sultan Nasiruddin Mahmud and carved out a permanent place for himself as well-wisher of the ruling family of Iltutmish. This was the greatest credit which paid him dividends in ample measures.

As an immediate reward, Balban received the title of the *Naib-i-mamlikat* from the ruling *junta* of the *Chalisa* on the recommendations of the sultan himself; this office had been held in abeyance during the first three years of Nasiruddin's reign by mutual agreement between the Shamsi nobles. Abu Bakr, who took over as the new *wazir* of Nasiruddin Mahmud, now took orders direct from Balban, thereby relieving the sultan from all anxiety to deal with two masters at a time. At a later stage, Balban's own son Bughra Khan was married to the only daughter of sultan Nasiruddin Mahmud from his second wife; thus the family line of Balban was almost completely merged in the ruling family of Iltutmish and Nasiruddin Mahmud.

Balban, on his part, took care to maintain formal dignity of the sultan as nominal ruler, and all the court ceremonials and royal prerogatives of the crown as constitutional head were scrupulously observed to maintain the high status of the exalted office. He also allowed the sultan 'to have his say in some non-controversial matters, particularly those in which the self-interest of the Shamsi nobles was not involved'.

In his capacity, earlier as *wazir* and after 1249 as the *naib-i-mulk*, Balban conducted the affairs of the state virtually as the *de facto* ruler. He held charge of these exalted offices all through the reign of Nasiruddin Mahmud except for a short break in 1253-54. He utilized this opportunity to strengthen his position gradually by promoting the interests of his blood-relations, friends and favourites. Balban promoted his younger brother Kishlu Khan as the *amir-i-hajib*, and later on sent him to Nagore as its governor. Similarly, one of his cousins, Sher Khan Sunqar held the governorships of the provinces of Bhatinda and Lahore for sometime with special supervisory powers to look after the defence of the northwestern frontier of the sultanate. It is a different matter that his above-mentioned real brother and the cousin both proved unworthy of the favours shown to them and put Balban to great inconvenience because of their insubordination at a later stage.

Achievements of Balban as *Wazir* and *Naib-i-Mulk* : When Balban took charge as the *wazir* of Nasiruddin Mahmud in 1246, the central authority of the sultans was totally crippled. Anarchy prevailed everywhere and 'there was no government worth the name'. The northwestern India had been laid waste by the Mongols, the entire Ganga valley, under the leadership of their respective Hindu chieftains was up in arms against the Turks and the Muslim governors of the distant provinces of the sultanate tended to break away from Delhi. To add insult to the injury, the royal court at the capital had become a hot bed of conspiracies and intrigues of the Shamsi nobles and the small fry even within the ruling family of Iltutmish and the royal *harem,* and political murders had become an order of the day. An atmosphere of fear and distrust prevailed in the royal camp as well as the Turkish bureaucracy. Law and order was the natural calamity and the people of Delhi suffered under the unbearable burden of a corrupt and inefficient administration.

Balban was an empire-builder and great administrator. The very first day he took over as the *wazir*, he launched a vigorous campaign to strengthen the forces of law and order in Delhi and made it known to the local bureaucracy as well as the public that he meant business. He conceived of an extensive plan to invigorate and expand the infrastructure of municipal functions and defences of the capital; provided adequate civic amenities to the royal palace, revised the court manual to impart a more disciplined and dignified appearance to the royal court, laid down strict rules to regulate entries into the Red Fort, made adequate provisions for the more dignified and comfortable life-style of the sultan, and, above all, strengthened the royal guards under his personal vigilant eye to ensure the protection of the sultan at the hands of the internal trouble-shooters or external threat. Being a *de facto* ruler, he did all this to set the standard and style of his administration and to provide stability and strength to the state. In a very short time, Balban gave a good account of himself as an intelligent and efficient administrator, thereby winning not only the confidence and respects of sultan

Nasiruddin and the citizens of Delhi but also applause from his fellow Shamsi nobles, who ungrudgingly accepted the sultan's proposal to confer the tile of *Naib-i-Mulk* on him.

Besides improving the civil administration and strengthening the defences of the capital, Balban simultaneously adopted measures to establish effective control over the governors of the various provinces and to restore law and order in the Turkish dominions. Minhaj-us-Siraj tells us that every winter, Balban moved out of the capital at the head of a large army, accompanied by the royal standards and the sultan Nasiruddin Mahmud, and launched a regular military campaign to fight against the Mongols or suppress the refractory Hindu chiefs or the rebellious Turkish nobles. Whatever the outcome of these annual expeditions, it accorded great confidence in the heart of the people of Delhi and kept all the forces of disorder on their toes, little knowing to which direction the punitive expeditionary army might turn its attention at the time of their choosing. It left every rebellious chief guessing and every *iqtadar* speculating about the sudden arrival of the royal standards to take them to task for their nefarious activities. The periodical visits of the royal entourage not only raised the prestige of the central government but also toned up the administration of the outlying provinces of the state.

(1) **Suppression of the Khokhars:** Balban signalled the beginning of the new reign under Nasiruddin Mahmud by leading the first such punitive expeditionary force, on the beating of the drum, into the Punjab. Passing through Lahore, he put up the 'royal standards' and the sultan Nasiruddin on the Ravi and himself pierced through the Salt Range to the Indus, taking the Khokhars and the Mongols totally unawares. The Khokhars had already exhausted their resources in their long and protracted struggle against the Mongol invaders; their crops and green foliage of their countryside had been ruined and their hearths and homes lay in shambles. Unable to muster their warriors in strength, they, therefore, offered feeble resistance and fled before the advancing Turkish forces. Balban destroyed their hamlets and took a heavy toll of their civilian lives. On the approach of Balban, the remnants of the Mongol hordes hurriedly retreated from the Indian soil; they had already devastated the region right up to Lahore and carried away immense booty besides thousands of the Indians as slaves, who were used by them as beasts of burden to carry the spoils to central Asia. It is said that Balban did not advance up to the Khyber and returned for want of fodder for his horses, besides food and other provisions for the army.

Minhaj-us-Siraj, the celebrated author of the *Tabaqat-i-Nasiri* records that he had also accompanied 'the royal standards' on this campaign; on his return to the capital, he was gratified to receive 'the gift of a coat and turban', besides 'a house with princely trappings' under His Majesty's orders.

(2) Suppression of the rebellious Hindu chiefs of the Doab: In 1247-48, Balban carried out a punitive expedition for the suppression of the rebellious Hindu *zamindars* of the Doab. A few refractory Hindu chieftains of the region were annihilated and their sympathizers crushed mercilessly. Minhajus Siraj gives an account of one such confrontation between the rebellious Hindus and the Turkish forces of Balban during this campaign as follows:

> 'In the neighbourhood of Kanauj, there is a fortified village called Naudana where there is a very strong fort vying with the walls of Alexander. A body of infidel Hindus shut themselves up in this place, and resolved to fight to the last extremity. For two days, the royal army carried out a murderous conflict at this village, but at length, the rebels were sent to hell, and the place was subdued'.

He further narrates that

> 'The author of this work (i.e. Minhaj-us-Siraj) celebrated the victory and all the events of the campaign in verse. The slaughter of the rebellious infidels, the capture of their fortifications, and the success of Ulugh Khan-i-Muazzam (i.e. Balban) in killing and taking prisoners Dalaki and Malaki (two Hindu chiefs), these and all the other incidents are celebrated fully in the poem to which the author gave the name of his gracious master, and called it *Nasiri Nama*. For this poem, the author received from the sultan the grant of a fine annual allowance, and from Ulugh Khan he received the grant in *in'am* (gift or prize) of a village near Hansi. (May God long maintain the seats of their empire and rule!)'—(*Tabaqat-i-Nasiri*—Book no. xx , entitled, *'The Muizziya Sultans of Hind'*, E&D. ii, Aligarh reprint, pp. 343-44).

(3) Collapse of conspiracy against Balban (1253-54): In 1253-54, Balban had to face much trouble at the hands of his own kinsmen and some influential members of the ruling dynasty. Unfortunately, his younger brother, Kishlu Khan, whom Balban had brought into the royal palace as *amir-i-hajib* or 'the lord chamberlain' with the illusion that he would act as his right-hand man in consolidating his hold over the central government of the state, was the first to betray him. Having developed intimate relations with the members of the royalty, he indulged in petty politics over minor administrative issues to score an edge over his elder brother- the *wazir*, to the great embarrassment of the latter. Balban, therefore, thought it prudent to send him out of Delhi as the governor of Nagore. Nevertheless, Kishlu Khan's ambitions soared high and he asked for the grant of viceroyalty of Multan and Sindh which was promptly denied to him by Balban. Thereafter, Kishlu Khan felt jealous of his elder brother and, by coincidence or design, came into contact with Malik Imaduddin Raihan—an Indian Muslim noble, and some other grumbling lot of the royal palace, and they poisoned the ears of Malika-i-Jahan, the mother of sultan Nasiruddin Mahmud, against Balban for his alleged ulterior designs to usurp the throne. So much so, these conspirators did not hesitate even making an unsuccessful bid to assassinate the *naib-i-mulk*.

Their conspiracy having been exposed, Balban, in his bid to remove the misgivings of the queen mother, voluntarily offered to resign his post. Thereupon, the sultan sent him to Hansi as its governor, and Imaduddin Raihan was asked to take charge as the *naib-i-mamlikat*. He, however, failed to run the administration effectively and the disaffected elements raised their ugly head in many parts of the state. The Shamsi nobles, who held important offices of the state, were in a quandary and confusion prevailed everywhere. Threatened with the disintegration of the empire, requests from well-wishers of the Turkish rule 'from all sides poured in upon the Sultan to dismiss Imaduddin'. The governors of 'Kara-Manikpur, Awadh, Tirhut, Badaun, Tabarhind (Bhatinda), Samana, Sunam, Kuhram, and the whole of the Shiwalik country entreated the exiled minister (viz., Balban) to resume the charge of affairs'. They made a common cause with Balban and staged a come-back by show of force.

The contemporary sources tell us that many of these chiefs mustered their respective troops and marched towards Delhi to measure their swords with Imaduddin Raihan, the ringleader of conspirators, now in command of the royal forces as *naib-i-mulk*. The rivals 'met in the vicinity of Tabarhindah. When both the advance guards encountered each other, disorder prevailed in the sultan's army, and it retreated towards Hansi without striking a blow. A compromise was afterwards effected by the leading *amirs* on both sides, and the Sultan was persuaded to order the dismissal of Raihan'. Raihan was relieved of his charge and Balban took control of 'the royal standards'. He returned with the Sultan to the capital in triumph on February 1, 1254. 'All hearts rejoiced at his return, and through the favour of God, the gates of the divine mercy opened and rain fell upon the ground, and all people looked upon his auspicious arrival as an omen of good to mortals'.

Balban was reinstated *naib-i-mulk* with absolute powers of government in his hands. His rivals were pardoned but sent out of the metropolis on provincial assignments. Raihan was sent to Badaun as its governor; Kishlu Khan was given charge of the distant provinces of Multan and Uchh with the duty to protect the northwestern region from the intrusion of the Mongols; while Qutlugh Khan, another co-accused, was assigned governorship of Awadh with full responsibility to suppress the disaffected Hindu chiefs of the region. The sultan was apprised of the unpleasant role played by his mother, *Malika-i-Jahan*, in the above conspiracy against Balban, but being the Queen-Mother, none dared to raise his little finger against her. Nevertheless, to the great chagrin of sultan Nasiruddin Mahmud, his mother created a sensation in the royal palace by entering into wedlock with Qutlugh Khan, who had been one of the co-conspirators against Balban. It embarrassed the sultan so much that he ordered her immediate banishment from the capital as 'her stay in the royal *harem* was thought undesirable and disgraceful'; on the advice of Balban, however, she was ordered to join her husband in Awadh, and her contacts with the royal family were completely cut off. - (*Ibid*; pp. 348-50).

(4) **Suppression of the Rebellious Turkish Nobles:** The troubles of Balban at the hands of his internal foes and conspirators did not end there, however. In 1255, Jalaluddin, the half-brother of sultan Nasiruddin Mahmud, who held the fief of Kanauj, aroused the suspicions of Balban about his fidelity to the state. When Balban prepared to take action against him, he deserted his charge and fled to northwestern India to join the Mongol camp. In 1257, we find him in possession of Lahore, seeking apologies from Delhi for his past misconduct. As a shrewd diplomat, Balban conferred on him the governorship of Lahore on behalf of sultan Nasiruddin Mahmud; having failed to take any punitive action against him, Balban's policy was 'to use him as a buffer between Delhi and the Mongols'.

Similarly, Imaduddin Raihan, now the governor of Badaun, also continued to nurture feelings of ill-will against Balban, and, in 1256, he raised a standard of revolt, in league with the *Malika-i-Jahan*, now his wife, with the declared object of ousting Balban from power to liberate sultan Nasiruddin Mahmud from his baneful influence. Balban at once marched upon Badaun with a huge force, accompanied by 'the royal standards' and sultan Nasiruddin Mahmud, of course. Raihan was killed in the battle and a large number of his associates and collaborators were liquidated. At Badaun, Balban received the intelligence that Raihan's old associate Qutlugh Khan, now the governor of Awadh, had also been hobnobbing with him. He at once issued orders for Qutlugh Khan's transfer to Baraich but the latter dilly-dallied in carrying out the command. Thereupon, Balban made straight for Awadh with a punitive expeditionary force to bring him to task. On the approach of royal armies, Qutlugh Khan fled to the Sirmur hills and took shelter in the court of a Hindu chief, Rana Ranpala of Santagarh. Balban demanded the custody of the rebellious Turkish noble from the Hindu ruler but the latter bluntly refused to oblige him, and, in consequence, large parts of his dominions were ravaged by the Turkish army.

The brewing of constant trouble by his adversaries against Balban has been interpreted by Dr. P. Saran differently. He opines that the very humble and docile character of Prince Nasiruddin Mahmud as made out by most of contemporary Muslim chroniclers does not seem to be correct. The prince was only a lad of seventeen when he was placed on the throne, purportedly on the condition that he would allow all powers of the state to be exercised by his king-makers. At that tender age, 'he could not be expected to become a recluse', and 'there is nothing to show that he had no interest in worldly affairs'. According to P. Saran, he 'began his reign with great enthusiasm but that was not palatable to Balban who wanted to keep all the powers in his own hands'. Being an intelligent person, he patiently 'waited for an appropriate opportunity to challenge Balban. A time came when Balban became unpopular with the Turkish nobility, including his relatives, and the Sultan took advantage of this opportunity to dismiss him from the post of *naib-i-mulk.* His substitute, Imaduddin Raihan, failed to win the confidence of majority of the powerful Shamsi nobles, however, and thereby brought about his fall. Otherwise, there was nothing special about the prevalent game of power-politics in which any and every Turkish noble felt tempted to indulge in. When Balban, backed by other Shamsi nobles, became strong once again and Raihan was ousted, Sultan had no hesitation in doing what he was ordered to do by Balban.

Well aware of the wretched fate of three of the preceding scions of Iltutmish, he readily banished his own mother, *Malika-i-Jahan*, because the hapless 'Sultan cared more for his own safety than for the life of his mother'.

To add insult to the injury, Kishlu Khan, the most unscrupulous younger brother of Balban, now the governor of Multan and Uchh since 1254, was still not reconciled to his fate. Minhajus Siraj (*Tabakat-i-Nasiri*, p. 354) has to say that, towards the close of 1257, when the Mongols made their appearance once again on the northwestern border, and intruded into the territories of Multan and Uchh, Kishlu Khan, instead of offering resistance to them, acknowledged the suzerainty of Halaku Khan, the Mongol ruler of Persia, and entered into a treaty with the leaders of Mongol hordes for a joint attack on Delhi. When Balban came to know of these developments, 'he made effective arrangements for the defence of the capital, and lost no time in establishing diplomatic contacts with Halaku Khan'. The envoys of Halaku Khan, who visited Delhi in 1258-59, were impressed so much by the military strength of Balban, and his competence to defend Delhi and the frontiers of his dominions that 'they refrained from entering into confrontation with him'. By his successful diplomatic parleys, Balban nullified the sinister designs of Kishlu Khan and other Turkish nobles from Delhi, who had joined the Mongol camp, but because of the perpetual Mongol menace on the northwestern frontier, he failed to bring the provinces of Lahore, Multan and Sindh under the effective control of Delhi during the reign of sultan Nasiruddin Mahmud.

(5) Unfinished Struggle against the Resurgent Hindu Powers: The partial success of Turkish arms against the resurgent Hindu powers of northern and central India during the reign of Iltutmish, and the feebleness of his weak successors had given further impetus to the refractory Hindu chieftains of the Doab. The Hindu subjects within the territories of the effective Turkish rule were simmering with discontent at the loss of their political and religious freedom, while a number of powerful Hindu states had re-emerged along the periphery of the Delhi Sultanate in central India and the Ganga valley. Balban was fully aware of the inherent threat posed to the stability and permanence of the Turkish rule by the resurgent Hindu India; and, most of his energies were devoted exclusively towards the suppression of the defiant Hindu chiefs. Year after year, he launched punitive military expeditions against the refractory Hindu *zamindars* of the Doab and in the Ganga valley, accompanied by 'the royal standards' and the puppet sultan Nasiruddin Mahmud, but his efforts were not crowned with much success. Because of the frequent revolts of Turkish nobles, Balban's policy to crush and demoralize the rebellious Hindus of these regions by the pursuit of the policy of 'blood and iron', enslavement of Hindu prisoners of war and even the unarmed civilian populace of the hostile villages and their forced conversions as an alternative to spare them from persecution failed to bear the desired results. As minister of Nasiruddin, Balban lacked the resources to deal with the hostile Hindu chiefs of the neighbourhood effectively; 'he led sporadic expeditions into Rajputana, Malwa and Bundelkhand but without any substantial gains'. The Chandellas of Bundelkhand were defeated in a number of running battles in 1248-49 but the stronghold of Kalinjar could not be re-conquered. In 1251-52, his attempt to recover Gwalior failed. Similarly, between 1248 and 1259, Balban made three unsuccessful attempts to re-conquer Ranthambhor from the hands of the Rajputs and the Turks failed miserably to establish their foothold in that region.

An important factor 'which very seriously hampered Delhi's striking power in Rajputana was the continuous depredation of the turbulent people of the northern Alwar region, designated as the *Koh-paya* (foot-hills) of Mewat'. They were the Yaduvanshi Rajputs who comprised the proud peasant proprietors of the region. 'Following the loss of their strongholds of Bayana and Tahangarh, they spread themselves over the countryside, and kept up an armed resistance against the Turkish rule, which intensified as the century progressed, and which increasingly tended to merge in the general Rajput offensive. They harried the districts of Shiwalik, Hariana (Hariyana or Haryana) and Bayana, and towards the end of Nasiruddin Mahmud's reign, territorised even Delhi itself'. (A.B.M. Habibullah in *History and Culture of the Indian People*, BVB, vol. v, p. 148).

The earlier attempts of Balban to contain the Meos—freedom-loving and boisterous Rajput peasant proprietors of Mewat, failed to deter them. Following Balban's preoccupations on other war-fronts, the Mewatis became bold enough to lay their hands on the Turkish military posts in the vicinity of Delhi, plundered the royal treasuries and posed a danger to the safety of the capital itself. Balban, therefore, launched two full-scale campaigns against them in 1258-59; a number of bloody battles were fought with the Mewatis but their power could not be crushed. Balban committed atrocities on the populace; but he 'could accomplish little beyond plundering a few Mewati villages and capturing some of their leaders. Although not directed by the Chauhans, the Mewatis yet appear to have operated as their spearheads which kept Delhi engaged in its neighbourhood while Ranthambhor accumulated strength and territory'. (*Ibid.*). These were the last military campaigns of Balban against the Hindu forces of resistance during his tenure as the *naib-i-mulk*; thereafter, he was constrained to adopt a defensive attitude towards them during the reign of sultan Nasiruddin Mahmud.

The Death of Nasiruddin Mahmud: The *Tabaqat-i-Nasiri* of Minhajus Siraj, the most important authority of the contemporary period, comes abruptly to an end about the middle of the year 1260, while our next first-rate authority on the subject , i.e., Ziauddin Barani's *Tarikh-i-Firozeshahi* begins its narrative from the accession of Balban in 1266. Therefore, no authentic information is available about the last days of Nasiruddin Mahmud. Isami, the celebrated author of *Futuhus Salatin*, and Ibn Batuta make us believe that Balban had poisoned his master to death and usurped the throne. But taking into consideration the facts that Nasiruddin was a son-in-law of Balban and that the latter had very close and affectionate relations with the sultan, it is difficult to believe their contention. It is generally held that sultan Nasiruddin Mahmud lived a peaceful life, free from all anxieties of the state, overshadowed by the ever-increasing Mongol menace, and the reverses suffered by his *naib-i-mulk* on the various diplomatic and warfronts, and died a premature but natural death on February 18, 1266. He left behind no male issue. Therefore, Balban, who, in his capacity as the *Naib-i-Mulk* or the Deputy Sultan was already adorned with the insignia of royalty, ascended the throne of Delhi without any opposition from any quarter. Probably, Nasiruddin Mahmud had nominated Balban to the throne before his death. According to A.B.M. Habibullah, 'For nearly twenty years, Mahmud (Nasiruddin) reigned but he never ruled. His piety and simplicity may have been overstressed but of his unassertive nature and weak resolution there can be little doubt. His excessive modesty ill-served the king of a conquering race, for a strong will was an essential pre-requisite for Iltutmish's representative. The king's lack of vigour threatened to destroy respect for the crown. A change on the throne became necessary even in his own lifetime but Mahmud escaped his brother's fate because of the loyal and devoted service of his *Naib*'—Ghiasuddin Balban.—(*The Foundation of Muslim Rule in India*; p. 160)

SECTION 3: THE SECOND ILBARI DYNASTY (1266-90)

Ghiasuddin Balban (1266-86)

Early life of Balban: Bahauddin *alias* Ghiasuddin Balban, who ascended the throne of Delhi on the death of Nasiruddin Mahmud in 1266, was also an Ilbari Turk to which his master Iltutmish belonged. Minhajus Siraj informs us that Balban's grandfather had been a great *khan* of above ten thousand *khanas* or families. In his boyhood, Balban, along with his younger brother Kishlu Khan, cousin Sher Khan Sunqar and many other members of their tribe had been carried away as slaves by the Mongol invaders and sold in the 'slave-markets of Central Asia'. After passing through various hands as slaves, they rediscovered one another in Delhi in 1232-33 when they were purchased by Iltutmish. To his good fortune, one of Balban's earlier masters, Khwaja Jamaluddin of Basra, being an educated man of virtue, had brought him up 'like a son' and provided for his education and training in swordsmanship. Minhajus Siraj writes that impressed by Balban's intelligence, robust health and well-cultured behaviour, Iltutmish 'made him his personal attendant (*khassa-dar*), placing, as one might say, the hawk of fortune on his head. So that in after times, in the reigns of this monarch's children, it might come to pass that this youth should save the kingdom from the violence and machinations of its foes, and raise it to a high pitch of glory and honour'. (*Tabaqat-i-Nasiri*, pp. 356-57). Balban rose quickly to become one of 'the Forty', the most trustworthy and powerful Turkish slave officers of Iltutmish. During the reigns of his weak successors, Balban's rise to power was phenomenal, and the narrative of his early career till his accession to the throne in 1266 merges into the chronicle of the preceding puppet sultans of Delhi from 1236 to 1266. Balban received the title of Ulugh Khan (the great Khan) from sultan Nasiruddin after successfully repelling a Mongol invasion in 1246 when he became the *de facto* ruler of Delhi in his new role as the *naib-i-mulk* or the deputy sultan. His achievements as *wazir* and *naib-i-mulk* from 1246-66 have been given in detail in the above narrative. By the time of Nasiruddin Mahmud's death, he had thoroughly consolidated his position as the de facto ruler of the state and was recognized as the most powerful and undisputed leader of the Shamsi slave officers or 'the Forty'. He ascended the throne with great pomp and show and enjoyed a long reign of twenty years.

Balban as King

Early difficulties of Balban: Balban was faced with numerous problems at the time of his accession to the throne. Because of a long era of weak and imbecile successors of Iltutmish, the prestige and authority of the crown had sunk very low. The military dictatorship established by the Turkish oligarchy of self-seeking and power-hungry nobles, of which Balban himself formed a part, held the semblance of authority at Delhi and kept the skeleton of the foreign Muslim state in northern India intact but their own sovereign or sultan, being a puppet in their hands, did not arouse much respect in the public esteem. The sultan was detested and held cheep, and his military generals as king-makers ruled the state by sheer force as usurpers; they could spread fear and awe in the hearts of their subjects but gave no confidence or sense of security to them on behalf of the state that they represented. The provincial governors were autocratic and aggressive, and they were usually insubordinate to the central authority. The treatment of foreign Turkish bureaucracy towards the people was generally arbitrary and cruel and the safety of life and property of the peace-loving subjects was a far cry. It spread discontent and distrust towards authorities and gave impetus to the anti-social elements to raise their ugly heads. In the words of Barani, 'fear of the governing power, which is the basis of all good government, and the source of the glory and splendour of states, had departed from the hearts of all men, and the country had fallen into a wretched condition'. (*Tarikh-i-Firozeshahi,* pp. 99-100). Therefore, 'the king's authority, more than a concern for the people's welfare, demanded a concentrated drive against this anarchy'. In the concluding years of Nasiruddin' reign, the revival of Mongol raids in northwestern parts of the sultanate kept Balban constantly on the tender hooks, and he was constrained to compromise even the sovereignty of Turkish rule over the regions of Lahore, Multan and Sindh by entering into truce with the Turkish nobles of doubtful integrity. 'Powerful Hindu states in Rajputana and central India had increased their military pressure on the southern borders of the sultanate, while the rebellious Hindu chieftains in the Doab and the Ganga valley threatened disintegration of the Turkish state from within. During the reign of Nasiruddin Mahmud, Balban had, no doubt, maintained the status quo without seeking permanent solutions to some of these problems'. The wearing of the crown by Balban was, therefore not a bed of roses. According to Habibullah, 'an effective solution of these multiplying problems called for a stable central direction which, in the circumstances, could only come from a strong king, realistic in approach and severely efficient in execution'. Balban was fully conscious of this fact that all the external dangers arose as a direct consequence of the internal weakness, which was 'due to the state's incomplete consolidation'. It goes to his credit that Balban proved himself equal to the occasion, and, without losing any time, came to grips with the real problems of state politics and governance to establish his position as an all-powerful sovereign ruler, who was his own master in the matter of providing political and military leadership to the bureaucracy and the ruling elite, besides securing due public recognition as their king, committed to the safety of their lives and properties as his subjects.

Balban's Theory of Kingship and His Style of Governance: No wonder, Balban's first task after his accession to the throne was 'to re-establish the prestige and authority of the state more than a concern for the people's welfare'. He was determined to present himself as the sovereign of 'an integrated and centralized state, symbolized by a strong, unquestioned monarchy'. His installation, therefore, marked a sharp contrast with the style of functioning, initiated by Qutubuddin Aibek in India as a faceless military conqueror without any regal titles and paraphernalia; instead, it imparted an entirely new spirit and vigour to the nascent Turkish rule in Delhi. It publicly demonstrated the end of power-hungry Turkish nobility and the puppet rulers, giving place to a despotic monarchy, for which he formulated his own theory of kingship on the lines of the 'Sassanian monarchy' to claim 'divine sanction for the office of the sultan, and fully exploited the religious sentiments of his people and the Muslim ruling elite to strengthen his hold over the state. The Khalifa of Baghdad was no more but Balban continued to inscribe his name on the coins so that his co-religionists might extend their unqualified obedience to him as *nasir amir-ul-momnin* or the right-hand man of the Khalifa'. Balban's theory of kingship was similar to the 'Theory of the Divine Rights of Kings' as propounded by the Tudor and Stuart kings of England. 'Balban traced his descent from the mythical Turkish hero Afrasiyab and attempted to create a halo of superiority round the monarchy'. Of the Muslim rulers of India, long before Akbar, Balban was the first to give currency to the epithet *Zil-i-Ilahi*, viz., 'the Shadow of God on Earth', which was inscribed on his coins. Thereby, Balban made out that, in his capacity as the Sultan, 'he was above law' as also the Turkish military generals and the Muslim bureaucracy who were instrumental in the very birth of the Muslim rule in India, and that he ruled by 'divine sanction and was not answerable to any worldly authority for the discharge of his powers and functions as a sovereign'. This regal claim, of course, contradicted his own loudly professed position as the king of an Islamic state and his duties towards the *Millat* in the traditional Islamic polity and his authority as the Muslim ruler of an Islamic state nor did it satisfactorily explain his legal position vis-à-vis the Khalifa of which he claimed to be the lieutenant. Nevertheless, Balban strove 'to raise the status and prestige of the crown by claiming divine powers for it'. K. A. Nizami tries to explain away this anomaly by the remarks that (*Comprehensive History of India*, Vol. V, p. 281) 'this was a subtle religious device to sanctify the exercise of his despotic authority'. As regards Balban's theory of kingship, J.L. Mehta observes that 'no sultan of Delhi ever laid stress on it in dialogue and court proceedings like Balban, not even Alauddin Khilji in the later period, who happened to be the most powerful despotic monarch of the sultanate. The funniest part of it was that Balban never felt tired of delivering sermons on this issue to those Shamsi nobles with whom he had once shared the power of the state as a slave officer of Iltutmish. By propagating such theories, Balban intended to exact reverence and loyalty from the common man *albeit* he made himself a subject of ridicule among his ex-colleagues who read in his rhetoric a blunt warning that they must not consider themselves 'king-makers' any longer, and that they would be dealt with severely if they poked their nose into the affairs of the Sultan'. (*Advanced Study in the History of Medieval India*, vol. I, pp. 118-19).

In the words of A.B.M. Habibullah,

> 'Acting on such ideas, matured during his deputyship, and in sharp contrast to the conduct of the weak, unassertive Mahmud, Balban inaugurated his reign by adapting the court ceremonial to the new conception. This included a rigid insistence on the *sijda* or *zaminos* and *paibos* (prostrating before and kissing the king's feet or the throne), two of the non-Islamic practices which Iltutmish was vainly requested by the jurists to regard with disfavour. Since the king's person was to be unapproachable, Balban surrounded himself with body-guards—a picked band of impressively uniformed, fearsome soldiers with drawn sabers glittering in the sun...Acting on the same motive, he gave up his earlier habit of drinking and prohibited the same to his

courtiers. The fear and dignity which he sought to earn by such frightful correctness of conduct was heightened by the effects of the Mongol conquests which sent princes and eminent soldiers flying for asylum to his court'. (*History & Culture of the Indian People*, v, pp. 149-50).

Balban was a typical oriental despot who displayed his autocratic powers and the regal grandeur, and the richness and prosperity of his realm through his court. The contemporary chroniclers sketch beautiful pen-portraits of Balban's magnificent *durbar*, which was organised on the Persian model; it became famous throughout Central Asia for its pomp and grandeur. His courtiers put on specified rich and shining bright 'costumes made of fine silken, woollen and cotton garments, studded with jewels, diamonds and gold ornaments which dazzled the eyes of the onlookers. Behind the Sultan stood his guards, tall and muscular Turkish slaves, in rich attire and heavily armed, with drawn-out swords. Stern discipline was enforced in the durbar; the courtiers and foreign dignitaries occupied their seats in a specified manner; all but two representatives of the Khalifa had to keep standing throughout the court proceedings'. Balban's word was law, and no body was permitted to interrupt the Sultan or defy his orders.

Though well-built and of healthy body physique, Balban was said to be rather ugly in appearance; perhaps it made him suffer from some inferiority complex, and he tried to make up for the deficiency by resorting to aloofness from the commoners and by assuming a very haughty posture. Barani writes that, after his accession to the throne, even the domestic servants of Balban never saw him without 'royal apparel, socks and the headgear'. We are told that no body was allowed to speak in the court without the permission of the Sultan; and he himself spoke but very little, and that too to the highest dignitaries through the Grand Chamberlain. Balban was never seen laughing by anybody, nor did he allow any of his courtiers or subordinates to smile in his presence.

Balban was a racialist to the core; he was extremely conscious of his superior racial birth, and discriminated between the high-born and the low-born people. He gave unequal treatment to his military officers and the Muslim subjects on racial considerations. In order of racial preference, he held the Arabs and the Turks in the highest esteem. Balban 'despised the company of the low and the vulgar, and nothing could ever induce him into unnecessary dalliance or familiarity either with friends or strangers. So punctilious was he in maintaining the prestige of his office that on one occasion, he refused a proffered gift of some *lakhs* from a rich upstart, who had accumulated a vast fortune, but who could not claim a lofty pedigree'. (Ishwari Prasad, *Early Medieval India*; p. 193). With Balban, low birth was the greatest disqualification for public office, and the Muslim nobles and officers never dared to recommend any but a well-born man for employment in the state during his reign. Noble pedigree, in fact, had become a fad with Balban. It is said that one Kamal Mahiya, a capable Muslim military officer and administrator, was not appointed *iqtadar* or governor of Amroha just because he turned out to be the son of a Hindu convert to Islam; 'even those high officials who had recommended his name for the appointment were reprimanded and punished'.

Balban conducted himself as an orthodox Sunni and a devout Muslim, fit to be recognized as the ideal ruler of an Islamic state; it was made out to the people at large that the Sultan offered prayers five times a day and observed other Islamic rituals with regularity. He is known to pay great respects to the *ulama* and the Muslim jurists who were well-provided by the state; he also used to hold discussions with them on *Shariat* and Islamic theology although, being an autocratic ruler, he never allowed them to indulge in the state politics nor brooked disobedience from them. It is said that Balban was always 'eager to make himself popular as the just monarch among his subjects'; the contemporary chroniclers record that he administered 'even-handed justice with extreme impartiality', but 'the slightest disregard of his authority was attended with a punishment which verged on cruelty'. According to Barani, 'two high-ranking officers—the governors of Badaun and Awadh, were given exemplary punishment for reported cruelty to their personal slaves'.

Obviously, there was no place of respect for the infidel Hindus, Buddhists or other non-Muslims in the sultanate, who, incidentally, comprised the majority of his subjects. No wonder, if they were hated and despised by the Sultan himself what to say of the foreign Turkish bureaucracy's treatment towards them; they were tolerated only as *zimmis* or 'the protected people' with limited rights of citizenship because they sustained the Turkish rule by payment of toll tax and other revenues on trade and agricultural produce. Otherwise, they were sternly dealt with and persecuted on the slightest pretexts. Firishta tells us that

> 'Balban made it a rule never to place any Hindu in a position of trust and responsibility. He threw all norms of justice, humanitarian or moral considerations to the winds while dealing with his opponents and committed inhuman barbarities on the innocent subjects under the pretext of restoring law and order'.

Firishta describes the atrocities committed by Balban on the innocent subjects of Bengal during the revolt of Tughril Beg, the governor of Lakhnauti, as follows:

> 'Ghiasuddin Balban, finding the enemy had dispersed, returned to Bengal, and put to death every member of the rebel's family. He did not even spare his innocent women and children; and he carried his rigour so far as to order the execution of a hundred holy mendicants, together with their chief *Qallandar*'.—(Briggs' trs. Indian reprint,Calcutta, 1966, i, pp. 147-48).

Reorganisation of the Army: The sultanate of Delhi was a police state whose very existence and stability depended exclusively on the military strength. The stability and solidarity of Balban's rule and the success of his despotic theory of divine rights of kingship, accordingly, depended upon a powerful army under the charge of his most trustworthy and loyal foreign Turkish nobility, fully committed to serve the Islamic state in India. Balban, therefore, immediately conceived of an elaborate plan to reorganize the armed forces on a war-footing. He separated the army establishment from the rest of the civil administration of the state by taking it out of the control of the *wazir* as well as the finance minister, and created a new post of the *diwan-i-ariz* or the army minister for this purpose. Imadul Mulk, a very competent military general and personal friend of Balban received appointment as the first *diwan-i-ariz* 'with powers equivalent to those of the other central ministers'. He was assigned the duty of recruitment, training and equipment of a powerful central army, under the control of competent foreign military generals, with their direct allegiance to the crown. The *diwan-i-ariz* had to perform multifarious duties in connection with his charge; he acted as the paymaster general of the central army, deployed the royal forces at strategic places, looked after the fortification of important forts and the military posts along the borders of the neighbouring Hindu states, and at many of the inter-state defences within the dominions, but he did not enjoy the actual command of the royal forces. The Sultan kept in his own hands the supreme command of the entire military force, and he nominated the senior commanders under his direct supervision and control in the respective fields of army operations.

Under Qutubuddin Aibek and Iltutmish, the military officers were authorized to recruit their own soldiers; they were trained, equipped and paid for by the respective officers concerned, and in lieu thereof they received land grants in the form of fiefs or *jagirs.* Many of these officers had since expired but their fiefs were still held by their families and successors who did not render any military service to the state. Balban ordered the resumptions of all such fiefs and made provisions for the grant of pensions to the widows and other dependents of the deceased fief-holders. It created discontent among the military officers and even the new-comers became apprehensive of their future prospects under the sultanate. Barani informs us that most of the fief-holders approached Fakhruddin, an elderly *kotwal* of Delhi and a personal friend of Balban, to intervene on their behalf against this measure. On his appeal, the Sultan withdrew his orders, and thereby the old practice of granting lands in lieu of military service to the Turkish nobility continued as before. As a result, the military officers in their capacity as fief-holders and provincial governors continued to recruit the soldiers for the central government as before though, after the creation of the office of the *diwan-i-ariz,* they were now put under greater obligations to recruit, train and equip them according to more stringent specifications; they provided military contingents to the central government as and when required. It did result in improving the efficiency and standard of performance of these feudal contingents. Of course, Balban failed to lay the foundations of a permanent standing army of the state under the direct supervision and control of the crown, but in order to make up this deficiency, he multiplied manifold the recruitment of royal guards, including the foot soldiers as well as the cavaliers, trained and equipped by the state with the latest weapons of offence and defence. Its horsemen comprised small but very fast-moving mobile units of archers, spearmen and the swordsmen, with firm commitment and allegiance to the crown. They, in fact, came to form a vast standing army under the direct control of the Sultan and stationed in the Red Fort and in the vicinity of the capital. The foundation of this military establishment had been laid by Balban during the reign of sultan Nasiruddin Mahmud, when, in his capacity as the *naib-i-mulk* or the deputy sultan, he started the practice of carrying the Royal Standards, including the puppet king, along with the central army, supplied by various fief-holders, for military operations. As this practice added to his personal safety and strength also, Balban slowly and steadily multiplied and expanded the regiments of the royal guards—foot soldiers as well as the horsemen, apparently for the safety of the sultan and the royal household; this policy paid him dividends when he himself became the sovereign monarch of the sultanate.

The Spy System: Balban organised a very efficient system of espionage to keep himself fully informed of the activities of the bureaucracy, law-enforcing agencies and the provincial governors. Well-organised bands of secret-service agents and fast-moving horsemen, paid and controlled by the central government, under the personal direction and control of the Sultan, were posted as secret news-agents and reporters throughout his dominions to apprise him of all that was going on at the district and provincial headquarters of the *Iqtadars* and in various parts of his kingdom. Balban thus acted as the fore-runner of Alauddin Khilji in the matter of organisation of the most efficient spy system to strengthen his position. These secret-service agents were authorized to report to the Sultan all sorts of abnormal and nefarious activities of the state officials, members of royalty and even the influential citizens, and neglect of official duties or violation of the state regulations by the bureaucracy in the performance of their functions. Stringent punishments were inflicted on those secret agents and the news-reporters who failed to perform their duty diligently; it is said that the news-writer of Badaun did not send the report about the unbecoming public conduct of the official dignitary, Malik Baqbaq, to Delhi; when the Sultan came to know of it, he ordered the defaulter to be hanged publicly at the main gate of the town.

Restoration of Law and Order: After his accession to the throne, restoration of law and order in and around the capital of Delhi and the Doab was the first priority of Balban. Therefore, after making a quick review of the internal security and defences of the Red Fort, Balban checked the antecedents of the military commanders in charge of the Royal Guards and contingents of the central army, then available, and launched a vigorous drive to restore law and order in and around Delhi.

Suppression of the Meos: As referred to earlier, the Meos or Mewatis, the inhabitants of Alwar and modern Haryana, were the Yaduvanshi Rajputs and peasant proprietors of the region, situated very close to Delhi. Being the sons of the soil, and freedom-loving and boisterous Hindu community of the region, they were never reconciled to the establishment of the Muslim rule at Delhi. No wonder, they had exhibited extreme hostility towards the Turkish sultans from the very inception of the Sultanate. According to Barani, the turbulence of the Meos or Mewatis had seriously hampered the defences of Delhi and endangered the life and property of its inhabitants at the time of Balban's accession; he writes that

> 'the Meos had become so daring that they sometimes carried their plundering raids within the capital, right beneath the walls of the royal palace....The people of Delhi were unable to sleep owing to the fear of the Meos, who had also plundered all the inns in the neighbourhood ...The roads (leading to and from the capital) were closed on all sides, and it was impossible for the caravans and the traders to come and depart ...Owing to the fear of the Meos; the western gates of the city were closed at the time of the afternoon prayer, and no one had the courage to go out of the city after that time either to visit the sacred tombs or to enjoy by the side of the Sultani (Shamsi) tank. But even before the afternoon prayers, the Meos molested the *bhishtis* (water-carriers) and slave-girls, who went to fetch water from the tank; the Meos took off their clothes and left them nude'. (*Tarikh-i-Firoze Shahi*, E&D.iii, Indian reprint ,Kitab Mahal, p. 104).

In our opinion,'if such was really the case, what had Balban been doing as the *naib-i-mulk* of sultan Nasiruddin Mahmud, to secure the defences of the capital? May be, the account of Barani is an exaggeration to highlight the achievements of Balban as the greatest of all the earlier sultans. May be, Balban had been marking time during the last few years to make the people feel the necessity of a strong and powerful monarch'. (*Advanced Study*, i, p.116 fn.). Balban launched an all-out offensive against the Meos. 'The thick jungles, which had grown all around Delhi, and the unreclaimed land of Hariana, covered with thorny herbs and shrubs, and the sand dunes were their main hide-outs'. Balban moved out of the capital and setup his military camp in the heart of the Meo-infested areas; the jungles on the periphery of the capital were cleared and the Mewatis were hunted out of their dens and killed in thousands. Roads were constructed to facilitate the movement of armies in hot chase of the trouble-shooters. A huge fort was built at Gopalgir and many police-posts were set in the infested areas which were heavily garrisoned by the Afghan militia under the charge of their ruthless and ferocious commanders with instructions to wipe out all the miscreants by complete destruction of their hearths and homes, crops, and all other means of their subsistence. Barani tells us that 'a hundred thousand males of the Meos, above the age of twelve, were massacred in cold blood; their women were enslaved, property pillaged and houses put on fire. Their lands were confiscated and distributed among the enterprising Turko-Afghan officers'.

Balban's policy of 'Blood and Iron' thus proved very fruitful, and within a year of his accession to the throne, he was successful in making the metropolis of Delhi safe from the menace of the Meos and other anti-social elements. Balban instructed his provincial governors to adopt equally stringent measures to restore law and order within their own respective regions by all means at their disposal.

Total destruction of the once powerful and influential Yaduvanshi Rajput community of the Meos or Mewatis at the hands of Balban had its natural consequences; persecution of their unarmed civilian population, accompanied by the general massacre of their men folk wiped out all Hindu resistance to the Turkish rule in and around Delhi. The genocide of the Hindus and enslavement of thousands of the Meo women (along with their minor children) implied their automatic conversion to Islam through coercion and their forced marriages to the Muslim soldiery, giving birth to the present-day Muslim community of Mewat. Barani's contention is correct that after this genocide of the Hindus and drastic demographic changes in the region, 'the people became tractable, obedient and submissive; self-assertion and self-will were thrown aside and all refrained from insubordination and insolence'.

Suppression of the Refractory Hindu Chiefs: After extirpation of the Meo miscreants, Balban turned his attention to the refractory Hindu chieftains of the Doab and Awadh (modern Uttar Pradesh). The Ganga valley had been overrun by the Turkish forces like a whirlwind but the sultans had failed to bring the heartland of the Hindu civilization and culture under their firm control because of tough opposition from its indigenous population. The inhabitants of these areas were rich and prosperous owing to the fertility of the soil, but being staunch Hindus, with the roots of their culture going back to the remote past, they deeply resented the establishment of the Muslim rule. The people as a whole felt indignation over the loss of their political and religious freedom, and they did not willingly pay taxes to the Turkish officials nor did they permit them establish their footholds in their habitats; they offered tough resistance even to the foreign Muslim settlers and Hindu converts to Islam in their midst.

During the reign of Nasiruddin Mahmud, Balban, in his capacity as the de facto ruler, failed to take effective measures against their rising power. After assuming the reins of government in his hands in 1266, he made up his mind to crush the forces of Hindu resistance for all the times to come. He, therefore, divided the whole of the Ganga valley into small administrative divisions or fiefs, and the *iqtas* or provinces which entrusted to the ambitious Turkish and Afghan officials, with full powers to crush the insubordinate Hindu (*kafir*) *zamindars* with an iron hand. He built very strong forts at Kampil, Patiali, Bhojpur and Jalali, all of which were fortified and heavily garrisoned with the semi-barbarous Afghan troops, who were frequently let loose for loot and plunder and to wreak their vengeance upon the refractory Hindu populace of the neighbouring villages to keep them under control. They were also kept in readiness to support the respective governors of the region in their punitive expeditions against the rebellious Hindu chiefs. Barani tells us that the Sultan himself 'went to Kampil and Patiali and stayed in these territories for five or six months. He put robbers and rebels unhesitatingly to the sword; the route to Hindustan (Awadh) was opened and caravans and merchants could come and go in peace. A lot of plunder of the region came to Delhi, where slaves and cattle became cheap'. (*Tarikh-i-Firoze Shahi*, p. 105).

While Balban was busy in the restoration of law and order in Awadh, he received the news of an uprising of the Bundellas in Katehar (Bundelkhand) which the Muslim governors of Badaun and Amroha failed to crush. He at once returned to Delhi for reinforcements and after making necessary arrangements, marched on Katehar with a fresh army without any loss of time. Balban issued orders for the total annihilation of the rebels by all means. Ishwari Prasad writes that during his expedition to Katehar, Balban 'ordered his men to attack the villages, to set fire to the houses, and to slay the entire adult male population. Innocent women and children were dragged into slavery. By these barbarous methods, he struck terror into the hearts of the people and depopulated the entire region. In every village and jungle, heaps of human corpses were left rotting. The remnants of the people, lurking here and there, were thoroughly cowed down'.(*Early Medieval India*; p. 79).

Stanley Lanepoole reproduces some of the extracts from the narrative of Barani to surmise that 'Balban pounced upon a disturbed district like a hawk, burnt and slew without mercy, till the blood of the rioters ran in streams, heaps of slain were seen near every village and jungle, and the stench of the dead even spread to the Ganges. Wood-cutters were sent to cut roads through the jungles, and, like the reform of Marshal Wade in Scotland, the road making did more to bring order among the wild tribes than even the massacre of their fighting men'. (*Medieval India*; pp. 71-72). At a later stage, Balban sent one such punitive expedition to the rebellious territories of Rajputana and another for the suppression of the Khokhars of the Salt Range in the Punjab but these campaigns met with partial success.

Destruction of *Chalisa* or 'the Forty': Balban had risen to power with the support of his fellow Turkish slaves of Iltutmish, which became known as the Shamsi slave officers or 'the Forty'. At the time of his accession to the throne, a number of them were holding high offices of the state as ministers, military generals and provincial governors. During the reign of sultan Nasiruddin Mahmud, Balban had consolidated his position as the deputy sultan and risen head and shoulders above all the other members of the *Chalisa* or 'the Forty'. Nevertheless, he was aware that they were highly ambitious and powerful military generals. Being proud of their superior status, they rightly considered themselves to be the share-holders and partners of Balban in the acquisition of royal powers. Therefore, Balban apprehended that, given the opportunity, they could join their hands together to establish their dominance over him, or any one of them might assume leadership of the *Chalisa* and claim the throne for himself. But Balban aspired to establish an absolute monarchy, confined to himself and his family, and the *Chalisa* naturally constituted the stumbling block in the fulfilment of his ambitions. He, therefore, was eager 'to remove the ladder by which he had once risen to the exalted office of the sultan'. Accordingly, soon after his accession to the throne, Balban began to pursue a subtle policy to curtail the powers and military strength of the Shamsi nobles one by one, on one pretext or the other but without provoking the rest of them or making them conscious of his evil designs. In the first instance, many of them were sent out of Delhi as governors of the outlying *iqtas* to safeguard the borders of the sultanate against the Mongol inroads and the hostile Hindu powers so as to reduce their power of mischief in the royal court. Secondly, he made frequent transfers of the Shamsi nobles from one place to the other so that they might not establish favourable contacts with the local bureaucracy and important public men or develop vested interests. Thirdly, the Shamsi nobles were frequently deployed on the most dangerous and risky assignments, usually on the war-fronts to keep them engaged against the heavy odds. Fourthly, he promoted very junior officers and even the new-comers from central Asia to important offices, previously reserved for the senior nobility, and placed them on a position of equality with 'the Forty', thus blurring the line of demarcation between the seniors and juniors. In consequence, with the passage of time, some of the senior Shamsi nobles died and the others were downgraded and disgraced or liquidated, and an entirely new class of Turkish nobility, came into existence which transplanted the Shamsi nobles. And, last but not the least, Balban adopted a highly arrogant and stern attitude towards each and every Shamsi noble, and inflicted severe punishments to them for the slightest faults or mistakes committed by them even inadvertently in the performance of their duties. It was done by him deliberately to tarnish their reputation and undermine their political status.

To cite but a few examples of Balban's harsh treatment towards his erstwhile colleagues—the Shamsi nobles or the *Chalisa*, who formed his props and support in his rise to power:

1. It was in this context that Balban had ordered Malik Baqbaq to be flogged publicly, disgraced and demoted just because he had caused one of his domestic servants to be beaten to death.
2. In another such incident, Haibat Khan, the governor of Awadh, was reported to have killed a man under the influence of drink. On the receipt of complaint against him, Balban took him to task and ordered him to be whipped publicly; as a punishment, 'he received 500 stripes on his bare body, which left him in a pool of blood. He was then handed over to the widow of the deceased person, who was authorized to stab him to death'. It is said that, according to the Islamic law, the relatives of Haibat Khan secured his release from the aggrieved woman by paying a compensation of twenty thousand *tankas,* but the unfortunate accused died of his wounds soon thereafter.
3. Sher Khan Sunqar, a cousin of Balban and his close ally since his early days as the slave of Iltutmish, was a capable military general, who, in his capacity as the governor of Multan and Uchh, had stood as a bulwark against the Mongol inroads into the northwestern frontier. He was said to be very ambitious but this

was not the cause of his disobedience towards Balban. Barani informs us that he incurred the displeasure of Balban because he had 'failed to turn up in Delhi and to pay personal salutations to him at the time of his coronation. The sultan, therefore, began to distrust him and, ultimately, got him poisoned to death' in 1270. (*Tarikh-i-Firoze Shahi*, pp. 108-09).

Tughril Khan's Revolt in Bengal (1279-81): Ever since the days of Muhammad bin Bakhtiyar Khilji, the control of Delhi over the outlying provinces of Bengal and Bihar had been very lax. The long distance from the imperial headquarters and the poor means of communication, coupled with 'the damp and malarious climate' of the region hampered the establishment of strict control over its eastern territories by the central government. According to Barani, 'the people of this country had for many long years evinced a disposition to revolt, and the disaffected and the evil-minded persons among them generally succeeded in alienating the loyalty of the governors'. Accordingly, taking advantage of the pre-occupation elsewhere of the sultans of Delhi, the successive governors of Bengal and Bihar, with their headquarters at Lakhnauti, had, more than once, declared their independence and defied the central authority with impunity. Iltutmish had to fight many a battle against the rebellious elements of Bihar and Bengal in 1226-30; his eldest son, prince Nasiruddin Mahmud had re-conquered both the provinces and was appointed their viceroy by Iltutmish, but he died a premature death, leaving the region in turmoil again. Ultimately, Iltutmish had separated the two provinces permanently and appointed separate governors for each. During the weak rule of the successors of Iltutmish, the governors of Lakhnauti had again asserted their independence. According to A.B.M. Habibullah, when Balban ascended the throne, Tatar Khan, the rebellious chief of Lakhnauti 'prudently submitted to Balban and, as a token of allegiance, sent a number of elephants to Delhi. Thereupon, he was presumably confirmed in the post'. (*Foundation of the Muslim Rule in India*, p. 172). But how long did he rule over Bengal as the governor of Delhi is not known. Probably, he was removed from this post by Balban after some time, when he appointed one of his own Turkish slave officers, named Tughril Khan as the governor of Lakhnauti.

Tughril Khan was said to be 'a brave and warlike man' and a trustworthy slave officer of Balban. He led several successful military expeditions against his neighbouring Hindu chieftains and compelled them to pay tribute; from these campaigns he secured 'enormous wealth' in the form of booty also which helped him in raising a large army without the knowledge of Delhi. With his state treasury full to the brim, and intoxicated with the possession of a formidable army, Tughril became overconfident of his military prowess; and on the ill advice of some over-ambitious and self-seeking Bengali officers, he raised a standard of revolt against Delhi in 1279. Taking advantage of the fresh Mongol incursions on the northwest frontier, and illness of the aged sultan, Tughril Khan withheld the payment of annual tribute to Delhi, and declared his independence. He formally ascended the throne of Lakhnauti by assuming the regal title of sultan Mughisuddin; he struck coins and got the *khutba* read in his name. To inaugurate the beginning of his sovereign rule, on a high note, Tughril Khan made an unprovoked attack on the neighbouring Hindu principality of Jajnagar (Orissa), which originally did not belong to him, and carried off a large booty from there, consisting of immense wealth in the form of gold, silver and other valuables, besides numerous horses and war elephants, to Lakhnauti, and kept it all to himself without making any reference to Delhi. Balban was shocked to hear of the treacherous conduct of his old Turkish slave. He flew into rage and at once directed another of his trustworthy slave officers, Amin Khan, the governor of Awadh, to take the field against Tughril. Amin Khan crossed the river Sarju, and proceeded towards Lakhnauti at the head of a large army but was intercepted and defeated by Tughril Khan 'near the Gogra in north Bihar', and fled the field. The vanquished royal army of Delhi fled pell-mell; some of the royal troops 'deserted their colours and went over to the enemy'; while the rest of the 'retreating army suffered heavy losses at the hands of the Hindu tribes of Awadh'. Amin Khan escaped alive from the battlefield, but the enraged sultan called him to Delhi and ordered him to be hanged. The later chroniclers record that 'the unjust execution of the Khan produced a feeling of consternation among the wise men of the age, who read in this atrocious decree the doom of the Balbani regime'.

The second royal expedition, sent by Balban under the command of Tirmiti or Tirmati Khan also met with a similar fate at the hands of Tughril Khan. In desperation, this vanquished Turkish general was also ordered to be hanged by Balban. According to Yahya bin Ahmad Sirhindi, Tughril Khan 'seems to have enormously increased in strength' because he defeated a third royal army, now sent by Balban under the command of Shihabuddin, the successor of Amin Khan as the governor of Awadh. The successive defeats of the royal armies at the hands of his erstwhile slave and once the capable and trustworthy military officer of the state, 'made Balban almost mad with rage. He was now in his eightieth year, and the Mongol pressure had by no means subsided. But he decided to lead the fourth expedition personally and thus stake his all to vindicate the crown's authority. And he swore never to return without the rebel's head'. (A.B.M. Habibullah, *The Foundation of Muslim Rule in India*; loc. cit; p. 173). After entrusting the affairs of Delhi to his most capable military general, Malik Fakhruddin, and deputing his eldest son, Prince Muhammad 'to keep a vigilant eye upon the Mongols', Balban started for Lakhnauti 'in spite of the rains'. Apart from a formidable force of the Royal Guards, the imperial army of invasion was strengthened by more than two *lakhs of* the additional horsemen and foot-soldiers, who were supplied by the *iqtadars* of the Doab and the Ganga valley. A huge fleet of thousands of boats sailed through the Ganga River to facilitate the movement of foot-soldiers and supplies.

On hearing of the full-fledged invasion of Bengal by the royal forces of Delhi, Tughril Khan lost his heart. He hurriedly collected his treasures and retreated with his family and the bulk of his army somewhere into the interior towards the southeast, in the jungles of Jajnagar. 'He depended on the climate and the waterlogged soil of the province to wear out the forces of Delhi and the King's patience when he hoped to emerge from his retreat and reoccupy the capital'. (*Ibid*; p. 174). Balban stormed Lakhnauti with a lightening speed and took possession of it without much difficulty. He was, however, not the man to rest contented with the flight of his foe. He spread his scouts into the interior to comb the jungles. Tughril Khan's hideout was discovered by one of his scouting parties, and he was taken unawares by the royal forces. The rebel army was completely destroyed; Tughril Khan fell fighting in his camp, and his head was presented to the sultan. All members of Tughril Khan's family, his relatives and friends and other supporters, besides the men-in-arms, who fell into the hands of the victors alive, were executed mercilessly on Balban's orders. Barani explains the aftermath of Tughril Khan's fall as given below:

> 'The sultan returned to Lakhnauti and there ordered that gibbets be erected along both sides of the *bazaar*, which was more than a *kos* in length. He ordered all the sons and sons-in-law of Tughril, and all men, who had served him or borne arms for him, to be slain and placed upon the gibbets...The punishments went on during the two or three days that the sultan remained at Lakhnauti, and

the beholders were so horrified that they nearly died of fear. I (viz., Barani—the writer) have heard from several old men that such punishment was inflicted on (*sic*) Lakhnauti as had never been heard of in Delhi, and no one could remember anything like it in Hindustan'. (*Tarikh-i-Firoze Shahi*, pp. 119-20).

Barani does not stop his narrative of Tughril's rebellion here. He continues that after the ghastly slaughter of Tughril Khan's associates at Lakhnauti was over, the sultan entrusted the governorship of Bengal to his second son, Bughra Khan, who had accompanied the royal army with him, and advised him to restore law and order in the region by adopting stern measures similarly. Many of the medieval chroniclers profusely reproduce the perceived dialogue, probably overheard by the eye-witnesses that took place between Balban and his son before the former's return to the capital; the sultan is said to have issued the stern warning to his son thus:

> 'If ever designing and evil-minded persons should incite you to waver in your allegiance to Delhi and to throw off its authority, then remember the vengeance which you have seen exacted in the *bazaar*. Understand me and forget not that if the governors of Hind or Sindh, of Malwa or Gujarat, of Lakhnauti pr Sonargaon, shall draw the sword and become rebels to the throne of Delhi, then such punishment as has fallen upon Tughril and his dependents will fall upon them, their wives, their children, and all their adherents'.

Bughra Khan felt so much dejected at the barbarous deeds of his father that he assumed total aloofness from the royal family at Delhi. So much so, on the untimely death of his elder brother, prince Muhammad, the eldest son of Balban and the warden of the marshes in northwestern India, Bughra Khan 'declined the offer of his dying father to accept nomination to the throne of Delhi' and became contented with the governorship of Bengal.

Defensive Measures against the Mongols: For the suppression of revolt in Bengal, Balban seldom moved out of Delhi for fear of the recurring Mongol incursions of northwestern India. Balban throws a very interesting light on Balban's policy to meet the Mongol menace. He tells us that

> 'The intimate friends and officers of Balban often said to him: *"How is it that with your well-equipped and disciplined army, you do not undertake any distant campaign, and never move out of your territory to conquer other regions?"*

The Sultan replied: "These accursed wretches (the Mongols) have heard of the wealth and prosperity of Hindustan, and have set their hearts upon conquering and plundering it. They have taken and plundered Lahore, within my territories, and no year passes that they do not come here and plunder the villages. They watch the opportunity of my departure on a distant campaign to enter my cities and ravage the whole Doab. They even talk about the conquest and sack of Delhi. I have devoted all the revenues of my sources ready and prepared to receive them. I never leave my kingdom, nor will I go to any distance from it". (*Tarikh-i-Firoze Shahi*, pp. 102-03).

Accordingly, Balban had adopted very elaborate arrangements for the protection of his northwestern borders against the intrusion of the Mongols from the beginning of his reign. His cousin Sher Khan Sunqar held the governorship of Multan and Uchh with special responsibility to protect the northwestern frontier. On his death in 1270, prince Muhammad, the eldest son of Balban, was assigned this charge. Balban created a second line of defence against the Mongols by placing the *iqtas* of Sunam, Samana and Dipalpur in southwestern and modern Haryana under the control of his second son Bughra Khan; he held this charge until 1279, when Balban deputed him to proceed to Bengal along with the royal armies for the suppression of Tughriḷ Khan's rebellion. At the same time, Balban himself preferred to stay in the capital as far as possible. He took care to keep a powerful contingent of 30,000 strong mobile cavalry permanently at Delhi to reinforce the royal forces of northwestern India to meet the Mongol challenge at a moment's notice.

In 1285, the Mongols, under the leadership of Timur Khan launched a major offensive in the Punjab. Prince Muhammad fought a number of actions against them and died fighting in one of the battles near Dipalpur in February 1286. It gave a serious setback to the aged sultan and considerably hampered his war operations against the Mongol marauders. The provinces of Lahore and Dipalpur, including the two major towns were plundered and devastated by them although the provinces of Multan and Uchh escaped their furry because of the heroic defence put up by Kai Khusrau, the youthful son of the deceased prince Muhammad. On the whole, Balban' policy to tackle the Mongol menace was defensive in nature because his first priority was to consolidate his position at Delhi and establish his strong foothold in the heart of Hindu-dominated regions of the Ganga valley, the Doab and the eastern provinces of Bihar and Bengal.

Balban's Death

The crown prince Muhammad was the most capable of all the children of Balban. He had already been nominated to succeed his father as the next monarch. His untimely death in harness, therefore, proved fatal for the octogenarian sultan. Barani writes that the grief-stricken sultan kept himself well composed and continued to transact the state business during the day as usual as if 'he was unaffected by the tragic blow that he had sustained, but in the night, cried out in bitter anguish, tore his garments and threw dust upon his head'. He called for his second son Bughra Khan from Bengal and offered him the crown of Delhi, but the latter spurned the offer 'and quietly left for Lakhnauti on the pretext of a hunting expedition'. The broken-hearted sultan died about the middle of the year 1287, leaving behind a '*will*', in which he had nominated his grandson Kai Khusrau, the son of the deceased prince Muhammad as his successor.

An Estimate of Balban

By all accounts, Ghiasuddin Balban was one of the greatest sultans of Delhi. Ziauddin Barani, the celebrated author of *Tarikh-i-Firoze Shahi* and the greatest of all the Muslim historians of the early medieval India, pays a handsome tribute to Balban in the following words:

> 'Sultan Ghiasuddin Balban was a man of experience in matters of government. From being a *malik*, he became a *khan*, and from being a *khan*, be became a king. When he attained the throne, he imparted to it new luster; he brought the administration into order, and restored to efficiency institutions whose power had been shaken or destroyed. The dignity and authority of government was restored, and his stringent rules and resolute determination caused all men, high and low, throughout his dominions, to submit to his authority. Fear and awe of him took possession of all men's hearts, but his justice and his consideration for his people won the favour of his subjects and made them zealous supporters of his throne'. (*Ibid*; p. 99).

A great warrior and capable administrator, Balban established an absolute monarchy of the Turkish conquerors in India. He did not resort to fresh conquests but, by the use of brutal force and the pursuit of 'blood and iron policy', he consolidated his rule and laid the foundations of the sultanate of Delhi very deep. He protected the nascent Muslim rule in India from internal revolts and external threats from the Mongols. Of course, his harsh treatment towards his own fellow Turkish slave officers, deliberate and willful humiliation and destruction of the Shamsi nobles, and cruel, rather inhuman, punishments inflicted on the guilty and not so guilty in the name of justice and fair play, struck awe and terror in the hearts of the nobility as well as the public. It suppressed all voices of opposition to his methods of highhandedness and enabled him to restore law and order in his dominions for the time being but it was not a permanent cure for uprooting opposition to the foreign Muslim rule by the indigenous population nor did it ensure the perpetuation of his family's rule at Delhi for a long time. A.B.M. Habibullah points out that 'in one aspect of his policy, Balban showed a lamentable lack of statesmanlike vision. This was his extreme racialism, which led him to make the sultanate an exclusively Turkish concern. He affected a great repugnance to associating with what he called 'men of low origin', and could not bear the sight of the native Mussalmans in his government'. Nevertheless, he was a Sunni Muslim by faith and behaved as a religious fanatic in his dealings with the Hindus and Buddhists, who comprised more than 90 per cent of his subjects. He held the Muslim *ulama* and theologians in high esteem, and in his clarion call to the Turkish nobility and the Muslim camp-followers, he exhibited firm commitment to convert the *dar-ul-harab* of India into *dar-ul-Islam,* and it was this line of approach which ensured him the unquestioned support of his co-religionists. Balban liberally granted asylum and huge privy purses to the central Asian fugitive Muslim princes and welcomed all the immigrant Arab, Turkish and Afghan soldiers of fortune; thereby, he not only earned their goodwill but also made his name famous in the far off lands. That is why, brilliant Muslim scholars, administrators and fighters flocked to his court to seek gainful employment and permanent settlement in India. It made Balban's court 'a centre of Islamic culture and learning' and added to the Muslim population in the country.

Sudden Collapse of Balban's Dynasty

As a despotic king, Balban aspired to perpetuate the rule of his family but the luck willed it otherwise. The untimely death of the crown prince Muhammad and the indifference of his second son Bughra Khan towards the throne proved Balban's undoing. His dying will to nominate his grandson, Kai Khusrau, son of the deceased Prince Muhammad, was contemptuously brushed aside by the Turkish nobility, under the leadership of Fakhruddin, the aged *Kotwal* of Delhi and *Wazir* of Balban, who preferred to place his second grandson Kaiqubad—the 17 years old son of Bughra Khan, on the throne. Kai Khusrau was sent out of the capital as governor of Multan and Uchh. It led to sharp division among the nobles and also created bitter enmity between the two rival factions of Balban's royal family which proved disastrous for the ruling house of Balban. In the revival of court intrigues and conspiracies, Kaiqubad, who was installed as the king with the title of Sultan Muizuddin, could not remain unaffected for long and the crown's authority slipped out of his hands, giving place to the short-lived regime of kingmakers once again.

Kaiqubad, an inexperienced and pleasure-seeking youth, proved absolutely worthless as a ruler. Being the offspring of Balban's second son, he was, perhaps, not expected to be trained for the role of a future monarch, unlike the children of the crown prince Muhammad. He was brought up under the personal care of his 'puritanical grandfather', who did not allow him to drink or taste the pleasures of life; according to Barani, the prince 'could not glance at a fair face or drain a goblet of wine'. Finding himself suddenly and unexpectedly elevated to the throne and made the master of his free will, with immense wealth and resources at his command, Kaiqubad lost his balance of mind. It aroused his pent-up desires and passions to enjoy the best things of life, and he plunged 'in unrestraint indulgence in wine, women and gaiety'. The example set by him was readily followed by his courtiers and ministers, with the resultant neglect of administration and weakening of the centre's hold over its military commanders and the bureaucracy. This unhealthy development undid the whole work of Balban to establish an absolute monarchy, and the pleasure-loving sultan was soon surrounded by self-seeking men of easy virtue. Malik Nizamuddin—an ambitious son-in-law of Fakhruddin, was one such unscrupulous and ambitious person who entered the inner circle of Kaiqubad's personal friends, and usurped all the powers of the crown.

Previously, Nizamuddin held only a subordinate judicial post as the chief magistrate in the metropolis, but taking advantage of his close relationship with Malik Fakhruddin, the senior most Turkish noble and *Kotwal* of Delhi, he carved out a personal friendship with Kaiqubad. Nizamuddin 'possessed the virtues of a shrewd and able administrator', and lost no time in gaining the confidence of the young sultan. Before long, he established his domination over Kaiqubad and reduced him to the position of a mere puppet in his hands. While Kaiqubad indulged in drunken revelries, Nizamuddin transacted the administrative business as the de facto ruler. He sent his wife to reside in the palace and to assume control of the sultan's *harem*. It was this 'intemperance and licentiousness' of the sultan which, ultimately, encouraged Nizamuddin 'to harbour designs of usurping the throne at a favourable moment'. It was, in fact, Nizamuddin, who apparently in the interest of sultan Kaiqubad, started the game of liquidating his political rivals. Kai Khusrau, the rival claimant to the throne of Delhi was put to death on the secret orders of Nizamuddin. It spread consternation and panic throughout the sultanate because Kai Khusrau, the governor of Multan and Uchh and the most capable of Balban's royal family, 'still commanded the respect and esteem of the nobility'. When Bughra Khan, the ruler of Bengal, came to know of such developments he became apprehensive of the safety of his son Kaiqubad. The contemporary chroniclers give widely different versions about the subsequent meeting that took place between Bughra Khan and Kaiqubad in Awadh in which the former advised Kaiqubad to protect himself from the evil intentions and intrigues of Nizamuddin. According to Ibn Battuta and Amir Khusrau, Bughra Khan intended to assert his claim to the throne of Delhi by ousting Kaiqubad from power but Abdul Qadir Badauni says that Bughra Khan, who had already assumed independent authority at Lakhnauti by the title of Sultan Nasiruddin, had no pretensions to occupy the imperial throne, which he had voluntarily declined to accept from the hands of his ailing father, Ghiasuddin Balban. From Badaoni's account, we infer that Bughra Khan had repeatedly warned his son of the designs of Nizamuddin through secret correspondence but Kaiqubad did not heed his advice. Ultimately, 'it was decided that Bughra Khan should leave Lakhnauti and Kaiqubad should start from Delhi, and that both should meet in Awadh'. After a cordial get-together between the father and the son, the two returned to their respective headquarters, and it was on the secret advice of Bughra Khan that Kaiqubad got rid of Nizamuddin by poisoning him to death through his agents. (*Muntakhab-ut Tawarikh;* i, S.A. Ranking, p. 222).

After the liquidation of Nasiruddin, Kaiqubad appointed Amir Jalaluddin Firoze Khilji as the *ariz-i-mumalik* or the 'paymaster general' of the royal army, and assigned him the important fief of Baran

(Bulandshahr). This appointment was not approved by the Turkish aristocracy of the capital and military generals of the regime who looked down upon the Khiljis as non-Turks. It created an open rift between the two rival factions of the court, one led by the privileged class of the Turkish and Arab aristocracy and the other that of the commoners or the non-privileged class of Muslim bureaucracy, including the Afghans, Khiljis and the Hindu converts to Islam. Caught in between the two factions, Kaiqubad failed to exercise his royal authority, and disorder and confusion prevailed everywhere. To his misfortunes, excessive indulgence in the sensuous pleasures had ruined Kaiqubad's health. About this time, he suffered from a stroke of paralysis and was incapacitated for all physical and mental work when he was hardly twenty. It triggered off the struggle for power between the ambitious military generals, and the rival factions came into open clash with each other. Being cut-throats, they started a horrible game of political murders and conspiracies to eliminate their opponents. It was in this struggle for power that Jalaluddin Khilji, then the governor of Samana and leader of one of the factions, took forced possession of Delhi early in 1290 and declared himself the sultan. Kaiqubad, who was confined to bed as a physical wreck, was kicked to death by a Khilji soldier and thrown into the Yamuna river, while his infant son Kaimurs died in the prison-cell of Jalaluddin Khilji in March 1290. It marked the end of Balban's ruling family and era of the 'Slave Sultans' of Delhi so-called.

❑ ❑

5

THE KHILJI DYNASTY (1290-1320)

SECTION 1: JALALUDDIN FIROZE SHAH KHILJI (1290-96)

The Khilji Revolution

Jalaluddin Firoze Shah, who ascended the throne of Delhi after the fall of the Slave Dynasty in 1290, belonged to the Khalji or Khilji tribe of the Turks. Usually misunderstood as non-Turks by the Turkish aristocracy of the thirteenth century India, the Khaljis comprised one of their 64 clans but they were not 'pure Turks'. The latest researches show that their forefathers had migrated to modern Afghanistan in the fourth century of the Christian era where they mixed up with the local inhabitants and adopted the Afghan socio-cultural traits long before their conversion to Islam. They joined the armies of Mahmud of Ghazni and Muhammad Ghori as ordinary soldiers and won applause from their masters for their bravery and martial qualities. Muhammad bin Bakhtiyar Khilji was the earliest known military general of their clan under Muhammad Ghori who conquered Bihar and Bengal and received appointment as the governor of the conquered territories. There is no doubt about it that the Khiljis belonged to the non-privileged class of ordinary Muslims, like the Hindu converts to Islam in India, and were treated as such by the foreign Turkish ruling elite of the period. They had no claim to political power in their original habitats of Turkistan or Afghanistan and formed a part of the common Muslim immigrants to India. Naturally, they were looked down upon by the privileged class of Turkish and Arab military officers who played a premier role in the foundation of the Muslim rule in India; as referred to in the previous chapter, racialism had been introduced in the Muslim Indian polity by none else but Ghiasuddin Balban, one of the founding fathers of the Sultanate of Delhi. Therefore, the rise to power of Jalaluddin Khilji was not a mere change of the ruling dynasty; it was a sort of political revolution in the history of the Muslim rule in India.

Early Career and Accession of Jalaluddin Khilji

Nothing is known about the parentage and early life of Jalaluddin Khilji. Ziauddin Barani in his *Tarikh-i-Firoze Shahi* introduces the founder of the Khilji dynasty by the simple observation that he 'came of a race different from that of the Turks and, consequently, he had no confidence in the Turks nor did the Turks own him as belonging to their tribe'. V. A. Smith, one of the early British historians of Indian history, likewise contented himself by referring to the Khiljis as Afghans but he advanced no reasons for it. We are also not sure as to when Jalaluddin's family migrated to India, and when did he start his career as ordinary trooper, whether under Iltutmish or Balban. During the reign of Balban, Jalaluddin was posted as military commander of a subordinate rank in the northwestern region. At the time of Balban's death, he had become the *iqtadar* of Samana. Jalaluddin was then an old man of 67 who had spent the whole of his life in the faithful service of the sultans of Delhi. A non-political man, he had earned reputation as a seasoned soldier and capable administrator. He had fought many successful battles against the Mongol invaders, and 'carved out a respectable place for himself among the old grandees of the Sultanate by dint of merit'.

We first find mention of Jalaluddin's name at the royal court of Delhi during the time of Kaiqubad (1287-90), when the young sultan made him *sar-i-jandar* or 'chief of the Royal Guards'; this charge was held by him in addition to the governorship of Samana. After the death of Nizamuddin, Kaiqubad offered him the post of *ariz-i-mumalik*, viz., the 'paymaster general', besides the command of the royal army, with the title of Shaista Khan, and bestowed the important fief of Baran (Bulandshahr) on him. Obviously, having been betrayed by Nizamuddin, the unscrupulous son-in-law of the senior most grandee of the old Turkish aristocracy, Kaiqubad had started looking towards the more faithful un-privileged class of the Muslim nobility for support to save himself from the domination of their aggressive Turkish rivals. It proved his undoing, however. The haughty and proud old Turkish guard disapproved of Jalaluddin's promotion and demanded his dismissal forthwith. The ensuing strife between the two rival factions, the one belonging to the privileged Turkish and Arab nobility and the other that of the commoners deprived Kaiqubad of all chances to establish his hold over the state affairs, and his untimely physical incapacitation because of the paralytic stroke, plunged the state into political anarchy. Nevertheless, in the course of this struggle for political power, Jalaluddin Khilji held fast to his charge as the governor of Samana and stood as bulwark against the inroads of Mongols into the interior. It earned him the credit of not only his friends and camp-followers but also his staunch rivals. He became leader of the *Taziks* (Freeborn Turks) and 'Indian Muslims' (Hindu converts to Islam and their offspring) and entered into the contest for domination with the other faction, which was led by Malik Aitmar Kachhan—the *amir-i-barbak*, and Malik Aitmar Surkha, the *vakil-i-dar*.

As the bed-ridden sultan Kaiqubad was under the protection of the royal guards, commanded by Jalaluddin Khilji, the rival faction of the old Turkish nobility, led by the two Aitmars kidnapped the infant son of Kaiqubad from the royal *harem* and placed him on the throne with the title of sultan Shamsuddin Kaimurs when Jalaluddin had gone out of the capital for the inspection of the royal army. They issued a hurried proclamation in the name of the infant sultan 'proscribing all the Khalji *amirs* and *maliks*, and Jalaluddin's name headed the opprobrious list'. Nevertheless, the vigilant sons of Jalaluddin Khilji 'took the wind out of the sails of their father's enemies'. They snatched the infant prince from the clutches of the Aitmars in a sudden assault, and safely carried him off to their father in the military camp. Jalaluddin Khilji thereupon took forced possession of the capital. It immensely enhanced the reputation and strength of the Khilji chief and finding further resistance impossible, most of the *amirs* and *maliks* went over to his side. Two days later, the Khilji troops stormed the Red Fort, where a Khilji Malik found the helpless Kaiqubad lying in his bed 'in the Palace of Mirrors, his favourite abode of pleasure'. He rolled up the Sultan in his bedding and kicked him to death; his corpse was thrown into the flowing Yamuna behind the walls of the palace; 'such was the inglorious end of the slave kings of Delhi'.

With the death of Kaiqubad and his infant son Kaimurs lodged safely at Kilugharhi or Kilokheri in the military camp of Jalaluddin Khilji—the leader of the revolution, the latter emerged as the undisputed master of the state. Nevertheless, Jalaluddin still hesitated in declaring himself the sultan all at once. He publicly offered the regency of the child-sultan first to Malik Chhajju, a nephew of Balban, and then to Malik Fakhruddin, the aged *Kotwal* of Delhi and once a personal friend of Balban, but both of them declined the offer. Jalaluddin then declared himself the Regent of the minor Kaimurs reluctantly and even issued the coins in the name of the child-king while assuming the reins of government in his hands. Barani makes no mention of the subsequent events of the child-king's short-lived reign. Yahya bin Ahmad Sirhindi states that he died in the custody of the Regent after about three months. It was, probably, after the death of Kaimurs when the youthful Khilji nobles had already strengthened their control over Delhi and become fully confident of their competence to wield regal powers and responsibilities that they persuaded their elderly leader to declare himself the Sultan in March 1290; he ascended the throne in his military camp at Kilugharhi in the vicinity of Delhi as Sultan Jalaluddin Firoze.

Jalaluddin as Ruler

A King with a Difference: All powers of the state had passed into the hands of the Khiljis but their septuagenarian leader Jalaluddin in his role as Sultan left much to be desired. The assumption of royal powers by him was not universally accepted. The Turkish nobility hated the Khiljis as they considered them to be low-born Afghans. And to the citizens of Delhi, who had been used to the stern discipline and awe-inspiring regal authority of the Turkish sultans for eighty years, the austere and colourless rule of the Khiljis was intolerable. 'The valiant governor of Samana, who had ably repelled the series of Mongol invasions', was very different from the Khilji king, who talked of peace and non-violence, and was not prepared to use his sword to punish even the rebels, thieves or thugs. He out rightly 'refused to shed the blood of any Muslim for political or territorial gains'. In the words of Lane Poole, 'the invincible clemency and humility of the sultan were incomprehensible to his followers. His was no ideal of kingship for an Eastern world. They resented his simplicity of life and even his familiar evenings with the old friends of his former obscurity. They did not appreciate his love of wit and learning. What they wanted was a fighting king inexorable in his judgments and unsurpassable in his pomp'. (*Medieval India under Muhammedan Rule*, London, 1903, p. 38).

In the same strain, Ishwari Prasad observes that Jalaluddin Khilji 'lacked the essential qualities of the thirteenth century kingship. His frugality and simplicity rendered him unfit for wielding the sceptre at a time when the voice of treason was still heard in the land, and the Mongols threatened the frontiers of the kingdom. His assumption of royal authority was looked upon as an act of usurpation by the nobles and the people, and it was for this reason that he crowned himself at Kilugharhi and not at Delhi'. The Muslim bureaucracy and inhabitants of the capital, in general, were not happy at this change of regime; and, consequently, Jalaluddin was constrained to stay at Kilugharhi for a whole year until the Khilji government was well-established, and the Sultan secured the confidence of the populace to safeguard their lives and properties. The 'preliminary measures' adopted by him 'went a great way in consolidating his power'. Barani writes that 'The Sultan, not being able to go into Delhi, made Kilugharhi his capital, and fixed his abode there. He ordered the palace, which Kaiqubad had begun, to be completed and embellished with paintings; and he directed the formation of a splendid garden in front of it on the banks of the Jumna (Yamuna). The princes and nobles and officers, and the principal men of the city, were commanded to build houses at Kilugharhi. Several of the traders were also brought from Delhi, and bazaars were established. Kilughahi then obtained the name of New Town. A lofty stone fort was commenced, and the erection of its defences was allotted to the nobles'.

Jalaluddin won over the aristocratic families of the capital by his virtuous conduct, generosity and good government. He accorded liberal treatment even to his political opponents and attempted to bridge the sharp divisions between the two factions of the nobility in the matter of distributing the higher offices of the state. He promoted the interest of the youthful Khilji officers, Taziks and the capable Indian Muslims but at the same time the stalwarts of the rival factions were all confirmed in their official assignments and privileges. The Sultan 'agreed to move to Delhi only when a deputation of the leading citizens of Delhi waited upon him and pleaded with him to grace the capital by his presence'. The contemporary chroniclers record that on reaching the gate of the royal palace, Jalaluddin alighted from his steed, and as he made it to the hall of the Maliks in the Red Palace of Balban, he stood with tears in his eyes 'as the melancholy thought arose in his mind how often he had stood in awe before the same throne'. The elderly Turkish nobles of Balban's regime were moved by the humility of the Sultan but the young Khilji officers felt disappointed at his emotional utterances and 'saw in his clemency and kindness the ruin of the prestige of the crown'.

Dignitaries of Jalaluddin's Court: The Sultan's generous distribution of offices reconciliated the Turkish nobility and they extended their support to the new regime. The Khilji revolution put an end to the supremacy of the Ilbari Turks but Jalaluddin did not exclude them from office. Malik Chhajju, a nephew of Balban and the only male survivor of Balban's ruling family, was confirmed in his old charge as the governor of Kara (Allahabad) and Manikpur (Awadh). The office of the prime minister (*wazir*) was conferred on Khwaja Khatir, who had held it under Balban as well as Kaiqubad. Similarly, Malik Fakhruddin, the aged *Kotwal* of Delhi since the days of Balban was confirmed in his position and conferred the title of *Malik-ul-Umara*. The court was, of course, dominated by the young Khilji nobles with important ministerial posts and military assignments. The Sultan's eldest son received the title of *Khan-i-Khana*; the second son that of *Arkali Khan*, and the third one was bestowed the title of Qadir Khan. For each of them a separate palace was provided. The Sultan's younger brother was entitled Yaghrish Khan, and he was made *ariz-i-mumalik*. Two nephews of Jalaluddin Khilji—Alauddin and Almas Beg, both of whom had also been made his sons-in-law by the Sultan by giving his daughters in marriage to them, likewise obtained important positions in the royal establishment, and all of them were assigned fiefs and special privileges befitting their royal status. Another name, worthy of mention here is that of the 'blunt and outspoken' Malik Ahmad Chap, a distant relative and personal friend of Sultan Jalaluddin Khilji, who was appointed the 'deputy lord chamberlain'.

Malik Chhajju's Revolt: Jalaluddin Khilji's reign lasted about six years, but he was always conscious of his weaknesses as a sovereign, and he used to take pride in his public utterances that he was not fit to occupy the exalted office of the sultan. His utmost humility won applause from the common people but it sent very wrong signals to the old Turkish aristocracy and the ambitious *iqtadars* of various provinces who looked down upon the Khiljis as usurpers and harboured ill-will against them; Malik Chhajju, the nephew of Balban was one of them. In the second year of Jalaluddin's reign, Malik Chhajju raised his standard of revolt at Allahabad. He declared himself as the sovereign ruler of Hindustan with the title of Sultan Mughisuddin and had the *khutba* read in his name. According to Barani, 'many of the inhabitants of Delhi and the environs, mindful of the benefits they had received from the ancestors of Malik Chhajju, heard of his approach with satisfaction and joy, and recognized him as the rightful heir to the throne, for they said that no Khilji had ever been a king, and that the race (of Khiljis) had no right or title to Delhi'.

In spite of his advanced age, the Sultan himself took the field against

Malik Chhajju. He left his eldest son Khan-i-Khana to deputise for him in the capital and marched from Kilugharhi at the head of the royal army to intercept Malik Chhajju's advancement towards Delhi. The latter was defeated and taken prisoner along with hundreds of his soldiers. The captives were presented before the Sultan for punishment, but Jalaluddin was overwhelmed to see the old aristocracy of Delhi and the ex-supporters of Balban's regime in chains, and ordered their release forthwith. They were all pardoned and entertained to a sumptuous feast at the time of their release; most of them were reinstated to their respective government assignments as before. As for Malik Chhajju, after granting pardon to him, he was sent to Multan to lead a comfortable retired life under the general surveillance of its governor, Arkali Khan, the second son of the Sultan. Malik Ahmad Chap, the master of ceremonies and counsellor of the Sultan, bluntly told him that 'a king should reign and observe the rules of government, or else be content to relinquish the throne …The punishments awarded by kings are warnings to men. Sultan Balban, who never forgot his dignity and power, visited rebellious and political offences with the greatest severity, and how much blood did he shed? If the Sultan (Jalaluddin) and his followers were to fall into their hands, no name or trace of the Khiljis would be left in Hindustan'. The Sultan heard his counsel with patience but excused himself with the remarks:

> 'Oh Ahmad! I am aware of what you say. I have seen the punishment of rebellion before you saw it, but what can I do? I have grown old among Mussalmans and am not accustomed to spill their blood. My age exceeds seventy and I have never caused one to be killed. Shall I now…act against the principles of the law and bring Mohammedans to the block?....If I cannot reign without shedding the blood of Mussalmans, I renounce the throne, for I could not endure the wrath of God'.

Of course, the ambitious Khilji and other Muslim nobles, who had helped Jalaluddin's rise to power, were frustrated and felt demoralised to see the unbecoming conduct of the Sultan in downgrading the dignity of the crown. They wanted to wipe out the entire old Turkish aristocracy, and restore the pomp and grandeur of Balban's regime under their control. No wonder, they were totally disenchanted with their old leader and wanted to replace him before it was too late. Jalaluddin was not lucky enough to see the writing on the wall; he failed to give a practical shape to his thoughts of actually renouncing the throne in favour of any one of his sons in time, and with the most tragic and disastrous consequences for himself and his entire family.

Deterioration of Law and Order: Jalaluddin Khilji showed similar weakness and clemency in his treatment towards the criminals and anti-social elements during his day-today administration at the capital. The Sultan undertook some preliminary measures to restore order but it did not produce the desired results. He did not adopt stern measures like Balban nor revived the 'blood and iron policy' of inflicting severe punishments on those criminals who were apprehended. We have it on the testimony of the medieval chroniclers that very often the thieves and thugs, who were captured by the law-enforcing agencies of the capital and presented for awarding the punishment, were set at liberty by the personal intervention of the Sultan after taking an oath from them that they would behave in future. It is said that once a thousand of the *thugs* were rounded off and brought before him for punishment, but the Sultan put them in the state-owned boats, provided them with food and other necessities of life, and then ordered them 'to be conveyed into the lower country to the neighbourhood of Lakhnauti, where they were to be set free' under the illusion that 'the *thugs* would thus have to dwell about Lakhnauti and would not trouble the neighbourhood of Delhi any more'.

The Sultan thereby made himself a laughing stock of the people. Barani records that 'a party of wicked, ungrateful nobles used to talk over their cups of killing him and setting him aside. This was all reported to the Sultan, but he sometimes dismissed it lightly, and at others used to say: "Men often drink too much, and then they say foolish things; do not report drunken stories to me". In a similar incident, some of the *amirs* held a social get-together 'in the house of Malik Tajuddin Kuchi, a nobleman of some distinction. When the wine had got into the heads of the guests, and they were intoxicated, they said to Tajuddin: *You are fit to be a king but the Sultan is not. If there is any Khilji fit to be a king, it is Ahmad Chap, not Jalaluddin.* This and similar absurdities they uttered, and all those, who were present there, promised to aid Tajuddin in acquiring the crown'. They thus openly talked of treason, and matter was promptly reported to the Sultan but the latter paid no heed to it, and pardoned the *amirs* after a stern warning.

The Affair of Sidi Maula: By way of an exception to the above-mentioned lenient policy of Sultan towards the miscreants, rebels and the anti-social elements, the case of a *Sufi darvesh*, Sidi Maula, who suffered at his hands, finds a special mention in the chronicles of almost all the medieval Indian writers. Sidi Maula came from Iran during the reign of Balban and setup a *khanqah* in the outskirts of Delhi. He lived a very simple and frugal life and attracted a large number of devotees from all walks of life. Amongst his followers were included a number of *amirs* and *maliks* who made rich donations to the *khanqah*, out of which free meals were provided to the visitors by a self-appointed committee of the local patrons and volunteers. According to Barani, in the community kitchen of the *khanqah*, 'twice a day, such bounteous and various meals were served as no *khan* or *malik* could furnish'. Naturally, the *khanqah* of Sidi Maula became the hub of capital's urchins and idlers who thronged the place and feasted themselves at the free kitchen. At the same time, it became a meeting place for the seditious and disaffected nobles and all those who were not reconciled to the establishment of the Khilji regime. Some of them actually hatched a conspiracy to assassinate the Sultan when he 'went in state to the *Jama Masjid* on *Sabbath*', and declare Sidi Maula as the Khalifa. In order to establish the claim of the *darvesh* to the throne of Delhi, Sidi Maula was to marry a daughter of the late Sultan Nasiruddin Mahmud. Sidi Maula was made a party to this conspiracy through 'a mischievous man', Qazi Jalal Kashani. To the good fortune of the Sultan, one of the conspirators divulged this secret to Jalaluddin; and the conspirators, including Sidi Maula were apprehended and produced in the royal court. As usual they denied the charge of conspiracy and the Sultan took the whole thing casually by inflicting mild punishments on them by way of a reprimand. However, the Sufi *darvesh* incited the wrath of some fanatical Sunni *mullas,* who charged him with heresy, and in a fit of anger, the Sultan issued the orders for his execution.

Encounter with the Mongols: In 1292, the Mongols invade India under the leadership of Abdullah, a grandson of Halaku Khan. About one and a half *lacs* of the Mongol marauders spread themselves in the northwestern areas and carried on destruction and devastation on a large scale; they penetrated as far as Sunam in the southwest of the Punjab and put it to plunder. In spite of his advanced age, Jalaluddin took the field against them in person and defeated them in a number of battles. Ultimately, Abdullah made peace with the Sultan of Delhi and returned to Afghanistan, heavily laden with booty. Thousands of the Mongols, who had been taken captives by the royal forces, were brought to Delhi; most of them embraced Islam, and were allowed to settle themselves in the outskirts of capital. In order to win their loyalty to the Sultanate of Delhi, Jalaluddin gave one of his daughters in marriage to their leader, Ulghu Khan, a descendant of Changez Khan. The Mongol converts to Islam became known as the New Mussalmans, and their colony, in the vicinity of Delhi, acquired the name of Mughalpura. The Mongol policy of the Sultan, therefore, met with considerable success.

Military Campaigns against the Hindu Rulers: As a devoted Sunni Mussalman, the new sultan pledged to inaugurate the beginning of his reign by launching a military campaign against the neighbouring Hindu rulers. His first choice was that of the Rana of Ranthambhor. Though conquered by Qutubuddin Aibek, the stronghold of Ranthambhor had been recovered by the Chauhan Rajputs after the death of Iltutmish. Jalaluddin led an expedition against Ranthambhor under his personal command in 1292. Unfortunately, his eldest son, Khan-i-Khana, had died a premature death soon after his accession to the throne; therefore, he had to appoint his second son, Arkali Khan, to be his vice-regent at Kilugharhi in his absence. On the way to Ranthambhor, the fortress of Jhain was stormed and captured by the royal troops. According to Barani, Jalaluddin 'plundered the town of Jhain and destroyed' its magnificent Hindu temples; he 'broke and burnt the idols, and obtained great booty, after which his army rested. The Rai of Ranthambhor, with his *Rawats* and followers, together with their wives and children, all took refuge in the fort of Ranthambhor. The Sultan wished to invest and take the fort. He ordered *manjaniks* to be erected, tunnels (*sabat*) to be sunk, and redoubts (*gargach*) to be constructed, and the siege to be pressed'. The Rajputs put up a tough resistance and compelled the Sultan to raise the siege. Jalaluddin ordered the return march of his troops to Delhi on the plea that 'the fort could not be taken without sacrificing the lives of many Mussalmans', and that ' he did not value the fort so much as the hair of one Mussalman'. Of course, the border town of Jhain was annexed to the Sultanate of Delhi, and the campaign boosted the morale of the Muslim troops by providing them an opportunity to loot and plunder the territories of the infidels besides the desecration and defiling of their places of worship, but 'the feeble-mindedness of the Sultan cast its reflections on his future policy against his Hindu antagonists.

In the year 1292, Jalaluddin organised yet another expedition against the Hindu chiefs. The fort of Mandor, situated close to the stronghold of Jodhpur, was snatched from the hands of Samant Singh Chauhan, but the Sultan did not pick up courage to launch an attack on his main citadel. Instead, the royal forces spread in the neighbourhood of Mandor for the loot and plunder of villages, and returned to Delhi with a huge booty. Afterwards, Jalaluddin Khilji 'marched a second time to Jhain, and after once more plundering the country, he returned in triumph'. That marked the end of his personal enthusiasm to fight against his Hindu rivals.

Alauddin's Appointment as Governor of Kara (Allahabad)

By far, the most important political event of Jalaluddin's reign was the appointment of his nephew, Alauddin Khilji—the future king emperor of Delhi, as the governor of Kara (Allahabad) after the defeat of Malik Chhajju in 1291. With his original name as Ali Gurshasp, Alauddin is said to have lost his father in his boyhood, and he, along with his younger brother Almas Beg, had been brought up with affection and care by their uncle Jalaluddin. The latter had further strengthened his family ties with the young Khilji upstarts by giving his daughters in marriage to them. Barani tells us that, after his appointment as the governor of Kara (Allahabad), Alauddin 'proceeded to his territory, and in the same year, he found there many of the officers and friends of Malik Chhajju, who had taken part in the rebellion. He set them free and took them into his service. These disaffected persons began at once to suggest to Alauddin that it was quite possible to raise and equip a large force in Kara, and through Kara to obtain Delhi. Money only was needed; but for want of that Malik Chhajju would have succeeded. Get only plenty of money, and the acquisition of Delhi would be easy'.

Like all the other adherents of the Khilji regime, Alauddin also felt dejected and humiliated to watch the clemency of Sultan Jalaluddin—his father-in-law and patron; the latter's weak and imbecile policy 'fostered disloyal ambitions' even in the hearts of the most loyal and trustworthy nobles, and Alauddin was no exception. Being an ambitious and shrewd person, he came to the conclusion that Jalaluddin's days as the sultan were numbered, and sooner or later he must fall a victim to one or the other of the conspirators. Therefore, he also started giving ears to the erstwhile conspirators and treacherous camp-followers of Malik Chhajju to try his luck. According to Barani, for sometime past, Alauddin had not been on good terms with his wife, the daughter of Jalaluddin, who had assumed a haughty and domineering posture towards him ever since his father became the sultan. She, in turn, poisoned the ears of his mother—the *Malika-i-Jahan*, the chief queen of Jalaluddin, against him. It furthered Alauddin's ambitions to tread the path of treachery, and he readily joined the ranks of the conspirators to bring about the fall of Jalaluddin Khilji.

Alauddin's Expedition to Bhilsa: Towards the end of 1292, when, after the capture of Mandor, Sultan Jalaluddin was aimlessly marching his royal army through the border territories of the neighbouring Rajput chiefs of Jodhpur and Ranthambhor, to collect booty and the trophies of war against the infidels, Alauddin sought his permission to organise a surprise raid on Bhilsa, situated on the road to Ujjain, and put it to plunder. After the success of his enterprise, Alauddin made straight for Delhi with the whole of his booty, which included enormous wealth in gold and silver, besides elephants and horses. A part of his booty consisted of 'some bronze idols, which the Hindus worshipped'; 'these were laid down before the Badaun gate to be trampled by the faithful'. The Sultan was so much pleased with the loyalty and daring exploit of his youthful nephew and the son-in-law that 'he was made the *Ariz-i-Mumalik* and awarded the *Iqta* of Awadh in addition to that of Kara. Hereafter, 'the centre of political gravity shifted from the old king to that of his ambitious nephew'. Having won the confidence and affections of the aged Sultan, Alauddin Khilji, before his departure for Kara, sought his permission for a similar raid into Chanderi in the near future, and also requested for 'the remission of the revenues of Kara and Awadh to enable him to raise a fresh army for the purpose'. His request was readily granted by the Sultan.

Alauddin's Expedition to Devagiri or Deogiri (1296): During his expedition to Bhilsa, Alauddin had heard of the richness and prosperity of the country of Devagiri or Deogiri (Daulatabad), in Maharashtra, situated between the Vindhya Mountains and the river Krishna. It was then ruled over by King Ram Chandra Deva (1271-1310) of the Yadava dynasty. The people of Maharashtra had enjoyed freedom from external invasions and internal security under the benevolent and popular rule of their indigenous monarchs for over a century, and they had flourishing trade and commerce relationships with overseas countries. According to Barani,

> 'The people of that country (Deogiri) had never heard of the Mussalmans; the Maratha land had never been punished by their armies (viz., by the armies of the Muslims). No Mussalman king or prince had penetrated (into Maharashtra) so far. Deogir was exceedingly rich in gold and silver, jewels and other valuables'.—(*Tarikh-i-Firoze Shahi*, p. 150)

Emboldened by the initial success of his raid on the Hindu town of Bhilsa, Alauddin had obtained a formal permission from the Sultan to organise a similar expedition to Chanderi but, in his heart of hearts, he aspired to lay his hands on the fabulous wealth of Deogiri. He, therefore, conceived of a very bold plan of organizing an expedition to the far-off Maratha stronghold of Deogiri, 'which is regarded as 'one of the most memorable feats' in the annals of the medieval Indian history. He made secret preparations for about two years to mature his plan with meticulous details; apart from strengthening his army, he gathered adequate information through his spies and the native travellers about the shortest southern route leading to Deogiri, besides the political geography of the region and the centres of armed resistance, that he was likely to encounter on the way to his prospective destination.

Alauddin left Kara with 8,000 picked horsemen on February 26, 1296. Though he had secretly resolved to march on Deogiri, 'he studiously concealed the fact' and made out that he intended to attack Chanderi; Malik Alaul Mulk, the uncle of Barani and one of the favourites of Alauddin Khilji was made deputy of Kara and Awadh in his absence. The latter kept Sultan Jalaluddin in the dark about the real designs and movements of Alauddin by sending fabricated reports to Delhi; while Alauddin's younger brother, Almas Beg, safeguarded his interests at the royal court.

Alauddin actually marched towards the neighbourhood of Chanderi, but, thereafter, he took a sharp turn towards the south, and 'all intelligence of him was lost. Accounts were sent regularly from Kara to the Sultan with vague statements, saying that he was engaged in chastising and plundering rebels, and that circumstantial accounts would be forwarded' shortly. As for Alauddin, after crossing the Vindhyas, he reached Ellichpur, 'the northern outpost' of the Yadava kingdom. 'In order to lull the suspicions of the neighbouring Hindu chieftains', he spread the rumour that he was a fugitive prince from the Sultanate, and that his relations with the Sultan of Delhi having been strained, he intended to seek refuge in the south. He actually gave full two days' rest to his fatigued soldiers and their horses at Ellichpur before he made a sudden assault on Deogiri. At the Lasura pass, about twenty kilometres from Deogiri, Alauddin met with stubborn resistance from Kanha, governor of the place, whose small contingent was supported by two brave women warriors; they died fighting against the intruders. To the misfortune of Raja Ram Chandra Deva, the best part of the Maratha army, under the charge of his eldest son Shankara Deva or Singhana, was engaged in some border dispute with a neighbouring state in the further south. Taken totally unawares by the invader, the Maratha chief hurriedly collected two or three thousand soldiers to stop him on the outskirts of Deogiri, but was defeated and took shelter in the fort, leaving the town at the mercy of the Muslim marauders. Alauddin thoroughly plundered the town, and put the fort under siege; he gave out that his contingent was but the advance guard of the Sultan's main force of 20,000 cavalry that was following. 'Suffering from lack of provisions and apprehending the enemy's strength', the Yadava king sued for peace and the release of his citizens on payment of huge ransom. Alauddin, in his eagerness to make an early exit from the south, accepted his proposal, but meanwhile, Shankara Deva, on learning of the Muslim invasion, hastened back with a large army, and 'ignoring his father's remonstrance not to violate the treaty' challenged the invader to surrender the booty. Alauddin was taken aback but took the field against the Maratha forces with only 7,000 fighters, leaving a thousand of his troops to continue the siege of the fort under the command of his lieutenant Nusrat Khan. Heavily outnumbered, Alauddin's soldiers were badly mauled after a day-long fight and were about to collapse when, Nusrat Khan, realizing the gravity of the situation, raised the siege of the fort and jumped into the fray. This turned the tide, as the Deogiri troops mistook it for the arrival of the alleged main army of Delhi, and they retreated in confusion. Alauddin quickly returned to the siege of the fort and, within another few days, brought the Yadava king to the knees. 'Undoubted courage, better war strategy and good fortune' brought victory to Alauddin, and he returned from Deogriri, heavily laden with booty, which, according to Firishta, included 600 maunds of gold, 1000 maunds of sliver, seven maunds of pearls, two maunds of diamonds, rubies and other precious stones, and 4,000 pieces of silk-stuff besides thousands of horses, elephants and captives as slaves, all of whom were used as beasts of burden to carry the spoils. Apart from the war indemnity, the vanquished Maratha chief pledged the annual revenues of the border district of Ellichpur as tribute, and had also to give the hand of a daughter in marriage to the Khilji adventurer.

Alauddin left Deogiri after 25 days of his arrival there. His return march to Kara was bound to be slow because of the heavy burden of the spoils, which were carried on thousands of the plundered horses, elephants and other animals, besides an equally large number of the slaves. On his way back, the Chauhans of Asirgarh tried to intercept the victor but they were repulsed by his mounted archers. He reached Kara in triumph on June 3, 1296.

Murder of Jalaluddin Khilji

Ziauddin Barani describes in detail Alauddin's successful expedition to Deogiri, and the subsequent events leading to the assassination of Sultan Jalaluddin Khilji at his hands. He writes that, in the year 1296, the Sultan was camping with his royal army in the neighbourhood of Gwalior to maintain pressure on the adjoining Hindu states. It was there that 'the rumours reached him that Alauddin Khilji had plundered Deogiri and obtained elephants and an immense booty, with which he was returning to Kara'. Jalaluddin 'was greatly pleased for, in the simplicity of his heart, he thought that whatsoever his son-in-law and nephew had captured, he would joyfully bring to him'. To celebrate this success, he 'gave entertainments' to his camp-followers and the soldiers, and himself also took wine in the company of his ministers and military commanders. Afterwards, he held a private council of his trustworthy advisers to discuss whether it would be advisable for him 'to go to meet Alauddin or to return to Delhi'. Malik Ahmad Chap, *Naib-i-Barbak*, 'one of the wisest men of the day', spoke before anyone else, and said:

> 'Elephants and wealth, when held in great abundance, are the cause of much strife. Whoever acquires them becomes so intoxicated that he does not know his hands from his feet. Alauddin is surrounded by many of the rebels and insurgents, who supported Malik Chhajju. He has gone into a foreign land without leave, has fought battles and won treasure. The wise have said: *Money and strife; strife and money*, that is, the two things are allied to each other....My opinion is that we should march with all haste towards Chanderi to meet Alauddin and intercept his return. When he finds the Sultan's army in the way, he must necessarily present all his spoils to the throne whether he likes it or not. The Sultan may then take the silver and gold, the jewels and pearls, the elephants and horses, and leave the other booty to him and his soldiers. His territories also should be increased, and he should be carried in honour to Delhi'. (*Tarikh-i-Firoze Shahi*, pp. 150-51)

Barani laments that 'unfortunately, the Sultan was in the grasp of his evil angel, so he heeded not the advice of Ahmad Chap'. Instead, he was taken in by the ill-advice of Malik Fakhruddin Kuchi and some other treacherous members of his court, who assured him of the fidelity of his worthy nephew and son-in-law, and the Sultan returned to Delhi 'to keep the Ramazan' in the fond hope of Alauddin's arrival at the court with all the booty, as he had done after the success of his earlier expedition to Bhilsa.

Nevertheless, the success of his Deogiri exploit turned Alauddin's head. He would not like to part with or share the fabulous wealth that he had 'acquired by his skill and at the risk of his own life'. He, therefore, evaded his visit to Delhi on various pretexts. Through 'treacherous correspondence' and personal agents, Alauddin convinced Jalaluddin about the danger to his life in Delhi at the hands of some hostile nobles of the court, who felt jealous of him and poisoned the ears of the sultan against him; Jalaluddin was also aware of the estranged relations between Alauddin and his first wife, viz., the daughter of the sultan, and her mother, the *Malika-i-Jahan*. With profound protestations of loyalty to the sultan, Alauddin expressed the desire to wait upon him and present the vast booty that he had brought from Delhi, if he paid a visit to Kara. Blinded by the affection for his nephew, and disregarding the sane advice and protests of his courtiers to the contrary, Jalaluddin decided to meet him at Kara.

The Murder Most Foul (July 20, 1296): Without suspecting any foul play, Sultan Jalaluddin proceeded in a flotilla of boats in the company of some nobles, while a small contingent of the Royal Guards, numbering a thousand horsemen, under the command of Malik Ahmad Chap, marched along the rough bank of the swollen Yamuna in the midst of the rainy season. Jalaluddin's boats reached Kara (Allahabad) on the southern bank of the Ganga on the 15th Ramazan. Meanwhile, Alauddin left the town with his family and the treasure, and crossed over the Ganga with his army to its northern bank. He drew out his army in a battle array. Barani records: 'When the royal en.ign came in sight, Alauddin was all prepared, the men were armed and the elephants and horses were harnessed. He sent Almas Beg in a small boat to the Sultan with directions to use every device to induce him to leave behind the thousand men he had brought with him, and to come with only a few personal attendants'. On the entreaties of the treacherous Almas Beg, the Sultan left behind all of his horsemen and bodyguards on the southern bank of the swollen river Ganga, 'whilst he, with two boats and a few personal attendants and friends', started moving to the other side. About this time, the traitor Almas Beg, requested the Sultan 'to direct his attendants to lay aside their arms, lest his brother should see them as they approached nearer, and be frightened'. Thus it was that the Sultan, with a handful of his unarmed attendants landed on the other side of the Ganga in the midst of Alauddin's army.

Barani records that 'the Sultan reached the shore before afternoon prayer, and disembarked with a few followers. Alauddin advanced to receive him. He and all his officers showing due respect. When he reached the Sultan, he fell at his feet, and the Sultan, treating him as a son, kissed his eyes and cheeks, stroked his head, gave him two loving taps upon the cheek, and said: *I have brought thee up from infancy; why art thouafraid of me?*' About this time, on receiving signal from their master, two of Alauddin' guards, Muhammad Salim of Samana and Ikhtiyaruddin Hud, struck down the Sultan with their swords, and chopped off his head. This murder was committed on the 17th Ramazan (July 20, 1296), and 'the venerable head of the Sultan was placed on a spear and paraded about'. To quote Barani,

> 'While the head of the murdered sovereign was yet dripping with blood, the ferocious conspirators brought the royal canopy and elevated it over the head of Alauddin. Casting aside all shame, the perfidious and graceless wretches caused him to be proclaimed king by men who rode about on elephants'. (*Ibid*; p. 155)

In deep anguish, Ziauddin Barani condemns this 'heinous crime' in the most pathetic terms. According to the contention of the author, the conspirators who were a party to this murder most foul did not escape retribution and received befitting punishments at the hands of nature sooner than later; he writes:

> 'Although these villains were spared for a short time and Alauddin for some years, still they were not forgotten (by nature) and their punishments were only suspended. At the end of three or four years, Ulugh Khan (Almas Beg—the younger brother of Alauddin), the deceiver, was gone; so was Nusrat Khan, the giver of the signal; so also was Zafar Khan, the breeder of the mischief, my uncle Alaul Mulk, *Kotwal*, and ... the bell-bound Salim, who struck the first blow, was a year or two afterwards eaten up with leprosy. Ikhtiyaruddin, who cut off the head, very soon went mad, and in his dying ravings cried that Sultan Jalaluddin stood over him with a naked sword, ready to cut off his head. Alauddin did not escape retribution for the blood of his patron. He shed more innocent blood than ever Pharaoh was guilty of. Fate at length placed a betrayer in

his path, by whom his family was destroyed..., and the retribution that fell upon it never had a parallel even in any infidel land'. (*Ibid*; pp. 155-56)

SECTION 2: ALAUDDIN KHILJI (1296-1316)

Early Career and Accession

The original name of Alauddin Khilji was Ali Gurshasp. His father Shihabuddin Masaud, the elder brother of Sultan Jalaluddin Khilji, died a premature death, leaving behind four sons, two of whom, Alauddin and Almas Beg, rose to prominence. Alauddin was born in c.1266. As described earlier, he was brought up by Jalaluddin with great affection and cares, and was made a permanent member of his family by a wed-lock with his daughter. Alauddin played an active part in the Khilji Revolution so-called, and was amply rewarded by his uncle by being made the governor of two most important provinces, Kara and Awadh, of the Sultanate, situated in the heart of the fertile Ganga valley.

Alauddin earned reputation among the Turkish nobility and the fanatical Muslim *ulama* by carrying out successful expeditions to the infidel strongholds of Bhilsa and Deogiri; besides, the fabulous wealth, that these enterprises yielded, filled the coffers of his treasury and enriched thousands of his soldiers and political adherents. That is why, after committing the heinous crime of Jalaluddin' assassination in cold blood, the conspirators acclaimed Alauddin as their king; the Turkish nobles and the entire Muslim ruling elite soon forgot the cruel murder of their venerable Khilji chief, and offered allegiance to the rising star.

After the murder of Jalaluddin at Kara on July 20, 1296, Alauddin was immediately declared the Sultan of Delhi, but it took him more than three months before he could make it to the royal capital and install himself on the throne. Barani records that, on hearing of the intelligence of the Sultan's murder in the army camp of Alauddin, Malik Ahmad Chap—the commander of the Royal Guards, who was stationed with his troops on the southern bank of the Ganga, decamped and made a hurried retreat towards Delhi, loosing many of his fighters and their horses in the rough and water-soaked terrain of the rainy season. Greatly depressed and shaken, most of his fighters deserted their commander and 'went to their homes'. Ahmad Chap held hurried consultations with the Jalali nobles and the *Malika-i-Jahan* for the future course of action. As luck would have it, *Khan-i-Khana*, the eldest son of Jalaluddin had died in 1290, soon after his father's accession to the throne, and Arkali Khan, the second son of Jalaluddin and heir-apparent to the throne, was at Multan—his provincial charge. In the absence of Arkali Khan, the *Malik-i-Jahan*, in her nervousness and anxiety not to leave the throne vacant, committed a fatal mistake in declaring her youngest son, Qadir Khan, as the sultan of Delhi, with the title of Ruknuddin Ibrahim, and herself setup as his Regent. On hearing of it, Arkali Khan felt 'so much affronted by this lapse on the part of his mother that he stayed back at Multan and did not come to the defence of the capital'. It led to sharp division among the Jalali nobles also which facilitated Alauddin's task in winning them over to his side by opening the chests of his treasures and by lavish distribution of gold and silver among all the high and the low.

Alauddin Khilji, accompanied by his grant army, reached Delhi with great pomp and show, on October 26, 1296; before his arrival, his generals had taken complete control of the capital, and all the members of the Jalali family had fled to Multan. The new monarch was accorded a grand reception by the populace of Delhi amidst great rejoicings; the festivities of the occasion, liberally financed by Alauddin's officials, and accompanied by distribution of sweets and free kitchens, continued for many weeks. Alauddin Khilji took his seat on the magnificent throne of Balban in the *Daulatkhana-i-Julus,* and was formally crowned with the title *Abul Muzaffar Sultan Alaud Duniya-wa-Din Muhammad Shah Khilji.* He accorded high offices to his friends and associates but many of the Jalali nobles, who had offered their allegiance to him, were also confirmed in their old positions; so much so that even Khwaja Khatir, the *Wazir* or Prime Minister of Jalaluddin was also allowed to continue in his office. Almas Beg, the younger brother of Alauddin Khilji now became the premier noble of his court with the title of Ulugh Khan; Malik Sanjar received the title of Alp Khan, Malik Hazbaruddin, now styled Zafar, received appointment as the *Ariz-i-Mumalik.* Nusrat Khan was made the *Kotwal* of Delhi, while Alaul Mulk was appointed the governor of Kara. All of his soldiers, who were on the pay-rolls on the day of his declaration as Sultan, were granted six months' additional salary as reward. Likewise, the Muslim theologians, *ulama* and the *sheikhs*, and all other nobles and subordinate officials received grants of land, titles and cash rewards, and even the visitors to the metropolis and its respectable citizens, who attended the various state ceremonies, were given valuable gifts by the Sultan. Barani concludes the narrative of Alauddin's accession to the throne with the remarks that follow:

> 'The people were so deluded by the gold, which they received, that no one ever mentioned the horrible crime which the Sultan had committed, and the hope of gain left them no care for anything else. Alauddin scattered so much gold about that the faithless people easily forgot the murder of the late sultan, and rejoiced over his accession... He had committed a deed unworthy of his religion and position, so he deemed it politic to deceive the people, and to cover his crime by scattering honours and gifts upon all classes of people'. (*Ibid.* p. 161)

Destruction of the Jalali Nobles

Alauddin had ascended the throne at Delhi but his position as a sovereign ruler was contested by the Jalali family, all the prominent members of which had retired to Multan along with their boy king, Qadir Khan, styled Sultan Ruknuddin Ibrahim. Alauddin felt himself insecure so long as his rival contender to the throne was at large. Therefore, immediately after his coronation at Delhi, he despatched a 40,000 strong army under the joint command of his younger brother Almas Beg, now styled Ulugh Khan, and Zafar Khan for their destruction. They made straight for Multan where their rivals were all concentrated. The stronghold of Multan was taken by them after much bloodshed and prolonged siege of two months. The whole family of Jalaluddin, including, *Malika-i-Jahan*, her sons Arkali Khan and Qadir Khan, and the family of Arkali Khan, besides Malik Ahmad Chap and many other Jalali nobles were taken captives. Qadir Khan, Arkali Khan and two sons of the later were handed over to the ***kotwal*** of Hansi, where they were put to death after some time. ***Malika-i-Jahan***, Malik Ahmad Chap and many other Jalali nobles were kept in confinement at Delhi, and nothing was known about them thereafter. Almas Beg (Ulugh Khan) was appointed governor of Multan and Uchh with responsibility to safeguard northwestern frontier against the Mongol invasions. All those who had collaborated with the family of Jalaluddin were severely punished, and their land-grants and properties were confiscated to the state. Alauddin did not rest contented until the Jalali family and all of its supporters and collaborators had been liquidated

Alauddin as Despotic Ruler

After the conquest of Multan and Uchh, and the destruction of the Jalali family, Alauddin Khilji 'assumed *a volte face* in his attitude towards the nobility'. In surprise move, he laid his hands on all the ex-Jalali nobles, whom he had won over to his side by offering monetary rewards and high offices after the murder of Jalaluddin. He charged them of greediness and treachery for having betrayed their old master, and denounced them as undependable and untrustworthy people. Alauddin dismissed them from their offices and 'took back the excessive gold and silver, which he had himself given to them, as a bribe so to say'; he 'deprived them of honours, blinded some and beheaded the others'; Alaul Mulk, the uncle of Barani, was recalled to Delhi, and made to surrender 'all the elephants and treasures which Alauddin had left with him at Kara'. Because of his fatty and bulky physique, he was thought unfit for active service, but, as an exception, the Sultan, keeping in view his very faithful services to him as a personal friend, allowed him to stay in Delhi as its *Kotwal*. Nusrat Khan, who had adopted stern measures to extract 'a crore of *tankas* for the state treasury by levying heavy fines on the ex-Jalali nobles and by the confiscation of their lands and properties, was sent to Kara as its new governor.

Alauddin's theory of Kingship: By such dictatorial commands and quick replacements of the higher bureaucracy and military officers, Alauddin chilled the spirits of even the best and the strongest of his courtiers and provincial governors. He frightened and over-awed them by the exercise of his autocratic powers. Alauddin had acquired the throne *ba-zor-i-shamshir*, that is, 'by the force of his sword', and he set up a despotic monarchy that surpassed the autocracy of Iltutmish and Balban. Before any of his ex-colleagues and friends 'could pause and think of his bilateral relationships with the Sultan, Alauddin Khilji had pulled himself far above their heads and shoulders and assumed the most dictatorial and autocratic powers'. He revived Balban's theory of *divine rights of kingship*, and claimed divine powers and virtues for himself as the Sultan 'who stood no comparison with the other human beings'. He styled himself as the *Zil-i-Ilahi*, and this title was duly inscribed on his coins. He regarded the king to be above the law of the land although this concept was not in conformity with the Islamic theology on which the Muslim state in India was originally founded.

Wild Aims of Alauddin Khilji

Ziauddin Barani records that, 'in the third year of his reign, Alauddin had little to do beyond attending to his pleasures, giving feasts, and holding festivals. One success followed another; despatches of victory came in from all sides; every year, he had two or three sons born, affairs of state went on according to his wish and to his satisfaction; his treasury was overflowing, boxes and caskets of jewels and pearls were daily displayed before his eyes; he had numerous elephants in his stables, and seventy thousand horses in the city and environs, two or three regions were subject to his sway, and he had no apprehensions of enemies to his kingdom or of any rival to his throne'. The learned historian continues that

> 'All this prosperity intoxicated him. Vast desires and great aims, far beyond him, or a hundred thousand like him, formed their germs in his brain, and he entertained fancies which had never occurred to any king before him. In his exaltation, ignorance, and folly, he quite lost his head, forming the most impossible schemes and nourishing the most extravagant desires'.
>
> 'Alauddin was a man of no learning, and (he) never associated with men of learning. He could not read or write a letter. He was bad tempered, obstinate, and hard-hearted, but the world smiled upon him, fortune befriended him, and his schemes were generally successful, so he only became the more reckless and arrogant'. (*Tarikh-i-Firoze Shahi*)

Alauddin talked of accomplishing two major projects of founding a new religion, and launching a military campaign for the world-conquest like Alexander the Great. About the first project, he argued that 'just as the Prophet Muhammad had four companions, namely, Abu Bakr, Umar, Usman and Ali, he had his four intelligent lieutenants —Ulugh Khan, Zafar Khan, Nusrat Khan and Alp Khan; and he alluded to his second project as follows:

> 'My wish is to place Delhi in charge of a Vice-regent and then I will go out myself into the world, like Alexander, in pursuit of conquest, and subdue the whole habitable world'.

In his haughtiness and pride as a great ruler, Alauddin Khilji styled himself as the *Sikander-i-Sani,* viz., 'the Second Alexander'; and he caused this title to be included in his *Khutba* and inscribed on his coins. It was Alaul Mulk, the *Kotwal* of Delhi, his old companion, who, boldly pointed out the hollowness of his illusions. As regards the founding of a new religion by Alauddin, Alaul Mulk told him that 'the Prophetic office has never appertained to kings, and never will so long as the world lasts, although some Prophets have discharged the functions of royalty'. And regarding his second project of the world-conquest, Alaul Mulk reminded him that, what to say of the world, there were as yet so many kingdoms and regions in India which were beyond his control; moreover, he had no intelligent minister of Aristotle's calibre to manage the affairs of his state during his absence from the capital, while his Sultanate faced grave danger from the Mongols. Alaul Mulk, therefore, advised Alauddin Khilji to concentrate his attention towards. the affairs of his state, and exercise restraint on sensual pleasures and indulgence in drinking bouts. Deeply impressed by Alaul Mulk's friendly exposition, the Sultan liberally rewarded him and promised to follow his advice. Barani tells us that this dialogue took place in the presence of all the four great *khans* of the Sultan, mentioned above, and just before the third Mongol invasion of India in 1299.

Alauddin's relations with Muslim Theologians and the *Ulama*: Alauddin was an orthodox Sunni Mussalman, who professed adherence to the faith, and who never disputed the injunctions of the Islamic law, although as a ruler, in practice, he was the law unto himself. Barani has preserved a detailed account of his dialogue with Qazi Mughisuddin of Bayana on his state policy, which culminated in Alauddin's political philosophy as follows:

> 'To prevent rebellion, in which thousands perish, I issue such orders as I conceive to be for the good of the state and the benefit of the people. Men are heedless, disrespectful, and disobey my commands; I am then compelled to be severe to bring them into obedience. I do not know whether this is lawful or unlawful; whatever I think to be for the good of the state or suitable for the emergency that I decree'. (*Ibid.*, p. 188)

As elaborated by Dr. J.L. Mehta, 'Alauddin's rhetoric on the state policy as given above can be understood better if we substitute *him* for *the state,* and *his self-interest* for *the good of the state.* So far as his position as head of *an Islamic state* was concerned, Alauddin continued to style himself *Yamin-ul-Khilafat Nasiri Amir-ul-Momnin*, but he never felt the necessity of invoking the *Khalifa's* name to justify and strengthen his claim to sovereignty. He never applied for investiture by the *Khalifa* nor regarded the latter to be his political superior; reference to the *Khalifa* in official records continued to be made simply to keep the tradition of *Khilafat* theoretically alive'. (*Advanced Study in the History of Medieval India,* I, Sterling, New Delhi)

Alauddin firmly believed in the theory that 'kingship knows no kinship'. He always kept a vigilant eye on his military commanders (*ahal-i-shamshir),* and did not allow any of them to grow too strong to become uncontrollable for him. He never brooked any disobedience on the part of his nobles and, like Balban, inflicted severe punishments on them for even petty offences. As for the *ulama* or the *ahal-i-qalam,* he kept them in good humour but firmly under his thumbs. The Muslim theologians, *mullas, shaikhs* and the scholars were paid liberally by the state for performing all of their religious and judicial functions but they were never allowed to interfere in the state affairs; all posts in the judicial and educational institutions were reserved for them. Alauddin fully exploited their zeal for Islam and religious fanaticism in his wars against the Hindu rulers and the Indian natives, Hindus and Buddhists, who were dubbed as the *kafirs* (infidels); those of them who came within the jurisdiction of the Sultanate were made the *zimmis.*

Alauddin's Imperialism

Alauddin was a great imperialist. His generals Ulugh Khan and Zafar Khan had recovered the provinces of Multan and Sindh from the Jalali family in 1296-97; Ulugh Khan was appointed their viceroy with the responsibility to checkmate the Mongol inroads. About this time, a horde of a hundred thousand Mongols, led by Kadar Khan, had made their first appearance on the northwestern frontier. They crossed the Indus in the winter of 1296-97 and started loot and plunder in the Punjab. Zafar Khan and Ulugh Khan confronted them in the Jalandhar Doab and repulsed them after bloody encounters. About 20,000 Mongols were killed or wounded in action while hundreds of them were captured and beheaded later on.

After consolidating his hold over Delhi, Alauddin first of all turned his attention towards the rich province of Gujarat, which had taken his fancy during his expedition to Deogiri (Maharashtra) early in 1296. Beginning with its conquest, he initiated a long and continuous campaign for the annihilation of the formidable Hindu kingdoms which surrounded the Sultanate of Delhi in central and south India. He was a great military genius, who had to maintain a large standing army to defend his dominions; and the success of his military arms, leading to one conquest after another in quick succession, opened a new chapter in the history of the Turkish conquests which, during the twenty years of his long reign, transformed his kingdom into a mighty Muslim empire in the country. A brief account of his imperial conquests is in order.

1. **The Conquest of Gujarat (1299):** Early in 1299, Alauddin ordered a two-pronged attack on Gujarat by Ulugh Khan and Nusrat Khan. Gujarat was then ruled over by Rai Karan Deva II of the Baghela or Vaghela clan of Rajputs, who had transplanted the Chalukya or Solanki dynasty of Gujarat in 1242; Anhilwara (modern Pattan) was his capital. Ulugh Khan marched with his forces from Sindh and Nusrat Khan led the contingents of royal army from Delhi. Ulugh Khan invaded Jaisalmer and, after giving a bloody nose to its Rajputs, made a junction with the army of Nusrat Khan in the vicinity of Chittor. They avoided a head-on collision with the Rajputs of Chittor, and, after making a show of strength to leave the neighbouring chiefs guessing, took a sudden turn towards the direction of Gujarat in a surprise move so that Rai Karan Deva was taken totally unawares. He clashed with the army of Ulugh Khan near Ahmadabad but suffered a defeat and fled towards the south. He took shelter in the court of Raja Ram Chandra Deva of Deogiri (Maharashtra) along with his daughter Deval Devi, but his chief queen Kamla Devi and his treasures fell into the hands of the victors. The Gujarati sources ascribe the Muslim success to the betrayal of Rai Karan's minister Madhava but nothing can be said about it with certainty.

Loot and Plunder in Gujarat: The victorious Muslim armies advanced as far as Surat, and then penetrated into Saurashtra, where they laid their hands on the historic town and temple of Somanatha which had once been plundered and desecrated by Mahmud of Ghazni. They put it to plunder once again, and its magnificent and invaluable idol, which had been installed after the invasion of Mahmud, was sent to Delhi 'where it was laid down for the faithful to tread upon'. In their bid to establish their control of the province, the two victorious generals took their troops by two different routes, and in the process, plundered as much wealth from the country as possible; those who offered resistance to the forces of occupation were 'ruthlessly slaughtered'. Nusrat Khan moved via the rich seaport of Cambay from where 'he obtained an immense booty'. The province of Gujarat, 'with its rich harbours of international fame, fell into the hands of Alauddin Khilji like a ripe fruit full of honey'. On the royal command, Alp

Khan received appointment as the governor of Gujarat and a strong army was posted there to help him in strengthening his control.

Mutiny in the Royal Camp: After the settlement of Gujarat, the victorious generals set out for the capital, but on the way, trouble broke out near Jalor over the distribution of the spoils. It so happened that the royal army from Delhi included a large number of the ferocious Mongol converts to Islam, called the New Mussalmans. According to the practice, the generals demanded a fifth of the valuable spoils from the soldiers as state's share and 'adopted harsh measures to extract the valuables, hidden by the latter in their personal baggage. It led to mutiny by a few thousand New Mussalmans, which was crushed by the generals with an iron hand. In the words of Barani,

> 'When the report of this outbreak reached Delhi, the crafty cruelty, which had taken possession of Alauddin, induced him to order that the wives and children of all the mutineers, high and low, should be cast into prison. This was the beginning of the practice of seizing women and children for the faults of men. Up to this time, no hand had ever been laid upon wives and children on account of men's misdeeds'.- (*Tarikh-i-Firoze Shahi*, p. 164)

According to Barani, the mutineers killed Nusrat Khan's brother and a nephew of the Sultan. Nusrat Khan and Ulugh Khan, however, proved themselves equal to the occasion. They rallied their loyal troops by the beat of drums, defeated the rebels and gave them a hot chase, accompanied by 'great slaughter'. Nusrat Khan, who was rewarded with the *wizarat* of Delhi after the conquest of Gujarat for some time, committed atrocities on the mutinous troops in the likeness of the Sultan himself as follows:

> 'He ordered the wives of the assassins to be dishonoured and exposed to most disgraceful treatment; he then handed them over to vile persons to make common strumpets of them. The children he caused to be cut to pieces on the heads of their mothers. Outrages like this are practised in no religion or creed. These and similar acts of his filled the people of Delhi with amazement and dismay, and every bosom trembled'.—(*Ibid.*, p.165)

An easy conquest of Gujarat, in fact, aroused Alauddin's imperial instinct, and he embarked upon a career of conquest against which the feudal Rajput polity of India stood no chances of success. In the words of J.L. Mehta, this victory 'increased the prosperity of the Sultanate through maritime trade and commerce and enhanced his reputation throughout the Muslim world. It prompted him to launch a full-fledged campaign of imperial conquests with the object of bringing the whole of the Indian subcontinent under his control. ..Having envisaged an imperial policy, he did not need any other plausible reason or excuse to invade the various Hindu states of the subcontinent. He carried on ruthless and unprovoked wars against them and, ultimately, transformed the kingdom of Delhi into a mighty Indian empire'. (*History of Medieval India*, I, Sterling, p. 147)

The conquest of Gujarat became memorable for Alauddin Khilji and his ruling dynasty for two special reasons. Firstly, Kamla Devi, the wife of Rai Karan Deva of Gujarat fell into the hands of the victors; she was brought to Delhi with due honour and presented to the Sultan. Alauddin Khilji was captivated so much by her beauty and the royal dignity that he entered her in his *harem* as his wife, and made her the *Malika-i-Jahan* or the Chief Queen soon thereafter. Secondly, a handsome Hindu eunuch, named Kafur, whom Nusrat Khan had acquired from a Muslim merchant of Cambay, became a military general of Alauddin Khilji and conquered Deccan for the Muslims; he also played a very crucial role in the family affairs of the ruling dynasty after the death of Alauddin.

2. **Conquest of Ranthambhor (1299-1301):** After the conquest of Gujarat, Rajputana, the impregnable citadel of the Rajput prowess and its tough resistance to the advancement of Muslim arms in central and south India, became the focus of Alauddin's attention. It was now surrounded on three sides by the territorial possessions of the Sultanate, which made its conquest comparatively easy. The two most formidable Rajput states of this region which stood as bulwark against the Muslim penetration were those of Ranthambhor and Chittor. Accordingly, in the pursuit of Alauddin's imperial policy, these two states stood on the top of the list of the infidel lands to be conquered and subjugated by him. It was 'with the full concurrence of his ministers and generals' that the Sultan resolved to invest the stronghold of Ranthambhor towards the end of 1299. This fort had been conquered first of all by Qutubuddin Aibek and then by Iltutmish but each time it had been lost to the Chauhan Rajputs. It was under the control of Rana Hamir Deva (Deo of Muslim chroniclers), the grandson

of Rai Pithaura (Prithvi Raj Chauhan III) of Delhi, who had died fighting against Muhammad Ghori in the Second Battle of Tarain in 1192. In the year 1291, Jalaluddin Khilji had also made an abortive attempt to conquer it; but he returned after the occupation and plunder of its border district of Jhain. A plausible excuse for the attack on Ranthambhor was that Rana Hamir Deva had given shelter to some of the fugitive Mongol deserters of the royal army during the Gujarat campaign.

Alauddin Khilji ordered the victors of Gujarat - Ulugh Khan, who held the fief of Bayana, and Nusrat Khan, then the governor of Kara, to assemble their forces and launch an attack on Ranthambhor together. The two armies made their junction in the district of Jhain and moved together to surround the stronghold from all the sides. The fort was promptly put under siege which was gallantly defended by the Rajputs. According to Barani, 'One day, Nusrat Khan approached the fort to direct the construction of a mound (*pashib*) and a redoubt (*gargaj*). A stone, discharged from a *Maghribi* by the Rajputs in the fort, struck him and so wounded him that he died two or three days after'. The frontal attack made by the Muslim forces on the fort was repulsed by the Rajputs with heavy losses. It constrained the Sultan to take the field in person; and he left the capital with reinforcements for Ranthambhor immediately.

The siege prolonged for over a year, putting the besieged Rajput garrison to great hardships. Hard-pressed, the Rana sent his minister Ranmal to negotiate the terms of peace, but having fallen into the trap of Alauddin, determined to take possession of the fort at all costs, the Rajput emissary 'deserted to the invader along with his companions' for the safety of their lives and those of their families in the fort. It was Ranmal who helped the besiegers to climb up the walls of the fort to spread consternation in the besieged garrison. Left with no other alternative, the Rajputs performed Jauhar; they 'lit fire at the top of the hill and threw their women and children into the flames', while all the males, led by Rana Hamir Deva, opened the gates of the fort and died fighting to a man in their hand to hand fight with the Muslim soldiers. Alauddin took possession of the fort on July 11, 1301.

Once the fort was captured, all of its magnificent buildings, including the palace of Rana Hamir Deva, were sacked and then put to flames. Ranmal, the traitor was not spared either; he and the other Rajputs, who had betrayed their master and their own people were put to death under the orders of the Sultan; that was, in fact, the befitting reward of the traitors. Alauddin conferred the fort of Ranthambhor and the surrounding country on Ulugh Khan and returned to the capital. However, Ulugh Khan was not destined to enjoy the fruits of his services to the crown for long; after about five months, when he was collecting a large army for an expedition to Telingana and the Malabar coast in the south, he was taken ill and died; his dead body was brought in state to Delhi and buried in his own mansion.

Alauddin's Discomfiture during the Siege of Ranthambhor: Incidentally, Alauddin had to face trouble from three different quarters during the siege of Ranthambhor in 1300-1301. In the first instance, on his way to Ranthambhor, an attempt was made on his life by Akat Khan, a nephew of the Sultan. In the course of a hunting expedition at Tilpat, Akat Khan- the *wakildar* of Alauddin, finding him seated on a lonely spot struck him down with arrows. Alauddin received two wounds in the arm and fell down unconscious, profusely bleeding, but his life was saved by the mental alertness of his slave attendants, who shielded their master by creating a human wall around him, and raised hue and cry that the Sultan was dead. The Sultan regained consciousness and recovered his position without much difficulty soon afterwards. The rebellious prince was captured along with his associates and all of them were beheaded.

In the second incident, when Alauddin was deeply engrossed in the siege of Ranthambhor, two sons of his sister, Umar Khan and Mangu Khan, who held the fiefs of Awadh and Badaun respectively, defied the imperial authority in connivance with some other conspirators, but they were defeated and taken captives by the central forces.

In the third incident, 'a man, called Haji—a *Maula* or slave of Fakhruddin, the late *Kotwal* of Delhi', who was 'a man of violent, fearless and malignant character', created a stir in the capital. According to Barani, Haji Maula was a guard of the royal treasury. He took up cudgels on behalf of the people of Delhi against the oppressive policies of the new *Kotwal* of Delhi, called Turmuzi, and taking advantage of the Sultan's absence from the capital, 'worked up popular passion to a fever heat' with the mischievous intentions of bringing about a revolution. On the authority of 'a forged royal order', Haji Maula collected round him a mob of unruly citizens, secured the city gates, and seized the royal treasure, which was distributed among his followers. It was the month of Ramazan when this uprising took place. Turmuzi, the Kotwal of Delhi, was called out of his house treacherously and put to death. Haji Maula placed a Sayyad, said to be the grandson of Shah Najaf, on the make-shift throne and compelled the chief men of the capital to offer him obeisance. On the receipt of intelligence, Alauddin deputed his half-brother Malik Hamid Amirkoh to bring the miscreants to book. He took possession of the Badaun Gate and inflicted a crushing defeat upon Haji Maula in an open engagement from street to street within the city. Haji Maula was killed, and the unfortunate Sayyad was beheaded in the Red Palace, and his head was sent to the royal camp at Ranthambhor; deterrent punishments were given to the miscreants and their families.

Dr. J.L. Mehta, in one of his earlier publications, entitled, *Advanced Study in the History of Medieval India* (Volume I, Sterling Publishers, 1979) gives his comments on the conquest of Ranthambhor by Alauddin Khilji as follows:

> The conquest of Ranthambhor, though hard-earned, gave an over-whelming confidence to Alauddin Khalji that none of the Hindu kingdoms, however strong, were invincible, when dealt with one by one. What the Rajputs of the neighbouring states, including that of Chittor, had been doing when the Chauhans of Ranthambhor were engaged in life and death struggle against *the armies of Islam*? No other Rajput chief came to the rescue of Hamir Deva during a year-long siege of his capital by the enemy; instead, he was confronted, in that hour of trial, with defections and treachery on the part of his own close associates. The Rajputs as a class, displayed utter lack of the feelings of collective security and self-defence; their clannish rivalries and narrow regional loyalties stood in their way of concerted action against the common enemy; as a result, they crumbled to dust and were defeated one by one by the imperial armies of Alauddin Khalji'. (pp. 148-49)

3. **Conquest of Chittor:** Emboldened by the success of his arms, Alauddin ordered the march of his armies on their next expedition against Mewar—'the land of the brave Guhila or Guhilot Rajputs'. Unlike the previous campaigns, which never disclosed beforehand their intended target, and usually preferred to launch their attack by taking the enemy unawares, the campaign against Mewar had been given wide publicity to highlight the imperial ambitions of the Sultan. So it was in January 1303 that 'the loud drums proclaimed the royal march from Delhi, undertaken with a view to the capture of Chittor'—the capital of Mewar. It was then

ruled over by the youthful Rana Rattan Singh, who had ascended the throne in 1301on the death of his father Samar Singh.

The Guhila Rajputs, 'who had held their sway in this region since the eighth century, had successfully withstood the invasions of the Muslims ever since the conquest of Sindh by the Arabs'. The physical features of Mewar rendered it very difficult for any aggressor to penetrate so deep into that secluded region, protected by long chains of mountains and the impregnable forests; and the stronghold of Chittor, situated on a hilltop, strongly fortified by nature had always defied the foreign invaders. In the near past, Rana Rattan Singh's grandfather, Rana Jaitra Singh (1213-33) had successfully repulsed an attack from the army of Delhi under Iltutmish. Amir Khusrau, the poet laureate of Alauddin's court, who had accompanied the Sultan on his expedition to Chittor, gives a graphic account of the fort, its physical description, siege and conquest by the imperial forces, and the aftermath of its fall to the Muslims in the *Khazain-ul-Futuh*. One of the declared objects of Alauddin Khilji in invading Chittor was to get hold of Padmini, 'the peerless queen of the Rana, renowned for her beauty all over Hindustan'. The siege lasted about eight months, accompanied by numerous skirmishes with heavy losses of life on both the sides. Ultimately, the Sultan resorted to a stratagem to achieve his objective. His treacherous plan centered round the Padmini episode, as described by Malik Muhammad Jayasi, in his epic poem *Padmavat*; composed in 1540, the story of Padmini seems to be based on historical truth.

The Padmini Episode: As per the medieval chroniclers and elaborated by Malik Muhammad Jayasi, Alauddin sent a message from his army camp to the Rana that he was willing to raise the siege of the fort if the Rana could give him a glimpse of his queen. The Rana obliged him. In a friendly gesture, Alauddin was admitted into the fort as a guest, and Padmini was shown to him in a standing posture from behind a glass screen. However, when the Rana and his nobles came out of the fort to see off the Sultan, they were treacherously taken prisoners by the Muslim soldiers.

What followed thereafter was most shameful for the Muslim monarch of Delhi and humiliating for the proud Rajput race. As the story goes, Alauddin sent a message direct to Rani Padmini that her husband would be released if she chose to come into his *harem*. The Rajputs 'could never brook this indelible stain on their national honour. They debated among themselves as to the course which was to be adopted. The Rani, 'like a brave Rajput matron, more anxious for the honour of her race than for her own safety', expressed her willingness to abide by their decision. The Rajputs now conceived of a bold plan to rescue their leader through a clever manoeuvre. At their bidding, Padmini sent a reply to the Sultan that she was prepared to come with her female attendants. The lustful Sultan, whose reason was clouded by base elements, permitted her to do so in a manner befitting her rank and dignity. Thereupon, 700 covered litters (*palakis* or *dolies*), said to be carrying the Rani's maid servants, but actually concealing within them the brave Rajput warriors, well-equipped with arms, entered Alauddin's camp on promises of strictest security, like Trojan horses and rescued Rana Rattan Singh. This was done by the heroic exploit of two young Rajput warriors, Gora and Badal, at the head of a small contingent of their daredevil companions. It was followed by a bloody clash of arms between the antagonists resulting in the collapse of the Rajput resistance. Rana Rattan Singh died fighting in the battlefield while Rani Padmini burnt herself along with the other Rajput ladies on the funeral pyre. J. Tod, on the testimony of Malik Jayasi, describes that horrible scene thus:

> 'The fire of *Jauhar* was lighted in a subterranean cavern, which still exists, and the Rajput ladies, led by Padmini, jumped into the flames...The fair Padmini closed the throng which was augmented by whatever of female beauty or youth could be tainted by Tatar lust. They were conveyed to the cavern, and the opening closed upon them, leaving them to find security from dishonour in the devouring element'.—(*Annals and Antiquities of Rajasthan*; revised by W. Crooke, 3 vols. London, 1920, I, p. 311)

The fort of Chittor was taken on August 26, 1303. Alauddin was so much enraged by the tough resistance put up by the Rajputs that, after its occupation, he ordered a general massacre of the entire population of the town of Chittor. As a result, above 30,000 Rajput men, women and children were massacred in cold blood in a single day. The town was, thereafter, renamed Khizerabad after the name of Alauddin's eldest son Khizer Khan, then hardly a young boy of about seven or eight years. The crown prince was declared the governor of Khizerabad and nominated as the heir-apparent to the throne of Delhi. The fort was heavily garrisoned by the Muslim forces under the command of competent and enterprising military generals who carried on the administration on behalf of the crown prince.

The Rajputs of Mewar did not reconcile themselves to the loss of their political and religious independence, however. They retreated to the interior of the mountains and dense forests and carried on their struggle for freedom against the Muslim occupation of their hearths and homes through guerilla warfare; as a result, the forces of occupation were compelled to confine themselves within the four walls of their fortifications and police-posts most of the time. About the year 1311, Khizer Khan was compelled to leave the place owing to the pressure of the Rajputs, and Chittor was made over to a puppet Rajput chief, Maldeo of Jalor—a kinsman of Rana Rattan Singh. The Rajputs of Mewar refused to recognise him as their ruler, and continued to fight for his ouster in spite of the heavy odds against them. Maldeo held the reins of government at Chittor under the tutelage of the Sultan of Delhi for about seven years before he was expelled from there by Rana Hamir (not to be confused with his namesake of Ranthambhor), a nephew of Rana Rattan Singh, belonging to the junior branch of the Guhila Rajputs, called the Sisodias, in 1318; Mewar thus secured its independence within two years of the death of Alauddin Khilji.

4. **Conquest of Malwa, Sevana and Jalor (1305-11):** The fall of Ranthambhor and Chittor sounded the death-knell of the Rajput supremacy in northern and central India for ever. It 'broke the backbone of the Rajput power' and had a very demoralising effect upon the other Hindu rulers of Rajputana. Alauddin was now free to take on any of the lesser Rajput chieftains at his convenience and demand his allegiance to Delhi on the pain of peril. He did not relax, however, and continued to exert his diplomatic as well as military pressure to bring them to knees at the earliest.

Malwa was the next target on the long list of Alauddin's prospective expeditions. The Muslim arms had penetrated into Malwa long before the rise of Alauddin Khilji. Iltutmish had captured Bhilsa and sacked Ujjain in 1231-32, in the course of which he had desecrated and destroyed the famous Hindu temple of Mahakali. In 1292, during the reign of Jalaluddin Khilji, Alauddin as a young upstart had won the affection and favours of his uncle by carrying out a successful plundering raid on Bhilsa. In 1305, he sent a strong contingent of well-armed 10,000 horsemen, under the command of Ainul Mulk Multani, with determination to conquer and annex the whole of Malwa to his dominions. Its chief Rai Mahlak Deva possessed 30 to 40 thousand cavalry and an innumerable infantry; his foster brother and minister Koka Pradhan was the commander-in-chief of his forces. In the first bloody encounter that took place between the antagonists, Koka

Pradhan, along with thousands of his soldiers, died fighting in the battlefield; his head was chopped off his dead body, and sent by the victorious commander to Delhi 'to be trampled under the feet of the horses below the palace gates'.

Thoroughly disheartened, Rai Mahlak Deva fled from the field and took shelter in the fort of Mandu. It was promptly put under siege by the Muslim troops. Mahlak Deva's youthful son died fighting against the foe on the outskirts of the fort, and to his further misfortune, a Rajput traitor from the town led the Muslim general to a private passage for entry into the fort in the darkness of the night. Mahlak Deva and his garrison were taken aback at the sudden appearance of the foe inside the fort, and, in the scuffle that followed, the Rai was killed and the fort fell into the hands of the Muslims on November 23, 1305. Soon afterwards, the historic cities of Ujjain, Dharnagri and Chanderi were also captured by the victorious Muslim general without much inconvenience, and the whole of Malwa was declared annexed to the Sultanate of Delhi. Ainul Mulk Multani, the hero of this exploit, was honoured with his appointment as the first Muslim governor of Malwa.

Conquest of Sevana (1308): After the conquest of Malwa, Alauddin Khilji ordered a vigorous diplomatic campaign in which he called upon all the other Rajput chiefs to acknowledge the suzerainty of Delhi. In 1308, Alauddin despatched his main army of invasion, under the command of Malik Kafur and Nusrat Khan, for the conquest of south India, and, at the same time, led an expedition, under his personal command, for the capture of Sevana. It was then ruled over by a Parmar chief, Rana Sital Deva, who had refused to offer his allegiance to Alauddin Khilji voluntarily. Alauddin invested the fort in July 1308, and its siege lasted about four months. The Muslim forces, ultimately, overpowered the besieged garrison by escalading the battlements of the citadel. The Rana escaped from the fort but 'ran into an ambush and was put to death on November 10, 1308. The Sultan entrusted the administration of Sevana to Kamaluddin Gurg before his return to the capital.

The fall of Jalor (1311): The Rajput principality of Jalor (ancient Javalipura) in the Marwar region was the last to be conquered and annexed to the Sultanate of Delhi in northern India by Alauddin Khilji. Situated at a distance of about 80 kilometres from Sevana, the fort of Jalor was conquered by Iltutmish in 1210 but it was lost to the Chauhan Rajputs after some time. .Its Chauhan ruler, Kanhar Deva, had voluntarily acknowledged the suzerainty of Alauddin in 1304, but his haughty demeanor irked the Sultan who made up his mind to annex the fort by abolishing the ruling dynasty of the Rajputs. In fact, after the conquest and annexation of the mighty Rajput states of Ranthambhor, Mewar and Malwa etc., the Sultan wanted to put an end to the semi-independent status of Jalor as a separate entity. Therefore, in 1311, Alauddin sent a royal army under the command of Malik Shahin, an illegitimate son of the Sultan from a slave girl, named Gul Bahisht, for the occupation of Jalor. Gul Bahisht also accompanied her son to Jalor in joint command of the royal army. The Rajputs fought desperately to retain their independence; and the siege of Jalor which dragged on for over a year, claimed the lives of Gul Bahisht, who died of fever, and her son Malik Shahin, who was killed in a skirmish. Ultimately, the fort of Jalor was conquered by Kamaluddin Gurg, the governor of Sevana; and he was granted the governorship of Jalor as a reward, in addition to that of Sevana.

Nothing is known about the fate of Raja Kanhar Deva, but, it is said that his brother Maldeo, who was related to the ruling family of Chittor, had betrayed his own people and helped the army of Delhi in the conquest of Jalor. As referred to earlier in this chapter, it was as a reward for these services that Maldeo was appointed the Rana of Chittor by Alauddin Khilji in 1311, when his son Khizer Khan had to leave the place under pressure from the Rajput freedom-fighters of Mewar.

Thus by the year 1311 all the important Hindu states of Rajputana had been brought under the subjugation of the Sultanate of Delhi; and, with the fall of Jalor, Alauddin Khilji became the undisputed imperial ruler of nearly the whole of northern India. Tod, therefore, makes a very appropriate observation that, with the collapse of the formidable Rajput states of the Parmars, Pratiharas, Chauhans and Chalukyas (Solankis), 'the entire Agnikula race' met with its doom, and the traditional Rajput glory of India departed for ever.

K.S. Lal, the celebrated author of *History of the Khaljis: 1290-1320* (The Indian Press, Allahabad, 1950) writes about the general character of the Rajput campaigns as follows:

> 'Ever since the Sultan (Alauddin Khilji) had embarked upon the conquest of Ranthambhor in 1300, till the fall of Jalor in 1311, his armies had constantly fought in Rajasthan (Rajputana). It was below the dignity of the Sultan to recall his forces once the siege of fortress had been begun, and the valour of the

Rajputs could not brook the insult of giving way to the enemy. The result was that bloody battles were fought before each and every fortress. To enumerate the various wars in Rajputana, then, is to repeat the horrors of blood and slaughter, of gallant fight, and of glorious martyrdom. Sometimes before a single citadel the contest prolonged for years, and ended in a general massacre of its population, accompanied by the gruesome destruction of the womenfolk in the fire of *Jauhar*'.—(pp. 139-40)

Causes of Collapse of the Rajput Power

The question, that has frequently been raised by the historians of Indian history, and baffled the political thinkers and analysts ever since the fall of the mighty Rajput kingdoms at the hands of their Muslim adversaries, still beggars description. We have already given a detailed analysis of the basic causes of the capitulation of the Rajputs in the face of the Muslim invaders in the conclusion of chapter three of this study, pertaining to the invasions and conquests of Muhammad Ghori. Here, we would like to record some observations of K.S. Lal to supplement and corroborate the evidence with specific reference to Alauddi's encounter with the Rajputs. The learned author writes that

> 'Unluckily, the Rajputs, who spurned life without freedom, possessed valour without the spirit of union. Individual fortresses offered stubborn resistance, but singly none of them was a match against the Sultanate of Delhi. Had even two or three Rajput princes combined against the Sultan, they would surely have succeeded in defeating him. But secure in their mountain fortresses, each one of them was content to mind his own affairs and exult in his own pride, while Alauddin raided and subdued one kingdom after another'.

The Rajput polity presented a house divided against itself. Lal cites the example of Sevana and Jalor to show the disunity among the Rajputs, and their contemptuous disregard towards the fate of their respective neighbouring chiefs; he observes that 'the case of Sevana and Jalor is a glaring example of the callous indifference of the Rajput chieftains towards one another. While the fall of Sevana was imminent, the ruler of Jalor, living only fifty miles from there, was unmoved, with the result that, after a couple of years, Jalor was also taken (by Alauddin) in another assault'.

The hill forts of the Rajputs, of course, formed an indispensable part of the ancient and medieval Indian defence system. These were well-maintained and abundantly supplied to meet any eventuality. The forts invariably served as the headquarters of the Rajput chiefs as also those of their provincial and district officers. They provided refuge in the face of enemy's aggression, and helped the Rajputs to store up military supplies, food and fodder. The forts could easily defy the sudden onslaught of the foreign invaders but they had their disadvantages in the face of their determined imperial foes like Alauddin Khilji, who could afford to put them under siege for a long time and be prepared for a protracted struggle to fight out the issue to the bitter end. K.S. Lal highlights this aspect of the forts with reference to the defeat of the Rajputs at the hands of Alauddin Khilji. To make up for this omission in the general treatment of the issue in the aforementioned chapter three of our book, the arguments of K.S. Lal may be reproduced below *ad valorem*:

> The hill forts 'were designed to protect women, children and cattle when the brave defenders sallied out to encounter a sudden invasion. And although it was difficult for the invaders to ascend step by step cliffs of the hillock, yet the citadel, when subjected to a siege, was always rendered separate and secluded from the plains below. Thus the corns and revenues of outlying districts automatically fell into the hands of the enemy.
>
> 'During investment, not all the people of the vicinity escaped in time to seek shelter inside the citadel; a large number of them were left on the plains below. Their distress though made them hate the enemy did in no way dispose them loyally towards their rulers inside the citadel.
>
> 'The conditions inside the fortress, again, were not very satisfactory. During an investment, the crowd far exceeded the number of the normal inhabitants, and there were no special arrangements for the extra provisions and vegetables.
>
> 'The enemy lying at the base of the hill, on which the fort stood, could easily cut off the convoy, and it was always the dearth of provisions that rendered defence impossible. The mighty fortresses of Ranthambhor, Chittor and Jalor—all surrendered to famine.
>
> 'Again, medieval conditions of sanitation were no preventive against outbreak of epidemics.
>
> 'To add to this, caste considerations and orthodoxy reigned supreme.

'The enemy was alive to these weaknesses of the Hindus and took full advantage. The instance of Ranthambhor is worth repeating. Through the services of some traitor, hides were thrown inside the grain cellars; provisions were thereby rendered *desecrate* and the fortress surrendered.'—(*History of the Khaljis*; pp. 140-41).

Alauddin's Unfinished Struggle against the Rajputs

The conquest of Rajputana by Alauddin Khilji proved short-lived, however. The campaigns against the Rajputs cost the Sultan very heavily in men and material with no parallel monetary or material gains. The peculiar topography of the region, which comprised a vast stretch of sandy deserts, interspersed with forests and dry hills, posed a great hindrance not only in the way of conquest but also in the consolidation of the conquered territories and the imperial bid to keep them under its control.

The Rajputs were great patriots; they loved their homeland or the country of their domicile; they had a strong affiliation to their hearths and homes and were ever ready to sacrifice their lives to maintain their political and religious freedom. When they had 'a country to love as their motherland, and an honour to maintain', how could they ever think of submitting to Alauddin's military dictatorship for long? In the words of K.S. Lal, 'if the day was irrevocably lost, they well knew how to deliver themselves and their families from the insulting invader, and as soon as the deluge of the invasion had ebbed, they reclaimed their territories'. Alauddin Khilji committed a serious mistake when he decided to bring them under his subjugation by brute force. The harsh and very-often humiliating treatment meted out by the Sultan towards the vanquished Rajput chiefs and the soldiers, and, whatever the provocation, the totally uncivilized and inhuman practice which tempted him to resort to the general massacre of the unarmed civilian population of the towns after the capitulation of the forts, proved counter-productive. No wonder, the Rajputs, even when their forts were captured and their military resistance completely shattered, never reconciled themselves to the loss of their political and religious freedom, and 'the liquidation of their clannish ruling houses'. It prompted them to start a counter-offensive against the victors. That is how the struggle for the independence of Chittor was launched by the populace of Mewar the very moment their stronghold was lost to the enemy. As a consequence, Alauddin's hold over Rajputana was very precarious; his conquest of the region, for the most part, lay on quicksand. To quote K.S. Lal, 'the occupation of Ranthambhor, after Ulugh Khan left it not more than six months after its capture, is uncertain. Khizer Khan had to vacate Chittor in Alauddin's lifetime. Bardic literature enumerates continual struggles between the Muslims and the Rajputs. Obviously, Rajputana had not completely submitted, and one or the other kingdom in that land of born warriors was always successfully defying the authority of the sultanate of Delhi'. According to J.L. Mehta,

> 'The misfortune of the Rajputs was that they had learnt nothing and forgotten nothing from their repeated failures in the long struggle against the Turks ever since the days of Muhammad Ghori. They possessed the same narrow and parochial outlook as ever before and failed to forge a united front against their common foe. Their isolated efforts to regain independence yielded some fruit at heavy costs to them, *albeit* the lack of coordination reduced the military efforts of the various Rajput clans to an exercise in futility in the long run'.—(Medieval India, *loc. cit*; I, pp. 151-52)

The Mongol Invasions

Before their conversion to Islam, the Mongols practised some form of Buddhism, intermingled with superstitions. They made their appearance on the northwestern frontier of India for the first time under Changez Khan in 1220-21. The rapid spread of Mongol domination in central Asia and Iran rendered India vulnerable to their frequent invasions, and posed a serious threat to the Sultanate of Delhi. Alauddin Khilji had to face six major Mongol invasions during his reign but he dealt with them with an iron hand, and saved his dominions against their onslaughts.

As referred to earlier, Alauddin had to face the first Mongol invasion soon after his accession to the throne in 1296-97, when Deva, the Mongol ruler of Mavar-un-Nahr sent an army of about a hundred thousand Mongols, under the leadership of Kadar Khan for an Indian invasion. They infiltrated into the Punjab and Sindh for loot and plunder. Zafar Khan and Ulugh Khan checked their advance in the Jalandhar Doab. Amir Khusrau records that about 20,000 Mongols were killed in a bloody battle somewhere near the confluence of rivers Satluj and Beas. Ulugh Khan sent the report of his victory to Alauddin Khilji, together with the chopped off heads of the Mongols, which enhanced his prestige, and helped him in stabilizing his position as the new Sultan of Delhi, who had usurped the throne by treacherously assassinating his own uncle very recently.

In the year following, the second invasion of the Mongols, under the leadership of Saldi took place in quick succession. They overran Sindh and captured the fortress of Siwistan—probably Sehwan, situated in the northwestern part of Sindh. On the orders of the Sultan, Zafar Khan took on them single-handed with his personal contingents only. Zafar Khan liberated Siwistan from the hands of the foe in a single assault, in his 'hand to hand fight' with the Mongol marauders. The entire army of Mongols was annihilated, and 'the valiant general returned to Delhi with hundreds of the Mongols of both sexes as captives; Saldi and his brother were also among them'. Barani records that

> 'This victory inspired awe of Zafar Khan in every heart, and the Sultan also looked at him in consequence of his fearlessness, generalship and interpidity, which showed that a Rustam had been born in India'.

Thereafter, Zafar Khan was entrusted the charge of Samana, a strategic military post in the Punjab to defend the capital against the sudden onslaught of the Mongols. Barani reveals that, instead of feeling pleased with Zafar Khan for the faithful and most meritorious services to the state, the Sultan and his younger brother Almas Beg, now styled Ulugh Khan, became jealous of him because he had earned reputation as a great hero, and 'eclipsed their own military exploits'. The Sultan was, however, awe-struck when 'the Mongols appeared on the northwestern frontier like locusts for the third time before the close of the year 1299'; they were led by Qutlugh Khwaja, the promising son of Deva Khan—the Mongol ruler of Transoxiana (Mavar-un-Nahr), and, according to the rough estimates of the contemporary writers, numbered about two hundred thousands (twenty *tumans*). It is said that Deva Khan had heard about the murder of Jalaluddin, and the object of sending his repeated invasions in quick succession was to wrest the throne of Delhi from the hands of its usurper Alauddin Khilji. That is why, this time 'the Mongols crossed the Indus and made straight for Delhi without molesting the people or engaging the Indian contingents stationed in the Punjab. Obviously, their object was to conquer Delhi and liquidate the Sultanate altogether'. It unnerved Alauddin Khilji, and he called upon all the provincial governors of his dominions to send their reserved forces for the defence of the capital against the Mongol invasion. According to Barani,

'Great anxiety prevailed in Delhi and the people of the neighbouring villages took refuge within its walls. The old fortifications had not been kept in repair, and terror prevailed, such as never before had been seen or heard of. All men, great and small, were in dismay. Such a concourse had crowded into the city that the streets and markets and mosques could not contain them. Everything became very dear. The roads were stopped against caravans and merchants, and distress fell upon the people'.

Battle with the Mongols: The panic and consternation that prevailed in the capital made the problem of defence and provisions all the more difficult. Some of the Sultan's counsellors advised him to fight a defensive war from within the city's fortifications, but Alauddin, like a dare-devil, preferred to challenge the invaders in the open. On the beating of the war-drums, he moved out of the capital and set up his army camp in the plain of Kili, at a distance of about ten kilometres to the north of the outskirts of Delhi. The main army was arranged in the battle-array and entrenched, with the river Yamuna on one side and the irregular wasteland of thorny bushes and shrubs on the other side. Strong contingents of war-elephants were stationed in front of each division as bulwark against a terrific assault by the Mongol chargers. With every passing day, the number of royal forces increased by fresh arrivals from the outlying provinces; the new contingents, on their arrival, were posted ahead of the main army at forward posts all around the capital. The Sultan, with Nusrat Khan and twelve thousand horsemen commanded the centre while Zafar Khan held the right wing and Ulugh Khan the left. A reserve force of picked royal guards was kept behind the battle-lines to be used in case of emergency.

Before the Mongols were sighted by the advance guards of Delhi, they had also arranged themselves into systematic battle-lines. They were engaged as soon as they showed their appearance on the bee-line. In the bloody encounter that took place, thousands lay dead on both sides. Before the sunset, the Mongol army, 'broken and routed' had commenced a hasty retreat. The Mongol attack had been successfully repulsed on all the fronts, but the royal troops were too tired to pursue the retreating enemy. To the great amazement of the Indian soldiers, many of the retreating Mongol horsemen 'continued to shower arrows behind their back on their pursuers - a practice in which the Mongols were past masters'. As an exception, Zafar Khan was the only Muslim commander, who 'broke through the enemy's lines, and gave a hot chase to the fleeing Mongols with about a thousand horsemen for eighteen *kos,* without any supporting force in his own rear'. Targhi Beg, a Mongol leader, 'who had placed his troops in ambush, saw through the game, and rushed forward to cut off Zafar Khan's party from its base camp. He entrapped the royal troops on their way back, and cut them to a man; Zafar Khan also fell fighting bravely'. According to Barani, Ulugh Khan knew that his colleague 'Zafar Khan was in trouble, but he did not send him reinforcements to save his life'.

Retreat of the Mongols: After a day-long battle, disengagement between the rival armies was natural, and the Mongols still had the upper-hand because they felt elated at having killed Zafar Khan, one of their most dreaded antagonists. But they were thoroughly disheartened by the dogged resistance put up the army of Delhi. According to Isami, having seen the mettle of the army of Hindustan, 'the Mongols hovered about Delhi for a few more days without daring to give a battle and then retired'. (*Futuhus Salatin*, ed. by Agha Mahdi Husain, Agra, 1938, pp. 258-60). According to Amir Khusrau, after disengagement, the Mongols retreated to a distance of about thirty *kos* from Delhi under the cover of the night, and then halted till the day-break when 'they returned to their country by continuous marches without stopping on the way'. Qutlugh Khwaja, the warrior son of Deva Khan, probably the crown prince, was taken ill and died on his way back to Transoxiana. (*Dewal Rani Khizr Khan*i, ed. by Muhammad Ismail, Aligarh, 1918, p.61).

The heroic defence of the capital, put up by Alauddin Khilji against the most dreadful assault of the Mongols under the leadership of Qutlugh Khwaja, saved it from the impending peril. The Sultan returned from Kili to Delhi in triumph, but 'by the irony of circumstances, nobody praised the hero of the battle, Zafar Khan, for his sacrifice and gallantry. On the contrary, Alauddin blamed him for fighting recklessly and pursuing the enemy without his orders. 'In his heart of hearts, he was happy, and considered his death another welcome event, only next in consequence to the defeat of the Mongols'. According to Barani, in a private conversation with his confidents, Alauddin is said to have remarked that 'Zafar Khan had been got rid of without disgrace'. (*Ibid.*, p. 168) Nevertheless, the terror created by Zafar Khan—in the hearts of the Mongols was so great that 'the dread of his name remained in the breasts of the Mongols for years, and when their cattle would not drink water they would ask: *What! Have you seen Zafar Khan that you do not drink water*?'. (Ibid)

Notwithstanding their repeated defeats, the Mongols did not stop their invasions on India; after a few years, they marked their presence on the northwestern frontier again in 1303. This gap was utilized by Alauddin Khilji to launch an extensive campaign for the conquest of Rajputana. He was engaged in the siege of Chittor in February 1303 when he received the intelligence about the appearance of the Mongols on the Indian borders. They numbered about 1,20,000 and were commanded by Targhi Beg, a reputed Mongol general, who had killed Zafar Khan in the previous invasion. Alauddin did not loose his cool to hear of it; he ordered the siege of Chittor to continue but himself returned to the capital, with whatever soldiers that he could spare from that engagement, and requisitioned fresh troops from the provincial governors. He made hurried arrangements for the defence of the capital 'which were far from being adequate.

Unlike the third invasion of the Mongols, Alauddin now adopted a defensive approach to deal with them, and the Mongols also avoided head-on collision with the royal forces because of their dread of the previous experience. They put Delhi under siege, while keeping at a safe distance from the Indian fortifications, and spread themselves in the countryside, where they resorted to destruction and devastation on an extensive scale. After about forty days, the Mongols suddenly decamped and retreated from India, carrying with them immense wealth, including precious metals, household goods and whatever they could lay their hands on, along with untold number of horses, cattle and the men and women as captives. In the words of J.L. Mehta, 'The Mongols, in fact, were very poor at laying siege to the fortified installations; they grew impatient and could not manipulate provisions or sustain their enthusiasm in the long drawn-out conflicts. Their failure to take Delhi by storm undid their enterprise and, with every passing day of the siege, Targhi Beg apprehended that his army might be encircled and destroyed by the Indian contingents from the provincial headquarters, which were gradually closing upon the capital. Hence the Mongols thought of their safety in retreat before it was too late'. (*Ibid.*, I, pp. 163-64).

In their fifth assault on India, 50,000 Mongol hordes, under the command of Ali Beg, a descendant of Changez Khan, accompanied by Targhi Beg and Khwaja Tash or Tartaq invaded India in 1305 with the sole object of loot and plunder. They ravaged Multan and spread themselves in the plains of the Punjab. Moving along the foothills of the Shiwaliks, they entered the Ganga-Yamuna Doab and carried destruction and devastation wherever they went. Having thoroughly understood the Mongol character and their real objectives, Alauddin now adopted new tactics to deal with them. He took the defence of the capital under his personal supervision, strengthened its fortifications, replenished its provisions, and always kept a strong standing army for its defence to meet any eventuality. With the emergence of a new military general in the person of Malik Kafur, now the *akhurbeg-i-maisrah* or 'master of the horse', he was assigned the duty to cut-off the lines of retreat of the Mongol marauders, and give them a hot chase from behind to bring about their destruction.

This is exactly what Malik Kafur did; instead of confronting them from the front, he followed their trail 'herded them together, as far as possible, by a flanking movement of the royal armies, and struck at them near Amroha with a terrible force'. As a result, Targhi beg was shot by an arrow of a Khilji trooper along with thousands of the Mongols, who were slaughtered in the battlefield, and 8,000 of them were taken prisoners along with their other two leaders, Ali Beg and Khwaja Tash. They were all sent in chains to the capital. Twenty thousand horses of the fallen Mongol soldiers were brought to Delhi by the victors and presented to the Sultan to his great delight. By the orders of Alauddin Khilji, the Mongol prisoners of war 'were paraded in the city on camels, after which they were beheaded; and their heads were used in the construction of towers outside the fort'. According to Firishta, '8,000 heads of the Mongol prisoners were used instead of stones and bricks to build the towers of Siri, which were then under construction'. His statement is also confirmed by Amir Khusrau who writes that 'the Mongols give blood to new buildings'.

According to Firishta, 'the worst fate awaited those Mongols, who had escaped from the trap laid by Malik Kafur'. About that time, Ghazi Malik (the later Sultan Ghiasuddin Tughluq, who founded the Tughluq Dynasty at Delhi) was the governor of Dipalpur in the Punjab; on the orders of the Sultan, he led his army towards the Indus and lay in ambush to entrap the Mongol fugitives during their retreat from Delhi and the Doab, and thousands of them were killed like rats. Those of the Mongols, 'who escaped the sword, finding it impossible to force their way home, retired into the desert, where thirst and the hot winds, which blow at that season, put an end to their miserable lives'. Amir Khusrau also adds that 'all the Mongol women and children, taken in this war, were sent to different parts of the kingdom, to be sold in the markets as slaves'. (*Tarikh-i-Firishta*; Briggs; I, p. 207).

The sixth and the last invasion of the Mongols during the reign of Alauddin Khilji took place in the winter of 1306. It is said that Deva Khan, the Mongol ruler of Transoxiana, had sent this expedition to avenge the deaths of his famous generals, Ali Beg and Khwaja Tash, who had been captured alive and put to death by the Sultan of Delhi. An army of 50,000 Mongols, under the commands of Kubak and Iqbalmand, spread itself into the Indian plains in two different groups. Kubak advanced towards Lahore while Iqbalmand adopted a more southerly course and reached as far as Nagor. Malik Kafur and Ghazi Malik herded together the contingents of Kubak by adopting the flanking movements and pounced upon them like hawks on the river Ravi; the whole of his army was annihilated, and many thousands of the Mongols were taken prisoners along with their leader, Kubak. They were all taken to Delhi in chains. Similarly, Iqbalmand was also defeated and repulsed by the Delhi troops near Nagor, but their leader probably escaped alive from the battlefield and fled to Afghanistan along with some other fugitives. According to Firishta, the Sultan was so much enraged at the persistent audacity of the Mongol invaders, who poured into the country year after year, that he ordered the captives, including their leader Kubak, 'to be thrown under the feet of elephants, and a tower to be constructed of their skulls in front of the Badaun Gate. Their women and children were sold in Delhi and the rest of Hindustan'.

Alauddin's Mongol Policy: Inspite of their repeated invasions, the Mongols failed to make headway on the Indian soil; it is because they had to reckon with a born warrior and war-lord that Alauddin Khilji was. A great imperialist and aggressive military general, he knew how to deal with the ferocious Mongol marauders. Like Balban, he also adopted a blood and iron policy to deal with the Mongol menace. He raised a large standing army for the internal defence of his capital and to fight against the Mongol invaders. It was well-equipped with superior quality of horses and the improved weapons of offence and defence. With Delhi as the nucleus, Alauddin converted the whole of northwestern India, into a defensive belt, which was divided into a number of powerful military posts, these were put under the charge of the most competent and dedicated generals who derived pleasure in bloodshed and slaughter of their foe with a vengeance. The governorships of Sirhind, Samana, Tabarhind, Lahore, Dipalpur, Multan and the Indus valley were all reserved for the men of steel among his nobility, who commanded vast armies and struck terror in the hearts of the invaders by their ruthless methods of warfare; they meted out the most inhuman treatment towards those who into their hands, and they did not spare even the women and children of the invaders, who were taken captives and sold as slaves in the markets of Hindustan. The whole of the northwestern belt was dotted with the massive forts and highly fortified military posts all along the roads and the routes of infiltration of the Mongols. All the military posts and installations were interconnected with broad roadways to facilitate the quick movement of armies. The Red Fort of Delhi was repaired, adequately fortified and furnished with enough provisions; it was defended by the best of the royal guards and made rather invincible against all attacks; so also was the main city of Delhi, which, as a fortified town, left nothing to be desired. To improve the defences of the capital, a new fort of Siri was constructed which safeguarded the royal palaces, imperial secretariat and the treasury. So long as the Mongol threat lasted, Alauddin preferred to stay put in Delhi and personally took command of the royal forces when the capital was under attack of the Mongols. It gave great confidence to the royal forces and sense of security to the people of Delhi and its surrounding areas at the time of danger. That is why Barani records with satisfaction that

> 'All fear of the Mongols entirely departed from Delhi and the neighbouring provinces. Perfect security was everywhere felt, and the *raiyats* (peasantry) of those territories, which had been exposed to the inroads of the Mongols, carried on their agriculture in peace'.—(*Tarikh-i-Firoze Shahi*, p. 199).

Deccan Campaigns of Alauddin Khilji

Alauddin had successfully checkmated the Mongol invasions with the help of his vast standing army during the earlier part of his reign. When the Mongol tide finally receded, this very army was helpful to him in the expansion of territorial jurisdictions of the Sultanate through his vigorous campaigns of conquests and annexations of the Hindu states. By the year 1311, nearly the whole of Rajputana lay within the imperial yoke of Delhi, while the success of his expedition to Devagiri of the yester years constantly impelled him to launch a full-fledged military campaign for the conquest of south India at the first opportunity. About this time, Alauddin had 4,75,000 well-equipped permanent standing army, credited with the subjugation of the proud Rajput race, besides numerous victories against the Mongol invaders. His magnificent standing army ought to be usefully employed if it was to be kept under effective control. The enormous wealth acquired from the Devagiri exploit of 1296 had made him the Sultan of Delhi, and the conquest of the Deccan now formed an irresistible part of his political ambitions to transform his kingdom into a mighty empire. Therefore, ever since he had become the ruler of Delhi, he had been keeping himself in touch with all the political developments of south India. From the caravans and travellers, and with the assistance of his own spies and scouts, he used to collect information about the topography of south India, ascertained the routes leading to the important towns, and learnt all about the military strength and wealth of the various Hindu states. It was to his knowledge that, in the beginning of the fourteenth century, Deccan, like north India, was also parcelled out into a number of big and small Hindu kingdoms, which did not see eye to eye with one another. Apart from numerous independent and autonomous Hindu principalities, there were four major Hindu states as follows:

1. The Kingdom of Devagiri (mod. Maharashtra); it lay to the south of the Vindhya mountains, and was ruled over by Raja Ram Chandra Deva of the Yadava dynasty.
2. The Kingdom of Telingana, with its capital at Warrangal; it was situated to the southeast of Devagiri. It was ruled over by Pratap Rudra Deva II of the Kakatiya dynasty.
3. The Kingdom of Dwarsamudra; it was ruled by Vir Ballala III of the Hoysala dynasty; and
4. To the far south lay the Kingdom of the Pandyas; this was ruled by Kulashekhra Pandya with his headquarters at Madura; this region was known to the Muslim chroniclers as the country of M'abar or Malabar.

After the conquest of Ranthambhor in 1301, the Sultan deputed Ulugh Khan to make preparations for an expedition for the conquest of Telingana, but, due to the untimely death of the latter, the plan did not materialise. In 1303, when Alauddin was engaged in his siege of Chittor, he ordered the *iqtadār* of Kara to organise an expedition to Telingana through the easterly route via Orissa but it did not prove successful; probably, the royal army was defeated by the ruler of Telingana.

Second Expedition to Devagiri (1307): By the year 1305, Alauddin's hands were free from the conquest of Malwa and Rajputana, and all the routes leading to south India had been ascertained and secured. Whereas, Alauddin's preparations for launching a major offensive for the conquest of south needed no explanation or excuse, Raja Ram Chandra Deva of Devagiri did provide some plausible causes for taking an initiative against him. For the last two or three years, he had failed to send the tribute in respect of the ceded district of Ellichpur to Delhi.

Secondly, he had granted asylum to the fugitive Rana Karan Deva Baghela of Gujarat. To the great annoyance of the Sultan, the fugitive was put up in the district of Ellichpur, which he had formally ceded to Delhi according to the earlier agreement of 1296. Karan Deva setup his headquarters at Nandurbar, a small town in the Baglana region, which contained a mixed population of Marathas and the Gujaratis.

Thirdly, according to Firishta, when the imperial armies were preparing to march on Devagiri, Kamal Devi, the ex-wife of Rana Karan Deva of Gujarat, now the chief queen of Alauddin, entitled, *Malika-i-Jahan*, had requested the Sultan to explore the possibility of securing her daughter Dewal Devi from her ex-husband. Firishta tells us that Kamla Rani had two daughters from her former husband; the elder one had died, but the younger one, named Dewal Devi or Dewal Rani, was about four years old when she was separated from her mother, who fell into the hands of the soldiers of Alauddin in 1296; Dewal Rani was rescued and brought up by her father, Rana Karan Deva.

These causes or excuses were more than enough for the dispatch of a vast 'army of the Deccan' to Devagiri under the command of Malik Kafur, now made the *Malik Naib* or 'the deputy sultan'; the nucleus of this army comprised 30,000 strong cavalry force, well-trained and provided with the latest sophisticated weapons of offense and defence. It was reinforced by the armies of Khwaja Haji, Ainul Mulk—the governor of Malwa, and Alp Khan—the governor of Gujarat. Their joint armies were to chastise the delinquent Maratha chief, to realize three years' tribute from him, and to obtain possession of Dewal Rani, the younger daughter of the fugitive Rai Karan Baghela, the ex-king of Gujarat, who had been sheltered by the Maratha king.

Recovery of Dewal Rani: Incidentally, while launching an attack on Devagiri (Maharashtra), the royal forces had to confront Rai Karan Deva, settled in its border territories. Accordingly, after crossing the Malwa, Malik Kafur sent a message to Rai Karan to hand over his daughter Dewal Rani to him or be prepared to face the consequences. The Rai 'spurned the humiliating alternative and prepared for defence'.

Thereupon, Malik Kafur asked Alp Khan to march with his army through the mountains of Baglana to secure the possession of the princess from him, and himself moved on towards Devagiri. Karan Deva was defeated and turned out of Ellichpur but his daughter, by chance, fell into the hands of Alp Khan's soldiers in the neighbourhood of the Ellora caves. Firishta gives in detail the story of Dewal Rani's recovery by the royal troops as follows:

Alp Khan, who was entrusted the job of securing Princess Dewal Rani from the hands of her father Karan Deva, was the maternal uncle and father-in-law of Khizer Khan, the eldest son of Alauddin Khilji. Karan Deva had fled before his army after suffering a defeat, and finding no trace of Dewal Rani, Alp Khan was encamped on the bank of a stream, in the vicinity of the famous Ellora caves, to give some rest to his tired soldiers. Nevertheless, a small party of about three or four hundred of his soldiers, without seeking his permission, slipped out of the camp to see the Ellora caves. By chance, they sighted a small Maratha contingent, which was promptly engaged and routed by them. It turned out to be an escort of the Princess Dewal Rani, who was being taken by them to Devagiri, where she was to be married off to Prince Singhana Deva, the son of Raja Ram Chandra Deva and heir apparent to his throne. The escort was being led by Bhillam, the younger brother of Singhana. In the fighting that took place, horse of the princess was wounded and she fell down on the ground. Thereupon, her female attendants disclosed the identity of the Princess to save her honour at the hands of the soldiers, and she was respectfully escorted to Alp Khan. The latter was so delighted by his prized catch, that 'he prosecuted his conquests no further, and hastened to Delhi with Dewal Rani'. The *Malika-i-Jahan* was very pleased to be reunited with her daughter, and Alp Khan was amply rewarded for his services. After a couple of years, Dewal Rani was married to the crown prince Khizer Khan. The rest of the romantic story of Dewal Rani and Khizer Khan, and the ultimate tragic end of both form the subject matter of the historic *masnavi* of Amir Khusrau, entitled, *Dewal Rani Khizer Khani* (ed. by Mohammad Ismail, Aligarh, 1918).

As for Malik Kafur, he pressed on with the siege of Devagiri with full force. Ram Chandra Deva was defeated and sued for peace. On the orders of Alauddin Khilji, he was treated leniently; and the Raja, along with his wives and children, was taken to Delhi to make personal submission to the Sultan. Alauddin treated him very generously; Ram Chandra Deva was restored his royal privileges, and stayed in the capital for six months as a state guest before his return to Devagiri to assume the reins of government as a feudatory of Delhi. Before his departure from the capital, the Rai had voluntarily given the hand of one of his daughters in marriage to the Sultan. Ram Chandra Deva returned to Devagiri by the end of the year 1308.

The Muslim rulers of India were notorious for getting hold of the Hindu ladies from their ruling families to be forcibly married and put into their *harems,* but this was an exceptional case, when out of gratitude for his generous suzerain, a vanquished Hindu chief had willingly given his daughter in marriage to the Sultan. The contemporary chroniclers record that the marriage was celebrated with great pomp and show in the royal palace, and Alauddin treated Ram Chandra Deva 'as his father-in-law in the right spirit'; he was granted a personal estate and one hundred thousand gold coins as a gift, besides the title of *Rai Rayan* or 'king of the kings' by the Sultan. Barani writes with satisfaction that 'the Rai was ever after obedient, and sent his tribute regularly as long as he lived'. Hereafter, Ram Chandra Deva collaborated whole-heartedly with the imperial forces from Delhi for the conquest of south India, and also placed all the recourses of his own state at their disposal.

A son, born of the wed-lock between Alauddin and the Rai's daughter, named Shihabuddin Umar, was nominated by the ailing Sultan to succeed him to the throne in 1316, when his eldest son, Khizer Khan, because of his purported rebellious intentions, was suffering confinement in the fort of Gwalior at the hands of the all-powerful Malik Naib 'apparently with the consent of the Sultan'.

According to some critics, the Yadava chief was 'a coward, who compromised his independence, honour and self-respect in order to preserve his throne and the other material gains...Having disgraced himself, he shamelessly helped the aggressors in trampling the whole of southern India under their heels. Ram Chandra Deva let down his own people, disgraced his religion and did incalculable harm to his own society and culture, of which he was expected to champion the cause. His cowardly conduct had a highly demoralising effect on the Hindus of south India, in general, and their rulers, in particular'. Whatever the criticism of the Hindu chief of Gujarat, it was a great triumph of Alauddin's diplomatic move. No wonder, his policy towards the Yadava chief was based on political expediency. As a shrewd politician and military strategist, Alauddin won over the loyalty of Ram Chandra Deva and exploited him as a tool in the fulfillment of his imperial designs.

The Conquest of Warrangal (1309-10): The abject surrender of the Yadava ruler of Devagiri paved the way for the fall of other Hindu chiefs of the south one by one. According to K.S. Aiyenger, 'Alauddin's object in these various invasions of the Deccan and the farther south appears to have gone no further than making them the milch-cow for the gold that he was often much in need of for the efficient maintenance of his army to keep Hindustan free from internal disturbance and the invasions by the Mongols from outside'. (*South India and Her Muhammadan Invaders*, Madras, 1921). Accordingly, on 31 October 1309, the Sultan ordered his Malik Naib 'to lead his lucky horses towards the south and reduce the kingdom of Telingana, with its capital at Warrangal'. Malik Kafur commanded an army of hundred thousand soldiers—cavalry as well as infantry, with the assistance of a number of seasoned military generals; being the 'deputy sultan' he was provided with a 'red canopy' and other royal insignia to signal his 'unquestionable supremacy and powers' to exercise control over the other nobles.

Telingana was then ruled over by Rai Pratap Rudra Deva II of the Kakatiya dynasty. The deployment of a huge army and the special precautions taken by Aladdin Khilji for an attack on Warrangal indicate the formidable military prowess of the Telingana chief, who had probably licked the royal forces in their previous attack in 1305. Rai Pratap Rudra Deva II was a kinsman of the ruler of Devagiri; his maternal grandmother Rudrambha Devi was a Yadava princess from Gujarat. Alauddin did not underestimate the strength of his foe, and gave the parting advice to Kafur not to push the matters too hard against him; Barani reproduces Sultan's instructions to his general as follows:

> 'If the Rai consented to surrender his treasure and jewels, elephants and horses, and also to send treasure and elephants in the following year, Malik Naib Kafur was to accept these terms and not to press the Rai too hard. He was to come to an arrangement and retire without pushing matters too far, lest Rai Ladar Deo (Pratap Rudra Deva) should get the better of him. If he could not do this, he was, for the sake of his own name and fame, to bring the Rai with him to Delhi'. (*Tarikh-i-Firoze Shahi,* p. 201).

Malik Naib led the royal forces through the old Chanderi route to Devagiri on his way to Warrangal. Ram Chandra Deva, now the most faithful ally of Alauddin Khilji in the Deccan, received Kafur and his lieutenants with great respects and rendered all sorts of help to the army of invasion, by procuring fodder for its horses and food supplies for its soldiers. While the army marched through his dominions, the Rai remained in constant attendance upon the Malik Naib and his staff and lavishly entertained them. On his instructions, the traders of Maharashtra setup markets all along the way so that the soldiers could purchase the necessities of life for themselves at rates fixed by the Sultan of Delhi. According to Barani, the Rai of Devagiri deputed scouts to guide the invaders en route to Warrangal and also contributed 'a force of Mahrattas (Marathas), both horse and foot, to Kafur's army of invasion.

On entering the borders of Telingana, Malik Kafur adopted the scorched-earth policy and ordered his army to ravage the towns and villages on the way. Firishta writes with dismay that 'this confounded the inhabitants, who had never injured their wanton enemies'. The first resistance was met by the invaders at the outpost of Sabar (Sirpur), where a small contingent of the Hindu soldiers attempted to check the advance of the invaders. The besieged soldiers fought valiantly, but, unable to withstand the terrible assault, burnt their women and children in the self-lit fire of Jauhar and themselves laid down their lives in the hand-to-hand fight with the invaders. Most of the *Rawats*, viz., 'the Hindu nobles' of Telingana, finding the futility of their isolated resistance against the aggressors in the countryside, preferred to retire to Warrangal to strengthen the hands of their master. By January 1310, the royal army made it to the outskirts of Warrangal. Malik Kafur sent a contingent of a thousand horsemen 'as a reconnoitering party' which took possession of the strategically located hill of Hanmuakonda 'from where all the buildings and gardens of Warrangal could be seen' clearly.

The massive fort of Warrangal was made of stone but it was encircled by a thick earthen wall which was perhaps stronger than the stone edifice'. The outer walls of the fort were further strengthened by a fairly wide and deep moat, full of water. It was one of the strongest forts in south India. Malik Kafur went round the fort twice to make a choice of fixing his tents, and then ordered the commencement of its siege. According to Amir Khusrau, the circumference of the fort, as enclosed by the royal tents was above nine kilometres ('twelve thousand five hundred and twenty-six yards').

Pratap Rudra Deva fought a defensive war from within his highly fortified fort, while some of his *Rawats*, who had been left outside, cut off the supply lines of the invaders, and disrupted 'the postal services of Delhi so much so that the Sultan did not receive any news for about six weeks from the front'. The guerilla fighters of the Rai launched night attacks from the countryside on the besiegers to their great embarrassment, as a protection against which Malik Kafur had to order the construction of a wooden defensive wall (*kath-ghar*) all around the royal camp for protection. After a brief but bloody struggle, accompanied by daily skirmishes between the rivals, the outer moat was filled up with earth, and the outer mud wall was breached by the digging of a tunnel through it. The besiegers had to cross yet another ditch, lying in between the two fort walls of fortifications; it was only thereafter that the besieged garrison was squeezed within the stone walls of the inner fort. At this stage, the Rai made overtures for peace to which Malik Kafur responded readily.

According to the terms of the settlement, the Rai had to part with 100 elephants, 7,000 horses and the entire wealth, then accumulated in the treasury of the Rai at Warrangal; it included 'unspecified quantity of gold, silver, jewels and other precious articles of incalculable value', which included the world-famous diamond, called *Koh-i-Noor*—'the mountain of light'. The Rai also promised in writing to send the annual tribute to Delhi regularly; which, in the estimate of Amir Khusrau, was Rs.10,000,000,000 or 'ten thousand million rupees per annum'. Here it is worthy of mention that the inner fortress of Warrangal had never capitulated, nor the Rai came out in person to acknowledge the suzerainty of Delhi. But he did send his 'man-size statue, made of gold, with a golden chain round his neck, in acknowledgement of his submission to the Sultan'. After the settlement, robes of honour, embroidered with jewels, were sent to Pratap Rudra Deva inside the fort.

With the laurels of victory on his brow, the Malik Naib ordered the return march of his forces by the middle of March 1310 via Devagiri, Dhar, Ujjain and Chanderi. Apart from what he had received from the vanquished Hindu chief by way of war indemnity, so enormous was the booty, captured by him from the Deccan, that he had carry it on 'a thousand camels groaning under the weight of treasure'. The Rai of Telingana had given 7,000 horses and 100 war-elephants to the victor, but the later brought 300 elephants to Delhi and innumerable number of horses; obviously, these 'animals of war' had been captured by the invader as booty in the course of the campaign. Malik Kafur had forwarded to Delhi, in advance, the detailed account of his victories, and the Sultan was delighted so much to know its contents that he ordered 'the public rejoicings' to be held, 'and the happy tidings of the success were read from the pulpits of the mosques'. On the approach of Malik Naib to the capital, on June 11, 1310, the Sultan himself came out to the *Chabutra Nasiri*, near the Badaun Gate, to receive him, and 'there the conqueror laid all the spoils at his sovereign's feet'.

The Conquest of Dwarsamudra and M'abar: The success of Warrangal expedition, which yielded fabulous wealth much beyond the imagination of the beholders, whetted the appetite of the Sultan and aroused the enthusiasm of his Malik Naib to give a repeat performance in the far south of India. It 'strengthened Alauddin's belief in his destiny', and he became impatient to extend the limits of his empire to the farthest extremity of the Indian peninsula. Accordingly, within four months of his Warrangal expedition, Malik Naib girded up his loins for the third expedition to the south. Above all, the Muslim soldiers, who had made the fortunes of their lifetime in their brief adventure into Telingana, vied with one another to get themselves enrolled in 'the Army of Islam' for *Jihad* against the infidels; 'everyone from the Sultan to the rank and file was tempted by the glamour of loot and plunder'.

The expedition was originally directed against the kingdom of Dwarsamudra, which was then ruled over by King Vir Ballala III (1292-1342) of the Hoysala dynasty. This powerful ruler held sway over the most fertile territories of the far south, including the Eastern and Western Ghats, a portion of Konkan and the whole of Mysore region. But, this time, Alauddin had set only the guide lines of the campaign, and given ample discretion to his general to execute the plan as he thought fit. Early in November, a vast army of invasion had assembled in the vicinity of Delhi, along the bank of the river Yamuna, where a review of the forces was held by the Sultan himself, accompanied by Malik Naib and his deputy commander, Khwaja Haji, for full two weeks before their departure for the south; as before, the Royal Standards and the Red Canopy marked out the official camp of the Malik Naib. The royal army was divided into regiments of ten thousands each, and each regiment was further split up into units of one thousand troopers, called the *tuman*, on the Mongol pattern, to ensure effectiveness of the command, and to facilitate its quick movements and deployment of the troops in action.

The army of invasion passed through the dominions of Devagiri in the month of February, 1311, and, as usual, was well-provided by Ram Chandra Deva. The latter also deputed his commander-in-chief, Parasuram Deva (Paras Deo Delvi of the Muslim chroniclers) to assist the Muslim army on its southward march; he collaborated with the army of Delhi in the conquest of Dwarsamudra and some other towns of the Hoysala kingdom. Vir Ballala III, like the other Hindu rulers of his day, had been wasting his valuable time and resources in the internecine conflicts with his neighbouring chiefs. At the time of Malik Kafur's invasion, he had gone with his army to the further south to meddle in the internal disputes of the Pandya kingdom. He lost his nerves to hear of the Muslim invasion on his dominions, and hastened back to Dwarsamudra for its defence. He fought short skirmishes with the invaders but hesitated in challenging them in a pitched battle. After a brief show of strength, Vir Ballala III offered his submission to the Malik Naib in person. The victorious military general of Alauddin was not satisfied with mere surrender of the Rai; instead, 'he gave vent to his bigotry' and demanded that the Rai must either embrace Islam or accept the position of a *Zimmi*. The Rai accepted the latter alternative, and acknowledged the suzerainty of Delhi with solemn commitment to send annual tribute to the imperial capital regularly. He had to pay a huge war indemnity, which included 36 elephants and numerous horses besides the entire treasure of Dwarsamudra, 'which was taken out from the cells for a whole night'. The triumphant Muslim army spread itself into the town of Dwarsamudra and its suburbs and sacked it thoroughly; the magnificent temples of the Hoysala kingdom were put to plunder and destroyed by the victorious Muslim forces.

Subjugation of the Pandya Kingdom: While at Dwarsamudra, Malik Naib came to know that the Pandya kingdom of the far south was a dependency of Dwarsamudra; therefore, after the subjugation of the former, the Pandya kingdom automatically came under the control of Delhi, and the power-drunk Malik Naib knew how to assert his imperial authority there. It was then ruled over by Kulashekhra Pandya (1268-1311), and Madura was his head quarters. To its bad luck, the Pandya kingdom was rocked by a fratricidal dispute between two half-brothers, Sunder Pandya and Vir Pandya, sons of the ruling chief. The king, because of his old age and precarious health, intended to nominate his successor to the throne before his death. He was more favourably inclined towards his elder but natural son Vir Pandya; therefore, he formally declared him the heir apparent. It excited the jealousy of his younger but legitimate son, Sunder Pandya, who, in a fit of anger, murdered his father and claimed the throne for himself. Vir Pandya, who enjoyed the support of majority of ministers and courtiers of the deceased king, took up arms against Sunder Pandya, and turned him out of Madura to claim the throne for himself.

Hard-pressed, Sunder Pandya appealed to Malik Kafur for help when the latter was stationed at Dwarsamudra. It provided a golden opportunity to the imperial commander to march upon the Pandya kingdom with the bulk of the Muslim army, apparently, in support of Sunder Pandya. As the Malik Naib was totally unacquainted with the country of the Pandya kingdom, 'he asked Vir Ballala III to lead him on the way towards M'abar'; the vanquished chief of Dwarsamudra 'had but to agree to what the victorious general said, and prepared to lead Malik Kafur towards the destruction of a sister state'. (K.S. Lal, The Khaljis, *loc. cit*; p. 206).

Amir Khusrau gives a graphic account of the progress of Malik Kafur's 'army of Islam' in those distant and inaccessible regions of the far south in his invaluable treatise, entitled, *Khazainul Futuh* or *Tarikh-i-Ilahi* (Eng. Trs. by M. Habib under the title, *The Campaigns of Alauddin Khalji*; Madras, 1931; extracts E&D III). It started from Dwarsamudra for the M'abar coast on March 10, 1311. 'The land through which the royal army marched was very unpropitious and hilly, so much so that the pointed stones tore the horses' hoofs; and every night the soldiers slept on ground, more uneven than a camel's back'. After five days of laborious marches, they reached the frontier of M'abar. They had to cross two passes to arrive at the first major town of Mardi. It was totally undefended, and all of its inhabitants were massacred without any provocation. Then starting from the river Kanobari, they advanced to Birdhul, which is generally identified by the historians with the old town of Virdachellam in south Arcot. It was also sacked and its magnificent temples were destroyed; the historic town, which now abounds in the ruins of old temples and relics of fortifications, has become a place of pilgrimage for the people of this region.

Vir Pandya fled from Madura on the approach of the army of Delhi, leaving the capital to the mercy of the intruders. On the pretext of capturing the fugitive prince, the Muslim forces sacked the Pandya capital, and desecrated and destroyed all of its temples, before it fanned out into the Pandya dominions and resorted to similar acts of vandalism wherever they went. The rains set in, but these did not dampen the spirit of the invaders, who merrily carried on their plundering sport in the absence of any armed resistance, apparently in the pursuit of the 'flying king' (Vir Pandya). Intelligence was brought that the Rai had fled to the city of Kandur (identified with modern Kannanur); and the imperial army dashed towards the town. To quote Amir Khusrau,

> 'The Malik Naib laid his hands on 120 elephants, on which he found some treasure also. In vain did he massacre the people of Kandur for the Rai had long before fled from that place. It was thought that he had fled towards Jat Kuta. Malik Naib marched in that direction but thorny forests forbade any persistent pursuit, and he again returned to Kandur where he searched for more elephants and treasure. Meanwhile, they had learnt much about the temples and treasures of the places lying in the vicinity of Kandur. The intelligence was received that Vir Pandya had kept his elephants at the famous golden temple of Barmatpuri (Barmastpuri—mod. Chidambaram); the temple was immediately raided and 250 elephants of the Pandya prince captured. The temple was assaulted and its idol *Ling-i-Mahadeo* broken...the foundations of the golden temple were dug up...the swords flashed where jewels had once been sparkling... and the heads of the Brahmans and idol-worshippers came dancing from their necks to their feet at the flashes of the sword'. (*Khazainul Futuh,* Habib's trs; pp. 103-05).

As all the Hindu temples in the region of Kannanur were plundered and desecrated by the Muslim soldiers under the command of Malik Kafur, the famous temple of Srirangam was no exception. The archaeological evidence shows that this historic temple was then under the charge of Arya Bhattas or 'the northern Brahmans'. They were overpowered and the entire wealth of the temple, including the golden idol of Lord Ranganatha, was taken away by the Muslim soldiers. In this connection, K.S. Lal observes that

> 'The destruction wrought by Malik Kafur can well be imagined from the fact that, in the search of Vir Pandya, the Muslim army went from place to place, and to some places many times over, and in their disappointment and rage at not finding the fugitive wherever they went, they destroyed edifices and killed people mercilessly... The temples were reservoirs of effluence and wealth. Hindu Rajas and other rich people presented them with gold and jewels, and endowed villages for the maintenance of their establishments. Thus wealth multiplied in a temple without being spent on a large scale. The result was that whenever the Muslims attacked a place, they sacked its temples, in particular, for despoiling them of their wealth. But in the

rage of warfare, fanaticism was naturally fanned and, besides looting the wealth of the temple, the invaders destroyed the very edifices and often threw their stones and idols at such places as could be trampled under the feet of the Musalmans'. (*Ibid.*,pp.211-12).

As a matter of fact, in his purported search for the run-away Vir Pandya, the real object of Malik Kafur was to allow a free hand to his soldiers to reap the maximum fruits of their plundering spree in the virgin land of the infidels, which in no way helped the other aggrieved party, led by the prince Sunder Pandya. 'Having realized his folly, though very late', Sunder Pandya also did not dare to approach the imperial commander, and, instead, sought his safety in his flight into the jungles. Thus both of the Pandya princes eluded the Malik Naib, and nobody came forward to offer his submission or allegiance to the imperial commander nor acknowledged the suzerainty of Delhi. However, Malik Kafur continued his march to target more and more villages and towns in the countryside, and had plundered and destroyed the towns and temples of Kum (Kham, probably Kadambavanam) and Jagnar (Jagnatha or Jagannatha) before he reached as far as Rameshwaram, where he erected a mosque in honour of the victory of Islam. According to Amir Khusrau, 'having searched the Rai for weeks and months', Malik Kafur was so much disappointed that, in his impotent rage, he set fire to many towns and temples. Nevertheless, the triumphant military general of Delhi 'now finding that he had become master of so much wealth, and had captured so many elephants, he decided to march back'.

Before marching homewards, Malik Kafur ordered all the spoils to be arranged and classified. His gains, according to Amir Khusrau, consisted of 512 elephants, 5,000 horses of the various foreign breeds like Arabi, Yamani and Syrian, 96,000 *maunds* of gold, and 500 *maunds* of jewellery of every description. Instead, Barani's narrative makes mention of 612 elephants and 20,000 horses of all breeds, obviously. No contemporary writer makes mention of silver as a part of Malik Kafur's spoils during this campaign. When so much of gold and pearls and jewels were on hand, the carriage of silver as booty was not considered worthwhile; it had ceased to be a valuable for the plunderers. With such fabulous rewards of his enterprise, 'he broke his camp on April 25, 1311, to the extreme joy of everybody' and reached Delhi on October 18 after an arduous journey of six months. The jubilant Sultan accorded a befitting reception to his victorious general and his forces by holding a grand *darbar* in the palace of *Hazar Satun* (of thousand pillars) in the fort of Siri, where the Malik Naib presented to him 'all he had brought from the Deccan'. According to Barani, Malik Kafur had brought so much wealth from Dwarsamudra and Madura that 'since the capture of Delhi by the Muhammadans, at no time had so much treasure been seized'; it defied all descriptions and estimates in terms of its monetary value. At such a happy occasion, Alauddin did not fail to exhibit his generosity either; he amply rewarded his military generals, ministers and *amirs* from one to four maunds of gold each.

The vanquished Hoysala chief of Dwarsamudra, Vir Ballala III, had accompanied Malik Kafur to Delhi to the great delight of the Sultan. Like Ram Chandra Deva, he was also accorded a very generous treatment by Alauddin, who thanked him for his fidelity and the whole-hearted assistance rendered by him to the royal forces in the south; the Hindu chief was awarded the robes of honour, a crown and a *chhatr* (canopy), besides a purse of ten *lacs* of gold tankas. The Hoysala chief stayed in Delhi for a couple of months as the state guest before his return to the south; all of his territories were restored to him. Vir Vallala reached Dwarsamudra on May 6, 1313, when he abolished most of the taxes by way of relief to his subjects to regain their confidence. After Ram Chandra Deva, the Yadava ruler of Gujarat, Vir Ballala III became the second most reliable and useful vassal of Delhi in south India.

Third Expedition to Devagiri (1313): According to the contemporary chroniclers, Ram Chandra Deva paid a second visit to Delhi early in 1312 to participate in the marriage ceremonies of the crown prince Khizer Khan and Dewal Rani, the daughter of Karan Deva, the ex-Rai of Anhilwara (Gujarat). He died after his return to Devagiri towards the end of 1312 or early in 1313 when he was succeeded by his eldest son Singhana Deva, also referred to as Shankar Deva by some of the contemporary writers. He was dead opposed to the penetration of the Muslims in the south, and had never approved of his father's abject surrender and later collaboration with the Sultan ofDelhi as his vassal. Moreover, Singhana had become an avowed enemy of Alauddin Khilji ever since Dewal Rani, his betrothed, fell into the hands of the army of Delhi, and was snatched away from him to be married to Khizer Khan. It is said that even his father, Ram Chandra Deva also felt embarrassed by the anti-Muslim attitude of his son, and had once requested the Sultan to restrain him 'from assuming open hostility against Delhi'.

Quite naturally, when Singhana became the king, he cut off all contacts with Delhi and tended to behave as an independent ruler. It necessitated the dispatch of Malk Kafur to Devagiri for the suppression of his revolt. Singhana was killed in a pitched battle; Devagiri was taken possession of by the Muslim forces and the Maratha kingdom was declared annexed to the Sultanate of Delhi. Malik Kafur stayed there for some time and administered the state with the object of strengthening the Muslim hold over it. The Malik Naib established his headquarters at Devagiri, took possession of some adjoining territories of Telingana and Dwarsamudra also with the tacit approval of the Sultan, and acted as the viceroy of the Deccan with the object of establishing effective control over the subordinate Indian chiefs. Nevertheless, Malik Kafur had become the personal counsel and most trustworthy lieutenant of Alauddin Khilji, who missed his company very badly. Moreover, the Sultan did not want outright annexation of the southern territories; therefore, when he suffered from ill-health, he called back Malik Kafur to Delhi; and the kingdom of Devagiri was given back to a prince of the Yadava dynasty, named Harpala Deva - the son-in-law of Ram Chandra Deva, as a vassal of Delhi.

The Rise to Power of Malik Kafur

The rise of Malik Kafur to power in the Sultanate of Delhi forms one of the most enigmatic chapters in the history of medieval India. It were the Turkish slave officers of Muhammad Ghori, followed by those of Iltutmish and Balban in succession, who had made the greatest contribution towards the establishment and consolidation of the Muslim rule in northern India or *Hindustan* of the medieval denomination. The credit for stepping into the south (*Dakshin* in Hindi and Sanskrit, and *Dakhan*, its corrupt form in Persian) or Deccan of the Muslim chroniclers goes to Alauddin Khilji—himself a half-Turk or *Tazik*, who was actually mistaken as a non-Turk by the predominant Turkish nobility of the times. Going by the logic of historical development, none could ever contemplate that a Hindu convert to Islam, a slave and an eunuch (neither a man nor a woman) would be destined to carry the banner of Islam into the Deccan, rather to the farthest end of the south Indian peninsula, as conqueror, Muslim fundamentalist and iconoclast, all rolled in one.

The readers are aware that Malik Kafur fell into the hands of Nusrat Khan, the military general of Alauddin Khilji, during his conquest of Gujarat. According to the Muslim chroniclers, he was acquired by him from a Muslim merchant (Khwaja) at Kambaya (Cambay). He was definitely a Hindu convert to Islam, and was an eunuch; whether he was so by birth or had been castrated and rendered impotent after having been captured and enslaved by the Muslims is not known. He was called a *Hazardinari,* but it is not certain whether Nusrat Khan had purchased him from the Muslim merchant for one thousand *dinars,* or the merchant had earlier purchased him for a similar amount from somewhere else. K.S. Lal is of the opinion that Kafur was 'forcibly snatched away from his master who had bought him for a thousand dinars'. (*History of the Khaljis,* p. 86*)*. The word Kafur means 'white', rather 'milky white', and this name he, probably, received from his previous master because of his fair complexion and extremely handsome physique. When he was presented to Alauddin Khilji by Nusrat Khan, the Sultan felt a special attraction for him; that is why he was put on his personal staff in the royal palace; Barani has to say the following about Malik Kafur in his *Tarikh-i-Firoze Shahi* when he makes mention of his name for the first time:

> 'Nusrat Khan proceeded to Kambaya (Cambay), and levied large quantities of jewels and precious articles from the merchants of that place, who were very wealthy. He also took from his master (a slave afterwards known as) Kafur Hazardinari, who was made Malik Naib, and whose beauty captivated Alauddin'.

Kafur seems to have been imparted good education and training in horse riding, swordsmanship and other arts of warfare by his previous master; being a man of robust health and impressive personality, he lost no time in winning the personal attention and confidence of the Sultan. His promotion from the rank of a domestic servant to that of an *amir* was based purely on personal merit. Alauddin was deeply impressed by his dedicated and selfless service as his personal attendant; and as a military officer, Malik Kafur won appreciation of his master by his superb intelligence, organising skill and refined manners, coupled with his capability to command the soldiers with enthusiasm and perfection in the martial arts. No wonder, within six years of his association with his royal patron, Malik Kafur had been found fit to acquire the exalted office of the *Akhurbeg-i-Maisrah* or 'the Master of the Horse'. In 1305, we find Malik Kafur being assigned the important duty to annihilate the Mongol marauders who had spread themselves in the plains of the Punjab and the Ganga-Yamuna valleys for destruction and devastation. He established ascendancy over all the other seasoned military generals of Alauddin Khilji and became the

Malik Naib or 'the Deputy Sultan' of Delhi. As detailed above, he made a signal contribution to the Sultanate of Delhi by the conquest of south India, which transformed it into a mighty Muslim empire of the country.

There are reasons to presume that Malik Kafur, because of his tremendous power and prestige, had excited the jealousy of some other nobles. *Malika-i-Jahan* and Alp Khan were not very happy with the growing influence of the Malik Naib in the court and family affairs of the sultan. Gradually they formed a clique in the royal court to oppose the interests of Malik Kafur, and they started poisoning the ears of the sultan against him on one pretext or the other. Their number gradually multiplied by the association of the old Muslim nobility of the regime who regarded Malik Kafur as an outsider. They rightly considered themselves to be the real custodians of the Muslim kingdom in India and did not want to be dictated by the deputy sultan. After his marriage with Dewal Rani, the crown prince Khizer Khan also took up their cause against Malik Kafur, and he became 'their pampered royal patron'. Being a Hindu convert to Islam and an eunuch, Malik Kafur had no filial attachments to the royal family and no social contacts with or permanent adherents among the old Muslim nobility or the Khilji bureaucracy. Therefore, he was no match for his political rivals in the struggle for power-politics at the court in the long run. That is why, when he was deputed by the Sultan to lead the third expedition to Devagiri for suppressing the revolt of Singhana Deva, he secured the consent of Alauddin Khilji to abolish the ruling house of the Yadava dynasty and annex the kingdom to Delhi so that he might stay back at Devagiri as its governor. His intention seemed to be to establish the nucleus of his power far away from Delhi, and setup as an independent ruler of the Deccan after the death of Alauddin Khilji, if possible. Nevertheless, Malik Kafur was the most trustworthy lieutenant of Alauddin Khilji, who could ill-afford to miss his company; therefore, when the Sultan fell ill, he called the Malik Naib back to carry on the administration on his behalf. This provided an opportunity to Malik Naib to play a crucial role in the family affairs of Alauddin Khilji. He set up as the kingmaker and played havoc with the members of the royal family, bringing about its ignominious fall.

The Last Days of Alauddin Khilji

The year 1312 marked the zenith of Alauddin's power and glory. Up to that year, the Sultan enjoyed a good physical as well as mental health and maintained firm control over the state machinery. As an autocratic ruler, he was his own master and all the strings of the state power were concentrated in his own hands. In his early years, when he maintained the balance of mind and had the power of discretion, he could usefully avail of the services of his capable counsellors to suit his own ambitious plans and policies of the state, but in his advanced age, with a deteriorating health, things took an ugly turn. In the words of K.S. Lal, 'like Aurangzeb in his old age, Alauddin also would listen to no advice, and would tolerate no opposition'. His passion for the centralization of power in his own hands remained unabated but he lacked the discretion and will-power to exercise it judiciously.

The last three years of his reign were, therefore, full of bitterness and anguish. The cunning fox of yesteryears, Alauddin Khilji could not get rid of his own unscrupulous and suspicious nature with the advancement of his age, and he became extremely peevish and suspicious of all around him. He did not trust his old, experienced and loyal officers; so much so he distrusted even his own chief queen (*Malika-i-Jahan*) and his own children. He, therefore, failed to utilize their valuable services for the long-range benefit of the state. A number of competent administrators, military officers and bureaucrats were at his beck and call, but the Sultan failed to call them to his aid when it was most needed.

During the absence of Malik Kafur from the capital, the party of Mahru—the favourite wife of Alauddin since his early life, now styled the *Malik-i-Jahan*, and her brother Alp Khan, the governor of Gujarat, acquired ascendancy in the royal court. In 1312, she arranged the marriage of her eldest son, called Shamsul Haqq, and surnamed Khizer Khan, with the daughter of Alp Khan, his maternal uncle. This marriage enhanced the prestige of Alp Khan in the court and ensured the nomination of Khizer Khan as the heir apparent to the throne. In the year following, the *Malika-i-Jahan* persuaded Alp Khan to give his second daughter in marriage to her second son Shadi Khan also with the object of strengthening the bonds of her parental family with the ruling house; at this occasion, on the insistence of Khizer Khan, he was also allowed to take Dewal Rani, the daughter of Kamla Devi, as another wife. It is said that 'the Sultan was keeping an indifferent health, but the *Malika-i-Jahan* was bent upon celebrating the nuptials'. She had sent out invitations to governors and nobles in far off provinces to participate in the royal weddings. Probably, it was on the second occasion that Malik Kafur, with head quarters at Devagiri, came to Delhi to attend the marriages of both the princes, Khizer Khan as well as Shadi Khan. It was then that he 'found the royal consort (*Malika-i-Jahan*), her brother Alp Khan and prince Khizer Khan in great ascendancy. An ambitious general like Kafur, who of late had been the only guiding spirit of the king, could now know well that he was lost if he did not stir betimes'. (K.S. Lal, *op.cit.*, p.299).

Meanwhile, the health of the Sultan had started deteriorating rapidly. According to Firishta, 'the Sultan had developed a very dangerous disease on account of excessive sexual indulgence'. Barani writes that he was suffering from dropsy and consequent fever but he was neglected by Khizer Khan and his mother, the beloved wife of Alauddin's youthful days. In fact, they hesitated in attending upon the Sultan in person because the latter did not trust them. To the misfortune of Alauddin Khilji, he had paid no adequate attention towards the education and training of his so many children from his different wives and concubines in the statecraft. 'Being left free at early days to do as they liked, they took to drinking and debauchery'. Therefore, none of them cared to attend upon the Sultan in his sick bed, nor anyone was capable enough to assist him in the state affairs what to say of undertaking responsibilities of administration in case of emergency. 'In utter helplessness, the Sultan recalled his favourite lieutenant from the Deccan and acquainted him with his troubles'. By the time Malik Kafur finally returned to the capital in 1315, Alauddin had been physically incapacitated and rendered totally unfit to attend to the affairs of the state.

Alauddin felt great relief on the arrival of Malik Kafur, who, in his capacity as the Deputy Sultan (Malik Naib) and Prime Minister (Wazir) at once undertook the reins of government in his own hands and set up as the *de facto* ruler. Unfortunately, the Sultan's 'infatuation for the eunuch Kafur had made the latter the most powerful man' of the Sultanate, and he thoroughly exploited the situation to serve his own selfish ends. It gave him an opportunity to play the role of a kingmaker, and he set in motion the sinister plans for the destruction of the ruling family of his master with the object of usurping the throne.

> As a first step towards this direction, 'the astute Malik Naib availed himself of the opportunity for overthrowing the Alp Khan Junta by poisoning the king's mind against Khizer Khan, his mother and his father-in-law. According to Amir Khusrau, 'One day, when Kafur was in a private audience with Alauddin, he

bitterly complained against his alleged enemies, and said that they wanted to put an end to his life simply because he was favoured by the king. They only waited for the Sultan's death when they would assassinate him. As Alauddin gave Kafur a patient hearing, the latter continued his plaintive rhetoric and accused Alp Khan of being the source of all the trouble. He said that Alp Khan had influence with the Queen and the Royal Princes, and that was the reason why he was reluctant to go back to his *Iqta* in Gujarat. He was simply waiting to usurp all power as soon as the Sultan's eyes were closed for ever. If Alp Khan could be killed, concluded Kafur, there would be no fear for him from the Princes'. (*Khazainul Futuh*, pp. 329-30).

Inspite of the fact that the Sultan was very favourably disposed towards his Malik Naib, 'he refused to listen to the false accusations levelled against his faithful governor', and told Kafur that 'he did not suspect anything from him'. Nevertheless, the crafty eunuch had made up his mind to make a short work of his arch rival, and one day, when Alp Khan was entering the royal apartments, he, in the company of his agent, Malik Kamaluddin Gurg, made a sudden assault on him and murdered him in cold blood. The news of his murder was withheld from Alauddin for quite some time, and, when ultimately, he came to know of it, he fretted and fumed but could do pretty little against his all-powerful Malik Naib, who had set up as the de facto ruler, and held the hapless Sultan in his virtual captivity.

Alp Khan's death cleared the way for the unchallenged ascendancy of Malik Kafur. He now openly charged prince Khizer Khan and his mother of hatching a conspiracy to kill Alauddin Khilji with the object of capturing the throne; and much against the will of the Sultan, the latter was compelled to sign the orders for the imprisonment of both of his sons, Khizer Khan and Shadi Khan, as state prisoners in the fort of Gwalior; of course, the Sultan had signed these orders most unwillingly and under coercion from his Malik Naib after obtaining repeated assurances from him that no harm would be done to the princes. A past master in the politics of assassinations, Alauddin Khilji was, in fact, being paid back in the same coin by nature at the hands of his most favourite and the most trustworthy servant. Dewal Rani, the favourite wife of Khizer Khan, was allowed to stay with him in the prison at Gwalior at her own request. The most celebrated queen of Alauddin and the mother of Khizer Khan, i.e., the *Malika-i-Jahan* also 'could not escape the rapacity of the cruel eunuch, and was kept as a state prisoner in the Red Fort of Delhi. After the death of Alp Khan, Malik Kafur had sent Malik Kamaluddin Gurg to Jalor to make a short work of its governor, Malik Nizamuddin, the brother of Alp Khan; he was also put to death treacherously.

By this time, Alauddin was seriously ill and lay helplessly in his sick bed, and the Malik Naib transacted all business of the state in the king's name. The last phase of Alauddin's reign was characterized by the slackening of the centre's hold over its provincial governors and the military generals, followed by a succession of open revolts in many parts of the empire. The un-called for assassinations of Alp Khan and his younger brother, Malik Nizamuddin, himself a seasoned military general, who had been bestowed the exalted title of Ulugh Khan by the Sultan, unnerved all the nobles and *amirs*, and spread panic and discontent among the people. It created a very dangerous situation in Gujarat, where the subordinate military officers and bureaucrats of Alp Khan raised their standard of revolt. Kamaluddin Gurg was sent there with a large force to crush the revolt but the rebels gave a crushing defeat to the imperial army and its commander, Kamaluddin, was killed in the battle. Gujarat was in turmoil at the time of Alauddin's death.

Taking a cue from disaffected Muslim nobles, the Rajputs of Chittor took up arms against the Muslim forces of occupation and Maldeo, the puppet of Delhi, was defeated and turned out of Chittor by them under the leadership of Rana Hammir Deva of the Sisodia dynasty before the death of Alauddin Khilji. Harpala Deva, the son-in-law of Ram Chandra Deva also declared his independence; and he liberated many forts of his kingdom by turning out the Muslim garrisons from there. On his initiative, the other Hindu chiefs of the south also defied the imperial authority, and stopped the payment of tribute to Delhi. According to the contemporary chroniclers, 'the intelligence of these insurrections used to set the dying king's body aflame with rage'; it turned him almost mad and 'he bit his own flesh with fury'. All of his life-work seemed to have been undone. According to Firishta, his grief and anger aggravated his illness 'which seemed to resist the power of medicine'.

About the time of his death, Alauddin Khilji had 'physically collapsed and lay unconscious, with his red tongue stuck up between his swollen cheeks'. It was in this state of affairs that the Sultan 'sought refuge in a silent death' on January 6, 1316; Barani presumes that he died from the fatal effects of slow poisoning administered by his most ungrateful slave eunuch, who had received the exalted status of Malik

Naib or 'the Deputy Sultan' of the Sultanate from the hands of the Sultan.

SECTION 3: ADMINISTRATION OF ALAUDDIN KHILJI

The Turkish sultans of Delhi had introduced a foreign system of government and administration in the country, and it was under the exclusive managerial control of a foreign bureaucracy. Whatever the Islamic theory of kingship or the Islamic polity, the sultanate of Delhi was essentially a police state, established on the barbaric principle of 'might is right'. Alauddin had occupied the throne by force and he could hold his own by his sword. He was an autocratic ruler and his despotism knew no bounds. In consequence, the working of government under him was deeply influenced by the personal character of the sultan. His ministers, counsellors and heads of various departments were all his creatures.

Political and Administrative Reforms of Alauddin

Alauddin was a good administrator but not an innovator like Sher Shah Suri or Akbar. So far as the central administration of his kingdom was concerned, he had copied the setup of Iltutmish and Balban without any basic change, and the efficient functioning of his state machinery depended almost exclusively on the personal factor of the sultan. Alauddin was a practical ruler and statesman rather than an administrator or technocrat; even otherwise he was an illiterate person and we cannot read much behind the successful working of his government and administration except that he possessed 'the rule of thumb knowledge of things'. His administrative reforms in the various civil as well as military fields can be understood only in this context.

Alauddin did not belong to the traditional foreign Turkish nobility. The readers are aware that the Khaljis or Khiljis belonged to the mixed Turkish-Afghan breed, and, during their own time, they were misunderstood as the non-Turks. As such, Alauddin had realized quite early the shortcomings and weaknesses of the Turkish aristocracy. As a diplomat and practical statesman, he knew the inherent dangers to which the preceding sultans of Delhi had exposed themselves by depending exclusively on the foreign Turkish nobility and bureaucracy in the matter of organisation of government and administration. He, therefore, did away with the Turkish nobility at the top level, and attempted to reduce its strength at the lower bureaucratic level as far as possible. The Khilji nobility took the lion's share of the higher state services, but they were as good as non-privileged Turks or commoners. Next to them he gave preference to the Turkish freemen, Afghans and other foreign Muslim immigrants of the non-privileged class or commoners and the Indian converts to Islam or the Indian Muslims. This brought about a radical bureaucratic change in the administrative set of the sultanate, which is usually characterized by the modern historians as the secularization of the state services. He threw open the government services to the commoners, including the Hindu converts to Islam and even the Zimmis (viz., the Hindu subjects) on merit, of course.

Alauddin had to face many revolts during the earlier years of his reign; these were engineered generally by the disaffected Muslim nobles and refractory Hindu chieftains; but to their categories was added yet another class of his ambitious kinsmen and blood relations. It was because there was no fixed law of succession among the Muslims, and Alauddin himself had been a usurper, who had no legal, moral or hereditary claim to the throne. It left the field open for any powerful and ambitious Muslim noble or any of his own near and dear ones to make a short work of him and declare himself the Sultan of Delhi. The accidental revolt of his ambitious nephew Akat Khan belongs to this category. As recorded by Ziauddin Barani,

> 'These revolts roused the Sultan from his dreams of security and pride. Therefore, after the reduction of Ranthambhor, he held consultations with his confidential advisers …arguing with them and inquiring into the causes of the insurrections, declaring that, if the real reasons could be ascertained, he would remove them, so that no revolt should afterwards occur. After considering for some nights and days, these great men agreed that the causes were four:

1. The Sultan's disregard of the affairs (both) of good and bad people;
2. Wine parties are formed for wine-drinking, and those who attend them talk openly of what passes in these meetings. They strike up friendships and excite disturbances;
3. The intimacy, affection, alliances, and intercourse of *maliks* and *amirs* with each other; so that if anything happens to one of them, a hundred others get mixed up in it; and
4. Money, which engenders evil and strife, and brings forth pride

and disloyalty. If men had no money, they would attend to their own business, and would never think of riots and revolts. And if rioters and rebels had no money, they could never count upon the assistance of low and turbulent people'. (*Tarikh-i-Firoze Shahi*, E&D III, p.178).

Accordingly, after the conquest of Ranthambhor in 1301, Alauddin Khilji launched a vigorous campaign to eliminate the afore-mentioned four causes. In the first place, he began to take keen interest in the day-to-day administration of his kingdom, and gradually consolidated his hold over the entire state machinery. He concentrated all powers of the state into his own hands and setup as an autocratic ruler. From the lowest level, pertaining to the appointment of a domestic servant or petty official to that of the most exalted office of the state, he would like to know all about it and give his clearance. Firishta writes that, as the Sultan was an illiterate person, the *ulama,* the sophisticated courtiers and nobility and the educated bureaucrats all assumed silence in his presence, and adopted 'a maxim not to talk upon subjects, beyond the king's knowledge'; Alauddin became conscious of his shortcomings and the consequent 'disadvantages, under which he laboured'. He, therefore, 'applied himself privately to study, and notwithstanding the difficulty of acquiring the knowledge of Persian, after he once bent his mind to it, he soon read all addresses, and made himself acquainted with the best authors in the language'. (Briggs, I., p. 197).

According to Firishta, it was 'after he had made such progress as to be able to take part in learned discourses', that Alauddin held parleys with his counsellors, promulgated his *firmans* on administrative reforms and inflicted severe punishments on the defaulters. The Sultan received regular reports about the working of his administration at the central and provincial levels, from the headquarters of his Iqtadars and district officers, from the army camps and the frontier outposts from three different sources: the officers in charge, *barids* or the news reporters and the *munhis* or the spies. All the civil and military officers of the state were under obligation to send reports of their day-to-day working to their respective departmental heads at Delhi, who, in turn, forwarded these to the office of the Sultan directly. The *barids* or news reporters, who ran the postal services, were known to the public but the *munhis* or spies worked secretly and were undetectable. The two direct outcomes of his personal interest in the state administration were (*a*) the organisation of the improved postal system; and (*b*) the espionage.

Ziauddin Barani has to say the following about the organisation of the postal services by Alauddin Khilji:

'It was the practice of the Sultan, when he sent an army on an expedition, to establish posts on the road, wherever posts could be maintained, beginning from Tilpat, which is the first stage. At every post relays of horses were stationed, and at every half or quarter *Kos*, runners were posted; officers and report writers were appointed. Every day, or every two or three days, news used to come to the Sultan, reporting the progress of the army, and intelligence of the health of the sovereign was carried to the army. False news was thus prevented from being circulated in the city or in the army; the securing of accurate intelligence from the court on one side, and the army on the other, was a great public benefit'. (*Ibid*; p. 123).

As for the espionage, the *munhis* or the spies reported direct to the Sultan, and they constituted 'the real terror to all the high and the low'. They were spread out all through the kingdom. They infiltrated the offices of the *Iqtadars*, district headquarters, and all the public places. Domestic servants of the aristocracy, soldiers, *amirs* and even the subordinate civil and military officers were assigned the duties of espionage to keep a watchful eye on their colleagues as well as the seniors, and their identification was well-nigh impossible. So much so that, in the social assemblies of the *amirs* and public men, an atmosphere of suspicion prevailed everywhere, and 'the right hand did not know the intentions of the left hand'. This subject is elaborated by Barani under the *second* administrative reform of Alauddin Khilji as follows:

'Secondly, he provided so carefully for the acquisition of intelligence, that no action of good or bad men was concealed from him. No one could stir without his knowledge, and whatever happened in the houses of the nobles, great men, and officials, was communicated to the Sultan by his reporters. Nor were the reports neglected, for explanations of them were demanded. The system of reporting went to such a length that nobles dared not speak aloud even in the largest palaces, and if they had anything to say they communicated by signs. In their own houses, day and night dread of the reports of the spies made them tremble. No word or action which could provoke censure or punishment was allowed to transpire. The transactions in the *bazars,* the buying and selling and the bargains made, were all reported to the Sultan by his spies, and were kept under control'. (*Ibid.*, pp. 179-80).

Accordingly, the dread of the Sultan's spies made the nobility and the state bureaucracy, including the ministers, courtiers, princes and all members of the royal household, from queens to the maid-servants, tremble to think of the Sultan's spies, and none could say with certainty which of his or her children, associates or servants might turn out to be a secret agent of the Sultan. It was on the bases of the reports received from these spies that Alauddin took his defaulting officials to task and liquidated the disaffected nobles and their collaborators.

Barani treats the subject of drinking wine by nobility and the people at large under the *third* administrative reform of Alauddin Khilji as under:

> Thirdly, he prohibited wine-drinking and wine-selling, as also the use of beer and intoxicating drugs. Dicing also was forbidden. Many prohibitions of wine and beer were issued. Vintners (wine merchants) and gamblers and beer-sellers were turned out of the city (of Delhi), and the heavy taxes which had been levied from them were abolished. The Sultan directed that all the China and glass vessels of his banqueting room should be broken, and the fragments of them were thrown out before the gate of Badaun, where they formed a heap. Jars and casks of wine were brought out of the royal cellars, and emptied at the Badaun Gate in such abundance that mud and mire was produced as in the rainy season. The Sultan himself gave up wine parties. He directed *maliks* to mount elephants and to go to the gates of Delhi, through the streets and wards, *bazars* and *sarais*, proclaiming the royal command that no one should drink, sell, or have anything to do with wine'.

Thus Alauddin Khilji introduced total prohibition in the capital and its adjoining territories, and ordered his provincial governors to do the same within their areas of jurisdiction. The use of wine in public functions, social get-togethers and parties by the people was made a penal offence, and severe punishments were inflicted on those who defied the royal injunctions. Nevertheless, selling and drinking of wine continued secretly, and we are all appreciation for the learned historian who gives an exhaustive account of how the laws of prohibition were violated by the lovers of wine and the anti-social elements. Barani records that

> Those who had any self-respect immediately gave up drinking; but the shameless, the dissolute and vile characters used to make and distil wine in the distilleries, and to drink and sell it

clandestinely at a great price. They put it into leather bottles, and conveyed it hidden in loads of hay, fire-wood, and such like. By hundreds of tricks and devices, and by all sorts of collusion, wine was brought into the city. Informers searched diligently, and city gate-keepers and spies exerted themselves to seize the wine, and apprehend the contrabandists. When seized, the wine was sent to the elephant stables and given to those animals. The sellers, the importers, and drinkers of wine, were subjected to corporal punishments, and were kept in prison for some days. But their number increased so much that holes for the incarceration of offenders were dug outside the Badaun Gate, which is a great thoroughfare. Wine-bibbers (drunkards) and wine-sellers were placed in these holes, and the severity of the confinement was such that many of them died. Many others were taken out half-dead, and were long before they recovered their health and strength'.

Barani dilates on the consequences of these harsh measures to enforce prohibition; he writes that 'the terrors of these holes deterred many from drinking'; but 'those who were unable to give up their habit went out to the fords of the Jumna, and to villages ten or twelve *Kos* distant to procure their liquor'. Nevertheless, 'the prevention of drinking having been found to be very difficult', 'the Sultan was, ultimately, constrained to permit a limited use of wine and spirits to the people in the privacy of their homes'.

Barani concluded the account of Alauddin's policy of prohibition with the remarks that 'after the prohibition of wine and beer in the city, conspiracies diminished, and apprehension of rebellion disappeared'. But the historian was totally disillusioned and mortified by the final outcome of the Sultan's much-touted political and administrative reforms, and he did not mince the matters while giving expression to his free and frank assessment of the Sultan's achievements and failures after his death in 1316. The writer was, particularly, critical about Alauddin's autocratic rule, based on tyrannical and cruel practices in utter disregard of all human and moral values. The success of his obnoxious 'universal system of espionage', which generated an atmosphere of suspicion and hatred all around, could never be made foolproof or perpetuated for ever; and it crumbled down to dust under the very nose of the Sultan when, in his advanced age, he became the slave of his vile nature, and when the evil traits of his personal character entered his psyche to make him a bad-tempered, cruel and blood-thirsty monster. Highly self-willed, suspicious, treacherous and aggressive by nature, 'his violent temper led him to displace experienced governors; his infatuation for Kafur bred envy and disunion, and caused the death or imprisonment of trusted counsellors, and his sons, prematurely emancipated from the schoolroom, took to drink and debauchery', leaving behind a political vacuum, which was readily filled up by his own favourite eunuch and his henchmen, flatterers and self-seeking persons of easy virtue. The Sultan's excessive indulgence into the sensuous pleasures of the royal *harem*, where he was surrounded by a huge crowd of his so many wives and concubines, with none of whom he could maintain a warm relationship of personal love and fidelity, left him a sex-hungry debaucher and a physical wreck, afflicted with incurable diseases. Ultimately, having lost all powers of discretion, and balance of mind, he became a virtual prisoner in the hands of his faithless Malik Naib, and that marked the end of his much-touted political and administrative reforms in his bid to exercise control over the state machinery and the disaffected nobility.

Fiscal Policy and Revenue Reforms of Alauddin

The money-power or accumulation of wealth was diagnosed by the 'wise counsellors' of Alauddin Khilji to be the fourth cause of revolts against the sultans or established governments of the day as mentioned above. As an adventurer himself, Alauddin Khilji knew by his personal experience the importance of wealth which had made him a powerful military commander and the Sultan. Therefore, the object of eliminating this 'source of trouble' to make his throne safe from the prospective rivals and perpetuate his rule, led him to think seriously of the financial matters, and to devise ways and means to enhance the financial powers of the state, on the one hand, and to lay his hands on the properties and wealth of his nobles and the well-to-do citizens of his state, on the other. According to K.S. Lal, Alauddin Khilji 'was perhaps the first sovereign of the Turkish line to have taken a keen interest in fiscal and revenue reforms. His predecessors, from Qutubuddin Aibek to Jalaluddin Khilji either did not get the time or did not possess the initiative to delve into this complicated branch of administration'.

To use a more sophisticated language, Alauddin adopted a new fiscal policy and introduced radical changes in the traditional revenue system of his state. He undertook the following measures to accomplish his above-mentioned two-fold objective:

1. Confiscation of Wealth and Property: To quote Ziauddin Barani *verbatim*,

The Sultan ordered that, wherever there was a village, held by proprietary right (*milk*), in free gift (*in'am*), or as a religious endowment (*waqf*), it should, by one stroke of the pen, be brought back under the exchequer. The people were pressed and amerced (fined), money was extracted from them on every kind of pretence. Many were left without any money, till at length it came to pass that, excepting *maliks* and *amirs*, officials, *Multanis* and bankers, no one possessed even a trifle in cash. So rigorous was the confiscation that, beyond a few thousand *tankas*, all the pensions, grants of land (*in'am wa mafruz*), and endowments in the country were appropriated. The people were all so absorbed in obtaining the means of living, that the name of rebellion was never mentioned'.

On the very face of it, the precise wording of the account by the celebrated historian reminds us of Morton, the Archbishop of Canterbury and minister of the Tudor King Henry VII (1485-1509) of England, who assisted his patron in amassing wealth at the cost of his subjects. Morton had a very clever way of extracting money both from the rich and poor. To a rich man he would say: 'You spend so much on yourself; why don't you give some money to the king?' To a poor man he would say: 'You spend so little; you must be saving a lot of money. Why don't you spare some for the king also?' This clever way of extracting money was called the 'Morton's fork'. As a result, when the king died, he had left behind 1,800,000 pounds sterling in his treasury, a really huge sum in those days. There are numerous instances to show that Alauddin Khilji also applied equally unscrupulous methods like those of the "Morton's fork' to rob people of surplus money on one pretext or the other.

Our readers are now aware how, at the time of his accession, Alauddin had to distribute gold and bestow land-grants on the influential military commanders and others to secure their sympathy and support; but after consolidating his position on the throne, he had laid his hands on the ex-Jalali nobles and confiscated all of their lands and wealth on the charge of their being disloyal to their former king and patron, Jalaluddin Khilji. Thereafter, he made this practice almost universal. In his wars against the disaffected Muslim nobles and the refractory Hindu rulers, Alauddin never hesitated in searching for the moles, self-seeking persons and traitors in the opposite camps, and went out of the way to win them over to his side through monetary gratification, but he never trusted them, and, after the fulfilment of his objectives, all such persons were done away with and their properties and wealth duly appropriated. In a way, he set a very good example for the treacherous folks but he enriched his coffers all the same, leaving the people penniless and destitute.

As regards the confiscation of land-grants, K.S. Lal holds that probably, all assignments were not confiscated, but their managements might have been taken over by the government. Nevertheless, 'the state officials were asked to treat the people as tyrannically as possible, and try to extort money from them on any and every pretext, so that nobody should be left in possession of much wealth. These instructions were literally carried out and people were compelled to surrender their property'. (*Ibid.*, pp. 242-43). Dr. P. Saran fully corroborates Lal's inference to say that 'originally, the ostensible and declared object of the step was to *render revolts in future impossible* by depriving the richer class of people of all their surplus wealth, which was supposed to be a potent cause of the prevalent spirit of turbulence. Nor did the Sultan, in pursuance of this objective, stop merely at this. He ordered the officers concerned to use all manners of excesses and cruel and ruthless extortions to make the peopled disgorge their wealth, and to *leave no one in possession of gold*. ...After making due allowance for the exaggeration of the chronicler, it is clear from the above account that the enforcement of this ordinance was made, in the beginning, or at any rate, without any restraint or moderation'. (*Studies in Medieval Indian History*; pp. 151-52).

Alauddin took drastic steps to cripple the power of his nobles and bureaucrats and never allowed them to amass wealth through fair or unfair means as far as possible. Nevertheless, whatever he attempted to do to enrich the state treasury, apparently 'to strengthen the hands of the central government', in fact, implied for his personal benefits. To our mind, 'Alauddin did absolutely nothing to create even a semblance of the central authority, apart from the person of the sultan himself, which could hold intact such a mighty state that he had brought into being through military prowess and forceful personal character'.

2. Economic Measures against the Hindus

Next to the Muslim nobility and other grandees of the sultanate, the Sultan turned his attention, particularly, towards his Hindu subjects, including the aristocracy, called the *rais*, *rawats* or *thakurs*, and hereditary landlords, referred to by Barani as the *khuts*, *muqaddams* and *chaudharis*, etc. According to the ancient traditions, the bulk of the cultivable land, under the sultans of Delhi, was held by the Hindu peasant proprietors or the *balahars* of Barani's denomination. So also was the case with their semi-official rural leaders and headmen of the villages, called the *khuts*, *muqaddams* and *chaudharis*, who occupied the position of landholders, or intermediaries for the collection of land revenue and other state levies from the villagers.

Barani records that, after enforcing the above measures regarding the confiscation of land-grants and properties, the Sultan called his counsellors a second time and asked them to 'suggest some rule or regulation whereby Hindus might be ground down, and their property or wealth, which is the source of rebellion and disaffection might no longer remain with them; and that one law respecting the payment of revenue might be instituted for all of them, whether landlords or tenants, so that revenues due from the strong might not fall upon the weak, and that so much should not be left to the Hindus as to admit of their riding horses, wearing fine dress and indulging in sumptuous and luxurious habits'. (*Ibid.*, pp. 287-291). In response to the Sultan's enquiry, his counsellors suggested two measures which were enacted immediately in the form of regulations (*zabitas*).

The First Regulation—Assessment of Land Revenue

The first Regulation (*Zabita*) prescribed that the land revenue or the government demand on the agricultural produce was to be fixed on the basis of two principles: (*a*) measurement of the cultivable land, by adopting *biswa* as the standard unit of measurement everywhere; and (*b*) the state demand was fixed at half of the produce in cash or kind, which was to be realised at uniform rate, and 'this rule was to apply to all the cultivators, including the *balahars* (peasants) and the *khuts* (landlords) without the slightest distinction'. The *khuts* were deprived of all special privileges.

The Second Regulation—Additional Levies

In the words of Barani, 'the second regulation related to buffaloes, goats, and other animals from which milk is obtained. A tax for pasturage, at a fixed rate, was to be levied, and was to be demanded for every inhabited house, so that no animal, however wretched, could escape the tax. Heavier burdens were not to be placed upon the poor, but the rules as to the payment of the levies were to apply equally to rich and poor'. According to P. Saran's interpretation, this regulation, in practice, imposed two additional levies, 'a grazing tax on all milch cattle from a cow to a she-goat, and a house tax on every inhabited house'.

It goes to the credit of Alauddin Khilji that he became the first Muslim ruler of Delhi to have thought of introducing agrarian reforms on a scientific basis though with the ulterior motives. The assessment of the land revenue on the basis of a uniform system of the measurement of land was a well-established custom in the pre-Muslim India, and *biswa,* as a standard unit of measurement, was also prevalent in the past; Alauddin only revived and implemented the traditional system of the land measurement in the sultanate. As regards the state demand, W.H. Moreland, the celebrated writer of *The Agrarian System of Moslem India*; (Cambridge, 1929) records that under the ancient Hindu sovereigns, it used to be 'one-fourth to one-sixth; the revenue rose to one-third or fell as low as one-sixth of the produce as the emergency required. During the rule of the early Muslim rulers, like Iltutmish and Balban, the rate does not seem to have risen above one-third'. Compare it with Alauddin's demand for half the produce as land revenue, and we can understand its importance, not as an agrarian reform but as a punitive measure to penalize his Hindu subjects. The Sultan deprived the *khuts* of their special privileges and abolished their *khuti* or the commission that they used to deduct out of the land revenue and other taxes, collected by them from the peasantry for onward deposit into the state treasuries. They were also made to pay land revenue and other taxes at the same rates at which the other peasants were taxed. According to Dr. J.L. Mehta,

> 'Barani's account on this point is not clear but it so appears that the *khuts* were expected to pay revenue on the land under their personal cultivation only, and not on behalf of or for the other peasants. If this is correct, then we conclude that Alauddin Khilji had abolished the *Zamindari* or Intermediary status of the *khuts, muqaddams* and *chaudharis*, and struck a serious blow to the traditional Hindu landed aristocracy. Therefore, they might have continued to hold their hereditary family titles, but we are not sure if they also continued to perform their old functions of revenue collection without the receipt of their collection fee. This conclusion seems to be correct in the light of meaningful statement made by Barani (*op. cit.,* pp. 182-83) in the course of his narrative. He says:
>
> The same rules for the collection of the tribute (taxes) applied to all alike, and the people were brought to such a state of obedience that one revenue officer would string twenty khuts, muqaddams or chaudharis together by the neck, and enforce payment by blows'. (*Ibid., I, pp. 172-73*).

Imposition of *Jaziya* (*Jizya*)

According to the traditional Islamic theory of taxation, which had become operational ever since the beginning of the Muslim rule in Delhi, all the non-Muslims, including the Hindus and the Buddhists, had been subjected to the imposition of *Jaziya* or *Jizya* in their capacity as the *Zimmis*. There is no denying the fact that the non-Muslims, who comprised the absolute majority of the sultanate, were deprived of the political and religious freedom, and they were not treated as the full-fledged citizens of the state. They had to pay the most obnoxious tax, called *Jaziya*, because of their religious disability, which was collected from the infidels and the idolaters *'as a punishment for their unbelief in order to humiliate them*, or it may be, by way of mercy, *as a price for the protection given them by the Muslim state'*. (P. Saran, *loc.cit.*, pp. 113-17).

Jaziya was collected from all the able-bodied males, from which there was no exemption even for a beggar or recluse. For the imposition of this tax, the non-Muslim population was divided into three grades on the basis of their economic standing; the richest among them paid 48 *dirhams*, the second grade 24 *dirhams* and the third 12 *dirhams* per annum. Shams-i-Siraj Afif, in his book, which is also entitled *Tarikh-i-Firoze Shahi* like that of Barani, records that 'the Sultans of Delhi generally charged ten, twenty and forty *tankas* as *Jaziya* from the poor, the middle class and the rich respectively.' (*E&D* III, p.383). *Jaziya* was definitely 'a regressive step, and bore more heavily on the poor than on the rich'. Dr. Satish Chandra's contention that 'the Hindus had stubbornly clung to their faith despite the prevalence of Muslim rule in large parts of the country for over four hundred years', and that 'during most of this period, they were required to pay *Jizya*', (*Ref. India's Islamic Traditions;* ed. by R.M. Eaton, OUP, 2003, p. 135) was all the more reason for Alauddin Khilji to adopt repressive measures for the collection of this tax to enrich his treasury. In our opinion, the Hindus, during the sultanate period, had to pay *Jaziya* as well as *Kharaj* as two distinct taxes; whereas, *Jaziya* was realised as a separate tax in the towns, it was, probably, collected along with *Kharaj* in the rural areas, and as a part of the *Kharaj* or tribute so-called from the subordinate Hindu chiefs of the south, particularly.

Of course, *Jaziya* was one of the major sources of the state income, and it was found handy by Alauddin Khilji to squeeze the Hindus by its vigorous collection through stringent measures. It is usually made out that the contemporary chroniclers throw no light on the estimated revenues collected from *Jaziya,* but 'they do not give figures for *Kharaj* and other taxes either'.

3. Harsh Measures for Revenue Collection

Alauddin Khilji adopted equally harsh measures for the collection of land revenue and other taxes from the people. He had a vast revenue establishment, and, probably, many of the old revenue collectors from among the Hindus like the *khuts*, *muqaddams* and *chaudharis* were still enrolled as revenue collectors on the new terms and conditions by the state government. The Sultan enforced strict discipline among them; and 'the collectors, clerks and other officers, employed in revenue matters, who took bribes and acted dishonestly, were dismissed'. Barani makes a mention of one Sharaf Kai—the *naib wazir-i-mamalik* in the capital, who 'exerted himself strenuously for some years in enforcing these regulations in all the villages and towns'. The chronicler records that

> 'Sharaf Kai so rigorously enforced his demands and exactions against the collectors and other revenue officers, and such investigations were made, that every single *jital* against their names was ascertained from the books of the *patwaris* (village accountants). Blows, confinement in the stocks, imprisonment and chains, were all employed to enforce payment. There was no chance of a single *tanka* being taken dishonestly, or as bribery, from any Hindu or Mussalman. The revenue collectors and officers were so coerced and checked that for five hundred or a thousand *tankas*, they were imprisoned and kept in chains for years. Men looked upon revenue officers as something worse than fever. Clerkship was a great crime, and no man would give his daughter to a clerk. Death was deemed preferable to revenue employment. Oft-times fiscal officers fell into prison, and had to endure blows and stripes'. (*Ibid.*, pp. 182-83)

The impact of these stringent measures for the collection of state revenues upon the Hindus is elaborated by Barani as follows:

> These measures 'were so strictly carried out that the *chaudharis* and *khuts* and *muqaddams* were not able to ride on horseback, to find weapons, to get fine clothes, or to indulge in betel... No Hindu could hold up his head; and in their houses no sign of gold or silver, *tankas* or *jitals* or of any superfluity was to be seen. These things, which nourish insubordination and rebellion,

were no longer to be found. Driven to destitution, the wives of the *khuts* and *muqaddams* went and served for hire in the houses of the Mussalmans'. (*Ibid.*)

4. Status of Hindus as *Zimmis*

Alauddin's attitude towards the Hindus as *kharaj-guzars*—'the payers of tribute' or *kharaj-dih* or 'givers of tribute' was determined by his incisive dialogue with Qazi Mughisuddin of Bayana, who explained that

> 'They (the Hindus) are called payers of tribute, and when the revenue officer demands silver from them, they should without question, and with all humility and respect tender gold. If the officer throws dirt into their mouths, they must without reluctance open their mouths wide to receive it. By doing so, they show their respect for the officer. The due subordination of the *Zimmi* (tribute-payer) is exhibited in this humble payment and by this throwing of dirt into their mouths. The glorification of Islam is a duty, and contempt of the religion is vain. God holds them in contempt, for He says: *Keep them under in subjection*. To keep the Hindus in abasement is especially a religious duty, because they are the most inveterate enemies of the Prophet, and because the Prophet has commanded us to slay them, plunder them, and make them captive, saying: *Convert them to Islam or kill them, enslave them, and spoil their wealth and property.* No doctor but the great doctor (Hanifa), to whose school we belong, has assented to the imposition of the *Jaziya* on Hindus. Doctors of other schools allow no other alternative but *Death or Islam*.' (*Ibid., pp. 187-88*).

Barani tells us that 'the Sultan smiled at this answer of the Qazi'; he must have been amused to hear the *Qazi*'s absurd interpretation of the Islamic law for the realisation of *Jaziya* from the Hindus. Nevertheless, going by the ferocious nature of Alauddin Khilji, the fact remains that his political and imperial motives also impelled him to adopt whatever harsh measures he could to extract the maximum from *Zimmis*.

5. Army Establishment of Alauddin

Alauddin had established a police state, the very existence and stability of which depended on a strong and well-equipped army. Being a great imperialist, he was ever eager to expand his kingdom by the conquest of his neighbouring Hindu states. At the same time, he was called upon to protect his dominions from the Mongol menace. In 1301, when he was engaged in the siege of Chittor, the Mongols also launched a major attack on India and threatened the safety of Delhi. 'Caught between the two whirlwinds', Alauddin faced the situation boldly and came out successful on both the fronts. Nevertheless, it prompted him to raise a permanent and well-equipped standing army not only for the defence of his territories against internal revolts and external invasions but also to carry on wars of aggression against the other Indian states for the territorial aggrandizement. As far as possible, he did not permit his military nobles to recruit their private armies, and he depended almost exclusively on the strength and prowess of his permanent standing army.

Alauddin's army consisted primarily of cavalry and infantry, but, in times of war, elephants and camels were also employed on an extensive scale. The *diwan-i-arz* or the 'muster master' maintained a descriptive roll of every soldier, and Barani tells us that he had also introduced the system of branding the state horses, so that, at the time of review, the soldiers should not cheat their commander by presenting one horse twice or replace it by an inferior quality of the animal. A periodical review of the state contingents was made very strictly, and the horses and weapons of the soldiers were examined.

Alauddin maintained a vast standing army on permanent basis, and did not disband his troops after the successful conclusion of a war or repulsion of the foreign attack, as was usually done by the Indian feudal chieftains in the medieval age. The precise strength of Alauddin's armed forces is not known, but Firishta informs us that, during the concluding years of his reign, he had on the state rolls a permanent standing army of well-equipped and trained 4,75,000 cavalry. Obviously, his soldiers were paid regular salaries in cash from the state exchequer all through the year which entailed a recurring expenditure on a very large scale. He, therefore, confronted a real problem to ascertain the substantial means to meet this huge expenditure on a permanent basis, and he sought the solution to this problem from his counsellors and advisers thus:

> 'If I settle a large amount of pay on the army, and desire to maintain the pay at the same rate every year, although the treasury is now full, five or six years will clear it out, and nothing will be left. Without money government is impossible. I am very desirous

of having a large army, well-horsed, well-accoutered, picked men and archers, ready for service year after year.' (Barani, *op. cit.*, pp. 191-92)

It is important to remember that Alauddin's soldiers, who comprised the 'army of Islam', could not be compared with the militia or ordinary soldiers of the feudal chieftains of the age. Even otherwise, raw men were not recruited and given formal training by the state in those days. They were, in fact, the most favoured children of the Sultanate, and their efficient and dedicated services ensured the safety of the crown. They were well-paid, materially rich and enjoyed much more comfortable family lives than the masses. The soldiers were paid salaries in cash; and Alauddin was anxious to raise the strength of his army but on the payment of moderate salaries without adversely affecting their standard of living. Because of the unending war operations and the presence of a large number of the defence personnel in and around the capital, the prices of commodities in the market had steadily been rising, and the prospects of more additions to their number were bound to lead to their further rise in the times to come.

The salary structure of Alauddin's soldiers, which was promulgated by him in 1303, has been given by all the contemporary chroniclers almost identically. The salary of a foot soldier was fixed at 78 *tankas* per annum, and the horseman, who was provided a horse by the state, received 156 *tankas* a year, viz., double the salary of the foot soldier. Very often, the horsemen brought their own horses for use in the army; in that case, if a cavalry man brought his own horse, he was given 78 *tankas* extra as the horse allowance per annum, and he was called *yak aspa* or 'the possessor of one personal horse'. These gentlemen soldiers were also encouraged to maintain an additional horse with them for use in emergency; if so, their additional horse allowance was automatically doubled, and they were called *du aspa* or 'the possessors of two personal horses'. Thus the total emoluments of a *du aspa* come to 312 *tankas* per annum. A *tanka* of silver was one *tola* in weight, and was equivalent to the silver rupee of the Mughal period.

The Sultan was keen that this salary structure should be frozen and made permanent. After considerable deliberations, 'his sagacious advisers made a unanimous report to the Sultan' that it could be possible only if his soldiers could buy from the open market 'the necessaries of life at low rates', as fixed by the state through regulations; and that 'the necessaries of life would never become cheap until the price of grain was fixed by regulations and tariffs. Cheapness of grain is a universal benefit'.(*Ibid.*) In consequence, Alauddin Khilji issued a number of regulations to fix the prices of food grains and other essential commodities, and ensure 'their regular supply to the people at fixed prices without any inconvenience'. Though an autocratic ruler, Alauddin did not fix the prices of grain and other goods arbitrarily but on 'the progressive principle of production-cost (*bar award*)'; it was not affected by 'the fluctuating supply and demand, good or bad weather, or the speculative trends of the business community who raised or lowered the prices with motives of making the maximum profits'. The successful implementation of these regulations also necessitated the adoption of elaborate measures for exercising stringent control of markets by the state as follows.

6. Price Control and Market Regulations

Barani's description of the various regulations (*Zabitas*), which dealt with the fixation of prices of corns and cereals, and the control of markets is incomplete. Though an official historian, he does not seem to have a complete set of all the original regulations of Alauddin Khilji with him when he wrote the *Tarikh-i-Firoze Shahi*. He has discussed all the economic reforms of Alauddin but with special reference to Delhi alone, though we have the reasons to believe that these regulations were made applicable to the other parts of the Sultanate also, may be with some modifications, through the *iqtadars* or provincial governors of his dominions, especially where the royal armies were put on active duty so that his soldiers could get the necessaries of life from the open markets at reasonable rates.

The first set of eight regulations dealt with corn and cereals. The first regulation (*Zabita*) fixed the prices of food grains as under:

Wheat...............7.5	*jitals*	per *maund*
Barley...............4	*jitals*	" "
Gram...............5	*jitals*	" "
Rice.................5	*jitals*	" "
Mash (*Urad*).......5	*jitals*	" "
Moth.................3	*jitals*	" "

It is not easy to calculate these prices in terms of modern currency and weights, but Firishta records that, during the times of Alauddin Khilji, a *maund* was equal to 40 *seers*, and a *tanka*, whether of gold or silver, was equal to one *tola* in weight. It is generally held that a *tanka* of silver was equal to 48 *jitals* of copper, and a *tola* was made-up of 96 *rattis*. He also informs us that a *jital* of copper, during the reign of Sher Shah Suri, was equal to one *tola* in weight but it might not have been so during the earlier period. This fractional currency, in fact, formed the basis of the later monetary changes in India when a *tanka* of silver became known as the silver rupee, with its fractional break-up as four *paisas* to an *anna,* and sixteen *annas* or 64 *paisas* to a rupee.

The second regulation dealt with the control of grain markets in the metropolis and the centrally administered areas, within the periphery of 100 *Kos* from Delhi. According to Barani, the Sultan appointed Malik Qabul—'a wise and practical man', a trustworthy servant of Ulugh Khan, as *Shahna-i-Mandi* or the Controller of Grain Markets. 'He received a large territory and used to go round (the markets) in great state with many horse and foot. He had clever deputies, friends of his own, who were appointed by the crown. Intelligent spies also were sent into the markets'.

The third regulation provided for the storage of corn in the *king's granaries*. The Sultan ordered the construction of government-owned store-houses or granaries for the' accumulation of grains'. These granaries were kept well-stocked. According to Barani, 'there was scarcely a *mohalla* where two or three royal stores filled with food-stuffs did not exist. These were different from the grain shops. They were godowns where grain was stored in reserve to be released in times of emergency'. In the words of Barani,

> 'The Sultan gave orders that all the *Khalsa* villages of the Doab should pay the tribute (*Kharaj*) in kind. The corn was brought into the granaries of the city (of Delhi)...Half the Sultan's portion (of the produce) was ordered to be taken in grain. In Jhain also, and in the villages of Jhain, stores were to be formed. These stores of grain were to be sent into the city in caravans. By these means so much grain came to Delhi that there never was a time when there were not two or three royal granaries full of grain in the city. When there was a deficiency of rain or when for any reason the caravans did not arrive, and grain became scarce in the markets, then the royal stores were opened and the corn was sold at the tariff price, according to the wants of the people. Grain was also consigned to the caravans from New City. Through these two rules, grain never was deficient in the markets, and never rose one *dang* above the fixed price'.

The other regulations similarly provided for the management of trade in grains and pulses to ensure the availability of these stuffs at the fixed prices to the soldiers and the general public. The grain market was run by two types of merchants or shop-keepers. The first category of those who dealt with this trade were retail shop-keepers or distributors, who had their permanent shops in the towns, and the second category was composed of the *carvanians* or the travelling merchants (*Banjaras*), who brought grain from the countryside and outstations to the towns and sold it to the shopkeepers as well as the public. Before the promulgation of these regulations, the *caravan*-merchants as well as the shop-keepers made huge profits on the food stuff, depending on the fluctuating demand and supply, weather conditions and the other speculative practices. Hereafter, they could have but only marginal profits, as fixed by the state, to the great relief of the people.

Barani reports that 'the shopkeepers looked with disgust at the new regulations, and the *carvanians* stopped coming into the city'. In order to make them tread on the path of righteousness, Alauddin Khilji issued regulation no. 4 'to bring all the grain carriers (*carvanians*) into a single corporation (*yak wujud*) under the charge of *Shahna-i-Mandi*'. All of them were to be registered and issued licences to bring grain from the far-off villages; and the provincial and local revenue officials were put under obligation to procure grain at fixed rates *from* the cultivators for them. Stringent measures were adopted to bring the *carvanians* under this regulation. The corn and cereals were 'either acquired by the state granaries or sold by the merchants in the open market at the rates, dictated by the government; the merchants were allowed to charge only a moderate profit plus the cost of carriage over and above their procurement price'. According to Barani, the defaulters were arrested and 'brought in chains before the Controller of the Markets, who was directed to detain them until they agreed upon one common mode of action and gave bail for each other. Nor were they to be released until they brought their wives and children, beasts of burden and cattle, and all their property, and fixed their abodes in the villages along the banks of the Jumna'. (*Ibid.*, pp. 193-94)

The fifth and sixth regulations made provisions against regrating (*ihtikar*), i.e. 'buying and hoarding of grain with a view to retailing at a profit'. In the words of Barani, 'this was so rigidly enforced that no merchant, farmer, corn-chandler, or anyone else could hold back secretly a *maund* or half a *maund* of grain, and sell it at his shop for *dang* or a *dirham* above the regulated price. If regrated grain were discovered, it was forfeited to the state, and the regrater was fined. Engagements were taken from the governors and other revenue officers in the Doab that no one under their authority should be allowed to regrate, and if any man was discovered to have regrated, the deputy and his officers were fined, and had to make their defence to the throne'. (*Ibid.*, p. 194)

In accordance with the seventh regulation, the Sultan received daily reports regarding the prevalent market rates for the sale and purchases of goods from three separate sources simultaneously - the *Shahna-i-Mandi* or 'the Controllers of the Markets', the *barids* and the *munhis*. If these reports showed any variation in their contents, enquiries were held and the defaulters were taken to task. Above all, the eighth regulation of Alauddin Khilji made provisions for the rationing of grain in his capital in the times of drought or famine. The Sultan was fully aware that, 'in favourable seasons, the people would buy as much grain as they liked, but the conditions were not the same in seasons of drought and famine. In seasons of drought, grain could not be sold to the people of Delhi in indefinite quantities, the more so because the people of the vicinity also flocked into the capital city. Consequently it was rationed'. In the words of Barani

> 'When the rains failed, a quantity of corn, sufficient for the daily supply of each quarter of the city, was consigned to the dealers everyday from the market, and half a *maund* used to be allowed to the ordinary purchasers in the markets. Thus the gentry and traders, who had no villages or lands, used to get grain from the markets; if in such a season, any poor reduced person went to the market, and did not get assistance, the overseer received his punishment whenever the fact found its way to the king's ears.'

During the times of Alauddin Khilji, the system of issuing ration cards did not exist; nor were the people numbered or counted for obtaining grain in fixed quantities. Because of influx of the people from the adjoining regions into the capital, its population fluctuated even otherwise, but whosoever went to the *bazaar* was permitted to purchase a reasonable quantity of grain. Under the circumstances, the task of the government officials to keep a strict watch over the pricing of goods by the merchants and shop-keepers was not so easy, but wherever 'the officials were found derelict in discharging their duty, they as well as the superintendent of the market (*Shahna-i-Mandi*) were taken to task by the Sultan'. Barani asserts that the specified rates of various goods were maintained in the capital during the lifetime of Alauddin, and 'all the wise men of the age were astonished at the unvarying prices' of corn and cereal in the markets irrespective of 'whether the rains were abundant or scanty'. Going by his assessment, 'this was indeed the wonder of the age, and no other monarch was able to affect it'. Barani narrates an incident that 'once or twice, when the rains were deficient, a market overseer reported that the price of grain has gone up by half a *jital*, and he received twenty blows with the stick'. It is really creditable that Alauddin's state machinery had a firm grip over the unscrupulous business community of the capital, who were not allowed to exploit the common man by raising the prices of goods arbitrarily even in times of scarcity.

Fixation of Prices for Groceries: Alauddin issued a second set of five regulations for the purchase of peace goods, garments and groceries. Barani omits the regulation about the groceries but Firishta reproduces a price list for the sale of groceries on fixed rates in the capital; he gives the list (Briggs, I, p. 204) as follows:

Sugar candy.....................one seer..............2...*jitals*
Coarse sugar (*shakar*).........one seer..........1...... *jital*
Coarse sugar *surkh* (*gur*)....one seer...............0.5....*jitals*
Lamp oil..........................3 seers............1 ....*jital*
Ghee........................one seer..........................0.5.. *jitals*
Salt.............................5 seers................1.... *jital*
Onions and Garlic.............one seer...........1.... *jital*

The contemporary chroniclers record that separate markets were setup for each major trade and each market was put under the charge of a *Shahna-i-Mandi*. According to Firishta, every thing that a soldier needed could be had by him at the specified rates, as fixed by the state, in every town and in the rowing markets of the *Banjaras* throughout the territories of the Sultanate. There were horse markets, slave markets, weapon markets, and markets for cattle and for sweets, spices, fruits, shoes, etc.

Cloth Markets: Next to food grains and groceries, the important item of price control was cloth. The administration of cloth market in the capital was regulated on the lines of the grain market. It was under the direct charge of Malik Yaqub—the *Diwan-i-Riyasat*, who enjoyed powers of supervision and control over the other markets, including the Grain Market; thus Malik Qabul Ulugh Khani, the controller or superintendent of Grain Market, was his *subordinate*.

'The Cloth Market of Delhi was located in the building known as 'the *Sarai Adl*, on the extensive lawns, near the Badaun Gate, which had not been used for years'. It was converted into an open market for the sale and purchase of cloth as well as groceries. A wing of this market was reserved for transactions in piece goods and garments, with special provisions to meet the requirements of the soldiers. 'The market was open from early morning till late in the night—the hour of the last prayer'. It was the only market in the capital which dealt in cloth since no trader was permitted to sell his goods secretly or at prices higher than those fixed by the Sultan. It was under the supervision of *Rais Parwana* (Permit Officer). All the cloth merchants, Indian as well as foreigners were required to bring every sort of cloth or garments to this market and sell it at the specified rates. They had to get their names registered and had to execute bonds to the effect that they will abide by the rules and regulations of the state.

Barani and others have given long lists of cotton and silk cloth and garments, the prices of which were fixed by the government; but unlike the food grains and groceries, and, with a few exceptions, it is not possible to identify them or ascertain their qualities and measures somewhat comparable to the modern stuffs. Suffice it to say, that the coarse cloth and garments were sold at the normal rates, based on 'the production-cost principle' but the superior qualities of cotton cloth and silks, and most of the indigenous as well as foreign textile products were very costly, and they 'had to be sold at the subsidized rates for the benefit of the nobility and aristocracy'. Barani informs us that there was a great demand for superior quality of cotton and silken piece goods and garments in Delhi. Therefore, the Multani traders, who were experts in cloth trade, were, at one time, advanced twenty *lacs* of *tankas* as loan by the Sultan to bring costly textile products from the far off centres of specialised production in Maharashtra, Gujarat, Rajasthan, Bengal and Kashmir etc. for sale in the cloth market of the capital. Ibn Batuta also refers to the occasional advancement of money by the Sultan to the merchants to procure merchandise, weapons, and horses etc from far off lands for sale in the capital on specified rates. After the close scrutiny of their statements, K.S. Lal infers that 'the Multani merchants and other traders, who were induced to trade in Delhi, were not traders in the true sense of the term, selling goods at profitable rates; but they were virtually (commission) agents of the government. They were advanced money to buy goods abroad and sell them in Delhi, and they received remuneration (or commission) for their services. It may be surmised that such transactions must have caused an immense loss to the state'. (*History of the Khaljis*; p. 282). The rates of a few common items of cotton cloth for general use, whose measures have been given by Barani, may be given below:

Chadar (ordinary bed sheet) : 10 *jitals*

Long cloth, coarse per 40 yards: one silver *tanka*

Long cloth, fine, per 20 yards: one silver *tanka*

Markets for Horses, Cattle and the Slaves: Alauddin issued a third set of four regulations for the sale and purchase of horses, cattle and the slaves at the prices fixed by the state. In India, horses of good breed were mostly imported from Arabia, Persia and Afghanistan, but with the beginning of the Mongol menace in Central Asia, their supply was considerably curtailed, and their prices rose sky high. Cavalry being the most important wing of Alauddin's army, the horses were much valued, and the Sultan was very keen that their prices needed to be controlled by the state by all means. Accordingly, the horses considered fit for use by the soldiers were divided into three grades according to their quality and breed. The price of the best quality horse ranged from 100 to 120 *tankas*, that of the second grade from 80 to 90 *tankas*, and the horses of third grade could be had from 65 to 70 *tankas* each. Those horses, which were not passed as fit for military service by the *Diwan-i-Riyasat*, or the ordinary breed of ponies (*tattoos*) priced from 10 to 20 *tankas* only. The government was aware of the frauds committed by the horse-brokers and the middle-men (*dallals*) who frequented the horse markets with the intention of purchasing the animals and then reselling them at the higher price to the private customers. To stop this evil practice, the state issued permits to the local dealers and the aristocracy for the purchase of a specified number of horses, according to their requirements, to make sure that these animals would not be resold by them at higher prices elsewhere. The whole business of the sale and purchase of horses was conducted at the specified place, called the *horse market*, which was frequently checked by the state officials, and was periodically reviewed by the Sultan himself. The contemporary chroniclers record that the defaulting horse dealers, who defied the government regulations, were severely punished. Firishta writes that 'every six weeks or two months, the Sultan sent inspectors to the horse market to inspect the horses of every variety to ascertain that such variety was sold at the price specified for it. If any variation was detected, the brokers had to suffer penalties and punishments. Fear kept the brokers vigilant and prevented them from trading upon the simplicity of customers; those who resorted to fraud, were either put to death or whipped out of the capital'. (Briggs, I, p. 204)

Cattle Markets: Likewise, the cattle and all the domesticated animals, including the milch cattle and those required for meet, like buffaloes, cows, camels, goats and sheep, or beasts of burden like asses, ponies and oxen were bought and sold in the cattle markets at the tentative rates fixed by the state. A cow for slaughtering could be had for a *tanka* and a half while the prices of milch cows, but without yielding milk, ranged from three to four *tankas* each. The average price of a cow or buffalo, actually yielding milk, ranged from 10 to 12 *tankas* each. Firishta informs us that a beast of burden, which was sold for 40 *tankas* in the times of Muhammad bin Tughluq or Firoze Tughluq, could be had for four or at the most five *tankas* each during the reign of Alauddin Khilji.

Slave Markets: The Muslims had brought with them the practice of enslaving the prisoners of war. The establishment of the Sultanate of Delhi was marked by constant wars and blood-shed between the Turkish armies of invasion and the Hindu rulers of the country. With the set up of the Khilji dynasty, this sphere of warfare was further extended by the repeated Mongol invasions and Alauddin's imperial wars of aggression against the Hindu chieftains of northern as well as southern India. These wars were accompanied by a lot of blood-shed on both sides, and usually a number of soldiers of either party fell into the hands of their enemies on the battle-fields. Their number increased manifold when the victorious party went in hot pursuit of the vanquished soldiers in flight. They were taken captives and treated as prisoners of war. Two special characteristics of these wars, which were fought by the Turkish sultans against the Hindu rulers and Mongols, are noteworthy. The Hindus were non-Muslims and so were the Mongols about that time. Whereas, the Muslim rulers invariably enslaved their prisoners of war and forcibly converted them to Islam, the Hindu rulers are not known to have resorted to this barbarous practice. The latter either exchanged the enemy's captive soldiers with their own men, taken prisoners by their antagonist, or disarmed them and set them free on humanitarian grounds, normally turning them out of their own dominions. On the other hand, the Muslim commanders, including Alauddin Khilji, who dreamed of establishing himself as the Lord Paramount over the Hindus and Buddhists of India, very often, in the course of war, let loose their 'armies of Islam' upon the unarmed civilian population, with freedom to put them to the sword or capture hundreds and thousands of them, men as well as women, and enslave them; they were dubbed as infidels (*Kafirs*) and idolators, and were compelled to embrace Islam. Thus it was that the Indian slave markets were flooded with the abundance of slaves, male and female, and they were sold and purchased at very nominal prices just like the cattle. As a matter of fact, the horses and cattle were regarded much more valuable than men and women slaves.

According to Barani, the standard price of a working slave girl or domestic servant was fixed at five to twelve *tankas*, and that of good-looking concubine from 20 to 30 and even up to 40 *tankas*. If a beautiful girl of a very high price, say of 100 or above *tankas*, was offered for sale in the market 'nobody dared to buy her for fear of the *munhiyans* (secret police), lest the Sultan should be informed that a particular person was rich enough to pay so high a price for a slave girl'. The slave boys were classified according to their looks, physique and working capacity. A handsome young lad could be had for 20 to 30 *tankas* while the price of slave labourers varied from 10 to 15 *tankas* each. In the words of Dr. J.L. Mehta, 'with the consumer's goods and domestic labour so cheap, a man of moderate means, say a horseman of Alauddin's army, could afford to enjoy a happy and comfortable life with one to four legally married wives, a number of concubines and a dozen of slave girls and slave labourers at his beck and call'. (*Advanced Study in the History of Medieval India*; Sterling Publishers, I, p. 179)

By all contemporary accounts, these economic regulations were enforced by Alauddin at least in and around the capital of Delhi with an iron hand. A schedule of the prices of various commodities was prepared and forwarded to the *Diwan-i-Riyasat* or 'the ministry of commerce' for wide publicity and enforcement; the office of *Nazir* - 'the superintendent of weights and measures' formed a part of his establishment. Malik Yaqub, the most successful *Diwan-i-Riyasat* of Alauddin, had held the post of the *Nazir* previously; he was an honest and capable administrator but was very notorious for severity and ruthlessness. He exercised the power of supervision and control over all the *shahnas* of the various markets. Malik Yaqub also held the office of the *Muhtasib* or 'the Censor of Public Morals' which imparted an aura of religious authority in the enforcement of the economic regulations by him.

As if the Sultan was not satisfied with the severe punishments, prescribed by him for the law-breakers, he took personal interest in the rigorous enforcement of his regulations. We are told that the Sultan occasionally used to send his slave boys with a few *jitals* to purchase small quantities of the necessities of life from the retail market. The Sultan would get these commodities weighed in his presence to see if any of them was found to be short-weight. If so, according to his regulation no. 4 of the third set, he sent his inspectors to cut 'a quantity of flesh, equal to the deficiency of weight from the haunches of the defaulting shop-keeper'. About its impact on the business community of the capital, Barani observes that 'the certainty of this punishment kept the traders honest, and restrained them from giving short weight, and other knavish tricks. Nay, they gave such good weight that purchasers often got somewhat in excess'. (*Ibid.*, p. 197). Only a creature of the medieval age could conceive of such like corporal punishments to keep the defaulters on the right track. As an autocratic ruler of the medieval age, Alauddin promulgated and enforced such measures with utmost severity and achieved success in his enterprise. Nevertheless, 'all the market regulations of Alauddin Khilji died with him'. In the words of Barani, 'the rules, the inquiries, the strictness with which the orders were carried out, and the punishments inflicted on the market people came to an end with the death of Alauddin, and his son, Qutubuddin was not able to maintain a thousandth part of them'. (*Ibid.*) This was the unceremonious end of Alauddin's fiscal policy or economic reforms so-called. As regards the immediate impact of his regulations during the lifetime of Alauddin Khilji, K.S. Lal observes that 'the people of Delhi, with the exception of the traders themselves, immensely benefited from these regulations. Prices were rendered cheap and stable. In times of scarcity, there was no danger of famine in the capital city. The terrible famines of the time of Sultan Jalaluddin and Muhammad Tughluq are not heard of in the reign of Alauddin, because the capital at least was never short of food; and if famine occurred in some isolated or distant part of the country, it surely escaped the notice of the contemporary chroniclers'. (The Khaljis; p. 203).

As a despotic ruler and aggressive imperialist, Alauddin conceived of such economic and administrative measures with the primary concern to keep his vast standing army in the enjoyment of a happy and comfortable life on moderate salaries, and he was fully successful in achieving that object. However, it would be wrong to fix these measures in the framework of any enlightened fiscal policy or economic reforms.

Alauddin was 'not learned enough to philosophise on the benefits of a far distant future and to foster trade, commerce and agriculture'. His personal ambitions, religious zeal and imperial instinct rendered the glory of conquest of the infidel lands much more appealing to him than the desire of making such laws for the amelioration of the condition of the peasantry, promotion of trade and commerce or for the prosperity of his subjects. All of his fiscal reforms and regulations were aimed at the filling of the coffers of his royal treasury and for the benefit of his army and the ruling elite of his dominions. Think of a peasant proprietor, who pays half of his hard-earned agricultural produce in land revenue, without having received any benefits from the state whatsoever; then he parts with some portion of the remaining produce to the farm labourers and menials, besides the payment of other sundry charges. Thereafter, he was not probably left with more than one-fourth of his actual produce. Obviously, he had to keep a part of the grain for his family consumption also; and whatever was left with him as surplus, he had to sell it to the government agents or merchants at the minimum rates, fixed by the state. It definitely speaks of the miserable condition of the peasants during the reign of Alauddin Khilji. Because of their vicinity to the state capital, where the Sultan's regulations were enforced with utmost severity, the peasants of the Doab were definitely ruined. K.S. Lal correctly observes that 'a peasant is not always a hoarder; he will not hoard if he is given a fair price for his produce. Just for the sake of safety, he stores up some grain as security against bad seasons, but even that was denied to him, and every *maund* of available grain was transferred to the Grain Market of Delhi'. (*Ibid.*, p. 291).

As a matter of fact, Alauddin did nothing to promote agricultural production. Unlike Sher Shah Suri, he made no attempt to reclaim the waste land or to clear the forests for bringing virgin land under the plough. The contemporary chroniclers do not give even the slightest hint that the Sultan ever thought of opening canals for irrigation or provided funds to the peasants, may be in the form of loans, for the digging of wells or construction of water tanks, nor he is known to have provided any other relief measure to them in times of drought or famine. Therefore, through such like regulations, as a tyrant that he was, Alauddin simply laid his hands on the lush-green standing crops of the peasantry to claim half the share of its produce as a state demand in kind, and his agents made a clean sweep of their fields by carrying away the government levis before its producers realised what was left with them. It was nothing short of a highway robbery, committed by their sovereign so-called; and indirectly, the Sultan discouraged the growth and development of agriculture; or was it that the absolute majority of the peasants, who were thus robbed of their hard-labours, happened to be Hindus and Buddhists, who could not claim full-fledged citizenship of the Islamic state of Delhi?

So also was the case with trade and commerce regarding the adverse effects of Alauddin's measures of price fixation and control of markets; his market regulations did not permit enough profits to businessmen and traders, from the petty shop-keepers of the capital and middlemen to the *carvanians* and foreign merchants, and hence discouraged the growth and development of trade and commerce. Leave aside the production or manufacture of anything, from the most ordinary commodities of daily use like the artisans' crafts and coarse cloth, woven by the indigenous weavers, to the fine cotton and silken textile goods and other luxurious commodities for use by the ruling elite and aristocracy of the capital, Alauddin Khilji again did absolutely nothing to promote production or encourage the skilled workers and manufacturers. Instead, his only concern seemed to be to procure and make available all such valuables to his army personnel and the nobility at the subsidized rates even at the cost of exorbitant expenditure from the state exchequer. We conclude the account of Alauddin's fiscal policy and economic regulations by referring to Barani's pathetic statement that the merchants and *carvanians*, responsible for the procurement and transportation of industrial goods and food stuffs were compelled to take up their abode in Delhi with families, and had to sign agreements, making them individually and collectively responsible for one another's good conduct. In a way, they were held to ransom to do the government's bidding, and the authority of the state extended even over their wives and children. Under the circumstance, how could trade and industry flourish? Therefore, there is nothing surprising if 'the grand edifice of state-controlled economy, built by Alauddin Khilji on brute force, tumbled down like a house of cards with the disappearance of that masterly hand; the whole lot of economic regulations died with the Sultan almost instantaneously, resulting in the spread of utter confusion and economic anarchy in the country'.

An Estimate of Alauddin Khilji

Alauddin Khilji was the greatest of all the sultans of Delhi and one of the most powerful rulers of medieval India; with the exception of Akbar and Sher Shah Suri, no other Muslim ruler of the country stands comparison with him. A born soldier and skilful fighter, he rose to be a successful military general and attained power from scratch by the sheer force of his strong willpower, personal ambitions and dare-devil nature, which inspired him to dream of attaining the most improbable, and encouraged him to challenge the most dreadful situations with utmost fearlessness and monstrous ferocity. As a shrewd politician and statesman, he correctly estimated the shortcomings and weaknesses of the feudal Hindu rulers, who were deeply engrossed in self-destructive fratricidal wars. They lacked over-all national consciousness, and were unable to take a united stand against the foreign Turkish invaders, their common foe. Alauddin was not a religious fanatic like Mahmud of Ghazni, but as head of the Islamic state of Delhi, he was committed to consolidate the Muslim rule in the heart of the land of infidels and expand the boundaries of his kingdom by the conquest of neighbouring Hindu states, for which he needed no other excuse. As an imperialist and political strategist, he did not allow religious sentiments to overshadow his state policy, but the main source of his strength lay in his religious affinity to Islam, and his imperial policy was whetted primarily by the prospects of raising a huge standing 'army of Islam' to fight against the infidel Mongols or the indigenous Indian rulers. The presence of vast tracts of the fertile and virgin lands, inhabited by the Hindus along the borders of the Sultanate of Delhi offered him a golden opportunity and incentive to launch a vigorous military campaign for the destruction and annihilation of the mighty Hindu rulers one by one. By his stubborn resistance to the Mongol invaders, Alauddin Khilji successfully protected the nascent Muslim state as well as the people of northern India from a fresh wave of destruction and devastation. Through his policy of 'blood and iron', he terrified and overawed the Mongol invaders as well as his political opponents and the rebellious nobles. Very often, he adopted the most unscrupulous and barbarous methods in his determined bid to defeat and subdue his neighbouring Hindu chiefs; and his blood and iron policy sometimes assumed the form of genocide of the Hindu populace of the conquered infidel lands when he resorted to wholesale massacre of the unarmed civilians. Cruel and aggressive by nature, Alauddin Khilji was a highly self-willed man, who pursued his imperial goal with steadfastness and set aside all human and moral considerations for the fulfilment of his objectives. The reign of Alauddin Khilji 'represents the high watermark of Muslim despotism' in India.

Alauddin Khilji was not an educated person but he knew the art of administration. His was a police state, the endurance and stability of which depended exclusively on the brute military power. And the main theme of his administrative policy was to maintain perfect peace and order with an iron hand, and to utilize all the financial resources of the state to enlarge and strengthen his armed might and fill the coffers of his treasury. As a shrewd person, he had the wisdom to select the right men for the right job, and also knew how to get the maximum out of them for efficient administration. Up to the year 1313, while he kept his balance of mind, he held all the strings of power in his own hands. All the courtiers, ministers and top bureaucrats were his creatures and he never allowed any of them to pursue an independent line of approach or exercise his own discretion in determining the state policy. He made adequate arrangements for the security of the capital and won the confidence of his subjects as a capable ruler, of course. Alauddin Khilji displayed great originality and mental vigour in organising his civil administration. He solved the various administrative problems 'with an air of professional competence' and earned the reputation as the just monarch among his co-religionists. His various economic measures, though undertaken with highly sectarian and selfish objectives, were the outcome of a really fertile brain. The innovative measures adopted by him in the fixation of prices, control of markets, and rationing of consumers' goods, though not based on very scientific principles, were, in fact, a unique contribution, made by an autocratic ruler, which carried the seeds of an original thinker far ahead of the times. Unfortunately, his fiscal policy was not intended to benefit his subjects, at large, majority of whom happened to be the infidel Hindus, who had to bear the brunt of his drastic economic reforms so-called. Alauddin Khilji setup no political, administrative or social intuitions nor cherished any public welfare ideals as a just and benevolent ruler. He was a typical medieval Indian despot who built up a powerful Muslim state in Delhi, and enjoyed the fruits of power so long as his personal energy and extraordinary zeal enabled him to do so. The moment he lost his health and power of discretion with the advancement of his age, he became a virtual prisoner in the hands of Malik Kafur, his own self-seeking slave eunuch, turned military dictator and the deputy Sultan; and died a miserable death in the first week of January 1316.

SECTION 4: THE IGNOMINIOUS END OF THE KHILJI DYNASTY

While Alauddin Khilji lay unconscious on his death bed, Malik Kafur, in his capacity as the deputy sultan (*malik naib*), had assumed all powers of the state and setup as the *de facto* ruler. Before the sultan breathed his last, the Malik Naib had already emerged as the most powerful Muslim noble in Delhi. He was determined to usurp the throne for himself, and brushed aside the claims of about half a dozen of Alauddin's sons for succession on one pretext or the other. Under the baneful influence and pressure of his ungrateful slave officer, Alauddin had issued the orders for the imprisonment of his two grown-up sons, Khizer Khan and Shadi Khan, in the fort of Gwalior, and their mother, the Malika-i-Jahan, was also held in captivity by the Malik Naib in the old fort of Delhi. Immediately after the death of Alauddin Khilji, Malik Kafur produced 'a spurious will of the late Sultan', according to which Alauddin Khilji was alleged to have disinherited Khizer Khan, the crown prince and most capable of his children, and nominated his minor son, named Shihabuddin Umar, then hardly six years old, as his successor; he was born of the daughter of the Maratha chief, Ram Chandra Deva of Devagiri. As there was none to challenge the contention of the Malik Naib, Umar was placed on the throne and Kafur himself assumed the reins of government as his regent. To add insult to the injury, Malik Kafur formally married the mother of the child sultan; who was the youngest widowed queen of Alauddin Khilji, although it was universally known that he was an eunuch.

Immediately after assuming the reins of government in his capacity as the Regent of the child sultan, Shihabuddin Umar, Malik Kafur commenced his shameful activities for the extermination of all the surviving sons and other important members of his master's family. On the very first day of the beginning of the reign of the child sultan, Malik Kafur despatched a villainous Malik Sambul to Gwalior to put out the eyes of Prince Khizer Khan, who was then held in captivity there. According to the poet laureate Amir Khusrau, Malik Kafur gave him Alauddin's most prestigious and invaluable ring, 'which he had removed from the dead Sultan's person', as a reward as well as an identification mark to secure access to the royal prison in the fort of Gwalior. 'Because of this royal insignia, Sambul was able to reach his prey without difficulty. Poignant were the tears that rolled down the prince's cheeks as he sat down to lose his sight; and the eyes that could not bear the touch of antimony, now bore the torture of a blinding needle'.

Prince Shadi Khan, the younger brother of Khizer Khan, had been shifted from Gwalior to the fort of Siri in Delhi a few days before the death of Alauddin. On that very day, when Malik Sambul was sent to Gwalior to commit this heinous crime, Kafur had sent a few *paiks*—'the slave guards or foot soldiers' of the late Sultan, to blind Prince Shadi Khan in the Kaushak-i-Siri, and they had accomplished this task instantaneously. In the words of Amir Khusrau, the eyes of prince Shadi Khan 'were cut out from their sockets with a razor, like slices of melon'. Their mother, *Malika-i-Jahan*, the eldest widowed queen of Alauddin Khilji, was robbed of all her jewels and property and was held in captivity indefinitely, nothing being known about her thereafter.

After the success of the above operations against the most prominent members of the royal family, Malik Kafur laid his hands on all the other surviving sons of Alauddin Khilji, including Mubarak Khan, Farid Khan, Usman Khan, Muhammad Khan and Abu Bakr Khan. All members of the royal household were cowed down by Malik Kafur, and all of these princes were rounded up and thrown into prisons at various places. With all the real contenders to the throne of Delhi now rotting in his prison cells, Malik Kafur felt quite secure and assumed airs as the virtual ruler of the state to assert his authority over the military officers and provincial governors. According to the contemporary chroniclers, he began to rule 'with a sense of security'. His style of functioning was quite typical. Every day, he would hold an open court in the fort of Siri. He 'seated the child-king on the throne on the terrace of the Hazar Satun for a show boy', and addressed the courtiers, military nobles and top-ranking bureaucrats of the capital in the fashion of Alauddin, making all grandees of the empire and dignitaries stand in his presence. In the day, he transacted the business of the state with a sort of professional competence, but at night used to drink, gamble and play dice in the company of his personal friends. 'When closeted with confidential associates, he used to discuss ways and means of removing Alauddin's scions and officers. Little did he know that his movements were spied by those, whose destruction he was planning'.

The ease with which Malik Kafur had established his control over the entire royal household and laid down his hands on all the prospective contenders to the throne without much opposition from the ministers and military generals of the capital, tempted him to liquidate his potential political rivals one by one. Accordingly, 'all the supporters of the late Sultan, the tried veterans, who had served Alauddin with rare fidelity, were removed , one by one, and in their places were pitchforked low-born men, who depended upon Kafur for favour and promotion to high office'. This policy of witch-hunt against the supporters and sympathisers of Alauddin's ruling family alarmed the old Turkish nobility and the Muslim aristocracy of the empire, and made them apprehensive about their own future and the future of the nascent Muslim State of Delhi. In consequence, there started a whispering campaign to dislodge the usurper from power before it was too late. Even otherwise, being a Hindu convert to Islam, Kafur had no permanent friends and sympathisers among the Turkish nobles and foreign Muslim immigrants, who were the real architects of the Muslim State in India. Hence, his plans to consolidate his power as the *de facto* ruler or install himself as the sultan boom-ranged earlier than expected. The situation came to a crisis when Malik Kafur attempted to blind the youthful prince Mubarak Khan, who had also been imprisoned in the fort of Siri. He once again commissioned the gang of hired *paiks*, under the leadership of Malik Mushir, the erstwhile commander of the slave guards of Alauddin Khilji, who had earlier taken out the eyes of prince Shadi Khan, and persuaded them to give their repeat performance in the case of the other princes too. They were now deputed to take out the eyes of prince Mubarak Khan for a hefty price. According to Firishta, as the agents of Malik Kafur, probably four in number, descended into the cells of the state prisoners, in the underground chambers of the Siri Fort, with malicious intentions, Mubarak Khan, who had earlier witnessed the ghastly scene of the youthful prince Shadi Khan being blinded by them, felt alarmed; and he started crying loudly while making entreaties for mercy from the ex-slave servants of his deceased father and their master, Alauddin Khilji. Simultaneously, 'he took out a jewelled necklace from round his neck, and throwing it before them reminded them of the duty they owed to the sons of the late king. Impressed by Mubarak's harangue, they not only left him untouched, but determined to finish the traitor'. (*Tarikh-i-Firishta*, p. 124). Accordingly, the *paiks*, retraced their steps towards the chambers of Malik Kafur, apparently to apprise him of the successful execution of their assigned job, and, instead, taking him unawares, made a short work of him. Malik Kafur was murdered only 35 days after the death of Alauddin Khilji. Firishta states that, the usurper was murdered by the *paiks* 'with the connivance of high military officers, who used to see the Regent waking up all the night in bolted chamber, discussing in secrecy'.

Qutubuddin Mubarak Shah (1316-20)

The news about the murder of Malik Kafur at once electrified the political atmosphere of the capital. It sent a wave of jubilation and relief among the Turkish nobles and the inhabitants of the capital. Prince Mubarak Khan was taken out of the prison cells by the ring-leaders of the anti-Kafur lobby in the midst of rejoicings from the crowds of Delhi, and was requested to take charge of the government on behalf of the child sultan Shihabuddin Umar as his Regent. Mubarak Khan conducted himself with utmost caution and dignity, and won over the confidence of the Alai nobles by assigning them important offices of the state. It was only after about two months, when law and order had been restored, and the government had started functioning smoothly under the guardians of the old regime, that Mubarak Khan himself ascended the throne with the title of Sultan Qutubuddin Mubarak Shah with the consent of the premier Alai nobles. At that time, he was only 17 or 18 years old, and his coronation was celebrated with a matching pomp and show amidst the rejoicings of the populace of Delhi. The child sultan Shihabuddin Umar was lodged in the fort of Gwalior as the state prisoner along with the other princes of the royal blood.

Mubarak Shah's reign lasted about four years. To begin with, he acted with commendable energy and moderation. To mark the beginning of his reign, he reversed most of the unpleasant and vindictive decisions of his father, the late Sultan Alauddin Khilji, and cancelled all the obnoxious appointments to the higher offices, made by Malik Kafur. The youthful Sultan 'ordered the release of political prisoners; the confiscated lands were restored to their owners, and the numerous tolls and taxes, which had hampered trade, were abolished'. Barani records with amusement and satisfaction that 'men were no longer in fear of hearing the words: *Do this but don't do that; say this but don't say that; hide this but don't hide that; eat this but don't eat that; sell such as this but don't sell things like that; act like this but don't act like that*'. The severe penal code of Alauddin Khilji was thus relaxed and all the economic regulations were scrapped. By the restoration of the confiscated lands to the old Muslim aristocracy and the *ulama*, Mubarak Shah revived the *jagir* system, and the old grandees of the empire readily 'rallied round the young Sultan and helped him in restoring law and order though for a short while'.

Re-conquest of Gujarat (1316): The first two years of Mubarak Shah's reign were quite eventful. In the person of the youthful sultan, the enthusiastic Turkish nobles visualized the rise of an enlightened monarch and forceful leader, who would usher in a fresh wave of imperial wars for re-consolidation and expansion of the Muslim dominions in India. Therefore, all the provincial governors and military officers cooperated with the new sultan and obeyed his orders with pleasure. The re-conquest of Gujarat and restoration of the Muslim hegemony in the south was the major contribution of his reign. As described earlier, the uncalled for murder of Alp Khan, the governor of Gujarat, by Malik Kafur had incited his subordinate Muslim officers to raise their standard of revolt against Delhi. On the eve of the death of Alauddin Khilji, Gujarat was in turmoil, and the Muslim army of occupation of the state was in open defiance of the imperial authority of Delhi under the leadership of two military generals, Malik Haider and Malik Vazirak. Kamaluddin Gurg, the imperial commander, who was sent there with a large army to suppress the revolt was defeated and killed in the battle. Taking advantage of the rift between the rival factions of the Muslim commanders of the Deccan and the political turmoil in Delhi, Harpala Deva, the son-in-law of Ram Chandra Deva of Devagiri, had also thrown off the imperial yoke and setup as an independent ruler of a part of Maharashtra. He had liberated many important forts from the hands of the Muslim officers during the hegemony of Malik Kafur.

Soon after his accession to the throne, Mubarak Shah, on the advice of his newly appointed team of the ministers and military generals, ordered the dispatch of military expedition to Gujarat to suppress its rebellious Muslim officers as well as the rebellious Hindu chieftain, Harpala Deva of Maharashtra. Malik Ghazi Tughluq (the later Sultan Ghiasuddin Tughluq), then the governor of Dipalpur (Punjab), was deputed to collaborate with Ainul Mulk Multani to accomplish this task. Their joint forces arrived in Gujarat and confronted the rebellious Muslim nobles Haider and Vazirak; they were being supported by a number of the local (Gujarati) Muslim as well as Hindu leaders with large contingents. Amir Khusrau writes that, Ainul Mulk Multani, as a seasoned military general, was convinced that 'there was no sense in the fighting of the two forces, professing the same religion'. Accordingly, he wrote secret letters to the Muslim officers of their rival camp not to fight against the royal forces of Delhi. His 'ruse worked well, and as the belligerent forces encountered each other, many Gujarati officers deserted to the side of the imperialists'. The rebellious Muslim officers, Haider and Vazirak, were defeated and fled the battlefield in panic; 'they took shelter with some Hindu chiefs and Zamindars in the far off provinces'. Thus, the ranks of the victorious army of Delhi swelled by the arrival of most of the Muslim camp followers of the rebels, and its task to fight against the refractory Hindu chieftains of Gujarat and Maharashtra was rendered comparatively easy.

After the conquest of Gujarat, Ainul Mulk and Ghazi Tughluq returned to the capital in triumph and were profusely rewarded by Mubarak Shah, while Malik Dinar, who had given his daughter in marriage to the young sultan and had been awarded the title of Zafar Khan, received appointment as the governor of Gujarat. Zafar Khan proved an able administrator, and within a few months, he restored order throughout the province by suppressing all the Hindu rebellious elements with an iron hand.

Expedition to Devagiri (1318): Early in 1318, Sultan Mubarak Shah himself proceeded towards the Deccan 'with a large number of officers and men' to recover the lost kingdom of Devagiri from Harpala Deva, the rebellious son-in-law of Raja Ram Chandra Deva, and 'to secure treasures from the Rai of Telingana and other Deccan princes'. Harpala was defeated in a pitched battle and fled from his capital. He retreated into the interior of the hills, where he was joined by another Hindu chieftain, Raghu, the ex-minister of Ram Chandra Deva; and they together continued the struggle against the Muslims for a few months. Mubarak Shah took possession of Devagiri without much opposition, and sent his new commander Khusrau Khan 'with a strong contingent to pursue the fugitive king and his minister'. According to Amir Khusrau, Raghu collected an army of 10,000 Hindu fighters and gave another battle to the Muslim armies in which he was defeated and badly wounded. He escaped from the battlefield and died an unknown death, but Harpala continued the struggle for some time more before he was defeated and taken prisoner by Khusrau Khan. On the orders of the Sultan, he was flayed alive—'a befitting punishment for an arrogant *Kafir* and *Zimmi*, who had dared to defy the authority of the Islamic state of Delhi'. His mutilated and torched body was hung on one of the gates of Devagiri as a warning to his Hindu subjects.

Mubarak Shah 'was overjoyed at this victory of his favourite general, and received him with a hundred flattering distinctions'. The Hindu temples of Devagiri were plundered and razed to the ground, and out of their material was built a mosque in the town to signal the annexation of the state to Delhi. A trustworthy Khilji officer, named Malik Yaklakhi—the ex-*naib barid-i-mamalik* of Alauddin Khilji, who had given his daughter in marriage to the young sultan, was appointed governor of Devagiri, and imperial officers were put in charge of its various districts. The sultan established outposts in Gulbarga, Sagar and Dharsamudra, and posted strong Muslim garrisons in many other important forts to avoid recurrence of any insurrection by the local populace in future.

Conspiracy to Assassinate Mubarak Shah: Mubarak Shah spent the rainy season at Devagiri and saw through the arrangements made for its proper settlement under his personal care. In September 1318, he ordered Khusrau Khan to lead an expedition to Telingana, and himself returned towards the capital. We have it on the testimony of Barani that the Sultan had taken his *harem* with him, and 'as was his disposition, he was always immersed in music and mirth. Moreover, the king had recently given posts of distinction to his favourites to the resentment of the senior nobility'. As a consequence, a conspiracy was hatched by some of the disgruntled nobles and kinsmen of the sultan, headed by Asaduddin, to assassinate him on the way back to Delhi. According to Barani, Asaduddin was a son of Malik Khamosh Yoghresh Khan, an uncle of Alauddin Khilji; he 'was a brave man, cliquish and influential. He won over to his side some enterprising desperadoes, and they decided to kill the king when he was about to cross the Ghati of Sakun, and to place Asaduddin on the throne'. To the good fortune of Mubarak Shah, one of the conspirators wavered in his commitment to the ringleader of the conspiracy, and apprised the sultan about it at the nick of time. Mubarak Shah 'at once stopped where he had arrived', and placed Asaduddin and his co-conspirators under arrest. On enquiry, the accused being found guilty were instantly executed. After the fashion of his father, the sultan sent orders to Delhi to kill all members of the family of Yoghresh, including young as well as old; 'they were about twenty-nine in number, and possibly none of them could have any knowledge of the plot, some of them being mere infants'.

The success of Mubarak Shah in his Deccan expedition had turned his head but the discovery of the above conspiracy to assassinate him swung him into violent action against his own people. He did not spare even his own father-in-law, Zafar Khan, one of the seasoned military generals, whom he had appointed the governor of Gujarat very recently. On a mere suspicion of his foreknowledge of the abortive conspiracy, he was executed, and similar fate was meted out to some other blood relations and nobles. In his bid to secure his position as the solitary claimant to the throne of Delhi, Mubarak Shah laid his hands on all of his half-brothers, the surviving sons of Alauddin Khilji, then languishing in the royal prisons, and slaughtered them in cold blood. Dewal Rani, the widow of Khizer Khan, was brought into his *harem* as his concubine. At the same time, the liberal policy, adopted earlier by Mubarak Shah in scrapping the economic reforms and harsh measures against the nobility to win over their sympathies, also produced adverse effects. The business community reasserted itself, and the prices of goods shot up. The bureaucracy became careless and corrupt, and the nobles began to show signs of arrogance and indifference towards the central authority. On the other hand, the young and inexperienced Sultan, shorn of adequate education or training in statecraft, readily fell into the company of the men of low tastes and loose moral character, who clustered around him as his well-wishers and favourites. Some of them were promoted to the high ranks in preference to the old and trustworthy officers of his father's regime; they mismanaged the affairs and brought bad name to the Sultan.

As luck would have it, just as Alauddin Khilji had showered special favours on the eunuch Kafur, Mubarak Shah took a fancy for one of his handsome slave boys, Khusrau Khan, a Hindu convert to Islam, 'with whom he had developed compromising personal relations'. Barani records that the 'Sultan's infatuation for this infamous and traitorous Parwari (a low caste Rajput) exceeded that of Alauddin for *malik naib* Kafur'. Like Malik Kafur, Khusrau Khan also gained the special consideration and attention of his master by the display of his competence as a successful military commander; and, as a reward for his services, was made the commander-in-chief of the army, besides being honoured with the exalted offices of the *wazir* as well as *malik naib*. Khusrau Khan earned his reputation as the most capable and trustworthy military general of Mubarak Shah during his Deccan campaign. Soon after the sultan's arrival in Delhi, he also returned with triumph from Warrangal after securing the re-submission of the Rai of Telingana; he brought with him a rich booty, besides a hefty tribute of 'more than a hundred strong elephants as large as demons, 12,000 horses, and immense quantities of gold, jewels and gems beyond compute'.

Firishta records that, pleased with the fidelity and personal attachment of Khusrau Khan to him, the sultan left the work of the state administration into his hands, and 'gave himself up entirely to wine, revelry and lust'. Khusrau Khan is alleged to have 'deliberately pushed the sultan into a life of dissipation'; who, 'overthrowing all decency and royal dignity to the winds, sometimes appeared in the court in a state of drunkenness, accompanied by the dancing girls and vulgar slave boys, who misbehaved with the courtiers and put everyone to shame'. It shocked the well-wishers of the state and spread wide-spread discontent among the provincial governors and other military officers.

The Reign of Khusrau Shah (April to September 1320)

By his foolhardy, arrogant and atrocious conduct towards his own kinsmen and their families, Mubarak Shah had already estranged the entire royal household of the Khilji family and friends; and, before long, he lost the goodwill and confidence of the Muslim nobility and well-wishers of the Islamic state too. Just as Alauddin had once placed himself entirely at the mercy of his favourite Malik Kafur, Mubarak Shah now came to depend exclusively upon his own slave-officer Khusrau Khan, who treacherously put him to death on April 20, 1320, and with it the famous ruling dynasty of Alauddin Khilji came to an ignominious end. Khusrau Khan ascended the throne with the title of Sultan Nasiruddin Khusrau Shah. It is said that the usurper laid his hands on the royal household and put it to plunder; all the surviving male members of the Alai family were put to death, and the women were distributed among themselves by Khusrau Khan and his camp-followers and kinsmen. Being a Hindu convert to Islam, he had no takers among the foreign Muslim nobility and the *mullas*, and he let loose a reign of terror to establish his dominance but met with a rebuff from most of the military commanders and the provincial governors. Ghazi Malik, the governor of Dipalpur and the grand old stalwart of the sultanate, bluntly refused to recognise Khusrau Khan as the Sultan, and called upon the other Turkish nobles to take up arms against him. As the rule of non-Turkish Indian Muslims was not acceptable to the Turkish nobility and the foreign Muslim aristocracy, his appeal had a profound effect, and, within a short span of time, a number of Turkish nobles rallied under the banner of Ghazi Malik with their contingents. Their combined forces marched upon Delhi to wrest it from the hands of Khusrau Khan. The latter was defeated and fled from the battlefield but was captured and beheaded on September 6, 1320; his reign lasted four months and a half. The victors re-occupied the imperial capital without any resistance. The supporters of Khusrau Khan were 'diligently traced out. They were charged with treason and made to suffer the fate which they so richly merited'. Ghazi Malik received the congratulations of all the assembled nobles, who had joined hands with him in the overthrow of Khusrau Khan, and 'offered him the keys of the royal palace'. According to Barani, 'the old leader shrank from the burden of the kingly office, and enquired if there was any survivor of the stock of Alauddin. The nobles answered in the negative, and dwelt upon the confusion and disorder that prevailed in the empire owing to the abeyance of authority. With one voice, they appealed to him to assume the insignia of sovereignty and placed him upon the throne'; Ghazi Malik ascended the throne with the title of Ghiasuddin Tughluq Shah. Thus, within five years of Alauddin's death, all of his descendants, kinsmen and associates were wiped out, leading to the foundation of the Tughluq dynasty at Delhi. As an orthodox Muslim chronicler, Barani concludes the account of the above narrative with the remarks that 'Islam was rejuvenated and a new life came into it. The clamour of infidelity sank to the ground. Men's minds were satisfied and their hearts contented. All praise for Allah'. (*Tarikh-i-Firoze Shahi*, p. 423).

❑ ❑

6

THE TUGHLUQ DYNASTY

SECTION 1: GHIASUDDIN TUGHLUQ (1320-1325)

Introduction

The contemporary sources provide us with two standard works on the history of the Tughluq dynasty, bearing the same title, *Tarikh-i-Firoze Shahi*; the one was written by Ziauddin Barani and the other by Sham-i-Siraj Afif. Both of them were accomplished historians, who adorned the courts of the Tughluq monarchs and enjoyed their royal patronage for many years in close association with each other. Afif was junior to Barani by four years, and he wrote this book long after the death of Sultan Firoze Tughluq, while Barani had traced the growth and development of the Muslim rule in Delhi from 1259 to the sixth year of Firoze Tughluq's reign. Whereas, Barani had given the most authentic critical as well as analytical account of the era of the Khilji Sultans, Afif, in his book, gives an exclusive treatment to the reign of Firoze Tughluq (1351-86), but his scholarly work, like that of Barani, is much more than a mere chronicle; 'it dwells in considerable detail on the state of the society and the common man in his reign, thus qualifying to be a total chronicle of the times'

Early Life and Accession of Ghiasuddin Tughluq

Ghazi Tughluq or Ghazi Malik, who ascended the throne of Delhi after the overthrow of Khusrau Khan in September 1320, with the title of Sultan Ghiasuddin Tughluq Shah, was a man of humble origin. According to the Muslim chroniclers, the word Tughluq was of an obscure origin as it did not form the name of any reputed clan or tribe of the Turks. It is now held that Ghazi Malik belonged to the community of 'Qarauna Turks', who inhabited the mountainous region 'between Sindh and Turkistan'; they were the people of a mixed ethnic stock, being the descendants of Turkish or Mongol fathers and non-Turkish mothers.

Nothing is known about the early life of Ghazi Tughluq. According to Firishta, his father was a Turkish slave of Balban, and his mother was a Jat (Hindu) woman from the Lahore region of the Punjab. He had three sons, Tughluq, Rajab and Abu, the eldest of whom was destined to lay the foundation of a ruling dynasty at Delhi, known after his name. Tughluq thus seems to be the personal name of Ghazi Malik or Ghazi Tughluq, and it did not refer to any family or clan of the Turks. Firishta correctly records that his original name was 'Qutlugh', which was vulgarised into 'Tughluq'. Accordingly, because of his parentage, Ghazi Tughluq typified in his character the salient features of the two races: the modesty and mildness of the Hindus and the virility and vigour of the Turks'. The three brothers came to Delhi during the Khilji regime and started their career as ordinary troopers. Tughluq was on the personal staff of Ulugh Khan, the younger brother of Alauddin; and he served his master in Multan and Sindh. He came into limelight as the bold and courageous warrior during the siege of Ranthambhor, and was promoted as *amir-ul-khail* or 'master of the horse'. After the death of Ulugh Khan, Tughluq joined the royal guards and earned reputation as a capable military officer in the wars against Mongols. At the time of Alauddin's death, he was the governor of Dipalpur and 'warden of the marches', who stood as a bulwark against the Mongol invasions. Ibn Battuta writes that he had seen an inscription of Ghazi Malik in the *Jama Masjid* of Multan, which ran as follows:

'I have fought twenty-nine battles with the Tatars (Mongols), and have defeated them. Hence, I have been named Malik-ul-Ghazi' -viz., leader of the Islamic crusaders in their fight against the infidels'.

Ghazi Malik was one of the most powerful and reputed military officers of Alauddin 'who kept himself aloof from the politics of the imperial court, and stuck to his post as faithful servant of the crown irrespective of who wielded power in Delhi'. During the reign of Qutubuddin Mubarak Shah, the name of Ghazi Malik was heard in the corridors of power at Delhi as the well-wisher of the Alai regime, who persuaded Ainul Mulk Multani and many others to rally to the support of the young Sultan after the fall of Malik Kafur. He played a leading role in the overthrow of Khusrau Khan, and, as all the male descendants of Alauddin Khilji had been done away with, the victorious military officers unanimously selected him to be their king. The coronation ceremony of Ghiasuddin Tughluq was performed with great pomp and show on the 7th or 8th of September 1320.

Ghiasuddin Tughluq as Ruler

The Sultanate of Delhi lay in shambles at the time of accession of Ghiasuddin Tughluq. The first priority of his reign, therefore, was to restore law and order and win the confidence of the Muslim nobles as well as the people at large as a competent ruler. He suppressed the supporters of Khusrau Khan and inducted many of his trusted followers in the ministry but took care to accord a liberal treatment towards the kinsmen and faithful associates of Alauddin's family and the other senior military commanders and bureaucrats, who were assigned offices of honour and importance according to their respective merit, of course. Most of the administrative officers and military officers were confirmed in their old assignments. As a result, the armed personnel were satisfied and the administration was put on the even keel.

Of the new entrants into the arena of state politics and administration may be mentioned the names of Malik Shadi Khan, a son-in-law of the Sultan, who was entrusted the charge of the *diwan-i-wizarat*; and two of his nephews, Malik Asaduddin and Malik Bahauddin, who became the *naib barbak*—'the deputy grand usher', and *ariz-i-mamalik* or 'muster-master or minister of the army' respectively. An old officer of Alauddin Khilji, named Bahram Aiba, who, like Ghiasuddin himself, had stood his ground firmly as the well-wisher of the Alai family, was formally addressed as 'the brother of the Sultan', and entrusted the governorship of Multan and Sindh with the title of Kishlu Khan. Malik Tajuddin Jafar received appointment as the *naib-i-ariz* or 'the deputy minister of the army' along with the governorship of Gujarat, while Kamaluddin, the old *qazi-ul-quzat*, viz., the chief justice of the empire, was confirmed in his office and conferred the title of *sadr-i-jahan*. At the same time, the capital of Delhi received its new *kotwal* in the person of Malik Burhanuddin and the reputed *mulla* Shamasuddin took over as the chief *qazi* of the metropolis.

Sultan Ghiasuddin had five grown-up sons, Jauna Khan, Bahram Khan, Zafar Khan, Mahmud Khan and Nusrat Khan. To begin with, none of them was given any administrative assignment though all of them were accorded high-sounding titles and dignified status in the royal court; his eldest son, Muhammad Jauna Khan, a promising young military officer, was honoured with the title of Ulugh Khan and entrusted a military command. Thus flanked by a host of young and old Muslim nobles, Ghiasuddin commenced his reign as mature administrator and capable ruler. He saved the tottering Sultanate of

Delhi from chaos and revived the memories of Balban and Alauddin Khilji, *sans* their autocracy and the aggressive blood and iron policies. Ghiasuddin took the entire royal family of Alauddin Khilji and his kinsmen under royal protection. All the surviving ladies of the Alai household were granted adequate pensions and restored their royal dignity and honour; the young girls were married to the responsible officers of dignity and status.

Ghiasuddin Tughluq gave a decent burial to all the fiscal reforms and economic regulations of Alauddin Khilji once and for all times to come. All those who had suffered during the previous regimes, including that of Alauddin Khilji, were suitably rehabilitated; and the *jagir* system, as revived by Mubarak Shah, was perpetuated to win the confidence of the Muslim aristocracy. The system of measurement of land for the purpose of determining the land revenue was also discarded and the elaborate land revenue establishment of Alauddin Khilji was done away with. Ghiasuddin encouraged agricultural production by relaxing the stringent state measures for the fixation of land revenue and its collection. The state demand was much reduced and the cultivators were encouraged to bring the unreclaimed lands under the plough. A principle was laid down that the *diwan-i-wizarat* should not enhance the land revenue demand beyond one-tenth or one-eleventh of the estimated produce at a time, in any year, to avoid hardships to the cultivators. Similarly, the harsh methods adopted by Alauddin's regime to collect the land revenue were also discarded. Ghiasuddin Tughluq was the first Muslim ruler of Delhi who took some interest in the construction of canals for irrigation. As a result, a lot of waste land was brought under the plough. The peasants were given relief in the seasons of drought. This sympathetic attitude of Ghiasuddin towards the peasant proprietors increased agriculture and enhanced the actual collection of revenues in cash as well as kind by the state. Nevertheless, from Barani's account it appears that all sections of the people were not treated alike; he records that 'some sections of the people (read Hindus) were to be so taxed that they might not be blinded with wealth and so become discontented and rebellious; nor, on the other hand, be so reduced to poverty and destitution as to be unable to pursue their husbandry'.

Ghiasuddin Tughluq paid attention to improve the general tone of the administration to make it more effective. The law and order machinery in and around the capital was overhauled, and the judicial organisation was also strengthened. The restoration of peace and order led to increase in trade and commerce also. Ghiasuddin Tughluq levelled and broadened the highways connecting the various big towns, which had been thrown into neglect by the state since the death of Alauddin. He further improved the means of communication by clearing forests and provided transit facilities to the caravans without imposing any additional financial burden upon the travelling merchants or the *Banjaras*. The Sultan revived the postal services of Alauddin's times also; and 'the posts were carried by runners and horsemen', who were so stationed at short distances along the highways that 'the news travelled at the rate of one hundred miles a day'.

Ghiasuddin Tughluq 'made his court more austere than it had ever been except probably in the time of Balban'. He acted with moderation and wisdom and always maintained the dignity of the crown in his dealings with his officers and the foreign visitors. Amir Khusrau (c. 1252-1325), the celebrated poet laureate of early medieval India, who had adorned the courts of all the Sultans of Delhi since the days of Balban, was now in his seventies, and was nearly of the age of Ghiasuddin Tughluq. He was held in the highest esteem by the Sultan, and occupied a very respectable position in his court as his friend, philosopher and guide. According to Barani, he received from the court a pension of one thousand *tankas* per month. Both of them, Sultan Ghiasuddin as well as Amir Khusrau, died in the year 1325, though it is not certain who preceded whom. As quoted by Barani in his *Tarikh-i-Firoze Shahi* (p. 230), 'the excellence of his government is said to have inspired this verse of Amir Khusrau':

He never did anything that was not replete
with wisdom and sense.
He might be said to wear a hundred doctors'
hoods under his crown.

Foreign Policy of Ghiasuddin

As capable military general, Ghiasuddin Tughluq was also an imperialist by instinct. Because of his advanced age, he felt handicapped in organising military expeditions under his personal command but he possessed the insatiable hunger for military adventures, and was eager to reclaim all those territories of south India over which Alauddin Khilji had once established his sway.

First Expedition to Warrangal (1321): The Kakatiya ruler, Pratap Rudra Deva II of Telingana, had stopped the payment of tribute to Delhi during the weak rule of Mubarak Shah Khilji. Therefore, soon after securing his position on the throne, Ghiasuddin sent an expedition to Warrangal, the capital of Telingana, under the command of the crown prince Jauna Khan, now styled as Ulugh Khan. The fort of Warrangal was besieged but 'the Hindus mustered strength to fight against the forces of Islam'. A fierce battle raged between the rivals in which large numbers of combatants were slain on both sides. Hard-pressed, the Rai sued for peace on the old terms but Jauna Khan haughtily rejected his appeal and, instead, demanded his unconditional surrender. Meanwhile, the guerilla fighters of Telingana disrupted the postal services of the invaders, and cut off their communications with Delhi. According to Barani, 'very nearly a month had passed since any couriers had arrived from the Sultan, although the Khan had previously received two or three letters every week. This want of intelligence from the court caused some uneasiness in the minds of the Khan and his officers', and a rumour spread that the aged Sultan had died. It resulted in large-scale desertions from the rank and file of the imperial army, and compelled Jauna Khan to raise the siege. He retreated in panic from Telingana with heavy losses in men and material. The prince came to know of the truth at Devagiri, however, and promptly hauled up some of the mischief-mongers of his camp, and sent them as captives to Delhi. Badly shaken, Jauna Khan hastened to Delhi to offer his apologies to the Sultan for the failure of his campaign, and was pardoned, but the rumour-mongers and conspirators were hauled up and executed; according to Barani, two of their ringleaders 'were impaled alive (*zindah bardar kardan*), and their wives and children were thrown under the feet of elephants'.

Second Expedition to Warrangal (1323-24): Failure of the expedition to the Deccan rankled in the mind of the Sultan. Therefore, within four months of his return to Delhi in 1323, the crown prince was ordered to lead the second expedition to Warrangal with a larger and well-equipped army but via Bihar. Jauna Khan overran the territories of some independent Hindu principalities in Bihar on his way to Warrangal. The border fortress of Bider in Telingana was stormed and captured by the army of invasion before Warrangal was reached and put under siege once again. The Hindus fought desperately but failed to take their stand for a long time, and 'Rai Laddar Deo (Pratap Rudra Deva II), with all his *rais* and *mukaddims,* their wives and children, elephants and horses, fell into the hands of the victors'. A dispatch of victory was sent to Delhi, and there were great rejoicings in the imperial capital. The Rai was sent as captive, with his family, and all the spoils of Telingana to Delhi, and the Kakatiya kingdom was declared annexed to the Sultanate; the name of Warrangal being changed to Sultanpur. The rule of the Kakatiya dynasty thus came to an end, and the territories of Telingana were parcelled out into small districts, each under the charge of a Muslim officer.

On his way back to Delhi, Jauna Khan overran and subjugated the Hindu state of Utkala in Orissa (Jajnagar of the Muslim chroniclers) also, and returned to the capital with a huge booty, including immense wealth, war elephants and thousands of horses.

Repulsion of the Mongols (1323): Before Jauna Khan returned to the capital after the conquest of Telingana, the Mongol hordes made their appearance on the northwestern frontiers of India. On the receipt of intelligence, Ghiasuddin at once sent a royal army under the command of Malik Shadi Khan to reinforce the border contingents at Samana, and the entire region from Delhi to the Salt Range was transformed into an army camp. According to Isami, the Mongols were defeated and repulsed although Firishta has to say that they were bought off.

The success of Malik Shadi Khan, his son-in-law, encouraged the Sultan to utilize his services for the reconquest of Gujarat, which had asserted its independence during the weak rule of Mubarak Shah Khilji. The expedition proved abortive, however, as Shadi Khan was killed by the rebels through a stratagem, and the badly mauled royal army returned to the capital in shambles.

Foundation of Tughluqabad—the new Township of Delhi: Just as Alauddin Khilji had built the fort and royal palaces of Siri, Ghiasuddin Tughluq thought of constructing yet another stronghold and the royal abode for himself at a distance from the old Hindu township and the Muslim enclaves of the earlier Sultans, for reasons of safety, of course. Situated to the east of the Qutub complex, it was named Tughluqabad. The selection of the venue and construction of the fortress capital of Tughluqabad was undertaken by Ghiasuddin immediately after his accession to the throne, and the fort and its township had become a reality a little before he received the news about the conquest of Telingana by Jauna Khan. Tughluqabad was a sort of fortified town, built on a hill top and protected by its own double or triple defensive walls. Quadrangular in shape, measuring about 2,000 metres on each side, and overlooking the entire Yamuna belt because of its elevation from the ground level, the township contained within it a magnificent royal palace and numerous other mansions of nobles and the Muslim aristocracy. According to Ibn Battuta, 'here were Tughluq's treasures and palaces, and the great palace that he built of gilded bricks, which when the sun rose, shone so dazzlingly that none could gaze at it steadily. There he laid up great treasures, and it was related that he constructed there a cistern (an underground reservoir for rainwater), and had molten gold poured into it so that it became one solid mass, and his son Muhammad Shah (Muhammad bin Tughluq) became possessed of all of it, when he succeeded him'. (*Kitab-ur-Rehla*; Eng. Trs. by A. Mahdi Husain). The township was surrounded by sharply sloping walls, made of huge irregular stones and having colossal circular bastions at close intervals, heavy battlements and a series of loopholes, which created an impression of great strength and solidarity. All of these building, except the massive outer walls of the township, now lie in ruins but it has rightly been said that 'few strongholds of antiquity look more imposing in their ruins than the town of Tughluqabad'.

Ghiasuddin Tughluq, 'the soldier Sultan', had built a mausoleum for himself, in red-sandstone with inlays of white marble, beneath the walls of the city. It was connected with the city by a bridge, carried on arches, and has survived the wears and tears of time, however. It is surrounded by a huge dome of marble, and the entire structure is enclosed by a battlemented sloping wall with a massive bastion at each corner, thus giving it the shape of a fortress.

Expedition to Bengal: The reverses on the warfront in Gujarat did not dampen the spirits of the old Sultan, however, and he stuck to his imperial pursuits all through his life. Bengal had become independent during the governorship of Bughra Khan, the second son of Balban. In 1322, after the death of Shamsuddin Firoze Shah, a descendant of Bughra Khan, there started a fratricidal war among his four sons for the possession of the throne. It provided an opportunity to Ghiasuddin Tughluq to to organise an expedition to Bengal under his personal command. He left for Bengal at the head of a large army, leaving Delhi under the charge of a council of regency, headed by the crown prince Jauna Khan, while his second son Bahram Khan accompanied the royal guards. A fugitive Bengali prince Nasiruddin joined the royal camp on the borders of Tirhut (Mithila) to fight against his rivals. On the orders of the Sultan, Bahram Khan and Nasiruddin marched on Lakhnauti; the town was captured after a fierce battle and its ruler Ghiasuddin was taken prisoner. Thereafter, the whole of Bengal was overrun by the royal forces. Pleased by Nasiruddin's services, the Sultan installed him as a vassal of Delhi at Lakhnauti, and the rest of Bengal was declared annexed to the Sultanate.

On his way back to Delhi, Ghiasuddin Tughluq led an expedition into the Hindu state of Mithila (Tirhut) in 1324-25; its ruler, Raja Harisimha Deva was defeated in an open battle but retreated into Nepal without offering submission to the Sultan. The fort of Tirhut was reached with great difficulty and put under siege but could not be conquered by the Muslim forces. According to Isami, the Sultan left his military general, Ahmad son of Talbaga, to carry on the siege and himself returned to Delhi. His commander took possession of the plains of Tirhut but failed to conquer the fort and returned to the capital after suffering a heavy loss in men and material; that is why Barani and other contemporary historians attach little importance to it.

Death of Ghiasuddin Tughluq (1325): Elated with victory, Ghiasuddin Tughluq returned from Bengal, heavily laden with booty, including a large number of horses, elephants and prisoners of war as slaves. On his triumphant return to the capital sometime in February or March 1325, the crown prince held a grand reception for his father at Afghanpura, near Delhi. He had constructed a huge wooden pavilion under which, the Sultan was received and entertained to a gala party. After the feast, the Sultan was requested by the prince to have a review of the elephants, brought by him from Bengal. As the elephants marched past the venue, the wooden pavilion collapsed suddenly, and Ghiasuddin Tughluq, along with about half a dozen other dignitaries, including prince Mahmud Khan, were crushed to death under the debris. Barani and Firishta regard his death accidental although Ibn Battuta and some other contemporary writers hold the crown prince Jauna Khan guilty of a conspiracy to kill the Sultan. According to them, the hastily constructed massive wooden pavilion was so designed as to crumble under their heavy weight, when trampled over by the elephants. Most of the modern historians subscribe to the second view and hold Jauna Khan responsible for the death of his father; he ascended the throne at Tughluqabad without any opposition with the title of Sultan Muhammad bin Tughluq.

Ghiasuddin Tughluq was a brilliant military general and successful ruler. An old servant of the Alai regime, he emerged as the saviour of the Sultanate of Delhi when it faced a sudden eclipse after the death of Alauddin Khilji. He was a man of character and integrity and did not suffer from the princely vices of his age. Unlike Alauddin Khilji,

Ghiasuddin Tughluq 'generated liberal tendencies in civil administration, and worked sincerely for the happiness and prosperity of his subjects according to the religious and moral standards of his times'. Though a devout Muslim and committed imperialist, ever eager to consolidate and strengthen the Islamic state of Delhi, Ghiasuddin was not very ambitious or power-hungry and ruled with moderation and dignity. His unnatural death was mourned by the Muslim nobility and populace of Delhi.

SECTION 2: MUHAMMAD TUGHLUQ (1325-1351)

Early Career and Accession

Sultan Ghiasuddin Tughluq was succeeded by his eldest son, Fakhruddin Muhammad Jauna Khan, designated variously as Muhammad Tughluq, Muhammad bin Tughluq or simply Muhammad Shah. He was the most highly educated of all the preceding Sultans of Delhi. Strangely enough, although we have a fairly detailed account of his accomplishments as prince and the important events of his reign from the hands of reputed contemporary chroniclers, none of them gives his exact dates of birth, accession and even the accurate chronology of his major projects and other controversial issues of his reign. The son of a self-made man and accomplished military general, Jauna Khan was brought up as an educated youngman, with proficiency in Persian as well as Arabic, and scholarly grounding in the secular subjects of astronomy, mathematics, medicine, philosophy and logic. A lover of fine arts and a poet of sorts, Jauna Khan was an adept in the art of calligraphy, which, in the absence of the printing press, was regarded as an accomplished scholarly trait by the medievalists. He was also imparted military training in horse riding and soldiery, and was enrolled as soldier when he was still in his teens. Jauna Khan lived an austere life like his father; and as a devout Sunni Muslim, he offered daily prayers regularly and abstained from drinking in public, though 'he was not unrelenting bigot like some of his predecessors'.

Jauna Khan was promoted as 'master of the horse' by Mubarak Shah Khilji; and confirmed in his assignment by Khusrau Shah, but he deserted his patron, and secretly apprised Ghazi Malik, then the governor of Dipalpur, of all about the manipulations of the usurper in the capital, and helped his father in bringing about his fall. Three days after the death of his father, the crown prince ascended the throne at Tughluqabad, and forty days later, he arrived at Delhi in state, where his coronation ceremony was held at the well-furnished and profusely renovated Red Palace of Balban amidst great rejoicings, accompanied by lavish feasting. According to Dr. Ishwari Prasad, 'no revolution, no palace intrigue, and no gubernatorial or popular insurrection marred the smoothness of his accession to the throne. The city was adorned and the streets were strewn with flowers. Money was thrown broadcast among the people, and to commemorate the auspicious occasion, large and generous gifts were made to loyal officers of the crown. The fame of his liberality travelled far and wide, and brought to Delhi learned and pious men, who were fitly honoured by their royal benefactor. Men's memories are proverbially short, and before the outflow of this generosity, the catastrophe which had befallen the late Sultan was completely forgotten, and in the minds of many the prince was perhaps, acquitted of all guilt'. (Medieval India, i, *loc cit*; p. 265).

Muhammad bin Tughluq—'a mixture of opposites'?

Muhammad Tughluq was exceptionally a lucky person to have inherited a vast empire from his father in which peace and tranquillity prevailed everywhere. He commenced his reign with great fanfare, and the Muslim nobility as well as the people of Delhi had great expectations from him. Worthy son of a worthy sire, he was unquestionably the ablest and the most learned of all the Muslim monarchs of early medieval India. Barani records that, 'in the calligraphy of books and letters, Sultan Muhammad abashed the most accomplished scribes...He knew by heart, a good deal of Persian poetry, and understood it well...No learned or scientific man, or scribe, or poet, or wit, or physician could have had the presumption to argue with him about his own special pursuits, nor would he have been able to maintain his position against the throttling arguments of the Sultan...He was an eloquent and profoundly learned scholar, a veritable wonder of creation, whose abilities would have taken by surprise such men as Aristotle and Asaf'. With these qualities of head and heart, he was expected to do better than the earlier Sultan of Delhi. Like Alauddin Khilji, he was also a great imperialist, and was eager to extend his sway over the whole of the Indian subcontinent. But he was an abstract thinker and idealist and not a practical statesman and administrator, who could comprehend the ground realities and see through the feasibility of the innovative administrative measures or the projects conceived by him for the extension and consolidation of his empire or the improvement of his administration. Accordingly, most of the projects launched by him failed to produce the desired results and earned for him the ridicule of his people.

Of all the good or bad Sultans of Delhi, Muhammad Tughluq was perhaps 'the most grossly misunderstood monarch'. The contemporary chroniclers, like Barani, Isami and Ibn Battuta, all misunderstood him and adopted a highly prejudicial outlook in making an assessment of his character and state policies. In his qualities of head and heart, or in his state policy and its applications in practice, he was alleged to be possessed of wide contradictions, and was dubbed as 'mixture of opposites'. Barani, who was the most competent scholar to give an objective and truthful account of his reign, was so much obsessed with the innovative character of his reputed 'five projects' and their failure, that he did not care to record even the important events of his rule in chorological order, which was the primary function of an historian.

Likewise, Ibn Battuta, the Arab traveller, who had enjoyed state patronage under him as the chief *qazi* of Delhi for eight years before suffering dismissal and imprisonment on charges of corruption, also gives a subjective assessment of his character 'as a man, who above all others, is fond of making presents and shedding blood. There may always be seen at his gate some poor person becoming rich or some living one condemned to death. His generous and brave actions, and his cruel and violent deeds, have obtained notoriety among the people. In spite of this, he is the most humble of men, and the one who exhibits the greatest equity. The ceremonies of his religion are dear to his heart, and he is very severe in respect of prayer and the punishment which follows its neglect'. (E&D, iii, pp.611-12). The Sultan was thus made out 'a mixture of opposites' but he was not really so. Of course, 'he was, like all other medieval despots, subject to great paroxysms of rage, and inflicted the most brutal punishments upon those who offended against his will, irrespective of the rank or order to which they belonged', but he was not a born tyrant, taking delight in the shedding of human blood for nothing. He was not an epileptic, and none of the contemporary writers has recorded even a single incident in which the Sultan inflicted punishment under fit of madness or without any rhyme or reason. As a matter of fact, the charge of blood-thirstiness was bolstered up by the bigoted Muslim fundamentalists whom the Sultan treated with open disregard.

The Mongol Invasion (1325)

As described earlier, the Mongols had invaded India during the reign of Ghiasuddin Tughluq in 1323, when Muhammad bin Tughluq, as the crown prince, was busy in the conquest of Telingana far away from Delhi. They were defeated and repulsed by Ghiasuddin but continued to hover around the northwestern frontier, and renewed their attack after the change of regime in Delhi. Just when Muhammad Tughluq ascended the throne and was striving to consolidate his rule, he received the intelligence about the Mongol invasion on Sindh; the leader of this onslaught was Tarmashirin, the Chaghatai ruler of Transoxiana. To the good fortune of the youthful Sultan, his father had already made adequate arrangements for the defence of the Sultanate, and 'the entire region from Delhi to the Salt Range had been transformed into an army camp'. Moreover, by this time, Tarmashirin and his followers had entered the fold of Islam, and were no more pagans to be dealt with harshly according to the tenets of Islam. Isami writes that Muhammad Tughluq defeated and repulsed the Mongols without much difficulty although Firishta records that they were bought off. Anyway, it was the first and the last foreign invasion that India faced during the reign of Muhammad Tughluq.

The Earlier Revolts (1326-27)

Muhammad bin Tughluq faced the first rebellion from a disaffected Turkish noble in the person of Bahauddin Gurshasp, a cousin of Ghiasuddin Tughluq (a son of his sister) who exercised considerable influence in the Deccan. The Sultan sent an army under the command of a reputed military general, Ahmad Ayaz, entitled Khwaja-i-Jahan, to crush the revolt, and himself also reached Devagiri to exert pressure on the neighbouring chiefs to support the royal army. Gurshasp suffered a defeat somewhere to the south of the Godavari River and took shelter with the Hindu ruler of Kampila, a town in the Tungbhadra valley, situated at a distance of about fifteen kilometres from the ruins of Vijayanagar.

The royal forces went in hot chase of Gurshasp to Kampila. The Rai of Kampila and the rebellious Turkish officer were defeated in an action but both of them escaped alive from the battlefield. The fort of Kampila was reduced after a siege that lasted about two months. The Rai fell fighting in a battle against the imperial army at Anegundi but Gurshasp was captured and brought in chains to Delhi, where he was flayed alive, and many of his friends and family members were inflicted severe punishments on the orders of the Sultan. All the eleven sons of the Rai of Kampila embraced Islam to save their lives, and some of them were enrolled in the royal guards. It was a great victory of Muhammad bin Tughluq at the very outset of his reign.

During his stay at Devagiri, Muhammad Tughluq was informed that Nag Nayak, the Rana of a small Hindu principality of Kondana (modern Singhgarh), situated near Poona, had stopped paying tribute to Delhi and showed signs of disaffection. The Sultan immediately sent a contingent of the royal army to chastise the rebel. The fortress of Kondana was besieged and taken after a prolonged siege that lasted about eight months. The Rana offered his submission and was allowed to retain his principality on payment of a huge war indemnity and the promise to pay enhanced annual tribute in future.

While at Devagiri, the Sultan came to know that Bahram Aiba, entitled Kishlu Khan, the viceroy of Multan, Uchh and Sindh, an old associate of Gurshasp, had lodged a strong protest against the inhuman treatment meted out to the rebellious Muslim noble by him, which was against the tenets of Islam. Muhammad bin Tughluq took his protest seriously, and hastened back to the capital to take stock of the situation. He mustered a strong army and proceeded towards Multan without any loss of time. Kishlu Khan was defeated and killed in fierce battle near Abohar, and the Sultan took possession of Multan without any opposition and returned to Delhi after making suitable arrangements for the governance of these frontier provinces.

The Visionary Projects of Muhammad bin Tughluq

Muhammad bin Tughluq was a great visionary. Just as Alauddin Khilji was once seized of the problem of revolts in the very beginning of his reign, and had arrived at his own conclusions to find ways and means for the suppression of these revolts; the youthful and energetic Tughluq Sultan was also put to thinking about similar problems that he faced in the revolt of Gurshasp in the Deccan. Like Alauddin, Muhammad Tughluq was also a great imperialist and a capable and enthusiastic military general, who was eager to consolidate the imperial gains of his predecessors. The political and administrative problems faced by him were also the same as those of Alauddin Khilji; these were - protection of the imperial capital from foreign invasions, suppression of internal revolts and the problem of exercising effective control over the outlying provinces of the state, besides the sufficient financial resources to meet the expenditure on the imperial army and to strengthen the infrastructure of the state. Alauddin was an unabashed political murderer, who had usurped the throne and held it illegally by wiping out all opposition as a tyrant. As a semi-literate political wizard, with an aggressive and unscrupulous character, he devised his own ruthless means to tackle these problems. Muhammad Tughluq, on the other hand, stood on a different level, however. Though alleged to be a subtle political murderer, he was the rightful claimant to the throne, and his accession was universally approved by the Muslim nobility and hailed by all and sundry. To his good fortune, he was much better placed than Alauddin Khilji as youthful sovereign, committed to uphold the banner of Islam and strengthen the Sultanate of Delhi. Being an intellectual and philosophical thinker, however, he was an idealist and a visionary who conceived innovative ways for the expansion and perpetuation of the Muslim rule in India. As luck would have it, his lofty designs and ambitious projects were beyond the comprehension of the Muslim bureaucracy and his subjects. He conceived his projects with the best of his intentions but his way to accomplish his half-baked schemes in a hurry, and without taking his ministers and bureaucrats into confidence, misfired; his officers were confused as they neither understood the significance of the Sultan's measures nor knew how to execute them properly. Likewise, the people at large were also surprised and puzzled by his 'hare-brained schemes'; they suffered and refused to cooperate with the state officials whole-heartedly in the successful execution of these projects. As observed by Stanley Lane-Poole, Muhammad Tughluq's 'idea of a central capital, and his plan of a nominal token currency, like most of his schemes, were good; but he made no allowance for the native dislike of innovations, and hurried his novel measures without patience for the slow adoption of the people, and when they grew discontented and rebelled, he punished them without ruth. To him what seemed good must be done at once, and when it proved impossible or unsuccessful, his disappointment reached the verge of frenzy, and he wreaked his wrath indiscriminately upon the unhappy offenders, who could not keep pace with his imagination. Hence with the best intentions, excellent ideas, but no balance or patience, no sense of proportion, Muhammad Tughluq was a transcendent failure. His reign was one long series of revolts, savagely repressed; his subjects, whom he wished to benefit and on whom he lavished his treasure, grew to loathe him; all his schemes came to nothing, and when, after twenty-six years, he died of a fever on the banks of the Indus, he left a shattered empire and an impoverished and rebellious people'. (*Medieval India*; *loc. cit*; pp. 124-25).

Muhammad Tughluq's projects were beyond the comprehension of the contemporary chroniclers either, and accordingly, instead of tracing the genesis of his visionary plans or analysing the causes of their failure, they unanimously harp on the untold sufferings of the people and the ruthless persecutions of the Sultan. A brief account of his major projects is given below.

1. Transfer of the Capital (1326-27): The first visionary project of Muhammad Tughluq was the change of his imperial capital from Delhi to Devagiri, which was renamed as Daulatabad. The plausible reasons for undertaking such a grandiose project by the Sultan need a careful analysis. To our mind, Muhammad Tughluq, as a great visionary, believed in the political unity of the Indian subcontinent, and as imperialist, he aspired to bring it under the effective control of a central authority. Barani's only explanation in support of the Sultan's project was that Daulatabad 'held a central position', and Firishta refers to its strategic importance as it was more centrically located than Delhi. Of course, this plan was conceived by Muhammad Tughluq during his frequent visits to Devagiri in the course of his military campaigns, first as the crown prince during the reign of his father, when he undertook two military expeditions for the conquest of Telingana, and then in the beginning of his rule when his army was engaged in the suppression of the revolt of Bahauddin Gurshasp. He realised the strategic importance of Daulatabad as the centre of imperial power to control south India, which comprised vast territories of rich and prosperous virgin lands, inhabited by the infidels, into which the armies of Islam could transgress with immunity and lay their hands at its immense wealth. The importance of south India, governed by a fragile Hindu polity, consisting of mutually hostile feudal monarchies, had become the centre of attraction and proved an invaluable treasure trove of gold, silver and precious stones for the Sultans of Delhi since the days of Alauddin Khilji and Malik Kafur. Daulatabad was in no way situated in the heart of the Sultanate, but it must have fascinated the Sultan with its pleasant climate, rich agricultural products and the flourishing maritime trade and commerce of Maharashtra which prompted him to make his imperial headquarters. Delhi was frequently exposed to foreign invasions but Daulatabad was free from this menace; the latter enjoyed a more strategic location and could be defended better.

Moreover, Mahdi Husain, a modern historiographer, on the testimony of *Siyar-ul-Auliya*, makes an observation that Muhammad bin Tughluq intended to solve 'the Deccan problem' by making Devagiri 'a centre of Muslim culture' through the plantation of 'a colony of the Musalmans' there. He writes: 'One of the factors controlling the situation in the Deccan was the scarcity of the Musalmans—a fact, which made it so tempting to the Hindu rulers to revolt, and so difficult for the emperor of Delhi immediately to control the situation from so great a distance. At the slightest outbreak of trouble in any part of the Deccan, either a capable general had to be sent from Delhi or the emperor himself had to march in person'. (*Tughluq Dynasty*, p. 144).

According to Firishta, when the Sultan unfolded his plan to his ministers, majority of them did not approve of it, but suggested that Ujjain was more centrally located to serve as the imperial headquarters of the Sultanate in place of Delhi, but as an autocratic and self-willed ruler, Muhammad Tughluq stuck to his project 'without carefully looking into the advantages and disadvantages on every side', and took the decision of his own to transfer the capital to Daulatabad in a hurry with the disastrous consequences.

The project was executed in two phases. To begin with, only the imperial court and the central government establishment shifted to Daulatabad in 1326-27. The ministers and military nobles 'moved but grudgingly' while the cream of the Muslim aristocracy, comprising the *saiyyads, sheikhs, ulema*, and the premier traders and businessmen showed disinclination to vacate Delhi, which, according to Barani, for over a century 'had grown in prosperity and rivalled Baghdad and Cairo'. It enraged the Sultan, who issued orders for the general .migration of the Muslim aristocracy of Delhi to Daulatabad; it was the second phase, and the incident took place about a year after the shifting of the royal court to the south. Nevertheless, it was not an *exodus en masse* of the populace of Delhi; the Hindus of Delhi, in general, were not affected by it, nor the Muslim masses were asked to migrate to the south. It were, in fact, the upper classes of the Muslim aristocracy, who were compelled to accompany the Sultan and his court to Daulatabad. Once the decision was taken, the Sultan made elaborate arrangements for the convenience of the emigrants all along the seven hundred miles (above 1100 kilometres) long *shahrah* or Trunk Road from Delhi to Daulatabad. This road had been widened and well-developed since the days of Alauddin Khilji to facilitate the movement of Muslim armies in the pursuit of his wars of aggression against the Hindu rulers of south India. On the orders of the Sultan, halting camps for the night-stay of the immigrants were setup at short distances along the road where free food, drinking water and all other amenities were made available at the state expense. All along the route, the state troops were posted and efficient arrangements for the postal and intelligence services were made for the protection of life and property of the emigrants. According to Ibn Battuta, the Sultan 'had purchased all the mansions and dwellings of those who were asked to shift to the south; they were provided free board and lodging on arrival in Daulatabad, and granted free land and other facilities for the construction of their houses and business concerns'. Barani tells us that 'the Sultan was bounteous in his liberality and favours to the emigrants, both on their journey and on their arrival' at Daulatabad.

Notwithstanding so much that Muhammad Tughluq had done to facilitate the smooth and comfortable journey of the emigrants from Delhi to Daulatabad and their rehabilitation there as privileged citizens of the Islamic state, many of them did not feel at home there, and suffered from severe hardships and mental strain. Barani records that 'they were broken-hearted. Many, from the toil of the journey perished on the road, and those who arrived at Deogir, could not endure the pain of exile. In despondency, they pined to death. All around Deogir, which is an infidel land, there sprang up graveyards of Musalmans'. In spite of the liberal patronage extended by the Sultan to the migrants from Delhi, 'they felt themselves as strangers in an infidel land, and continued to grumble against him'. They lost their confidence in Muhammad Tughluq, giving birth to a permanently disgruntled and hostile lobby of the Turkish nobles, who did not cooperate with the bureaucracy in the running of state administration smoothly. It had an adverse effect on the administration and brought a bad name to the Sultan.

Daulatabad did not prove an ideal capital for the vast Turkish empire of India, however. Being situated far away from the northwestern frontier and Bengal, it was not suitable as the base for an effective control over northern and eastern India. Moreover, the historic importance of Delhi, which was associated with the foundation of the Sultanate, could not be under-rated by the sudden change of its imperial headquarters. Muhammad Tughluq realised his folly after a few years and, probably in 1335-36, shifted his imperial court to Delhi 'without any fanfare; and general permission was granted to the emigrants to return to Delhi with full assistance from the state, if they so desired.

It is now fully established that Delhi was never discarded or neglected as the strategic political headquarters of northern India, even when the Sultan and his court functioned from Daulatabad.

Infrastructure of the state administration in Delhi was always kept intact, and its defence was never neglected. Ibn Battuta came to Delhi in 1334 and found the metropolis 'in a fairly flourishing condition'. Abbas, the author of *Masalik-ul-Absar*, an Arabic treatise, written sometime in 1336-37, records that the Islamic state of India had two capitals, Delhi and Devagiri or *Qubbatul Islam*—'the Metropolis of Islam'. 'The two cities were connected with each other by a broad and well-maintained highway. All along the route, there had been placed huge beating drums at hundreds of the posting stations, situated at short distances from each other. Whenever something special happened in a city, or when the gates of the capital, where the Sultan was not present, were opened in the morning and closed at night, the drums were beaten in rapid succession from posting station to posting station. In this manner the Sultan came to know of the opening and closing of the gates of the capital, lying at a distance of about seven hundred miles from his place of residence'. (Quoted by Mahdi Husain, *Tughluq Dynasty*, *loc. cit*; p. 145). The discovery of a few coins, minted simultaneously at Delhi and Daulatabad, during the reign of Muhammad Tughluq, and bearing the inscriptions on them as *Takhtgah-i-Delhi* and *Takhtgah-i-Daulatabad* respectively fully corroborate the version of Abbas that, while shifting his court to Daulatabad, the Sultan had never overlooked the importance of Delhi as the imperial capital of the Sultanate. About the transfer of capital from Delhi and its evacuation or ruination by Muhammad Tughluq, 'We have reasons to believe that the unprecedented project conceived by Muhammad bin Tughluq was not scrapped altogether. The original plan misfired and was universally condemned by the people essentially because of its dictatorial execution; the Sultan crippled a wise project by its hasty implementation and the use of brute force. However, notwithstanding the personal and autocratic element, which constituted a part of the general nature of medieval Indian monarchical hierarchy, the importance of Daulatabad as the second headquarters of the empire was confirmed by experience, and the original plan was modified to suit the exigencies of the times. The ancient Indian monarchs did have more than one capital to control their vast Indian dominions. Considered from this angle, Muhammad bin Tughluq made a great contribution to the concept of medieval Indian polity, and anticipated the British, who started with Calcutta as the capital, situated on the eastern fringe of the country, and subsequently developed Simla to be the second headquarters of their Indian empire'. (Advanced Study, i, pp. 202-03).

Of course, the immediate effect of Muhammad Tughluq's visionary project proved catastrophic; the state treasury was emptied; the Muslim aristocracy of Delhi were uprooted from their prized possessions and comfortable abodes, and had to suffer much in their bid for rehabilitation in the midst of a new segment of the hateful infidels, with yet another unfamiliar language and abhorrent cultural traits over whom they were expected to establish their dominance as the ruling elite. No wonder, they felt themselves as strangers in the entirely new geographical as well as socio-political environment in which they were called upon to settle down and acclimatize themselves to the new 'land of the infidels'. They rightly cursed the Sultan for having put them to great inconvenience and turned their wrath against him. As a result, Muhammad bin Tughluq lost in the estimation of his people and could never win back their confidence all through his life. Thus the bad execution of the well-conceived project resulted in the greatest personal loss to the Sultan.

Nevertheless, 'the long-range effects of this experiment proved marvellous'. It broke the socio-cultural barriers between the North and the South. A large number of the Muslim elite migrated to the South and settled down permanently there. They being the privileged citizens of the Islamic state were assigned free land grants and estates and appointed to the lucrative bureaucratic posts. As a consequence, they gradually came to acquire a dominant position among the 'native aristocracy' of the Deccan, including the Hindu converts to Islam or 'the Indian Musalmans'. The propagation of Islam among the natives received impetus and population of the Muslims beyond the Vindhyas increased considerably. Thus, south India also became the stronghold of Muslim power before long. Irrespective of whether Muhammad Tughluq had originally conceived it or not, he became indirectly responsible for the plantation of the Muslim faith and Islamic culture in the South.

2. Introduction of Token Currency (1330-32): Introduction of token currency was the second 'unprecedented' and rather 'strange' hair-brain measure of Muhammad Tughluq which baffled his contemporaries and made him a laughing stock of his nobles as well as the business community who robbed the state exchequer through the production of spurious stuff. The plan of such a modern concept, authored by Muhammad Tughluq, establishes his credibility as a very original thinker and a genius who was far ahead of his times. It is essentially a modern concept that needs no elaboration; we belong to the age of token currency in which the mere thought of calculating the intrinsic value of the material of paper notes and coins would be dubbed idiotic. That a medieval Indian monarch had conceived of such an advanced measure to revolutionize the Indian currency is really praiseworthy; it prompted Edward Thomas (*Chroniclers of the Pathan Kings of Delhi*; London, 1871) to describe him as the 'Prince of Moneyers' though the unfortunate man, for making such a novel experiment, had earned the title of a 'fool' from his subjects.

Soon after his accession to the throne, Muhammad Tughluq introduced many reforms in the prevalent currency. He fixed the relative values of gold and silver and issued new coins with the object of facilitating their exchange and circulation to promote trade and commerce. In place of the gold and silver *tankas* of the Alai regime, which weighed 175 grains each, Muhammad Tughluq introduced a gold *dinar* of 200 grains and a silver coin, called *adali,* of 140 grains. It shows that there was an abundance of gold and a relative scarcity of silver in the country about that time. The fractional currency in copper or bronze was also made available to meet the daily transactions of the masses. With the recruitment of a large standing army, territorial expansion of the empire, and increase in trade and commerce, the demand for silver to mint the coins also increased considerably. Alauddin Khilji had met this problem by fixing the salaries of his soldiers at moderate rates and state control of the prices of goods with an iron hand. Muhammad bin Tughluq refrained from reviving the Khilji horror, and, instead, met the problem of scarcity of silver by three methods. Firstly, he raised the price of silver in relation to gold. The relative value of gold and silver was reduced to the ratio of seven to one instead of ten to one which generally prevailed during the reigns of earlier Sultans. Secondly, he increased the weight of gold coins and reduced that of the silver coins. And thirdly, he conceived the novel scheme of token currency

As a well-read man, the Sultan was aware of the concept of token currency, as introduced by Kublai Khan (1260-94) of China and Gai Khatu (1293) of Persia; and he took the decision to introduce this visionary project in c.1330-31. Following their example, he ordered the minting of *tankas* of bronze, which were to be used for and at par with the silver *tankas.*

The contemporary chroniclers, who failed to comprehend the significance of the token currency, advanced varied reasons which compelled the Sultan to undertake this measure primarily to replenish the state treasury by defrauding or cheating the people. Barani, who erroneously mentions it as Muhammad Tughluq's 'third project', writes that 'the Sultan in his lofty ambition had conceived it to be his work to subdue the whole habitable world and bring it under his rule. To accomplish this impossible design, an army of countless numbers was necessary, and this could not be obtained without plenty of money. The Sultan's bounty and munificence had caused a great deficiency in the treasury; so he introduced his copper money, and gave orders that it should be used in buying and selling, and should pass current, just as the gold and silver coins had passed'. But Barani's argument that it was on account of the failure of his taxation policy in the Doab, and the subsequent famine in northern India, which emptied the state treasury, and compelled the Sultan to undertake this measure, is wrong. It is now established that the taxation in the Doab, which was treated by Barani as the very first project of Muhammad Tughluq, which was introduced in 1335-36, much after the failure of the experiment in token currency. It is, however, acknowledged by Barani and the other contemporary writers that, on the withdrawal of the token currency, 'the Sultan had paid back to the public, gold and silver coins in return for the token currency, to their full satisfaction', and thus managed a most difficult situation with astonishing success; it leads us to the conclusion that 'the financial stringency was not the reason for the introduction of token currency; on the other hand, the failure of the experiment must have resulted in the financial bankruptcy of the state'.

Muhammad Tughluq made the bronze coins as the legal tender and put them at par with the silver coins. The basic principle of his token currency was the same as that of the modern paper and metallic currency. The intrinsic value of the bronze coins was insignificant but they were issued on government credit. The scheme was on the whole quite good and statesmanlike but bad implementation led to its failure in spite of the best intentions of the Sultan. Unfortunately, Muhammad Tughluq could not adopt measures to make the mint a state monopoly, nor there was any specialized machinery to prepare the standard coins. Any goldsmith could produce as good a coin as the royal token. As observed by Edward Thomas, 'there was no special machinery to make the difference of the fabric of the royal mint and the handiwork of the moderately skilled artisan. Unlike the precautions taken to prevent the imitation of the Chinese paper notes, there was positively no check on the authenticity of the copper token, and no limit to the power of production by the masses at large'. (*Chronicles of the Pathan Kings*, p. 245).

Barani does not exaggerate the point when he says that 'the house of every Hindu was turned into a mint'; of course, as an orthodox Muslim, he condones the offences of his co-religionists. There is no shadow of doubt that the Hindus as well as Muslims, without exception, must have resorted to forgery on a large scale. In the words of Barani, they 'turned their utensils into coins, and with these they paid their tribute (taxes) and with these they purchased horses, arms and fine things of all kind. The *rais,* the village headmen and landowners grew rich and strong upon these copper coins but the state was impoverished. ...In those places, where fear of the Sultan's edict prevailed, the gold *tanka* rose to be worth a hundred of the copper *tankas.* Every goldsmith struck copper coins in his workshop, and the treasury was filled with these copper coins. So low did they fall that they were not valued more than pebbles or potsherds. The old coin, from its great scarcity, rose four-fold and five-fold in value. (*Tarikh-i-Firoze Shahi*, p. 240).

As a result, trade was interrupted on every side, and all transactions in money came to a standstill. In utter dismay, the Sultan repealed his former edict and ordered the withdrawal of token currency after it had been in use for about two years. He recalled all the token coins, exchanging each for the silver one, and the people got gold and silver in exchange for all such coins whether genuine or forged. According to Barani, 'So many of these copper *tankas* were brought to the treasury that heaps of them rose up in Tughluqabad like mountains. Great sums went out of the treasury in exchange for the copper, and a great deficiency was caused. When the Sultan found that his project had failed, and that great loss had been entailed upon the treasury through his copper coins, he more than ever turned against his subjects.' (*Ibid.*, p. 241).

It marked the end of the much-maligned visionary project of Muhammad Tughluq in the field of Token Currency. Never was so wise a measure of reform so cruelly frustrated than this experiment in token currency. The Sultan, who meant no deception, was defrauded by his own people; the state treasury was emptied and the country's economy was totally ruined. The discredited token currency having been recalled with full compensation to the subjects, all forgery was stopped and the credit of the government restored. The storm blew over, the panic ended, and the people grew rich at the cost of the state so much so that not even a murmur about the affair was heard by Ibn Battuta, who came to India shortly afterwards.

3. Visionary Plans of World Conquest: After the failure of above two major projects, when the state treasury was already in a deplorable condition, the Sultan ought to have exercised restraint in launching his wild plans of conquest, but this was not to be. It is because, ever since the days of Alauddin Khilji, a vast standing army had become a regular feature of the Islamic state, which had to be paid and kept engaged in offensive or defensive wars by the Sultans for the safety of their vast dominions and to guard against their inherent foes, the neighbouring Hindu rulers. The substantial part of the Indian subcontinent, inhabited by the infidel Hindus, was an open invitation to the Sultans to engage them in eternal strife for the extension of their dominions and the glory of Islam. Like Alauddin, Muhammad Tughluq also had the grandiose plans of new conquests. The proposed Khurasan expedition was one of them.

The Abortive Khurasan Expedition (1332-33): The Khurasan expedition was a part of international Muslim politics. Situated adjacent to the northwestern frontiers of India and Afghanistan, the country of Khurasan was included in the Persian empire of the Ilkhan Mongols. Abu S'aid, then the Mongol emperor of Persia, being a minor, this region was coveted by Tarmashirin, the Chaghatai ruler of Transoxiana as well as the Sultan of Egypt. In fact, Tarmashirin had already taken possession of Afghanistan and, in 1325-26, he invaded Khurasan but suffered an unexpected defeat at the hand of the Persian forces, and entered Sindh with 40,000 Mongol troops to establish his foothold there. The Mongol attack was repulsed, and Tarmashirin made a hasty retreat from the Indian borders. But before his return to Transoxiana, he is said to have made a friendly gesture to Muhammad Tughluq to wrest Khurasan from the hands of the Persians in a joint operation. After his return to Bukhara, the capital of Transoxiana, Tarmashirin Khan sent his son-in-law, Amir Nauroz, with a number of Mongol chiefs to the court of Muhammad Tughluq as his representatives. On the persuasion of the Sultan, they enrolled themselves in the state army, and Amir Nauroz remained in the service of the Sultanate of Delhi till the death of the Sultan in 1351. Barani records that it was on the 'instigation' of these foreign emigrants that the Sultan conceived the wild project for the conquest of 'Khurasan and Iraq' in collaboration with the rulers of Transoxiana and Egypt. Tarmashirin opened Ghazni to direct communications with Delhi for this purpose. Barani repeatedly deplores that Muhammad Tughluq spent lavishly on his diplomatic missions to Ghazni for negotiations with the kings of Transoxiana and Egypt, and formed a triple alliance with them, with the object of carving out a 'common sphere of political influence' in central Asia. The Sultan of Delhi had developed a rapport with many of Tarmashirin's local officials at Ghazni; so much so the chief *qazi* of Ghazni was said to be 'into his pay'. Accordingly, the Sultan assembled a special army of 3, 70,000 horsemen, called 'the army of Khurasan', 'on very liberal and attractive terms', which was, obviously, 'over and above the regular imperial army of Delhi and the contingents of the provincial governors'. This incident took place sometime in 1332-33.

To the bad luck of Muhammad Tughluq, this expedition had to be cancelled because of the sudden deposition of Tarmashirin Khan of Transoxiana by one of his cousins, with the support of his rebellious nobles. Simultaneously, the court of Persia restored friendly relations with the Sultan of Egypt, and Muhammad Tughluq having been isolated, had to call off the proposed expedition. In consequence, 'the Army of Khurasan' was disbanded after one year of its enrollment at a tremendous cost to the state exchequer. As observed by Dr. Ishwari Prasad, 'the expedition had little chance of success. The Muslims had hitherto encountered the disunited Hindus but to try conclusions with their co-religionists in their own native land was a task beyond the strength of the armies of Delhi at this period. It was an act of wisdom on the part of Muhammad Tughluq to abandon the scheme and to concentrate his attention upon India'. (Medieval India, p. 280).

The Qarachil Expedition (1333-34): Out of the Khurasan army, about a *lakh* of the soldiers were retained for the next Qarachil expedition, and the rest of them were disbanded. The soldiers, suddenly having been thrown out of employment, took up to loot and highway robbery and proved a source of great trouble to the people as well as the state. Firishta, who did not know the exact nature of the expedition, wrongly mentions that it was directed against China. Barani declares the Sultan's object to conquer the mountain of 'Qarajal' or 'Qarachal', which has rightly been identified by the modern writers with Kurmachil, the old name of Kumaun. It is obvious that the imperial army was sent against some of the independent Rajput states in the Kumaun-Garhwal region of the Himalayas. The Hindu princes of these hill states refused to acknowledge the imperial authority of Delhi, and usually served as the places of refuge for the rebels against the Sultanate. Khusrau Malik, a nephew of the Sultan was the commander of the Qarachil army. He was instructed by the Sultan to setup military posts all along the route through the mountains so as to keep in touch with the base camp;

these posts were intended to serve a two-fold purpose; to facilitate the transport of supplies to the army of invasion, and to serve as places of refuge in case of retreat on any account.

The initial attack of the imperial army was successful. It defeated a hostile formation of the infidels and 'conquered the fortress of *Jidya* (un-identified)) and its surrounding country at the foot of the Himalayas'. 'The treasures and lands were seized, and a written intimation of the victory was conveyed to the Sultan, who despatched a *qazi* and a *khatib* to take charge of the civil administration of the newly acquired territories'. Flushed with this initial success, Khusrau Malik marched into the mountains towards the Indo-Tibetan border, 'when his army was suddenly overtaken by ice-cold winds and rains, followed by the outbreak of plague'. The panic-stricken army begged a hasty retreat, and 'encamped in various places but the Hindus closed the passes and cut off its retreat...The mountaineers, having got the upper hand, hurled blocks of stones from the hill tops on to the retreating troops in the valley below, and the posts, established previously to safeguard the retreat, fell into disorder'. As a result, the whole of the Muslim army, including its commander, perished, and 'out of the chosen body of men', only ten horsemen, according to Barani, and three as per the narrative of Firishta, returned to Delhi to tell the tale of their misery to the frustrated Sultan, 'who immediately got them hanged'. This was the fourth wild project of Muhammad Tughluq.

The Qarachil expedition proved an utter failure, but Firishta concludes its account by making a significant statement in this connection as follows: 'After this the Sultan made peace with the inhabitants of the hills on the condition that they should pay him a certain amount; since these people held possession of the territory lying at the foot of the hills, they were unable to use it without his permission'. (Mahdi Husain, The Rehla; *loc cit*; p. 145). A few years later (1337-38), Muhammad Tughluq sent yet another expedition to the Mountains, and his army defeated and subjugated the Hindu ruler of Nagarkot (Kangra); the historic Hindu temple of Nagarkot had been plundered by Mahmud of Ghazni but this town never formed a part of the Sultanate of Delhi before.

The Fifth Project: Taxation in the Doab (1333-34)

The failure of the above four visionary projects of Muhammad Tughluq, in quick succession, must have ruined the state treasury, to replenish which, the Sultan was constrained to enhance the taxation in the Doab. Nevertheless, Barani reckons it as the very first of his wild projects, thus placing a cart before the horse. Mahdi Husain, after a careful analysis of the whole material available on the subject, has come to the conclusion that it was not the first but the last project of Muhammad Tughluq. The Sultanate had become bankrupt because of the repeated follies of its autocratic ruler; and the only alternative left with the Sultan was to device ways and means for increasing the revenues of the state. As luck would have it, because of its bad implementation, as usual, this measure also ended in smoke with disastrous effects on the fortunes of the Tughluq empire.

Unlike Alauddin Khilji, Muhammad Tughluq was very liberal in his treatment of the cultivators, and he is known to have made at least one experiment in the reclamation of barren lands and the improvement of agricultural production through rotation of crops. For this purpose, he had created a department of agriculture, called the *diwan-i-kohi*, which was managed by the agricultural experts and officials of the revenue establishment in collaboration with the peasants. The department was wound up after about three years without producing any tangible results, however; and no more is heard of Muhammad Tughluq's interest in the improvement of agriculture or reforms in the field of revenue administration as such. Taxation in Doab was not a visionary project either as Barani has attempted to show.

The arbitrary enhancement of taxes in the Doab by Muhammad Tughluq rested on two major considerations: Firstly, situated so close to Delhi, the imperial capital of the Sultanate, this region was enclosed between and irrigated by the two premier rivers of northern India, the Ganga and the Yamuna. Accordingly, its land was very fertile, and there was abundance of agricultural production, leading to the general well-being and prosperity of its peasantry. Secondly, there was concentration of the Hindu population in the Doab, and this region was notorious for the refractory and rebellious conduct of its landed aristocracy. As narrated earlier in this study, 'Alauddin had also harshly dealt with the *khuts, muqaddams*, and *balahars* of the Doab, who gave not a little trouble to the administration'. (Barani's *Tarikh-i-Firoze Shahi*, p. 291). Barani's version of the Doab episode is rather vague as he does not specify the actual increase in the prevalent rates of revenue assessment; therefore, his statements like 'the taxes were doubled' or 'increased ten or twenty timers' do not help us to visualize the true picture. Nevertheless, Barani, whose parents had settled in the district of Baran, modern Bulandshahr in the Uttar Pradesh, which suffered from the effects of this enhanced taxation, bitterly criticizes the Sultan for his cruel treatment of the peasantry of the region. All the contemporary chroniclers, without exception, record that the land revenue in the Doab was 'raised out of all proportions to the income of the people', and some oppressive *abwabs* or additional levies, such as *ghari* or 'the house tax', and *charai* or 'the pasture tax' were also imposed. Unfortunately, this measure was adopted when the northern India was engulfed in a severe famine because of the failure of rains, and the distress of the people was greatly exaggerated by its disastrous effects. In the words of Barani,

'The cesses were collected so rigorously that the *raiyats* were impoverished and reduced to beggary. Those who were rich and had property became rebels; the lands were ruined, and the cultivation was entirely arrested. When the *raiyats* in distant countries heard of the distress and ruin of the *raiyats* in the Doab; they threw off their allegiance and betook themselves to the jungles, through fear of the same evil befalling them. The decline of cultivation, and the distress of the *raiyats* in the Doab, and the failure of convoys of corn from Hindustan, produced a fatal famine in Delhi and its environs, and throughout the Doab. Grain became dear. There was a deficiency of rain, so the famine became general. It continued for some years, and thousands upon thousands of people perished of want. Communities were reduced to distress, and families were broken up. From that day, the glory of the State, and the power of the government of Sultan Muhammad, withered and decayed'. (*Ibid.*, pp.291-92)

Discontentment and Revolts against the Sultan

The enhanced taxation in the Doab, capped by the failure of his innovations and visionary schemes, in quick succession, made Muhammad Tughluq totally unpopular among his subjects as well as the Muslim bureaucracy and the military commanders. It led to widespread discontent against him throughout his dominions. The heavily-taxed peasants of the famine-affected Doab refused to pay the revenues and picked up quarrels with the tax collectors who used force for the realisation of the state dues. About the 'tug-of-war between the unimaginative Muslim bureaucracy and the peasants of the Doab', Hajji-ud-Dabir has to say that 'when the collectors treated the peasants harshly, the latter killed them. On this, the Emperor sent the *Amiran-*

i-Sadah (foreign Muslim military commanders) against them. They killed the peasants. Then the peasants seized the opportunity and killed the *Amiran-i-Sadah*. As a result, the region (of the Doab) was completely ruined'. (Quoted in Mahdi Husain, *Tughluq Dynasty*, p. 232). The Sultan realised his folly but he was too late in the enforcement of remedial measures. He ordered the collection of revenue to be suspended and the liberal relief operations followed. The provision was made to dig wells for irrigation, and the cultivators were offered loans for the purchase of bullocks and seeds. But the corrupt and unsympathetic tax collectors continued to oppress the starving peasants for the extraction of the state dues. As a result, many of the poor peasants deserted their lands and fled into the wild for their lives; and they could not be persuaded to return to their villages and take up cultivation once again. It so appears that the bondage of goodwill and faith between the Sultan and his bureaucracy had broken completely; that is why, none of his ministers and counsellors dared to apprise the Sultan of the need to change his taxation policy in time. As a result, the Doab episode was silently merged into the general discontent and upsurge of the nobility against his unpopular rule leading to insurrections and revolts of his military generals, provincial governors, and the subordinate Hindu princes. According to Mahdi Husain, starting with an uprising in the Ma'abar or the eastern coast of the extreme southern peninsula, he faced as many as sixteen rebellions in various parts of the Sultanate till his death in 1351. The main object of all the refractory Hindu chieftains and Muslim nobles, who took up arms against Muhammad Tughluq since 1335, was to cut off relations with the imperial authority of the Sultans of Delhi, and setup as independent rulers.

Saiyyad Hasan, the governor of Ma'abar in the far south, was the first ambitious Muslim noble to take advantage of the discomfiture of Muhammad Tughluq because of the prevalent famine in northern India and the discontent of the heavily taxed peasantry of the Doab. He cut off all contacts with Delhi and defied the imperial authority. A royal army sent for the suppression of his revolt took six months to reach there but changed sides and strengthened the ranks of the rebellious chief instead. The Sultan himself marched towards the south with a large army to restore order there, but the extension of famine conditions and the outbreak of plague in his army camp at Bidar (Telingana) took a heavy toll of life of the royal soldiery. A number of his officers also fell victims to plague, and, as a result, the imperial army was badly crippled.

The Sultan too was taken ill though 'he escaped death by divine providence', and retraced his steps to Daulatabad. It gave an opportunity to Saiyyad Hasan to setup as sovereign ruler with his capital at Madura; he assumed the title of Sultan Saiyyad Ahsan Shah. After hanging on in the south for about two years, Muhammad Tughluq returned to Delhi in July 1337 to find that he had lost his control over the civil and military administration altogether. Following in the footsteps of Saiyyad Hasan, Malik Hushing, governor of Daulatabad, had revolted in 1335-36 and was replaced by Qutlugh Khan. Saiyyad Ibrahim, son of Saiyyad Hasan of Ma'abar, who held the governorship of Hansi, also raised his standard of revolt but was defeated and killed, but by that time, the insurrections had become general and the Sultan was simply unable to cope with the situation. To quote Lane-Poole, 'Piece by piece the empire dropped away. One province after another revolted, and though the Sultan was usually victorious, and punished the rebels without mercy, he could not be everywhere at the same time; and whilst one insurrection was being crushed, another sprang up at the other end of his dominions... Some of them were never suppressed, and Bengal and the Deccan were lost to the kingdom'. (*loc. cit.*, p. 137)

The rebellions of the Muslim nobles against Muhammad Tughluq were folloed by the uprisings of the Hindu princes of the south to regain their lost independence. Of the old ruling families, Krishna Nayak, son of Pratap Rudra II of Telingana, took possession of Warrangal in 1343-44 and declared his independence though his success proved to be short-lived. Similarly, Vir Ballala III, who died in 1342, and his son, Vir Ballala IV, carried on the struggle for independence in the teeth of opposition from the Sultans of Madura. Meanwhile, two enterprising brothers, Harihar and Bukka Rai, who were associated with the erstwhile ruling dynasty of Telingana, laid the foundation of the town of Vijayanagar in 1336, and carved out a small principality, which rose to become the famous Vijayanagar Empire in the times to come.

It was, however, the revolts of *Amiran-i-Sadah*—the foreign Muslim nobles in the service of the Sultanate, whose leaders held the governorships in Malwa, Gujarat and Daulatabad, particularly, which sounded the death-knell of the mighty Muslim empire of India. In desperation, Muhammad Tughluq sought sanction of the Abbasid Khalifa of Cairo (Egypt) to his title as the sovereign Muslim ruler of India; and he did receive 'the mantle and diploma of investiture' from him in 1343, but 'nothing could restore the loyalty of the people or his governors' to the discredited Sultan. The *Amiran-i-Sadah*, who had grown rich and prosperous because of the Sultan's bounties, and who held high offices of the state, became restless and entered into a sort of general understanding among themselves to throw off the allegiance to Delhi and setup as independent regional rulers. They challenged the imperial authority of Muhammad Tughluq and engaged him in a deadly struggle which lasted full ten years till the death of Muhammad Tughluq. Qutlugh Khwaja, the rebellious noble of Daulatabad, was the ringleader of the disgruntled *Amiran-i-Sadah* in the Deccan. The Sultan recalled him to the court in 1341, and ordered Nizamuddin, the governor of Gujarat, to take additional charge of Daulatabad as the viceroy of the Deccan. On the bidding of the Sultan, Aziz Khumman, the newly appointed governor of Malwa, put to death as many as 89 members of the foreign Turkish nobility through a treachery; while engaged in a state-organised get-together, 'they were suddenly caught hold of and beheaded in front of his palace with a view to terrorise others'. It led to a general uprising against Muhammad Tughluq throughout his dominions. The Sultan rushed to Daulatabad to retrieve the situation but failed to crush the revolts, led by different nobles simultaneously, and the Deccan was lost to the empire.

The end of Sultan's troubles came, when having lost all hopes of the discovery of the Deccan, Muhammad Tughluq directed his attention towards the rebellious Muslim nobility of Gujarat and Sindh. Malik Taghi, the rebellious chief of Gujarat, was defeated by the Sultan in a number of encounters and hotly pursued towards the mouth of the Indus; he took shelter with the Jam of Thatta. The Sultan stayed in Gujarat for over two years, and after restoring law and order there, marched upon Sindh to reckon with the rebellious chiefs but, on the way to Thatta, he was taken ill and died on the banks of the Indus on March 20, 1351, and so it was that 'the king was freed from the people and they from their king'. The mighty Sultanate of Delhi, which once comprised as many as 23 provinces (*iqtas*), and extended from Lahore and Delhi to Dwarsamudra and Ma'abar in the south, and from Lakhnauti and Gaur in the east to Thatta and the Indus in the west, broke up into pieces; giving place to a number of Hindu as well as Muslim regional kingdoms. The Ma'abar rebellion of the year 1335 thus comprises a watershed in the history of the Sultanate of Delhi which signalled the decline and slow disintegration of the Turkish empire of early medieval India.

An Estimate of Muhammad Tughluq

Opinions have been sharply divided about the character and personality Muhammad Tughluq. His subjects misunderstood him, the Muslim nobility and bureaucracy failed to comprehend his state policies and programmes, and the contemporary Muslim historiographers, in their confusion, were found wanting in making an objective assessment of his achievements and failures as a ruler. He was an 'unlucky monarch' but the verdict of his contemporaries, that declares him cruel and bloodthirsty tyrant, does little justice to his great genius. A scholar and soldier, Muhammad Tughluq was an idealist and a visionary who wanted to bring about radical changes in the administrative setup of the Sultanate, and as imperialist, he was ever eager to extend the Muslim sway over the whole of the Indian subcontinent. But as self-willed autocrat, he seldom cared to take the sane advice of ministers and counsellors. Over-confident of his capabilities, he formulated abstract schemes, which he executed in haste without taking into consideration the pros and cons of their implications. He failed as a ruler because he lacked discretion and knew no moderation. The visionary schemes of Muhammad Tughluq carried the seeds of modernity in the background of political unification of the country, and stability and credibility of the Muslim state to ensure its economic prosperity; but he failed to convince his people of their significance, and himself lacked the common sense and skill to implement them for the benefit of the state as well as its subjects. According to an estimate, 'the period of rule of Muhammad bin Tughluq constitutes one of the most tragic chapters in the history of early medieval India; it is a sad commentary on the self-intentioned but incompetent monarch and corrupt, selfish and short-sighted bureaucracy, who were called upon to rule the unimaginative and backward masses'. As a result, the Sultan failed as ruler and administrator and lost in the estimation of the people, particularly, the Muslim ruling elite of the country. He came to be hated and despised by them but stubbornly held out against his political adversaries and the rebellious provincial governors and the military generals till the bitter end.

SECTION 3: FIROZE TUGHLUQ (1351-1388)

Muhammad Tughluq had no male issue nor did he nominate a successor to the throne. His sudden death in the army camp near Thatta, therefore, created a crisis. The leaderless military commanders panicked and their soldiers hurriedly decamped to retrace their steps towards Delhi in disorder. A large number of the Mongol mercenaries, who had been hired by the deceased Sultan to suppress rebellions, 'assailed the royal army in front with the object of acquiring booty', while the rebels of Sindh pounced upon the baggage train of the retreating army in the rear to carry off with whatever fell into their hands. In that hour of crisis, the military commanders and Muslim saints and scholars of the royal camp, with near unanimously, decided to install Firoze Tughluq, an elderly cousin of Muhammad Tughluq, who was present in the camp, as Sultan to save the empire. Barani, who was an eye witness to all these developments, records that Firoze Tughluq had actually been nominated as his heir-apparent by the deceased Sultan. Accordingly, he was formally crowned as the king on March 23, 1351, in a simple ceremony, held somewhere on the bank of the Indus where the retreating army had halted for the night before. He immediately took command of the army and conducted it safely to the imperial capital.

The Parentage of Firoze Tughluq: Firoze Tughluq, the third great ruler of the Tughluq dynasty, was the son of Rajab, the younger brother of Ghazi Malik (Ghiasuddin Tughluq)—the founder of the dynasty. He was born of a Bhatti Rajput mother from Abohar in the Punjab in 1309. Shams-i-Siraj Afif, in the very first chapter of his book, *Tarikh-i-Firoze Shahi*, gives an account of the marriage of Rajab with the daughter of a subordinate Hindu chieftain of Ghazi Malik under coercion which throws a flood of light on the aggressive style of functioning of the Muslim ruling elite and the miserable plight of the Hindu subjects under the Sultanate of Delhi. Afif narrates the story as under:

> 'Sultan Tughluq (Ghazi Malik—then the governor of Dipalpur) thought of marrying Rajab with the daughter of any *Raja* (*Rai*) of Dipalpur. While on the lookout for such a match, some well-known person brought to his notice that the daughter of *Rai* Ran Mal Bhatti was extremely beautiful, accomplished, and embellished with every good manner. During those times, due to the design of Allah, the entire estate of the caste of Bhatti and Matra was located in the town of Abohar, which was an appendage of the administration of Dipalpur, and the forest land was also included in the same tract of the kingdom. At that time, the administration of Abohar Township was under

the charge of the great grandfather of the author (Shams-i-Siraj Afif), Malik Saad-ul-Mulk Shahab Afif. In consultation with the latter, Sultan Tughluq dispatched a few wise messengers with the marriage proposal to the court of Ran Mal. The messengers conveyed the message of Sultan Tughluq but Ran Mal responded with great pride and haughtiness and made uncharitable remarks. On coming to know of it, the Sultan consulted Saad-ul-Mulk and after great deliberation, it was decided that Tughluq should proceed to the ancestral holding of Ran Mal and demand the annual tribute in one go instead of installments. Accordingly, the next day Tughluq reached the ancestral *Jagir* of Ran Mal and demanded in cash all the tribute in one installment. All the *Chaudhries* and *Muqqadams* of the area were also summoned and put under pressure to make payment in cash in one installment at once. The tracts and territories of Ran Mal were put to great harm and the people suffered greatly. Being the reign of Alauddin Khalji, no one dared raise the standard of rebellion. Within a couple of days, the subjects of Ran Mal were fully exhausted. One truthful and reliable source himself narrated to the author that at prayer time in the evening, Ran Mal's mother, a very old woman, went to the residence of Ran Mal, crying and wailing in despair and started weeping ceaselessly. In such a situation, the august daughter of Ran Mal, i.e. the kind mother of Sultan Firoze, was standing in the courtyard. Seeing the grandmother weeping, she asked for the cause of her misery and lamentations. The mother of Ran Mal replied: "*This is due to you, and if you had not been the cause, Tughluq would not have descended to oppress our subjects.*" The truthful and reliable person had stated that on hearing the reason, the daughter replied: "*If by offering me, the troubles of the subjects can be obliterated and the calamity postponed, then accept their demand and think that Mongols had taken away one of the daughters.*" The mother went to the apartment of Ran Mal and acquainted him with what his daughter had said. Ran Mal also liked the offer and sent a message through the great grandfather of the author, accepting the marriage proposal of his daughter to Rajab. The marriage was solemnized and the bride taken to Dipalpur at an auspicious moment. The lady i.e. Firoze's mother was known as Bibi Naila before her marriage. After the marriage, she was named Bibi Kad Banu by Sultan Tughluq.'

The Accession of Firoze Tughluq

Before the arrival of Firoze Tughluq at Delhi, *Khwaja-i-Jahan,* the *wazir* (prime minister) of Muhammad Tughluq—the eighty-year old grandee of the Sultanate, who held charge of the imperial capital, had placed an infant on the throne and declared him to be the son and successor of the deceased Sultan. It created a piquant situation though the Khwaja could not be charged with treason as he was said to have done so 'in public interest just to maintain law and order' in the dominions. As Firoze Tughluq approached Delhi with the royal troops, the Khwaja hastened to offer his submission to him at Hansi. He was pardoned by the Sultan and assigned the estate of Samana to spend the rest of his life in retirement. Nevertheless, the Tughluq nobility, who had played the role of king-makers for a while, did not approve of the Sultan's action, and on their insistence, the Khwaja was put to death before he could make it to Samana. Firoze Tughluq entered Delhi without any opposition and was coronated with great pomp and show on August 25, 1351.

The Nature of His Rule

Firoze Tughluq was about 46 years old at the time of his accession to the throne. He strengthened his legal position as 'the rightful successor of Muhammad bin Tughluq' by obtaining an investiture from the *Khalifa* Al-Hakim of Egypt and assumed the title of *Naib-i-Amir-ul-Momnin*. The *Khalifa*'s name was inscribed on the coins. The accession of Firoze Tughluq was hailed by the orthodox Sunni public because 'it marked the beginning of that religious reaction, which became a prominent feature of his administrative policy.' He enjoyed a long reign of 37 years (1351-88). A poor military general and not so competent an administrator, he failed to maintain a strong and efficient army which was the backbone of the Sultanate. He was unable to utilize his long era of peace for developing the institutions of civil administration on healthy lines so as to ensure the stability of the central government and administration. By all accounts, Firoze Tughluq was 'an uncompromising bigot, who followed the straightest path of orthodoxy, and in the management of the government, employed the theocratic principles of the Quran. He observed the Holy Law with great strictness, and onthe occasion of religious festivals, behaved like a fanatic Muslim. He encouraged his 'infidel subjects' (viz., the Hindus) toembrace Islam and exempted the converts from the payment of Jaziya.

Fully in the grip of the orthodox school, he sanctioned the persecution of those whom he considered heretic or infidels'. In his memoirs, entitled, *Futuhat-i-Firozeshahi,* the Sultan, as a pious but fanatic Muslim ruler declares his state policy as under:

> 'My desire is that, to the best of my human power, I should recount and pay my thanks for the many blessings Allah has bestowed upon me, so that I may be found among the number of His grateful servants. First, I would praise Him because when irreligion and sins opposed to the Law prevailed in Hindustán, and men's habits and dispositions were inclined towards them, and were averse to the restraints of religion, He inspired me—is humble servant, with an earnest desire to repress irreligion and wickedness, so that I was able to labour diligently until, with His blessing, the vanities of the world, and things repugnant to religion, were set aside, and the true was distinguished from the false.'

The public disposition of Firoze Tughluq as a bigoted Muslim chief and 'a humble servant of Islam' did earn him the applause of the orthodox *ulema* and his Sunni camp-followers, but it did not amuse the majority of his subjects, including the *zimmis* or *kafirs* (Hindus), Shias and other liberal-minded Muslims. His policy of religious intolerance and persecution of non-Muslims and those, who did not conform to the tenets of orthodox Islam, badly marred his philanthropic activities, and his policy of peace and public welfare foundered against the rock of religious fanaticism. The evil effects of his 'poor administration, weak foreign policy and defective military organisation' began to show their ugly face before long, and the last seventeen years of his reign comprised an era of rapid decay and disintegration of the Sultanate.

Domestic Affairs

Firoze Tughluq commenced his reign on a very happy note. The people of Delhi, after having suffered a lot during the much-maligned rule of his predecessor, extended a warm welcome to him on his arrival at the imperial capital. As narrated by Afif,

> 'Firoze Shah entered the city at an auspicious moment on a fortunate day... and drums of joy were beaten all around. The whole city was decorated with all kinds of fine and pleasant buntings and (six) cupolas were erected... in the city as Firozabad had not yet been founded. Under each cupola, there were

festivities for twenty-one days, and nearly one *lakh tankas* were spent on each... The festivities were open to all, and people from various cities turned up to see the cupolas. As ordered by the Sultan, whosoever came to see the cupolas was provided free meals of his choice. Under each cupola, music and dance parties were taking place...The Sultan rewarded and showered kindness upon the entire populace from his merciful hands...(he) showered his favours like a rain cloud on the whole community, which included the high born as well as commoners, free men and slaves. The entire kingdom became a garden and the Sultan condoned all major and minor crimes...Firoze Shah's grants and obligations were so much that the amounts, due from the subjects since the times of previous Sultan were also written off.'

On the day of his coronation, he declared the appointment of a Hindu convert to Islam, named Malik Maqbul, as his *wazir* or prime minister with the title of *Khan-i-Jahan*. He belonged to an educated and well-placed Brahman family of south India, and, in his early life, was attached to the court of Raja Pratap Rudra Deva II of Telengana. His original name was Kattu or Kannu. After the conquest of Telengana in 1323-24 by Prince Jauna Khan during the reign of Ghiasuddin Tughluq, he was brought as a prisoner of war to Delhi, where he was forcibly converted to Islam and enslaved by the name of Maqbul. Nevertheless, when his captor, Prince Jauna Khan ascended the throne of Delhi styled as Muhammad bin Tughluq, he 'perceived in him (Maqbul) many marks of sagacity and intelligence' and promoted him as the *naib wazir* (deputy prime minister). At the time of the death of his patron, he held this exalted office along with the governorship of Multan when Khwaja-i-Jahan was the *wazir*. He had established his reputation as capable administrator, who 'had issued many rules and regulations to restore the health of *diwan-i-wizarat* (revenue ministry)' and was very popular among the bureaucracy of the metropolis. After the fall of Khwaja-i-Jahan, Firoze Tughluq conferred the *wizarat* on Maqbul although 'he was not one of the king-makers of the imperial camp, who had been instrumental in raising Firoze Tughluq to the throne'.

Khan-i-Jahan Maqbul rightly deserved the exalted office of the prime minister on merit. He fully justified the trust and confidence reposed in him by Firoze Tughluq, and 'the two acted in perfect harmony with each other. Whenever the Sultan went out of the capital for hunting or on military expeditions, Khan-i-Jahan deputized for him and carried on the administration with such wisdom and alacrity that the long absence of the Sultan had no adverse effect on the functioning of the central government'. He rendered a very commendable service to the crown and died at the ripe old age of eighty during the 18th year of Firoze Tughluq's reign. Afif pays the following tribute to Khan-i-Jahan:

> 'When Khan-i-Jahan grew old and attained the age of eighty, his frame and body were afflicted. The approach of death was imminent and Khan-i-Jahan experienced immense pain...When Khan-i-Jahan died, all people in Delhi mourned. Every soul who was in banquet, went to the mosque or tomb in mourning...(he) was a *Wazir* with wisdom and policy. Fear of God was ingrained in his personality. He managed the affairs of the state and the army with great effort. All the time, he worked for the welfare of the subjects. He did not victimize any one even a bit...all sections of the society mourned his death.... When the Sultan got the news of the Khan-i-Jahan's death, he declared with tears in his eyes: *Now onwards, I will never undertake any journey for big conquests.* He wept bitterly and often remembered him. Such was the greatness and popularity of Khan-i-Jahan'.

In recognition of the meritorious services rendered by the deceased, one of his sons, Jauna Khan, was promoted *wazir* and granted the title of his father. He was 'no match to his father in calibre' but held this post with unflinching loyalty to the Sultan for the next twenty years. The services of Maqbul and his family to Firoze Tughluq ensured law and order at the metropolis and accorded a semblance of relevance and dignity to the otherwise dwindling authority and dimensions of the *Sultanate* of Delhi.

The actual decline and disintegration of the *Sultanate* had begun during the concluding years of the reign of Muhammad Tughluq, and Firoze Tughluq had received in heritage but a small kingdom only. The civil services were crippled, anti-social elements had raised their ugly head, and the royal treasury was empty. The people of northern India had suffered much on account of famine and pestilence, and were simmering with discontent under the oppressive regime of Muhammad Tughluq. The immediate task of Firoze Tughluq was to pacify the estranged provincial governors and military officers, and provide the much-needed relief to the people at large. After burying the deceased (Muhammad Tughluq) with all honour, the 'pious and merciful' Sultan handled the situation tactfully, and initiated a state policy on a very conciliatory note. He traced the victims of his predecessor's ferocity or their descendants and 'endeavoured as far as possible to indemnify them for their sufferings and losses'. In return, he obtained the 'deeds of satisfaction' from them, in which they had duly acknowledged the reparation that they had received to their full satisfaction. All these documents were 'buried in the tomb' of the deceased in the pious hope 'to ensure peace to the departed soul' and help it 'on the Day of Judgement'. There is no denying the fact that 'this action of Firoze Tughluq, though based on a blind religious conviction, proved very helpful to him in winning the confidence and support of the masses; in a way, the Sultan recounted the oppressive deeds of his predecessor and made amends for them'. (*Advanced Study,* i, p.227)

Muhammad Tughluq had advanced a staggering sum of money to the tune of about two *crores* of rupees, by way of loans, to the inhabitants of Delhi, after the Daulatabad debacle, for their resettlement in the capital; all these debts were cancelled by the Sultan on the sane advice of his newly appointed *wazir,* Khan-i-Jahan Maqbul, who came forward with 'a wonderful response' as follows: 'When a ruler departs from this world and is succeeded by another one, then the new ruler bestows favour upon his subjects, like nobles and commoners, and pardons their major and minor sins. If someone had been exiled on account of his treachery' he too is permitted to return'. Accordingly, the Sultan wrote off all the debts of the citizens of Delhi, agriculturists and all others; and, on the further suggestion of his *wazir*, 'publicly destroyed' the official documents and deeds of agreements, signed by the people, 'to relieve their anxiety'. He also 'did not take any action against those who had collaborated with Khwaja-i-Jahan nor asked them to return the wealth they had acquired from him' by way of gratification. These measures added to the popularity of the new Sultan and his reputation soared high as 'just and benevolent ruler'.

Administrative Reforms

With the active assistance and guidance of his able prime minister, Khan-i-Jahan Maqbul, Firoze Tughluq ushered in an era of peace and prosperity for his subjects. Unlike his predecessor, who had shown scant regard to the Muslim divines, he eagerly sought and enlisted the support of the *ulema*; revived the *Jagir* system and enhanced the salaries of his soldiers and military officers beyond all proportions; his *khans* and *maliks* received from four *lac* to eight *lac* tankas. His *wazir* Khan-i-Jahan Maqbul was in the receipt of thirteen *lacs* of *tankas*, and 'additional grants were given to him for each son or daughter born to him'. Afif applauds the Sultan for 'the deference' paid by him 'to the learned and holy men' in the court, and talks of 'the harmony and good feeling which subsisted between Firoze Shah and his *amirs*, a blessing which could not have been attained without a complete overhaul of the policy and administration of the preceding reign'. The Sultan conferred new titles and offices on the *amirs*, and obtained the whole-hearted cooperation and support of the *imams*, *maulvis* and the *mullas*, by liberal grants of *madad-i-muash* and other state privileges.

The contemporary chronicles give a profuse account of the high principles which formed the basis of Firoze Tughluq's state policy. Probably, he is the only Muslim ruler of medieval India, who frankly admits the brutality and horrors of inhuman torture which formed a part of the traditional Islamic penal code, and declares his intention to reduce its intensity. He revised the penal code by softening the punishments which were made more humane; the brutal punishments, based on physical torture and amputation of organs were abolished. We quote *verbatim*, the very first of his accomplishments as Sultan, in the *Futuhat-i-Firozeshahi* as follows:

> 'In the reigns of former kings, the blood of many Musalmans had been shed, and many varieties of torture employed. Amputation of hands and feet, ears and noses; tearing out the eyes, pouring molten lead into the throat, crushing the bones of the hands and feet with mallets, burning the body with fire, driving iron nails into the hands, feet, and bosom, cutting the sinews, sawing men asunder; these and many similar tortures were practised. The great and merciful God made me, His servant, to hope and seek for His mercy by devoting myself to prevent the unlawful killing of Musalmans, and the infliction of any kind of torture upon them or upon any men.
>
> 'Through the mercy, which God has shown to me, these severi-ties and terrors have been exchanged for tenderness, kindness, and mercy. Fear and respect have thus taken firmer hold of the hearts of men, and there has been no need of executions, scourging, tortures, or terrors. But this blessed result is altogether due to the mercy and favour of the Creator.
>
> 'By God's help I determined that the lives (*khún*) of Musalmans and true believers should be in perfect immunity, and whoever

transgressed the Law should receive the punishment pre-scribed by the book and the decrees of judges.'

The contents of the above paragraph and, in fact, the whole text of the *Futuhat-i-Firozeshahi*, makes it clear in un-ambiguous terms that all the reforms, including the administrative, civil, judicial or financial, of Firoze Tughluq were made applicable to the 'Musalmans', who comprised the rightful citizens of the Islamic state of Delhi; how far the non-Muslims or Hindus, who formed the bulk of the Sultanate as *zimmis* or second-rate citizens, benefitted from it is only a matter of conjecture. The evident from the contemporary sources, including the *Futuhat-i-Firozeshahi* itself, does not warrant the universal application of his reform measures, however. As a devoted and pious ruler of a truly Islamic state, Firoze Tughluq adopted numerous measures of austerity and simplicity in his style of functioning, In consequence, his royal court was bereft of all the pomp and show of the bygone days of Iltutmish and Balban or the magnificence and aristocracy of Alauddin; the musicians and singers were turned out and the nobles were not allowed to put on gaudy robes; gold brocades and embroidery were sparingly used. In *Futuhat-i-Firozeshahi*, the Sultan proudly records *inter alia* as follows:

> 'It had been the practice in former reigns to use vessels of gold and silver at the royal table, and sword-belts and quivers were ornamented with gold and jewels. I forbade these things, and I ordered the fittings of my arms to be made of bone, and I commanded that only such vessels should be used as are recognized by the Law (*Sharia*).' (Para 14)
>
> 'In former times it had been the custom to wear ornamented garments, and men received robes as tokens of honour from kings' courts. Figures and devices were painted and dis-played on saddles, bridles, and collars, on censers, on goblets and cups, and flagons, on dishes and ewers, in tents, on curtains and on chairs, and upon all articles and utensils. Under Divine guidance and favour I ordered all pictures and portraits to be removed from these things, and that such articles only should be made as are approved and recognized by the Law (*Sharia*). Those pictures and portraits which were painted on the doors and walls of palaces I ordered to be effaced.' (Para 15)
>
> 'Formerly the garments of great men were generally made of silk and gold brocades, beautiful but unlawful. Under Divine

guidance I ordered that such garments should be worn as are approved by the Law of the Prophet, and that choice should be made of such trimmings of gold brocade, embroidery, or braiding as did not exceed four inches (*asábi'*) in breadth. Whatever was unlawful and forbidden by, or opposed to, the Law (*Sharia*) was set aside.' (Para 16)

Fiscal Reforms

Firoze Tughluq was much worried about the economic health of the state. On his accession, he was 'surprised to learn' that the royal treasury was almost empty, and all the accumulations of the previous Sultans in gold, silver, pearls and other precious metals had completely vanished. On enquiry, Khwaja Fakhr Shadi, who held the post of 'accountant general of the war department' under Muhammad Tughluq produced, among other transactions, the detailed records of the squandering away of wealth among his friends and favourites by Khwaja-i- Jahan to win the support of *amirs* and civil servants of the capital. It necessitated the introduction of fiscal reforms to replenish the state treasury and restore the credit of the government. According, on the advice of Khan-i-Jahan Maqbul, the Sultan deputed Khwaja Hisamuddin Junaid 'to prepare a rough estimate of the public revenues of the state'. He, accompanied by a large body of the staff of the revenue establishment, traversed the kingdom for six long years and, after examining the revenue records of the various *Iqtas* (provinces), assessed the annual revenues, expected from the *khalsa* lands, at 'six *crore* and eighty-five *lakh tankas*'.

Unlike Alauddin Khilji, Firoze Tughluq did not adopt the scientific principles for the measurement of land and assessment of the state demand on the actual produce of the soil. On the other hand, in the absence of any guidelines from the Sultan or the central government, revenue officers made use of the various rough and ready methods, based on local traditions and customs, to determine the revenue due to the state in cash or kind. Of course, Firoze Tughluq was keen to 'prescribe the state demand on a more or less permanent basis to ensure the steady flow of revenues into the treasury. It enabled him to regulate the expenditure in accordance with the income'.

Simultaneously, Firoze Tughluq was very keen to overhaul the entire taxation policy of the state to bring it in conformity with the injunctions of the *Shariat.* The Sultan gives a long list of more than twenty 'frivolous, unlawful and unjust' taxes, which were collected by the preceding Sultans of Delhi but were abolished by him as these were not approved by the Islamic law. Firoze Tughluq was not an expert in financial affairs but he imparted a theocratic tinge to the fiscal policy of his predecessors 'with the twin objects of ensuring adequate state revenues and reducing the burden on the tax payers'. According to the Islamic law, only four taxes were permissible—*Kharaj, Zakat, Jaziya* and *Khams*; and these were retained. The rate of *Kharaj,* i.e. the land revenue was considerably reduced by being brought to one-tenth of the estimated produce, to the great relief of the agriculturists. As usual, it was payable in cash or kind to the state. The tributary Hindu chiefs paid tribute or *Kharaj* in lump sum.

The earlier Sultans of Delhi, particularly, Alauddin Khilji used to demand from his soldiers four-fifths of the booty, obtained during the war, as *Khams*; but Firoze Tughluq following the Islamic tradition, reversed the ratio and allowed his soldiers to pay only one-fifth of such spoils to the state. The soldiers, who constituted the backbone of the Sultanate, must have benefitted immensely from this measure. Obviously, this was done by the Sultan with communal considerations with the sinister object of encouraging his Muslim soldiery to indulge in wanton loot and plunder during the military campaigns into the non-Muslim territories, as is evidenced by the actual language used by him to elaborate this reform measure in his memoirs thus:

> 'Before my time it was the rule and practice that in re-pressing infidelity four-fifths of the spoil was appropriated to the public treasury and one-fifth was given to the captors; but the rule of the Law is that one-fifth should be taken by the State, and four-fifths allotted to the captors. The provisions of the Law had thus been entirely subverted. As the Law was thus set at naught, every man looked upon himself as the lawful owner of the spoil he captured. Hence, children borne by female captives were the offspring of fornication. To prevent these irregularities I decreed that one-fifth (of the spoil) should be taken by the State, and four-fifths given to the captors.' (*Futuhat-i-Firozeshahi*, Para 4)

Jaziya or poll tax was charged from all the non-Muslim subjects of the Sultanate, who refused to convert to Islam. They were not granted full-fledged citizenship of the state but were assured of the protection to their lives and properties on the payment of this religious tax. Accordingly, they were called *zimmis* or the 'protected subjects' of the Islamic state. In the earlier reigns of the Sultans, it was compounded with the land revenue in the rural areas, and recovered along with other cesses on trade and commerce from the inhabitants of towns and cities. Similarly, it was compounded with *Kharaj* or tribute, which was realized from the tributary Hindu chieftains. Firoze Tughluq created a separate department for the collection of this tax exclusively from his Hindu subjects. It was collected from all able-bodied grown-up males. Only women, children, the disabled and the indigent, who had no means of livelihood, were exempt from it.

In order to show his religious zeal, Firoze Tughluq extended the scope of *Jaziya* by levying it on the Brahmans also. Previously, the non-earning Brahmin priests, who depended exclusively on the charities of the Hindu devotees, were exempt from the payment of this tax. The Sultan was advised by 'truthful *Ulema* and *Shaikhs* in the court' that 'the Brahmans and sacred thread-holders were the key to the citadel of infidelity, and infidels follow them (trust them or have faith in them)'; therefore, 'they should not be exempt and *Jaziya* must be imposed upon them first'. Afif records that, on hearing of this news, 'all the Brahmins from all around' went to the royal palace and pleaded with the Sultan to exempt them from the payment of this tax but the later did not oblige them. The Brahmins 'resorted to hunger strike for a few days, endangering their lives', but when some of them collected a heap of firewood beneath the palace and prepared to immolate themselves, the Sultan retorted:

> '*They should immolate themselves at once and die (but) the Jaziya can, in no case, be exempted. They should remove such thoughts from their minds.*'

To quote Shams-i-Siraj Afif *verbatim*,

> 'When they realized that the Sultan was steadfast in his resolve, the Hindus of the city gathered around and told them unanimously that it was not desirable on their part to put their lives in danger for the sake of *Jaziya*. The groups of Hindus took the burden of *Jaziya* due to the Brahmans on themselves. There were three grades of *Jaziya* in Delhi: first grade was forty *tankas*; the second twenty *tankas*, and the third ten *tankas* per head per *annum*. All the Brahmans expressed their inability and helplessness and requested the Sultan that some concession be given to them. The Sultan ordered that on each Brahman ten *tankas* of fifty *jitals* be imposed. After issuing this order, the Sultan appointed officials to collect the said amount.'

Firoze Tughluq directed his officials to collect *Jaziya* through coercive means; otherwise, they were under strict instructions not to make demands 'in excess of the regular government dues', and those found guilty of 'any such exaction' were punished severely.

Firoze Tughluq did all, that he could, to improve the agricultural production of the state. He constructed four or perhaps five canals in the region of Delhi, Hissar and Alwar to irrigate large tracts of arid land. We have it on the testimony of Afif that 150 wells were sunk at state expense to provide drinking water to the travellers and for irrigation. After the construction of these irrigation works, the Sultan introduced, with the approval of theologians, of course, an irrigation tax at ten percent of the produce of the lands which benefitted from them. Firoze Tughluq's agrarian policy was not in any way progressive or scientific but it benefitted the peasantry irrespective of their religious beliefs and practices. Instead of introducing any progressive reforms in the matters of revenue assessment and collection, the Sultan allotted the work to the bidders, contractors and middlemen. The revenue officials were liberally provided through rent-free land grants. As a matter of fact, 'Firoze Tughluq revived the *Jagir* system with a vengeance; the whole kingdom was parcelled out into *fiefs*, and the *fiefs* into districts, which were held by the regional and local government officials almost as personal estates. In addition to the land-grants, the nobility as well as the bureaucracy received fat allowances, which enabled them to accumulate large fortunes. The nobles enjoyed considerable powers in the internal administrative affairs of their rent-free holdings, which cut at the very roots of the uniformity of administration and integrity of the central authority. The system of granting lands or assignments (*Itlaq*) upon the revenues were extended even to the junior ranks which did an incalculable harm, in the long-run, to the army establishment as well as the state. The soldiers on active duty were unable to collect the revenues by themselves and sold out their assignment deeds at a discount to the professional revenue collectors or middlemen." (Advanced Study, i, p. 230)

Firoze Tughluq made many improvements in the minting of coins. The experiment of token currency, as attempted by Muhammad Tughluq, had failed miserably, but the state currency had its own sanctity. The Sultan was fully conscious of the fact that 'gold and silver coins, though based originally on the intrinsic value of the metals contained therein, ought to be such that they should not lose credibility of the people with the fluctuations in their price level year after year'. When asked by the Sultan to express his opinion on the subject, Khan-i-Jahan Maqbul, his *wazir*, observed that 'the coinage of kings is like an unmarried daughter, whom no one would seek after, however beautiful and charming she might be, if any aspersion had, either rightly or wrongly been cast upon her character. So also (is the case) with the royal coinage; if any one honestly or falsely, from interested motive, alleged a deterioration of the coinage, the insinuation would spread, the coinage would obtain a bad name, and no one would like it.' – (Firishta, Briggs; i, p. 454) Accordingly, Firoze Tughluq carried out extensive reforms in the technique of minting, and issued varieties of standard coins. Apart from the gold and silver *tankas,* he manufactured a lot of fractional currency of middle denominations in between the copper *jital* and the silver *tanka.* These coins were of the respective value of 48 *jitals* (*chihal-o-shashgani*), 25, 24, 12, 10, 8 and 6 *jitals* (*shashgani*), which contained silver in due proportions, mixed up with other metals. Similarly, he produced in abundance the fractional currency of the lowest denomination below *jital,* which comprised half a *jital* (*adha*) and a quarter *jital* (*bikh*) to facilitate buying and selling by the commoners at the lowest level of the society; it was a wonderful production which fascinated the masses and left no scope for the imitators and forgers to let down the state currency.

Religious Policy

Sultan Firoze Tughluq eagerly sought the cooperation and support of orthodox Muslim theologians to strengthen the foundations of the Sultanate as an Islamic state. He went over backwards 'by proclaiming that he was a true Muslim king and that the state under him was a truly Islamic state'. According to Satish Chandra,

> 'Actually, right from the time of Iltutmish's accession to the throne, there was a tussle between the orthodox theologians and the Sultans regarding the nature of the state, and the policy to be adopted by the state towards the non-Muslims... from the time of Iltutmish, and especially under Alauddin and Muhammad Tughluq, the Turkish rulers did not allow the theologians to dictate the policy of the state. They waged *jihad* against the Hindu rulers, whenever it was convenient for them to do so. In order to keep the theologians satisfied, a number of them were appointed to high offices. The judiciary and the educational system, of course, remained in the hands of the theologians.' (*Medieval India*; NCERT, New Delhi, pp. 70-71)

Firoze Tughluq seems to have 'learnt a good lesson from the reactions and revolts of the preceding reign'. As observed by R.C. Majumdar, 'he had been heretofore a passive instrument in the hands of the reactionary *ulema* and saints; and he continued to play the same role throughout the period of his rule. Thus the state under him came under the influence of the theologians, and this is perhaps the reason of his popularity.' (*History and Culture of the Indian People*; BVB, vi, pp. 97-98) The Sultan took pains to enumerate his manifold accomplishments in his memoirs, entitled, *Futuhat-i-Firozeshahi*, to prove his adherence to the afore-mentioned state policy in his bid to restore the regime of true Islam in the *Sultanate.* Being a 'fanatically orthodox Muslim like Aurangzeb' Firoze Tughluq was intolerant towards the Shias and certain heretical Muslim sects, whose leaders were punished and the so-called anti-Islamic practices put down with a strong hand. In paragraph five of the *Futuhat-i-Firozeshahi*, he mentions one of his accomplishments as under:

> The sect of *Shí'as*, also called *Rawáfiz*, had endeavoured to make proselytes. They wrote treatises and books, and gave in-struction and lectures upon the tenets of their sect, and traduced and reviled the first chiefs of our religion (on whom be the peace of God!). I seized them all, and I convicted them of their errors and perversions. On the most zealous I inflicted punish-ment (*siyásat*), and the rest I visited with censure (*tázír*) and threats (*tahdíb*) of public punishment (*tashhír-i zijr*). Their books I burnt in public, and so by the grace of God the influence of this sect was entirely suppressed.'

Likewise, in the sixth paragraph of the memoirs, Firoze Tughluq refers to 'a sect of the heretics (*mulhids*) and sectarians (*abah-rivan*)' among the Muslims, 'who laboured to seduce the people into heresy and schism'; the Sultan 'cut off the heads of the elders of this sect, and imprisoned and banished the rest, so that their abominable practices were put an end to'. In the next two paragraphs, Firoze Tughluq refers to two other sects of the heretics and atheists of Delhi, led by Ahmad Bahari and Ruknuddin, the self-styled Imam Mahdi, who led the Muslims astray by preaching the anti-Islamic practices among them; they were inflicted exemplary punishments 'to put them on the path of righteousness' As observed by Ishwari Prasad, by his 'constant association with *Muftis* and *Maulvis*', the Sultan had made himself a mere tool in the hands of the *ulema* and the theologians, and 'he never transacted any business of the state without referring to the Quran for an augury'.

So much so good; the contemporary historians like Barani and Afif are full of praise for Firoze Tughluq and describe him as 'a just, merciful and benevolent ruler'. Yahya bin Ahmad Sirhindi, the author of *Tarikh-i-Mubarak Shahi*, regards him as an ideal monarch who tried to rule strictly according to the Quranic injunctions. He writes that under his benevolent rule, 'all kinds of oppression, tyranny, highhandedness, and violence ceased', and claims that 'decline of the realm and rebellion of the people– a curse with which the reign of the late Sultan Muhammad bin Tughluq had been afflicted, were replaced by justice, equity, peace, prosperity and consolidation'. The actual record of his performance as ruler and the chronicle of his reign prove it otherwise, however. As a matter of fact, Firoze Tughluq was a weak and imbecile ruler who miserably failed to stem the rising tide of the forces of ultimate decline and disintegration of the Sultanate that had already begun during the reign of his predecessor. To add insult to the injury, his religious bigotry as orthodox Muslim ruler, strictly delimited the benefits of his so-called 'benevolent rule' to a small fringe of his subjects, which did not include even all the Muslims. In the words of R.C. Majumdar, 'the blackest spot on his character...was the intolerance of any faith other than orthodox Islam. It is evident from his book (*Futuhat-i-Firozeshahi*) that the Sultan divided mankind into two groups – Musalmans (by which he meant Musalman of the approved orthodox type), and non-Musalmans, and regarded the former alone as his special concern.' As a result, the Hindus, who comprised the bulk of his subjects, and all those Muslims who did not conform to the orthodox tenets of Sunni Islam, were deprived of his much-publicized measures of public welfare and the state patronage. The following extracts from *Futuhat-i-Firozeshahi* give an idea of his bigoted attitude towards his Hindu subjects:

> The Hindus and idol-worshipers had agreed to pay the money for toleration (*zar-i zimmiya*), and had consented to the poll tax (*Jaziya*), in return for which they and their families en-joyed security. These people now erected new idol temples in the city and the environs in opposition to the Law of the Prophet which declares that such temples are not to be tolerated. Under Divine guidance I destroyed these edifices, and I killed those leaders of infidelity who seduced others into error, and the lower orders I subjected to stripes and chastisement, until this abuse was entirely abolished. The following is an instance:—In the village of Malúh there is a tank which they call *kund* (tank). Here they

had built idol-temples, and on certain days the Hindus were accustomed to proceed thither on horseback and wearing arms. Their women and children also went out in palanquins and carts. There they assembled in thousands and performed idol worship. This abuse had been so overlooked that the *bazaar* people took out there all sorts of provisions, and setup stalls and sold their goods. Some graceless Musalmans, thinking only of their own gratification, took part in these meetings. When intelli-gence of this came to my ears my religious feelings prompted me at once to put a stop to this scandal and offence to the religion of Islam. On the day of the assembling I went there in person, and I ordered that the leaders of these people and the promoters of this abomination should be put to death. I forbade the in-fliction of any severe punishments on the Hindus in general, but I destroyed their idol temples, and instead thereof raised mosques. I founded two flourishing towns (*kasba*), one called Tughuqpúr, the other Sálárpúr. Where infidels and idolaters worshiped idols, Musalmans now, by God's mercy, perform their devotions to the true God. Praises of God and the summons to prayer (*azans*) are now heard there, and that place which was formerly the home of infidels has become the habitation of the faithful, who there (*sic.*) repeat their creed and offer up their praises to God.' (Para 11)

'Information was brought to me that some Hindus had erected a new idol-temple in the village of Sálil1, and were performing worship to their idol. I sent some persons there to destroy the idol temple, and to put a stop to their pernicious in-citements to error.' (Para 12)

In the same breath, the Sultan continues:

'Some Hindus had erected a new idol-temple in the village of Kohána, and the idolaters used to assemble there and perform their idolatrous rites. These people were seized and brought before me. I ordered that the perverse conduct of the leaders of this wickedness should be publicly proclaimed, and that they should be put to death before the gate of the palace. I also ordered that the infidel books, the idols, and the vessels used in their worship, which had been taken with them, should all be publicly burnt. The others were restrained by threats and punishments, as a warning to all men, that no *zimmí* could follow such wicked practices in a Musalman country.' (Para 13)

The contemporary chronicles are replete with numerous such examples of the persecution of Hindus, Shias and the other non-Sunni Muslims by Firoze Tughluq throughout his period of rule. The Hindus, publicly dubbed as *kafirs* or non-believers, were the worst sufferers during his reign. They were held in contemptuous disregard by the Sultan, and deprived of all the higher state services as far as possible. With or without any pretext or provocation, they were insulted and humiliated, and their temples, holy shrines and centres of education and learning were defiled and pulled down In two respects, the Sultan was more oppressive to the Hindus than his predecessors. Previously, the Brahmans, who depended exclusively on the charities of their co-religionists as priests, and were not formal bread-earners, were exempt from the payment of *Jaziya*, but Firoze Tughluq imposed *Jaziya* on them also. In the second place, the Sultan himself boasts that he adopted every means to induce the Hindus to embrace Islam. This is evident from the following assertion that he makes in his autobiographical treatise:

> 'I encouraged my infidel subjects to embrace the religion of the Prophet, and I proclaimed that everyone who repeated the creed (*Kalma*) and became a Musalman should be exempt from the *Jaziya*, or poll-tax. Information of this came to the ears of the people at large, and great numbers of Hindus presented themselves, and were admitted to the honour of Islam. Thus they came forward day by day from every quarter, and, adopting the faith, were exonerated from the *Jaziya*, and were favoured with presents and honours.' (*Futuhat-i-Firozeshahi*, Para 10)

According to Shams-i-Siraj Afif, intelligence was received by the Sultan that in the suburbs of Delhi, 'a wicked Brahman was openly carrying on the worship of idols, and had built a temple in his house'. The Brahman 'had prepared a wooden seal and decorated it with different kinds of engravings' of Hindu gods and goddesses, which were worshipped by the devotees, 'belonging to different castes, who assembled there on fixed days for the purpose. A report was also received that the said Brahman had induced a Muslim woman (obviously belonging to a family of the Hindu converts to Islam) to reconvert to Hinduism. The accused was summoned to the Sultan's court. The latter called for 'the *Ulema* and the *Shaikhs* to look into the matter and pronounce their verdict'. The Brahman was asked to embrace Islam, and 'on his refusal to convert, was condemned to be burnt alive'. Afif, who was an eye-witness to the public execution of the said Brahman, gives a graphic account of that ghastly incident as follows:

'Every effort was made to persuade the confused Brahman to embrace Islam but the Brahman did not listen to any argument and flatly refused to convert. The Brahman was presented before the royal court and a heap of firewood was made. The hands and feet of the Brahman were tied, and he was thrown on to the heap of the firewood. His wooden seal (idol) was placed on top of the wooden heap and fire was lighted from beneath. The author Afif was present on the occasion at the court and saw the whole scene, himself. After the *Zuhr Namaz* (early afternoon prayers), the wooden seal of the Brahman was put to fire from both ends; one side was towards the head of the Brahman and the other towards the feet. Since the firewood was dry, it first caught fire from the direction of feet. The Brahman cried in pain, and while he was crying, fire from the direction of his head also burnt speedily, and the Brahman was quickly burnt. Thanks to the majesty of *Shariat*, the Sultan, the follower of Islamic path, never deviated a bit from *Shara*.' (*Tarikh-i-Firoze Shahi;* Eng. Trs. by R.C. Jauhri, pp. 214-15),

The public disposition of Firoze Tughluq as a bigoted Muslim chief and 'a humble servant of Islam' did earn him the applause of the orthodox *ulema* and his Sunni camp-followers but it could not have amused the majority of his subjects, including the *zimmis* or *kafirs* (Hindus), Shias and other liberal-minded Muslims.

Expeditions

Unlike his predecessor, Firoze Tughluq was a poor military general; he lacked the courage and marshal qualities of a warrior to lead the armies and indulge in wars of conquest. On his accession to the throne, he was 'faced with the problem of preventing the imminent break-up of the Delhi Sultanate', but he failed to bring the rebellious chiefs to book and helplessly watched the slow disintegration of his dominions. Most of the military expeditions, undertaken by the Sultan, for the recovery of his lost territories failed miserably, but as a self-proclaimed 'man of peace', he timidly pretended to console himself with the public pronouncement that he was 'resolved never more to make war upon Muslims'.

Bengal had asserted its independence under a local Muslim dynasty during the reign of Muhammad Tughluq. It was ruled over by Haji Ilyas, entitled Sultan Shamsuddin Ilyas Shah, at the time of Firoze Tughluq's accession; Lakhnauti was his capital The Sultan launched two full-fledged military campaigns, under his personal command, for its recovery but each time had to cut a sorry figure. During the first campaign, organised by him against Bengal in 1353-54, Firoze Tughluq remained absent from the imperial capital for eleven months while his *wazir*, Khan-i-Jahan Maqbul, deputized for him. Haji Ilyas lost the battle and took shelter in the fort of Ikdala in East Bengal which was promptly besieged by the victorious royal troops. In spite of his best efforts, Firoze Tughluq failed to conquer the fort, and, on the beginning of the rainy season, made peace with Ilyas, virtually recognizing his independence, and raised the siege. Nevertheless, Shams-i-Siraj Afif, the biographer of the Sultan, defends his patron with the argument that when the victory was in sight, 'the shrieks and wails of women in the fort, who pathetically demonstrated their grief, moved the compassionate heart of the Sultan, and he forthwith decided to abandon the fruits of a hard-earned victory', on the plea that 'to storm the fort, put more *Musalmans* to the sword, and expose honourable women to ignominy, would be a crime for which he could not answer on the Day of Judgement and which would leave no difference between him and the Mongols'. Firoze Tughluq returned to Delhi empty-handed in spite of the fact that no less than 1,80,000 Bengalis were said to have been slain in this expedition. He was not an imperialist by instinct, and Afif's contention seems to be true that he was fully contented by the extension of the Muslim sway in Bengal even though it was not under his control.

On the death of Ilyas in 1359, his son Sikander Khan became ruler of Bengal. About this time a deputation of the Bengali fugitives, headed by one Zafar Khan, the son-in-law of the ruling chief, waited upon Sultan Firoze Tughluq at Delhi and pleaded with him to intercede on their behalf to save them from the highhandedness of Sikander Khan. It tempted the Sultan to make a renewed attempt to subdue Bengal. In his second expedition, Firoze Tughluq marched out of the imperial capital with a grand army, consisting of 70,000 cavalry, innumerable infantry, 470 war elephants, a large number of boats for sailing through the Yamuna and Ganga, and all the paraphernalia of war, We have it on the testimony of Afif that the Sultan proceeded on his mission leisurely, rather majestically, and took six months to reach Bengal. Instead of giving an open fight, Sikander Khan shut himself in the fort of Ikdala like his father, and offered a stubborn resistance to the besiegers. After a protracted siege that lasted many months, Firoze Tughluq failed to conquer it. To the great disappointment of his military commanders, the Sultan raised the siege and recognised the independence of Bengal which was cut off from the Sultanate forever. According to contemporary sources, Sikander Khan promised to rehabilitate Zafar Khan and his party at Sonargaon, and send an annual tribute of elephants to Delhi.

On his return from Bengal, Firoze Tughluq diverted his army into the interior of Bihar and Orissa to plunder and subjugate the Hindu states of the region, obviously, 'by way of boosting the morale of his otherwise demoralized and disheartened soldiers'. The Hindu chief of Sikhar in the Manbhum district, put up 'a stern fight' before his garrison was overpowered and annihilated. From there, Firoze Tughluq headed towards the south with a large cavalry force and 'reached Tinanagar, within the frontier of Orissa, which had never before been invaded by any Muslim army'. After the sack of this town, the invaders marched on and put to plunder the towns of Kinianagar- identified with Khiching, the capital of the old Mayurbhanj state, and Keonjhar before reaching the frontier of Cuttack, the capital of Orissa. According to Afif, 'the movement of the Muslim army was so swift' that Rai Bhanudeva III of Orissa, referred to by the medieval chroniclers as Jajnagar, 'was frightened' and 'took shelter in the midst of the sea'. The garrisons of Saranghar and Cuttack put up resistance but were defeated. To quote Afif,

> 'The entire kingdom of the *Rai* was despoiled and large numbers of his people were arrested, and many left to take shelter in the hills. Innumerable animals, along with forest wealth, were captured. It is said that so many animals were gathered that no one was interested to have more. The cost of a slave fell to two *jitals;* it was impossible to count them. At every halt, the army men would capture many sheep and slaughter them for eating; and would leave those found extra in the camp itself before departing for another halt. More animals were always available at subsequent halts. The object of penning down these lines is to indicate the excess of worldly goods in that region'. (*Tarikh-i-Firoze Shahi*, p. 109)

After the sack of Cuttack, Firoze Tughluq proceeded to the holy city of Puri, where he demolished the temple of Jagannatha and desecrated the images. In the words of Afif, 'inside the palace-fortress, there was a stone idol, which the Hindus called Jagannath. The idol was worshipped by them. The Sultan, following the example of Sultan Mahmud Ghazni, uprooted the idol from its base and foundations, and took it to Delhi, and put it to humiliation on the pavement'. (*Ibid.*, p. 111). The author of *Sirat-i-Firoze Shahi* adds to our information regarding Firoze Tughluq's expedition to Jajnagar or Orissa by the remarks that 'two of his objectives' in undertaking this venture were 'massacring the unbelievers and demolishing their temples.' According to R.C. Majumdar, the detailed account given in this book, which was written by an anonymous author 'either at the dictation or at the dictates of Firoze Shah himself, leaves us with no doubt that these objects were pursued by him with relentless severity'. About the sack of Jagannatha temple at Puri, *Sirat-i-Firoze Shahi* records as follows:

> 'Allah, who is the only true God and has no other emanation, endowed the king of Islam with the strength to destroy this ancient shrine on the eastern sea-coast and to plunge it into the sea, and after its destruction, he ordered the nose of the image of Jagannath to be perforated and disgraced it by casting it down on the ground. They dug out other idols which were worshipped by the polytheists in the kingdom of Jajnagar, and overthrew them as they did the image of Jagannath, for being laid in front of the mosques along the path of the Sunnis and way of the *musallis* (the multitude, who offer their prayers) and stretched them in front of the portals of every mosque, so that the body and sides of the images might be trampled at the time of ascent and descent, entrance and exit, by the shoes on the feet of the Musalmans'. (Quoted by R.C. Majumdar in *History and Culture of the People of India*, vi, pp. 105-6)

In continuation of the narrative, *Sirat-i-Firoze Shahi* describes that, after having achieved 'his cherished object', the Sultan proceeded to an island (identified with the Chilka Lake) near the sea-coast, where 'nearly one hundred thousand men of Jajnagar had taken refuge with their women and children. The Sultan converted the island into a basin of blood by the massacre of the unbelievers'. Those, who survived the massacre, particularly women were enslaved. 'Women with babies and pregnant ladies were haltered, manacled, fettered and enchained, and no vestige of the infidels was left except their blood'. After this, the 'jubilant' Sultan concluded his victorious campaign by an elephant-hunt at Padamtala, in the old Baramba state of Orissa. (*Ibid.*, p. 93)

On their return journey, the royal forces lost their way in the thickly forested mountainous tracts of Orissa and were put to great hardships. Bengal was lost but, nonetheless, the campaign, which lasted two years and seven months, was hailed as a great success. The *Rai* of Orissa had offered nominal submission to the Sultan in absentia and agreed to furnish some elephants to Delhi by way of tribute. In the words of Afif, the Sultan had achieved 'strange and wonderful success', which was, perhaps, not originally conceived or contemplated by Firoze Tughluq or any of his camp-followers. Firoze Tughluq had brought with him a fresh lot of 73 elephants, which were captured during his expedition to Jajnagar. In the course of celebrations of this victory at Delhi, these animals 'were painted and decorated with various colours and displayed like goats in the city without their *mahavats* or riders'; besides, the state's share of the booty of this campaign (viz., one-fifth of the plunder only), as collected by the Sultan from his soldiers, included 75,000 Hindu captives as slaves. Of course, while proclaiming the abolition of tortures and mutilations of the criminals, Firoze Tughluq had taken care to adopt 'liberal and humane attitude towards slaves' as follows:

> 'The Sultan commanded his great fief-holders and officers to capture slaves whenever they were at war, and to pick out and send the best for the service of the court. The chiefs and officers naturally exerted themselves in procuring more and more slaves and a great number of them were thus collected. When they were found to be in excess, the Sultan sent them to important cities. In all cases, provision was made for their support in a liberal manner. Arrangement was made for educating the slaves and training them in various arts and crafts. In some places, they were provided for in the army. It has been estimated that in the city and in the various fiefs, there were 1,80,000 (state-owned) slaves for whose maintenance and comfort the Sultan took special care. About 12,000 slaves became artisans of various kinds, and 40,000 worked as military guards to Sultan. The Sultan created a separate department, called the *Diwan-i-Bandagan,* with a number of officers for administering the affairs of these slaves. Gradually, the slaves increased to such a degree that they were employed in all sorts of domestic duties, so much so that there was no occupation in which the slaves of Firoze Tughluq were not employed. By order of the Sultan, the great feudal chieftains also treated the slaves like children, providing them with food and raiment (clothing), lodging them and training them, and taking every care for their wants'. (Afif's *Tarikh-i-Firoze Shahi,* p.157)

In 1360-61, Firoze Tughluq decided to subdue the disaffected Muslim nobles of Daulatabad, and actually moved up to Bayana for the purpose, but 'wiser counsel prevailed' and he directed forces for the conquest of Nagarkot (Kangra) instead. The Hindu chieftain of Nagarkot had earlier been defeated and subjugated by Muhammad Tughluq but re-asserted his independence after his death. The Raja was besieged in the fort which was heavily fortified. The army of Delhi took possession of the town of Nagarkot and put it to plunder. The historic temple of Jawalamukhi was also sacked and desecrated. As usual, the Sultan failed to conquer the fort by force. According to Afif, 'the imperial siege lingered on for six months, and the combatants' brave soldiers tried very hard to overpower the other. After a period of six months, the signs of victory of the imperial side became visible due to Divine grace', when the *Rai* of Nagarkot offered his nominal submission on the promise to pay annual tribute to Delhi. The triumphant army returned to the capital, laden with 'costly presents as tribute' besides a rich booty and 'countless slaves'. (*Ibid.*, p. 120)

In 1362-63, Firoze Tughluq undertook his last military expedition for the re-conquest of Sindh, which had been lost to the Sultanate of Delhi during the concluding years of his predecessor's reign. Muhammad Tughluq had died a broken-hearted man in the course of his armed struggle to subdue the Sindhi rebels. It is said that this campaign had originated in Firoze Tughluq's 'desire to avenge the wrong done by the people of Sindh to his predecessor'. Jam Babaniya, the Amir of Sindh, had setup as independent ruler with his headquarters at Thatta. Firoze Tughluq set out with a huge army of 90,000 cavalry and 480 elephants. He himself sailed through the river Sindh by a large fleet of boats, while his army marched along the river banks to reach Thatta. The fort was promptly put under siege but the royal troops failed to conquer it. Meanwhile, the prevalent famine made the royalists suffer from the shortage of provisions while the outbreak of plague took a heavy toll of their men and horses. It encouraged the Jam to take the initiative. One dark night, he came out of the fort all of a sudden and made a frontal attack on the besiegers with 20,000 horse and four *lakh* foot soldiers to the great bewilderment of the royalists. The Jam was beaten and made to take shelter within the fort again, but the Sultan panicked. Unwilling to take the risk of another engagement against the antagonist, he ordered the retreat of his troops to Gujarat as a measure of relief. To his misfortune, some of the local guides misled the army of Firoze Tughluq into the Rann of Kutch, where the non-availability of drinking water claimed the lives of many more soldiers and beasts of the Sultan. But for the timely dispatch of provisions and reinforcements from Delhi by Khan-i-Jahan, the royal army might have perished in the marshes of the Ran. The Jam Babaniya also thought it prudent to offer his submission to the Sultan. He was replaced by a member of his family as the new Amir of Sindh under the nominal suzerainty of Delhi. The expedition, which lasted more than two years and a half, was claimed to be a great success; in the words of Afif, 'for twenty-one days, the drums of joy were beaten and cupolas erected. in the capital'. Nevertheless, the Sultan, who 'felt disheartened and demoralized' because of his incompetence and failure to lead the military expedition successfully, regretted to have undertaken this venture in which numerous Musalmans had lost their lives from both the sides, and he swore never again to launch any such campaign in future. As the matters stood, the military power of the Jams of Thatta remained unbroken; the successor of Babaniya re-asserted his independence after a few years while Firoze Tughluq was still at the helm of affairs, and Sindh was cut off from the Sultanate of Delhi forever. So also was the case with the southern peninsula. The Deccan was allowed to become independent under a Muslim chief, named Hasan Gangu—the founder of the Bahmani kingdom, whose successor states – Ahmadnagar, Bijapur, Golconda, Berar and Bidar, ruled over the erstwhile provinces of the Sultanate for 180 years. Indirectly, it also facilitated the rise of independent Hindu states, including that of Vijayanagar, on the ruins of the Sultanate. According to Afif, Firoze Tughluq formally renounced war against the rebellious Muslim chiefs when, in defiance of his *firman,* the people of Mabar (Malabar Coast) declared their independence under the leadership of a relative of Hasan Gangu from Daulatabad. However, he kept his options open to wage war against 'the infidels and wicked' who, according to his conviction, 'must be destroyed and extra effort be made to conquer territories'.

Public Welfare Works

Firoze Tughluq 'was not made for the glories of conquest' but it has universally been acknowledged that he was 'a great philanthropist'. From the time of his accession to the throne, he was engaged in the public welfare activities. As an intensely religious man, he usually 'spoke in the tone of a bigot' who was concerned with the happiness and welfare of Muslims alone, but, in the exercise of his functions as a sovereign, his works of public utility benefitted most of his subjects, including the Muslims as well as Hindus. According to Afif, the Sultan constructed four canals for the irrigation of agricultural lands. The first canal emanated from the river Satluj and ran up to Ghaghar, covering a distance of more than 150 kilometres. Thesecond canal originated from the neighbourhood of Mandavi and Sirmur Hills; it carried the waters of as many as sevenstreams to Hansi and the newly constructed fort of Hissar Firoza. The third canal was taken out of the river Ghaghar for the irrigation of Hariana region; it carried waters to the newly built town of Firozabad; and the fourth canal was taken out of the river Yamuna, which flowed to Firozabad, and from there 'its waters were carried further after filling a huge tank, constructed near the town.

Firoze Tughluq dug many wells to provide drinking water to the travellers and the villagers. He laid out 1200 state-managed-fruit gardens in the neighbourhood of Delhi. Their fruits were sold in the open market which brought handsome income to the royal treasury besides providing delicious and nutritive food to the royal household as well as the inhabitants of the capital. Firoze Tughluq also paid attention towards the extension and promotion of internal trade and commerce by abolishing the 'vexatious taxes and reducing the octroi duties'. All these measures benefitted the kingdom of Delhi, though sharply reduced in territorial dimensions; agricultural production increased, the interests of cultivators were well-protected, trade and business revived. It warded off the famines and the inhabitants of Delhi became prosperous and satisfied. Afif, the biographer of the Sultan, records that

> 'Contentment attained its climax during the blessed reign of Firoze Shah. The cheapness and abundance was not limited to the capital city only but was all pervasive in the entire kingdom. During the forty years of Sultan's reign, no one ever saw famine. People forgot the abundance and cheapness of Alauddin's reign. The Sultan had laboured hard to usher in cheapness and its description is found in all books of history. Alauddin advanced money to the traders and conferred upon them wealth and gold, and even stipends and other benefits. Hence there was so much cheapness but during the reign of Firoze Shah, the cheapness of grain and other commodities resulted without any endeavour and effort.' In the same strain, Afif continues: 'The cheapness of food grains was so much that the price of wheat in the city of Delhi was eight *jitals* per *maund*, and gram and barley - four *jitals* per *maund*, Coarse grain meant for the horses was available

at ten *seers* for a *jital.* Similarly, the price of sugar was one *jital* per *maund*...the price of cloth, whether white linen or soft linen, was also very low. Firoze Shah ordered that the price of the sweets should also be reduced as all other commodities were cheap.'. (*Tarikh-i-Firoze Shahi,* p. 170)

Firoze Tughluq created a separate department of public charities, called the *Diwan-i-Khairat* to provide succor to *fukara-wa-maskin*, i.e. the poor and the needy. As a God-fearing man of very humble disposition, the Sultan 'paid regard to the holy men, repaired the tombs of the Sufi saints, built *Khanqahs* and looked after the comforts of the *fakirs* (beggars) and all those devoted to religious pursuits.' He introduced the practice of granting old-age pensions, and opened an employment bureau to find work for the unemployed Muslim young men. One of the functions of the *Diwan-i-Khairat* was to provide for the weddings of poor Muslim girls at state expense; a 'charity house' was established in Delhi exclusively for this purpose. The officials of this department verified the condition of those who sought help and divided them into three categories in the ascending order of poverty; the poorest people received fifty sliver *tankas*; the next above them-thirty *tankas* and those in the third category were granted twenty *tankas.* According to Afif, the 'needy Muslims and miserable widows flocked to the capital from all directions, got the names of their daughters recorded, and obtained enough financial support enabling them to purchase necessary provisions for the marriages. Thus due to Sultan's kindness and benevolence, a few thousand lucky girls were married and a large number of people employed.'—(*Tarikh-i-Firoze Shahi*, pp. 197-98). Firoze Tughluq opened charitable kitchens in and around the metropolis to provide free food to the poor, built *serais* along the roads for the travellers, and also established rest houses for the pilgrims on their way to the *khanqahs* of the *Sufi* saints. In the words of the Sultan:

'For the benefit of travellers and pilgrims resorting to the tombs of illustrious kings and celebrated saints, and for pro-viding the things necessary in these holy places, I confirmed and gave effect to the grants of villages, lands, and other endowments which had been conferred upon them in olden times. In those cases where no endowment or provision had been settled, I made an endowment, so that these establishments might for ever be secure of an income, to afford comfort to travellers and wayfarers, to holy men and learned men.'—(*Futuhat-i-Firozeshahi*).

Afif adds to our information that the Sultan 'awarded stipends and salaries for the *Ulema, Hafiz* (Quran reciters) and *Shaikhs*. Reliable persons have told the author Afif that an amount of 36,00,000 *tankas* was spent by way of stipends and nearly 42,000 people, who were poor and helpless, were paid salaries from the royal treasury. There were separate officials for taking care of these activities. With Firoze Tughluq's bounty, everyone lived comfortably.' Nevertheless, as an orthodox Muslim, Firoze Tughluq was desirous of confining the women of his community to the four walls of their *harems*. He did not approve of their free movement in public even during the social festivities or in the course of pilgrimages to the shrines of the holy saints. In his memoirs, the Sultan records as under:

> 'A custom and practice unauthorized by the Law of Islam had sprung up in Musalman cities. On holy days, women riding in palanquins, or carts, or litters, or mounted on horses or mules, or in large parties on foot, went out of the city to the tombs. Rakes and wild fellows of unbridled passions and loose habits took the opportunity, which this practice afforded, for improper riotous actions. I commanded that no woman should go out to the tombs under pain of exemplary punishment. Now, thanks to the great God, no lady or respectable Musalman woman can go out on pilgrimage to the tombs. The practice has been entirely stopped'. - (*Ibid.*, Para 10)

Firoze Tughluq established a magnificent charitable hospital, called *Dáru-sh shifá* or *Sehat Khana* (Health Department) in the capital 'for the benefit of every one of high or low degree, who was suddenly attacked by illness and overcome by suffering'. In the words of the Sultan 'physicians attend there to ascertain the disease, to look after the cure, to regulate the diet, and to administer medicine. The cost of the medicines and the food is defrayed from my endowments. All sick persons, residents and travellers, gentle and simple, bond and free, resort thither; their maladies are treated, and, under God's blessing, they are cured.' (*Ibid.*)

Not only this; the provincial officers were instructed 'to emulate the example of the Sultan in opening such charitable institutions and hospitals within the areas of their jurisdiction'. Shams-i-Siraj Afif tells us that Firoze Tughluq 'donated lands and villages for the maintenance of the *Diwan-i-Khairat* and *Shafa Khana*', and 'further ordered the officials to establish hospitals for the commoners (general public), and post proficient surgeons, doctors and physicians therein. Money was sanctioned for the purchase of medicines, food and drink, and other necessities to be provided to the patients.'

Firoze Tughluq was an accomplished scholar of Persian and Arabic, and took keen interest in the advancement of education and learning. He liberally funded the state-owned educational-system. Apart from the numerous *maktabs* (schools) attached to the *masjids;* he opened a large number of primary schools and as many as thirty *madrassas* in the various towns of his kingdom. The *madrassa* of Sultan Iltutmish in Delhi had since been closed and its building was in ruins. Firoze Tughluq ordered the reconstruction of the building, 'furnished it with sandal-wood doors' and made it functional once again. The newly-constructed Firozeshahi Madrassa at the Firozabad campus of the capital 'rose to be a magnificent university, which surpassed all other Islamic institutions of the time in academic attainments,' Highly qualified teachers of Persian and Arabic languages, especially the specialists in Islamic studies, from Iran and other Muslim countries of Central Asia were employed on the teaching staff of these institutions; they received handsome salaries from the state exchequer. The grants of teachers were raised from 100-200 *tankas* to 400-500, and even up to 1000 *tankas* for the learned scholars. Education was free. The students were charged no fees, and even the cost of their board and lodging was borne by the state; 'the students, who earlier did not receive even ten *tankas* as stipends, were given grants of 100 or 200 or 300 *tankas*'.

The Sultan was fond of the subject of history; he not only penned an autobiographical account of his own activities as a dedicated Muslim ruler of the Islamic state of Delhi but also liberally patronized the celebrated historians of his time suchas Ziauddin Barani, Shams-i-Siraj Afif and the author of *Sirat-i-Firoze Shahi*. He was perhaps the only Sultan of Delhi who showed some interest in the literature of the Hindus. During his expedition to Nagarkot (Kangra), he found a fine library of the Hindus, containing 1300 books, at the temple of Jawalamukhi; he is known to have caused some of the Sanskrit works to be translated into Persian, with the title, *Dalayal-i-Firoze Shahi*.

Firoze Tughluq was a great builder. In his *Futuhat-i-Firozeshahi*, the Sultan records with a feeling of satisfaction and pride that 'among the gifts which God bestowed upon me—His humble servant was a desire to erect public buildings. So I built many mosques and colleges (*Madrassas*) and monasteries (*Khanqahs*), that the learned and the elders, the devout and the holy, might worship God in these edifices, and aid the kind builder with their prayers'. He founded a number of new cities like those of Fatehabad, Hissar Firoza (mod. Hissar in Haryana), Ferozepur, Jaunpur and Firozabad, now called Kotla Firozeshah – a part of the city of Delhi. Afif credits him with the construction of nine palaces in the various towns for the stay of royalty, and civil and military officers, besides 120 *khanqahs* where the travellers and pilgrims were provided free board and lodging for three days at the state expense. Firoze Tughluq took keen interest in the preservation of old monuments of the earlier Sultans, and carried out extensive repairs to many of them. The long list of public buildings and the tombs of the preceding Sultans and saints which were repaired and renovated by him included among others, 'the *Masjid-i jámi'* of old Delhi', which was built by Muhammad Ghori 'but had fallen into decay from old age, and needed repair and restoration', *Hauz-i Shamsí* or tank of Iltutmish, *Hauz-i-Ilahi*, or tank of Alauddin Khilji and the *Madrassa* (college) of Iltutmish.

Firoze Tughluq's interest in the preservation of old monuments fascinated him to take notice of two Ashokan pillars, one found near Tobra or Topra village in the Ambala district of modern Haryana, and the other at Meerut in Uttar Pradesh; he removed and transplanted them in the metropolis of Delhi. Afif has it on record that

> 'After his return from Thatta, Sultan Firoze often frequented the vicinity of Delhi as a pleasure and engaged the infidels in battles. There were two stone pillars – one in the neighbourhood of Shiq Salora and Khizerabad at the village Tobra, and the other near the town of Meerut. No ruler of Delhi had the good fortune of transferring these pillars to the city of Delhi. Firoze Shah was blessed enough to have worked hard to re-erect both these pillars at Delhi. One pillar was re-erected in the palace at Firozabad near the Jama Masjid and named Golden Minar. The other pillar was brought to the palace *Koshak-i-Shikar* with great skill and effort.' – (*Tarikh-i-Firoze Shahi*, p. 175)

His biographer informs us that Firoze Tughluq had setup 36 state-owned *karkhanas* or factories for the manual production of weapons of war and accessories of life for use by the army, royal household and the public. They were managed by a separate wing of the *Diwan-i-wizarat*, called the *Diwan Khana*. These factories were put under the charge of high-ranking *khans* or *amirs* and were manned by thousands of skilled and unskilled workers. Each of these factories specialized in the production of certain special type of goods and served as ware-houses for the collection, production as well as storage of those commodities.

Apart from weaponry, these *karkhanas* or 'store-workshops' met the requirements of 'elephant stables, cavalry, camels, candlesticks & light, kitchen accessories, wine cellar, water works and so on. All these factories were a permanent charge on the state exchequer. The second category of *karkhanas,* which had no fixed grants, included 'the wardrobe store, royal standards, furniture, tents and carpets, saddles and harness store, etc. The most outstanding and conspicuous part of this fruitful public activity of Sultan Firoze Tughluq is the revelation that almost the entire labour force or man-power for these *karkhanas* was provided by the Sultan's slaves (enslaved Hindus, forcibly converted into Muslims) many of whom were imparted technical training and skill for production.

The Concluding Years of Firoze Tughluq's Reign

Firoze Tughluq was lucky enough to have enjoyed a long reign of comparative peace and tranquillity. It remained free from external dangers from central Asia; and as for the internal revolts, after a few highly expensive but poorly organized military expeditions, which proved only partially successful, Firoze Tughluq renounced warfare. He abandoned the chances of victory against the rebellious provincial governors and others 'on account of either incapacity or religious scruples' and was contented with the shrinking of his dominions into a small kingdom of Delhi. At the same time, his humane and benevolent reign, marked by many works of public utility, also foundered against the rock of religious bigotry. 'Lacking a broad philosophical base such as Muhammad Tughluq had,' observes Dr. Satish Chandra, 'he interpreted religion in a narrow sense, and indulged in acts of bigotry and oppression, against sections of both the Hindus and the Muslims. This weakened rather than strengthened his concept of a benevolent state'. (*Medieval India.*, New Delhi, 3rd ed. 2004, p. 113).

Though a pious and devoted Musalman, Firoze Tughluq was known to be a disciple of the liberal-minded *Sufi* Saint Shaikh Alauddin, grandson and successor of Shaikh Fariduddin Ganj Shaker of Ajodhan. According to Afif, he used to pay obeisance to the saints of Delhi before proceeding on any journey outside the metropolis. But in the year 1374-75 (776 A.H.), the Sultan went to Bahraich and offered obeisance at the tomb of an orthodox Sunni saint, *Sipahsalar* Masud Ghazi. It is said that 'the spirit of the saint' appeared to him in a dream and 'stroked his beard, suggesting that it was time to take stock of oneself as the old age was overtaking, and provisions must be made for the last journey (*aakhrat*)'. Thereupon, 'the Sultan had his head shaved' as a holyman or *darvesh*, and many of his nobles followed suit. Thereafter, the Sultan decided to forbid all practices which were against the *Shara*', and ended as a fanatic proselytizer. Most of his acts of religious bigotry, as referred to in the preceding pages of this study, were committed by him after this incident. He assumed the role of a missionary of Islam, and all of his habitual clemency and mildness vanished into thin air while dealing with the Hindu infidels and liberal-minded Muslims, including the Shias.

The infirmities of old age compelled Firoze Tughluq to delegate his royal powers to his trustworthy and highly ambitious *wazir*, Khan-i-Jahan II, the son and successor of Khan-i-Jahan Maqbul, in 1375-76 (777 A.H.) but his zeal to restore the pristine glory of orthodox Islam by the elimination of *kufar* and annihilation of the *kafirs* from his dominions spurred him to renewed activity and preoccupied his attention till his death. Though weak and irresolute in his fight against the rebellious Muslim chiefs because of his narrow religious affinities, Firoze Tughluq picked up 'courage, resolution and firm determination', and assumed the role of a blood-thirsty monster in the persecution of the Hindus, Shias and other non-conformist Musalmans. A glaring instance of this contradiction in his character is provided by his 'barbaric method' of handling the disaffected Hindu *zamindars* and chieftains of Etawa and Katehr, particularly after the renunciation of war by the Sultan, in sharp contrast to his timid behaviour and humane attitude in the face of the Muslim rebels of Bengal and elsewhere, In 1376-77 (778 A.H.), the Hindu *zamindars* of Etawah 'threatened to revolt' against the oppression and highhandedness of the Muslim officers but they were crushed with an iron hand on the instructions of the Sultan. At the same time, Firoze Tughluq himself 'went on a hunting excursion' so-called towards Katbar or Katehr (Rohilkhand), where a *raja* (Hindu feudatory chief), referred to by the contemporary chroniclers as Kharku, was said to have 'treacherously murdered' Sayyid Muhammad, the governor of Badaun and his two brothers. The rebels were engaged by the royal troops. The Sultan returned to the capital after some time while a number of Afghan contingents were left behind by him to chastise the rebels. Two years later, in 1379-80 (781 A.H.), Firoze Tughluq went on a similar expedition again into 'the infidel territories' and the royal forces 'perpetrated almost a wholesale massacre of the Hindus.' The rebellious Hindu chief, after suffering a defeat, fled to the Kumaon hills. The Sultan gave a hot chase to the fugitive, and although he could not lay his hands on the rebel, 'a very large number of Hindus were killed and 23,000 captured and enslaved'. Before his return to the capital, Firoze Tughluq deputed a powerful Rohilla Afghan general at Badaun to muster a powerful and well-equipped force 'to devastate Katehr annually for the next five years'; it was tantamount to the total annihilation or genocide of the Hindus in the region. Not only this; the Sultan himself undertook such 'hunting excursions' year after year, which actually implied the hunting down of infidels, in the heart of northern and central India, and to oversee the compliance of his orders by his lieutenants, till he fell ill and was confined to bed in the year 1387 (789 A.H.).

The concluding years of Firoze Tughluq's reign were clouded by troubles and turmoil. He had many sons and grandsons. Two of his sons had predeceased the Sultan while his third eldest son, Prince Muhammad was jealous of the prime minister and distrusted him. In the game of power-politics, the crafty *wazir* conspired to liquidate the prince but was himself disgraced and killed instead. Prince Muhammad assumed royal powers for a while, but he was not acceptable to majority of the nobles, including the slave officers of Firoze Tughluq, who attempted to play the role of kingmakers. It triggered off a fratricidal war between the rival claimants to the throne while the Sultan had not yet closed his eyes. Firoze Tughluq nominated his grandson, Tughluq Shah II, 'to administer the realm' on his behalf a few days before his death on September 20, 1388 (the month of *Ramzan*, 790 A.H.). According to orthodox Muslim standards, he was 'an ideal king' though he sat on the throne of Delhi and saw through the rapid disintegration of the Sultanate. He was the last great Sultan of the Tughluq dynasty, and his weak and imbecile successors were reduced to the stature of petty chieftains of the principality of Delhi.

❑ ❑

7

DISINTEGRATION OF THE SULTANATE

SECTION 1: THE LATER TUGHLUQS

The decline and disintegration of the Sultanate of Delhi had begun during the reign of Muhammad bin Tughluq. A poor administrator and incompetent military general, Firoze Tughluq failed to establish effective control over the ambitious provincial governors and hastened the process of its decay. He had neither the will nor capacity to check the forces of disruption and depended heavily upon his prime ministers and orthodox *ulema* in the administrative affairs. His excessive mildness and clemency towards the bureaucracy, revival of *jagirdari* system, and excessive feudalization of the state army bred lethargy and corruption in the civil and military services, and his saintly disposition as devout Muslim degenerated into religious bigotry and persecutions of the Hindus and all those who did not conform to the orthodox tenets of Islam. These factors struck at the very roots of a strong and stable state, and, no wonder, Firoze Tughluq haplessly watched the dismemberment of the Sultanate in spite of his appreciable record of public welfare activities and concern for the poor and the needy.

Firoze Tughluq was succeeded on the throne of Delhi by six princes of his royal family, including one son and five grandsons in quick succession, but they were all weaklings. None of them could assert his full authority as sovereign ruler in the face of his respective band of ambitious and all-powerful nobles, who played the role of kingmakers. On the death of Firoze Tughluq, one of his grandsons—Tughluq Shah, son of the crown prince Fatah Khan, who had predeceased the Sultan; ascended the throne and assumed the title of Ghiasuddin Tughluq II. The pampered grandchild of the late Sultan, he turned out to be a debauch and pleasure-seeking ruler, who could not handle the state affairs effectively. He failed to establish his control over the royal household and many of his courtiers and military generals openly defied his authority. His claim to the throne was immediately contested by prince Muhammad Shah, the third surviving son of Firoze Tughluq who was then residing at Sirmur. The latter was defeated and turned out of Sirmur but he took possession of the stronghold of Nagarkot (Kangra) and could not be dislodged from there.

Meanwhile, Ghiasuddin Tughluq II was assassinated by one of the rival factions of nobility at the court in February 1389. They placed another grandson of Firoze Tughluq, named prince Abu Bakr, on the throne; he was the son of Zafar Khan, the second son of Firoze Tughluq, who had also died during the lifetime of his father. Meanwhile, his uncle, prince Muhammad Shah had descended from Kangra and setup as independent ruler at Samana in April 1389; he was supported by a party of the *Amiran-i-Sadah*. The Sultanate of Delhi now came to be ruled over by two Sultans of the Tughluq dynasty. Confusion and chaos prevailed everywhere and all the provincial governors as also the *zamindars* even in the neighbourhood of Delhi did not know to whom they should acknowledge their ruler or extend their support. It led to a civil war between the two rival claimants to the throne in which most of the provincial governors and refractory *zamindars*, including the Hindus as well as Muslims, held aloof. Prince Muhammad came out victorious in the civil war and entered the capital in triumph in August 1390. He ascended the throne at Firozabad with the high-sounding title of Sultan Nasiruddin Muhammad Shah II while Abu Bakr was taken prisoner and held in confinement in the fort of Meerut where he died a few months later.

This was not the end of the fratricidal struggle between the various scions of the Tughluq dynasty, however. Muhammad Shah II (1390-94) ruled for about four years and showed some semblance of royal authority, but he failed to win the support of the provincial governors. Farhat-ul-Mulk, the governor of Gujarat, threw off the imperial yoke of Delhi and declared his sovereignty; Gujarat was thus lost to the Sultanate forever. He died of ill health in January 1394. His son and successor Humayun, styled Alauddin Sikander Shah, died within six weeks of his accession under suspicious circumstances. A faction of the nobles put up the younger brother of Humayun, a ten years old boy, on the throne of Delhi with the title of Sultan Nasiruddin Mahmud Shah, but their rivals immediately brought out another sibling of the royal family, named Nusrat Shah and installed him as the Sultan at

Firozabad, a suburb of the capital; he was a grandson of Firoze Tughluq and a brother of Ghiasuddin Tughluq II. It created a very funny situation in which the two puppet Tughluq Sultans sat on two different royal thrones within the metropolis of Delhi. To the great bewilderment and inconvenience of the people, 'the rival factions grinned at each other with drawn-out swords and occasionally the streets of Delhi were smeared with blood while their puppet Sultans wore the crowns like the clowns, and played hide and seek with each other like the proverbial 'kings of the game of chess'. Taking advantage of the confusion that prevailed at Delhi, the provincial governors of Jaunpur, Malwa and Khandesh also cutoff their contacts with the central government and declared their independence. According to Firishta, this anomalous state of affairs lasted about three years 'with astonishing equality; for if one Sultan's party had at any time the superiority, the balance was soon restored by the neutral chiefs, with the consequence that the government fell into anarchy; civil war raged everywhere; and a scene was exhibited, unheard of before, of two kings in arms against each other residing in the same capital'. (*Tarikh-i-Firishta*; Briggs, i, p. 481)

In the winter of 1397, the news spread that Amir Timur, the ruler of Samarqand, had made his appearance on the northwestern frontiers of India with a huge army of invasion. His advance-columns crossed the Indus and, following a southwesterly course, moved towards Delhi after the conquest of Uchh and Multan. On the approach of the invader, Sultan Nusrat Shah fled from the capital and took shelter in the Doab. The child Sultan Mahmud Shah, accompanied by his mentor, Mallu Iqbal Khan, put up a feeble resistance against Amir Timur in mid-December 1398, but they were defeated and fled for their lives, leaving the capital at the mercy of Amir Timur's marauders. The town was sacked and thousands of its inhabitants were slaughtered like animals; and those who survived were humiliated and disgraced, and 'made to suffer all sorts of indignities 'as if for having tolerated, with an attitude of indifference, the misrule of incompetent and worthless successors of Firoze Tughluq'.

Headquarters of the 'Sultanate of Hindustan' lay at the feet of Amir Timur, but like Mahmud of Ghazni, the victor did not want to stay here for reasons, explained elsewhere in this study. He, however, annexed the northwestern provinces of Multan, Lahore and Dipalpur to his central Asian empire; these provinces were put under the charge of Sayyad Khizr Khan (later the founder of the Sayyad dynasty in Delhi), erstwhile subordinate of Sultan Firoze Tughluq, who had held the governorship of Multan at the time of his master's death. Khizr Khan was ousted from Multan in 1395 by Mallu Iqbal Khan and his brother, Sarang Khan, during the nominal rule of the phantom Tughluq Sultan Mahmud Shah. At the time of Amir Timur's invasion, he joined the invader's camp and faithfully collaborated with him in his onslaught on India. As no scion of the Tughluq dynasty dared or had the resources to establish contacts with the victor even by way of acknowledging his suzerainty. Khizr Khan was nominated by Amir Timur as his viceroy in Delhi, on the eve of his departure for Samarqand, in March 1399.

After the departure of Amir Timur, Delhi lay in shambles, and confusion and chaos prevailed everywhere in northern India. The Tughluq Sultan Nusrat Shah was the first to step into the almost deserted town midst the vale of tears and cries of the wounded and the sick and claimed sovereignty over it. The other Tughluq contender, Sultan Mahmud Shah was wandering about as a fugitive in Malwa and Gujarat but his lieutenant Mallu Iqbal descended on Delhi and Nusrat Shah was beaten out of the capital by him. Nusrat Shah died a broken-hearted man somewhere in Mewat. Mallu Khan took possession of the ruined capital and some adjoining districts of the Doab and setup as *de facto* ruler without assuming any royal title. In 1401, he called back Mahmud Shah to Delhi and tried to exploit him as a puppet Sultan once again, but the latter, having grown up into manhood, refused to play the second fiddle to Mallu, thus triggering off yet another civil war, now between Mahmud Shah and his mentor and kingmaker Mallu Khan. In the struggle that ensued, Mahmud Shah left Delhi and setup his court at Kanauj, leaving behind Mallu Khan as the undisputed master of the capital.

By this time, Sayyad Khizr Khan, the nominee of Amir Timur as viceroy of northwestern India, had consolidated his position at Multan; he declared Mallu Khan the usurper and prepared to take action against him. Mallu Khan died fighting against Khizr Khan some time in 1405 (808 A.H.) but the latter, having been dubbed as traitor by the Hindustani Musalmans, failed to establish a popular base in Delhi, and resisted the temptation to gatecrash into the capital. It provided an opportunity to Mahmud Shah to stage a comeback to Delhi once again. To his misfortune, in this game of hide and seek, 'a new set of kingmakers, led by one Daulat Khan, emerged on the scene and compelled Mahmud to be content with his position as the puppet Sultan of Delhi as before. Totally disheartened and disillusioned by these developments, Sultan Mahmud resorted to drinking and debauchery and died a physical and mental wreck in 1412 at Kaithal after a fruitless reign of twenty years. He was the last scion of the Tughluq dynasty and the last Turkish Sultan of Delhi.'(*Advanced Study,* i,pp. 241-42). Daulat Khan continued to hold Delhi as its *de facto* ruler for another year and a half but without assuming any royal title. By this time, the once mighty Sultanate of Delhi had been reduced to the position of a small estate. The whole region was engulfed in anarchy, and, in the absence of any powerful central authority, most of the fief-holders and *zamindars* of the adjoining areas, whether Hindus or Muslims, were left to fend for themselves. Daulat Khan continued to strike coins in the name of the Tughluqs till March 1414 when Khizr Khan finally made an assault on Delhi. Daulat Khan was defeated and taken prisoner. Khizr Khan ascended the throne of Delhi on June 6, 1414, and laid the foundation of the Sayyad dynasty, and Daulat Khan died a state prisoner in the fort of Hissar soon thereafter.

SECTION 2: THE INVASION OF AMIR TIMUR (1398-99)

Amir Timur – 'the Scourge of God on Earth', who took Delhi by storm in 1398-99, was one of the greatest Muslim rulers of central Asia, and 'the second most barbaric, blood-thirsty and awe-inspiring warrior after Changez Khan, who sat on the throne of Samarqand'. He 'had already overrun all Persia and Mesopotamia to the frontiers of the Ottoman empire in Asia Minor on the west, and occupied Afghanistan on the east, before the wealth of India drew him to the invariable road of central Asian invaders.'- (Stanley Lane-Poole, *Medieval India,* pp.154-55). He was born in April 1334 at Kech or Kesh, popularly known as *shahr-i-sabz* ('the green city'), situated about 80 kilometres to the south of Samarqand. He was the son of Amir Turghay, chief of the Gurgan or Chaghtai branch of the Barlas Turks; the epithet Gurgan was derived from the word '*gurg*' (a wolf) which was the insignia of the ruling family of Timur. Turghay ruled over a small principality with its capital at Kesh. He died in 1361 but Timur had to fight against his own kinsmen for nine years before he established himself as the chief of the Chaghtai Turks and ascended the throne of Samarqand in 1370. Thereafter, his rise to power was very rapid. Timur's lust for power and domination involved him in a long struggle and wars of aggression for over thirty years which made him the overlord of the whole of central Asia, including Persia and Afghanistan. In 1363, he was wounded in the leg by an arrow during an encounter with Siestani army, which maimed him for life; thereby, he earned the nickname of *Aksak* (one who limps) from his Turkish foes while the Persians called him Timur-i-Lang (Timur the Lame), and the European writers corrupted this name into *Tamarlane.* It is said that in his long career of struggle and strife, he had never suffered defeat in any battle.

Objects of Timur's Invasion on India

It was towards the end of his career that Amir Timur thought of organizing an expedition to India. In his memoirs, under a forthright heading - *The history of my expedition against Hindustan,* he narrates the story of the invasion, in the first person, as follows:

> 'About this time there arose in my heart the desire to lead an expedition against the infidels, and to become a *ghází*; for it had reached my ears that the slayer of infidels is a *ghází*, and if he is slain he becomes a martyr. It was on this account that I formed this resolution, but I was undetermined in my mind whether I should direct my expedition against the infidels of China or against the infidels and polytheists of India. In this matter, I sought an omen from the Quran, and the verse I opened upon was this, *"O Prophet! Make war upon infidels and un-believers, and treat them with severity."* (*Tuzuk-i-Timuri*)

Accordingly, Timur summoned a council of his premier generals and the *ulema* to take a decision regarding the projected expedition. After deliberations, India was selected as the target of his onslaught with the twin objects of waging a holy war (*Jehad*) against the infidels and laying his hands on its fabulous wealth. Maulana Yezdi, the celebrated author of *Zafarnama,* explains the underlying reason that led to this choice; he writes that Amir Timur 'had previously heard that the standards of the faith of Islam had been raised in Dehli and other places, and that its profession of faith was impressed upon the coins, but that the country in general was polluted by the inhabitants being infidels and idolaters. Impelled by the desire of waging a religious war, he resolved to march against Multan and Delhi. He consulted with his nobles and chiefs, and they concurred in the propriety of making the invasion'.

The primary object of his invasion, which was quite evident from the introductory paragraph of his memoirs, was further elaborated by Amir Timur on its re-affirmation by his advisers with the observation that 'We may convert to the true faith the infidels (*kafirs*) of that country, and purify the land from the filth of infidelity and polytheism; and that we may overthrow their temples and idols and become *ghazis* and *mujahids* before God'. To this was closely allied the second and the more tempting prospect of loot and plunder. Prince Muhammad Sultan, in his speech, alluded to the richness and prosperity of the vast country of Hindustan, inhabited by idol-worshippers and infidels and pleaded with the Amir to kill two birds with one stone by organising an expedition against India; he argued his case in the words that follow:

> 'The whole country of India is full of gold and jewels, and in it there are seventeen mines of gold and silver, diamond and ruby and emerald and tin and iron and steel and copper and quicksilver, etc., and of the plants which grow there are those fit for making wearing apparel, and aromatic plants, and the sugarcane, and it is a country which is always green and verdant, and the whole aspect of the country is pleasant and delightful. Now, since the inhabitants are chiefly polytheists and infidels and idolaters and worshipers of the sun, by the order of God and his Prophet, it is right for us to conquer them'. (*Ibid.*)

Amir Timur's appetite for gold and silver was thus sharpened when he was informed by his ministers that the estimated amount of the revenue of India was '*six arbs*' or six hundred crores of rupees (silver *miskals*) per annum. He became rather emotional to hear of this staggering amount and attempted to split it up like a child by way of calculating it arithmetically as follows:

> 'Now each *arb* is a 100 crores, and each crore is a 100 *lacs*, and each *lac* is a 100,000 *miskals* of silver'.

Some of the nobles talked of 'the four great defenses of Hindustan' which had to be overcome for the success of their venture; these were: (1) 'five great rivers (of the Punjab) to cross'; (2) 'dense forests and trees, which, interweaving stem with stem and branch with branch, render it very difficult to penetrate into that country'; (3) 'the soldiery, and landholders, and princes, and Rájas of that country, who inhabit fastnesses in those forests, and live there like wild beasts'; and (4) 'the elephants, for the rulers of that country, on the day of battle, equipping elephants in mail, put them in the van of their army, and place great confidence in them; and they have trained them to such a pitch that, lifting with their trunks a horse with his rider, and whirling him in the air, they will dash him on the ground'. But the other counsels recalled of the heroic exploits of Mahmud of Ghazni—'the Idol-breaker', and

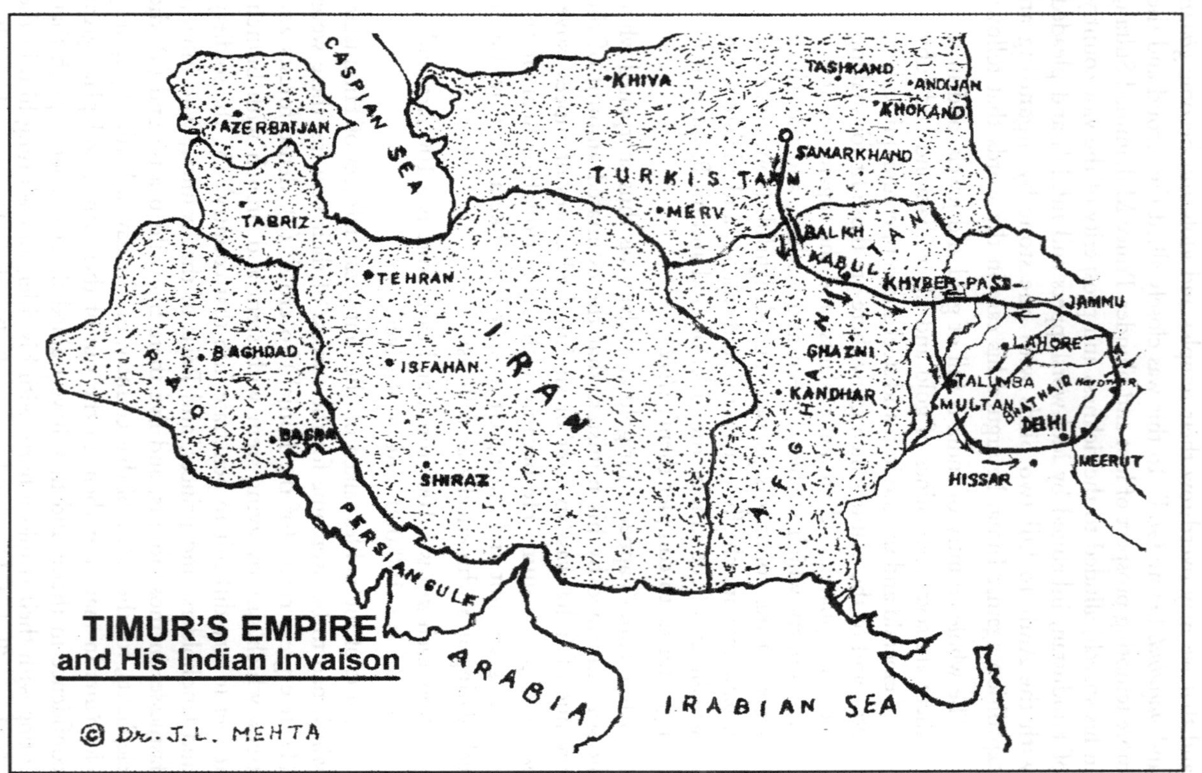

TIMUR'S EMPIRE
and His Indian Invaison

© Dr. J.L. MEHTA

called upon Amir Timur to emulate his example. Nevertheless, as regards the subjugation of Hindustan – 'the land of Hindu infidels', which implied their prospects of permanent settlement in India, there was much difference of opinion among the courtiers of Amir Timur. Those of his advisers, who struck a note of discord said,

> "By the favour of Almighty God we may conquer India, but if we establish ourselves permanently therein, our race will degenerate and our children will become like the natives of those regions, and in a few generations their strength and velour will diminish."

It clinched the issue and the afore-mentioned two-fold object of Amir Timur's Indian invasion was clearly defined. Thus it was that Timur, true to his pre-planned solemn resolve, stormed India like a tsunami, drenched Delhi in pools of human blood and swept away with all of its gold and silver, imperial glory and much besides; he was 62 at the time of his invasion.

The Invasion

Prince Pír Muhammad Jahangir, a grandson of Timur, who held the viceroyalty of Kabul, Ghazni, and Kandahar, 'with all their dependencies as far as the confines of India', crossed the unguarded Khyber Pass with his advance-columns, towards the end of 1397. He captured the towns of Uchh and Dipalpur and setup his military posts there. Elated with his initial success, Pir Muhammad moved along the Indus in the southwesterly direction, and laid siege to Multan. It was then held by Sarang Khan, a brother of Mallu Iqbal, the *de facto* ruler of Delhi. Sarang Khan offered a tough resistance to the invaders, however, and the siege of Multan dragged on for many months. According to *Tuzuk-i-Timuri*, it was from Multan that Pir Muhammad wrote to Timur and apprised him of the political anarchy that prevailed in northern India, ever since the death of Sultan Firoze Tughluq, and 'sought his advice and support'. It confirmed Timur's resolve to invade India strictly in the spirit of a *Jihadi*; and hearing his 'edifying words', the hearts of his nobles 'were setupon a holy war in Hindustán, and throwing themselves on their knees, they repeated the *Chapter of Victory*.'

Amir Timur left Samarqand in the month of March 1398 'with an army as numerous as the leaves of the trees'; it comprised '92,000 regiments of a thousand horse each'. According to *Zafarnama*, when he reached Indrab, 'the chiefs of that country came and cast themselves at his feet, saying that they were Musalmans, and that the infidel Kators (Katurs) and *Siyah Poshan* exacted sums of money every year as tribute from them; and in default of payment, the infidels slew the men, and made their women and children prisoners...The infidels of this country are tall, stout, and vigorous. Their chiefs are called Uda and Udashu. Most of them know no language but their own. Their statements kindled the anger of the emperor, and he resolved to suppress these infidels'. Accordingly, Amir Timur's first priority was to chastise the remnant of the Hindu tribes of the Pamirs—the inhabitants of Katur, and the *Siyah Poshan.* Amir Timur crossed the high mountains surrounding Katur, 'struggling over the stony girdles of the earth...through ice and snow...in pursuit of the infidel tribes', and

> 'When he arrived at Kháwak, (he) ordered the fort of that place, which was in ruins, to be repaired. The soldiers and many of the *amirs* left their horses there, and ascended the mountain of Kator on foot...After three days' continuous fighting Timur's troops prevailed, and the enemy sued for quarter. Timur sent to them Ák Sultán, proposing that if they would surrender and become Musalmans, he would spare their lives and property, and confirm them in the possession of their country. When they were informed of these terms by means of interpreters they, on the fourth day, hastened with Ák Sultán to the court of Timur, made their profession of the faith, and with tears offered excuses for their conduct. They declared themselves to be his slaves, and ready to obey his commands. Timur, in his kingly generosity, gave them robes and dismissed them. When night came on, these black-hearted renegades made an attack upon Amir Shah Malik. Some few of them, wounded and maimed, escaped, but 150 of them were taken prisoners, and were despatched to hell with the sword. The whole army of Islam then ascended the mountain and put all the men to the sword, and carried off the women and children. On the summit of the mountain pyramids were built with the heads of these infidels, who had never bowed their heads in adoration of Allah. An account of the victory was engraved upon stone, with the date of the month Ramzan 800 H., together with the date used in the locality'. (*Zafarnama*)

Timur's action against the *Siyah Poshan* (the Black Robes) proved a failure, however. His general, Burhan Ughlan, who was sent to chastise them, suffered a humiliating defeat at their hands and 'fled back like a coward'. This campaign, which had to be waged on foot, lasted 18 days.

After 'the settlement' of newly conquered territories of non-Muslim tribes in Afghanistan, and the adoption of 'measures for the protection of the roads' to his satisfaction, Timur's main army moved through the Khyber Pass, while he, in spite of his old age, personally jumped across the Suleiman Ranges with a body of royal guards on foot; and 'exterminated' the infidel 'predatory tribes of the Aghánís' (Afghans), before descending down the hills by way of Bannu on the Indian side of the border. In September 1398, Timur crossed the Indus by a bridge of boats, defeated the Khokhars and then proceeded along the Jhelum towards Multan. The stronghold of Multan was conquered by Pir Muhammad before Timur's arrival there, but with the onset of the monsoons, the Prince, having lost a large number of his horses, was put to great straits by the local populace who had been plundered by the invaders. The prince joined Timur's camp at the village of Janjan, by the side of the river Beas, and was given thirty thousand horses for his soldiers. Thereafter, Timur sent the bulk of his army via Dipalpur while he himself adopted a more southerly route. After the annihilation of the Rajputs of Bhatnair, he proceeded through Sirsa and Sunam to join his main camp at Samana (in modern Haryana). Delhi being the major target of his attack, he 'had no time for long sieges' and avoided most of the well-fortified towns.

The pages of Timur's memoirs are replete with the fearful stories of loot and plunder, torture and massacre of unarmed populace of villages and towns, destruction of their hearths and homes, chase of the fleeing fugitives, and capture of their women and children. For instance, the town of Tulamba (Talmi) was situated at the junction of the rivers Jhelum and the Chenab about seventy miles from Multan. According to the *Tuzuk-i-Timuri*, the garrison of Tulamba fort and inhabitants of the town made an unconditional surrender. They were asked to pay a ransom of two lakhs 'as the price of their safety', but on the representation by 'the *Sayyads*, *Ulema* and the *Shaikhs*', they were exempted from it; Timur 'sent them away, having filled their hearts with joy and triumph by presents of costly dresses of honour, and Arab horses'. This exemption from ransom and plunder was extended to all those who could prove their identity as the Muslims; and the discrimination between the Indian populace on religious grounds was generally exercised by Amir Timur and his army as far as possible throughout his campaign. In the same context, it is worthwhile to mention that, ever since Timur crossed the Indus, he had been receiving offers of support from many local Muslim nobles, and small bands of the Muslim deserters from the armies of provincial governors had started trickling into his camp, thereby swelling his ranks. Timur did not depend upon them nor put them to use as combat troops. Instead, he utilized their services as scouts and guides to facilitate the march of his regiments, and deputed them to collect provisions for his fighters and fodder for his horses.

Zafarnama records that 'some of the chief *zamindars* of the environs of Tulamba', who had earlier offered their submission, revolted and took refuge in the jungles along with their families and treasures. On the receipt of information, Timur immediately ordered two of his officers 'to march with their *tumáns* and *kushúns* against these rebels, and to inflict condign punishment upon them'. Accordingly, they 'taking a guide with them, instantly commenced their march, and having arrived at the jungles in which these wretches, forsaken by fortune, had taken refuge, they dismounted, and entering the jungle slew two thousand of these ill fated Indians with their remorseless sabers, carrying off captives their women and children, and returned with a great booty of kine (cows), buffaloes, and other property'.

The inhabitants of Dipalpur, who had killed the military commander and Tatar soldiery of Pir Muhammad, had fled for their lives, and the town was nearly depopulated. According to *Tuzuk-i-Timuri,* thousands of them took refuge in the Rajput stronghold of Bhatnir (Bhatnair), which was surrounded by a vast stretch of sandy desert of Chaul; it was under the control of Rai Dul Chand. On his way to Bhatnair, Timur reached Ajodhan where he halted for the night. He writes

> 'I was informed that the blessed tomb of Hazrat Shaikh Faríd Ganj-Shaker (whom may God bless) was in this city, upon which I immediately set out on pilgrimage to it. I repeated the *Fátiha*, and the other prayers, for assistance, and prayed for victory from his blessed spirit, and distributed large sums in alms and charity among the attendants on the holy shrine.'

The town of Ajodhan was also found deserted by most of its inhabitants, and Timur left it the next morning on his march to the fortified town of Bhatnair. Passing through Rudanah and Khális Kotlí, he made a three-pronged attack on Bhatnair; while his generals advanced upon it from right and left, he himself commanded the centre with ten thousand picked horsemen. On the approach of the invaders, the

Rai shut himself up within the fort and prepared to give a fight. According to *Zafarnama*, innumerable refugees from Dipalpur, Ajodhan and the countryside had sought shelter in the walled city of Bhatnair for fear of the invaders; 'so much so that the city would not contain them, and carts and vehicles with large quantities of goods and furniture had been left outside in the vicinity of the fort...All that was outside of the city was plundered immediately by the army of Islam' and the ground was cleared for an attack on the walled city. Timur deputed two regiments of his army to take on the town, and he himself prepared to invest the fort. 'At the very first assault the fortifications and walls were wrested from the hands of the Hindus, and the town was taken. Many Rajputs were put to the sword, and all the enormous wealth and property, which was in the city, fell as spoil into the hands of the soldiers'. The Rajput resistance collapsed after two days, and Dul Chand came out of the fort to offer his submission to the Amir in his camp. Meanwhile, all the strangers, including the Hindu and Muslim fugitives from Dipalpur and Ajodhan, were hauled up and inflicted severe punishments. More than 500 men from Dipalpur alone, who were suspected of having killed Pir Muhammad's lieutenant and his Tatar solders, were put to the sword in cold blood, their properties and goods, including 300 Arab horses were confiscated, and women and children distributed among his soldiers as slaves.

This 'fearful retribution' filled Dul Chand's brother, said to be a Musalman, named Kamaluddin, and son with dismay and they fled back to the fort and shut its gates. It enraged Amir Timur who placed the *Ráo* in confinement, and the fighting re-started. Although the defenders of the fort submitted again but there arose a dispute about the collection of ransom money, and the fort was taken by an assault. What followed thereafter and described by Timur in his memoirs and the author of *Zafarnama* in so many words is summarized as under:

The *gabrs* (Hindu fighters) set fire to their houses, and cast their wives and children into the flames to be consumed by fire. A party of them, who claimed to be Musalmans, cut off the heads of their wives and children with the sword like so many sheep. The two parties then joined and fought together against the invaders. They were very numerous, and very resolute and savage. Timur's soldiers stormed the fort from all sides, and shouting their war cry fell upon the defenders. A desperate conflict ensued, and many of the assailants (viz., Timur's soldiers) were slain and many wounded. Timur concludes the description of this event with the remarks:

> 'In a short space of time all the people in the fort were put to the sword, and in the course of one hour the heads of ten thousand infidels were cut off. The sword of Islam was washed in the blood of the infidels, and all the goods and effects, the treasure and the grain which for many a long year had been stored in the fort became the spoil of my soldiers. They set fire to the houses and reduced them to ashes, and they razed the buildings and the fort to the ground'.

According to Yezdi, besides the fort, the whole town of Bhatnair was also set ablaze and razed to the ground. 'The whole place was destroyed. Nothing was left but a few heaps of ashes. The gold and silver, and horses and spoil of every sort that fell into the hands of the captors were by order of Timur divided among the soldiers. He solaced the wounded by his royal munificence'. As 'the air was polluted by the putrefying bodies of the slain', Amir Timur left the place the very next morning for the onward march towards Delhi, plundering the villages and killing the people as they fell his way. After passing through Fatehabad, Timur arrived at the town of Sirsutí, probably modern Sirsa, which was found abandoned by its inhabitants. We have it from the horse's mouth as follows:

> 'When I made inquiries about the city of Sirsutí, I was informed that the people of the place were strangers to the religion of Islam and that they kept hogs in their houses and ate the flesh of those animals. When they heard of my arrival, they abandoned their city. I sent my cavalry in pursuit of them, and a great fight ensued. All of these infidel Hindus were slain, their wives and children were made prisoners, and their property and goods became the spoil of the victors. The soldiers then returned, bringing with them several thousand Hindu women and children who became Muhammadans, and repeated the creed'.

Tohana, the heart-land of Jats, was Timur's next target of attack. Timur was told that they were very aggressive and dangerous people, who organized themselves into bands of robbers and threatened the security of the highways leading to the capital. Their town, though found abandoned, was plundered and destroyed, and thereafter, Timur's soldiers searched for them 'in the jungles and sugarcane crops of the neighbourhood, and put 2,000 of these wild demon-like men to the sword; their wives and children he took captive, and their cattle and effects he plundered'. In contrast, the author of *Zafarnama* records that 'in that neighbourhood (of Tohana) there was a party of distinguished *Sayyads* who had taken up their abode in a certain village and sustained the honour of their religion. They came full of hope and confidence to wait on Timur, who received them kindly and bestowing on them his princely bounty, he gave them a governor to protect them from the violence of (his) soldiers'. The other towns of the region, including Kaithal, Sunam and Asand were also ravaged by the invader; he met with no resistance anywhere.

The Conquest and Sack of Delhi

In the third week of November 1398, the main army of Timur, which had followed a more northerly route, joined him at Samana. Timur now reorganized his forces for the final assault on Delhi, and moving through Panipat, reached the neighbourhood of the metropolis. The town of Panipat and its entire countryside was depopulated; 'the inhabitants having taken flight, not a soul was found there'. Timur, therefore, did not find any difficulty in collecting fodder for his horses and huge stocks of wheat, more than 10,000 *maunds* of which were found by him in the godowns of Panipat alone. He prepared to cross the Yamuna, on 11 December, near the village of Palla, preceded by a division of his best horsemen with orders 'to plunder and destroy and to kill every one whom they met' on the sight of their landing. Next day, Timur took possession of the palace of *Jahan-numa*, situated at a distance of 'two *farsakhs*' (about ten kilometres) from Delhi. It was 'a fine building, erected by Sultán Firoze Sháh on the top of a hill by the banks of the Jumna'; its guards and inhabitants were either killed or taken prisoners. Timur resided there for about two weeks during his stay at the capital. The fort of Loni, situated in its vicinity, was also taken by him but after a fight with its defenders. The inhabitants of Loni were mostly Hindus; the Muslim *kotwal* of the place, named Maimun, offered to make an unconditional surrender on the advice of an elderly Sayyad, but most of his soldiers, who happened to be Hindus, as well as the citizens of Loni, 'unmindful of the consequences' and 'in their folly and presumption, resolved to defend the place'. Accordingly, they had to face the gauntlet. Before the evening, the fort was captured by Timur but after the annihilation of its defenders. 'The Hindus set fire to their houses in the fort and burnt their women and children; then they rushed to the battle and were killed.' Timur 'remained outside of the fort that night'. He ordered that of the captives, the Muslims 'should be set aside' and 'all the infidels be despatched to hell with the proselytizing sword'. The fort of Loni, though ruined, was subsequently put to use by Timur for the storage of supplies for his forces.

About this time, the child Sultan Mahmud Shah Tughluq and his mentor Mallu Iqbal Khan were in control of Delhi, but, so far, they had taken no steps to oppose the invader. On the 12th of December 1398, Mallu made his appearance in the neighbourhood of *Jahan-numa* palace with 4,000 horse, 5,000 foot and 27 elephants but, after a brush with a detachment of Timur, hurriedly retreated towards Delhi. It was a signal for the final combat between the adversaries. At this occasion, two officers of Timur apprised him of the danger of keeping in his camp a hundred thousand Hindu prisoners, captured from the northwestern India, who were being used as beasts of burden to carry their baggage and to take care of their supplies and animals. They were reported to have 'shown delight at the idea of being rescued' in case of defeat of the invader. Accordingly, they were all mercilessly slaughtered like goats and sheep on the orders of Timur 'lest they might create trouble for them' during their conflagration with the foe. In the words of Yezdi,

> 'In pursuance of this order, 100,000 infidel Hindus were put to the sword. Maulana Nasiruddin, a most distinguished ecclesiastic, had fifteen Hindus in his train, and he, who had never caused a sheep to be slaughtered, was obliged to have these fifteen Hindus killed. Timur also issued an order that one man out of every ten of his combatants should be left in the camp to guard the wives and children of the prisoners, and the captured cattle'. (*Zafarnama*)

The water of Yamuna must have turned red with the blood of so many innocent children of the soil, and their dead bodies and broken limbs being carried by the Yamuna-Ganga Rivers to the Bay of Bengal must have horrified the whole of northern India. Timur got full one week to set his camp in order. The battle royal between the foes was fought on December 17, 1398 (8th Rabi'u-s sání, 801) in the vast plain at the foot of the *Jahan-numa* Palace, along the bank of the Yamuna, where he had stationed his forces in the battle array; the ground was levelled to suit the horses, all the obstructing shrubs and trees were cut off and dumped into deep ditches, dug around the open side of the battle-formations. We would not like to withhold, from our readers, the knowledge of yet another amazing but dreadful crime that the blood-thirsty Tatar warrior of central Asia committed in his bid to win the battle of Delhi. To have it from the horse's mouth:

> 'It had been constantly dinned into the ears of my soldiers that the chief reliance of the armies of Hindustán was on their mighty

elephants; that these animals, in complete armour, marched into battle in front of their forces, and that arrows and swords were of no use against them; that in height and bulk they were like small mountains, and their strength was such that at a given signal they could tear up great trees and knock down strongly built walls; that in the battlefield they could take up the horse and his rider with their trunks and hurl them into the air. Some of the soldiers, in the doubt natural to man, brought some little of what they had heard to my attention, so when I assigned their respective positions to the princes and *amírs* of the right and left wing and of the centre, I enquired of the learned and good men that accompanied my army, such as * * * where they would like to be placed in the day of battle. They had been with me in many campaigns, and had witnessed many a great battle, but the stories about the elephants of India had so affected them that they instantly replied that they would like to be placed with the ladies while the battle was in progress'.

'So to allay the apprehensions of this class of men', writes Amir Timur, 'I gave orders that all the buffaloes which had been taken and placed with the baggage should be brought up; I then had their heads and necks fastened to their legs, and placed the animals inside the *abattis* (ditches).'

Thus we are given to understand that the ditches, around the battle-lines, which were filled with the trees and shrubs and the bundled buffaloes, were, particularly, designed to keep the war elephants of the foe at a safe distance from his horsemen. At the same time, Amir Timur had got prepared, out of the fallen trees, a big lot of the wooden planks to be placed over the ditches for his horsemen to cross over them in the course of fighting. The ingenuity of Amir Timur in planning for the victory really deserves all appreciation.

On the fateful day of the battle, Mallu Iqbal Khan, accompanied by the child Sultan, confronted the invaders with only 10,000 horsemen, 40,000 foot and 125 elephants. Mallu's army emerged from the environs of Delhi a little before dawn and straightway marched on the adversary's right wing with a thunder. As 'the two armies confronted each other, the drums were beaten on both sides, shouts and cries were raised, a trembling fell upon that field, and a great noise was heard'. (*Tuzuk-i-Timuri*). The advance guard of the Indian elephants vanished into Timur's ditches without any accomplishment. The Indian soldiers 'showed no lack of courage' and held the ground till afternoon, but they could not withstand the repeated assaults of Timur's horsemen, 'Seeing their own plight and that of the soldiers and elephants around them, their courage fell and they took to flight'. (*Ibid.*) The victors gave a hot chase to the fleeing soldiers up to the gates of Delhi. Many of the fugitives were killed and others taken captives, but Mallu and his puppet Sultan escaped alive into the city and shut the gates behind them. Having lost the opportunity for making a formal surrender, they fled in the darkness of night from the hind gates of the capital. Mallu retreated towards Bulandshahr while the child Sultan was taken away to safety by his kinsmen and well-wishers in Gujarat. The whole night was spent by the victors in the encirclement of the city with the object of securing its gates 'to prevent the escape of anyone'. All the suburbs of Delhi were put to plunder and much booty was obtained by Timur's soldiers

The next day, on the 18th of December 1398, Amír Timur made a triumphant entry into Delhi and alighted at the *Idgah*, close to the *Haus-i-Hhas* (Alai Tank); he ordered his royal tents to be pitched in the open ground there. The leading citizens of Delhi and the *ulema*, led by Fazlullah Balkhi, the deputy of Mallu Iqbal, waited upon him and sought mercy for the inhabitants of the city. As soon as Timur heard about the flight of the phantom Sultan and Mallu Khan, he deputed 15,000 of his soldiers, under the command of senior officers, to take possession of all the public buildings, including the treasury, palaces, stores and armoury. Two days later, he held the court in which all the nobles and officials of *diwn-i-wazarat*, besides the Sayyads, Shaikhs, *Qazis* and other notables of the capital proceeded to offer their *nazrs* and make submission. *Khutba* in his name as the overlord of Hindustán was read on Friday, the 21st of December 1398. The people of Delhi took it as a change of regime and sought amnesty for all the subjects; they lost no time in making substantial contributions voluntarily to the 'safety money' demanded by the victor. But the evil genius of Amir Timur induced him to plunder the whole city and denude it of everything, including not only the fabulous wealth of its ex-rulers and nobility, including invaluable treasures, horses and elephants, but also the gold and silver of bankers and businessmen, accumulations of the rich and the poor, Hindus as well as Muslims without discrimination, and even the men and women of Delhi, who were to be taken away in chains as his slaves, He hesitatingly agreed to spare the life and property of the 'citizens of Delhi' but with the mental reservation that the innumerable outsiders and fugitives, who had taken refuge there with their families and valuables, were excluded. It was a mere ruse played upon the unsuspecting people of Delhi to absolve himself of the moral responsibility for what took place a couple of days later.

To begin with, after having taken possession of the royal palaces and public buildings, instead of safeguarding them, Timur's soldiers began to despoil them of their wealth and invaluable material assets, including even the furniture and baggage, manufactured goods and garments, corn and cereal, and whatever they could lay their hands on. All these spoils were carried away by the victorious soldiery to their camp, outside the city, by means of captured wheeled carts, horses, animals and men and women captives, who were used as beasts of burden. More than a hundred thousand outsiders, who had choked the public buildings, open spaces and streets of the walled city, were all hauled up with their families and valuable assets and taken away as spoils of war; those who dared to resist were put to the sword. *Tuzuk-i-Timuri* and *Zafarnama* both have apologetically and in self-defence, attempted to describe the causes and circumstances which led to the general massacre of the populace and loot and plunder of the capital on the orders of Amir Timur. To quote *Tuzuk-i-Timuri* verbatim,

> A party of fierce Turk soldiers had assembled at one of the gates of the city to look about them and enjoy themselves, and some of them laid violent hands upon the goods of the inhabitants. When I heard of this violence, I sent some *amírs*, who were present in the city, to restrain the Turks. A party of soldiers accompanied these *amírs* into the city. Another reason was that some of the ladies of my *harem* expressed a wish to go into the city and see the palace of *Hazár-sutún* (thousand columns) which Malik Jauna (Muhammad bin Tughluq) (had) built in the fort called *Jahán-panáh*. I granted this request, and I sent a party of soldiers to escort the litters of the ladies. Another reason was that Jalál Islám and other *diwans* had gone into the city with a party of soldiers to collect the contribution laid upon the city. Another reason was that some thousand troopers with orders for grain, oil, sugar, and flour, had gone into the city to collect these supplies. Another reason was that it had come to my knowledge that great numbers of Hindus and *gabrs* (men-in-arms, the Rajputs), with their wives and children, and goods, and valuables, had come into the city from all the country around, and consequently I had sent some *amírs* with their regiments

(*kushúns*) into the city and directed them to pay no attention to the remonstrance of the inhabitants, but to seize and bring out these fugitives. For these several reasons, a great number of fierce Turki soldiers were in the city. When the soldiers proceeded to apprehend the Hindus and *gabrs* who had fled to the city, many of them drew their swords and offered resistance. The flames of strife were thus lighted and spread through the whole city from *Jahán-panáh* and *Sírí* to Old Dehli, burning up all it reached. The savage Turks fell to killing and plundering. The Hindus set fire to their houses with their own hands, burned their wives and children in them, and rushed into the fight and were killed. The Hindus and *gabrs* of the city showed much alacrity and boldness in fighting. The *amírs* who were in charge of the gates prevented any more soldiers from going into the place, but the flames of war had risen too high for this precaution to be of any avail in extinguishing them. On that day, Thursday (December 27, 1398), and all the night of Friday, nearly 15,000 Turks were engaged in slaying, plundering, and destroying. When morning broke on the Friday, all my army, no longer under control, went off to the city and thought of nothing but killing, plundering, and making prisoners. All that day the sack was general. The following day, Saturday, all passed in the same way, and the spoil was so great that each man secured from fifty to a hundred prisoners, men, women, and children. There was no man who took less than twenty. The other booty was immense in rubies, diamonds, garnets, pearls, and other gems; jewels of gold and silver; *ashrafis, tankas* of gold and silver of the celebrated 'Aláí coinage; vessels of gold and silver; and brocades and silks of great value. Gold and silver ornaments of the Hindu women were obtained in such quantities as to exceed all account. Excepting the quarter of the *sayyads*, the *'ulema*, and the other Musalmans, the whole city was sacked. The pen of fate had written down this destiny for the people of this city. Although I was desirous of sparing them I could not succeed, for it was the will of God that this calamity should fall upon the city.

'On the following day, Sunday, it was brought to my knowledge that a great number of infidel Hindus had assembled in the *Masjid-i-jámi'* of Old Dehli, carrying with them arms and provisions, and were preparing to defend themselves. Some of my people who had gone that way on business were wounded

> by them. I immediately ordered Amír Sháh Malik and 'Alí Sultán Tawáchí to take a party of men and proceed to clear the house of God from infidels and idolaters. They accordingly attacked these infidels and put them to death. Old Dehli then was plundered'.

Timur concludes the narrative regarding the sack of Delhi by the remarks:

> 'By the will of God, and by no wish or direction of mine, all the three cities of Dehli, by name Síri, Jahán-panáh, and Old Dehli, had been plundered. The *Khutba* of my sovereignty, which is an assurance of safety and protection, had been read in the city. It was therefore my earnest wish that no evil might happen to the people of the place. But it was ordained by God that the city should be ruined. He (God!) therefore inspired the infidel inhabitants with a spirit of resistance, so that they brought on themselves that fate which was inevitable'.

The facts speak for themselves and need no qualification or comment except that 'when a *lakh* of the hungry wolves (*gurgans*!) were let loose upon the defenseless citizens of the metropolis, it is difficult to perceive how they could discriminate between Hindus and Muslims among the common folk; may be some *sayyads* and *maulvis,* because of their distinct physical make-up and garments, were spared their lives. Of course, the prisoners included a large number of masons and craftsmen, both Hindus and Muslims, who were taken to central Asia to slave for the victors'. (Advanced Study, i, p. 245).

Plunder of Meerut, Haridwar, Kangra and Jammu

Timur stayed at Delhi for fifteen days only. The route for his return march through India was determined by two considerations; firstly, to secure a safe passage for his vast army, heavily overladen with the booty, he wanted to avoid any serious confrontation or resistance from the hostile Indians; and, secondly, to strengthen his cause of waging a holy war (*Jihad*) against the infidels of India, he was eager to lay his hands on some famous Hindu temples or centres of their power, so that his soldiers might get the thrill of some more loot and plunder. According to *Tuzuk-i-Timuri*, before Timur and his marauders retraced their steps across the Indus and 'disappeared up the Afghan valleys', they were credited with many victories 'in the land of the infidels', that was Hindustan, under the following sub-headings:

1. Campaigns against the infidels after the conquest of Delhi;

2. Battles on the Ganga;
3. Victories in the Shiwalik Hills;
4. Plunder of Nagarkot (Kangra);
5. Conquest of Jammu; and
6. The Hunting of Rhinoceros.

Probably, on the first of January 1399, when his 'mind was no longer occupied with the destruction of the people of Delhi', Amír Timur 'took a ride' round the three ruined cities of the metropolis, and 'met a congregation of the assembled *sayyads*, lawyers, *Shaikhs*, and other principal Musalmans in the *Masjid-i jámi'* . He consoled them, treated them with every respect, and bestowed upon them many presents and honours. He appointed an officer (from among them) to protect their quarter of the city, and guard them against annoyance'. He then 'remounted and returned to his camp'; it was the time to leave Delhi. After offering a prayer in the mosque of the Firozabad fort, on the Yamuna, he ordered the return march of his troops, and sent several contingents 'to plunder the country and vex the infidels' in the villages and towns along the Yamuna and the Ganga rivers, while they moved. Next day, he crossed the Yamuna and personally led a division of 10,000 horse to storm the fortified town of Meerut on the 8th of January. Though defended bravely by its besieged garrison, its defence collapsed suddenly 'for some un-explained reasons', and the Turks made a forced entry into the town the next day. Its Hindu chief died fighting while two of his Muslim collaborators were presented to Timur in chains. Most of the inhabitants of Meerut were put to the sword and their women and children enslaved. To display his sheer vandalism and brutality, the *Sahib-Kiran* (Timur) ordered his men 'to raze all the towers and walls of the city to the earth and set fire to the houses of the infidels'.

Thereafter, Timur 'placed the left wing of the army under the command of Amír Jahan Sháh, with orders to march up the Jumna, to take every fort and town and village he came to, and to put all the infidels of the country to the sword', while he himself directed his operations 'against the infidels on the Ganges'. Timur usually took under his personal command a division of his cavalry, consisting of ten regiments of a thousand horsemen each, in his assaults on select targets. With these picked horsemen, he proceeded towards the Ganga, which was then said to flow 'fourteen *kos* from Mírat (Meerut).' The entire countryside and all the human habitats which fell his way were ravaged before he crossed the river to its northern bank. The bulk of his army, which had been separated from him 'to ravage the country and plunder the infidels and fire-worshippers', joined his camp at Haridwar, which was the main target of their attack. The town was thoroughly sacked, and all of its temples and other holy shrines were put to plunder and desecrated. It is needless to add details to the devil-dance of his Turkish marauders; 'the progress of his armies was marked by rapine, massacre, and plunder of the Hindus'; the adult males were slain; the women and children were taken prisoners and converted into Islam while being carried as slaves. The road to Shiwaliks was clear. This highly fertile region was dotted with petty Hindu principalities and estates. Its prosperous and peace-loving *rais* and the villagers were driven to fight the Turkish robbers 'in sheer desperation' and were destroyed. *Tuzuk-i-Timuri* refers to the capture of seven forts and as many as twenty battles fought by the Timurids against the infidels of this area in the months of January-February 1399, accompanied by the same inhuman atrocities being committed by them, which make the civilized world hang its head in shame. Among the numerous temples destroyed by Timur's forces, *Tuzuk-i-Timuri* and *Zafarnama* both make a special mention of one shrine of the infidels where they used to worship a 'stone cow'. It was situated in 'the valley of Kupila, at the foot of a mountain by which the river Ganges passes'. It had a big stone 'in the form of a cow and the water of the river flew out of the mouth of that cow'. In the words of Yezdi,

> 'The infidels of India worship this cow, and come hither from all quarters, from distances even of a year's journey, to visit it. They bring here and cast into the river the ashes of their dead whose corpses have been burned, believing this to be the means of salvation (probably, Kankhal near Haridwar). They throw gold and silver into the river; they go down alive into the river, bathe their feet, sprinkle water on their heads, and have their heads and beards shaved. This they consider to be an act of devotion, just as the Muhammadans consider the pilgrimage to Mecca a pious work....It was the will of Heaven that these infidels should perish, so in the pride of their numbers and strength they awaited his (Amir Timur's) approach, and had the temerity to resolve upon resistance. At the rising of the sun, our army reached the valley. The right wing was under the command of Prince Pír Muhammad and Amír Sulaimán Sháh, and the left under some renowned leaders. Amír Sháh Malik and other officers

with the centre began the attack. When the cries of our men and the noise of our drums reached them, the courage of the infidels failed. In their terror they fled for refuge to the mountains, but they were pursued and many were slain. A few, who, half-dead, escaped the slaughter, were scattered all around. All their property and goods became the spoil of the victors'.

After the Shiwalik territories were ravaged to his heart's content, Timur 'turned back victorious and triumphant, laden with spoils', in which, apart from invaluable treasures, 'every Tatar soldier obtained 100 to 200 cows and 10 to 20 slaves.' He crossed the Ganga and after his 'mid-day prayers in the congregation, on the bank of that river', ordered the westward march of his troops along the foothills. His temptation to lay his hands on yet another holy town of the Hindus at Nagarkot (Kangra) and the Jawalamukhi temple, in the footprints of Mahmud of Ghazni, took him into the interior of the Shiwaliks. Leaving his main army at the foothills, with his officers deeply engrossed in the packing of booty and safeguarding of their staggering spoils in the form of elephants, horses, cows, buffaloes and slaves, Timur made up his mind to organize an expedition to 'demolish this centre of infidelity' with a part of his army. In order to convince his *amirs* about the urgency of this venture, Timur reiterated his commitment to his earlier twofold objective with which he had come to India. To reproduce his solemn vow verbatim,

> "My principal object in coming to Hindu-stán, and in undergoing all this toil and hardship, has been to accomplish two things. The first was to war with the infidels, the enemies of the Muhammadan religion; and by this religious warfare to acquire some claim to reward in the life to come. The other was a worldly object; that the army of Islám might gain something by plundering the wealth and valuables of the infidels: plunder in war is as lawful as their mothers' milk to Musalmans who war for their faith, and the consuming of that which is lawful is a means of grace."- (*Tuzuk-i-Timuri*)

According to *Tuzuk-i-Timuri*, the fort of Nagarkot was said to be situated at a distance of about thirty *kos* from the base camp of Timur but the passage lay 'through jungles, and over lofty and rugged hills'. 'Every *Rai* and *Raja* who dwelt in these hills had a large number of retainers';' and they were all ready to fight for the defence of their holy shrine. Timur was informed that 'the people of these forts and countries had formerly paid the *Jaziya* (poll-tax) to the Sultán of Hindustán; but for a long time past they had grown strong, and casting off their allegiance to those sovereigns, they no longer paid the *Jaziya*, but indulged in all sorts of opposition. They had posted themselves on lofty mounds which were all covered with an impenetrable forest'. On hearing of this, Timur 'set spurs to his horse and wended his way thither' with a strong body of the Tatar soldiers and officers of his army who had voluntarily offered to join this expedition against the infidels. With the help of the local guides, he ordered the advance of his troops at night 'under torch-light, and when the Hindus heard of the approach of his army, they fled without making even a show of resistance'. Early next morning, 'by a rapid march', they reached the vicinity of Nagarkot 'and sighted the infidels'. According to *Tuzuk-i-Timuri*,

> 'Like a pack of hungry sharp-clawed wolves, they fell upon the flock of fox-like infidels, and dyed their swords and weapons in the blood of those wretches till streams of blood ran down the valley. I went to the front from the rear, and found the enemy flying on all sides, and my braves splashing their blood upon the ground. A party of the Hindus fled towards the mountain, and I taking a body of soldiers pursued them up that lofty mountain, and put them to the sword. After mounting to the summit I halted. Finding the spot verdant and the air pleasant, I sat myself down and watched the fighting and the valiant deeds my men were performing. I observed their conduct with my own eyes, and how they put the infidel Hindus to the sword. The soldiers engaged in collecting the booty, and cattle, and prisoners. This exceeded all calculation, and they returned victorious and triumphant. The princes and *amírs* and other officers came up the mountain to meet me and to congratulate me on the victory'.

According to Timur, about two thousand Hindu soldiers died fighting in the battle. The garrison of Nagarkot was soon overpowered and all of its defenders were put to the sword but their women and children were taken prisoners. Building of the temple and houses of the people were ravaged and razed to the ground. Next morning, the invaders, heavily laden with booty, including slaves and herds of cows and buffaloes, were descending down the hills to their base camp in triumph.

Before his departure from Delhi, Timur had already sent his ambassadors to the rulers of Jammu, Kashmir and other hill chiefs to make unconditional surrender and pay tribute to him. The Hindu ruler of Jammu had paid no heed to his demand but Iskander Shah, the Sultan of Kashmir, had offered his submission to Amir Timur and had agreed to come down the hills to meet him. After the successful conclusion of his campaign in the Shiwaliks, Timur 'resolved to march against the country of Jammu.' He carried fire and sword all through the forests and hilly tracts en route to Jammu, crossing a number of rivulets and streams, and ravaging all the villages and hamlets of the region. The town of Jammu was situated 'in a valley, where the river Jammu (Tawi) rises'. Timur's army passed the river below the town and encamped at the foot of a mountain on its left. According to *Zafarnama*,

> 'The Rai of Jammu, with a force of bold and fearless men, had taken his stand in a strong position on the mountain, where they discharged their arrows and kept on shouting like dogs baying the moon. Timur resolved to proceed against them by stratagem, so he gave orders that they should be left alone, and that the village of Manu (situated on the right side of his camp) should be attacked. The soldiers accordingly plundered that village, and as they were returning they entered the town of Jammu, and carried off a large quantity of grain and provisions. Timur then ordered several regiments of active men to place themselves in ambush in the groves, and to remain there while he marched away with the (rest of the) army'.

Next day, Timur apparently decamped from Jammu, as a part of the strategy; he crossed back the river Jammu Tawi, and marching about 'four *kos* through cultivated lands, encamped in pasturage on the banks of another rivulet. The author of *Zafarnama* records that

> 'As Timur left the valley of Jammu and Manu, the Hindus, like foxes, thinking that the mighty lion had left the field, came out of their holes in the jungle, quite unaware of the ambuscade prepared for them. They were suddenly assailed by the concealed troops, who put numbers of them to the sword....The *Rai* of Jammu was defeated and seriously wounded when he was taken prisoner along with fifty other soldiers. These men were put in chains and bonds, but the *Rai*, who was wounded, was carefully tended, for the sake of getting the ransom-money. By hopes, fears, and threats, he was brought to see the beauty of Islám. He repeated the creed, and ate the flesh of the cow, which is an abomination among his compatriots. This obtained for him great

honour, and he was taken under the protection of the emperor (Timur)'.

Timur stayed in the vicinity of Jammu for about two weeks awaiting the arrival of his contingents from Lahore and submission of the Sultan of Kashmir, and utilized his time in hunting while his army was preparing for the return march to Central Asia. To his dismay, when Iskander Shah of Kashmir was conveyed through his ambassador to contribute 30,000 horses and one *lakh* of silver coins of 2.5 *misqals* each, he hurriedly retraced his steps towards the valley on the pretext that he will meet Timur after having made arrangements for his demands. Timur had neither time nor inclination to pursue the matter. After a few days, prince Pir Muhammad and other officers 'returned from Lahore with much wealth and property and were received with all honour'. They had brought with them Malik Shaikha Kokhar, a Gakhar Hindu convert to Islam, in chains. He was the brother of Nusrat Kokhar, formerly the governor of Lahore on behalf of Sultán Mahmud of Dehli. After the defeat of Nusrat Kokhar at the hands of Timur's contingents, Shaikha had joined his camp and was entrusted the governorship of Lahore. He was allowed to take charge of Lahore on the promise of collecting adequate contributions for the victor but, subsequently, changed his mind and defied Timur's authority. It had necessitated the dispatch of a fresh expeditionary force under Pir Muhammad to Lahore, 'which ravaged his territory' and brought him as prisoner. Nothing is known about his fate; perhaps he was put to death instantaneously.

About this time, Timur had received 'disturbing news from the western part of his empire' and his presence was eagerly sought at Samarqand to settle the affairs of Central Asia. As all of his men and detachments had rejoined his camp after the accomplishment of their respective missions, Timur held 'a splendid court' in the outskirts of Jammu wherein he bestowed many rewards on the *sayyads* and *ulema*, *zamindars* and gentlemen natives of Hindustan, who had joined and accompanied his camp, and then 'issued orders for them all to return' to their respective homes and assignments. As no other prominent chief of the country had joined his camp in the Indian campaign, Sayyad Khizer Khan, the ex-governor of Multan and Uchh during the regime of Sultan Firoze Tughluq, was granted the fiefs of Multan, Dipalpur and Lahore. It is not mentioned specifically by *Tuzuk-i-Timuri* or *Zafarnama* but some other contemporary sources allude to his nomination as Timur's viceroy or plenipotentiary at Delhi.

Thereafter, leaving the bulk of his forces to proceed towards home by their prescribed routes at a leisurely speed, Timur preceded them with the nucleus of his army, and moving swiftly through the southwestern territories of Jammu and Kashmir, crossed the river Chenab on March 3 and reached the Jhelum, variously known as Dandana or Jumb river. From the confines of Jammu to this place, Timur had the pleasure of hunting one lion and a number of rhinoceroses. He crossed the Jhelum by a bridge of boats, 'which was a great relief' to his troops for taking with them huge cargo of plunder, provisions and slaves, particularly. He posted a strong contingent of the soldiers and engineers to safeguard this bridge for the rest of his army to cross over it in due course of time. Timur moved down the Jhelum about 23 *kos* along its outer bank to reach the fort of Baruja. From there he turned westward through the sandy tract to reach the Indus at breakfast time on March 19, 1398. He crossed this river also by a bridge of boats and rested on its outer bank till noonday prayer. This bridge had been built by his men, under the command of Amir Allahdad, who had been sent there in advance. He was asked 'to guard the bridge for the transit of the forces and baggage which were following'. Timur 'travelled ten *kos* more before halting for the night'. Next day, he 'marched again, and, travelling rapidly', reached the fort of Banu in the northwest frontier. It marked the end of his Indian campaign.

Effects of Amir Timur's Invasion

The effects of Amir Timur's invasion were disastrous. He came as 'a scourge of God' and inflicted untold miseries on the people of India. We are in accord with Professor Mohammad Habib's observation that 'among the *killers*, who have claimed to belong to the Prophet's creed, Amír Timur Gurkan (Gurgan), entitled the Sahib Kiran (Lord of Fortune), has surpassed all others with reference to the murder of peaceful non-combatant Muslims and...non-Muslims who were beheaded by his orders or put to death' (*Comprehensive History of India, v, p.101*) in cold blood. He was, in fact, a blood-thirsty monster, who thoroughly exploited the name of religion to commit atrocities on the peace-loving and innocent citizens of not only India but many other countries of central Asia. This is also true that *Zafarnama*, an official history of his career and achievements, as prepared by Yezdi under the patronage of his descendants, to present him as an apostle of Islam, if peeled off 'the sugar-coating', 'becomes a charge-sheet against one of the world's greatest criminals'. (*Ibid.*)

Amir Timur and his Turkish marauders descended on India in the true form and spirit of the *Mlechhas* or *Rakshashas* and trampled under the heels of their horses the whole of northwestern India, including the Punjab, Delhi, a substantial part of the Doab, and the Shiwalik Hills, besides Jammu and southwestern borders of Kashmir, and carried out destruction and devastation wherever they went. As sworn enemies of the civilized world, they sacked scores of big towns and thousands of the villages, massacred the unarmed and defenseless citizens like sheep and goats, enslaved their women and children, desecrated their holy places, destroyed the schools, public libraries and cultural institutions, razed the magnificent buildings to the ground and set fire to their dwellings to wipe out all signs of a civilized and cultured society of which the Indians were proud of. According to a conservative estimate, half a million of the Indians died fighting or were massacred by Timur's blood-thirsty soldiers, two hundred thousand men and an equally large number of women and children were taken away as slaves, and more than two millions of the people were uprooted from their hearths and homes. The city of Delhi was converted into debris of ruined buildings, with hundreds and thousands of the stinking dead bodies, scattered all around the households and streets, in close proximity to hundreds of the badly bruised and seriously wounded men and women, crying in vain for succor. No official or voluntary organisation of the public-spirited persons made its appearance to help the wounded or the hungry, with the result that the city of Delhi was struck by famine and pestilence, and those of the inhabitants, who were left behind, were made to die of hunger and disease 'while for two months, after the departure of Timur, not a bird moved a wing in the capital'.

As a result of the drainage of its wealth and ruination of its agricultural and industrial sources, the economic and industrial development of northwestern India came to a standstill. Timur had denuded this region of its entire love-stock and the labour force, including hundreds and thousands of the craftsmen and artisans, mechanics and architects, skilled and semi-skilled workers, and destroyed the famous *karkhanas* of the time of Sultan Firoze Tughluq. The Turkish soldiers of Timur behaved as murderers and highway dacoits, who robbed the country of its fabulous wealth in men and material; destroyed the standing crops of the fertile lands of the Punjab and the Yamuna-Ganga valleys, and carried away with them the accumulated stocks of corn and cereal along with the herds of innumerable live-stock, leaving behind poverty and hunger all around.

Timur gave a death blow to the tottering Tughluq dynasty and the civil administration of all the territories overrun by his armies collapsed. As he failed to provide an effective alternative to the political vacuum thus created by him, anti-social elements raised their ugly heads and created anarchy all through this region. Timur's nominee, Sayyad Khizr Khan held a precarious position as the governor of Multan but, being the agent of a foreign renegade, who was hated and despised even by his own co-religionists for the destruction of the Muslim rule in Delhi, did not find favour with the native Muslim bureaucracy of the country. In consequence, all the people who had escaped death or enslavement at the hands of Timur's soldiery, were left without adequate protection of their lives and properties. The regional chiefs and the local *zamindars*, having been deprived of their power and prestige, were unable to restore law and order and were left to fend for themselves. Agricultural production received a serious setback and the crippling of all fruitful economic activities led to the scarcity of food grains and the soaring of prices. 'Timur left behind famine, disease and misery for the inhabitants of northwestern India. Never before had so much harm been done by any invader to the country in a single onslaught; the vandalism displayed by Mahmud of Ghazni during his Indian campaigns pales into insignificance before the atrocities committed by the marauders of Amír Timur on the unarmed and defenseless citizens'. (Advanced Study, i, p. 246.). Timur wanted to earn the title of Ghazi by annihilating the Hindu infidels and wiping out the infidelity from Hindustan, but 'his army, like a steam-roller, knocked down all the Indians alike, whether Hindus or Muslims. As a matter of fact, Amír Timur insulted India and its people as a whole, and like Mahmud of Ghazni, did more harm to the cause of Islam than to the Hindu *kafirs* in the subcontinent; it was the Muslim Sultanate of Delhi which was left prostrate and bleeding by him, beyond all hopes of recovery.' (*Ibid.*, p. 247). He died in 1405 and was buried in a mausoleum, built by the Indian victims of his atrocities—the architects and masons, whom he had carried away from their hearths and homes as slaves, like the dumb-driven cattle, to Samarqand.

SECTION 3: THE SAYYAD DYNASTY (1414-50)

As described earlier, Sayyad Khizr Khan, the founder of the Sayyad dynasty at Delhi, had started his political career as the governor of Multan during the reign of Sultan Firoze Tughluq. He was defeated and expelled from Multan in 1395 by Sarang Khan, the younger brother of Mallu Iqbal Khan, the prime minister of Sultan Mahmud Tughluq and the *de facto* ruler of Delhi. He had escaped to Mewat but re-emerged to join the camp of Amir Timur in 1398, and was awarded the governorship of Multan, Dipalpur and Lahore as a reward of the valuable services rendered by him to the invader. Yahiya bin Ahmad Sirhindi, the author of *Tarikh-i-Mubarak Shahi*, who is the only contemporary authority on the Sayyad dynasty of Delhi, confirms that Khizr Khan was a *Sayyad* and that he was granted the viceroyalty of Delhi by Timur before his departure from India. Nevertheless, Khizr Khan had no support base in the metropolis. The capital of the erstwhile Sultanate was utterly ruined and denuded of most of its Muslim nobility, but it still remained the battle-ground for the scions of the Tughluq dynasty and their kingmakers for more than a decade as narrated in the first section of this chapter.

Mallu Iqbal Khan was defeated and killed in a battle in the *khitta* of Ajodhan by Khizr Khan on November 12, 1405 (19th *Jumadal-awwal*, 808 H.), and Sultan Mahmud, the last scion of the Tughluq dynasty, died in 1412 (815 H.) but the rise to power of Daulat Khan, an Afghan noble of the old regime, spoiled the chances of Khizr Khan to take possession of Delhi, After the death of Sultan Mahmud, Khizr Khan openly claimed the throne of Delhi as 'the plenipotentiary of Amír Timur' and started penetration into the territories of modern Haryana and the Doab around Delhi. In December 1413, he marched on the capital with full force, put his tents on its outskirts and called for Daulat Khan's surrender. Delhi remained in a state of siege for about four months but none of the adversaries dared to challenge his rival for an armed conflagration. Meanwhile, some supporters of Daulat Khan deserted him and joined the camp of Khizr Khan, who took forced possession of the *Naubat-Khana* gate of Delhi, opposite the fort of Sírí. A few days later, Daulat Khan was defeated and overpowered; he was pardoned and sent as state prisoner to the fort of Hissar where he died after some time. According to Yahiya bin Ahmad, Khizr Khan 'accomplished the conquest of Delhi' on May 30, 1414 (15th *Rabiul awwal*, 817 H.); he entered the fort of Sírí and took his residence in the palace of Sultan Mahmud Tughluq on June 6, 1414. It marked the beginning of a short-lived Sayyad dynasty of Delhi. There were only four kings of this dynasty who sat on the throne of Delhi for about 37 years.

Sayyad Khizr Khan ruled over Delhi independently for about seven years but he did not assume any sovereign title as *Sultan* or *shah* nor struck coins in his name. In his official records, he was addressed as *Rayat-i-Ala*; and he professed to rule Delhi as the viceroy of Amir Timur and his descendants. He publicly declared his allegiance to Sultan Shah Rukh, the son and successor of Amir Timur at Herat, and used to send him money and costly gifts by way of tribute every year. This acknowledgement of foreign tutelage by Khizr Khan did not materially alter his position as sovereign ruler of Delhi but gave him an edge over his Turkish and Afghan rivals and helped him to frighten the rebellious Hindu chieftains in the neighbourhood of Delhi by invoking the name of Amir Timur.

Though a seasoned military general, Khizr Khan was not a man of high calibre to restore the lost fortunes of the Sultanate as an empire, but he restored law and order in Delhi, and won the goodwill and confidence of his subjects. According to Yahiya bin Ahmad Sirhindi, immediately after taking control of the metropolis, he pacified its Muslim nobility by assigning positions of importance and responsibility to them in the administrative setup. He conferred the office of the *wazir* or prime minister upon Malikus-Shark Malik Tuhfa with the title of Tajul Mulk—'a selection which was justified by subsequent events'. Sayyad Salim, chief of the Sayyad community of Delhi, was entrusted the governorship of Saharanpur 'who at once proceeded to his charge to set things in order'. Similarly, the fiefs of Multan and Fatehpur were assigned to Abdur Rahim with the title of Alaul-Mulk; and Malik Sarwar was appointed the governor (*Shahna*) of the capital with powers to act as his vicegerent in his absence. Likewise, Malik Daud became Dabir (secretary), Malik Khairuddin was made *Ariz-i-Mamalik* (muster-master), Malik Kalu – 'keeper of the elephants', and Ikhtiyar Khan was appointed the *shikdar* of the Doab. 'The state officials were confirmed in the *parganas,* villages and *iqtas*, which they had held in the reign of Sultan Mahmud Tughluq, and were sent to look after them. Thus the affairs of State were all properly arranged.' (*Tarikh-i-Mubarak Shahi*).

The kingdom of Delhi under Khizr Khan included within its fold the territories of the Punjab, Sindh and a part of the Doab. Though fairly large, it was just one of the so many regional states which had come into existence in Bengal, Jaunpur, Rajputana, Malwa, Gujarat, Khandesh and the southern peninsula, on the debris of the erstwhile Sultanate of Delhi. Throughout his reign, he continued to fight against the hostile neighbours or the rebellious Hindu and Muslim chiefs within his own kingdom for his bare survival. Unlike the typical Muslim nobility of his times, Khizr Khan was a man of character and 'lived like a true Sayyad'. He tried to establish his reputation as an ideal ruler of an Islamic state and emulated Sultan Firoze Tughluq as a pious Musalman of peaceful disposition. But totally unlike Amir Timur or Firoze Tughluq, 'he never shed blood unnecessarily, nor did he ever sanction an atrocious crime either to cement his own power or to wreak vengeance upon his enemies'. The author of *Tarikh-i-Mubarak Shahi* records that 'the people of the city, by force of late events, had become impoverished and needy, so he settled allowances and made provision for them. By this kindness, they were all made easy and happy'. Khizr Khan thus provided liberal government aid to the people of Delhi for their rehabilitation; of course, it is not known if the Hindu residents of the capital were also beneficiaries of his state bounties because we do not find the name of even a single Hindu in the long list of his newly appointed officers, as given by Yahiya bin Ahmad Sirhindi.

In the concluding year of his reign, Khizr Khan remained busy with the suppression of revolt in Mewat and destroyed the fort of Kotla. Thereafter, he overran Gwalior and exacted tribute from its Hindu chief. But he fell ill during the campaign and returned to Delhi. He died on May 20, 1421; three days before his death he had nominated his son Mubarak Shah as his heir-apparent. According to Firishta, 'Khizr Khan was a great and wise king, kind and true to his word; his subjects loved him with a grateful affection so that great and small, master and servant, sat and mourned for him in black raiment till the third day, when they laid aside their mourning garments, and raised his son Mubarak Shah to the throne'.

Mubarak Shah assumed the title of Sultan 'with the approval of the *amirs* and *maliks*', and, like his father, confirmed almost all of them in their landed possessions and official assignments. Yahiya bin Ahmad, an inhabitant of Sirhind, titled his chronicle after the name of Sultan Mubarak Shah, although his personal status and connection with the royal court of Delhi is not known; probably, he was an important official of the state administration, and was well-educated and knowledgeable. Mubarak Shah ruled for over 13 years. He attempted to provide the semblance of regal authority at Delhi but it was an uphill task to maintain the integrity and stability of his small kingdom in the face of rebellious Hindu *zamindars* and the fissiparous tendencies of the Muslim nobility. As a good military general, he suppressed revolts of some of the disaffected Muslim chiefs like Jasrath Khokhar and the Turk-Baccha in the Punjab, but the rising power of the Rajputs and the ambitious designs of the newly born Muslim states of Jaunpur and Malwa seriously threatened the kingdom of the Sayyads. Mubarak Shah fought almost incessantly against the internal rebels and external foes throughout his reign; he was able to preserve his kingdom intact but without adding an inch to its territories. In the fourteenth year of his reign, he fell a victim to the conspiracy hatched by his over-ambitious *wazir*, Malik Sarwar (Sarwarul Mulk)—an old grandee of the Sayyad dynasty, who held the office of *Shahna* of Delhi during the days of Khizr Khan. According to Yahiya bin Ahmad, on the 19th of January 1434 (9th Rajab, 837 H.), the Sultan, accompanied by a handful of his escorts, was on a leisurely visit to the new township of Mubarakabad, under construction on the banks of the Yamuna. As he was getting ready for the prayer, he was taken unawares and murdered by the agents of Malik Sarwar.

The all-powerful *wazir* and ring-leader of the conspirators placed Muhammad Shah, a nephew of Mubarak Shah, on the throne, and himself usurped all powers of the state as its *de facto* ruler; he assumed the title of *Khan-i-Jahan* and forthwith proceeded to distribute the highest offices of the state among his fellow conspirators. As a consequence, the power and prestige of the Sayyads took a nose dive. After the initial bonhomie between the *wazir* and the puppet Sultan was over during the first six months, the latter began to garner the secret support of his loyal nobles to liberate himself from the clutches of the kingmaker. It created feelings of distrust between the Sultan and his prime minister, and the court was divided into two hostile camps. An abortive attempt on the part of king's friends, led by Malik Kamal-ul-Mulk, to liquidate the *wazir*, triggered off a civil war between the rival factions and the administrative machinery was totally paralyzed. On August 14, 1434 (8th of Muharram, 838 H.), the crafty *wazir* and his hirelings secured an entrance into the royal palace with the intention of assassinating the Sultan, but because of the vigilance of Muhammad Shah, the *wazir* was immediately struck down 'with blows of the sword and dagger', and his accomplices were seized 'and put to death publicly before the *Darbar*'.

Next day, Muhammad Shah reconstituted his court by offering

the office of the *wazir* to Kamal-ul-Mulk, who received the title of Kamal Khan, and high offices were distributed among his associates; but the Sultan failed to exercise control over the forces of distrust and disaffection among his nobles, with the result that confusion and disorder prevailed everywhere. On hearing of the internal dissentions among the nobility of Delhi, the neighbouring rulers of Jaunpur, Gwalior and Malwa felt encouraged to encroach upon the border territories of the Sultanate. The ruler of Gwalior and many Hindu *zamindars* of the Doab stopped paying tribute to Delhi. In 1440 (844 H.), Sultan Mahmud Khilji of Malwa, on the invitation of a few disgruntled nobles of Delhi, made a surprise attack on the capital with the intention of taking possession of it. But the timely arrival of Bahlol Khan Lodhi, the governor of Sirhind, with 20,000 cavalry, to the aid of Muhammad Shah saved the situation. The first day's battle, that was fought at Talpat, within ten miles of Delhi, remained inconclusive. Early next morning, Muhammad Shah, without taking any of his *amirs* into confidence, sent his emissary with 'proposals of peace' to his antagonist. During the intervening night, the Khilji Sultan had received intelligence about the threatened invasion on his capital, Mandu, by Sultan Ahmad of Gujarat. He, therefore, immediately accepted the terms of peace and retraced his steps towards Malwa.

According to the author of *Tarikh-i-Mubarak Shahi*, 'this peace degraded Muhammad Shah still lower in the estimation of all men'. Bahlol Lodhi felt affronted by the Sultan's timid behaviour. He retrieved the prestige of his soldiers and that of Delhi by making a frontal attack on the retreating soldiers of Malwa; he killed many of their men and carried off a part of their baggage and valuable effects. The stupefied Sultan of Delhi felt ashamed of his cowardice and 'joined the chorus of praise' for Bahlol Khan; he addressed Bahlol as his son and conferred the title of *Khan-i-Khanan* on him. It aroused the ambitions of Bahlol Lodhi, and, taking advantage of the disorders in the Punjab, he began to encroach upon the territories of Dipalpur and Lahore on the pretext of restoring law and order there. In 1441, the Sultan of Delhi readily 'acquiesced in Bahlol's occupation of major part of the Punjab and formally appointed him as the governor of Lahore and Dipalpur with special instructions to subdue the rebellious Jasrath Khokhar, who was still at large. The crafty Khokhar leader 'made peace with Bahlol Khan and flattered him with hopes of the throne of Delhi'. Accordingly, 'aspirations of sovereignty' now spurred Bahlol Khan to enlist the support of other Afghans of northwestern India in the trial of strength at Delhi. In 1444, 'on a slight pretence', Bahlol 'declared war against Sultan Muhammad' and marched upon the capital in great force. His first attempt to wrest the city of Delhi from his hands proved abortive, but it badly shattered the administrative setup and prestige of the Sayyad chief. According to Yahiya bin Ahmad, 'the business of the state day by day fell into greater confusion, and affairs came to such a pass that there were *amirs* at twenty *kos* from Delhi who shook off their allegiance, and made pretensions to independence'. Sultan Muhammad died a broken-hearted man in 1445 (849 H.).

Prince Alauddin Sayyad, the son and successor of Muhammad Sayyad, ascended the throne of Delhi with the high-sounding title of Alam Shah but he proved to be the last and the most unworthy ruler of the Sayyad dynasty. By this time, the Sultanate of Delhi had practically ceased to exist, and it was reduced to the position of a petty principality. The Sultan's writ did not extend beyond the municipal boundaries of the city which was surrounded by numerous local and regional Hindu as well as Muslim kingdoms and semi-autonomous *jagirs* and estates. To his further misfortune, the Sultan did not pull on nicely with his ambitious *wazir*, named variously as Hisam Khan or Hamid Khan by the author of *Tarikh-i-Mubarak Shahi.* Unable to cope with the administrative problems and mutual jealousies and intrigues of his courtiers, who fought for petty pecuniary gains, Alam Shah retired to his personal *jagir* at Badaun in 1447, and 'gave himself up to pleasure, resting satisfied with the little territory that remained to him'. It provided an opportunity to Bahlol Lodhi to take possession of Delhi, in connivance with none else but Hamid Khan, the all-powerful *wazir*. It is said that because of the long absence of Sultan Muhammad from Delhi, the *wazir* became apprehensive that some powerful ruler of a neighbouring state might take forcible possession of the capital; therefore, he, 'of his own accord', invited Bahlol Lodhi to take control of Delhi with the illusion that the sturdy Afghan noble might 'agree to play the puppet king' while he himself retained all powers of the state as *wazir.* Accordingly, Bahlol marched on Delhi with a huge force with the declared object of restoring law and order there. Hamid Khan collaborated with him for a short while but was treacherously overpowered and thrown into prison by Bahlol Khan, who declared himself the ruler of Delhi. According to Yahiya bin Ahmad Sirhindi, before formally ascending the throne, Bahlol Lodhi wrote to Sultan Alauddin Alam Shah Sayyad, stating that he had overthrown the usurper 'for the Sultan's benefit, and that he was his devoted servant'. To this Alauddin replied:

'My father called you his son, and I have no means of resisting you. I will content myself with the single district of Badaun, and resign the sovereignty to you.'

Thus it was that Bahlol Lodhi ascended the throne of Delhi, with the apparent consent of Alâuddin, on April 19, 1451, and 'clothed himself with the garments of royalty'; he adopted the title of Bahlol Shah Ghazi. All the nobles, who had stood by Alauddin, were confirmed in their assignments and privileges. Alauddin, now divested of his regal powers and privileges, was permitted to retain his estate, under the protection and care of the new regime, and died a happy and fully contented man in 1478.

SECTION 4: THE LODHI DYNASTY (1451-1526)

Bahlol Lodhi (1451-89)

Bahlol Khan Lodhi laid the foundation of the first Afghan dynasty at Delhi. Northern India was ruled by the Turks ever since the establishment of the Sultanate of Delhi. Daulat Khan, who rose to power and acted as the *de facto* ruler of Delhi in 1413-14 after the death of Sultan Mahmud Tughluq, was also an Afghan noble, but he did not assume any regal title; he was soon defeated and deposed by Khizr Khan, the founder of the Sayyad dynasty. Thereafter, Sher Shah Sur or Suri and his descendants provided the second and the last Afghan dynasty of Delhi from 1540 to 1555.

Bahlol Khan belonged to the Lodi or Lodhi clan of the Ghilzai tribe of the Afghans. He was the son of Malik Kala Khan and grandson of Behram, a merchant, who had migrated to Multan during the reign of Sultan Firoze Tughluq. Behram had five sons, two of whom, Sultan Shah and Kala Khan, joined as soldiers under the provincial governor of Multan and rose to be capable military officers with the titles of *maliks*. At the time of Amir Timur's invasion, they extended their support to the invader and were able to safeguard their landed estates. Malik Kala Khan, who had earned reputation for having once defeated Jasrath Khokhar, lost his life at the hands of his foes, and his son Bahlol, then a small child, was brought up by his uncle, Malik Sultan Shah, who had received the governorship of Sirhind in 1419 with the title of Islam Khan from Khizr Khan Sayyad. Bahlol was brought up by his uncle with affection and care, and, on attaining majority, was given his daughter in marriage. Islam Khan consolidated his position almost as an autonomous ruler of the fief of Sirhind under the nominal suzerainty of the Sayyads, and, before his death, made Bahlol Khan the commander of 12,000 and nominated him as his successor 'on merit, in preference to his son Qutb Khan'. By the time Alauddin Alam Shah ascended the throne of Delhi, Bahlol had become the master of nearly the whole of the Punjab. The story of his occupation of Delhi and the declaration of sovereignty by him in April 1451 has already been narrated above.

As a shrewd politician, Bahlol Shah commenced his reign on a very low key. He neither wanted to alienate the Sayyads, the Turks and other foreign nobles by his haughty demeanour nor adopted autocratic or dictatorial attitude towards his turbulent Afghan leaders but treated them all with respect and gave them the impression that he highly valued their opinions in the running of the state administration. He setup a sort of Afghan tribal monarchy and his court was quite different in composition and character from that of the Turkish Sultans of Delhi. He did not sit on a magnificent throne 'bedecked with jewels and diamonds in gorgeous robes' or decorated chair on a raised platform in the traditional style of the medieval rulers but sat on a carpet in the midst of his ministers and other prominent nobles, presenting the sight of an Afghan *Jirga*, 'in such a way as to show that he was the popularly chosen leader of his people and held the regal powers at their pleasure. According to Yusuf Hussain, Bahlol Lodhi occupied the status of *primus inter pares* among his Afghan nobles, and the Afghan monarchy of Delhi was, in fact, 'a feudalistic tribal oligarchy'. (*Indo-Muslim Polity*, p. 174).

Bahlol Lodhi enjoyed a long reign of 39 years. He restored law and order in his small tribal kingdom with the enthusiastic support and cooperation of his Afghan nobles. He gradually distributed all the important civil and military offices among his trusted Afghan officers. Following the example of Firoze Tughluq, he revived the *jagir* system with a vengeance, and parcelled out his kingdom into small *jagirs* and feudal estates, which were handed over mostly to his kinsmen and other Afghans. The feudal chiefs were authorized to raise their local militia for the maintenance of law and order within their areas and to support the central government in time of need; usually they recruited the people of their own community and tribe for reasons of loyalty to them. Bahlol Lodhi encouraged large-scale migration of the Afghans into India and extended liberal patronage to the immigrants. The moment they arrived at Delhi or reported their presence to any of the district or local officials, they were provided with residential accommodation and state services to settle down comfortably. Bahlol Lodhi was ever eager to increase the population of Afghans in India and to *afghanise* his administration as far as possible. By doing so, he did arouse the jealousies and opposition of the Turks, Persians and other Muslim immigrants from central Asian countries but they were suppressed with an iron hand. Taking advantage of the disorders and political instability at Delhi, most of the fief holders and *zamindars* in the neighbouring regions, including the Doab, Mewat and central India had become lukewarm in their loyalties towards Delhi. The rise of Sharqi dynasty at Jaunpur had posed a direct threat to the very existence of a Muslim state at the erstwhile imperial capital of the Sultans. Therefore, Bahlol Lodhi's throne was not a bed of roses. He had to fight continuously against his external foes and the rebellious Muslim nobles and disaffected *zamindars* within and in the neighbourhood of his kingdom. Accordingly, he organised a punitive expedition against the rebellious Mewati chief Ahmad Ali Khan and annexed a part of his possessions to Delhi. He led successful expeditions against Dariya Khan of Sambhal, Isa Khan of Koil (Aligarh), Mubarak Khan of Saket, Qutb Khan of Rapri and Raja Pratap Singh of Kampila and Patiali, and compelled them to acknowledge his suzerainty as his feudatory chiefs. Nearer home, Bahlol Shah was called upon to tame the *zamindars* of Etawa, Chandwar and other districts of the Doab which had caused much trouble to the preceding regimes by their insubordination; so much so, he had to interfere even in the internal administration of Sirhind, his parental *jagir*, to ensure its allegiance to Delhi.

Bahlol Lodhi was conscious of his limitations as a regional ruler and never harboured imperial designs. He did not adopt aggressive postures against the other powerful regional states like those of Jaunpur and Malwa, but much against his will, he was dragged into a protracted war against Sultan Mahmud Shah of the Sharqi dynasty at Jaunpur. Mahmud Shah was the son-in-law of Alauddin Alam Shah Sayyad, the ex-Sultan of Delhi. It was distasteful to him to see the discomfiture of his father-in-law at the hands of the Afghan chief, and he immediately disputed Bahlol's claim to the throne of Delhi. According to Abdulla, the author of *Tarikh-i-Daudi* (E&D, iv, pp. 434-513), the Sharqi Sultan's Sayyad wife pestered him to dislodge the Afghans from Delhi who had usurped her father's throne and even threatened that 'if he hesitated, she would herself lead an expedition against Bahlol'. It was, therefore, that during the very first year of Bahlol's reign, when he had gone to

Multan to settle its affairs, the Sharqi Sultan marched on Delhi at the head of a large army, consisting of 170,000 cavalry and 1,400 elephants and put the capital under siege. On the receipt of information, Bahlol hastened back to Delhi and defeated Mahmud Shah at Narela, about 30 kilometres from Delhi. It was made possible because of the desertion of Mahmud's commander, Darya Khan Lodhi, who was chided by Bahlol's agents for fighting against his own people.

Mahmud Shah returned to Jaunpur in a huff but the struggle was not over. Before his death in 1457, he had fought two more inconclusive battles with Bahlol on the borders of their respective kingdoms at Etawa and Shamsabad respectively. After the death of Mahmud Shah, there started a fratricidal feud between his three sons about their succession at Jaunpur, but all the three of them considered themselves to be the rightful claimants to the throne of their maternal grandfather at Delhi, and their relations with Bahlol Lodhi were usually strained. Of them, Hussain Khan, who proved to be the last Sharqi king of Jaunpur, suffered a defeat at the hands of Bahlol Lodhi at Rapri in c.1479 and fled the battlefield to seek refuge with the Hindu ruler of Gwalior. Bahlol Lodhi took possession of Jaunpur but he did not annex it to Delhi. Instead, he installed Barbak Shah Lodhi, his eldest son, on the throne of Jaunpur and maintained its separate identity, thus 'creating a fraternity of two Afghan kingdoms in fraternal relationships with each other'. It was the greatest and the most important achievement of Bahlol Lodhi.

In the concluding years of his reign, Bahlol Lodhi subdued the Hindu fiefdoms of Kalpi, Dholpur, Bari and Alapur up to the borders of the Gwalior state; and, in the year 1488, declared war against Raja Man Singh of Gwalior. The latter was defeated and compelled to acknowledge the suzerainty of Delhi. Bahlol Lodhi realized a tribute of 80 *lakh tankas* from the Gwalior chief, but was taken ill during his return march to Delhi and 'died at a place called Malawali near the township of Jalali in the *parganas* of Saket'. Bahlol Lodhi deserves credit for having revived the fortunes of the Sultanate of Delhi; He restored law and order in the kingdom, extended its boundaries by reclaiming some of its adjoining districts and *parganas*, and gave it the semblance of a central administrative authority once again. His pre-occupations with the military engagements did not spare much time for him to introduce administrative reforms but he earned the reputation of a just and generous king, who ruled over his subjects with moderation and enjoyed their respect?

He was 'scrupulous in adhering to the tenets of Islam, but was not intolerant of other creeds'. Bahlol Lodhi was not a man of learning but he valued his association with scholars and saints and extended liberal patronage to them. He was always keen about the happiness and welfare of his subjects. Abdulla, the author of *Tarikh-i-Daudi*, is all praise about the high moral character of Bahlol Shah Lodhi; he writes:

> 'In his social meetings, he (Bahlol Lodhi) never sat on a throne, and would not allow his nobles to stand; and even during public audience, he did not occupy the throne, but seated himself upon a carpet. Whenever he wrote a *firman* to his nobles, he addressed them as *Masnad Ali*; and if at any time they were displeased with him, he tried so hard to pacify them that he would himself go to their houses, ungird his sword from his waist, and place it before the offended party: nay, he would sometimes even take off his turban from his head and solicit forgiveness, saying—"*If you think me unworthy of the station I occupy, choose someone else, and bestow on me some other office*'. He maintained a brotherly intercourse with all his chiefs and soldiers. If anyone was ill, he would himself go and attend on him'.

Thus it was Bahlol Lodhi's modesty and non-assuming nature and the spirit of compromise that enabled him to lay the foundations of a stable Afghan dynasty on the throne of Delhi. In the course of his grim struggle against the Sharqis of Jaunpur, he had to depend very heavily upon the co-operation and support of his Afghan camp-followers, thousands of whom had migrated to India especially from the region of Roh in Afghanistan in response to his express call for help; this region extended roughly from the valleys of Swat and Bajaur to Bhakkar, and from Hasan Abdal to Kabul and Qandahar.

Sikander Lodhi (1489-1517)

Bahlol Lodhi had nine sons and a number of grandsons from about half a dozen wives belonging to different tribes and communities. He had accommodated his eldest son Barbak Khan in the new Lodhi regime of Jaunpur, and, after his death, the Afghan nobles elected his third son Nizam Khan to be his successor; he ascended the throne on July 17, 1489, with the title of Sikander Shah. Sikander was known to be a religious bigot by temperament, and it was, probably, this trait of his character which influenced most of his selectors to exercise this discretion. Sikander Lodhi was a tall and handsome young man of thirty-one at the time of his accession to the throne. Like Firoze

Tughluq, he was the son of a Hindu goldsmith's daughter, a disability which initially provoked some of the Afghan nobles to oppose his claim to royalty; and to overcome which he exhibited religious orthodoxy and intolerance towards the Hindus to prove his credentials as the rightful king of an Islamic state. Otherwise, he was the ablest and the most capable of all the surviving sons and grandsons of Bahlol Lodhi.

Sikander Lodhi's greatest problem was to liberate himself from the negative effects of the concept of Afghan tribal monarchy bequeathed from his father and assert his status as the sovereign ruler. The whole of his kingdom had been parcelled out among his brothers and other kinsmen who posed a potential danger to his throne, and Sikander Lodhi was ever eager to establish his integrity as the ruling monarch. Unlike his father, Sikander styled himself as the Sultan, and 'imparted a bit of glory to his royal court'; he occupied a seat on an elevated throne like the traditional Sultans of Delhi and did not allow the senior Afghan nobles to claim equality with him. His eldest brother Barbak Shah, who had already assumed the title of the Sultan of Jaunpur, preferred his claim to the Sultanate of Delhi and fought a pitched battle with him near Kanauj. He was defeated and fled to Badaun but Sikander Lodhi pardoned him and reinstated him as the Sultan of Jaunpur under the suzerainty of Delhi. Similarly, Sikander Lodhi, as a shrewd politician, won over his brother Alam Khan to his side but had to fight a battle with his uncle Isa Khan and his son Azam Khan to bring them under his subjugation. A faction of the Afghan nobles of his court hatched a conspiracy to overthrow him in favour of his younger brother Fateh Khan. On the receipt of intelligence, Sikander Lodhi took drastic action to bring the conspirators to book; as a consequence, twenty-two Afghan nobles were dismissed and inflicted severe punishments. It enabled him to consolidate his position as the sovereign ruler of Delhi.

Amir Timur had done a great harm to the splendour and aristocratic political environment of Delhi as the imperial capital. To the almost ruined metropolis, was added the atmosphere of Afghan tribal oligarchy by Bahlol Lodhi. Delhi had, therefore, lost its charm for the youthful Sultan Sikander Lodhi, who visualised the revival of royalty as an absolute monarchy. It was, therefore, that he shifted his residence to Sambhal in 1499 where he lived for about four years. Meanwhile, he conceived of a project for the construction of a new capital town. In 1504 (910 H.), he laid the foundation of a new township at the village of Agra on the Yamuna and shifted his court there; not far away from Delhi, it was situated at a more central place from where he could exercise better control over the governors of Etawa, Bayana, Kol (Aligarh), Gwalior and Dholpur. Agra developed into a beautiful town during the very lifetime of Sikander Lodhi. He revived the concept of absolute monarchy and setup a net work of espionage to keep himself well-informed about all the developments and the activities of his civil and military officers. Sikander Lodhi was a good military organiser; he raised a strong army under his personal command and did not depend much on the subsidiary forces of his feudal chiefs. He pursued a policy of aggressive intervention into the affairs of his fief-holders as well as the neighbouring chiefs to maintain law and order in his kingdom and to safeguard his political interests against the outsiders. Barbak Shah, the Sultan of Jaunpur, was unable to keep the turbulent *zamindars* of his state under control. It necessitated repeated intervention of Sikander Lodhi to restore law and order there; ultimately, Barbak Shah was deposed and Jaunpur was declared annexed to the Sultanate of Delhi. In 1494-95, Sikander Lodhi conquered south Bihar and pushed the boundaries of his kingdom to the borders of Bengal; he also concluded a treaty of peace and friendship with Sultan Alauddin Husain Shah of Bengal.

Sikander Lodhi was a capable administrator and he did much to tone up the revenue and judicial establishments. He enforced discipline among the services and improved the machinery of law and order to safeguard the life and property of his subjects. Like Firoze Tughluq, he introduced the Islamic law as a matter of state policy and paid special attention towards the public welfare activities. He did everything for the promotion of agriculture and production of sufficient food products; he ordered the repair and reconstruction of roads to facilitate the movement of traffic and goods and abolished several duties to give impetus to agriculture as well as internal trade. Unfortunately, he was not free from religious bias and was intolerant of other faiths. On the testimony of the contemporary chroniclers, Professor Hameeduddin writes that

> 'Born of a Hindu mother and anxious to marry a Hindu princess, his (Sikander Lodhi's) attitude towards this religion of a vast majority of his subjects appears to be rather baffling and inexplicable, for, it was bound to prejudice the realization of his political aims. Even as a prince, he had been dissuaded from raiding the Hindu tanks at Thaneswar (Kurukshetra) by a verdict

of the famous divine, Mian Abdullah of Ajodhan, who had also ruled against the demolition of non-Muslim places of worship. Sikander, as a king, however, frequently razed temples to the ground and erected mosques and public utility buildings in their place, as illustrated by his behaviour at Mandrail, Utgir and Narwar. At Mathura, he prevented the Hindus from bathing at their sacred *ghats* or having themselves shaved. The stones of broken images of Hindu idols, brought from Nagarkot, were given away to butchers to be used as weights. ...It may, however, be stated that Sikander, in conformity with his opposition to idolatry, stopped some of the semi-idolatrous practices that had grown up among the Muslims also, such as the annual procession of Salar Masud Ghazi's lance, the visits to the tombs of saints by Muslim women, and the carrying of *taziyas* during Muharram.'
– (*History and Culture of the Indian People*, BVB, v, pp. 146-47.)

Thus, in spite of Sikander Lodhi's competence as capable administrator, and his good intentions as well-wisher of his subjects, the state under him 'once again assumed a theocratic character and officially imposed Islam upon Hindus. Once a Brahmin (named variously as Bodhan, Budhan or Laudhan by various contemporary authorities), was burnt alive simply because he had made an innocent remark in the presence of certain Muslims of his village that his faith, i.e. Hinduism, was as good as that of the Prophet. To illustrate the point, we reproduce below the narration of this incident *verbatim* as recorded by Abdulla, the author of *Tarikh-i-Daudi*,

'There was a Brahmin, by name Laudhan, who dwelt in the village of Kaner (near Lucknow), who had one day asserted in the presence of Musalmans that Islam was true, as was also his own religion. This speech of his was noised abroad, and came to the ears of the *Ulama*. Qazi Piyara and Shaikh Badr, who resided at Lakhnauti, gave *fatwas* which did not coincide respecting the merits of the case. Consequently, Azam Humayun, the governor of that district, sent the Brahmin, the Qazi, and Shaikh Badr, all three into the King's presence at Sambhal. Sultan Sikander took great pleasure in disputations on religious questions, and on this occasion, summoned all the wise men of note from every quarter. *Mulla* Abdulla, the son of *Mulla* Ilahdad, *Sayyad* Muhammad, and *Mian* Kadam from Delhi, all the *Mullas* in short of his empire, were summoned to Sambhal, and the assembly of the learned who were always attached to the stirrup of his Majesty, were also present on this occasion. After investigating the matter, the *Ulama* determined that he (the accused Brahmin) should be imprisoned and converted to Muhammadanism, or suffer death, and, since the Brahmin refused to apostatize, he was accordingly put to death by the decree of the *Ulama*. The Sultan, after rewarding the learned *casuists*, gave them permission to depart'.

The use of the word *casuists* in the above statement, obviously, refeers to 'the persons, who use clever but false reasoning' to prove their point. It is very significant that the celebrated author of *Tarikh-i-Daudi*, while recording this incident, was himself not convinced of the wisdom or rationality of the *Ulemas'* verdict and its compliance by the Sultan, According to Professor Hameeduddin, 'such an irrational policy is indefensible in modern times, even though it be granted that, in the age in which Sikander lived, tolerance was not the order of the day.' We are in full accord with Dr. Ishwari Prasad that 'to men like Bodhan, the Hindu martyrs of the middle ages, who cheerfully suffered death for the sake of their convictions, the Brahmanical religion in India owes not a little of its vitality and vigour.' Sikander Lodhi died of 'a disease of the throat' on Sunday, the 7th *Zilkada*, 923 A.H. (November 21, 1517).

Ibrahim Lodhi (1517-26)

Sikander Lodhi had left behind five surviving sons. After his death, his eldest son Ibrahim Lodhi ascended the throne of Delhi with the consent of the Afghan nobles and assumed the title of Ibrahim Shah. He was doomed to be the last ruler of the Lodhi dynasty and the last of the Sultans of Delhi, however. Ibrahim Lodhi was hardly nineteen at the time of his accession, and to his misfortune, his claim as the sole monarch of the entire Afghan kingdom was immediately disputed by his younger brother Jalal Khan, who held the governorship of Kalpi at the time of his father's death. Jalal Khan was born of a different mother and was supported by a powerful faction of the self-seeking nobles who wanted to re-assert their influence in the state affairs. Ibrahim acquiesced in his brother's demand, and agreed to parcel out his dominions into the twin Afghan states of Delhi and Jaunpur respectively on the old model of Bahlol Lodhi. Accordingly, while Ibrahim was coronated at Delhi, Jalal Khan, accompanied by his mother's kinsmen and the army, left for Jaunpur.

This suicidal policy of dividing the Afghan kingdom was condemned by Khan Jahan Lohani, the governor of Rapri, who warned the other Afghan leaders about the folly of their decision which stood to weaken their hegemony in northern and central India. On his advice, the august assembly of the Afghan nobles at Delhi reversed its earlier decision and declared Ibrahim Lodhi to be the sole monarch of the entire kingdom. They dispatched posthaste a powerful military general, Haibat Khan –'the wolf-slayer', to persuade Jalal Khan to withdraw from Jaunpur but the latter refused to give up his claim to royalty. Nevertheless, the mischief had been done, and Jalal Khan, though not successful in taking possession of Jaunpur, was coronated as Sultan Jalaluddin at Kalpi. It led to a civil war between the two brothers. To safeguard his position, Ibrahim Lodhi placed all the three of his minor brothers into confinement in the fort of Hansi, and himself marched upon Kalpi with full force. In the struggle that ensued, Jalaluddin was, ultimately, defeated and the fort of Kalpi was captured and dismantled by Ibrahim but the former fled from there and took refuge with the Raja of Gwalior. It compelled Ibrahim to declare war against Gwalior. After a lot of bloodshed, the fort of Gwalior was taken by Ibrahim but Jalal made good his escape towards Malwa. The struggle came to an end when the fugitive Afghan prince fell into the hands of the *zamindars* of Gondwana who sent him in chains to Delhi. Jalaluddin was sent as a captive to Hansi but murdered on the way by the secret orders of Ibrahim Lodhi.

The fratricidal war was won by Ibrahim but at the cost of the solidarity and stability of the Afghan state. The Lodhi monarchy was considerably weakened by the individualistic tendencies of its short-sighted and selfish Afghan chiefs who did not like to be dictated by a despotic monarch. Sikander Lodhi had held them under control by tactfulness and firm policy but, when the crown passed on to a man, who was much inferior to him in ability and political skill, the fissiparous tendencies of the Afghans once again broke loose and destabilized their monarchy. Ibrahim Lodhi was young and inexperienced but 'he was not so incapable and inefficient a ruler as he has usually been made out'. However, having been brought up in the affluent and aristocratic environment of the royal household as 'a born prince', he had no idea of the strenuous efforts put in by his predecessors in carving out the 'feudal monarchy' of their community in India. The civil war with his brother had made him distrustful of his kinsmen and the other Afghan chiefs alike; he lost his faith in the Lodhi, Lohani and Farmuli nobles who held major fiefs of the kingdom and important offices of the state, and began to penalize them on mere suspicion. Ibrahim's initial success against his younger brother and the Hindu ruler of Gwalior made him overconfident of his military prowess, and he committed the blunder of challenging Rana Sangram Singh of Mewar. To his great horror, the mighty army of Delhi, comprising 30,000 horses and 300 elephants was routed and annihilated by the valiant Rajputs. The Sultan lacked the courage and resources to retaliate against the Rajputs which gave a serious setback to his power and prestige and made him a subject of ridicule among his nobles. It signalled revolts in various parts of his kingdom.

To make up for the loss of face, Ibrahim adopted a still more dictatorial attitude towards his seasoned military generals and grandees of the Afghan monarchy. He displeased his ministers and provincial governors by his irritant and arrogant behaviour which alienated the Afghan nobility and spread disaffection among them. In consequence, they did not cooperate with the Sultan wholeheartedly in the solution of various political and administrative problems. Some of the hereditary provincial governors setup as *de facto* rulers of their territorial possessions and instigated the others to follow suit. Like Muhammad bin Tughluq, Ibrahim Lodhi also meted out revengeful and cruel treatment towards the disaffected nobles, who fell into his hands, and thus terrified the rest of them to carry on their struggle against him relentlessly till the bitter end. For instance, a powerful Afghan noble, Azam Khan Sarwani, who had collaborated with Jalal Khan, had offered his submission and was granted royal favours. But the Sultan continued to harbour ill-will against him, and got him murdered through his agents after some time while his son Islam Khan died fighting against the royal forces. Mian Bhuwah, the aged *wazir* of Sikander Lodhi's time, was dismissed by Ibrahim Lodhi for expressing his views which were not to the liking of the Sultan; he breathed his last in the royal prison. Similarly, Mian Husain Khan Farmuli had once disobeyed Ibrahim Lodhi but was later pardoned and reinstated as the governor of Chanderi; nevertheless, the revengeful Sultan got him assassinated through his agents soon thereafter. No wonder, it made the old grandees of the Afghan monarchy apprehensive about 'the perfidious designs' of Sultan Ibrahim Lodhi, and they began to take defensive measures for their own safety.

The things came to a head when Khan-i-Jahan Lodhi, one of the senior most military generals of the Sultanate, and Darya Khan Lohani, the governor of south Bihar, assumed leadership of the rebellious

Afghans in the eastern part of the kingdom. Nasir Khan Lohani, the governor of Ghazipur, was ordered by the Sultan to march against Darya Khan but he changed sides and himself raised the standard of revolt against Delhi. After the death of Darya Khan, his son, Bahadur Khan, declared his independence as the Sultan of Bihar; he assumed the title of Sultan Muhammad Shah and struck coins in his name. The other disaffected Afghan nobles flocked to his court and the ranks of his armed forces swelled to over a hundred thousand fighters. Ibrahim Lodhi could do nothing against the rebels, and the eastern half of his kingdom, including the erstwhile state of Jaunpur, was lost to him.

On the northwestern side of Delhi, the Punjab formed a part of the Sultanate since the period of Bahlol Lodhi. The whole of the Punjab and the northwestern frontier posts, including the fiefs of Multan and Lahore, besides the strategic posts of Jalandhar, Sultanpur Lodhi, Dipalpur, Sirhind, Samana, Kaithal and Hissar had been entrusted to their kinsmen by the Lodhi Sultans. Tatar Khan, the governor of Lahore, who held over-all responsibility for the defence of northwestern India, was a cousin of Bahlol Lodhi. His son Daulat Khan Lodhi, the hereditary governor of Lahore, was a capable administrator and seasoned military general, who had under his control 80,000 strong army, and a long purse. Ibrahim Lodhi felt affronted with him on the ground that he had not paid a personal visit to the court of Delhi at the time of his coronation, apparently because of his old age. Instead, he had sent his son Dilawar Khan with 5,000 horsemen to attend on the new Sultan, but Dilawar fled back to Lahore after some time to escape arrest at the hands of Ibrahim Lodhi. The Sultan suspected Daulat Khan Lodhi of harbouring rebellious intentions; therefore, when Dilawar Khan was in Delhi, he was taken by the Sultan to the royal prison in the underground cellars of his palace where the state 'prisoners were suspended from the walls', and by way of warning to him and his father, said: *Have you seen the condition of those who have disobeyed me?* Dilawar Khan was frightened by the humiliating treatment received at the hands of Ibrahim Lodhi; 'he offered his humble submission before the Sultan but somehow managed to escape to his father and told him all that he had seen and experienced at the capital'. It was under these circumstances that Daulat Khan sent an invitation to Babar at Kabul to invade India and overthrow Ibrahim Lodhi.

About this time, another disaffected Lodhi chief, Alam Khan, the ex-*faujdar* of Dipalpur, and a maternal uncle of the Sultan, 'who had been biding his time in Gujarat and was much sought out by the disaffected *amirs* to replace Ibrahim on the throne of Delhi, also arrived at Kabul to seek Babar's support'. The Punjab was thus in open revolt against Ibrahim Lodhi when Babar appeared on the scene. Zahiruddin Muhammad Babar was a promising Mughal leader, who claimed descent from Changez Khan as well as Amir Timur. Having been up-rooted from his ancestral land of central Asia, he had entered Afghanistan as a fugitive and conquered Kabul by a stratagem in 1504. After consolidating his position as the king of Afghanistan, he directed his attention towards India. The weakness of Lodhi Sultans and the prevalent political disorders in northern India encouraged him to fish in the troubled waters. From 1519-20 to 1525-26, he organised five military expeditions in quick succession, and conquered Delhi after killing Sultan Ibrahim Lodhi in the historic battlefield of Panipat on April 21, 1526. He laid the foundation of the Mughal rule in India, and, with the death of Ibrahim Lodhi, the Turko-Afghan Sultanate of Delhi came to an end.

SECTION 5: DOWNFALL OF THE SULTANATE

The decline and disintegration of the Sultanate of Delhi had begun during the concluding years of Muhammad bin Tughluq's reign. It gained momentum during the period of Firoze Tughluq, and, by the time of his death, almost all the outlying provinces of the kingdom had thrown off the imperial yoke of Delhi. By the year 1388, the erstwhile Sultanate of Delhi had, in fact, shrunk to the position of a small state like so many regional kingdoms and principalities of the country. The Sultanate was a police state and its foundation was based on the virus of Islamic fundamentalism; its ultimate downfall lay in the logic of history; *albeit* 'the most distressing part of the story is that its ghost continued to haunt the historic capital of India for so long after the death of Firoze Tughluq and the invasion of Amir Timur'. The manifold and diverse causes that led to the decline and dismemberment of their dominions during the reigns of Muhammad bin Tughluq and Firoze Tughluq respectively have already been explained in details in the preceding pages of this study; here suffice it to say that 'they were not exclusively responsible for the downfall of the Sultanate. There were many inherent defects and causes which were bound to have their adverse effects on the foreign autocratic regime that the Sultanate was. There was no conventional law of succession among the Sultans of Delhi. The right of succession to the throne depended on the general law of nature, i.e. 'the survival of the fittest'. In fact, it was the major factor which had helped the foreign Muslim invaders in consolidating their territorial possessions and expanding their dominions in India generation after generation. Nevertheless, the repeated application of this 'law of the jungle' proved counter-productive in the long run. It aroused the ambitions of the Turkish slave officers and other foreign Muslim nobles to aspire for the crown and spread disaffections among them. The wearing of the crown thereby no longer remained a bed of roses even for the best administrators and organisers of victories. In the game of power-politics, very often, the most dishonest and crafty princes and ambitious military generals, supported by a committed band of equally self-seeking nobles, were able to usurp the crown at the cost of the rightful and deserving claimants. It has rightly been said that the 'the Sultans of Delhi, on the whole, comprised a race of cut-throats; the princes and ambitious nobles killed their near and dear ones and liquidated the entire families of their parents, friends and patrons for the attainment of the throne'. This rat-race for power-politics cut at the very roots of the Turko-Afghan monarchy as, very often, it brought into the forefront the weaklings and unworthy princes who were placed on the throne as puppet Sultans, to be exploited by the kingmakers and power-brokers. Secondly, the Sultanate was essentially a police state, which had been setup by the foreign conquerors by use of force and aggression; it had no roots among the people of the country and did not enjoy their support. Moreover, it was declared an Islamic state in which the Hindus, including the Buddhists and Jains,viz., the non-Muslims, were not considered eligible for the grant of full-fledged citizenship. Apart from the loss of political freedom, they were dubbed as *kafirs* or infidels and deprived of their religious and cultural freedom as well. With a few exceptions, most of the Sultans of Delhi behaved as foreign autocratic rulers who did not bother to win the goodwill of their Hindu subjects. The Hindu *kafirs*, in the capacity of *zimmis*, were called upon to pay *Jaziya* or poll tax for their very survival, and they usually suffered persecution at the hands of the Muslim officials. In consequence, they generally maintained an attitude of indifference towards the government and took no interest in the rise and fall of the Sultans or their ruling dynasties. Therefore, at the very first opportunity, the vanquished Hindu princes and *zamindars* defied the authority of the Sultans and took up arms against them to regain their lost freedom. The survival of such a state depended upon the powerful and aggressive military machine of the Sultans, the moment their military organisation became weak, the powerful provincial governors and feudal nobles raised their standards of revolts against the Sultans and setup as regional rulers usually with the support of the local ruling elite.

Firoze Tughluq was the last sovereign ruler of Delhi though he had inherited a fast disintegrating empire, engulfed in widespread revolts and political disorders. He professed to be an ideal Muslim ruler of peaceful nature but, in fact, he was an incompetent military general, who had neither the resources nor the courage and will-power to bring back the break-away provincial governors under his control. He was, accordingly, content with the Sultanate of Delhi which had been reduced to the status of a regional kingdom. It was governed well during the first half of his reign by his capable *wazir*, Khan-i-Jahan Maqbul. But after his death, the civil and military administration of the state deteriorated rapidly under the unimaginative and weak policy of Firoze Tughluq, which was based upon religious bigotry and persecution of his Hindu subjects. Strange though it may seem, the excessively long life enjoyed by the Sultan, unchallenged by any rival claimant to the throne, did an incalculable harm to the interest of his own ruling family. His first two grown-up and capable sons predeceased Firoze Tughluq, thus leaving the burden of the state upon the shoulders of his younger sons and grandsons, none of whom was educated or trained enough to hold his own as a sovereign ruler. This gave birth to the kingmakers among the ambitious Muslim nobles, who came to dominate the state politics and held the princes as puppets in their own hands. It infested Delhi with a protracted civil war and made the phantom Tughluq Sultans of Delhi a mockery of the people. No wonder the Sultanate collapsed soon after the death of Firoze Tughluq and was reduced to a petty principality of Delhi.

Above all, Amír Timur struck a fatal blow to the tottering Tughluq kingdom. He trampled Delhi under his feet and sounded the death-knell of the Sultanate. He was, however, not interested in establishing himself as the ruler of Delhi and left for Samarqand, leaving northern India in ruins and political anarchy. He left behind a political vacuum at Delhi, once the imperial capital of the Turkish rulers. It is amazing, however, that not a single Hindu or Muslim military general or leader emerged on the Indian political horizon for over a century and a quarter, who could establish himself at Delhi and claim as the sovereign ruler of the country. Meanwhile Delhi continued to be ruled by Lilliputians styled as Sultans. It showed some signs of recovery under the tribal monarchy of the Lodhi Afghans but, because of the inherent individualistic and fissiparous tendencies of the ruling race, stood little chances of developing into an all-India power. It was left to Babar, the great Mughal, to take possession of Delhi in 1526 as a result of his victory on the historic battlefield of Panipat, which, ultimately, revived 'the glory of Delhi as the imperial capital of Hindustán' under his worthy successors.

❑ ❑

8

ADMINISTRATIVE SYSTEM OF THE SULTANS

SECTION 1: THE NATURE OF MUSLIM RULE IN INDIA

The Islamic Theory of State

The Sultanate of Delhi was founded by the foreign Muslim adventurers. The Turko-Afghan rulers of India declared it as 'an Islamic state'. It necessitates a brief analysis of the Islamic theory of state and the treatment of non-Muslims therein. The Muslims had brought with them an exotic concept of state, according to which the head of the state was also regarded as the religious leader of his people, called 'the *millat*' or the Muslim Brotherhood, and was believed or presumed to derive his position and authority from Allah, the Merciful. The genesis of this concept can be traced back to the Prophet Muhammad, the founder of Islam, who, on his *hijrat* or migration from Mecca to Medina, was called upon to assume the political leadership of his followers for the protection of their lives and properties; he thus laid the foundation of the first Muslim state in the world, and assumed a double role as founder of the Islamic creed as well as temporal head of 'the faithful'. According to Dr. Ishwara Topa,

> 'The Prophet of Islam founded a theocratic state. It was a system of political and social control, based on divine sanctions. It reflected the will of God (Allah) in its movements (*sic.*) and activities. Its desire was to islamise life in accordance with the law of God. Its dictates were divine laws to be imposed on human beings for their guidance. The aim of the Prophet was to organise and discipline people into a nation in which religious diversions, social inequality, political disunity and economic exploitation

should not exist...The law of Islam was the law of the Islamic state'. (*Politics in Pre-Mughal Times*; Allahabad & London, 1938, p.39).

Thus, Islam does not separate religion from politics; in fact, the concept of religion in Islam emerged first, and the state was 'an after-thought'. According to U.N. Day, the traditional Islamic law does not acknowledge 'the independent existence of state, nor is state regarded as a primary condition of human society'. (*Mughal Administration*; Munshirasm Manoharlal, p.1) It makes the state completely subservient to the religion of the Prophet. As such, the Islamic state is an instrument to serve the Islamic creed in the attainment of its objectives or fulfilment of ideals of the Muslim Brotherhood. The Islamic theory of state was, therefore, based on a three-fold vision of one scripture, one sovereign and one nation; scripture was the holy *Quran*, sovereign was the *Imam* (leader), also called *Khalifa*, i.e. 'the political successor to the Prophet', and nation was the *Millat* or 'the Muslim Brotherhood'. The basic feature of the Islamic state, according to this theory, was its 'indivisibility' in all the three aspects. It contemplated the establishment of a theocratic state based on Islamic law, and recommended only one sovereign- the *khalifa,* to rule over the whole of the Muslim world. The *khalifa* was styled as the *amir-ul-momnin* or 'leader of the faithful'; and his office was thus a political institution, based on Islamic injunctions. The Islamic government was, therefore, one which was composed of the Muslims, by the Muslims and existed for the happiness and welfare of the Muslims alone. Obviously, such a state was not confined within any geographical boundaries or delimited by any territorial jurisdictions. The monarchical form of government, the basic feature of the Sultanate of Delhi, was an extra-Quranic growth which had evolved and entered the fold of Islam on the Persian soil.

The Sultanate of Delhi, without any shadow of doubt, was a foreign regime; and from its very inception, it functioned as an Islamic theocracy *par excellence*. Its rulers, the dominant nobility and the higher administrative hierarchy belonged to the Muslim faith. Theoretically, the Sultan was expected to enforce the Islamic law (*Shariat*) in the land and administer his dominions in a way as to transform the *dar-ul-harb* of Hindustan (the land of the Hindu *Kafirs*) into *dar-ul-Islam.* He professed nominal allegiance to the *Khalifa* (whosoever he was) and felt pride in obtaining investiture from him. With the exception of Alauddin Khilji and Mubarak Shah Khilji, all other Sultans styled themselves as deputies of the *Khalifa* with the titles such as *nasir-i-amir-ul-momnin*—'assistant to the leader of the faithful', or *yamin-ul-*

khalifa – 'the right-hand man of the *khalifa*'. In actual practice, however, the Sultans were sovereign rulers who did not derive their powers from, nor depended upon any external force; they were independent rulers of their territorial possessions and did not owe their sovereignty to any other worldly power. Nevertheless, they owed their existence to the strength of their armed forces or 'the Army of Islam' to be very precise, which can rightly be called the armed-wing of the *millat*. Otherwise, the overwhelming majority of their subjects (*raiyyat*) happened to be Hindus, including the Buddhists and Jains, or the non-Muslims, and the so-called *millat* constituted but a microscopic part of it. Being foreign adventurers, they were called upon to rule over vast territories of Hindustan, inhabited primarily by the Hindus; therefore, they thought it politically expedient to maintain active contacts with the Islamic world beyond the Khyber so as to draw the maximum number of foreign Muslim immigrants to strengthen their armed forces and increase their population. It also helped them to produce a psychic of fear among the Hindus by alluding to the potential sources of their strength.

Some of the Sultans formally introduced the Islamic law within their dominions but most of them were despotic rulers who did not always conform to the orthodox Islamic principles. They were invariably influenced by the Indian traditions and customs and incorporated many elements of the Rajput polity with or without modifications. Alauddin Khilji, backed by a powerful standing army could afford to defy the Islamic principles of government and administration, while keeping the *ulema* in good humour. The founding fathers of the Sultanate of Delhi did not belong to any traditional ruling house or families of high social status; they started their careers as slaves, not even as ordinary freemen. Therefore, they usually did not claim any noble pedigree or hereditary right to hold the crown; even if they did, none took them seriously. There was no fixed law of succession among them; the acquisition of the crown depended on the laws of the jungle such as 'survival of the fittest' and 'the might is right'. The Sultanate of Delhi was, therefore, a police state or foreign military dictatorship whose strength or weakness depended exclusively on the armed might and personality of its despotic ruler.

Treatment of Non-Muslims in an Islamic State

The Islamic theory of state did not permit the existence of any religion other than Islam; and none but the Muslims were considered to be its rightful citizens. Nevertheless, the existence of some non-Muslim subjects, who refused to be converted to Islam, had to be tolerated within the territorial jurisdictions of an Islamic state from its very inception under the leadership of the Prophet himself. These 'non-believers' were divided into two categories: *ahl-e-kitab*—'men of the book' or those who possessed some sort of revealed scriptures, and *kafirs* or 'the infidels'. To begin with, the Jews and Christian inhabitants of Medina were recognised by the Prophet as *ahl-e-kitab* and granted the protection and partial religious toleration in return for the receipt of *Jaziya*—'the poll tax' from them. They were called the *Zimmis.* All the rest of the non-Muslims, who were usually referred to as *kafirs* or *mushriks*, viz., the infidels or idolaters, were denied the right of existence in a truly Islamic state. They were dubbed eternal enemies of Islam and condemned as *kable-e-garden- zadni* or 'those who were fit to be beheaded or extirpated'; they were confronted with either of the two alternatives – 'Islam or death'. The Holy Quran issues the following instructions to 'the faithful':

'Say thou to the unbelievers,

If (even now) they would desist (from infidelity), the past will be forgiven them;

But, if they still persist (there starteth then) the example of those who had preceded them.

Then fight ye them until there is left no harassment, and the worship of Allah is altogether feasible'. (sura 8, verses 38 & 39)

The Concept of *Zimmi* in Islam

The birth of the concept of *Zimmi* in Islam dates back to the year 628 A.D., when Hazrat Muhammad arrived at an agreement or *zimma* with the Jews of Khaybar situated 140 kms from Mecca. Those of the Jews, who had refused to convert, were allowed to stay within the Islamic state on the payment of a tax, called *Jaziya* (*Jizya*), a poll tax; it enabled them to save their religion and cultivate their land. Otherwise, according to the Quranic doctrine, 'any land, property or life captured as a result of a *jihad* belonged to the (Muslim) conquerors'. The Jews, who had accepted the terms of this agreement, were called the *Zimmis*, i.e. the 'the people under contract of protection by the Islamic state'. The Quran says:

'Fight ye those who believe not in Allah, nor in the Final Day;

Who do not make taboo that which has been made taboo by Allah and his Apostle;

Who follow not the teachings true among the Peoples of the Book;

Until they willingly offer Jaziya and are quite subdued.' (sura 2, verse 29)

The first clear enunciation of the status of a *Zimmi* was written down in a contract, signed a little before 720 A.D. between Khalifa Umar II and the local Jewish and Christian leaders. The English translation of this document has been given in a recent publication, entitled, *Why I am not Muslim,* by Ibn Warraq (Prometheus Books, New York, 1995). The terms of the agreement were as follows:

(1) We shall not build in our cities or in their vicinity any new monasteries, churches, hermitages, or monks' cells. We shall not restore, by night or by day, any of them that have fallen into ruin or which are located in the Muslims' quarters.

(2) We shall keep our gates wide open for the passerby and travellers. We shall provide three days' food and lodging to any Muslims who pass our way.

(3) We shall not shelter any spy in our churches or in our homes nor shall, we hide him from the Muslims.

(4) We shall not teach our children the Quran.

(5) We shall not hold religious ceremonies in public. We shall not seek to proselytize anyone. We shall not prevent any of our kin from embracing Islam if they so desire.

(6) We shall show deference to the Muslims and shall rise from our seats when they wish to seat down.

(7) We shall not attempt to resemble the Muslims in any way.

(8) We shall not ride on saddle.

(9) We shall not wear swords or bear weapons of any kind, or even carry them with us.

(10) We shall not sell wines.

(11) We shall clip the forelocks of our head.

(12) We shall not display our books anywhere in the Muslims' thoroughfares or in their marketplaces.

(13) We shall only beat our clappers in our churches very quietly. We shall not raise our voices when reciting the service in our churches,

nor when in the presence of Muslims. Neither shall we raise our voices in our funeral processions.

(14) We shall not build our houses higher than those of the Muslims.

(15) *The Oxford History of Islam* (OUP, Hong Kong, 1999) adds one more interesting aspect of the above covenant, which was not listed in the terms of the agreement but was all the same applicable to the *Zimmis*. It reads as follows:

'A Muslim woman was not allowed to marry a Christian or Jew man although the Quran does allow the marriage of a Muslim man to a Christian or Jew woman. Nevertheless, Islamic law, from its very inception, stipulated a great range of conditions under which such a marriage might take place. The children of a mixed marriage were always considered Muslim. A Muslim could own a *Zimmi* slave but never the opposite.'

Accordingly, *Jaziya* was originally levied upon non-Muslims 'as a sign of humiliation, and compensation for security of life and property in a Muslim state', and also as 'compensation for military service' from which they, 'being unbelievers', were exempt. (U.N. Day, *Administrative System of Delhi Sultanate*; Kitab Mahal, 1959, p. 88). To begin with, only Jews and Christians were given the status of *Zimmi* but, at a later stage, the Zoroastrians, who were declared to be ***musahab ahl-e-kitab*** or 'those who resembled the possessors of revealed scriptures, were also included in this category. It is now a part of history that, during the very lifetime of the Prophet, the Jews and Christians of Medina, who had, in all humility accepted their inferior status as *Zimmis* and begun to pay *Jaziya* to 'the first Muslim state', proved irksome to the 'true believers' and the Prophet was constrained to turn them out of Medina. Umar I (634-44), the most famous of the Pious Khalifas, following in the footprints of the Prophet, expelled the Jews and Christians from the whole of Arabia, thus converting the homeland of the Arabs into a true *Dar-ul-Islam*.

The Prophet and the Khalifas had already set the example of religious intolerance towards their non-Muslim subjects, which was treated as an ideal by the orthodox Muslim rulers. The Umayyad Khalifa Umar II discriminated against his Christian subjects; they were expelled from all public offices. The first Abbasid Khalifa, Saffah, was a 'narrow-minded bigot' who persecuted all the non-Muslim subjects of his empire. Even the great Harun-al-Rashid, under the influence of orthodox *ulema*, felt obliged to deprive the Christians of their socio-religious liberties. In 807 A.D., he issued an ordinance by which all churches 'in the border countries' were to be demolished and the non-Muslims were to dress differently from Muslims. In Africa, Ibrahim ibn Aghlab passed severe law against the Christians and the Jews. (For details, refer to K.D. Bhargava, *A Survey of Islamic Culture and Institutions*; Kitab Mahal, Allahabad, 1961).

Recognition of Hindus as Zimmis

This is an historic fact that the Hindus, including the Buddhists and Jains, viz., all the indigenous inhabitants of India, who were subjugated by the Muslim conquerors, were deprived of an honourable place within the jurisdiction of the Muslim state as its full-fledged citizens. Muhammad bin Qasim, who conquered Sindh and Multan in 711-12, secured the status of *Zimmi* for his Hindu subjects from the Khalifa and accorded protection to their lives and property on the receipt of *Jaziya*. Obviously, this step was necessitated as a matter of political expediency because, in spite of the loss of political freedom, the Hindu masses, in general, offered dogged resistance to forced conversions. It was physically impossible for Qasim and handful of his Arab soldiers and camp-followers to compel the vanquished multitude 'to choose between Islam and death', particularly, when they were 'armed to the teeth'. (A.B.M. Habibullah, *Foundation of Muslim Rule in India*). Recognition of Hindu 'idolaters' as *Zimmis* by Qasim proved to be 'a momentous decision' as such a concession had earlier been denied to the idolaters of Arabia. His example was followed by the Turko-Afghan rulers of Delhi in their dealings with their Indian subjects, almost all of whom happened to be non-Muslims; they were granted the status of *Zimmis*. Thus, they were not recognised as the full-fledged citizens of the Sultanate like the Muslims, and were granted only partial civil liberties which made them suffer from many socio-religious and economic disabilities so as 'to prevent them from growing strong'. As a matter of fact, all the Muslim jurists were never in favour of granting this status of *Zimmi* to the Hindus, who were invariably dubbed as *kafirs* (infidels) and idolaters. There had developed, with the passage of time, four schools of Islamic thought for the authoritative interpretation of *shara* or the Islamic law. These were known as Mulakite, Shafiite, Hanbalite, and Hanafite schools of thought after the names of their founders – Malik ibn Anas (715-95 A.D.), Ash-

Shafi (767-820), Ahmad bin Hanbal (780-855) and Abu Hanifah (699-766). Exponents of the first three schools offered no other alternative but death to 'the idolaters', including the Hindus, on their refusal to embrace Islam. The jurists of the Hanifah School alone permitted the existence of Hindus in an Islamic state as *Zimmis*. That explains the intense hatred of the Hindus by the orthodox Muslim fanatics, in general; and, whenever a Muslim ruler fell under the spell of such orthodox *ulema*, he adopted the policy of religious intolerance and persecution of his Hindu subjects. It created a permanent gulf between the Hindus and the Muslim inhabitants of India which could never be bridged effectively for a long time.

The mamluk Sultans had reserved all the higher posts for the foreign Muslim immigrants; they exercised religious as well as racial discrimination in the matter of recruitment to such services. This policy was discarded by Alauddin Khilji who threw open the public services to commoners, including the non-privileged Muslim immigrants, Indian converts to Islam and even the Hindus. It made him quite popular with his subjects.

Ever since the inception of the Sultanate, Persian (Farsi) had been introduced as the court language as well as the medium for the transaction of the state business. To begin with it proved a handicap to the Indians, including the Hindu converts to Islam, in securing employment under the Sultans. With the passage of time, however, they took up the study of this language with enthusiasm; and, gradually, were followed in this direction, though hesitatingly, by the Hindus as well. The fiscal policy of Alauddin Khilji, though not based on scientific principles, including the land reforms, price control and market regulations revived the Indian economy considerably and promoted trade and commerce which benefitted his subjects, both Hindus as well as the Muslims; his administrative policy carried the seeds of a progressive and secular state.

SECTION 2: THE CIVIL ADMINISTRATION

The Sultanate of Delhi had come into existence as a result of the armed victory of foreign Muslim invaders whose number was not very large. During the first two centuries of their rule, particularly, the Sultans of Delhi were constantly engaged in warfare against their hostile neighbouring Hindu rulers and the vanquished and disgruntled native inhabitants who had lost their political as well as socio-religious freedom. 'The state, under such circumstances', writes A.B.M. Habibullah 'was bound to resemble the organisation of an army in occupation and hence had to be, in the main, military. The civil functions emerged only gradually and at a converse ratio to the disappearance of security problems'. Moreover, 'the continuity of the occupation process, spreading over generations, permitted little governmental planning'. (*The Foundation of Muslim Rule in India*; pp. 197-98). Accordingly, there was no distinction or demarcation between the civil and military services in the administration of the Sultanate. Almost all the higher offices of the state, excluding judiciary and subordinate services in the revenue establishment, were usually held by the military commanders. The princes of royal household and seasoned military generals formed the ruling *junta* or royal court of the Sultans at Delhi, and held all the important civil and military assignments, including the governorships of the provinces, called *fiefs* and *iqtas*. All the district officers, heads of civil and military supplies, *karkhanas* or centres of production and manufacture, and police chiefs or *kotwals* of big towns were military officers.

The Sultan

The Muslim rulers of Delhi assumed the title of 'Sultan' or king, which remained in vogue throughout the early medieval period of Indian history; this title was quite popular even among the local and provincial Muslim monarchies which sprang up on the ruins of the Sultanate. Babar, the founder of the Mughal dynasty at Delhi, was the first Muslim ruler of India, who styled himself as *Padshah* or emperor in 1526. The Sultans of Delhi were independent and autocratic rulers of their territorial possessions but their formal allegiance to the *Khalifa* was a socio-political necessity. Theoretically the Islamic sovereignty resided in the *millat*, which was supposed to elect the Sultan, but in actual practice, the *millat* served as the mainstay of the Muslim monarchy in general. The *millat* could voice its approval or disapproval of the policies and administration of a particular Sultan but it could neither elect a Sultan according to the modern democratic norms nor depose an unworthy and incompetent ruler. In fact, the Muslim state of Delhi had been carved out and expanded by some of the capable and ambitious military generals by force of arms, it was essentially a police state, and 'a well-knit army of Islam' was its real strength.

The government of the Sultanate was based on highly centralized despotic principles. The Sultan was the chief executive, supreme commander of the army of Islam, sole legislator and fountain-head of justice. In the exercise of their powers, the Sultans generally professed to abide by the Islamic law; but in actual practice, there was no rule of law in the Sultanate, and word of the Sultan was treated as law. A powerful Sultan, like Alauddin Khilji, backed by a strong standing army, could make the *ulema* subservient to him and afford to defy the Islamic principles of government, particularly in his dealings with his Muslim political rivals and other co-religionists. He made appointments to all the top civil and military offices and the entire bureaucracy functioned under his personal direction and control. The Islamic law assigned ten major functions or duties to the Sultan in his capacity as the chief executive of an Islamic state; these were –

1. Protection of the faith;
2. Defence of the Muslim territories;
3. Protection of the frontiers of the state against foreign aggression;
4. War against the infidels or enemies of Islam;
5. Enforcement of the Islamic criminal code and maintenance of law and order;
6. Administration of justice according to the Islamic law;
7. Collection of revenues as per the Islamic injunctions;
8. Disbursement of grants and wages to those who deserved an allowance from the public exchequer;
9. Appointment of trustworthy and capable counsellors and administrators,
10. And control of the public affairs through personal inspections and supervision of the administrative machinery.

The Sultan forfeited his claim to the throne if he failed to perform these duties deliberately or disregarded them willfully. There was no difference between religion and politics and Islam pre-dominated every sphere of the state activity. The rights or duties of the Sultan towards his non-Muslim subjects were also well-defined by the Islamic law. The Hindus, having been dubbed as infidels and idolaters, were not treated as full-fledged citizens of the Sultanate. Nevertheless, once they offered their submission and agreed to pay the *Jaziya*, they acquired the status of the *Zimmis*, and the Sultan was under obligation to protect their lives and properties and grant them partial civil liberties as per the Islamic law. Accordingly, the Muslim theologians or the *ulema* – 'the conscious keepers of the Islamic state', wielded great influence in the court and acquired a substantial share in the state bounties as well as the civil services. No Sultan could feel secure on the throne unless he had obtained formal investiture from the *Khalifa* and consolidated his position by the active support and collaboration of the *ulema*. Whenever any Sultan faced a serious difficulty in the solution of his political problems on the home front or received reverses in the military campaigns, he at once evoked the religious zeal of his camp-followers and soldiers by making out that he was merely waging a holy war against the infidels.

The Central Government

The Sultan was assisted in the discharge of his functions by a number of ministers and other dignitaries who adorned his court. Ever since the foundation of Muslim rule in northern India, Delhi had become an important centre of Islamic culture which attracted rich talent from all over the Muslim world. The rulers of Delhi welcomed with open arms soldiers and scholars, administrators and Islamic jurists, traders and businessmen, craftsmen and men of learning and literature from Arabia, Persia and other Muslim countries of Central Asia and Africa, and readily absorbed them in the Central and state services according to their qualifications, competence and experience. It enabled them to consolidate their position with the active support and assistance of the foreign soldiery, military commanders and bureaucrats. As a result, reputed military generals, experienced administrators and renowned scholars and theologians of the Muslim world flocked to their courts and received liberal royal patronage. The Sultans, therefore, found no difficulty in selecting the wisest and the best of them as ministers, counsellors and heads of the various civil and military departments.

The business of the state was transacted in a magnificent *durbar.* The Sultans organised their court on the Persian model and spent lavishly on its maintenance as they felt that the magnificence and splendour of the court will automatically force the public to bow down or prostrate before the Sultan. Every noble was allotted a specific place and seat according to his position and status, and he had to attend the court in specially prescribed dress. Every attempt was made to observe all the ceremonies and etiquettes of the court after the fashion of the Persian model.

The Ministers

In the beginning of the Muslim rule, the mamluk Sultans of Delhi were assisted in the discharge of their royal functions by four senior ministers and counsellors at the top level; they were the *Wazir*, the *Ariz-i-Mumalik*, the *Diwan-i-Insha* and the *Diwan-i-Risalat*. The *Wazir* also referred to as *Vakil* or *Vakil-i-Sultanate* was the prime minister, and his department was called the *Diwan-i-Wizarat*. He held charge of the finance department and exercised general supervision and control over the entire administrative setup of the state. But like all the other ministers and office-bearers, he was also a mere nominee of the Sultan and held his office at the pleasure of the king; accordingly, he had no disciplinary control over the other central ministers. As head of the finance department, he laid the fiscal policy of the state in consultation with the Sultan, tapped various sources of income and exercised control over the expenditure on civil as well as military establishments. The *Naib Wazir* acted as deputy to the prime minister. The prime minister was also assisted in the discharge of his functions by two other junior ministers, called *mushrif* and *mustafi* respectively; whereas, the *mushrif* could be defined as the accountant-general, the *mustafi* acted somewhat like an auditor-general.

With the gradual expansion of the Sultanate and multiplication of the duties and functions of the Sultan, there came into existence an extraordinary office of the deputy Sultan, who was called the *Naib-ul-Mulk* or *Malik Naib*. This office was usually held by the princes of the royal blood or the most powerful and influential members of the ruling *junta* next after the Sultan. The *Malik Naib* deputized for the Sultan and exercised all the royal prerogatives during his absence from the capital and acted as a sort of regent. Sometimes, the offices of the *wazir* and *malik naib* were held by one and the same person, particularly when the Sultan happened to be a minor or weak and imbecile; otherwise, under the normal circumstances, the *malik naib* enjoyed fewer powers than the *wazir*. When the Sultanate was well-established, two more heads of departments were raised to the status of the central ministers; they were the *sadr-us-sadur* and the *diwan-i-qaza*. The commander of the royal forces, next after the Sultan, the crown prince-if so nominated, and the afore-mentioned six or seven dignitaries, constituted the council of advisers, called the *Majlis-i-Khlawat* to aid and advice the Sultan in determining the state policies, but it had no constitutional validity, and its decisions were not binding on the Sultan.

Nevertheless, the wise Sultans preferred to carry their counsellors with them in the formulation and implementation of the important state policies.

The *Ariz-i-Mumalik* was head of the army establishment or the ministry of defence, which was known as the *Diwan-i-Arz*. He was responsible for the recruitment, training and equipment of the royal forces, usually referred to as 'the Army of Islam'. His duties included the fixation of salaries of the soldiers, and preparation of the muster rolls, branding of the horses and review of the army also formed a part of his functions. The *Ariz-i-Mumalik* made all provisions for the soldiers and exercised disciplinary control over the entire army establishment. It was his duty to construct, repair and garrison the forts. In time of war, the Ariz-*i-Mumalik* equipped and prepared the contingents for action and was responsible for the deployment of the fighting units at the capital and other strategic places along the borders, but he did not act as the commander-in-chief. Very often, he accompanied the Sultan or other senior military generals on the war fronts and acted in subordination to them. After the military operations, the *Ariz-i-Mumalik* took charge of the booty and secured the state's share from the soldiers. The military officers always looked to him for promotions, enhancement of their emoluments and other privileges. The strength, efficiency and discipline of the royal armies depended much on the character and competence of the *Ariz-i-Mumalik*; like the prime minister, he was also provided with one or more *naibs* or deputies to facilitate the discharge of his duties.

Diwan-i-Insha comprised the department of correspondence and records of the royal court. Its minister in charge was known as *Dabir-i-Mumalik* or simply *Dabir*. It functioned like the central secretariat which maintained complete records of the communications between the royal court and the provincial and local governments, military commanders, feudatory chiefs and the foreign rulers. The Dabir had under his charge a large number of Persian and Arabic scribes and was assisted in the drafting of royal *firmans* and other official correspondence by many Islamic jurists and linguistic scholars. Accordingly, the office of the *Dabir-i-Mumalik* was entrusted to an outstanding scholar of Persian and Arabic, reputed as expert in Islamic jurisprudence and diplomacy who commanded respect among the *ulema* of the regime.

The *Diwan-i-Risalat* formed the fourth pillar of the central administration of the Sultanate. It dealt with the ecclesiastical affairs of the Islamic state. This department was entrusted many types of religious functions during the period of various ruling dynasties. Under the mamluk Sultans, it was headed by the *Sadr-us-Sadur*. He held charge of all the religious endowments, and disbursed grants and stipends to *ulema, sheikhs* and other holy men. He acted as the religious adviser or *rasul* of the Sultan, and received complaints and appeals from the Muslim community pertaining to the religious and social matters, particularly, and redressed their grievances. In his capacity as the chief theologian of the state, the *Sadr-us-Sadur* was sometimes called upon to receive ambassadors and envoys from the foreign Muslim rulers and introduce them to the Sultan. It so appears that during the reign of Alauddin Khilji, this department was probably renamed or replaced by the *Diwan-i-Riyasat* and entrusted the additional function of enforcing the economic regulations and the exercise of control over the markets and prices of goods. Nevertheless, after the death of Alauddin, the office of the *Sadr-us-Sadur* as the chief executive of the ecclesiastical affairs was revived and restored to its pristine glory. The department of justice, called the *Diwan-i-Qaza*, was headed by the *Qazi-ul-Qazat* or *Qazi-i-Mumalik*; he was the chief justice as well as the officer-in-charge of the judicial establishment. Sometimes, the offices of the *Sadr-us-Sadur* and *Qazi-ul-Qazat* were held by one and the same person.

The rule of the Sultans comprised a highly despotic monarchy; therefore, there were some departments and services of the central government, the heads of which functioned under the direct supervision and control of the Sultan. They included the offices of *Barid-i-Mumalik* – 'head of the information and intelligence department'; *Vakil-i-Dar* – 'the officer in charge of the royal household'; and *Amir-i-Hajib*, who kept an eye on all the visitors to the royal court and presented them to the Sultan in accordance with the court etiquette. Similarly, there were a number of other central services, the heads of which usually functioned under the supervision of the prime minister but had also direct access to the Sultan. For instance, *Amir-i-Barbak* was the superintendent of the royal court; he assigned places to the nobility in the court in accordance with their ranks and status, and maintained the dignity of the court. *Amir-i-Majlis* made arrangements for the meetings of the royal assembly and organised special celebrations and feasts. The personal bodyguards, usually the slave men-in-arms, of the Sultan were called *jandars;* they were headed by the *Sar-i-jandar*. Likewise, the *Amir-i-Shikar* organised the royal hunts and formed an important part of the royal entourage. The police chief, called the *Kotwal,* and *Qazi* or the

'Justice of Peace' of the capital, were also treated as important imperial officers of the state. The *Qazi* looked after the administration of justice and *Kotwal* maintained law and order within the metropolis, while the *Muhtasib* or 'the censor of morals' kept a watch on the social and religious conduct of the Muslim masses to ensure that they conducted themselves as 'true Musalmans' in their day-to-day lives; he inflicted punishments on the persons of easy virtue, and also regulated weights and measures to bring the cheats among the shopkeepers to book. Nevertheless, all the high dignitaries of the state, including the *wazir* or prime minister, were mere creatures of the Sultan, and there was no law of the land; the word of the Sultan, supported by Quranic injunction or purported to be in accordance with the Islamic tradition, was the law.

Provincial and Local Government

With a few exceptions, the Sultans of Delhi paid little heed to the administrative infrastructure of the state. According to Habibullah, because of the 'limited (Muslim) manpower, the setting up of a uniform civil administration over all parts of its dominions was out of the question. Familiarity with the details and problems of day-to-day administration could not be expected of the newly-arrived Turks, even if such officers were available in their ranks and could be spared from military work. Retention of the existing governmental machinery in the form of vassal states and the employment of non-Muslims for such essential civil work, as the assessment and collection of the land-revenue in villages directly within the military area, were thus unavoidable. Direct annexation of territories, requiring large civil and military personnel to administer them was mostly to be avoided'. (*Ibid.*, pp. 241-61).

The territorial possessions of the Sultanate were divided into two broad divisions, the *khalsa* or the land held under the direct administrative control of the Sultans, and the *jagirs* or the territories of the tributary Hindu states and 'the rent-free estates', held by the Muslim nobility in lieu of state service. The *khalsa* land, in its maximum dimensions, comprised the northwestern region, including the provinces of Lahore and Multan, the territories of the Ganga-Yamuna Doab and the Ganga valley up to the borders of Bihar and Bengal. The local governors of this region, called variously as *walis* and *muqtas* or *muqtis* (fief-holders) were under the direct administrative control of the Sultans under normal circumstances. The distant provinces of Malwa, Gujarat,

Bihar, Bengal and parts of the Deccan were ruled by the Muslim governors, who enjoyed considerable autonomy in their internal administration. The whole of the Sultanate was interspersed with numerous hereditary possessions of the Hindu feudal chiefs and estates of the Hindu landlords and the Muslim fief-holders. The central government did not interfere in the internal administration of the distant provinces and the *jagir* lands.

The provincial government of the Sultans was not well-defined as that of the imperial Mughals, beginning with Akbar; it was organised more or less on the central pattern. The governor was invariably a military officer of repute who recruited his own army or militia and rendered military service to the king in times of need. He held a miniature court like that of the Sultans, and was assisted in the discharge of his work by a large number of signatories like the provincial *vakil, ariz, sadr* and the *qazi*; who were generally appointed by the governor with the approval of the Sultan, though, in some cases, nominees of the central government were also posted there to control the provincial revenues and exercise a sort of check on the powers and activities of the governors. The powerful Sultans usually maintained a large number of spies and news reporters at the provincial headquarters to keep themselves informed of local developments and nefarious activities of the provincial governors, if any.

The local administrative units of the provincial government of the Sultanate were very vague and undefined. Some of the provinces were roughly divided into *shiqs* or districts which were administered by the *shiqdars*; each *shiq* consisted of a few *parganas*, the number of which was not fixed. Wherever this division existed, the *shiqdar* acted as the police chief of the territory under his charge; he recruited his own local militia to maintain law and order and to suppress the refractory *zamindars*, including the local revenue collectors like the *khuts* and *muqaddams*. He helped the *amil* to collect land revenue and other taxes. According to Ibn Battuta, a *pargana* was 'an aggregate of about one hundred villages'. The important government officials of a *pargana*, after its officer-in-charge, called *shiqdar*, were an *amil, mushrif, khazandar* and *qazi*; the *amil* collected revenues; the *mushrif* kept the accounts, and *khazandar* held charge of the treasury. The *qazi* decided the civil suits while the *shiqdar* administered criminal justice. The military officers in charge of the forts and their adjoining territories were called the *faujdars*. All these government posts, excluding the *khuts* and *muqaddams*, who belonged to the category of the local Hindu *zamindars*, were reserved for the Muslims. Of course, at the lowest level, the ancient Indian villages, inhabited mostly by the Hindus, were the self-supporting and self-dependent administrative units, which maintained their precarious existence with the help of their local *panchayats* in spite of the unbearable political stress and strain of the early medieval period.

The Iqta System

The *Iqtadari* was a unique type of the land distribution system, evolved by the Turkish rulers of Delhi for the extension and consolidation of Muslim rule in Hindustan It was quite distinct from the feudal estates of the pre-Muslim Rajput period or the *Jagirdari* system of the imperial Mughals. The *iqtadari* was the system of allotment of vast tracts of partially conquered and unspecified lands, inhabited by the Hindu population, and territorial possessions of the well-established Hindu rulers in the neighbourhood of the Sultanate of Delhi, among the ambitious Muslim military officers by the Sultans with freedom to carry on *jihad* or wars of aggression against the *kafirs* until they were overpowered and completely subjugated by the *iqtadars*. The prospective military commanders were expected to muster their own armed resources and carry on such warfare at their own initiative and risk but with the moral support of the central government of Delhi and the promise of active military support if necessary. All such territorial acquisitions made by the iqtadars were declared annexed to the imperial government and permitted to be held as rent-free grants by the respective *iqtadars*. The *iqtadari* system thus denoted the official sanction for the perpetual *Jihad* against 'the hostile infidel lands' and their forced possession by the destruction of 'the enemies of Islam'. We have described elsewhere the evolution of this legalized practice of unprovoked aggressive warfare (read *Jihad*), introduced by the Muslim adventurers against the poorly equipped and ill-organised Hindu *zamindars* and the undefended leaderless Hindu populace of the countryside around the urban centres of their power as follows:

> "As we know, the conquest of India by the Turks is a paradox of Indian history. A handful of the Turkish nobles, assisted by thousands (but not *lakhs*) of the adventurers, apparently strangers to the land and its people, scored a military victory and setup as rulers. The number of the victors was very small, rather

> insignificant, as compared with the teeming millions (of the non-Muslim Indian populace) who had been subjugated by them. The conquerors established their military hold over important towns and fortifications *albeit* the vast land mass of the countryside, with the bulk of the Indian population, was yet to be explored and conquered. In order to facilitate this task, the Sultans of Delhi parcelled out their vague and undefined dominions into *iqtas* and distributed these among their ambitious and enterprising nobles. The latter, called the *iqtadars* or *muqtas*, were instructed to carry on aggressive campaigns against the powerful and refractory Hindu *zamindars* and chieftains in their region and bring them under effective subjugation. The *iqta* was a half-conquered and poorly administered territory over which the assignee was expected to establish a firm hold, and introduce civil administration there as he thought fit or feasible. The *iqtadar* recruited his own army which was made self-supporting by utilizing the resources of his possessions. He held the *iqta* almost as a rent-free grant in lieu of the state service. He paid to the sovereign a specified amount of *kharaj* or offered presents in cash or kind, including gold, silver, horses, elephants or other precious articles, every year and rendered military service to the state when needed.
>
> 'The *iqtadars* were not ordinary *jagirdars* or holders of rent-free assignments; they made personal contribution towards the expansion and consolidation of the Turkish rule in India in the thirteenth century. Most of them were self-made men who held the *iqtas* as their personal estates which were passed on to their descendants in heritage. The emergence of hereditary *iqtadars* or feudal lords among the Turkish nobility laid the foundations of their rule very deep in the Indian soil.' (*Advanced Study in the History of Medieval India*; Sterling, 1979, i, pp. 307-8).

Balban had to face considerable difficulty in bringing the powerful hereditary *iqtadars* under the control of the central authority of Delhi. Alauddin Khilji and Muhammad bin Tughluq, being great imperial rulers, were ever keen to exercise complete control over all the centres of Muslim power in the country; they, therefore, made an attempt to abolish the traditional system of *iqtadari* or *jagirdari* by drastically curtailing the powers and functions of the *iqtadars*. They retained the *iqtas* as administrative units but changed the method of appointment and character of its holders. Traditionally, the *iqtadars* were under the charge of major regional or provincial governors. But as the provincial government of the Sultanate was not well-developed, some of the *iqtadars* were now brought under the direct control of the central government at Delhi, and were treated as provincial governors for all intents and purposes. Politically important or prosperous *iqtas* were given to the princes of the royal blood as their personal estates. Nevertheless, this system was revived by the successors of Alauddin Khilji, and subsequently made universal by Firoze Tughluq who parcelled out the whole of his kingdom into *iqtas* or *fiefs* which were distributed among the nobles as rent-free assignments. Theoretically, the *iqtadars* were under obligation to remit their surplus revenues to the state treasury and get their accounts checked by the royal editors of the *diwan-i-wizarat*. Of course, within each *iqta*, Firoze Tughluq further granted villages, agricultural lands or residential places as rent-free grants to the *ulema*, saints and other Muslim dignitaries which were excluded from the jurisdiction of the *iqtadars*. The *iqtadars,* in turn, were fully authorized to grant free assignments to their blood relations, subordinates and brilliant lieutenants, thus strengthening and perpetuating the feudal element in the administrative hierarchy of the Sultanate. We have it on the testimony of Shams-i-Siraj Afif that Firoze Tughluq formally renounced war against the rebellious Muslim nobles and facilitated the rise of many Muslim ruling dynasties on the ruins of the erstwhile Sultanate of Delhi. It led to the decentralization of the Muslim power all through the country and saw the emergence of numerous local and regional states and principalities ruled over by them.

Fiscal Policy of the Sultans

The revenue establishment of the Sultanate was based on the Islamic theory of taxation as proposed by the Hanafite school of thought; it prescribed the levy of four major taxes – *Zakat, Kharaj, Khams*, and *Jaziya*. The *Zakat* was a religious tax, paid by the Muslims in *khairat* or charity—'as an act of piety', for the benefit and welfare of the poor sections of their community. It was charged at the rate of 2.5 per cent of the actual income of the householders. The *Kharaj* was the land revenue, which varied from 10 to 50 per cent of the agricultural produce in the regimes of various Sultans, and was payable in cash or kind. The tributary Hindu chiefs also paid *Kharaj* or tribute in lump sum. The *Khams comprised* the state's share of the booty, acquired by the soldiers in the course of war. The Islamic law required the soldiers to surrender one-fifth of their spoils to the king, although some of the powerful Sultans were not content with it; Alauddin Khilji was known to demand as much as the four-fifth of it from his soldiers. As referred to earlier, all the non-Muslim subjects of the Sultanate, including the Hindus, Buddhists and Jains, had to pay *Jaziya* or poll tax as the price for their stay in their own ancestral hearths and homes in the role of *Zimmis* or second-class citizens of the Islamic state. *Jaziya* was collected from all able-bodied grown-up males. For this purpose, the Hindu population of the Sultanate was divided into three grades on the basis of their economic standing: the richest among them had to pay 48 *dirhams* per head per annum; while a middle class Hindu male paid 24 *dirhams* and the one of the poor sections had to part with 12 *dirhams* per annum irrespective of whether he had any regular means of livelihood or not.

The so-called extensive economic and agrarian reforms of Alauddin Khilji and Muhammad bin Tughluq were all based on unscientific and irrational principles; they failed to develop a progressive land revenue system based on the measurement of land and assessment of the state demand in proportion to the actual produce. Their reforms 'fizzled out in the hands of their less imaginative and shortsighted successors', and Firoze Tughluq revived the *jagir* system with a vengeance with disastrous consequences.

The Judicial Organisation

Diwan-i-Qaza or the 'department of justice' was the weakest and the most poorly organised wing of the Sultanate's civil administration. The Sultans transplanted the foreign law and legal institutions in India which did not take deep roots during the early medieval period. The Sultan being the fountain head of justice was responsible for the implementation and upholding of the Islamic law of crime and punishment, which, in theory, was the only law recognised by the Sultanate of Delhi. The main sources of this law were the Holy *Quran*, the *Hadis* and the *Ijma;* the *Quran* contained the 'divine revelations', the *Hadis* was composed of the traditions and precepts of the Prophet in the matters of law and religion, while the *Ijma* or the 'consensus of opinion' referred to all the legal decisions, ever taken by the Muslim jurists (*mujtahids*) on the authority and by the interpretation of the first two sources.

The judicial organisation of the Sultanate was not very complex.

The Islamic law was treated as personal and indispensable for the Muslims while the *Zimmis* or non-Muslims were exempt from the application of the religious part of it. Nevertheless, a Hindu was subjected to the Islamic law when the rival party in dispute happened to be a Muslim or the state. The Sultan comprised the highest judicial authority of the state, and usually dispensed justice to earn reputation as the just monarch of an Islamic state; his *durbar*, therefore, constituted the highest court of civil and criminal justice which took up original as well as appellate cases without any set procedure. While dealing with the religious cases, the Sultan was assisted by *sadr-us-sadur* or the chief *sadr* but in secular cases he had the assistance of the *qazi-ul-qazat* or the chief *qazi* of the dominions. During the Sultanate period, both of these offices were usually held by one and the same person.

The chief *qazi* was formally designated as the head of the department of justice though, in actual practice, he was only its nominal head. The chief *qazi* was appointed by the Sultan and held office at his pleasure; he lived and held his court at the capital of Delhi and was assisted by a *mufti* – 'legal interpreter' in the administration of justice. The court of the chief *qazi* was treated as the highest court of appeal only when the Sultan's court was not in session; even otherwise when the chief *qazi* acted as the highest court of appeal, his decisions were liable to be taken up and revised by the Sultan. As incharge of the judicial organisation, the chief *qazi* recommended the appointment of the provincial *qazis* by the Sultan, issued rules and regulations for the proper functioning of the provincial and local courts and exercised disciplinary control over the judicial services. All the important towns of the state had a *qazi*'s court. *Muhtasib*, the censor of public morals, acted as police officer-cum-magistrate in the observance of the canon law by the Muslims. At a later stage, we also hear of another judicial institution, called the *Diwan-i-Mazalim* in big cities which was headed by the *amir-i-dad*; his office seems to correspond to that of the modern city magistrate. He performed two duties; he apprehended the criminals like a police officer and also tried the cases with the help of the *qazi*. He thus acted as judge as well as an executive officer; in the latter capacity, he was required to enforce the *qazi's* decisions and to cooperate with the *Muhtasib* in enforcing his regulations. The provincial governors, *iqtadars* and other executive officers, like the *faujdars* and *kotwals*, all possessed some judicial powers within the jurisdiction of their administrative assignments, and were authorized to settle criminal cases and inflict punishment on the defaulters. Ordinarily, the high executive officers did not discriminate between the exercise of their executive and judicial functions. The *amils a*nd other revenue officers decided the revenue disputes. The government left small towns and rural areas, which comprised more than ninety per cent of the state's population, untouched, and appointed no judicial officers of its own to administer justice. Fortunately, the Hindus, who comprised the bulk of this population, 'were happy to be left undisturbed by their foreign masters, whose rule over the villages existed only for the collection of land revenue and the Jaziya.' Their village *panchayats,* with the tacit approval of the government, administered justice according to their personal law and the local traditions and customs,

The Islamic penal code was very severe; physical torture and capital punishment formed an essential part of it. The usual practice was to make use of force and torture to extort confession from the accused and the culprits were punished with the mutilation of their limbs; the cutting of hands, feet, or noses of highwaymen and thieves or those found guilty of immoral practices was a common affair. Deterrent punishments were inflicted on the rebels and enemies of the state.

A careful perusal of the contemporary chronicles reveals glaring defects in the administration of justice in the Sultanate of Delhi. There was no proper classification or grading of the courts, and their territorial jurisdictions were also left undefined. Accordingly, an aggrieved person or party could lodge a complaint or file his suit anywhere he liked; he could seek justice from the *qazi* of the town or go straight to the court of the provincial *qazi,* or even knock at the gates of the Sultan's court, depending upon his social status and resources. The judicial procedure of trial was not uniform; very often the cases were investigated and disposed off without proper enquiries. Proceedings of the court were not recorded and the practice of allowing the accused to have their *vakils* or counsels to plead their case was unknown. Disputes between the Hindus and Muslims were decided by the *qazi* on the basis of the Quranic law and the posts of *qazis* or judicial officers were reserved exclusively for the Muslims. The chronicles of early medieval India do not throw out the name of even a single Hindu who ever might have been appointed as the *qazi;* obviously, great injustice must have been done to the *Zimmis* (the Hindu subjects) of the Sultanate who must have suffered religious discrimination even in the matter of settlement of their secular disputes. By every standard, the judicial organisation of the Sultans marked a rudimentary setup of semi-civilised social order for the benefit of a microscopic Muslim community which did not comprise more than five to ten per cent of the total populace of the Sultanate during the early medieval period; it was tantamount to the denial of justice to the majority of their Hindu subjects, reduced to the status of *Zimmis* or second class citizens of the state.

The Army Establishment

The Sultanate of Delhi was a foreign 'military dictatorship; it owed its genesis to the military victory of the Turks over the Indian rulers in the twelfth and the thirteenth centuries, and its strength and stability depended primarily on its strong and efficient army'. The entire political structure of the Sultanate was, in fact, cast in the Islamic mould and manned by 'the army of Islam'. The army of Sultans was based on the Turkish and Mongol models. The Sultan and all the *grandees* of the kingdom were basically men-in-arms, whose titles denoted the socio-political status by way of a military gradation. Changez Khan is known to have classified his nobility on decimal basis. According to his classification, a *Khan* commanded 10,000 horsemen, a *Malik* 1,000 and an *Amir* 100; and somewhat this type of classification of the Muslim nobility remained in vogue throughout the Sultanate period although the precise numerical strength of the soldiery commanded by them was not fixed. A Turkish military officer or noble was called *Amir*, and collectively, they were referred to as *Umara* (plural of the term *amir*). The Sultanate was based on the active support and cooperation of the *Umara,* who were professionally styled as the *Ahl-i-Shamshir* or *Ahl-i-Saif* – viz., 'the men of the sword'. They constituted the backbone of the Sultanate and formed a part and parcel of the sovereign power. The nobles commanded the armies and contributed towards the establishment as well as expansion and stability of the Sultanate. They supplied ministers, provincial governors, *iqtadars* and other high executive officers from among them and exercised great influence on the state policies; even the crown was not beyond the reach of a capable and ambitious noble. A.B.M. Habibullah, in his valuable treatise, entitled, *The Foundation of Muslim Rule in India*, makes a very forthright comment on the army of the Turko-Afghan conquerors of India as follows:

> 'Contemporary writers lay great emphasis on the need for maintaining a strong and efficient army, for a state can never

function without a coercive instrument. Originally, the army (of the Muslim conquerors) was, perhaps composed of every able-bodied man who immigrated to India, but there soon grew up the idea of a division of labour. As the conquerors gradually assumed the duties of civil government, a functional division of society (Muslim community) took place and fighting became more or less a profession. While potentially all Muslims were members of the state's fighting forces, normally, professional soldiers in the state's employ manned the army'. (*loc. cit.*, pp.262-63)

Army of the Sultanate belonged to four major categories:

(*a*) Regular troops, under the direct control of the Sultan and in permanent employment;

(*b*) Troops of the nobles recruited and employed permanently in their service by the feudal chiefs, including the provincial governors, *fief*-holders and *iqtadars*;

(*c*) Mercenary troops or irregular army, recruited and employed in time of war and expeditions; and

(*d*) The Muslim volunteers, enlisted for fighting against the infidels, 'who were expected to bear their own arms and enroll, for no pay but a share in the booty, for participating in what was called a *Jihad*'.

The royal guards or troops of the Sultan at Delhi were known as *Hashm-i-Qalb*. They belonged to two categories; those who were permanently attached to the Sultan, and the others who were in the service of the nobles at Delhi. The royal guards or the troops under permanent service of the Sultan were known as *Khasah Khail*; they included the royal slaves, the slave-guards, known as the *jandars*, and regular troopers, called the *afwaj-i-qalb*, who were directly under the royal command. Though numbering quite a few thousands, the royal guards were meant for the personal safety of the Sultan and the royal household and could not be labelled as a 'standing army'. The credit for raising a large standing army, recruited, equipped and commanded by the military officers directly under the central government goes to Alauddin Khilji His standing army numbered 4,75,000 horsemen besides a large number of the foot-soldiers and war elephants. It was supplemented by the feudal armies of the provincial governors and nobles in time of war. After the death of Muhammad bin Tughluq, the institution of standing army melted away, giving place once again to the feudal setup of the military establishment which carried all the inherent defects of the system with it. The whole of the army, including the troops supplied by the nobles and provincial governors, were under the general supervision and control of the *Ariz-i-Mumalik*, who headed the ministry of defence, called the *Diwan-i-Arz*. There were no fixed rules for the recruitment, training and promotion of the soldiers. Firoze Tughluq failed miserably in maintaining the standard and efficiency of the royal troops and did away with the system of cash payment to them. Instead, he popularised the feudal practice of granting *jagirs* or rent-free assignments in lieu of state service and made military service life-long and hereditary; he also did away with the system of branding of the horses and taking of the descriptive rolls of the soldiers, and was thus personally responsible for the decay and deterioration of the once mighty standing army of the Sultanate. Army of the Lodhi Sultans was organised on clannish basis; it primarily consisted of the tribal hordes of the Afghans and was weak and ill-organised. The weakening of the central authority of the state and downfall of the Sultanate was its natural consequence, but it led to the decentralization of Muslim power under the leadership of numerous regional and provincial feudal chiefs who setup independent states in different parts of the country side by side with those of the Hindus as in Malwa, Gujarat, Jaunpur, Bengal and the southern peninsula. The *Ariz-i-Mumalik* had one or more *naib-i-ariz* under his charge to assist him in the discharge of his functions.

The provincial forces, though recruited by the respective military governors, called *muqtas* or *muqtis* personally, were also graded and maintained on the central model; they were under the control of the provincial *ariz* and were presented to the Sultan through the local representative of the *naib ariz-mumalik*. According to Shams-i-Siraj Afif, all the troops employed permanently at the centre and in the provinces were known as the *wajhi* or 'regulars'.

The recruitment of special militia or temporary forces in times of war and for the purpose of some specific expeditions was also 'an established practice'. They comprised the third wing of the armed forces of Delhi. These troops were hired on contract and disbanded after the fulfilment of the assigned task. For instance, in 1241, when the Mongols marched on Lahore, Minhaj-us-Siraj, the celebrated historian who held the office of the *Sadr-us-Sadur*, 'was directed by the king to deliver an exhortation urging the people to enroll in the army for fighting the infidels' According to Habibullah, such recruitments were most probably 'confined to Muslims only'. But in many other cases, while organizing expeditions against the disaffected Muslim nobles, or fighting their political rivals, the Sultan and even the other contenders for power did not hesitate in recruiting the Hindu soldiers temporarily. When Sultana Razia marched from Bhatinda with her husband Iltuniah to recover the throne of Delhi, she is said to have been accompanied by a large number of mercenaries from the Hindu Jat and Khokhar tribes of the Punjab. Similarly, when Balban marched from Delhi to quell the rebellion of Muslim nobles at Lakhnauti (Bengal), he enrolled about two *lakhs* of the mercenaries from *Awadh as* 'archers, carriers, and also as horsemen and infantry', a large number of whom were Hindus. Nevertheless, when the non-Muslims were recruited as mercenaries in the army, they did not resort to loot and plunder in the course of the war nor were they entitled to any share in the booty.

The fourth wing of the army of the Sultanate was formed by the Muslim volunteers or *Jihadis* to fight against the infidels. The *Muslims* were invariably encouraged to enlist themselves as volunteers whenever the Sultans or their provincial governors and *iqtadars* waged war against any Hindu ruler or organised expeditions against the disaffected Hindu *zamindars* within their territories. Such armed encounters were widely publicized and the *maulvis* and the *ulema* were sent around the country to exhort the Muslim youth to participate in the holy war. They brought their own horses and weapons of war and were paid no salaries from the state treasury; instead, they were assured of a handsome share in the booty, and were accorded a great honour by the state as well as the Muslim society as *Ghazis*. Barani makes mention of a special class of gentlemen troopers in the Sultan's army who supplied their own horses and weapons of war. Minhaj-us-Siraj records that in 1259, when the Mongol envoys of Halaku Khan arrived in Delhi, the royal army of Delhi, under the command of Balban,—then the *malik naib* of Sultan Nasiruddin Mahmud, numbering about 2,00,000 infantry and 50,000 horsemen was assembled for the purpose of display; it was supplemented by many thousands of armed volunteers from the Muslim citizens, who appeared in their own arms and horses and were drawn up along with the regulars.

The army of the Turko-Afghan rulers was composed of cavalry, infantry and elephants. The cavalry occupied a place of pride in it and constituted the very backbone of the Muslim military establishment; India was, in fact, overrun and ravaged primarily by the horsemen of

Mahmud of Ghazni, Muhammad Ghori and Amir Timur. As the worth of a trooper depended much upon the quality and fitness of his horse, many of the fighters preferred to have one or two additional horses ready for service. Accordingly, the horsemen were divided into three grades; ordinarily, a cavalryman or *swar* had a single horse, but an enterprising fighter who could muster one additional horse was called *du-aspa,* and the one with two led horses was known as the *murattab*; and these soldiers were paid handsome extra allowance by the state for the maintenance of their beasts. Great care was taken by the Muslim military generals that their soldiers should not run short of horses, and the Sultans of Delhi, of necessity, kept thousands of extra horses in the royal stables ready for service. They ensured regular supply of good horses from Arabia, Turkistan and other countries of Central Asia. A cavalryman was usually armed with two swords, a dagger and a shield besides the Turkish bow with a rich stock of arrows with poisoned tips; some of them carried maces too. The horseman and his horse were well protected in the battlefield; the soldier wore a coat of mail and even leather jacket, quilted with fibrous material like cotton, and his horse was also provided with iron trappings so as to cover the whole of its body. The Turkish horsemen and camel-riders were reputed as excellent archers who could aim at their targets with precision while moving at full speed on the backs of their animals. The flying columns of the archers on their horses and camels could play havoc in the enemy's camp in time of war. The use of elephants in the war was learnt by the Turkish invaders from their Indian adversaries, and it goes to their credit that they made a much better use of the war elephants against their foes. Normally, the Turks used the elephants as beasts of burden to carry armament and the foot soldiers on the war fronts. A trained war elephant was clad in plates of steel and large scythes were attached to his trunk and tusk; it could carry on its back about half a dozen armed men, seated safely inside the wooden *hauda*. During the Sultanate period, the possession of an elephant was regarded as a royal prerogative, and all the beasts found with the people, including the Hindu *sadhus* or forest hermits, were confiscated; very rarely, some celebrated noble or provincial governor was likely to be granted permission to keep an elephant for use on ceremonial occasions as a mark of honour. The forts were a prized possession of the Turks and infantry was of great use to them in laying siege to the strongholds of the enemy. The use of modern artillery was not known but the catapults and other mechanical means were employed for hurling big stones on the besiegers and for battering the walls of the fortresses, while combustible material like naphtha balls, hand-grenades and fireworks were used for setting fire to the enemy's camp.

The Turks were the masters of military strategy. They fought for victory and not for the vain display of their military prowess and martial talent. The art of ambushing and surprise attacks formed the normal techniques of their war strategy. Instead of challenging the enemy in the open fight, they invariably preferred to employ false military maneuvers, deceit, and feigning retreat before the foes, in battle array, to create confusion in their ranks, and then struck hard against them when they were found off the guard. Before the actual conflagration, the prospective theatre of war was carefully surveyed by their leaders to guess the war strategy of the enemy, his battle formations, entrenchments and the geographical hazards of the landscape. The adversary's troops, deeply entrenched and awaiting head-on collision with the Turks for a pitched battle, were avoided as far as possible, and every effort was made to draw them out of their trenches and break their battle formations before making a frontal attack on them. On the battle-field, the Turkish army was usually divided into several divisions, which included the advance guard and the centre, the right wing and the left wing, the rear guard or the reserve, and the right and the left flanking parties. The elephants were usually stationed on the frontline but they were put to some selective use also to take on the enemy's formations of hosemen and infantry in the thickest of the battle. Numerous parties of scouts and advance columns of expert archers as camel riders and horsemen were employed for reconnaissance to collect intelligence about the location and movements of the enemy and to ascertain the weak spots for a surprise attack on him.

The *Ulema*

Together with the nobles or *Ahl-i-Shamshir*, the Muslim intellectuals and theologians, commonly referred to as *Ulema* or *Ulama* comprised the first two estates of the Muslim socio-political order. Styled as the *Ahl-i-Qalam*, they provided the second set of the *Umara* to the Sultanate and exercised a great influence on the politics and functioning of the Islamic state of Delhi. They interpreted the Islamic law and regarded themselves as the religious and spiritual guardians of the state. They manned the judicial and ecclesiastical services and held an exclusive control over the mosques, religious establishments and educational institutions. The *Sadr-us-Sadur* and *Qazi-ul-Qazat* were usually their high priests. The Sultanate being a theocratic state, the construction, maintenance and upkeep of the *masjids* and other educational and religious institutions was regarded as one of its important functions, and all the *imams, maulvis,* and religious preachers and teachers in the *madrassas* were liberally provided by the state exchequer through salaries in cash in the form of *madad-i-muash, inaam* and rent-free land grants. Vast tracts of land, including many villages, were attached to the *masjids* as endowments. The *Ulema* enjoyed respect and influence among the Muslim masses and, because of their popular appeal, demanded attention of the Sultan and the ruling elite. The Sultan always felt obliged to treat them with due deference and kept them fully satisfied by extending liberal state patronage to them. Even the despotic and most autocratic ruler like Alauddin Khilji, who did not want them to interfere in the state affairs, had to keep them in good humour by lavish state bounties, while Muhammad bin Tughluq had to pay heavily when he incurred the displeasure of the *Ulema* as a class. Under the weak and orthodox rulers like Firoze Tughluq, the *Ulema* established their predominance in the state politics and converted it into an instrument for proselytization.

❑ ❑

9

THE BAHMANI AND VIJAYANAGAR KINGDOMS

The signs of decline and downfall of the Sultanate of Delhi made their appearance in the concluding years of Muhammad bin Tughluq's reign, and Firoze Tughluq's period of rule saw its rapid disintegration. In the course of its dismemberment from 1335 to 1400, it gave birth to a large number of regional and provincial monarchical states and feudal principalities besides the two mighty kingdoms of Bahmani and Vijayanagar in south India. The Sultanate as a binding force between the distant provinces and regions having ceased to exist, the country was once again parcelled out into 'congeries of states' of Dr. Ishwari Prasad's denomination. The post-Sultanate period of Indian history thus came to present the almost identical picture of the Indian polity of the pre-Muslim era with the only difference that now the conglomerate of the Indian feudal states were ruled over by the Hindu as well as Muslim ruling houses and the feudal lords side by side with one another. The provincial and regional states comprised among others, the well-established and prosperous Muslim states of Malwa, Gujarat, Jaunpur and Bengal along with equally powerful Rajput states of Mewar and Marwar in Rajputana. In between them were interspersed numerous small principalities and feudal estates of Hindu as well as Muslim hereditary landlords. The territorial boundaries and spheres of influence of these big and small states were not fixed, and the big states were usually in perpetual warfare with one another while the small fry, in between them, 'suffered and wavered in their feudal loyalties towards their more influential neighbours'.

Northern and central India thus presented a dismal political picture in the fifteenth century while the fortunes of the south Indians were determined by the rise of the Bahmani and Vijayanagar kingdoms, the one ruled over by the Muslims and the other by the Hindu ruling dynasty. Both of these kingdoms came into existence almost simultaneously; the ruling dynasty of the Bahmani kingdom of Gulbarga was provided by the Muslim nobility of the erstwhile Sultanate of Delhi while the ruling house of Vijayanagar belonged to the indigenous Hindu stock. 'Together they determined the destinies of south India for over two centuries and provided a long era of peace and prosperity to their subjects when the inhabitants of Delhi had been suffering under the misrule of their lilliputian Sultans. The age of the Bahmani and Vijayanagar kingdoms, therefore, constitutes a distinct epoch in the socio-cultural history of the southern half of the country from the decline of the Sultanate to the rise of the Mughal Empire as an all-India power'. (*Advanced Study*; i, p.266).

SECTION I: THE BAHMANI KINGDOM

Amiran-i-Sadah—the Founders

The Bahmani kingdom of the Deccan was the most powerful of all the independent Muslim states which came into existence on the ruins of the Sultanate of Delhi. It was during the reign of Muhammad bin Tughluq that the foreign Muslim nobility, popularly known as the *Amiran-i-Sadah* – 'the centurions', and including in their ranks most of the *walis, shiqdars* and *iqtadars* of the Deccan, joined their hands together and raised a standard of revolt against Delhi. They took forced possession of Daulatabad, a provincial capital of the Sultanate, and declared one of their senior colleagues, named Ismail Makh, as their king. Because of his advanced age with ease-loving habits, however, Ismail voluntarily resigned in favour of Hasan Gangu, entitled Zafar Khan, a more enterprising member of their party, who had meanwhile conquered Gulbarga by inflicting a crushing defeat on the imperial troops from Delhi. Accordingly, the *Amiran-i-Sadah* installed him on the throne at Gulbarga with the title of Sultan Muzaffar Alauddin Bahman Shah on August 3, 1347. The ruling dynasty of Gulbarga, founded by him came to be known as the Bahmani dynasty.

To assert his high pedigree, Hasan claimed his descent from the Persian hero Bahman-bin-Isfandiyar but Firishta records an interesting story about the origin of his dynasty. He writes that, in his early life, Hasan was a servant of Gangu—a prominent Brahman astrologer of Delhi, who enjoyed the confidence of Muhammad bin Tughluq. Pleased with his honesty, the astrologer recommended him to the Sultan for favours who conferred the title of *amir* on him with the command of 100 horsemen. It facilitated his subsequent rise to power as a senior military general in a short span of time. The astrologer is said to have once predicted royalty for Hasan and expressed a wish to become his minister in that eventuality. His prophecy having come true, Hasan was beholden to his Brahman patron, whom he appointed his first minister and also named his kingdom after him on his elevation to the throne. The Bahmani dynasty produced 18 Sultans and their rule lasted 180 years from 1347 to1527; some of them were very capable monarchs who made substantial contributions towards the advancement of their people and prosperity of their kingdom.

Alauddin Hasan Bahman Shah ruled for about ten years from 1347 to 1358 and proved a very successful and powerful ruler. With his capital at Gulbarga, he waged a continuous warfare against the neighbouring chieftains and compelled them to acknowledge his suzerainty. Because of wide-spread revolts in other parts of the Sultanate, Muhammad bin Tughluq failed to take effective steps to dislodge the Bahmanis from the Deccan, and ,after his death in 1351, Bahman Shah was relieved of much anxiety and took up to his career of conquests with a fresh vigour. His outstanding conquests included the towns and territories of Bidar, Goa, Dabhol, Kolhapur and a part of Telengana. Towards the close of his reign, he had divided his kingdom into four provinces, called *Tarafs*, with their headquarters at Gulbarga, Daulatabad, Berar and Bidar respectively. Each of these provinces was entrusted to an *amir*, called *Tarafdar*, who received a personal jagir in heredity in lieu of his service. The entire administration was based on feudal principles; and his provincial governors recruited their own armies and rendered military service to the centre in time of need. HK Sherwani, the author of *The Bahmanis of Deccan* (Hyderabad, 1953) writes about the founder of the dynasty as follows:

> 'There is not a single campaign either against the partisans of the Tughluq faction or against the Hindu *Rajas* and *Muqaddams* in which he showed the slightest hint of cruelty, and it invariably happened that after the campaign was over, the king or his representatives made a gift of the territory back to the erstwhile enemy to be held as a *jagir*. This was the reason why such powerful rulers as the *Raya* of Warangal accepted the king's hegemony without any blood being shed, and began to be regarded as honoured friends and allies of the new state'. (pp. 262-63)

Though at peace with the newly emerged Hindu state of Vijayanagar and tolerant towards his non-Muslim subjects, Alauddin Hasan, nonetheless, took up cudgels as the champion of Islam in the Deccan and claimed the fidelity and support of *Amiran-i-Sadah* for him on this account. He died at the age of 67 on February2, 1358.

Muhammad Shah I (1358-75)

Muhammad Shah, the son and successor of Alauddin Hasan, organised the civil administration of the Bahmani kingdom on sound footing with the assistance of his able prime minister (*wazir*) and father-in-law Saifuddin Ghori. He created the civil departments, each of which was put under the charge of a separate minister. Apart from the *wazir* or *vakil*, Muhammad Shah had three other ministers of cabinet rank; they were the *amir-i-jumla* or 'the finance minister', *wazir-i-ashraf* or 'the foreign minister', and *sadr-i-jahan* or 'head of the ecclesiastical and judicial establishments'. There was a deputy prime minister, called the *peshwa*, while *nazir* performed the functions of deputy finance minister. All the big towns of the kingdom had a *kotwal*, who headed the police department and was responsible for the maintenance of law and order.

Like his father, Muhammad Shah I remained busy all his life fighting against the neighbouring chiefs and the refractory *zamindars* for the consolidation and expansion of his dominions. But unlike his father, being a man of haughty demeanour and addicted to drinking, he professed to establish the supremacy of Islam in the Deccan; he displayed religious fanaticism towards his Hindu subjects and adopted authoritative attitude towards his Hindu political rivals. Muhammad Shah was not on good terms with the Muslim states of Malwa, Khandesh and Gujarat but his foreign policy was marked, particularly, by hostility towards the neighbouring Hindu states of Telengana (Warangal), Orissa and Vijayanagar. The Raja of Warangal had voluntarily entered into a friendly subordinate alliance with the founder of the Bahmani kingdom but Muhammad Shah went out of the way to assert his dominance over him by demanding exorbitant tribute. According to Firishta, 'enraged at an insult, offered or supposed to have been offered by the Rajah of Warangal' Muhammad Shah made an unprovoked attack on the border town of his dominions, called Vellunputtun, 'slaughtered its inhabitants without mercy, and captured the unfortunate prince Vinayaka Deva' on the orders of the Sultan, 'a pile of wood was lighted before the citadel', and the prince was burnt alive therein. 'After a few days' rest, the Sultan retired, but was followed and harassed by large bodies of Hindus and completely routed. Only 1500 men returned to Kulbarga (Gulbarga), and the Sultan himself received a severe wound in his arm'. (Robert Sewell, *A Forgotten Empire*; London, 1900, pp.30-31)

Unable to digest this humiliation, Muhammad Shah I 'assembled fresh forces, and despatched them in two divisions against Warangal and Golconda. The expedition was successful, and the Rajah submitted, the Sultan receiving Golconda, an immense treasure and a magnificent throne as the price of peace. The throne was set with precious stones of great value, and being still further enriched by subsequent sovereigns, was at one time valued at four million Sterling. Warangal finally fell in 1424 (during the reign of Sultan Ahmad Shah), and was annexed to the Bahmani kingdom, thus bringing the Muhammadans down to the river Krishna all along its length except in the neighbourhood of the east coast'. (*Ibid.*, p. 32)

Similarly, Alauddin Hasan had established friendly relationships with the rising power of the Hindu chiefs at Vijayanagar but Muhammad Shah entered into a deadly conflict with them, which acquired the overtones of a religious frenzy, being styled as *Jihad* or 'the holy war against the infidels'. The protracted war between the political, rather religious adversaries lasted two hundred years, and 'became a common feature of the southern politics throughout the period of existence of the two rival kingdoms – Bahmani and Vijayanagar; and, in the long run, ruined both of them'. Muhammad Shah triggered off the conflict with Vijayanagar on very flimsy grounds. It originated with the dispatch of a messenger by him, sometime in 1365, to demand money from Bukka Raya, the sovereign ruler of Vijayanagar, who was otherwise said to be on friendly terms with the Sultan. Affronted at this insult, and to forestall an attack by the Muslims, the Raya of Vijayanagar marched into the Sultan's territories with a large force, took possession of the border fortress of Mudgal and put its Muslim garrison to the sword. On the receipt of this news, Muhammad Shah opened his first regular campaign against Vijayanagar early in 1366 with a solemn vow that 'till he should have put to death one hundred thousand infidels, as an expiation for the massacre of the faithful, he would never sheathe the sword of holy war (*Jihad*) nor refrain from slaughter.' The Sultan personally led the attack on Vijayanagar; Bukka Raya was defeated and there was a terrible carnage in which men, women and children were not spared. The war ended only after a holocaust in which, according to Firishta, 'the victims on the Hindu side alone numbered no less than half a million; the Sultan had so wasted the districts of Carnatic that for several decades, they did not recover their natural population'.

Mujahid Shah (1375-78)

Muhammad Shah died on April 21, 1375, and was succeeded by his son Mujahid, then nineteen years old. He continued his father's policy of maintaining hostile attitude towards the neighbouring Hindu state of Vijayanagar, Shortly after his accession, Mujahid wrote to Bukka Raya that 'as some forts and districts between the Krishna and Tungabhadra rivers were held by them in participation, which occasioned constant disagreements, he must for the future limit his confines to the Tungabhadra, and give up all on the eastern side to him, with the fort of Beekpore (Bankapur) and some other places'. The fortress of Bankapur, situated to the south of Dharwar was always coveted by the Bahmani Sultans 'as it lay on the direct route from Vijayanagar to the sea, and its possession would paralyse Hindu trade'. (R Sewell, op. cit., p. 40). The Raya replied by a counter-demand that the Sultan should evacuate the whole of Raichur Doab and surrender the forts of Raichur and Mudgal to Vijayanagar 'as they had always belonged to the Anegundi family'. He declared that, in the interest of peace, the Krishna river should be recognised as the true boundary between the Bahmani and Vijayanagar kingdoms, and that 'the elephants, taken by Sultan Muhammad Shah should be restored'.

The Raichur Doab, in fact, was the eternal bone of contention between the two states; therefore, Mujahid Shah responded by organizing a surprise attack on Vijayanagar. He laid siege to the fort but failed to take it in spite of his best efforts, and had to beg a hasty retreat on the arrival of the Raya's brother with reinforcements from the neighbouring district. According to Firishta, the Sultan 'retreated from Vijayanagar and sat down before Adoni; but, after a siege lasting nine months, the attempt was abandoned, and he retired to his own territories in disgust'. In fact, Vijayanagar had by this time grown into a powerful kingdom which commanded the allegiance of a large number of dependent princes of south India, who all looked upon it as a great bulwark against the Muslim aggressors. Firishta records that 'the princes of the house of Bahmani maintained themselves by superior valour only, for in power, wealth, and extent of country, the Roys of Vijayanagar were greatly their superiors'.

Mujahid Shah's second expedition to Vijayanagar to settle his scores with the Raya also proved abortive. The Muslims suffered a crushing defeat in 'a highly contested engagement, which was fought outside the walls of the town of Vijayanagar'. The vanquished Sultan had a narrow escape from the battle-field, and an 'uneasy truce' was concluded by him with Bukka Raya through the agency of his veteran prime minister Saifuddin Ghori, Nevertheless, after having been weakened and discredited because of his failure in the self-provoked war against Vijayanagar, Mujahid Shah fell a victim to a conspiracy, hatched by his ambitious uncle, Daud Khan. During his retreat from Vijayanagar, when the Sultan had entered his own territories and was halting at a place en route to Gulbarga, he was stabbed to death in his sleep by Daud Khan and his henchmen on the night of April 16, 1378. Daud at once proclaimed himself Sultan, being 'the nearest of his kin' as the deceased had left no child behind him; he was acknowledged as such by the military officers of his camp and proceeded to Gulbarga where he formally ascended the throne. But the assassination of the youthful Sultan was resented by a section of the nobles who refused to recognise the usurper as the rightful claimant to the throne. In the confusion that followed, Daud Khan was also murdered 'while at prayers in the great mosque of the capital' by a hired slave of Ruh Parvar Agha, a foster sister of Mujahid Shah, on May 21, 1378. As a matter of fact, during the reign of Mujahid Shah, the nobility of the Bahmani kingdom had came to be divided into two rival factions; the *Amiran-i-Sadah* or the foreign nobility and bureaucracy and the *Dakhinis* or the native Muslim nobles. The Sultan extended liberal patronage to the foreign immigrants, particularly, the Turks and the Persians, which excited the jealousies of the natives, viz., the south Indian Muslims. Like the mutual conflict of Bahmani and Vijayanagar kingdoms, the rivalry between these factions of the nobility became very acute in the years to come and proved detrimental to the interests of the state.

Taking advantage of the political crisis at Gulbarga, Bukka Raya, the Vijayanagar chief, overran the Raichur Doab, advanced as far as the river Krishna, and invested the fortress of Raichur; it made the confusion worse confounded. To the good fortune of the Bahmani kingdom, Saifuddin Ghori, the grand old father-in-law and *wazir* of Alauddin Hasan, was still alive and held the administrative charge of the government at Gulbarga. On his sagacious advice, the rival factions of the nobles at the court agreed to install on the throne the youngest surviving son of Alauddin Hasan, as the Sultan with the title of

Muhammad Shah II; being 'a man of peace' he was 'welcome to all the parties' as the consensus candidate. An eight-year old son of Daud Khan was blinded 'in order to prevent dissension' among the nobles.

Muhammad Shah II (1378-97)

Like Nasiruddin Mahmud of the Mamluk dynasty of Delhi, Muhammad Shah II (1378-97), seems to have been a man of religious disposition who had passed his early life in obscurity, and was fond of literary pursuits. He offered a hand of friendship to the Raya of Vijayanagar, and the latter, having been alerted by the display of unity by the court of Gulbarga, thought it prudent to raise the siege of Raichur and vacate the Bahmanide territories. Muhammad Shah II entered into a friendly relationship with Vijayanagar, and 'during the whole of his reign of nearly twenty years, there was peace and tranquillity at home and abroad'. The Sultan devoted much of his time for the welfare and prosperity of his subjects. He built *masjids, madrassas* and *dargahs* for the propagation of the faith and encouraged conversions to Islam. He welcomed Muslim saints and scholars from all parts of Asia and offered liberal patronage to them. It is said that the Sultan sent a personal invitation to Hafiz, the celebrated *Sufi* poet of Persia, and the latter 'accepted the invitation and actually started for India' but, the fear of 'the sea in storm' and inclement weather, held him back. The poet, however, sent an ode to the Sultan, which greatly pleased him and the latter reciprocated by sending 'a handsome reward' to the poet in his native country. Muhammad Shah II lived a simple and frugal life like Nasiruddin Mahmud of Delhi, and sincerely believed that 'the king was merely a trustee of the wealth of the people, and any careless or unnecessary expenditure (from the state treasury by him) amounted to a breach of trust'. His period of rule witnessed a drought and famine in the Deccan, in the course of which 'he employed 5,000 bullock carts to import food grains from Malwa and Gujarat to mitigate its severity'; it is a different matter that 'the corn was sold at low rates to the Muslims only'. Likewise, many *maktabs* and orphanages were established by him at Gulbarga, Bidar, Qandhar, Ellichpur, Daulatabad, Chaul, Dhabol and other cities for free education and board and lodging of the Muslim children at the state expense. Special allowances were given to the readers of the Quran, reciters of the Traditions and the blind students. According to Firishta, the Sultan 'did nothing that is prohibited in the Quran except drinking wine and listening to music, but he used to say that he did the first because it saved him from evil thoughts, and the second because music helped him to think of God'. Saifuddin Ghori, the oldest *grandee* of the Bahmani kingdom, lived long to serve the first five Sultans of Gulbarga, including Muhammad Shah II; he died in early 1397 at the age of 104. The closing years of Muhammad Shah's life were saddened by the estrangement of his relations with his sons, who hatched a conspiracy to get rid of him, 'perhaps because of their impatience to get the throne'. Nevertheless, the Sultan held them in check and died a natural death after a brief illness on April 20, 1397.

Tajuddin Firoze Shah (1397-1422)

Muhammad Shah II was succeeded by his two sons, Ghiasuddin and Shamsuddin one after another in quick succession but their rule lasted for a brief period of six months only. Ghiasuddin, a young lad of seventeen, was overpowered and blinded during an entertainment by the henchmen of his younger brother Shamsuddin, and the latter was, in turn, blinded and thrown into prison by means of a *coup d'état* by Firoze Khan, another grandson of Alauddin Hasan, who ascended the throne with the title of Tajuddin Firoze Shah in November 1397. He ruled for a period of about twenty-five years up to 1422. A devout Muslim, Firoze Shah, in his early life, is said to have made his living by copying the Quran while the ladies of his *harem* used to augment the family's resources by embroidering the garments. But, after his accession to the throne, we find him indulging in heavy drinking, debauchery and music; and he is known to have builtup a large *harem* which consisted of 'women of several nationalities'. According to Firishta, as the sacred law of the Muslims did not permit more than four wives, the Sultan, on the advice of a close confident, 'had recourse to the device of multiplying his *harem* through '*muta* marriage'- 'a custom which permitted a marriage for a fixed term', and that 'about 800 women were daily admitted into his royal seraglio in this manner'. Being a religious fanatic, Firoze Shah revived the conflict with Vijayanagar and launched three successive campaigns against it during his period of rule. He defeated the armies of the Raya in the first two expeditions, but, in the third 'unprovoked attack on the fort of Pangal' in 1420, the Sultan received a crushing defeat and fled the field. At this juncture, when the defeat and discomfiture weighed so heavily on Firoze Shah's mind and he was taken ill, his younger brother Ahmad

Shah took forced possession of Gulbarga and barred his entry into the capital. Realising the gravity of the situation, Firoze voluntarily abdicated in favour of Ahmad Shah, who ascended the throne on September 22, 1422; Firoze Shah died a broken-hearted man a few days later.

Ahmad Shah (1422-36)

Immediately after his accession, Ahmad Shah took effective command of the royal forces in his hands and declared war on Devaraya II of Vijayanagar to avenge the defeat of his predecessor. Firishta writes that, in his war of vengeance, 'Ahmad Shah, without waiting to besiege the Hindoo Capital, overran the open country, and wherever he went, put to death men, women and children, without mercy, contrary to the compact made between the Raya of Vijayanagar and his uncle Muhammad Shah (II). Wherever the number of slain amounted to twenty thousand, he halted three days, and made a festival in celebration of the bloody event. He broke down, also, the idolatrous temples, and destroyed the colleges of the Brahmins. During these operations, a body of five thousand Hindoos, urged by desperation at the destruction of their religious buildings, and at the insults offered to their deities, united in taking an oath to sacrifice their lives in an attempt to kill the Sultan as the author of all their sufferings'.

The band of armed but leaderless Hindu villagers, mentioned above, found the opportunity to surround the Sultan when 'he was engaged in a hunting expedition. They chased him with tremendous fury, and reduced him to the extremity of distresses'. Pressed hard, Ahmad Shah took refuge within a mud enclosure, where he was assailed by his pursuers, who were at last driven out by his *Jandars*. Freed from danger, he made a frontal attack on Vijayanagar. Devaraya II had called the king of Warangal and some other Hindu princes for help, but the allied forces deserted the Raya on the eve of the battle. The Raya suffered a defeat at the hands of the Bahmanis on the bank of the river Tungabhadra and retired into the fort of Vijayanagar. Ahmad Shah besieged the stronghold and 'reduced its people to such distress that Devaraya was compelled to sue for peace. He agreed to pay all arrears of tribute, and sent his son with 30 elephants, laden with money, jewels and other articles of untold value to the royal camp, where he was cordially received by the Sultan'.

Flushed with victory, Ahmad Shah declared war upon Warangal

in 1424. His general, Khan-i-Azam fought a successful battle in which the Hindus were defeated and their chief was slain. The Hindu ruling dynasty of Telengana was extinguished; the state of Warangal was declared annexed to the Bahmani kingdom, and its sovereignty was lost forever. This rapid success encouraged Ahmad Shah to engage in wars against the Muslim rulers of Malwa and Gujarat also, apparently, to establish his hegemony over them. Sultan Hushing Shah of Malwa suffered a crushing defeat at his hands and fled from the battle-field. The last military expedition of Ahmad Shah was directed against the rebellious Hindu *zamindars* of Telengana. Thereafter, because of his advanced age and poor health, Ahmad Shah entrusted the reins of government to the crown prince and heir-apparent, Prince Zafar Khan, and retired from public life with 'directions to his nobles, ministers and generals to swear allegiance' to his successor. According to an inscription, found on his magnificent tomb on the outskirts of Bidar, he died of illness on April 17, 1436.

Ahmad Shah's reign was marked by two other important events. Firstly, he transferred his capital from Gulbarga to the newly constructed township at Bidar in 1425. According to Dr. PM Joshi, 'after the conquest of Warangal, the Bahmani kingdom extended in the east and Bidar was the most central point for this augmented dominion. The three linguistic areas of the kingdom converged on this city; it had moreover a far better climate than Gulbarga and strategically a far stronger position' (*History & Culture of the Indian People*; BVB, vi, p. 258)

Nevertheless, Dr. N Venkataramanayya has his own opinion about this change of the capital by Ahmad Shah, when he was still engaged in war with Vijayanagar. Referring to the 'political motive' of the Sultan, he writes:

> 'The Transfer of his capital from Gulbarga, near Vijayanagar frontier, to Bidar, situated in the hilly tract farther north in the interior of his dominions, is not without significance. Ahmad Shah's war on Vijayanagar did not perhaps end as favourably to the Sultan as the Muslim historians would have us believe. Some unrecorded Vijayanagar attack on Gulbarga probably compelled the Sultan to remove the seat of his government to a safer distance. That the war did not end in an absolute victory for the Sultan is made clear by an epigraph from South Kanara district dated 1429-30 AD, which refers to the defeat of the large and powerful *Turushka* cavalry by Devaraya II. As there was but one war between Vijayanagar and the Bahmani kingdoms in the time of

Ahmad Shah (1422-36), Devaraya II's victory over the *Turushkas,* mentioned in the record, must have been won during the Bahmani invasion of 1423 A.D.' (*Ibid.*, pp. 289-90)

Secondly, the rivalry between the two political factions of his court, the *Amiran-i-Sadah* and the Deccan party (*Dakhinis*) became accentuated. The Deccan party was composed of local Muslim nobles and was supported by the African Muslim immigrants who did not enjoy high posts in the kingdom, while the other party, called the *Amiran-i-Sadah,* consisted of the foreign Muslim immigrants from Persia, Turkistan and other countries of Central Asia. As it happened, the *Amiran-i-Sadah* were the founding fathers of the Bahmani kingdom, and the long line of its Sultans, including Ahmad Shah, were the leaders and spokesmen of that party. They held most of the prestigious positions and assignments in the court as well as in the provinces. The *Dakhinis* or the south Indian Muslims, to be very precise, were treated as inferior to the ruling junta and suffered discrimination in the allotment of higher offices in the civil as well as military organisations. They naturally felt jealous of the foreign Muslim bureaucracy. Moreover, some religious differences were also added to this political rivalry between the two factions at this stage; whereas the *Dakhinis* were Sunnis, a big segment of the *Amiran-i-Sadah,* belonging to the Persian stock, professed Shia faith. Owing to the dissensions at the court, administration of the Bahmani kingdom was much weakened. According to Sherwani, Ahmad Shah 'encouraged the influx of learned men, poets, statesmen, soldiers and others from over the seas, which, to a certain extent, led to a greater cleavage between these new-comers and the older colonists.' (The Bahmanis of Deccan, *loc.cit.*, pp. 211-12)

By all accounts, Ahmad Shah, like Amir Timur, was a fanatical Muslim and a tyrant who took delight in ruthlessly shedding the blood of unarmed and innocent people in the name of Islam. It is creditable that 'he loved the company of the learned (read Muslim scholars), and that he awarded seven lacs of *Deccani tankas* to Shaikh Azari, a native of Khurasan, for writing two verses in praise of the Sultan at Bidar'; but, presuming that he was 'a pious Muslim', we do not accept Professor Sherwani's other observations about him that 'his disposition was adorned with the ornament of clemency and temperance and with the jewel of abstinence and devotion'. For instance, in his fight against Hushang Shah, the Sultan of Malwa, when the latter suffered a defeat and fled from the battle-field, the victorious Bahmani Sultan, besides plundering his deserted army camp which yielded rich booty in wealth, war material and a large number of horses; put to the sword two thousand of his men, who had committed the mistake of offering their surrender. 'Such wanton massacres', writes Dr. Ishwari Prasad, 'commemorated the victories of this tyrant, who had assumed the title of *Vali* or 'Saint' as a reward for his services to the cause of Islam'. To cite yet another example of his base character and blood-thirsty nature, we reproduce below a paragraph from the *Tarikh-i-Firishta*, which reads as follows:

> 'In the year 829 H (1425-26 AD) Ahmad Shah marched to reduce a rebellious (Hindu) *Zamindar* of Mahoor, who still retained several strong places which held out against his troops. The rebel soon submitted; but Ahmad Shah, though he had assured him of pardon, put him to death in violation of his promise, as soon as he fell into his hands, together with five or six thousand of his followers, compelling, at the same time, all the captive women and children to embrace the true faith. During this campaign, the King obtained possession of a diamond mine at Kullum, a place dependent on Gondwana, in which territory he razed idolatrous temples, and erecting mosques on their sites, appropriated to each some tracts of land to maintain holy men and to supply lamps and oil for religious purposes'.

Alauddin II (1436-58)

After the death of Ahmad Shah, the crown prince, who had already taken charge of the government as its caretaker, formally ascended the throne under the title of Sultan Alauddin Ahmad. Known to history as Alauddin II, he 'held out the promise of a glorious reign' and built the magnificent dome over the grave of his father at Bidar whose walls and the ceiling were decorated with beautiful paintings in bright colours, composed of calligraphic devices and floral designs. It is said that he had performed a grand religious ceremony, accompanied by festivities and liberal public charities, while starting the construction of his father's tomb, to commemorate which a fair is held there every year 'in honour of the *Vali*'. Alauddin II ruled from 1436 to 1458 and had to face the rebellion of his younger brother, Prince Muhammad, soon after his coronation; the rebel was defeated and taken captive but pardoned and given the governorship of the Raichur Doab. After a few years, Prince Muhammad, on the instigation of 'some evil-minded persons', again raised the standard of revolt, but surrendered after a pitched battle, accompanied by heavy slaughter on both sides. 'Contrary to the practice of his time', the Sultan readily pardoned his vanquished and remorseful brother again, and allowed him to retain the district of Raichur as his personal *jagir*; thereafter, he 'remained faithful to Alauddin for the rest of his life'. It enhanced the reputation of the Sultan as the noble and kind-hearted king. In the earlier years of his reign, Alauddin II 'acted like a good king'; though not deeply religious himself, 'he enforced the observances of the faith' and ordered the *kotwals* and *muhtasibs* 'to educate the people in rites and customs of Islam, and the laws regarding lawful and unlawful things'. But, at a later stage, we find Alauddin II leading a life of luxury 'in debauchery and gratification of lust'.

Having overcome his initial domestic dissensions, Alauddin II undertook an expedition against a Hindu chieftain of Konkan – 'the strip of land which lay between the ghats and the sea' and reduced him to submission. Thereafter, the Sultan compelled the Raja of Sangameshwar to acknowledge his suzerainty and give his beautiful daughter in marriage to him. This lady, known to the Muslim chroniclers as *Pari-chehra* (Fairy face) became the youthful Sultan's favourite queen. Alauddin II was infatuated with his Hindu queen so much that it aroused the jealousy of his chief queen, the daughter of Sultan Nasir Khan of Khandesh, and she appealed to her father 'to save her from disgrace and humiliation'. Nasir Khan, in turn, sought the advice and support of Sultan Ahmad Shah of Gujarat, and with his help, declared war upon his son-in-law. He invaded Berar but was defeated and had to cut a sorry figure. War against Vijayanagar was not on the agenda of Alauddin II but, the Raichur Doab being a perpetual bone of contention between the two neighbouring states, he had to maintain an aggressive posture against his hereditary Hindu foe. The Muslim chroniclers record two brief wars between the adversaries during the reign of Alauddin II; one was fought in the year of his accession, and the other in 1443-44. These wars were in the nature of border skirmishes and remained confined to the Krishna-Tungabhadra Doab, and the clashes between the rivals centred round the forts of Mudgal and Raichur without producing any decisive result. Peace was ultimately concluded between them and 'the Raya agreed to pay the stipulated tribute'.

According to the Muslim chroniclers, 'in spite of his loose life', Alauddin II was 'a champion of Islam' and he was very considerate towards the Muslims. He constructed the *masjids,* public schools and charitable institutions, among which was 'a hospital of perfect elegance and purity of style', which he built in his capital. Nevertheless, the concluding years of his rule were much disturbed by the rivalry between the

Amiran-i-Sadah and the *Dakhini* factions of his nobles which led to the 'perpetration of an atrocious crime'. In 1454, a noble of the *Amiran-i-Sadah* faction, named Khalaf Hasan Malik-ul-Tujjar, who commanded a regiment, composed exclusively of the *Pardesi* (foreign immigrants) officers and the soldiery, in the royal army, suffered a crushing defeat at the hands of a Hindu chief, Raja Sankar Ráo Shirke of Khelna in the Konkan region; and the remnant of the unlucky soldiers, led by Hasan, fled to the town of Chakan in the district of Poona to save their lives. The Deccani ministers and the nobles misrepresented this affair to the Sultan by ascribing the defeat to the treachery and inefficiency of the *Pardesis,* dubbed the surviving fugitives of Chakan as deserters, and obtained orders for their extirpation as a punishment, Hasan and his fugitive soldiers were then lured out of Chakan by the *Dakhini* ministers and slaughtered in cold blood. As a result, 'besides Hasan, about 1,200 Sayyids of pure lineage and nearly 1,000 other *Pardesi* soldiers lost their lives because of the jealousy and perfidy of their political rivals. According to Firishta, a few *Pardesi* soldiers, who escaped from the holocaust, apprised the Sultan of the deception that had been practised on them. The Sultan wept to hear of the true story; duplicity of the *Dakhini* ministers having been exposed, the culprits were awarded capital punishment and the *Amiran-i-Sadah* regained their ascendancy in the court.

The massacre of Chakan sent shock-waves in the Muslim states of Malwa and Gujarat, discredited the Sultan in the eyes of his own people, and bred disaffection among them. In 1455, he had to face the rebellion of Jalal Khan, his brother-in-law and governor of Telengana, who headed a party of the rebellious nobles and proclaimed his independence. Alauddin II, though suffering from 'a festering wound in one of his shins', marched against him with full force but the latter, on the approach of royal forces, took refuge in the fort of Nalgonda, and sent his son Sikander towards Malwa to beseech the help of its ruler. Prince Sikander did secure the support of Sultan Mahmud Khilji of Malwa by making out that the Bahmani chief was dead and the kingdom was engulfed in political anarchy. At this critical juncture, Alauddin entrusted the charge of Nalgonda's siege to a newly recruited foreign military officer, *Amir* Mahmud Gawan, and himself rushed towards Malwa 'to meet the danger created by the conduct of Sikander'. As soon as the Sultan of Malwa came to know that he had been misled by the false information about the death of the Bahmani Sultan, he turned against Sikander and his agents from Telengana and retired to his kingdom. At the same time, Mahmud Gawan displayed his diplomatic skill to persuade Jalal Khan, the besieged noble at Nalgonda, to offer his unconditional surrender to Alauddin II, and secured royal pardon for him as well as his son and their rebellion was over. It was the first occasion when Mahmud Gawan, who rose to be the greatest prime minister and statesman of the Bahmani kingdom in the years to follow, came into lime light. Alauddin II thus came out of this crisis with flying colours and died of his 'malignant wound' but as a fully contented man, a few months later in April 1458.

Humayun Shah (1468-61)

Alauddin II was succeeded on the Bahmani throne at Bidar by his eldest son Humayun. He ruled from April 1458 to October 1461, for less than three years and a half, and earned notoriety as a tyrant (*zalim*) who struck terror in the hearts of his people. His short period of rule was, in fact, marred by dissensions among the members of royal household and unrest and rebellions in the kingdom. His father had formally nominated him as the heir apparent to the throne before his death, but, a powerful band of the 'New-comers' among the foreign nobles (*Pardesis*), who had gained ascendancy at the court after the 'Chakan episode', had their own nefarious designs. In violation of the deceased Sultan's express desire, they brushed aside the claim of the crown prince and, instead, put his younger brother, Hasan, on the throne with the ulterior motive of exploiting him as the puppet king, and actually 'sent a mob at the residence of Prince Humayun to murder him and plunder the royal palace'. The conspiracy hatched by them was foiled by the timely intervention of Humayun's confidents and supporters, however. The mob was dispersed and their ring-leaders were taken prisoners by the Royal Guards but Hasan and some other members of the royalty, who were drawn into this controversy, though segregated and kept under royal surveillance, were pardoned. According to Firishta, about six or seven thousand men were imprisoned after the failure of the first revolt of Prince Muhammad.

Humayun was not allowed by the miscreants to rule in peace. Jalal Khan, the governor of Telengana and his son Sikander Khan, who had earlier revolted during the reign of Humayun's father but pardoned and restored to their original assignments, showed their signs of disaffection again. In fact, Jalal Khan was one of the foreign nobles, belonging to the party of 'New-comers'. While appointing him the governor of Telengana, Alauddin II had also struck a matrimonial alliance with Jalal Khan by offering the hand of his sister in marriage to him. But the self-seeking *Pardesi* betrayed the trust reposed in him by his master and his royal family. The defiance of central authority by Jalal Khan and Sikander Khan necessitated the organisation of a punitive expedition against them into Telengana. A pitched battle was fought near Nalgonda but it remained indecisive. After a day's bloodshed, however, Humayun offered to make peace with the rebels on the plea that he did not want to shed the blood of more Muslims in this strife. Sikander died an untimely death in the course of the struggle and Jalal Khan was, ultimately, defeated but the Sultan spared his life on the intercession of his *wazir*, Mahmud Gawan, and some other foreign nobles.

In the light of what has been written above, we come to the conclusion that Humayun had been sinned more against than sinning. We are in accord with HK Sherwani's inference that 'all this does not depict Humayun in the colours of a wanton cut-throat'. (The Bahmanis; *loc.cit.*, pp. 264-67) Of course, there is nothing during the first two years of his reign to warrant his condemnation by the contemporary chroniclers. There was not a single campaign of aggression against his neighbours during this period. To his good fortune, Humayun had secured the services of a very capable minister, Mahmud Gawan, who maintained perfect law and order in the state and protected it from the adverse effects of the Sultan's domestic feuds and weaknesses of his personal character and conduct. Be his nature as it was, Humayun became desperate and lost his balance of mind in the third year of his rule when some other 'New-comers', led by Yusuf Turk, forcibly secured the release of Hasan and his associates from the royal prison and Hasan proclaimed himself the king at Bir. It dragged Humayun into yet another life and death struggle in which his failure or clemency implied his own death and the destruction of his entire family. No wonder, Humayun crushed this uprising with an iron hand and gave vent to his cruel propensities towards his rivals as narrated by Firishta and the author of *Burhan-i-Maasir*. Firishta, on the authority of some other contemporary sources, writes about Humayun Shah Bahmani that after the defeat and surrender of Hasan and his accomplices, the Sultan meted out the following treatment to the rebels:

> 'Humayun Shah, now abandoning himself to the full indulgence of his cruel propensities, and mad with rage, directed stakes to be setup on both sides of the King's *chouk* (marketplace) and caused vicious elephants and wild beasts to be placed in different

parts of the square; in other places the cauldrons of scalding oil and boiling water were also prepared as instruments of torture. The King, ascending a balcony in order to glut his eyes on the spectacle, first cast his brother, Hussun Khan, before a ferocious tiger, who soon tore the wretched Prince to pieces, and devoured him on the spot. Yusuf Turk and his seven associates were then beheaded in the King's presence, and the females of their innocent and helpless families, being dragged from their houses, were violated and ill-treated in the palace-square by ruffians, in a manner too indecent to relate. Tortures were now invented by the King, who inflicted on the young and old of both sexes, torments more cruel than ever entered the imagination of Zohak and the tyrant Hijaj. About seven thousand persons, including females and servants, none of whom had the most distant concern in this rebellion, besides the menials, such as cooks, scullions, and others, were put to death—some being stabbed with daggers, others hewn in pieces with hatchets, and the rest flayed by scalding oil or boiling water. This tragedy happened in the month of *Shaban*, in the same year as the rebellion'.

The Sultan, who had, by this time, completely lost the balance of his mind, continued to perpetrate atrocities on all and sundry without any rhyme or reason. Firishta has it on the record that

'Alarmed at the example of Hussun Khan, he put to death several innocent persons of the royal family who were confined in different fortresses. Nor did his suspicions rest here; many other persons of his own court became the innocent victims of his indiscriminate cruelty. From this moment, Humayun threw off all restraint, and seized at will the children of his subjects, tearing them from their parents to gratify his passions. He would frequently stop nuptial processions in the street, and seizing the bride, after enjoying her, send her to the bridegroom's house. He was in the habit of putting the females of his royal *harem* to death for the most trivial offences; and when any of the nobility were obliged to wait upon him, so great was their dread, that they took a last leave of their families, as if preparing for death'.

Humayun died sometime in October 1461; according to Firishta, he was murdered by the domestic servants of his royal palace in a state of drunkenness. It is probable that, although fatally wounded, the Sultan survived the assault but died a short while later. It is because we are told that Humayun had left the question of succession to be settled by his prime minister, Khwaja Mahmud Gawan. His death afforded relief to his subjects 'who had groaned under his tyranny in utter helplessness'. According to Ali bin Azizullah Tabataba, the author of *Burhan-i-Maasir*, a contemporary poet 'Naziri only voiced their feelings when he composed the following chronogram:

Humayun Shah has passed away from the world,
God Almighty, what a blessing was the death of Humayun!
On the date of his death, the world was full of delight,
So, 'DELIGHT OF THE WORLD' gives the date of his death.'

The Persian phrase *Zuq-i-jahan*, used by the poet in this couplet, means 'delight of the world', and the numerical value of the letters of this phrase comes to 865 H. (1460-61 A.D.)—(Quoted in *the Bahmanis of Deccan* by Sherwani).

The Successors of Humayun

Humayun was survived by two minor sons. After his death, Mahmud Gawan, in consultation with the influential nobles of the court, placed an eight-year old son of the deceased Sultan, named Nizam Shah, on the throne under a Council of Regency, headed by the Dowager Queen, Makhdumah-i-Jahan; she was ably assisted in the discharge of her royal functions by two of the ablest nobles of the royal court, Mahmud Gawan and Khwaja Jahan Turk. The Queen-mother, a grand-daughter of Sultan Tajuddin Firoze Shah (1397-1422), and a highly educated lady, 'was one of the few remarkable women that have appeared in the Muslim ruling dynasties of Medieval India'; she energetically set herself to the task of removing the evil effects of her husband's misrule. 'Though she did not appear in public', writes Dr. PM Joshi, 'she kept herself in close and constant touch with her colleagues of the council from whom, and from her personal agents, she received daily reports of the affairs of the kingdom. She directed that her son, the boy king, should sit every day in the hall of audience and preside over the royal *durbar* so that he should gain full knowledge of current affairs and familiarity with the details of administration'. The Council of Regency declared a general amnesty for all those who had been thrown into prisons by Humayun, and the servants of the state, who had been dismissed without cause, were reinstated in their offices.

Taking advantage of the minority of the Sultan, the Hindu chiefs of Orissa and Telengana intruded into the Bahmani territories but were defeated and repulsed with heavy losses. Soon thereafter,

Mahmud Shah Khilji of Malwa invaded the Bahmani kingdom. Mahmud Gawan and Khwaja Jahan attempted to hold him back but were defeated, and the Deccan army fled from the field in panic. The invader marched forward in triumph and threatened Bidar, but the timely intervention by the Sultan of Gujarat on behalf of the Bahmanis compelled him to retrace his steps.

Nizam Shah met with a sudden death under mysterious circumstances on July 30, 1463, and was succeeded by his younger brother Muhammad Shah III (1463-82). During his minority, the Council of Regency, headed by the Queen-mother continued to function as before. Playing an active role in the state affairs, she entrusted the charge of the royal army to Mahmud Gawan and asked Khwaja Jahan to act as her *Vakil* or the chief executive of the civil administration. The Khwaja abused his office and embezzled funds by keeping the Queen-mother in the dark about the major transactions. It constrained the Queen-mother to get the minister's conduct censured in the open court through the boy Sultan; and, ultimately, she got him murdered by one of the trustworthy nobles of her court. Thereafter, Mahmud Gawan was bestowed the title of Khwaja-i-Jahan and made the chief authority in the state on behalf of the crown.

Mahmud Gawan's Services to the Bahmani Kingdom

Mahmud Gawan, the celebrated *wazir* or 'prime minister' of the Bahmani kingdom, was by far the greatest Muslim administrator and statesman of the Deccan in the history of medieval India; he held this exalted office under three Sultans and steered the ship of the Bahmani state through the most troublesome times for more than three decades. He belonged to a reputed bureaucratic family of the Persian stock, and his ancestors hailed from the Qawan or Gawan region of Iran. Khwaja Mahmud Gawan went to the Deccan as a trader at the age of 45. He arrived at Dabhol in 1453 and, finding his way to Bidar, attracted royal notice as an influential man of means who plied the trade in quality steeds. Being fond of horse riding and interested in martial arts, Gawan struck personal friendship with Sultan Alauddin II (1436-58) who persuaded him to settle down in India and ennobled him as an *Amir* of a hundred soldiers at his court. After the unfortunate massacre of Chakan, in which more than two thousand foreign military commanders and soldiers of the kingdom lost their lives because of the treachery of the Deccani officers, the Sultan depended heavily on the remnant of the foreign (*Pardesi*) nobility for support to meet the danger posed by the internal rebellions and threats from the external foes. As described in the preceding pages of this study, in 1455, Mahmud Gawan was attached to the Sultan's camp when the latter was called upon to fight against Jalal Khan, his own rebellious brother-in-law and the governor of Telengana. Jalal Khan was besieged in the fort of Nalgonda and the Sultan was personally conducting the siege when he heard the alarming news about the hostile movements of the Sultan of Malwa against him. At that critical moment, Alauddin II, probably on the initiative and suggestion of Mahmud Gawan—then a very junior subordinate officer on his staff, left the command of the besieging contingent at Nalgonda in his hands while the Sultan himself proceeded with the bulk of his forces against the army of Malwa. The Sultan had, in fact, taken a great risk in calculating the competence and fidelity of a newly recruited foreign military officer of a junior rank, but in his first major assignment, Gawan acquitted himself creditably, and his subsequent rise at the Bahmani court was very rapid.

Sultan Humayun, the son and successor of Alauddin II, appointed Khwaja Mahmud Gawan his *wazir* and conferred the title of Malik-ul-Tujjar upon him. It goes to the credit of Humayun that, irrespective of his whimsical character and barbarous nature, he seldom interfered in the day-to-day administration which was left exclusively in the hands of the prime minister. He was fully convinced of the administrative competence and diplomatic skills of Mahmud Gawan and reposed confidence in him as the most reliable and trustworthy servant of the state. The Sultan, in fact, held his prime minister in the highest esteem as an elder and the senior most *grandee* of the kingdom. Mahmud Gawan, in his wisdom, devoted himself exclusively in the discharge of his ministerial functions and always took the Sultan into confidence before undertaking important decisions. Prior approval of the Sultan was sought by him before initiating major reforms. Moreover, Mahmud Gawan, most scrupulously, segregated the state affairs from the personal whims and orgies of the Sultan, and did not poke his nose into the internal feuds of the royal household. As prime minister, Mahmud Gawan's primary concern was to maintain law and order and ensure the stability of the state, and he did not allow the baneful influence of Sultan's personal misdeeds to cast their shadow on the proceedings of the court or administration.

Mahmud Gawan was a capable civil and military administrator. Because of the full confidence reposed in him by the Sultan, he was able to carry out extensive administrative reforms without depending upon or aligning himself with any faction of the court. He organised the finances and improved the administration of justice. He built mosques and *khanqahs* for the Muslim saints, and opened numerous primary schools to encourage public education. Agricultural lands of the villages were surveyed to ascertain the state demand on just and equitable basis. Corrupt practices in the determination of the state demand and collection of revenues were curbed with an iron hand and those found guilty were severely punished. Mahmud Gawan reorganised the military department of the state and introduced better discipline among the soldiers as well as the nobility; he gave the entire control of the army into the hands of the Sultan in order to weaken the position of the military officers and provincial governors. The mutual dissensions of the *Amiran-i-Sadah* and the *Deccani* nobles were a source of great trouble; and the quarrels for loaves and fishes among them were further complicated by sectarian differences. The natives were all *Sunnis* but the foreigners included among them a large segment of the Persian stock, who professed *Shia* faith. The feuds among them were not confined to mere intrigues for place and power but frequently found expression in armed conflicts, rebellions and bloody massacres. Mahmud Gawan kept himself aloof from their sectarian politics and scrupulously strove to maintain a balance between them in assigning the places of importance or determining the state policies.

After the death of Humayun, Mahmud Gawan became one of the three members of the Council of Regency during the minority of the boy Sultan, Nizam Shah. In that capacity, he acted in perfect unison with the Queen-dowager and held firm control over the army establishment to curb any indiscipline or defiance of central authority by the nobles. After the untimely death of Nizam Shah, his younger brother Muhammad Shah III was placed on the throne as the child Sultan but Mahmud Gawan continued to exercise the powers and responsibilities of the state with equal devotion as before. When Khwaja Jahan, the third member of the regency, was assassinated, Mahmud Gawan was entrusted the entire civil as well as military administration of the state and bestowed the title of *Khwaja-i-Jahan* by the Queen-mother, and was granted unlimited powers, including the exercise of royal prerogatives but the sagacious Mahmud Gawan always behaved with moderation and never displayed arrogance as the *de facto* head of the state. 'With a singleness of aim, which was unparalleled in the history of the Bahmani kingdom, Mahmud Gawan devoted himself to the service of the State; he fought wars, subdued the foes and increased the Bahmani dominions to an extent never reached before'.

On attaining the age of thirteen, Muhammad Shah III was formally given the reins of government in his own hands; the Queen-mother retired from the public life and the Council of Regency came to an end. The boy Sultan signalled the beginning of his sovereign authority to mark the end of the regency, by initiating a holy war (*Jihad*) against the Hindu chieftains of the Konkan. On his directions, Mahmud Gawan, who commanded the royal army, organised several expeditions into the Konkan region, conquered many forts, and compelled the Raja of Sangameshwar to surrender the premier stronghold of Khalna (modern Visalgarh) to the royal army. The triumphant Bahmani minister and commander-i-chief, returned to Bidar with an immense booty, where 'the Sultan loaded him with titles and accorded him precedence over all other nobles of the court'. Thereafter, Gawan led an expedition against the Raja of Orissa and obtained hefty tribute and many elephants from him for the Bahmani Sultan; the royal army freely resorted to loot and plunders in the border towns and villages of Orissa and returned to the capital with a rich booty. In 1474-76, the Deccan was engulfed in a severe famine which took a heavy toll of human and animal life. Mahmud Gawan utilized the resources of the state to help the famine-stricken people as far as possible. The most important military campaign of Mahmud Gawan was directed against the kingdom of Vijayanagar. The Raya was defeated in a well-contested pitched battle and made to surrender the marine province of Goa, a prestigious possession of the Vijayanagar state. Besides, one of Mahmud Gawan's lieutenants captured the forts of Rajahmundry and Kondavir in another part of the Vijayanagar kingdom.

The Tragic End of Mahmud Gawan

Nevertheless, the administrative reforms and military exploits of Mahmud Gawan, accompanied by resounding victories and acquisition of immense wealth in the form of tribute and booty from the neighbouring Hindu states, aroused the jealousy of the Deccani nobles against him. Being a Persian immigrant and a *Pardesi*, he was supposed to be more favourably inclined towards the foreigners; therefore, a conspiracy was hatched to bring about his fall. It is said that, once during the absence of Mahmud Gawan from the capital, the ring-leaders of the Deccani party, led by Hasan Nizam-ul-Mulk Bahri, the governor (*Tarafdar*) of Telengana, bribed the keeper of the official seals of Gawan and induced him to affix the seals of the *wazir* to a blank sheet of paper, on which a letter was subsequently written, purportedly by Mahmud Gawan to the Raya of Vijayanagar with treasonable contents against the interests of the Bahmani kingdom. This forged letter was laid before the Sultan whose ears had already been poisoned by his rivals. Firishta and some other chroniclers narrate the legendary tale of Mahmud Gawan's miserable death as under:

> 'On his return to the capital, the Sultan called the prime minister to his private apartment and asked:
>
> *If a slave of mine is disloyal to his benefactor and his crime is proved, what should be his punishment?*
>
> Like a loyal servant, the Khwaja replied:
>
> *The unfortunate wretch who practises treachery against his lord should meet with nothing but the sword.*
>
> Thereupon, the Sultan showed him the letter, on seeing which the Khwaja said that it was a clear forgery although the seals were his. He protested his innocence but in vain. The intoxicated king signalled to his slave Jauhar, the Abysinian, and he severed the Khwaja's head from his body'.

Mahmud Gawan was put to death at the age of seventy-eight on April 5, 1481. His death spread a wave of consternation and resentment throughout the state. 'With him departed all the cohesion and power of the Bahmani kingdom'. The small fry among the conspirators were exposed soon afterwards, and Muhammad Shah III inflicted severe punishments on them but their ring-leaders remained behind the veil and escaped his notice. The execution of Mahmud Gawan became the immediate cause of the downfall and disintegration of the Bahmani kingdom. The foreign *amirs* left the royal court and returned to their personal *jagirs* in the provinces without the formality of obtaining the Sultan's permission. Even the responsible nobles of the Deccani party openly denounced the conspirators, and joined the camp of Yusuf Ádil Khan, a foreign noble and right-hand man of Mahmud Gawan, who had been duped by the conspirators by being sent out of the capital on an expedition as a part of the conspiracy. Before Muhammad Shah III could identify the real culprits, he was held as a virtual prisoner by them in his own palace. Deserted by the foreigners and some of the prominent Deccani nobles, the Sultan was forced to throw himself at the mercy of the conspirators. He wept and cried over his folly but all in vain. As a consequence, Hasan Nizam-ul;-Mulk, the mastermind behind the conspiracy, secured from the hapless Sultan, his appointment as the *Malik Naib* or 'deputy Sultan'. He usurped all powers and prerogatives of the Crown and setup as the *de facto* ruler. The Sultan cursed himself for having shed the innocent blood of his prime minister and thereby sounded the death-knell of his kingdom itself; isolated from his friends and sympathizers, he began to indulge in excessive drinking 'to drown his remorse in wine' and died a grief-stricken man on March 22, 1482.

Downfall of the Bahmani Kingdom

Muhammad Shah III was succeeded by his son Mahmud, a young lad of twelve. Being at the helm of affairs in his capacity as the 'deputy Sultan', Hasan Nizam-ul-Mulk retained all powers of the state in his hands. As Prince Mahmud was a minor, the crafty *Malik Naib* claimed exclusive authority to act as his Regent and kept all other nobles, *Pardesis* as well as the *Deccanis*, guessing about the game of his power politics. No assembly of the senior nobles, ministers or courtiers was held to mourn the death of the late Sultan or discuss the constitution of regency and formalities of coronation of the new Sultan. According to Firishta, on the eve of the coronation ceremony, when all the *amirs* had assembled at the capital, the crooked *Malik Naib* hatched a conspiracy to assassinate Yusuf Adil Khan and destroy the power of the *Amiran-i-Sadah*. To their good fortune, the *Pardesis* were apprised of the impending threat to their lives by some of their well-wishers among the Deccanis. Thus forewarned, the *Amiran-i-Sadah* disrupted the court ceremonies, withdrew from the royal camp and refused to acknowledge the authority of the *Malik Naib* to wield all powers of the state. The feud between the two factions came into the open and 'for no less than twenty days, Bidar was a scene of conflict between the rival factions; when peace was restored, Yusuf Adil Khan agreed to retire to Bijapur and Malik Naib was left at the helm of affairs in the Bahmani capital. (Briggs; ii, p. 527)

The *Malik Naib* thoroughly abused his powers as the regent of the boy Sultan. It is believed that, while pretending to act as the best friend and well-wisher of the Prince, the power-hungry Regent contrived to spoil the character and ruin the physical and mental health of the innocent boy Sultan; his agents in the garb of the king's attendants drugged him and induced him to adopt perverted sexual habits to seek pleasure. As a result, by the time he attained manhood, Sultan Mahmud had become a drug edict and imbecile. 'He spent all his time in the company of the buffoons and fiddlers who flocked to his court from all quarters'. Obviously, they were brought there by the agents of Hasan to keep the company of the idiotic Sultan. It facilitated the task of the *Malik Naib* to exercise royal prerogatives and authority with impunity. Meanwhile, the feuds between the *Deccani* and the Pardesi nobles continued. The rival provincial governors and nobles cared for their own interests as against the interests of the state. Taking advantage of the prevalent confusion they declared their independence as regional rulers, and the nominal authority of the Bahmani king was confined to a small area around the capital of Bidar.

The regency of *Malik Naib* did not last long. He was feared and hated by the *Amiran-i-Sadah* and disliked by many of his own camp-followers for his ignoble role in the murder of Mahmud Gawan. His persistent policy of contemptuous hatred towards the foreigners 'made him intensely hated by a section of the *Deccanis* also'. As a result, intrigues and counter-intrigues became a routine feature of the Bahmani politics in which all sections of the Muslim nobility were badly caught, making it difficult to comprehend as to who was intriguing for or against whom. According to Firishta, in such an environment of distrust and political anarchy, 'Malik Naib lost his nerves and fled from the capital for safety, but was lured into a trap and done to death by the Abyssinian governor of Bidar'. Thus the notorious '*Malik Naib* shared the fate of the great *Pardesi* noble, Mahmud Gawan, whose death he had basely contrived'. (Briggs; ii, pp. 531-32.). Firishta gives a graphic account of what followed thereafter. Once again, the swing of the pendulum brought the *Pardesis* to power at Bidar. Once again, their political rivals conspired to destroy their power. One dark night, in the month of October 1487, a body of the *Deccani* troops, led by the conspirators, sneaked into the royal apartments with the intention of killing the imbecile Sultan but the latter 'was saved by the vigilance and valour of his Turkish guards'. Early next morning, the *Pardesi* nobles descended on the capital with their forces and 'ordered the conspirators to be put to death. The slaughter lasted for three days and the *Pardesis* took a terrible retribution on the *Deccanis* for the wrong they had suffered'. (Briggs; ii pp. 532-34).

After these events, Mahmud Shah, the puppet Bahmani Sultan, was relegated into the background, and the responsibility of government passed into the hands of Amir Qasim Barid-ul-Mulk, a Turkish noble of Sunni denomination. He held his office formally as the *Wazir* and *Malik Naib* but, in practice, acted the *de facto* ruler of the state. After his death in 1510, his son Amir Ali Barid also held the Bahmani Sultan as virtual prisoner and continued to exercise the supreme authority at

Bidar. Nevertheless, 'the power and prestige of the Bahmani kingdom was gone forever' and its provincial governors refused to recognise the authority of the Baridis. The first to declare his independence in 1489 was Yusuf Adil Khan at Bijapur, and he was followed by Malik Ahmad Nizam-ul-Mulk, the son of Hasan Malik Naib, the governor of Daulatabad, who founded the Nizam Shahi dynasty of Ahmadnagar in 1490. Fatehullah Imad Shah, a Hindu convert to Islam and the governor of Berar since 1484, also asserted his independence and caused the *Khutba* to be red in his name at Burhanpur by 1490, and thus laid the foundation of the Imad Shahi dynasty. Qutb-ul-Mulk, the governor of Telengana, setup as an independent ruler with his headquarters at Golconda in 1512 and became the founder of the Qutb Shahi dynasty, thereby reducing the Bahmani kingdom to the province of Bidar and its adjoining territories only. Amir Ali Barid continued to govern Bidar as its *de facto* ruler, apparently as the *Wazir* and *Malik Naib* of the Bahmani kingdom till 1527. Mahmud Shah died in 1518 and was followed by three more weak and incompetent princes of the ruling house who were held as puppets in the hands of their all-powerful Baridi ministers. The last Bahmani prince, Kalimullah, who ascended the throne in 1524, 'disappointed in his hopes to recover his shattered fortunes', fled to Ahmadnagar. It was then that his minister Amir Ali Barid formally deposed the Bahmani Sultan and declared his independence; thus the Bahmani dynasty was itself transplanted at Bidar in 1527 by the Barid Shahi dynasty. Kalimullah died a fugitive in 1538, but, much before his death, the erstwhile Bahmani kingdom had ceased to exist, and was split up into five well-established and compact Muslim states, four of which had been founded by the *Pardesis* or the foreign immigrants. These five succession states were as follows:

1. The Adil Shahi dynasty of Bijapur;
2. The Nizam Shahi dynasty of Ahmadnagar;
3. The Imad Shahi dynasty of Berar;
4. The Qutb Shahi dynasty of Golconda; and
5. The Barid Shahi dynasty of Bidar.

SECTION 2: THE VIJAYANAGAR EMPIRE

The Foundations

The Empire of Vijayanagar in the Deccan came into existence almost simultaneously with the Bahmani kingdom of Gulbarga. It was the direct outcome of the Hindu reaction against the Muslim domination in south India. Before the penetration of Muslim arms into the Deccan, the southern peninsula was under the rule of four major Hindu dynasties – the Yadavas of Devagiri, the Kakatiyas of Warangal, the Hoysalas of Dwarasamudra and the Pandyas of Madura. Alauddin Khilji successfully utilized the services of Malik Kafur, a Hindu convert to Islam, to overrun all these states in the first quarter of the fourteenth century, and Muhammad bin Tughluq made an all-out effort to consolidate the Muslim rule in the south by transferring his capital from Delhi to Devagiri, now renamed as Daulatabad in modern Maharashtra. His administrative-cum-political venture failed but the forced migration of the foreign Muslim nobility (*Amiran-i-Sadah* or *Pardesis*) to the Deccan had its desired results in the long run; it showed the direction to the foreign Muslim adventurers and fortune seekers to make their way to south India to exploit the rich resources of the country and lay their hands, through wars of aggression, on the fertile lands and untold wealth of its Hindu infidels in the name of Islam. Nevertheless, 'the Muslim conquest of the Deccan', writes Dr. Ishwari Prasad, 'was nothing more than a mere military occupation. Fired by the lust of domination and plunder, the Muslims carried death and destruction wherever they went, and reduced the Hindus, even of the far south, to a state of misery and helplessness. No institutions were devised for the better government of the conquered people and religious toleration was not extended to them. An empire, consisting of alien races, having vast differences in their social and religious outlooks, and representing different stages of civilization, cannot permanently rest upon physical force; and the great disorders of Muhammad Tughluq's reign were only a vindication of this principle, which has been slowly recognised by mankind. It was not merely Muhammad's severity and turbulence of the foreign *Amirs* (Pardesis) that led to the convulsions of his reign but the inherent impossibility of keeping under firm control such distant territories from Delhi in the utter absence of means of communication'. (Medieval India; *loc.cit.*, pp. 413-14).

The rise of Vijayanagar formed a part of the Hindu national upsurge against the Turkish (*Turushka*) wars of aggression in south India. The Hindu reaction to throw off the Muslim domination had assumed the form of a movement in the coastal districts of Andhra well before the founding of the Vijayanagar kingdom. According to RC Majumdar, 'the uprising of the Hindus in Telengana, Andhra and the region to the south of the Krishna-Tungabhadra assumed serious proportions during the reign of Muhammad Tughluq'. Though the major ruling dynasties and numerous Hindu noble families had perished on account of the persistent Muslim onslaughts from the north, some of the Hindu princes, who had survived the catastrophe, joined their hands together with the object of liberating their country from the Muslim yoke. According to contemporary Hindu records, Prolaya Nayaka was one of them. He 'made himself lord of the Andhra region between the Godavari and Krishna rivers', and 'restored to the Brahmans their *agraharas*, which had been granted to them by former kings but forcibly taken away from them by the *Turushkas*'. After his death, the mantle fell on his cousin, Kapaya Nayaka. In 1335, after the failure of Muhammad Tughluq to suppress the rebellion of Saiyyad Hasan, the Muslim governor of Ma'abar in the far south, Kapaya Nayaka felt encouraged to launch an offensive against Warangal. He defeated and expelled Malik Maqbul, the Muslim governor of Telengana, and assumed the titles of *Andhradesadhisvara* and *Andhrasuratrana.* Maqbul, like Malik Kafur, was a Hindu general of the old Kakatiya kingdom and his original name was Nagaya Gauna; after his defeat at the hands of the army of Delhi, he was taken prisoner and converted to Islam before he was entrusted the governorship of his own native country. Like Alauddin Khilji, Muhammad Tughluq had also adopted the policy of honouring the vanquished Hindu princes, nobles, and outstanding warriors and bureaucrats by the award of high offices of the state if they converted to Islam; this was the best device adopted by the Sultans of Delhi to consolidate the imperial hold over the newly conquered territories; besides, it set the precedent and gave an incentive to their Hindu subjects to throw off the burden of *Jaziya* by embracing Islam.

The Hindu national uprising now spread to the old kingdom of Kampili, where the natives under the leadership of Somadevaraja took up arms against the Muslim governor of Delhi. The names of two brothers, Harihar and Bukka Rai – the founders of Vijayanagar kingdom, find mention in the annals of Muslim chroniclers about this time. Robert Sewell, the author of '*A Forgotten Empire (Vijayanagar)*', gives seven traditional versions about the origin of the kingdom of Vijayanagar, of which the story of Harihar and Bukka Rai seems to be more plausible. Harihar and Bukka Rai were two of the five sons of Sangama, a kinsman of Raja Pratap Rudra Deva II, the Kakatiya ruler of Warangal. They held 'positions of authority' in the revenue establishment of the state when Warangal was overrun in 1323-24 by the Turkish army of Delhi, but they escaped to Anegundi (Kampili) and entered the service of its local Hindu Prince as his ministers. Anegundi also fell into the hands of the Muslim armies after some time, and the two brothers were taken to Delhi as prisoners of war. They were subsequently released by Muhammad Tughluq when they agreed to embrace Islam; and were sent 'as the imperial agents of Delhi' to restore order in Kampili. According to Barani, the Sultan had taken 'oaths of loyalty' from them before sending them to pacify the region 'but they turned against him' and 'apostatized from Islam'. Harihar and Bukka Rai were re-admitted to the Hindu fold by the celebrated sage Vidyaranya of Sringeri *Math* and they turned freedom-fighters who championed the cause of liberation of the south from the Muslim domination. As observed by N. Venkataramanayya in the *History and Culture of the Indian People* –

> 'Their path was not free from obstacles. The Hindu Society was chary in re-admitting within its fold those who were forced to embrace Islam. Moreover, they were treated with suspicion on account of their connection with the Musalmans. They, however, got over these difficulties with the help of Vidyaranya, who arranged for their reconversion to Hindu religion. He convinced Vidyatirtha, his own *guru* and the chief pontiff of the *Advaita-matha* at Sringeri, that the reconversion of his disciples was necessary for saving the Hindu *Dharma*, and secured his approval. Harihara and Bukka were then taken back to Hinduism; and to mitigate any suspicion that might still lurk in the minds of the people, it was declared that Harihara was not ruling the kingdom in his own right but as a vice-regent of the god Sri Virupaksha to whom it actually belonged. To lend colour to this declaration, Harihara was persuaded to adopt the name of the god Sri Virupaksha as his sign manual with which he had to sign all the state documents.' (BVB; vol. vi, pp. 271-72).

Harihar commenced his rule with his headquarters at Anegundi. The ancient town of Anegundi (Kampili), situated in the Raichur district on the southern bank of the Tungabhadra, which formed the nucleus of the Hindu resistance against the Muslim rule, was said to have been founded by Vir Ballala III sometime before 1336. It was taken possession of by Harihar and Bukka Rai in 1334 to the great joy of its people, who hailed them as their liberators and extended whole-hearted cooperation to them in consolidating their hold in the region. The two brothers thus found them in the possession of territory which originally belonged to the Hoysala kingdom; that is why, they seem to have some Ḳarnataka connection also, and are regarded as the 'legitimate successors' to the Hoysala dynasty.

The Sangama Dynasty of Vijayanagar

According to the Kapaluru and Bagepalli grants, in 1336, Harihar and Bukka Rai, with the assistance and blessings of the great sage and scholar Vidyaranya, founded a new township at a strategic location, surrounded by hills and dense forests, on the bank of the Tungabhadra River, as a place of protection against the sudden onslaught of the Muslim invaders; it was named Vijayanagar. Its foundation was laid by Harihar on the inaugural day of his reign and it took seven years to become habitable with the transfer of his court there. The Sangama brothers built a magnificent temple in the heart of the city in honour of the sage Vidyaranya after his death. Harihar became the first ruler of Vijayanagar and, on his death in 1356, his brother Bukka Rai succeeded him; he also enjoyed a long reign of twenty-one years (1356-77). They laid the foundations of what is known to history as the Sangama dynasty of Vijayanagar after the name of their father. The two brothers worked in perfect harmony with each other, and preferred to be known as the leaders of popular Hindu reaction against the Muslim domination of the south; nevertheless, the use of the epithet *Raya* (*Rai*) by them denotes their royal status as this word was used for *Raja* or King, particularly, in the Kanarese region of the far south. According to Sewell, 'the city of Vijayanagar speedily grew in importance and became the refuge of the outcasts, refugees, and fighting men of the Hindus, beaten and driven out of their old strongholds by the advancing Muhammadans'.

The reign of Harihar I (1336-56) saw the foundation and consolidation of the kingdom of Vijayanagar in the teeth of opposition from the Sultans of Delhi and the local Muslim as well as Hindu feudatory chiefs in south India. The small principality of Vijayanagar, which to begin with comprised a couple of Telugu and Kannada districts, expanded considerably in dimensions by the conquests and territorial acquisitions of Harihar and Bukka Rai. The substantial part of their acquisitions included the Hoysala territories, the conquest of which had been undertaken by them sometime after 1338, during the last years of Vir Ballala III. The Hoysala chief, often described as 'the champion of the Hindu resistance movement in the far south', had failed to prevent the emergence of an independent Muslim state at Madura, in the heart of his ancestral kingdom. He and his son, Virupaksha Ballala, carried on relentless struggle against the Sultans of Madura but could not dislodge them from power. It brought the

Sangama brothers into the struggle with the two-fold object of overthrowing the Muslim rule from Madura, and taking possession of the Hoysala territories lest these fell into the Muslim hands. The stronghold of Penugonda in the Anantapur district was conquered by them in c.1340, which served the Sangama brothers as a base of operations against the Hoysalas. In 1342, the Sultan of Madura, under the cover of a truce ' with Vir Ballala III 'suddenly made a treacherous attack on his camp, destroyed his army, and having taken him prisoner, murdered him after extorting from him all his wealth'. It weakened the Hoysala dynasty beyond all recovery. In 1344, Harihar I joined the confederacy, organised by Krishna Nayaka of Warangal to drive out the Muslims from the Deccan. Virupaksha Ballala, the son and successor of Vir Ballala III and the last ruler of the Hoysala dynasty, died fighting against the Sultan of Madura in 1346, but the Sangama brothers were quick to overrun all the Hoysala territories before the Sultan could lay his hands on them; the local Hindu populace and their ruling elite eagerly sought the protection of Vijayanagar chiefs to save themselves from the tyrannical domination of the *Turushkas* or the foreign Muslim adventurers.

Vijayanagar was not the only fort built by Harihar. According to N. Venkataramanayya, he strengthened the fortifications of the old Chalukyan capital Badami, and posted there a strong garrison under a capable officer to safeguard his kingdom from any possible attack by the Sultans of Delhi via Devagiri (Daulatabad). Harihar treated his brothers very well. He appointed his second younger brother Bukka as his *Yuvraja* (the heir apparent) and co-regent, and placed him in charge of the fortress of Gooty in the Anantapur district to protect the western frontier. He also made the famous fort of Udayagiri, in the Nellore district, the headquarters of his eastern province, and entrusted its administration to his third brother, Kampa, From the inscriptions of the Vijayanagar dynasty we come to know that the two youngest brothers of Harihar, named Marappa and Mudappa respectively, also held important political and military assignments and assisted Harihar in the extension and consolidation of his kingdom by conquests and annexations. Harihar laid the foundations of a strong and stable system of civil administration with the help of his capable and trustworthy Brahman minister, Anantarasa Chikka Udaiya, which, with few modifications, lasted until the very end of the Vijayanagar Empire.

The intermittent struggle between the founders of the Vijayanagar kingdom and the Sultans of Madura lasted almost four decades. In

1352-53, Harihar I made two-pronged attack on Madura, apparently to secure the release of some vanquished Hindu princes from his clutches, The Sultan of Madura was defeated and taken prisoner, and all the Hindu captives, including the prince Sambuvaraya, were liberated and restored to their fortunes but the intervention of the Bahmani Sultan against Vijayanagar, on behalf of his counterpart of Madura, restrained Harihar to pursue the success of his arms to its logical conclusion. Nevertheless, within the lifetime of Harihar, the kingdom of Vijayanagar extended from the Krishna in the north to the neighbourhood of the Kaveri in the south, and comprised the whole peninsula from east to west between the Gulf of Bengal and the Arabian Sea. He parcelled out his dominions into provincial and local divisions like the *sthalas, nadus* and *simas,* and entrusted the administration of these units to his brothers, kinsmen, brilliant lieutenants and the surviving princes of the old Hindu states, thus creating a sort of feudal hierarchy of officials with all the inherent defects. During the concluding years of his reign, Harihar remained busy at Vijayanagar with the organisation of civil administration primarily while Bukka Rai wielded command of the royal armies, and, actively assisted by his younger brothers, pursued a vigorous plan of military campaigns and conquests.

Alauddin Hasan Gangu or Bahman Shah, the ruler of the newly founded Bahmani kingdom at Gulbarga, was hostile to Vijayanagar from its very inception, the foundation of which checked the advance of the Vijayanagar Empire towards the north. As the rulers of these two mutually hostile states pursued 'similar schemes of territorial expansion, they frequently came into head-on collision and fought with each other with a ferocity and vigour which has no parallels in the annals of medieval india'.

After the death of Harihar in 1356, Bukka Rai I completed the construction of the city of Vijayanagar and added considerably to the territorial dimensions of his kingdom. He engaged the Bahmani Sultans in the north while his son, Prince (*Kumara*) Kampana successfully fought against the Sultans of Madura. The Muslim principality of Madura, which had come into existence in 1335-36, was conquered and annexed to Vijayanagar by Bukka Rai in 1377. He rebuilt many Hindu shrines, destroyed earlier by the Muslim aggressors, and reinstated the divine images in the Rajasimheswara temple at Kanchi and the Ranganathaswami temple at Srirangam. The Vijayanagar Empire now extended over the whole of south India up to Rameshwaram and included in its fold Tamil lands as well as Kerala; he is described in the inscriptions as 'the master of the Eastern, Western and Southern oceans'. He sent a friendly mission to Tai-tsu, the King-emperor of China in 1374, and waged a protracted bloody war against Muhammad Shah and Mujahid Shah, the Sultans of Bahmani kingdom, a brief account of which has been given in the preceding pages of this study; here suffice it to say that these gruesome wars, though cost hundreds and thousands of men on both sides, remained indecisive; According to N. Venkataramanayya,

> 'Bukka Rai I contended with the Bahmanis on equal terms, and struck blow for blow. In the end, the Bahmani Sultan had to sign a treaty which left Bukka I master of the whole of the Krishna-Tungabhadra Doab excepting some *mahals* on the southern bank of the Krishna, which were to be governed jointly by the two monarchs. The terms of this treaty...clearly show that the war ended practically in a victory for Vijayanagar. As the war had commenced on account of the refusal of Muhammad Shah I to recognise the river Krishna as the boundary between Vijayanagar and the Bahmani kingdoms, and as the river Krishna, according to the terms of the treaty, was fixed as the boundary between the two kingdoms, though a few *mahals* on the southern bank of the rive were subjected to the joint authority of the two governments, it is obvious that Bukka Rai I got the better of his rival'. (*loc.cit.*, p.278)

Bukka Rai was the real architect of the Vijayanagar Empire. Though a devout Hindu and worshipper of Shiva, he was very liberal-minded and tolerant towards all the other religions. In an age marked by religious bigotry and fanaticism, he adopted a policy of tolerance towards all the religious minorities of his State. 'Taking advantage of the dispute between the Vaishnavas and the Jainas', writes Venkataramanayya, 'Bukka Rai issued an edict, copies of which were setup in important centres, proclaiming that from the standpoint of the State, all religions were equal and entitled to protection and patronage. The policy of religious concord, indicated in this edict, was followed by all his successors. All religious communities of the kingdom including the Jews, Christians and Muslims, looked upon the Raya as the guardian of their religious rights and privileges.' (*Ibid.*, p.280). Bukka Rai took keen interest in the revival of the Vedic *Dharma*. He invited all the Vedic scholars of south India, and having placed them under his *Kula-Guru* Madhavacharya Vidyaranya, persuaded them to compose fresh commentaries on the Vedas, and also to expound the meaning of the Vedic literature to the masses through the local Tamil, Telugu and other vernaculars. Nachana Soma, the greatest Telugu poet of the age adorned the court of Bukka Rai.

Bukka Rai had several sons who distinguished themselves on the field of battle and held important administrative assignments, but his eldest and the most accomplished son, Kumara Kampana, having predeceased his father in 1374, he nominated one of his younger sons, named Harihar II by his queen Gaurambika, as his successor on the eve of his death in February 1377.

Harihar II (1377-1404)

Harihar II, the third ruler of the Sangama dynasty, assumed the imperial titles of *Maharajadhiraja* and *Raja-Parmeshwara.* He consolidated his possessions into a well-knit and compact kingdom by eliminating many feudal aspects of its territorial divisions, and extended his dominions by the conquest of Kanara, Mysore, Trichinopoly and Conjeevaram or Kanchi. He had to fight sporadic wars against the Bahmanis also but in retaliation. From his inscriptions we find that, in 1380, the *Turushkas* repeated their incursions in the Raichur Doab and took possession of the hill-fort of Adoni, situated in the Bellary district on the road from Bangalore to Secundarabad; but, after their initial victory, they were beaten back and the fort was recovered from their hands. The Vijayanagar Empire now spread over the whole of the southern peninsula and exercised control over a number of seaports –'the flourishing centres of maritime trade'.

The concluding years of the reign of Harihar II were marked by peace and tranquillity as he had to face no internal troubles or foreign invasions. But he suffered from ill-health and was confined to bed for over a year before his death in August 1404. His succession was disputed by his three sons, Virupaksha I, Bukka II, and Devaraya I, and their war of succession lasted about two years to the great detriment of the interests of the state; Virupaksha I crowned himself king after the death of his father but was overthrown by Bukka II after about a year, and the latter, in turn, was ousted from power and deposed by Devaraya I, who ascended the throne in 1406 and ruled for 16 years before his death in 1422.

Devaraya I (1406-22)

Taking advantage of the mutual dissensions among the princes of the ruling dynasty, Tajuddin Firoze Shah, the Bahmani Sultan, revived the conflict with Vijayanagar and organised three successive expeditions against Devaraya I. The army of Vijayanagar was worsted in the first two raids, but in the third such expedition, when the Sultan made an unprovoked attack on the fort of Pangal in 1420, he suffered a defeat and fled for his life. The last two years of Devaraya's reign were peaceful. Devaraya had been associated with the administrative and military affairs of Vijayanagar since his early life during the reign of his father 'He was the first king of his family', writes N. Venkataramanayya, 'to realize the value of cavalry, which contributed greatly to the success of medieval armies. By purchasing, on a large scale, horses from Arabia and Persia, and recruiting suitable troopers to man them, he enhanced the strength and the fighting capacity of his forces. Devaraya I was also the first ruler of Vijayanagar to employ in his service Turkish bowmen whom he attracted to his court by liberal grants of land and money. Under the fostering care of Devaraya I, the Vijayanagar army became an efficient instrument for victory, and enabled him to emerge successfully from the long-drawn contest with the Bahmani Sultan Firoze Shah'. (*Ibid.*, pp.287-88).

Devaraya I is celebrated in the history of South India for his public welfare projects, including the construction of dams across the Tungabhadra and Haridra rivers for irrigation. As a Shaivite by faith, he was devoted to the worship of the Goddess Pampa of the *Tampi-tirtha*. He built several temples in various parts of the Vijayanagar Empire, some of which still survive though in dilapidated condition. Devaraya was fond of the company of men of letters, Vedic scholars, philosophers and artists, whom he liberally patronized and with whom he held public discourses on the arts and sciences in which they specialized. In the words of N. Venkataramanayya,

> 'The *Pearl Hall* of the palace, where he honoured distinguished poets, philosophers and artists by bathing them in the showers of gold coins and gems is immortalized in literature and is still remembered in the Telugu country. Under Devaraya I, Vijayanagara became the chief centre of learning in the whole of South India to which gravitated all seeking public recognition and fame. Vijayanagara had indeed become Vidyanagara, the city of learning and the abode of the Goddess Sarasvati'. (*Ibid.*, p.288).

Devaraya II (1423-46)

There is some confusion about the order of succession among the rulers of Vijayanagar after the death of Devaraya I in 1422. He seems to have been followed, in quick succession, by his two sons, Ramchandra—the governor of Udayagiri, and Vijayabhupati or Vijaya I before the accession of one of his grandsons, Devaraya II, who ascended the throne in 1423. He was the last great ruler of the Sangama dynasty. He overhauled the civil and military organisation of the state and waged many successful wars against his foes. According to Firishta, Devaraya II had a mighty army, composed of 60,000 cavalry and two *lacs* of infantry besides a regiment of two thousand Muslim archers; he fought three bloody wars with the Bahmani Sultan Ahmad Shah (1422-36), with heavy losses on both sides. Ahmad Shah proclaimed *Jihad* against the Hindus of Vijayanagar and killed about a *lac* of the unarmed Hindu civilians, including men, women and children in the course of this conflict, at the end of which both parties agreed to maintain status quo on the frontiers. The Venetian traveller Nicolo Conti and Abdur Razzak, the Persian envoy, visited the Vijayanagar kingdom during his reign and left valuable accounts of their visits.

Devaraya II died in 1446; his successors, Mallikarjuna (1446-65) and his brother Virupaksha II (1465-85) proved to be weak and incompetent rulers, during whose period the powers of the crown were usurped by their ambitious nobles. A period of court intrigues, disorders and rebellions ensued, as a result of which Mallikarjuna was assassinated and his younger brother Virupaksha II usurped the throne. It gave a further impetus to the forces of disintegration, and the military commanders and subordinate ruling chieftains to defy the central authority of the state with impunity. This political anarchy was finally put an end to by Saluva Narasimha, a powerful chief of Chandragiri and commander-in-chief of the royal forces, who deposed Virupaksha II, the last ruler of the Sangama dynasty, and, later on, made a short work of him in captivity. He usurped the throne and laid the foundation of the Saluva dynasty of Vijayanagar.

The Saluva Dynasty (1485-1505)

The last inscription of Virupaksha II is dated July 29, 1485, and the first known inscription of Saluva Narasimha as the sovereign ruler of Vijayanagar was issued on the first of November, 1486; the deposition of the last Sangama king, therefore, must have taken place in the intervening period. The short-lived Saluva dynasty of Vijayanagar lasted only two decades from 1485 to 1505. The princes of the Saluva family had been ousted from their ancestral possessions by the Bahmanis. They joined the camp-followers of Harihar and Bukka Rai in their struggle to liberate South India from the Muslim rule and setup their headquarters at Chandragiri in Chittur district. Narasimha, the founder of this dynasty, was the eldest son of Saluva Gunda, the chief of Chandragiri; he succeeded to the family estate in about 1456. Saluva Gunda is known to have rendered active military service to the state during the reigns of the earlier monarchs. Saluva Narasimha, the founder of the new dynasty, was a seasoned military general and proved himself a very capable ruler. His period of rule lasted only five years but he utilized this opportunity to overhaul the state administration to stop the rot that had set in during the weak rule of his Sangama predecessors. He improved the system of revenue collection to restore the financial credit of the state, and waged incessant war against the foes of Vijayanagar. Before his death in 1490, he had recovered most of the territories which had been lost to the Bahmani Sultans and the king of Orissa during the reign of the weak successors of Devaraya II. N. Venkataramanayya pays tribute to Saluva Narasimha in the following terms:

> His services to the kingdom of Vijayanagar can hardly be over-estimated. It is true that he expelled the old dynasty and usurped the throne. But it is possible to construe his action in a more favourable light and to regard the act of usurpation as due not so much to his ambition to sit upon the Diamond Throne as to a desire to protect the Hindu kingdom and thereby save the Hindu *Dharma* from the neighbouring Muslim kingdom'. (*loc.,cit.*, p. 308)

Saluva Narasimha had no time to consolidate his position and establish himself firmly on the throne. He died a premature death, the real cause of which is not known. He left behind two minor sons but, just before his death, had nominated his prime minister Narasa Nayaka as the guardian of his sons and regent of the kingdom, with instructions to hand over the reins of government to either of the two princes 'whom he considered more worthy to rule'. Narasa Nayaka placed the elder Saluva prince, *Yuvaraja* Timma, on the throne, took effective command of the royal army into his own hands, and, apparently in his capacity as the Regent, gave an excellent account of himself as a capable military general, administrator and well-wisher of the kingdom. The boy king died after some time for unknown reasons and was replaced by his younger brother, Prince Immadi Narasimha, as the next ruler of Vijayanagar under the regency of Narasa Nayaka; it is alleged by the Muslim chroniclers that the minor king Timma of Vijayanagar was murdered by his Regent.

Nevertheless, Narasa Nayaka started on a career of vigorous conquests, and during his regency of thirteen long years, restored the power and glory of the Vijayanagar kingdom by his victories against the Bahmani Sultans and other foes. Besides, he subdued not only Chera, Chola, Pandya and other Hindu principalities in the Far South but also defeated Gajapati Prataparudra, the king of Orissa, one of the traditional antagonists of Vijayanagar. Narasa Nayaka died in 1503, and was succeeded by his eldest son, Vira Narasimha, as the *de facto* ruler of the Vijayanagar kingdom; he concentrated all the powers of the State into his own hands in his capacity as the Guardian of the Saluva King, Immadi Narasimha, commander-in-chief of the Royal forces and the Regent of the State. By this time, Immadi Narasimha was growing fast into manhood with promising qualities of head and heart but his youthful Regent was not in a mood to relinquish powers to his 'ward and master'. In a stratagem, the boy king was got hold of and thrown into prison in the fort of Penugonda in 1505 while his Regent, Vira Narasimha, proclaimed himself emperor at Vijayanagar; the unfortunate Saluva prince was put to death in captivity after some time. This is called the 'second usurpation' after the 'first usurpation' of Saluva Narasimha in 1485.

The Tuluva Dynasty

Vira Narasimha (1505-09), the founder of the Tuluva dynasty, got the opportunity to rule over Vijayanagar for about five years. His short period of rule was full of internal revolts and foreign wars. The treacherous conduct of the usurper and, particularly, the cold-blooded murder of the Saluva prince by him, aroused deep resentment and opposition from all quarters and his authority was defied by some of the powerful provincial governors which threatened the disruption of the State. Taking advantage of the internal revolts, the rulers of the Bahmani kingdom and its succession states organised a confederacy to fight against the Vijayanagar kingdom and 'declared *Jihad* (holy war) against the infidels' Vira Narasimha was hard-pressed to fight against them on different fronts simultaneously and lost many territories of his kingdom in quick succession. Nevertheless, as a competent military general, he enjoyed the confidence of and exercised complete control over the royal forces, and left no stone unturned in improving the strength and efficiency of his army by introducing changes in the methods of recruitment, training of the soldiers and their equipment. To improve the cavalry wing of his army, Vira Narasimha offered tempting prices to the horse-dealers and attracted them to Bhatakal and other Vijayanagar ports. About this time, the Portuguese had setup their footholds along the Arabian Sea-coast. Vira Narasimha sent his envoys to Almeida, the Governor of the Portuguese possessions at Goa, and 'concluded a treaty with him for purchasing all the horses that they imported for sale from abroad'. The incessant wars of aggression against Vijayanagar by Muslim confederates of the Bahmani kingdom and its break-away states attracted the public attention before long and their earlier hatred against the usurper was quickly replaced by their concern for the safety and integrity of their Hindu state and the protection of their hearths and homes; it led to the birth of a wave of sympathy and cooperation for the Tuluva dynasty. To quote Venkataramanayya about the increasing popularity of the Tuluva ruler with his subjects:

> 'Vira Narasimha infused warlike spirit among his subjects by encouraging all kinds of military exercises. Men of every social rank and profession became thoroughly war-minded, and cowardice was condemned as the most disgraceful thing among the Raya's subjects. They delighted in military exercise and flocked to the standards of the Raya to fight against the Muslims'. (*Ibid.*, pp.308-09)

Krishnadeva Raya (1509-30)

On the premature death of Vira Narasimha in 1509, in the prime of his life, obviously, because of his excessive civil and military pre-occupations and mental strain, his half-brother Krishnadeva Raya ascended the throne of Vijayanagar. His reign inaugurated a new epoch in the history of Vijayanagar 'which attained under him a height of greatness and prosperity never reached before'. He was one of the greatest and most distinguished monarchs of Vijayanagar, whose account needs to be given in a bit detail. His coronation took place on the auspicious day of the *Sri-Jayanti* of Saka Era 1432, corresponding to August 8, 1509. Krishnadeva Raya did not inherit a peaceful kingdom. Irrespective of what Vira Narasimha had done to suppress the internal revolts and destroy the power of his foes, a number of the rebellious chieftains were still at large and the authority of the central government was not yet fully respected. The Bahmani kingdom had virtually ceased to exist but the rise of successive Muslim states on its ruins like the hydra–heads had posed a still greater danger to the precarious existence of a Hindu state in their midst. To add insult to the injury, the Gajapati chief of Orissa still held in his possession the eastern districts of the Vijayanagar Empire and, unmindful of the threats from the fanatical Muslim powers of the Deccan, was far from reconciled with his Hindu counterpart. The history of Krishnadeva Raya's reign is, therefore, 'a record of sanguinary conflicts between the rival powers for supremacy' in which the Vijayanagar monarch gave a good account of himself as a capable military general and organiser of victories, civil and military administrator, diplomat and statesmen all rolled in one. Domingos Paes, a Portuguese traveller, who visited the court of Krishnadeva Raya sometime in 1520-22, and was granted interview by the king, has to say the following about him:

> 'The King is of medium height, and of fair complexion and good figure, rather fat than thin; he has on his face signs of small-pox. He is the most feared and perfect King that could possibly be cheerful of disposition and very merry; he is one that seeks to honour foreigners and receives them kindly, asking about all their affairs whatever their condition may be. He is a great ruler and a man of much justice, but subject to sudden fits of rage, and this is his title: *Crisnarao Macacao..., the King of Kings and Lord of the Greater Lords of India, Lord of the three Seas and of the Land.* He has this title because he is by rank a greater lord than any by reason of what he possesses in armies and territories but it seems that he has (in fact) nothing compared to what a man like him ought to have, so gallant and perfect is he in all things'. (Narrative of Paes in Sewell, *A Forgotten Empire*, pp. 246-47)

From the indigenous records and accounts of the Muslim chroniclers and foreign visitors, we get a glimpse of Krishnadeva Raya's character and personality. He was a capable and energetic ruler of magnetic personality. According to Robert Sewell,

> 'He was physically strong in his best days, and kept his strength up to the highest pitch by hard bodily exercise. He rose early, and developed all his muscles by the use of the Indian clubs and the use of the sword. He was a fine rider, and was blessed with a noble presence, which favourably impressed all who came in contact with him. He commanded his enormous armies in person, was able, brave and statesmanlike, and was withal a man of much gentleness and generosity of character. He was beloved by all and respected by all' (*Ibid.*, pp. 121-22)

(1) War with the Muslim States (1509-12)

After the treacherous assassination of Mahmud Gawan, the ablest prime minister and the greatest Muslim administrator and statesman of medieval India, in 1481, the fortunes of the Bahmani kingdom took a nose-dive. On the death of Sultan Muhammad Shah III in 1482, his minor son, Mahmud ascended the throne at Gulbarga under the regency of his all-powerful *Wazir* and *Malik Naib*, Hasan Nizam-ul-Mulk, whose reign saw the rapid split up of the Bahmani kingdom into the independent Muslim states of Bijapur (1489), Ahmadnagar (1490), Berar (1490) and Golconda (1512), while the old Bahmani dynasty itself was transplanted by the Barid Shahi dynasty of the *Malik Naib's* family at Gulbarga in 1527. Incidentally, the rulers of all these five succession states of the Bahmani kingdom were *Pardesis* or foreign Muslim adventurers; they were all fanatic Sunni Musalmans, who hated and despised the Hindu *Kafirs*, the indigenous inhabitants of the land, and were the staunch enemies of the Hindu kingdom of Vijayanagar. The whole history of the Bahmani and Vijayanagar kingdoms is, in fact, replete with the bloody wars of Hindu-Muslim conflict for supremacy in South India which saw the massacre of quite a few *lacs* of innocent men, women and children, desecration and destruction of their temples and holy shrines, the torching of their schools and libraries, and the loot and plunder of their hearths and homes. According to the author of *Burhan-i-Maasir*, in 1501 (907 H.), on the initiative of Yusuf Adil Khan, who had setup as independent ruler of Bijapur, styled as Adil Shah, the religious spokesmen and representatives of all the Muslim states of the Deccan assembled at Bidar where it was resolved that 'once in each year, all of the *amirs* and *wazirs* (of these states) should come to the royal court of Gulbarga, and join in a *Jihad* against the idolaters of Vijayanagar, and, hoisting the standards of Islam, should use their utmost endeavours to eradicate the infidels and tyrants'. (Quoted in *Ibid.*, p. 268)

Accordingly, the immediate predecessors of Krishnadeva Raya suffered much at the hands of their Muslim antagonists. The Bahmani kingdom had declined but not so the religious fanaticism of the foreign Muslim Sultans of its succession states. In the post-Bahmani era, the credit for the organisation of full-fledged *Jihad* (Holy War) against the infidels of Vijayanagar, in 1502, goes to Adil Shah. Mahmud Shah, the puppet Bahmani Sultan of Gulbarga, under the regency of Amir Qasim Barid-ul-Mulk, was persuaded by him to assume the leadership of the break-away Muslim states of the Deccan to pool their resources for this purpose. Thus Vijayanagar confronted the first *Jihad* of the corporate Muslim combination during the concluding year of the regency of Narasa Nayaka. By all accounts, the Army of Islam met with little or no opposition; Mahmud Shah overran the whole of the Raichur Doab, took possession of the two Hindu strongholds of Raichur and Mudhal, and handed them over to Adil Khan as a reward.

The acquisition of the Raichur Doab by Yusuf Adil Shah of Bijapur whetted his appetite for more territorial gains at the cost of the Vijayanagar kingdom, and he became the chief exponent of the concept of *Jihad* against the infidels of South India. The usurpation of the throne by Vira Narasimha and the defiance of his authority by some of the Hindu governors of his dominions, afforded a glorious opportunity to him to open a perpetual war-front against Vijayanagar to achieve his objectives. In collaboration with the governor of Adoni on the Tungabhadra, he marched upon the territories of Vijayanagar with threatening postures towards the stronghold of Kandanavolu (Kurnool). Vira Narasimha sent his Arevidu feudatory chief, Ramraja I and his son Timma to oppose him. Adil Shah was defeated and expelled from the Vijayanagar territories with heavy losses by them. Thereafter, Ramraja invested the fort of Adoni and wrested it from the hands of the Muslims. Vira Narasimha felt obliged to bestow the forts and districts of Kurnool and Adoni to his subordinate chief, Ramraja I of Arevidu, and decorated Prince Timma as the 'Hero of Vijayanagar'.

Nevertheless, war with Bijapur and its other Muslim allies of the Deccan was far from over when Krishnadeva Raya ascended the throne. He fought against his Muslim adversaries and other political rivals 'on equal terms and avenged the wrongs that had been done to his predecessors'. At the very outset of his reign, Krishnadeva Raya had to reckon with the confederacy of the Muslim rulers. Adil Shah of Bijapur was licking his wounds after his humiliating defeat at the hands of Vijayanagar; therefore, immediately after the death of Vira Narasimha, he stirred into action to retaliate in collaboration with his other Muslim allies. Early in 1510, Amir Qasim Barid-ul-Mulk, the *Malik Naib* of Gulbarga also breathed his last and was succeeded by his youthful son, Amir Ali Barid as the new 'deputy Sultan' and *de facto* ruler of the Bahmani kingdom. Now, Adil Shah and Amir Ali contrived to persuade Mahmud Shah, the puppet Bahmani Sultan, to assume the leadership of the *Jihadi* campaign against Vijayanagar once again, and declared *Jihad* against Krishnadeva Raya; they did not want the new ruler of

Vijayanagar to stabilize his position. The armies of Gulbarga and Bijapur *were* supported by thousands of the unpaid *Jihadi* volunteers from all the Muslim states of the Deccan, to collect the trophies of war in the form of loot and plunder of the infidel territories. The vast army of Islam, headed by the Bahmani Sultan Mahmud Shah, invaded Vijayanagar; it was intercepted by Krishnadeva Raya on the Vijayanagar frontier in the vicinity of Dony. The Muslims 'suffered a crushing defeat'; and the Sultan himself being wounded, and his nobles and associates 'being unable to face the victorious enemy, beat a hasty retreat towards Kovelakonda'. Undaunted, Krishnadeva Raya gave them a hot chase and forced yet another battle on them. In the battle of Kovelakonda that followed, the Muslim army was totally destroyed and dispersed; Adil Shah was killed in action while the Bahmani Sultan and the remnant of his vanquished troops fled towards Gulbarga.

The death of Yusuf Adil Shah threw the newly founded state of Bijapur into confusion and anarchy. He was succeeded on the throne of Bijapur by his minor son Ismail Adil Khan under the regency of Kamal Khan. Taking advantage of the prevalent situation, Krishnadeva Raya invaded the Krishna-Tungabhadra Doab and recovered the stronghold of Raichur from the Bijapuris in 1512.

Flushed with these victories, he marched on the Bahmani kingdom and took possession of the strongholds of Gulbarga and Bidar after crushing the power of the *Malik Naib*, Amir Ali Barid, and his associates. At this hour of victory, the Bahmani kingdom lay at his feet, but, as a shrewd politician and diplomat, he did not think it prudent to annex Gulbarga and other conquered territories of Bidar to Vijayanagar to avoid the hostility of the break-away Muslim states of the Deccan. In his wisdom, Krishnadeva Raya set the puppet Sultan, Mahmud Shah, at liberty and restored him to power on the throne of Gulbarga, apparently to befriend the rightful scion of the Bahmani dynasty. According to Venkataramanayya, 'this was not a whimsical step'; in doing so, 'he wanted to weaken his Muslim neighbours by throwing an apple of discord in their midst. He knew that so long as the shadow of the Bahmani monarchy persisted, there would be no peace among the Muslim rulers of the Deccan'. In commemoration of this great victory, Krishnadeva Raya assumed the title of *Yavana-rajya-sthapan-acharya*. (History & Culture of the Indian People; BVB, vi, pp. 309-10).

(2) Conquest of Ummattur

The Palaigars of Ummattur and Talakadu in western Karnataka, the erstwhile vassals of the Hoysala kingdom, had defied the imperial authority of Vijayanagar during the reign of Vira Narasimha. Ganga Raja, the ruling chief of Ummattur in the upper Kaveri valley, had declared his sovereignty and was inducing some other chieftains of the region also to break away from Vijayanagar; his strength lay in his possession of the strongholds of Seringapatam (Srirangapattana) and Sivasamudra (Sivansamudram), which, being situated on small islets between two branches of the Kaveri, 'were considered impregnable'. Anticipating reprisal from Vijayanagar, Ganga Raja had shifted his headquarters to Sivasamudra and further strengthened its fortifications by amassing troops and stockpiling ammunition and provisions. Krishnadeva had kept him under surveillance ever since his accession; and, after his triumphant return from Gulbarga, he lost no time in organizing an expedition against him. The fort of Seringapatam fell after a long siege but Ganga Raja escaped to Sivasamudra, which was defended by him against heavy odds for more than a year. Ultimately, he had to abandon the fort but, while attempting to escape to a place of safety, he was drowned in the river Kaveri; Krishnadeva Raya took possession of the fort and dismantled its fortifications. He occupied all the territories of the Ummattur principality and annexed them to the empire; it was constituted into a separate province with its headquarters at Seringapatam.

(3) War with Orissa

After restoring law and order within his dominions, Krishnadeva Raya turned his attention towards Gajapati Prataparudra of Orissa, who had wrested two provinces of Udayagiri and Kondavidu from Vijayanagar during the weak rule of his predecessors. Krishnadeva commenced the hostilities with him by leading an expedition into the province of Udayagiri, under his personal command, in January 1513. The Oriya king was defeated in a well-contested battle and the stronghold of Udayagiri, situated in the interior of the hills, covered with dense forests, was taken after a brief siege. From within the fort of Udayagiri, an uncle and aunt of the Gajapati were taken captives but treated very kindly. Krishnadeva then returned to the capital after entrusting the charge of the campaign to his *senapati,* Saluva Timma, for the conquest of Kondavidu. He fought many successful battles with the army of Orissa and captured about half a dozen forts of the province, including those of Kandukur, Addanki and Vinukonda, etc, before investing the stronghold of Kondavidu, but it held out against the besiegers for over three months. It necessitated the return of Krishnadeva to the scene of action in person with reinforcements. He applied ingenious war techniques to invest the fort as did Akbar at a later stage. 'The fort was surrounded and ingress was completely blocked. The Raya ordered several *nada-chapparams,* i.e. wooden platforms to be constructed, and when they were ready, he caused his soldiers to be mounted on them so that they might stand on a level with the defenders and fight with them. Krishnaraya's forces demolished the walls of the fort in some places, and, ultimately, captured it by escalade'. The victors obtained a rich booty from the fort and took captives a large number of soldiers along with their military officers and members of the Oriya royal family; they included Prince Virabhadra, the Crown Prince of Orissa, his two younger brothers and the queen-mother, i.e. the wife of the Gajapati.

In spite of all these reverses, the Gajapati showed no inclination to acknowledge the suzerainty of Vijayanagar. Krishnadeva Raya was equally determined to settle the issue with his Hindu contender for supremacy in the Deccan once and for all times to come. After the fall of Kondavidu, he had returned in triumph to Vijayanagar to celebrate victory. The royal Oriya captives were treated very kindly by Krishnadeva with the hope that the Gajapati would see to the reason to unite the Hindu forces in their fight against the Muslim domination. But this was not to be. Disgusted with the adamant attitude of the Gajapati, he ordered his victorious troops to take on the Oriya territories also. The fall of Kondavidu, therefore, was followed by the conquest of the coastal region up to the river Krishna. Krishnadeva Raya now joined his forces on the war front for the third time and ordered them to march on the Oriya stronghold Bezwada, on the Krishna, which was promptly invested. The Gajapati Prataparudra also took the field in person against his adversary with all the forces at his command, and their gruesome struggle continued up to the year 1518. There was a heavy loss of life and property on both sides; the Gajapati was defeated in a number of well-contested battles and lost ground with every battle that was fought. The impregnable forts of Bezwada, Kondapalli and Rajahmundry fell before Krishnadeva Raya like ripe fruits; and the Vijayanagar forces overran all the territories of Telengana and Vengi. As a last resort, Krishnadeva ordered the march of his troops upon Cuttack, the capital of Orissa, and the Gajapati was besieged therein. At this critical juncture, Prataparudra heard the sad news about the death by suicide of his son, Prince Virabhadra, in the captivity of

Vijayanagar. Having lost his heart, the hard-pressed Gajapati sued for peace which was granted to him on offering his daughter in marriage to Krishnadeva Raya. Thereafter, the terms of the treaty between the two monarchs were most liberal and edifying; all the conquered Oriya territories were returned to the Gajapati; the victor and the vanquished embraced each other like friends, and the matrimonial alliance between them, instead of humiliating the vanquished, cemented the bonds of friendship between the two ruling houses under the leadership of Vijayanagar. 'Thus ended', writes N. Venkataramanayya, 'one of the most brilliant episodes in the military history of the sixteenth century'. (*Ibid.*, p. 313)

(4) War with Golconda

Quli Qutb Shah, entitled, Qutb-ul-Mulk, the Bahmanid governor of Telengana, had declared his sovereignty in 1512, and laid the foundation of the Qutb Shahi dynasty with his headquarters at Golconda. He was no friend of the Hindus of Karnataka and was ever eager to subjugate the Telugu country. Taking advantage of the war between Vijayanagar and Orissa, he prepared an ambitious plan to fish in the troubled waters. In a surprise move, he overran the Vijayanagar's outposts of Pangal and Guntur, and also wrested the fort of Warangal from its Muslim governor, Shitab Khan, who had sided with the Gajapati of Orissa. While the two Hindu adversaries had locked their horns elsewhere, Qutb Shah marched on the coastal region, took forced possession of the forts of Kondapalli, Ellore and Rajahmundry, and 'compelled the Gajapati to cede to him the whole of the territory between the mouths of the Krishna and Godavari'. So much so that he felt bold enough to attack the stronghold of Kondavidu also which had recently been liberated by Krishnadeva Raya from the hands of the Gajapati. It drove the Vijayanagar monarch into action. He despatched a strong army of two hundred thousand men under the command of Saluva Timma, to Kondavidu to deal with the situation. Timma defeated the Qutb Shahi army and expelled it from the Vijayanagar dominions; the Muslim commander, Madar-ul-Mulk and a large number of his military officers and soldiers were taken captives and sent as prisoners of war to Vijayanagar. Timma stayed in Kondavidu for some time for making suitable administrative arrangements before his return to the capital.

(5) War with Bijapur

As narrated earlier, Krishnadeva had wrested the fort of Raichur from Bijapur during the minority of its Sultan Ismail Adil Khan in 1512.

The Bijapuris were not reconciled with this loss. On attaining majority, Ismail aspired to regain control over the Raichur Doab, but the discomfiture of the Sultan of Golconda at the hands of Vijayanagar held him in restraint. It was only after the return of Saluva Timma from Kondavidu that he invaded the Doab and re-took possession of the fort of Raichur. This renewed war with Bijapur was the most important episode of Krishnadeva's life. According to the contemporary accounts, he descended upon the Doab with a million strong army and hundreds of war elephants. Adil Shah crossed the Krishna with 1, 40,000 army for the defence of the Raichur fort, and entrenched himself near the village of Gobbur. In the fierce engagement that took place on May 19, 1520, the Sultan suffered a crushing defeat and fled for his life, 'abandoning his camp and war equipment to be plundered by the victorious Vijayanagara forces'. Apart from those who fell fighting on the battle-field, hundreds of the fleeing Muslim troops were given a hot chase and massacred, while an equally large number of them were drowned in the river while attempting to escape. The fort of Raichur was taken after a tough fight in which the Muslim governor of the stronghold was killed; thereafter, the besieged garrison made an unconditional surrender. Krishnadeva returned to his capital with a rich booty and hundreds of the Muslim soldiers as prisoners of war.

The vanquished Sultan of Bijapur sent his envoy to Vijayanagar for a settlement but Krishnadeva, much elated with his victory, 'proposed the most humiliating terms' as the price of peace by demanding that 'the Sultan should pay a personal homage to him by kissing his feet'. On the receipt of information, Adil Shah agreed to do so, and it was decided that the ceremonial meeting between them will be held at the Vijayanagar's outpost of Mudgal on the frontier between the two kingdoms. Krishnadeva reached Mudgal on the appointed day but the Sultan did not turn up. It provoked Krishnadeva to march on Bijapur to teach him a lesson. On the arrival of the Vijayanagar's forces, the Sultan lost heart and fled from his capital in panic. Krishnadeva took possession of Bijapur without a fight and stayed there for several days. The royal treasury, armoury and the court properties were plundered but, unlike his Muslim adversaries, the Hindu monarch had no intention of laying his hands on the royal palace or sacking the city. Nevertheless, the fugitive Sultan failed to arrive at an amicable settlement with the victor because of the treachery of his second envoy, Asad Khan Lari, the governor of Belgaum. In consequence, the victorious army of

Vijayanagar sacked the capital of Bijapur, and spread itself into the countryside, 'burning and plundering' as it proceeded; the towns of Firozabad and Hasanabad were captured and sacked. The Sultan re-assembled his forces and fought an action with Krishnadeva near the town of Sagar but was defeated and again fled before the victors. He fought two more unsuccessful running battles with the Vijayanagar's army in pursuit, one at Sholapur and another at Kemba, in the Gulbarga district, before making his final exit from the scene of action. Krishnadeva Raya marched upon Gulbarga and took it by an assault for the second time. The district of Gulbarga had treacherously been wrested by the Sultan of Bijapur from Bidar, sometime earlier, to deprive the latter of his connection with the historic capital of the erstwhile Bahmani kingdom.

The conquest of Gulbarga by Krishnadeva for the second time in quick succession was an historic victory of the Vijayanagar monarch which established his undisputed sway over the whole of the Deccan in the teeth of the Muslim opposition. His victory over Ismail Adil Shah, the Sultan of Bijapur, was complete, although severally defeated and on the run, the fugitive foe had made no settlement with the victor, and, technically and potentially, was at perpetual war with Vijayanagar like the vanquished Sultan of Golconda. Hence, even at this hour of victory, Krishnadeva Raya wavered in his resolve to annex Gulbarga and Bijapur to the Vijayanagar Empire. Instead, on the advice of his council of ministers, he, for the second time, made a futile attempt to revive the defunct Bahmani dynasty on the throne of Gulbarga. He set at liberty the three sons of Mahmud Shah II, the last Sultan of the Bahmani dynasty, 'whom Adil Khan had kept in confinement in the fort of Gulbarga'; he placed the eldest Bahmani prince on the throne of Gulbarga and took the other two to Vijayanagar where 'they were kept in safety, bestowing an annual pension of fifty thousand gold *paradaos* on each of them.' As a matter of policy, Krishnadeva Raya did not intent to annex the well-defined territories of any of his neighbouring Muslim states though it did not cut ice with his inherent foes. In the opinion of Venkataramanayya,

> 'This step (of Krishnadeva Raya, like that of his earlier one) was (also) prompted by motives of policy. The continuance of the Bahmani monarchy, even in a shadow form, was a source of potential danger to the stability of the new Deccani Muslim states; and if Adil Khan or any other Muslim ruler of the Deccan imprisoned or made away with the prince whom he (Krishnadeva) setupon the throne, he held the other two in

reserve to make use of them, as he deemed fit, in any new situation that might arise in the future'. (*Ibid.*, p. 316)

The Gulbarga campaign marked the end of Krishnadeva Raya's foreign wars. He was successful in humbling the pride of his hostile neighbours. For the time being, the victory of Krishnadeva's arms so frightened the Sultan of Bijapur and his other Muslim associates that none of them dared to transgress the territories of the Vijayanagar Empire during his lifetime. Robert Sewell, while analyzing the political outcome of Vijayanagar's triumph over its Muslim rivals in the Deccan, opines that it had 'far-reaching effects'. He writes that

> 'The Hindu victory so weakened the power and prestige of Ismail Adil Shah that he ceased altogether to dream of any present conquest in the south, and turned his attention to cementing alliances with the other Muhammadan sovereigns—his neighbours. The victory also caused all the other Muhammadan Powers in the *Dakhan* seriously to consider the political condition of the country; and this eventually led to a combination without which nothing was possible, but by the aid of which the Vijayanagar Empire was finally overthrown and the way to the south opened'. (*A Forgotten Empire*; p. 155)

Firishta informs us that, in his conflict with Vijayanagar, Ismail Adil Shah had constantly raised the cry of *Jihad* against the Hindu and Christian infidels as the Portuguese of Goa had also offered their services to Krishnadeva in his fight against the Muslims. He gave his sister in marriage to Burhan Nizam Shah of Ahmadnagar to cement his bond of friendship with him. Similarly, he offered the hand of another sister in marriage to Alauddin Ummad, a scion of the Barid Shahi dynasty of Bidar, and called upon him to join the army of Islam under his leadership to fight against the Hindus of Vijayanagar. Nevertheless, at this critical juncture, the brothers-in-law of Adil Shah were not willing to acknowledge his political leadership. The enraged Ismail Adil Shah fought two wars, in 1523 and 1528 respectively, against Burhan Nizam Shah, the youthful Sultan of Ahmadnagar and his brother-in-law, to dictate terms to him. Likewise, the aged Sultan Amir Barid of Bidar did not feel strong enough to open a joint front with Adil Shah against Vijayanagar, and invited his wrath. In desperation, Adil Shah made a frontal attack on Bidar. The Sultan of Bidar was defeated in a pitched battle and taken prisoner by him in c.1529. Thus we see that the Muslim states of the Deccan also indulged in mutual warfare, like the feudal Hindu states of medieval India, in their bid to establish their domination over one another but, unlike the Hindu chieftains, did not fail to join their hands together and form a league to fight against their common foes, the Hindu infidels of Vijayanagar, when the situation so demanded. Of course, all the Muslim powers of the Deccan 'had begun to plan measures to break the preponderance of the Vijayanagar Empire'.

Extent of the Vijayanagar Empire

The Vijayanagar Empire acquired the maximum territorial dimensions and reached the apex of its glory during the reign of Krishnadeva Raya. As a result of his military conquests, his authority now extended as far as south Konkan in the west, Vizagapatam in the east and the extremity of the Indian Peninsula in the south. Whereas the River Krishna separated it from the Muslim states on the north, the boundaries of the empire stretched up to Cuttack on the eastern coast, Salsette in the Arabian Sea, and the pre-historic centres of ancient Indian culture and civilization, like Madura, Cochin, Kanya Kumari, Rameshwaram and the Rama Settu were included in the domain of Vijayanagar; some of the islands in the Indian Ocean also acknowledged its suzerainty.

Relations with the Portuguese

The Portuguese discovered the sea-route to India via the Cape of Good Hope during the age of the Bahmani and Vijayanagar kingdoms. Vasco da Gama, a Portuguese navigator, sponsored by his Government, reached the seacoast of Malabar in 1498; he cast anchor at a small village, named Kappad, situated at a distance of 16 kms to the north of the beautiful town of Calicut (Kozhikode in Kerala) on 17 May with three well-built vessels and a crew of 170 seamen, and three days later shifted his ships to the Calicut harbour. He received a very cordial treatment from its local Hindu king, Nediyiruppu Svarupam or simply the Zamorin of the European nomenclature. He was granted permission by the Zamorin to trade in his dominions without any restraint. Nevertheless, the Portuguese did not endear themselves to the inhabitants of Calicut because of their haughty demeanour and religious prejudice especially against the Muslims, who were called 'Moors' by them. They adopted an aggressive and violent attitude towards the Asians, in general, and resorted to slave trade, the Arab traders being the special targets of their attacks. Albuquerque seized Goa by force from its Bahmani governor in 1510 and converted it into a permanent Portuguese base on the Indian soil; the pockets of Diu and Daman were acquired by him soon afterwards. After having defeated and expelled the Arab and Persian merchants from the Arabian Sea, they enjoyed the monopoly of the eastern trade for over a century until they received an effective challenge from the other European powers, like the Dutch, the French and the English in the seventeenth century. On the whole, they maintained friendly relations with the emperors of Vijayanagar and sought trade privileges from them.

By the time of Krishnadeva Raya, the Portuguese were well-established at Goa and were plying a flourishing trade along the eastern seacoast of India. Krishnadeva was very favourably disposed towards them especially because it enabled him to secure the much-needed horses of good quality for his army. The Portuguese, on their side, were equally anxious to secure the favours of the Vijayanagar monarch, the most powerful ruler of south India. Therefore, with his accession to the throne, there commenced a period of intimate intercourse between Vijayanagar and Portugal, and streams of Portuguese merchants, travellers and adventurers started making their appearance in the Hindu kingdom to explore the prospects of trade and commerce and seek the favours of the Raya and his couriers for concessions. Krishnadeva's desire to cultivate friendship with the Portuguese notwithstanding, he never supported their political designs. He sent a message of congratulations to Albuquerque in 1510 on his conquest of Goa from Bijapur but refused to enter into an alliance with them against the Sultan of Bijapur or the Zamorin of Calicut. In 1523, the Portuguese encroached upon some territory of the mainland near Goa, belonging to the Bijapur State, but he sent a small contingent of troops under his minister Saluva Timma (Timmarasa), 'to notify his protest against the Portuguese aggressions on the mainland'. The Portuguese did not heed to his warning and the Timma's mission proved a failure, but, because of the prevalent 'mutual feuds of the Hindu and Muslim rulers of the Deccan', the Raya did not press the issue to the breaking point, and normal relations of friendship were resumed between Vijayanagar and the Portuguese.

The Concluding Years of Krishnadeva's Reign

The concluding years of Krishnadeva's reign, though free from the foreign wars, were full of anxiety and unrest for him. To his misfortune, he had no male issue for a long time. At long last, in his advanced age, his chief queen, Tirumaladevi, gave birth to a son in c. 1518; he was named Tirumaladeva-Maharaya. Krishnadeva was overwhelmed so much by having obtained his successor that, after the successful conclusion of the Gulbarga campaign, he decided to end the hostilities with his Muslim foes, and returned to the capital for celebrations. To ensure the succession of his infant son after his death, he formally 'abdicated the throne and having crowned the young Prince, assumed the office of his Prime Minister, and carried on the administration in the name of the Prince'. As luck would have it, the child king fell ill and died after a reign of eight months only. From a secret agent of his court, the Raya learnt that his son was poisoned to death by Timma Dandanayaka, the son of his Prime Minister Saluva Timmarasa. Without confirming the truth of the report, he got hold of the suspect along with his father and uncle, i.e. the Prime Minister and his younger brother Saluva Gangaraja, and threw them into the prison. It immediately deprived him of the invaluable services of his capable Prime Minister, and the political vacuum thus caused could never be filled up during his lifetime. To add to his voes, Timma Dandanayaka escaped from royal captivity after three years, and raised a standard of revolt in collaboration with his two cousins, Nandendla Appa and Gopa, who held the governorships of Gooty and Kondavidu respectively. After a lot of trouble, the rebel was, ultimately, defeated and brought to Vijayanagar in chains. On the orders of the Raya, Timmarasa and his son Dandanayaka were blinded; Dandanayaka died soon thereafter but his father and uncle, Saluva Gangaraja, both languished in the royal prison long after the death of Krishnadeva Raya. The uncertainty of succession and the absence of any capable minister of the calibre of Saluva Timmarasa badly affected Krishnadeva's health and threw the state administration out of gear. The exact date of the Raya's death is not known, but it is presumed that he fell ill towards the end of 1529 and was confined to bed for quite some time before he breathed his last.

Character and Personality of Krishnadeva Raya

Krishnadeva Raya was the last great ruler of the Vijayanagar Empire. He was a great warrior and leader of men who always loved to lead his troops under his personal command. Unlike the typical egg-headed Rajput leadership of medieval India, Krishnadeva was a seasoned military general and great organiser of victories, who carefully planned and fought to win the battles and knew no defeat. He was always found in the front line of his forces and enjoyed love and respect of his soldiers. He thundered at the capitals of his foes and challenged them to measure their swords with him on their turf. His victorious armies smashed the strongest known strongholds of Cuttack, Bidar, Golconda and Bijapur and trampled under their feet the territories of Vijayanagar's hereditary foes with comparative ease to the great bewilderment of his much confused and stupefied enemies. According to Venkataramanayya,

> 'Krishnaraya's success must be ascribed to his capacity for organisation and the extraordinary skill which he displayed in leading his forces. He showed amazing resourcefulness in overcoming obstacles besetting his path. He smashed rocks and boulders for making a road for his soldiers to reach the fort of Udayagiri, setup movable wooden platforms around Kondavidu to enable his men to fight on an equal footing with the garrison defending the fort, cut canals to drain the waters of a river swollen with floods to seize the stronghold of the rebel chief of Chittur, and put to the sword his own soldiers who turned their backs on the enemy at Raichur and converted a disaster into a brilliant victory'. (History and Culture of the Indian People, *loc.cit.*, pp.318-19)

Much more than his personal bravery and organizational skill, it was his personal attachment with and concern for the safety and happiness of his troops which won him their devotion and fidelity. From the contemporary records we find that

> 'Krishnaraya was accustomed, after the conclusion of every battle, to go about the battlefield, looking for the wounded. He would pick them up and make arrangements to give those medical help and other conveniences needed for their recovery. Those who specially distinguished themselves in the fight were placed directly under his supervision so that he might bestow particular attention on them and help them to regain their health as quickly as possible. The care with which Krishnadeva Raya nourished the wounded soldiers and warriors did not go unrewarded. It won him the affection of the rank and file of his army. The soldiers as well as officers were prepared to throw themselves into the jaws of death in executing his commands'. (*Ibid.*, p. 319)

Krishnadeva Raya was a great empire-builder and administrator. Born in an atmosphere of political and religious hostility with the neighbouring Muslim rulers of the Deccan, he had inherited the monarchy with the solemn resolve to maintain the integrity and sovereignty of the Hindu state of Vijayanagar. He was a devout Brahman, well-educated and trained in the state-craft, and, as a king, was committed to the maintenance of high standards of justice and morality. Unlike his Muslim antagonists of the neighbouring states, he was very liberal in his treatment towards his Muslim subjects and granted them complete religious and economic freedom to build places of worship, own properties and pursue their professions and trades as they pleased. As for his personal devotion to Hinduism was concerned, an inscription in the Pampapati temple at Hampe states that, 'on the occasion of a festival in honour of the coronation of Krishnadeva Raya, the king had built a hall of assembly and a *gopura* or tower there'. The monarchs of Vijayanagar were the defenders of Hindu religion and culture. The Portuguese traveller Fernao Nuniz, in his observations about the Vijayanagar Empire, made in 1535-37, writes that

> 'The king of Bisnaga (Vijayanagar) is a Brahman; every day he hears the preaching of a learned Brahman, who never married nor ever touched a woman. He urges in his preaching (obedience to) the commandments of God, that is to say, that one must not kill any living thing, nor take anything belonging to another, and as with these, so with the rest of the commandments. These people have such devotion to cows that they kiss them every day... and with the droppings of these cows they absolve themselves from their sins as if with holy water'.

Elsewhere, Nuniz informs us that, during the war operations, when the king was stationed with his troops in the army camp, 'his tent was surrounded by a great hedge of thorns, with only one entrance, and with a gate at which stood the guards. Inside this hedge, lodged the Brahman who washes him and has charge of the idol that he always carries about with him'. Many other observations of Nuniz about the characteristics of the Hindu society of Vijayanagar are worth remembering. He writes *inter alia* as follows:

> 'This kingdom of Bisnaga is all heathen. The women have the custom of burning themselves when their husbands die, and hold it an honour to do so...And in this kingdom of Bisnaga there is a class of men, natives of the country, namely Brahmans, who the most part of them never kill or eat any living thing, and these are the best there are amongst them. They are honest men, given to merchandise, very acute and of much talent, very

good at accounts, lean men and well-formed, but little fit for hard work. By these and by the durties they undertake the kingdom is carried on. They believe that there are Three Persons (Divinities) and only One God (*Parmatama*), and they call the Persons of the Most Holy Trinity' (Three attributes of the Divine manifestation, namely, Brahma – 'the Creator', Vishnu – 'the Preserver", and Mahesh – 'the Destroyer') . (For details, refer to *Chronicle of Fernao Nuniz* in Sewell's *Forgotten Empire*; pp. 291-395).

The Brahmins acted as ministers as well as political and religious advisers of the Vijayanagar monarchs and held key positions in the administrative hierarchy of the State. Nuniz further informs us that apart from the Brahmans, 'there is another class, called the Canarese who have pagodas in which are the images of monkeys and cows, and buffaloes, and devils to whom they pay much honour...because of this, neither in the kingdom of Bisnaga (Vijayanagar) nor in all the land of the heathen are any monkeys killed, and there are so many in this country that they cover the mountains'. Krishnaraya was an administrator par excellence; in spite of his incessant military engagements, he paid considerable attention to the civil administration of the empire. Vijayanagar was a Hindu state, with its deep roots in the Indian soil and the indigenous socio-cultural institutions; therefore, its organisation and civil administration was based on the law of the land. Most of the powers and functions of its governance were decentralized among the age-old national and local civil and socio-cultural institutions, which helped the king in maintaining perfect law and order and accorded an element of stability to the State without much strain. The king and his ministers abided by the national Hindu traditions and local customs in making the bureaucratic appointments and determining the state policies. Of course, they had to work hard to make the administration run smoothly. Krishnadeva was a hard task master and did not allow the corruption and lethargy to grow under the feet of his provincial governors and civil administrators. He utilized the resources of the state for the happiness and welfare of his subjects and adopted a policy of religious toleration towards them. Following the practice of his predecessors, Krishnaraya, when not engaged in actual warfare, would carry on extensive tours in the interior of his dominions to redress the grievances of the peasants and men in the streets and punish the dishonest, corrupt and inefficient government servants who oppressed them, He established contacts with the multitude, listened to their problems and complaints and tried to improve the tone of his government and administration. According to the contemporary records, he took considerable interest in constructing irrigation tanks and digging canals to increase agricultural production.

Krishnadeva was a great scholar and patron of art and learning; he promoted Sanskrit as well as Telugu literature. The learned Brahmans, famous scholars, artists and poets of the age were received with open arms and extended liberal patronage by him. Known to history as 'the Andhra-Bhoja, and true to his name, he never failed to load with presents the numerous scholars, poets, philosophers and theologians that flocked to his court in search of patronage'. Apart from Sanskrit, Krishnadeva contributed much to the development of Telugu language and literature. As observed by N. Venkataramanayya,

> 'The Augustan age of Telugu literature, which began with the accession of Saluva Narasimha, burst forth in full splendour in the reign of Krishnadeva Raya, and his court became the centre of light and learning in the country. Himself a poet, the author of the *Amukta-malyada*, one of the greatest poems in the Telugu language, he loved to surround himself with poets and men of letters. His literary court was adorned by a group of eight eminent Telugu poets, called the *Ashtadiggajas* or the elephants, supporting the eight cardinal points of the literary world. Apart from his great encouragement to the Telugu poets and men of letters of his day, Krishnadeva Raya rendered an important service to the cause of Telugu literature which had far-reaching consequences. He created the ideal of a scholar-king, one of whose important duties was to protect poets and men of letters and foster the growth of language and literature. It was recognised ever since by all the Telugu monarchs that one of their principal duties as rulers was to patronize Telugu poets and learned men and encourage the growth of literature. As a consequence, notwithstanding the numerous political changes through which the country passed, learning flourished without hindrance, and Telugu literature became what it is at present, owing to the patronage of the generations of princes and chiefs who bore sway over the land'. (*Ibid.*, p. 320)

Weak Successors of Krishnadeva Raya

In ancient and medieval Indian monarchies, the issue of hereditary succession to the throne posed serious problems; it usually weakened the successive generations of the rulers, triggered off fratricidal wars of succession and very often led to the downfall of the ruling dynasties and the empires. The Vijayanagar Empire was not free from this dilemma. Krishnadeva Raya was survived by a second infant son, aged eight months only and born after the death of his first one, and a nephew, the son of his elder brother Vira Narasimha. Besides, he had kept two of his half-brothers, Ranga and Achyuta, in royal captivity to avoid any dispute about his own succession. Ranga had predeceased Krishnadeva, leaving behind a son, called Sadashiva. When Krishnadeva fell ill towards the close of 1529, he overruled his infant son as well as his nephew for succession as he did not want them to be maltreated or exploited by any other unscrupulous prime minister and regent. At the time of his death, Krishnadeva ignored the claim of Sadashiva also, and, instead, took out Achyuta from the prison and declared him his successor. Accordingly, on his death, Krishnadeva was succeeded by Achyuta Raya whose coronation was celebrated early in the year 1530; he held the reins of government for about twelve years from 1530 to 1542. Achyuta Raya proved to be a weak and incompetent ruler who was 'ill-fitted to control the destinies of such a large empire'. Having languished in the royal prison all his youthful life, he turned out to be a physical and mental wreck; he lacked self-confidence and depended too much on the advice of his two ambitious brothers-in-law, Tirumala and Venkatadri, who had been married to two daughters of Krishnadeva Raya, for running the affairs of the state. Taking advantage of this change of regime at Vijayanagar, Ismail Adil Shah, the Sultan of Bijapur, lost no time in overrunning the forts of Mudgal and Raichur by a sudden assault. Firishta states that

> 'The Sultan, who had made preparations to recover possession of these strongholds before the death of Krishnadeva Raya, put his army in motion, attended by Ummad Shah and Amir Barid with their forces; when the affairs of Vijayanagar were in confusion owing to the death of the Raya...Raichur and Mudgal were taken after a siege of three months, by capitulation, after they had been in possession of the infidels for seventeen years'.

Achyuta Raya lost his nerves to hear of it and did not dare to organise a punitive expedition to expel the invader. Nuniz ascribes it to Achyuta's cowardice and lack of will-power owing to his 'craven spirit and utter unworthiness'. Achyuta was certainly not a war-like prince and he had no experience of commanding the armies; moreover, he did not want to move out of the capital lest he became a victim to some court intrigues in his absence.

On the death of Achyuta Raya in 1542, his infant son, Venkatadri or Venkata was crowned king but he died after six months and the crown passed to Sadashiva, son of Ranga and a nephew of Achyuta Raya. Sadashiva Raya, who ruled from 1542 to 1570, also proved to be a figure-head and the real power of the State was usurped by his ambitious Brahman Prime Minister, Ram Raya Saluva, son of Krishnadeva Raya's famous Prime Minister Saluva Timma, and his two younger brothers- Tirumala and Venkatadri. Ram Raya was a man of considerable ability, but being arrogant and over-confident of his diplomatic skills, 'he never based his state craft on an astute calculation of chances and risks, and gave needless provocation to his allies as well as opponents' by clever manipulations and haughty demeanour. Highly ambitious and tactless, Ram Raya began to poke his nose into the mutual disputes of the Muslim rulers of the Deccan in the vain hope of reviving the power and prestige of Vijayanagar. For a while, his Brahmanical ingenuity had his way and he made them fight with one another; but his over-indulgence in this wily statecraft boomeranged in the long run and invited their wrath against Vijayanagar. A series of political complications arose which finally prepared the way for the ruin of Vijayanagar.

Ismail Adil Shah of Bijapur, the most powerful and ambitious of all the Muslim rulers of the Deccan of his time, had died in 1534, but, in his eagerness to establish his domination over the other Muslim chiefs of the Deccan, he had caused them much annoyance and humiliation. His son and successor, Ibrahim Adil Shah (1535-57) lacked the diplomatic and aggressive qualities of his father, but, being a man of religious prejudice, he was unable to keep the rival factions of his nobles under his effective control. As a consequence, many of the foreign nobles of his court, particularly, the Shias had migrated to Vijayanagar, where they were received with kindness and accommodated in the state services. As a shrewd politician, Ram Raya took to his head the idea of exploiting the situation to his advantage. In 1543, he forged an alliance with Burhan Nizam Shah of Ahmadnagar and Jamshed Qutb Shah of Golconda and declared war upon Bijapur to settle their territorial disputes. To cross the religious barriers in the politics of South India was a great diplomatic victory of Ram Raya but it proved very short-lived. After some initial reverses, Asad Khan, the astute prime minister of Bijapur, patched up a truce with Burhan by ceding some border territories to Ahmadnagar, and also detached Ram Raya from the alliance by promises of compensation to meet his demands. Having thus broken up the alliance, he marched upon Golconda; its aged Sultan, Jamshid Qutb Shah, was defeated and seriously wounded in the battle-field; and Bijapur established its domination over Golconda once again.

The Communal Politics in South India

Ibrahim Adil Shah of Bijapur died in 1557. His son and successor, Ali Adil Shah (1558-80) restored Shia faith in his dominions which had earlier been discarded by his predecessor, but he did it in such a clumsy manner that the Sunni bureaucracy, who held majority of the key posts and dominated the state politics, felt discontented; as a result, wide-spread disaffection spread among the grandees of the kingdom because of his changed religious policy. Husain Nizam Shah, the son and successor of Burhan Nizam Shah of Ahmadnagar, since his death in 1553, taking advantage of this change of succession and dip in the popularity of Ali Adil Shah, invaded Bijapur territories and recovered the fortresses of Kalyan and Sholapur. In order to retrieve the lost territories, the new Sultan of Bijapur, thereupon, entered into an alliance with Golconda and Vijayanagar and invaded Ahmadnagar. Thus Ram Raya, the all-powerful Prime Minister of Sadashiva Raya, and the *de facto* ruler of Vijayanagar, had started active participation in the mutual disputes of his neighbouring Muslim chiefs unmindful of its long-range consequences. The fort of Ahmadnagar could not be conquered by them because of the tough resistance put up by its defenders, and Firishta is silent about the participation of Golconda in this alliance, but he describes this episode as follows:

> 'In the year 966 H. (October 14, 1558 to October 3, 1559), Ali Adil Shah having called Ram Raaje (Ram Raya) to his assistance, they in concert divided the dominions of Husain Nizam Shah, and laid them waste in such a manner that from Porundeh to Khiber, and from Ahmadnagar to Daulatabad, not a mark of population was to be seen. The infidels of Vijayanagar, who for many years had been wishing for such an event, left no cruelty unpractised. They insulted the honour of the Muslim women, destroyed the mosques, and did not even respect the sacred Quran'.

Earlier, the army of Krishnadeva Raya, following the example of its Muslim counterparts, was accused of loot and plunder of the conquered Muslim territories; the victorious Hindu soldiers of

Vijayanagar had resorted to vandalism in Bijapur and the historic fort of Gulbarga was sacked and demolished by them. Now Ram Raya was charged of displaying religious fanaticism and vandalism during his military campaigns which incurred the indignation of the Muslim population of the South as a whole. As observed by Robert Sewell,

> 'This behaviour on the part of the Hindus so incensed the followers of Islam, not only the hostile subjects of Ahmadnagar but even the allied troops and inhabitants of the Bijapur territories, that it laid the foundation for the final downfall and destruction of Vijayanagar'.

As a result, 'the existence of a powerful Hindu kingdom in their midst, vastly superior to them in wealth and military resources, was gall and wormwood to the Muslims; and as no single power could cope with the Hindu state, the Muslim rulers sank their differences and formed the grand alliance to bring about its overthrow'.

The Portuguese Atrocities on the Indians

Robert Sewell, while narrating the story of communal conflict between Vijayanagar and the Muslim rulers of South India about the middle of the sixteenth century, does not fail to dwell at length the display of religious intolerance and the atrocities committed by the Portuguese on the Indians during their war of aggression in the Malabar region from their base at Goa. We intend to reproduce below the verbatim account of his narrative as follows:

> 'In 1558, Dom Constantine de Braganza became Viceroy of Goa, and his period of government was signalized by every kind of violence and aggression. In 1559, Luiz de Mello carried fire and sword into the towns along the Malabar Coast. He attacked Mangalore, set fire to the town, and put all the inhabitants to death. Later in the year he destroyed in similar manner a number of towns and villages on the same coast, and desolated the whole seaboard.
>
> 'In 1560, the Sea of Goa was elevated into an archbishopric, and the Inquisition, the horrors of which even excelled that of Spain, was established. The inhabitants of Goa and its dependencies were now forced to embrace Christianity, and on refusal or contumacy were imprisoned and tortured. In this year also, and those following, the predatory excursions of the Portuguese were continued. In 1564, the Viceroy sent Mesquita

with three ships to destroy a number of ships belonging to the Malabarese. Mesquita captured twenty-four of these, by twos and threes at a time, sunk them, beheaded a large number of the sailors, and in the case of hundreds of others, sewed them up in sails and threw them overboard. In these ways, he massacred 2,000 men.

'This resulted in a serious war in Malabar, as the wretched inhabitants of the country, driven to desperation, determined at all hazards to destroy the ruthless invaders of their land. The Portuguese were attacked at Cannanore, and a series of desperate struggles took place, in the course of which Noronha, the commandant, desolated the country and ruined many people by cutting down forty thousand palm trees. At last, however, peace was made.' (*A Forgotten Empire*, pp. 194-95).

The rulers of Vijayanagar and the Muslim states of the Deccan were too engrossed in their own territorial disputes and the Hindu-Muslim rivalry to pay any attention to what was going on along the western borders of their states on the Malabar seacoast.

Quadruple Alliance against Vijayanagar

The internecine feuds between the succession Muslim states of the Deccan seemed to be unending. To pick up the thread of the story, after Husain Nizam Shah's dominions were ravaged by the armies of Bijapur and Vijayanagar in 1558-59, peace was made by the Sultan of Ahmadnagar by the restoration of Kalyan to Bijapur. But as soon as the Allies retired to their respective territories, Husain Nizam Shah entered into an alliance with Ibrahim Qutb Shah of Golconda and again marched upon Bijapur to wreak his vengeance against Ali Adil Shah. The latter, in turn, again called Ram Raya for help. The rivals confronted one another at Kalyan and the territories of Bijapur were once again turned into the battle-field and desolated. On the eve of the battle, Adil Shah once again won over Qutb Shah to his side, and Husain Nizam Shah having been isolated was compelled to withdraw to Ahmadnagar. There was no fight but Ram Raya had to be placated by ceding to Vijayanagar the forts of Ghanpura and Pangal by the Sultan of Golconda. According to Firishta, it was 'the last gain' of Ram Raya, obtained as a reward for his involvement to settle the internal disputes of the Muslim rulers. It put the warring Muslim chiefs to think afresh in terms of their Islamic conceptions and religious pride. The presence of a Hindu *Kafir* in their midst, and his recognition as their co—equal, rather superior, was simply irritating to them. In the words of Firishta:

> 'Ram Raaje daily continuing to encroach on the dominions of the Musalmans, Adil Shah at length resolved, if possible, to punish his insolence and curtail his power by a general league of the faithful against him, for which purpose he convened an assembly of his friends and confidential advisers'.

They pressed the Sultan not to allow the *Kafirs* of Vijayanagar to poke their nose into the internal affairs of the Islamic states, and 'form a federation' of all the Muslim rulers of the *Dakhan* to wage *Jihad* (Holy War) against them. 'Ali Adil Shah heartily concurred in their opinion, and began by dispatching a secret embassy to Ibrahim Qutb Shah' to play the role of a mediator between them. Thus, the grandiose plan of forming an enduring alliance between the Muslim rulers of the Deccan to defeat and wipe out the Hindu kingdom from their midst was the brain-wave of Ali Adil Shah, and Ibrahim Qutb Shah of Golconda readily accepted his role as the mediator and high-priest of this confederacy. Qutb Shah persuaded Husain Nizam Shah of Ahmadnagar to give his daughter, Chand Bibi, in marriage to Ali Adil Shah of Bijapur, and the fort of Sholapur was to be given by him in dowry to his son-in-law. In return, to cement this matrimonial alliance between the two ruling houses, Adil Shah agreed to give his daughter in marriage to Prince Murtaza, the eldest son of Husain Nizam Shah. The latter died soon after solemnizing the mutual matrimonial alliance between the two ruling families in 1565, and his son, Murtaza Nizam Shah succeeded him to the throne of Ahmadnagar, who was already committed to this confederacy. In the second chain of these alliances, the Sultan of Berar was invited to join the confederacy; he expressed his inability to become its active partner but extended full moral support to the confederates. The Sultan of Bidar welcomed this development, however, and became a full-fledged member of the Alliance. Thus the Sultans of Bijapur, Golconda, Ahmadnagar and Bidar formed the Grand Quadruple Alliance to fight against Vijayanagar. According to Firishta,

> 'The marriages were celebrated in due course, and the Sultans began their preparations for the Holy War. Ali Adil Shah, preparatory to the war, and to afford himself pretence for breaking with his ally (Vijayanagar), despatched an ambassador to Ram Raaje, demanding restitution of some districts that had been wrested from him. As he expected, Ram Raaje expelled the ambassador in a very disgraceful manner from his court; and the united Sultans now hastened the preparations to crush the common enemy of the Islamic faith'.

Vijayanagar's Reaction

Ali Adil Shah's unusual and sudden move, without any provocation on the part of Ram Raya, to break the most cordial relations between Bijapur and Vijayanagar, ought to have alerted the crafty Brahman Prime Minister of Vijayanagar to read between the lines, but Ram Raya and his court did not heed to the warning shots. The *de facto* ruler of Vijayanagar, as usual, treated the movements of the Muslim confederates with indifference and utmost scorn, 'deriving strength from the thought that no Muslims had ever been able, in the past, to ravage the city of Vijayanagar and its environs' The prosperous and ease-loving Hindu population of Vijayanagar had no presentiment of the approaching doom; and the military demonstrations of the Muslim rulers in their neighbourhood did nothing to disturb the placid serenity of life in the town. As observed by Robert Sewell,

> 'At Vijayanagar, there was the utmost confidence. Remembering how the Muslims had vainly tempted to injure the great capital, and how for over two centuries, they had never succeeded in penetrating to the south, the inhabitants pursued their daily avocations with no shadow of dread or sense of danger; the strings of pack-bullocks, laden with all kinds of merchandise, wended their dusty way to and from the several seaports as if no sword of Damocles was hanging over the doomed city. Sadashiva, the king, lived his profitless life in inglorious seclusion, and Ram Raya, *King de facto*, never for a moment relaxed his attitude of haughty indifference to the movements of his enemies'.

Ram Raya, who had 'a marvellous faculty for self-deception, remained indifferent', and in the words of Firishta, 'treated the ambassadors of the allies with scornful language, and regarded their enmity as if of little moment'. Such a state of 'fancied security' did not last long, however, and, when he was convinced of the imminent danger, he ordered the marshalling of his troops. He sent his younger brother, Tirumala, with twenty thousand cavalry, a hundred thousand infantry and 500 elephants to guard the passages of the Krishna at all points. His second brother, Venkatadri, followed him with a large force of combatants to support Tirumala and block the enemy's passage on any front, wherever needed, while he himself proceeded with the main army of Vijayanagar, close upon their heels, for measuring his swords with the foes.

The Battle of Talikota so-called (January 23, 1565)

The Allied forces issued forth from their respective headquarters towards the south on the 20th of Jamad-ul-Awwal 972 H., corresponding to Monday, December 25, 1564. Moving along the different prescribed routes through the Bijapur territories, they made a junction with the army of Ali Adil Shah near the small fortress and town of Talikota, situated about 40 kms. to the north of the River Krishna, on the rivulet Don—a northern tributary of the main river. As inferred by Sewell from the contemporary records, the Sultan of Bijapur, playing the host to the 'Armies of Islam', accorded complete freedom to the Allied troops to 'traverse through the now dry plains of the *Dakhan* country, where the cavalry, numbering many thousands, could graze their horses on the young crops...The country at that time of the year was admirably adapted for the passage of large bodies of troops, and the season was one of bright sunny days, coupled with cool refreshing breezes'. He writes that at Talikota,

> 'Ali Adil Shah, as Lord of that country, entertained his allies in royal fashion, and they halted (there) for several days, attending to the transport and commissariat arrangements of the armies, and sending out scouts to report on the best locality for forcing the passage of the River.'

The scouts returned to inform their masters that 'all the passages of the river were defended and that their only course was to force the ford immediately in their front'. After playing hide and seek with their Hindu foes, concentrated along the southern bank of the river, for three successive days, the Muslims crossed the water barrier one dark night with the whole of their army and proceeded towards Ram Raya's camp. The Raya, though surprised was not alarmed, and adopted all possible measures for defence. Early in the morning of Monday, January 22, 1565, the enemy was cited within fifteen kms of the his camp but both of his brothers, Tirumala and Venkatadri, were successful in effecting a junction with Ram Raya's camp along with their forces before the beginning of the battle.

The fateful battle, which was fought on the day following, has wrongly been ascribed to the place of Talikota. In fact, the actual battle between the antagonists took place about fifteen kms. from the camp of Ram Raya, setup somewhere to the south of the River Krishna, far away from Talikota. Robert Sewell suggests that it might have been in the plain of Mudgal, an historic fort of strategic importance in the region, and 'the ford crossed by the Muslim Allies would appear to be that at the bend of the River at Ingaligi, and the decisive battle seems to have been fought in the plains around the little village of Bayapur or Bhagalpur, on the road leading directly from Ingaligi to Mudgal'. (*A Forgotten Empire*; pp. 199-200 fn.)

An estimate of the rival combatants, who took part in this historic battle of Talikota so-called, cannot be ascertained with precision because of the very wide variations in the accounts of various chroniclers. Firishta, on the authority of various sources, gives considerably exaggerated strength of the Vijayanagar army, which, according to him, comprised 9,00,000 infantry, 45,000 cavalry, 2,000 elephants and 1,000 field pieces, besides 15,000 auxiliaries, though he himself is not sure about the accuracy of these figures. The imperial army of Vijayanagar was supplemented by 'large drafts from all the provinces – Canarese and Telugus of the frontier, Mysoreans and Malabarese from the west and centre, mixed with the Tamils from the remoter districts to the south; each detachment was under its own local leaders, and formed a part of the levies of the provincial governors'. According to the conservative estimates of the Portuguese sources, the royal army of Vijayanagar numbered 6,00,000 infantry and 1,00,000 cavalry, and their Muslim adversaries had about half the number. Nevertheless, it cannot be denied that more than a million of the Hindu and Muslim warriors had once encountered each other in the holocaust of Talikota, in 1565, in their bid to establish their dominance in the Deccan.

Truth is stranger than fiction; though surprising, the fact remains that, on the fateful day of the battle, Sadashiva Raya, the *de jure* emperor, was held as a prisoner in his own royal palace at Vijayanagar, far away from the scene of action; while Ram Raya, who was supposed to be in effective command of the Hindu forces on the battle-field, was himself 'a very old man', said to be in his nineties, 'but as brave as a man of thirty'. He was, perhaps, ceremoniously mounted on an elephant for a short while, but much 'against the entreaties of his officers, preferred to superintend operations from a litter'. According to the contemporary Portuguese and Muslim records, 'he was so confident of victory that he had ordered his men to bring him the head of Husain Nizam, but to capture the Adil Shah and Ibrahim of Golconda alive, that he might keep them the rest of their lives in iron cages'.(*Ibid*., pp. 203-04)

When face to face with each other, separated only by a distance of fifteen kms between them, the antagonists took a whole day to arrange their troops in battle array. The battle commenced in the wee hours of

23rd January with a frontal attack by the Vijayanagar forces on the Allied formations. The left wing of the Vijayanagar army was commanded by Tirumala, the right wing by Venkatadri, and Ram Raya was in personal command of the centre. Opposed to Tirumala was the army of Bijapur under the command of Ali Adil Shah; the Allied centre was directed by Husain Nizam Shah, while the left wing of the Allies was composed of the armies of Ahmadnagar and Golconda under the command of two Sultans, Ali Barid and Ibrahim Qutb Shah respectively. As sketched by Sewell, 'the Allied forces drew up in a long line with their artillery in the centre, and waited the enemy's attack, each division with the standards of the twelve *Imams* waving in the van. The Nizam Shah's front was covered by six hundred pieces of ordnance, disposed in three lines, in the first of which were heavy guns, then the smaller ones, with light swivel guns in the rear. In order to mask this disposition, two thousand foreign archers were thrown out in front, who kept up a heavy discharge as the enemy's lines came on. The archers fell back as the Hindus of Ram Raya's division approached, and the batteries opened with murderous effect on the assailants'.

By this time the battle had become more general in which the field-gunners played havoc on both sides; but the Hindu troops attacked with desperate fury and drove back the right and left wings of the Muslim army. A second similar attack by the Vijayanagar troops on the enemy's centre seemed likely to put the whole of the Allied army to rout, but the tables were turned when the Muslim gunners suddenly opened fire on the assailants with bags of copper money instead of ammunition at very close quarters, 'which proved so destructive that 5,000 of them lay wounded or dead in front of the batteries'. It was followed by a determined attack by the Allied elephants and cavalry in waves, who charged through the intervals of their gunners and pierced through the Hindu lines to overwhelm the central spot where Ram Raya was seated. It so appears that the Allied generals had received intelligence about the exact location and physical incapacitation of the supreme Hindu commander on the battlefield, and made straight for him. In the confusion that ensued, a war elephant of Nizam Shah struck down the litter-bearers, dropping their commander on the ground, and, before Ram Raya had time to mount a horse, a body of the picked Allied cavalry overpowered him. It goes to the credit of the Allied strategy that, in the thickest of the battle, their horsemen got hold of Ram Raya, immobolised him and carried him away, through the Hindu combatants, very swiftly to their own battle-lines. According to the Portuguese records, Ram Raya was immediately beheaded by Husain Nizam Shah with his own sword, and his blood-soaked head was elevated on a long spear, accompanied by the beating of the drums. The news of the fall of Ram Raya spread in the battlefield like wild fire, and the Vijayanagar forces, seized with panic, fled pell-mell in all directions. By the evening, 'the battle ended not in a defeat but a complete rout; no attempt was made by the Hindu commanders of various wings to stop the panic'; according to Firishta, about a hundred thousand of the Hindu soldiers fell in the battle or were slain in their flight by the victors on that day. What about the remaining nine *lacs* of the disorganized and leaderless fighters of Vijayanagar? Obviously, they had dispersed and vanished into thin air for want of direction and poor leadership. There were no reserves, and we have no information about any general, having been nominated as the second-in-command, to take charge of war operations in case of death of the supreme commander. Venkatadri died fighting on the battlefield and Tirumala, deserted by most of his troops, fled towards Vijayanagar, not as a defeated general in retreat but as a fugitive. To our knowledge, no arrangements had been made for the defence of the capital city and 'invincible stronghold' of Vijayanagar in case of defeat in the open battle.

The Destruction of Vijayanagar

According to most of the contemporary chroniclers, the victors reached the city of Vijayanagar on the third day after the battle. Firishta makes a startling statement, however, that 'the Allied armies halted for ten days on the field of action, and then proceeded to the capital of Beejanuggur (Vijayanagar)'. He refers to the re-organisation of their troops and sack of the Hindu camp which yielded incalculable treasure, arms, horses and much besides. After careful examination of the sources, Robert Sewell comes to the conclusion that both of the above versions seem to be correct. According to him, 'the advanced Muhammadan troops are almost certain to have been pushed on to the capital. The main body, after the Sovereigns had received information that no opposition was offered, might have struck their camp on the tenth day'. What followed the debacle of Talikota was much more horrible and gruesome. As described by Sewell,

> 'The story of this terrible disaster travelled apace to the city of Vijayanagar. The inhabitants, unconscious of danger, were living

> in utter ignorance that any serious reverse had taken place; for their leaders had marched out with countless numbers in their train, and had been full of confidence as to the result. Suddenly, however, came the bad news. The army was defeated; the chiefs slain; the troops in retreat. But still they did not grasp the magnitude of the reverse; on all previous occasions, the enemy had been either driven back or bought off with presents from the overstocked treasury of the kings. There was little fear, therefore, for the city itself; that surely was safe! But now came the dejected soldiers hurrying back from the fight and amongst the foremost the panic-stricken princes of the royal house.
>
> 'Within a few hours, these craven chiefs hastily left the palace, carrying with them all the treasures on which they could lay their hands. Five hundred and fifty elephants, laden with treasure in gold, diamonds, and precious stones—valued at more than a hundred million sterling, and carrying the state insignia and the celebrated jewelled throne of the kings, left the city under convoy of bodies of soldiers, who remained true to the crown. King Sadasiva (Sadashiva Raya) was carried off by his jailor Tirumala, now the sole regent since the death of his brothers, and in long line the royal family and their followers fled southward towards the fortress of Penukonda'. (*Ibid.*, p. 206)

It was a great betrayal of the Hindu populace of Vijayanagar by their ruling elite and defenders who had left them at the mercy of their deadly foes. 'A panic seized the city' when it became known to the people that they had been deserted by their leaders. 'No retreat, no flight was possible except to a few, for the pack-oxen and carts had almost all followed the forces to the war, and they had not returned. Nothing could be done but to bury all treasures, to arm the younger men, and to wait'. Next day, the town became a prey to the robber tribes and anti-social elements of the neighbourhood, who are said to have made as many as six concerted attacks on the terror-stricken inhabitants and 'looted the stores and shops'. The advance columns of the victors must have made their approach to Vijayanagar rather very cautiously but were thrilled to find the metropolis and its fort undefended, and pounced upon its hapless citizens like hawks. In the words of Sewell again,

> 'The third day saw the beginning of the end...From that time forward for a space of five months, Vijayanagar knew no rest. The enemy had come to destroy, and they carried out their

object relentlessly. They slaughtered the people without mercy; broke down the temples and palaces; and wreaked such savage vengeance on the abode of the kings, that, with the exception of a few great stone-built temples and walls, nothing now remains but a heap of ruins to mark the spot where once the stately buildings stood. They demolished the statues, and even succeeded in breaking the limbs of the huge Narasimha monolith. Nothing seemed to escape them. They broke up the pavilions standing on the huge platform from which the kings used to watch the festivals, and overthrew all the carved work. They lit huge fires in the magnificently decorated buildings forming the temple of Vithalasvami near the river, and smashed its exquisite stone sculptures'. (*Ibid.*, pages 207-8)

Caesaro Federici (Caesar Frederick), an Italian traveller, who visited the place two years later, describes the destruction of Vijayanagar at the hands of the Muslim invaders as follows:

> 'The victors entered the unguarded city of Vijayanagar with their minds full of revenge. With fire and sword, with crowbars and axes, they carried the day after day their work of destruction. Never perhaps in the history of the world has such havoc been wrought and wrought suddenly, on so splendid a city and industrious population in the full plenitude of prosperity one day, and on the next seized, pillages, and reduced to ruins, amid scenes of savage massacre and horrors, beggaring description'. (Quoted in M N Venkata Ramanappa, *Outline of South Indian History*; Vikas, 2nd ed; 1976 reprint, p.181)

Caesaro Federici makes a very sensational statement in the course of his travelogue which seems to have escaped the notice of modern historians of medieval Indian history; he writes that 'Ram Raja (Raya) perished through the treachery of two Musalman generals in his service, who turned against him in the middle of the battle'. It is well-known that Ram Raya, as a shrewd politician, did not hesitate in extending patronage to the Muslims, including the foreign immigrants, and did have a small contingent of Muslim archers and gunners in his employ. It gave him credentials as a liberal-minded Hindu chief in his dealings with his Muslim neighbours. Whether he trusted them so much that some of them were attached to the inner circle of his servants or guards is not known. If so, there is nothing surprising that he was captured from the inner well-protected centre of his military camp in the thickest of the battle and dragged away to the enemy lines by the Muslim horsemen of the Allied commander. Similarly, on the eve of the battle of Talikota, Ram Raya had also received a small company of the Portuguese musketeers by way of a friendly gesture from their Viceroy of Goa; what was its impact on the attitude of his Muslim employees is also a matter of conjecture.

We have it on the testimony of Firishta that the Allies stayed in the territories of Vijayanagar for five months. After the thorough sack of Vijayanagar, 'which they plundered, razed the chief buildings, and committed all manner of excesses', they spread their armies in different parts of the 'infidel territories' for loot and plunder. The people fled before the 'faithfuls', and those 'wretched *Kafirs*', who fell into their hands, were either put to the sword or enslaved. They overran and pillaged all the big and small towns and villages of the region within the periphery of about a hundred kms from Vijayanagar, and the standing crops in the countryside were eaten up and destroyed by their horses. Firishta concludes his narrative of Vijayanagar as follows:

> 'When the depredations of the Allies had destroyed all the country around, Venkatadri (named erroneously for Tirumala), who had escaped from the battle to a distant fortress, sent humble entreaties of peace to the Sultans, to whom he gave up all the places which his brothers had wrested from them; and the victors being satisfied, took leave of each other at Raichur and returned to their respective dominions'.

The Aftermath

Of course, the battle of Talikota, like the famous battles of Panipat, was one of the most decisive battles in the history of India. It sounded the death knell of the Vijayanagar Empire and shattered all prospects of the Hindu domination in South India. Nevertheless, after their victory, there arose mutual jealousy among the four Sultans which prevented them from combining together to wipe their vanquished Hindu adversary out of existence. Their confederacy or league foundered on the rocks of the leadership issue; being hereditary feudal lords of their respective ruling dynasties and co-equals, none of them was prepared to acknowledge the other as his superior, and there was no tradition or precedent to claim joint proprietorship of the Vijayanagar's territories overrun by them. They had taken a united stand on the emotional issue of waging *Jihad* against the infidels but this unity could not be maintained in the face of their personal political ambitions and self-interest. It enabled Tirumala, the sole survivor of the erstwhile power brokers of Vijayanagar to establish himself at Penukonda or

Penugonda. With Sadashiva Raya, the *de jure* ruler of Vijayanagar in his captivity, he transplanted the Tuluva dynasty there and setup as his Prime Minister and the *de facto* ruler of the State. The lacklustre and badly mauled political authority of the now defunct Vijayanagar Empire evoked no confidence or fear amongst its provincial governors and subordinate feudal chieftains, who 'began to throw off their allegiance, and one after another, started asserting their independence. The country was in a state of anarchy. The empire, just now so solid and compact, became disintegrated, and from this time forward it fell rapidly to decay'. Sewell correctly concludes: 'There is no more striking example of Nemesis in medieval Indian history'.

Tirumala, the usurper of political powers and captor of the wretched Tuluva king, Sadashiva Raya, was hated by the people and held in contempt by the ruling elite of the erstwhile Vijayanagar Empire because of his anomalous position. To retrieve the situation, he murdered his sovereign in c. 1570 and seized the throne for himself. Thus came into existence, what is known to history as the 'Third Dynasty' of the usurpers, called the Aravidu dynasty. Gradually, he recovered a part of the kingdom, and the city of Vijayanagar and its neighbouring districts were also reclaimed by him but the whole of this region had so thoroughly been desolated and depopulated that for more than a century after this holocaust it showed no signs of recovery. Caesaro Federici, who visited the ruins of Vijayanagar only two years after the battle of Talikota, and stayed there for more than six months in 1567-68, records that Tirumala had taken possession of the place immediately after the exit of the Muslim armies from there, and 'he tried to re-populate the city but failed, though some few people were induced to take up their abode there'. According to him,

> 'The Musalmans spent six months (and not five as mentioned by Firishta) in plundering the city, searching in all the directions for buried money. The city of Bezeneger (Vijayanagar) is not altogether destroyed; yet the houses are still standing but they are empty, and there is dwelling in them nothing but tigers and other wild beasts. The court has moved from Bezeneger to Penukonda which is eight days' journey to the south; the inhabitants have disappeared and gone elsewhere.'

The surrounding country of Vijayanagar was so infested with thieves and highway robbers that there was no trade or free movement of the people in the region; 'which compelled him to stay six months longer at Vijayanagar than he intended'. When at last he set out for Goa, he was frequently waylaid and had to pay a ransom at each occasion. Similarly, Firishta, the celebrated author of *Gulshan-i-Ibrahimi* or simply the *Tarikh-i-Firishta*, who visited Bijapur in 1589, writes about Vijayanagar as under:

'The *Raaje* (kingdom) of Beejanuggur (Vijayanagar), since this battle, has never recovered its ancient splendour; and the city itself has been so destroyed that it is now totally in ruins and uninhabited, while the country has been seized by the *zamindars* (petty chiefs), each of whom hath assumed an independent power in his own district'.

Tirumala, on his death in 1575, was succeeded by his second son, Ranga II (1575-86) and he was followed by his brother Venkata II who ruled from 1586 to 1614. All of them styled themselves as the kings of Vijayanagar and claimed to be the rightful inheritors of the great Vijayanagar tradition. Venkata II was a man of some ability and character who attempted to revive the glories of the Vijayanagar court at Penugonda, of course, by extending patronage to poets and men of letters. But he committed the mistake of recognizing the complete autonomy of the Mysore state which was founded by Raja Oedyar in 1612. He transferred his capital from Penugonda to Chandragiri. On his death in 1614, there was a war of succession which led to the final disruption and dismemberment of his kingdom. Ranga III, who ascended the throne, was unable to keep the disaffected hereditary provincial governors of the kingdom under his control; and they proved to be the worst enemies of the Hindu unity. Among them, the important feudal governors of Seringapatam, Bednur and Naiks of Madura and Tanjore threw off the imperial yoke of the central government and setup as independent rulers. It was under these circumstances that the kings of Vijayanagar, now established at Chandragiri, were reduced to the position of petty chieftains like many others of their erstwhile feudatories and the Empire of Vijayanagar met with its ignominious end.

SECTION 3: THE IMPACT OF BAHMANI RULE ON THE SOCIETY AND CULTURE OF SOUTH INDIA

Nature of the Bahmani Rule

Just as the Turko-Afghan rulers of Delhi had struck a fatal blow to the ancient Hindu society and culture of northern and central India in the thirteenth and fourteenth centuries, the foundation of the Bahmani kingdom exercised a profound influence on the society and culture of South India in the fourteenth and fifteenth centuries. South India, beyond the Vindhyas, had served as a repository of Hinduism and ancient Indian socio-cultural traditions for centuries until Alauddin Khilji gate-crashed into the Deccan with his 'armies of Islam'. Alauddin and Muhammad bin Tughluq penetrated deep into the far south, overthrew the age-old Hindu monarchies, and 'uprooted the indigenous social and cultural institutions'. They set in motion the entirely new foreign political forces and exotic socio-cultural traditions which were to shape the life and condition of the people there beyond all recognition. The Bahmani kingdom provided a powerful base to the Islamic fundamentalists in the Deccan, and the rule of its foreign Muslim adventurers implied the loss of political and religious independence by the Hindus; it bore no comparison with the Vijayanagar kingdom wherein the indigenous inhabitants of South India had regained their political independence from the imperial Muslim yoke of the Sultanate of Delhi under the inspiring leadership of their native ruling elite.

The Bahmanis, following in the foot-prints of the Sultans of Delhi, established in the Deccan what was called 'an Islamic state' in which all the powers were concentrated in the hands of the Muslim nobility; some of its rulers were religious fanatics who persecuted their Hindu subjects, encouraged conversions to Islam by fair means or foul, fanned the feelings of communalism, and gave preferential treatment to the Muslims in the state services in order to retain their predominance in all walks of life though they constituted but a microscopic minority of their subjects. The non-Muslims were dubbed as *Zimmis*; they had to pay *Jaziya* and suffered from many socio-religious and civil disabilities. Influx of Foreigners from the Muslim countries. In order to makeup the deficiency of the Muslim population, the Bahmani Sultans threw the gates of their kingdom open to the foreign immigrants, who were readily absorbed in the government services and rehabilitated by the grants of free lands and stipends. According to Haroon Khan Sherwani,

> 'The handful of the Muslims of the Deccan had to get moral and material help from over the seas, and we find an increasing influx of a vigorous human element in the shape of newcomers from the coasts round the Persian Gulf and from further north round the Caspian Sea, i.e. from Iran, Iraq and Arabia,. They comprised all sorts of men, including poets, litterateurs, saints,

artisans, merchants, soldiers and adventurers, and came to settle down in the Deccan, some at the invitation of the Bahmani Sultans, others of their own accord. They were called *Pardesis* (foreigners) or *Afaqis* (cosmopolitans)'. (Bahmanis of the Deccan; *loc.cit.*, pp. 113-14).

Malik Saifuddin Ghori, 'the right-hand man' of as many as five Bahmani Sultans, provided many incentives from out of the royal treasury and other resources of the state to attract the best warriors and the most talented Muslims from abroad. Sultan Muhammad Shah II (1378-97), 'himself a scholar of Arabic and Persian', invited 'the Arab and Persian poets to the Deccan to make the country the seat of learning and culture'. (*Ibid.*, p. 116). Of course, the large-scale influx of the foreign blood, with strong exotic cultural traditions was bound to have 'a great effect upon the culture and future history of the Deccan'. Sherwani writes:

'It is remarkable how, while the northern cultural influences are visibly declining, foreign influences are having their direct play on the Bahmani kingdom...it was because of these newcomers, who really came to settle down in the Deccan...An evidence of the influx of Iranians, Transoxianians and Iraqis can be found in the surnames of the civil and military personnel of the Bahmani State even in the time of Muhammad Shah I (1358-71), and Seistanis, Tabrizis, Mozendranis, Kirmanis and others of the same nature abroad'. (*Ibid.*, p. 114)

Rivalry between the *Pardesis* and the *Dakhinis*

The influx of foreigners was felt seriously not by the Hindus or the original inhabitants of the land, who carried no weight in the state affairs but by the old Muslim nobility of the Deccan, including the Hindu converts to Islam and the Muslim immigrants from Delhi. They were called *Dakhinis* (southerners) in comparison with the newly arrived foreigners, who were called the *Pardesis* or *Afaqis*. It gave rise to rivalry between the two factions of the Muslim ruling elite, which caused its evil shadow on the fortunes of the Bahmani kingdom in the long-run.

Evolution of the Indo-Muslim Culture of the Deccan

The indigenous Hindu cultural forces of South India, though under great strain from the pressure of exotic religion and diverse foreign cultural elements, refused to die down. In spite of the loss of political independence and economic disabilities, accompanied by occasional persecution of the Hindus, they stuck to their ancestral religion and culture with steadfastness. Even those, who under the force of circumstances, were compelled to embrace Islam, did not give up the ancient culture of their motherland. It ultimately initiated a process of interaction between three types of cultural influences—local, north Indian and foreign. The outcome of their interaction, which lasted about two hundred years, was the birth of a peculiar Bahmani or *Dakhani* culture. Synthesis between these diverse cultural traits started about the time of Sultan Tajuddin Firoze Shah (1397-1422), who made a conscious attempt to strike 'a balance between various elements which went to make the Bahmani state'. He also 'took the bold step' of opening the state services to the Hindus, especially the educated Brahmans. Bahman Shah, the founder of the dynasty, had already adopted a liberal policy towards the Hindu landlords to retain their landed estates and *jagirs* on the acknowledgement of suzerainty and payment of *Jaziya* on behalf of their Hindu subjects. It was, however, Firoze Shah who began to offer them positions of honour and responsibility in the royal court. Rai Narasimha of Kherla was appointed 'a peer of the Bahmani kingdom' by the Sultan, who is also said to have received enthusiastic support from 'some Keddis of the east' in his struggle against Vijayanagar. Once the gates of higher civil and military services were thrown open to the Hindus, there was no going back, and before long, they became the companions-in-arms of the *Dakhani* Muslim nobles in their conflict with the *Pardesis*. At the same time, the inflow of the foreign elements reached its saturation point, and the stage was set for synthesis between the indigenous and exotic cultural traits without prejudice against either. It radically changed the racial and religious composition and character of the Bahmani nobility and the court which was shifted from Gulbarga to the newly constructed township of Bidar by Sultan Ahmad Shah in 1429. Thus the Bahmani court at Bidar acquired a unique cultural personality of its own because it showed thorough intermixture of South Indian Hindu and exotic Muslim traits in every respect. The trade and commerce was already in the hands of the Hindu bankers and businessmen. They had entered even the overseas trade in a big way, and supplied 'horses from Urmuz, elephants from Ceylon, and musk and fur from China' to the court of the Bahmani Sultans; they had become *Dakhinis* from every point of view.

Development of Education and Learning

The Bahmani Sultans were great patrons of education and learning. They invited Persian and Arabic scholars from other parts of India and abroad to come and settle down in their dominions. Like the Sultans of Delhi, they also declared Persian as the court language, and granted liberal stipends and land grants to the scholars to promote Persian and Arabic languages. The whole of the kingdom was dotted with numerous *masjids* to which were attached *maktabs* or elementary schools at the state expense to provide free education to the people at large while the *madrassas* of the high school and university standard were opened in big towns for higher learning. Mahmud Gawan opened a *madrassa* and a magnificent library at Bidar for the promotion of Persian and Arabic studies. The famous historian Firishta belonged to an aristocratic family from Persia; born in c.1570, he migrated to South India in his early youth and spent most of his time at the Nizamshahi court of Ahmadnagar. The towns of Bidar, Ahmadnagar, Bijapur and Golconda had become great centres of Persian and Arabic education and learning much before the rise of the regional Muslim states of these places. The history of the Bahmani kingdom and that of the Nizamshahi dynasty of Ahmadnagar has been well preserved in the *Burhan-i-Maasir* of Sayyad Ali Tabataba who was an official at the court of Ahmadnagar. It is said that the influx of the foreign scholars to Golconda during the reign of Sultan Ibrahim Qutb Shah was so great that it became difficult to find accommodation for them within the walled city; it prompted the Sultan to found a new city of Hyderabad in 1592.

The Urdu language, which was born in the north, found a more fertile ground for its growth and development in the Deccan. As the Bahmani kings used it as a means of communication with their local population, it drew its vocabulary freely from the south Indian languages like the Marathi, Tamil, Telugu and Kanarese, and with the passage of time, itself became known as the Deccani language. Khwaja Band Nawaz Gesui Daraz was the first scholar of *Dakhan* to produce a treatise in Urdu in the Persian script, entitled, *Mirat-ul-Ashiqin*. The Sultans of Ahmadnagar, Bijapur and Golconda allowed Urdu to be used freely at their royal courts while Ibrahim Adil Shah II was the first to make it the official language of Bijapur. Many of the Muslim rulers of the Deccan were themselves poets and scholars of Urdu. Wajabi, the celebrated author of *Qutub Mushtri* and *Sabras*, and Faiz – the author of *Ruzwane Shah-o-Ruhafza*, were the luminaries of the court of Golconda. The *Sufi* saints of the Deccan produced religious treatises and wrote *masnavis* on spiritualism in the Urdu language; for instance, Shah Miran authored *Khushnuma* and Shah Aminuddin Ala composed *Rumuz-us-Satikin* and Muhammad Nusrat produced *Gulshan-i-Ishaq*, *Alinama* and *Tarikh-i-Sikandri* in the Urdu language.

Art and Architecture

The Indo-Muslim art and architecture of Tughluq style was introduced into the Deccan when Muhammad bin Tughluq transferred his capital to Daulatabad (old Devagiri or Deogiri) but an independent Indo-Muslim style of architecture came into existence with the foundation of the Bahmani kingdom. It passed through three phases of its growth corresponding to those of the political developments there. The first phase lasted with the Gulbarga period (1347-1429) and the second corresponded to the Bahmani rule at Bidar. The third phase of the *Dakhani* Art and Architecture, when it reached a stage of maturity, covered the era of five succession states of the Bahmani kingdom. The construction of forts at all the strategic places in the kingdom formed one of the major architectural activities of the Bahmani Sultans, The *masjids*, minarets, domes, royal palaces and public buildings, besides the tombs formed the other major forms of architecture. In the construction of these buildings, the Sultans showed 'the unrestricted and unbiased use of all sorts of architectural concepts and technology, indigenous and foreign, 'Hindu" or 'Muslim' alike'. Therefore, the Bahmani or Dakhani Art and Architecture was the outcome of free intermingling of all the best that was available to the architects.

Amongst the monuments of the Bahmani period, mention may be made of the mausoleums of the first three Sultans at Gulbarga; they show marked influence of the Tughluq style reflected by 'thick walls with a sharp slope and very little surface decoration' although the tomb of Bahman Shah is characterized by 'a beautiful band of deep blue enamel tiles of the purely Persian style' The Persian influence on the *Dakhani* art and architecture increased successively which differentiated it from the monuments of the Sultans of Delhi The *Jama Masjid* of the Gulbarga fort, with its 'square base supporting the dome', and 'broad squat arches' set the style of the first phase of the Bahmani art. "Unlike the mosques of northern India, it has no open courtyard, and the whole of its area has been covered, permitting the light to trickle through its perforated side-walls and arches'. To begin with, the Bahmani Sultans, because of their superiority complex, looked down upon everything indigenous or 'Hindu' as it belonged to 'the vanquished infidels'. Their attitude changed gradually by the considerations of the availability of material and the concepts of beauty and utility. *Haft Gumbad* or 'the seven tombs' of Sultans Mujahid Shah, Daud Shah and their family members at Gulbarga, were built on a new plan with decorative variations showing 'the Hindu influence in the carvings of the prayer niche, doorways of polished black-stone, carved in Hindu fashion, and beautiful brackets supporting the cornice or the horizontal projections' for the first time.

The second phase of the Bahmani art and architecture began at Bidar with the construction of the massive fort and its mosques and palaces. They show increasing Persian imprint side by side with the indigenous or Hindu influences. The twelve tombs of the latter Bahmani rulers at Bidar show the partially digested intermingling of the Persian and indigenous styles in equal proportions. They are much larger than their counterparts at Gulbarga and contain more 'arched recesses, screen windows in the façade and decorative columns besides richly decorated enamel tiles and paintings in many and varied colours'. The tomb of Sultan Ahmad Shah I is the best of these monuments which 'sets the fashion' at Bidar; 'its exterior, having a lofty and impressive entrance archway on each side, is divided into three storeys by recessed arches and windows while its dome illustrates a happy combination of the flat dome of the Delhi style and the sound conical domes of Persia...Its interior is decorated with paintings in bright gold, vermilion and green colours'. (Ziyauddin A Desai, *Indo-Islamic Architecture*; p. 31). Mahmud Gawan's *Madrassa* at Bidar has been built in the typical Persian style; it is a three-storey building with a rectangular plan, and contains a mosque, lecture rooms, a library hall and the residential flats for the teachers. In the words of Ziyauddin

> 'On its front side are two minarets, one at each corner, while semi-octagonal structures with bulbous domes project, one each, from the middle of the remaining three sides. The whole building is remarkable for the perfect symmetry and proportion of its various parts. Its front side was lavishly decorated with encaustic tiles of various colours and designs, and the minarets were also adorned with glazed tiles arranged in a zigzag pattern'. (*Ibid.*, p. 30)

In the opinion of Ziyauddin, the *Sola Khamba* (i.e. the building with sixteen pillars) mosque of the Bidar fort is one of the best specimens of the second phase of development of Bahmani architecture. Its spacious prayer-hall is divided into 'a number of aisles by massive circular columns'. Its roof is 'crowned by a majestic dome of fine shape, raised on a high clerestory with windows of fine perforated screen-work in different geometrical patterns. A parapet of pleasing design above the imposing arcade of its facade adds to its picturesqueness'. (*Ibid.*)

Daulatabad (old Deogiri) possessed a very rich Hindu architectural heritage; it contained intact many of the public buildings and palaces of the Yadava kings which were put to use by the Muslim rulers without any prejudice to its 'infidel architecture'. And some of the new buildings erected by them also showed a free blending of the indigenous, north Indian and the Persian styles. The Chand Minar at Daulatabad, constructed in 1445, is a solitary example of a building which was designed in a typical Persian style.

The third phase of the Bahmani art and architecture corresponds to the era of the five succession states of the Bahmani kingdom. It was marked by complete synthesis between the 'foreign Muslim' and the 'indigenous Hindu' styles of art and architecture and rightly became known as the Deccani art style. In this art style, the foreign and indigenous or Muslim and Hindu traits of art are totally intermixed and become indistinguishable; rather they develop further to assume regional variations from state to state. The Deccani art style retained a number of Persian traits in their modified form but it showed a much greater influence of the local traditions from state to state, thus imparting to each a freshness and individuality of its own. The best specimens of Bijapur art style of the age are provided by the tomb of Ali Adil Shah, Mehtar Mahal, Gagan Mahal, Gole Gumbad, the Zanjiri and Andu *masjids* of Bijapur, besides the Sunehri *masjid* of Shahpur and *Kali masjid* at Lakshmeshwar. The Nizamshahi buildings of Ahmadnagar were influenced by the neighbouring Gujarat and Malwa styles 'reflected in the fine quality of their building material and other architectural and decorative features; their extant monuments include the Damri *masjid* and tombs of Ahmad Nizam Shah, Rumi Khan and *Do-Boti-Chira* at Ahmadnagar, the tombs of Malik Amber and *Zachcha Bachcha* at Daulatabad, besides the water palace-cum-pleasure resort of *Farah Bagh* at Ahmadnagar. Like Bijapur, Golconda also provided fine local traits to the Deccani art style. The monuments of the Qutb Shahi dynasty impart a unique historical personality to the towns of Golconda and Hyderabad. The *Char Minar* of Hyderabad, which was the main entrance to the royal building complex, is one of the best specimens of the medieval Indian architecture. It consists of a central square building structure with lofty arched openings on all the four sides. There arises a beautiful *Minar* from each of its four corners, showing unique synthesis of indigenous and foreign art styles. The state of Berar, having been annexed by Ahmadnagar could not develop an individualistic art style of its own though some of its monuments, like the *masjids* at Gwaligarh, Ellichpur and Malikapur, and *Houza Katora* - a beautiful building, now standing in partial ruins in the centre of a water tank at Ellichpur, remind us of the brief but imaginative architectural activity of the Imadshahi Sultans of Berar. The Burhanshahi dynasty which transplanted the Bahmanis at Bidar, also gave a new local touch to the Deccani art style. On the whole, the Muslim rulers of the Bahmani kingdom and its succession states made a positive contribution towards the development of the Indo-Muslim art and architecture of the medieval period.

SECTION 4: LIFE AND CONDITION OF THE PEOPLE IN THE VIJAYANAGAR KINGDOM

Nature of the Vijayanagar State

Unlike the Bahmani Sultans, the founders of the Vijayanagar kingdom were 'the sons of the soil'. They were freedom-fighters who liberated their people from the foreign Muslim domination and secured religious and cultural freedom for them; hence they commanded the love and obedience of their subjects. Though Hindus by faith, they adopted a policy of religious toleration towards the non-Hindu subjects of their dominions and granted complete civil liberties to them in the true ancient Indian traditions. Like the Muslim rulers, they were oriental despots but unlike them, they implemented the law of the land, abided by the time-honoured customs and traditions, and safeguarded the indigenous religious and socio-cultural institutions while paying due regards to the customs and beliefs of their Muslim subjects. Despotism of the Vijayanagar kings, therefore, bore no comparison with the despotic rule of the Bahmanis who had established an alien military dictatorship in the Deccan by crushing the civil liberties of its original inhabitants. The Vijayanagar monarchs were benevolent despots who understood the happiness and welfare of their subjects as a whole to be their primary duty.

The kings of Vijayanagar were aided and advised in the discharge of their functions by a council of ministers and their court was composed of the most talented men of the land, including the diplomats and statesmen, provincial governors and hereditary feudal chiefs, military generals and Brahman theologians, saints, scholars and artists. They were formally the nominees of the king but, in their own right, they were usually men of public reputation and acclaim. The prime minister's office invariably belonged to a learned Brahman and diplomat of repute. The functions of the court were advisory in nature but the kings were morally bound by the unanimous or collective decision of their council of ministers.

The civil and military administration of the Vijayanagar kingdom was based on the Hindu feudal system of the pre-Muslim days which seems to have been faithfully preserved along with all of its inherent defects. The state of Vijayanagar, during the heydays of its glory, was roughly divided into 200 provinces or feudal estates (like *jagirs* or fiefs of the Sultanate polity) which were usually allotted to the trustworthy and capable military generals as hereditary governors; important governorships were held by princes of the royal blood, their kinsmen and scions of the old dynasties and the traditional ruling elite. Like the monarchs, they were all bound by the law of the land and abided by the local customs and traditions of the people, but enjoyed considerable autonomy in the discharge of their administrative functions. They held their own miniature courts in the likeness of the Vijayanagar monarchs, recruited their armies and rendered military service to the central government when required. The provinces were divided into districts, called *nadus* or *kottams,* each of which comprised a couple of towns and some villages. The village *panchayats* maintained law and order within their charge without much interference from the state officials who usually made their appearance at the time of collecting the land revenue in cash or kind.

Glimpses of the Vijayanagar City and the Royalty

South India was visited by a number of adventurers, traders, scholars and dignitaries from foreign countries, Muslims as well as Christians, during the age of the Bahmani and Vijayanagar kingdoms. Some of them have left very valuable accounts of the political, social, cultural and economic condition of the people which help us a lot in the reconstruction of the history of these states. They include among others, the chronicle of Abdur Razzak, a Persian ambassador to the court of Vijayanagar, and the travelogues of Nicolo Conti, Duarte Barbosa, Fernao Nuniz and Domingos Paes, etc. Nicolo Conti, a Venetian traveller, who visited south India in c. 1420-21, gives an eye-witness account of the city of Vijayanagar as follows:

> "The great city of Bizengaalia (Vijayanagar) is situated near very steep mountains. The circumference of the city is 97 kms. Its walls are carried up to the mountains and enclose the valleys at their foot, so that its extent is thereby increased. In this city,

there are estimated to be ninety thousand men, fit to bear arms'. (Travelogue of Nicolo Conti in R H Major, *India in the Fifteenth Century*; pp. 1-39).

Abdur Razzak, who visited the court of Vijayanagar twenty years later, in 1442-43, as an envoy of Sultan Shah Rukh of Khurasan, gives an eye-witness account of the splendour of the Vijayanagar court during the reign of Devaraya II, and draws a pen-portrait of the character and personality of the reigning monarch. He describes the magnificence of the royal processions and the festivals at the capital and is amazed to see the fabulous wealth and luxurious life-style of the nobility. Like Nicolo Conti, he also gives the description of Vijayanagar in his own way as under:

'The city of Bisanugur (Vijayanagar) is such that eye has not seen nor ear heard of any place resembling it upon the whole earth. It is so built that it has seven fortified walls, one within the other. Beyond the circuit of the outer wall there is an esplanade extending for about 250 metres, in which stones are fixed near one another to the height of a man; one half buried firmly in the earth, and other half rises above it, so that neither foot nor horse, however bold, can advance with facility near the outer wall'. (Eng. Trs. by R H Major in *Ibid.*).

Domingos Paes, writing about the city of Vijayanagar about a century later (c. 1520-22) gives his observations as follows:

'Two leagues before you arrive at the city of Bisnaga (Vijayanagar) (from the direction of Goa), you have a very lofty *Serra* (a range of hills) which has passes by which you enter the city. These are called 'gates' (*paratas*). You must enter by these for you will have no means of entrance except by them. This range of hills surrounds the city with a circle of twenty-four leagues. And within this range, there are others that encircle it closely. Wherever these ranges have any level ground they cross it with a very strong wall in such a way that the hills remain all closed, except in the places where the roads come through from the gates in the first range, which are the entrance ways to the city'. (Narrative of Domingos Paes in Sewell; *A Forgotten Empire*; p. 235).

About the population of Vijayanagar and their wealth and prosperity, Domingo Paes has to say that:

'The people in the city (of Vijayanagar) are countless in number, so much so that I do not wish to write it down for fear it should be thought fabulous; but I declare that no troops, horse or foot could break their way through any street or lane, so great are the numbers of the people and elephants'.

Elsewhere in his travelogue, Paes records that 'in this city, you will find men belonging to every nation and people because of the great trade which it has, and the many precious stones there, principally diamonds'. The Portuguese traveller is unable to give an exact estimate of 'the size of the city' because 'it cannot all be seen from any one spot'. Paes writes with confidence, however, that

"This is the best provided city in the world; and it is stocked with provisions such as rice, wheat, grains, Indian-corn, and a certain amount of barley and beans, *moong*, pulses, horse-gram and many other seeds which grow in this country, and which are the food of the people, and there is large store of these and very cheap... The streets and markets are full of oxen without count so that you cannot get along for them, and in many streets you come upon so many of them that you have to wait for them to pass, or else have to go by another way'. (*Ibid.*, p. 248)

By all accounts, Vijayanagar was the most extensive and richest of all the states of India in the fifteenth and the first half of the sixteenth century. It owed its prosperity to the growth and development of agriculture and industry, trade and commerce, including the voluminous maritime trade with the foreign countries. According to Abdu Razzak, there were 300 seaports in the Empire which established its commercial contacts with Persia, Arabia, Africa, Malaya Archipelago, Burma, China and the numerous islands in the Indian Ocean. South India exported cloth, rice, indigo, iron, salt petre, diamonds, sugar, and spices, and received in return, horses, pearls, copper, china-silk and velvets, etc. Shipping industry flourished in the coastal towns. The foreigners, who visited the court of Vijayanagar, were simply amazed to observe the fabulous wealth of the ruling elite and richness of its people. The huge quantities of gold, diamonds and material wealth, possessed by the inhabitants of Vijayanagar was beyond the comprehension or estimation of Domingos Paes and other foreigners. Abdur Razzak refers with bewilderment to the existence of underground chambers in the royal treasury of Vijayanagar, which were said to 'have been filled with molten gold to form one mass'; and Paes tells us that the citizens of Vijayanagar, 'high or low, even down to the artificers of the *bazaar*, wear jewels and gift ornaments in their ears, and around their necks, arms, wrists and fingers'. No wonder, south India was 'a golden sparrow' of the east during the age of the Vijayanagar Empire, and it rightly excited the curiosity and envy of the foreigners who visited its coasts in that age.

Socio-Cultural Life of the People

Hindus, the indigenous inhabitants of the Vijayanagar Empire, constituted the bulk of its population though a fairly large number of Muslims and Jews besides some Portuguese and other European traders and businessmen had also settled there; they were welcomed by the local inhabitants and 'enjoyed happy and comfortable lives under the benevolent rule of the Hindu monarchs'. The latter adopted a policy of religious toleration towards all and did not discriminate between their Hindu and Muslim subjects. The Brahmans were held in high esteem by the Vijayanagar rulers and they wielded great influence on the socio-political life of the people. The upper strata of the society, including the bureaucracy, landed aristocracy and traders and the Brahmans, in general, were rich and prosperous. Within the city of Vijayanagar, 'each class of men belonging to each profession' had their cluster of shops or distinct markets for plying their business or trade. Abdur Razzak writes that the jewellers have their separate market or shopping centre where they sell publicly pearls, rubies, emeralds and diamonds. Vijayanagar was a very big centre of domestic as well as international trade and commerce which was thronged by hundreds and thousands of the Indian and foreign traders every day.

The Hindus, in general, practised monogamy although the royalty and the aristocracy showed laxity in morals. Nicolo Conti tells us that 'those who could afford marry as many wives as they lease,' and that 'they are burnt with their dead husbands'. It shows the prevalence of the practice of *Sati* among the Hindus, and the Brahmans are known to commend this kind of 'self-immolation' forcibly. According to Nicolo Conti,

> 'The king's palace has as many as '12,000 women, of whom 4,000 follow him on foot wherever he may go, and are employed solely in the service of the kitchen. A like number, more handsomely equipped, ride on horse-back. The remainder are carried by men in litters, of whom 2,000 or 3,000 are selected as his wives, on condition that, at his death, they should voluntarily burn themselves with him, which is considered to be a great honour for them'.

Nevertheless, the general condition of Hindu women in the Vijayanagar era is said to be fairly good. The girls of the upper castes received higher education and some of them took up to the scholarly studies in theology, literary pursuits and state-craft, while the ladies of the middle and lower-middle classes engaged themselves in useful arts and crafts like their men folk. While Nicolo refers to women body-guards and soldiers of the Vijayanagar monarchs, we are told by other writers that the capital of Vijayanagar had women wrestlers, astrologers, soothsayers, and a staff of women clerks and accountants to maintain the accounts of the royal household. Nuniz is simply amazed to see the heathen women scholars and writers, poets, musicians and singers at Vijayanagar and observes that the king has in his employment, 'women judges as well as bailiffs', and female guards, who every night perform the watch and ward duties at the royal palace'.

As most of the Hindus were vegetarians by food habits, Abdu Razzak, during his stay at Vijayanagar, found much difficulty in procuring ready-made non-vegetarian food for him in the city's open market or guest houses; it is, therefore, that he made special enquiries about the food habits of the people and writes with satisfaction that the Hindus, in general, love to take fruits, cow's milk, corns and cereals and all sorts of vegetables besides fish, but some of them do 'take meat of all kinds except that of oxen or cows'. Likewise, Nuniz writes as under:

> 'These kings of Bisnaga (Vijayanagar) eat all sorts of things but not the flesh of oxen or cows, which they never kill in all the country of the heathens because they worship them'.

But he hastily adds that 'everything has to be sold alive so that each one may know what he buys – that at least so far as concerns game, and there are fish from the rivers in large quantities'. He further tells us that 'the markets are always overflowing with abundance of fruits- grapes, oranges, limes, pomegranates, jackfruit and mangoes, and all very cheap'. Abdur Razzak, in a foreign land, on the other hand, finds something of his taste, that was, 'the brothels in the city of Vijayanagar', which were, of course, 'duly licensed by the state'.

Education and Learning

The kings of Vijayanagar were great patrons of education and learning. 'Their period of rule was made glorious by the renaissance in Sanskrit –the language of higher culture in south India, and the Vedic literature. It also witnessed tremendous growth and development of Dravidian languages – Tamil, Telugu, Kannada and Malayalam, which owed a great deal to Sanskrit'. According to Nilakanta Sastri, 'Sanskrit language acted as the magic vand whose touch alone raised each of these Dravidian languages from the level of a patois (the dialect of a particular region, especially one with low status in relation to the standard language of the country) to that of a literary idiom'. (History of South India; *loc. cit.*, p. 340).

Bukka Raya, one of the founding fathers of Vijayanagar and the second ruler of the Sangama dynasty, took keen interest in the rehabilitation of the Hindu religion and the cultural institutions which had suffered a serious setback during the period of Muslim rule. Under his inspiring leadership, the *pundits* of Sanskrit and Vedic literature and philosophy, poets and artists flocked to the court of Vijayanagar and initiated the process for the revival of indigenous education and learning. Most of the Vijayanagar rulers and many other members of the royalty were well-educated, and some of them actually made substantial literary contributions. The scholars and artists came from all parts of south India and received patronage from the Vijayanagar court without any regional or sectarian prejudices; and they worked in perfect harmony with one another to produce 'the synthetic indigenous culture of south India'; this was the greatest cultural achievement of the Vijayanagar empire. A galaxy of Sanskrit scholars, headed by Sayana, reproduced religious scriptures and rewrote commentaries on all the four Vedas and some of the *Brahmanas* and *Aranyakas*. Similarly, the profuse literature produced in Tamil under the Vijayanagar rulers was next only to the Sanskrit literature of south India. The religious literature in Tamil during the Vijayanagar Empire was produced by *Shaivites*, *Vaishnavites* and the *Jain* saints and scholars; it included the translations of ancient scriptures from Sanskrit to Tamil and preparation of commentaries thereon, and recasting of the Puranic literature and religious philosophy. Meykandar prepared *Siva Nana Bodam* – 'a short treatise of a dozen *sutras*, translated from some Sanskrit original'. The *Siva Nana Sittiyar* of Arunandi comprises 'a great classic of *Saiva* (*Shaivite*) doctrine in Tamil'. Two great scholar-saints, Svarupananda Desikar and his pupil, Tattuvarayar, wrote two anthologies on the philosophy of *Advaita*, captioned, *Sivaprakasa Perundirattu* and *Kurundirattu* in the early fifteenth century; these voluminous productions 'conserve much of the religious and philosophical literature of the silver age of *Saivism* in the Tamil country that would otherwise have been lost'. Yet another work on Saiva philosophy was produced by Velliyambla Tambiran under the title, *Nanabharana Vilakham*.

According to Nilakanta Sastri, *Tanjai Vanam Kovai* of Poyyamoli and *Nalavenba* of Pugalendi are outstanding Tamil productions in the long list of secular literature, while the *Bharatum* of Villiputturar, prepared in c.1400, is an epic of great merit which describes the whole story of the *Mahabharata* in 4350 Tamil verses; 'the narrative style of its author', writes Nilakanta, 'and his rich diction, marked by a profuse admixture of Sanskrit words and expressions, make the poem a very attractive reading'. (*Ibid.*, p. 383).

Nilakanta Sastri gives an interesting story about the development of Telugu as a language of literary merit; it started in the eleventh century when Nannaya made an attempt to translate the *Mahabharata* into Telugu during the reign of Rajaraja Narendra (1090-61). His work remained incomplete but Tikkana (c. 1220-1300), the greatest poet of his times, resumed the versification of the great Epic from where Nannaya had left. Somehow, he also could not complete the work which, ultimately, received finishing touches from another great scholar and poet, Yerrapragada (1280-1350); the latter writes that Tikkana had appeared to him in a dream and asked him to complete the *Mahabharata*. Yerrapragada, who earned reputation as *Prabandha Parameshwara*, proved his capability as the master of Sanskrit and Telugu languages and showed his poetic skills in versification; 'he begins his work in the style of Nannaya but, imperceptibly, passes into that of Tikkana'. All these poetic translations of the *Mahabharata* are held in the highest esteem by the Telugu scholars of the medieval and modern ages alike. The work of translation and adaptation of Sanskrit scriptures and secular literature preoccupied the scholars of that language during the vijayanagar period. Thus Vemana and Virabhadra earned their fame by versifying Kalidasa's *Shakuntala* into Telugu. More original and standard works in this language started coming forth during the reign of Krishandeva Raya, who was himself a genius as a scholar of Sanskrit and Tamil. A born poet with love for music and philosophy, he wrote five books in Sanskrit besides the one in Tamil. He opened schools and colleges for the promotion of Sanskrit and Dravidian languages, and provided opportunities to the talented men and women of his age for the display of their literary and artistic skills for the benefit of the masses. Allasani Peddana, a celebrated Telugu poet of Krishnadeva's court was honoured by the monarch with the title of *Andhrakavita-pitamaha* –'the Grandfather of Telugu Poetry'.

Likewise, the era of the Vijayanagar rulers constitutes 'the formative age' in the development of Kannada and Malayalam languages also.

The first Kannada scholar of this age was Madhura who wrote *Dharmanathapurana* on the 15th Jain *Tirthankara* during the reigns of Harihar II and Devaraya I. Palkunki Somanatha wrote many books on *Vira-Saivism* in Telugu and Kannada languages. Of course, the scholarship in Sanskrit was a prerequisite for attaining recognition or competence in the Dravidian languages. *Karnataka Sabdanusasana* of Bhattakalanka Deva, compiled in 1604, was the most comprehensive grammar of Kannada in 592 Sanskrit *sutras* with a glossary (*Vriti*) and commentary (*Vyakhya*) in the same language. (Nilakanta Sastri, *op.cit.*, pp.404-5). Similarly, *Unnunili Sandesam* – a poem by an anonymous poet, belonging to the early fourteenth century, is the first standard literary work in Malayalam; it is based on the model of Kalidasa's *Meghaduta.* Nambudiri *Brahmans* introduced a new class of Malayalam literature, called *Chakkiyarkuttu*, which aimed at a dance-recital of the famous literary works; usually the Puranic stories and other literary traditions of the past formed the themes of this literature. Rama Panikkar, one of the Niranam poets, and characterized by the critics as the 'Chaucer of Malayalam', composed a number of classical pieces of literature, including *Ramayanam, Bharatagatha, Savitri Mahatmyam, Brahmandapuranam* and *Bhagavatam.* Among the other scholars of Malayalam may be mentioned the name of Madhava Panikkar, who versified Bhagawad Gita from Sanskrit into Malayalam, and Cherusseri Nambudiri- the celebrated author of *Krishnagatha,* who is said to have heralded the age of modern literature in Malayalam.

Art and Architecture

The ancient Indian art and architecture, which had reached the pinnacle of its glory in south India during the pre-Muslim age, received barbarous treatment at the hands of the 'Armies of Islam', led by Alauddin Khilji, Muhammad bin Tughluq and their lieutenants. One of the declared objectives of the founders of Vijayanagar kingdom was to safeguard and preserve 'all that had remained of Hinduism against the onslaughts of Islam'. The revival of Brahmanism, therefore, was the immediate outcome of 'the Vijayanagar revolution in the Deccan'. Accordingly, the kings of Vijayanagar undertook to reclaim and reconstruct the old temples and religious shrines, which had been ruined by the Muslim invaders, and initiated a vigorous policy of temple building; they extended liberal patronage to the revival of ancient Indian arts, including architecture, sculpture, painting, music and dancing. 'The partially ruined temples were repaired and enlarged, and given new face-lift;

and new temples on very elaborate plans were constructed over the ruins of the old and elsewhere. The different schools of ancient architecture of south India pooled their resources to evolve new art forms and architectural plans. The newly constructed temples were usually of massive structure, lofty stature and very extensive in dimensions to accommodate hundreds and thousands of the devotees within their premises. Among the new additions to the temple architecture may be mentioned the *kalyanamandapa* or 'the ornate pillared pavilion' built in the left corner of the courtyard, varied and most artistic use of the pillars for the extension of buildings and construction of huge audience halls, and profuse ornamentation giving vent to the entire range of ancient Indian sculptural and ornamental forms and paintings, etc. A thousand pillared *Mandapa* became an ideal form of the Vijayanagar style of temple architecture'. (Advanced Study; i, p. 289-90).

Nilakanta Sastri, in his vivid account of the destruction of Vijayanagar by the fanatical Muslim invaders, does not fail to mention a few partially ruined monuments of exquisite beauty which defied the club and hammers of the vandals; they are the Vitthala and Hazara Rama temples, the Throne Platform and the King's Audience Hall, supported by ten rows of ten pillars each. We had elsewhere concluded the narrative of Vijayanagar with the following observations:

> 'Most of the magnificent temples of modern India, situated to the south of the Tungabhadra, were constructed during the Vijayanagar era; the town of Kumbakonam, Kanchipu-ram, Srirangam, Tadpatri, Vellore and Virinchipuram are adorned with such historic temples which constitute the places of pilgrimage and worship for the millions. The last phase of the Vijayanagar architecture is represented by the Madura style which continued to flourish even after the fall of the empire; the specimen temples of this style are found at Madura, Rameshwaram, Srirangam, Jambukevvara, Tiruvalur, Chidambaram, Tinnevelly and many other places in the extreme south'. (*Ibid.*, p. 290)

❑ ❑

10

INDIA ON THE EVE OF BABAR'S INVASIONS

Disintegration of the Sultanate

The decline and disintegration of the Sultanate of Delhi, once the mighty Indian empire, had begun during the concluding years of Muhammad bin Tughluq's reign. It gained momentum under the rule of Firoze Tughluq, and within a decade of the latter's death, rapidly disintegrated and passed into oblivion. Still known as 'the Sultanate of Delhi', it was reduced to the position of a small regional state on the eve of Babar's invasions in the beginning of the sixteenth century. Amir Timur had struck a fatal blow to the Sultanate in 1398-99 and left a political vacuum in the country, but, as elaborated in the preceding pages of this study, the Indian polity had deteriorated to such an extent that not a single Hindu or Muslim chieftain or military stalwart emerged on the political horizon for over a century and a quarter to hold Delhi for long and claim his sovereignty over the country.

The successors of Firoze Tughluq from 1388 onwards were never allowed to rule independently by their more ambitious military generals; the latter usurped the powers of the crown and played the kingmakers, while Timur's invasion 'took away the last semblance of royalty' professed by the puppet Sultans of Delhi. Mahmud Tughluq, the last scion of the Tughluq dynasty, died a fugitive in 1412 at Kaithal in the Punjab, and Delhi was, in fact, without a king for two years, when Khizer Khan, 'the viceroy of Amir Timur' took possession of it and setup the Sayyad dynasty in June 1414. Nevertheless, all the four Sayyad rulers (1414-50) were petty chieftains of Delhi – 'the Lilliputians, styled as Sultans', and their writ did not run beyond the metropolis and its suburbs. The Sultanate showed some signs of recovery under the first two Lodhi Sultans, Bahlol (1451-89) and Sikander Lodhi (1489-1517) but it was like 'the last flicker of the dying lamp'; the tribal monarchy of the Afghans, based on feudal principles and weakened by the fissiparous and individualistic tendencies of its nobles, stood little chance of developing into a all India power.

Ibrahim Lodhi (1517-26)

Babar, 'the great Mughal', started invasions on India in 1519. His adversary on the throne of Delhi was Sultan Ibrahim Lodhi, the eldest son and successor of Sikander Lodhi. He was a young lad of nineteen at the time of his accession. At the very outset, his claim to the throne as the sole ruler of the Afghan tribal monarchy was disputed by his younger brother, Jalal Khan who, supported by a strong lobby of the nobles, simultaneously installed himself as the independent king with his headquarters at Kalpi. It led to a fratricidal war between the two brothers, in which Jalal Khan was ultimately defeated and liquidated, but this episode sharply divided the Afghan nobility and led to wide-spread disaffections among them. In spite of his best efforts, Ibrahim Lodhi failed to establish his control over Jaunpur which was lost to the Sultanate of Delhi forever. Because of his haughty demeanour and tactless policy, Ibrahim alienated the sympathies of most of his camp-followers as well as the traditional Turkish nobility. Khan-i-Jahan Lodhi and Darya Khan Lohani became the ring-leaders of the rebellious Afghans in south Bihar, while Nasir Khan Lohani, the governor of Ghazipur, who was directed by the Sultan to march against them, changed sides and himself raised the standard of revolt. After the death of Darya Khan, his son Bahadur Khan declared himself the Sultan of Bihar with the title of Muhammad Shah and struck coins in his name. The other nobles flocked to his court and the ranks of his armed forces swelled to over one *lakh*. Similarly, the Punjab was held by Daulat Khan Lodhi and his successors as hereditary governors whose loyalty to the Sultan of Delhi was very doubtful.

To add insult to the injury, within the territorial limits of the fief or province of Delhi there prevailed total political anarchy (*tewaif-ul-maluki*), and its petty *jagirdars* and district officers were hard-pressed to maintain their precarious existence. For instance, Ahmad Khan, the *faujdar* of Mewat, who held the territories up to Mehrauli – a suburb of Delhi, defied the authority of the Sultan, while the *faujdar* of Sambhal, on the opposite side, 'to the very suburbs of Delhi' was threatened by the Lohani chiefs of Jaunpur. Likewise, a part of the Yamuna-Ganga Doab was under the control of a rebellious Muslim officer, named Isa Khan Turk, while Rewari was held by Qutb Khan

Afghan, Kampila and Patiali by Raja Pratap Singh, and Bayana by Daud Khan Lodhi, none of whom could be depended upon in time of danger to the capital of Delhi.

In the course of its disintegration, the Sultanate of Delhi, 'in conformity with the traditional Indian pattern', was split up into numerous regional and provincial states and feudal principalities. They comprised, among others, the two powerful regional kingdoms of the Deccan – Bahmani and Vijayanagar; the first was setup by the Muslims and the second by the Hindus. Similarly, the rest of India was divided into a number of well-established and powerful regional and provincial states ruled over by the Hindus as well as Muslims. These states were usually in conflict with their neighbours and fought wars with one another for territorial aggrandizement or to establish their dominance over the rivals; they also suffered from internal revolts and political upheavals, leading to the change of their rulers or the ruling dynasties. Of course, many of the provincial and regional rulers of India, in the beginning of the sixteenth century, whether Hindus or Muslims were enlightened and benevolent monarchs who worked for the happiness and welfare of their people; they had, in fact, to earn the goodwill and confidence of their subjects to stay in power. They were usually good builders; they patronized scholars and artists, promoted trade and commerce, and were, in general, helpful in the socio-cultural, moral and material advancement of their people.

The history of the rise and fall of the Bahmani and Vijayanagar kingdoms of south India has been given in the preceding chapter of this study; and a brief review of the other important provincial and regional states of the country, and their prominent rulers, on the eve of Babar's invasions, is as follows:

The Punjab

The Punjab formed a part of Bahlol Lodhi's dominions. From the administrative point of view, it could be divided roughly into five parts- the *iqtas* or provinces of Lahore and Multan, the no-man's land of the northwestern frontier, the autonomous territory of the Gakhars (Hindu tribesmen, who became known as Khokars on embracing Islam) in the Salt Range, and the defensive belt of military posts, setup by the Sultans of Delhi for the protection of the capital. The first or outer line of the capital's defence comprised the military posts of Jalandhar, Sultanpur Lodhi and Dipalpur while the second or inner line included the forts of Sirhind,

Samana, Kaithal and Hissar (also called Hissar Firoza). All these military posts were heavily garrisoned by the royal troops under the command of centrally recruited and trustworthy generals. Because of the strategic importance of the region, the governor of Lahore was granted the powers of general supervision and control over the whole of the Punjab and northwestern frontier around the Khyber and Bolan passes – the traditional gateways to India.

Bahlol Lodhi had entrusted the governorship of Lahore and viceroyalty of the Punjab to his kinsman Tatar Khan; he was a cousin of the Lodhi Sultan and the second most powerful man after him in the Afghan kingdom. His son and hereditary successor, Daulat Khan Lodhi, was at the helm of affairs at Lahore at the time of Ibrahim's accession to the throne. A great warrior and seasoned military general, Daulat Khan had an 80,000 strong army and huge purse at his command. Ibrahim felt annoyed with him as he had failed to present himself in person at Delhi at the time of his coronation, apparently because of his advanced age, and, instead, sent his son, Dilawar Khan, to pay obeisance to the new Sultan. The latter was ill-treated by Ibrahim Lodhi and an attempt was made to put him under arrest. Alarmed at the evil intentions of the Sultan, Dilawar Khan fled to Lahore with his 5,000 troops to save his life. Ever since, the relations between Daulat Khan Lodhi and Sultan Ibrahim Lodhi were strained, and the crafty viceroy of the Punjab was contemplating measures for his self-defence. About this time, Babar, then the king of Kabul, started his expeditions to India, and 'Daulat Khan Lodhi was caught between the two whirlwinds. As a shrewd diplomat, he attempted to play the one against the other for a short while. He invited Babar, through his son Dilawar Khan, to invade Delhi and offered his services to the invader in return for control of the Punjab as his vassal'.

There was nothing unusual about Daulat Khan's friendly overtures to the Mughal chief; the latter had already established himself as the sovereign ruler of Afghanistan- 'the homeland of the Afghans', and Daulat Khan would have been trigger happy to acknowledge his suzerainty if Babar could become the master of Delhi as well provided he (Daulat Khan) could be allowed to retain the viceroyalty of the Punjab. Babar welcomed Daulat Khan's offer though he did not trust the self-seeking Afghan chief nor depended upon him during his fight against Ibrahim Lodhi. Babar had to reckon with yet another rebellious Afghan noble in the Punjab, named Alam Khan Lodhi; he was the *faujdar* of Dipalpur and a maternal uncle of Sultan Ibrahim Lodhi. Alam Khan had about 8,000 horsemen under his command and aspired for the throne of Delhi; he had a number of supporters among the disaffected Afghan nobles and courtiers of Delhi. It is said that he sought Babar's help in taking possession of Delhi and was prepared to cede the whole of the Punjab to Ghazni as the price for this help. Babar was simply amused to receive the self-contradictory proposals of these Afghan nobles and did not fall into their trap. Thus there was a sort of triple contest for supremacy in which Babar came out victorious; he not only crushed the power of these rebellious Afghan nobles of the Punjab but also defeated and killed Ibrahim Lodhi in the first battle of Panipat in April 1526 and established himself at Delhi.

Sindh

The province of Sindh was the first to be conquered by the Arabs in the beginning of the eighth century. It formed a part of the Sultanate of Delhi till the concluding years of Muhammad bin Tughluq's reign. The latter died in the course of his expedition to Sindh in his bid to subdue the Sindhi rebels. Their first independent ruler, Jam Khairuddin of the Samma tribe - Hindu converts to Islam, laid the foundation of a local ruling dynasty at Thatta. His son and successor, Jam Babaniya, called the Amir of Sindh, put up a heroic defence against Firoze Tughluq in 1362-63, but was, ultimately, defeated and deposed. He was replaced by a member of his family as the feudatory chief under the nominal suzerainty of Delhi but the new Jam asserted his independence during the very lifetime of Firoze Tughluq and Sindh was lost to the Sultanate of Delhi forever. In 1520, Shah Beg Arghun, the erstwhile governor of Kandahar, having been driven out of Afghanistan by Babar, made his way to Sindh with his army intact; he wrested Thatta from the hands of the Jams and laid the foundation of the Arghun dynasty there. His son and successor, Shah Hussain, had consolidated his position by the conquest of Multan from a local chieftain in 1526 just when Babar marched upon Delhi to reckon with Ibrahim Lodhi.

Jaunpur

The town of Jaunpur, situated on the Gomati, a northern tributary of the River Ganga, in eastern Uttar Pradesh, was founded on the ancient ruins of the famous Rajput fort of Manaich, in the heart of the Hindu territories, by Sultan Firoze Tughluq, during his return march from the second Bengal expedition in 1359-60; it was named Jaunpur in

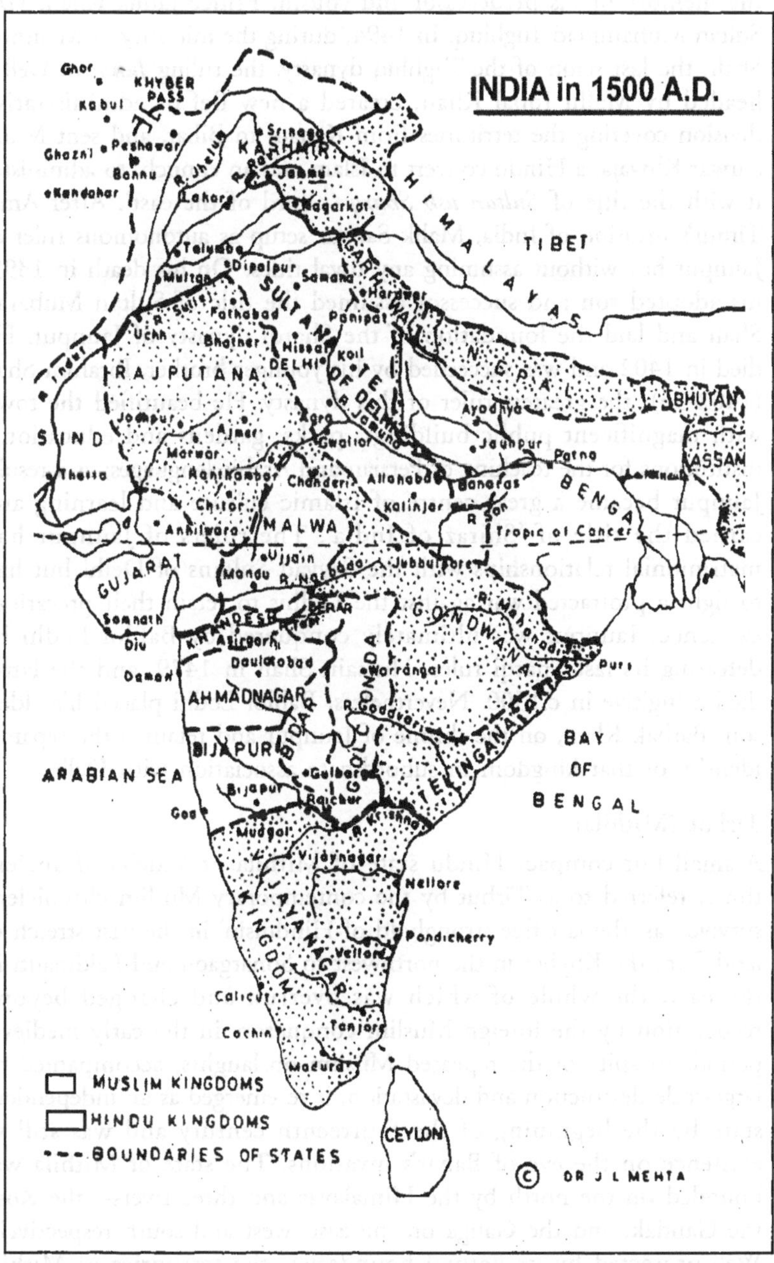
INDIA in 1500 A.D.
Ghor
KHYBER PASS
Kabul
Ghazni
Peshawar
Bannu
Kandahar
Srinagar
KASHMIR
Jammu
R. Jhelum
R. Ravi
Lahore
Nagarkot
HIMALAYAS
TIBET
Talumba
Dipalpur
Multan
Samana
Hardwar
R. Sutlej
Fathabad
Panipat
Uchh
Bhatner
Hissar
Koil
DELHI
SULTANATE OF DELHI
GARHWAL
NEPAL
BHUTAN
Indus
RAJPUTANA
Ayodhya
Jodhpur
Ajmer
Agra
R. Jamuna
SIND
Marwar
Gwalior
Jaunpur
Patna
ASSAM
Thatta
Ranthambor
Chanderi
Allahabad
Banaras
BENGAL
Chitor
Kalinjer
R. Son
Anhilwara
MALWA
Tropic of Cancer
Ujjain
Jubbulpore
GUJARAT
Mandu
R. Narbada
BERAR
Somnath
KHANDESH
Asirgarh
Diu
GONDWANA
R. Mahanadi
Daulatabad
Daman
Warrangal
Puri
AHMADNAGAR
R. Godavari
TELINGANA
BIDAR
GOLCONDA
BAY OF BENGAL
BIJAPUR
ARABIAN SEA
Gulbarga
Bijapur
Raichur
Goa
R. Krishna
Mudgal
Vijaynagar
Nellore
VIJAYANAGAR KINGDOM
Pondicherry
Vellore
Calicut
Tanjore
Cochin
Madura
CEYLON
MUSLIM KINGDOMS
HINDU KINGDOMS
BOUNDARIES OF STATES
© DR J L MEHTA

the memory of his predecessor and cousin, Prince Jauna Khan, viz., Sultan Muhammad Tughluq. In 1494, during the minority of Mahmud Shah, the last scion of the Tughluq dynasty, the ruling *Junta* of Delhi, headed by Mallu Iqbal Khan, created a new fief or administrative division covering the territories from Kanauj to Bihar, and sent Malik Sarwar Khwaja, a Hindu convert to Islam and an eunuch, to administer it with the title of *Sultan ush Sharq* – 'lord of the east'. After Amir Timur's invasion of India, Malik Sarwar setup as autonomous ruler of Jaunpur but without assuming any royal titles. On his death in 1399, his adopted son and successor assumed the title of Sultan Mubarak Shah and laid the foundation of the Sharqi dynasty of Jaunpur. He died in 1402 and was succeeded by his younger brother, Ibrahim Shah (1402-36), the greatest ruler of this dynasty. He beautified the town with magnificent public buildings, parks, gardens and educational institutions for the teaching of Persian and Arabic languages; as a result, Jaunpur became a great centre of Islamic culture and learning and earned the title of 'Shiraz of India'. The rulers of Jaunpur had matrimonial relationships with the Sayyad Sultans of Delhi but had to fight a protracted war against the Lodhis to retain their precarious existence. Jaunpur was ultimately conquered by Bahlol Lodhi by defeating its last Sharqi ruler, Hussain Shah in 1479, and the latter died a fugitive in c.1500. Nevertheless, Bahlol Lodhi placed his eldest son, Barbak Khan, on the throne of Jaunpur and retained the separate identity of that kingdom in subordinate association with Delhi.

Tirhut (Mithila)

A small but compact Hindu state of Mithila or Videha of ancient times, referred to as Tirhut by the contemporary Muslim chroniclers, survived as 'the last free stronghold of Hinduism' in the vast stretch of land from the Khyber in the northwest to Sonargaon and Lakhnauti in the east, the whole of which was overrun and changed beyond recognition by the foreign Muslim conquerors in the early medieval period. In spite of the repeated Muslim onslaughts, accompanied by large-scale destruction and devastation, it re-emerged as an independent state by the beginning of the fourteenth century and was still in existence on the eve of Babar's invasions. The state of Mithila was bounded on the north by the Himalayas and three rivers—the Kosi, the Gandak, and the Ganga on the east, west and south respectively. Well-protected by its natural boundaries, the territories of Mithila were covered by thick jungles and *chows* or deep-bedded streams of rainy water in the midst of intervening low-lying hills with narrow passes, which were made almost inaccessible in the absence of public highways and modern means of communication. It served as a repository of ancient Indian civilization and culture for a very long time.

In 1097, a Hindu chieftain 'of the Karnataka origin', Nanyadeva, laid the foundations of a new dynasty in Mithila; his descendants were 'ruling over Tirhut when Muslim Turkish invaders swept over the whole of North India'. Hemmed in between the Muslim provinces of Oudh (Awadh) on one side and Lakhnauti (Bengal) on the other, Tirhut was not immune from their attacks but its rulers and their determined people fought desperately against the *Turushkas* and the *Mlechhas* to safeguard their political and socio-religious freedom. Ghiasuddin Iwaz Khilji, the governor of Bengal, after declaring his sovereignty, is said to have realized tribute from Tirhut, but, according to R.C. Majumdar, 'this vague claim is not supported by any actual invasion'. Similarly, another rebellious governor of Bengal, Izzuddin Tughril, who reportedly pillaged Awadh, also 'made an inroad into Tirhut and acquired much valuable booty, but no submission... Barring occasional raids and temporary occupation of parts, or even assertion of nominal suzerainty by some Sultans, Tirhut seems to have escaped the fury of Muslim attacks...though the principality lay on the way from Delhi or Awadh to Lakhnauti, the Muslim forces seem to have systematically avoided it...The rulers of Mithila maintained their independence, while every other Hindu principality in the Gangetic valley crashed beneath the heels of Turkish cavalry'.

Harisimha Deva, who ascended the throne in c. 1280, enjoyed a long reign of about 45 years. He was the greatest but the last ruler of the Karnata (Karnataka) dynasty of Mithila. According to the indigenous Sanskrit records, Chandesvara, the *Maha-sandhi-vigrahika* (Minister of War and Peace), of Harisimha, 'conquered Nepal for his master, and performed the great religious gift of *tula-purusha* (gift of gold of the donor's weight), in November 1314. In 1324-25, Harisimha suffered a defeat at the hands of Sultan Ghiasuddin Tughluq of Delhi and was compelled to retire into Nepal which had already acknowledged his suzerainty, but Tirhut did not fall to the Muslim forces. The throne of Tirhut was occupied by a new Brahmanical dynasty of the local kings; they acknowledged the nominal suzerainty of Delhi but threw off the imperial yoke in the concluding years of Muhammad Tughluq's reign once again. From 1353 to 1526, the rulers of this dynasty continued to ruler over Tirhut independently 'in an unbroken line of succession'. In the words of R/C. Majumdar,

> 'The survival of the small state of Tirhut, a tiny Hindu island in the Muslim ocean, must be regarded as an event of the highest importance from the point of view of medieval Hindu culture. It gave refuge to a number of Pundits and students, flying from the flames of foreign invasions that burnt up the neighbouring centres of learning. Sanskrit learning flourished under the patronage of the Hindu rulers in Mithila, such as it did nowhere else in Northern India during the seven hundred years that followed the establishment of the Delhi Sultanate. Mithila School was not only instrumental in preserving the old Sanskrit works and traditions, dealing particularly with laws and usages, but also contributed a great deal that was new, especially in the branch of *Nyaya*....during the period under review, Mithila produced famous scholars like Chandesvara Thakkura and Vachaspati Misra, whose names are even now remembered all over India. Thus the contribution of the small State of Tirhut or Mithila to the preservation and development of Hindu culture during the medieval age, exceeds far in importance, and gives a special value to the annals of its political history.' (*History and Culture of the Indian People*; BVB, vi, p.410).

Bengal

Bengal had been conquered by the Muslims at the very beginning of their rule in Delhi but its governors enjoyed considerable autonomy in the exercise of their powers. They recruited their own armies and were granted complete freedom by the Sultans of Delhi to wage wars of aggression against their neighbouring Hindu chiefs for the 'glory of Islam' and extension of their territories. In consequence, they usually behaved as *de facto* rulers of their charge and did not hesitate to defy the central authority as and when they found the opportunity. Their repeated revolts against Delhi ultimately led to the foundation of two independent Muslim states in Bengal during the reign of Muhammad bin Tughluq in 1338-39; one was headquartered at Sonargaon under Sultan Fakhruddin Mubarak Shah, and the other at Lakhnauti which was ruled by Haji Ilyas. After a brief struggle against his Bengali rival, Haji Ilyas overran Sonargaon also and emerged as the sovereign ruler of the united Bengal with title of Shamsuddin Ilyas Shah. Firoze Shah made two abortive attempts to bring Bengal into subjugation, and, instead, had to recognise its independence. The throne of Bengal changed many hands in its domestic conflicts but it always lay beyond the pale of the Sultans of Delhi. In 1493, Bengal was ruled over by Sultan Alauddin Hussain Shah when Sikander Lodhi made an unsuccessful attempt to conquer it, and ended, instead, by making a treaty of friendship with him on equal footing. At the time of Babar's invasions, Bengal was under the control of Sultan Nusrat Shah (1518-33), the son and successor of Hussain Shah, who was known to the invader as 'a capable and powerful ruler'.

Orissa

The ancient Hindu kingdom of Orissa (old Kalinga) spread along the seacoast from the delta of the Ganga to that of the Godavari and was separated from the mainland by the densely forested mountains and marshy land. One of its rulers, Ananta Varman Choda Ganga (c.1076-1148) is credited to have built the famous Jagannatha temple at Puri. During the Sultanate period, its rulers had to fight frequently against the Turkish invaders from Delhi and their governors in Bengal and Bihar to safeguard their independence. For a very long time, the Hindu state of Orissa served as a wedge between the Muslim rulers of Bengal and the Deccan, and exercised a check on the penetration of the Muslim arms from the side of Bengal and Bihar. On the eve of Babar's invasions on India, it was ruled over by Raja Prataparudra Deva (1497-1540).

Assam

The term Assam is derived from the Sanskrit word '*Asoma*', meaning peerless or unparalleled because of its natural beauty, although, according to some, it is a derivative of *Ahom*—a Hinduised Shan tribe of the northeast, which ruled over this region for about six hundred years before the establishment of the British rule. Nevertheless, in the beginning of the thirteenth century, the valley of Brahmaputra in Assam, known as Kamarupa in ancient times, had still preserved the old regime of the Brahman dynasty, whose ruler Bhaskar Varman was the feudatory of Maharaja Harsh Vardhana. Incidentally, the Sanskrit word *Kamarupa* also implies something of exquisite beauty and charm like *Kamadeva,* the legendary Hindu 'god of love and beauty'. Its western borders were, as usual, contiguous to those of Bengal though its eastern boundaries varied from time to time. At the extreme east of

Assam, in the upper Brahmaputra valley, the Hinduised Shan tribe, known as the Ahoms, had made their settlements. In between them, Assam had a number of other tribal principalities, including those of the Chutiyas and the Cacharis. In 1185, Kamarupa was ruled by king Vallabhdeva, whose descendants successfully repulsed the Muslim attacks from Bengal, beginning with that of Bakhtiyar Khilji in 1205. Towards the end of the thirteenth century, Durlabh Narayan was the king of Kamarupa with his capital at Ganpati on the Brahmaputra. Early in the fourteenth century, Shamsuddin Firoze of Bengal wrested the town of Sylhet and the district of Mymensingh from Kamarupa while the districts of Tippra and Chittagong fell to the Muslims in 1326-27. The kingdom of Kamarupa, though considerably reduced in size, maintained its precarious existence till the beginning of the fifteenth century when the Khens, a primitive Hinduised tribe of Assam, transplanted its old ruling dynasty, and shifted their capital to a new township, called Kamatapura or Kamata, situated to the southeast of Cooch Bihar. The last ruler of this dynasty was overthrown by Alauddin Husain Shah of Bengal in c. 1498, but Kamarupa, now known as Kamata, regained its independence from the Muslim rule under the leadership of Vishasimha of the Hinduised Koch tribe of Assam in 1515. Wedged in between the Ahoms in the east and the Muslim rulers of Bengal, it was gradually swallowed by its neighbours and seized to exist in 1539. Nevertheless, the major part of Assam, including the old kingdom of Kamarupa or Kamata, and eastern India continued to flourish under the Hindu regime of the Ahoms and stood as a bulwark against the inroads of the Muslims from Bengal for over six hundred years.

Malwa

On the eve of the Muslim invasions, the Malwa region of central India had a flourishing Hindu kingdom of the Parmar Rajputs with their headquarters at Ujjain. It suffered from repeated Arab and Turkish attacks from Sindh and Delhi respectively ever since their arrival in India and was finally conquered and annexed to the Sultanate by Alauddin Khilji in 1305. It remained a part of the Sultanate up to 1398 when its governor, Dilawar Khan Ghori, cut off his contacts with Delhi and asserted his independence with his capital at Dhar. The Ghori ruling family was replaced by the Khilji dynasty of Malwa by Mahmud Khan Khilji, an erstwhile minister of the state, in 1436. The Sultans of

Malwa, in their bid for the extension of their territories, were usually engaged in warfare against their neighbouring Hindu chiefs and the Muslim rulers of Gujarat and the Bahmani kingdom. The fourth ruler of this dynasty, Mahmud II, entered into a deadly conflict with the Sisodia Rajputs of Mewar and suffered many defeats at the hands of Rana Sangram Singh. Malwa was conquered by Bahadur Shah of Gujarat in 1531 and, thereafter, its separate entity came to an end.

Gujarat

Gujarat was conquered and annexed to Delhi by Alauddin Khilji in 1297. Its Muslim governors and the local Hindu princes made repeated attempts to throw off the imperial yoke of Delhi during the Tughluq period; and after Amir Timur's invasion, its governor, Zafar Khan - son of a Hindu convert to Islam, declared his independence by assuming the title of Sultan Muzaffar Shah in 1401. His son and successor, Ahmad Shah (1411-42), setup his headquarters at a new township, named after him as Ahmadabad. The sixth ruler of this dynasty, Mahmud Shah *alias* Baghera (1451-1511) was the greatest ruler of Gujarat though he failed to stop the Portuguese from establishing their factory at Diu during his reign. The eighth Muslim ruler of Gujarat, Bahadur Shah (1526-37), was a contemporary of Humayun, the son and successor of Babar on the throne of Delhi; he conquered Malwa from the hands of its local Muslim chief in 1531 but lost it to Humayun in 1536-37. He fought desperately against the Mughal emperor to maintain his hold over Gujarat but fell a victim to the treachery of the Portuguese, who drowned him in the Arabian Sea in February 1537; his successors, though considerably weakened, continued to have their precarious existence till Gujarat was conquered by Akbar in 1572.

Rajputana

The conquest of Rajputana and subjugation of Rajputs was by far the greatest military achievement of Alauddin Khilji. The fall of two most formidable Rajput strongholds, Ranthambhor (1299-1301) and Chittor (1303) was a signal for the other Rajput chiefs of the region to acknowledge the suzerainty of Delhi to save their hearths and homes, but they did not reconcile themselves to the loss of their freedom, and, before long, there started a counter-offensive against the Muslim armies of occupation. As a result, within two years of Alauddin's death, Chittor was liberated from the Muslim rule by the Sisodia clan of the Rajputs, who belonged to the junior branch of the Guhilas. It was followed by a general uprising of the Rajputs against Delhi which gave birth to many new Hindu states, of which the two premier states of Mewar and Marwar need a bit detailed treatment.

Mewar

The fort of Chittor was liberated by the Rajputs from the imperial yoke of Delhi under the leadership of Rana Hamir (Hammir), probably, a nephew of Rana Rattan Singh, in 1318; during his long reign of 46 years (1318-64), he revived the glory of ancient Mewar by his military exploits and maintained the sovereignty of his state in the teeth of opposition from Delhi. One of his successors, Rana Kumbha (1433-68) was a great warrior who transformed Mewar, a small but compact Rajput kingdom, into one of the most powerful and influential states of central India. It was he who built the famous *Kirtistambha* or *Vijayastambha*, viz., 'the Tower of Victory' of Chittor in 1448 in commemoration of his victory against the Sultan of Malwa. He beautified Chittor by the construction of public buildings, temples, parks and educational institutions. Rana Kumbha was a great scholar of Sanskrit and patron of education and learning. In the beginning of the sixteenth century, Rayamalla (Rai Mal) was the sovereign ruler of Mewar (1473-1509) with his headquarters at Chittor. It was his illustrious son and successor, Rana Sangram Singh *alias* Rana Sanga (1509-28), who challenged the establishment of Mughal rule at Delhi and died fighting against Babar in the battle of Khanua or Kanwaha in March 1527.

Marwar

The kingdom of Marwar was ruled by the Rathor Rajputs - the descendants of the Rashtrakutas; it acquired prominence during the reign of Rana Chunda (1394-1421). His successor Rana Jodha built a new fortified township, named after him as Jodhpur, which became the capital of Marwar. He enjoyed a long reign of fifty years (1438-88) which ushered in an era of peace and prosperity for his people. One of his enterprising sons, named Rana Bika, founded the township of Bikaner which became the capital; of yet another powerful state in Rajputana in due course of time. The Rajputs of Marwar had to fight a life and death struggle against the royal forces of Sher Shah Suri during the reign of Rana Maldeva (1532-62).

Khandesh

The *Iqta* or fief of Khandesh came into existence in the valley of the River Tapti with the extension of the Muslim arms into south India during the reign of Muhammad bin Tughluq; it was wedged in between the Vindhya and Satpura mountains in the north and the Deccan Plateau in the south while the province of Berar lay to its east and that of Gujarat to its west. Its governor, Malik Raja Farruki, broke all contacts with Delhi after the death of Firoze Tughluq, and his son and successor, Malik Nasir (1399-1438), extended his territories by the conquest of the famous fort of Asirgarh from its Hindu chief; but, soon afterwards, suffered a defeat at the hands of the Sultan of Gujarat and had to acknowledge his suzerainty. One of its chiefs, named Adil Shah II (1457-1501) was credited with the conquest of Gondwana also, but being wedged in between the powerful Muslim neighbours, Khandesh could never flourish as a sovereign state. The fort of Asirgarh was conquered and annexed to Delhi by Akbar in 1601.

Kashmir

The valley of Kashmir, because of its isolation from the plains, was not much influenced by the political upheavals in northern India. The Kashmiri Brahmins, the indigenous inhabitants of the valley, who comprised the bulk of its population, retained the sovereignty of their homeland till the fourteenth century. In spite of the frequent dynastic changes and internal feuds, they produced a number of powerful and capable rulers who foiled all attempts of the Muslim invaders to establish their foothold in Kashmir; Srinagar was their capital. In 1003, Samgramaraja laid the foundation of the first Lohara dynasty of Kashmir; he was the son of king Udayaraja of Lohara (Lohkot, mod. Lohrin in the territory of Poonch) and was related to the Hindu Shahi ruling family of Waihand. He extended support to Trilochanapala, the fugitive Hindu Shahi prince, against Mahmud Ghazni and, in return, invited the attention of the marauder. In 1015-16, Mahmud made an abortive attempt to carry fire and sword into the valley but his army lost the way in the hills, and suffered a huge loss of life in men and horses. In 1101, Prince Uchchala of Lohara, a scion of Samgramraja's uncle, founded the second Lohara dynasty in Kashmir. By this time, Afghanistan had been overrun, first by the Arabs and then by the Turks, and the Muslim adventurers had started trickling into Kashmir through Swat valley and northwestern mountain ranges but their territorial encroachments went un-noticed. The second

Lohara dynasty came to an end with the death of Raja Vantideva in 1172 but the valley of Kashmir did not face major threat from the Muslim intruders for another century and a quarter, and continued to enjoy sovereignty under its Brahmin rulers. The Kashmiri Pandits offered no resistance to the peaceful settlement of the *Mlechhas* (Muslim immigrants)—hill men or shepherds, whether *Tajikas, Turushkas*, or Afghans, in the sparsely populated mountainous tracts of the valley; and meted out a friendly treatment towards them without any religious or cultural prejudices. The Brahmin kings of Kashmir and even their local officers and regional feudal chieftains, in spite of the language barriers, did not hesitate in transacting business with them according to the old traditions of the pre-Muslim days; even some of the well-behaved and enterprising Muslim immigrants were recruited as mercenaries also.

The year 1286 constitutes a water-shed in the history of Kashmir when it faced a full-fledged invasion from the Muslim hordes (*Mlechhas*) through the Swat valley under the leadership of one Kajjala; Lakshmadeva, the Brahmin ruler of Srinagar, died fighting on the battlefield against them, and a part of the valley, including the metropolis, was sacked; it led to the outbreak of anarchy in Kashmir. A military general, called Simhadeva, ultimately took possession of the capital and restored a semblance of authority but lost his life as a result of court intrigues soon thereafter, and the valley was once again plunged into disorders and lawlessness. In 1301, we find Raja Suhadeva, a brother of the deceased king, at the helm of affairs in Kashmir. During his reign, the ruler of Kandahar, in the spirit of Mahmud Ghazni and Amir Timur, despatched a 60,000 strong army of Tatars, under the command of Dalju (Dulucha) for *Jihad* against the *Kafirs* of Kashmir. Suhadeva, attempted 'to induce the invader to retreat by paying a large amount of money', but in spite of having received incalculable wealth from the king and his subjects, the *Mlechhas* did not relent and took Srinagar by storm. On their approach, Suhadeva, like a coward, fled from the capital without a fight, leaving the inhabitants of the city at the mercy of the invaders. He retreated with his army and treasures into the inaccessible mountains but lost his life at the hands of some of his own dejected camp-followers in 1320. (D.C. Ganguly in *History and Culture of the Indian People*, BVB, v, p. 102). Srinagar was sacked, and, thereafter, the Muslim marauders spread themselves into the valley and carried out loot and plunder, destruction and devastation, and performed all sorts of vandalism to their heart's content.

For the first time, thousands of the Kashmiri men, women and children were carried away as slaves and sold like sheep and goats in the slave markets of central Asia.

Close upon the heels of the Muslim invasion, 'a Western Tibetan noble', Rinchana, descended upon the valley with a large army. Ramachandra, probably a blood-relation of the deceased king, gave him a battle in the vicinity of Srinagar and blocked his entry into the city but 'was treacherously murdered by his adversary'. Rinchana took possession of the town, lying in partial ruins, and assumed royal powers; he took the family of the deceased Brahman warrior, Ramchandra, under his protection and married his young daughter to strengthen his claim to the throne of Kashmir. He was not a Muslim, as erroneously made out by some of the writers, but a Buddhist by faith. According to Jonaraja, one of the associate authors of *Rajatarangini*, once he expressed his desire to embrace Brahmanism but the assembly of Kashmiri Pundits, led by Sri Devaswami, declined 'to initiate him in the *mantras* of Siva as he was a Bhotta'; they 'feared that the king was unworthy of such initiation, and did not favour him'. (Quoted by A.K. Majumdar in *Ibid.*, vi, p. 373). Jonaraja writes that Rinchana was a capable ruler who restored law and order in the valley and won the confidence of the hapless Kashmiris who had suffered a lot at the hands of the Muslim invaders.

Rinchana had recovered a part of the valley and the feudal chieftains of the outlying provinces had gradually started offering their allegiance to him but, unfortunately, he fell victim to a conspiracy, hatched by some of his own camp-followers, who had accompanied him from Tibet to Kashmir, out of mere jealousy. Though seriously wounded, he survived the attack of the assassins and was saved by the vigilance and timely action of a few Brahman attendants and a subordinate Muslim military officer of the old regime, named Shah Mir, referred to as Sahamera by Jonaraja. The Brahman nobles and the inhabitants of Srinagar at once rallied to the support of the king, and Shah Mir, though a *Mlechha* and an outsider, instantaneously rose into prominence as their leader and 'saviour'. (*Ibid.*, vi, pp. 373-75). The king 'took terrible vengeance on the traitors'. Apart from the culprits, many other Tibetan suspects were also hauled up with their families, and all of their male members were put to death; even their pregnant womenfolk were not spared. Shah Mir, apparently as the supporter and well-wisher of the king, played a prominent role in wiping out the powerful lobby of the Tibetan courtiers and military officers and emerged as the commander of royal forces and most trustworthy and reliable minister of the state.

As luck would have it, 'a wound, inflicted on the head of the king, was not completely healed, and he died, probably of its effect', on November 25, 1323. Rinchana left behind his widowed Brahmin queen Kotadevi and an infant son, who were formally placed by him under the protection and care of Shah Mir just before his death. Thus the latter, a foreign Muslim immigrant, suddenly found him at the helm of affairs as the regent and guardian of the infant prince and the youthful but widowed queen dowager. According to Jonaraja, Sahamera (Shah Mir) was a *Mlechha* adventurer, who had come from Swat to Kashmir along with some of the Afghan hill men and shepherds in Saka 1235 (1313 A.D.). He took up service under king Suhadeva as a mercenary trooper and raised a small contingent of his kinsmen who gave a good account of themselves as faithful servants of the crown When Rinchana took possession of Srinagar in 1320, Shah Mir readily joined his camp and rendered a great service to him in establishing his foothold in Srinagar. The decadent political condition of the valley and good fortune led to his meteoric rise to power, and within a decade of his association with the royal court, he stood head and shoulders above all the nobles of the state. But, with a handful of his Muslim mercenary troopers, with no social or political roots in the valley, and without a supporting lobby in the court, Shah Mir did not feel strong enough to usurp the royal powers in his new role as the guardian and regent of the infant son of the deceased king. Moreover, we have the reasons to believe that, being a Muslim, he could have no direct access to the Queen Dowager and her infant son all at once; Kotadevi belonged to the royal family of the Lohara dynasty, and the powerful lobby of the Kashmiri Brahmins, who were left with no political rivals at the court after the elimination of the Tibetan nobility, could never allow Shah Mir to mix up freely with the members of the royal household or establish his domination over them. That is why he humbly consented to the unanimous decision of the august assembly of the Kashmiri Pandits to offer the crown jointly to Kotadevi and Udayana, the leader of the Brahman nobility at Srinagar, who was also related to the royal family of the Lohara dynasty. After their coronation, King Udayanadeva and Kotadevi were united together in the wedlock to the great joy of the people of Kashmir.

According to Jonaraja, King Udayanadeva was 'a pious orthodox Hindu, who spent his time in bathing, penance and prayer, and gave all the golden ornaments in his treasury to God Vishnu. The king's administrative ability was not, however, equal to his piety, and the queen seems to have exercised the real power and authority'. (*Ibid.*, p. 374) Be as it may, in political terminology it implies that the new king took little interest in or was forced to keep himself away from the strenuous state affairs by his crafty prime minister and commander of the forces who played the role of a king-maker and *de facto* ruler; he cunningly concentrated all powers and functions of the state into his hands, apparently to take the administrative worries off the shoulders of the monarch though he kept the queen in good humour to win her favours. Thus the royal couple was reduced to the position of ceremonial heads of the state. Shah Mir gradually consolidated his position by creating a strong lobby of his supporters in the royal court, established direct contacts with the provincial governors, subordinate feudal chieftains and other high officers of the state, and earned reputation as capable administrator and well-wisher of the people.

King Udayana's reign lasted about fifteen years and Shah Mir got sufficient time to entrench himself deeply in the echelons of power at Srinagar. The king died in 1338 and, by that time, the Muslim Prime Minister had established his complete hold over the royal court, now bereft of all opposition to the exercise of his powers, and all the ministers and high officers of the state were his nominees or yes-men, none of whom dared to defy his authority. Besides, he held the supreme command of the state's army which now contained a large segment of the foreign Muslim immigrants. According to Jonaraja, Sahamera had 'further extended his position by matrimonial relations with powerful chiefs in Kashmir, his military abilities, and his possession of extensive territories including some strong forts'. (Ibid.,) We are not sure if some of the Kashmiri Pandits had established 'matrimonial relationships' with the Muslim dignitary or his family because, as yet, there was no scope of inter-religious marriages between Hindus and Muslims or large-scale conversions of Hindus to Islam in the valley. Of course, taking advantage of the weakness and adamant attitude of the Kashmiri Pandits, he might have coerced some of the Hindu *zamindars* and officials to give their daughters and sisters in marriage to Shah Mir and his kinsmen for free land-grants or promotions in civil and military services, and thus created a new class of the hybrid families, possessed of landed estates and in control of strategic hill forts and military posts.

According to Jonaraja, such being the case, on the death of King Udayana, 'the queen Kotadevi was placed in a great dilemma. Her elder son by Rinchana was under the influence of Sahamera, and the queen rightly feared that if he (viz., her elder son) became king, Sahamera would rule the kingdom through him. Her younger son by Udayana was a mere boy. Therefore, she kept the death of the king a secret for four days and then assumed the sovereign authority. Sahamera and other ministers obeyed her but the queen was afraid of this Muslim upstart and placed her chief confidence on Bhatta Bhikshana. This enraged Sahamera, and he treacherously murdered Bhikshana. Although Kotadevi displayed great ability in administering the affairs of the kingdom, she was no match for the wily Muslim'. (*Ibid.*, p. 374)

Jonaraja continues the narrative with the remarks that the queen 'was neither favourable to, nor angry with the powerful Sahamera'. In other words, she had estranged Sahamera but did not take adequate precaution against him. A.K. Majumdar sums up 'the inevitable result' of the queen's lapse as follows:

> 'Taking advantage of the absence of the queen, Sahamera seized the capital and besieged the fort of Kotta where the queen had taken shelter. He offered the queen to share the throne with him by becoming his wife, and she foolishly agreed. After spending one night with Kotadevi, Sahamera imprisoned her in the morning and then imprisoned her two children also. Sahamera thus became the undisputed master of Kashmir and founded a Muslim dynasty of rulers about 1339 A.D.' (*Ibid.*, pp. 374-75).

What was the fate of the hapless queen Kotadevi and her two sons from her previous husbands is not known. If she survived the shock and lived her third life as the queen of Shah Mir, now styled as Sultan Shamsuddin Shah of Kashmir, is only a matter of conjecture, because after having entered the royal *harem* and conversion to Islam, her public life was sealed behind the veil. May be she and her sons languished in the captivity of the usurper and breathed their last or were done to death after some time. The contemporary Muslim historians, including Nizamuddin and Firishta, summarily dispose of this episode with the remarks that 'Rinchana was an infidel' and that his widowed 'Queen Kota embraced Islam after she had married Shah Mir as the first Muslim Sultan of Kashmir'. Some of them do refer to the elder son of Kotadevi from Rinchana as Haider but it is a Muslim name and cannot be taken to be the original name of the incumbent according to the Buddhist or Hindu traditions; just possible, her elder son, who had been placed under the guardianship of Shah Mir by his dying father, might have been spared his life and converted to Islam.

One of Shamsuddin's grandsons, Sikander (Iskander) Shah (1394-1416), who enjoyed the epithet of *Butshikan*, viz., 'the Idol-breaker', like Mahmud of Ghazni, was the ruler of Kashmir at the time of Amir Timur's invasion of India. As narrated in the preceding pages of this study, he had formally acknowledged the suzerainty of Timur and actually commenced his march down the hills from Srinagar to offer personal submission to the invader at Jammu, but on hearing of the exorbitant demand for tribute through his envoys, returned to the valley without meeting him. Sikander Shah's son and successor, Ali Shah (1414-20) was deposed by his younger brother Shah Khan in June 1420; the latter ascended the throne with the title of Zainul Abidin who enjoyed a long reign of 49 years up to 1470 and earned a name for himself as the most enlightened and popular Muslim ruler of Kashmir. He adopted a policy of religious toleration towards the Hindus and engaged himself in the public welfare activities; he is known to the modern historians as the 'Akbar of Kashmir'. The valley suffered from a series of weak rulers thereafter and was plunged into political anarchy. It was conquered by Akbar in 1585.

The Himalayan Belt of Independent Hindu States

Besides Kashmir, Nepal, Bhutan and Sikkim were the other major centres of ancient Indian culture and civilization in the great Himalayan belt which flourished under the sovereign Hindu and Buddhist ruling dynasties throughout the ancient and medieval periods. Apart from these, the gigantic Himalayan ranges, including their northwestern and southeastern offshoots, from the Pamir Plateau to the Khasi, Garu and Jaintia hills, contained within their folds, habitable plateaus and beautiful valleys, such as Gilgit, Chitral, Ladakh, Jammu, Kulu, Kangra, Tehri Gharwal and Kumaon, called the Duns, in the north, and Arunachal Pradesh, Assam, Nagaland, Manipur, Meghalaya, Mizoram and Tripura in the northeast. Thickly populated and intensely cultivated, these were dotted with numerous big and small independent and autonomous Hindu states and principalities. Many of these states, particularly in the Shiwalik hills and the interior of modern Himachal Pradesh, were setup by the fugitive Rajput princes of the plains when northern India was under attack from the Turko-Afghan hordes of Mahmud Ghazni and Muhammad Ghori and their slave lieutenants. Some of them, lying in the northwestern India, like the Hindu Shahis of Waihand, Gakhars of the Salt Range,

Jammu and the Kangra valleys in the Shiwalik hills were overrun and subjugated by the Muslim invaders, and the historic Hindu temples, including that of Nagarkot (Kangra), were plundered and desecrated by Mahmud Ghazni, but many more of them retained their sovereignty in the teeth of opposition from the Muslim rulers of northern India Muhammad Tughluq's so-called Qarachil expedition to subjugate the hill chiefs of Kumaun-Garhwal region, in 1333-34, ended in smoke but it did not desist him from sending yet another expedition for the conquest of Nagarkot, which had been plundered by Mahmud earlier but never formed a part of the Sultanate of Delhi before.

Babar's Description of 'Hindustan'

Babar, the founder of the Mughal rule in India, was not a mere fighter and empire-builder; he was well-educated in Persian and Turki languages and used to maintain a diary in which he recorded the important events of his daily life. His career was full of adventures and his autobiography, entitled, *Tuzuk-i-Baburi, Waqiat-i-Baburi* or simply *Babarnama*, comprises the most authentic primary source of our information about his life and the history of his times. It throws a flood of light on the geographical, political, social and economic condition of India in the beginning of the sixteenth century. The conquest of Kabul in 1504 brought him close to the Indian borders, and kindled in his heart a desire to invade 'the land of infidels', but, unlike his ancestor Amir Timur, his object was not mere loot and plunder or 'the glory of Islam' but to bring it under his imperial control. He mentions in his diary, *inter alia*, as follows:

> 'As it was in my heart to possess *Hindustan*, and as these several countries...had once been held by the Turk, I pictured them as my own and was resolved to get them into my hands, whether peacefully or by force'. (Babar's Memoirs; Beveridge; p. 380).

Such being the aspirations of Babar to conquer *Hindustán*, it was but natural that he must have kept himself well-informed about the political developments which had been taking place in India ever since he became the king of Kabul. The un-protected Khyber Pass comprised a busy highway for the two-way flow of public traffic and the *caravans* of merchants, travellers and adventurers to and from India, without any obstruction on either side; therefore, Babar had ample means of apprising himself of the Indian topography, climate and the means of communication, cutting across the mighty rivers of the Punjab and the northern plains. He took his time to prepare himself for a long drawn out struggle to crush the military power of the Indian princes, Hindus as well as Muslims, and bring them under his subjugation on the basis of very authentic sources of information. Hence his exhaustive observations about the land and the people of his *El Dorado* and its socio-political condition, as reproduced below, were not only accurate but also very original and fascinating.

The Indian Landscape

Babar was overwhelmed by the vastness of the country and its beautiful landscape; he commences the description of *Hindustan* (the land of the Hindus) thus: 'The country of *Hindustan* is extensive, full of men, and full of produce. On the east, south and even on the west, it ends at its great enclosing ocean.' (*Ibid.*, p. 480). He writes with a sense of wonder and excitement that '*Hindustan* is of the first climate, the second climate, and the third climate; of the fourth climate it has none. It is a wonderful country. Compared with our countries, it is a different world; its mountains, rivers, jungles and deserts, its towns, the cultivated lands, its animals and plants; its peoples and their tongues, its rains, and its winds, are all different...Once the water of Sindh (the Indus River) is crossed, everything is in the *Hindustan* way – land, water, tree, rock, people and horde, opinion and custom'. Babar makes mention of the Himalayan Mountains 'on the north, which connect with those of *Hindu-kush* and *Kafiristan*.' He describes the geographical boundaries of the country as if he is eager to learn all about India like a school boy. He writes:

> 'The Range of Mountains, which in Kabul is known as *Hindu-kush*, comes from Kabul eastwards into *Hindustan*, with slight inclination to the south. The *Hindustan* are to the south of it. Tibet lies to the north of it....The Hindus call these mountains *Savalak-parbat*. In the Hindi language *sawalak* means one lac and a quarter; that is, 1,25,000 and *parbat* means a mountain, which makes 1,25,000 mountains. The snow on these mountains never lessens; it is seen white from many districts of Hind, as, for example, Lahore, Sirhind and Sambal'. (p. 485)

Babar writes with frankness that he knows nothing about the hill-men of India and expresses his desire to know more about them in the words that follow:

'After crossing the Sindh River eastward, there are countries in the northern mountains mentioned above, appertaining to Kashmir... Beyond Kashmir, there are countless peoples and hordes, *parganas* and cultivated lands, in the mountains. As far as Bengal, as far indeed as the shore of the great ocean (the Bay of Bengal), the peoples are without break. About this procession of men no one has been able to give authentic information in reply to our enquiries and investigations. So far people have been saying that they call these hill-men *Kas*. It has struck me that as a *Hindustani* pronounces *shin* as *sin* (i.e. *sh* as *s*), and Kashmir is the one respectable town (*sic.*) in these mountains, no other indeed being heard of, *Hindustanis* might pronounce it as Kas or Kashmiris. These people trade in musk-bags, saffron, lead and copper'. (*Ibid.*, pp. 484-85)

Rivers, Rains and the Climate

Babar had acquired adequate knowledge about the major Indian rivers of northern and central India which posed the greatest hurdle in crossing them in the course of travelling. He knew well about the River Sindh and its five major tributaries of the Punjab – Jhelum, Chenab, Ravi, Beas and Satluj, as also the River Ganga, Yamuna and their tributaries, but makes no mention of the rivers of southern peninsula or the River Brahmaputra. He was well aware of the material benefits of these rivers to the *Hindustanis* which were a 'a gift of the Himalaya"; he takes particular note of the fact that 'whereas, there are four seasons in those countries (of central Asia) there are three in *Hindustan*, namely, four months of summer, four months of the rains, and four those of winter'. Babar writes that during the rainy season, the Indian weather becomes very pleasant although it would be a great folly to undertake any military expedition into the country during this season.

After the conquest of Delhi and his settlement in India, Babar's knowledge of Indian geography increased manifold on the basis of his personal experience. According to him, 'sometimes it rains ten, fifteen or twenty times a day; torrents pour down all at once and rivers flow where no water had been. While it rains, and through the rains, the air is remarkably fine, not to be surpassed for the healthiness and charm'. His description of the defects of the rainy season, in his memoirs, makes a very interesting reading. He writes that during the rains 'the air becomes very soft and damp. A bow of those (Transoxianian) countries, after going through the rains in *Hindustán*, may not be drawn even; it is ruined; not only the bow, everything is affected—armour, book, cloth, and utensils all; a house even does not last long'. As a true lover of nature, Babar never feels tired of making repeated observations about the special peculiarities of the Indian weather in poetic rhythm. He writes *inter alia* as under:

> 'Not only in the rains, but also in the cold and the hot seasons, the airs are excellent; at these times, however, the north-west wind constantly gets up laden with dust and earth. It gets up in great strength every year in the heats, under the Bull and Twins when the rains are near; so strong and carrying so much dust and earth that there is no seeing one another. People call this wind, *andhi*, i.e. 'darkness of the sky'. (*Ibid.*, p. 520)

The Flora and Fauna

Babar was a great lover of nature, and he took keen interest in the description of the flora and fauna of Hindustán in his memoirs. He had an inborn passion for the objects of nature, like the animals and birds, gardens, trees and flowers, rivers and torrents, valleys and dense forests, lofty hills and snow-clad mountains and never felt tired of narrating their charms. 'To him India looked like a beautiful garden where multicoloured and sweet-smelling flowers grow through all the seasons of the year'. Of the fruits, Babar considered mango to be 'the best fruit of Hindustan'. Of its fauna, he was fascinated by the very sight of an elephant and he took keen interest in collecting the trained beasts as 'the trophies of war'; and a word about the sighting of a rhinoceros in the neighbourhood made him restless and he ran after the game even at the risk of his life. He gives a penportrait of the beast as follows:

> 'The rhinoceros is a large animal, equal in bulk to perhaps three buffaloes. The opinion current in those countries (of Transoxiana) that it can lift an elephant on its horn seems mistaken. It has a single horn on its nose, more than nine inches long...The hide of rhinoceros is very thick; an arrow shot from a stiff bow, drawn with full strength right up to the arm-pit, if it pierces at all, might penetrate four inches. From the sides of its fore and hind legs, folds hang which, from a distance, look like housings thrown over it. It resembles the horse more than it does any other animal... It is more ferocious than the elephant and cannot be made obedient and submissive. There are masses of it in the Parashawar (Peshawar) and Hashnagar jungles, so too between the Sindh River and the jungles of the Bhira (Bhera) country'.

Indian Society and Culture

In his early career, Babar had to fight a life and death struggle against his own Mongol and Turk kinsmen and the Muslim co-religionist political rivals; therefore, he did not suffer from the religious prejudice against the Hindus or non-Muslims (*Kafirs*) of Hindustán. Here he had to fight against the Hindus as well as the Muslims both and he did not bother to discriminate between them on religious grounds; for him, they were all *Hindustanis* or *Hindis* irrespective of whether they were Hindus or Muslims; 'perhaps, he did not observe any sharp socio-cultural difference between the two communities during his brief contact with the Indians. Be as it may, Babar did not find the Muslims of India to be superior to the Hindus of the day; he was rather deeply impressed by the intellectual attainments, industrial and administrative skills, and admirable socio-cultural traits of the Hindus. He writes:

> 'Most of the inhabitants of Hindustan are *Kafirs* (pagans); they call a *Kafir* a Hindu. Most Hindus believe in the transmigration of souls. All artisans, wage-earners, and officials are Hindus. In our countries, dwellers in the wilds (viz., the nomads) get tribal names; here the settled people of the cultivated lands in the villages get tribal (caste) names. Again, every artisan here follows the trade that has come down to him from forefather to forefather'. (*Ibid.*, p. 518)

Babar was deeply impressed by the scientific mode of reckoning the time and the classification of days into weeks, months and the year by the Hindus. He writes:

> 'The people of Hind divide the night-and-day into 60 parts, each called a *ghari* (watch in Persian is a *pas*). A watch and watchman (*pas-u-pasban*) had been heard about (by us) in those countries (Transoxiana) but without these details. Agreeing with the division into *pahrs*, a body of *gharials* (gangmen) is chosen and appointed in all big towns of Hindustán. They cast a broad brass-plate, perhaps as large as a tray and about two hands' thickness; this they call a *gharial* and hang it up in a high place. Also they have a vessel perforated at the bottom like an hour-cup and filling in one *ghari*. The *gharialis* put this into water and wait till it fills. For example, they put the perforated cup into water at day-break; when it fills the first time they strike the gang once with their mallets, when a second time twice, and so on ...' (*Ibid.*, pp. 516-17)

Babar was simply amazed to note the public consciousness about time and its value, and the universal mode of informing every citizen about it when they did not have the benefit of possessing the modern wrist watches. He is all praise for the Hindus who had learnt to classify the days into seven days' week, and the weeks into twelve months which constituted a year; he makes a specific mention of the Hindu nomenclature of the week days and months in his memoirs, and also explains the variations in their normal calendar when 'every three years', he elaborates, 'they add a month to the year; if one had been added to the rainy season, the next is added three years later to the winter months, the next, in the same way, to the hot months. This is their mode of intercalation (to harmonize it with the solar year)'. Similarly, Babar gives the tables of 'the well-arranged' weights and measures of the Hindus and speaks highly of their 'excellent mode of reckoning'. He writes:

> 'The Hindus call a sum of 100,000, a *lakh*; 100 *lakhs* a *crore*, 100 *crores*, an *arb*; 100 *arbs*, one *kharab*; 100 *kharabs*, one *neel*; 100 *neels*, one *padam*; and 100 *padams*, one *sang*'.

And, thereafter, he observes with bewilderment that 'the fixing of such high reckonings as these is proof of the great amount of wealth in Hindustán'. (*Ibid.*, p. 518). Nevertheless, under a special headline, 'defects of Hindustán', Babar takes note of some shortcomings in the socio-cultural life of the Indians. He writes *inter alia* as under:

> 'Hindustán is a country of few charms. Its people have no good looks; of social intercourse, paying and receiving visits there is none of genius and capacity none; of manners none; in handicraft and works there is no form or symmetry, method or quality. There are no good horses, no good dogs, no grapes, musk-melons or first-rate fruits, no ice or cold water, no good bread or cooked food in the *bazaars*, no hot-bath, no colleges, no candles, torches or candlesticks. In place of candle and torch they have a great dirty gang, they call lamp-men (*divatis*), who in the left hand hold a smallish wooden tripod to one corner of which a thing like the top of a candlestick is fixed, having a wick in it about as thick as the thumb. In the right hand they hold a gourd, through a narrow slit made in which oil is let trickle in a thin thread when the wick needs it. Great people keep a hundred or two of these lamp-men. This is the Hindustan substitute for lamp and candlesticks. If their rulers and *begs* have work at night needing candles these dirty lamp-men bring these lamps, go

close up and there stand. Except their large rivers and their standing waters, which flow in ravines or hollows, there are no running waters in their gardens or residences. These residences have no charm, air regularity or symmetry...Peasants and people of low standing go about naked. They tie on a thing called *lunguta*, a decency-clout which hangs two spans below the naval...Women also tie on a cloth (*lung*), one-half of which goes round the waist; the other is thrown over the head'. (*Ibid.*, pp. 518-19)

Babar's comments, though interesting, are deficient in many respects. It shows that, during the short span of his four years' rule in Delhi he did not get the opportunity to establish friendly contacts with the upper strata of the Indian society, including the Muslim ruling elite, Hindu businessmen and bankers, and educated and well-cultured caste Hindus. Lane-Poole makes a correct observation that Babar 'might have modified this sweeping condemnation of Indians if he had lived longer in the country and seen more of its people'. It must be said to his credit, however, that 'during his short stay in India, he had come to like this country *albeit* the Indians had as yet no reason to be happy about the establishment of the Mughal rule; even long after the death of Babar, the Mughals were dubbed as foreigners by the Indians, whether Hindus or Muslims, who fled their hearths and homes on the approach of the Mughal armies. That was one of the reasons why the Afghan chief, Sher Khan (later Sher Shah Suri) could muster public support in his conflict with Humayun.' (*Advanced Study*; ii, p. 111). Nevertheless, Babar is justified in complaining about the ugliness of the Indian towns and villages which were nothing more than cluster of houses, constructed without any regard to proper town-planning, the layout of streets and lanes and a suitable drainage system; the Indians seemed to have forgotten all about the grandeur of the Indus Valley culture of their remote ancestors. Babar records with disgust that 'the towns and country of Hindustán are greatly wanting in charm. Its towns and lands are all of one sort; there are no walls to the orchards, and most places are on the dead level plain. Under the monsoon-rains, the banks of some of its rivers and torrents are worn into deep channels, difficult and troublesome to pass through anywhere. In many parts of the plains, jungle grows, behind the good defence of which, the people of the *pargana* become stubbornly rebellious and pay no taxes'.(Ibid., p. 487) The following observations of Babar about the Indian habitats are particularly noteworthy:

> 'In Hindustán, hamlets and villages, towns indeed, are depopulated and setup in a moment. If the people of a large town, one inhabited for years even, flee from it; they do it in such a way that not a sign or trace of them remains in a day or a day and a half. On the other hand, if they fix their eyes on a place in which to settle, they need not dig water-courses or construct dams because their crops are all rain-grown, and as the population of Hindustán is unlimited, it swarms in. They make a tank or dig a well; they need not build houses or setup walls; *khas*-grass abounds, wood is unlimited; huts are made, and straightway there is a village or a town'. (*Ibid.*, pp. 487-88)

It reminds us of the unstable political condition of the times, resulting in near anarchy. Colonel Wilks draws a dreadful picture of the miserable plight from which the Indian masses had to suffer because of the absence of a strong and stable central government which could safeguard their lives and properties. He writes:

> 'On the approach of a hostile army, the unfortunate inhabitants of India bury underground their most cumbrous effects, and each individual, man, woman, and child above six years of age (the infants being carried by their mothers), with a load of grain proportioned to their strength, issue from their beloved homes and take the direction of a country (if such can be found), exempt from the miseries of war, sometimes of a strong fortress, but more generally of the most unfrequented hills and woods, where they prolong a miserable existence until the departure of the enemy, and if this should be protracted beyond the time for which they have provided food, a large portion necessarily dies of hunger'. (quoted by Beveridge in Babar's Memoirs, p. 488).

Indian Economy

Babar was deeply impressed by the vastness of India and its incalculable material wealth. He repeatedly makes mention of this fact in his autobiography that Hindustán is a very large country and that 'it has masses of gold and silver'. Of course, the Indian economy on the eve of Babar's invasions, as far as its agricultural and material wealth was concerned, was quite sound, and there was general economic prosperity. Agriculture, which constituted the backbone of the Indian economy, was fairly developed, and the land produced enough and to spare. Babar showed great interest in understanding the agricultural life of the Indian peasantry. In the later part of his memoirs, he gives a detailed account of the various methods employed by the Indian cultivators for irrigation to increase their production; he writes *inter alia* as follows:

> 'The greater part of the Hindustán country is situated on level land. Many though its towns and cultivated lands are, it nowhere has *running waters* (viz., irrigation canals). Even where, as for some towns, it is practicable to convey water by digging channels (*ariq*) this is not done ...To young trees, water is made to flow by means of buckets or a wheel (water pulley). They are given water constantly during two or three years, after which they need no more. Some vegetables are watered constantly. In Lahore, Dipalpur and those parts people water by means of a wheel. They make two circles of ropes; long enough to suit the depth of the well, fix strips of wood between them, and on these fasten pitchers. The ropes with the wood attached pitchers are put over the well-wheel. At one of the wheel-axles a second wheel is fixed, and close to it another one on an upright axle. This last wheel the bullock turns; its teeth catch in the teeth of the second, and thus the wheel with the pitchers is turned. A trough is set where the water empties from the pitchers and from this the water is conveyed everywhere.' (*Memoirs*; pp. 486-87).

Babar did not appreciate the method employed by the peasants of Agra, Chandwar and Bayana for irrigating their crops. He writes that they use 'buckets for this purpose which is a very laborious and filthy way'. (*Ibid.*, p. 487). Babar speaks highly of the Indian trade and commerce, which, according to him, was 'very well-developed' though the currency in circulation was scare because of 'low prices'. Babar writes with appreciation:

> 'Another good thing in Hindustan is that it has unnumbered and endless workmen of every kind. There is a fixed caste for every sort of work and for everything, which has done that work or that thing from father to son till now...680 men worked daily on my buildings in Agra and of Agra stone-cutters only; while 1491 stone-cutters worked daily on my buildings in Agra, Sikri, Dhaulpur, Gwalior and Koil. In the same way, there are numberless artisans and workmen of every sort in Hindustán.' (*Ibid.*, p. 320).

In the estimate of Babar, the revenues of the territories held by him in 1528, amounted to 52 *crores*, including eight or nine *crores* of the sum realised as tribute from the subordinate Hindu chiefs. According to Erskine (1854), the estimated revenues of Babar's dominions in India were 4,212,000 pounds sterling – 'a very large sum, when the working of the American mines had not yet produced its full weight'. (*History of India*; *op. cit.*, i, p. 542)

Political Condition

Unlike Mahmud of Ghazni or Amir Timur, Babar did not think of India merely to be 'a land of the infidels' to be overrun and sacked by 'the armies of Islam' or 'a treasure-trove' to dip his hands into it. He was an ambitious adventurer and empire builder who treated India as a land of fortunes and permanent settlement, if possible. After the first battle of Panipat and the occupation of Delhi, he wrote in his memoirs that

> 'From the date 910 A.H. (1504-5 A.D.), when the country of Kabul was conquered (by me), down to now (1526 A.D.), (my) desire for (the conquest of) Hindustán had been constant, but owing sometimes to the feeble counsels of *begs* (Mughal military officers), sometimes to the non-accompaniment of elder and younger brother, a move on Hindustán had not been practicable and its territories had been unsubdued. At length, no such obstacles were left; no *beg* great or small or of lower birth, could speak an opposing word'. (*Memoirs;*Beveridge, p. 478)

With such aspirations of Babar to conquer Hindustán, it was but natural that he must have kept himself well-posted with the political developments which had been taking place in India ever since he became the ruler of Kabul. His understanding of the prevalent political situation, the military resources of the various Hindu and Muslim states, and their points of strength and shortcomings, is really remarkable. As a mature politician, he writes that 'Dihli is held to be the capital of Hindustán. From the death (1206 A.D.) of Shihabuddin Ghuri (Muhammad Ghori) to the latter part of the reign of Sultan Firoze Shah Tughluq (d. 1388 A.D.) the greater part of Hindustán must have been under the rule of the Sultans of Dihli.' (*Ibid.*, pp. 480-81). Thereafter, he writes that 'at the time of my conquest of Hindustán, it was governed by five Mussalman and two *Kafir* (Hindu) rulers. These were the respected and independent rulers, but there were, in the hills and jungles, many *Rais* and *Rajas*, who held lesser esteem'. (*Ibid.*, p. 481)

The five prominent sovereign Muslim rulers of India, according to Babar, were Sultan Ibrahim Lodhi of Delhi, Sultan Muhammad

Muzaffar Shah II of Gujarat, the Bahmanids of the Deccan, Sultan Mahmud II of Malwa and Nusrat Shah of Bengal, while the King of Vijayanagar and Rana Sanga of Mewar headed the list of the most famous Hindu rulers. 'Babar's rating of these rulers was based on the latest intelligence received by him from his own agents as well as the Afghan citizens and the *caravans* of traders and businessmen, who had been frequently visiting Kabul on their way to and from India. He gives an apt description of the territorial jurisdictions and military prowess of each of his Indian counterparts, though only two of them actually came into conflict with him during his Indian campaigns.' (Advanced Study; ii, p. 115).

Babar records with appreciation that the most powerful of all the Indian rulers, including the Muslims and the *Kafirs*, was the king (Krishnadeva Rai: 1509-30) of Bijayanagar (Vijayanagar). He refers to his great military exploits, like the humbling of the pride of the *Kafir Raja* of Orissa as also the conquest of Raichur Doab by defeating Sultan Adil Shah of Bijapur. (*Memoirs*; p.483). Babar was fully aware of the valiant Rajputs and their prominent chief Rana Sanga, and, in his memoirs, repeatedly alludes to the military prowess of the Rana, who, according to the Mughal chief, 'had grown great by his own valour and sword.'

❑ ❑

11

FOUNDATION OF THE MUGHAL RULE IN INDIA

SECTION 1: WHEN THE MONGOLS TURNED MUGHALS

Ancestors of Babar

Zahiruddin Muhammad Babar, the founder of the Mughal rule in India, was connected by blood with the Mongols as well as the Turks – 'the two most barbaric and ferocious nomadic races of the Tatar or Tartar tribes', who once inhabited the vast steppes of northern Asia in the remote past. The Tatars comprised two major subdivisions – the Mongols and the Turks; and Babar claimed descent from Changez Khan (c. 1162-1227 A.D.) and Amir Timur (c. 1336-1405 A.D.)—the two great leaders and conquerors of the Mongols and the Turks respectively. He belonged to the fifth generation of Amir Timur's family from his father's side, and was thirteenth in descent from Changez Khan from the side of his mother.

Because of 'the global climatic changes', these nomadic tribes gradually descended down into the plains of Central Asia, preceded by the Turks, and the Mongols followed close upon their heels. According to the *Encyclopaedia of Islam* (London, 1913, p. 856) 'they were the people who, in the first half of the thirteenth century, shook the foundations of every kingdom from China to the Adriatic Sea in their campaigns'. The Mongols occupied chiefly the middle portion of Asia, north of the Gobi desert, now called Mongolia, and the Turks inhabited the Asian lands situated to the west of the Gobi desert which became known as Turkistan. They were not Muslims.

The Turks were, obviously, the first to enter into a deadly conflict with the Arabic protagonists of Islam after the latter's conversion to

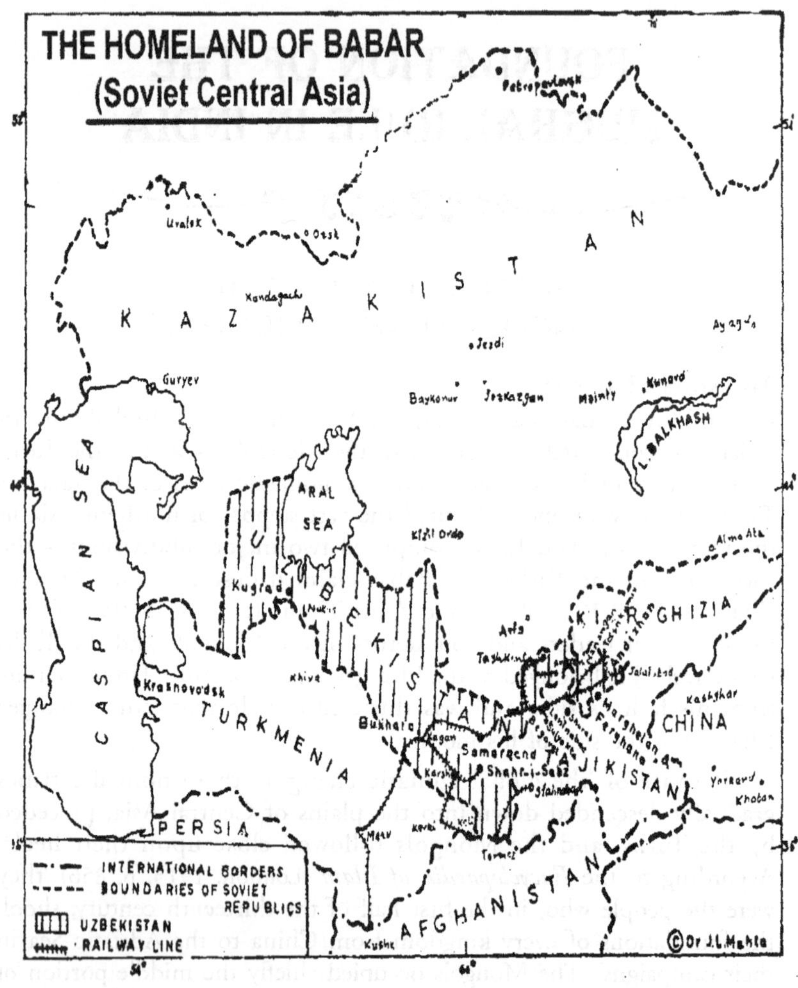
THE HOMELAND OF BABAR
(Soviet Central Asia)
KAZAKISTAN
CASPIAN SEA
ARAL SEA
UZBEKISTAN
TURKMENIA
KIRGHIZIA
TAJIKISTAN
CHINA
PERSIA
AFGHANISTAN
L. BALKHASH
Uralsk
Gurjev
Krasnovodsk
Khiva
Bukhara
Samarqand
Shahr-i-Sabz
Kashghar
Yarkand
Khotan
Termez
Kushk
INTERNATIONAL BORDERS
BOUNDARIES OF SOVIET REPUBLICS
UZBEKISTAN
RAILWAY LINE
©Dr J.L.Mehta

the new faith by the Prophet Muhammad (c.570-632 A.D.). Soon after the death of Muhammad, the Arabs invaded Turkistan as *Jihadis.* Hundreds and thousands of the Turks perished in their struggle against the Muslim fanatics; their hearths and homes were destroyed and innumerable men, women and children taken prisoners. They were enslaved, forcibly converted to Islam and sold like cattle in the markets of Central Asia. No wonder, it swelled the 'armies of Islam' to spread their aggressive campaigns for territorial aggrandizement and proselytization in the far-off lands, including India, now under the leadership of their newly emerged Turkish slave officers of the Arabs.

The Mongs or Mongols acquired the status of the ruling tribes with the emergence of Changez Khan as 'the empire-builder' in the thirteenth century. Like Turks, they were also not originally Muslims but professed a varied form of Buddhism, called *Shamanism*, which had spread in Central Asia since long. The word Mongol was changed into Moghul or Mughal when they came into contact with the Persian culture and entered the fold of Islam much later. They made their first appearance on the northwestern borders of India in 1220-21 during the reign of Iltutmish. Changez Khan was then engaged in a deadly struggle against his adversary, named Alauddin Muhammad –'the greatest Muslim monarch of the age'; the latter was defeated at the hands of Changez Khan and fled towards the Caspian Sea while his eldest son, Jalaluddin Mankbarni retreated into Afghanistan. The vanquished Muslim prince was followed in hot chase by his victor. At this critical juncture, Jalaluddin rushed through the Khyber Pass to take shelter in the Indus valley and sent an express appeal to Iltutmish, his co-religionist at Delhi, to fight against the Mongols. Nevertheless, as a shrewd politician, Iltutmish set aide the religious considerations, threw the emissary of Mankbarni into prison and refused to oblige the fugitive Muslim chief with the diplomatic reply that 'the climate of India would not be suitable for him'. At the same time, he hurriedly assembled his troops and prepared to fight against the intruder. Utterly disappointed, Mankbarni turned his attention towards Sindh, which was then under the control of Nasiruddin Qabacha, a Turkish 'slave officer' of Muhammad Ghori and adversary of Iltutmish, to the great relief of the Sultan of Delhi. Thus it was that Iltutmish saved his nascent Turkish kingdom of Delhi from the invasion of Changez Khan, who, after the retreat of Mankbarni towards Seistan and Iran, retraced his steps towards Central Asia to consolidate his hold there. Iltutmish was so much scared of the Mongols that he gave up the idea of conquering the western Punjab or Sindh and did not make any attempt to bring Qabacha under his control until after the death of Changez Khan in 1227.

The Sultanate of Delhi was somehow saved from the fury of Changez Khan but the spread of Mongol sway in Central Asia, Persia and Afghanistan rendered India vulnerable to their occasional onslaughts and created a permanent danger to the Sultanate. To begin with, the Mongols were dead enemies of the Muslims. Before starting their invasions on India, they had already overrun almost all the prominent Muslim states in central and western Asia. They carried destruction and devastation wherever they went and slaughtered the vanquished people like sheep and goats. Their appearance on the Indian frontiers, therefore, spread a wave of horror in the country; and it posed a serious threat to the infant Muslim state of Delhi. Halaku Khan, a grandson of Changez Khan, founded the ruling house of the Ilkhan Mongols in Persia, and their lieutenants invaded India off and on up to the period of the Sultan Jalauddin Khilji. By the time Alauddin Khilji ascended the throne, Deva Khan (1272-1306), the Chaghtai ruler of Transoxiana, had acquired a premier position among the other Mongol chiefs. He snatched Afghanistan from the Ilkhans and began to look forward towards India with greedy eyes.

The Mongol attacks on India started during the reign of Balban. He was, therefore, called upon to adopt stringent measures for the protection of the northwestern frontiers of his dominions against the Mongol menace. He deputed his cousin Sher Khan Sunqar, a brilliant military general and strategist, to hold charge of that region. On his death in 1270, the Crown Prince Muhammad became 'the warden of the marches' with general powers of supervision over the provinces of Lahore, Multan and Uchh. Balban created a second line of defence against the Mongols by placing the *iqtas* like those of Sirhind, Sunam, Samana and Dipalpur as special military posts under the overall charge of his second son Bughra Khan Moreover, ever since he was alerted about the presence of the Mongol hordes along the northwestern frontiers of India and Afghanistan, he preferred to stay put in Delhi and maintained a well-equipped and strong army of 30,000 horsemen at the capital for its defence. In spite of all these protective measures, the Mongols marched on the Punjab and ravaged large tracts of the region, including the towns of Lahore and Dipalpur, and Prince Muhammad died fighting against them in 1285-86. Of course, Balban's policy to tackle the Mongol menace was defensive in nature because the consolidation of a Muslim state in the heart of the Hindu-dominated country was his first priority.

The Khiljis had to face the repeated invasions of the Mongols. Jalaluddin, the founder of the Khilji dynasty, built his reputation, in his early life, as a great warrior who had fought many successful battles against them. He started as a junior military commander in northwestern India during the reign of Balban and, by the time of Kaiqubad (1287-90), had become the governor of Samana and warden of the marches to defend the capital of Delhi against the Mongol onslaughts. Soon after Jalaluddin ascended the throne, Abdulla, a grandson of Halaku Khan, invaded India at the head of 1,50,000 Mongols. They spread themselves all over the northwestern region and started loot and plunder. In spite of his old age, Jalaluddin moved swiftly from the capital and personally took the field against them. The Mongols were defeated in a number of engagements and compelled to retrace their steps towards Afghanistan. Thousands of the Mongols, who were taken prisoners, were brought to Delhi as captives and compelled to embrace Islam. Most of them did it and were allowed to settle down in the suburbs of the capital while those, who refused to do so, were murdered in cold blood. In order to win the loyalty and support of the converted Mongols, now called Mughals or New Mussalmans, the Sultan gave one of his daughters in marriage to their leader, Ulghu Khan – a descendant of Changez Khan, who was assigned a respectable position in the royal court. Jalaluddin's policy of dealing with the Mongol problem thus proved very successful.

When Alauddin Khilji ascended the throne, Deva Khan (1272-1306), the Chaghtai ruler of Transoxiana, organized as many as six expeditions against India, the detailed account of which has been given at its appropriate place in the preceding pages of this study. Here suffice it to say that all of these invasions were repulsed by Alauddin with an iron hand. He adopted Balban's policy of 'blood and iron' to tackle the Mongol menace and struck terror in their hearts by inflicting the most barbaric punishments on them. Shortly after Alauddin's accession to the throne, a vast horde of 100,000 Mongols, led by Kadar invaded the Punjab and advanced as far as the environs of Lahore. Ulugh Khan and Zafar Khan defeated them near Jalandhar and drove them back with heavy slaughter. Ulugh Khan, sent the report of his victory to the Sultan at Delhi together with the chopped off heads of thousands of them which raised the latter's prestige and helped him to secure the confidence and approval of the people of the capital after having usurped the throne by assassinating his own uncle Jalaluddin Khilji. In the year following, the whole army of Mongols, numbering above 50,000 and commanded by Saldi, which overran Sindh, was annihilated by Zafar Khan. The victorious Khilji general returned to Delhi with thousands of the Mongols as captives, who were enslaved and forcibly converted to Islam; those who refused to convert were put to the sword.

In their third invasion, about two hundred thousand Mongols under the command of Qutlugh Khwaja, son of Deva Khan, crossed the Indus in the winter of 1299 and made straight for Delhi without resorting to loot and plunder or engaging the Indian troops stationed at various strategic places in the Punjab. Nevertheless, they were defeated in a pitched battle, fought by Alauddin Khilji with them in the plain of Kili near Delhi and made to return with heavy losses. They were given hot chase while passing through the Punjab by the provincial forces of Lahore and Dipalpur, and thousands of them were put to the sword while their leader, Qutlugh Khwaja, was said to have been taken ill and died on his way back to Transoxiana. In February-March 1303, more than a hundred thousand Mongols, led by Targhi Beg, laid siege to Delhi and made an abortive attempt to conquer it for the second time. Alauddin, who had returned from Chittor barely a month ago, could not face the enemy in an open battle and was forced to stay put in the fort of Siri. Though the capital was heroically defended by the Sultan, the Mongols plundered the environs of Delhi and very often raided even the streets of Delhi. Being ignorant of 'the art of siege war', however, they failed to conquer the metropolis but returned after plundering and devastating large tracts of the adjoining Doab territories and the Ganga valley.

Thereafter, in the two subsequent invasions, the Mongols avoided Delhi and all the fortified posts of the region with the primary object of loot and plunder, and Alauddin also allowed them unchecked to penetrate into the interior of the Doab and the Ganga valley before they were encircled, herded together and annihilated. Alauddin did not encourage the large-scale conversion of Mongols to Islam because of their infidelity to the new faith and disloyalty to the Sultanate of Delhi. In the early years of his reign, the Mongol converts to Islam or the New Mussalmans, who had settled down in the colonies of Delhi and Lahore, called *Mughalpuras*, had put him to great trouble. A large number of them had been recruited by Alauddin in the royal army which was sent by him under Nusrat Khan and Ulugh Khan for the conquest of Gujarat in 1299. After the conquest of that province, when the victorious army, laden with rich spoils, was returning to the capital, the generals, according to the practice, demanded from the soldiers a fifth of the spoils as the state's share, and adopted harsh measures to extract the valuables hidden by the latter in their personal baggage. It was resisted by a few thousand defiant soldiers, mostly *New Mussalmans*. They revolted and killed a brother of Nusrat Khan and a nephew of the Sultan. The mutiny was crushed with an iron hand by the royal commanders but many of the rebels, including their ring-leaders escaped to the courts of the neighbouring Hindu chieftains. On the receipt of report at Delhi, the Sultan immediately ordered the wives and children of the rebels to be imprisoned. Even this did not pacify the enraged Nusrat Khan; on his return from Gujarat, he officiated as *wazir* (prime minister) for some time, and he utilized this opportunity to commit most inhuman atrocities on the families and relatives of the rebellious New Mussalmans. According to Barani, he handed over the wives of the mutineers to the scavengers of Delhi while their children were hacked to pieces in the presence of their mothers. It sent a wave of unrest among the entire community of Mongol converts to Islam in India, and their colonies, called Mughalpuras, at Delhi and Lahore, became the centres of conspiracies and intrigues against Alauddin Khilji and his government. Akat Khan, another nephew of the Sultan, who made an unsuccessful bid on the life of Alauddin Khilji in a hunting expedition at Tilpat during the siege of Ranthambhor in 1301, was also supported by a large body of the disgruntled soldiers, belonging to the community of the New Mussalmans. In consequence, the Mongol converts became *persona non-grata* among the ruling elite of Delhi, and they were dismissed *en mass* from the state services; a large number of them left India for their country and their colonies of Lahore and Delhi were completely destroyed. Babar, on his establishment at Delhi, after his victory at Panipat in 1526, did not receive even a single representative or spokesman of the Mongol converts to Islam or New Mussalmans who might have preceded his arrival in India.

Conversion of Mongols to Islam

One of the descendants of Chaghtai Khan was Tughluq Timur who became the *Grand Khan* of Mongolistan in 1324; it was he, who having fought many battles against the Muslim *Jihadis,* felt deeply concerned about their obsession for Islam and was impressed by their zeal for obtaining converts to this faith. Under the influence of some Muslim divines, therefore, he voluntarily embraced Islam along with thousands of his camp-followers in 1353, and spread this religion among his people. The Mongols secured many benefits there from. Firstly, their incessant warfare against the Turks, Arabs and Iranis (Persians)—the other three predominant races of Central Asia on the pretext of religious considerations alone came to an end, and it facilitated their reconciliation, particularly, with the Turks, who together belonged to the same Tatar tribal stock. Secondly, it reduced the destruction and devastation of their habitats and territorial possessions at the hands of the Turkish and other Muslim *Jihadis* on religious considerations and saved the lives of hundreds and thousands of the Mongols in their wars against them simply on the grounds that they were *Kafirs.* Thirdly, it secured them a place of respect and dignity for their community as political rivals to their Muslim adversaries of Central Asia by the elimination of the stigma of *Kufr* from their foreheads, and thus legitimatized their wars of aggression against the others. And, fourthly, they were known to be the most ferocious, aggressive, cruel and brutal war-mongers among the wild tribes of the world, and all these attributes became their positive assets after their conversion to Islam as these qualities enabled them not only to continue with their notorious habits of destruction and plunder, now in the name of religion, and facilitated the establishment of their predominance among the other aggressive Muslim racial communities. No wonder, they became the ruling race of the world and established their vast empires in Central Asia, China, India and wherever they went. The advent of Mughals in India under the leadership of Babar lay in the logic of history.

SECTION 2: BABAR'S INVASIONS ON INDIA

Early Life of Babar

Zahiruddin Muhammad Babar, the founder of the Mughal rule in India, was the son of Umar Sheikh Mirza and grandson of Sultan Abu S'aid Mirza—a descendant of Amir Timur, who had assumed the premier position among all the Turkish chiefs of Transoxiana with his headquarters at Samarqand. Umar Sheikh, being the fourth and the youngest son of Abu S'aid, held the governorship of a petty principality of Ferghana in Samarqand. Babar was born on 14 February 1483 at Andizhan, the capital of Ferghana. His mother, Qutlug Nigar Khanum, was a daughter of Yunus Khan—a descendant of Chaghtai Khan, who had became the *Grand Khan* of Mughlistan in c.1470. Umar Sheikh died in the prime of his life on 8 June 1494 through an accidental fall, and Babar, being the eldest of his three sons, acquired the parental heritage as the chief of Ferghana at the tender age of eleven. We are told by Babar about this 'strange event' in his *Memoirs* in an amusing style that his father was fond of pigeon-flying. One day, he climbed up the wooden pigeonry, raised close to the outer wall of the fort of Andizhan, and 'was feeding the birds when a strong wind blew; the wooden platform flew away and so did his father along with the pigeons and their house, and became falcon'; Umar Sheikh fell upon the rocks outside the walls of the fort and breathed his last.

Though a minor, Babar also inherited, along with Ferghana, the perpetual rivalry of his own uncles and cousins, who held positions of power all around him. Immediately after the death of Umar Sheikh Mirza, Babar's paternal uncle, Ahmad Mirza, the ruler of Samarqand and Bukhara, declared Ferghana annexed to his dominions and marched upon Andizhan to take possession of it but the Turkish begs of the state stood solidly behind Babar like a rock to safeguard the independence of Ferghana. At this critical juncture, Babar's maternal grand parents, Yunus Khan and his wife Aihsan Daulat Begam, in spite of their advanced age, came all the way from Mughlistan, to extend their support to Babar. In consequence, Ahmad Mirza had to retreat from Andizhan without a fight. It encouraged Babar to assume the reins of government directly in his own hands without the formal appointment of a council of regency, which enhanced his popularity and prestige as the young and energetic ruler of Ferghana. After the death of Ahmad Mirza, Babar aspired to conquer Samarqand, once the imperial capital of his ancestors. His first attack on it in July 1496 proved a failure, but he marched upon Samarqand for the second time in early 1497, now with full military support from his maternal kinsmen, and after a siege of seven months took possession of it in November. Nevertheless, Babar was not destined to hold Samarqand for long. After a 'hundred days' rule' there, he fell ill, which triggered off a revolt in Ferghana. It compelled Babar to return to Ferghana with the bulk of his army, but before he reached there, the capital of Andizhan had fallen into the hands of the rebels. Babar returned to Samarqand for reinforcements but found to his dismay that it had also slipped out of his hands. 'For the sake of Andizhan', writes Babar, 'I had lost Samarqand, and found that I had lost the one without preserving the other'.

Having lost Andizhan and Samarqand both, Babar became a homeless exile who held only a small tract of land in Khojend where his army was encamped. Babar describes his helpless condition in his *Memoirs* thus:

> 'It was very hard and vexing to me; for why? Never since I had ruled, I was cut off like this from my retainers and my country. Never since I had known myself, had I known such annoyance and such hardship...It came very hard on me; and I could not help crying a good deal'. (*Memoirs*, Beveridge, pp. 90-91)

Nevertheless, Babar was not disheartened. After taking stock of the situation for a couple of days, he was again on the march towards Andizhan, and, by the month of June 1499, had recovered it from the hands of the rebels. To his misfortune, however, his own selfish Turkish kinsmen of the Chaghtai clan were divided in their loyalties towards different contenders for power, and he was constrained to make an exit from the town in early 1500 to save his own life. Undaunted, he retraced his steps towards Samarqand which had since fallen into the hands of Shaibani Khan Uzbeg, the rival of Chaghtai Turks. He at once entered into secret contacts with his vanquished kinsmen of the town, and, with their assistance, expelled the Uzbek chief from Samarqand.

Babar was not destined to stay at Samarqand for long, however, as Shaibani Khan returned from his wanderings with a massive Uzbek following and inflicted a crushing defeat on him in the historic battle of *Sar-i-Pul* (bridgehead), in 1502, and compelled him to flee from Samarqand after eight months. Babar recalls with dismay in his diary that on that unlucky day of the battle, when the darkness began to fall and defeat stared him in the face, his Mughal troopers, 'instead of fighting, betook themselves to dismounting and plundering' their own companions. Babar saved his life by hurriedly crossing the river Kohik with a handful of his faithful bodyguards. His mother and two wives escaped with him, but, in the confusion that followed, one of his sisters fell into the hands of the enemy, and later entered the *harem* of Shaibani Khan Uzbeg.

Babar spent the next three years as a fugitive. After wandering about hither and thither in Transoxiana for sometime, he bade good-bye to his homeland in 1504, and accompanied by a handful of the followers, set out for Afghanistan where the political situation was said to be quite fluid because of the unchecked inflow of the foreign Muslim adventurers including the Mughals. Always haunted by his real or potential foes, he avoided the fortified towns and thickly populated habitats, and advised his followers to travel in small groups, usually through the uninhabited hilly tracts and barren lands to avoid the suspicions of the people. Nevertheless, it was the strong willpower and the inborn 'princely instinct' which kept the flame of ambition and hope burning in the heart of Babar. The hardships of life had made a poet of him who once expressed his sentiments in the following couplet:

'What though the field is lost, all is not lost –

The unconquerable will and the courage never to submit or yield.'

It was during these wanderings that Babar came to know of India and its fabulous wealth for the first time. While staying with the headman of a village, called Dikhit (Transoxiana) in 1503, he heard an eye-witness account of Timur's invasion of India from the 111 years old grandfather of his host. He was thrilled to hear that story and makes a mention of it in his *Memoirs* (*Ibid.*, pp. 149-50)

Babar as King of Kabul (1504 A.D.)

The Turks had held their sway in Afghanistan since the days of Amir Timur. About the turn of the century, the territories of Kabul and Ghazni were ruled by a paternal uncle of Babar, Ulugh Beg, but, after his death in 1501, the throne of Kabul was wrested from the Chaghtai Turks by an Arghun chief, Muhammad Muqim. He was, however, unable to bring the rebellious chiefs of the country under his control and disorder prevailed everywhere. Taking advantage of the situation, Babar sneaked into the town of Kabul with about 400 men in small groups apparently as migrants. One dark night, he made a surprise attack on the fort of Kabul and took possession of it under very dramatic circumstances. Most of the Chaghtai Turks and followers of his deceased uncle readily rallied to his support and almost overnight he became a king of Kabul. The town of Ghazni passed under his control soon thereafter, and with it Babar's days of wanderings were over. He consolidated his hold over the country and won the confidence of his subjects by efficient administration. In 1507, he assumed the title of *Badshah* (emperor). Next year he was blessed by the birth of his first son, Humayun, from his third wife Maham Begam. In October 1511, Babar recovered Samarqand once again in collaboration with the Persians but he was expelled from there by a nephew of Shaibani Khan Uzbeg within a year. It was after having lost all hopes of the recovery of Samarqand that Babar began to think seriously about seeking new pastures on the Indian soil.

Indian Invasions

Ever since his occupation of Kabul, Babar had been contemplating to invade India though sometimes 'from the misconduct' of his *amirs* and sometimes 'from the opposition' of his brothers, he was prevented from undertaking this venture. He writes in the *Memoirs* that 'as it was in my heart to possess Hindustán, and as these several countries... had once been held by the Turk, I pictured them as my own and was resolved to get them into my hands, whether peacefully or by force'. Because of his preoccupations elsewhere, however, he could not give it a practical shape for long. He utilized this period for collecting information through people and caravan leaders, travelling between Afghanistan and India for trade and commerce, and was well-acquainted with the topography, climatic variations and political condition of Hindustan.

Babar launched his first expedition to India in January 1519 to suppress the turbulent Yusafzai tribesmen along the Indo-Afghan border ranges. Finding the Khyber Pass undefended, he ventured to pass through it and took possession of the first fortified town of Bajaur after a brief but bloody encounter in which at least 3,000 Indian defenders lost their lives. Proceeding further, he overran Bhera on the bank of the river Jhelum without much resistance. He records that he meted out a very generous treatment towards the citizens of Bhera and issued orders to his soldiers ' not to hurt or do harm to the flocks and herds of these people, nor even to their cotton-heads and broken needles'. Some of his soldiers, who were reported to have misbehaved towards the Indians, were put to the sword. Babar halted at Bhera to feel the pulse of the Indian-powers-that-be and familiarize his soldiers with the topography and socio-political environment of their new ventures. From Bhera, he sent his envoy with two letters, one for Sultan Ibrahim Lodhi of Delhi and the other for Daulat Khan Lodhi, the governor of Lahore, demanding that 'the countries, which of old had depended on the Turk', should be handed over to him. Babar's envoy was detained by Daulat Khan at Lahore and he never returned to report the outcome to his master. After waiting for a couple of months he returned to Kabul with the Khyber Pass firmly under his control.

After the rainy season, in September 1519, we find Babar on the Khyber once again ready for his second expedition. To his delight, there was none to challenge him on the Indian side. After subjugating the Khizr-khail Afghans, he took possession of Peshawar and converted it into a base camp for the onward march. He took full four months in consolidating his hold over the north-west frontier between the Khyber Pass and the Jhelum before his return to Kabul in January 1520 on hearing of an uprising in Badakhshan. Revolt in Badakhshan having been crushed, Babar marched upon India for the third time in September-October 1520. Peshawar had been held firmly by his troops. Passing through Bajaur and Bhera, he overran Sialkot without much difficulty. The inhabitants of Sayyadpur (Eminabad) put up resistance but were mercilessly crushed. Babar returned from there on hearing of a revolt in Kandahar.

Fourth Invasion (1524 A.D.)

Babar took about two years in settling the affairs of Kandahar to his full satisfaction. He had now made up his mind to conquer Lahore and Delhi. Hitherto Daulat Khan Lodhi had pretended to be totally indifferent towards Babar's expeditions. But on hearing of his preparations for a full-fledged invasion on India, he hastened to send his son Dilawar Khan to Kabul to formally invite Babar for the conquest of Delhi. Daulat Khan offered his services to Babar for the overthrow of Ibrahim Lodhi with the hope that the Mughal chief, after taking possession of Delhi, would permit him to retain the Punjab as his vassal. According to Ahmad Yadgar, Alam Khan Lodhi, a self-seeking uncle of Ibrahim Lodhi, and the governor of Dipalpur, is also said to have reached Kabul with 8,000 soldiers to seek his help in securing the throne of Delhi in return for the surrender of the Punjab to the invader. Babar must have been amused to know the mutually contradictory motives of the selfish Afghan nobles who were ready to betray their own master and kinsman, the Sultan of Delhi. Nevertheless, he gave no help to either of the Afghan nobles and, instead, directed them to proceed ahead and challenge Ibrahim Lodhi to pave the way for his onward march.

Babar commenced his fourth invasion as per his own pre-conceived plan. After taking possession of the northwestern territories, he overran the towns of Sialkot and Sayyadpur, and was preparing to march on Lahore with confidence when he heard the news that Daulat Khan had already been defeated by the royal army of Ibrahim Lodhi and retreated into the interior of the southwestern Punjab with his main army almost intact. The fort of Lahore was defended only by a small garrison of 5,000 soldiers, left behind by Daulat Khan. After a feeble resistance, they surrendered to Babar but it annoyed the latter and he inflicted a severe punishment on them. On hearing of the Mughal occupation of Lahore, Ibrahim's army hurriedly retreated towards Delhi. It encouraged Babar to proceed from Lahore towards Delhi. He conquered the military posts of Dipalpur, Jalandhar and Sultanpur Lodhi. Daulat Khan came to pay his respects to Babar at Dipalpur along with his two sons, Ghazi Khan and Dilawar Khan, 'apparently as a fugitive'. Babar received them well but, instead of recognizing Daulat Khan as the governor of the Punjab, offered him the charge of Jalandhar and Sultanpur Lodhi as reward of his services, and entrusted the fief of Dipalpur to Alam Khan Lodhi. Daulat Khan felt insulted, and tried to make a fool of the invader by advising him to divide his army into two parts, one to proceed towards Delhi through Panipat, and the other via Hissar and Rohtak. According to Erskine, Babar had nearly fallen into his trap when' he was secretly warned by Dilawar Khan against his father's advice as he had done so with 'the treacherous intentions of dividing his army'. It incensed Babar so much that he at once ordered the imprisonment of Daulat Khan. He was reprimanded by Babar for betrayal but pardoned and released on the profession of loyalty to him. Babar now asked Daulat Khan to take charge of Jalandhar while Dilawar Khan was entrusted the governorship of Sultanpur Lodhi. Daulat Khan took leave of Babar but, instead of proceeding towards Jalandhar, fled towards the Shiwalik hills with the whole of his army. In desperation, Babar handed over both the districts of Jalandhar and Sultanpur Lodhi to Dilawar Khan, and gave up the idea of attacking Delhi. Alam Khan was re-confirmed in the governorship of Dipalpur. Babar stationed small contingents of Mughal troops at Lahore and Sialkot and thought it prudent to retrace his steps towards Kabul to make better preparations for reckoning with the treacherous Afghan nobles of the Punjab and the conquest of Delhi.

Soon after Babar's return, Daulat Khan re-emerged from the hills and overran all the three military posts of Jalandhar, Sultanpur Lodhi and Dipalpur; Dilawar Khan patched up with his father and Alam Khan Lodhi fled to Kabul to join Babar's camp. In the face of Daulat Khan's advance, the Mughal garrisons of Lahore and Sialkot retreated towards Peshawar and the whole of the Punjab once again passed under the control of Daulat Khan. Babar could not trust any of the Afghan nobles of the Punjab.

The Fifth Invasion (November 1525)

Babar had now made up his mind to conquer Delhi by all means. He organised his fifth and the last invasion to India in November 1525. He reached Peshawar with twelve thousand fresh troops on December 10 to find his officers and strong concentration of his armed forces there fully prepared for the onward march. Humayun had already reached there with his contingents from Badakhshan. Next day, while their armies were ferrying across the Indus, Babar and Humayun led a hunting expedition 'downstream', and killed three rhinos; the young prince, who had seen rhinos for the first time in his life was thrilled with the game.

An army sent by Ibrahim Lodhi to chastise Daulat Khan was defeated and repulsed by him but, on the approach of Babar near Lahore, he and his sons retreated towards Malout in the district Hoshiarpur. Babar gave them a hot chase and they were besieged in the fort. Dilawar Khan escaped but Daulat Khan offered submission, still making pretensions of friendship. The Mughal chief was not to be taken in, however. After reprimanding Daulat Khan for his repeated perfidy, Babar sent him in chains to Bhera but he died on the way. Nothing was known about the sons of Daulat Khan after the debacle of Malout; Alam Khan stood by Babar till after the first battle of Panipat, but, thereafter, he also deserted him and took shelter with the ruler of Gujarat. Most of the soldiers and officers of Daulat Khan readily joined the ranks of Babar and were confirmed in their positions. They rendered a great service to Babar in the conquest of Delhi. Having got rid of the selfish Afghan nobles of the Punjab, Babar marched upon Delhi via Sirhind with full confidence. He halted at Sirhind for several days, from where he sent small parties of scouts to collect intelligence about the whereabouts of Ibrahim's camp. There he started receiving the agents of many other disaffected nobles of Ibrahim's court with messages of support. Babar is also said to have received an envoy from Rana Sanga of Mewar with the invitation for a joint invasion of Delhi for the overthrow of Ibrahim Lodhi but nothing came out of it. In order to divert the attention of Babar, Ibrahim Lodhi ordered Hamid Khan, the *faujdar* of Hissar-Firoza to intercept the invader but an advance guard of the Mughals, led by Humayun, defeated him on February 26, 1526. Simultaneously, a cavalry division, sent by Ibrahim towards Panipat, was routed by Babar's men. It was a signal for Babar to prepare for the final confrontation. He ordered the march of his forces almost in battle array towards Delhi.

The First Battle of Panipat (April 21, 1526)

At Shahabad Markanda, Babar came to know that Ibrahim Lodhi had marched out of Delhi at the head of a hundred thousand men-in-arms and a thousand war elephants, and had started movement by measured paces towards the Mughal camp. Babar also moved forward slowly but steadily while the foraging parties of his horsemen spread themselves in the countryside for collection of fodder and food. Ultimately, he selected the vast span of level ground, covered with herbs and shrubs, between Panipat and the river Jamuna, as the battlefield, and ordered the entrenchment of his forces. In those days, the river Jamuna used to flow at a distance of about four or five kilometres from the town of Panipat. Babar had with him at least 25,000 fighters, mostly cavalrymen, on the eve of the battle, and he got full one week at Panipat, from April 12 to 19, to arrange his forces in battle formations. He gives a graphic account of his fighting technique at Panipat and the historic battle in his Memoirs (Beveridge, pp. 272-74) which made him the king of Delhi. He personally commanded the centre (*ghul*), which was protected by a long line of mutually chained 700 wheeled carts, previously used by his army for the transport of their baggage. Babar's artillery was commanded by two famous gunners of central Asia- Ustad Ali-quli and Mustafa. He had fourteen pieces of heavy field-guns, which were carried on wooden gun-carriages in pairs; they were installed in front of the centre, just behind the chain of carts. In between the sets of carts, he left sufficient space for his horsemen to charge the foe. Interestingly, the vast space in front of his formations had been levelled and cleared of all obstacles by the felling of the trees and the shrubs to allow the forward movement of his cavalry in the thickest of the battle. The right wing of the Mughal army, commanded by Humayun and Khwaja Kalan, was hidden behind the town of Panipat while the left wing, under the charge of Muhammad Sultan Mirza and Mahdi Khwaja, was posted in the dry bed of the river. A very special feature of Babar's formations was the posting of flanking parties of mobile cavalry beyond the right and left wings, intended to wheel round the enemy's camp and to hit his soldiers on the right, left as well as the rear to create confusion among them. Behind the battle-lines, Babar had kept a strong body of the reserves under the charge of Abdul Aziz, the Master of the Horse. On the other hand, Ibrahim's vast and unwieldy army was divided into four traditional divisions, the advance guard, the centre, the right wing and the left wing, and there were no reserves. Ibrahim was supported by his ally Raja Bikramajit of Gwalior at the battle of Panipat. The historic battle is described by Babar, *inter alia*, as under:

> 'When the incitement to battle had come, the Sun had risen spear-high....From the time that Sultan Ibrahim's blackness (mass of his troops) first appeared, he moved swiftly, straight for us, without a check, until he saw the dark mass of our men, when he pulled up and, observing our formation and array, made as if asking: "To stand or not? To advance or not?" They could not stand, nor could they make their former swift advance'.

After giving details of the battle bit by bit, Babar concludes:

> 'Till mid-day, fighting had been in full force; noon passed, the foe was crushed in defeat; our friends rejoicing and gay. By God's mercy and kindness, the difficult affair was made easy for us. In half a day that armed mass was laid upon the earth.'

On the fall of Ibrahim Lodhi, his army broke up in flight; and the victorious Mughals pursued the fleeing soldiers relentlessly up to the very gates of Delhi; hundreds and thousands of them were slaughtered before the nightfall. According to Babar, about fifteen to sixteen thousand of Ibrahim's soldiers died on the battlefield while many more of them fell as fugitives; Raja Bikramajit died fighting in the battle. Babar writes that 'it came to be known later in Agra from the statements of Hindustanis that 40 to 50 thousand Indian soldiers had perished at Panipat.' It is generally held that the first battle of Panipat was fought on April 21, 1526; but, the Persian manuscript of *Tuzuk-i-Baburi*, used by Mrs. A S Beveridge for its translation into English, specifically carries the date as Friday, the eighth of Rajab, which falls on April 20, 1526. (*Ibid.*, p. 472).

Occupation of Delhi and Agra

Just after the battle, when his troopers were in hot pursuit of the fugitives, Babar ordered Mahdi Khwaja and his party to rush towards the capital 'and keep watch on the treasures', while Humayun was asked to proceed towards Agra without any loss of time. On April 27, Babar was accorded a grand reception by the citizens of Delhi when *Khutba* was read in his name as the Emperor of Hindustan. Meanwhile Humayun had taken possession of the Agra fort and Babar was received there in the royal palace of Ibrahim Lodhi on the 10th of May. Among the rich treasures, presented by Humayun to his father, was included the famous *Koh-i-Noor* diamond, which he had received from the family

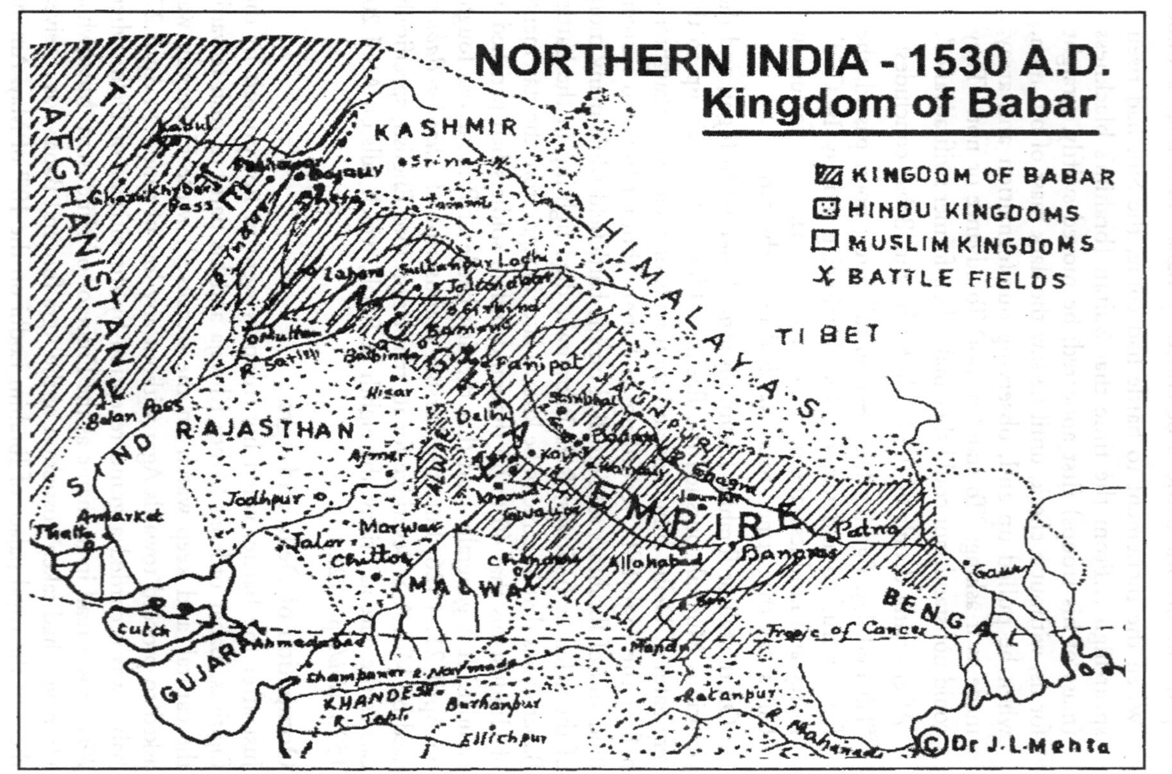
NORTHERN INDIA - 1530 A.D.
Kingdom of Babar
KINGDOM OF BABAR
HINDU KINGDOMS
MUSLIM KINGDOMS
BATTLE FIELDS
TIBET
HIMALAYAS
KASHMIR
AFGHANISTAN
Kabul
Khyber Pass
Lahore
Sultanpur Lodhi
Multan
R. Satluj
Hisar
Panipat
Bolan Pass
SIND
RAJASTHAN
Ajmer
Jodhpur
Delhi
Sambhal
Agra
EMPIRE
Gwalior
Marwar
Jalor
Chittor
MALWA
Allahabad
Banaras
Patna
Gaur
BENGAL
Tropic of Cancer
Cutch
GUJARAT
Ahmedabad
Champaner
R. Narmada
KHANDESH
R. Tapti
Burhanpur
Ellichpur
Ratanpur
R. Mahanadi
© Dr J.L. Mehta

of the deceased Raja Bikramajit of Gwalior in gratitude for his chivalrous protection. . To quote Stanley Lane-Poole,

> 'The spoil of the royal treasuries at Delhi and Agra was immense, and the first business was to divide the booty among the expectant troops. To his eldest son Humayun, who had played his part like a man in the great battle, he gave seventy *lacs* of *dams*, i.e. about 20,000 pounds sterling) and a treasure which no one had counted. His chief begs were rewarded with six to ten *lacs* apiece. Every man who had fought received his share, and even the traders and camp-followers were remembered in the general bounty. Every man and woman, slave and free, young and old, in Kabul, was sent a silver coin in celebration of the victory. When Humayun brought his father the glorious diamond, one of the famous historical jewels, valued at *'half the daily expenses of the world'*... Babar gave it back to the young prince as a reward'. (*Medieval India*, pp. 203-4)

Babar accorded royal protection to the family of Ibrahim Lodhi but his mother, out of jealousy, administered poison to him in his meals through the connivance of her cooks. Babar 'vomited but was saved by the timely treatment and good fortune'. The culprits were apprehended; they admitted their crime and were inflicted capital punishments, while Ibrahim's mother was kept in prison till her death.

Significance of the Battle

The battle of Panipat proved to be one of the most decisive battles of medieval Indian history. It put an end to the Lodhi dynasty and gave a crushing blow to the degenerate Turko-Afghan polity of the Sultanate period. It led to the foundation of the Mughal rule in India whose monarchs gradually shed the foreign outlook and gave birth to a new socio-cultural pattern of the Indian society based on mutual cooperation and harmony between the Hindus and Muslims. The Mughals like the Turks were foreign conquerors but Akbar transformed his ruling dynasty into a national monarchy and laid the foundation of a secular nation-state in India. Incidentally, the battle of Panipat added to the political and military importance of Panipat which made it the venue of two more such decisive battles of Indian history in the times to come. According to Badaoni, the town of Panipat became notorious as a haunted and ' uncanny spot which no man dared to pass after dark' He writes that, long after the event, the terrifying noise of conflict and shouts of combatants proceeding from that field of battle would strike the ears of travellers at night and make them tremble in their bones.

Causes of Babar's Success

Many factors contributed to Babar's success against Ibrahim Lodhi. Though called a Mughal, Babar rode to Delhi for the first time but not as a stranger among the aliens. He came as a rightful claimant to the imperial heritage of Amir Timur and the ferocious Turkish conquerors who had preceded him on the throne of Delhi. The burly sun-torched faces of the turbulent Afghans, who welcomed him in the erstwhile imperial capital of the Sultanate, were sad and gloomy but they accorded timid reception to the Mughal chief as the well-established and benevolent monarch of their homeland that was Kabul. Therefore, Babar needed no formal introduction to demand their absolute surrender and obedience. As a successor to the recently established Afghan tribal monarchy, dominated by extremely selfish, proud and short-sighted clannish nobles, Ibrahim Lodhi stood no chance of success against him. Even otherwise, he was a haughty young man of no experience of warfare or statecraft; 'he was negligent in all of his movements; he marched without order; retired or halted without plan, and engaged in battle without foresight'. Ibrahim's army, which was hastily assembled, consisted of the heterogeneous elements of poorly equipped raw and inexperienced soldiers. They were not animated by any religious, regional or national sentiments; instead, having been recruited on clannish basis by the various Afghan nobles, the individual soldiers obeyed their immediate chiefs and not the supreme head of the army. Babar correctly records in his diary that 'the Indian soldiers knew how to die and not how to fight'. On the other hand, Babar was a seasoned military general who turned the scales against his antagonist through very skilful disposition of his army in the battlefield. 'The effective use of artillery, the flanking manoeuvres of his *Tulughma* parties, and perfect coordination of action between the various parts of his army, assured his victory'. Babar's accurate gun-fire terrified Ibrahim's elephants of his advance guard, and they turned upon their own men, trampling thousands of them under their feet. Above all, Ibrahim Lodhi had to pay heavily for the disloyalty of his prominent Afghan nobles, including his own self-seeking kinsmen; his was the case of an Afghan tragedy of high intentions, self-defeated.

SECTION 3: BABAR AS THE KING OF DELHI (1526-30)

The victory at Panipat made Babar the king of Delhi but 'not yet the King of Hindustan, much less of India'. Even the kingdom of Delhi, which was supposed to extend from the Indus to Bihar and from Gwalior to the Shiwaliks, was not under his firm control. Ibrahim Lodhi had been killed but the end of the Lodhi dynasty was still in doubt. He had left behind a brother to claim the throne of Delhi, and the land remained un-subdued east and south of Agra. Babar records with dismay: 'When I reached Agra, it was the hot season. All the inhabitants of the town fled from terror, so that we could find neither grain for ourselves nor fodder for our beasts. The villagers, out of mere hatred and spite to us, had taken to anarchy, thieving and marauding. The roads became impassable. I had not had time, after the division of the treasures, to send fit persons to occupy and protect the different *parganas* and stations. The heats this year chanced to be unusually oppressive, and many men dropped at about the same time, as though struck by the *samum* (sun-stroke), and died on the spot'.

Lane-Poole correctly observes that 'the people were hostile to the strangers of uncouth tongue, and each town and petty ruler prepared for obstinate resistance. The strongholds of the Doab and Rajputana were all fortifying against attack, unanimous in rejecting the newcomers'. (*loc. cit.*, p. 204). The Afghan power was broken but a large number of the Turko-Afghan nobles, with huge armies under their control, were at large. Qasim set himself up as the chief of Sambhal; Nizam Khan became the Sultan of Bayana while Hasan Khan Mewati that of Mewat. Among the other autonomous Afghan chiefs may be mentioned the names of Muhammad Zaitun of Dholpur, Tatar Khan of Gwalior, Hussain Khan Lohani of Rapri, Qutub Khan of Etawa and Alam Khan of Kalpi. Nasir Khan Lohani, Maruf Farmuli and some other nobles held Kanauj and the neighbouring territories on the other side of the Ganga, while Bahar Khan, son of Dariya Khan Lohani, setup as the king of Bihar under the title of Sultan Muhammad.

Babar took prompt steps to force most of them to submission. He divided the unconquered towns, fortresses and districts among his officers and sent them with their troops to take possession of them. His policy proved eminently successful. Humayun conquered Sambhal; Muhammad Ali Jang-Jang captured Rapri, Mahdi Khwaja took possession of Etawa, while Sultan Muhammad acquired Kanauj and Junaid Barlas took Dholpur. Babar spent about six months to establish a semblance of his authority at Delhi and Agra. By the beginning of the year 1527, there remained two formidable groups of his rivals to challenge his authority; the Afghan chiefs of Awadh and Bihar, and the Rajputs. Mahmud Lodhi, the younger brother of Ibrahim Lodhi, had escaped to Bihar to garner the support of the other Afghan nobles, and they were actively supported by Nusrat Shah, the ruler of Bengal. Nearer the capital, however, Babar faced the most serious threat to his newly conquered kingdom by Rana Sangram Singh *alias* Rana Sanga of Mewar. Babar proved himself equal to the task, however, and, within the course of the next three years, fought three more bloody battles to settle his scores with them.

Conflict with the Rajputs

Over the centuries, the Turko-Afghan conquerors had repeatedly trampled the whole of northern and central India under the iron heels of 'their armies of Islam' so as to leave no pockets of resistance among the Rajput chiefs and Hindu *Zamindars*. Those, who survived the repeated shocks, were compelled to have their precarious existence as the *Zimmis*, and had to pay hefty tributes, including *Jaziya* on behalf of their Hindu subjects, to the Islamic state of Delhi. It was only in the fifteenth century, when the decline of the Sultanate set in, that some of the Rajput states showed signs of revival; the state of Mewar being one of them. And it was perhaps the first and the last time in the history of medieval India, that Rana Sangram Singh of Mewar was in a position to organise 'a confederacy of most of the kings of Rajputana with the clear object of recovering Delhi from the hands of the Afghans.' It is said that the Rana was preparing to march on Agra and Delhi to overthrow the Lodhi dynasty just when Babar launched a full-fledged invasion for the conquest of Delhi. The Rana's envoy to Babar suggested a joint invasion on the Lodhi dominions but nothing came out of it. Babar has it that

> 'While we were still in Kabul, Rana Sanga had sent an envoy to testify to his good wishes and to propose this plan:
>
> "If the honoured *Padshah* will come to near Dihli from that side, I from this will move on Agra". But I beat Ibrahim. I took Dihli and Agra, and up to now that Pagan has given no sign whatsoever of moving'. (*Memoirs*, p. 529)

It is surmised that, perhaps, Rana Sanga suffered from an allusion that like Amir Timur, Babar would 'return to Afghanistan after loot and plunder, and thus facilitate the establishment of his sway in the north. Babar's decision to settle down in India, however, dashed his hopes to the ground, and he began to prepare himself for a contest with the Mughals. Babar also knew that, in order to secure his Indian kingdom, a clash with the Rajputs was inevitable; therefore, immediately after the occupation of Delhi and Agra, he also began to prepare for war with Rana Sanga'.

The Battle of Khanua (March 17, 1527)

Rana Sangram Singh was by far the most powerful ruler of northern India about that time. He had once defeated the royal army of Ibrahim Lodhi and aspired to establish Hindu rule in the country. The Rana was a younger son of Raymal and a grandson of the famous Rana Kumbha. He ascended the throne of Chittor in 1509. He rose to be a warrior of great fame and his heroic military exploits were known all over India. Having to his credit about a score of brilliant victories against his Rajput and Muslim neighbouring chiefs of Malwa and Gujarat, he bore eighty scars of wounds, sustained during these wars, and had lost one arm, one eye, and was lame of one leg. In fact, he had been left as 'a fragment of a warrior' and epitomized the Rajput chivalry; no wonder, the Indian rulers trembled in their bones to hear of his name. He commanded eighty thousand soldiers and a thousand war elephants, and was accompanied in the battlefield by as many as 120 Rajput chieftains of rank; 'the lords of Marwar and Amber, Gwalior, Ajmer, Chanderi, and many more brought their retainers to his standards' as symbolic of the Rajput unity in their fight against yet another foreign Muslim invader. The war between Babar and the Rajputs was inevitable.

Notwithstanding the fact that the Rana had earlier invited Babar to invade India, he could not bear to see the Mughals entrench themselves at Delhi and provide fresh blood to the tottering Muslim power of the country. Accordingly, when Babar had defeated Ibrahim in the battle of Panipat, Rana Sanga made up his mind to take up arms against the Mughal invader. He lost no time in declaring war against Babar early in 1527, and the latter also followed suit by declaring '*his first Jihad (holy war) against the infidels*'. On the eve of the battle with the Rajputs, Babar had under his command no less than two hundred thousand fighters, 'the maximum number of soldiers ever commanded by him in any single action'. The ranks of the Mughal forces had been swelled by the addition of the troops of numerous Afghan nobles who had offered their submission to the Mughals by that time.

The rival forces came face to face with each other, early in February 1527, at Khanua or Kanwaha, a small village, situated at a distance of about 60 kilometres from Agra. The Rana despatched a strong contingent for the occupation of the intervening town of Bayana, and Babar pushed forward to Sikri, afterwards Akbar's favourite palace-city of Fatehpur. The advance guard of the Mughals was defeated by the Rajputs, which disheartened the *amirs* of Babar and his troops began to murmur. They were afraid of fighting against the Rajputs, 'the warriors of a higher type than any Babar had encountered'; he writes in his Memoirs with dismay:

> 'Our people, great and small, had been made very anxious and timid by past occurrences. No manly word or brave counsel was heard from anyone. What bold speech was there from the *wazirs* who are to speak out or from the *amirs* who will devour the land? None had advice to give, none a bold plan of his own to expound'. (*Memoirs*, p. 556.)

The position was made still worse by the currency of a prophecy, made by Muhammad Sharif, an astrologer from Kabul, that Babar would not be successful in his fight against the Rajputs. He, however, rose to the occasion; and, in order to boost the morale of his troops, raised the cry of *Jihad* against the *Kafirs*. He writes that 'after I had made enquiry concerning people's want of heart, and had seen their slackness for myself, a plan occurred to me; I summoned all the *Begs* and braves and addressed them thus:

> 'My Lords (*Begs*) and Comrades-in-arms!
>
> 'By the labours of several years, by encountering hardship, by long travel, by flinging myself and the army into battle, and by deadly slaughter, we, through the Grace of God, beat these masses of enemies in order that we may take their broad lands. A mighty enemy had been overcome, and a rich and powerful kingdom is at your feet.
>
> 'And now, having attained our goal and won our game, are we to turn back from all we have accomplished and fly to Kabul like men who have lost and are discomfited? ...What force compels us? What necessity has arisen that we should, without cause, abandon countries taken at such a risk of life? Was it for us to remain in Kabul, the sport of harsh poverty?...

'Do you know that there lies a journey of some months between us and the land of our birth and our familiar city? If our side is defeated (God preserve us from that day! God forbid it!!), where are we? Where is our birth-place? Where is our city? We have to do with strangers and foreigners. Henceforth, let no man who calls himself my friend ever again moot such a thing. But if there be any one of you who cannot bring himself to stay, then let him go. ...

'Who comes into the world, will die;
What lasts and lives will be God. (Persian)
He who hath entered the assembly of life,
Drinketh at last of the cup of death. (Turki)
He who hath come to the inn of life,
Passeth at last from Earth's house of woe. (Turki)

Better than life with a bad name, is death with a good one.

Well it is with me, if I die with good name;
A good name must I have, since the body is death's. (Persian)

'God the Most High has allotted to us such happiness and has created for us such good fortunes that we die as martyrs if we kill as Avengers of his Cause. Therefore, must each of you take oath upon his Holy Word (the *Quran*) that he will not think of turning his face from this foe, or withdraw from this deadly encounter so long as life is not rent from his body'. (*Ibid.*, pp. 556-57)

In a most dramatic manner, after his address, Babar offered prayers to God (*Allah*) for success, renounced wine for life, broke all the wine pots, destroyed and threw away precious gold and silver vessels, carried in his camp,, and above all, declared the 'abolition of *Tamgha* (stamp duty) on all the Muslim subjects of his dominions . Babar's appeal had the desired effect; his *begs* and soldiers swore on the *Quran* and by the divorce of their wives that they would fight to the bitter end, and Babar, in turn, held out a promise that, after the victory, he would grant leave to all those desirous of going back to their homes in Afghanistan.

After the initial debacle, Babar was not in a hurry to take on the Rajputs. He spent more than a month in setting his forces in battle-formations. His battle-plan was similar but with many improvements upon that of Panipat. He took special care to keep an exceptionally strong army in reserve behind his lines for safe retreat to Delhi or Afghanistan in case of defeat. After a few skirmishes, spread over a week, the rivals, ultimately, clashed on the morning of March 17, 1527 beginning with the charge by the left wing of the Rajputs. It was followed by the heavy gunfire by Mustafa which created consternation among the elephants of Rana Sanga but, in the long run, the artillery and the flanking parties of Babar, failed to stem the advance of the Rajputs. They pierced through the Mughal centre by sheer strength and spread themselves within the enemy's ranks to give a tough fight for ten hours without yielding ground. For a while, the victory seemed to hang in the balance when Babar's reserves plunged themselves in the battlefield and turned the scales against their foe. Rana Sanga 'was seriously wounded and taken to safety by his followers in a state of unconsciousness'. After the hard-earned victory, the Muslim soldiers were left with neither strength nor courage to give a chase to the fleeing Rajputs. The victorious army stayed at the battlefield for the night, looking out for the trophies of war. The next day, Babar mounted a platform over the dead bodies of the Rajputs and proclaimed his victory by assuming the title of *Ghazi*, i.e. 'the Victor in *Jihad* against the *Kafirs*'.

In spite of his crowning victory at Khanua, Babar did not dare to enter the interior of the Rajput territories. Chittor was defended heavily by the lieutenants of Rana Sanga, who setup his abode in the nearby hills with a vow not to enter the town without avenging his defeat, suffered at the hands of Babar. The Rana was incapacitated by the injuries sustained at Khanua; nevertheless, when he heard of the siege of Chanderi by Babar early next year, he directed his officers to take him to the place with an army to help Medni Ráo. As luck would have it, Rana Sanga died *en route* to Chanderi, a few days before the stronghold capitulated to Babar. According to Dr. J L Mehta, 'the defeat of Rajputs at Khanua deprived them of the opportunity to regain political ascendancy in the country for ever'. (Medieval India; ii, p. 140) The Mughal rule was established at Delhi and did not face any danger during the lifetime of Babar. In the words of Rushbrook Williams, 'the occupation of Hindustán might have been looked upon as a mere episode in Babar's career of adventure, but from henceforth, it became the keynote of his activities for the remainder of his life'. (An Empire Builder; *loc. cit.*, p. 156)

The Battle of Chanderi (January 21, 1528)

After the battle of Khanua, Medni Ráo, the ruler of Chanderi and camp-follower of Rana Sanga, escaped to his stronghold and prepared to defend it against the Mughals with a small contingent of 5000 soldiers. The fort of Chanderi was situated near Bhopal, on the border of Bundelkhand and Malwa. The remnants of the Rajput fighters also fled from Khanua and assembled at Chanderi to fight against Babar under the banner of Medni Ráo. Babar, on the receipt of intelligence, lost no time in marching upon Chanderi with full force to crush the Rajputs before it was too late. He stormed the fort early in 1528 and pressed on with the siege vigorously. When the upper fort fell to the Mughals, the besieged garrison, considerably reduced in numbers, opened the main gate of the fort on January 21, 1528, and performed the ghastly rite of *Jauhar* in the true Rajput spirit; they killed their women and children, put on the saffron-coloured garments and fell upon the foe like hawks. They wreaked terrible vengeance upon the Mughal army before being killed to a man. Thus it was that the handful of freedom-loving Rajput warriors gave the Mughals a real taste of their chivalry. It marked the end of Rajput resistance to Babar.

The Battle of Ghagra (May 6, 1529)

This was not the case with the Afghans, however. Beaten at Delhi, they were still strong in Bihar, and had even resumed the offensive when they saw Babar engaged in life and death struggle against the Rajputs. They were led by Mahmud Lodhi, the younger brother of Ibrahim Lodhi and claimant to the throne of Delhi. In spite of the numerous Afghan stalwarts having submitted to Babar, he did not take their insurgent counterparts in Awadh and Bihar lightly. He proceeded direct from Chanderi via Agra, in February 1528, to reduce the eastern territories. On the approach of Babar with threatening postures, the Afghans fell back from Kanauj and assembled at the confluence of the Ghagra with the Ganga. Babar struck against them on May 6, 1529. After a brief encounter, the Afghans melted away and Babar had an easy victory. Mahmud Lodhi escaped towards Burma where he was put to death by the Makh tribesmen after some time. Babar took possession of Bihar but allowed the local chieftains to retain their estates on professions of loyalty to him. He concluded a treaty of peace with Nusrat Shah of Bengal on the basis of equality of status and returned to Agra for the rainy season. It was his last military exploit; in four battles, fought in as many years, he had conquered and established himself as the king of northern India.

Illness and Death of Babar (1530)

Babar outlived the battle of Ghagra by about a year and a half. The strain of his continuous warfare and the administration of his newly conquered alien lands and the people had badly told upon his health, and, notwithstanding his vow at Khanua to give up drinking, he had resumed this pastime apparently to drown his anxieties. His Memoirs reveal that he also began 'to suffer from home-sickness, and occasionally could not help weeping'. After the battle of Khanua, he had sent his eldest son, Humayun, to Badakhshan as its governor to safeguard the dominions against their Central Asian foes, but the latter, as a pampered prince, failed to bear the burden of this tough assignment and returned to Delhi without his father's permission. Much annoyed with the crown prince, Babar divested him of all the official duties and sent him to take charge of his personal estate at Sambhal where he fell ill. Humayun was consequently brought back to Agra, and he recovered from his illness after some time, but this incident caused an adverse effect on Babar's own state of physical and mental health.

There is an interesting story about Babar's death. It is said that, when the physicians felt concerned about Humayun's slow recovery, Abu Baqa – a reputed saint, advised Babar 'to pray for his recovery from God and give away in charity the most valuable thing in his possession'. Thereupon, Babar, declaring 'his life to be the most valuable possession', walked three times round the bed of Humayun and prayed to God to take his illness upon himself. The contemporary Muslim writers have to say that, 'after this dramatic incident, Humayun began to get well while Babar was taken ill and died'. In fact, Babar was bed-ridden and died nearly six months after the recovery of Humayun but the psychological effect of that event on his mind cannot be over-ruled. He died at Agra on December 26, 1530, at the age of forty-eight, but, moments before his death, he had declared Humayun to be his successor to the throne. His body was first buried at *Arambagh* in Agra, but afterwards it was taken to Afghanistan and laid to rest in a garden, by the side of a small stream near Kabul – 'a beautiful spot, which had earlier been selected by Babar himself for the purpose'.

Character and Personality of Babar

Babar was one of the most fascinating characters in the history of Medieval India. He was a born soldier and an empire-builder. His cousin, Mirza Haider, records with appreciation that he was 'adorned with various virtues and clad with numberless excellences, above all of which bravery and humanity had the ascendance... None of his family before him ever surpassed such talents; no one of his race performed such amazing exploits or experienced strange adventures'. (Elias & Ross, *Tarikh-i-Rashidi*; loc. cit., pp. 173-74). Babar was highly proud of his superior birth and displayed a high standard of catholic morality befitting his royal dignity; even during his wanderings as a homeless fugitive, he behaved as a king to claim the respect of his camp-followers. Physically well-built and stout, he had learnt to bear the stress and strain of life with cheerfulness. Babar was a scholar of sorts and had a flare for writing in his mother tongue Turki; his autobiography, *Tuzuk-i-Baburi*, has established his reputation as the 'Prince of Autobiographers'. He was fond of horse-riding, hunting and swimming. A lover of nature, 'he took delight to be in the lap of natural environment where verses flowed like torrents from his lips'. (*Ibid.*, p. 174). 'As obedient son, a sincere friend, a devout husband and a loving father, Babar could always be relied upon by his near and dear ones in times of need'.

Babar was a brave and fearless warrior. As a shrewd military general, he thoroughly understood the character and qualities of his own men as well as the weaknesses of his rivals and made the best use of his knowledge to attain his objectives. He always maintained strong discipline among his men and was ever ready to undergo hardships and sufferings along with his soldiers. He was a staunch Sunni Muslim and a man of faith who always attributes his success to the grace and mercy of God though his belief in Sunni orthodoxy did not prevent him from making an alliance with Shah Ismail Safavi, the Shia ruler of Iran, who was notorious for his persecution of the Sunnis in his dominions. Babar was not a religious fanatic but he could not rise above the circumstances of his age in India. He did not follow an enlightened and liberal religious policy towards the Indians. He described the death of Raja Vikramajit of Gwalior and of other Hindu *Kafirs* as their going to hell (Memoirs, p. 477), declared *Jihad* (holy war) against Rana Sanga and called upon his men to fight against him as their religious duty. After his victory against the Rajputs at Khanua, he ascended the pyramid of the bodies of the slain Hindu soldiers and assumed the title of *Ghazi* ('slayer of the infidels'). Against the Rajput chieftain, Medni Ráo of Chanderi, too, he fought a 'holy war' (*jihad*). Babar discriminated against the Hindu traders and businessmen when he abolished the stamp duty for all Muslim merchants in his dominions while allowing it to remain intact for the non-Muslim sections of the trading community of his subjects. His Memoirs are replete with many references to the destruction of Hindu temples, forced occupation of their hearths and homes, and 'mutilation and defacement of beautiful statues in the fort of Gwalior'; the demolition of the Hindu shrine at Ayodhya, called 'Vishnu-Hari temple' and the construction of a *masjid* 'on the spot which was revered by the millions of Hindus as the birth-place of Shri Ram Chandra', was one of them. According to a renowned archaeologist, B.B. Lal, the demolition of the Babari Masjid so-called at Ayodhya on December 6, 1992 by the Hindu '*kar sevaks*', 'though regrettable, brought to light a great deal of archaeological material from within the thick walls of the Masjid. From the published reports, it is gathered that there were more than 200 specimens, including many sculptured panels and architectural components, which must have once constituted parts of the demolished temple.' (*Rama—His Historicity, Mandir and Setu: Evidence of Literature, Archaeology and other Sciences;* New Delhi, 2008; pp. 61-62). Besides, there were recovered three inscriptions, one of which, engraved on a stone slab in the chaste and classical Nagari script of the eleventh-twelfth century A.D., and consisting of twenty lines, composed partly in high-flown Sanskrit verse and partly in prose, reveals that the magnificent temple of Vishnu-Hari, built with chiseled stones and beautified with a golden spire, had been constructed there. This wonderful temple was built in the temple-city of Ayodhya, situated in the district *(mandala)* of Saket, of which Ayodhya formed a part. Nevertheless, in fairness to Babar, it may be added that his attitude towards his newly-conquered Hindu subjects in India was not as bad as that of the rulers of the Sultanate period.

❑ ❑

12

HUMAYUN (1530-1556)

SECTION 1: ACCESSION AND EARLY DIFFICULTIES

Early Life

Babar was succeeded on the throne of Delhi by his eldest son, Nasiruddin Muhammad *alias* Humayun – 'the fortunate', though he proved to be the most unlucky of all the imperial Mughal rulers of India. His mother, Maham Begam, whom Babar married in 1506, belonged to a noble Shia family of Khurasan. The three younger half-brothers of Humayun, born of different mothers, were Kamran, Askari and Hindal. He was born at Kabul on March 6, 1508. Babar had been well-established as the ruler of Kabul by that time; therefore, Humayun was brought up 'in a princely atmosphere of peace and plenty' and excellent arrangements were made for his education and training in statecraft; he was a good horse-rider and had learnt to read and write in Turki, Persian and Arabic languages.

Humayun received his first assignment as the governor of Badakhshan at the age of twelve; he was sent there in the company of his trusted and most competent military officers and administrators to assist him in the discharge of his duties, and his mother, being a well-educated and intelligent lady, was also sent along with him to Badakhshan to train him in the art of governance. Humayun took active part in the historic battles of Panipat and Khanua along with his own contingent and gave a good account of himself as a soldier. As a reward for his services, he was assigned the *jagir* of Sambhal for life to meet his personal expenditure but sent back to Badakhshan to hold the northwestern border post against their Central Asian foes. Nevertheless, after having tasted the soft and comfortable life of royalty at Delhi and Agra for a short while, and being the crown prince, he did not want to stay away from the imperial seat of governance, and returned to India in 1529 without permission from his father. It enraged Babar who, instead of assigning him any official duty, ordered him to go to Sambhal to manage his personal estate, but the latter had to be brought back to Agra after some time when he fell ill. As described earlier, Babar gave a proof of his unbounded filial affection for his son by offering his famous self-sacrificial prayer to God to take the illness of his son upon himself. Humayun recovered from his illness soon and Babar was taken ill and confined to bed six months later but, just before his death, he had declared Humayun to be his successor.

Accession at Agra

Babar died at Agra on December 26, 1530 and Humayun ascended the throne three or four days later which needs an explanation. It was because some of the influential nobles of Babar's court, including his *wazir* Amir Nizamuddin Ali Khalifa, did not hold a good opinion of Humayun 'because of his pleasure-seeking and ease-loving habits, particularly, his addiction to opium at a young age'. They hatched a conspiracy to install Mahdi Khwaja, a brilliant military general and husband of Babar's elder sister, to the throne. Because of Humayun's alertness and timely action by his well-wishers, the *wazir* realized his folly, and the conspiracy was nipped in the bud. Nizamuddin Ahmad, the author of *Tabakat-i-Akbari* writes that his father, Khwaja Muhammad Muqim Harawi, then in the service of Babar, 'played an important role in warning the Khalifa that he should not betray the family of his royal patron'. (E&D.v, pp. 187-88). Humayun was coronated at Agra probably on December 29 or 30, 1530.

Early Difficulties and Follies of Humayun

Humayun did not find the throne of Delhi a bed of roses. He was hardly twenty-three years old at the time of accession but not without experience. He had governed the outlying province of Badakhshan beyond the Hindukush with success and had commanded under his father in the battles of Panipat and Khanua. According to Lane Poole, 'the young prince was indeed a gallant and loveable fellow, warm-hearted and emotional...personally brave, as indeed were all the princes of his house, and capable of great energy on occasions; but he lacked character and resolution. He was incapable of sustained effort, and after a moment of triumph would bury himself in the *harem* and dream away the precious hours in the opium-eater's paradise whilst his enemies were thundering at the gate'. (Medieval India, *loc. cit.*, pp.218-19).

In our opinion, along with the newly carved-out Mughal empire, 'Humayun had inherited many difficulties for which he did not owe any personal responsibility. The Mughal rule had not yet taken deep roots into the soil of the country. The Mughals were still treated as foreigners, and were hated and despised by the Indians, both Hindus as well as Muslims. Babar had done little to consolidate his Indian possessions; these were hurriedly parcelled out among the ambitious nobles (*amirs*) who had made sacrifices along with Babar in the conquest of India. Their attachment to Babar had been very much personal *albeit* their loyalty to his successor could not be guaranteed as a matter of course. The civil administration of Babar was far from satisfactory and the royal treasury was almost empty at the time of his death'. (Advanced Study, ii. P. 148). Obviously, it was no easy throne that Babar had left to his son, nor was Humayun strong enough to hold it with comparative ease. The newly founded Mughal state in India faced numerous internal as well as external enemies. Its precarious existence at the time of Babar's death required a firm grasp of the political and military situation and resolution to meet it. But Humayun failed to rise to the occasion and committed many blunders in handling the matters of the state.

Humayun's most formidable rivals were his own Turkish and Mughal relatives and camp-followers, especially the Timurids who claimed kinship with Babar and were styled as the Mirzas. His cousins Muhammad Sulaimán Mirza and Muhammad Sultan Mirza, his brother-in-law Muhammad Zaman Mirza and uncle Mahdi Khwaja, all of whom held vast tracts of partially conquered and unspecified territories as governors adopted an attitude of hostility towards Humayun. To add insult to the injury, his brothers also did not exhibit loyalty towards him and tried to put him to great inconvenience at every stage of his life. On his death-bed Babar had advised his successor to treat his brothers with kindness. Accordingly, as soon as Humayun ascended the throne, he confirmed them in the possession of various territories held by them in governorships and personal estates but it did not satisfy them. Kamran, who was junior to Humayun by six years, held the governorship of Kabul and Kandahar. After the death of Babar he started behaving as an independent ruler and took forced possession of the Punjab, including Lahore and Hissar, but, Humayun, out of sheer modesty, refrained from taking any action against him and 'was at once deprived of about half of his father's dominions'. The Mughals used to draw their Muslim camp-followers and troops from

Central Asia; but the emergence of Kamran as the *de facto* ruler of Afghanistan and the Punjab cut off Delhi from contact with its main source of manpower and deprived Humayun of the best recruiting ground for his army. He granted Mewat (south of Delhi) and Alwar to Mirza Hindal and Sambhal (Rohilkhand) to Askari; but they were deceitful, and, being minors and weaklings, usually played in the hands of Kamran and other ambitious Mughal nobles. As if not content with dividing the empire among his brothers, Humayun extended the personal estates (*jagirs*) of all of his *amirs* apparently to please them but, much against his expectations, it encouraged insubordination among them and led them to defy the central authority before long.

Among the external foes of Humayun, the Muslim rulers of Bengal and Gujarat posed the greatest danger to the Mughal dominions. Babar had entered into friendly relations with them but, after his death, they adopted hostile attitude towards his successor. Nusrat Shah of Bengal once again began to instigate and support the Afghan nobles of Bihar against the Mughals. The Afghans regarded the Mughals as usurpers and were eager to re-establish their rule at Delhi. In the south, Bahadur Shah, the Afghan ruler of Gujarat, 'a soldier of fortune', had also become very powerful by the conquest and annexation of Malwa to his dominions. After the death of Babar, he became bold enough even to aspire for the throne of Delhi and entered into an understanding with the rebellious Afghan nobles of Bihar to cooperate with him for the expulsion of Mughals from India. He gave shelter to the enemies of Humayun and gave liberal patronage to the fugitive Afghan nobles. Bahadur Shah carried on relentless war against Humayun in collaboration with the brilliant Afghan upstart Sher Khan (later Sher Shah Suri) of South Bihar till Humayun was thoroughly beaten and expelled from India.

In his life and death struggle against his internal and external foes, Humayun proved himself to be a very poor military general; he failed to exercise effective control over the Mughal army which was composed of heterogeneous elements of foreign adventurers – Chaghtai, Uzbeg, Mughal, Persian, Afghan and Hindustani Musalmans. He could not discipline the nobles who were 'too conscious of their own importance and authority, while the more important of them did not consider the throne beyond the range of their ambition'. Above all, Humayun was his own worst enemy; devoid of military genius and strong will-power, he lacked wisdom and insight into political and military affairs, and was found wanting in the qualities of quick decision and execution when confronted with the heavy odds. He never stuck to anything, but always did things by halves.

He left one enemy subdued behind him while turning to meet another. Humayun did not possess the energy and sagacity of his father and was given to pleasure, and often wasted much useful time in merry-making. In short, he was devoid of the essential qualities of a good ruler and failed to command the respect and loyalty of his subjects as well as soldiers.

SECTION 2: STRUGGLE TO MAINTAIN THE PARENTAL HERITAGE (1530-40)

Expedition to Kalinjar (1531)

During his chequered career as ruler of Delhi for about a decade, Humayun mishandled the state affairs and made numerous mistakes, rather committed serious blunders one after another in quick succession which, ultimately, cost him his throne. He signalled his accession to the throne by dispatching an expedition to Kalinjar in Bundelkhand whose Hindu chieftain was suspected to be in league with the rebellious Afghans of Bihar. The conquest of this stronghold was deemed essential to strengthen the eastern frontier of the Mughal dominions and safeguard the passage of troops from Delhi to the territorial possessions of Bahadur Shah in Malwa. The Mughal army laid siege to the fortress but failed to conquer it. Humayun was constrained to make peace with the Hindu chief and lifted the siege after about six months on the acknowledgement of a nominal submission and payment of indemnity by the latter. Humayun hailed it as a great victory but, in fact, the Raja could not be beaten, and, instead, the weakness of the Mughal army was exposed. On the other hand, it is believed that the Raja could have been befriended by Humayun if he had handled the situation tactfully.

First Encounter with the Afghans

Finding Humayun engaged in the siege of Kalinjar, the Afghans of Bihar had started encroachments on the Mughal province of Jaunpur. An Afghan army, led by Mahmud Lodhi, the younger brother of Ibrahim Lodhi, was defeated by Humayun at Dauhria in August 1532. Encouraged by this victory, Humayun pushed forward and laid siege to the fort of Chunar on the Ganga; it was situated at a distance of about 25 kilometres from Varanasi (Banaras) and was held by Jalal Khan, the son of a local Afghan chieftain, Sher Khan (the future Sher Shah Suri). The siege lasted about four months from September to

December 1532 but, like Kalinjar, this fort also could not be conquered by Humayun while Sher Khan constantly 'hovered round the Mughal camp with the double purpose of harassing the besiegers and providing succor to the besieged'. Ultimately, Humayun lifted the siege of Chunar on the offer of 'a purely perfunctory submission' by Sher Khan. The latter was undoubtedly the rising star among the Afghans, and it proved to be a cardinal mistake on the part of Humayun to let him go unpunished. This was the most appropriate time for the Mughals to crush the power of the Afghans in South Bihar, 'the nerve-centre of Afghan power in India, but Humayun was not the man to avail himself of the opportunity'. Instead, apparently elated with his false victory, he returned to Agra and wasted more than a year in enjoyment and merry-making. This provided an opportunity to the Afghans to re-organise themselves while Bahadur Shah of Gujarat strengthened his position by the conquest of Malwa and Raisen.

The Conquest and Loss of Malwa and Gujarat (1535-36)

Bahadur Shah, the ruler of Malwa and Gujarat, was a sworn enemy of the Mughals. He regarded the Mughals as foreign aggressors and aspired to become the king of Delhi after expelling them from India. He was known to give shelter to the internal foes of Humayun, including his rebellious kinsmen, the Mirzas; therefore, war with him was inevitable. In July 1534, Muhammad Zaman Mirza, who had been assigned the governorship of Bihar by Humayun, raised a standard of revolt in alliance with Muhammad Sultan Mirza and Wali Khub Mirza. They were all defeated by Humayun while Zaman Mirza was taken prisoner and ordered to be blinded. But he managed to escape from being blinded by bribing his royal captors and fled to the court of Bahadur Shah in Gujarat in November 1534. Humayun asked Bahadur Shah to surrender Zaman Mirza and the other Mughal fugitives but the latter refused to do so. It left Humayun with no other alternative but to invade Gujarat.

About that time, Bahadur Shah was engaged in the siege of the famous Rajput citadel of Chittor; it was then ruled over by the Sisodia chief, Rana Vikramaditya, who was a minor. His mother Rani Karameti of the medieval chroniclers (Karmavati or Karnavati) sent a *rakhi* to Humayun with the appeal to help her in the time of distress like a brother. It is said that Humayun accepted the offer and at once proceeded towards Chittor but stopped short at Sarangpur in January

1535 on the ill-advice of some religious fanatics. Bahadur Shah was alarmed, but he, 'correctly relying on his conviction that the Mughal chief would follow the Muslim tradition of refraining from an attack on a brother-in-faith engaged in a war against the Kafirs', pressed on the siege of Chittor. The stronghold fell after a heroic resistance on the 8th of March when the ladies of the badly-thinned besieged garrison committed *Sati* en-mass and their men folk died fighting to a man by performing the dreadful rite of *Jauhar*. Bahadur Shah put the city to plunder for three days and acquired huge booty but he was no match for the Mugahl army and begged a hasty retreat from the site on the approach of Humayun. The Mughal prince took possession of the Rajput citadel in ruins but he had lost the splendid opportunity of winning the Rajput sympathies as friends and allies, 'the inestimable worth of which was later realized by his son and successor Akbar'.

Humayun gave a hot chase to the retreating army of Bahadur Shah; the forts of Mandasor, Mandu and Champaner fell into the hands of the Mughals in quick succession and Bahadur Shah fled to Cambay and from there escaped to and took refuge in the island of Diu. Humayun followed close upon his heels up to Cambay but returned from there to Champaner. The conquest of Malwa and Gujarat was a great achievement of Humayun but he lost the fruits of his victory earlier than expected. He appointed Askari as the governor of the newly conquered territories and himself returned to Agra in triumph. But as soon as his back was turned, Bahadur Shah came out of his hiding at Diu and, with the active support of his nobles and the subjects, expelled the Mughal armies from his dominions within a year. Lane-Poole correctly remarks that

> 'Malwa and Gujarat, the two provinces, equal in area to all the rest of Humayun's kingdom, had fallen like ripe fruit into his hands. Never was conquest so easy. Never too was conquest more recklessly squandered away'. (*Medieval India*, p. 225)

While Bahadur Shah staged a comeback to Gujarat and swept across his lost territories like a hurricane, Askari and his Mughal troops fled before him in panic, vacating one town after another in quick succession. Humayun could do pretty little to save his newly conquered prized possessions; gloating over the vast spoils of Bahadur Shah's camp, of Champaner, and of Cambay, he indulged in festivities, and 'wasted a whole year at Agra in merrymaking and opiated idleness'. He could never again think of challenging Bahadur Shah because of the danger posed by Sher Khan (the future Sher Shah Suri) who had emerged as a formidable rival of the Mughals in Bihar.

War with Sher Khan (1537-39)

As described earlier, Sher Khan had submitted to Humayun after the first siege of Chunar in 1532. As a part of the treaty, Humayun had brought his younger son, Qutb Khan, with a contingent of 500 troops to Agra to be in attendance upon him. During the Gujarat campaign, Humayun wanted him to join the Mughal army of invasion but, instead, Qutb Khan slipped away from the Mughal camp and rejoined his father in Bihar. It so appears that Sher Khan had arrived at a secret understanding with Bahadur Shah 'to foment trouble in the east while Humayun was busy in Malwa and Gujarat'. He utilized the period of Humayun's absence from Agra to strengthen his position in Bihar and Bengal. He won over most of the Afghans and their chieftains of Bihar to his side, expelled Mahmud Lodhi, the younger brother of Ibrahim Lodhi and pretender to the throne of Delhi, from Bihar, defeated Sultan Ghiyasuddin Mahmud—the successor of Nusrat Shah and king of Bengal, twice in 1534 and 1536 respectively, and took most of their camp-followers and soldiers under his service. Humayun woke up from slumber and was stirred to action only when he received an express appeal from the king of Bengal for assistance against Sher Khan.

The Second Siege of Chunar (1537—1538): Humayun took the field against Sher Khan in July 1537. His campaign against the Afghan adversary was full of blunders from the beginning to the end and it proved fatal for him. Humayun had seventy to eighty thousand troops and well-equipped artillery under his command which could have helped him in overrunning the whole of south Bihar within a couple of months, but, like a foolhardy person, he moved leisurely and wasted four valuable months before making himself to the scene of action. Thereafter, instead of marching upon Sher Khan, he halted at the border post of Chunar which was put under siege for the second time. Humayun did not care to send timely aid to Ghiasuddin Mahmud either, resulting in the utter ruin of the Bengal's ruler at the hands of Sher Khan's forces. The stronghold of Chunar was defended gallantly by Jalal Khan, the second son of Sher Khan, and his seasoned military general, Khwas Khan, and the siege dragged on for six long months from October 1537 to March 1538 while Sher Khan kept the indolent Mughal prince engaged in a fruitless dialogue for peace. Humayun came to know of Sher Khan's perfidy and raised the siege of Chunar on hearing the news of the fall of Gaur at his hands on April 6, 1538. The vanquished king of Bengal reached the Mughal camp as a fugitive where he died of his wounds soon thereafter.

Humayun, in desperation, ordered his forces to march upon Bengal but his passage was blocked by Jalal Khan at the Teliagarhi Pass for over two months while Sher Khan's men transferred all the treasures from Gaur to the fortified and well-protected fort of Rohtas in Bihar. After successful completion of the task, Jalal Khan stealthily retired to Bihar, leaving the pass open for the Mughal forces to enter Bengal. Humayun moved forward and took possession of the badly ransacked town of Gaur without any resistance on August 15, 1538; he was simply 'delighted to find huge quantities of wine, opium and other articles of enjoyment in the royal palaces which had deliberately been left there by Sher Khan's men'. Niamutullah, the author of *Tarikh-Khan Jahan Lodhi*, writes that 'the royal palaces of Gaur had been furnished with an exquisite variety of ornaments and embellishments, including the magnificent carpets and costly silk-stuffs, in the hope that Humayun, charmed with it, would be induced to prolong his stay there'. (E&D, v, pp. 112-13)

Sher Khan had guessed right; Humayun was fascinated so much with his easy victory over Bengal that he prolonged his stay at its capital for no less than eight months from August 1538 to March 1539 while his adversary was busy in strengthening himself for the final assault on the Mugahl intruders. Jauhar records that 'Humayun divided Bengal into *jagirs* among his officers, after which he, very unaccountably, shut himself up in his *harem*, and abandoned himself to every kind of indulgence and luxury. The town was renamed by him as Jannatabad (Paradise). Meanwhile, Sher Khan brought under his control all the territories between Teliagarhi and Kanauj and cut off Humayun's contacts with Agra'. (*Tazkirat-ul-Waqiat*; E&D, v, p. 141)

The Debacle of Chausa (June 26, 1539)

Humayun became apprehensive of the danger when his royal couriers to and from Agra began to disappear in the transit and all news from his imperial capital were blocked out for over two months. The major towns of Kara (Allahabad), Kanauj and Sambhal were overrun by Sher Khan, and Humayun's brother, Hindal, who had been assigned the duty of defending this region, abandoned his charge and retired to Agra; he assumed the imperial titles and began to behave as a sovereign ruler. Shocked by this development, Humayun hastened to return to Agra with all of his troops; only 5000 soldiers, under the charge of a junior military officer, were left behind by him for the defence of Gaur. On the way back, Humayun committed a serious mistake of shifting the whole of his army to the southern bank of the Ganga, apparently with the twin object of 'making use of a better route along the Grand Trunk Road (*Shah rah*) to Agra, and putting pressure on Sher Khan'. Incidentally, this route passed through a low-lying area which was always flooded during the rainy season. To Humayun's further misfortune, this region of South Bihar was under the firm control of Sher Khan which enabled the latter to acquire first-hand information about the striking power and movements of the Mughal troops through his scouts.

To the great chagrin of Humayun, with the first shower of the pre-monsoon rains, the route adopted by him became muddy and unfit for the movement of troops, necessitating the immediate transfer of Mughal army to the northern bank of the Ganga once again; this clumsy scene was enacted near Bihiya in modern Bhojpur district at the great inconvenience of the Mughal soldiers and made Humayun the laughing stock of his own people. Sher Khan, who was lurking in the neighbourhood, watched the development with amusement; it encouraged him 'to stall the Mughal army and prepare for a showdown' without any loss of time. Accordingly, he made an appearance on the southern bank of the river with threatening postures. It provoked Humayun who, 'without visualizing the full implications of his action', ordered his armies to re-cross the river to its southern bank for the second time. It was done at Chausa, situated at a distance of about 16 kms from Buxar, near the confluence of the Ganga and the Karmansa. According to the contemporary chroniclers, 'this action would have been justified if Humayun had ordered an immediate attack upon the enemy'. The Afghan troops were no match for the well-equipped Mughal army. About that time, they were far less in number than their rivals and 'were thoroughly tired because of forced marches from the south'; therefore, they were likely to be put to rout by the Mughal soldiers in a sudden assault but Humayun did not pick up courage to take such an initiative. Instead, he encamped at Chausa, and the rival forces lay face to face with each other for two months. It gave sufficient time to Sher Khan to reinforce and reorganize his army for the contest.

As apprehended, with the onset of the monsoons in June 1539, the Mughal camp was inundated and put its defences out of gear. On June 25, Sher Khan suddenly decamped and pretended a show of retreat from the battle-field. It was made out by him that he was proceeding to suppress the rebellion of Maratha Chero, an aboriginal leader of

Shahabad district in Bihar. That put Humayun off his guard, and he also decamped with the object of seeking some elevated ground for the protection of his men and material from the flood. After the nightfall, Sher Khan returned to Chausa, however, and made a surprise attack on the disorganized Mughal camp from three quarters. Taken completely unawares, the Mughal soldiers fled helter shelter in utter confusion; thousands of them were put to the sword by Afghans while over eight thousand of them were estimated to have been washed off by the flooded Ganga in their bid to cross it.

When confusion prevailed everywhere, Humayun also made a desperate bid to cross the swollen Ganga on his horseback. His horse was drowned in the mid-stream but his life was saved by a water carrier, Nizam *saqqa* (*mashki*), who offered him his *mashak* (the inflated skin bag) for swimming across the river. Jauhar records that, on reaching Agra, the emperor richly rewarded the water carrier and allowed him to sit on the imperial throne for two hours with the blessings: "I will make your name as celebrated as that of Nizamuddin Auliya". (*Tazkirat-ul-Waqiat*; E&D, v, p.143). Similarly, Firishta says that 'Humayun rewarded the water-carrier with the grant of kingship for half a day, and permitted him to sit on the throne and distribute rich presents to his friends and relatives according to his desire'. (Briggs's Firishta, II, p. 88). Gulbadan, on the other hand, writes that Nizam *saqqa* was granted royalty for two days. (Beveridge's *Humayun Nama*, p. 140) Ladies of the royal *harem* in the Mughal camp were also put to great straits. Two queens of Humayun and one of his daughters were either killed or drowned in the Ganga. Those of the ladies, who fell into the hands of the Afghan soldiers, included Humayun's chief queen Bega Begum also. It goes to the credit of Sher Khan, now styled as Sher Shah that he afforded them full protection, and, after the battle of Chausa, returned them to Humayun under an escort, with full honours.

The Battle of Kanauj (May 17, 1540)

The defeat of Chausa crippled the Mughal power in India. After this historic victory Sher Khan assumed the insignia of royalty as the Emperor of India under the name of Sher Shah and started vigorous preparations to expel the Mughals from Agra and Delhi. Humayun reached Agra in distress but was soon joined by many nobles and thousands of the Mughal troops who had made good their escape from Chausa. Hindal, who had done little to help him in his encounter with the Afghans, hastened to apologize for his misconduct but Kamran, who had come to Agra from Lahore with 20,000 troops, struck a note of discord with his elder brother and demanded supreme command of the Mughal army as the price for offering a joint front for resistance against Sher Shah. Many other Mughal nobles refused to acknowledge Humayun as their king and demanded a change of leadership, but the latter was in no mood to oblige them and adopted stringent measures to curb all opposition to his accession. Thereupon, Kamran refused to cooperate with him and returned to Lahore with his soldiers and many other disaffected Mughal nobles early in 1540.

By this time Sher Shah had become the master of Bihar and Bengal and extended his sway up to Kali and Kanauj towards Delhi. Humayun mustered his forces and set up his army camp at Bhojpur in the vicinity of Kanauj in April 1540 for another showdown with the Afghans, and Sher Shah lost no time in showing his presence opposite to the Mughal camp on the southern bank of the Ganga. Like a foolhardy person, Humayun again committed the folly of ordering his army to cross over to the southern bank of the river without taking into consideration the approaching monsoons. The rival forces lay face to face with each other for over a month. During this time, the Mughal camp swelled to over two lacs of the fighters though many of them lacked the qualities of warriors and were poorly equipped. As a poor military general Humayun simply failed to utilize their services effectively, and allowed the fateful story of Chausa's debacle to be repeated with a vengeance. On May 15, 1540, Humayun's camp was flooded by heavy rainfall and the field guns were submerged in water. When the Mughals were busy in shifting their camp to a higher place, Sher Shah struck against them with full force on May 17. It spread consternation in Humayun's camp and most of the Mughal soldiers fled for their dear lives without a fight but, unlike the debacle of Chausa, Humayun stood the ground and fought desperately against the foe. The battle that ensued is known to history as the battle of Kanauj. Nevertheless, in the confusion that followed, thousands of the Mughal soldiers were either trampled under the feet of their own horses and elephants or washed away by the flooded Ganga. The Mughal artillery could not be put to use at all and fell into the hands of Sher Shah intact. Abbas Khan, the famous biographer of Sher Shah, pays a personal tribute to Humayun for the courage with which he fought in this 'fateful battle' in the words that follow:

> 'The Emperor Humayun himself remained firm like a mountain in his position on the battlefield, and displayed such valour and

> gallantry as is beyond all description. But when he saw supernatural beings fighting against him, he acknowledged the work of *Allah*, abandoned the battle to these unearthly warriors, and turned the bridle of his purpose towards his capital of Agra. He received the wound himself but escaped safe and sound out of the blood-thirsty whirlpool. The greater part of his army was driven into the River Ganga'. (*Tarikh-i-Sher Shahi*; E&D. iv, pp. 382-83).

After the decisive battle of Kanauj, the triumphant Afghans gave a hot chase to Humayun in flight and did not allow him to take respite at Agra or Delhi. Humayun fled to the Punjab with the hope of persuading Kamran to make a combined effort against Sher Shah. All the four brothers met at Lahore and wasted five months in fruitless deliberations. Mirza Haider Dughlat, a cousin of Babar, made earnest endeavour to compose their differences but 'in spite of the danger of losing all they possessed', the brothers failed to forge a united front against the Afghans. The treacherous Kamran foolishly believed that, if he refrained from cooperating with Humayun, he might be allowed by Sher Shah to remain unmolested in his possession of the Punjab and Hissar Firoza, but Sher Shah contemptuously turned down his offer. Meanwhile, Sher Shah reached Sultanpur Lodhi in the Jalandhar Doab and, as his army crossed the Beas, Humayun, with his panic-stricken followers, decamped from Lahore with the intention of retiring towards Afghanistan but Kamran blocked his passage. Humayun's plan to find his way to Kashmir was also foiled by Kamran. In desperation, he fled towards Sindh as a fugitive. From there, he made a futile attempt to come to some understanding with Sher Shah in his presumed capacity as the ruler of Kabul and the Punjab but received no response from the latter. In November 1540, Kamran also fled from Lahore on the approach of Sher Shah's army and retired to Kabul, thus allowing the Afghans to take over the whole of the Punjab and the northwestern frontier up to the Khyber Pass without a fight. Askari joined Kamran's camp and was rewarded with the governorship of Kandahar from him. Hindal accompanied Humayun to Sindh but he also deserted him after some time and was received with open arms by Kamran in Afghanistan.

SECTION 3: HUMAYUN IN EXILE (1540-55)

As Fugitive in Sindh and Rajputana (1540-43)

Humayun wandered about as fugitive with a handful of his camp-followers in the desert regions of Sindh and Rajputana for about three years. He tried to conquer the towns of Thatta and Sehwan but Shah Husain Arghun, the chief of Sindh, foiled all of his attempts to set his foothold on the Indian soil. Ultimately, he got rid of Humayun by offering him some monetary help and safe passage through his territories to Kandahar, and from there he made it to Persia as a refugee. The Mughals were turned out of India lock, stock and barrel.

A few events of Humayun's miserable life pertaining to the period of his wanderings in Sindh and Rajputana are, nonetheless, of great historical significance. As referred to earlier, Hindal had remained loyal to Humayun and accompanied him to Sindh. Humayun had a meeting with Hindal at Patar in the Rohri region, where he chanced to see a beautiful Persian girl of fourteen, named Hamida Banu, in his camp. She was the daughter of a *Shia maulvi*, Mir Baba Dost *alias* Alí Akbar Jami—the tutor and spiritual guide of Hindal. Because of his lecherous habits, Humayun felt a liking for her and, 'in spite of his brother's bitter protest' married her on August 29, 1539 though he had already a number of ladies in his *harem*. Hamida Banu Begum was destined to be the mother of Humayun's illustrious son and successor Akbar. Again, Akbar was born under the most peculiar circumstances in the course of Humayun's wanderings in Sindh; Hamida Banu gave birth to him on October 15, 1542 in the Hindu palace of Rana Virsala of Amarkot in Sindh where Humayun's womenfolk had been lodged by the courtesy of the Rana.

Humayun in Exile (1543-55)

Humayun entered Afghanistan in July 1543 through the Bolan Pass where the scouts of Kamran were already on the lookout for him. Having been sighted by them, he lost his nerves but escaped from falling into their hands under the most dramatic circumstances. Leaving behind his camp-followers and the womenfolk at the mercy of his hostile brothers, and, accompanied by Hamida Banu and some of his trusted servants, including Bairam Beg (later Bairam Khan) and Mulla Pir Muhammad, Humayun took to flight on the horseback at the dead of night. Even his infant child, Akbar, then hardly nine months old, who was with his nurse, had to be left behind in the hurry of his flight for his dear life. Bairam Beg was a Persian *Shia* who had fought in the battles of Chausa and Kanauj as an ordinary soldier. On his initiative, the idea of going to Kandahar had also to be given up as it was then under the control of Kamran who had appointed Askari as its governor with instructions to oppose him. Humayun, therefore, escaped towards Persia and sought refuge from its monarch, Shah Tahmasp. The latter gave him a cordial reception and offered him military help to re-conquer Afghanistan provided the fugitive Mughal prince adopted *Shia* faith and returned Kandahar to Iran after its recovery from the hands of his brothers. Humayun stayed in the Persian court for a few months, converted to the *Shia* faith with the promise to promote this cult of Islam in his territories, and, reinforced by 14,000 Persian troops, marched on Kandahar.

The fort of Kandahar was invested by Humayun towards the end of March 1545. As the siege went on, he sent Bairam Beg, now called Bairam Khan, on a diplomatic mission to Kabul 'with a view to winning the Timurid princes and nobles to his side' but, apparently nothing came out of it. Askari surrendered the fort of Kandahar to Humayun on September 3, 1545. According to S. Roy, the stronghold was handed over to the Persian commander as stipulated, but 'the Persian troops declined to render any further help to Humayun, who was now being joined by his followers but had no shelter. Pressed by sheer necessity, Humayun made a sudden attack on the fort of Kandahar one month later, expelled the Persian garrison, and took the fort in violation of his agreement with Shah Tahmasp'. The Shah's army returned to Persia empty-handed. (*History and Culture of the Indian People*, BVB, VII, p. 59)

The occupation of Kandahar proved a turning point in the otherwise dull and dreary career of Humayun. It provided a base for his further operations which ended his period of exile and led to his restoration as the king of Afghanistan as well as Delhi. The fort of Kabul was wrested by him from the hands of Kamran in November 1545 when the latter, after suffering a defeat in a few skirmishes, fled towards Sindh by way of Ghazni, and Humayun entered the town without any opposition. Kamran, who had married a daughter of Shah Husain Arghun earlier, found a safe haven in Sindh and was fully supported by his father-in-law. The child Akbar, who had fallen into the hands of Kamran and kept a sort of hostage by him 'along with his half-sister Banu Begam and some other destitute ladies of Humayun's *harem*', was reunited with his parents at Kabul after an interval of about two years.

The occupation of Kandahar and Kabul encouraged Humayun to think seriously of recovering his kingdom in Afghanistan and ultimately his dominions in India. Nevertheless, his selfish brothers continued to give him a lot of trouble for some time more 'until they were finally liquidated'. In March 1546, Humayun set out on a campaign from

Kabul against Suleiman Mirza in Badakhshan (northern Afghanistan) but, on the way, he fell ill and was bed-ridden for about two months of severe winter. It triggered off a fresh wave of desertions from his army. On hearing of these developments, Kamran staged a come-back from Sindh stealthily, with reinforcements from Shah Husain, to try his luck in Afghanistan once again. He recaptured the forts of Ghazni and Kabul with the assistance of his secret agents without much resistance and commenced 'a reign of terror, by brutally killing and executing many of the followers of Humayun. To his misfortune, the child Akbar again fell into the hands of his cruel uncle along with most of the ladies of Humayun's palace. 'This time, Akbar was treated very shabbily by being placed under house arrest in the supervision of Kamran's own men'. Winter was at its best but Humayun had to hurry back towards Kabul. He led his second expedition to Kabul in November 1547 and put the stronghold under siege which continued for several months. It was at this occasion that, having lost all hopes of success, Kamran placed Akbar on the rampart of the main gate of the fort and exposed him to the gunfire of Humayun's artillery. It is said that Humayun and his gunners took note of the child, and changed the target of their attack without stopping the artillery operation. 'Akbar's survival at that critical moment was a matter of mere chance and good luck'. Kamran fled from Kabul but did not give up his claim of sovereignty as the successor of Babar, and, in league with his other two brothers, continued to foment trouble against Humayun even thereafter. In the last resort, he retreated towards the Khyber Pass and assumed the leadership of the Afghan tribes in the region between Kabul and the Indus to oppose Humayun. Askari, who had surrendered to Humayun at Kandahar and forgiven, also changed sides to join hands with Kamran. He was finally taken prisoner and exiled to Mecca in 1551 and nothing was heard of him afterwards. Similarly, Hindal had also joined the camp of Humayun after his occupation of Kabul in 1545 but again revolted and made a common cause with Kamran; he fell fighting in a bloody encounter that took place between Humayun and Kamran on November 23, 1551. Kamran was defeated but still unrelenting. He fled to the Punjab and sought refuge with Islam Shah—the son and successor of Sher Shah Suri, but was cold-shouldered by him. Thereafter, Kamran went into hiding in the Gakhar territory, and took refuge with their chief, Sultan Adam. The latter betrayed Kamran and, 'after some hesitation, surrendered him to Humayun', who had reached the Indus in hot pursuit. Nevertheless, in spite of the advice of his nobles to put him to death, Humayun forgave his brother but blinded him and sent him to Mecca. Not prepared to challenge his Suri antagonist at Delhi, he retraced his steps to Kabul in December 1553.

SECTION 4: RESTORATION AND DEATH OF HUMAYUN (1555-56)

The second Afghan dynasty (after the Lodhis) established by Sher Shah Suri in Delhi proved very short-lived. Sher Shah was injured and died during the siege of Kalinjar (Bundelkhand) in May 1545. His son and successor Islam Shah, though a mediocre ruler, held his dominions intact and ruled for eight years. But, after his death on October 30, 1553, disintegration set in during the rule of his weak successors. Firoze Shah, a twelve years old son of Islam Shah, who was expected to succeed him, was put to death by his maternal uncle, Mubariz Khan, within three days of his father's death. Mubariz Khan ascended the throne with the title of Muhammad Adil Shah but he proved to be an incapable ruler. His claim to the throne was contested by two of his own brothers-in-law—Ibrahim Khan and Sikander Shah. Ibrahim Khan Suri defeated and turned out Adil Shah from Delhi and Agra and declared himself the Emperor of India, while Sikander Suri, the governor of Lahore, set up as an independent ruler of northwestern India.

The Suri Empire was thus threatened with disintegration because of the fratricidal war which broke out between the rival Afghan claimants to the throne. It prompted Humayun to try his luck on the Indian soil once again. On the advice of Bairam Khan, who had now become his prime minister as well as the commander-in-chief, he organised an invasion of India during the winter of 1554. The main army of invasion was put under the formal charge of Akbar, then a promising young boy of thirteen, but controlled on his behalf by his tutor Bairam Khan. Humayun himself reached Peshawar in December 1554 and was joined by Bairam Khan and all other Mughal nobles for a major attack on India. The Gakhar chief Sultan Adam, who had previously submitted to Humayun but later shifted his loyalties to Sikander Suri, had to be dealt with first. Humayun, therefore, proceeded through the Gakhar territory. Tatar Khan, who held the fort of Rohtas for Sikander Suri, fled on the approach of the Mughal army and the stronghold fell into the hands of Humayun without a fight.

Occupation of Lahore and Dipalpur: Moving along the foothills of the Punjab, Humayun reached Kalanaur in the Gurdaspur district from where he descended on the plains of the Punjab in a three-pronged military operation; one division of his army was sent to Lahore, and the other towards the Afghan centre of power at Dipalpur while he, accompanied by Bairam Khan, conducted the main army through the Jalandhar Doab. Lahore was occupied by the Mughal troops without much resistance in February 1555 and Dipalpur was taken after a fierce fighting with Shahbaz Khan Afghan in March. Meanwhile, Bairam Khan overran the Jalandhar Doab.

The Battle of Machhiwara (May 15-16, 1555): About this time, Sikander Suri was at the helm of affairs in Delhi. He despatched an army of 30,000 cavalry towards Sirhind to intercept the invader. On hearing of the intelligence about it, Bairam Khan hastened from Jalandhar with full force and crossed the Sutlej before the arrival of the enemy. The rival armies met at Machhiwara, about 30 kilometres from Ludhiana, on May 15, and the battle between them began instantaneously. It was one of the most unusual battles fought in the darkness of night with very poor visibility. It is said that 'an accidental fire broke out in the village in which the Afghan army had drawn up. It enabled the Mughals to see clearly every motion of the Afghans and discharge arrows at them, whereas the Afghans, who had no view of the foe, shot at random, and, ultimately failed to maintain their ground'. The Afghan ranks broke up and fled from the field in the early hours of the morning. Bairam Khan marched forward and took possession of Sirhind and its adjoining territories without any loss of time.

The Battle of Sirhind (June 22, 1555): Alarmed at the success of the Mughal arms at Machhiwara, Sikander Suri marched from Delhi with a huge army, including 80,000 horse, a big train of artillery and war elephants and arrived in the vicinity of Sirhind. By this time. Humayun had also come from Lahore with reinforcements to join his main army at Sirhind. The rivals remained encamped opposite each other for about three weeks and engaged themselves in minor skirmishes to gauge the strength and weaknesses of each other. The Mughal troops took the initiative in starting the battle on June 22, 1555. The Afghans concentrated their main attack on the centre of the Mughal army, commanded by Bairam Khan, who stood on the defensive, while the two Mughal divisions under Shah Abul-Maali and Tardi Beg wheeled round the enemy, and, within a few hours, the Afghan army 'became a mass of confusion and took to flight'. According to Jauhar, the Mughal troops, 'who were vastly inferior in number', gave a chase to the fleeing Afghans and killed many of them. In the words of S. Roy, 'Machhiwara and Sirhind undid the work of Chausa and Kanauj, which had put an end to the empire of Babur; they sealed the fate of the Afghan empire of Sher Shah'. (*Ibid.*, p. 63). Sikander Suri fled to the Shiwalik hills, and Bairam Khan, accompanied by Akbar, was sent behind him in hot pursuit.

Occupation of Delhi and Agra: Humayun entered the town of Sirhind after his victory on the battlefield and from there proceeded to Samana where he stayed for a few days until the Mughal army had taken firm possession of Delhi. He re-entered the metropolis at an auspicious moment on July 23 and ascended the throne after an interval of about fifteen years. Agra was occupied soon thereafter. Humayun thus became the emperor of India once again and the *Khutba* was read in his name. "Under his orders, a dispatch of victory was drawn in which the honour of the victory was ascribed to Prince Akbar, who was designated heir-apparent to the throne and governor of the Punjab; he had already been sent along with Bairam Khan, to put down Sikander Suri. This step was deemed necessary in order to deal effectively with Sikander Suri on military as well as political grounds, because 'his army had been swelling' and he was still determined not to allow the Mughals to re-establish themselves in India. The war against the Afghans was yet half-finished.

Humayun had recovered his kingdom but he was not destined to rule over it for long after his restoration. Immediately after his accession, he distributed offices and commands to faithful military officers and camp-followers and sent them to establish their control over the various parts of his kingdom, the conquest of which was far from complete. Atga Khan wrested the control of Hissar from the Afghan garrison after a siege of 23 days while Ali Quli Khan was sent to Badaun to establish law and order there. A Mughal officer, named Haider Muhammad Akhta Begi, took Bayana after treacherously putting to death its governor Ghazi Khan, the father of Ibrahim Suri, one of the Afghan claimants to the throne of Delhi, though the latter had made his surrender on the promise of being pardoned by the Mughal monarch. Soon thereafter, two prominent Mughal nobles, Shah Abul Maali and Haider Muhammad had to be punished by their dismissal because of their insubordination.

Death of Humayun (January 26, 1556)

Humayun was, in fact, not firmly established on the throne when, on January 24, 1556, he met with an accidental fall while descending down the stairs of his personal library, situated in the imperial buildings, called Din Panah or Sher Mandal in Delhi. Abdul Qadir Badaoni, the celebrated author of *Muntakhab-ut-Tawarrikh*, writes that,

> 'On that fateful evening, as the Emperor was descending, the *Muezzin* uttered his call to prayer, and he knelt out of respect for the *Azan*; and as he rose, his staff glanced aside and his foot slipped, and he rolled down several steps to the ground. When he recovered a little, Nagar Shaikh Juli (variant Jumali) was sent to the Punjab to summon the Prince (Akbar) and to tell him exactly what had happened'. (George Ranking, i, pp. 600-601)

Nizamuddin Ahmad and some other chroniclers add to our information that, as a result of his fall from the stairs, 'the Emperor fractured his skull' and was carried into the palace in a state of unconsciousness. On recovering consciousness, 'he rallied and spoke. The Court physicians exerted all their powers, but in vain. Next day he grew worse and his case was beyond medical help'. A messenger was then sent to the Punjab to summon Prince Akbar. The injury proved fatal and Humayun breathed his last at the setting of the sun on January 26, 1556. The news of his death was kept a secret for seventeen days until Akbar had been apprised of it and proclaimed as the Emperor of India.

An Estimate

The medieval as well as modern historians have written profusely about the interesting but pathetic character and personality of Humayun which 'attracts but does not dominate'. In the hyperbolic words of Nizamuddin Ahmad, 'Humayun's angelic character was adorned with every manly virtue, and in courage and heroism, he excelled all the princes of his time. All the wealth of Hindustan would not have sufficed to maintain his generosity. In the sciences of astrology and mathematics, he was unrivalled. He made good verses, and all the learned and great and good of the time were admitted to his society and passed the night in his company. Great decorum was observed in his receptions, and all learned discussions were conducted in the most orderly manner...such was his clemency that he repeatedly pardoned the crimes of Mirza Kamran and the Chaghtai nobles when they were taken prisoners and were in his power. He was particular about his ablutions and never allowed the name of God to pass from his tongue until he had performed them'. (*Tabakat-i-Akbari*; Vol. II).

Nevertheless, it is admitted by most of the medieval chroniclers that the indecisive temperament of Humayun was partly due to his habit of eating opium. He took delight in merry-making and wasted the precious time which he ought to have utilized in crushing the power of his enemies. In spite of his manifold virtues as a man, he proved to be a total failure as ruler, administrator and military general. In our opinion, 'Humayun was a misfit in the line of imperial Mughal rulers of India, He was not competent to hold the exalted office of a monarch and he made very little contribution towards the advancement of Indian society in any form It would not be wrong to say that he failed even to uphold the honour and dignity of the imperial house to which he belonged. The only redeeming feature of his life was reoccupation of the throne of Delhi just before his death. But for his restoration and the subsequent achievements of his brilliant son and successor, Akbar the Great, Humayun would have gone down in Indian history as a nonentity'. (*Advanced Study*, ii, pp. 160-61)

Humayun died of an accidental fall in the forty-ninth year of his life which prompted Lane-Poole to observe humorously though correctly that 'his end was of a piece with his character. If there was a possibility of falling, Humayun was not the man to miss it. He tumbled through life, and he tumbled out of it'. (*Medieval India*, p. 237).

❑ ❑

13

THE AFGHAN INTERREGNUM (1540-56)

SECTION 1: THE RISE OF SHER SHAH SURI

The Ancestors of Sher Shah

The rise of Sher Shah Suri as leader of the Afghan reaction against the Mughals and the establishment of the short-lived second Afghan dynasty (after that of the Lodhis) in India splits up the reign of Humayun into two parts by an interlude of 15 years. The original name of Sher Khan, who emerged as the founder of the Suri dynasty with the title of Sher Shah, was Farid. He was the son of Hasan and grandson of Ibrahim, who belonged to the Sur or Suri tribe of the Afghans and hailed from the region of Roh in the Suleiman ranges of Afghanistan; probably, they inhabited the Indo-Afghan border in the vicinity of Peshawar. They migrated to India in search of a livelihood during the reign of Bahlol Lodhi (1450-88).

Hasan, a horse-dealer by profession, settled down at Bajwara, near Hoshiarpur, in the Punjab, and took up service under a Hindu landlord, Rai Mall. Later on, he joined the retinue of an Afghan noble, named Jamal Khan Sarankhani of Hissar Firoza (mod. Hissar in Haryana) as a guard. We are not sure about the exact date and place of birth of Farid. According to one version, he was born at Bajwara in 1472 although Qanungo has reasons to believe that his birth took place at Hissar in 1486 after his parents had shifted there. In 1494, Jamal Khan was transferred to south Bihar and promoted as the *faujdar* of Jaunpur by Sultan Sikander Lodhi. Jamal Khan took Hasan along with him, who, on his commendation, was granted a *jagir* of three villages-Khwaspur, Sehasram and Tanda, by the Sultan.

Early Life of Faríd (Sher Khan)

Faríd spent his youth at Sehasram, situated in a beautiful landscape on the river Son, a tributary of the Ganga, but his early life was far from happy. Though a petty cavalryman, Hasan had four wives and eight sons, and Farid was born of his eldest wife, who was no longer in the good books of her husband. Hasan was greatly under the influence of his youngest wife, a concubine, who felt jealous of Faríd, and did not allow him to win the favours of his father as his eldest son. Fed up with the ill-treatment of his step-mother and neglect of his father, Farid left his parental home at Sehasram at the age of 22 and went to Jaunpur to carve out an independent career for himself. About that time Jaunpur had become an important centre of Islamic education and culture and was called 'the Shiraz of India'. Education, including board and lodging for the boys being free in the Muslim institutions, Faríd devoted himself to the study of Persian and Arabic languages and literature and soon made his presence felt among the intellectuals of the town as a scholar of sorts.

As Manager of his Father's *Jagir*

Jamal Khan, the *faujdar* of Jaunpur and the ex-master of Hasan, also took note of Faríd. He reconciled him with his father and persuaded the latter to appoint him as the manager of his parental *jagir* in c.1497. Farid held this charge for about 21 years, long enough to gain excellent experience in the civil and military administration of the estate from the grass-roots. He organised militia for its internal defence, suppressed the rebellious *zamindars* and evolved a good land revenue system, based on the measurement and classification of the land according to its fertility, and fixation of the revenue on the actual production. It stood him in good stead when he assumed the reins of government as the sovereign ruler of India in the concluding years of his life. Abbas Khan Sarwani, the celebrated biographer of Sher Shah, makes him to express his attitude and treatment towards the peasantry in the first person as follows:

> 'The cultivators are the source of prosperity. I have encouraged them and sent them away, and shall always watch over their condition that no man may oppress and injure them; for if a ruler cannot protect humble peasantry from the lawless, it is tyranny to exact revenue from them'. (*Tarikh-i-Sher Shahi,* E&D.iv, p. 314)

The success of Faríd as the manager of his father's *jagir* did not end the dispute about his succession and, instead, aroused the jealousy of his step-mother and half-brothers as they apprehended that, after the death of Hasan, he might appropriate the whole of the estate to himself. This domestic feud compelled Faríd to leave Sehasram once again. Now he made his way to the court of Sultan Ibrahim Lodhi at Agra and appealed to him for the grant of his parental *jagir* to him in succession. The Sultan did not oblige him as he was not much impressed by Farid's complaint against his own father. But Faríd did not lose hope and hanged on at Agra for a couple of years until his father's death when his request was granted by the king.

Armed with the royal *firman*, Faríd returned to Sehasram to claim the exclusive proprietorship of Hasan's estate in c.1520-21. He joined the service of Behar Khan Lohani, the Afghan governor of south Bihar, to strengthen his position against his rival claimants to his parental heritage. Once on a hunting expedition in the entourage of Behar Khan, Faríd killed a tiger with his sword single-handed and received the title of Sher Khan from his master. Thereafter, his rise to power was very rapid. Before long, he received appointment as the deputy governor of the province and tutor of his infant son, Jalal Khan, from Behar Khan Lohani.

As Deputy of Bihar Khan Lohani

After the first battle of Panipat and fall of the Lodhi dynasty in 1526, Behar Khan Lohani declared himself independent ruler of south Bihar with the title of Sultan Muhammad Shah. It automatically enhanced the power and status of Sher Khan as the deputy Sultan and enabled him to emerge as one of the prominent Afghan leaders. No wonder, it aroused the jealousy of the Lohani and Farmuli nobles who dominated the Afghan politics of south Bihar because they regarded Sher Khan as an outsider and an intruder. They, therefore, resorted to conspiracies to bring about his fall and charged him of disloyalty to the Lohani chief by spreading rumours that Sher Khan was secretly preparing to join the camp of Mahmud Lodhi, the younger brother of Ibrahim Lodhi, who had sneaked into Bihar to re-unite the Afghans against the Mughals. Sultan Muhammad Shah was taken in by these rumours and turned against Sher Khan with the result that the latter had to flee from Bihar for his dear life.

In the Service of Babar

About this time, Babar had broken the power of the Rajputs and launched a major military-cum-diplomatic offensive against the defiant Afghans of eastern India. Thoroughly disgusted with the malicious conduct of his Afghan colleagues, Sher Khan was left with no other alternative but to join the Mughal camp like many other Afghans in distress. He sought an interview with Babar through the courtesy of Junaid Barlas, an official of the Mughal court at Agra, and remained in the service of Babar from April 1527 to the end of 1528. He is said to have rendered a useful service to Babar in his eastern campaign and was restored his parental *jagir* of Sehasram, Khwaspur and Tanda. The association of Sher Khan with Babar proved very short-lived, however. Abbas Sarwani refers to an incident which estranged the relationships between the two. He writes that

> 'One day Sher Khan waited upon the Emperor (Babar) at an entertainment, when it happened that they placed before him a dish of solid meat, which he did not know the customary mode of eating. So he cut it into small pieces with his dagger, and putting them into his spoon easily disposed of them. The Emperor took note it and wondered at Sher Khan's ingenuity, and said to Khalifa (Nizamuddin Ali), his minister, who was at his elbow:
>
> *Keep an eye on Sher Khan; he is a clever man, and the marks of royalty are visible on his forehead. I have seen many Afghan nobles, greater men than he, but they never made any impression on me. But as soon as I saw this man, it entered into my mind that he ought to be arrested, for I find in him the qualities of greatness and the marks of mightiness.*
>
> Sher Khan also sagaciously perceived that the Emperor had spoken something concerning him. When he got to his own quarters, he said to his men: *The Emperor today looked much at me, and said something to his minister; and cast evil glances towards me. This is not a fit place for me to remain. I shall go away.*' (*Tarikh-i-Sher Shahi*, E&D; iv, pp. 331-32)

'Mounting at once, Sher Khan left the Mughal camp', and made good his escape before Babar's men could take hold of him. 'Nature had, however, preordained that Babar's prophecy must come true, and with a vengeance indeed! Babar could never contemplate even in his dream that this Afghan youth, whom he wanted to languish in his prison, was destined to transplant his own imperial dynasty' before long.

As Leader of the Afghans in South Bihar

After deserting the Mughals, Sher Khan became homeless once again but the news about his sudden flight from Babar's camp alerted the other Afghan chiefs who had rallied to his support. During his absence from Bihar, his self-seeking rivals at the court of Sultan Muhammad Shah had also been exposed and discredited. Therefore, when the latter heard of

Sher Khan's rupture with Babar, he at once invited him to re-join his court, and re-appointed him as the tutor and guardian of his minor son Jalal Khan. Muhammad Shah died in October 1528, and his widowed Queen, Dudu Bibi, in her capacity as the regent of her minor son Jalal Khan, appointed Sher Khan as her *vakil* and placed the administration of the state in his hands. Sher Khan made the best use of this opportunity to consolidate his position by entrusting the higher civil and military offices to his trustworthy friends and favourites. It considerably raised the power and prestige of Sher Khan among the Afghans of South Bihar.

On the call of unity among the Afghans against the Mughals, Sher Khan did extend his support to Prince Mahmud Lodhi, the claimant to the throne of Delhi, but his association with him was only half-hearted and nominal; he supplied but only a small contingent of troops to support the Lodhi prince against Babar in the battle of Ghagra on May 6, 1529. After the defeat of Mahmud Lodhi at the hands of the Mughals and his flight from Bihar, Jalal Khan and his minister Sher Khan offered their submission to Babar and were restored to their previous positions of power in Bihar on the condition of paying tribute to the Mughal court at Agra. Sher Khan quickly restored law and order within the territories under his charge, and reorganised the civil and military setup of the state to further strengthen his position. After the death of Dudu Bibi early in 1530, he became the *de facto* ruler of South Bihar as the regent of the minor Sultan. At this stage, the Lohani nobles made a desperate bid to oust Sher Khan from power but he stood the ground firmly. He was willing to share power with the kinsmen of Jalal Khan but the latter took hold of the boy Sultan and fled to Bengal to seek help from Nusrat Shah for fighting against Sher Khan who was dubbed as usurper by them. It left the field open for Sher Khan to declare himself the independent ruler of South Bihar. He avoided adopting any high-sounding royal title, however, and was content to style himself simply as *Hazrat-i-Ala*. He strengthened his position militarily as well as financially by acquiring the famous stronghold of Chunar by his marriage with Lad Malika, the widow of Taj Khan, a former Afghan governing chief of the fief. By the time of Humayun's accession to the throne at Delhi in December 1530, Sher Khan had emerged as the most prominent leader of the Afghans in India who stood to re-organise his people against the Mughals. According to Abbas, Sher Khan, while in the service of the Mughals, is once boasted to have confided to his Afghan friends that 'if luck and fortune favour me, I will very shortly expel the Mughals from Hind, for the Mughals are not superior to the Afghans in mettle or single combat; but the Afghans have let the empire of Hind slip from their hands, on account of their internal dissensions. Since I have been amongst the Mughals, and know their conduct in action, I see that they have no order or discipline, and that their kings, from pride of birth and station, do not personally superintend the government, but leave all the affairs and business of the State to their nobles and ministers, in whose sayings and doings they put perfect confidence. These grandees act on corrupt motives in every case, whether it is that of a soldier's or a cultivator's, or a rebellious *zamindar*'s. Whoever has money, whether loyal or disloyal, can get his business settled as he likes by paying for it; but if a man has no money, although he may have displayed his loyalty on a hundred occasions, or be a veteran soldier, he will never gain his end.'(*Ibid*., pp. 329-30)

Initial Conflict with Humayun

The untimely death of Babar so soon after the establishment of his rule in northern India encouraged the various Afghan chieftains of Bihar, Bengal and Gujarat to renew their struggle against the Mughals. Sher Khan was equally committed to the forging of a united front of all the Afghan chiefs of eastern India against the Mughals but his undisputed leadership was not acceptable to many. Some of his political rivals still looked towards Mahmud Lodhi, the last scion of the Lodhi dynasty, who was hovering around as a fugitive, and invited him to assume the command of the Afghan bands that were ready to march upon the Mughal province of Jaunpur. Sher Shah extended moral support to them as usual but refrained from offering any substantial assistance. They were defeated by Humayun at Dauhria in August 1532.

The First Siege of Chunar by Humayun: Flushed with victory, Humayun moved forward and laid siege to the fort of Chunar on the Ganga, then held by Jalal Khan, the eldest son of Sher Khan (not to be confused with Jalal Khan, the son and successor of Bahar Khan Lohani). The first siege of Chunar by Humayun lasted about four months but he failed to conquer it. In January 1533, Sher Khan made peace with Humayun by offering nominal submission and agreed to send his third son Qutub Khan, with 5,000 horsemen, to Agra to be in attendance upon the Mughal emperor. Humayun lifted the siege and returned to Agra, apparently as a victor, although Sher Shah's prestige soared high among the Afghan insurgents for having put up the heroic defence of

Chunar. It was only after his initial success at Chunar and the final exit of Mahmud Lodhi from the scene of action that the Afghan nobles of Bihar and Bengal offered their whole-hearted support to Sher Khan.

Like Sher Khan's earlier service under Babar, Qutub Khan's association with Humayun also proved very short-lived. He deserted the Mughal camp at Agra and returned to Bihar when Humayun was engaged in the conquest of Malwa and Gujarat.

Conquest of Bengal by Sher Khan (1533-37)

Nusrat Shah, the reputed Afghan ruler of Bengal died in December 1532. His son and successor, Alauddin Firoze Shah, was assassinated by one of his Afghan nobles, who ascended the throne of Bengal with the title of Sultan Ghiasuddin Mahmud Shah in May 1533. It gave an opportunity to Sher Khan to settle his scores with his Lohani rivals, who had taken refuge with the ruler of Bengal and sought his help to fight against Sher Khan, the usurper of power in South Bihar so-called. Now that the new ruler of Bengal, though an Afghan, was also a usurper, the Lohani nobles lost their argument and moral support of the Afghans, in general, to oppose Sher Khan's rise to power. Sher Khan exploited this situation to his benefit and launched a full-fledged offensive against Ghiasuddin on the plea of reuniting the Afghans against the Mughals. He inflicted a crushing defeat to his rivals in the decisive battle of Surajgarh in 1534. It proved a turning point in the career of Sher Khan and whetted his appetite for further conquests. As a result of this victory, writes Abbas Sarwani, 'the whole of the treasure, elephants, and train of artillery of the Bengal chief fell into the hands of Sher Khan, who was thus supplied with munitions of war, and became the master of the kingdom of Bihar and much besides'. Mahmud Shah could not be ousted from power and the war against him was protracted for another three years, He was repeatedly defeated by Sher Khan and was made to lose the territories of Bengal bit by bit. In vain did the Bengal chief seek help from the Portuguese of Chinsura to fight against Sher Khan as the later proved 'too clever for both' the allies. In 1536, Sher Khan invaded Bengal for the second time. The army of Bengal blocked his passage at the Teliagarhi Pass, but leaving a detachment there under his son, Jalal Khan, Sher Khan marched 'through the unfrequented Jharkhand route' and surprised the Sultan of Bengal by making a sudden appearance before Gaur, the capital of Bengal'. Fear-struck, Mahmud Shah sued for peace by offering 13,00,000 gold coins as tribute and ceding a large slice of the Bengal territory to him.

Sher Khan was not content with the acknowledgement of formal subjugation by Mahmud Shah. He was eager to conquer the whole of Bengal while Humayun was still engaged in his conflict with Bahadur Shah of Malwa and Gujarat. Early in 1537, he marched upon Bengal for the third time on the pretext that Mahmud Shah had 'failed to pay the annual tribute and had not given up unfriendly policy'. Besieged in the stronghold of Gaur, Mahmud Shah appealed to Humayun for help. The latter responded to his call in July 1537 but, instead of marching upon Gaur direct in support of the Bengal chief, resorted to the second siege of Chunar as if to atone for his earlier omission to conquer the stronghold. The second siege of Chunar by Humayun, which dragged on for six months, from October 1537 to March 1538, also proved a failure. As referred to in the preceding chapter, Sher Khan cleverly engaged the Mughal emperor in a futile talk for a settlement while exerting himself to the full for completing his task in Bengal. Humayun heard about the fall of Gaur to Sher Khan in the first week of April 1538 and lifted the siege of Chunar for forward movement towards Bengal, but Mahmud Shah, the vanquished Sultan of Bengal, reached his camp as refugee and died of his wounds a few days later.

Renewal of Conflict with Humayun

In the renewed conflict with Humayun, as described elsewhere in this study, the passage of the Mughal army was blocked at the Teliagarhi pass for over two months by Jalal Khan while Sher Khan's men transferred all the treasures of Gaur to the stronghold of Rohtas, situated in the inaccessible mountainous region of Bihar on the banks of the river Son, and vacated Bengal. Humayun overran Bengal without much resistance and wasted more than eight months in festivities and merry-making at Gaur while Sher Khan utilized this period to cut off his communications with Agra by taking possession of the intervening territories of eastern U.P. and northern Bihar, including the major towns of Tirhut, Jaunpur and Banaras. His troops started raids into the Mughal territories as far as Kanauj and Kalpi. On his return from Bengal, Humayun was defeated in the historic battle of Chausa on June 26, 1539. Abbas writes that after this momentous victory, Sher Khan himself went in hot pursuit of the fleeing Mughal soldiers; the vanquished Mughal emperor was also hotly pursued but allowed to escape to Delhi. The whole country as far as Kalpi and Kanauj was taken possession of and contingents of troops were despatched to destroy the country around Agra and Delhi in preparation for the final contest with Humayun.

According to Dr. K.R. Qanungo, the victory of Chausa had far-reaching results; it brought about 'a radical change in Sher Khan's objective in life'. Whereas, before this victory, he would have been contented with the possession of Bihar and Bengal as a Mughal vassal, he had 'now won by this single stroke the whole territory of the Sharqi kingdom of Jaunpur in addition to the kingdoms of Bengal and Bihar in independent sovereignty, and could legitimately claim equality with the (Mughal) Emperor. So Delhi was no longer such a far cry for the future.' (*Sher Shah and His Times*, 2nd edn; Bombay, *i*, pp. 24-25). A brief coronation ceremony, of Sher Khan which, took place at Chausa, was followed by the immediate dispatch of a strong army to Gaur to expel the Mughal garrison from there. After the victory of Chausa, Sher Khan was proclaimed emperor of Hindustan with the express desire and approval of the Afghan nobles and camp-followers who had assembled there soon after the battle to offer their felicitations to him. He assumed the insignia of royalty and Khutba was read in his name with the title of Sher Shah. He struck coins in his name and issued letters of victory to his officers in the form of *firmans*. Abbas tells us that he had initially taken the new title of 'Shah Alam' although some of the coins issued in the name of Sher Shah carry the title of 'Sultan-i-Adil' as well.

As for Bengal, Jahangir Quli Beg had been left by Humayun there with a token force of 6,000 soldiers only for its defence. He had setup his post at Garhi which was taken by the Afghan troops in a single assault. Jahangir Quli was defeated and offered to surrender but was treacherously slain along with his camp-followers. Gaur fell to the Afghans without a fight, and Sher Shah reached there in person soon thereafter to complete the conquest of Bengal. Sher Shah did not have much time to establish his undisputed sway over the whole of Bengal but it appears that his rule extended over the country around Gaur, Satgaon and Chittagong. His second coronation ceremony, accompanied by profuse display and rejoicings was celebrated during his stay at Gaur. Sher Shah's ambitions soared high, and he now began to chalk out plans for driving out the Mughals from India lock, stock and barrel. He welcomed all the deserters from the Mughal army and sent his emissaries to the important Muslim chieftains of northern and central India to garner support against Humayun.

The final issue between the antagonists was settled in the battle of Kanauj which was fought on May 17, 1540; it resulted in the defeat of Humayun and total annihilation of his army. After his victory at Kanauj, Sher Shah gave a hot chase to the fugitive Mughal emperor and did not allow him to enter Agra and Delhi which were taken possession of by the Afghan troops without any loss of time. The Afghan forces entered Lahore in November 1540 and the whole of northwestern India, including the southwestern Punjab, Multan, northwestern frontier and Sindh up to the Khyber pass, was brought under effective control by them by the end of 1541. Sher Shah and his successors held their sway as the imperial rulers for fifteen years and left behind a valuable legacy of efficient civil and military administration over which Akbar, the illustrious son of Humayun, built the grand edifice of a strong national government in medieval India

SECTION 2: SHER SHAH SURI AS EMPEROR OF INDIA (1540-45)

Sher Shah Suri became the emperor of India at the advanced age of sixty-eight and was destined to rule for a brief span of five years only. He often used to lament that he had been blessed with sovereignty by God 'in the evening of his life'. But even at this age, he did not hesitate in commanding the royal forces in person when the circumstances so demanded; he used to attend to the business of the State for long hours every day, and continued to exercise strict supervision and control over the civil and military affairs till his very death.

Occupation of Agra, Delhi and Lahore

The victory of Kanauj had uprooted Humayun and provided an opportunity to Sher Shah to step into the shoes of his adversary but the occupation of Agra, Delhi, and Lahore to legitimatize his claim to the imperial throne was yet a far cry. It goes to the credit of Sher Shah that he not only humbled the pride of the Mughal emperor in the decisive battles of Chausa and Kanauj but also moved with swiftness and determination thereafter and smashed all pockets of resistance throughout the erstwhile Mughal dominions of India. He wrested from the hands of Humayun and Kamran not only the strategic towns of Agra, Delhi and Lahore but also a substantial part of northwestern India upto the Khyber Pass during the first one year and a half of his imperial regime. He was in effective personal command of his forces all this time.

Conquest of the Punjab and Northwestern Frontier

Following close upon the heels of his advancing detachments, Sher Shah marked his personal presence at Agra and Delhi, and after making quick arrangements for the restoration of civil government, moved on and reached Lahore by November 1540. At Lahore, Sher Shah came to know that the Mughal princes, having failed to re-unite even at this hour of peril, had dispersed in different directions, viz., Humayun towards Sindh, Hindal towards Multan by a different route, and Kamran towards Kabul. Sher Shah lost no time in dispatching Afghan detachments of mobile cavalry and light artillery in their hot pursuit and himself also moved westward quickly, frightening and driving away the fugitive Mughal princes to deprive them of any respite. On reaching the bank of the river Chenab, Sher Shah sent yet another detachment to pursue Hindal; then he went to Bhera and from there to Khushab where he halted. Khwas Khan had been sent against Humayun with instructions not to engage the fleeing Mughal emperor but only drive him out of his dominions. Likewise, Qutb Khan was sent against Kamran with similar instructions. Khwas Khan gave a chase to Humayun as for as Mithankot, situated on the confluence of the Sutlej with four other rivers of the Punjab, and then returned to rejoin Sher Shah at Khushab. Here the Baluch chiefs – Fath Khan, Ismail Khan and Ghazi Khan made their submission to Sher Shah.

Suppression of the Gakkhars

From Khushab, Sher Shah sent an expedition for the conquest of the Gakkhar country lying between the upper courses of the Jhelum and the Indus. The Gakkhars, a freedom-loving tribe of the Hindus, 'inhabited a mountainous region between the upper courses of the Jhelum and the Indus. They were inimical to the Afghans and their country occupied a strategic position through which an invader from the northwest might suddenly enter the Punjab which was then in Sher Shah's possession. So, for security and safety of his dominion, an offensive had to be undertaken.'(J. N. Chaudhuri in *History and Culture of the Indian People*, BVB, vii, p.47). The Afghan army ravaged their country but failed to bring the Gakkhars under complete subjugation. A few of their chiefs, particularly Rai Sarang Gakkhar, refused to acknowledge the overlordship of Sher Shah. To tackle the problem, Sher Shah conceived of a plan to build a strong military post there. 'A proper site was then found out for the construction of a fortress with a view to guarding the northern frontier and keeping the Gakkhars under control. A gigantic and impregnable fort was built 16 kilometres northwest of the town of Jhelum and named Rohtas, after his famous strong fortress in Bihar. It was completed by his son Islam Shah.' (*Ibid*). In March 1541, Sher

Shah had to leave the northwestern frontier in a hurry to deal with Khizer Khan, the rebellious governor of Bengal, and the task of completing the conquest of Multan and Sindh was left to his military generals.

Settlement of Bengal

Sher Shah had recovered Bengal from Jahangir Quli Khan, Humayun's lieutenant, immediately after the defeat of the Mughal emperor at Chausa. Before proceeding towards Kanauj to face his imperial adversary, he had appointed Khizer Khan, one of his reputed military generals, as the governor of Bengal and posted a strong Afghan contingent at Gaur under his charge for its defence. In March 1541, when Sher Shah was stationed at Khushab and engaged in the Gakkhar campaign, he received the intelligence about the rebellious activities of Khizer Khan. During Sher Shah's absence from Bengal for over a year, Khizer Khan had married a daughter of the deceased Sultan Mahmud Shah to enlist the support of the sympathizers of the erstwhile ruling family and was suspected of misappropriating the government funds to strengthen his army with intent to declare his independence.

On receipt of reports, Sher Shah, while keeping his mission a top secret, set out from Khushab at the head of a large mobile cavalry at once, and thundered at the gates of Gaur unannounced. He took Khizer Khan by surprise, put him in chains and inflicted severe punishments on his disaffected advisers and camp-followers; he believed in nipping the evil in the bud. As a shrewd politician and experienced administrator, 'he decided to do away with the military governorship of Bengal to avert the danger of a future rebellion. He remodeled the administration of Bengal by dividing it into as many as 47 *sarkars* or districts, placing each of them under a district officer, called the *shiqdar-i-shiqdaran or chief shiqdar*, with a small militia, to maintain law and order and run the civil administration of the territory under his charge. These officers-in-charge of the *sarkars*, viz., the chief *shiqdars* were recruited by and put under the direct supervision and control of the imperial court. The office of the provincial governor was abolished and, in his place, a civilian nominee of the Emperor, called *Qazi Fazilat*, was posted at the provincial capital who supervised the work of *shiqdar-i-shiqdaran* and settled disputes among them. The *Qazi Fazilat* does not seem to have a strong military force under his command nor did he enjoy independent executive powers but saw to it that the districts were properly administered, the revenues were collected and submitted regularly to the central treasury, and above all, he exercised vigilance over the activities of the district officers to ensure that they did not enter into any conspiracy or nurtured rebellious intentions. The system, which was based on the highly centralized bureaucratic machinery, was at once original in principle and proved very efficient in its working because it struck at the very roots of the chronic rebellions in the far off province of Bengal. Sher Shah's hold on the administration of Bengal was further strengthened by the establishment of military posts or *thanas* of imperial troops, under the trustworthy and promising military officers of the junior ranks in the fortresses and other places of strategic importance throughout Bengal.

Conquest of Malwa (1542)

In 1542, Sher Shah led a military expedition for the conquest of Malwa which was then ruled over by Mallu Khan. He had taken possession of Malwa in 1537 after the death of Bahadur Shah and assumed the title of Sultan Qadir Shah. Sher Shah coveted Malwa because its independence had always been irksome to the monarchs of Delhi and Agra. As it controlled the road from the north to the south, its possession was all the more necessary. Sher Shah proceeded towards Malwa by way of Gwalior, which was still held by a Mughal noble. After the battle of Kanauj, Sher Shah had despatched Shujaat Khan, one of his Afghan officers, to besiege the fort but he had failed to conquer it. On the approach of Sher Shah's army, the Mughal commandant of the fort made an unconditional surrender to him and was meted out very lenient treatment by Sher Shah. Similarly, Mallu Khan also submitted without a fight and accorded a warm reception to Sher Shah at Ujjain, the capital of Malwa. Sher Shah intended to send him as the *faujdar* of Kalpi but Qadir Shah thought it beneath his dignity to accept a subordinate position and, suspecting foul play, fled to Gujarat and sought refuge with its ruler Mahmud III. After making suitable arrangements for the governance of Malwa, Sher Shah returned to Agra. On the way back, he passed through Ranthambhor and persuaded its Mughal officer to surrender the fort in return for a suitable service under the central government.

Conquest of Multan and Sindh

After expelling Humayun, Kamran and other Mughal princes from the Punjab and northwestern frontier, Sher Shah had to return from Khushab in 1541 to suppress the revolt in Bengal. He had left behind two Afghan generals, Khwas Khan and Haibat Khan Niyazi to administer the region and hold the Gakkhars under check. Khwas Khan was subsequently recalled but Haibat Khan proved successful in the suppression of the refractory chiefs. He is credited to have completed the conquest of Multan and its dependencies. Upper Sindh with its famous forts of Bhakkar and Sehwan also fell into the hands of Sher Shah's forces in1543.

War against the Hindu Rulers

The Conquest of Raisen (1543): The Hindu principality of Raisen situated about forty-five kilometres to the east of Bhopal, in Central India, had risen to a state of importance during the later days of Humayun's reign. Its ruler, Puran Mall Chauhan, son of Rai Silhadi, wrested the stronghold of Chanderi from its Mughal governor and strengthened his position by compelling many Muslim landlords of the region to acknowledge his over-lordship. With the rise of Sher Shah to power and the conquest of Malwa by him, the existence of a sovereign Hindu state so close to the imperial Muslim authority, became untenable. Therefore, during Sher Shah's campaign into Malwa, Puran Mall had voluntarily offered his submission and was allowed to retain his state as a tributary, Nevertheless, Sher Shah as an imperialist did not want that a strong nucleus of Hindu power should take its roots within the fold of the Muslim empire. Accordingly, Sher Shah's unprovoked attack on Raisen in 1543 had political motivations though Puran Mall was falsely accused of ill-treating his Muslim subjects. Puran Mall and his soldiers 'fought gallantly, but when defeat stared them in the face, they agreed to vacate the fort on the express promise made by Sher Shah that their lives and property would be fully safeguarded. Sher Shah was ill-advised, however, by some fanatic Muslim divines to break his promise'. This incident took place in June 1543. According to Abbas, '*Ulama*, who accompanied the victorious army, pronounced a decision for the death of Puran Mall', and Sher Shah allowed his men to attack the Hindus when they were making preparations to vacate the fort. Abbas writes, *inter alia*, as follows:

> 'At night, orders were given to Isa Khan Hajib, that he should desire his troops to collect with the elephants in all haste at a certain spot, for that Sher Shah intended to make a forced march towards Gondwana. To Habib Khan he gave secret orders that he should watch Bhaia Puran Mall and take care he did not fly, and not to speak of a word of this to any living creature, for that he (Sher Shah) had long entertained this design'.

When the elephants and troops were at the appointed spot, they reported it. Sher Shah ordered that at sunrise, they should surround the tents of Bhaia Puran Mall. Puran Mall was told that they were surrounding his encampment, and going into the tent of his beloved wife Ratnavali who sang Hindi melodies very sweetly. He (Puran Mall) cut off her (Ratnavali's) head, and, coming out, said to his companions: *"I have done this; do you also slay your wives and families".*

When the Hindus were engaged in putting their women and families to death, the Afghans on all sides commenced the slaughter of the *Kafirs*. Puran Mall and his companions, like hogs at bay, failed not to exhibit valour and gallantry, but in the twinkling of an eye all were slain. Such of their wives and children as were not slain were captured. One daughter of Puran Mall and three sons of his elder brother were taken alive, the rest were all killed. Sher Khan gave the daughter of Puran Mall to some itinerant minstrels (*bazigaran*), that they might make her dance in the *bazaars*, and ordered the boys to be castrated, that the race of the oppressor might not increase. He made over the fort of Raisen to Munshi Shahbaz Khan Achakhail Sarwani, and returned himself towards Agra, and remained at the capital; during the rainy season'. (*Tarikh-Sher Shahi*, E&D. iv, pp.402-3).

War against Marwar: The conquest of Raisen encouraged Sher Shah to wipe out other Hindu states and principalities of northern India one by one. Marwar, with its capital at Jodhpur, had risen to occupy the first place among the sovereign Hindu kingdoms in Rajputana after the death of Rana Sangram Singh *alias* Rana Sanga of Mewar; its boundary at Jhajhar in the north was only about 50 kilometres from Delhi. Maldeva Rathor, the reigning chief of Jodhpur, ascended the throne after the death of his father, Rao Gangaji, in 1531. Taking advantage of the fall of the Lodhi dynasty and early death of Babar soon thereafter, the Hindu rulers of northern India picked up some courage to overthrow the Muslim domination and regain sovereignty. Maldeva, being a capable military general and energetic ruler, aspired to step into the shoes of Rana Sanga as leader of the numerous Hindu states and principalities into which Rajputana was then divided. He conceived a bold plan of increasing his power and expanding the boundaries of his kingdom by absorbing the neighbouring small principalities by persuasion or force, and by extending his sphere of influence among the other states of the region. He started by annexing the traditional Rajput estates of Merta, Jaitaran,

Bilara, Mallani, Siwana, Didwana, Pachbhadra and Bali. He also waged war against Bikaner and deprived it of a big slice of its territory. Thereafter, he joined issue with Jaipur and compelled its chief to renounce the suzerainty over its tributary states of Jalor, Tonk, Toda and Malpur, the chiefs of which transferred their loyalties to Jodhpur. When Humayun was engaged in his life and death struggle with Sher Shah, Maldeva laid his hands on the Muslim governorships of Nagaur and Ajmer as well and annexed them to his dominions.

The contemporary chroniclers inform us that after the debacle of Kanauj, when Humayun was wandering about in Rajputana and Sindh in his bid to find a foothold somewhere, Maldeva Rathor, being an ambitious diplomat, invited him, in July 1540, to come to Jodhpur and make an attempt to recover the throne of Delhi with his assistance. Perhaps, Maldeva's object seemed to be 'to have on the throne of Delhi a ruler who should be his friend and ally'. Humayun took more than a year to think of availing the hospitality of Maldeva's offer, however. By that time, the political situation in the country had undergone a sea-change as Sher Shah had consolidated his position as the master of northern and northwestern India Therefore, by the time Humayun proceeded towards Jodhpur to seek the help of Marwar chief; the latter had changed his mind. The Mughal envoy who went to the court of Maldeva to apprise him of Humayun's intended arrival, was taken aback to notice the agents of Sher Shah at Jodhpur. Suspecting a foul play, he rushed back to his master and advised him to leave Marwar at once. Obviously, the Rajput chief had been warned by Sher Shah not to give shelter to the fugitive Mughal emperor but arrest and deliver him to the Afghan monarch. Under the circumstances, Maldeva adopted a neutral attitude for fear of offending Sher Shah or Humayun. The fugitive Mughal emperor, in panic, had to retrace his steps towards Sindh 'suffering unspeakable hardship and privation' in the month of August 1541, during the hottest days of the season, in the desert of Rajputana; though harassed on the way back, Humayun was yet left unmolested by the Rathor troops.

Sher Shah was annoyed by Maldeva's dubious conduct; 'he wanted absolute friendliness and submission from the Rajput chief'. Maldeva had failed to capture and hand over the fugitive Mughal emperor into his hands. Moreover, Sher Shah could not brook the thriving of a powerful Hindu ruler as that of Jodhpur, though under the suzerainty of Delhi, so close to the imperial capital. According to Abbas Sarwani, the Muslim *ulama* could not tolerate that a Hindu chief should hold under sway the governorships of Nagaur and Ajmer which once formed a part of the

Sultanate of Delhi. By all accounts, the powerful Rajput state of Jodhpur posed a serious threat to the safety of the Muslim regime at Delhi and Agra, and the war between Sher Shah and Maldeva was inevitable. Hence after the rainy season of 1543, Sher Shah marched upon Marwar 'with the largest and the most magnificent army that he had ever led into the field'; it numbered about 60,000 cavalry and 3,00,000 infantry, as estimated by the author of *Makhzan-i-Afghani*. Sher Shah invaded Jodhpur all of a sudden before Maldeva, who was encamped near Ajmer, could take steps for the protection of his capital or stop him at the borders of his kingdom.. Abbas narrates that

> 'When Sher Shah marched from the capital of Agra and arrived at Fatehpur Sikri, he ordered that each division of the army should march together in order of battle, and should throw up an earthen entrenchment at every halting ground. On the way, they encamped one day on a plain of sand, and in spite of every labour, they could not, on account of the sand, make an entrenchment. Sher Shah considered by what contrivance the entrenchment could be completed. Mahmud Khan, grandson of Sher Shah, said: *Let my Lord order that sacks should be filled with sand, and that they should make the entrenchment with the bags.* Sher Shah praised his grandson's contrivance, and was greatly delighted, and ordered that they should make the fortification of bags, filled with sand; and accordingly, at that halting place, they did so.' (*Tarikh-i-Sher Shahi*)

Maldeva came to know of Sher Shah's invasion when the Afghan army, passing through Didwana, had already reached Merta. The Rajput chief was frightened, and hastened back from Ajmer towards Jodhpur with his 50,000 cavalry to face the enemy in the open battle. On hearing of Maldeva's rapid advance from Ajmer, Sher Shah, instead of proceeding towards Jodhpur diverted his direction towards the Rajput columns and the rivals confronted each other at the village of Sumel, near Jaitaran, situated about 90 kilometres to the east of Jodhpur. 'For a month, the two armies lay opposite to each other, and, in the meantime, the position of Sher Shah became critical owing to difficulties of food supplies for the huge army. The ruler of Marwar was in an advantageous position and the initiative of action lay with him.' (J. N. Chaudhuri in *History and Culture of the Indian People*, BVB, VII, p. 82). To get rid of this uncomfortable position, Sher Shah took recourse to a stratagem to create dissensions between the Rajput chief and his nobles. According to Abbas,

'Having caused the letters, written in the name of Maldeo's nobles (and addressed to himself), to this effect, viz., *Let not the king permit any anxiety or doubt to find its way to his heart. During the battle, we will seize Maldeo, and bring him to you;* and having enclosed these letters in a *Kharita* (Silken bag), he gave it to a certain person, and directed him to go near to the tent of the *Vakil* of Maldeo and drop the *Kharita* there (as if it had fallen there by accident), and conceal himself. Sher Shah's agent did so as he was ordered. And when the *Vakil* of Maldeo saw the *Kharita* lying, he picked it up, and sent the letters to Maldeo. When the latter learnt their contents, he was much alarmed and (suspecting treachery on the part of his officers) fled without fighting. Although his nobles took oaths of fidelity, he did not heed them'.

Accordingly, before the dawn, Maldeva Rathor had decamped to the great relief of Sher Shah and rejoicing of his army. When the truth about the ruse played on the Rajput chief became known to his lieutenants, who were alleged to have written the purported letters for the foe, and were suspected of treachery, they separated themselves from the main Rajput army, and with their 12,000 troops, made a frontal attack on the Afghans to prove their innocence. They pushed through the Muslim camp and made their way to the very royal tents of Sher Shah. Abbas writes that

'Some of the Rajput chieftains, such as Jaya Chandel and Goha, and others, came and attacked Sher Shah and displayed exceeding valour. Part of the (Afghan) army was routed, and a certain Afghan came to Sher Shah and abused him in his native tongue, saying; *Mount, for the infidels are routing your army.* Sher Shah was then performing his morning devotions, and was reading the *Musta-abi-i'ashr*. He gave no reply to the Afghan but by a sign ordered his horse and mounted'.

The Rajput intruders fought desperately but they were overwhelmed and cut to a man. Jaya and Goha were slain by Khwas Khan and his troops. When Sher Shah 'learnt about the valour and gallantry of Jaya and Goha, he said: I had nearly lost the Kingdom of Delhi for a handful of *Bajra* (millet)'.

Maldeva retreated from the battlefield to Jodhpur, and after collecting his family and treasures from there, retired to the fort of Siwana on the borders of Gujarat. The jubilant Afghans attacked

Jodhpur and took it after a brief but bloody encounter with its defenders. Sher Shah did not pursue or challenge the Rathor chief but his army took possession of the Rajput territories from Ajmer to Mount Abu. Before his return to Agra, he deputed Khwas Khan as the governor of Jodhpur to consolidate his hold over the region.

Khwas Khan took his residence at Jodhpur but the town had been deserted by most of the Rajput families, including the ruling elite and the business community, and the Muslim army of occupation faced non-cooperation and hostility from the Rajput subjects, in general. Khwas Khan did not think it safe to reside in the royal palace of the Rajput chiefs, situated in the heart of the town, and felt constrained to build a new township, named after him as Khwaspur, in the vicinity of Jodhpur, for his stay and the setup of his court, and the stationing of his officers and camp-followers. The strongholds of Jodhpur, Ajmer and Mount Abu were refortified and heavily garrisoned by the Muslim troops but many other forts and fortresses, situated in various towns and the countryside were demolished to avoid their re-occupation by the Rajput insurgents.

Subjugation of Mewar: Earlier it was believed that, after the fall of Jodhpur in 1544, Sher Shah had proceeded directly towards Mewar for the reduction of Chittor to keep the momentum of easy success attained by him against Maldeva; but a careful study of the contemporary chronicles reveals that from Jodhpur he did return to Agra for a couple of months to manage the affairs of the state and to collect reinforcements and supplies for an assault on the other Rajput states. Abbas informs us that 'Sher Shah's nobles represented to him that, as the rainy season was near at hand, it was advisable to go into cantonments. Sher Shah replied: "I will spend the rainy season in a place where I can carry on my work"; and marched towards the fort of Chittor. When he was yet twelve *Kos* from the fort of Chittor, the Raja, who was its ruler, sent him the keys'.

The author of *Tarikh-i-Daudi* records that, before proceeding on the Chittor expedition, Sher Shah prayed for his success at the shrine of Khwaja Muinuddin Chishti for his success; probably, he led the army of invasion via Ajmer. The unconditional submission of Chittor to Sher Shah needs a brief review of its recent past. The readers are aware that Rana Sanga, the adversary of Babar, had raised the power and prestige of Mewar to the pinnacle of its glory. Babar scored a victory over Rana Sanga in the historic battle of Kanwaha in March 1527 but he did not follow up his success by advancing upon Chittor, the premier citadel of the Sisodia Rajputs. Rana Sanga died of his wounds sustained in the battle of Kanwaha, a couple of months later. The state of Mewar was ruled over by three *ranas* in quick succession from 1528 to 1537 but they failed to restore law and order in the state. In 1537, Udaya Singh, the minor son of Rana Sanga, was installed on the throne of Mewar under a council of regency. It was during his period of minority that Sher Shah, after his occupation of Jodhpur in 1544, turned his attention towards Mewar. About this time, Mewar was passing through a dark period of its history. Banbir, a Rajput renegade and usurper, had assassinated Rana Vikramajit and now planned to kill the infant Udaya Singh, the father of the future Rana Pratap. Mewar had not yet recovered from the evil effects of the mutual dissensions and intrigues, the natural consequences of its period of adversity. Therefore, when Sher Shah, flushed with his recent victory over Marwar, made his appearance at Chittor, the keys of the fort were meekly delivered to him by the guardians and defenders of the minor boy-king without any resistance.

Sher Shah placed the control of Chittor in the hands of Shams Khan, a brother of Khwas Khan, and for the administration, Chittor and its dependencies were formed into a separate *Sarkar* (district) of Jodhpur. The Rajput commandant of Ranthambhor offered his submission to Sher Shah on demand thereafter, and the latter sent his son, Adil Khan, to take charge of it. Thus within a short period of about two years Sher Shah had established his suzerainty over a substantial part of Rajputana; the two powerful Rajput states of Jaisalmer and Bikaner held out against him and zealously maintained their sovereignty but Sher Shah had no time to challenge their authority. He adopted a lenient attitude towards the vanquished Rajput chiefs or those who had voluntarily offered their submission to him. They were allowed to remain in possession of their states and lands without demanding their abject surrender and refrained from adopting the policy of annexations. He did not interfere in the internal administration of the Rajput states and estates (*jagirs*) so long as their chiefs or hereditary landlords were willing to pay tribute. Nevertheless, Sher Shah's hold over the Rajput states proved very short-lived. Within two months of his death, Maldeva Rathor returned from Siwana and recovered his lost dominions from the clutches of the Afghans in July 1545. Similarly, on attaining majority, Udaya Singh setup as sovereign ruler of Mewar and revived its ancient glory through the pursuit of successful military career. So much so that Mewar, with its capital at

Chittor, came to occupy once again the premier position among the Rajput states.

The Siege of Kalinjar (November 1544 to May 1545): Sher Shah's next and the last military expedition was directed against Kalinjar in Bundelkhand In November 1544, he laid siege to the fort of Kalinjar which was then ruled over by Raja Kirat Singh. The motive behind this expedition has been explained differently by the various medieval chroniclers. Abbas gives us no plausible reason for Sher Shah's decision to march on Kalinjar soon after taking possession of Chittor. He writes that after the submission of Chittor, Sher Shah sent his son Adil Khan to take possession of Ranthambhor and himself went to Kachwara with his main army, and from there marched towards Kalinjar. What was the urgency that directed Sher Shah's attention towards Kalinjar is not explained. Abbas narrates an absurd story that led him to attack Kalinjar as follows:

> 'The Raja of Kalinjar, Kirat Singh, did not come out to meet him. So he ordered the fort to be invested, and threw up mounds against it, and in a short time, the mounds rose so high that they over-topped the fort. The men who were in the streets and houses were exposed and the Afghans shot them with their arrows and muskets from off the mounds. The cause of this tedious mode of capturing the fort was this: Among the women of Raja Kirat Singh was a Patar slave girl, that is, a dancing girl. The king had heard exceeding praise of her, and he considered how to get possession of her, for he feared lest if he stormed the fort, the Raja would certainly make a *Jauhar*, and would burn the girl'.

Firishta, on the other hand, writes that the Raja of Kalinjar, 'who had witnessed the treachery of Sher Shah against Rai Puran Mall of Raisen', refused to offer his submission to him when called upon to do so, 'and assumed a hostile attitude'. It was Ahmad Yadgar, the author of *Tarikh-i-Salatin-i-Afghana*, who gives a specific reason for Sher Shah's attack on Kalinjar; he writes that it was the refusal of Raja Kirat Singh of Kalinjar to hand over a hostile Bundela chieftain who had taken refuge with him. J. N. Chaudhuri identifies this fugitive with Raja Bir Bhan of Arail, which was situated on the right bank of the Yamuna in the vicinity of Allahabad; he was said to have been friendly to Humayun, a cause enough to offend the Afghan monarch. To our mind, Sher

Shah had imperial instincts and the campaign against the ruler of Kalinjar formed a part of his general policy of aggression against the local and regional rulers, who acted as road-blocks towards the expansion and consolidation of his dominions or posed a threat to the safety of his empire. According to Abbas, on his way to Kalinjar, Sher Shah halted in the Doab for some time and saw to the defeat and destruction of a rebellious Mughal officer also by his lieutenants; he was Alam Khan Miana, 'who having created a disturbance in the Doab, and having raised the province of Mirath (Meerut), had ravaged great part of the neighbouring country'. He was defeated and killed by Bhagwant, a Hindu convert to Islam, who had been appointed as the governor of Sirhind by Sher Shah.

The fort of Kalinjar was invested by Sher Shah in November 1544 under his personal command. Despite his best efforts, it could not be captured and the siege lingered on for many months. It compelled Sher Shah to adopt many unusual measures, as alluded to by Abbas, to attain his object. He issued orders for digging mines to blow up the walls of the fort and built high mounds of earth overlooking the inmates of the fort for shooting them down. At the same time, arrangements were made to erect covered lanes (*sabat*) with the object of protecting the assault troops. It was then that, on the fateful day of Friday, the 9th of Rabi-ul-awwal, 952 A.H (May 21, 1545), when the besiegers were engaged in throwing hand-grenades or loaded-rockets (*hukkaha pur az atish*) inside the fort, one of the rockets loaded with gunpowder, after striking the gate of the fort, exploded, and rebounding, fell into a heap of ammunition near the place where Sher Shah was standing. The ammunition caught fire and Sher Shah was most seriously burnt. He was immediately carried to his tent but, while 'hovering between life and death' did not fail to order his men to assault the fort from all sides and capture it. Accordingly, as per the version of Abbas in *Tarikh-i-Sher Shahi,* 'Men came and swarmed out instantly on every side like ants and locusts; and by the time of afternoon prayers captured the fort, putting everyone to the sword and sending all the infidels to the hell. About the hour of evening prayers, the intelligence of the victory reached Sher Shah, and marks of joy and pleasure appeared on his countenance'. Thus Sher Shah had received the happy news about the conquest of the fort of Kalinjar by his men before he died in the wee hours of the next morning, viz., the 22nd of May 1545. The date was discovered in the words: *as atash murd,* viz., 'He died from fire'.

The Extent of his Empire

Starting as the son of a petty *jagirdar*, Sher Shah had conquered the provinces of Bihar and Bengal before the beginning of his contest with Humayun for the imperial throne of Delhi. Within a few years of Humayun's defeat at his hands in the battles of Chausa and Kanauj, Sher Shah established himself as the emperor of practically the whole of northern India excluding Assam, Kashmir and Gujarat. A part of central India had also been overrun by him. At the time of his death, his empire extended from Sonargaon (now in Bangladesh) in the east to the river Indus and the Gakkhar country in the northwest. It was roughly bounded in the north by the Himalayas and touched the Vindhya Mountains at certain points in the south.

SECTION 3: ADMINISTRATIVE REFORMS OF SHER SHAH SURI

Sher Shah—the Forerunner of Akbar

Sher Shah Suri was an empire-builder and a great administrator. Unlike Humayun he was a self-made and self-propelled man. Once on the throne, he proved himself worthy of the exalted office which he had attained by dint of his ability, life-long experience and great military skill. William Erskine, the celebrated author of the *History of India under Babar and Humayun* (2 vols; London, 1854) had once opined that Sher Shah, the Afghan adversary of the Great Mughals, exhibited 'more of the spirit of a legislator and guardian of the people than any other medieval (Muslim) ruler before Akbar'. He anticipated, in many respects, the work of Akbar and has rightly been called the forerunner of the great Mughal monarch as empire-builder and administrator. It would not be wrong to say that the genesis of all the administrative reforms and to a great extent the state policy of Akbar can be traced back to the regime of Sher Shah; these were faithfully adopted, improved upon and executed in a more refined and mature style by the latter. The land revenue system of Akbar, for which he is specially known, was a carbon copy of the revenue system of Sher Shah; it owed its evolution, experimentation and development to the genius of Raja Todar Mall, a seasoned bureaucrat of the Afghan regime. Similarly, the military administration of Akbar was like that of Sher Shah Suri sans the detailed classification of the Mansabdari system. The practice of branding the horses and entering the identification marks of the troops in their muster rolls was also a legacy of his Afghan predecessor.

Sher Shah's administrative reforms and public welfare activities constitute an excellent record for a stormy reign of five years. 'Few men', writes H.L.O. Garret, 'have crowded more into the short span of five years than this able and conscientious man'. (Edwards and Garret: *Mughal Rule in India*, p. 18). It has been suggested that 'had Sher Shah been spared a few more years as the emperor, he could have established his dynasty, and the Great Mughals would never have reappeared on the stage of Indian history.' (V.A. Smith in Oxford *History of India,*, Vol. II, Oxford, 1920, p. 329).

Dr. K.R. Qanungo, in his valuable treatise, entitled, *Sher Shah and His Times* (loc.cit.) had put forth a new thesis; he suggested that 'Sher Shah was a greater constructive genius and a better nation-builder than even Akbar the Great' but his claim has since been challenged by many other historians. It is now universally acknowledged that 'Although Sher Shah was one of the greatest administrators of medieval India yet he was not an administrative genius like Akbar. He has to his credit a number of administrative reforms but many of these were such as had already been conceived and successfully tried in the country by the preceding rulers. He did not introduce any innovation in the structure of central administration which was simply a copy of the Old Persian model, brought to India by his Muslim predecessors. He did not evolve the concept of the office of the Prime Minister or of a compact central ministry as was done by Akbar or Shivaji later. Unlike Akbar, Sher Shah did not introduce new administrative divisions like the provinces. The local sub-divisions of the civil administration, for the success of which his name is especially celebrated in the history of India, were not his original work but had been borrowed by him from the past. Similarly, his military reforms such as the branding of the horses and the practice of taking down the descriptive rolls of the soldiery had been tried by Alauddin Khilji much earlier. Thus it is not correct to call Sher Shah as an innovator in the field of administration though he was an excellent administrator. He was endowed by nature with a remarkable executive as well as administrative acumen which enabled him to administer the old institutions in an entirely new spirit so as to make them function efficiently and for the welfare of his subjects'. (*Advanced Study*, ii, Sterling, pp. 173-74).

Benevolent Despotism

Like all the Muslim rulers of the Sultanate period, Sher Shah Suri was also an autocratic ruler but he was an enlightened despot who regarded administration of the state as a part of his duty. Abbas Sarwani writes that 'Sher Shah attended to every business concerning the administration of his kingdom and the revenues, whether great or small, in his own person'. As a devoted Muslim, 'he did not permit his temporal affairs to be unmixed with devotion; day and night he was employed in both works. Abbas records, *inter alia*, the daily working schedule of Sher Shah thus:

> 'He had his assistant in waiting to awake him when two-thirds of the night were passed; and bathing himself every night, he employed himself in prayer and supplication until the fourth watch. After that he heard the accounts of the various officers, and the ministers made their reports of the work to be done in their respective departments, and the orders, which Sher Shah gave they recorded for their future guidance, that there might be no necessity for inquiry in future.
>
> 'When the morning had well broken, he again performed his ablutions, and with a great assembly went through his obligatory devotions, and afterwards read the *Mustaabi-ashr*, and other prayers After that his chiefs and soldiers came to pay their respect, and the 'heralds' (*nakibs*) called out each man by name. ...so he employed himself in personally discharging the administration of the kingdom, and divided both day and night into portions for each separate business, and suffered no sloth or idleness to find its way to him. For he said: *It behoves the great to be always active, and they should not consider, on account of the greatness of their own dignity and loftiness of their own rank, the affairs and business of the kingdom small or petty, and should place no undue reliance on their ministers.*' (*Tarikh-i-Sher Shahi*; E&D, iv, pp. 410-11).

Central Government

As a despotic ruler, Sher Shah had concentrated all civil and military powers of the state into his own hands. Accordingly, he setup highly centralized machinery for running the administration of the imperial government. Though theoretically committed to implement the Islamic law, Sher Shah was an absolute monarch whose word was law and his ministers were his mere creatures who owed their nomination, promotion and dismissal to the goodwill of the sovereign. They enjoyed no discretion in the discharge of their official duties and performed their administrative functions strictly according to his directions and under his personal supervision like his secretaries or dignified clerks. In fact, Sher Shah is not credited with any reform in the constitution of the central government which continued to be based on the Old Persian model as had been brought to India by the preceding Sultans of Delhi.

Sher Shah setup four major central departments, called *diwans*, on the model of the Sultanate period. The most important of these was known as the *diwan-i-wizarat*, which was headed by his chief minister, called the *wazir*. His office cannot be compared with that of the prime minister of a state though, in theory, the *wazir* of Sher Shah Suri did have some powers of general supervision and control over the other ministries. It is doubtful if Sher Shah had ever nominated any of his ministers to act as his prime minister, *Vakil* or the deputy Sultan. In fact, his *wazir* was expected by Sher Shah to hold a firm control over the state exchequer and look after the income and expenditure– the functions, which in modern times fall within the domain of the finance ministers. That is why, during the Muslim rule, the offices of the *diwan-i-wizarat* and the finance ministries were usually indistinguishable; so much so that even during the period of the imperial Mughals, the prime minister or *Vakil* of the empire was also sometimes called the *Diwan-i-ala*. As Sher Shah happened to be an expert in land-revenue and financial affairs, he used to take keen interest in the functioning of the *diwan-i-wizarat*.

The second important department of Sher Shah's empire was called the *diwan-i-ariz* and its minister in charge was called the *ariz-i-mamalik*. His office may be compared with that of a modern defence minister who exercised control over the defence establishment, including the recruitment, training, equipment and organisation of the army. He looked after the deployment of the armed forces in the forts and other strategic parts of the empire but did not enjoy the powers to command the troops on the battlefield. Sher Shah was his own commander-in-chief, and all the senior commanders of his forces were under his direct supervision and control.

The third important ministry was called the *diwan-i-risalat* or *diwan-i-muhtasib* whose minister-in-charge dealt with the foreign affairs and the diplomatic correspondence. He remained in close touch with the ambassadors and envoys sent to and received from the foreign powers. Sher Shah seems to have entrusted the work of charity and endowments also to this department. The fourth important ministry which handled the drafting of royal proclamations and despatches to the imperial officers and administrators was called the *diwan-i-insha;* it communicated with the provincial governors and other executive officers. This department maintained the government records and formed the imperial secretariat.

Apart from the above, the imperial government of Sher Shah had some other central departments, the heads of which were appointed by the king himself and were directly responsible to him in the discharge of their duties. The department of justice was called the *diwan-i-qaza* and was headed by the *qazi-ul-qazat* or the chief *qazi* of the empire although the king himself was considered as the chief judicial authority and was known as the 'fountain of justice'. The intelligence department was called the *diwan-i-barid* and its officer was called the *barid-i-mamalik;* the organisation and maintenance of the postal services also formed a part of his functions. The officer-in-charge of the royal household and the various workshops (*karkhanas*) attached to it was called the *amir-i-saman* or 'the lord high steward'. Being closely attached to the king, the *amir-i-saman* happened to be one of the most trustworthy and capable public servants, upon whom the personal safety and comforts of the sovereign and his family rested. It was an autocratic government, and the classification of powers and functions of the various central departments and their ministers was not well-marked; hence their successful functioning depended primarily on the personality and wisdom of the emperor himself. By all accounts, Sher Shah was known to be 'a great judge of human character'. He selected men of virtuous habits and integrity to take charge of the administration. He always exercised close supervision over the work and activities of his ministers and 'imposed a very high code of conduct over them'. Abbas, his biographer, makes Sher Shah to speak for himself as follows:

> 'The corruption of ministers of contemporary princes was the means of my acquiring the worldly kingdom I possess. A king should not have corrupt *vakils* or *wazirs*; for a receiver of bribes is dependent on the giver of the bribes; and one who is dependent is unfit for the office of *wazir*, for he is an interested personage, and to an interested person, loyalty and truth in the administration of the kingdom are lost'. (*Tarikh-i-Sher Shahi*, E&D. iv, p. 411)

Provincial and Local Administration

It is now universally recognised that Akbar was the founding father of modern provincial administrative units, called the *subas* or provinces, as 'the uniform and exactly alike administrative units', and that, like the central administrative structure, Sher Shah's provincial administration also did not show much impact of his administrative zeal. Dr. R.K. Qanungo, once misreading the administrative reforms of Sher Shah in Bengal, (*Sher Shah; loc.cit.*, p. 357) had expressed the opinion that he had abolished the provincial subdivisions and divided the whole of his kingdom into 47 *sarkars* or districts which were placed under the direct control of the central government. Subsequent researches have proved, however, that his observations were not correct. Sher Shah had taken this drastic step in the case of Bengal only because of the repeated revolts there by its local hereditary chieftains and scions of the erstwhile vanquished ruling dynasty. It was the province of Bengal which was parcelled out into as many as 47 *sarkars*, administered by centrally recruited district officers, called *shiqdar-i-shiqdaran.*

As a matter of fact, like the Sultans of Delhi, he had divided the whole of his kingdom into fiefs or the provincial subdivisions, called the *iqtas*. They could be compared roughly with the *subas* or provinces although their composition or administrative machinery was not based on any well-defined principles or uniform pattern. Vastly differing in size, some of the outlying *iqtas* were simply military governorships, held by his war veterans with the help of huge armies. For instance, Haibat Khan, the governor of the Punjab, had 30,000 troops under his command, and enjoyed vast powers of conferring *jagirs* on his own men. Similarly, Khwas Khan, the governor of Rajputana, commanded 20,000 soldiers. Besides, Sher Shah's empire was interspersed by a large number of powerful Hindu states which enjoyed complete internal autonomy and acknowledged only nominal suzerainty of the Suri regime. In spite of all these facts, major part of Sher Shah's kingdom, particularly in the Indo-Gangetic plain, including the Doab, modern Uttar Pradesh, Bihar and Bengal, had been brought under the direct civil administration of Delhi by the time of Sher Shah's death in 1545. Heads of the *iqtas* were variously known as *hawkims* (rulers, viz., the governors), *faujdars* (military officers in-charge) or *momins* to emphasis their religious denomination as a mark of distinction from the local *bajguzar* (tributary) *rajas, ranas* and other Hindu chieftains, subordinated to them. The *iqtadars*, like *jagirdars*, recruited and maintained their own armed forces, a part of which had to be placed at the disposal of the imperial commanders during war operations. They were responsible for the maintenance of law and order in their *iqtas* and carried on the civil administration in accordance with the royal *firmans* and directions of the central government.

Of course, Sher Shah made a positive contribution towards the development of civil administration at the local level. He carried out radical reforms in the administration of the districts (*sarkars*), tehsils (*parganas*) and the villages. The *iqtas* were divided into *sarkars* or districts. Each *sarkar* was headed by two Muslim officers – *shiqdar-i-shiqdaran* or chief *shiqdar* and *munsif-i-munsifan* or the chief *munsif*. The *shiqdar-i-shiqdaran* was the officer incharge of the civil administration and police-cum-military chief of the district; he held under his control a small contingent of two to five hundred locally recruited militia or soldiers to maintain law and order. He undertook punitive expeditions against the refractory *zamindars* of the region, supervised the work of *shiqdars* of the *parganas* and administered criminal justice. Unlike the chief *shiqdars* of Bengal, who were appointed by the imperial government directly, their counterparts in the *iqtas* were appointed by the *iqtadars* and performed their functions under their supervision. The chief *munsif*, on the other hand, was primarily a judge and revenue officer of the district; he held charge of revenue collections, maintenance of accounts and civil justice. He supervised the work of the *munsifs* or *amins* of the *parganas*.

Each *sarkar* was divided into two or three *parganas*. A *pargana* usually centered around and was named after a medium-sized city or town of the region and included in its fold a cluster of villages. According to Abbas Sarwani, every *pargana* had 'a God-fearing *shiqdar*' a *munsif* (*qazi*), a *fotdar* (treasurer) and *karkuns* (scribes) to write in Hindi and Persian. A *shiqdar* may be called the police chief or a junior military officer who held charge of the *pargana* under the direct supervision of the chief *shiqdar* of the *sarkar*. He maintained law and order in the *pargana* and helped the *munsif* in the discharge of his work of measurement of land and settlement of proprietary rights of the peasants. He also helped the *munsif* in the collection of land revenue and its safe custody and transfer to the royal treasury. A *munsif* was sometimes addressed as *amin* (revenue officer) or simply *amir*, a common connotation for the state officers.

A village, as usual, comprised the lowest and by far the most important and stable administrative unit of the state in medieval India. 'Sher Shah accepted the time-honoured custom of recognizing the autonomy of the villages which were governed by their own *panchayats*. The *Panchayati Raj* was treated as law of the land and Sher Shah accorded a legal recognition to it.' The *panchayat* of a village was composed of all of its able-bodied adult men who looked after the interests of its people. They arranged the municipal functions, appointed *chaukidars* for the safety of their life and property, administered justice and even inflicted punishments to the defaulters to regulate their social lives, particularly. The headman of the village, a semi-government official, acted as a coordinator between the village *panchayat* and the higher state administration. *Patwari* and the *chaukidar* were the other two semi-government officials of the village.

Sher Shah's Army

Whatever the administrative achievements of Sher Shah Suri, we must not forget that, like other rulers of medieval India, he was a typical oriental despot who had come to occupy the throne by sheer force of arms; therefore, the importance of army to him cannot be overemphasized. 'His empire was at the best a police state whose stability and progress depended primarily on military strength'. Sher Shah was a great fighter and excellent military organiser; it were these qualities which helped him in recruiting a large army with the help of which he drove out Humayun and subjugated practically the whole of northern India. The exact estimate about his total military strength is not available and his biographer Abbas is content to dispose of the subject with the remark that Sher Shah's army was beyond all limits or numbering'. (*Tarikh-i-Sher Shahi*; E&D, IV, pp.414-15). According to one estimate, Sher Shah's permanent standing army, held under his personal command and stationed at Delhi and Agra alone, numbered 1,50,000 cavalry, 25,000 foot soldiers, 5,000 war elephants and a big stock of heavy field guns. It was supplemented by quite a few lacs of the feudal forces, recruited and maintained by his *iqtadars* and military officers in various parts of his empire and at the strategic military posts along the borders. Sher Shah invited Afghan fighters from every part of India and Afghanistan and gave them the highest posts in the army. He took keen interest in the recruitment of soldiers at the grass-roots and very often personally fixed their emoluments. The military officers were promoted on merit and, no wonder, he was able to raise a well-equipped, strong and reliable army. Most of his soldiers were equipped with matchlocks or bows and were commanded by young and brilliant officers recruited by Sher Shah himself. Higher ranks in the army were usually given to the Afghans or Muslim youth from Central Asia who came in thousands to seek their fortunes in India. Therefore, it would not be wrong to say that Sher Shah's 'army which was instrumental in maintaining his hold over the country, was foreign in character'. The soldiers were usually paid in cash while the officers were granted *jagirs* in lieu of their salaries.

Sher Shah laid great emphasis on the cavalry. Following in the foot-steps of Alauddin Khilji, he reintroduced the two-fold system of *Chehra* and *Dagh* in the recruitment of soldiers and the state horses; the first related to the preparation of descriptive rolls of his soldiers, which included the record of their physical identification marks also while the *Dagh* system implied the branding of horses.

Land Revenue Reforms

Sher Shah Suri made his regime memorable by the introduction of extensive land revenue reforms which not only increased the agricultural produce of the country and enhanced the revenues of the state but also won the love and gratitude of the peasantry for him. The experience gained by him in his youth as the manager of his father's *jagir* had given him first-hand knowledge of all the problems of the cultivators, agricultural production and the fixing and collection of land revenue. He had already done a lot of work in improving the land revenue collections of his parental estate on a small scale, and, after ascending the throne, lost no time in introducing radical land revenue reforms to ensure the prosperity of the peasants and stability of the state. His reforms were based on a three-fold objective—improved agricultural production, prosperity of the peasants and increase in the revenues of the state. He carried out a survey of all the land in the territories brought under his direct civil administration, adopted a uniform method for the measurement of the cultivable land, and determined the exact proprietary rights of the cultivators. For the purpose of measurement, Sher Shah used what was called the *Sikandri gaz* (the yard used by Sikander Lodhi for measurement) which was probably equivalent to ¾ of the modern metre. A *jarib* of rope was treated as a standard unit for measurement and a *bigha* (60 by 60 square yards) as the standard unit for the fixation of land revenue.

All cultivable land was divided into three categories – good, middling and bad, and the annual produce per *bigha* of land in case of each crop and each category was ascertained. It was then added up and divided by three to determine the average produce per *bigha* of land in case of each crop. One-third of this average was fixed as the land-revenue which could be paid by the cultivator in cash or kind. For the purpose of determining the value of land-revenue in cash, the government prepared and made public the rate lists of various crops, prevalent in different parts of the empire from time to time. On the basis of this scientific method, land revenue was determined and each cultivator was given two documents by the government; the first was called the *patta* or 'title deed', which recognised his proprietary rights over the various categories of land held by him, and the rate of land revenue payable by him thereon in respect of various crops. The second document was called the *qabulayat* or 'the deed of agreement' according to which the cultivator made a promise to pay a particular amount of land revenue to the state.

Of course, it was not possible for Sher Shah to introduce a uniform method of land revenue assessment throughout his dominions in the short span of his reign. There is an evidence to show that he made an exception in the case of Multan where he did not insist on the survey of land. Similarly, it was not possible for his officials to carry out a systematic survey of the cultivable land in Rajputana. The most significant feature of Sher Shah's land revenue system was the elimination of the middlemen or intermediaries, like the *zamindars,* agents (*dalals*) or contractors for the purpose of collection of the land revenue. Instead, his government established direct contacts with the *ryots* or cultivators and thus saved both of the parties—state as well as the peasants, from being exploited by the middlemen. That is why his land revenue system has been called the *Ryotwari System*, viz., the 'the system of the *ryots* or cultivators'.

Sher Shah gave special incentives to the peasantry for the reclamation of land to increase agricultural production. He remitted the state demands in times of drought and famine, and advanced *taqavi* loans to the cultivators for the purchase of seeds and cattle. He introduced many schemes of canal irrigation and rendered help to the villagers for the digging of wells. He was aware of the prevalence of corruption in the land revenue establishment, particularly, and took steps to reduce it as far as possible. He was always eager to safeguard the interests of the peasants and protected them from the exploitation of the government officials. According to Abbas Sarwani, he issued a warning to his revenue officials as follows:

> 'I know the oppression and exactions of which you have been guilty towards the cultivators; and for this reason, I have fixed the payments for measurements and the tax-gatherer's fees; that if you exact from the cultivators more on this account than is fixed, it may not be credited to you in making up your accounts. Be it known to you that I will take the accounts of the fees in my own presence.' (*Tarikh-i-Sher Shahi*, p. 313)

It was not possible for Sher Shah to eliminate corruption from the land revenue establishment altogether but his attempts did have some salutary effect on the attitude and actions of the public servants; he used to transfer the revenue officials from one place to the other very frequently. At the same time he also saw to it 'that the cultivators behaved as honest and law-abiding citizens and paid the government dues regularly. His standing instructions to the revenue officials were that 'they should show leniency to the cultivators at the time of measurement, and have a regard for the actual produce; but when the time of payment comes, they should show no leniency but collect the revenue with all strictness'. (*Ibid.*) He further ordered that 'if they perceived that the cultivators are evading payment, they should so chastise them as to be an example to others not to act in the same way'. (*Ibid.*, p. 314)

In addition to the land revenue, the peasants were also required to pay certain additional cesses such as *jaribana* or 'the surveyor's fee' and *muhasilana* or 'the tax-collector's fee' at the rate of 2.5 and 5 per cent of the land revenue respectively.

Law and Order

In those days no distinction was made between the civil and military duties of public servants or between the police and military functions. Therefore, as usual, the duty of maintaining law and order or the police functions were also performed by the soldiers in the time of Sher Shah. All of his civil and military officers were under obligation to maintain perfect law and order in the territories under their jurisdiction, and they enjoyed wide powers of punishing the law-breakers. The *shiqdars*, the chief *shiqdars*, the *amirs* and *faujdars* were all regarded as the custodians of peace in the territories which they were called upon to administer. Abbas writes that Sher Shah being a 'God-fearing man' regarded the establishment of law and order and protection of the honour and property of his subjects as his 'religious and moral duty'. He used to say that 'Crime and violence prevent the development of prosperity. It behoves kings to be grateful for the favour that Allah has made His people subject to them, and, therefore, not to disobey the commandments of Allah'. (*Ibid.*, 410). Sher Shah was said to have been 'adorned with the jewel of justice' and meted out even-handed justice to all. He did not spare even his near and dear ones if they resorted to any criminal deeds. Beginning with the village *panchayats* and the courts of *munsifs* in the *parganas* most of his government officers were armed with judicial powers in their respective fields. Simultaneously, there was an ascending hierarchy of the courts of the *qazi* and *amir-i-adl,* culminating in the highest court of the chief *qazi* at Delhi, and, above all, the King's court constituted the supreme original as well as appellate court of the empire.

In the administration of justice, the Islamic Law of Jurisprudence prevailed wherein, by definition, 'the subjects' implied the *millat* or the Muslims alone, but, in the civil suits, particularly, 'the law of the land' was paid due consideration so that his non-Muslim subjects also received just treatment according to their own customs and traditions. Punishments were harsh, and mutilation of limbs, hanging by public execution and flogging were in vogue. To ensure the establishment of law and order in the countryside and to bring the culprits to book speedily, Sher Shah had introduced a novel principle – 'local responsibility for local crime' According to this principle, the local *muqaddams* and *chaudhries* were held responsible for tracing out the culprits because Sher Shah believed that murders, thefts and highway robberies could not take place without the knowledge and connivance of the local elements. His standing orders were that 'If a *muqaddam* (the village headman) harbours thieves and robbers unknown to the *amir* (governor), it is fit he should be punished or even be put to death'. Abbas Sarwani is all praise for the effectiveness of Sher Shah's judicial policy as follows:

> 'Travellers and way-farers, during the time of Sher Shah's reign, were relieved from the trouble of keeping watch, nor did they fear to halt in the midst of a desert. They encamped at night at every place, desert or inhabited, without any fear. They placed their mules to graze, and they slept with minds at ease and free from care, as if in their own house; and the *zamindars*, for fear any mischief should occur to the travellers, and that they should suffer to be arrested on account of it, keep watch over them. And in the time of Sher Shah's rule, a decrepit old woman might place a basket full of gold ornaments on her head and go on journey and no thief or robber would come near her for fear of punishment which Sher Shah inflicted'. (*Tarikh-i-Sher Shahi, E&D.* iv, pp.432-332)

Public Welfare Works

Sher Shah was fully aware of the fact that the affluence and stability of his monarchy depended very much upon the richness and prosperity of his subjects besides the enforcement of law and order and the reign of justice within his dominions. He, therefore, encouraged the growth and development of trade and commerce by abolishing numerous taxes, local cesses and custom duties levied at the ferries and borders of the various states and *iqtas* within his empire and its external boundaries. In our opinion, 'it so appears that, after the foundation of the Mughal rule Babar and Humayun had done nothing to facilitate the free flow of goods within the boundaries of their own dominions. It was left to Sher Shah to remove such road-blocks by simplifying the tariff. During his reign only two duties were levied on the goods; a custom duty of not more than 2.5 per cent of the price of goods was charged on the frontiers of the empire at the time of entry while a sales-tax was charged at the time of their first sale in the market.' (Advanced Study, ii, p. 182).

Sher Shah was a great road-builder. He immensely improved the means of communication and transport by the construction of roads throughout his empire to facilitate the free movement of goods and traffic. The system of building the *pacca* tar-coal roads was unknown in those days, but he repaired the old *kacha* pathways, and widened and solidified the highways (*shahrahs*), in use by the wheeled carts and *caravans* since ages, and inter-connected them to make it a network of roads running from one corner of the country to the other. Within the short span of five years of his rule, he had caused to be built four national highways; the first of these was the old Grand Trunk Road, which ran from Sonargaon in Bengal to Attock in the Northwest Frontier and rightly earned the name of *Sher Shah Shahrah* or *Sarak-i-Azam.* It was 1500 *kos* or 5,000 kilometres in length (*Kos* being roughly equal to two miles or 3, 25 kms.) on the main track of which has been laid out the modern National Highway No. 1. The second highway ran from Agra to Mandu, the third from Agra to Jodhpur and Chittor, and the fourth one connected Lahore with Multan. Sher Shah Suri can rightly be called the Father of modern national highways of India and Pakistan. He planted green trees and constructed no less than 1700 *caravan sarais* along these roads for the convenience of the travellers. The *sarais* provided suitable accommodation, cooking facilities and drinking water for the travellers and their beasts of burden. These *caravan sarais*, being situated on the main highways, gradually developed into magnificent centres of trade and commerce, and formed the nuclei of many of the modern towns and cities of India. They served the purpose of *dak chaukis* or 'resting places for the news-carriers of the postal department. Two horsemen were stationed at each *sarai* who carried the royal mail in the up and down direction respectively. According to Abbas, 'the postal arrangements of Sher Shah were so swift that the royal *firmans* could be delivered from one place to another with great speed'. Of course, these postal arrangements were meant only for the official communications and the idea of providing this facility to the public had not yet been conceived. In fact, the postal department of Sher Shah formed a part of his Intelligence services. We have it on the testimony of the medieval chroniclers that 'apart from thousands of the news-writers, news-carriers, and news-runners, Sher Shah also employed numerous scouts and well-trained spies throughout the length and breadth of his empire with the object of keeping himself abreast of the latest developments in various parts of his dominions, he had revived the elaborate espionage system of Alauddin Khilji'. (*Ibid.*, p. 183).

The system of currency which regulated trade and commerce and monetary transactions of the people was in a hopeless condition at the time of Sher Shah's accession to the throne. He introduced radical reforms therein to improve the economic health of the country. Numerous types of old and debased coins belonging to the preceding regimes were removed from the market and replaced by new and better-minted gold, silver and copper currency of various denominations. He minted a new copper *dam* (*paisa*) of 322 grains and a silver rupee (*rupiah or rupaya* – i.e. 'round-edged coin') of 180 grains which contained 175 grains of pure silver. Both of these coins had their fractional currency, equal to ½, ¼, 1/8 and 1/16 of the original value. The silver rupee of Sher Shah, which was equal to 64 copper *dams* remained in vogue in our country even during the early part of the British rule up to 1835 A.D., with changed inscriptions thereon, and it formed the basis of the British Indian currency till after the dawn of Independence in 1947.

Sher Shah was a great philanthropist. He gave liberal patronage to the public welfare activities. He opened *maktabs* and *madrassas* for the promotion of education and learning and made liberal grants to the *imams* and the Muslim saints and scholars. Special grants were given to the *Madrassas* and *masjids* and the *ulama* and the *maulvis* were paid fat salaries and stipends. Education in the *maktabs* and *madrassas* was free and the students were provided with free board and lodging besides the books in the state-run hostels. Sher Shah strengthened the department of public charities in order to help the poor and the needy and established dispensaries at state expense for the treatment of human beings as well as animals. Free kitchens were run by the *masjids* and *khanqahs* with liberal funds received in charity from the public and the state grants.

Buildings of Sher Shah

Sher Shah exhibited much interest in the building activity as well. He had a refined taste in architecture which manifested itself especially in the mausoleum at Sehasram (Sasseram) in Bihar which he got prepared for himself. It is octagonal in shape and 'has been built on a lofty plinth in the middle of a lake'. Among the other extant architectural monuments of his regime may be mentioned the magnificent fort of Rohtasgarh that he had constructed on the Jhelum, in the Punjab, for the defence of his northwestern frontiers. The *Purana Qila* (old fort) of Delhi is also said to have been built by Sher Shah in the enclosure of which he erected a lofty mosque; it has survived the wear and tear of time and presents one of the best examples of the Indo-Islamic architecture. Percy Brown showers praise on Sher Shah's buildings 'for their exquisite design, excellent execution and artistic decoration'.

Religious Policy

There is a difference of opinion among the modern scholars regarding the religious policy of Sher Shah Suri. Some of the modern 'leftists' and so-called 'secularist' historians of modern India had put forth the thesis that the Afghan monarch of Delhi had adopted 'a policy of religious toleration towards his Hindu subjects,' and that 'his attitude towards them was not contemptuous sufferance but respectful deference'. Principal Sri Ram Sharma, the celebrated author of the *Religious Policy of the Mughal Emperors* (OUP, 1940), did not agree with them, however. He maintained that

> 'Sher Shah was a great ruler– undoubtedly the greatest Muslim ruler before Akbar, but he cannot be credited with a religious policy which he never dreamt of pursuing....If the Muslim chroniclers do not praise him for his religious fanaticism as they do Alauddin, Firoze Shah or Sikander Lodhi, they simply bring him to the level of the general run of Muslim rulers who had been governing India before his time. The only positive evidence in his favour is the presence of a Hindu commander of doubtful standing and the provision for Hindus in the postal houses (*dak chaukis*) which he established. The first does not prove much, as Hindu commanders were found even in the army of Mahmud of Ghazni to whom nobody could attribute liberal religious policy. The second brings us to the question of the nature of these rest houses. They were essentially part of a working postal

system. The postal runners might well have been Hindus for whom provision was necessary in these rest-houses. There is a separate caste of Hindus which even today (1931) works as carriers. It is doubtful whether Muslims in general could have been found willing enough to undertake this humble work. Thus the provision for the Hindus at rest-houses was in the nature of a provision for a class of state servants. Hindu caste rules would not admit of the arrangements described being utilized by high class Hindus and the places seem clearly to have been utilized, if at all, by Hindus of a lower caste, most probably public servants'.(pp. 10-11)

Thus infers Sri Ram Sharma, that 'in his religious views and conduct, Sher Shah did not rise above the Turko-Afghan rulers of the Sultanate of Delhi'. By all accounts of the contemporary writers, Sher Shah Suri was 'an orthodox Sunni Mussalman. He was punctilious in saying his five daily prayers, in keeping the fast of *Ramzan* and in going through various observances enjoined by his faith. He was, moreover, an upholder of the dignity and supremacy of Islam'. In his fight against the formidable Rajput rulers, rebellious Hindu chieftains and refractory *zamindars,* he invariably exploited the religious sentiments of his Muslim camp-followers and soldiers by declaring *Jehad* or holy war against the *Kafirs.* His expedition against Raja Maldev of Jodhpur, though dictated by political and military considerations, was, nevertheless, motivated by the feelings of religious fanaticism, and, after his victory, Sher Shah demolished temples in the fort of Jodhpur and built a mosque on their ruins. The same could be said about his siege of Kalinjar. His treachery towards Raja Puran Mal, asserts Qanungo, was not the act of a fanatic religious leader, forcing his opinions upon an unwilling Hindu king. But, argues Sri Ram Sharma that

'It had been planned by Sher Shah beforehand, discussed by him with his officers and was deliberately done to earn religious merit for exterminating that arch-infidel. Sher Shah said prayers of thanks after this religious deed. No amount of mere rhetoric can enable us to get over the accounts of the expedition, especially, when we find Sher Shah, who got up, on the eve of the battle, inviting his officers and confiding in them that, ever since his accession, he had been anxious, in the cause of his religion, to defeat Puran Mal. All accounts give this expedition a religious significance which no argument can destroy'. (*Ibid.*, pp. 11-12)

SECTION 4: SHER SHAH'S PLACE IN HISTORY

Sher Shah Suri has been adjudged as 'a remarkable ruler' of medieval India who surpassed all the preceding Muslim kings of Delhi in his administrative capabilities, strength of character and actual achievements. He was a self-made man who rose to be a great empire-builder. Alauddin Khilji stands heads and shoulders above Sher Shah as conqueror and administrator but in constructive statesmanship he cannot claim equality with this Afghan monarch; the latter's administrative work and public welfare activities were more enduring and beneficial to his subjects. VA Smith had correctly observed that 'if Sher Shah had been spared, he would have established his dynasty, and the 'great Mughals' would not have appeared on the stage of history'. According to Sir Wolseley Haig,

> 'Sher Shah was, in truth, one of the greatest rulers who ever sat upon the throne of Delhi. No other (Muslim) ruler, from Aibek to Aurangzeb, possessed such intimate knowledge of the details of administration, or was able to examine and control public business so minutely and effectively as he. Sher Shah restrained the turbulence and quelled the tribal jealousies of the Afghan chiefs, reformed the land revenue administration, introduced a system of great trunk roads, furnished with caravan *sarais,* wells and every convenience for the comfort and safety of the travellers, and maintained throughout his dominions such order that 'none dared to turn the eye of dishonesty upon another's goods'....Himself a pious Muslim, he suffered none to be persecuted in the name of religion; and, (being) far wiser than Akbar, (he) made no attempt to assume spiritual power but left each to seek God after his own fashion. Badaoni, the orthodox Muslim historian, thanks God that he was born in the reign of so just a king. Of his wise and judicious measures of administration many were adopted or imitated by Akbar without acknowledgement, and he was far more successful than any who followed him in checking corruption, peculation and frauds on the public treasury.' (*Cambridge History of India*, iv, pp. 261-62)

Nevertheless, despite 'Sher Shah's indefatigable industry, devotion to duty, numerous reforms and love of justice', which 'secured for him a place of distinction in Indian history', he was only a product of his age as far as his religious policy was concerned. Like Firoze Shah Tughluq before him, he combined administrative zeal with religious intolerance. It would be, therefore, not fair to compare him with Akbar who was definitely superior to him both as a ruler and a man. We do not agree with Sir Wolseley Haig's contention that Sher Shah was 'the greatest of the Muslim rulers of India'. His place in history also does not depend upon his initiating a policy of religious toleration or neutrality as made out by some of the modern writers. He had, in fact, nothing to do with the founding of 'a united nation in India,' which is 'yet in the making even today'. The opinion that Sher Shah may justly dispute with Akbar the claim of being the first who attempted 'to buildup an Indian nation' by reconciling the followers of the rival creeds like Hinduism and Islam, as suggested by some does not find favour with most of the modern non-sectarian and objective researchers. No doubt, however, that Sher Shah ranks with the greatest sovereigns of India, and, in the history of medieval India, he occupies a place next to that of Akbar, who, as Dr. K R Qanungo rightly asserts in *Sher Shah and his Times* (2nd edition, Bombay, 1965) 'is justly entitled to a higher place in history than Sher Shah'.

SECTION 5: THE SUCCESSORS OF SHER SHAH

Qutb Khan, the youngest of Sher Shah's three sons, had died during the lifetime of his father. None of his other two sons—Adil Khan and Jalal Khan, was available on the spot at the time of Sher Shah's accidental death in the siege of Kalinjar on May 22, 1545. Both of them had been entrusted independent commands of troops and were actively engaged against the Rajputs; Adil Khan, was posted at Ranthambhor and Jalal Khan at Rewa, about 25 kilometres to the south-east of Kalinjar. The news of Sher Shah's death was, therefore, kept a closely guarded secret for a few days while arrangements were in the offing to apprise the princes of the sad demise of their father. According to Abdulla, the author of *Tarikh-i-Daudi* (E&D, IV) Adil Khan, being the eldest of Sher Shah's sons, had already been nominated as his heir-apparent by the Afghan monarch, but his nobles in the army camp at Kalinjar, headed by Isa Khan Hajib, preferred Jalal Khan, who was said to be 'industrious and skilled in arms while his elder brother was ease-loving and devoted to pleasures'. Moreover, Jalal Khan was 'nearer at hand', and it was thought 'dangerous to keep the throne vacant for long'. Hence, a messenger was sent post-haste to Jalal Khan at Rewa to come immediately and take his father's place as King. Thus it was that Adil Khan was deliberately superseded and his younger brother Jalal Khan was the first to reach the royal camp and 'was proclaimed emperor on the 15th of the month *Rabi-ul-awwal*, 952 A.H (May 25, 1545 A.D.). He assumed the title of Islam Shah and this verse was engraved on his seal:

"The world, through the flavour of the Almighty,
Has been rendered happy;
Since Islam Shah, the son of Sher Shah Sur,
Has assumed sovereignty."

Islam Shah was a fairly educated man and a poet in Persian but he was primarily a soldier who had given sufficient proof of his military skill on more than one occasion in his early youth. He had gained sufficient experience as military officer under the personal supervision and care of his father and had played a heroic role in Sher Shah's struggle against Humayun. The author of *Tarikh-i-Daudi* tells us that

> "The common people call him Salim Shah. On the day of his accession to the throne, he ordered two months' pay to be distributed in ready money to the army: one month of this he gave them as a present; the other as subsistence money. Moreover, he resumed all the *jagirs* in the provinces of his government, and allowed their holders a stipend in money from his treasury instead. He entirely abolished, with one stroke of the pen, all former regulations respecting jagirs. After his accession, he ordered the Raja of Kalinjar, who had been captured with seventy of his adherents, to be put to death, and directed that not one of them should be spared." (*Ibid.*, p. 479)

Islam Shah was 'a mediocre' as ruler but he kept his parental heritage intact for eight years. According to Abdulla, 'Islam Shah resembled his father in his pomp and splendour and in his desire of dominion and conquest'. He even extended the boundaries of his empire by the annexation of East Bengal and the establishment of his sway over the Kashmir valley. Following in the foot-steps of his father, Islam Shah also exhibited interest in promoting the public welfare activities. To quote the author of *Tarikh-i-Daudi* again,

> "His father had erected *sarais* at a distance of one *Kos*, one from the other. Islam Shah built others between them, so that there was a *sarai* at every half Kos. He caused two horses and some footmen to be stationed at each *sarai*, for the purpose of acting as posts, and bringing him every day the news from Bengal, after the manner of *dak-chaukis*. During the time of Sher Shah,

a place had always been established in the royal camp for the distribution of alms to the poor. Instead of this, Islam Shah directed that arrangements for the giving of alms should be made at each of the *sarais*, and that indigent travellers should be supplied with whatever they needed, and that mendicants should receive a daily pittance, in order that they might be contented and at ease." (*Ibid.*)

Conflict between Adil Khan and Islam Shah

Nevertheless, the supersession of Adil Khan, the rightful claimant to the throne of Delhi, had sown the seeds of eternal discord between Islam Shah and his elder brother Adil Khan which proved ruinous to the nascent Afghan monarchy. The latter was formally confirmed in the governorship of Ranthambhor but there was no dearth of nobles and the military officers in the army camp who considered Islam Shah as a usurper. Obviously they nurtured inborn sympathies with the Crown Prince and Islam Shah was also suspicious of their loyalty towards him. In his bid to raise a fresh crop of youthful guards for his personal protection, he promoted all the 6,000 soldiers of his personal contingent that he had maintained as a prince; it was the case of the ordinary soldiers being raised to the status of commanders and *amirs*. This unwise step caused dissatisfaction among the old nobility and *grandees* of the Afghan empire and turned some of the disaffected nobles secretly towards Adil Khan whose loyalty to his younger brother was already suspected. The author of *Tarikh-i-Daudi* describes in details this sad tale of the estrangement of relations between the two brothers, which led to the disintegration of the Afghan, empire as under:

"Islam Shah, being a monarch of vindictive disposition, wrote to his elder brother, saying: *Because I was near, and you were distant, to prevent disorder in the affairs of the State, I have taken charge of the army until your arrival. I have nothing to do but obey you, and attend to your orders.*

"He (Islam Shah) feigned to wish to gratify his affection by a personal interview with his (elder) brother.

"Adil Khan wrote in reply to Islam Shah, saying: *If these four persons, viz. Kutb Khan – the Naib, Isa Khan Niazi, Jalal Khan Jalu, and Khawas Khan come and insure my safety, I will proceed to visit you.*

"(Accordingly), Islam Shah sent all of these nobles to his (elder) brother; and after removing his fears for his safety by oaths and protestations, they promised him that he should be permitted to depart after the first interview, and that he should be allowed to choose any *jagir* in Hindustan which suited him.

"Adil Khan went, accompanied by his nobles, to see his brother (Islam Shah, since proclaimed emperor of Hindustan). When he reached Fatehpur Sikri, Islam Shah came forth to meet him in the village of Singarpur, the place prepared for the meeting of the two brothers, and they had an interview there. They made professions of affection one to the other, and after sitting together for a short time, set off for Agra. Islam Shah, intending treachery towards his brother, had given directions that only two or three persons were to be allowed to enter the Fort (of Agra) with Adil Khan. When they arrived at the gate of the Fort, Islam Shah' men forbade their entry; to this Adil Shah's people paid no attention, and a great number of them went in with Adil Khan.

"When Islam Shah saw that his plot against his brother had been unsuccessful, he was obliged to speak courteously to him. He said: *I have a number of Afghans in my service, who are very unruly, and whom I will now make over to you.*

"After which Islam Shah seated his brother on the throne, and treated him with all possible civility. Adil Khan was a man who loved ease and comfort (but) he was aware of the deceit and cunning of Islam Shah, and would not consent to this. He rose up, and after causing Islam Shah to seat himself on the throne, he first of all made him an obeisance and did homage, and congratulated him on his accession to the throne. The chief nobles, after paying their customary compliments, retired to their appropriate places. The four nobles before mentioned then informed the King that an oath and a promise had been made that Adil Khan should be allowed to depart after the first interview, and that a *jagir* should be allotted to him.

"Islam Shah ordered this to be done, and Isa Khan and Khawas Khan were directed to accompany Adil Khan to Bayana (his newly allotted *jagir*). Two months afterwards, Islam Shah sent Ghazi Mahali, one of his attendants, with golden chains, and ordered him to seize Adil Khan. The latter, on the receipt of timely intelligence, fled to Khawas Khan in Mewat, before the arrival of Ghazi Mahali, and informed him of the perjury of Islam Shah. Khawas Khan was enraged. He sent for Ghazi Mahali, and caused the fetters to be fastened on his own legs, and thus raised the standard of revolt." (*Ibid.*, pp. 481-83)

Disintegration of the Afghan Empire

The revolt of Khawas Khan was a signal for all the disaffected nobles and ambitious provincial governors to defy the imperial authority of Islam Shah. Adil Khan, supported by a number of powerful nobles, including Khawas Khan, proceeded to attack Agra but 'was defeated in a battle in the outskirts of the town and fled towards Patna. He 'was not heard of any more'; but the dye had been cast. It enkindled the fissiparous tendencies of the Afghan nobles and triggered off the forces of disintegration and dismembership of the Afghan dominions. Caught in the whirl-wind of conspiracies and intrigues to dislodge him from the throne, and unable to cope with his rebellious and untrustworthy Afghan nobles, Islam Shah died in harness on October 30, 1553. His son and successor Firoze Shah, who was hardly a lad of twelve summers, was put to death by his own maternal uncle, Mubariz Khan, within three days of the death of Islam Shah. Mubariz Khan ascended the throne with the title of Muhammad Adil Shah but he proved to be an incapable ruler. His claim to the throne was contested by two of his own brothers-in-law, Ibrahim Suri and Sikander Shah Suri. Ibrahim Suri turned out Adil Shah from Delhi and Agra and declared himself as the emperor of India, while Sikander Suri, the governor of Lahore, setup as an independent ruler of the northwestern region. As narrated in the preceding pages of this study, both of them were defeated and dislodged from power by Humayun in 1555, which restored the Mughal rule in India.

❑ ❑

14

AKBAR—'THE GREAT MOGUL' (1556-1605)

SECTION 1: EARLY CAREER AND ACCESSION

Birth and Boyhood

Jalaluddin Muhammad Akbar, the son and successor of Humayun, styled by VA Smith as 'the Great Mogul', in his historical treatise, entitled, *Akbar the Great Mogul* (Oxford, 1917) was destined to be the greatest and the most celebrated national ruler of medieval India. He was born of Humayun's Persian *Shia* wife Hamida Banu Begam on October 15, 1542 at Amarkot (Sindh) in the house of its Rajput chieftain, Rana Virsal. There is a lot of controversy about his exact date of birth which is given variously as Rajab 5, 949 A. H. by Jauhar and Shaban 14 (November 23) by Firishta but we accept the well-considered opinion of his latest biographer, A. L. Srivastava (*Akbar the Great*, 3 vols, 1962, i, pp. 1-6).

The birth of Akbar, 'a foreigner in blood, religion and culture', in the royal palace of a Hindu chief in the midst of an orthodox Kshatriya ruling family had had a very special bearing on his upbringing and the moulding of his thoughts and character as a man as well as ruler. After having been ousted from power by Sher Shah, the fugitive Mughal emperor Humayun had been wandering about in the inhospitable regions of Sindh and Rajputana with a handful of his followers. At this time of distress, when Humayun was deserted by his kinsmen and the Muslim nobility, he was offered protection by the Rana of Amarkot, and his family was given shelter within his royal palace by the Rajput chief. Needless to say that the fugitive Mughal family was treated as guests and provided with all the comforts and luxuries of the Rajput household in which the royal family of the Rana played the hosts. Accordingly, Akbar was born in the family and social environment of a

Rajput royal household and received all the filial affection and care of his Hindu hosts. Even his father Humayun was not present at Amarkot at the time of his birth. A few days before his birth, Humayun, assisted by a contingent of 7,000 soldiers of the Rana had marched out of Amarkot on an expedition to the districts of Bhakkar and Thatta against Shah Husain Arghun. He was encamped in a garden on the bank of a water tank, about fifty kilometres southwest of Amarkot when Tardi Beg Khan, one of his horsemen, brought him the happy news of the birth of his son. Jauhar writes that the fugitive emperor thanked the Almighty for having blessed him with a son and heir, and celebrated the occasion by distributing bits of musk among his associates with the prayer that the fame of the child might 'one day spread all the world over like its perfumes.' (*Tarikh i Humayuni*; Eng. trs. by Charles Stewart, p. 66).

Akbar's childhood was spent in adversity. His father Humayun could make little progress in his expedition. He took possession of a fortified town of Jun, in the vicinity of Thatta, from the hands of Shaibani Khan's *faujdar*; but his repeated attempts to conquer Thatta and Sehwan were foiled by the tough resistance put up by the Arghun chief. Hamida Banu with her infant son joined Humayun at Jun sometime in December 1542. Meanwhile, the Rajput contingent was recalled by Rana Virsal to Amarkot and the Mughal ranks were also considerably thinned by ever-increasing desertions. Shah Husain Arghun ultimately got rid of the fugitive emperor in July 1543 by offering him some material help and a safe passage through his dominions to Afghanistan.

Akbar in the Captivity of his Uncle Kamran

After crossing the Bolan pass, Humayun reached Mastung on the frontier of Kandahar which was then governed by his younger brother Askari on behalf of Kamran, the ruler of Kabul. Humayun lost nerves on the sudden appearance of Askari's men at Mastung, and fled for his dear life towards Persia along with his wife Hamida Banu and one or two helpmates. The infant Akbar was left behind in the camp with his nurses—Maham Anaga and Jiji Anaga, and fell into the hands of Askari. The latter carried his nephew as a hostage to Kandahar and lodged him in the servants' quarters. Askari's wife took a fancy to the child, however, and made suitable arrangements for his upbringing. When Humayun invaded Kandahar with the help of Persian contingents early in 1545, Akbar was shifted by his uncle to Kabul in disguise and held as captive, along with his half-sister Banu Begam and some other destitute females of Humayun's *harem*. A mere pawn in the hands of nature, Akbar spent his childhood under conditions of adversity, tension and uncertainty; at occasions, his fate hung him in the balance between life and death.

Akbar was liberated and reunited with his father in November 1545 when Humayun captured the fort of Kabul from Kamran. Akbar's mother Hamida Banu, later officially designated at Mariam Makani, came from Kandahar to Kabul a couple of months afterwards when the circumcision ceremony of Akbar was performed. Akbar's reunion with his parents proved, however, very short-lived.

In 1546, Humayun led an expedition to Badakhshan. On the way he fell ill and remained confined to bed for about two months, thus giving rise to the rumours about his death. It encouraged Kamran to come out of his hiding and try his luck. He recaptured the fort of Kabul, and, to his misfortune, the child Akbar fell into the hands of his cruel uncle once again. This time, Akbar was treated very shabbily; he was placed under house arrest in the supervision of Kamran's own men. Humayun organised the second invasion of Kabul in November 1547. It was at this occasion that, having lost all hopes of success, Kamran showed his utmost meanness and heartlessness by placing Akbar at the rampart of the main gate of the fort and exposed him to the gunfire of Humayun's artillery. It is said that Humayun's gunners took note of the child and changed the target of their attack but the artillery fire was not stopped. At that critical moment, the survival of Akbar was a matter of mere chance and good luck.

Akbar's Reunion with his Parents

Akbar was a child of nature in the real sense of the term. He was reared up in an atmosphere of utter neglect and adversity, far beyond the control of his parents. It would not be wrong to say that in his days of infancy, he was brought up in the lap of nature. Arrangements for his formal education were made by Humayun after his restoration to the throne of Kabul. However, when attempts were made to teach him, he simply refused to learn; and the efforts of his tutors, like Mulla Pir Muhammad and Bairam Khan failed to inculcate in his heart any taste for the formal education in reading and writing. Instead, he showed his fondness for sports and took greater interest in the company of the beasts than men. Akbar, therefore, was the finest product of Negative Education, received from the Mother Nature, of which Rousseau was to talk about two centuries later, on the eve of the French Revolution. As a young lad of eight or nine, Akbar was skilled enough to ride and control horses, camels and even elephants unaided. He freely indulged in the use of sword, spear and other deadly weapons of war, as if these were toys, and would fearlessly ride a horse to join the soldiers of his father on the battle-fronts. He had seen enough of life and its vicissitudes, much beyond the scope and comprehension of the boys of his age. Akbar received his first official assignment as governor of Ghazni in November 1551 at the age of nine. About this very time, he was married to Ruqaiya Begam daughter of his uncle Hindal, who had fallen in battle near Ghazni while fighting against Humayun's forces. Humayun's second son Mirza Muhammad Hakim, from his wife Man Chuchak Begam, was younger than Akbar by a couple of years.

Humayun's Restoration and Akbar's Nomination as the Heir Apparent

On the eve of Humayun's Indian campaign which resulted in his restoration to the throne of Delhi, he put Muhammad Hakim in nominal charge of the kingdom of Kabul under the care of capable Mughal nobles while Akbar was declared to be in nominal command of the army of Indian invasion. In the official records, Akbar was given the credit of Humayun's victory at Sirhind on January 22, 1555. After his occupation of the throne of Delhi, Humayun declared Akbar to be the heir apparent and assigned him the governorship of the Punjab.

Akbar's Formal Accession at Kalanaur (February 14, 1556)

Akbar was actively engaged against Sikander Suri in the Punjab under the supervision of his tutor and guardian Bairam Khan when Humayun had an accidental fall from the wooden stairs of his library, under construction, at *sher mandal* in Delhi on January 24, 1556. Though grievously injured, he was conscious enough to dispatch a messenger to the Punjab the next day to summon Prince Akbar to his presence. Two days later he expired, thus necessitating the dispatch of another messenger to the Punjab the next day to summon Prince Akbar to his presence. The news of Humayun's death was kept secret for 17 days. A man named Mulla Bekasi, whose features resembled that of Humayun, was dressed up in the royal costumes and shown to the people from the terrace of the palace until the formal proclamation of accession of Akbar to the throne of Delhi. Akbar and Bairam Khan received the news of Humayun's death on February 14 when they were encamped at Kalanaur in district Gurdaspur. In the words of VA Smith, 'the formal enthronement took place in a garden at Kalanaur. The throne, a plain brick structure, eighteen feet long, three feet high, resting on a masonry platform, still exists....the throne platform has been recently enclosed in a plain post-and-chain fence, and a suitable inscription in English and Urdu has been affixed. (*Akbar, op. cit*, p. 6.) After due observance of the rites of mourning, Bairam Khan, 'with the concurrence of' the Mughal nobility, declared Akbar to be the emperor of India and held a brief ceremony to mark the occasion. *Khutba* had already been read in the name of Akbar at Delhi three days earlier (viz., on February 11) when the news of his father's death became known to the people. A formal coronation *darbar* was held a few days later, somewhere in the Punjab, in which Akbar adorned a golden throne and gave an audience to the public with due state ceremonial. The 'nobles of the Chagatai tribe were made joyful by the gift of expensive dresses of honour and regal presents, and promises of future favours were likewise made to them, and 'letters of grace and favour were sent to all parts of Hindustan'. At this occasion, Akbar assumed the regal title of *Shahinshah* while Bairam Khan received appointment as *Vakil-us Sultanate* i.e., the Prime Minister with the designation of *Khan-i-Khanan*. Bairam Khan assumed the reins of government on behalf of Akbar during the period of his minority.

Akbar as *'King of no Land'*

Akbar's formal accession to the throne, however, had nothing to do with the realities of the situation. As a matter of fact, he was *king of no land* at the time of his coronation as the emperor of Hindustan. Soon after Humayun's death, Agra and Delhi were occupied by Hem Chandra, nicknamed Hemu Baqqal (viz., Baniya), the brilliant prime minister and 'indomitable' commander-in-chief of Muhammad Adil Shah Sur. Originally; he belonged to a Brahman family of Rewari. He started his career as an ordinary employee in the royal court of the descendants of Sher Shah Sur and rose to power purely by dint of his hard work, personal talents and good fortune. He earned reputation as the best military leader of northern India who had successfully fought no less than twenty-two pitched battles against his foes. As soon as he came to know of Humayun's demise. Hem Chandra moved out of Chunar, the headquarters of his master Adil Shah, and stormed Agra at the head of a large army with the declared objective of driving out the Mughals from India. He quickly gathered immense strength in men and material from the enemies of the Mughal cause. The Mughal armies at Agra were defeated and routed while Delhi fell into the hands of Hem Chandra without a fight; its Mughal defender Tardi Beg fled the capital on the approach of the former's armies. Hem Chandra declared himself the emperor of India and ascended the throne at Delhi with the title of *Vikramaditya*. Akbar's claim over the Punjab was contested by Sikander Shah Sur while the dominions of Afghanistan, including Kandahar and Badakhshan, were held under the charge of Mirza Muhammad Hakim. He became virtually independent of Delhi under the tutelage of his ambitious mother Man Chuchak Begam and guardian Munim Khan. All the outlying provinces of the empire slipped out of the hands of the Mughal forces immediately after Humayun's death. About this time, the territories in the neighbourhood of Delhi and Agra fell in the grip of severe famine and plague which added to the miseries of the people and resulted in the collapse of the administrative structure. Thus political anarchy prevailed throughout northern India, and the public had to suffer untold hardships. Such was the deplorable condition of the country when Akbar was called upon to assume the crown as a young lad of thirteen; needless to say that the Mughals were as yet treated as foreigners, and were hated and despised by the Indians, Hindus and the Muslims alike. Akbar was encamped at Jalandhar when the news of the fall of Agra and Delhi reached him. The first task before him, therefore, was to recover the lost parental heritage. He was ably assisted in the fulfilment of this task by his tutor and guardian Bairam Khan who acted as the commander-in-chief of the Mughal armies and Regent of the empire till 1560. Many Mughal officers were of the view that they had no chance of success against Hem Chandra and other political opponents in India, and that they should retreat to Afghanistan immediately lest they might be annihilated by their Indian adversaries. Being an ambitious, fearless and self-reliant young boy, Akbar declared his determination to stay and try his luck in India; he was promptly supported by Bairam Khan in the fulfilment of his resolution. One of the reasons as to why did Akbar take this vital decision was that his future in Afghanistan was equally bleak where his half-brother Mirza Muhammad Hakim was already well-established as the virtual ruler of the country.

The Second Battle of Panipat: (November 2, 1556)

Akbar deputed a small contingent of troops at Lahore under the charge of Khizr Khwaja to keep a watch on the movements of Sikander Sur, and himself left for Delhi at the head of 20,000 soldiers in October 1556. At Sirhind, the fugitive Mughal officers and soldiers from Agra, Delhi and other parts of the empire also joined him. They included among others, Tardi Beg, the ex-governor of Delhi. He became the spokesman of the majority of the Mughal nobles who were anxious to return to Kabul forthwith for the safety of their lives. Through a strategic move and with the secret permission of Akbar, Bairam Khan put him to death after fabricating a charge of treason against him. This drastic action terrified the other dissidents and rallied them to the cause of Akbar. Badaoni narrates this incident as follows:

> 'The *Khan-i-Khanan*, who, although he was in disposition, alienated from Tardi Beg Khan, still in spite of this, used to call him *Toqan*—'the elder brother', perceiving the cause of the defeat of that army to have been the treachery of Tardi Beg, and having succeeded in impressing this on the emperor's mind by bringing Khan Zaman and many others as witnesses to substantiate his accusations, obtained a sort of permission to put him to death. So at the time of afternoon prayer, he went to the house of Tardi Beg Khan, and took him to his own abode in the tent; afterwards, at the time of evening prayer he rose up on the pretence of performing the ablutions, and gave to some men, who were held in readiness for the purpose, the signal to slay him. So they made an end of Tardi Beg Khan. And in the morning, when Khwaja Sultan Ali and Mir Munshi did not come to the Diwan, he suspecting them also of treachery, had them imprisoned together with Khanjar Beg, a relation of Tardi Beg Khan. But some time after they regained their liberty.'—(*Muntakhab-ut Tawarikh;* W H Lowe, ii, p. 7.)

The incident of Tardi Beg's cruel treatment at the hands of Bairam Khan needs an explanation. The question of Tardi Beg's delinquency and the particulars of his encounter with Hem Chandra, while defending Delhi, are a subject of controversy. Firishta, who brought out his book, entitled *Gulshan-i-Ibrahimi or Tarikh-i-Firishta* in 1612, during the reign of Jahangir, justifies the action taken by Bairam Khan against Tardi Beg. According to him, the writer had 'understood from the well-informed men of the times that had Tardi Beg not been executed by way of example, such was the condition of the Mughal army and its panic-stricken officers that 'the old scene of Sher Shah might have been enacted'. In consequence of this prompt, though severe measure, however, 'the Chagatai officers, each of whom before esteemed himself at least equal to Kaikubad and Kaikos, now found it necessary to conform to the orders of Bairam Khan, and to submit quietly to his authority.'(Briggs. II, pp. 186-87) VA Smith supports the contention of Firishta with the observation that 'failure to punish the dereliction of Tardi Beg from his duty would have cost Akbar both his throne and his life,' (*Akbar*, p.36)

Crowned with success at Delhi, Hem Chandra got ready to settle his scores with the Mughals who were regrouping themselves for an assault on Delhi. According to Firishta, he was said to possess 1500 war elephants and one *lakh* strong army—'as numerous as the locusts and ants of the desert.'(Briggs. ii, p.187) He dispatched small contingents of troops and his artillery towards Panipat in advance to stall the Mughals. To his misfortune, Bairam Khan made a dash for the historic battle-field of Panipat where he reached first and arranged his forces for the battle-array. One of the Mughal generals, Ali Kuli Khan, led a surprise attack on Hem Chandra's advance guard and annihilated it without much difficulty; the entire artillery of Hem Chandra fell into the hands of the Mughals intact.

The major encounter between the adversaries took place on November 5, 1556. The Mughal army was under the personal command of Bairam Khan. Akbar was not permitted by his lieutenants to take the field in person; instead, he was provided with a special guard of 5,000 well trained and most faithful troopers, and was stationed at a safe distance, far behind the battle-lines. He was instructed by Bairam Khan to flee towards Kabul for life in case the Mughal army was routed in the battle-field. The Mughals successfully withstood the sudden onslaught of Hem Chandra's elephants; and, by their vigorous artillery attack, made them turn their backs and trample their own men under their feet. Hem Chandra and his Indo-Afghan army had to suffer terribly at the hands of their own artillery which had been lost to the Mughals earlier. In spite of the desperate fight put up by the Mughals, they were overpowered by Hem Chandra's forces, *albeit* the scales were turned in their favour by an incidental arrow shot which hit Hem Chandra in the eye and made him unconscious. It created panic among his soldiers who, taking him to be dead, fled the field. The *mahavat* of Hem Chandra's elephant tried his best to save his master by withdrawing from the battlefront, but Shah Kuli Mehram, a Mughal soldier, gave him a hot chase and overpowered him.

Hem Chandra's body was covered with blood when he was presented before Akbar in a state of unconsciousness. Badaoni and Firishta write that Bairam Khan requested the young Prince 'to do a meritorious act by killing the infidel with his own hands'. In deference to the wishes of his nobles, Akbar drew out his sword and touched the head of his foe so as to earn the appellation of a ghazi *albeit* the refused to kill him on the plea: 'Why should I strike him now that he is already as good as dead? If sensation and activity were left in him, I would do so.' (*Muntakhab ut Tawarikh,* W H Lowe, ii, p. 9). Thereupon, Bairam Khan drew out his sabre and severed the head of Hemu from his body with a single blow.

The Second Battle of Panipat, proved to be as much decisive as the first one that had been fought between Babar and Ibrahim Lodhi on April 20, 1526. It broke the backbone of the Indo-Afghan power for all times to come and re-installed the Mughals on the throne of Delhi. The issue was apparently decided by a mere accident or chance, because Hem Chandra, who was visible to his soldiers from the *howdah* of his huge elephant, fainted in the thickest of the battle; *albeit* there were certain inherent causes which led to the defeat of his forces. The most important single factor which led to his fall was his ignorance of the war strategy and his shortsightedness as military general. As a matter of fact, immediately after his occupation of Agra and Delhi, he could have chased the handful of Mughals out of India without much difficulty; it was because the Mughals, at that time, were regarded as foreign intruders while Hem Chandra enjoyed the confidence and support of various sections of the Indian society—Hindus and Muslims alike. The bulk of his army was composed of Muslim soldiers, including hundreds of the Afghans nobles and their personal contingents. His unnecessary delay in turning out the Mughals from the Punjab, his dispatch of artillery far ahead of the main army, with insufficient number of troops to protect it, are some of the factors which betray his incompetence as statesman and military general to handle the situation at the all-India level. Perhaps it was pride and overconfidence in his power and resourcefulness that he made a straight and face-to-face onslaught on the Mughals who were deeply entrenched at Panipat. Had he studied the history of the first battle of Panipat and the one fought by Babar at Khanua against Rana Sanga, he would not have allowed his armies to be caught in the trap laid by Bairam Khan in that historic battlefield. In spite of all the odds against Hem Chandra, the Mughal forces were no match for his men, *albeit* it is doubtful if he had kept himself well-informed of the actual strength, resources and the movements of the enemy. Above all, the leader-worshipping Indo-Afghan army did not have any second-in-command to safeguard their interest in case of sudden death or incapacitation of their leader, and thus the outcome of the encounter depended primarily on the personal wellbeing and active participation of their supreme commander, the fall of whom meant the ruination of the whole mighty army, and the total collapse of the entire political fabric which it represented.

The longrange effects of the Second Battle of Panipat proved far more important than the mere change of the ruling dynasties. Akbar, who benefited from the victory of Panipat and acquired the throne of the Delhi, was destined to play the most significant role in the history of medieval India as an empire-builder and national ruler. He amply proved himself worthy of the exalted office of the monarch that he had come to occupy as a consequence of this battle. Akbar transformed the entire socio-political structure of the country by his radical reforms and secular outlook, and thus laid the foundation of a nation-state in India. The victorious Mughal armies entered Delhi the very next day of the battle, and Agra was taken soon afterwards. From Mewat was captured Hem Chandra's family and huge treasure. Abul Fazl states that the old father of Hem Chandra also fell in the hands of Mulla Pir Muhammad, commander of the local Mughal contingent; the latter gave him a choice between conversion and death, and on the refusal of the formal to embrace Islam made a short work of him.

SECTION 2: BAIRAM KHAN AS THE SAVIOUR OF MUGHAL MONARCHY

Bairam Khan, the Regent of Akbar during his period of minority, was Persian by race and *Shia* by faith. He came to India as an immigrant in search of livelihood and sought service with Humayun as ordinary soldier. But, in the course of time, he was destined to render a great service to Humayun and Akbar in the re-establishment and consolidation of the Mughal rule in India. We do not know much about Bairam Khan's early life. He was a bold and courageous soldier with a tall and well-built body and attractive personality; He took part in the battle of Kanauj (1540) but escaped alive from the debacle, and had no contacts with Humayun thereafter. Like Humayun, he also wandered about in India as a homeless foreign immigrant for a couple of years until he met the fugitive Mughal emperor at Amarkot in 1542 and introduced himself as his old soldier.

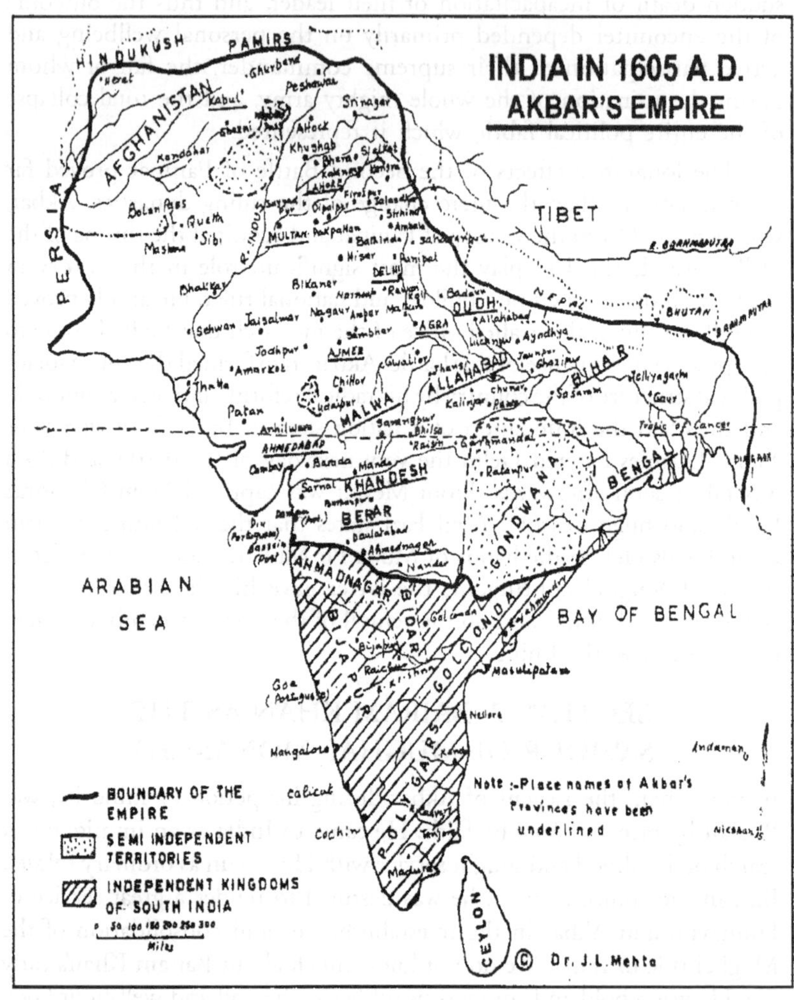
INDIA IN 1605 A.D.
AKBAR'S EMPIRE
HINDUKUSH
PAMIRS
AFGHANISTAN
PERSIA
Kabul
Peshawar
Srinagar
Attock
Kandahar
Bolan Pass
Quetta
Sibi
LAHORE
MULTAN
Bhatinda
Hisar
Panipat
DELHI
Bikaner
Jaisalmer
Nagaur
Amber
Sambhar
Jodhpur
AJMER
AGRA
Gwalior
Amarkot
Thatta
Chittor
Udaipur
Patan
Anhilwara
AHMEDABAD
Cambay
Baroda
Mandu
MALWA
ALLAHABAD
Allahabad
Lucknow
Ayodhya
Jaunpur
Ghazipur
Chunar
Kalinjar
Patna
Sasaram
OUDH
TIBET
NEPAL
BHUTAN
R. BRAHMAPUTRA
BIHAR
Gaur
Tropic of Cancer
BENGAL
Garhmandal
Ratanpur
GONDWANA
KHANDESH
Burhanpur
Surat
Daman (Port.)
Diu (Portuguese)
Bassein (Port.)
BERAR
Daulatabad
Ahmednagar
Nander
AHMADNAGAR
BIDAR
BIJAPUR
GOLCONDA
Golconda
Bijapur
Raichur
R. Krishna
Masulipatam
Rajahmundry
Goa (Portuguese)
Nellore
POLYGARS
Mangalore
Calicut
Cochin
Tanjore
Madura
CEYLON
ARABIAN SEA
BAY OF BENGAL
Andaman
Nicobar
BOUNDARY OF THE EMPIRE
SEMI INDEPENDENT TERRITORIES
INDEPENDENT KINGDOMS OF SOUTH INDIA
0 50 100 150 200 250 300
Miles
Note :-Place names of Akbar's Provinces have been underlined
© Dr. J. L. Mehta

Humayun took him under service at once and this reunion between them proved to be everlasting. Bairam Khan became a personal friend and associate of Humayun and won his confidence as his trustworthy follower. A man of courage and conviction, he proved to be a shrewd statesman and diplomat who possessed well-cultured and dignified social manners and the spirit of self-sacrifice towards his friends.

Bairam Khan stood by his royal patron and friend through thick and thin and earned his gratitude in ample measures. It was on his advice that Humayun took the decision to seek shelter with Shah Tahmasp of Persia. Bairam Khan escorted the fugitive emperor safely to Persia and acted as his chief bodyguard during his period of exile. Humayun being a scion of orthodox *Sunni* Turko-Mongol royal lineage, was ordinarily suspect in the eyes of the Persians, *albeit* Bairam Khan played the cards with utmost patience and diplomatic skill in enhancing the respect and royal dignity of his hapless master. So much so that he not only secured substantial military aid for Humayun for the re-conquest of his lost dominions but also persuaded the Shah to give the hand of a Persian princess in marriage to the fugitive Mughal emperor; the girl who was united in wedlock with Humayun was the daughter of the Persian Emperor's sister. Bairam Khan played an important role in the re-conquest of Kandahar and Kabul. He helped Humayun in getting rid of his selfish brothers and restoring law and order in the kingdom of Kabul. But for his initiative, Humayun might not have contemplated the recovery of his lost Indian empire. Bairam Khan played a heroic role the re-conquest of Delhi and Agra by Humayun. As a reward for his services, Humayun appointed him his *wazir, i.e.*, the Prime Minister, and Commander-in-Chief of the Mughal armies.

Bairam Khan was attached to Akbar from his very birth. He was appointed the tutor (*ataliq*) of the crown prince soon after Humayun's restoration to the throne of Kabul when Akbar was just a small child of five. Bairam Khan treated him with affection and care and gave him complete freedom to pursue the sports and engagements of his own inclination; he imparted practical training to the young prince in soldiery and statecraft. As a consequence, Akbar developed a sort of emotional attachment with his tutor.

The contributions made by Bairam Khan in the recovery of the kingdom of Delhi by Akbar, after the death of Humayun, have already been described in preceding pages of this chapter. The credit for victory by Akbar in the Second Battle of Panipat and the re-conquest of Delhi and Agra by the Mughals goes entirely to Bairam Khan. There is no doubt that,' but for Bairam Khan, chances of Akbar's survival as ruler of India were very remote; he might have even lost his life in the struggle against his rivals'. The appointment of Bairam Khan as the prime minister and regent of Akbar on the death of Humayun was, therefore, in the fitness of things; the young prince reposed full confidence in his guardian, and, out of affection for him, conferred the title of '*Khan Baba*—viz., the father,' upon Bairam Khan.

During his period of regency, Bairam Khan held the reins of government and exercised undisputed control over its administration for over four years from 1556 to 1560. He quickly despatched Mughal officers to take charge of the various districts and restored law and order with an iron hand. Within a month of the battle of Panipat, he made suitable arrangements to deal with the Sur claimants to the throne of Delhi. The Mughal army, led by Akbar personally for a short while, gave a hot chase to Sikander Suri who had retired into the Shivalik hills. He was besieged in the fort of Mankot and 'reduced to such straits that he was compelled to sue for peace.' He surrendered the fort to the Mughals in May 1557 and was granted *jagir* for his decent upkeep. This victory was briefly celebrated by Akbar and Bairam Khan at Jalandhar where they were joined by the ladies of the royal household from Kabul. It was here that Akbar expressed his gratitude to Bairam Khan by allowing him to marry his cousin, Salima Sultan Begam, daughter of Humayun's sister Gulrukh Begam, and 'a lady of great charm and accomplishment'. It enhanced the prestige of Bairam Khan among the Mughal nobles as a kinsman of the ruling house.

Bairam Khan now directed his attention towards Muhammad Adil Shah, the other Suri adversary of Akbar. A vigorous military campaign was launched against the rebellious Afghan chiefs in the Ganga valley; Lucknow was overrun and Adil Shah was compelled to retreat towards Bengal where he was killed in an encounter with the Bengalis towards the close of 1557. The fort of Ajmer was conquered by the Mughal forces in 1558 without a fight while the fort and the state of Gwalior was conquered the year next. Before the fall of Bairam Khan in 1560, Jaunpur had also been wrested from hands of the Afghan rebels.

The Fall of Bairam Khan

'The rise of Bairam Khan to power was gradual and well-deserved but his sudden fall from power in 1560 came as an anticlimax.' Most of the Mughal nobles were Sunnis by faith; therefore, given the opportunity, they would not have approved of Bairam Khan's promotion to the exalted office of the regency. The fact that Bairam Khan happened to be a Persian *Shia* was enough to excite the jealousies of many. To his misfortune, Bairam Khan made many enemies in the court by his haughty behaviour and misuse of his powers to further the interests of his friends and favourites. Once at the helm of affairs, Bairam Khan was surrounded by a crowd of self-seekers, opportunists and flatterers who turned his head as the virtual ruler of the state. To some extent Akbar was personally responsible for it. The whole responsibility for administration was taken over by Bairam Khan but Akbar did not realise the significance of the royal charge that had befallen his shoulders. He neglected his royal duty and freely indulged in hunting and merry-making. He seldom bothered to understand the intricacies of the state problems and never questioned Bairam Khan about the state policies pursued by him. As a result, Bairam Khan became used to exercising royal powers without any interference from the boy king. He acquired complete hold over the Mughal court and the royal household, made all appointments to high offices and exercised even the royal prerogatives without the knowledge or consent of the young monarch. The things came to such a pass that Akbar became almost a non-entity whom his Regent did not feel the necessity to take into confidence in the administration of the state.

Bairam Khan acted as a *de facto* ruler and treated Akbar as mere puppet in his hands. He dealt with all the high dignitaries of the state, the subordinate Indian princes and the foreign ambassadors directly and always tried to undermine Akbar's authority as the sovereign ruler by making out that he was a child. The regent and his family lived in state while Akbar and his royal family received no privy purse and had to look towards the hands of Bairam Khan for meeting their daily needs. Akbar's personal servants, relatives and friends were not treated well while Bairam Khan's friends and favourites wielded power and rolled in wealth. Akbar's mother Hamida Banu Begam, foster-mother Maham Anaga and her son Adham Khan felt very sore about it and pleaded with Akbar to wake up from slumber before it was too late. Bairam Khan had adopted a very haughty and unsympathetic attitude even towards the domestics and personal friends of Akbar. He did not allow other high officers, ministers and nobles to develop close contacts with Akbar and his royal family and felt jealous of the old, experienced and most trustworthy camp-followers of Humayun. Very often he adopted a haughty demeanour even towards Akbar; he made no attempt to apprise the youthful monarch of the day-today developments in the court and injured his sentiments by various acts of high-handedness. Abul Fazl gives two instances to illustrate this point. One day 'a royal elephant became *mast* and got out of the control of its *mahavat*. It attacked one of Bairam Khan's elephants and struck it so hard that the latter's entrails came out.' Bairam Khan put the *mahavat* to death although he was not to blame for it.

In another such incident, Bairam Khan struck terror in the hearts of Akbar's domestics soon thereafter. One day, another elephant of Akbar's royal stables got *mast* in the Yamuna River and attacked Bairam Khan's pleasure boat. The *Khan-i-Khanan* was 'much alarmed' but the *mahavat* managed to control the elephant just in time to avert the accident. When Akbar came to know of this incident, he promptly got its *mahavat* bound in chains and sent him to Bairam Khan for action against him although 'he was innocent'. To add insult to the injury, Bairam Khan, without taking Akbar into confidence, appointed Sheikh Gadai, a *Shia* scholar of doubtful loyalty towards the crown, as the *sadr-i-sadur*, which excited the sectarian rivalry of all the *Sunni* nobles. The Sheikh was also 'exempted from the ceremony of homage' to the monarch and given precedence over all the other *ulama* and the *sayyids*. Accordingly, he held Akbar in low esteem and began to endorse the royal decrees by his own seal. The majority of the Mughal officers at the court felt offended and publically charged Bairam Khan of having pushed up his unworthy favourite to the exalted office of the *sadur*. 'Bairam Khan did not attempt, however, to pacify the frayed tempers nor did he advice the Sheikh to behave with discretion.'

The situation took a serious turn when a rumour was set afloat by the antagonists of Bairam Khan that he was hatching a conspiracy to do away with Akbar and place his cousin Abul Qasim, son of Mirza Kamran, on the throne. Akbar and his well-wishers felt alarmed and decided to strike against the conspirators before they could mature their sinister designs. Some of them took the courage to warn Akbar about the sinister designs of his Regent. Another incident about the misconduct of Bairam Khan soon provided an opportunity to them to plead their case before the young emperor to take action against him. Bairam Khan did not see eye to eye with Mullah Pir Muhammad—an old teacher of Akbar, whose association with the Mughal royal house had been as old as that of Bairam Khan. He held an important office in the royal court with the title of *nasir-ul-mulk*. Bairam Khan ordered his dismissal on very flimsy grounds and asked him 'to proceed to Mecca on pilgrimage'. Pilgrimage to Mecca was a sort of punishment, which was imposed by the medieval Indian rulers upon their defeated rivals or hostile nobles by way of banishment from the country.

Akbar was shocked to know of this development. He was clearly made to understand by his well-wishers that Bairam Khan was gradually eliminating all the supporters of the Mughal crown from the positions of power and influence. By this time Akbar had entered the eighteenth year of his life, and felt himself quite mature to take up the reins of government in his own hands. It aroused 'the King' in him and he made up his mind to remove Bairam Khan from his office all at once. He resorted to a strategy for the success of his objective. He took his wet-nurse (in Turki termed as *Anka* or *Anaga*) Maham Anaga, his son, Adham Khan, and some of their most trustworthy nobles and provincial governors into confidence to inform them that he would like to assume sovereignty and dismiss his Regent. According to Abul Fazl, Maham Anaga, 'who was a marvel for sense, resource and loyalty, played a prominent role in this enterprise; she communicated this secret to her son-in-law, Shihabuddin Ahmad Khan Atka, the governor of Delhi. Shihabuddin at once swung into action and prepared a 'detailed plan to oust Bairam Khan from power'. Through his efforts, the governors of Lahore, Kabul, and many other military officers were secretly won over to the cause of Akbar. The queen-mother Hamida Banu was already in Delhi. On March 19, 1560, Akbar left Agra with only 350 soldiers of his personal guard, apparently for hunting in the neighbourhood of Aligarh, and went across the Jumna. At Sikandra, he was joined by Maham Anaga and some other members of the royal family. From there Akbar made straight for Delhi and sent a message to Bairam Khan that he was going to see his mother who was said to be seriously ill. At Khurja, in the vicinity of Delhi, Akbar was welcomed by Shihabuddin, the governor of Delhi, and some other friends of Akbar with their small contingents, which were placed at his disposal. They held a royal reception for the young king amidst great public rejoicing in Delhi on March 27, 1560. We have it on the testimony of Abul Fazl that "some of' the personal favourites and suspected agents of Bairam Khan were taken into custody in a swoop while the rest fled the town. The fort of Delhi was well-defended (by Shihabuddin) and the army kept in a state of readiness for war. Confidential messages were sent to important provincial governors and military officers regarding the resumption of sovereign power by Akbar and the dismissal of Bairam Khan; and everyone was made responsible for the protection of territories and the treasures under his charge for the crown." (*Ibid; p. 142*)

All the state officials and respectable citizens of the metropolis were asked to present themselves at the imperial court in Delhi and offer their personal allegiance to the crown. Shamsuddin Atka received appointment as the governor of the Punjab with the title of *Khan-i-Khanan*, while one of his subordinates, Mir Muhammad Kalan, defended the fort of Lahore for the emperor. Munim Khan, the governor of Kabul, was faithfully attached to Akbar, and was summoned to the court at Delhi. Akbar nominated Shihabuddin Atka, the governor of Delhi, as his *Vakil* or the Prime minister also, and he took charge of this exalted office immediately. Abul Fazl records that immediately on the receipt of information, "right-minded novices and devoted seniors, and experienced men came trooping in from all parts of the Empire to the sublime court…In a short time, the report of the alienation of the sacred disposition from Bairam Khan was spread far and near. There was a rit (restraint) in his sway and men began to separate from him. The first man to leave the *Khan i Khanan* and to proceed to the throne, and on the path of rectitude, was Qaiya Khan Gang. He was a capable old officer. After him men came, one by one and two by two, to the sublime threshold…Everyone who brought sincerity to the threshold was exalted by fitting officers and titles and fiefs.' (*Akbarnama*, ii, pp. 143-44).

After making his position secure on the throne of Delhi, Akbar sent one of his tutors, Mir Abdul Latif, to Agra with the following orders for Bairam Khan: 'Your services and your fidelity to this great family are known to mankind. As owing to our tender age, we gave our attention to promenading and hunting, we did not cast our glance on political and financial affairs, and all the business of sovereignty was entrusted by us to your excellent capacity and knowledge. Now that we have applied our own mind to the affairs of government, and administration of justice, it is right that this sage well-wisher (Bairam Khan), who ever boasted of his sincerity and devotion, should recognise a Divine gift in truth, and offer up endless thanks for it. He should for a time gather up his skirts from business and turn his attention to the bliss of pilgrimage to Mecca of which he was always desirous, and with regard to which he was constantly in public and in private, expressing his great longing to obtain such a boon. We shall grant him whatever place and whatever extent of land he may wish for (as *jagir*) in India, so that his servants may remit him the proceeds, harvest by harvest and year by year." (*Ibid.*)

Akbar's order 'came as a bolt from the blue to Bairam Khan'. Some of his more hot-tempered camp-followers suggested trial of strength with Akbar but Bairam Khan kept his cool. 'He did not want to tarnish the glorious record of his lifelong services to the Mughal crown by assuming the role of a traitor'. After some hesitation, he offered his unqualified submission to Akbar and prepared to leave for Mecca. He left Agra for Nagor from where he sent all the insignia of royalty, consisting of kettledrums and the royal standards, etc., to Akbar's court at Delhi. According to Badaoni, at this critical juncture, even Sheikh Gadai, whose appointment as *sadr-us-sadur* and misconduct had hastened Bairam Khan's fall, broke off with his patron and 'sought forgiveness at the feet of Akbar'. (*Muntakhhab ut Tawarikh*, ii, p. 33)

The Revolt of Bairam Khan and its Aftermath

For a while, Bairam Khan hesitated in relinquishing the charge of his personal contingent, which numbered quite a few thousands. He moved at a leisurely pace from Nagor to Bikaner and delayed his departure for Mecca. It was rumoured that he intended to visit the Punjab with the object of collecting his personal treasure which had been lodged at Sirhind and Lahore. Akbar did not like his movements which were not free from suspicions. As a precautionary measure, he himself marched towards Punjab at the head of royal armies and despatched Mulla Pir Muhammad, whom Bairam Khan had dismissed from service a short while ago, with 5,000 troops to hasten the ex-Regent out of the Mughal dominions. Bairam Khan was already feeling very angry and dejected. 'When he heard of Pir Muhammad's arrival as his chastiser, his pride was touched to the quick'. Badaoni writes that in desperation, and 'at the instigation of some demon-like men', he 'turned to the Punjab, lodged his family at Bathinda (Bhatinda) and raised a standard of revolt'. The royal army led by Shamsuddin Atka challenged him at Tawara, on the bank of the Beas in the foothills of Shivalik. After a half-hearted resistance, Bairam Khan fled from the field, and soon thereafter, sent his letter of submission to Akbar through one of his officials.

Bairam Khan was produced in the court of Akbar at Lahore. Nizamuddin has to say that, on his arrival, 'all the *Amirs and Khans* went out by the Emperor's orders to receive him; and they conducted him to the Emperor with every mark of honour. Bairam Khan fell at the feet of the monarch and burst into tears. Akbar received him with the princeliest grace and made him sit on the right hand side at the head of the *grandees* of the empire'. Akbar invested him with a splendid robe of honour and offered him three alternatives regarding his future career; (1) the governorship of the districts of Kalpi and Chanderi; (2) the post of confidential adviser to the crown at the royal court, or (3) departure for Mecca. Bairam Khan observed that after having lost his master's confidence once, it was not appropriate for him to continue in the royal service any more. He thanked Akbar for his forgiveness which according to him 'was more than a reward for his former services.' He, therefore, expressed his desire to go to Mecca and spend the rest of his life there. Two days later, Bairam Khan was allowed by the Emperor to start for Gujarat, *enroute* to Mecca, with a strong military contingent and sufficient money to meet the travelling expenses.

The Tragic End of Bairam Khan

To his misfortune, Bairam Khan was not destined to reach Mecca. He was assassinated at Patttan (Gujarat) on January 31, 1561, by a party of turbulent Afghans, led by one Mubarak Khan, whose father had died fighting against Bairam Khan in the battle of Machchiwara in 1555. Bairam Khan's camp was put to plunder and his widow Salima Begam, along with her infant son Abdur Rahim, reached Ahmadabad in distress. Nizamuddin tells us that 'the dead body of Bairam Khan was picked up in the *jungle* by some Muslim ascetics (*fakirs*) who gave it a burial'. Akbar was shocked to hear of this tragic end of Bairam Khan – his revered teacher and guardian. Bairam Khan's family was brought to the court under royal escort. Akbar married his widow as a mark of respect to the memory of the deceased, and reared up Abdur Rahim under his personal care just like his own son. Abdur Rahim grew up to be a outstanding military officer and scholar of his times and was honoured by Akbar with the title of *Khan-i-Khanan,* held by Bairam Khan previously.

SECTION 3: AKBAR'S LIBERATION FROM THE '*PETTICOAT GOVERNMENT*'

Akbar had secured freedom from the tutelage of Bairam Khan through a stratagem, organised by the *harem* party so-called. Maham Anaga, the foster-mother of Akbar, had played a major role in this affair. It gained for her an important position in the state politics. It is recorded by most of the contemporary chroniclers that, after the fall of Bairam

Khan, Maham Anaga came to wield great influence at the royal court; and she acted as the personal adviser of the youthful king for about four years. Accordingly, VA Smith opines that 'Akbar shook off the tutelage of Bairam Khan only to bring himself under the monstrous regiment of unscrupulous women'. He observes that Maham Anaga held the reins of government in her hands, bestowed offices on her favourites and 'cared for nothing except her own interests.' In other words, she tried to play the role of a king-maker and brought into existence 'the petticoat government of the worst kind.' (*Akbar*, p. 48).

The important members of the *harem* party, who constituted the so-called 'petticoat government', were Hamida Banu Begam – the Queen Mother, Maham Anaga, Adham Khan, Shihabuddin Atka Khan, Munim Khan and Mulla Pir Muhammad. Adham Khan, the son of Maham Anaga, who was older than Akbar by about a year, was the most intimate and trustworthy friend of the young emperor as they had been 'brought up together by Maham Anaga, whether in the servants quarters or in the royal place. It is, therefore, not surprising that Akbar loved Adham Khan and treated him as his brother,' Shihabuddin Atka Khan, the governor of Delhi, was son-in-law of Maham Anaga., while Mulla Pir Muhammad had been a tutor of Akbar, who used to teach Persian to the young prince. Above all, the elderly Munim Khan, the governor of Kabul, was a seasoned military general who had been one of the most trustworthy camp-followers of Humayun. All of them enjoyed the confidence of the queen mother and were liberally patronized by her. All the above-mentioned persons were held in the highest esteem by Akbar who consulted them in determining the state policies but VA Smith's contention that, after the fall of Bairam Khan, Akbar was used as puppet by this *Petticoat Government* or *Parda Regime* is, not borne out by the facts of history. No doubt, Akbar loved Maham Anaga like his mother and had great regard for her people. Very kind-hearted and noble by nature, he felt obliged to all those who had stood by him in the trial of strength with his formidable Regent. It was, therefore, quite natural that they should be richly rewarded by the grateful monarch. Abdul Fazal states very clearly that 'everyone who brought sincerity to the threshold was exalted by fitting offices and title and fiefs.' Accordingly, on the sudden removal of Bairam Khan and his protégés, all the high offices of the state and the military commands were redistributed, the lion's share of which went to the leaders of the *harem* party. But Akbar never obliged anybody under pressure nor did he permit anyone to convert his or her privileges into a right. None could dictate the terms to him on any account. Once he had taken the reins of government in his own hands, Akbar set up as an absolute king who never allowed any one to interfere in the exercise of his sovereign powers. He was the master of his own will. As soon as he became conscious of the fact that some ambitious or unscrupulous officer, friend or kinsman was attempting to encroach upon his sovereignty, he acted swiftly to cut him or her to size. This is amply borne out by the course of events during the first four years (1560-64) after the fall of Bairam Khan when members of the *harem* party held positions of influence in the court.

Akbar's Hold Over his Prime Ministers

After the fall of Bairam Khan, Akbar never allowed his *Vakils* or Prime Ministers to exercise powers arbitrarily. On assuming the reins of government in his hands, he began to exercise vigilance and control over his Prime Ministers and did not permit them to adopt an independent course of action. Within six months of Bairam Khan's fall, Akbar appointed, in quick succession, as many as four persons to hold the office of the prime minister and did not allow respite to anyone to develop vested interests therein. On the formal dismissal of Bairam Khan, Shihabuddin Atka Khan, the governor of Delhi, was the first to be entrusted with this exalted office on March 27, 1560. It is alleged that Maham Anaga had started interfering with the state affairs but Abul Fazl makes a very interesting statement that she was formally associated with Shihabuddin by His Majesty to officially represent matters to him for orders; it legalized her position as the Joint or associate Vakil of the King. Akbar thus tried to establish dual prime ministership, the incumbents of which were held collectively responsible to him. But this experiment did not prove successful as Maham Anaga, because of her closeness to the sovereign, usually over-ruled her colleague and attempted to use him 'as the second fiddle'. Even otherwise, the Mughals had no tradition of being governed by a woman prime minister, however capable. Shihabuddin was replaced as the *Vakil* by Bahadur Khan Uzbeg, the leader of a powerful faction of the Turkish nobility at the court, but he was not found competent to hold this exalted office and was relieved of the ministerial charge. Maham Anaga continued to act as the joint *Vakil* with Bahadur Khan also but, on September 10, 1560, she was also politely asked by Akbar to hand over the charge of the *vakalat* to Munim Khan, another important member of the *harem* party, who became the fourth Prime Minister of Akbar with the title of *Khan-i-Khanan*. Thus by repeatedly changing the incumbents of this office, he reduced the status of the *Vakils* or *Prime Ministers* to his mere nominees who held office at the pleasure of the Crown. It was the first achievement of Akbar towards the establishment of absolute monarchy.

Conquest of Malwa

To signal the beginning of his sovereign rule, Akbar chalked out a plan for the conquest of Malwa as an experiment to test the competence and loyalty of his new supporters of the *Harem Party*. Bahadur Shah, the ruler of Malwa and Gujarat, had put Humayun to great trouble. Malwa and Gujarat were conquered by Humayun but he failed to establish his permanent hold over them for long, and they were lost to Bahadur Shah again. Malwa formed a part of the Suri Empire but its governor, Shujaat Khan, had became independent of Delhi during the reign of Muhammad Adil Shah Sur; Sarangpur was his capital. On the death of Shujaat Khan, his son Baz Bahadur became the sovereign ruler of Malwa in early 1556. Akbar sent the royal forces for the conquest of Malwa in the winter of 1560 under the charge of Adham Khan while Mulla Pir Muhammad Khan was put second in command. Baz Bahadur was defeated near Sarangpur and fled towards Khandesh and Malwa was conquered by the Mughals. A rich booty, including invaluable treasures, war elephants and horses fell into the hands of Adham Khan. A number of the ladies of Baz Bahadur's *harem*, including his most accomplished wife Rupmati, were also captured by Adham Khan. Rupmati saved her honour by poisoning herself to death but Adham Khan appropriated the major part of the booty, including the ladies, and sent only a few elephants and horses to the court of Akbar. He also tarnished the Mughal victory by committing atrocities on the defeated foe. On the receipt of intelligence of his misdeeds, Akbar ordered Munim Khan and other senior officers to look after the affairs of the state; and, without informing any one of them about his plan of action, left Agra on April 27, 1561. He rushed towards Sarangpur with a strong contingent of mobile cavalry. Abul Fazl writes that Adham Khan was 'amazed at the sudden appearance of the Emperor, who had marched so fast that he outstripped the messengers sent by Maham Anaga to warn her son.' (*Akbarnama*, ii, p. 218). Maham Anaga apprehended some trouble, and she followed close upon the heels of Akbar's army. 'She reached Sarangpur just in time to intervene and apologies on behalf of her defaulting son'. Akbar got hold of the treasure and all the other spoils and granted pardon to Adham Khan 'in consideration of his past services to the crown'.

Liquidation of the *Harem Party*

By this time Akbar had become fully conscious of the growing power of the *Harem Party* which had liberated him from the clutches of his unscrupulous Regent. Therefore, after his return from Malwa, he undertook the next step to curtail the powers of his new supporters of the *Harem Party* so-called. Akbar was not satisfied with the competence and general conduct of Munim Khan. In November 1561, he relieved him of the ministerial charge and appointed Shamsuddin Atka Khan as his fifth Prime Minister; he was the husband of Jiji Anaga, another wet-nurse of Akbar. At the same time, Akbar recalled Adham Khan from Sarangpur and promoted his lieutenant, Mulla Pir Muhammad, as the governor of Malwa. It gave a serious set-back to the powers and prestige of the *Harem Party*.

Death of Adham Khan: The misconduct of Adham Khan and dishonesty displayed him in the discharge of his duties in Malwa had badly shaken the faith of Akbar about the honesty and integrity of his closest and apparently the most reliable friends. After the recall of Adham Khan to Agra, Akbar treated him with the traditional warmth and consideration. He was allowed to attend the imperial court with full honour and dignity befitting a member of the royal family as before. But Adham Khan, 'failed to reconcile himself to the loss of power and prestige'. Abul Fazl records that 'a tragical event' then took place on May 16, 1562. In the evening of that fateful day, Shamsuddin Atka Khan, the new Prime Minister was transacting official business in a small room in the Royal Palace, adjoining the sleeping chamber of Akbar, at Agra. Adham Khan went to his room with a few men-in-arms and murdered Shamsuddin. Thereafter, he tried to enter Akbar's sleeping chamber 'with the blood-stained sword'. His attempt was foiled, however, by a eunuch who quickly bolted the door from within the royal chamber. On hearing of the noise, however, Akbar woke up and rushed out of his chamber from the backdoor; he 'had a scuffle with the assassin and overpowered him with the help of his domestics'. Akbar had a narrow escape. He immediately ordered Adham Khan to be put to death. Accordingly, 'on the orders of His Majesty, the assassin was bound hand and foot and twice thrown down the terrace of the Palace so that his neck was broken and his brains destroyed.' (Abul Fazl, *Akbarnama*, ii, p. 272). His accomplices fled from the palace but were soon apprehended and inflicted severe punishments.

Death of Maham Anaga: At the time of the above incident, Maham Anaga was also present in the royal apartments at Agra. She was, however, struck down by illness and was confined to bed in her own chamber near the royal palace. According to Abul Fazl, Akbar conveyed to her the news of the tragic event, on the receipt of which Maham Anaga, 'by virtue of her wisdom, preserved her respect for His Majesty and did not complain or lament', and replied, "Your Majesty has done well." She was not permitted to see the dead body of her son for the sentimental reasons. 'The corpses of Shamsuddin and Adham Khan were sent to Delhi and given a burial with full state ceremonial'. Maham Anaga could not bear the shock of her son's death, however, and, 'forty days after this occurrence' breathed her last. Her dead body was also sent to Delhi and given a state burial near the grave of her son.' With the orders of His Majesty, a lofty building was erected over the tombs of Maham Anaga and Adham Khan'. Akbar 'accorded a very generous treatment' to the family and dependants of the deceased. Munim Khan was forgiven and reinstated as the Prime Minister and he continued to serve the Crown with distinction till his death.

Death of Mulla Pir Muhammad: Mulla Pir Muhammad, who had replaced Adham Khan as the governor of Malwa, proved to be an incapable administrator. His haughty and unsympathetic treatment of the subjects made the Mughal rule unpopular in Malwa. It created disorder and anarchy and the oppressed peasantry and zamindars began to defy the state authority. It gave an opportunity to Baz Bahadur to stage a come-back with the active support of the neighbouring chiefs of Khandesh and Berar. Mulla Pir Muhammad defeated and retreated towards Mandu. While fleeing across the river Narbada, Pir Muhammad fell off his horse and was drowned. Abul Fazl describes this event as follows:

> "Mounted as Pir Muhammad was, he flung himself with confusion into the swellings of the Narbada. It chanced that a string of mules was then crossing rapidly. They came near the horse and kicked it on the side. Pir Muhammad's horse, as well as his sense, departed from their place. He fell from his horse into the water, and his comrades who were close by, did not in their wickedness exert themselves to draw him out of that

whirlpool of destruction. He was drowned and went to the ocean of annihilation, either as a retribution for the oppression which he had committed in this expedition, or for his conduct (rather misconduct)...By heaven's decree, so loyal, able and gallant a man underwent such a fate." - (*Akbarnama*, ii, pp. 258-59).

With the death of Mulla Pir Muhammad, the last pillar of the *Harem* Party or the 'Petticoat Government' so-called met his end and Akbar 'emerged from behind the veil'.

Death of Khwaja Muazzam: After the deaths of Adham Khan, Maham Anaga and Pir Muhammad, Akbar had to deal with yet another disloyal and wicked member of the Mughal family; he was Khwaja Muazzam, a half-brother of the queen mother, Hamida Banu Begam. He held an important position in the royal court. It is said that he was found 'guilty of several disgraceful actions' during the reign of Humayun. In spite of repeated warnings from Akbar, this 'half insane monster' did not mend his ways. In March 1564, he put his wife Zuhra Agha Begam to death in a domestic quarrel. Akbar paid a personal visit to his 'farm house', situated on the bank of the Jumna, and 'ordered his guard to well thrash him, and then to put him in a boat and souse him several times in the river. As the assassin survived this shock treatment, he was sent a captive to the fort of Gwalior where he died in confinement'. In the opinion of VA Smith, 'this incident marks the date of Akbar's final emancipation from the influence of the Petticoat Government and his kith and kin'. Akbar held the queen mother in the highest esteem but she never interfered in the state affairs against his will.

SECTION 4: AKBAR'S IMPERIALISM

EARLY CONQUESTS (1556-62)

At the time of his formal accession to the throne early in 1556 at Kalanaur in district Gurdaspur of the Punjab, Akbar had no territorial possessions and was literally a '*king of no land*'. Bairam Khan helped him in the recovery of Delhi and Agra as a result of his victory at the Second Battle of Panipat. The Punjab was occupied by the Mughals after the surrender of Sikander Suri at Mankot in May 1557. Ajmer was occupied towards the end of 1557, while the state of Gwalior was conquered and annexed to the Mughal kingdom in 1558-59. Muhammad Adil Shah Suri was defeated and Jaunpur wrested from the hands of the Afghan rebels in 1559-60. Bairam Khan also organised an expedition to Malwa but, due to the sudden flaring up of his conflict with Akbar, it was called off. After the fall of Bairam Khan, Akbar sent an army for the conquest of Malwa, the detailed account of which has been given above. Malwa was conquered and annexed to Delhi but the victorious Mughal generals failed to consolidate their hold over it. Adham Khan, the first Mughal governor of Malwa was recalled by Akbar on charge of misrule while the second governor Mulla Pir Muhammad was defeated at the hands of Baz Bahadur, and was drowned in the Narbada during his hurried retreat. Akbar sent a fresh army under the command of Abdullah Khan Uzbeg who recaptured Malwa from its ruler Baz Bahadur; Abdullah Khan was appointed the governor of Malwa with his headquarters at Mandu.

Suppression of Disaffected Nobles and Rebellions

Akbar was a bold and courageous warrior; he possessed high moral character and fine qualities of leadership. He had inherited strong imperial instincts from his grandfather Babar. He was not satisfied with a small and shaky kingdom but, before he could enter upon a regular career of military conquests or envisage an imperial policy, he had to deal with a number of his turbulent Turko-Afghan nobles and hostile relatives who posed a grave threat to his very survival as a sovereign king. Therefore, he was called upon to organise quite a few military expeditions to bring the rebellious Muslim nobles and zamindars to book in quick succession.

Rebellion of Khan Zaman Uzbeg (1560): Of all the Mughal officers, the Uzbegs, because of their traditional hostility towards the Ruling Family of Babar, were the most restless and aggressive people. They nurtured feelings of disloyalty towards Akbar and their leaders, in spite of their professions of loyalty towards the Mughal monarchy, were most unreliable and untrustworthy. Nevertheless, Akbar kept them in good humour and always tried to secure their cooperation with politeness and skilfulness. Their seniomost leader, Khan Zaman Uzbeg, had earned distinction at the Second Battle of Panipat. He led the Mughal army against the Afghan rebels in eastern India and, in recognition of his services, received appointment as governor of Jaunpur. In 1568, the Afghan rebels from Bengal entered the Ganga valley. They were led by Sher Shah II—the son of Muhammad Adil Shah Suri. Khan Zaman repulsed their attack and acquired huge booty, including treasure and war elephants. He, however, withheld the major part of the spoils and submitted a false report about their depredations instead. On the receipt of intelligence, Akbar marched upon Jaunpur in person with a large army to take the culprits to task. Khan Zaman lost his nerves and hastened to surrender the entire booty with apologies. As the Uzbegs formed a big slice of the powerful immigrant community in India, Akbar could ill-afford to earn their active hostility; therefore, he deemed it expedient to pardon Khan Zaman who was allowed to retain his ministerial charge intact because he stood as bulwark to keep the turbulent Afghan chiefs of Bihar and Bengal in check.

Rebellion of Abdullah Khan Uzbeg (1564): Abdullah Khan Uzbeg, the governor of rich and fertile province of Malwa, amassed wealth and raised a strong army, and started hob-knobbing with the disaffected Afghan companions of Baz Bahadur in the region with the evil intentions of throwing off the imperial yoke of the Mughals. On the receipt of intelligence, Akbar marched upon Malwa in person with a huge force in the month of July 1564, in the midst of the heavy rains, and took Abdullah by surprise. The rebel suffered defeats in a number of skirmishes, fought against the Mughal army, and fled towards Gujarat. Kara Bahadur Khan was appointed the new governor of Malwa by Akbar before his return to Agra in October 1564. Baz Bahadur, he wandered about as a fugitive in the courts of various rulers of central and south India for about fifteen years and, ultimately, sought shelter at the Mughal court. Akbar enrolled him as *mansabdar* of one thousand and granted him a suitable *jagir* for passing the rest of his life in peaceful retirement.

Revolts of Uzbeg Chiefs, Afghans and Mirzas (1565-67): Abdullah Khan Uzbeg, the rebellious governor of Malwa had taken shelter in Gujarat. From there he sneaked into Jaunpur and was accorded protection by its governor Khan Zaman. They once again raised a standard of revolt against Akbar in 1565 by making a common cause with some other rebellious Uzbeg and Afghan nobles. Akbar personally took the field against them but he had to return to Agra without achieving much success on hearing of serious political developments on the northwestern frontier. It was because Akbar's half-brother, Mirza Muhammad Hakim, had been driven out of Kabul by Suleiman Mirza of Badakhshan. The latter retreated towards the Punjab with his army to seek help from Akbar. But, finding the latter engaged against the rebellious Uzbegs and Afghans in the east, he assumed aggressive postures. He plundered Bhera and laid siege to Lahore. It was very difficult for Akbar to fight his enemies on two fronts, widely separated from each other. He, therefore, advised his trusted officers 'to maintain superficial pressure upon the Uzbeg rebels without engaging them in the open field, and keep a watch over their movements'. Akbar secretly returned to Agra, and after collecting fresh troops from there, reached Delhi for onwards march towards Lahore. On hearing of Akbar's sudden arrival, Mirza Muhammad Hakim lost his nerves. He hurriedly raised the siege of Lahore and fled towards the Khyber. Akbar sent the royal army in hot chase of Muhammad Hakim as far as the Indus. Thereafter, Akbar again made his appearance on the eastern front to reckon with the Uzbeg and Afghan rebels. In a surprise attack, he struck at the Uzbeg camp at Mankuwal, near Allahabad, and spread consternation in their ranks. Khan Zaman was killed in the battle while many of his associates were taken prisoners and inflicted severe punishments. All the traitors in the ranks of the Mughal camp, including Abul Qasim, were also apprehended and executed. Jaunpur was re-conquered by the Mughal forces by July 1567 although it took another five years to identify and destroy all the rebellious Afghan and Uzbeg chiefs in Bihar and the Ganga Valley before the Mughal rule was consolidated there.

Akbar's Policy of Imperialism

Akbar was always anxious to extend the boundaries of his kingdom and acquire dominance over the other rulers. He was an imperialist by instinct. Therefore, he was ever eager to raise a strong standing army to fight wars of aggression. His earlier victories and the success in the suppression of revolts of the rebellious nobles and selfish friends and kinsmen gave him a great; confidence; it aroused the imperial instincts in him, and gave birth to his policy of imperialism for the establishment of a vast Indian empire for himself. 'Akbar evolved out a systematic plan for the expansion of his dominions. This plan received a fillip from his successful dealings with the Rajputs both as friends as well as foes. As a matter of fact, the adoption of a specific Rajput policy by Akbar and his liberal religious outlook, resulting in the emancipation of his Hindu subjects, were the two pillars upon which the grand edifice of his imperialist policy was laid. These two factors nurtured his imperialist instincts and provided a political philosophy to his military campaigns. Akbar now evolved an ambitious plan for the conquest of the whole of the Indian subcontinent with the objective of establishing an all-powerful imperial or central government under the Mughal ruling house. The political unification of the country and the establishment of an all-powerful central government with a uniform system of administration throughout the land became the ideals of his life. During the second half of his reign, it was not his land-hunger or the thrill of exploits which prompted his military actions; instead, he was guided by the political idea to establish himself as the Lord Paramount of the whole of the country and earn reputation as the national monarch of its entire people. His career of military exploits which started with the expedition to Malwa in 1560 and culminated in the conquest of Asirgarh in 1601, forms a glorious chapter in the annals of the military history of India. Akbar stood for the political unification of the country and the national integrity of its people. Regionalism, racialism or religious considerations were totally superseded by the national sentiments in his scheme of conquests. This was exactly the political ideal of the ancient *chakravartin* monarchs of India. Akbar spent the whole of his life in the fulfillment of this objective and the same ideal was pursued by his successors, Jahangir and Shah Jahan, with unabated zeal.' (Advanced Study; ii, pp. 220-21).

The important military conquests and territorial acquisitions of Akbar which led to the gradual expansion of his Empire were as follows.

(*a*) CONQUEST OF RAJPUTANA

Marriage with the Daughter of Raja Bihari Mal of Amber

The adversities of his early life had made Akbar a young man of high moral character and sober temperament. From his very early youth, he had a spiritual bent of mind. In January 1562, he went on a pilgrimage to the mausoleum of Sheikh Muinuddin Chishti at Ajmer. His route lay through the Rajput state of Amber (modern Jaipur). The trespassing into the territories of a neighbouring sovereign chief posed a serious problem. Raja Bihari Mal Kachhwaha, the ruling chief of Amber could permit him to pass through his territories only as a friend otherwise Akbar must fight his way through the Rajput state. After some hesitation, the Rajput chief adopted the first course of action. With a view to safeguarding his own position, he offered his submission to Akbar at Sanganer, on the outskirts of his state, and, voluntarily, proposed his daughter's marriage with the young Muslim chief. Akbar readily accepted the offer, and on his return from Ajmer, marriage was solemnized at Sambar, the whole army contingent of Akbar being received and entertained as the marriage party. Bihari Mal gave a rich dowry to his daughter and sent his son Bhagwan Dass with 5,000

Rajput soldiers to escort his newly married sister to Agra according to the Hindu custom. Akbar was deeply impressed by the highly dignified, sincere and princely conduct of his Rajput relations. He took Man Singh, the youthful son of Bhagwan Dass into the royal service. Akbar was deeply impressed by the cordial and respectful conduct of his Rajput relatives who belonged to the most chivalrous warrior class of the Hindus. He was still more fascinated by the charm and accomplishments of his Rajput wife. He developed real love for her and raised her to the status of the Chief Queen. She, in turn, exercised 'a profound impact on the socio-cultural environment of the entire royal household and changed the life-style of Akbar'. Prince Salim (later Jahangir), the son and successor of Akbar, was born of this Rajput wedlock on August 30, 1569.

Akbar's Rajput Policy – Its Evolution

Akbar's marriage with the Rajput princess of Amber had a profound effect on the outlook and state policy of Akbar. He was simply amazed to find the emotional and sincere attachment of the Amber Rajputs to him. They were always prepared to lay down their lives for the personal protection of Akbar and the honour of the Mughal throne. Up till now, the Rajputs were regarded as sworn enemies of the Muslim rulers in India. But by befriending them and by paying due regard to their sense of honour and self-respect, Akbar had won over their love and services beyond all contemplations. The Rajputs once comprised the 'Sword-Arm of Hindustan' and stood as bulwark against the Muslim invaders; but by a single stroke of diplomacy, they readily became 'the Props and Supports' of the Mughal crown. 'This new revelation prompted Akbar to adopt a rational approach to the problem of his relationships with his Hindu subjects, in general, and the Rajputs, in particular. Akbar was formally the head of an Islamic state in India from which the Hindus were kept at an arm's length. They suffered from numerous socio-religious disabilities and were denied full rights of citizenship, at par with the Muslims, although they constituted the bulk of the population. They were treated as non-entity in the matters of state policy. The entire political and military powers of the Mughal state belonged to the Muslims; most of them were foreign immigrants, and unfortunately, Akbar had a very bitter experience at their hands. His father had suffered at the hands of his Muslim rivals and, particularly, his brothers. The challenge to Akbar's authority came from within the ranks of his own nobility. He had to fight a life and death struggle against his kinsmen, disaffected nobles and self-seeking friends and associated, all of whom were Muslims. Within their ranks, the Mughal nobility constituted a house divided against itself. There was intense rivalry between the Turko-Afghans and the Mughals, between the Chaghatais and the Uzbegs, between the Persians and all the rest. The dominant majority of the *Sunnis* did not see eye to eye with the *Shias*. The considerations of race and religion all paled into insignificance in Akbar's grim struggle for survival as the sovereign ruler. He was all the time worried about the safeguarding of his interests against the aggressive tendencies and encroachments of his own people. In the Rajputs he found at once an alternative source of authority for himself, a counter-force against his selfish kinsmen and turbulent Mughal nobles. Guided by his happy experience with the Rajputs of Amber, Akbar formulated an intelligent and well-calculated Rajput policy to befriend and subjugate all the Rajput states, without interfering in their internal affairs. The cardinal principles of his policy were 'enlightened self-interest, recognition of merit, justice and fair play', based on honourable and equitable treatment with the Rajputs. His plan was to bring the Rajputs into the main stream of national political life under the leadership of the Mughal dynasty. He wanted the Rajputs to serve as his right-hand men for the protection of his throne and the defence of the Mughal Empire. In the long run, he successfully utilised their services for the fulfillment of his imperialist policy that was to bring about the political unification of the country.' (Advanced Study, ii, pp. 222-23).

Of course, Akbar extended his hand of friendship to the Rajputs from a position of strength. He wanted to assert himself as the Lord Paramount of the whole country. Therefore, he adopted a 'carrot and rod' policy to bring the Rajputs under his subjugation; 'so to say, he held a flower in one hand and sword in the other'. Those of the Rajput chiefs who willingly submitted to him were absorbed into 'the imperial system' while most of them adopted an attitude of reservation towards him. They were challenged on the battle-field one by one and were left to draw their own conclusions. In fact, as a great warrior, having full confidence in his military prowess, Akbar was always ready to challenge them for an open fight to establish his superiority, and he had started unprovoked war of aggression against the various Rajput states from the beginning of his sovereign rule.

Conquest of Merta (1562)

During his very first visit to Ajmer in 1562, Akbar had issued instructions to his local Mughal commanders to organise an expedition to the fort of Merta which was under the control of Jai Mal Rathor, a tributary of Rao Maldev of Jodhpur. Jai Mal was taken aback by the sudden appearance of the Mughal forces at the borders of his principality. His suzerain could not provide any assistance to Jai Mal who put up a tough fight for the defence of Merta, single-handed, but failed to protect it. The Rajput defenders, who were heavily outnumbered by the invaders, were annihilated and the fort fell to the Mughals in March 1562. In distress, Jai Mail retreated towards Chittor and took shelter with Rana Udai Singh of Mewar. At a much later stage, he sacrificed his life while fighting for the defence of Chittor against the Mughal forces.

Invasion of Gondwana and Fight with Rani Durgavati (1564)

Akbar started a systematic war of aggression against the other powerful Rajput chiefs with effect from 1564. He organised an unprovoked attack on the Hindu state of Gondwana which constituted the northern part of modern Madhya Pradesh; its capital was Chauragarh, which was located about 47 kilometres to the southwest of Narsinghpur. This state was then called by the double name of 'Garh-Katanga', because of the historic importance of its two headquarters- Garh (Chauragarh) and Katanga respectively. Abul Fazl records that its boundaries 'extended from Ratanpur in the east to Raisin in the west and from Rewa in the north to edge of the Deccan plateau.'(*Akbarnama*, II, pp. 323-24). It was ruled by Rani Durgavati, the Chandel princess of Mahoba, on behalf of her minor son Vir Narayan. The charge of the Gondwana expedition was entrusted to Asaf Than, the governor of Kara. The Mughal army of invasion comprised 50,000 mobile cavalry under the charge of Asaf Khan, while the Rani commanded 20,000 soldiers and 1000 war elephants. She checked the advance of the aggressors at the Nardhi Pass and fought bravely for two days until she was fatally wounded and incapacitated. She stabbed herself to death to save her honour. Two months later, Asaf Khan attacked Chauragarh, which was heroically defended by its minor ruler Vir Narayan until he fell fighting in the battle. Asaf Khan acquired huge booty which included about a thousand elephants and immense treasure. Abul Fazl writes that 'When the fort was taken, there fell into the hands of Asaf Khan and his men incalculable amount of gold and silver. There were coined and uncoined gold, decorated utensils, jewels, pearls, figures, pictures, jeweled and decorated idols, figures of animals made wholly of gold and other rarities. I have heard from reliable informants that among the goods and treasures of Chauragarh which Asaf Khan took sole possession, there were one hundred *degs* full of Alauddin *ashrafis*. There were also other things which could not be calculated.' (*ibid.*, p. 332). It is said that Asaf Khan sent only a part of the booty with 200 elephants to the imperial court at Agra. Akbar had received the intelligence about the dishonest conduct of his high-placed commander and grandee of the Empire but because of his pre-occupation with other more serious problems of the state, he thought it expedient to keep silent about it.

War against Mewar: The Conquest of Chittor (1567-68)

Unfortunately, the powerful Rajput rulers of Mewar (Chittor), Marwar (Jodhpur) and Ranthambhor had remained silent spectators when Akbar launched an unprovoked attack on the reputed Hindu state of Gondwana – the home of the sturdy freedom-loving Gonds. It encouraged Akbar to go ahead with his plans of aggressive warfare against these formidable Rajput states as well and at the time of his choosing. The revolts of the turbulent Uzbegs, disaffected Afghan nobles and some of his personal political rivals engaged his attention for about two years (1565-66), but, by the beginning of 1567, he was free to measure his swords with the Rajput rulers. Akbar was fully conscious of the fact that without crushing the power of the Rajputs, he could not justly claim to be the undisputed overlord of northern India. 'His war with the Rajputs lay in the logic of history'.

Strategic Importance of Chittor: According to VA Smith, Akbar launched his regular war operations against the major Rajput chiefs with effect from September 1567 when he 'resolved on the most famous and tragically interesting of his martial enterprises - the siege and capture of Chittor, the capital of Mewar'. (*Akbar, op. cit.*, p. 81). In retrospect, Rana Sanga, the contemporary of Babar, had raised the power and prestige of Mewar to the pinnacle of its glory. Babar defeated him in the historic battle of Kanwaha or Khanua on March 13, 1527, but he did not dare to march on Chittor, the capital of the Sisodia Rajputs. From 1528 to 1537, the throne of Mewar was occupied by three *Ranas* in quick succession, but none of them could restore law and order in the state. In 1537, Udaya Singh, the minor son of Rana Sanga, was placed on the throne of Mewar under a Council of Regency. So long as Udaya Singh was a minor, the Sisodia *sardars* thought it prudent to acknowledge nominal suzerainty of Sher Shah Suri after his victory at Jodhpur in 1544. On attaining majority, however, Udaya Singh took the reins of government in his own hands and restored his prestige as the sovereign ruler of Mewar. Before long, he revived the ancient glory of the Sisodia state through his successful military exploits, and Mewar came to occupy a premier position among the Rajput states once again..

Akbar had many reasons to settle his scores with Mewar first. He did not stand to gain much by the annexation of barren and unfertile sandy lands of Rajputana but he looked upon the fertile province of Gujarat with greedy eyes. 'The conquest of Gujarat could transform the Mughal kingdom into a mighty maritime state and also establish its direct contacts with the Islamic world through the sea route. And Chittor lay on the route to Gujarat; it controlled the lines of communication between Delhi and the Arabian Sea'. Moreover, Rana Udaya Sing had publically denounced the Mughals as 'unclean foreigners'. He looked down upon Raja Bihari Mal of Amber for having entered into 'a humiliating matrimonial alliance' with a Muslim ruler which was a direct challenge to the imperial authority of Akbar. Besides, the Rana of Mewar had annoyed Akbar by giving shelter to Baz Bahadur—the fugitive ruler of Malwa.

The Siege of Chittor: After making elaborate preparations, Akbar marched upon Mewar at the head of a huge army under his personal command when the Rajputs were busy in the celebrations of Dussehra and the other seasonal festivals; he was accompanied by the cream of his seasoned military generals and political advisers. The Rajputs woke up from slumber when it was too late. Worn down by their mutual rivalries and suffering from their inflated sense of pride and haughtiness, neither the Sisodia Rajputs requested their neighbouring rulers of Marwar or Ranthambhor for help nor did the latter bother to come to their aid voluntarily. The Mughal forces reached the outskirts of Chittor on October 20, 1567. Realizing the gravity of the situation; the Sisodia nobles thought it advisable to send their minor ruler, Rana Udaya Singh with family and treasures to a place of safety in the inaccessible forests of the Aravali hills, and Jai Mal Rathor, the former chief of Merta, undertook the defence of the stronghold of Chittor with only seven or eight thousand men. The description of the historic fort of Chittor, as given by the contemporary Muslim chroniclers, is worth reading. Nizamuddin records that 'the fort of Chittor is seated (*sic.*)

on a hill, which is about one *Kos* in height, and has no connection with any other hill. The length of the fort is three *Kos*. It contains plenty of running water.' (*Tabakat-i-Akbari* E&D. v, p. 325). Similarly, Abul Fazl mentions that 'the surveyors who are always in attendance on the royal stirrup (of Akbar), found by measurement that the circumference (of the fort of Chittor) was more than two *Kos* while it was five *Kos* at the part used by the general public'.(*Akbarnama*, ii, p. 464). According to Nizamuddin, the Mughal forces, equipped with heavy field guns, took full one month in laying a total siege of the stronghold; and the entire 'circuit' of the fort 'was hermetically sealed' by them. The chronicler records that 'upon His Majesty's orders, the ground round the fort was portioned out among the different *amirs*. The royal forces was ordered to plunder and lay waste the country. Asaf Khan (the victor of Gondwana) was sent to Rampur (about 50 miles southeast of Chittor), a prosperous town of the province. He attacked and captured the fort, and ravaged all the neighbourhood... Husain Kuli Khan was sent with a detachment towards Udaipur and Kambalmir (34 miles northwest of Udaipur) which is one of the chief fortresses in the country and is the residence of the Rana. He ravaged several towns and villages, but finding no trace of the Rana, he returned to the imperial camp.' (*Tabakat-i-Akbari*, E&D.v, pp. 325-26).

Construction of *Sabats* by the Invaders: Jai Mal, the commander of the besieged Rajput garrison defended the fort with great courage and determination but, being shorn of adequate fighters, 'it was beyond his capacity to stop the investment of the fort by the Mughals which was affected by the most scientific way then known'. For the first few days, some of the hot-blooded Mughal commandoes, headed by small contingents, challenged the Rajput warriors in their sorties at the main gate of the fort for hand-to-hand fights, but the latter fought like dare-devils and slaughtered, on the average, about 200 Mughal soldiers every day. Akbar, on realising the futility of such wasteful ventures stopped his soldiers from the display of such misplaced enthusiasm. Instead, he ordered the construction of two *sabats* or covered passages from the foothills to the walls of the fort about which Abul Fazl and Nizamuddin Ahmad both give us the minutest details. According to Abul Fazl, about 5,000 builders, carpenters and stonemasons were employed for the purpose. A *sabat* was partly an underground tunnel and partly a covered pathway above the surface of the ground. It was cut through the hills; the natural hill, earth-work, and stones provided the protective walls on either side of the passage, while the gaps or low hill was covered with 'broad mud wall, such that balls could not penetrate it.' The roof of the passage was made up of wooden planks 'strongly fastened together and covered with raw hides', thus forming a safe passage or corridor (*kucha*) from the base of the hill to the walls of the fort. (*Akbarnama*, II, p. 468). Nizamuddin adds to our information that while the *sabats* were under construction, the besieged Rajput garrison kept up such a fire of guns and muskets that more than 100 of the workmen and labourers employed in it were killed daily although they covered themselves with shields of bull-hide. Corpses were used in the walls like bricks,' (*Tabakat-i-Akbari*, E&D.v, pp. 326-27). He records further that 'the *sabat* which was conducted from the royal battery was so extensive that ten horsemen abreast could ride along it, and it was so high that an elephant rider with the spear in his hand could pass under it.'(*ibid;* p. 326). Abul Fazl attaches the greatest importance to the technique of constructing such sabat or under-cover pathways for overwhelming the fortified Indian strongholds. He continues the narrative to say that 'once the first *sabat* was ready, it became safe for the Mughal soldiers to move up to the walls of the fort unseen and unhurt by the enemy. The Mughal miners now made two excavations contiguous to each other under the wall of the fort, and in one of these they put 120 *mans* and, in the other, 80 *mans* of gunpowder.' Thereafter, 'an order was given that the brave and enterprising should stand armed, and in readiness, and be on the watch so that when the mines were fired, and the wall broken down, they should rapidly take possession of the fort.' The mines were, ultimately, fired on December 17, 1567 with the following results.

> 'The bastion was pulled up from its foundation and sprang into the air with all the ill-fated soldiers who were on it. The match of the second excavation had not taken fire when the assailants, seeing that the wall had been demolished, rushed on heedlessly to the breach in order to enter by it. All at once, the second mine exploded and the troops who were entering, and also a body of their opponents, who were preparing to prevent them, were involved in the catastrophe and their souls severed from their bodies by the fierce storm. Their limbs were blown here and there, and stones were carried for leagues. The report of the explosion extended to fifty *Kos* and more, and astonished those who heard it.'(*Akbarnama, ii*, p. 468).

According to an estimate of Nizamuddin, about 500 Mughal soldiers were killed in this mine blast, and the number of the Rajput defenders who lost their lives was much more. According to Abul Fazl 'There was one train for both mines and so it was fired from one place. One mine took fire after the other, and the brave men made their attack without noticing this and without reflection.' (*ibid.*). Nizamuddin narrates with dismay that in spite of this mishap and huge loss of life on both the sides, 'all attempts of the Mughal soldiers to force an entry into the fort were foiled by the besieged Rajput soldiers who sacrificed their lives in one place, and, in the other, exerted themselves in raising up a wall, till in a short time, they succeeded in building another broad wall as high as the former one.'(*ibid.*, p. 469).

Akbar takes on Jai Mal in a chance shot: On the night of February 22, 1568, the fort of Chittor was 'under attack from all sides and several breaches were made in the walls.' Akbar was seated in a gallery which had been constructed behind a ridge on the *sabat*, very close to the wall of the fort. He noticed 'a prominent man on the rampart of the fort' who was supervising the repair of a breach in the wall and issuing directions to his soldiers. Akbar took aim at him and fired a shot; the victim, who probably died on the spot, happened to be Jai Mal. The besieged garrison was disheartened by the fall of their leader.

The Rajputs commit *Jauhar*: Within an hour of the incidence, their ladies lit the funeral pyres 'at several places in the fort' and committed mass suicide. In the early hours of February 23, the Rajputs, in the true spirit of *Jauhar*, opened the gates of the fort and took the offensive. Akbar ordered a general assault on the fort from all sides; the royal war elephants played an important role in it. The Rajputs were led by Fatha or Phattah (viz., Fateh Singh Sisodia of Kailwa)—'a young lad of sixteen summers', who descended the rock, flanked by his mother and the youthful wife, all clad in the yellow robes, on horse-backs. In their hand-to-hand fight with the Mughal soldiers, both the ladies died fighting before Fatha was fatally wounded and crushed to death by an elephant. The Rajput soldiers fought recklessly and were killed to a man. Akbar ordered general massacre of the survivors of the fort; as a result, about 30,000 of the non-combatant civilians including old and infirm men and women, and children were murdered in cold blood.

Abul Fazl records that 'a wonderful thing happened when the emperor made a triumphant entry into the fort on the royal elephant called Madhukar the next day. There was none to make a formal submission and surrender the fort to the victor on behalf of the vanquished except one wounded soldier, Isar Dass Chauhan. Apparently unarmed, he made a move towards the royal elephant and asked the name of the beast. Within a moment when the Mughal officers in attendance upon the emperor answered his question, Isar Dass, with daring rashness seized the trunk of the elephant with one hand, and struck off his dagger with the other, and shouted: *Be good enough to convey my respects to the world-adorning appreciator of merit.*' (*Akbarnama*, ii, p. 475). Abul Fazl comments on the horrors of that bloody battle for the conquest of Chittor in verse as follows:

'No one ever saw such battles,
Nor ever heard of such from the experienced.
What shall I say of that battle and engagement?
I cannot mention one item out of a hundred thousand.'

The Fall of Chittor and Its Aftermath: The fort of Chittor and some of its adjoining territories fell into the hands of Akbar. The Sisodia warriors dispersed and disappeared into the ravines and dry mountainous tracts of Mewar, and so did the Rajput population of the countryside; the villages and hamlets were deserted and their inhabitants seemed to have vanished into thin air. But the Mughal nobles and their fighters were exhausted and rather panic-stricken; they did not dare to stray into the countryside on the lookout for booty nor forage for their horses and other beasts of burden. Akbar declared the town of Chittor and its suburbs annexed to the Mughal Empire; it was created a *sarkar* (district) and handed over to Khwaja Abdul Majid Asaf Khan for the purpose of administration. The fort of Chittor was converted into a base-camp for the imperial armies to carry on further operations against Rana Udaya Singh who held sway over major part of the state of Mewar. We have it on the testimony of Abul Fazl that at the commencement of the siege of Chittor, Akbar had taken a vow that, after his victory, 'he would go on foot to the shrine of Khwaja Muinuddin Chishti at Ajmer'. He fulfilled this vow with all humility by paying a visit to Ajmer before his return to Agra. Akbar was deeply impressed by the undaunted courage and the spirit of sacrifice displayed by the Rajputs of Chittor. As a great warrior himself, 'he commemorated their heroism by installing the stone (marble) statues of Jai Mal (Jaimal) and Fatha (Fateh Singh), seated on elephants, on either side of the inner entrance of the main gate (Delhi Gate) of the Agra fort'. Rana Udaya Singh built a new capital at

Udaipur, and carried on the struggle against the Mughals until his death on March 3, 1572. He was succeeded by his illustrious son Maharana Pratap. In passing reference it may be mentioned here that it was Aurangzeb who demolished these statues of Jaimal and Phatha, along with the elephants of marble, after the escape of Shivaji from his captivity at Agra in 1666.

Conquest of Ranthambhor (1568-69)

After Chittor came the turn of Ranthambhor which was considered to be 'the second invincible stronghold' in Rajputana; it was ruled by Rana Surjan Rai who belonged to the Hara community of the Chauhan Rajputs and was a vassal of Mewar. Akbar organised an expedition to Ranthambhor in April 1568. It proved abortive, however, because of the sudden recall of the Mughal army from Rajputana owing to an uprising of the Mirzas in Malwa. In February 1569, Akbar took charge of the Mughal army of invasion in person. On the basis of the experience gained at Chittor, the Mughals quickly besieged the fort and constructed a *sabat* without losing many lives. The siege lasted for about six weeks only and the fort was surrendered to the Mughals by the Rajputs on March 18, 1569.

There are two versions about the early fall of Ranthambhor. According to Tod, the Rajputs waged such a hot war that Akbar and his Rajput generals, Bhagwan Das and Man Singh, thought it prudent to initiate a diplomatic move to persuade the Rana for surrender to avoid unnecessary blood-bath. Accordingly, Bhagwan Das went into the fort as the imperial envoy and Akbar accompanied him in disguise as one of his associates. The Rajputs recognised him, and thereupon Akbar disclosed his identity and negotiated peace with Surjan Rai in person. This story is accepted by VA smith. According to the second version, as given by Badaoni, on the intervention of Bhagwan Das and Man Singh, Surjan Rai sued for peace and sent his two minor sons, Duda and Bhola along with the Rajput chiefs to Akbar as hostages. Akbar received the young princes with great courtesy and granted very liberal terms to the Rajput chief. Thereafter, Surjan Rai waited upon Akbar near the gate of the fort and handed over the keys of the fort to him. He entered the imperial service and received appointment as the *Qiladar* (*faujdar*) of Garhkantaka; later on, he was appointed the governor of Banaras.

Tod, in his learned treatise, *Annals and Antiquities of Rajasthan*, gives a graphic account of the treaty of peace signed between the two parties. The fort of Ranthambhor was surrendered to the Mughals but the township and the principality of Bundi - the second major habitat of the Hara Rajputs, was allowed to retain its sanctity as an exclusive reserve of the Hara Rajputs as before. It was recognised that 'Bundi was to the Haras what Delhi was to the Mughal Emperor'. To mention but a few of these terms – (1) Although under the suzerainty of the Mughals, 'the Chiefs of Bundi were exempted from the custom of sending the *Dola* to the royal harem'; it implied that they were not to be compelled to give their females in marriage to the Mughal princes as a bond of submission. (2) *Jaziya* had already been abolished by Akbar in his dominions in 1564 but this fact was re-emphasised in the treaty of peace that the Rajput chiefs of Bundi were exempt from the payment of this obnoxious poll tax. (3) They were not under obligation to send their wives or other females of their clan 'to hold a stall in the Meena Bazaar' at the Royal Palace on the Nauroz festival. (4) Even when on the state service, their horses were not to be branded with the imperial *Dagh*. (5) The Hara chiefs, when on state visit to the imperial capital, were allowed to beat their kettle-drums in the streets of the mtropolis as far as the Lal Darwaza or the Red Gate of the Royal Palace. (6) They were not under obligation 'to make prostration' on entering the Presence (of His Majesty). And (7) The Hara Rajput soldiers of the Mughal army were 'not to be compelled to cross the Attock (viz. the Indus River)'; in other words, they were exempt from posting in Afghanistan or other northwestern and Central Asian parts of the Mughal empire.

Kalinjar, Jodhpur, Bikaner and Jaisalmer Acknowledge Mughal Suzerainty (1569-70)

The conquest of Chittor and Ranthambhor by Akbar, in quick succession, established the superiority of Mughal arms and terrified all the other Hindu rulers of northern India. In his bid to maintain the tempo of the victorious Mughal forces, Akbar ordered an attack on the historic Hindu stronghold of the Bundellas at Kalinjar, now situated in the Banda district of modern Uttar Pradesh; it was during the siege of Kalinjar that Sher Shah Suri had lost his life. This fort was held by Raja Ram Chandra of Rewa. The Mughal army under the command of Majnun Khan besieged Kalinjar in August 1569. After some resistance, Ram Chandra offered submission and was granted a *jagir* in the neighbourhood of Allahabad. His state was annexed to the Mughal Empire and Majnun Khan was appointed the first Mughal governor of Kalinjar.

The fall of Kalinjar broke the backbone of the Hindu resistance against the Mughal rule in northern India. Thereafter, most of the big and small Hindu chieftains of northern and central India hastened to offer their submission to Akbar as their overlord. In November 1570, two Rajput rulers, Raja Chandra Sen, son of Raja Maldev of Jodhpur, and Kalyan Mal of Bikaner, acknowledged the suzerainty of Akbar at Nagaur through the agency of Raja Bhagwan Dass of Amber. Akbar took a Rajput princess of Bikaner in marriage and absorbed Rai Singh, son of Kalyan Mal, into the imperial service. In December 1570, Rawal Har Rai of Jaisalmer also came forward to acknowledge the suzerainty of the Mughal Emperor and gave his daughter in marriage to Akbar. Thus by the end of 1570, the whole of Rajputana, with the exception of Mewar and its tributary states of Dungarpur, Banswara and Pratapgarh, was brought within the sphere of the Mughal hegemony.

Triumph of Akbar's Rajput Policy

As an imperialist, Akbar had come to the conclusion that without crushing the power of the formidable Rajput states in northern and central India, the stability and integrity of the Mughal Empire was a far cry. He, therefore, carried on relentless warfare on military as well as diplomatic front against the Rajputs until they were compelled to acknowledge his overlordship. Akbar came into contact with three categories of the Rajput states and its people. The first category included the Rajputs of Amber, Bikaner and Jaisalmer, who voluntarily acknowledged his suzerainty and were promptly absorbed in the imperial system. The second category included the Rajput states like those of Ranthambhor and Merta which offered dignified resistance but, ultimately, made an amicable settlement with Akbar on the receipt of honourable treatment. And the third category of the Rajput chiefs were represented by Rana Udaya Singh of Mewar and his associates 'who stubbornly refused to compromise their regional and tribal independence, dignity and self-respect for any other consideration'. Akbar was hard-pressed to reckon with them, but, according to SR Sharma, 'they contributed their 'own quota to the strength and nobility of our national character.'(Mughal Empire, *op. cit.*, pp. 170-71). As observed by Tod, 'Akbar was the first successful conqueror of Rajput independence...but generations of the martial races were cut off by his sword, and lustres rolled away ere his conquests were sufficiently confirmed.', (*Rajasthan*, *op. cit.*, i, p. 338).

The establishment of hegemony over the Rajput states of northern and central India formed but a part of Akbar's Rajput Policy. In our opinion, 'the second and more important aspect of this policy was to heal the wounds of the vanquished and pacify their injured pride. Akbar was more generous and humane in his treatment towards the Rajputs than all the other Muslim rulers of India who preceded him. With the exception of his massacre of the civilian population at Chittor, for which Akbar made suitable amends, he never insulted or humiliated the vanquished Rajput soldiers, nor persecuted the Rajput subjects or ravaged their lands'. (Advanced Study, ii, p. 233). Similarly, in his 'reflections on Akbar's Rajput policy', Dr. Ishwari Prasad has to say that 'Akbar was endowed with the higher qualities of statesmanship, and he resolved to base his Empire on the goodwill of both, the Hindus as well as Muslims.' (*A Short History of Muslim Rule in India*, p. 334). Therefore, he adopted a policy of conciliation towards the Hindus and did not treat them 'as inferiors' just because they happened to be *kafirs*—viz., 'the infidels'. Akbar led vigorous military campaigns against the Hindu rulers, but 'once they offered submission, he sheathed his sword with pleasure'. As observed by Ishwari Prasad:

> 'No desecration or religious persecution marred the glory of his triumphs, and he refrained from doing anything that might wound the feelings of his Rajput enemies. Equality of status with the Muslims steeled the loyalty of the Rajput chiefs and they shed their life-blood in the service of the Empire in distant and dangerous lands. This friendship was further cemented by matrimonial alliances which brought advantages to both sides, and opened new avenues of honour to the Rajput princes. They found scope for themselves as soldiers who might have otherwise lived out their life in glorious obscurity in their mountain or desert fastnesses. The rapid growth of the Empire and the success of their mighty hero, a worthy object of devotion and loyalty, stirred their martial spirit, and led them on to new fields of glory and renown, and made them forget whatever humiliation their discomfiture or surrender implied.' (*Ibid.*, pp. 334-35).

The contribution made by Rajputs in the process of political unification of the country and national integration under Akbar and his successors proved beneficial from many points of view. 'As the Rajputs comprised the socio-political leadership of the Hindus, they readily secured the support and goodwill of the entire Hindu society for the Mughal throne. It was primarily because of the Rajput association with the political power-structure that the Hindu masses became reconciled to the Mughal imperialism and wished for its welfare. Moreover, the Rajput princes were great patrons of art and literature. They not only appreciated but also whole-heartedly supported Akbar's state enterprises for the socio-cultural advancement of their people. Their participation imparted strength to the imperial armies and added to the magnificence of the imperial Mughal court which became famous throughout Asia and Europe. The Rajputs were instrumental in bringing about the synthesis of religions and cultures of the land. The Rajputs identified themselves with Akbar and the men of his school of thought who stood for national integration and secularism; they adopted the Muslim ideas of social and political organisation, and thus facilitated national integration between Hindus and Muslims. In short, the Rajputs appeared in the new role as the pioneers of Indo-Muslim culture, the greatest legacy of the Mughal rule to India'.

(*b*) THE EMPEROR AKBAR AND MAHARANA PRATAP (1572-97)

Most of the modern historians regard Akbar as 'the founder of a secular-nation state in India'. The Mughals were foreign conquerors but Akbar transformed his ruling house into a national monarchy. Nevertheless, some exponents of Akbar's policy of 'the political unification of India' 'usually attempt to underrate the character and personality of Rana Pratap and even condemn the fruitless resistance put up by him against the forces of national integration'. There is no denying the fact that most of the Muslim chroniclers, the religious fanatics as they were, used derogatory words for Rana Pratap but that was their universal way of referring to the Hindu rebels or antagonists of the Muslim rulers;. All of them were invariably dubbed as *Kafirs*. But we sincerely believe that was no contradiction between Akbar's commitment to the political unification of India and Rana Pratap's dogged resistance to fight for the independence of his state and the people. Rana Pratap 'was the son of the soil, the illustrious offspring of the great ruling house of Bapa Rawal, whose account is worth recording in letters of gold in the annals of medieval Indian history. It, in no way, belittles the importance of Akbar as the national monarch of India. Rana Pratap embodied in his person the true spirit of Rajput valour and freedom. He was the true representative, in blood as well as spirit, of the people called Rajputs, after whom the Indian history and culture of the post-Harsha era has been designated as the *Rajput Period.* Rana Pratap was an ideal hero of the great Rajputs, with all of their virtues and faults, who had given us the *Rajput Culture,* and the glorious *Rajput Tradition* of the medieval times. It were the valiant Rajputs like Rana Pratap who constituted 'the sword arms' of the pre-Muslim India. It goes to the credit of Akbar as imperialist, statesman, diplomat and nationalist ruler who not only established his military dominance over the Rajputs but also won over the love and cooperation of most of them to his cause. The invaluable contribution made by Raja Man Singh and the whole horde of the Rajput chiefs towards the expansion of the Mughal Empire and consolidation of the nation-state of medieval India can be appreciated better when we bear in mind that Rana Pratap, just one of the Rajput chiefs, stood out and certainly outdid Akbar, the Lord Paramount of India. What if a few other Rajput chiefs had also started protracted guerrilla warfare against Akbar in the way that Rana Pratap did? It was Akbar's good fortune that he had already conquered Gondwana and Malwa before coming to clash with the Sisodias of Mewar, otherwise, even his hard-earned victory over Chittor would not have proved very fruitful. Had Akbar reckoned with the Sisodias first, the fate of his imperial policy, in spite of its nationalistic overtones, might have been sealed'. (*Advanced Study*; ii, p. 235).

VA Smith, while showering all praises on Akbar 'the Great Mogul' for the political unification of India under the Mughal rule, does not fail to notice the heroic struggle carried on by the Sisodia Rajputs of Mewar to retain the traditional freedom of their ancestral lands and culture. In his words, 'none but the bravest of the brave could have dared to match the chivalry of poverty-stricken Mewar' against the all-powerful Mughal Empire. There was no comparison between the man-power and meager resources of Rana Pratap and those of the Mughals. No doubt, in this 'uneven struggle' between the antagonists, 'the vanquished, it may be, were greater than the victor,' (Akbar, p. 254).

Akbar's Unfinished Struggle against Mewar

To pick up the threads of the story from the conquest of Chittor by Akbar in February 1568, the Sisodia Rajput chiefs of Mewar had lost the battle of Chittor but refused to surrender to the Mughal emperor. Before the battle of Chittor began, the Sisodia nobles had sent their minor ruler, Rana Udaya Singh, to a place of safety into the interior of Mewar. After the occupation of the capital and 'the eastern part of Mewar', Akbar made a settlement of the district (*sarkar*) of Chittor, and diverted his attention towards other state affairs but it would be wrong to presume that he had relaxed his pressure upon the vanquished Rajput chief of Mewar. The armed struggle between the adversaries continued, though at a low intensity, and did not allow respite to the Rana Udaya Singh and his camp-followers. Meanwhile, Udaya Singh built a new capital, known after his name as Udaipur; the major portion of the Mewar kingdom remained under his control and he continued his resistance to the Mughals until his death in early 1572.

Early Life and Accession of Rana Pratap

Not much is known about the early life of Rana Pratap, the son and successor of Rana Udaya Singh. According to one version, he was born on May 6, 1540. His accession to the throne was disputed by his younger half-brother, named Jagmal, but he was supported by majority of the Sisodia nobles. He was formally Coronated at Gogunda, situated about 30 kilometres to the northwest of Udaipur on March 3, 1572. In the midst of 'unequal life and death struggle' against the imperial Mughal armies, Rana Pratap 'took a solemn vow in the name of his worthy ancestors- Bapa Rawal, Rana Kumbha, Rana Rattan Singh and Rana Sanga, never to barter away the centuries' old freedom of his homeland for any price whatsoever'. According to VA Smith,

> 'the patriotism of Rana Pratap was his offence. Akbar had won over most of the Rajput chieftains by his astute policy and could not endure the independent attitude assumed by the Rana who must be broken if he would not bend like his fellows.'

Rana Pratap, 'a regional ruler of war-ravaged Mewar, cut off from its original capital, Chittor, and shorn of all resources, was no match for the mighty Mughal emperor who was the richest and the most powerful monarch of the world during the last quarter of the sixteenth century.' He fought not only against the Mughals but also against many of the leading Rajput chieftains of his day who had acknowledged the suzerainty of the Mughal Emperor. Some of them, like Raja Man Singh of Amber, had been publicly insulted by Rana Pratap, and 'they bore personal grudge against him'. On the other hand, Akbar was fully determined to conquer Mewar by all means. He arrayed the Rajput princes of Amber, Marwar, Jaisalmer, and Bikaner against Rana Pratap who had vowed, in the words of the bard, 'to make his mother's milk resplendent'.

Desertion of Shakti Singh

It is not that all the Sisodia Rajput nobles stood behind Rana Pratap in his 'uneven' and rather hopeless and suicidal fight with the Mughals. Even his younger brother Shakti Singh alias Sagar also deserted Rana Pratap and acknowledged the suzerainty of Akbar. The Mughal Emperor was immensely pleased to hand over the charge of Chittor to him 'as the price of treachery' and conferred upon him all the royal titles of the Sisodia Ruling House. It did not un-nerve Rana Pratap and the handful of his dedicated camp-followers, however. To quote Tod again,

> "The magnitude of the peril confirmed the fortitude of Pratap and he amply redeemed his pledge. Single-handed, for a quarter of a century (1572-97), did he withstand the combined efforts of the Empire; at one time carrying destruction into the plains, at another, flying from rock to rock, feeding his family from the fruits of his native hills, and rearing the nursling heir Amar Singh (his son) amidst savage beasts and scarcely less savage men, a fit heir to the prowess and revenge. The bare idea that '*the son of Bapa Rawal should bow the head to mortal man*,' was insupportable; and he spurned every overture which had submission for its basis, or the degradation of uniting his family by marriage with the Tarter (Akbar), though Lord of countless multitudes' (*Annals and Antiquities of Rajasthan; loc. cit.*, I, p. 347)

Construction of the New Capital at Kumbhalgarh

By this time, Udaipur had also become vulnerable to the repeated Mughal attacks. Pratap, now styled as Maharana by his camp-followers, took his abode at Kumbhalgarh (or Kumalmair) and made it the seat of his government. Kumbhalgarh was situated on a mountain at a distance of about sixty-five kilometres to the north of Udaipur. The landscape of the stronghold was not within the easy reach of the horsemen and ground troops as it was covered with dense forests, traversed by inaccessible ravines. Maharaṇa Pratap remodelled his government by 'adapting it to the exigencies of times and to his slender resources.' He raised a new crop of dedicated and self-sacrificing young Rajput fighters and bureaucrats to manage the affairs of the poor inhabitants of Mewar with barren lands and meager sources of subsistence. New rules and regulations were issued to sustain the protracted struggle against the Mughals and fresh grants of land were made to the most devoted and energetic peasants to raise the crops, if possible. As Maharana Pratap was 'unable to keep the field in the plains of Mewar, he followed the system of his ancestors, and commanded his subjects, on pain of death, to retire into the mountains' on the approach of the hostile forces. (*Ibid., pp. 347-48*). He and his associates took a solemn vow 'to eat in *Patras* or leaves, sleep on beds of straw, and keep their beards untouched until the liberation of Mewar'. Tod informs us that with the object of reminding them of 'their fallen fortune' and 'to stimulate its recovery', Maharana Pratap ordered that 'the martial *nakkaras,* which always sounded in the van of battle of procession, should follow in the rear.'(*Ibid.*) It must be admitted that 'it was very difficult to beat such desperadoes'.

After the conquest of Gujarat (1572-73, Akbar ordered an all-out attack on the territories of Mewar under the control of Maharana Pratap to bring him to the knees. This marked the beginning of the final phase of the Mughal operations against the rebellious Rajput chief. Accordingly, the Mughal forces penetrated into the interior of Mewar from different directions in which the Muslim governors and the vassal Hindu chieftains of all the surrounding provinces and states were actively involved. They started exerting slow but steady military pressure on Maharana Pratap from all quarters. The Sisodia chief held his sway over the mountainous and forested areas of Mewar. It is said that 'while the plains and the desert regions of Mewar were ruled during the day by the Mughal armies, at night they were taken over by the guerrilla bands of Rana Pratap'. Tod writes that during the protracted war between Maharana Pratap and the Mughals, the fertile tracts of land, watered by the rivers Banas and the Beris, from the Aravalli Mountain Ranges in the west, to the eastern tableland, all became '*bechiragh,*' i.e., 'without a lamp or human settlement'. The villages and towns of Mewar were ravaged by the Mughal troops, and deserted by their inhabitants who sought shelter with Maharana Pratap in the jungles and the hills.

After the conquest of Bihar and Bengal (1574-76), Akbar diverted his personal attention towards 'the Mewar problem' and further intensified his efforts. We have it on the testimony of Mulla Abdul Qadir Badaoni that Akbar declared *Jehad* (holy war) against Maharana Pratap, and, actually welcomed volunteers from among the Muslims to join military operations against Mewar. Badaoni then held the post of an *imam* at the imperial court. Being a fanatic *Mulla,* he sought special permission of Akbar to join 'the holy war' against 'the infidels' to earn the title of a *ghazi*', i.e.' the slayer of infidels'. There is no doubt that Akbar 'scorned at the religious bigotry of Badaoni and his tribe' but, at that critical juncture, he did not hesitate in utilizing their services to beat his Hindu foe. On the orders of Akbar, the Mughal armies adopted scorched-earth policy to destroy the whole of Mewar if its chief did not submit to him. In April 1576, he shifted his headquarters to Ajmer to exercise personal supervision over the war operations. He employed all the resources of the state to liquidate the Rana. Acting on the principle that 'Iron cuts Iron', Akbar appointed Raja Man Singh of Amber, the arch enemy of Maharana Pratap, as the commander-in-chief of the Mughal army of invasion, while Asaf Khan, then the *Mir Bakhshi* of the Empire and victor of Gondwana, was put second in command; they were assisted in the enterprise by a number of other reputed Mughal generals and Rajput chiefs.

The Battle of Haldi Ghati (June 18, 1576)

An eye-witness account of the military campaign, which culminated in the historic battle of Haldi Ghati, has faithfully been preserved in the *Muntakhab ut Tawarikh* (Volume II, pp. 233-42) by Badaoni as he had participated in it as a fighter in the train of Asaf Khan. We would, therefore, like to give a summary with a few glimpses of the historic battle of Haldi Ghati, fought between Maharana Pratap and the Imperial Mughal forces as given by Badaoni in his well-written historical treatise. According to him, 'an unaccountable army of invasion' marched from Ajmer towards Gogunda via Mandalgarh. Once in 'the hostile territory, it moved very cautiously in perpetual battle-array'; its advance guard was preceded by a small band of skirmishers or scouts, about 80 to 100 in number, who were commanded by Sayyad Hashim Barha; they were called 'the Chickens of the Front Line, and 'they acted as the tentacles of the advance-guard in making the forward moves through measured paces'. The imperial army apprehended danger at the Pass of the Haldi Ghati—'a spur of the Aravalli Chain' leading to the town of Gogunda, and halted near the deserted habitat of Darah, distant about seven *koses* or about 23 kilometres (a *pacca Kos* was approximately equivalent to two miles) from Gogunda. It was here that Rana Pratap, nicknamed Kika by the Muslim chroniclers, emerged out of the Haldi Ghati Pass with only three thousand horsemen and challenged the imperial army. The battle of Haldi Ghati was fought on June 18, 1576. The Rana had divided his small army into two divisions, one of which was commanded by himself and the other by his most trusted lieutenant Hakim Sur Afghan. In the words of Badaoni,

> 'One division (of Maharana Pratap's army, which was commanded by Hakim Sur Afghan) came straight from the

direction of the mountains, and attacked our advance-body. On account of the broken and uneven state of the ground, and the quantity of thorns, and the serpentine twisting of the road, the skirmishers and the advance-body of our troops became hopelessly mixed up together, and sustained a complete defeat." (*Muntakhab-ut-Tawarikh*, II, pp. 236.37)

Badaoni continues:

"And the Rajputs of our (Mughal) army, the leader of whom was Rajah Loun Karan, and who were most of them on the left, ran away like a flock of sheep, and breaking through the ranks of the advance body, fled for protection to our right wing. At this juncture, the author (Badaoni), who was with some of the special troops of the advance-body, said to Asaf: *How are we now in these circumstances to distinguish between friendly and hostile Rajputs?*' He (Asaf Khan) answered: *They will experience the whiz of the arrows, by what way. On whichever side they may be killed, it will be a gain to Islam.* So we kept firing away and our aim (*shist*) at such mountain like mass of men never missed...and it became certain that my (Badaoni's) hand prospered in the matter, and that I (Badaoni) attained the reward due to one who fights against infidels:" (*Ibid.*, p. 237).

To our mind, the words put by Badaoni into the mouth of Asaf Khan, were probably not correct. Asaf Khan was a seasoned Mughal general, who fully understood and appreciated the liberal religious and the state policy adopted by Akbar. He could not be expected to display such religious fanaticism as attributed to him by Badaoni. We have the reasons to believe that the orthodox Mulla took shelter behind the name of Asaf Khan to justify his immoral and treacherous conduct. In the opinion of Dr. J.L. Mehta, it may not be wrong to presume that Badaoni might not have been able to shoot down even a single fighter of Maharana Pratap but it follows from his statement that, in the heat of the battle, he might have killed a number of Rajput soldiers of the Mughal army, to earn the title of a *Ghazi*. Otherwise, so far as the battle of Haldi Ghati was concerned, it was not fought between the Champions of Islam and the *Kafirs*; it was primarily a clash of arms between the Rajputs—one party fighting for the Mughal Empire and the other for regional independence; likewise, the Muslims also constituted a part of both the sides. To continue the description of the battle, as given by Badaoni,

'The other (the second) division of Rana Kika's army, under his personal command, charged out of the Pass, and meeting Qazi Khan, who was at the entrance of the Pass, swept his men before them, and, bearing them along, broke through his centre. Then the *Shaikh* sons from Sikri all fled at once. And an arrow struck *Shaikh* Mansur (a commander of the Mughal unit) as he was in the act of flight; and he bore the wound for a considerable time. But Qazi Khan, although he was but a *Mulla*, stood his ground manfully, until receiving a cimetar blow on his right hand, which wounded his thumb; being no longer able to hold his own, he recited (the saying) *Flight from overwhelming odds is one of the Traditions of the Prophet*, and followed his men (in their retreat).' (*Ibid.*, ii, p. 238). Badaoni writes further that 'those of the (Mughal) army, who had fled on the first attack, did not draw their rein till they had passed five or six *koses* (about 20 kms.) beyond the River Banas.' The chronicler, on the other hand, is all praise for the fighters of Maharana Pratap who spread consternation in the ranks of the imperial army. He writes with appreciation that 'Rajah Ram Shah of Gwalior, who always kept in front of the Rana (Pratap), performed such prodigies of valour against the Rajputs of Man Singh, as baffle description. And these (Rajputs of Man Singh) were those who, on the left of the advance-body, fled and thereby caused also the flight of Asaf Khan....' (*ibid.)*.

Of course, Raja Man Singh and the hard core of his Rajput soldiers fought with determination and secured victory in the long-run. To give a few highlights of their performance, Badaoni says that

> "With regard to the elephants—two strong *mast* elephants singled each other out and fought together......and Man Singh, springing into the place of the elephant-driver, exhibited such intrepidity as surpasses all imagination...... Then the young heroes, who acted as the body-guard of Man Singh, performed such exploits as were a perfect model; and that day, through the generalship of Man Singh, the meaning of this line of Mulla Shiri (a Muslim diplomat) became known (was confirmed), "*A Hindu wields the sword of Islam*."—(*Muntakhab ut Tawarikh*, ii, pp. 238-39)

After describing all about the Mughal camp and its dramatis personae Badaoni writes, apparently in derogatory terms, about the dogged resistance put up by the soldiers of Maharana Pratap on the historic battlefield of Haldi Ghati. He mentions by name some of the prominent Rajput lieutenants of the Rana; they included Ram Dass

Rathor—'the son of Jaimal of Chittor', Bhama Shah, and Ram Shah - the Rajah of Gwalior and his three sons; probably, all of them fell fighting valiantly on the battlefield. While making mention of the fall of Ram Shah – the ruler of Gwalior, and his three sons, Salibahan, Bhan Singh and Pratap Singh, in the battle of Haldi Ghati, Badaoni has to say that they 'showed extreme obstinacy of resistance, went to hell; and of the clan of the Rajputs there was not left one fit to be his (Ram Shah's) successor; good riddance of bad rubbish'. (*Ibid.*, p. 239). Brushing aside the sentiments of religious bigotry as expressed by Badaoni, it must be admitted that 'he has paid the best tribute to all the Rajput leaders, Raja Man Singh, Maharana Pratap and their fearless associates and soldiers, who, true to their class, fought against one another and sacrificed their lives for the respective causes they stood for. Badaoni writes that 'by midday Kika's contingent was considerably reduced in numbers and overwhelmed by the imperial armies'. To turn the scales against Maharana Pratap, Raja Man Singh threw the reserves into the battle and rumour spread that the Emperor Akbar had personally arrived at the scene of action with reinforcements. It 'considerably boosted the morale of the Mughal troops' and they began to re-assemble in formations. On the other hand, the Rana was badly wounded and incapacitated; thereupon, his men who, according to Badaoni, 'had fought from early morning till midday, when it was so extremely hot that the very brain boiled in the cranium', turned their backs and 'betook themselves to the high mountains.' Later on, it became known that before their retreat, Maharana Pratap had been taken to a place of safety behind their lines in a state of unconsciousness by his faithful followers. There was heavy loss of life on both the sides. About half of the Rana's soldiers died fighting in the battle and most of the remnants were wounded and incapacitated. The Mughal troops were too exhausted and terrified to give a chase to the retreating soldiers of the Rana. Badaoni, accordingly, concludes the account of the battle with the following remarks:

> "When the air was like a furnace, and no power of movement was left in the (imperial) soldiers, the idea became prevalent that the Rana, by stealth and stratagem, must have kept himself concealed behind mountains. This was the reason why they made no pursuit." (*Muntakhab-ut-Tawarikh*, ii, p. 239)

The Aftermath of the Battle

The Mughals had won the battle but they were not sure of the whereabouts and intentions of Maharana Pratap. They were so much terrified by the valour and the unpredictable movements of their adversary that their commanders did not deem it fit to break their battle-formations. They stayed put at the battlefield and passed the night in fear of a surprise attack. It was only next morning that they ordered the forward march of their troops.

The Occupation of Gogunda: The victorious Mughal army took possession of Gogunda without a fight as 'it had already been evacuated by the entire population bag and baggage'. Nevertheless, Badaoni makes mention of stray incidents of violent attacks on the imperial troops in the otherwise deserted town of Gogunda. The victors encountered about twenty Rajput desperadoes, the 'devoted servants' of Maharana Pratap,' who had been posted in twos and threes at the place of the Rana and temples of the town, to offer *Jauhar* on the approach of the enemy'. Badaoni records that 'in accordance with an ancient custom of the Hindus, when they are compelled to evacuate a city, they should be killed to save their honour; accordingly, these men in saffron clothes, coming out of their houses and temples, performed the sacrificial rite' and were killed to a man'. (*Ibid*; p. 240)

The Mughals converted the town into an army camp; but their commanders were so much afraid of Maharana Pratap that 'as security against a night attack on the part of the Rana, they barricaded the streets, and drew a trench, and a wall of such a height round the city of Kokanda (Gogunda) that the horsemen could not leap over it, and then settled down quietly.'(*Ibid.*). According to an assessment, 'the hard earned victory of Man Singh at the battle of Haldi Ghati did not fulfil the imperial objective of Akbar. The occupation of Gogunda added a feather to the cap of Man Singh for a short while, *albeit* he failed to conquer the mountainous territories of Mewar which were still held firmly under the control of Rana Pratap. He did not dare to launch an attack on Kumbhalgarh, the next stronghold of Rana Pratap, and even the occupation of Gogunda could not be sustained for long owing to want of provisions and the perpetual threat to the imperial troops from the Rana from behind the mountains'. (*Advanced Study*; ii , p. 243).

Badaoni informs us that, in the months of October-November 1576, Akbar paid a visit to Mewar, apparently 'on a hunting expedition'; but his real intention was to see the site of the battle of the Haldi Ghati. He actually encamped at that historical place to visualize the clash of arms between his forces and those of Maharana Pratap. After making his own assessment of the situation, Akbar supplied 'the much-needed provisions and reinforcements to the imperial armies on the Mewar front'. But he did not think it safe to go forward to examine his 'advanced military post at Gogunda'. Instead, from Haldi Ghati, he ordered an expedition against Raja Narain Dass of Idar, an ally of Maharana Pratap. Narain Dass, with a few hundred soldiers at his command, fought desperately against the locust swarm of the Mughal forces. After the annihilation of his entire contingent, he was compelled to vacate the fort with a handful of his followers; and he retreat to the jungles to seek the shelter of Maharana Pratap. Badaoni pays the following obituary to the Rajah of Idar:

'The Rajah of Idar, like the Rana (Pratap),
after the fashion of robbers,
Kept wandering from mountain to mountain,
and from jungle to jungle.
What does the Moon that
the Halo does not imitate?' —(*Muntakhab ut Tawarikh*, ii, p. 249).

The Last Days of Maharana Pratap

Leaving behind a massive imperial army in Mewar, Akbar left the field of Haldi Ghati with his personal guards in his onward march to Malwa. The whole of Mewar was converted into a sort of the Mughal army camp. As was apprehended, Maharana Pratap resumed his operations against the Mughals and recovered the town of Gogunda and many other parts of Mewar from their hands before long. Raja Man Singh held the supreme command of the imperial army of occupation but he had become the most hated and despised person among the Rajputs and he never dared to venture outside the imperial camp without adequate protection. He felt thoroughly demoralized because of his failure to hold his ground in Mewar and was, ultimately, recalled to the imperial court by Akbar.

Fresh War Operations against Maharana Pratap: Raja Man Singh relinquished the command of imperial troops in Mewar but Akbar did not relax his military-cum-diplomatic pressure on Maharana Pratap and his supporters. Banswara and Dungarpur—the two other feudatories of Mewar, when threatened by the Mughal invasion, were compelled to acknowledge the suzerainty of Akbar, though on very liberal terms. The Mughal governors of Malwa and Gujarat were under strict orders not to relax their vigilance against Maharana Pratap and his associates. As a result, the forts of Sirohi and Bundi were also conquered by the Mughals before the end of 1577. The theory, put forth by some of the modern writers that, 'moved by sentiments of chivalrous regard for his great adversary' Akbar had left Rana Pratap 'unmolested for the rest of his life' has since been exploded by the latest researches. According to A. L. Srivastava, Akbar 'had made the reduction of Rana Pratap a question of prestige,' (*Akbar the Great*; i, p. 217) to which we must add that his determination was perfectly in consonance with 'the fulfilment of his ideal to bring about the political unification of the country'. Akbar's repeated attempts to subjugate or destroy Maharana Pratap did not prove successful, however. We have it on the testimony of Abul Fazl that as late as in October 1577, Akbar had despatched a fresh imperial army 'to extirpate the Rana;' he writes that 'as the most choice form of devotion in the social state is to cause the obedience of the proud and stiff-necked by suitable admonitions and vigorous plans, and if advice and rebuke were not successful, to remove such from existence so that there may be no crevice in unity, and that the pleasant abode of the world may not be stained by the confusion of plurality, Rajah Bhawant Dass, Kanwar Man Singh, Painda Khan Mughal, Sayyid Qasim, Sayyid Raju, Ulugh Asad Turkman, Gajra Chauhan and other loyal warriors were...despatched to carry this great work; Shahbaz Khan, Mir Bakhshi was appointed to command the force, and the execution of the task was committed to him.' —(*Akbarnama*, iii, p. 307).

The Siege of Kumbhalgarh by Shahbaz Khan: The Mughal commanders were spread out in various parts of the occupied Mewar to keep a strict watch over the movements of Maharana Pratap and his freedom-fighters. One of the imperial commanders, Shahbaz Khan picked up the courage to penetrate deep into the forested tracts of western Mewar. He located the Maharana at Kumbhalgarh and promptly put the stronghold under siege. The latter held out against the Mughals for about five months. Hard-pressed, Shahbaz Khan called for reinforcements from Ajmer 'to hold the passes in the Rana's territory' and the fort of Kumbhalgarh was conquered in April 1578. Badaoni supplements Abul Fazl's description of the campaign by informing us that, 'ultimately, the imperial troops were victorious and ravaged that district. One night the Rana affected his escape from the fortress, and took refuge in another mountain fortress.' (*Muntakhab-ut-Tawarikh*, ii, p. 275).

Maharana Pratap 'lost Kumbhalgarh but not so the indomitable will to continue the struggle against the Mughals'. Off and on, he made his sudden appearance in the plains and spread consternation in the Mughal camps. Now, instead of the Mughals, it was the Maharana who adopted the *scorched-earth policy* of devastating his own territory. 'in the Mughal-occupied Mewar', so as to make it inconvenient and unprofitable for the imperialists to hold it. Shahbaz Khan had now been entrusted the supreme command of the Mughal forces of occupation in Mewar. He received fresh contingents of troops from Ajmer in December 1578 and launched his second major campaign against the Maharana.

In November 1579, Akbar paid his second visit to Mewar. According to Abul Fazl, the Emperor reviewed the Mughal troops at Sambhar and expressed his satisfaction with their performance. On his directions, Shahbaz Khan received yet another (the third) imperial army, with adequate provisions, to be posted under his command in Mewar but with the primary object of consolidating the imperial hold in the region. During the *crisis of* 1581, when Akbar was engaged in his conflict with Mirza Muhammad Hakim of Kabul, the fanatic Mullas and the rebellious Muslim nobles of Bihar and Bengal, Maharana Pratap launched an offensive against the Mughals. He organised raids on the Mughal camps in Mewar as far as Mandalgarh and Chittor; the Rajput desperadoes usually laid their hands on the Mughal armoury and provisional stores and set fire to their habitats and tents to spread panic among the soldiers. In consequence, Akbar was constrained to dispatch the fourth imperial army, now under the command of Rajah Jagannath Kachhwaha. Like Man Singh, he also spread a military-cum-diplomatic network of his agents to woo the local populace of Mewar to submit to the Mughal authority for security and the material benefits. He 'played a fruitless hide and seek game' against Maharana Pratap for quite some time before his recall to the imperial court. All attempts of Akbar to reckon with Maharana Pratap and the defiant people of Mewar had proved futile. After the recall of Rajah Jagannath Kachhwaha from Mewar, we do not hear of any high Mughal dignitary, military general or diplomat, Hindu or Muslim, for his special posting in Mewar, with any specified objective; the plains of Mewar had been converted into a vast Mughal camp, the maintenance of which depended upon the constant supply of provisions and armament from Delhi and Agra. The Mughal armies gradually lost ground to Maharana Pratap and were put on the defensive. The Rana built-up a new capital at Chavand in the teeth of opposition from the Mughals and, before his death on January 19, 1597, he had recovered from the hands of the Mughals 'the whole of western Mewar and a part of the eastern Mewar, including the garrison towns of Mohi, Udaipur and Mandalgarh'. Akbar could do pretty little against him.

After the death of Maharana Pratap, his youthful son and successor, Rana Amar Singh Rathor, also carried on relentless struggle against the Mughals with a renewed pledge. As observed by Tod, 'the last moments of Pratap were an appropriate commentary on his life which he terminated, like the Carthaginian, swearing his successor to eternal conflict against the forces of his country's independence...Thus closed the life of a Rajput whose memory is even now idolized by every Sisodia, and will continue to be so...There is not a Pass in the Alpine Aravalli that is not sanctified by some deed of Pratap...some brilliant victory, or oftener, more glorious defeat.' (*Rajasthan*, i, pp. 345-63).

In 1599, for the last time, Akbar called upon Prince Salim (future Jahangir) and Raja Man Singh to try their luck against Mewar once again, but their reaction to the Emperor's plans was lukewarm. The Prince was an unwilling partner in this affair; he simply stayed back at Ajmer, and asked Raja Man Singh to adopt whatever measures he thought fit to win over the cooperation and loyalty of the people of Mewar. And to the Sisodia Rajputs, Man Singh and his ilk were the *persona non grata.* The latter, because of having suffered a personal insult and humiliation at the hands of Maharana Pratap, could think of nothing else but the revengeful pursuit of a policy of destruction and devastation in Mewar which aroused the anger and hostility of the entire population of the state who had started reclaiming their deserted lands and habitats since 1585. Rana Amar Singh challenged the imperial armies in the plains but suffered a defeat and retreated to the hills. But the inhabitants of the scarcely populated villages and towns stubbornly refused to submit to the Mughal rule and made the stay of the imperial armies in Mewar impossible. The rebellious Mewar always rankled in the eyes of Akbar but his desire to make it a part of his vast Indian Empire did not bear fruits during his life-time. It was left to his son and successor, Jahangir, to solve the Mewar problem in the long-run.

(*c*) ESTABLISHMENT OF THE MUGHAL HEGEMONY IN THE NORTH

Conquest of Gujarat (1572-73)

After the conquest of Malwa and Chittor, Akbar invaded the maritime province of Gujarat in 1572. Ever since the death of Bahadur Shah,

Gujarat had been passing through a period of troubles and turmoil. About this time, it was under the control of Muzaffar Shah III, who was an incompetent and unpopular ruler. His authority was defied by about half a dozen feudal chieftains who set up as rival claimants to the throne of Gujarat. Because of the near political anarchy that prevailed in Gujarat, it was also converted into a place of refuge by the rebellious Mirzas - the kinsmen of Akbar, who had carved out their own estates in various parts of the province. In July 1572 Akbar received an appeal for help from Itimad Khan, one of the political adversaries of Muzaffar Shah III. Akbar immediately ordered the dispatch of an imperial army of 10,000 horsemen as advance guard under the charge of *Khan i Kalan* (viz; Mirza Muhammad Khan Atka), and himself followed close upon its heels with the main army of invasion towards Ahmadabad, the capital of Gujarat. On the approach of the Mughal troops, Muzaffar Shah fled from Ahmadabad and the stronghold fell into the hands of Akbar without a fight. Muzaffar Shah was found hiding in a corn field and brought a captive to Akbar; the emperor spared his life and granted him a small pension. His rival Itimad Khan also sought Akbar's protection and was allowed to retain the command of his army as an ally of the Mughals. But much against Akbar's hopes, these Gujarati chiefs started hatching conspiracies against the Mughal rule; and their perfidy having been exposed, both of them were apprehended and thrown behind the bars.

Akbar entrusted the governorship of Gujarat to his foster-brother Mirza Aziz Koka with his headquarters at Ahmadabad, and himself overran various parts of the province to establish Mughal control. At Cambay he saw the sea for the first time; and he enjoyed his first naval excursion in a ship where he received homage from the Indian and foreign merchants, including the Portuguese. The rebellious Mirzas were defeated by Akbar in the battle of Sarnal (Gujarat) in December 1572. After making suitable arrangements for the civil administration of Gujarat, Akbar returned to Sikri in March 1573; he renamed the town as Fatehpur Sikri to commemorate the conquest of Gujarat and ordered the construction of buildings there for his royal residence.

Six months later Akbar was called upon to organise a second expedition to Gujarat for the suppression of a revolt of the local disaffected nobles who had put the Mughal governor under siege at Ahmadabad. It is regarded as one of the swiftest military campaigns in history. Akbar left Fatehpur Sikri on August 23, 1573, with 3,000 mobile horsemen only, and reached Ahmadabad on September 2, thus covering a distance of over 725 kilometres in eleven days. 'He reached the bank of the Sabarmati at night and immediately ordered his troopers to cross the river, with himself in the lead'. He charged the besiegers, who numbered about 20,000, 'like a fierce tiger' and took a heavy toll of their lives. Though dangerously exposed, Akbar had scored a clear victory over the rebels and dispersed their forces' before the besieged Mughal garrison could find time to come out of the fort and make junction with his troops. After restoring law and order in Gujarat, Akbar returned to Fatehpur Sikri in triumph within forty-three days.

Conquest of Bihar and Bengal (1574-76)

Sulaiman Kararani, the Afghan governor of Bihar, had asserted his independence after the death of Sher Shah Suri; he overran the provinces of Bengal and Orissa also and set up his headquarters at Tanda. In 1568 he was compelled to acknowledge the suzerainty of Akbar but after his death in 1572, his eldest son and successor Bayazid was murdered by the Afghan nobles. They installed Daud, the second son of Sulaiman on the throne who tended to act as an independent ruler. According to Badaoni, he possessed 40,000 well-mounted cavalry, 1, 40,000 infantry, 20,000 guns of various calibers, 3600 elephants and several hundred war-boats. Akbar took personal command of the royal armies against Daud and defeated him at Patna in August 1574. Bihar was conquered and declared annexed to the Mughal Empire. Daud fled to Bengal but the Mughal forces gave him a hot chase. Daud suffered another defeat and fled towards Orissa while Tanda fell into the hands of the imperial troops. He was, ultimately, defeated and killed in an action fought with the Mughals at Rajmahal on August 12, 1576, and his head was sent as a trophy of war to Akbar. With this victory, the provinces of Bengal and Bihar became the part and parcel of the Mughal Empire.

The Crisis of 1581

The Mughals were orthodox *Sunnis*; therefore, the establishment of their rule in India implied the dominance of the Sunnis in the state politics as before. Most of the Muslim nobles, accordingly, disliked Akbar's policy of religious toleration, as adopted by him since 1562. But they did not raise their voice of protest against him forcefully as they were fascinated by his strong imperial ambitions which led to the rapid expansion of the Muslim empire, particularly at the cost of the

Hindu regional ruling chiefs and the Afghan principalities. Akbar's grant of complete religious freedom to the Hindus and their recruitment in the civil and military services was considered by some to be an assault on Islam because it narrowed their scope for monopolizing the power of the state. Accordingly, some of the disgruntled military officers, at the instigation of fanatical *ulama*, hatched a conspiracy, in 1581, to depose Akbar and install his half-brother, Mirza Muhammad Hakim of Kabul, on the throne of Delhi. Khwaja Mansur, the imperial *diwan or* 'the Finance Minister' of Akbar, was the ring-leader of these conspirators at the court; and he entered into 'treasonable correspondence' with Muhammad Hakim under the very nose of Akbar. Mulla Muhammad Yazdi, the *qazi* of Jaunpur, issued a *fatwa* (religious decree) that Akbar had 'ceased to be a true *Mussalman*, and, therefore, rebellion against him was a religious duty of the faithful'. It led to a general uprising of the orthodox Muslim nobles who were publicly backed by a number of fanatic *mullas*. They read a *khutba* in the name of Mirza Muhammad Hakim and instigated the Muslim masses to join against Akbar. The Mughal governor of Jaunpur was besieged by the rebels in the fort of Tanda, and the royal army, which was sent by Akbar to his aid, was defeated and repulsed.

The violent protest against his religious policy took Akbar by surprise but he did not lose his cool at this critical juncture. It was not an ordinary armed uprising in which his military strength alone could carry the day. Instead, it posed 'a direct challenge to his integrity as the rightful successor to the Mughal throne. The Indian Muslims, though in minority, constituted, nevertheless, the backbone of the Mughal Empire; and Akbar was called upon to regain their confidence and prove his credibility as their leader *par excellence*. It goes to the credit of Akbar that he proved himself equal to the occasion. He not only suppressed the uprising with an iron hand but also solved the delicate issue of his credibility as the national monarch of India to the satisfaction of all his subjects—Hindus as well as Muslims'. In fact, Akbar emerged out of this crisis of 1581 as the most powerful and respected emperor of his times in the whole of Asia. Akbar acted with swiftness and tactfulness in dealing with the situation. Through a clever maneuver, he got hold of Mull Muhammad Yazdi and Mir Muizul Mulk- two of the ring-leaders of the rebels in eastern India and made a short work of them.

Mirza Muhammad Hakim had received the charge of Afghanistan

from his father Humayun; and, on assuming the reins of government in his own hands in 1560, Akbar had confirmed him in his possessions He was, therefore, enraged to find Muhammad Hakim in league with the rebels of Bihar and Bengal. Abul Fazl tells us that Muhammad Hakim wanted to capture the throne of Delhi by deposing Akbar. He had established secret contacts with the rebellious nobles of Bihar and Bengal as well as the traitors among the Mughal officers at the imperial court and at Lahore. After the declaration of *Fatwa* against Akbar by the Qazi of Jaunpur, Muhammad Hakim crossed the Indus with his army and marched upon Lahore but the Mughal officers of the Punjab did not support him as had erroneously been supposed by him. Meanwhile Akbar reached the Punjab at the head of a strong imperial army. Shah Mansur and his accomplices, who had been suspected of treason, had deliberately been put by him on the royal entourage, and their activities were watched closely. At Shahabad (modern Haryana) they were publicly exposed and promptly executed. It gave a serious setback to Muhammad Hakim who had contemplated occupation of the Punjab through treachery of Akbar's own officers. On hearing of Akbar's arrival in the region so soon, Muhammad Hakim lost his nerves and retraced his steps towards Kabul. Akbar gave him a hot chase by marching straight to the frontier. On the approach of the imperial troops, Muhammad Hakim fled from Kabul to Ghurband; and Akbar was accorded a royal reception at Kabul on August 10, 1581. Nevertheless, on the intervention of ladies of the royal *harem,* Muhammad Hakim was pardoned and restored to the governorship of Kabul but under the supervision of his sister, Bakht-us-Nisa Begam. On his death in July 1585, Kabul was brought under the direct control of Delhi and Raja Man Singh was appointed its governor.

Occupation of Kashmir (1585-86)

Akbar always looked upon the valley of Kashmir with coveted eyes. In 1581, its ruler, Yusuf Khan, did not respond favourably to Akbar's overtures to acknowledge the Mughal suzerainty. In 1585, Akbar visited the northwestern frontier to facilitate the smooth takeover of the government of Kabul by Raja Man Singh on the death of Mirza Muhammad Hakim. From his military camp at Attock, he sent an army of invasion in December 1585, under the command of Raja Bhagwan Dass and others, for the conquest of Kashmir. Hard-pressed, Yusuf Khan made peace with the Mughal generals on the condition that 'he would mint the coins and get the *khutba* read in the name of

Akbar, and that the imperial officers would be permitted to take charge of the Kashmiri mint, saffron cultivation, manufacture of shawls and the regulation of game' in the valley. He and his eldest son, Yaqub accompanied the Mughal envoy to offer their personal homage to the emperor. Akbar had, however, made up his mind to annex the valley; therefore, he placed Yusuf Khan under arrest although his son managed to escape. The latter fought a couple of well-contested battles with the Mughals which necessitated the dispatch of a fresh imperial army to reduce the valley. Yaqub was captured and sent as a prisoner along with his father to Bihar. Both of them died in captivity and Kashmir was annexed to the Mughal Empire. Akbar paid his first 'visit of pleasure' to the valley in the summer of 1589. During his brief stay there, he ordered some administrative reforms and adopted measures for public-welfare as also for the beautification of the valley. To quote Frederick Augustus, 'the Emperor did not leave his new territory without trace of his genius but displayed great activity during his brief visit. Irrigation channels were cleansed and many orchards laid out. From his day date the avenues of spire-like poplars and the groups of giant plants, in shadow of which, even now, the traveller resting at...Srinagar, sees in their leafy glories a memorial of Akbar's sense of beauty and love of well-doing." (F Augustus, *Akbar*, ii, p. 215)

Conquest of Sindh (1591)

The Upper Sindh, including the island fort of Bhakkar, had been overrun by the Mughal troops in 1574. In 1590 Akbar appointed Abdur Rahim *Khan-i-Khana* as the governor of Multan with instructions to complete the conquest of Sindh up to the month of the Indus. A large imperial army, inclusive of 'a hundred elephants and a train of artillery,' was placed at his disposal for the purpose. Mirza Jani Beg, the Turkoman chief of Thatta (Lower Sind) was defeated and compelled to surrender. His territories were annexed to the Mughal Empire. Jani Beg was offered a *mansab* of 3,000 in the imperial service which the latter gladly accepted. Later on, Jani Beg became a member of the *Din-i-Ilahi* also and earned the personal friendship and association of Akbar as his faithful camp-follower.

Conquest of Orissa (1592)

In 1586, Raja Man Singh was recalled from Kabul and entrusted the government of Bihar and Bengal. He was ordered by Akbar to extend boundaries of the Empire along the Gulf of Bengal by the conquest of

Orissa; it was then ruled over by an Afghan family of the Lohani tribe. Man Singh marched upon Orissa in 1590 and secured the submission of its ruler Nisar Khan. The latter ceded the territories of Puri, including the famous Hindu temple of Jagannath, to Delhi in lieu of tribute. In 1592 Nisar Khan displayed rebellious intentions which called for another expedition from Man Singh. The rebel was killed and Orissa was annexed to the Mughal Empire; it was made a *Sarkar* (district) of the province of Bengal.

Conquest of Baluchistan (1595)

Some of the Baluchi chiefs had voluntarily acknowledged the vassalage of Akbar in 1586. In order to consolidate the imperial hold over Baluchistan, Akbar deputed Mir Masum, the celebrated author of the *Tarikh-i-Sind,* to conquer Baluchistan, which was then held by the Pani Afghans. He led an attack on their stronghold of Sibi (Siwi), situated to the northeast of Quetta, and defeated them in a pitched battle. Simultaneously, he exerted diplomatic pressure for their future security to acknowledge the imperial authority of Delhi. As a result, 'the whole of Baluchistan, including Mekran—the region lying along the seacoast, as far as the frontiers of the Kandahar', was incorporated in the Mughal Empire.

(*d*) SPREAD OF MUGHAL IMPERIALISM IN THE SOUTH

After the annexation of Sindh in 1591, Akbar became the undisputed overlord of the whole of northern and northwestern India. Nevertheless, while the Mughal arms were gradually penetrating into Kandahar with the object of establishing their influence in Central Asia, Akbar had a special fascination for India, the southern half of which was yet beyond his control. Therefore, soon after his victory in Sindh, he sent from Lahore, in August 1591, four diplomatic missions to the four major regional kingdoms of the Deccan—Khandesh, Ahmadnagar, Bijapur and Golconda.

Submission of Khandesh: Raja Ali Khan, the Sultan of Khandesh, whose territories lay in the Tapti valley, and touched the borders of the Mughal Empire in the south, lost no time in acknowledging the suzerainty of Delhi. Burhanpur was the capital of Khandesh which was defended by the mighty fort of Asirgarh, situated on a spur of the Satpura range to the north of Burhanpur. Asirgarh commanded the main road to the Deccan and, according to VA Smith, 'it was regarded as one of the strongest and best equipped forts in Asia or Europe'.

As for the rulers of the other three states, they sent diplomatic replies and asserted their hereditary right of sovereignty in the South. It is a different matter, however, that they, like the Rajput rulers of the North, were at daggers drawn with one another and presented the sight of a house divided against itself. Even in the face of the common threat for annihilation, posed by Akbar's warning to them in 1591-92 to accept his lord paramountcy, they did not cooperate with one another to safeguard their sovereignty.

War with Ahmadnagar—the First Siege of Ahmadnagar: Taking advantage of the disunity among the South Indian rulers, Akbar ordered the dispatch of two Mughal armies to subjugate Ahmadnagar by force in 1593; one was commanded by Abdur Rahim *Khan-i-Khana* and the other by Prince Murad, then the governor of Gujarat. Because of lack of cooperation between the two Mughal commanders, they took quite some time to start the expedition. Meanwhile, the ruler of Ahmadnagar, Burhanul Mulk, died in April 1594, and his son and successor Ibrahim was attacked and killed in action by the Bijapuris. It gave rise to a number of claimants to the throne. The court of Ahmadnagar was, accordingly, divided into a number of factions, each supporting the claim of its own puppet to be the Sultan. It led to the outbreak of civil war in Ahmadnagar. Mian Manju, the prime minister of Ahmadnagar, supported the claim of Bahadur Shah, an infant son of Ibrahim, whose candidature was put forth by Chand Bibi, a sister of *Burhan-ul-Mulk* and widow of Sultan Ali Adil Shah of Bijapur. Mian Manju and Chand Bibi were opposed by three other rival factions of the court. In his bid for personal survival, the Mian committed the mistake of sending an appeal to the Khan-i-Khana, then in Malwa, to come to his aid. Akbar was very happy to know of it, and, on his orders, Prince Murad and the Khan-i-Khana proceeded with their armies from Gujarat and Malwa respectively. They made a junction at Chand, about 130 kilometres from Ahmadnagar, and reached the vicinity of the metropolis in an aggressive mood in November 1595. Mian Manju, who became apprehensive of the Mughal designs, changed his mind and prepared to defend the freedom of his state from the hands of the imperialists, whom he had himself invited as allies a short while ago The Mughals laid siege to the fort which was heroically defended by Chand Bibi for over three months, from December 1595 to February 1596; earned her the legendary fame as Chand Sultana, 'the invincible Lady of Ahmadnagar'. About this time it became known to the Mughal commanders that the fugitive freedom-fighters of Ahmadnagar, accompanied by the combined armies of Bijapur and Golconda were heading fast towards the place of siege in support of Chand Bibi. Prince Murad, the supreme commander of the Mughal forces, took alarm; he hurriedly concluded peace with Chand Bibi and raised the siege on February 23, 1596. According to the terms of the treaty, the Mughals accepted Bahadur Shah, the infant grandson of Burhan-ul-Mulk, as the rightful ruler of Ahmadnagar under the regency of Chand Bibi. In turn, Ahmadnagar accepted the suzerainty of Delhi and ceded the territory of Berar to the Mughal Empire. Thereafter, the Mughal army proceeded towards Ellichpur, the most important fort of Berar, which was occupied by them without much difficulty; it was converted into a permanent military headquarters by the Mughals.

Renewal of War with Ahmadnagar: The treaty of peace with Ahmadnagar proved a non-starter. Immediately after the departure of the Mughal forces, Ahmadnagar was overwhelmed by the soldiers of Bijapur and Golconda, and all the fugitives of the state, including Mian Manju. It led to the revival of old feuds between the rival factions for control of the Ahmadnagar state. Chand Bibi, being unable to bring about reconciliation between them, resigned her authority, and the nobles of Ahmadnagar, much against her advice, repudiated the treaty of peace with the Mughals. Accompanied by the allied troops, they marched upon Berar with the object of turning out the Mughals from there. Prince Murad and Khan-i-Khana were hard-pressed to keep the Deccanis at bay. In January 1599, Akbar ordered Shahrukh of Badakhshan, now in the imperial service, to take charge of the Deccan campaign and Prince Murad was recalled to the court. The unfortunate prince, who suffered from depression and excessive indulgence in drinking, was not destined to reach Agra; he breathed his last near Daulatabad on May 2, 1599. Thereafter, Akbar sent Prince Daniyal to take charge of the Deccan affairs..

Rebellion in Khandesh: While the Mughals were preparing to take on Ahmadnagar for the second time, Khandesh posed a fresh problem to them. Raja Ali Khan of Khandesh had died fighting for the Mughals in the first siege of Ahmadnagar in early 1599 but his son and successor, Miran Bahadur, resented the Mughal domination. Encouraged by the successful resistance put up by Ahmadnagar, Bijapur, and Golconda against the Mughals, he defied the imperial authority. When prince Daniyal reached Burhanpur enroute to Ahmadnagar, Miran Bahadur did not come out of Asirgarh to receive him. The prince felt offended and prepared to attack the Asirgarh fort first, but he was directed by the emperor that Daniyal 'should proceed with his expedition against Ahmadnagar' and leave the settlement of dispute with Miran Bahadur to the imperial court. The Mughal forces, now led by Prince Daniyal, invaded Ahmadnagar and put it under siege for the second time.

Death of Chand Bibi and the Fall of Ahmadnagar: In the conquest of Ahmadnagar, the scenes of Chittor were frequently re-enacted with the display of valour and sacrifice of lives by both the parties. Hard-pressed, Chand Bibi opened negotiations with the Mughals for peace on old terms but a section of her diehard followers opposed this move, and, in a fit of anger, 'Jita Khan, an eunuch, with some evil persons inside the fort' put Chand Bibi to death; this tragedy took place on July 3, 1600. Thus Chand Bibi fell 'a victim to the folly of her own men'. The culprits were immediately apprehended and put to death by the angry soldiers, but, being convinced of their total annihilation, the entire besieged garrison took a solemn vow that, *like the Hindus*, they would die to a man in the defence of Ahmadnagar and thus uphold the honour of the deceased lady'. They fulfilled this vow in the true spirit of the Rajputs and fell fighting against the foe after taking a heavy toll of the Mughal lives. The fort fell on August 19 'after a siege of four months and four days'. The minor Sultan, Bahadur Shah, was captured along with some members of his family and sent to Gwalior as a state prisoner; he died in captivity soon thereafter. Just like Chittor, the conquest of the stronghold of Ahmadnagar by the Mughals did not lead to the subjugation of the entire state; some of the vanquished nobles and soldiery of Ahmadnagar declared yet another member of the royal family to be the Sultan, and continued the struggle for freedom from the Mughals yoke.

The Siege of Asirgarh: The fort of Asirgarh was invested by the Mughal armies in February 1600. By this time, Akbar had shifted his military camp from Ujjain to Burhanpur, the capital of Khandesh, which was captured by him in a single assault, but Asirgarh 'proved to be the most formidable of all the forts conquered by Akbar in his life'. It was because 'the mountainous nature of the ground prevented the besiegers from using the mines or constructing *sabats*. The siege, therefore, became little more than a blockade, and mere blockading operations directed against a fortress so amply supplied with food, water, and munitions, offered little prospect of success within a reasonable time.' (VA Smith, *Akbar*, p. 275). Akbar was, therefore, constrained to take charge of the operations in his own hands. Having failed to take the fort by force, he 'resorted to bribery and conceit' for the attainment of his objective. According to one version, 'Sultan Miran Bahadur's military commanders and envoys were bribed, and on an assurance of safe conduct, he was induced to come out of the fort for talks with the Mughal emperor. Miran Bahadur was detained, however, in the Mughal camp and coerced to sign a letter to the besieged garrison to surrender the fort to the besiegers. Muqarrab Khan, son of the Abyssinian commandant of the fort, who came to the Mughal camp as one of the envoys, was put to death without any reason'. In spite of all this, the besieged garrison continued to hold on against heavy odds for full two weeks before its surrender on January 6, 1901. Khandesh was annexed to the Mughal Empire and Miran Bahadur was sent as a state prisoner to the fort of Gwalior. The credit for this victory was given to Prince Daniyal who received appointment as the viceroy of Malwa, Gujarat, and all the Mughal possessions in the Deccan, including Khandesh, which was renamed as Dandesh after the name of the Prince. This was the last military conquest of Akbar. Sultan Ibrahim Adil Shah of Bijapur was totally disheartened to see the sad plight of his neighbouring state; he voluntarily offered his submission to Akbar and gave his daughter in marriage to Prince Daniyal. Akbar returned to Fatehpur Sikri with great satisfaction on the 1st of August 1601, and ordered the construction of the famous Darwaza to commemorate his victory.

Administrative Divisions of Akbar's Empire

The conquest of Asirgarh in 1601 concluded Akbar's successful military career which was spread over more than forty years. It goes to his credit that, beginning with the conquest of Malwa in 1560, Akbar was personally associated with the conduct of almost all the military operations throughout his life. He carved out a vast Empire which was divided into fifteen provincial divisions, called the *Subahs.* Most of these provinces were named after their capitals. The twelve *Subahs* of the North, from east to west, were, Bengal, Bihar, Allahabad, Oudh, Agra, Delhi, Lahore, Multan, Kabul; Ajmer, Malwa and Ahmadabad (Gujarat), while the Mughal territories in the Deccan were parcelled out into three provinces of Khandesh, Berar and Ahmadnagar; they formed a single viceroyalty under the charge of a Prince Besides, Orissa was made a *sarkar* (district) of Bengal, while Kashmir and Kandahar were treated as *sarkars* of the *Subah* of Kabul (Afghanistan). Similarly, the territories of Baluchistan and Sindh, then called Thatta by the

Muslim chroniclers, were included in the province of Multan. In addition to the above, the Mughal Empire, included within its fold, a large number of Hindu states and some Muslim principalities which enjoyed considerable internal autonomy in the administrative affairs.

SECTION 5: AKBAR'S RELIGIOUS POLICY AND DIN-I-ILAHI

The Background

Medieval India of Akbar's age showed great diversity in the matter of religious beliefs and practices of its people. By this time, Islam was rooted in the soil, and the Muslims, though in minority, formed the predominant section of the Indian ruling elite. The Turko-Afghan rulers had setup an orthodox Muslim polity in the country but, much before the coming of the Mughals, some sort of conciliation between the Hindus and Muslims had started taking place. The Hindus were dubbed as Zimmis by the Sultans and the regional Muslim rulers but they had perforce to associate them in the state administration. 'The Hindus, in general, had proved to be very conservative in outlook, and too devoted to their ancestral faith to change it for any price whatsoever. As a result, by the time of Akbar, conversions to Islam had practically come to stop; so much so that even the fanatical *mullas* had also given up much of their enthusiasm and craze for proselytization'. M L Roychoudhury, in his learned treatise, entitled, *Din-i-Ilahi or the Religion of Akbar* (University of Calcutta, 1941, p. 49) writes that by the time of Akbar, a 'community of political and economic interests was gradually asserting its inevitable superiority over difference of faith' between the Hindus and the Muslims, and the ground for the socio-cultural synthesis had already been prepared by the *Sufi* saints and reformers of the Bhakti movement all over the country. In our opinion, 'the discrimination between the two communities, though well marked in the political sphere, tended to disappear for all practical purposes because of the establishment of sovereign Hindu states, often in the teeth of Muslim opposition, in many parts of the country; the existence of these states acted as a sort of deterrent to the neighbouring Muslim rulers to face the consequences if they ill-treated their Hindu subjects. For want of numbers of their coreligionists, the Muslim chiefs had to recruit the Hindus even in their armed forces. The invasion of Timur in 1398 brought about a close unity of political interests between

Hindus and Muslims of northern India. We, therefore, find that, in the beginning of the sixteenth century, regionalism, instead of religion, had become the predominant factor in determining the loyalties of the people to their local rulers. The Mughal invasion threw the Indian Muslims completely into the arms of their Hindu fellow-brethren. The rise of Hem Chandra, a petty Hindu of obscure origin, to the supreme command of the army of Muhammad Adil Shah Sur, is a proof of the rapport which had been established between Hindus and Muslims of the land in safe-guarding their political interests on the eve of the advent of the Mughals". (Advanced Study; ii, pp. 278-79).

Add to the above historical background 'the parental and social heritage of Akbar and the solid foundations of the grand edifice of his state policy of secularism would become at once visible and also intelligible'. The Mughals were orthodox *Sunnis* but Babar was by nature very liberal in his religious outlook; even otherwise, he was always very kind and generous in his treatment towards his subjects. Similarly, Humayun bequeathed to his son the princely virtues of liberalism and broad-mindedness. He did not hesitate in adopting some of the *Shia* practices of the Persian ruler, who had not only given him shelter and military aid in the time of adversity but also the hand of a Persian *Shia* lady in marriage, who was destined to be the mother of Akbar. Above all, Akbar himself was born and reared up for about a month in a Hindu house where 'the chief queen of his parents' host, treated Humayun as her brother; something unknown to the Muslim culture of Central Asia.' Akbar's teachers and guides, including Abul Latif, Mulla Pir Muhammad and Bairam Khan, incidentally happened to be men of unorthodox religious views. This parental and social heritage exercised a profound impact on the evolution of Akbar's liberal religious policy.

Above all, Akbar had had a very bitter experience at the hands of his kinsmen, styled the Mirzas, and many other self-seeking and disloyal Muslim officers besides his political rivals and the deadly Muslim foes. On the other hand, his devoted, well-groomed and intelligent Rajput wives and their relatives won his love and regards by their selfless love and loyal service to him. The Rajputs, in fact, emerged as the props and supports of the Mughal throne upon whom Akbar could depend in his fight against his Muslim rivals. All these factors served as ingredients to shape his religious views and the secular state policy.

Evolution of Akbar's Religious Policy

The historians have discerned four distinct stages in the process of evolution of Akbar's religious policy. Akbar had a religious and spiritual bent of mind. He had a great experience in spiritual awakening after his marriage with the first Rajput princess from Amber in January 1562. It secured him the voluntary and selfless services of the Rajput warriors as his relatives. He was amazed to see for the first time, at the siege of Merta, how the friendly Rajput soldiers of Raja Bhagwan Das fought with enthusiasm for the Mughal throne against their own people. He was impressed so much by the undaunted courage and bravery of the Rajputs, including his friends as well as foes, that he 'stopped the practice of enslaving the prisoners of war and their forcible conversion to Islam'. This was the first step of its kind taken by a Muslim ruler of India purely 'on the humanitarian considerations'. It was against the traditional Islamic law and practice. This marked the first stage in the evolution of his religious policy which earned him the goodwill of Hindus, including his arch enemies among the Rajput chiefs.

The second step in this direction was taken by Akbar when he was encamped at Mathura sometime in 1563. He came to know that, the preceding Muslim rulers had imposed a tax on the Hindu pilgrims who wanted to have a dip in the 'holy' waters of the Jumna. Akbar's conscience did not allow the imposition of such restrictions on the religious beliefs and practices of the Hindus and he abolished the pilgrims' tax throughout his dominions. Soon thereafter, Akbar took the most revolutionary step on March 15, 1564 when he granted complete religious freedom to the Hindus by the abolition of *Jaziya*. 'This was a poll tax, charged from the Hindus in their capacity as *Zimmis*, whereby they were denied the right of full-fledged citizenship of the state under their Muslim rulers'. The abolition of *Jaziya* caused a huge financial loss to the state and met with opposition from his own Muslim officers and the orthodox *ulama* for the violation of 'the Islamic theory of state'. But Akbar faced the opposition with patience and tried 'to cool the frayed tempers with arguments that the solidarity and stability of the Mughal state depended very much on the goodwill and cooperation of his Hindu subjects'. Abul Fazl, who joined Akbar's court much later, defends his action on the ground that 'When owing to the blessings of abundant goodwill and graciousness of the Emperor, those who belong to other religions (i.e. the non-Muslims), have, like the Muslims, bound up their waist of devotion and service, and exert themselves for advancement of the dominion, why should they be classed with that old faction which cherished mortal enmity, and be the subjects of contempt and slaughter?' (*Akbarnama*, ii, pp. 203-4).

Akbar was not fully contented with the grant of complete religious freedom to his subjects. His next attempt was 'to create a spirit of love and harmony among his people by eliminating all the racial, religious and cultural barriers between them'. The noble company of Sheikh Mubarak and his sons—Abul Fazl and Faizi, diverted Akbar's attention 'from the world of politics into the domain of spiritualism'. In the first instance, Akbar showed eagerness to understand the basic principles of Islam, his own religion. For this purpose, he ordered the construction of *Ibadat Khana*—'the house of worship' at Fatehpur Sikri, in January 1575, 'to adorn the spiritual kingdom'. (*Ibid.*, II, p. 157). Here he commenced the practice of holding religious discourses with the learned *ulama* and the *Sufi* saints of the age. The discourses were held on Thursday nights, and very often continued till the wee hours of the next morning. To begin with, Akbar used to invite only the Muslim theologians and saints, including the *ulama, sheikhs, Sayyads*, and the religious-minded Mughal nobles, to take part in these discussions. According to Abul Fazl,

"The *Ibadat Khana* had for *aiwans* (verandahs), and there were four noble sections in that spiritual and temporal assemblage. In the eastern chamber of worship (*Ibadatkada*) were the great leaders and high officers who were conspicuous in the courts of society for enlightenment. In the southern compartment, the keen-sighted investigators, both those who gathered the light of day (i.e., the illuminati) and those who chose the repose of the night-halls of contemplation, sat in the school of instruction. In the western compartment, those of lofty lineage practiced auspicious arts. In the northern compartment were the *Sufis* of clear heart who were absorbed in beatific visions.' (iii, pp. 158-59).

Akbar was a God-fearing man and took keen interest in these religious assemblies. The mutual discussions and arguments were allowed to be carried on by the scholars even in the absence of the Emperor long after midnight. His sleeping chamber was attached to the *Ibadat Khana.* From the very beginning, the Muslim theologians came to be divided into two groups – the Sunnis and the Shias, who differed with each other on various religious issues and the interpretation of the Islamic Canon. Sheikh Makhdum-ul-Mulk and Sheikh Abdun

Nabi were leaders of the orthodox *Sunni* party while Sheikh Mubarak, Faizi and Abul Fazl were spokesmen of 'free-thinkers and liberal-minded theologians'. Very often, they failed to arrive at agreed opinions on many Islamic beliefs and practices, and, in the course of discussions, displayed a spirit of intolerance towards each other. Badaoni, himself an orthodox Mulla, informs us that 'the *Mullas* quarrelled among themselves and drew the sword of the tongue, called their opponents names, and even attributed motives to one another'. One night, Akbar's sleep was disturbed when the two rival factions of the Muslim divines 'actually drew their swords to settle the religious issues at stake'. Akbar was totally disappointed with 'the irresponsible behaviour of those self-conceited, greedy and intolerant *Mullas*'. They 'had failed to give satisfactory answers to his yearnings for spiritual enlightenment'. It was after that unpleasant incident that Akbar threw open the gates of the *Ibadat Khana* to the theologians and scholars of other religious faiths, including Hinduism, Jainism, Zoroastrianism and Christianity. In the company of these holy men, saints and scholars, Akbar sought enlightenment about God, His Creation and the Universe in the true spirit of 'a Searcher after Truth'.

The Issue of Mahzar or 'The Infallibility Decree': The second stage in the evolution of Akbar's religious policy was marked by the issue of Mahzar or 'the infallibility decree'. The religious discourses, held at the *Ibadat Khana*, shook Akbar's belief in the orthodox *Sunni* Islam. And the orthodox *Sunni Mullas* were holding pre-dominant position in the state politics ever since the assumption of powers by him. Abdun Nabi, their chief spokesman, was the *Sadr-us-Sadur or* 'the minister for ecclesiastical affairs and religious endowments' of the Empire. As leader of the *ulama* or the *ahl i saadat*, he wielded great influence at the imperial court. Akbar noted with concern that Abdun Nabi had been persecuting the *Shias* and the heretics among the *Mussalmans* under his very nose, misused his official position to promote the interests of his friends and favourites. He was dead opposed to the grant of religious freedom to the Hindus, and actually put up a tough opposition to his liberal religious policy. According to S M Jaffar, 'The *ulama* were not only narrow-minded, but their influence in the State was wholly schismatic. The implicit obedience, which they exacted from the Boy-Badshah, intoxicated them, and the unbounded reverence they received from the orthodox sect blinded them to the interests of the State. They could not tolerate the honest difference of opinion in religious matters. Power, pride and prejudice alike governed their passions. Under the charge of heresy, a number of *Mussalmans* suffered death at their hands, many died in dungeons, and a good many more escaped with their lives and lived as exiles. Their hatred against the *Zimmis*, particularly, against the Hindus, knew no bounds. They could not tolerate any concession accorded to them by the Emperor.' (*The Mughal Empire*, op. cit., pp. 118-19).

Akbar was totally alienated from the partisan attitude and exercise of religious fanaticism by Abdun Nabi, his *Sadr-us-Sadur*, and the other orthodox Sunni *ulama*, and he made up his mind to curtail their powers in determining the state policies. To begin with, he removed the *Waiz* - 'the head priest' of the *Jama Masjid* at Fatehpur Sikri, himself mounted the pulpit on June 22, 1579, and read the *Khutba* in his own name just as the Prophet Muhammad and his succeeding *Khalifas* used to do. The *Khutba*, which was composed in verse by the Poet Laureate Faizi, was thereafter repeated by the *Imams* in the *Jama Masjids* of all the important towns and cities of the empire. it read as follows:

> "In the name of Him who gave us sovereignty, who gave us a wise heart and a strong arm, who guided us in equity and justice, who put away from our heart aught but equity; His praise is beyond the range of our thoughts, Exalted by His Majesty, Allah hu Akbar". (Abul Fazl, *Akbarnama*, iii, p. 369).

The introduction of Akbar as the sovereign in the above words 'struck a serious blow at the prestige of the *Mullas* who considered themselves to be the moral and spiritual guardians of the State'. They did not like the Emperor to have direct contacts with his subjects (read the *Millat* or the Muslim subjects), with whom he was expected to communicate only through the agency of the *Imams* – the spokesmen of Islam. They felt enraged at the so-called un-Islamic practice of Akbar who had attempted to ignore the presence of the Muslim theologians. They 'started a whispering campaign against Akbar on the ground that the latter was striving to assume the role of the *Khalifas*, as the spiritual and temporal head of the state'. Akbar was ready to meet their challenge. He paid no attention to their voice of protest and went ahead with his plans to reduce the power and influence of the *Mullas* in the state politics. It led to the issue of a proclamation, called the *Mahzar*, in September 1579. Literally implied as pronouncement, declaration, or a petition, the *Mahzar* was prepared by Sheikh Mubarak, and signed by almost all the prominent Muslim theologians and divines of the Mughal Empire; it recognised Akbar, in his capacity as the Just Monarch and *Amir-ul-Momnin*, to be the *Imam-i-Adil*, i.e., 'the

Supreme Interpreter or Arbiter of the Islamic Law' in all the controversial issues pertaining to ecclesiastical or civil matters. Earlier, the *Mullas* used to act as the sole arbiters of all such disputed questions in their capacity as *Mujtahids* or 'the Interpreters of Islamic law'. The *Mahzar* proclaimed Akbar to be higher in rank than the *Mujtahids* as the Supreme Arbiter of the controversial religious issues. It clearly implies that the *Mahzar* did not deprive the *Mullas* of their basic right to act as the *Mujtahids*, except that Akbar placed himself at their head as the Chief Judge, thus assuming the powers which previously belonged, by delegation, to *Sadr-us-Sadur* or *Qazi-ul-Qazat* - the Chief Justice of the Mughal empire. (For the English translation of the complete document, refer to J.L. Mehta, Advanced Study in the History of Medieval India; *ii*; pp. 291-92).

SM Jaffar defines the *Mahzar* as 'the Act of Supremacy' which 'reveals most unmistakably the statesmanship of Akbar, who caught the ferocious lions (the *Ulama*) in their own dens...Like King John's Magna Carta, it was a Petition to the King from the most influential *ulama* but unlike it, it increased rather than diminished the Royal Prerogative'. No wonder, the *Mahzar* came as a bolt from the blue to the orthodox *Sunni* Muslims. They raised a hue and cry against Akbar's interference in the religious affairs, and accused him of having assumed the role of the Prophet. But Abul Fazl absolves Akbar of this charge with the remarks that he was an absolute king who 'did not brook the infringement of his sovereign powers at the hands of the *ulama*'. Therefore, his belief in the 'theory of Divine Rights of Kingship' should not be confounded with the charge that he wanted to play the Prophet. Nevertheless, as a result of the vicious propaganda of the orthodox *Mullas* and intrigues of the disaffected courtiers and military nobles, there took place the crisis of 1581 which was faced by Akbar with courage and determination as described earlier. Akbar's 'success against the rebellious Muslim fanatics and their political protégés marked the triumph of absolute monarchy as also the end of the baneful influence of the orthodox Muslims in the state-politics'. It set the stage for the establishment of a secular national monarchy in the country in which majority of the people were non-Muslims.

The Genesis of *Din-i-Ilahi*: The attainment of 'spiritual enlightenment' by Akbar did not distract him from this materialistic world. He was a religious-minded and God-fearing person but, being a man of action, his attachment to the worldly affairs was very much real. Akbar was a *Sufi* or mystic by nature but not an ascetic. He made use of his 'spiritual visions' to utilise the powers and resources of the state for the happiness and welfare of his subjects. Besides, he showed his eagerness to establish more cordial and enduring relationships of fraternity and brotherhood between the various sections of his subjects by eliminating all elements of friction and discord between the Hindus and Muslims. As religion predominated the Indian society, Akbar 'conceived a plan in terms of religion to counter the divisive religious forces which stood in the way of Hindu-Muslim unity.' It led to the promulgation of the *Din-i-Ilahi* early in 1582. It was not a new religion, nor did Akbar attempt to play the prophet or missionary in the spread of his 'divine faith' so-called. His real object was to unite the people of his Empire into an integrated national community by providing a common religious-cum-spiritual platform or the meeting ground. In our contention, 'Akbar was not so *naive* as to envisage a plan for the elimination of the powerful religions of the world like Hinduism and Islam, and their replacement by the *Din-i-Ilahi* as a new religion. Rather his real desire seemed to be to create a connecting bond or bridge between the two major religions of the country by breaking the age-old socio-cultural barriers which had divided them into water-tight compartments of the Indian society. The *Din-i-Ilahi* was a socio-religious association of the like-minded intellectuals and saints who had transcended the barriers of their orthodox religious beliefs and practices, and shaken off the religious prides, prejudices and superstitions which were the hallmarks of the character of the medieval Indians, whether Hindus or Muslims. In the absence of any specific treatise or manual available on the subject, it is very difficult to define the *Din-i-Ilahi* as it was understood by Akbar'. (*Ibid*; pp.299-300)

Abul Fazl, who played a major role in the promulgation of the *Din-i-Ilahi*, does not attach much importance to it as being worthy of mention in his historical treatise, entitled, *Akbarnama*, that preserves 'the classical account of the life history and achievements of his royal patron.' He makes only a casual reference *to Din-i-Ilahi* in the *Ain-i-Akbari*, the third volume of *Akbarnama*, where it is presented 'in the form of a *Sufi* order or assembly of saints and religious divines who were formally enrolled as the regular members of the *Ibadat Khan*'. They were made out as 'the forceful exponents of Akbar's liberal religious policy, and sought moral and spiritual guidance from him'. According to him, the organisation of the *Din-i-Ilahi* functioned as sort of an association of the like-minded God-fearing men who frequently assembled together to dilate upon the various social or moral and religious or spiritual issues of the day for the purpose of promoting the concepts of religious harmony and universal brotherhood.

Abul Fazl describes 12 principles of the *Din-i-Ilahi* in *Ain*-77, which are preceded by the statement that the Emperor has now become 'the spiritual guide of the nation' who 'sees in the performance of this duty a means of pleasing God (Allah).' None of these principles can be interpreted as 'a fundamental doctrine, religious dogma or belief which can form the basis of any new faith' opposed to or a replacement of the prevalent religions - Hinduism, Islam, or Christianity. These principles explain the initiation ceremony and the rules of conduct to be observed by the members of the *Din-i-Ilahi*. A person who wanted to become the member of this organisation, approached Abul Fazl for the purpose. The applicant was presented to Akbar with the turban in his hands. He performed the *Sijdah* (prostration) by placing his head at the feet of the Emperor, and the latter took him in his embrace. Then the Emperor placed the turban back on the head of the prospective member of *Din-i-Ilahi* and gave him his own portrait (*shast*), on which were engraved the words *Allah-u-Akbar*. The members of *Din-i-Ilahi* were called the *Ilahias*, and they greeted each other with the words – *Allah-u-Akbar* and *Jalle-Jalal-e-Hu*.

The members of *Din-i-Ilahi* abstained from meat as far as possible, did not dine with or use the utensils of the butchers, fishermen and bird catchers, nor did they marry old women or minor girls. They practiced charity. The *Ilahias* celebrated their birth anniversary by throwing a feast to their associates, and, also gave a dinner (*ziafat*), once in their lifetime in celebration of their death, which would ultimately liberate them from this mortal world. There were four grades of devotion to Akbar 'as the Spiritual Guide of the *Ilahias*'; these were in the ascending order of importance, (1) Property; (2) Life; (3) Honour, and (4) Religion. A person, who pledged to sacrifice only one of these things for his Spiritual Guide possessed one degree of devotion, so on and so forth. Obviously, Religion was the last and the most important thing, the surrender of which was not at all essential for enrollment as member of the *Din-i-Ilahi*.

Of course, there was nothing wrong with the prescribed method of presentation of the prospective members of *Din-i-Ilahi* to Akbar. He was an absolute king who claimed himself to be 'the Shadow of God on Earth' on the basis of the 'Theory of Divine Rights of Kingship'. It is quite apparent that he had introduced *Sijdah* as 'a custom' in his capacity as the *Zill-i-Ilahi* or 'the Lord Emperor', and not as a religious obligation as the founder of *Din-i-Ilahi.* In fact, everyone who presented himself before Akbar had to perform the *Sijdah.* It is a fact of history that *Zaminbas* was introduced in India by Balban; and *Paibos* was also one of the court customs of the Sultans of Delhi. According to RP Tripathi, Islam Shah Suri, the son and successor of Sher Shah Suri, 'would not be satisfied till he had received homage to his 'shoes by the noblemen of his court'. (*Some Aspects of Muslim Administration*; Allahabad, 193, p. 61). It can be said without any shadow of doubt that '*Din-i-Ilahi* was not a new religion; it had no holy book of its own, no priests or missionary organisation to propagate it, and no religious dogmas or beliefs to be enforced by it'. *Ain-i-Akbari* mentions all-told eighteen names of the prominent persons who had adopted the *Din-i-Ilahi* in all; they included only one Hindu, Raja Birbal. The total number of the *Ilahias* of all grades did not exceed a few thousands. Badaoni tells us that Raja Bhagwan Dass and Man Singh bluntly refused to enroll themselves as members of the *Din-i-Ilahi*; and Akbar is never known to have expressed his displeasure with them on this account. 'When the prominent Hindu officers of the imperial court who had rendered invaluable services to the state and who were known for their unflinching loyalty to the person of Akbar, refused to oblige him by accepting the membership of the *Din-i-Ilahi*, its significance as a vehicle for the promotion of Hindu-Muslim unity or national integration was also lost forthwith. The *Din-i-Ilahi* as an association or institution of a handful of the liberal-minded and God-fearing intellectuals and saints set the model before the people in the light of which they could generate the forces of national integration by overcoming their respective religious prides and prejudices and other separatist or divisive tendencies. Akbar provided not only the political but also moral and spiritual leadership to the Indians of his day; he deserves a place of honour and pride in the annals of Indian history for all times to come". (Advanced Study; ii, p. 305).

SECTION 6: AN ASSESSMENT OF AKBAR'S CHARACTER AND PERSONALITY

The Concluding Years of Akbar's Life

The conquest of Asirgarh in January 1601 marks the end of Akbar's active military career. He returned to Fatehpur Sikri from the Deccan in August where he stayed only for eleven days before shifting his headquarters to Agra again. The concluding years of his life were spent at Agra. They were made unhappy because of his fast deteriorating health and untimely death of his near and dear ones, and other personal setbacks. Unfortunately, his own sons proved to be the greatest source of anxiety to him. Akbar had raised a fairly large *harem* like the typical oriental monarchs, and enjoyed a rather very happy and carefree family life until his old age set in. Of his children, three sons and three daughters, from different wives and concubines, attained majority. As regards his daughters, none of them took any part in the state affairs. In fact, the ladies of Akbar's *harem* were never mentioned in the court except the dowager queens, and most of the contemporary writers knew nothing about them. His sons, in the decreasing order of their age, were prince Salim, his eldest surviving son, who succeeded him to the throne as emperor Jahangir, was born of his first Rajput wife, the illustrious daughter of Raja Bihari Mal of Amber while Murad and Daniyal were born of two different concubines of Akbar on June 8, 1570 and September 10, 1572 respectively. In spite of Akbar's efforts to the contrary, all of his sons were inflicted with the traditional princely vices of their age. His second son, prince Murad, had died of *delirium tremens* in 1599, and his third son, prince Daniyal, died of excessive drinking at Burhanpur in April 1604. The crown prince Salim, 'the child of many prayers and pilgrimages', was equally guilty of excesses but he survived probably because of his well-built body and good health.

Conspiracy to Disinherit Prince Salim

As referred to earlier, Salim had also fallen in the estimation of his father and prominent nobles of his court, including Abul Fazl—the prime minister, because of his sedative habits and insubordination. He got Abul Fazl murdered in cold blood through his henchman, Bir Singh Bundella of Orchha, on August 19, 1602. Sheikh Mubarak had died in 1593, followed by Faizi who expired in 1595. Therefore, the untimely death of Abul Fazl in the fifty-second year of his life came as a terrible shock to Akbar. His assassination, writes VA Smith, 'made Akbar furious with rage and distracted with grief. For three days he abstained from appearing in public audience, a dangerous omission in a country where the non-appearance of the sovereign for a single day might be the signal for a revolution.' (*Akbar the Great Mogul*, p. 307).

About that time, Salim held the viceroyalty of the eastern provinces with his headquarters at Allahabad. The relations between the father and the son were totally strained and the crown prince had started behaving as virtually independent ruler. He escaped punishment, however, by the intervention of his grandmother, Sultana Salima Begam (a stepmother of Akbar). In February 1603, she went to Allahabad and persuaded Salim to come to Agra and seek pardon from his father. Salim abided by her advice and was forgiven by Akbar. The prince was allotted separate apartments to live in state at Agra, while the administration of the eastern provinces was carried on by his lieutenants.

The death of Daniyal in April 1604 left Salim as the only surviving son of Akbar who was entitled to succeed him to the throne. As luck would have it, his nomination as the heir-apparent did not go unchallenged. His own seventeen years old son, Khusrau, from his Rajput wife, the sister of Raja Man Singh, had grown up to be a handsome young man of accomplishments under the affection and care of Akbar. Taking advantage of the discredited prince Salim, some of Khusrau's personal friends and self-seeking scions of the senior nobles, fed 'the crazy idea into his head that he could supersede his father as the emperor of India after the death of his grandfather, Akbar. It gave birth to a conspiracy. Khusrau's maternal uncle, Man Singh, and father-in-law, Mirza Aziz Koka—the two influential nobles of the court, supported his claim and actually began to poison the ears of Akbar against Salim. On getting the wind of it, Salim slipped away to Allahabad without permission from Akbar and openly declared himself to be the emperor. Akbar felt annoyed but, because of filial weaknesses, failed to take any action against his rebellious son.

On the death of Akbar's mother in September 1604, Salima Begam, Salim did come to Agra to offer condolences to his father but' his real intention was to be near his father with shattered health and broken heart, to acquire the throne in the case of the latter's death'. Akbar received him affection and stately regards in the court but, 'on his arrival in the royal apartments, burst out in anger and displayed his parental wrath by slapping the prince in the face'. Akbar kept Salim in a sort of confinement in his spacious bathroom for ten days. He deputed the royal physician, Raja Salivahan; to monitor his health while the prince was 'denied the use of liquor and opium'. It humbled the remorseful Prince Salim to offer regrets for his irresponsible conduct; he 'resigned himself to the will of his father'. He was now allotted separate apartments for his *harem* within the royal palace, and was granted 'the viceroyalty of all the western provinces, including Malwa, Gujarat, and the three provinces of the Deccan'.

Illness and Death of Akbar

On October 3, 1605, Akbar was taken ill and confined to bed. He had an attack of diarrhea which prolonged for eight day. The royal physicians, having failed to diagnose the exact ailment, 'refrained from prescribing any medicine.' Thereafter, the emperor was administered a strong dose of medicine, 'which stopped the dysentery but, as a result of the side-effects, Akbar suffered from fever and strangury. It was quickly followed by the sudden loss of vitality which was probably aggravated by the loss of Akbar's will to live'. During all these days, Prince Salim, 'who had lived in the same palace, next door to Akbar's apartments, was not allowed to see the ailing monarch, lest he should make short work of him'. It was only on October 21, when Akbar's condition became serious, that Salim was formally declared heir-apparent to the throne on the bidding of the emperor. That day, he was formally escorted to Akbar's apartments, where the emperor, having lost his power of speech, and with his mouth swollen, was lying on his sick-bed. All the principal ministers and courtiers were in attendance upon him. Prince Salim paid respects to Akbar by touching his feet and, on the receipt of an indication from his ailing father, 'put on the royal turban and girded himself with the sword of Humayun'. He received salutation as the new emperor by all the *grandees* of the empire then present there, and promptly placed them under his command. Salim set up as the 'acting emperor' and instantaneously issued *firmans* to the provincial governors and imperial bureaucracy to hold their respective assignments with full responsibility. The royal guards were ordered to secure the imperial treasury; and entry of the persons, including certain senior members of the nobility and their followers into the royal palace, was watched and strictly regulated to ensure the safety of the new emperor and members of the royal family. Akbar died on the midnight of October 25-26, 1605, and was buried in state at the mausoleum of Sikandra near Agra; he had himself planned and started the construction of this mausoleum during his lifetime and Jahangir completed it by spending lavishly on its beautification. Akbar lived and died as a Muslim and was given a state funeral according to the Muslim custom.

An Assessment

Akbar was not formally educated but it would be wrong to presume that 'he had not learnt even the elements of reading and writing.' V A

Smith correctly observes that 'Indian rulers have always been accustomed to dictate orders and to leave most of the actual writing to subordinate professional secretaries and clerks'. (*Akbar*, the Great Mogul; p. 338). Akbar was, in fact, a highly learned man who had acquired vast and multifarious knowledge in the lap of nature; 'he possessed a memory of almost superhuman power, which enabled him to remember accurately the contents of books read to him.' According to V A Smith,

> 'Akbar was intimately acquainted with the works of many Muhammedan historians and theologians, as well as with a considerable amount of general Asiatic literature, especially the writings of the *Sufi* or mystic poets. He acquired from the Jesuit missionaries a fairly complete knowledge of the Gospel story and the main outlines of the Christian faith, while at the same time learning from the most accredited teachers - the principals of Hinduism, Jainism and Zoroastrianism; but he never found an opportunity to study Buddhism. As a boy he took some drawing lessons, and he retained all his life an active interest in various forms of arts. The architecture of the reign unmistakably bears the impress of his personal good taste. A man so variously accomplished cannot be considered illiterate in reality. He simply preferred to learn the contents of books through the ear rather than the eye and was able to trust his prodigious memory, which was never enfeebled by the use of written memoranda. Anybody who heard him arguing with acuteness and lucidity on a subject of debate would have credited him with wide literary knowledge and profound erudition, and never would have suspected him of illiteracy.' (*ibid.*, pp. 337-38)

Akbar was a vegetarian by choice; he did not relish non-vegetarian food. He was fond of outdoor sports and hunting. Polo, horse-riding, animal combats and the taming of elephants were some of his cherished amusements. He frequently organised *qamargha* hunts which involved the engagement of 'hundreds of village folk as beaters to drive animals from far-off places into a ring where the emperor and his most intimate friends hunted the wild beasts with all sorts of weapons, including swords, spear, bows and arrows and guns'. These hunting expeditions were not organised by him just for fun and amusement; Instead, he indulged in this hobby 'to increase his knowledge', and 'to inquire, without having first given notice of his coming, into the condition of the people and the army'. In the words of Abul Fazl, 'the emperor travels *incognito*, and examines into matters referring to taxation, or to *sayurghal* lands, or to affairs connected with the household. He lifts up such as are oppressed, and punishes the oppressors. On account of these higher reasons His Majesty indulges in the chase, and shows himself quite enamored of it'. (*Akbarnama*, iii, Ain 27, p. 292).

Akbar was a religious-minded and God-fearing person. He understood that every religion is based upon some elements of Truth, and, therefore, did not discriminate between the people on the basis of differences in their religious beliefs and practices. He adopted the policy of religious toleration', secularism and universal brotherhood as a matter of conviction. As a gentleman, Akbar left nothing to be desired although he was not a perfect man as Abul Fazl portrays him to be. He took liquor and opium in moderation and allowed himself latitude in his sexual life. He had quite a few wives and concubines in his *harem* which was manned by a huge army of the maid-servants and the *khwaja saras*. Akbar was an affectionate husband, a loving father and very sociable by habits. He was considerate and generous in his treatment towards the common people and earned the gratitude of his subjects in ample measures. Akbar was a sincere friend and reliable companion of the like-minded people, and loved to keep the company of his subordinates like Sheikh Mubarak, Faizi, Abul Fazl and Birbal without any pride or prejudice.

Akbar as Conqueror and Nation Builder

Akbar was a born soldier and great conqueror like his grandfather Babar. Imperialist by instincts, he transformed a small and shaky Mughal kingdom into a mighty empire. He reorgnised the Mughal army by introducing the *mansabdari* system and increased its fighting skill and efficiency by making use of the latest techniques of warfare then known to the Asians. Akbar imparted a political philosophy to his aggressive warfare and the territorial conquests; it was the political unification of India and the establishment of an all-powerful central government with a uniform system of administration throughout the country Although a foreigner by blood, 'Akbar was every inch an Indian who, like the ancient imperial rulers of India, had developed a firm faith in the principle of *one country, one government, and one people*'. He granted complete religious freedom to his subjects and threw upon the gates of imperial services to all without discrimination. Under him, the Mughal state retained its traditional character as the police state which was ruled predominantly by the foreign Muslim nobility and the alien bureaucracy, but, according to K.T. Shah, Akbar himself was 'thoroughly Indianised' and 'his genius perceived the possibilities, and his courage undertook the task of welding the two communities - Hindus and Muslims, into a common nation by the universal bond of common services and equal citizenship of a magnificent empire.' (*The Splendour That was India*, Bombay, 1932, p. 30).

Akbar was an innovator in the field of administration. He laid the foundations of an imperial structure of administration under which the country was successfully governed by his descendants for over a century after his death. He was a great patron of art and architecture. He took keen interest in the planning of palaces, mosques, tombs, forts and even the new townships and had his own ideas about the construction of buildings by the free amalgamation of the Turko-Afghan and indigenous styles. It resulted in the evolution of what was called the Mughal architecture which was, in fact, the national Indian architecture of that age. Akbar created an elaborate public works department for undertaking the construction of public buildings, gardens, roads, *sarais*, wells and canals. He was a great lover of fine arts, including calligraphy, painting, music, dancing and the like. He nationalized all these arts by extending liberal patronage to the artists of all communities and races, and by encouraging them to evolve out new forms by complete synthesis of foreign and indigenous traits. Akbar identified himself completely with the land and its people and did his best to impart socio-cultural unity to the country. Persian as court language was compulsory for recruitment to the imperial civil services; but the translation department of the central government rendered into Persian ancient Indian scriptures; including the *Vedas, Ramayana, Mahabharata,* and other Sanskrit literature. Arabic and Turki literature was also translated into Persian to make it available to the scholars of all communities. Besides Persian and Arabic, Akbar also patronised Sanskrit, Hindi and regional languages. Urdu, the offspring of Persian and Hindi, received due attention from him although its use was confined to the common people during his days.

❑ ❑

15

NURUDDIN JAHANGIR (1605-1627)

SECTION 1: ACCESSION AND EARLY DIFFICULTIES

Prince Salim, the son and successor of Akbar, ascended the throne with the title of Nuruddin Muhammad Jahangir Padshah Ghazi. He was born of the first Rajput wife of Akbar, the daughter of Raja Bihari Mal of Amber, on August 30, 1569, and thus carried fifty percent of the Hindu blood in his veins. As referred to earlier, he was named after Sheikh Salim Chishti, and was known as 'a child of many prayers'; Akbar affectionately used to call him as 'Sheikhu Baba'. Salim's two younger half-brothers, Murad and Daniyal, had predeceased their father although Jahangir's accession did not go unchallenged.

Jahangir was well-educated in Persian, Turki, Arabic and Hindi languages. As a student, he had taken scholarly interest in the study of various subjects like arithmetic, history, geography and general sciences. He was fond of music, painting and fine arts, and was a poet of sorts, who composed verses in Persian and sang Hindi lyrics in the true spirit of a lovelorn young man. The story of romantic love-affair between Prince Salim and Anarkali, as preserved in the fictional literature even today, whether true or false, can be traced back to the actual traits of Jahangir's character and lifestyle. Before his accession to the throne, Prince Salim took keen interest in horse-riding, hunting and swordsmanship; and rose to be 'a fine warrior who could handle all weapons of offence and defense affectively'. He was actively associated with the civil and military affairs of the state and was loved by his soldiers. Very often, the Prince was sent on military expeditions under the care of the state's most accomplished and reputed generals. Abdur Rahim *Khan i Khana*, a renowned soldier-scholar of the day, was one of his tutors. Salim was conferred the *mansabdari* of Ten Thousand

(*Dah-Hazari*), the highest military rank of the empire after that of the emperor, and was adorned with royal insignia, flags and drums. Salim held independent charge of a regiment in the Kabul campaign of 1581 when he was hardly twelve years old. His *mansab* was raised to Twelve Thousand in 1585 at the time of his betrothal to his cousin Man Bai, daughter of Raja Bhagwan Dass of Amber; and their marriage took place on February 13, 1585 amidst great celebrations. Later on, he married quite a few accomplished princesses belonging to the reputed Muslim and Rajput families.

Jahangir's erratic conduct as prince and the circumstances leading to the illness and death of Akbar, as detailed in the preceding chapter, need no repetition. Here suffice it to say that Salim was formally nominated heir-apparent to the throne and assumed the reins of government on behalf of his ailing father on October 21, 1605; Akbar expired four days later. After observing state mourning for a week, Salim ascended the throne in the fort of Agra on November 3, 1605. Jahangir's coronation is said to have been celebrated in the most unusual way. It included 'no anointing, no oath and no sermon'; instead, 'he put the crown on his head with his own hands, read the *khutba* and singalised his accession by the issue of new coins and grant of general amnesty to the prisoners'.

Twelve Ordinances of Jahangir

Jahangir issued Twelve Ordinances to mark his coronation. The issue of some of these ordinances was a necessity while the others were formally proclaimed to declare his aims and objects as the new monarch. They were in the form of public regrets for his past irresponsible conduct as a prince and expressed his resolve to follow in the footprints of his father to govern the country for the happiness and welfare of his subjects. All the nobles and government officials, big or small, were confirmed in the positions, privileges and the posts held by them. Jahangir 'pledged his faith in the liberal and benevolent state policy' of Akbar and offered to make amends for his past acts of omission and commission. His biographer, Beni Prasad has to say that Jahangir did not suffer from the evil of religious bigotry, and being 'endowed with plenty of that most uncommon commodity, called common sense, he was admirably qualified to work the liberal polity bequeathed by his father. His doings during the last five years had aroused serious misgivings, but responsibility restored his sobriety and equillibrium.' (*History of Jahangir*, OUP, 1922, p.129). Jahangir abolished some unpleasant taxes on trade and commerce, and curtailed the powers of government officials to overcharge the goods or seek gratification from the traders. He prohibited the manufacture and sale of wine and intoxicating drugs and, following in the footsteps of his father, banned the slaughter of animals on many days in the year, including two days in every week; these were, Sunday—the day of Akbar's birth, and Thursday—the day of his own coronation. He held out the promise to continue the public welfare activities, initiated by his predecessor; these included among others, the construction of *caravan sarais, masjids,* and wells for drinking water along the highways, and civil hospitals for the treatment of men as well as the beasts in big towns. The public charities were to be extended. Jahangir pledged to abolish the inhuman corporal punishments, like the cutting of nose and ears of the culprits throughout the Mughal dominions, and ordered the government officials 'not to confiscate the property of the deceased if his heirs and successors could be traced out; otherwise, his property should be acquired and utilized for the construction of public buildings'. Jahangir lost no time in acquiring firm hold over the entire state machinery and restored confidence among the people about his capability 'to govern the country in the likeness of his father'. In order to establish his reputation as the 'Just Monarch', Jahangir ordered the preparation of a *Zanjir-i-Adl*—'the chain of justice', made of pure gold, to hear public grievances against the corrupt and oppressive government officials. Jahangir gives the description of the chain and the method of its use in *Tuzuki Jahangiri* as follows:

> 'If those engaged in the administration of justice should delay or practice hypocrisy in the matter of those seeking justice, the oppressed might come to this chain and shake it so that its noise might attract attention. Its fashion was this: I ordered them to make a chain of pure gold, 30 *gaz* in length and containing 60 bells. Its weight was four Indian *maunds,* equivalent to 42 Iraqi *maunds.* One end of it they made fast to the battlements of the Shah Burj of the fort at Agra and the other to a stone post fixed on the bank of the River (Yamuna)". (Trs. by Rogers & Beveridge, i, p.7).

Revolt of Prince Khusrau (April-May 1606)

As narrated in the previous chapter, a conspiracy was hatched by some of the Mughal nobles in favour of Prince Khusrau to disinherit his father, Prince Salim, on the eve of Akbar's death. It proved abortive and Jahangir forgave all of his political opponents, including his estranged son and his kinsmen. Having been brought up and educated at Agra under the personal care of his grandfather Akbar, Khusrau was very popular with the imperial nobles and citizens of the metropolis. With the active support of his maternal uncle, Raja Man Singh, and father-in-law, Mirza Aziz Koka, 'he had become a serious candidate for succession to the throne and had posed a real threat to the very existence of his own father, now the Emperor Jahangir'. Therefore, Beni Prasad is correct in his estimation that 'Khusrau had but narrowly missed the goal.'(*Jahangir*,op.cit., i, p. 38).

Jahangir had forgiven Prince Khusrau for his past misconduct and reserved separate apartments for his family at Agra. Nevertheless, the bond of filial love and attachment between the father and the son had been cut off and they distrusted each other. Accordingly, Khusrau was allowed to attend the imperial court but he was not conferred any rank or *mansab* befitting a crown prince. The erstwhile rebel remained 'a suspect in the eyes of his father, and was treated as nonentity in the state affairs'. None of Khasrau's personal friends or associates ever received any recognition or consideration from the Emperor, and 'they were treated as conspirators and intriguers by the members and guards of the royal household'. Obviously, it was Jahangir who was to blame for this indifferent and humiliating treatment meted out to Prince Khusrau and his youthful friends most of whom belonged to highly respectable and influential Mughal families. Their kinsmen and well-wishers vouchsafed for their loyalty to the crown and pleaded for better treatment towards them but the emperor smelt a rat, and Khusrau was placed under house-arrest within the royal apartments in the fort. It unnerved Khusrau, who became restless by 'the dark prospect of lifelong detention' and, 'in desperation, sought liberation from his father's confinement'.

On the evening of April 6, 1606, Khusrau sought permission to leave the Fort of Agra along with about 350 personal guards and associates on horsebacks, 'on the pretext of visiting the mausoleum of Akbar at Sikandra'. At Mathura, he was joined by Husain Beg, a junior *mansabdar* and a personal friend of Khusrau, with 300 horsemen. It prompted him to take to flight towards Delhi with the hope of gaining support from his well-wishers. On the way, he laid his hands on the royal treasure of a hundred thousand rupees which was being escorted to Agra. The news about his escape from confinement spread like wild fire, and a large number of his well-wishers and sympathizers, including soldiers and peasants, joined his ranks which swelled to 12,000 by the time he reached the neighbourhood of Delhi. As the metropolis was heavily guarded by the royalists, Khusrau sneaked into the Punjab. Abdur Rahim, the *Diwan* of Lahore, was the only important Mughal officer who supported the cause of Khusrau, and joined his camp with a few thousand soldiers, but Dilawar Khan, the governor of Lahore, held out against the rebellious prince and foiled his attempts to take possession of the stronghold. Khusrau appointed him as his *wazir* and laid siege to the fort of Lahore but it was strongly defended by its governor Dilawar Khan.

On the receipt of intelligence, Jahangir's *Vakil,* Sharif Khan, 'sought permission to mount and give a hot chase' to the rebellious prince immediately. The Emperor permitted him to do so, but 'after a moment's thought, changed his mind. He summoned Sheikh Farid, the Mir Bakhshi, and commanded him to start off at once and to take with him the *mansabdars* and *ahadis* who were on guard. Aihtimam Khan, the *kotwal* of Agra, 'was made scout and intelligence officer'. (*Tuzuki Jahangiri,* pp. 51-54) He sent express messengers to all the provincial governors and feudatory chiefs of the north, east and west to apprehend the rebel and his supporters. All police posts, situated on the route to Bengal, were also alerted lest Khusrau might attempt to escape to the east and take shelter with his maternal uncle Raja Man Singh. Accordingly, 'the imperial guards, led by the Mir Bakhshi, gave a hot chase to the rebel. Jahangir put the Prime Minister in charge of the capital, and himself left Agra at the head of all the imperial troops which could be assembled by the day-break' of the 7th April.

Having failed to take the fort of Lahore, Khusrau lost his nerves and fled towards the interior of the Punjab. He was hotly pursued by the imperial troops. Khusrau fought a bloody battle with the royalists at Bhairowal but was defeated and fled from the battlefield with a handful of his followers. The fugitives were captured by the men in pursuit with the help of some village folk while they were trying to cross the River Chenab at the ferry of Sodharah. They were brought in chains to Lahore on the 1st of May, and produced before Jahangir in an open court. The success of the operation was attributed to Sheikh Farid, the Mir Bakhshi, who was honoured by the emperor with the title of Murtaza Khan. Khusrau was condemned to royal captivity as the state prisoner and 'barbarous punishments were inflicted' on his accomplices. According to *Tuzuk-i-Jahangiri,* Khusrau's right-hand men, Husain Beg and Abdur Rahim, were 'stitched in the fresh skins of an ox and ass respectively. Mounted on asses, with their faces to the tails, they were paraded through the streets of Lahore'. Husain Beg died of suffocation within twelve hours while Abdur Rahim, 'who was in the ass's skin, and to whom they gave some refreshment from outside', remained alive at the end of an ordeal of twelve hours; he was pardoned and 'restored to his old dignities' later on. A few days later, about two to three hundred of Khusrau's camp-followers were 'publicly hanged on the gibbets, which were put up on each side of a mile long road leading from the garden of Mirza Kamran to the city of Lahore'. To complete the tail of barbarity, Prince Khusrau 'in chains, was led on a filthy elephant through the gibbets to receive the homage of his followers.' (pp. 68-69). Whosoever had been directly or indirectly associated with Khusrau was traced out, and received 'cruel and inhuman treatment' from Jahangir. The execution of Guru Arjan Dev, the fifth Guru of the Sikhs, at Lahore on May 30, 1606, is directly related to the incident of Khusrau's rebellion.

The end of Prince Khusrau was very tragic. He remained in captivity within the fort of Agra for over 16 years under the personal supervision of the emperor. His mother Man Bai, the first wife of Jahangir and the daughter of Raja Bhagwan Dass of Amber, had already committed suicide because of the estranged relations between father and the son. In 1607, Khusrau was blinded on the orders of Jahangir as he was suspected of having developed intimacy with some royal guards and disaffected nobles through two eunuchs, Itibar Khan and Nuruddin. In 1616 he was put under the custody of Asaf Khan, the brother of Nur Jahan, who was then the Prime Minister of the empire. In 1620, Prince Khurram (future Shah Jahan), the younger half-brother of Khusrau, was entrusted the charge of the Deccan campaign; before proceeding to the South, 'he demanded that his elder brother Khusrau be put under his personal custody because he considered the latter to be his political rival'. Khusrau was taken by him to the Deccan and kept in captivity in the fort of Burhanpur; there he was treacherously put to death sometime in March 1622. Jahangir was shocked to hear of the news 'but assumed silence about the sordid affair for which he was himself partly to blame'. Such was the fate of the unfortunate Mughal prince – the eldest son and prospective successor of Jahangir as the future emperor of India.

Martyrdom of Guru Arjan Dev (May 30, 1606)

Guru Arjan Dev, the fifth Guru of the Sikhs, lived at Goindwal when the revolt of Prince Khusrau took place. He was summoned by Jahangir at Lahore on the ground that 'he had supported an enemy of the state'. It is said that Khusrau had visited the Guru's *dera* at Goindwal during his flight from Agra and Delhi to Lahore. It is surmised that Khusrau had already been familiar with the Sikh Gurus through Akbar. Perhaps, in his early boyhood, he might have visited the abode of the Gurus in the company of his grandfather. That is why 'he sought the blessings of the saint' in his hour of distress. According to the Sikh tradition, Guru Arjan received the prince just like his other devotees and admirers in the midst of a Sikh congregation. He applied a *tilak* mark with saffron on his forehead, and the Sikh *sangat* gave a sum of five thousand rupees to the prince by way of help. Accordingly, the Guru was dubbed by the Mughal emperor as an accomplice of the rebellious prince, and was asked to pay a fine of two *lakhs* of rupees for having supported a state criminal. The Guru denied the charge and expressed his inability to pay the fine on the ground that 'he was a recluse with no material possessions and that the property of the Sikh shrines belonged to his *Sangat* (the devotees)'. Jahangir, who had no soft corner for his own erratic son and his associates, was not the man to be appeased by the arguments of a recluse, especially the one who belonged to the community of the non-believers or *kafirs*. In fact, from the *Tuzuki Jahangiri* (R&B, i, pp. 72-73), we find that Jahangir was well aware of the peaceful missionary activities of Guru Arjun Dev and his Sikh followers, but unlike his father, Akbar the Great, he did possess some element of religious bigotry in his character, which induced him to award death sentence to the Guru for his purported crime. Jahangir writes in his memoirs as under:

> 'In Gobindwal, which is on the river Biyah (Beas), there was a Hindu named Arjun, in the garments of sainthood and sanctity, so much so that he had captured many of the simple-hearted of the Hindus, and even of the ignorant and foolish followers of Islam, by his ways and manners, and they had loudly sounded the drum of his holiness. They called him Guru, and from all sides stupid people crowded to worship and manifest complete faith in him. For three or four generations (of spiritual successors) they had kept this shop warm. Many times it occurred to me to put a stop to this vain affair or to bring him into the assembly of the people of Islam'. (*ibid.*, p.72).

Obviously, the Sikh Guru was condemned to death not because of any heinous crime committed by him but for other reasons which were recorded by Jahangir without mincing the words. The Guru's execution, which took place at Lahore on May 30, 1606, was accompanied by barbarous torture. Thus, 'unmindful of the exalted position held by Guru Arjan as a divine with a huge following of the devotees, and in spite of his innocence, Jahangir treated him like an ordinary criminal and meted out an inhuman treatment to him'. We are of the opinion that 'the martyrdom of Guru Arjan proved a turning point in the history of Sikhism which changed the entire character and course of development of a peaceful religious reform movement, launched by Guru Nanak when the foundations of the Mughal rule were being laid in India. It gave birth to the *new policy of miri and piri* under the spiritual guidance and leadership of Guru Hargobind, son and successor of Guru Arjan, according to which the Guru assumed the role of spiritual as well as temporal head of his followers. The peace-loving and non-violent disciples of Guru Nanak were constrained to take up to arms for their self-protection and, in the long-run, were transformed into soldier-saints. The execution of Guru Arjan estranged the relations between the Mughal government and the Sikhs and, ultimately, led to open confrontation, which proved one of the causes of the downfall of the Mughal rule in India". (Advanced Study, ii, p.384)

SECTION 2: 'THE EMPRESS NUR JAHAN': HER INFLUENCE ON THE MUGHAL POLITICS

In May 1611, the marriage of Jahangir with Nur Jahan, a widow of one of his subordinate military officials, and the latter's meteoric rise to power forms one of the most fascinating and romantic chapters of the Mughal history. She was born of the Persian parents. She was the daughter of Ghiyas Beg of Teheran; whose father, Khwaja Muhammad Sharif, had held a ministerial post during the reign of Shah Tahmasp Safawai. After the death of his father in 1577, Ghiyas Beg 'fell on evil days and decided to migrate to India in search of livelihood'. He came to India with family in the caravan of a wealthy merchant, named Malik Masud. On their way to India, Ghiyas Beg's wife, Asmat Begam, gave birth to a girl at Kandahar, who was named Mehr-un-nisa, the future Nur Jahan. Ghiyas Beg was introduced to Akbar by Malik Masud at Fatehpur Sikri, and he was immediately taken into service. Ghiyas Beg became known as Mirza although he did not belong to the house of the Timurids. He rose to be the *diwan* (superintendent) of the royal household by dint of his personal merit and 'virtuous character'.

By virtue of her father's employment, Mehrunnisa was brought up in an aristocratic environment of the Mughal ruling elite at Agra. She grew to be a model of the pearless Persian beauty with sophisticated tastes, and was married, at the age of 17, to a handsome Persian military officer of junior rank, named Ali Quli Astajlu. The latter was put on the personal staff of Prince Salim in 1598-99. Ali Quli received the title of Sher Afghan from Salim for having killed a lion (*sher*) single-handed.

It is said that Sher Afghan did not take sides in Salim's conflict with his father, Akbar. But it was no disqualification, and we find the prince, now the emperor Jahangir, promoting Sher Afghan as the *faujdar* of Burdwan when Raja Man Singh was confirmed in the governorship of Bengal. It was the unexpected revolt of Prince Khusrau, which aroused the feelings of suspicion and doubt in the heart of Jahangir against those officers who had not stood by him during his confrontation with his father; and Sher Afghan's name was included in the list of such suspects. After suppressing the revolt of Khusrau, Jahangir recalled Raja Man Singh from Bengal in August 1606, and his place was taken by Qutubbuddin Khan as the new governor of Bengal. It was during his official tour to Burdwan, when Qutubbuddin called for Sher Afghan in his camp for cross-examination. In the arguments that followed, Sher Afghan lost temper and murdered the governor, while he himself was put to death by the governor's men; this tragedy took place on April 9, 1607. Jahangir was shocked at the murder of Qutubbuddin, a competent and trustworthy Mughal officer, but he could do nothing about it. Of course, he heaps curses on Sher Afghan in his *memoirs*, and feels a sense of relief to note that 'the black-faced scoundrel' had been 'sent to hell'. (*Tuzuk-i-Jahangiri*; R&B, i, pp.114-15).

Nevertheless, there was nothing unusual about the fact that Mehrunnisa, the widow of Sher Afghan, along with her infant daughter, Ladli Begam, was brought or came to reside at Agra where her father Ghiyas Beg was employed. As a normal practice, and by way of an official relief and compensation to the bereaved family of a Mughal official, Mehrunnisa was put in attendance upon the Queen Dowager, Salima Begam, who had brought about reconciliation between Prince Salim and his father. Jahangir saw Mehrunnisa at the Nauroz festival in March 1611. He fell for her at the first sight and married her in May 1611. About that time, Jahangir was 42 years old and a much married man while his consort was thirty-four. In our opinion, 'the interesting story of Jahangir's love-affair with Mehrunnisa and Akbar's obstruction in the way of their marriage constitutes but a part of colourful legends and myths which have been woven round the otherwise romantic personalities of the royal couple. The arguments advanced forward by Ishwari Prasad and A. L. Srivastva in support of the legend are too far-fetched and abstract to be taken as correct. No contemporary Persian source mentions that Prince Salim had ever seen or expressed the desire to marry Mehrunnisa. A shrewd judge of human character like Akbar, having once refused the hand of a beautiful damsel in marriage to his sex-hungry son, could never commit the mistake of putting Ali Quli on the staff of his wife's paramour. Vice versa, knowing fully the character and habits of Salim- a drunkard and sensual prince royal, slave of his passions and pleasures, extremely aggressive and arrogant in his conduct towards the highest officers of the state, and, above all, an over-ambitious and impatient person who could dare to raise the standard of revolt against an all-powerful and renowned monarch like Akbar, it cannot be satisfactorily explained how and why did he spare the life of Ali Quli when the latter was under his own thumb for quite some time. The man who could secure the murder of the Prime Minister Abul Fazl could easily have liquidated Ali Quli without taking an iota of blame on his own shoulders; Salim had the guts to remove and destroy the stumbling block between him and his lady love, if there was any. The Emperor Jahangir who could exercise the indiscretion of charging Guru Arjan with high treason, unmindful of its effect on the majority of his subjects, was definitely ill-disposed towards Sher Afghan who had deserted him in his hour of confrontation with Akbar. The death of Sher Afghan was, however, purely accidental for which the deceased himself was to blame'. (Advanced Study, ii, pp.390 91)

Motamad Khan gives a simple and the most trustworthy account of Mehrunnisa's marriage with Jahangir in the words that follow:

> 'The officials of Bengal, in obedience to royal command, sent to the court the daughter of Ghiyas Beg, who had been exalted to the title of Itimadud Daulah, and the king entrusted her to the keeping of his own royal mother. There she remained for some time without notice. Since, however, Fate had decreed that she should be the Queen of the world and Princess of the Times, it happened that on the celebration of New Year's Day in the sixth year of the Emperor's reign (March 1611) her appearance caught the emperor's far-seeing eye, and so captivated him that he included her among the inmates of his select *harem*'. (*Iqbalnama-i-Jahangiri*; E&D. vi, pp. 403-4).

Thus marriage between Jahangir and Mehrunnisa was a non-event but, for all that followed thereafter, full credit must be given to the meritorious character of the beautiful Persian lady and her good fortune. Nur Jahan 'won the heart of Jahangir by her feminine charms, personal devotion, and intelligence', and quickly rose into prominence. In spite of her advanced age, she had retained the freshness and vigour of a youthful lady. 'No gift of nature seemd to be wanting to her. Beautiful with the rich beauty of Persia, her soft features were lighted up with a sprightly vivacity and superb loveliness. Nature had endowed her with a quick understanding, a piercing intellect, a versatile temper, and sound common sense. Education had developed the gifts of nature in no common degree. She had a fine aesthetic taste and possessed, in a high measure, those graces and accomplishments which are supposed to be the glory of her sex.' (Beni Prasad, *Jahangir*, p.184) A Scholar of Persian, she composed verses which she recited in her own melodious voice to the great joy of the emperor. On the death of the Queen Dowager in 1613, she became the *Padishah Begam*—'First lady of the Realm', and mistress of the imperial household; originally styled as Nur Mahal, the title of Nur Jahan was conferred on her by Jahangir in March 1616.

Nur Jahan as Power behind the Throne

It is held by the chroniclers that Jahangir attained maturity of character as responsible family man and householder only after his marriage with Nur Jahan. It was she who 'fully satiated his intense hunger for life' and all the princely pleasures; and, as a result of Nur Jahan's magical charm, he was gradually drawn away from all the other wives and concubines, 'until he belonged exclusively to her and to none else'. It was, in fact, a great personal achievement of Nur Jahan 'to have tamed the beast in Jahangir'. As highly intelligent and shrewd lady, with a political bent of mind; she started taking interest in the state politics, and Jahangir willingly made her a partner in running the government. Very often, she would sit in the balcony of her palace along with Jahangir, while the nobles would present themselves, and listen to her dictates. Coin was struck in her name and the *firmans* were countersigned by Nur Jahan, the Queen Begam, along with the imperial seal and signatures of Jahangir.

Accordingly, Jahangir's period of rule from 1611 to 1627 was marked by the ascendancy of Nur Jahan in state affairs. She became a power behind the throne. She began to participate actively in state affairs, and worked very hard in mastering the details of administration. She was actively supported and assisted in the discharge of administrative functions by her kinsmen who received rapid promotions to the highest offices of the state. According to Beni Prasad, her Persian mother, Asmat Begam, was an intelligent and shrewd lady, who 'exercised a steadying influence on her imperious, restless daughter and contributed not a little to her greatness'. (*Jahangir, pp.187-88*).

Nur Jahan's father, Mirza Ghiyas Beg, had received the title of Itimadud Daulah with a *mansab* of 2,000 *zat* and 500 *swar* from Jahangir; and his rise to power after Nur Jahan's marriage with Jahangir was very rapid. In 1615, he was bestowed 'the standard and drum', originally reserved for princes of the royal blood, and made a *mansabdar* of six thousands. The very next year, Itimadud Daulah was promoted to the exalted *mansab* of seven thousands, the highest honour bestowed on any *grandee* of the empire after the princes. Similarly, Nur Jahan's brother Abul Hasan was appointed *mir i saman-* 'master of the royal household', with a cabinet rank, in 1611. Originally, he was granted the title of Itiqad Khan, but three years later, he was honoured with the title of Asaf Khan and the personal *mansab* of three thousands, which was raised to six thousands when he was promoted the Prime Minister of the Empire. Nur Jahan's two younger brothers were military generals, one of whom (Ibrahim Khan) became the governor of Bihar in 1615. Prince Khurram, the third son of Jahangir, was married in April 1612 to Arjamand Banu Begam, daughter of Asaf Khan; since then the Prince became a favourite of Nur Jahan and rapidly rose into prominence at the imperial court as the prospective successor of Jahangir. The Queen and her kinsmen, as mentioned above, now including Prince Khurram, comprised the 'Nur Jahan Junta' so-called, which usurped almost all the powers of the state. Not only this; many other Persian immigrants of Nur Jahan's clan, including her friends, favourites and acquaintances, were absorbed in the imperial services and they were always at the beck and call of the Queen. Francisco Pelsaert, an eye-witness to the proceedings of the imperial Mughal court under Jahangir records that

> 'Nur Jahan's former and present supporters have been well rewarded, so that now most of the men, who are near the King, owe their promotion to her and are consequently under such obligations to her that he (Jahangir) is King in name only, while she and her brother Asaf Khan hold the kingdom firmly in their hands'. (*Jahangir's India- The Remonstrantie of Francisco Pelsaert*; p.50).

Thus it was that Nur Jahan's influence over Jahangir and the state politics increased to that extent that the emperor became 'servile to her will and wishes'. He 'leaned more and more to ease and sloth' and left the administration of the state exclusively in the hands of Nur Jahan. To the good fortune of the Mughal subjects, Nur Jahan governed the country with competence with the support of the 'Nur Jahan Junta'. 'She developed a real taste for power and having acquired the power; she stuck to it till the death of Jahangir'. According to Motamad Khan, Jahangir expressed his satisfaction with the oft-repeated remarks: 'I have bestowed sovereignty on Nur Jahan Begam. So long as she holds the reins of government in her hands, I require nothing beyond a *seer* of wine and half a *seer* of meat to make merry'. *Iqbalnama-i-Jahangiri*; E&D. vi, p. 405.

By the year1622, Jahangir was physically incapacitated because of excessive indulgence in intoxicants and Nur Jahan's father and mother, 'who used to exercise sobering influence over their daughter, were no more'. Besides, Nur Jahan's relation with her brother Asaf Khan—the Prime Minister, and his son-in-law, Prince Khurram (future Shah Jahan) were also strained. It was because her daughter Ladli Begam (from Sher Afghan) was married to Shahryar, the youngest son of Jahangir from a concubine, in April 1621. Thereafter, she set up Shahryar as a political rival against Prince Khurram for accession to the throne. Thus the Queen and her *Junta*, which once wielded sovereign powers on behalf of the Emperor, was itself put in disarray. The Queen and the Prime Minister did not see eye to eye with each other, and so also was the case with the two princes, Khurram and Shahryar. Of course, in her dealings with Asaf Khan, Nur Jahan still had an upper hand because she was better placed to secure the royal consent to her manipulations.

Nur Jahan's influence on Jahangir and her emergence as a power behind the throne proved beneficial for the Mughal Empire for a while although, in the long run, it proved counter-productive. She did exercise a very healthy influence on the personal life of Jahangir. With 'devotional attachment to the emperor, she put a damper on his violent temper and uncontrolled emotions. She improved his moral character and changed his outlook towards life'. Nur Jahan was a highly cultured and educated Persian lady; she had 'very refined tastes and an inventive brain'. According to an opinion, in her capacity as the first lady of the empire, she 'set the standards in socio-cultural values for the aristocracy of her times'. She became a model in the world of fashion; 'she revolutionized male and female dresses, and brought about innovations in the design of gold and silver ornaments, household furnishings and decorations and what not. Under her supervision, the imperial court as well as the royal household was changed in architectural designs and decorative set-up beyond all recognition. She enhanced the beauty of the court, prescribed elegant dresses for the courtiers, and added to the grandeur and magnificence of the *darbar*, while at the same time affecting economy in the expenditure which was previously incurred on its maintenance. The innovations introduced by her in the organisation of the *darbar* and conduct of its proceedings elicited praise from all quarters. The world of fashions owes the invention of the *otto* of the roses either to Nur Jahan or her illustrious mother. From aristocratic and aesthetic points of view, Nur Jahan imported a fairy's touch to the court in much less extravagant ways than before, and transformed the awe-inspiring men-in-arms into impressive personalities of the most elegant yet invincible warriors of a dream-land'. (Advanced Study, ii, pp. 396-97)

Nur Jahan was a capable ruler. She improved upon the method and style of working of the Mughal administration. The partial vacuum created by the lack of interest in state affairs by Jahangir was fairly made good by her active participation in the work of administration with the able guidance and support of her parents and brother Asaf Khan. Nur Jahan was a soft-spoken and kind-hearted lady. She was very generous in the distribution of royal charities. She ordered the construction of *masjids, sarais* and charity houses; she created religious endowments and granted liberal stipends and allowances to outstanding scholars, artists and saints. But her excessive interference in state affairs produced bad results, particularly, towards the concluding years of Jahangir's reign. At first, she aroused the ambitions of Prince Khurram by grooming him as the crown prince, but, later on, made him a rebel by withholding the support to him. Shahryar, the son of a concubine of Jahangir, was no match as the political rival to Prince Khurram which led to the emergence of hostile factions at the imperial court. Nur Jahan was to blame for the loss of Kandahar at the hands of Persia in 1622; and she was responsible for the unpleasant and dangerous revolts of Khurram and Mahabat Khan. Jahangir suffered humiliation at the hands of Mahabat Khan simply because of Nur Jahan's outrageous proceedings against the most influential and trustworthy general of the empire. It goes to the credit of Nur Jahan, however, that Jahangir, ultimately, secured his liberation from the clutches of Mahabat Khan by the Queen's presence of mind and strategy.

SECTION 4: IMPORTANT EVENTS OF JAHANGIR'S REIGN

Revolt in Bengal (1612 A.D.)

Ever since the recall of Raja Man Singh from Bengal, in August 1606, the eastern frontier of the empire was suffering from law and order problems. As ever before, Bihar and Bengal were the trouble-spots of disaffected Afghan nobles. Jahangir Quli Khan, who succeeded Qutubbuddin as the Mughal governor of Bengal, was incapable and too old to suppress the refractory Afghan *Zamindars*; he died in harness within a year of his appointment. Islam Khan, the next Mughal governor, was a capable military general and administrator who shifted his headquarters from Rajmahal to Dacca. Nevertheless, in 1611-12, Bengal faced the general uprising of the Afghan insurgents under the leadership of Usman Khan. Referred to as 'the last of the Afghans', Usman Khan was defeated and killed during his attack on Dacca in March 1612. Thereafter, Jahangir, on the advice of Nur Jahan, adopted a very sympathetic attitude towards the vanquished Afghan nobles of Bengal; and most of them were absorbed in the imperial services to secure their loyalty to the Mughal regime.

Jahangir and the Rajputs

Jahangir scrupulously followed the Rajput policy of his father, Akbar the Great. Born of a Rajput princess, he had half of the Hindu blood in his veins, and was very liberal and broadminded in his religious outlook. He adopted and continued the secular state policy in running the state administration on the lines of his predecessor; it has been estimated that 'all the fundamentals of the Mughal policy, evolved laboriously by Akbar, bore their pleasant fruits during the reigns of Jahangir and Shah Jahan'. Jahangir's uncomplimentary remarks, in his *memoirs*, about Guru Arjan Dev, which display his attitude of religious intolerance, are interpreted by historians as 'an exceptional outburst of an angry despot whose very existence had been endangered by the revolt of his own son'. Jahangir never displayed the sentiments of religious intolerance thereafter. He granted complete religious freedom to his subjects and never attempted to impose *Jaziya* or socio-religious restrictions on the non-Muslims. The temporary estrangement of his relations with Raja Man Singh on the Khurram episode did not have any adverse effect on the attitude or policy of Jahangir towards the Hindus, in general, or the Rajputs, in particular. Raja Man Singh was kept away from the imperial court but he did not suffer any loss of his official status, position or the fortunes. He expired in June 1614 while on active duty in the Deccan. Just like his father, Jahangir had also married a number of Rajput princesses, and he maintained very cordial relationship with the Rajput ruling houses. Prince Khurram, the successor of Jahangir, was, in turn, born of a Rajput princess, an accomplished daughter of Raja Udai Singh of Jodhpur (Marwar), who had a very strong lobby of the Rajput nobles and military generals at the court. Jahangir's court was thus adorned by generals, scholars and artists of all communities and the civil and military services were wide open for the Hindus on merit.

Confrontation with Mewar (1606-15)

The First Phase of the Struggle: Mewar was 'in a state of war' with Delhi when Jahangir ascended the throne. In the concluding years of Akbar's reign, Jahangir had defied the imperial command to lead an expedition to Mewar. To atone for this lapse, he, immediately after his accession to the throne, ordered a military expedition to Mewar under the charge of Prince Parvez, his second son. It was directed against Rana Amar Singh, who had become the leader of the Sisodia Rajputs of Mewar after the death of his father, Maharana Pratap, in 1597. The Mughal forces were accompanied by Sagar, an uncle of Rana Amar Singh, who had deserted his people and was living at the Mughal court as a pensioner. A bloody but indecisive battle was fought between the Rana and the Mughal troops at the Pass of Dewar. The Mughals declared Sagar as their protégé as the Rana of Mewar at Chittor with the intention of creating dissensions between the Rajputs but the people refused to acknowledge the traitor as their Rana and Sagar had to vacate Chittor in disgrace soon thereafter. The Mughal armies were recalled by Jahangir from the Mewar front on the sudden outbreak of Khusrau's revolt. It marked the end of the first phase of struggle between Mewar and the Mughals during the reign of Jahangir.

Perpetual War against Mewar (1608-15): After the settlement of Khusrau affair, Jahangir directed his attention once again to the problem of Mewar. He was fully determined to conquer Mewar by all means, fair or foul. Therefore, from 1608 to 1615, he sent as many as four military expeditions for its conquest. In 1608 Mahabat Khan led the Mughal army of invasion into Mewar. He overran all the plains of Mewar but the Sisodia Rajputs, under the leadership of Rana Amar Singh, held out against the Mughals in the hilly tracts and the forested valleys. Mahabat Khan was recalled to the court after a year of his futile struggle to bring the Rana to the knees. In 1609, Abdullah Khan carried fire and sword into Mewar but failed to bring the Rana to book. Likewise, in 1611, Mirza Aziz Koka and Prince Khurram were directed to lead the imperial troops against Mewar but they did not see eye to eye with each other, and their mutual wrangles led to the failure of their expedition.

The repeated failure of the military expeditions against Mewar made Jahangir desperate. In 1613, he declared a perpetual war on Mewar under his personal command. He took charge of the imperial forces, and shifted his headquarters at Ajmer to direct the operations against Mewar. Thereafter, 'the entire might' of the imperial armed forces was directed against Mewar. On the advice of Nur Jahan and Asaf Khan, Prince Khurram was credited with the exclusive command of the army of invasion. The Prince adopted 'a scorch-earth policy' in Mewar. According to this policy, the Mughal forces 'ravaged the towns, razed the villages to the ground and destroyed the standing crops, and the territories, infested and defended by the Rajputs, were put under a state of blockade. All supplies from outside to those areas were stopped; so much so that even the water channels, which fed that region, were chocked and diverted'.

Treaty of Peace with Mewar (1615): To the great misfortune of the people, Mewar was caught in famine and epidemic about this time. As a consequence, the people living in the plains of Mewar were uprooted and threatened with total annihilation. The hot war between the tiny state of Mewar and the mighty Mughal Empire was not only unequal but also 'undesirable' because, if protracted beyond limits, it was likely to adversely affect the respectability and credibility of the Mughal state among its non-Muslim subjects. Hard-pressed, Rana Amar Singh and his camp-followers also realised the futility of dragging on the struggle which had already 'destroyed the whole state and heaped untold miseries on its people'. Therefore, in 1615, the Rana sent his maternal uncle, Shubh Karan, to make a settlement with the Mughals on honourable terms. Prince Khurram and Jahangir were both overjoyed to see a turn in the tide; and, on the recommendations of the Prince, Jahangir 'ratified a treaty of peace with Mewar on the most liberal terms ever granted to any Rajput vassal state by the Mughals'. According to the terms of the treaty,

(i) Rana Amar Singh recognised Jahangir as his suzerain.

(ii) The Mughals restored to the Rana all the territories of Mewar, including Chittor, which had ever been annexed by them since the beginning of the conflict with Mewar under Akbar.

(iii) No limit was imposed on the armed forces to be kept by the Rana but, as a point of prestige for the Mughal Empire, it was agreed by the Rana that the fort of Chittor would not be repaired or fortified so that it might not be used as a place of resistance against the imperial Mughal government in future.

(iv) Rana Amar Singh was not obliged to attend the imperial court or join the imperial service nor was he required to enter into a matrimonial alliance with the Mughal ruling house.

Jahangir mentions in his *memoirs* that, when Rana Amar Singh paid a visit to Prince Khurram in his military camp somewhere in Mewar, the Mughal prince 'behaved to him with perfect kindness.' He writes: "When the Rana clasped his feet (viz., paid a soldier's salute; not a *sijda* or *zaminbas*) and asked forgiveness for his faults, he (the Prince) took his head and placed it on his breast, and consoled him in such a manner as to comfort him. He (the Prince) presented him with a superb dress of honour, a jewelled sword, a horse with a jewelled saddle, and a private elephant with silver housings, and as there were not more than one hundred men with him (the Rana) who were worthy of complete robes of honour (*saropa*), he gave one hundred *saropas*, fifty horses and twelve jewelled *khapwas* (daggers)." (*Tuzuk-i-Jahangiri* R&B, i, p. 276).

There was prevalent a custom among the Rajputs that 'the son who is the heir-apparent should not go with his father to pay respects to a king or prince.' The Rana observed this custom, and did not bring with him Karan, his son, who had received the *tika*'. Therefore, prince Karan came to pay homage to prince Khurram after some time, and was received with equal warmth. He accompanied Khurram to pay personal respects to the emperor Jahangir who was stationed at Ajmer. The affectionate treatment meted out to Karan, the crown prince of Mewar, by Jahangir exhibited not only a great stroke of diplomacy and statesmanship but also his honest and sincere desire like that of Akbar to win over the love and cooperation of his Hindu subjects in general, and the Rajputs in particular.

The Treaty of Peace with Mewar (1615 A.D.) was a great landmark in the history of the Mughal rule in India. It marked the success of Akbar's policy of political unification of India and the set up of a nation-state in the country on secular lines. The Rajput policy of Jahangir was thus crowned with success. Jahangir and his son prince Khurram, later the emperor Shah Jahan, had correctly imbibed the national policy of their great ancestor Akbar, and they pursued it in the right spirit. It was Aurangzeb who reversed the liberal and secular policy of his ancestors which led to wide-spread revolts by the subordinate Hindu chieftains in their bid to break away from the Mughal Empire.

Jahangir and the Deccan

Like Akbar, Jahangir also aspired to conquer the whole of south India so as to complete the political unification of the country. His Deccan policy was, therefore, a continuation of Akbar's policy which prompted him to wage wars of aggression against all the regional states of the south. Akbar had established his sway over a part of the Ahmadnagar kingdom, including its headquarters, but the major part of the state remained under the control of the Nizamshahi ruler. After the fall of Ahmadnagar in 1601, one of the Nizamshahi generals, Malik Ambar, had put up a scion of the ruling family as the sultan of Ahmadnagar with the title of Murtaza II Nizam Shah and acted as his Prime Minister and Regent with his new capital at Khirki (Khadki). During the reign of Jahangir, he declared war upon the Mughals, and, within a few years, wrested all of the territories, including the historic fort of Ahmadnagar, from their hands. It gave a serious set-back to the Mughal prestige in the south. In 1608, Jahangir ordered Abdul Rahim *Khan i Khana* to take up arms against Ahmadnagar but he failed to accomplish anything in the face of tough resistance put up by Malik Ambar. In 1610, prince Parvez was appointed viceroy of the Deccan and asked to launch a fresh attack on Ahmadnagar but to no avail. A number of other Mughal generals, including *Khan i Jahan* Lodhi and Abdulla Khan, were sent to the south to deal with the situation. In 1611-12, the Mughal forces launched a three-pronged attack on Ahmadnagar but had to eat a humble pie at the hands of Malik Ambar. As a result, Malik Ambar emerged as the champion of struggle for the liberation of the Deccan from the imperial Mughal yoke.

Malik Ambar was an erstwhile Abyssinian slave of a Muslim military officer of Ahmadnagar, named Changez Khan. 'A true Deccani by adoption', he rose to be a brilliant administrator and courtier of the Nizamshahi ruler. He liberated the territories of Ahmadnagar state from the clutches of the Mughals, introduced extensive administrative reforms, and won the hearts of his people by his public-welfare activities.

He strengthened the army of Ahmadnagar by the extensive recruitment of Marathas as guerilla fighters. Malik Ambar is rightly said to be the forerunner of Shivaji in the matter of introducing guerilla warfare, called *bargi-giri*, in south India. He became a formidable foe of the Mughals on the south Indian front.

It was the success of Mughal arms in Mewar which encouraged Jahangir to assume aggressive posture on the southern front. Accordingly, following in the foot-steps of Akbar, he shifted his court to Burhanpur in 1616 and placed prince Khurram in charge of the army of invasion. Extensive arrangements were made by the Mughals to overrun Ahmadnagar like a steam-roller. Prince Khurram exhibited a great diplomatic skill in opening negotiations with Malik Ambar from a position of strength. It un-nerved Malik Ambar, who, for his survival, sued for peace in 1617 which was granted on very liberal terms. The sultan of Ahmadnagar paid personal homage to prince Khurram and presented a sum of sixteen lakhs of rupees as tribute. According to the Treaty of Peace, the Nizamshahi ruler acknowledged the suzerainty of Delhi and ceded the territories of Balaghat along with the fort of Ahmadnagar to the Mughal emperor. It marked yet another great achievement of prince Khurram, who was honoured by the emperor with the 'high sounding title' of Shah Jahan and the grant of 'the unprecedented' *mansab* of 30,000 *zat* and *swar*.

Nevertheless, the power of Malik Ambar could not be crippled. In his wisdom, he warded off the Mughal threat for the time being while continuing to build his strength to challenge them at an appropriate occasion. Within a few years, he defied the Mughal authority once again, and reconquered the territories of Balaghat. In 1620, he laid siege to the fort of Ahmadnagar with the assistance of contingents from Bijapur and Golconda. Prince Khurram, now styled Shah Jahan, was asked to resume the command of the Deccan campaign for the second time but, before the arrival of the Mughal troops, Malik Ambar raised the siege of Ahmadnagar.

At Burhanpur, Shah Jahan came to know that Nur Jahan was conspiring to put up her son-in-law, Shahryar, in the role of his rival for nomination as heir-apparent to the throne. It made the Mughal prince apprehensive of his own future and he hurriedly concluded peace with Malik Ambar and his allies on easy terms. The sultans of Ahmadnagar, Bijapur and Golconda accepted the nominal suzerainty of the Mughal crown, and paid sums of twelve, eighteen, and twenty lakhs of rupees respectively as tribute. Thereafter, Shah Jahan put to death his elder brother Prince Khusrau, then held in his captivity, and himself left for the north with most of the imperial troops under his command. Taking advantage of the subsequent revolt of Shah Jahan, Malik Ambar once again consolidated his position and took up arms against the Mughal armies of occupation in Ahmadnagar state. He continued the resistance till his death in 1626 in the eightieth year of his life. He 'was remembered long by his friends and foes alike as a man of action who served his state and its people with utmost devotion'.

Subjugation of Kangra (1620 A.D.)

Akbar had made two abortive attempts to conquer the fort of Kangra which guarded the town of Nagarkot and the sacred temple of the Hindus at Jawalamukhi. The temple was desecrated and plundered by Mahmud of Ghazni in 1009 but the Hindu chiefs of Nagarkot successfully defied the sultans of Delhi and retained their independence for long. The existence of a sovereign Hindu state in the Kangra valley so close to the centre of Mughal power at Delhi wrankled in the eyes of Jahangir but he was considerably restrained in laying his hands on it. In 1615, Jahangir deputed Murtaza Khan, the Mughal governor of Lahore, to invest the fort but he failed to conquer it. In 1618, Prince Khurram was entrusted this task and he set up his camp at Lahore to direct the operations against Kangra with the assistance of some other Hindu chieftains of the hills. The Raja of Kangra after his submission on November 16, 1620 after 14 months of the Mughal siege of the stronghold.

Loss of Kandahar to the Persians (1622 A.D.)

Kandahar had been 'a bone of contention' between Persia and the Mughals throughout the medieval period. Akbar had recovered it from the Persian hands in 1595 through diplomatic skill, but the Persians were not reconciled to its loss. At the time of prince Khusrau's revolt, Shah Abbas of Persia made an abortive attempt to take over Kandahar but, having failed to do so, offered apologies. Thereafter, as many as four Persian missions visited Agra from 1607 to 1621 with rich presents to keep the Mughal emperor in good humour. Nevertheless, taking advantage of Jahangir's physical incapacitation and withdrawal from state affairs, Shah Abbas ordered a surprise attack on Kandahar in 1622 and took possession of the stronghold. By that time, Nur Jahan had begun to conspire against Prince Khurram, now styled Shah Jahan, to deprive him of the nomination as successor to Jahangir. Therefore, when she secured orders from her husband for Prince Shah Jahan to lead an expedition to Kandahar, the latter refused to obey and raised the standard of revolt. This helped the Persians to consolidate their hold over Kandahar and its adjoining territories to the great chagrin of the Mughal emperor.

The Revolt of Prince Shah Jahan (1523-25)

The great Mughals were well-established in India but they had no fixed law of succession to the throne. Akbar had faced this problem of succession during his very lifetime when prince Salim, later the emperor Jahangir, set a very bad precedent by raising a standard of revolt against his father. Jahangir was paid back in the same coin when his own son, Khusrau, took up arms against him immediately after his accession to the throne. Khusrau was disgraced and liquidated but Jahangir could not stop his other three sons, Parvez, Khurram and Shahryar, from harbouring feelings of mutual jealously and strife in their bid to secure their nomination as the next rulers. While dealing ruthlessly against the rebellious Khusrau and his associates, Jahangir had firmly established that 'kingship knows no kinship'. Therefore, it was not surprising if his sons bade farewell to all the brotherly affections and bonds of kinship between themselves to improve their respective chances of succession to the throne.

As narrated earlier, Khurram had won the initial race against Parvez with the support of Nur Jahan and Asaf Khan, as he was married to the daughter of the prime minister. But, by the year 1620, he fell out of favour with Nur Jahan when the latter gave her daughter Ladli Begam in marriage to Shahryar, the youngest son of Jahangir, in April 1621. Thereafter, she began to prepare Shahryar as the political rival to Parvez and Khurram in the race for succession. Accordingly, she conspired to disgrace prince Khurram in the eyes of the emperor. In 1621-22, Khurram, in his capacity as the viceroy of the Deccan, had earned reputation and prestige by bringing Malik Ambar and the sultans of Bijapur and Golconda to acknowledge the Mughal suzerainty. At that moment of Khurram's triumph, Nur Jahan conspired to dislodge him from the Deccan which had become the stronghold of his power. She secured orders from the emperor for him to proceed on the Kandahar expedition. Prince Khurram (future Shah Jahan) suspected a foul play and refused to obey the royal command. It gave an opportunity to the Queen to poison the ears of Jahangir against the prince. The murder of prince Khusrau in captivity by Shah Jahan also came handy to her to frighten the emperor about the violent behaviour and sinister designs of the power-hungry prince. Accordingly, Nur Jahan induced the emperor to order 'the recall of Shah Jahan to the court with his personal troops, which implied *ipso facto* that he had been removed from the viceroyalty of the Deccan, and that he should hand over the charge of the imperial armies'. Shah Jahan disobeyed the royal command and raised the standard of revolt. He mustered all the imperial troops at his command and marched on Fatehpur Sikri to secure the possession of the royal treasury but his attempt was foiled by Nur Jahan's diplomacy. Shah Jahan then turned the direction of his armies towards Delhi but was defeated by the royalists, led by Prince Parvez and Mahabat Khan, at Bilochpur.

Without losing heart, Prince Shah Jahan hastened towards the Deccan with the bulk of the imperial troops still under his command. Nur Jahan secured the emperor's orders to dispatch Mahabat Khan behind the rebellious prince in hot chase. The latter proved more than a match for Shah Jahan, however. He wrested the Mughal provinces of the Deccan from his hands and made him to run about as a fugitive, first to Gujarat, and from there to the territories of Bijapur and Golconda. Passing through Telingana, Shah Jahan marched upon the provinces of Bihar and Bengal which passed into his hands without much resistance. thereafter, contingents laid siege to the fort of Allahabad in modern U.P. but the timely arrival of the royal armies from Delhi, uner the command of Prince Parvez and Mahabat Khan, compelled them to retrace their steps. Shah Jahan suffered a defeat and retreated towards the Deccan campaign once again. The Mughal garrison of Ahmadnagar, which had been posted there by none else but the prince himself some time ago, willingly passed under the control of Shah Jahan to his great relief. He now established his foothold at Ahmadnagar and entered into an alliance with Malik Ambar against his father Jahangir, the reigning Mughal emperor.

It created an amusing situation in which most of the Mughal and Deccani nobles and soldiers of south India hesitated in taking sides. They watched the political developments with interest but could not guess the ultimate outcome of the internal strife of the imperial household. With the active support of Malik Ambar, Shah Jahan laid siege to the fort of Burhanpur whose Mughal commander had refused to join his camp. But within days the rumour spread that Prince Parvez and Mahabat Khan had crossed the Vindhyas in their southward march with massive imperial forces. On the receipt of intelligence, Shah Jahan lost his heart and raised the siege of Burhanpur. At this critical moment, he was taken ill and his personal troops also started deserting him. 'Faced with total annihilation at the hands of the imperial armies, Shah Jahan offered unconditional surrender' to the emperor and sought forgiveness for his acts of omission and commission. The terms of peace were dictated by Nur Jahan in April 1526. The prince was forgiven and allowed to retain the control of Balaghat region, then under his control, in governorship when he agreed to send his two minor sons, Dara and Aurangzeb, aged ten and eight respectively, as hostages to the imperial court along with ten *lakhs* of rupees as war indemnity. The fort of Asirgarh, the only citadel of importance under the control of Shah Jahan, was also surrendered by him to the imperial Mughal officers. Dara and Aurangzeb were presented to Jahangir in the open court, held at Lahore in June 1526, and were kept in the royal *harem* under the personal supervision of Nur Jahan. Shah Jahan's revolt caused an incalculable loss to the state exchequer and created numerous law and order problems for the government. Thousands of the imperial soldiers perished in the futile royal feud which gave a serious set-back to the Mughal power and prestige. And all these ugly developments took place primarily because of Nur Jahan's excessive indulgence in the Mughal politics.

Revolt of Mahabat Khan (1526)

Having cut Shah Jahan to size, Nur Jahan directed his attention towards Prince Parvez, the only other political rival of Shahryar in the game of nomination as heir-apparent to the throne. Mahabat Khan, the most reputed and influential Mughal general, had been attached to Prince Parvez for the last many years. Parvez 'was a weakling as a prince'. He had 'ruined his health as well as reputation by excessive indulgence in sensual pleasures' and was 'no match for Prince Khurram in the game of power-politics'. Nevertheless, the emperor had bestowed 'the unprecedented rank' of 40,000 *Zat* and 30,000 *Swar* on Parvez 'ostensibly to put him higher in rank and prestige than the rebellious prince Shah Jahan'. The power-hungry Queen, Nur Jahan, was fully aware that the Lilliputian Shahryar would never be acceptable to the Emperor Jahangir as his successor in preference to Parvez. And Mahabat Khan—the right-hand man of Prince Parvez, stood behind his royal ward in shining armour to strengthen his claim to royalty. Hence Mahabat Khan became a victim to the political ambitions and intrigues of Nur Jahan. Instead of feeling beholden to the most capable and trustworthy imperial commander for the meritorious services rendered by him to the crown, the wily Queen became jealous of Mahabat Khan and conspired to bring about his fall.

What followed thereafter was most uncharitable and disgraceful action on the part of the all-powerful and the most magnificent Mughal Queen. When Prince Shah Jahan made his unconditional surrender to the Mughal emperor, Mahabat Khan and Prince Parvez were stationed at Burhanpur, the headquarters of the Mughal viceroys of the Deccan. In order to break the association of Mahabat Khan with Parvez, she secured the orders from Jahangir for the former's appointment as the governor of Bengal. It came as a surprise to Mahabat Khan but, being a faithful servant of the crown, he readily obeyed the royal command and was preparing to leave for Bengal when he received yet another *Firman* from the Imperial Court in which 'uncalled-for charges of disloyalty, embezzlement and insubordination were framed against him'. It is presumed that Nur Jahan had cunningly poisoned the ears of Jahangir against Mahabat Khan. In fact, she was bent upon provoking Mahabat Khan into an open revolt 'so that he could be charged with high treason and then punished'.

What prompted Nur Jahan to levy such serious allegations against Mahabat Khan? It is said that an excuse was taken of 'a minor lapse' on the part of Mahabat Khan that, while at Burhanpur, he had celebrated the engagement of his daughter to one Barkhurdar—the son of another premier noble, Khwaja Usman Naqshbandi, without obtaining the 'customary' imperial permission. Motamad Khan informs us that Nur Jahan did not wait for the receipt of an explanation from the accused noble. Instead, she summoned Barkhurdar to the court where he was insulted and humiliated for nothing; 'his hands were bound to his neck and he was taken bare headed to the prison'. All the valuables given by Mahabat Khan to his would-be son-in-law by way of wedding-portion or dowry were ordered to be confiscated. (*Iqbalnama-i-Jahangiri*; E&D, vi, pp. 419-20).

It is amazing to note the fertility of Nur Jahan's brain and her capacity to hatch conspiracies and intrigues to reckon with her potential rivals for the attainment of her selfish political ends; she had initiated proceedings against Mahabat Khan in the beginning of the year 1626 when he and Prince Parvez had overwhelmed the rebellious Shah Jahan and compelled him to appeal for unconditional surrender to the imperial court. No wonder, Mahabat Khan's blood boiled to hear of the above incident. In despair, he decided to present his case in person to the emperor when the royal standards were on the customary move from Kashmir to Lahore and from thence to Kabul. The royal entourage included Nur Jahan and Asaf Khan—the prime minister. Asaf Khan himself had been let down by the crafty Queen by bringing disrepute to his son-in-law, Prince Shah Jahan. Therefore, he encouraged her in her manipulations against Mahabat Khan as he was equally eager to weaken the friends and sympathisers of Prince Parvez.

Mahabat Khan reached the Punjab with about 5,000 Rajput soldiers of his personal contingent. He made it to the imperial camp when it was being shifted across the river Jhelum sometime in March 1626. When Nur Jahan came to know of his arrival, she sent orders to him on behalf of the emperor to keep his soldiers at a safe distance from the royal camp. At the same time, she served him with yet another provocative notice to explain as to 'why he had betrothed his daughter to another noble's son without permission from the emperor'. It proved the proverbial 'last straw on the camel's neck'. Having gauged the import of the Queen's sinister designs, the soldier in Mahabat Khan made him to pounce on the foe unmindful of the consequences. He resorted to a *coup de main* by getting hold of the physically incapacitated Emperor from the royal camp when Nur Jahan had already crossed the Jhelum while Jahangir was waiting to be carried across the river. It created a piquet situation. Nur Jahan gave in after making a futile attempt to liberate Jahangir by force and voluntarily joined the emperor in the captivity of Mahabat Khan. Realising the gravity of the situation, Asaf Khan–the Prime Minister, also offered his submission to Mahabat Khan at Attock.

By the travesty of circumstances, Mahabat Khan had emerged as the *de facto* ruler of the Mughal Empire. He had no other alternative but to play his role as the 'virtual dictator' to keep the things going. Mahabat Khan took charge of the administration in the name of the Emperor although he treated the Monarch and the Queen with utmost courtesy and respect. 'Being a commoner, he could never dare to ill-treat the royal couple or undermine their royal prestige'. He was not 'a man of destiny', however. Though a seasoned military general, he lacked the qualities of state craft and diplomatic skills. It was but natural that he should excite the jealousy of most of the bewildered courtiers and military officers who commanded the imperial troops. It was beyond his power to stop the spread of all sorts of rumours among the people which dubbed him as the usurper.7

Meanwhile, Nur Jahan resorted to studied silence, diplomacy and whispering campaign to overthrow the dictatorship of Mahabat Khan.

'The royal couple adopted a very conciliatory attitude towards their captor; they pretended to show that they had resigned themselves to their fate and were very happy to play the puppets in his hands. They thus lulled the suspicions of Mahabat Khan and put him completely off his guard. On Nur Jahan's suggestion, the schedule of royal tour to Kabul remained unchanged; it covered the whole of the Indian rainy season. In the meantime, Nur Jahan made use of her royal influence to win over most of the courtiers and military commanders of the Empire by establishing secret contacts with them through her domestics, including the females and eunuchs. Her plan to end the servitude of Mahabat Khan attained maturity during the return march from Kabul to Lahore. On reaching the fort of Rohtas, Nur Jahan took Mahabat Khan by surprise by making a sudden announcement to the effect that His Majesty the Emperor would review the imperial troops early next morning; obviously, the step had been taken by her after taking some of the prominent military generals into confidence. Mahabat Khan was warned to keep his Rajput soldiers away from the imperial troops so as to avoid communal tension. Jahangir was brought before the royal troops on an elephant; as soon as he reached the military lines, he placed himself at the head of the imperial army and was hailed by the soldiers with shouts of joy and clatter of arms' (*Advanced Study*, ii, pp. 414-15).

Terror-stricken Mahabat Khan fled with his Rajput soldiers to Lahore; from the position of a virtual dictator, he sank to the level of a mere state rebel and fugitive in the twinkling of an eye. Before taking to flight, Mahabat Khan had taken Asaf Khan and some other members of the royalty with him as hostages. Nur Jahan's men gave a hot chase to him and demanded his surrender. Mahabat Khan had no way of escape from the dragnet of the imperial Mughal forces. At Lahore, he set free Asaf Khan and all other royal prisoners. The rebellious Mughal noble treated Asaf Khan with full regards due to him as the Prime Minister, explained his conduct with an open mind and tendered his unconditional surrender to the Emperor through him. Mahabat Khan was promptly forgiven by Jahangir and ordered to proceed against Prince Shah Jahan, who had laid siege to the fort of Thatta about that time. Mahabat Khan begged a hasty retreat towards Sindh via Rajputana with great relief, but, instead of fighting against Shah Jahan, won over the friendship of the rebellious prince and joined his camp. His arrival came as a windfall to Shah Jahan. He was trigger happy to secure the association and support of Mahabat Khan as both of them had suffered humiliation and discomfiture at the hands of the wily Queen Nur Jahan. At the imperial court, Nur Jahan was dumfounded to see the turn of the events while Asaf Khan, her brother and prime minister of the empire, laughed in his sleeves to watch the backfiring of her wicked manipulations. Meanwhile, Prince Parvez died of excesses in October 1626 which removed the last element of obstruction between the friendship of Mahabat Khan and Shah Jahan. Thereafter, Mahabat Khan made a common cause with Shah Jahan and enabled him strengthen his position in the south.

The Death of Jahangir

After the conclusion of Mahabat Khan's episode, Jahangir stayed at Lahore during the winter of 1626-27. His health was totally shattered and he remained confined to his bed as an invalid person most of the time. What to say of his riding a horse, Jahangir was unable even to stand on his feet, and was carried about in *palki*. In March 1627, he was taken to Kashmir to protect him from the scorching heat of the plains in summer but, during his return from the valley, he died of exhaustion near Bhimbar on October 28, 1627. His dead body was taken to Lahore and buried in state in a beautiful garden at Shahdra. His widowed queen Nur Jahan subsequently built a magnificent mausoleum over his grave. The political wrangles that took place between Nur Jahan and Asaf Khan over the problem of succession and the circumstances leading to the ascendancy of Shah Jahan form the subject-matter of the next chapter.

There are divergent views about the character and personality of Jahangir. According to some European writers, he was a mixture of opposites. In the words of VA Smith, "Jahangir was a strong compound of tenderness and cruelty, justice and caprice, refinement and brutality, good sense and childishness'. He is thus made out as 'a fickle-minded tyrant, fond of wine and women' who proved 'successful both as a man and ruler'. A.L. Srivastava does not regard him 'a great king' or 'a statesman and administrator of outstanding calibre' although he admits that Jahangir 'was a successful and benevolent ruler who cherished the well-being of his subjects and was deservedly popular with them'. Captain W Hawkins and Sir Thomas Roe, who visited India during the reign of Jahangir, have written a lot about the Mughal emperor and his times. Hawkins tells that Jahangir showed himself publicly three times a day to hear petitions of the people and give justice to them. But he was 'a drunkard; when he got angry, terrible results followed'. 'He might order a man to be flayed alive or torn to pieces by elephants or tortured to death in many ways. On one occasion, he might order the murder of a person, and on another occasion, he may forgive generously or intervene to save the life of some innocent person'. Likewise, Sir Thomas Roe's journal gives a pen-portrait of the Mughal court and important persons at the helm of affairs during the reign of Jahangir. He tells us that the imperial court observed a lot of pomp and show. He describes the festivities in which the nobles took part. Thomas Roe was struck by the fact that there were no written laws in India and the word of the king was law. The control of the central government over the provinces was very weak. Local administration was inefficient and corruption and bribery prevailed everywhere. Thomas Roe is said to have obtained trade concession for the English by bribing Asaf Khan, the prime minister. Nevertheless, Thomas Roe is all praise for Jahangir who was said to be very straightforward and plain in his dealings with the people; he did not suffer from the evils of 'pride or conceit'.

❑ ❑

16

SHAH JAHAN (1628-1658)

SECTION 1: EARLY CAREER AND ACCESSION

Early Life (1592-1627)

Shah Jahan, the son and successor of Jahangir, was born of his Rajput wife, Jagat Gosain, daughter of Mota Raja Udai Singh of Jodhpur, on January 5, 1592 at Lahore. His original name was Khurram. He was the third of Jahangir's five sons, each from a different wife or concubine. Of Jahangir's other four sons, Jahandar, the youngest one, born of a concubine in 1605, had died in infancy, while the eldest one, named Khusrau, proved to be the most unfortunate person. He was put up as political rival to his father in the race for succession to the throne on the eve of Akbar's death by the influential nobles with vested interests which proved his ruin. He fell a victim to Jahangir's wrath and languished in the royal custody as state prisoner for the rest of his life until he was strangulated to death by Prince Khurram in 1622.

Each of the other three other sons of Jahangir – Parvez, Khurram and Shahryar had an ambitious though violent career. Prince Khurram, later styled Shah Jahan by Jahangir in 1622, was destined to succeed him to the throne as the most magnificent monarch of the imperial Mughal dynasty whose reign has been hailed as the Golden Age of the Mughal period. His early career and rise to power with the active support and patronage of his father-in-law, Asaf Khan – the Prime Minister, and Nur Jahan has been discussed in detail in the preceding chapter of this study. Prince Parvez died of *delirium tremens* in 1626; leaving behind only Shah Jahan and Shahryar as the only two contenders for succession to the throne.

Accession to the Throne and Coronation (February 1628)

To pick up the threads of the story, Asaf Khan setup a separate ministerial camp immediately after Jahangir's death, and avoided all contacts with Nur Jahan. On the inducement of the crafty Queen, Shahryar proclaimed himself Emperor of India at Lahore but the Prime Minister stood for Prince Shah Jahan. As a diplomatic manoeuvre, he formally installed Dawar Bakhsh, son of Khusrau, as the emperor and refused to recognise Shahryar as the rightful successor; most of the courtiers and senior military officers of the imperial camp were won over by Asaf Khan to approve his actions and Nur Jahan was isolated.

Asaf Khan had secretly 'despatched a fast courier, Banarsi, with his (own) signet ring to Prince Shah Jahan in the Deccan' with the message to reach the imperial capital without any loss of time. On the receipt of this symbolic signal from his father-in-law and prime minister of the state, Shah Jahan played his cards well. As a shrewd person, he did not declare himself emperor of India all at once, but, issued secret directions to all the provincial governors and military generals to offer their allegiance to him. Dawar Bakhsh was to continue on the throne till the arrival of Shah Jahan from the Deccan. Meanwhile Shahryar had setup his court in the fort of Lahore and started issuing decrees as the emperor of the Mughal Empire. He had taken possession of the royal treasury at Lahore, confiscated the property of those nobles who had refused to accept him as the ruler and recruited a large army 'by a lavish distribution of money'. Nevertheless, Shahryar and his royal patron, Nur Jahan–now the Queen Dowager, were both no match for Asaf Khan, who had started making vigorous preparations to take on them on behalf of Shah Jahan. In a surprise move, Asaf Khan marched on Shahryar's army camp near Lahore and inflicted a severe defeat on him. Shahryar's attempt to make good his escape was foiled and he was promptly taken a prisoner. Nur Jahan was also placed under virtual house-arrest and kept under personal surveillance by Asaf Khan till the arrival of Shah Jahan.

Shah Jahan lost no time in marching towards the north through Rajputana. On the way he took care to take all the provincial and local Mughal officers under his personal supervision and control. Men with doubtful fidelity were promptly overwhelmed and replaced. He was welcomed on the way by a number of Rajput chiefs including Rana Karan of Mewar. While yet on the way, Shah Jahan sent secret instructions to Asaf Khan to liquidate all the royal contenders for power.

On the receipt of his communication, Asaf Khan at first blinded Shahryar in the prison, and then put him and four other male members of the royal family, including Dawar Bakhsh, to death on January 23, 1628, so as to leave Shah Jahan as the sole claimant to the Mughal throne; the other three royal weaklings to lose their life at this juncture included Gurshasp, the second son of Khusrau and the younger brother of Dawar Bakhsh, besides Tahmurs and Hoshang – the two sons of Daniyal.

By this time, *Khutba* had been read in the name of Shah Jahan at Delhi on January 19, 1628. Under instructions from Shah Jahan, Asaf Khan, in his capacity as the Prime Minister of the new regime, assumed the administrative charge of the imperial government with renewed vigour. He moved from Lahore to Delhi and placed all the high officers of the state in the north under his effective control. As Asaf Khan 'had been a reputed Prime Minister of Jahangir's reign, very few persons dared to defy his orders'. Meanwhile, Shah Jahan consolidated his hold over the southern, central and western India. He reached in the neighbourhood of Agra in February 1628 and entered city of Agra in state at an auspicious moment on the 14th of February and celebrated his coronation ceremony amidst great public rejoicings. Asaf Khan, the prime minister, reached Agra from Delhi on February 27, 1628 when a grand reception was held by the Emperor Shah Jahan in his honour; he had already been awarded official title of 'Uncle' with the most exalted ***mansab*** of 8,000 ***zat*** and ***swar du-aspa seh-aspa***. Shah Jahan was more lavish than his predecessors in the distribution of honours, titles and wealth among those who had stood by him during his period of struggle against Nur Jahan. Mahabat Khan received the next highest *mansab*, after Asaf Khan, of Seven Thousand *zat* and *swar* with the title of *Khan-i-Khana*. Faithful and trustworthy officers and provincial governors were confirmed in their posts while the suspect and disloyal were removed to make room for the younger blood. Shah Jahan had become very popular during the days of his father; therefore, his accession to the throne was hailed by the people all over the country. Nur Jahan retired from public life and was granted a pension of two lakhs of rupees *per annum* for her comfortable living. She adopted Lahore as her abode where she lived a very simple and austere life in the company of her daughter Ladli Begam, the widow of Shahryar. Like a typical Indian widow, she abstained from all the social functions and public festivities and was always clad in white clothes. The major portion of her pension was spent by her in public charities. She died in 1645 and was buried in a tomb beside Jahangir's grave at Shahdra over which she had built a beautiful mausoleum with the funds received from the Emperor Shah Jahan.

SECTION 2: THE CHRONICLE OF SHAH JAHAN'S REIGN

The Nauroz Festival (March 1628)

Shah Jahan's reign began in style with the celebration of the festival of Nauroz (New Year's Day) by him in the month of March 1628 'as a part of the extended coronation ceremonies'. The open lawns of the Red Fort of Agra were utilised for the purpose. This was the first magnificent display of the royal festivities ever witnessed by the citizens of Agra. Apart from the usual setting up of the numerous stalls and stages for public performance by the wives and ladies of royalty and the ruling elite in the fashion of the Meena Bazaar, a huge canopy was installed in the courtyard of the royal palace where the Emperor gave an audience to the distinguished citizens, courtiers and outstanding nobles and military generals. Shah Jahan was seated on a richly decorated throne on the four corners of which stood his four sons. Members of the royal family and high officers were given a grand feast and bestowed rich presents and titles. Asaf Khan was promoted to the *mansab* of Nine Thousand *zat* and *swar* in recognition of the meritorious services rendered by him to the throne. The citizens of the metropolis joined the celebrations by lavishly illuminating the town at night, and the public charities were distributed on an extensive scale. The festival of *Nauroz* cost the state exchequer nearly two *crores* of rupees.

Khan Jahan Lodhi's Rebellion (1628-31)

Shah Jahan had to face a few revolts and defiance of imperial authority by some of the un-reconciled nobles and disgruntled elements in different parts of his dominions 'as an after-effect of the mini civil war which preceded his accession to the throne'. Khan Jahan Lodhi's rebellion was the first such incident. A distinguished military commander, Khan Jahan had been faithfully attached to Nur Jahan's entourage for many long years. His original name was Pir Khan. Because of his meritorious services to the crown he was bestowed the title of Khan-i-Jahan with the *mansab* of Five Thousand *zat* and *swar*. After the revolt of Mahabat Khan, early in 1526, Khan Jahan Lodhi was posted as the lieutenant of Prince Parvez in the Deccan. On the death of Parvez in October 1526, Khan Jahan was appointed the Mughal viceroy of the Deccan with Burhanpur as his headquarters. He owed this exalted position to the patronage of Nur Jahan, and was, obviously, at the beck and call of the all-powerful Queen. On receiving the news of Jahangir's death, he consolidated his hold over the Mughal Deccan and suppressed all the supporters of Asaf Khan and his party. At the same time, he entered into an alliance with the Nizamshahi ruler of Ahmadnagar by surrendering the territories of Balaghat to him as a price of friendship. He stood up against Shah Jahan and invaded Malwa with the object of obstructing his march from Gujarat to Agra, the imperial capital. He suffered a defeat at the hands of Shah Jahan's supporters and fled back to the Deccan.

After his accession to the throne, Khan Jahan Lodhi was forgiven by Shah Jahan and confirmed in the viceroyalty of the Deccan. But he was ordered to recover the territories of Balaghat from the Nizam of Ahmadnagar. This he failed to do and was recalled to the court while Mahabat Khan was sent to the Deccan as the new Mughal viceroy. Khan Jahan was allowed to retain his personal contingent and the *mansab* and was treated with consideration at Agra but he distrusted the new Emperor and 'lived in perpetual fear of being liquidated with family'. After a few months, he fled to the south with his five thousand troops. The imperial army overtook him near Dholpur and defeated him in a pitched battle although Khan Jahan made good his escape and took shelter with the Nizam of Ahmadnagar.

Khan Jahan proved to be the most dangerous enemy of Shah Jahan and his revolt lasted about three years. Though repeatedly defeated, he did not lose heart and carried on relentless struggle against Delhi with the support of the ruler of Ahmadnagar and other disaffected elements of the Deccan. In consequence, 'the whole of the Mughal Deccan was ravaged and laid waste by the movements of armies of the adversaries'. In the long run, the chief of Ahmadnagar withdrew his support to Khan Jahan Lodhi and turned out his men from his territories which were being used as base of operations by them against the Mughals. Khan Jahan attempted to make his way to the Punjab with intentions to arouse the Afghan nobles against the Mughal rule but his path was blocked by the royal troops. He fell fighting at Tal Sehonda near Kalinjar and his head was sent to Agra to the great relief of Shah Jahan. Besides Mahabat Khan, the other Mughal generals, who rendered valuable service to Shah Jahan in the suppression of

Khan Jahan's revolt, included Abdullah Khan, who was bestowed the title of Firoze Jung with the *mansab* of six thousand, and Muzaffar Khan, who was honoured by Shah Jahan with the title of Khan Jahan (*Khan-i-Jahan*) with the *mansab* of five thousand, as was held by the fallen Lodhi rebel.

Uprising in Bundelkhand

Jujhar Singh, son of Bir Singh Bundella—the murderer of Abul Fazl, was one of the senior officers of Jahangir. He held, in parental heritage, the state of Bundelkhand and enjoyed complete autonomy in its administration; Orchha was capital. Jujhar Singh was in the good books of Nur Jahan; and his relations with Prince Khurram *alias* Shah Jahan were very good so long as Nur Jahan was favourably disposed towards the prince. When Nur Jahan turned against Shah Jahan, Jujhar Singh lost all contacts with him. Accordingly, when Jujhar Singh presented himself in the court of Shah Jahan on the occasion of his coronation, the latter showed no favours to him and, instead, asked him to submit the previous accounts of the revenues of his state. The youthful Bundella chief 'could not brook this ill-treatment', and, on his return to Orchha, raised his standard of revolt. Incidentally, his revolt synchronized with that of Khan Jahan Lodhi. Therefore, Shah Jahan lost no time in ordering an all-out invasion of Bundelkhand from three directions and himself shifted to Gwalior to supervise the military operations against the Bundella rebel.

Jujhar Singh fought against the imperialists with dauntless courage and determination for about a year before offering his submission in February 1629. As he had nothing to do with the rebellion of Khan Jahan Lodhi, Shah Jahan promptly forgave him and restored him to the royal dignities. In gratitude, the Bundella chief cooperated with the Mughal emperor in his fight against Khan Jahan Lodhi and other rebellious elements in the Deccan. He conquered Daulatabad for the Mughals. Having regained the confidence of the Mughal emperor, Jujhar Singh amassed huge wealth and strengthened the defenses of his own state. On his return to Bundelkhand in 1635, he prepared an ambitious plan to conquer Gondwana, situated to the south of Bundelkhand, which was not under the direct control of the Mughal emperor. Without the knowledge of Shah Jahan, he organised an unprovoked attack on Chauragarh and put its *raja* Prem Narain, the Mughal vassal, to death. His son, in distress, appealed to Shah Jahan for help. The emperor adopted 'unethical approach' to settle the dispute. Instead of sending the imperial troops in support of the Gondwana chief, he ordered

Jujhar Singh either to surrender Gondwana to the imperialists or cede a part of his own territories to the Mughal dominions in lieu thereof, besides paying a fine of five *lakhs* of rupees. Jujhar Singh refused to obey Shah Jahan's orders, recalled his son Jagraj Singh from the imperial service in the Deccan, and declared his sovereignty once again.

It necessitated a fresh invasion of Bundelkhand by Shah Jahan. The Mughal army of invasion was now commanded by Aurangzeb—the first such assignment held by the young prince who was then hardly 17 years old. Assisted by seasoned military officers, Aurangzeb conquered Orchha and Dhamoni, and Jujhar Singh retreated towards Chauragarh. The Mughal armies followed close upon his heals. It so happened that Jujhar Singh and one of his sons, Bikramajit, fell into the hands of Gonds by chance and were put to death by them; their heads were sent to Shah Jahan at Agra in December 1635. Jujhar Singh's treasure, worth fifty *lakhs*, and his family fell into the hands of Aurangzeb. The Mughal prince displayed his religious fanaticism by forcibly converting two sons of Jujhar Singh to Islam, while the third one, who refused to do so, was executed. Not only this; all the women of Jujhar Singh's family were enslaved and made to serve as menials in the houses of nobles. The magnificent Hindu temple of Orchha was desecrated and converted into a mosque. Thus Aurangzeb, in his very early age, gave the first proof of his religious intolerance in Bundelkhand, and, 'unfortunately, his policy was endorsed by Shah Jahan' to the great encouragement of the orthodox Muslims who had been lying low since the days of Akbar. B P Saksena, a modern biographer of Shah Jahan, holds the emperor personally responsible for initiating the policy of religious intolerance. He writes:

"The fact of the matter is that it was Shah Jahan who encouraged his Mussalman officers to indulge in their religious frenzy, and it was he who ordered the demolition of the magnificent temple of Orchha. That he was able to reverse so far the conciliatory policy of his grandfather was due to the fact that he expected little opposition. The Hindu officers in his employ, though some of them were not lacking in courage, were smaller in number, lower in rank, and hopelessly degenerate in character." (*History of Shahjahan of Dihli*; Allahabad, 1958, pp. 89-90).

Shah Jahan installed Devi Singh, a kinsman of Jujhar Singh, as a puppet ruler of Bundelkhand at Orchha but 'the Bundellas dubbed him a traitor and defied his authority as a protest against the display of religious intolerance, and ill-treatment meted out to the ruling family of Orchha by Shah Jahan'. Champat Rai of Mahoba, one of the vassals of Orchha, refused to submit to Devi Singh and single-handed continued to fight against the Mughals for many years. Likewise, his son Chhatrasal, following in the footprints of his deceased father and the Maratha leader Shivaji, waged a long war of liberation against Aurangzeb's oppressive regime.

Famine and Plague (1630-32)

The war-ravaged Deccan, Khandesh and Gujarat were engulfed in a severe drought and famine in 1630-32 which took a heavy toll of human as well as cattle life. The crops were ruined, food prices soared sky high, and the village folk left their habitats with cattle and beasts of burden in search of water, food and fodder. The famine was compounded by the outbreak of the epidemic of plague which laid its icy hands on the survivors. Peter Mundy, who passed through the Deccan in November 1630, saw numerous deserted villages and ruined towns with scanty population of food-starved human beings and the animals. He records that, 'the highways were strewn with corpses which emitted foul smell'. The people 'dragged 'off the dead bodies 'by the heels, stark-naked, and left them out of the city-gates so that the way was half barred-up'. (*Travels of Peter Mundy*, Hakluyt Society, London, 1908, II, p. 14). Abdul Hamid Lahouri in *Badshahnama* gives an account of the measures adopted by Shah Jahan to provide relief to the famine-stricken people. He talks of the state-run free *langars* at Burhanpur, Ahmadabad and many other places to feed the poor. According to him, 'every day sufficient soup and bread was prepared by the state officials to feed the hungry. The royal treasuries were thrown open for distribution of money among the poor and the destitute; thus 50,000 rupees were given in charity at Ahmadabad and one *lakh* at Burhanpur over a period of four or five months. Land revenue, amounting to seventy *lakhs* of rupees was remitted; it constituted about one-eleventh of the land revenue of the whole empire'. (E&D, VII, pp. 24-25). 'According to the medieval standards, the relief measures adopted by Shah Jahan' government, though inadequate, were highly commendable'.

Death of Queen Mumtaz Mahal (1631 A.D.)

Arjmand Banu Begam, styled Mumtaz Mahal – the chief queen of Shah Jahan, died an untimely death in the prime of her life, on June 7,

1631 at Burhanpur, when he was stationed there to restore law and order in the Deccan after the fall of Khan Jahan Lodhi. It came as the most unforgettable personal loss to Shah Jahan. Mumtaz Mahal was the daughter of Asaf Khan, the prime minister of Jahangir and brother of Nur Jahan. Born in 1594, she was a highly educated and accomplished lady of parts. In her 'natural beauty and charms', she was in no way inferior to her aunt Nur Jahan. She was married to Prince Khurram (later Shah Jahan) in April 1612 and was his second wife but Shah Jahan made her the Chief Queen with the title of *Malika-i-Zamani* after his accession to the throne and the imperial seal was entrusted to her custody. Nevertheless, 'unlike Nur Jahan, Mumtaz Mahal was least interested in politics and she never interfered in the state affairs. So much so that even the formal possession of the royal seal looked like an unbearable burden on her shoulders, it is said that, at the first opportunity afforded to her, she requested the emperor to transfer it to the custody of her father, the prime minister of the empire'.

Mumtaz Mahal was a soft-spoken lady of noble virtue. She was intensely religious-minded and pious lady who endeared herself to her husband by her devotional attachment and fidelity. She played the role of a real life-partner of Shah Jahan and shared his joys and sorrows in full measure. On the other hand, Shah Jahan, although a polygamist had also developed intense love and attachment towards her; and they, in fact, lived like a common monogamous couple during his times of troubles and wanderings as state rebel against his father. Mumtaz Mahal bore 14 children to Shah Jahan, of which eight died in infancy or minority; and she expired at the time of her fourteenth child, a girl, at Burhanpur. Her six children who attained majority were: Jahan Ara Begam, Dara Shikoh, Shah Shuja, Roshan Ara Begam, Aurangzeb and Murad Bakhsh. Immediately after her death, Mumtaz was buried in a garden at Burhanpur, but a few years later, her remains were brought to Agra and buried on the bank of the Jumna over which now stands the world famous Taj Mahal which, according to AL Srivastava, 'reflects in a superb manner the feminine grace of the royal lady in whose memory it was built. It is a frozen lyric in which is sung the story of an emperor's passionate devotion to his queen.' (*Medieval Indian Culture*; Agra, 1964, p. 229). It is said that whenever Shah Jahan 'visited the tomb of Mumtaz Mahal, streams of tears rolled out of his eyes, and that his beard which had but a few grey hair before the queen's death, became silvery grey soon after this tragedy'.

Punitive Measures against the Portuguese (1631-32)

By the beginning of the sixteenth century, the Portuguese had established their settlement on the banks of the Hugli River in Bengal. They had started misusing their privileges to carry on trade and commerce and had become aggressive in their dealing with the local people. They made forced conversions to Christianity, and even resorted to piracy and slave trade. It was reported by Qasim Khan, the governor of Bengal, that the Portuguese had fortified their settlement on the Hugli. They levied tolls on the Indian merchant boats and defied the authority of the local Mughal officials. The matters came to a head when two slave-girls of Queen Mumtaz Mahal were abducted by them from the royal boats and enslaved. Shah Jahan felt enraged to hear of it. He was apprised of the fact that the Portuguese had failed to pay him homage and offer customary presents to him even at the time of his accession. The emperor, therefore, ordered his governor to take punitive action against them. Accordingly, Qasim Khan organised an expedition against the Portuguese settlement from land and water. His initial attack was repulsed by the Portuguese with a heavy toll of the Mughal soldiers by their artillery fire. Thereupon, Qasim Khan reorganized his troops and invested their settlement with determination and force. The siege lasted more than three months but the Portuguese were, ultimately, overwhelmed and destroyed. About ten thousand of the Portuguese men, women, and children were either killed or drowned in the river in their bid to escape to the sea and 'the Hugli was cleared of the pirates'. It is estimated that '4,400 persons of both sexes, including Europeans, slaves and slave girls, who had forcibly been converted to Christianity, were taken prisoners, and about 10,000 inhabitants of the neighbouring *parganas* and villages, who had fallen into the hand of the Portuguese, obtained their freedom'. The Portuguese prisoners were brought to Agra and asked to embrace Islam; those who accepted the offer were liberated while the rest were made to languish in jails and tortured according to the Islamic law; it was done in retaliation of what the Portuguese had been doing towards the Indian inhabitants. According to BP Saksena, 'their piracy, their proselytising zeal, and their dishonesty, are mentioned in every contemporary chronicle, foreign as well as native. The fate which they suffered was what they deserved, but too severely carried out'.(*Shahjahan*; pp. 112-13).

Shah Jahan and the Deccan Affairs

Shah Jahan was committed to the Deccan policy of his predecessors, Akbar and Jahangir. It involved a persistent struggle against the south Indian states to bring them under the Mughal imperial fold. The best part of his life as a prince had been spent in the south where he earned reputation as warrior and statesman, and received the title of Shah Jahan from his father. Again, it was his southern base which gave him strength to challenge Nur Jahan's perfidy to deprive him of his accession to the throne. Therefore, he was determined to bring the whole of south India under his subjugation. Moreover, as an orthodox Sunni Muslim, he had no soft corner for the Shia rulers of Ahmadnagar, Bijapur and Golconda. The rebellion of Khan Jahan Lodhi and other disaffected elements of south India compelled him to adopt aggressive attitude towards the Deccan affairs from the very beginning of his reign.

Conquest of Ahmadnagar: The state of Ahmadnagar had been the target of Mughal aggression since long. During the reign of Shah Jahan, it was ruled by Murtaza II Nizamshah. Assisted by his capable minister Malik Ambar, he had been fighting against the Mughals for years. Malik Ambar had given his daughter in marriage to the Sultan to strengthen his bonds of unity with the Nizamshahi dynasty. As referred to above, the rebellious general, Khan Jahan Lodhi, had surrendered the territories of Balaghat to Nizamshah to create a joint front against the Mughals. No wonder, Shah Jahan himself had to direct the military operations against them. Therefore, he stayed at Burhanpur for about two years in 1630-31 for this purpose. To the good fortune of Shah Jahan, Malik Ambar had died just before the former's accession to the throne, and his son Fateh Khan, the new minister of Ahmadnagar, though an ambitious young man, was not so capable as his father to take a firm stand. In his bid to establish his pre-dominant role in the state politics Fateh Khan fell out with his Sultan and was put behind the bars by his master. The minister secured his release by the intervention of the queen, but he, in turn, placed his master under confinement.

It proved very helpful to the Mughals in overcoming the resistance of Nizamshahi kingdom. Fateh Khan developed secret contacts with Asaf Khan, the Mughal prime minister then stationed at Burhanpur, and, on the instigation of the latter, put Nizamshah to death while giving out that 'he had died a natural death'. He placed Nizamshah's minor son Husain on the throne, and himself setup as his Regent. It led to factionalism among the nobles of Ahmadnagar and weakened their opposition to the Mughals considerably. Meanwhile, Mahabat Khan was put in charge of the Mughal army of the Deccan. He overran many parts of the Ahmadnagar state on the pretext of wiping out pockets of resistance to the Mughals, and Fateh Khan made peace with the Mughals by acknowledging the Mughal suzerainty. He read the *khutba* and struck coins in the name of Shah Jahan and offered 'jewellery and valuables of the late king, worth eight *lakh* rupees' besides a number of war elephants and horses to Shah Jahan at Burhanpur as *nazrana*. Fully satisfied with the outcome, the Mughal emperor returned to Agra in triumph in March 1632.

The opponents of Fateh Khan bore a grudge against him for his treachery towards the ruling dynasty of Ahmadnagar. They refused to acknowledge the abject surrender to the Mughal authority and Ahmadnagar was plunged into a state of civil war between the two rival factions. Incidentally, Shahji Bhonsla, the father of future Chhatrapati Shivaji, also happened to be one of the leaders of the rival faction of Ahmadnagar. He secured the support of Bijapur in his fight against Fateh Khan. As a counter-reaction, Fateh Khan surrendered the fort of Daulatabad, along with the boy Sultan of Ahmadnagar, to Mahabat Khan in return for the Mughal protection and a 'substantial reward (bribe) of over ten *lakhs* of rupees'. The minor Nizamshahi Sultan, Husain Shah, was sent to Gwalior as the state prisoner and Fateh Khan was admitted into the imperial service.

The treacherous change of sides by Fateh Khan gave a serious setback to the defenders of Ahmadnagar. Shahji Bhonsla put up another scion of the Nizamshahi family as the Sultan of Ahmadnagar and himself played the role of a king-maker for many years. He rallied round him many other nobles and fugitive soldiers of the erstwhile Ahmadnagar state, and the war between the antagonists dragged on beyond expectations. Mahabat Khan, the renowned Mughal viceroy of the Deccan, died in October 1634. Thereupon, Shah Jahan felt obliged to march to the south for the second time. He reached Burhanpur in January 1636 and personally directed the operations against Shahji Bhonsla. The Maratha noble was, ultimately, defeated and compelled to surrender the puppet Nizamshahi Sultan and six forts of Ahmadnagar state, which were still in the hands of his men, to the Mughals as the price of peace with them. Nevertheless, Shahji was allowed to retain his personal assets and permitted to take up service under Sultan Adil Shah of Bijapur who had acknowledged the suzerainty of the Mughal emperor a short while ago. Adil Shah assigned the territories of Poona and Supa as personal *jagirs*, in perpetuity, to Shahji Bhonsla. With the exit of Shahji the state of Ahmadnagar ceased to exist for ever.

Submission of Bijapur and Golconda (1636 A.D.)

Muhammad Adil Shah, the Sultan of Bijapur, had always been sympathetic towards the struggle of Ahmadnagar against the Mughals, and Shahji Bhonsla enjoyed a liberal patronage from the court of Bijapur. Adil Shah had a large body of the Marathas in his army who played havoc in the Mughal territories by their guerilla tactics. Therefore, after the submission of Fateh Khan of Ahmadnagar in 1631, Shah Jahan directed his attention towards Bijapur. In December 1631, the Mughal forces, under the command of Asaf Khan, launched a major offensive against Bijapur. They overran Gulbarga, and put the stronghold of Bijapur under siege. Nevertheless, the outbreak of famine and plague took a heavy toll of the imperial troops and their horses while Adil Shah engaged Asaf Khan in the futile talks for peace for too long to break the Mughal morale. Shah Jahan ordered the recall of the Mughal armies from Bijapur and returned to Agra. Thus the first military expedition against Bijapur proved a failure. The death of Mahabat Khan and Shah Jahan's pre-occupations elsewhere, 'gave a lease of life to the Bijapuris' but 'they failed to make use of the opportunity to strengthen their defenses'. Shah Jahan made his reappearance in the Deccan in January 1636 for the second time. He immediately issued stern warning to the Sultans of Bijapur and Golconda to make their submission or face destruction, and strengthened his demand by dispatching the imperial troops to invest both the states instantaneously.

Sultan Adil Shah of Bijapur offered his submission after some hesitation. He acknowledged the suzerainty of Delhi, and *khutba* was read and coins stuck in the name of Shah Jahan. Twenty *lacs* of rupees were paid by him as war indemnity, and he further promised not to support Shahji Bhonsla in his fight against the Mughals. In return, Shah Jahan not only handed over the entire state of Bijapur to Adil Shah but also gave him additional control of fifty *parganas* of the erstwhile state of Ahmadnagar. This Treaty of Peace, which was signed between Bijapur and the Mughals on May 6, 1636, remained in force for twenty years.

As for Golconda, its ruler Muhammad Qutub Shah had died on January 31, 1626, and was succeeded by his minor son Abdullah Shah, then hardly twelve years old. The nobles of Golconda, therefore, adopted a conciliatory attitude towards Shah Jahan. During his first visit to the Deccan in 1630-32, a deputation from the court of Golconda had waited upon the Mughal emperor with rich presents even though the question of acknowledging the suzerainty of Delhi was tactfully held in abeyance by the agents of the Qutbshahi Sultan. In 1636, Shah Jahan's envoy was received by Abdullah Shah with due respects and entertained lavishly. Meanwhile the Mughal army had also arrived at the Golconda borders to press for complete submission. The Sultan of Golconda, therefore, opened negotiations for peace on amicable terms. As soon as he received the news about the submission of Bijapur, he hastened to offer his submission on the terms dictated by the Mughals. By the Treaty of Peace, which was signed on May 26, 1636, Golconda acknowledged the suzerainty of Delhi. The name of Shah of Persia, which previously appeared in the *khutba*, was deleted and substituted by that of the Mughal emperor. Golconda agreed to pay an annual tribute of two hundred thousand *huns*, equivalent to six *lakhs* of rupees, with retrospective effect. All arrears of the tribute, amounting to thirty-two *lakhs* of rupees were to be paid in installments. The Sultan of Golconda professed loyalty to the Mughal throne on oath by the Quran and promised to assist the imperialists against Bijapur if ever hostilities broke out between them. Shah Jahan received tribute and presents from the envoys of Bijapur and Golconda personally at Burhanpur, and his south Indian campaign met with complete success. It extended the boundaries of the Mughal Empire to the far south.

Aurangzeb as the Mughal Viceroy of the Deccan (1636-44)

Aurangzeb, the third son of Shah Jahan, then aged eighteen, had accompanied his father to the Deccan in 1636. After the conclusion of the Deccan affairs to his satisfaction, Shah Jahan appointed Aurangzeb as the viceroy of the Deccan and himself returned to Agra in July 1636; Burhanpur, the provincial capital of Khandesh was his vice regal capital. The Mughal territories in the south were divided into four provinces, namely, Khandesh, Berar, Daulatabad and Telingana. Khandesh comprised the Tapti valley with its capital at Burhanpur with its formidable fort of Asirgarh. The provincial capital of Berar was Ellichpur and its second major fort was at Gwaligarh. The province of Daulatabad included in its fold the heart of the Maratha land, including the historic fort of Ahmadnagar and its adjoining territories. For some time, its provincial capital was located at Ahmadnagar which was subsequently shifted to Daulatabad. The province of Telingana included the region of Balaghat, extending from Chand and the Waingangâ River to the north and north-eastern frontiers of Golconda. Nanded, now the famous Sikh shrine, where Guru Gobind Singh had been stabbed to death by a disgruntled Afghan in 1708, was included in this province.

Aurangzeb governed the Deccan with success for about eight years. He restored law and order within the territories under his control, introduced administrative reforms and consolidated the Mughal hold there. The Shia states of Bijapur and Golconda were held by the Mughals in suzerainty but Aurangzeb's treatment towards them rather harsh. His viceroyalty of the Deccan came to an abrupt end in March 1644 when he went to Agra to enquire about the health of his ailing sister, Jahan Ara Begam. It is said that the emperor had received complaints about the policy of excessive religious fanaticism displayed by him towards Hindus as well as *Shias* of the south. Nevertheless, Aurangzeb received fresh appointment as governor of Gujarat in May 1644.

Aurangzeb's Second Viceroyalty of the Deccan

Eight years later, Aurangzeb received the viceroyalty of the Deccan for the second time in November 1652. By this time, he had earned reputation as excellent administrator and seasoned military general though 'an uncompromising religious fanatic who regarded the *Shia* Sultans of Bijapur and Golconda as heretics, worthy of being extirpated'. No wonder, Aurangzeb began to interfere into the affairs of Bijapur and Golconda on one pretext or the other. Bur for the restraint exercised by the imperial court, he would have liked to destroy both the ruling houses and annex their territories to the Mughal Empire immediately. Abdullah Qutubshah, the Sultan of Golconda, was not on good terms with his ambitious prime minister Mir Jumla who was an orthodox Sunni Mussalman. Aurangzeb entered into secret understanding with Mir Jumla and declared war on Golconda in January 1656 on the ground that it had failed to pay annual tribute regularly. The Mughal army led by Prince Muhammad, the eldest son of Aurangzeb, invaded Golconda. It conquered the fort of Hyderabad and laid siege to the fort of Golconda. Hard-pressed, the Sultan sent his envoys to Shah Jahan to seek his personal intervention for restoring peace. Shah Jahan sent express orders to Aurangzeb to stop aggression against Golconda forthwith; but the latter did not divulge his orders, and pressed the siege of Golconda with full force until the Sultan was compelled to sue for unconditional surrender. A fresh Treaty of Peace was, accordingly, signed by Golconda. The Sultan cleared all the arrears of tribute and paid a war indemnity of fifteen *lakhs* of rupees. Besides, he gave his daughter in marriage to Prince Muhammad, accompanied by ten *lakhs* of rupees as dowry. And treacherous Mir Jumla, who had become the cause of humiliation of his own master, secured all of his assets within the state of Golconda while being admitted to the imperial Mughal service. He was destined to rise to the exalted office of Aurangzeb's prime minister in due course of time.

Aurangzeb's war of aggression against Golconda had a sobering effect on Adil Shah, the Sultan of Bijapur. He became extremely humble in his dealings with the Mughal prince and always tried to keep him in good humour. Adil Shah died in November 1656 and was succeeded by his son Ali Adil Shah II, then a young boy of eighteen. Aurangzeb declined to recognise him as the real son of the deceased Sultan, and secured permission from Shah Jahan to intervene in the affairs of the state on this account. He made a sudden attack on Bijapur on the advice of Mir Jumla, who was, obviously,' an expert in the affairs of the Deccan'. The forts of Bidar and Kalyani were captured by the Mughals, when they made a final assault on the defences of the Bijapur fort. About this time, the envoys of the Sultan Ali Adil Shah II secured peace by the direct intervention of the Mughal emperor in August 1657. Nevertheless, Aurangzeb thrust a new Treaty of Peace on Golconda but on very hard terms. Large territories of the Golconda state, including the forts of Bidar, Kalyani and Parenda, were annexed to the Mughal empire and the Sultan was called upon to pay a sum of one crore of rupees as war indemnity. As luck would have it, the timely conclusion of peace with Bijapur and Golconda proved very helpful to Aurangzeb in fighting the War Succession that broke out between the sons of Shah Jahan soon thereafter.

The Kandahar Affairs

The Mughals had lost Kandahar (Qandahar or Qandhar) to the Persians in 1622 because of Prince Shah Jahan's irresponsible conduct. No wonder, as emperor, Shah Jahan felt very bad about it but the Deccan affairs kept his hands full for a long time. Nevertheless, the recovery of Kandahar from the hands of the Persians was a matter of prestige and honour with Shah Jahan. He had instructed Sayyad Khan, the Mughal governor of Kabul, to keep an eye on the Persian governor and other dignitaries of Kandahar, and persuade them to change sides for securing the patronage of the mighty Mughal Empire which provided vast avenues for civil and military services to the Muslim immigrants from all over the world. Ali Mardan, the governor of Kandahar, sounded a note of warning to his Persian monarch that he apprehended danger from Kabul. But the Persian ruler disbelieved and distrusted his own governor and sent a military commander to arrest him. Ali Mardan was distressed 'at the false allegations levelled against him', and decided to betray his master. He joined hands with the Mughal agents, secretly admitted a Mughal contingent of 1,000 troops into the fort of Kandahar in February 1638, and handed over its control to the Mughal commander. Ali Mardan read the *Khutba* in the name of Shah Jahan on February 28, 1638; and all the pro-Persian elements were promptly turned out of the fort to avoid bloodshed. Sayyad Khan, the Mughal governor of Kabul, marched on Kandahar with full force within a couple of days and took possession of the stronghold. The Mughal troops quickly spread themselves into the countryside and acquired control of the whole region without much resistance. The Mughal officials, who had recovered Kandahar through this bloodless coup, were richly rewarded by Shah Jahan and Ali Mardan and his accomplices were absorbed in the imperial Mughal services. Ali Mardan was granted a very high *mansab* so as to join the ranks of the *grandees* of the empire, and he held the governorships of Kashmir and the Punjab during the next two decades.

Central Asian Policy

The expansion of the Mughal sway in the Deccan and re-occupation of Kandahar spread the name and fame of Shah Jahan all through the Muslim world. It prompted him to adopt a forward policy on the Central Asian front. He was ill-advised by some of his short-sighted courtiers and flatterers to go ahead and conquer 'the homeland of his ancestors' in Central Asia. It gave birth to what is known as the Central Asian policy of Shah Jahan. He chalked out wild plans for the conquest of Balkh and Badakhshan, situated beyond the Hind Koh as the first step. These countries formed a part of the empire of Nazar Muhammad Khan, the Uzbeg ruler of Bokhara. Taking advantage of the internal conflict between Nazar Muhammad and his son, Abdul Aziz, in 1646, Shah Jahan sent a strong Mughal force, composed of 50,000 horsemen and 10,000 foot soldiers under the command of Prince Murad and Ali Mardan for the occupation of Balkh. On the approach of the Mughal armies, Nazar Muhammad hurriedly patched up with his rebellious son, and they put up joint front against the invaders. Nevertheless, the Mughal forces overran the regions of Balkh and Badakhshan in July 1646, and seized huge booty from the retreating Uzbeg troops, which included 2,500 horses, 500 camels, and gold and silver worth twelve *lakhs* of rupees. It was a great victory of the Mughal arms. For a while, the Central Asian policy of Shah Jahan seemed to have been very successful.

Unfortunately, Prince Murad, being a man of ease-loving habits, did not relish the hardships of camp life in the far-off lands with severe climate. He sought Shah Jahan's permission to return home, and without waiting for reply from the emperor, handed over the charge of conquered territories to Ali Mardan and, himself returned to Kabul. It disappointed his father, who relieved Prince Murad of his high *mansab* and the royal titles, and recalled him to the court. He sent his prime minister, Sadullah Khan, to Balkh to review the situation. On his recommendations, Shah Jahan sent reinforcements to Balkh under Aurangzeb in 1647, and himself moved to Kabul to supervise the new setup.

The conquest of Balkh by the Mughals alarmed all the Muslim powers of Central Asia. The ferocious tribesmen of Hindu Kush and the Uzbegs stood up en masse to defend their homelands against their intrusion. Despite their tough resistance, Aurangzeb reached Balkh and defeated the Uzbegs in a pitched battle in September 1647. It was, however, impossible for the Mughals to establish their permanent hold over Balkh because of the bitter opposition and non-cooperation of its inhabitants. Nazar Muhammad was willing to accept the Mughal vassalage provided they withdrew their troops from Balkh and allowed the Uzbegs internal autonomy. At long last, Aurangzeb handed over the charge of Balkh intact to Nazar Muhammad with the permission of Shah Jahan and returned to Kabul with the entire Mughal force in the winter of 1647. On the return march, the Mughal army was waylaid by the Hazara tribesmen of the Hindu Kush and put to plunder. The Uzbeg chief, Nazar Muhammad, professed loyalty to Shah Jahan until his abdication in favour of his son in 1650, but the Mughals got nothing from him by way of tribute. This expedition cost the Mughal government more than four crores of rupees. A thousand of the Mughal soldiers were killed in action while more than 500 of them, besides thousands of horses and beasts of burden perished on their return march through the Hindu Kush; they either killed by the Hazaras or 'tumbled into the deep ravines and were frozen to death'. War material and provisions worth *lakhs* of rupees were plundered by the tribesmen or buried under snow.

The ill-conceived Central Asian policy of Shah Jahan proved a complete failure. It proved counter-productive. The hard-earned reputation of the power and prestige of the Mughal Empire met with a nose dive, and the Mughal emperor, Shah Jahan, became a laughing stock of the entire Muslim world.

Loss of Kandahar to the Persians (1649)

It is held by the contemporary Muslim chroniclers that 'the loss of Kandahar at the hands of Persians was the direct outcome of the failure of Central Asian Policy of Shah Jahan'. The failure of the Mughals to hold on in Balkh encouraged Shah Abbas of Persia to recover Kandahar by force. He shifted his army camp to Herat and launched a frontal attack on Kandahar under his personal supervision. The Persians overran the countryside and laid siege to the fort of Kandahar in December 1648. The besieged Mughal governor, Daulat Khan, held out for 57 days before his surrender on February 11, 1649, because of the non-receipt of reinforcements from Kabul. Kandahar was thus lost to the Mughals forever. Shah Jahan fretted and fumed and dispatched as many as three full-fledged expeditions for its re-conquest during the next six years in quick succession but they all proved unsuccessful. These expeditions cost the Mughal exchequer over twelve *crores* of rupees besides the loss of five thousand lives of the Indian soldiers.

SECTION 3: WAR OF SUCCESSION BETWEEN THE SONS OF SHAH JAHAN (1657-58)

According to Khafi Khan, Shah Jahan suffered from eternal constipation and urinary disorders – very common ailments of which the medical science today provides an instant relief through medication or operation but, unfortunately, the most magnificent Mughal emperor lost his throne and much besides on this account. He felt intense pain and irritation at the base of the urinary bladder at the time of urination. On September 8, 1657, Shah Jahan was struck down by total blockage of his stools and urine. The royal physicians tried all the remedies but to no effect. The Crown Prince Dara Shikoh, who had already been kept by Shah Jahan at the imperial capital to assist him in the discharge of his royal functions, was now called upon to deputise for the ailing emperor; 'even otherwise, under the normal circumstances, he was expected to succeed his father as the rightful successor to the throne'. To his misfortune, however, Dara failed to send the timely information about the illness of the emperor to his brothers. It was his foolishness as the inability of the emperor to show himself at the *jharokha darshan* had already set afloat all sorts of speculations about his illness. Long silence of Dara to clarify the exact position spread the rumours that Shah Jahan had either breathed his last or done to death by poisoning by the Crown Prince. It triggered off a bloody war of succession between all the four surviving sons of Shah Jahan in which Aurangzeb ultimately came out successful.

The Four Contestants for Power

As described earlier, Shah Jahan had six surviving children—four sons, Dara Shikoh, Shah Shuja, Aurangzeb and Murad Bakhsh, and two daughters, Jahan Ara Begam and Roshan Ara Begam, all from his wife Mumtaz Mahal. And, in the fratricidal war, all of them, including the two princesses, took part vigorously. Jahan Ara supported Dara Shikoh while Roshan Ara stood for Aurangzeb. The four brothers were respectively 43, 41, 39 and 33 years old at the time of this self-destructive conflagration. All of them were well-educated and trained in diplomacy and statecraft. Again, all of them held substantial administrative assignments and personal *jagirs* in various parts of the empire, and were ably assisted in the discharge of their functions by competent military officers and bureaucrats. Dara was the viceroy of North-Western India, including the provinces of Lahore, Multan and Kabul although his presence at the imperial court was deemed essential by his father. He had entrusted the work of administration of his provinces to the respective provincial governors and *diwans* as his assistants. Shah Shuja was the governor of Bengal while Aurangzeb held the viceroyalty of all the four Mughal provinces of the Deccan. Shah Jahan's youngest son Murad was the governor of Gujarat.

All the four brothers possessed unlimited resources in men and material. They maintained huge personal armies, and 'there was none to question them about the way they utilised the revenues of their provinces'. The imperial troops posted in the provinces under their respective governorships, could be readily brought under their personal control without much difficulty. Above all, every one of these princes had a strong lobby at the imperial court which kept him posted with the latest developments at the capital. Roshan Ara played this role for Aurangzeb within the imperial *harem* also. It is said that she, being an orthodox Sunni by faith, did not approve of Dara's liberal ideology; she spied on the Crown Prince and reported all about his activities and his supporters to Aurangzeb through secret agents. Dara Shikoh was a capable administrator but not a good military general or statesmen. According to an assessment, Dara was 'a man of character and scholarship, he was cast in the mould of Akbar in his religious views and state policy. Very broad-minded and generous, he believed in *suleh-i-kul* and the concept of a secular nation-state for India, so ably espoused by Akbar. Shah Shuja, the governor of Bengal, possessed Shia ideology and was a good administrator and brave warrior but, because of his addiction to drugs and ease-loving habits, his health was badly impaired. And Murad, the youngest of Shah Jahan's sons, was the least capable as a man, administrator or military commander. He was addicted to sensual pleasures and was known to be an idiot or 'a fool in politics, who played in the hands of Aurangzeb to bring about Dara's fall, and, as a reward for his services to his crafty brother, lost his head instead'.

Aurangzeb, the third son of Shah Jahan, was well-educated in Islamic religion and theology. He was a capable administrator, warrior and statesman. He lived a simple and austere life unlike the princely order of the day to which he belonged. He was possessed of 'cool courage, unflinching determination and dogged perseverance' – the qualities which 'won him the admiration, if not always the devotion, of his contemporaries'. As a prince, Aurangzeb had been performing his civil and military duties with great success. Twice he had held the viceroyalty of the Deccan besides the governorship of Gujarat. His successful command of the Balkh and Badakhshan expeditions had established his reputation as the seasoned military general. But, as luck would have it, Aurangzeb had grown up as orthodox religious fundamentalist and was extremely 'narrow-minded, suspicious and reserved by nature'.

Nevertheless, Shah Jahan had no doubts or allusions about his future successor. He was fully convinced that his eldest son, Dara Shikoh was fully competent and the most suitable person to be his rightful successor. Formal nomination of Dara as the heir-apparent to the throne had not yet been made but he was the favourite and trustworthy sons of Shah Jahan. On merit, Aurangzeb was the nearest rival to Dara Shikoh in the race for succession to the throne, although, in his mental make-up and political ideology, Aurangzeb was an antithesis of Dara Shikoh. On the other hand, each of the four sons of Shah Jahan aspired to step into the shoes of his father as the next emperor of India. In the race for kingship, they were equal contestants and, in the absence of any fixed law of succession, each one of them was prepared to take any risk; they were all cut-throats.

Shah Shuja Blows the Bugle

On the receipt of intelligence about Shah Jahan's illness and Dara's failure to apprise them of the correct position, the other three princes suddenly realised that 'their day of reckoning had come'. They rightly suspected that Dara Shikoh 'would not allow the news of his father's death to leak out until he had consolidated his position on the throne'. So it was that none of them bothered to confirm the rumour about the death of Shah Jahan, and they set the ball to civil war rolling. Shuja was the first to snatch the initiative. He made out that Dara Shikoh had poisoned the emperor to death and; therefore, did not deserve to be his successor. From his headquarters at Rajmahal in Bengal, he read the *khutba* and struck coins in his name as the emperor of India. Without losing any time, he marched out with his army and the fleet of boats towards Banaras along the Ganges on the way to Delhi and Agra.

Prince Murad Declares his Independence

Almost simultaneously, Prince Murad also declared his sovereignty in Gujarat. He put his *Diwan*, Ali Naqi, to death as he was suspected to be a supporter of Dara Shikoh and started hectic preparation to march towards Agra.

Aurangzeb Stoops to Conquer

In this game of power-politics, Aurangzeb resorted to cunning diplomacy to overpower his brothers. He quickly strengthened his firm control over all the provinces under his viceroyalty by deputing his most trustworthy officers at the helm of affairs, removed all the non-partisan or doubtful imperial nobles, and hurriedly made amicable settlements with the states of Bijapur and Golconda. His personal army was always kept in readiness to take the field at the moment's notice. He showed wonderful skill in acquiring control over all the imperial troops then stationed in the Deccan. Mir Jumla, an orthodox Sunni and an intimate friend of Aurangzeb, then held the charge of the imperial artillery and war material in the Deccan. Nevertheless, Aurangzeb 'played a ruse upon the central government, then under the charge of Dara Shikoh, by placing Mir Jumla under arrest', apparently to take personal possession and command of the imperial artillery. VA Smith observes that 'probably, Mir Jumla connived at his own arrest to befool Dara Shikoh' (*Oxford History*, pp. 228-29). It was because the latter 'did not resent his arrest, nor did he fail to continue to give his ally (Aurangzeb) invaluable support when released'. His artillery proved extremely useful to Aurangzeb in his struggle against his brothers.

At the same time, Aurangzeb entered into correspondence with Shuja and Murad to inflame their wrath against Dara Shikoh. While doing so, he concealed his own evil designs to deceive his brothers. In his letters, Aurangzeb addressed his elder brother Shuja with utmost humility and respect as 'Bhai Jiyo, and wished him success in his plans for the occupation of the throne in which, according to his own profession, he was least interested'. On the other hand, he ridiculed Prince Murad by assuming the role of his elder brother, and advised him to make a very cautious approach in his struggle against Dara Shikoh and Shah Shuja. He incited Murad by suggesting him like a pontiff that 'the Mughal throne must be saved from falling into the hands of the heretics like Dara and Shuja'. In his wickedness, Aurangzeb made a secret offer to Murad to divide the Empire between themselves in case of their collective efforts; Murad was to get one-third of the spoils and sovereignty over the North-Western part of the Mughal Empire, including the provinces of Punjab, Sindh, Kashmir and Kabul, while Aurangzeb was to occupy the throne of Agra. In his foolhardiness, Murad fell into his sinister trap and was fully convinced of Aurangzeb's sincerity to form a united front to fight against their other two brothers.

Murad Joins Aurangzeb's Camp

Aurangzeb crossed the River Narbada at the head of a well-equipped army and heavy artillery on his march towards Agra but without any fanfare. He falsely gave out that he was going to the North to see his ailing father. On the other hand, Murad marched out with his armies from Gujarat with the open declaration to fight against Dara Shikoh. Their forces made a junction near Ujjain in April 1658.

Important Events of the War

Dara Shikoh at Agra seems to have been ill-prepared to meet the challenge from his brothers in the hot contest. He was assured of his regal status as the Crown Prince and rightful successor of Shah Jahan, and was confidently deputizing for his ailing father. He never assumed sovereignty nor adopted strong diplomatic measures to refute the baseless allegations of his brothers against him. He was, in fact, the *de facto* ruler of the empire at Agra, and had prepared his own plans to deal with the situation. He fell for the false public pronouncements and propaganda of Aurangzeb regarding his disinterest in the problem of succession, and was put off his guard towards him, at least for the time being.

Defeat of Shah Shuja at Bahadurpur (February 1658): Meanwhile, Suleiman Shikoh, the elder son of Dara Shikoh, and Raja Jai Singh of Amber were dispatched to confront Shah Shuja. The latter was defeated by the imperial troops at Bahadurpur near Banaras in February 1658 and begged a hasty retreat towards Bengal. The imperial army pursued him up to the borders of Bengal.

The Battle of Dharmat (April 25, 1658): Dara sent another army, under the command of Kasim Khan and Raja Jaswant Singh of Jodhpur, to deal with Murad. The imperial commanders were totally ignorant of the hostile but secret march of Aurangzeb towards the north. It was only at Ujjain that they came to know that armies of Murad and Aurangzeb had joined together to make a common front against Dara Shikoh. It made them nervous and indecisive about their plans of action. They were not equipped with sufficient men and armour to face the combined armies of the two princes. Kasim Khan and his men wavered but Raja Jaswant Singh and his Rajput soldiers pressed forward and made a frontal attack on the armies of Aurangzeb and Murad which had already been arranged in battle-array. A pitched battle was fought at Dharmat, situated about 25 kilometres to the southwest of Ujjain on April 25, 1658. The Rajputs fought valiantly but Kasim Khan's soldiers put up a half-hearted fight and fled the field. As a result, the battle was lost to the royal army; Jaswant Singh was himself wounded seriously and was removed from the battle-field by his faithful followers. Having been deserted by Kasim Khan's men altogether, the Rajputs retreated towards Jodhpur. It is said that when the Queen of Maharaja Jaswant Singh came to know of their defeat at Dharmat, she refused to admit her husband and the vanquished fighters into the stronghold until they explained to her the true nature of the strife between the Mughal princes.

The Battle of Samugarh (May 29, 1658): The victorious forces of Aurangzeb and Murad swiftly marched on Agra via Gwalior. By that time, Shah Jahan had recovered from illness, and he wanted to face his rebellious sons in person, but to his misfortune, Dara Shikoh, being at the helm of affairs, did not accept his father's advice. Being overconfident of his secure position and strength, he was determined to confront his brothers in person 'so as to decide the issue of succession once and for all'. It proved his ruin. It is believed that 'if the soldiers of Aurangzeb and Murad had come to know that the Emperor Shah Jahan was still alive, and if Shah Jahan had simply made his appearance on the battlefield, they would have refused to fight for the princes. But the fate had willed it otherwise'. Dara Shikoh assembled 50,000 royal troops under his personal command and camped outside Agra to meet his rivals. So confident was he of his sure victory that he did not wait even for the arrival of a huge segment of the imperial army, under the command of Raja Jai Singh, which was fast approaching Agra on the receipt of news about the advance of Aurangzeb and Murad.

The armies of Aurangzeb and Murad made their appearance in the neighbourhood of Agra on May 28, 1658. Their soldiers were dead tired because of their long and strenuous march from Central India. To his misfortune, Dara, whose forces were set in battle array, did not take the initiative to make a frontal attack and thus allowed a much-needed rest to the adversaries. The fateful battle was fought at Samugarh, about 13 kms to the east of Agra Fort early next morning. When the battle was raging with full fury, Dara's elephant was seriously wounded, and, on the ill-advice of his lieutenants, he left his elephant and mounted a horse. The sight of an empty *howdah* of the Royal Elephant was enough for the soldiers to panic. They broke up and fled for their lives, thus converting their near victory into clear defeat. Deserted by his men because of his own folly, Dara had no alternative but to take to flight. According to an estimate, about ten thousand soldiers of Dara died fighting at Samugarh while the loss of life among the troops of his adversaries was equally great.

Dara in Flight: The debacle of Samugarh sealed the fate of Dara Shikoh. He fled to the Agra Fort but, being ashamed of his defeat, did not dare to meet his father. Instead, he collected his family and the treasure and fled towards Delhi, accompanied by a handful of his faithful friends and followers. In his utter foolishness, Dara left the old and bed-ridden 'emperor in the lurch and deprived him of all chances to handle the situation with courage and tact at that critical moment'. By his hasty action and cowardly flight from the imperial capital, Dara Shikoh 'converted his personal defeat at Samugarh into an imperial catastrophe and the defeat of the Emperor Shah Jahan himself'.

Aurangzeb Plays a Ruse on Murad: The victorious Aurangzeb and Murad encamped at the battlefield of Samugarh for some time. They had come to know that the emperor Shah Jahan was alive. Murad regretted his action and declared that 'had he known this fact before, he would never have taken up arms against the imperial forces'. He wrote two letters of regrets to his father about his misconduct and sought his permission to meet him at the earliest. But 'Aurangzeb was too clever to let Murad slip out of his hands at the moment of his triumph'. He attributed the victory of Samugarh to Murad, and made a public pronouncement that the reign of Murad as the sovereign ruler (of North-Western India, obviously) would begin soon after Aurangzeb took possession of Agra. It was at the call of Aurangzeb that Murad agreed to give him company for a joint attack on Agra; nevertheless, he kept his army at a safe distance from that of Aurangzeb. They attacked the imperial capital from two separate sides; occupied the town and invested the fort. As Dara Shikoh had made sudden exit from the capital and the sick and much-bewildered emperor Shah Jahan could not summon the imperial court in time, Aurangzeb put up his royal tents in the *Bagh-i-Noor* on the outskirts of the metropolis and setup as the virtual emperor of India while Murad was stationed within his army camp away from the city. Aurangzeb moved swiftly to establish personal contacts with the important courtiers and civilians of the capital to win their support, apparently against Dara Shikoh, and started conferring high *mansabs*, honours, and titles, besides rich presents on those who came forward to acknowledge him as the sovereign.

Aurangzeb's Treachery against his Father: Shah Jahan was fully aware of Aurangzeb's wickedness. He shut the gates of the Agra Fort against him and prepared to defend it with the assistance of the Royal Guards. He called upon Aurangzeb to meet him and make a settlement but the latter put the imperial fort under siege and ordered artillery fire 'to frighten the guards into submission'. The 'royal abode' was well-defended, however, and could not be taken by storm. Aurangzeb, thereupon, 'cut off water supply from the Yamuna to the fort to compel his father to surrender. The water of the wells within the fort being brackish was unfit for drinking; it put the royal *harem* and guards to great straits'. Nevertheless, having failed to take the fort by storm, Aurangzeb resorted to cunning diplomacy to achieve his object without much delay. He professed loyalty to his father, and agreed to meet the emperor Shah Jahan in the fort for deliberations. The main gate of the imperial stronghold was, accordingly, opened on June 8, 1658, to admit Aurangzeb and his personal guards into the fort. True to his wile nature,

Aurangzeb sent his son Prince Muhammad who, through a strategy, overpowered the guards of the main entrance and took forced possession of the fort. The fort of Agra was thus occupied by Aurangzeb through treachery and deceit. The supporters of Dara Shikoh, who fell into his hands, were put to the sword. Aurangzeb immediately took into his possession the royal treasury and all the imperial assets. Shah Jahan was isolated from his *harem* and put into confinement within his own palace. It made Aurangzeb the *de facto* ruler of the country and most of the courtiers and imperial officers made a bee line to offer their congratulations and allegiance to him. So also was the case with the Royal Guards, provincial governors, imperial troops and their military generals, who flocked to Aurangzeb's court or sent messages of congratulations while offering their allegiance to him. After taking over the Agra fort, Aurangzeb lost no time in dispatching two armies, one to Bengal and the other to Delhi to bring Shah Shuja and Dara Shikoh to book.

Treacherous Imprisonment and Liquidation of Murad: Aurangzeb took the reins of government in his hands and setup as the emperor of India, and Murad, stationed within his army camp away from the imperial capital, 'was left high and dry'. Aurangzeb never bothered to take Murad into confidence while executing his plans regarding the occupation of the Agra fort or placing Shah Jahan into confinement, particularly. Murad's name was never mentioned in any of Aurangzeb's court proceedings or royal decrees, nor did any of the state ministers; imperial officers or military generals pay any attention to him. Totally isolated, Murad became desperate and separated himself from the army camp of Aurangzeb with his 20,000 men, apparently to chalk out an independent programme of action. The wily Aurangzeb was quick to pacify him on the ground that he should wait for a while until their real enemies, Dara and Shuja, were apprehended. He argued that without the extirpation of the other contenders for power, the proposed partition of the empire could not be affected. Khafi Khan writes that Murad 'was deluded by flattering promises and the presents of money' by Aurangzeb, who sent to his camp cart-loads of gold, silver and other valuables worth *lakhs* of rupees as his share of the spoils. According to the chronicler, these 'were deposits or loans rather than gifts' for which Murad had to pay by his dear life. (*Muntakhab-ul-Lubab* E&D. vii, pp. 228-29).

After consolidation of his position at Agra, Aurangzeb marched towards Delhi with a large army, and Murad also followed him but 'in a separate formation'. Aurangzeb invited Murad to a joint dinner in which the latter was served with strong drinks and then treacherously put in golden chains on June 25, 1658. His senior military commanders and advisers were bribed to surrender his camp with Murad's family, entire treasure, and property intact. When apprised of this occurrence, almost all of Murad's military officers and soldiers changed their sides and were absorbed in the imperial service by Aurangzeb. Murad was first taken as captive to Delhi and from there shifted to Gwalior. Later on, he was charged with the alleged murder of Ali Naqi, the *diwan* of Gujarat, and executed at Agra on December 4, 1661.

The Fate of Dara Shikoh and his Family: On hearing of the above tidings, Dara's lieutenants at Delhi and Lahore deserted him. On receipt of express summons from Aurangzeb, most of the Mughal nobles and bureaucrats of northwestern India professed their loyalties to him and refused to cooperate with Dara. Therefore, on the approach of Aurangzeb's troops, Dara fled to Lahore, and Delhi fell into Aurangzeb's hands without a fight. He made a triumphant entry into the imperial metropolis on July 21, 1658, and promptly assumed all the formal imperial titles as the Emperor of India. It marked the end of Shah Jahan's reign. He celebrated his regular coronation ceremony long afterwards, in June 1659, when all of his political rivals had either been done to death or were held as state prisoners.

Meanwhile, Aurangzeb's troops gave a hot chase to Dara and his camp-followers. All the provincial governors, *diwans* and other high officers of northwestern India had been warned by Aurangzeb to stall the fugitives. Dara fled from Lahore to Gujarat and from there went to Rajputana to seek help from his erstwhile Rajput associates like Maharaja Jaswant Singh and Mirza Raja Jai Singh but they had already been won over by Aurangzeb to his side. Dara was overtaken and defeated by the imperial troops at the pass of Deorai near Ajmer. Thereafter, most of his soldiers and friends deserted him and he was left with only his family, including his younger son Siphir Shikoh and a few others. He again fled to Gujarat from where he intended to migrate to Persia via Sindh and Kandahar. On the way, Dara took shelter with a Baluchi chief Malik Jiwan of Dadar, whom he had once saved from the displeasure of his father Shah Jahan. Nevertheless, his host and beneficiary betrayed Dara Shikoh and party for fear of his own future and handed them over to Aurangzeb's agents. They were all brought to Delhi as prisoners on September 1, 1658. It is said that 'Dara, in rags, was paraded through the streets of Delhi while seated on a filthy elephant. He was charged with apostasy from Islam, and beheaded'; His dead body, soaked in blood, was again placed on a howdah (of a dirty elephant), and was carried round the city for public exposure. He was buried in the tomb of Humayun while his son Siphir was sent to Gwalior as state prisoner. All the accomplices of Dara were condemned to death. The sympathisers of Dara and the citizens of Delhi, who witnessed 'this shocking and dastardly action' of Aurangzeb, wailed and cried but could do nothing to save his life. According to Khafi Khan, 'the traitor Malik Jiwan, though condemned by the people, received a robe of honour and a *mansab* of 1,000 with 200 *swar* rank' from the new sovereign. Suleiman Shikoh, the eldest son of Dara, had taken shelter in Garhwal. He was also captured after some time and lodged in the fort of Gwalior, where he was poisoned to death in May 1662.

The Liquidation of Shah Shuja: Shah Shuja was defeated by Aurangzeb's army at Khajwaha in the Fatehpur district of modern U.P. on January 5, 1659. He retired towards Bengal, followed close on his heels by Aurangzeb's troops, and fled for his dear life to Arakan where he was killed by the Meghs in May 1660. Siphir Shikoh, the younger son of Dara, was lucky to escape the wrath of Aurangzeb. After the extirpation of his elder brother Suleiman Shikoh, he was liberated and brought to the imperial *harem* in Delhi where Aurangzeb married his daughter to him; he was the only Mughal prince of royal blood, other than his own family, to have been spared his life by Aurangzeb Alamgir.

The Imprisonment and Death of Shah Jahan: The erstwhile Mughal emperor, Shah Jahan – the most magnificent and world-famous Great Mogul, who had recovered from his earlier ailment, languished in the jail of his most malicious, cold-blooded, disobedient ungrateful son, Aurangzeb, throughout the rest of his life. He was confined in the Shah Burj of the Agra Fort for about seven years and a half. Having been totally cut off from the outside world, he was deprived of even the writing material, 'lest he might smuggle some information about him out of the prison'. The personal jewellery and all other valuables of Shah Jahan were also taken away from him by force. Jahan Ara Begam—the eldest child of Shah Jahan, who had not been married 'for reasons of state', voluntarily joined her aged father in the prison to look after him. Prolonged detention in close confinement completely shattered Shah Jahan's health. He was taken ill and confined to bed early in 1662 and died on 22nd of January. It is said that the only thing that attracted his attention outside the Shah Burj was the sight of Taj Mahal, and that, on the eve of his death, he had fixed his gaze on that historic monument – the mausoleum of his wife at the Taj till his last moment. Aurangzeb never met his father during his confinement within the royal palace in the Agra Fort. None else was allowed to meet the erstwhile Mughal emperor, now a state prisoner. Even after the death of Shah Jahan, Aurangzeb did not come to pay homage to the deceased nor permitted the state funeral for him. On the other hand, Shah Jahan's dead body was carried by eunuchs and menials from a back-door of the fort and buried by the side of the grave of Mumtaz Mahal in the Taj. So long as Shah Jahan was held in confinement at Agra, Aurangzeb preferred to stay in Delhi where his harem was lodged and the imperial court was held. He entered the Fort of Agra one month after the death of his father; and, before his arrival, all the buildings of the Fort were renovated after eight years of neglect.

The Last Days of Jahan Ara Begam: As regards Jahan Ara Begam, 'the embodiment of human virtue and the spirit of self-sacrifice', she was, of course, received with respect by Aurangzeb but requested to go away to Delhi, where she was allowed to stay with all the royal honours and dignities. She was acclaimed as 'the most respected First Lady of the Realm' till her death on September 16, 1681. She was buried in the shrine of Sheikh Nizamuddin Auliya. She had Sufi inclinations and was said to have been a disciple of Mian Mir; she used to spend most of her time in meditation and prayers. Nearly the entire pension, received by her from the state exchequer, was given away by her in charity. Beale pays his homage to her by the remarks that 'her name will ever adorn the pages of history as a bright example of filial attachment, and heroic self-devotion to the dictates of duty.'(Quoted in B P Saksena, *Shahjahan*, pp. 341-42).

The Fate of Prince Muhammad—the eldest rebellious son of Aurangzeb: The narrative of the civil-war victims of Aurangzeb includes the name of Prince Muhammad Sultan – his eldest son also. As referred to earlier, he had been sent by Aurangzeb along with Mir Jumla to fight against Shah Shuja. The latter was defeated and pushed back to Bengal. However, the prince hated his father's mean role in the war of succession. He developed a soft corner for his uncle Shah Shuja and, finding a suitable opportunity, defected to him along with some other Mughal nobles. Shah Shuja received them with open arms and gave his daughter in marriage to Prince Muhammad. The defection of Prince Muhammad shocked Aurangzeb but he kept this news as a closely guarded secret, and directed Mir Jumla to liberate Bengal from the hands of Shah Shuja. This was promptly done by the much-embarrassed Mughal general and Shah Shuja fled towards Arakan. Thereafter, Prince Muhammad Sultan returned to the Mughal camp to the great joy of Mir Jumla. He at once reported the matter to Aurangzeb, on whose orders, the prince was sent to the imperial court while his accomplices were thrown in jail.

Shah Jahan had soiled his hands with the blood of his two ambitious brothers and four other innocent princelings of the royal blood to make it to the throne, and nature inflicted a severe punishment on him during his very lifetime the like of which could never be contemplated by a sovereign of his stature.

SECTION 4: SHAH JAHAN'S REIGN 'THE GOLDEN AGE OF MUGHAL HISTORY'

Golden Age of Medieval India

The Mughal rulers of India, particularly, from Akbar to Shah Jahan (1556-1657) gave a century of peace and prosperity to the people of the country. The name and fame of the mighty Mughal monarchs of India spread throughout the civilised world and attracted hundreds and thousands of the foreign adventurers, businessmen and Christian missionaries to this 'golden sparrow of the world'. They were 'dazzled by the wealth, magnificence and grandeur of the Indian monarchs and their ruling elite. During this period, the reign of Shah Jahan (1627-57), especially, 'represented the height of kingly splendour'. The magnificence of his imperial court 'surpassed the imagination of the foreign visitors', like Bernier, Tavernier and Manucci, who have left very valuable accounts of their visits to India. The Mughal Empire attained its maximum territorial dimensions under Aurangzeb, but it is universally acknowledged by the historians that it had reached 'the zenith of its prosperity and affluence' during the reign of Shah Jahan. Accordingly, the period of his rule is considered to be 'the Golden Age of Mughal India or the medieval Indian history; and there are many sound reasons to uphold this view.

The Era of Peace and Tranquillity

Shah Jahan inherited a vast and well-consolidated empire from his predecessors. The policy of political unification of the country, conceived by Akbar, was being carried out to its logical conclusion.

The armed strength of the empire, built so consistently by Akbar and Jahangir, ensured slow but steady expansion of the Mughal dominions; and the occasional 'grossly mismanaged expeditions and undesirable foreign wars of aggression' waged by Shah Jahan could not weaken the military prowess and resources of the state beyond repairs. Therefore, during the reigns of these three magnificent emperors—Akbar, Jahangir and Shah Jahan, the people enjoyed a long era of peace and tranquillity. The Mughal Empire remained free from internal revolts and foreign wars and there was almost perfect law and order. The internal and foreign security of the empire was well looked after by Shah Jahan. The foreign travellers testify to the prevalence of perfect law and order in the Mughal Empire during the days of Shah Jahan. The roads were safe and the movement of traffic and trade was brick. The dacoits and thieves were inflicted severe punishments and the anti-social elements were held in check. Stern measures were adopted by the Mughal government to protect the life and property of his subjects.

Good Government

Akbar and Jahangir had bequeathed to Shah Jahan 'a well-knit, prosperous and the best-administered empire of Asia'; therefore, Shah Jahan had nothing to worry about any sort of political or administrative problems. For every political or administrative problem there was a technique or precedence ready at hand for its solution. The uniform system of administration, evolved by Akbar for his dominions, had attained maturity and the functioning of the state machinery had become almost automatic by the time of Shah Jahan. The manifold strings of the far-sighted state policy, as conceived by Akbar, were now deeply rooted into the soil, and the minor strains on the body politic, such as 'the occasional display of religious intolerances by Shah Jahan, could not do irreparable or incalculable harm to it until his successor Aurangzeb struck, like a mad man, at its very roots'. In fact, Shah Jahan's only concern seemd to be 'to wield the scepter and maintain peace and order within his dominions; and he was well-equipped, by virtue of his education, training and experience, to perform this function most successfully'.

Shah Jahan was a very capable, conscious and active ruler. He took keen interest in the state affairs and did everything systematically, methodically and diligently. Sir Jadunath Sarkar correctly observes that the Mughal throne was not a bed of roses; its occupant 'had his duties and his division of time showed he knew the fact'. Like Akbar, Shah Jahan also 'strictly adhered to the daily routine whether he was in camp or at the capital'. The contemporary sources provide evidence to prove that 'he led a strenuous life and divided his time evenly between government and sport' Unlike Jahangir, Shah Jahan 'did not throw the burden of administration on his ministers or favourites nor did he play the second fiddle to any political faction or clique at the court'.

During the concluding years of his reign, Shah Jahan had deliberately decentralized the royal authority among his four sons 'as a matter of state policy and in good faith'. To his misfortune, in the age of despotism, 'the latitude given by him to his sons, within the spheres of their influence, proved a folly for which he had to pay a terrible price'. Nevertheless, Tavernier, who had repeatedly visited many parts of India, records that Shah Jahan 'reined not so much as a king over his subjects, ***but*** rather as a father over his family and children'. On the testimony of the unbiased observations of foreign travellers, MS Elphinstone comes to the conclusion that Shah Jahan's 'treatment of his people was beneficent and paternal'. (*History of India—The Hindu and Mahometan Periods*; London, Murray, 1889, p. 603).

Administration of Justice

Like Akbar and Jahangir, Shah Jahan also 'enjoyed reputation as a just monarch who administered even-handed justice to all high and low'. Rai Bhara Mal, the celebrated author of *Lubbut Tawarikh-i-Hind* records with appreciation that

"It was owing to the great solicitude evinced by the king towards the promotion of the national weal and the general tranquillity, that the people were restrained from committing offences against one another and breaking the public peace. But if offenders were discovered, the local authorities used generally to try them on the spot where the offence had been committed according to law, and in concurrence with the law officers; and if any individual, dissatisfied with the decision passed on his case, appealed to the governor or *diwan*, or to the *qazi* of the *Suba*, the matter was reviewed, and judgment awarded with great care and discrimination, lest it should be mentioned in the presence of the King that justice had not been done. If parties were not satisfied even with these decisions, they appealed to the chief *diwan*, or the chief *qazi* on matters of law. These officers instituted further inquiries. With all this care, what cases, except those relating to blood and religion, could become subjects of references to his Majesty? (E&D, vii, pp. 172-73).

Flourishing Trade and Commerce and General Prosperity

A long era of peace and order, absence of foreign invasions, good government and efficient administration, provided by Shah Jahan led to the rapid advancement of material prosperity and enrichment of its the people. W H Moreland, the celebrated author of *Agrarian System of Moslem India,* .is all praise for the excellent financial administration of Shah Jahan which raised the income of the state 'beyond all precedents' without causing much strain on the peasantry; he calls his reign 'a period of agrarian tranquillity', during which the land revenue system of Raja Todar Mal was extended to the Deccan also (p. 131). Similarly, Elphinstone forcefully asserts that 'Shah Jahan was the most magnificent prince that ever appeared in India. His retinue, his state establishments, his largesse and all the pomp of his court, were much increased beyond what they attained to under his predecessors. His expenses in these departments can only be palliated by the fact that they neither occasioned any increase to his exactions nor any embarrassment to his finances'. (*History of India,* loc. cit., pp. 602-3).

In fact, the concept of public welfare state in the medieval age was very much limited in its scope; therefore, the Mughal emperors did not know how to make the best use of the imperial reserves for the benefit of his subjects. The court historian Abdul Hamid Lahouri writes that 'the imperial jewel house' was full of so many valuable gems that 'in the opinion of far-seeing men, the acquisition of such wonderful brilliants can only render one service, that of adorning the throne of the Empire. (*Badshahnama*; E&D, VII, p. 45-46). So it prompted Shah Jahan to spend lavishly for his personal comforts or superfluous display of wealth. The construction of the historic *Takhat-i-Taus* or the Peacock Throne by Shah Jahan for his use in the imperial court is one such example of vulgar display of wealth by him. It was made of '*one lakh tolas*' of pure gold, and studded with 'rubies, garnets, diamonds, rich pearls and emeralds', exceeding 50,000 *mishkals* in weight.' The throne was nine feet in length, 7.5 feet in breadth and fifteen feet in height. Its canopy, again made of solid gold, stood on twelve emerald columns. The outside of the canopy was of enamel work with occasional gems while the inside was thickly set with rubies, garnets and other jewels. On the top of each column of the canopy, there were two peacocks of gold, thickest with gems, and between each two peacocks there was a tree, decorated with rubies and diamonds, emeralds and pearls. The throne stood on four legs of solid gold and its ascent consisted of three steps, set with jewels of the rarest quality. The throne was completed in the course of seven years under the care of Bebadal Khan, the superintendent of the royal goldsmithy. According to an opinion, a conservative estimate of the cost of its construction, as given by Abdul Hamid, to be a crore of *rupees*, according to the metallic value of gold in those days, was yet a gross under-estimate of the true value of the priceless jewellery which was utilised in the preparation of the throne' No wonder, the invaluable Peacock Throne fell into the hands of Nadir Shah, an erstwhile dacoit turned the emperor, in 1739, who took it away to Iran.

Nevertheless, this unlimited and incalculable wealth, possessed by the Mughal emperor and his ruling elite, was not raised by them through questionable means. They spent lavishly and rather extravagantly, but they were not known to run after money. The Mughal emperors 'never employed Morton's fork to fleece their subjects. None of the imperial Mughals is known to have extorted money and valuables from the indignant peasantry or the indignant businessmen and traders. The immense wealth of the Mughal treasury represented the surplus revenue of the state, collected through peaceful means and according to the law of the land. This wealth belonged to the nation as a whole while the Mughal emperors and the *grandees* of the empire were its custodians; it is a different matter that neither the people nor their masters knew how to make the best use of it for more beneficial public activities. The wealth of the country was unevenly distributed; it was certainly concentrated in the hands of a microscopic minority. (*Advanced Study*; ii, p. 464).

The Glorious Age of Mughal Art and Architecture

The reign of Shah Jahan marks the culmination of its attainments in the fields of the Mughal art and architecture. Shah Jahan loved to live in style. To him the royal forts, palaces and public buildings left behind by his ancestors looked like old and out-dated monuments for which he showed little interest. He was a builder *par excellence* and had an inborn taste for it. We are told that even in his early youth he was very selective in the matter of his residential apartments. He never felt satisfied until he would get his place of residence thoroughly renovated and beautified for his stay. After his accession to the throne, Shah Jahan displayed his passion for architectural activity without restraint, and, as a result, the development of architecture reached the zenith of its excellence and magnificence during his reign. B P Saksena, the biographer of Shah Jahan, opines that 'the two natural traits' of Shah Jahan's character, viz., 'vanity and ambition', were primarily responsible for his persistent attachment to the architectural activity; he writes that 'vanity always hankers after popular applause; and it may have struck him that he could secure this for all time by erecting magnificent buildings. Secondly, his ambition always goaded him to achieve the unsurpassable. It was impossible to improve upon painting (which had reached its stage of perfection under the patronage of Jahangir) and so naturally he turned to architecture which provided an extensive field for improvement. And the buildings of his reign must have satisfied both his vanity and ambition'(*Shahjahan,* P. 263).

Shah Jahan had inherited a rich and prosperous state. The coffers of the royal exchequer were full to the brim and the government officials were hard-pressed to provide safe storage facility for the fresh arrivals of state revenues year after year. The accumulation of immense wealth and unlimited resources at the command of the Mughal emperor sharpened his appetite to spend on his architectural activities as much as he pleased; and, no wonder, he was successful in engraving 'the sermons in stones' which have faithfully preserved 'the glories of his reign in marble edifices'. He had a refined taste for architectural designs and loved white marble and other rare types of building materials, He did not like the 'massive buildings erected by Akbar in red sandstone at Agra, Lahore and elsewhere'. Accordingly, he demolished many of the old royal structures and raised in their place new buildings of white marble, which was available in abundance from the quarries of Makrana near Sambhar.

Akbar had built the Red Fort of Agra on the bank of the Yamuna where the old brick fortress of Sikander Lodhi was once located. It took eight years (1564-72) to complete the fort with its entire complex which is said to have contained as many as 500 palaces, public buildings, royal stables, servants' quarters and other structures within its enclosure to accommodate the imperial court, *harem* and the guards. Shah Jahan razed to the ground many of these and added new buildings, like the Diwan-i-Aam, Diwan-i-Khas, Musamman Burj, Moti Masjid, Shish Mahal, Khas Mahal, Machhi Mahal and many other apartments for the royal ladies. The Musamman Burj is actually a beautiful building made of marble; it faces the river side of the fort and was originally decorated with precious stones. It was here that Shah Jahan spent the last days of his life as prisoner of his son Aurangzeb. The Moti Masjid is considered to be the most beautiful of all the architectural monuments of the Agra Fort; made of white marble, it is situated on an elevated terrace in the courtyard to the north of the *Diwan-i-Aam*; it was built in seven years (1645-53) at a cost of three *lakhs* of rupees. Originally there was an open space in front of the Agra Fort which was converted into a beautiful *chauk* with grassy lawns and flower-beds by Shah Jahan. His elder daughter Jahan Ara Begam built a beautiful mosque within these lawns for public use.

The Mughal emperors frequently held their imperial courts at Agra but the importance of the historic metropolis of Delhi as the imperial capital of the empire was never lost upon them. Agra was used by them as their second or supplementary headquarters for a change only. Shah Jahan celebrated his coronation at Agra and held his court there for many years but was, ultimately, fed up with the saline water, dry climate and dusty winds of Rajputana, lying so close to Agra, and made up his mind to shift his royal court and the *harem* to Delhi. Being a lover of architectural beauty and style, he would not like to make use of the old buildings of his predecessors' there. Thus it was that Delhi became the second avenue for Shah Jahan to engage himself in the magnificent architectural activity. He ordered the construction of an entirely new imperial township at Delhi. After an extensive survey of the landscape in its neighbourhood along the banks of the Jumna, he selected a vast stretch of land, outside the existing township, where the foundations of the new city of Delhi, called ShahJahanabad, were laid by him at' an auspicious hour' and 'with the approval of architects and astrologers', on May 12, 1639. It is now located by the famous Red Fort and the Jama-i-Masjid, in the vicinity of *Chandani Chauk*. The Red Fort was completed and made fit for occupation after nine years and three months. Some of the buildings constructed within its premises were the Diwan-i-Khas, Diwan-i-Aam, Rang Mahal, Moti Mahal, and Hira Mahal, everyone of which had its own ornamental garden with flower-beds, water-channels and fountains. Besides the imperial buildings, there were provided within the walls of the fort, spacious residential accommodation for the royal guards, store houses, recreation chambers, kitchens, and stables for horses and elephants. The Diwan-i-Khas of the Red Fort, adorned with the *Takhat-i-Taus* or the Peacock Throne, was one of the most ornamented buildings of Shah Jahan; a couplet of Amir Khusrau, inscribed on one of its walls, pays a befitting tribute to the grand edifice as follows:

Agar firdaus bar ru i zamin ast,
Hamim ast o hamin ast o hamin ast.

It means: 'if there is a paradise on earth, it is this, it is this, none but this'. Among the other extant architectural monuments of Shah Jahan may be mentioned the mausoleum of Jahangir at Lahore, and the beautiful marble tomb of Nizamuddin Auliya in Delhi. To crown them all, there is the Taj Mahal – 'the most celebrated of Shah Jahan's architectural monuments', said to be one of the 'seven wonders' of the world. It took twenty-two years to complete the whole structure at a cost of three crores of rupees; the principal marble dome alone took twelve years to finish. Its chief designer, Ustad Ahmad Lahouri, was honoured by the emperor with the lofty title of *Nadir-ul-Asar*. The architectural beauty of the Taj beggars description. The mausoleum of Mumtaz Mahal, with its allied garden and the building complex is in the form of a rectangle measuring 1,900 by 1,000 feet. It is enclosed by a high wall, surmounted by four arcaded marble pavilions, one at each of its four corners. The principal structure of the mausoleum stands on a rectangular marble platform with twenty-two feet as its plinth-level while the mausoleum itself is square in form and stands 108 feet above the plinth; it is situated on the short side of the rectangle along the southern bank of the Yamuna, and its only ornamental entrance, made of red sandstone, lies on its southern side. On each of the four corners of the platform, there is a minaret, crowned by a kiosk although the central dome towers above all the surrounding cupolas and the minarets. The vast space within the enclosure has been laid out into a beautiful garden with marble pathways, water course, and the fountains. In the opinion of B P Saksena,

'The buildings constructed in Shah Jahan's reign stand as a living monument of unsurpassed engineering skill. They have maintained their charm and freshness in its full vigour, and the sumptuously feast the eyes of visitors from all corners of the world. They breathe sublimity, peace, elegance and grandeur, and though over-elaboration in some of them appears a little grotesque to an expert, yet the untrained eye is simply enchanted by their all-round beauty. Even if the entire mass of historical literature had perished and only these buildings had remained to tell the story of Shah Jahan's reign, there is little doubt that it would have still been pronounced as the most magnificent in history.' (*Shahjahan*, pp. 261-62).

Development of Education and Literature

Like Akbar and Jahangir, Shah Jahan was also a great patron of education and learning. The liberal educational policy, as introduced by Akbar for the socio-cultural, economic and intellectual advancement of the people remained in full operation till the end of Shah Jahan's reign. The development of Persian, Arabic and Sanskrit languages and literature in India, which had started during the reign of Akbar, continued un-interrupted during the reigns of Jahangir and Shah Jahan. The 17th century is known, particularly, for the growth and development of Hindi language and literature in India. Shah Jahan and his eldest son, Dara Shikoh, loved to speak in Hindi; they composed verses in the spoken language of the people and were fond of listening to the Hindi songs and music. A number of Hindi scholars and poets, including Sunder Dass, Chintamani and Kavindra Acharya enjoyed the state patronage. Jagan Nath, the celebrated musician of Shah Jahan's reign, was also a born poet in Hindi; he was honoured by the emperor with the title of *Maha Kavi Rai*. The subjects of astronomy, mathematics, general sciences, historiography and the translation of Sanskrit works into Persian continued to receive encouragement from the Mughal court as ever before. Ibn Har Karan translated Ramayana and Munshi Banvali Dass *Prabodh Chandrodaya* into Persian. Abdur Rashid translated *Bij Ganit* from Sanskrit into Persian. Abdul Hamid Lahouri, Khafi Khan and a number of other historians, whose works have been cited in this study, flourished during the reign of Shah Jahan. Mulla Farid, the greatest astrologer of the age, produced the astral chart, entitled *Zich-i-Shajahani*, while Ataullah wrote a treatise on Arithmetic, Algebra and menstruation which was dedicated by him to Shah Jahan and Darashikoh. At certain occasions, Shah Jahan is known to have displayed religious orthodoxy in his treatment of the people but, being a very 'shrewd and sagacious statesman, he never allowed religion to override the liberal and secular state policy' of his predecessors.

❑ ❑

17

AURANGZEB ALAMGIR (1658-1707)

SECTION 1: EARLY CAREER AND ACCESSION

Aurangzeb, the successor of Shah Jahan, was 'the last of the Great Mughals of India'. 'The history of Aurangzeb', writes his biographer Sir Jadunath Sarkar 'is practically the history of India for sixty years. His own reign covers the second half of the seventeenth century and stands forth as a most important epoch in the annals of our country'. Under him the Mughal Empire reached its greatest dimensions, and, for a while, it emerged as 'the largest single state, ever known in India from the dawn of history to the rise of the British power'. It was during his reign that 'Islam made its last onward movement in India' but his desperate attempts to convert this 'land of infidels' into *Dar-ul-Islam* by the application of force and by injecting the virus of 'Islamic fundamentalism and religious intolerance' in the Indian polity boomeranged and proved counter-productive. In consequence, Aurangzeb's life became 'one long tragedy, the story of a man battling in vain against an invisible but inexorable fate. And this tragedy in history was enacted with all the regularity of a perfect drama'. (*History of Aurangzeb*; 5 vols. Calcutta, 1912-25)

Aurangzeb was the third son of Shah Jahan and Mumtaz Mahal. He was born on October 24, 1618 at Dohad, in the army camp of his father, Prince Khurram, when the latter held the viceroyalty of the Deccan. His early career has been described in sufficient details in the previous chapter. He came out victorious in the war of succession (1657-58) against his brothers. After his brilliant victories in the battles of Dharmat (April 25, 1658) and Samugarh (May 29, 1658) against Shuja and Dara Shikoh respectively, he took possession of the Red Fort of Agra by playing a ruse upon his ailing father; and the ruling monarch Shah Jahan was kept by Aurangzeb as prisoner in the Shah Burj within the fort till his death. Delhi and Lahore also fell into the hands of Aurangzeb without a fight, and he ascended the throne in the Red Fort of Delhi without any fanfare on July 21, 1658 although he held his formal coronation in abeyance until all of his brothers and other claimants to the throne were totally liquidated.

Aurangzeb's Coronation

After eliminating all the opponents to his succession, and consolidating his position as the undisputed sovereign of the Mughal Empire, Aurangzeb held his Coronation *Darbar* at the Red Fort of Delhi on June 5, 1659 with great pomp and show and assumed the lofty title of Abul Muzaffar Muhiuddin Muhammad Aurangzeb Bahadur Alamgir Badshah-i-Ghazi. To make the inhabitants of Delhi to gloss over the questionable means through which he had acquired the throne by shedding the blood of his own near and dear one, Aurangzeb spent lavishly on his coronation ceremony so as 'to make the occasion go down in history as one of the grandest coronations ever celebrated by a Mughal monarch'. The royal festivities continued for over two months and 'the chests of the royal treasury were thrown open to be distributed among the courtiers, government officers, scholars, holy men, beggars and the spectators without discrimination of creed or religion'. According to Khafi Khan, when the emperor entered the Hall of Audience (*Diwan-i-Aam*) and mounted the Peacock Throne 'at the auspicious hour of three hours and fifteen minutes from the sunrise', as fixed by the court astrologers, 'there was a loud burst of joyous notes from the imperial band in attendance. The musicians began their songs and the *nautch* girls began their dances.' And, 'when the *Khutba* was read' in the name of Aurangzeb, 'the trays of gold and silver coins and plates heaped over with pyramids of pearls and jewels were showered in the emperor's name among the assembled courtiers who picked them up as tokens of good luck'.

As a part of the coronation ceremonies, Aurangzeb, accompanied by his sons, and the new crop of his ministers, courtiers and nobles, led the royal procession through the bazaars of Delhi seated on richly decorated elephants to the accompaniment of music and dance. From the backs of the elephants handfuls of gold and silver coins were incessantly flung among the crowd right and left as the procession moved on.' (*Muntakhab-ul-Lubab*, E&D, vii, p. 241). Aurangzeb ordered his reign to be formally reckoned with from the first of Ramzan 1068 A.H. viz., May 23, 1658 in all official records although his 'grand coronation' had taken place 'on the fourth of Ramzan in the year 1069 A.H'.

Aurangzeb's Education, Character and Lifestyle

Aurangzeb had received the best education and training along with his brothers befitting the royal princes of his age. In his boyhood, he had shown more interest in literary education and religious studies, however. He acquired proficiency in three languages—Persian, Arabic and Chaghatai Turki, mastered the *holy Quran* and *Hadis* by *rote memory* and grew up as a devoted Muslim under the influence of orthodox *Sunni* tutors. Of course, Aurangzeb's mother-tongue was *Hindustani* or *Hindavi*, later known as Urdu, which had already become 'the spoken language of the imperial Mughals at the court and the royal household although it was not employed in the official proceedings. Aurangzeb was 'an excellent calligraphist'; he used to copy the Quran which, in the absence of the printing press, helped in its public circulation, and was regarded as 'a deed of piety' among the orthodox Muslims. It is said that, as a puritan, Aurangzeb 'plied the trade of copyist and cap-maker to earn his livelihood'. Two beautifully written copies of the *Holy Quran Majid*, duly bound and illuminated, are said to have been sent by him to Mecca and Medina respectively.

Aurangzeb was an introvert by nature. He grew up as a narrow-minded and orthodox young man with a 'highly prejudiced and pessimistic outlook towards life'. Nevertheless, Shah Jahan, as a caring father, accorded very liberal and generous treatment towards his children. He fixed 500 rupees as daily allowance for every one of his sons until they were bestowed the imperial *mansabs* befitting the princely order. Thus Aurangzeb received the high *mansab* of 10,000 *zat* and 4,000 *swar* in 1634 when he was hardly sixteen years old. In 1634-35, he successfully crushed the uprising of Bundellas under Jujhar Singh, and then acted as the viceroy of the Deccan for about eight years (1636-44).

Aurangzeb's first marriage took place at Agra on May 8, 1637, amidst great rejoicing, in the nineteenth year of his life. His first wife, Dilras Banu Begam was the daughter of Shah Nawaz, a *Sayyad* of high pedigree, who belonged to the ruling family of Shah Tahmasp of Persia. Unlike the other princely order of the age, Aurangzeb did not build a large *harem*. Thoroughly conservative and self-disciplined by nature, 'he was not a slave to luxurious or sensual pleasures of life'. As a puritan, he strictly abided by the Islamic tradition in the matter of his conjugal relations and never had more than four living wives at a time. All through his life, he did not have more than two formally or legally married wives besides four or five concubines, who were actually known by their humble titles of *mahals* or *bais*. His consorts left him with ten children, including five boys and five girls. He was outlived by three of his sons, Prince Muazzam *alias* Shah Alam, Azam and Kam Bakhsh, who fought their next suicidal war of succession, after the death of their father in 1707, to establish their claim to the Mughal monarchy.

As a prince, Aurangzeb was known to be very humble, reserved, and soft-spoken in his social contacts with the people at large. He assumed 'utmost humility and courtesy' in his dealings with the ministers and military generals of his father to win their admiration and support. After his accession to the throne, Aurangzeb treated his ministers and nobles with dignity but adopted a stern, extremely reserved and despotic attitude so that none could dare to defy his commands. He proved to be an extremely narrow-minded, prejudiced, suspicious and cold-brooded autocrat who did not trust his ministers and nobles; in fact, he lacked affection, sympathy, and magnanimity of heart which are the basic attributes of a gentleman. The inhuman treatment meted out by him towards his father, brothers and other kinsmen had already tarnished the fair name of the Mughal ruling dynasty; unfortunately, Aurangzeb failed to give a better treatment even towards his own wives and children. As a 'highly self-willed man, Aurangzeb suffered from the complex of self-righteousness who lived for himself alone and for none else'. He treated his sons and daughters very shabbily when they did not come up to his expectations.

Two Distinct Periods of Aurangzeb's Reign

Aurangzeb enjoyed a very long period of reign which can naturally be divided into two almost equal parts of about 25 years each. He spent the first half of his rule, from 1658 to 1681, in the North. During this period, northern and central India, known to the Muslim invaders as Hindustan or 'the Land of the Hindus,' engaged the main attention of Aurangzeb because it formed the nucleus of the Muslim power in India. Aurangzeb was a great imperialist. He spent almost the whole of his time, energy and recourses of the state for the consolidation of his rule and expansion of his dominions by successfully organizing military expeditions against the internal rebellious elements and the neighbouring princely states. He received the cooperation and utilised the services of all the old grandees of his father's regime and showed remarkable skill in adopting various civil and military measures to strengthen the Mughal Empire. Under the leadership of an otherwise energetic and dynamic monarch, like that of Aurangzeb, his occasional display of religious orthodoxy, discrimination between the nobles on sectarian considerations and personal whims went unnoticed for quite some time. His belief in Islamic fundamentalism and the practice of Puritanism characterized him as a 'pious Muslim' for which he won applause from the orthodox Sunni circles and none bothered about his occasional deeds of religious intolerance so long as it did not become his declared state policy. During the first two decades of his rule, he did not pay special attention to the affairs of the Deccan which were left by him to his viceroys.

During the second half of his reign, from 1682 to 1707, Aurangzeb's' role as administrator and military general as also his field of operations and the targets of attack were completely reversed. His policy of imperialism was now coloured by the ideology of Islamic fundamentalism and religious orthodoxy. This period was spent by him in the Deccan exclusively where he fought decisive wars against the so-called heretic Shia states of Bijapur and Golconda to bring about their destruction besides declaring *Jihad* against the Marathas, being dubbed as 'Kafirs,' with disastrous results. We would like to deal with the achievements and failures of Aurangzeb during these two periods under separate sections as follows.

SECTION 2: AURANGZEB AND NORTH INDIA

1. Early Measures

The war of succession between the rival claimants to the throne had created disorders and anarchy throughout the Mughal dominions. It had a very demoralizing effect on the civil and military services, and the state administration was almost paralyzed. The robbers, thieves and anti-social elements raised their ugly heads and the lives and properties of the people became unsafe. Aurangzeb was fully aware of this problem. Therefore, immediately after his accession to the throne, he adopted stern measures to restore law and order in his dominions. He brought all the provincial governors, military generals and civil administrators under his firm control. The bureaucrats of integrity and good reputation were confirmed in their assignments and were liberally rewarded while the others were downgraded or dismissed. His strong measures to establish law and order and ensure the life and property of his subjects were widely appreciated and added to his popularity as capable and 'the just monarch'. By the time he celebrated his coronation, there was all calm and quiet within the Mughal dominions. Aurangzeb had proved himself as 'a painstaking and efficient administrator'; he 'was not found wanting when the situation so demanded

2. Remission of Taxes

Aurangzeb's second priority was to win the confidence and loyalty of his subjects. Accordingly, he initiated many relief measures to reduce the burden of taxes upon the people. Quite a few taxes, 'not permissible by the Islamic law', were abolished. They included among others, the *Pandari* or the octroi duties and *Rahadari* or the tax charged on the inland transport. The people of the towns and cities were provided relief by the abolition of the House Tax while the inhabitants of villages were exempted from the payment of *Abwabs* or 'the miscellaneous taxes other than the Land Revenue'. Similarly the tax on corn and cereals was abolished with the object of bringing down the prices of the food grains. The long list of the taxes, said to have been abolished by Aurangzeb, also included two taxes, which were previously levied on the Hindus exclusively, one 'at the birth of a son', and the other when they immersed the remains of their dead into the River Ganga. It assured the non-Muslim subjects of the Mughal Empire about Aurangzeb's commitment to the policy of secularism as had been pursued by his predecessors. Of course, Khafi Khan informs us that 'with the exception of the *Pandari*, the royal decrees had no effect, and *faujdars* and *jagirdars* in remote places did not withhold their hands from these exactions'. (*Muntakhab-ul-Lubab*, E&D, vii, pp. 247-48).

3. Banning of Un-Islamic Practices

Aurangzeb was a 'devout Muslim' and orthodox Sunni by faith. As such, he did not like to see the prevalence of some un-Islamic practices and ceremonial in the state administration. Accordingly, he stopped the practice of engraving *kalima* on the coins 'so that it might not be desecrated in the hands of the non-Muslims'. He gave up the practice of celebrating the Nauroz or the 'New Year Day' festival which belonged to the Persian tradition. Similarly, the use of Solar Calendar in the state affairs was given up as 'it resembled the system of the fire-worshippers'. Instead, in his zeal to establish the regime of Islam, Aurangzeb issued the instructions that 'the year of his reign should be reckoned by the Arab Lunar Year and months and that in the revenue accounts also the Lunar Calendar should be preferred to the Solar.' Khafi Khan condemns Aurangzeb for introducing this major change purely because of his religious orthodoxy; he writes:

> 'Mathematicians, astronomers, and men who have studied history, know that the recurrence of the four seasons, summer, winter, the rainy seasons of Hindustan, the autumn and spring harvests, the ripening of the corn and fruit of each season, the *tankhwah* of the *jagirs*, and the money of the *mansabdars*, are all dependent upon the solar reckoning, and cannot be regulated by the lunar; still his religious Majesty was unwilling that the Nauroz and the year and months of the Magi should give their names to the anniversary of his accession.' (*ibid.*, pp. 241-42).

4. Revival of the Islamic Theory of Kingship

Aurangzeb's accession to the throne led to the revival of the influence of the orthodox *mullas* in the state politics. Aurangzeb sincerely believed in the Islamic theory of state. He regarded the Mughal Empire as 'an Islamic state' and, as such showed his eagerness to act as 'an ideal Muslim ruler'. He looked upon the non-Muslims as *kafirs* (infidels) and had no soft corner for the *Shias* and *Sufis* also who, according to him, were not true Mussalmans. He had no regards for his forefathers – Akbar, Jahangir and Shah Jahan, who, according to his conviction, 'had adopted un-Islamic practices in the state affairs, encouraged the heretical tendencies among the Muslims' and that 'the grant of religious freedom and civic liberties to the idol-worshippers at par with the faithful had given a serious set-back to the growth and development of Islam in India'. As observed by Dr. J. L. Mehta elsewhere in his studies, 'it was Aurangzeb's honest and sincere desire to convert the *dar-ul-harb* of India into *dar-ul-Islam* but he 'did not allow these dangerous opinions to become generally known in the early years of his rule. Aurangzeb was an anti-thesis of Akbar in thought, word and deed. He would like to reverse the entire state policy of Akbar, but being a clever politician, he took a hundred precautions before showing his true colours. The presence of powerful Rajput generals like Raja Jaswant Singh and Raja Jai Singh, and the immense influence wielded by the

Hindus and *Shias* in the state affairs, acted as a deterrent to the fulfilment of his heart's desires all at once'. (*Advanced Study*; ii, pp. 486-87).

Instead, as an initial step towards the fulfilment of his theological convictions, Aurangzeb, 'as a pious Muslim' assumed the role of a 'Defender of the Faith'. It involved a two-fold process, (*a*) to enforce the Islamic law in statecraft slowly and steadily; and (*b*) to make the Muslim population of his dominions 'conform to the orthodox *Sunni* standards'. Towards the achievement of his objectives, Aurangzeb re-affirmed 'Islam's premier position as the State Religion' and 'the Muslims began to be treated as the favourite children of the Islamic state in India'. The orthodox *mullas* were assigned high state offices and the positions of dignity and influence at the imperial court. The traditional powers and functions of the Chief *Sadr* and his establishment at the central and provincial levels were redefined according to the orthodox principles of the Sunni faith. All the *masjids* and religious institutions of the Muslims were granted state protection and patronage on preferential basis. The *imams* and *mullas* of the *masjids* and various Muslim institutions were declared to be the government servants, and they began to receive sumptuous salaries from the state exchequer. Thereby they once again acquired their respectable status as the official dignitaries. The coffers of the state treasuries were thrown open for the propagation of Islam. The old mosques received a face-lift and many new mosques were ordered to be built at state expense. Ordinances were issued to make the Muslims conform to the orthodox rules of socio-religious conduct. The office of the *Muhtasib* regained its importance with its traditional religious powers and functions, and the *muhtasibs*, as 'Censors of Public Morals', began to be appointed in all important towns to enforce Islamic law and practices with the object of 'improving the moral and spiritual tone of the Muslim society'. Their main function was to instruct the Muslims to lead lives according to the behests of the Holy *Quran*. The *muhtasibs* kept a watch on the adult Muslims of the areas under their charge to make sure that they offered five prayers a day and kept the fast of Ramzan. These Censors of Public Morals 'were authorized to inflict punishments on those who contravened the Islamic principles'. Accordingly, the heretics and atheists among the Muslims began to receive corporal punishment at their hands; sometimes they were got hold of and flogged in public 'to bring them to the path of righteousness'. The *Shias* and *Sufis* were also persecuted. Sheikh Sarmad, one of the prominent *Sufi* associates of Dara Shikoh, with a large following, was put to death on the charge of heresy. Many converts to Islam who were suspected of having reverted to the old faith were punished. The worst sufferers among the Muslims were, however, the members of Ismailia or Bohra community of Gujarat. Through these measures, the Muslims of the Mughal dominions were made to realise that 'the reign of Islam had begun; it was hailed as a great event in the history of the Mughal rule in India by the orthodox *mullas* and the devout Muslim monarch who had ever sat on the Mughal throne'. Nevertheless, the Hindus, Buddhists and other non-Muslims, who comprised the majority of the Mughal subjects,' had no reason to object or cause to worry about the religious leanings of the new monarch so long as they enjoyed socio-religious freedom and were not discriminated against the Muslims in the state affairs. On the basis of a long tradition, they looked upon the Mughal Empire as a nation-state which belonged to them as much as to their Muslim fellow-brethren. For over a century, they had enjoyed civic liberties as full-fledged citizens of the Mughal state. They looked to the Mughal emperor with hopes and expectations and continued to offer their whole-hearted services and cooperation for quite some time until Aurangzeb resorted to religious bigotry and struck at the foundation of the secular state policy of his predecessors'. (*Ibid.*, pp. 488-89).

5. Invasion of Assam (1661-63)

After the expulsion of Shah Shuja from Bengal, Mir Jumla was appointed its governor by Aurangzeb in June 1660. During the war of succession, the Ahom ruler of Cooch-Behar in Assam had taken possession of the Hindu state of Kamrup, with its capital at Gauhati, which was under the suzerainty of the Mughals. The Ahoms were an off-shoot of the Shan tribes of Burma who had setup their rule in the eastern and central parts of Assam in the thirteenth century; they had adopted Hindu faith.

Aurangzeb signalled the beginning of his rule by ordering Mir Jumla to launch a full-fledged campaign for the conquest of Assam. Mir Jumla invaded Assam in 1661 at the head of a well-organised Mughal army; it consisted of 12,000 cavalry, 30,000 infantry and 300 war boats for use in the Brahmaputra delta. The Ahoms were defeated and their capital Garhgaon fell to the Mughals but they failed to maintain their hold over the conquered territories because of difficult terrain and hostile climate. The Ahoms took the offensive with the beginning of the rainy season when most of the areas under the Mughal control were flooded and their military out-posts isolated. Handicapped for want of provisions, a large number of the Mughal soldiers died of starvation and disease or fell victims to the Ahom attacks. Mir Jumla ordered his troops to retreat via Dacca but himself died of fever on the way in April 1663. Aurangzeb's first expedition against Assam thus proved a failure.

6. Conquest of Arakan

After the death of Mir Jumla, Aurangzeb appointed his material uncle Shaista Khan, son of Asaf Khan, as the governor of Bengal. He carried on war on the eastern front for over a decade. He fought against the Portuguese pirates who had intruded into the Arakan region along the eastern seacoast; Chatgaon (modern Chittagong) was their stronghold from where they used to raid Bengal. In 1663, Shaista Khan captured Chatgaon and expelled the Portuguese from the delta of the Brahmaputra. During the next three years, he overran the whole of the Arakan region. Nevertheless, in 1666-67, Chakradhwaja, the Ahom chief retaliated with force and put the Mughals on the defensive. He liberated many parts of Assam from the hands of the Mughals. The Mughal campaign on the eastern front proved a failure in the long run as the central government failed to provide sufficient reinforcements to the governor of Bengal to carry on the struggle. Gauhati was finally lost to the Mughals in 1681 but as result of 'this long and strenuous warfare' the Ahom chief of Cooch-Behar accepted nominal suzerainty of the Mughals.

7. Suppression of the Portuguese Pirates

The Bay of Bengal was infested with the Portuguese pirates in the seventeenth century. Shah Jahan had adopted stern measures against them but the Mughal government failed to build a strong naval force to safeguard its seacoasts. As a result, the Portuguese made their appearance in Bengal again and resorted to piracy with a vengeance. They plundered the merchant boats of the Indians, raided the villages along the seacoasts, and kidnapped the Indians to be sold as slaves. Shaista Khan, the governor of Bengal, was, therefore, called upon to adopt strong measures against them. He prepared a flotilla of 300 boats and stormed the Portuguese bases by land and sea. He expelled them from the town of Chatgaon and took possession of the island of Sandwip in January 1666. The contemporary chroniclers inform us that Shaista Khan had 'secured the release of thousands of the Bengali village folk, including men and women, who had been held as slaves by the Portuguese'. The Sandwip Island was converted into a military post by Shaista Khan.

8. War with the Frontier Tribes

Aurangzeb adopted a 'forward policy' against the turbulent Afghan tribes of northwestern India out of political and economic considerations. Though an orthodox Muslim, he 'had to wage war with equally fanatical Muslim tribes of the northwestern frontier region'. The Afridi tribes of the frontier pursued highway robbery as their profession. They descended down the hills to plunder the fertile plains of the Punjab; the travellers, traders and their *caravans*, proceeding to and from Afghanistan through the Khyber, Bolan and other passes usually fell victims to their plundering raids. To begin with, Aurangzeb attempted to pacify them through bribery. It is said that the Mughal emperor paid the frontier chiefs six lakhs of rupees per annum 'to maintain peace and to keep the frontier open to peaceful traffic' but this policy proved a failure as 'fresh leaders arose amongst the tribesmen' to resume the plundering raids. In 1667, Bhagu, a leader of the Yusufzai tribe, plundered Attock and Peshawar districts and attempted to hold the ferry on the Indus to block the passage of the Mughal forces but was defeated and repulsed. In 1672, the Afridi chief Akmal Khan crowned himself king and declared *Jihad* against the Mughals. He defeated the Mughal governor of Afghanistan at Ali Masjid. His victory was followed by a widespread 'national uprising' against the Mughal domination in which 'the whole of the Pathan land from Attock to Kandahar' rose in arms. Shujaat Khan, the Mughal commander, died fighting against the Afghans in February 1674. It compelled Aurangzeb to proceed to the war front in person. He setup his military camp at Hasan Abdal in July 1674 and brought the situation under control by use of force and diplomacy. Many of the Afghan nobles were won over by liberal grants of subsidies, *jagirs*, and the imperial services. Amir Khan, the new Mughal governor of Kabul, following the instructions of Aurangzeb, adopted a very conciliatory policy towards the people to win their cooperation and support.

SECTION 3: GRADUAL UNFOLDING OF AURANGZEB'S RELIGIOUS POLICY

Aurangzeb unfolded his real intentions to convert the liberal Mughal monarchy into an orthodox Islamic state but very gradually. His early steps to eliminate un-Islamic practices at the Mughal court and his resolve to act as the 'defender of the faith' were taken lightly by the grandees of the empire and the people at large, Hindus as well as Muslims. Every individual has his beliefs and convictions, and Aurangzeb, being 'a devout Muslim', seemed to impart 'a personal touch' to the commencement of his new regime.

Similarly, his attempts 'to patronize Islam on preferential basis also went unnoticed by the Hindus so long as the government did not discriminate against them on religious grounds'. In fact, the Shias, Sufis and other liberal-minded Muslims were the first to suffer silently because of Aurangzeb's disregard of 'the time-honoured secular state policy' of his predecessors. They felt bewildered but did not raise their voice of protest and thus Aurangzeb implemented the first phase of his religious policy without any trouble.

The second phase of Aurangzeb's religious policy began when he started making deliberate attempts to let down and belittle the importance of the liberal-minded Muslim officers, Hindu bureaucrats and the Rajput chiefs and military officers, particularly at the imperial capital and the court. They were gradually removed from the offices of importance and replaced, downgraded or dispersed to the far off areas of the empire or put on the most dangerous and difficult official assignments on the borders or war fronts. The vacancies thus caused were filled by him with the appointments of *Sunni ulama* and the orthodox Muslim civil and military officers.

With the emergence of this new order of the Mughal bureaucracy and the nobility, Aurangzeb became more outspoken about his orthodox religious views year after year. By the beginning of the second decade of his rule, he started giving expression to his religious emotions by making a sharp distinction between the Islamic and the anti-Islamic features of the traditional Mughal administrative set-up. Under the guidance of 'the religious bigots', he openly declared to impart 'an Islamic touch' to his court on the pattern of the Khalifas. He hated the 'infidel atmosphere' so-called. Aurangzeb 'found fault with the decorative and architectural designs of the *darbar* and public buildings, organizational setup and working of the court, the court etiquette, dress and liveries of the courtiers and nobility, and so on and so forth. In the process of hair-splitting of the things Islamic and un-Islamic, the narrow-minded and bigoted *mullas* found that many a socio-cultural aspect of the court, which had been acquired whole-sale or was an adaptation of the Hindu culture, or which could be traced back to the indigenous culture of the land, was un-Islamic and, therefore, ought to be discarded by the Muslims. In other words, the fruits of centuries of the socio-cultural developments, on the Indian soil, by the Indo-Muslims, must be given up. The Islamic touch of Aurangzeb, therefore, boiled down to an anti-Hindu or rather anti-Indian stance which aimed at establishing the superiority and dominance of the foreign traits of the Indo-Muslim culture. This campaign for the purification of Islam and its institutions from the pagan influence in India marked the second phase of Aurangzeb's religious policy'. (Advanced Study; ii, pp. 492-93)

Aurangzeb's Religious Orthodoxy Assumes Anti-Hindu Overtones

Aurangzeb publicly adopted anti-Hindu policy after the escape of Shivaji from his captivity at Agra in 1666. Adolf Waley, the learned author of *A Pageant of India* writes that 'it was as though Aurangzeb's vindictive nature wished to make the entire Hindu population of India responsible for Shivaji's cunningly devised escape... and his intense bigotry from early youth—one of his most powerful characteristics, began to exercise an over-whelming influence on his entire policy of government.' (Delhi reprint, 1975, p. 473). According to Adolf Waley, Aurangzeb used the episode of Shivaji's escape from his prison as a ploy to show his true colours as a religious fanatic. 'As if to express his intense grief at the escape of his dreaded foe, Aurangzeb banned music at the imperial court on the plea that he had no time for amusements; he dismissed all the musicians and singers employed at the court and stopped the stipends of all the masters of fine arts. By a royal decree, the frescoes on the walls of some of the palace pavilions, both at Delhi and Agra, were destroyed. The statues of Jaimal and Phatta (Fateh Singh), seated on elephants, which had been installed by Akbar at the Agra fort, were demolished. The earlier emperors used to celebrate Holi and Diwali with great enthusiasm and love; Aurangzeb banned the celebration of these and other Hindu festivals at the court. The play of music was not to be allowed in the celebration of the Muslim festivals either. The art galleries were deprived of the best portraits, and the furnishings of the court as well as the *harem* which smacked of Hindu designs were removed. The Hindu astrologers were turned out of the court unceremoniously although the Muslim astrologers continued to enjoy the royal patronage. *Jharokha darshan* was stopped because it was thought to be an imitation of the Hindu tradition. The birthday and coronation festivals of the emperor were also simplified;

the ceremony of *tuladan* or weighing of the emperor on his birthdays was given up. The Muslim ladies were prohibited to visit the shrines of the holy men. In 1670, the Mughal courtiers were ordered that they should neither shake nor wave their hands by way of salutations to each other but simply speak out *salaam-a-lekam*—'peace be on you'. As regards the use of intoxicants like wine and *bhang*, it was 'banned by Aurangzeb on pain of mutilation of limbs'; this step was otherwise appreciable although the mode of its restraint is highly objectionable.

Thus, by the year 1678 'a perfectly Islamic atmosphere' prevailed at the Mughal court. Most of the Shias, Sufis and other broad-minded Muslim courtiers, seasoned Hindu administrators and Rajput nobles had either died or shunted out of the positions of power and pelf, and the imperial court had come to be dominated by orthodox Sunni *ulama* and the religious bigots who acted as the emperor's counsellors in determining the state policy. Under their influence Aurangzeb declared the Mughal Empire as the Islamic state in which the Hindus and other non-Muslims could not be treated at par with the Muslim subjects. And he expressed his resolve to convert the *Dar-ul-Harb* of India into *Dar-ul-Islam* by all means

Re-imposition of Jaziya (April 2, 1679)

On April 2, 1679 Aurangzeb issued a public Proclamation of *Jehad* (Holy War) against all the Hindus of India with the object of converting 'the land of infidels' into *Dar-ul-Islam*. It was signalled by the re-imposition of *Jaziya* on them which had been abolished by Akbar in 1564. It at once reduced the Hindus to the position of *Zimmis* who were deprived of the civil liberties. They were no more to be treated as full-fledged citizens of 'the Islamic State of India'. This marked the third phase of Aurangzeb's religious policy which aimed at the persecution of Hindus at state level.

The sequence of events preceding the imposition of *Jaziya* by Aurangzeb makes a sensational revelation. As described in the preceding pages of this study, Aurangzeb hesitated to declare his hostile intentions against the Hindus as such so long as the powerful and influential Rajput chiefs of Shah Jahan's times adorned his court as grandees of the empire. Instead, he utilised their services and exploited their resources in men and material to the maximum. They were put on the most dangerous and risky military duties until they met with their own destruction for the cause of the empire. On Aurangzeb's orders,

Mirza Raja Jai Singh of Amber, the grandson of Raja Man Singh, thrust his entire manpower in his deadly fight against the Marathas and brought Shivaji to his knees at Purandhar in 1665. Immediately after that, he was sent to the Bijapur front to destroy the *Shia* kingdom. Totally exhausted and worn out by age, Jai Singh was recalled to the court from Aurangabad in May 1667. He died a broken hearted man at Burhanpur enroute to Delhi on July 2, 1667. According to Manucci, he was poisoned to death by the orders of Aurangzeb.

Similarly, Maharaja Jaswant Singh of Jodhpur had been sent by Aurangzeb to fight against the turbulent Pathan tribes of the North-Western Frontier with intentions that 'he might end his career there'. Two of his sons, who held junior commands under their father, died fighting the tribesmen for the Mughal throne. Meanwhile, the state of Jodhpur had been left under the charge of Jaswant Singh's eldest son and heir-apparent Prithvi Singh. It is said that Aurangzeb summoned Prithvi Singh to the imperial court where 'at the end of a flattering entertainment, he was presented by the emperor with a poisoned Dress of Honour; he wore the dress and died of poison that very day'. The old and grief-stricken Maharaja Jaswant Singh expired at Jamrud on December 10, 1678. On the receipt of information, Aurangzeb at once despatched the Mughal troops to annex the state of Jodhpur (Marwar), and he himself shifted his court to Ajmer to facilitate the task. As most of the seasoned Rajput fighters of Jodhpur were on the northwestern war front, and no male member of their ruling family was there to provide leadership, yet the people of Jodhpur, who were taken aback to know of the sinister designs of Aurangzeb, offered a tough resistance. The Marwari youth, peasants and small bands of the warriors fought the Mughal armies of invasion desperately and sacrificed their lives in thousands but they were overwhelmed by the massive imperial forces. The treasure and assets of the ruling family of Jodhpur were confiscated and the state was annexed to the Mughal Empire. Aurangzeb returned from Ajmer to Delhi on April 2, 1679 after the annexation of Marwar and, that very day, he re-imposed Jaziya over his Hindu subjects throughout the Mughal empire. Persecution of the Hindus was its natural consequence and it became the corner-stone of his future policy.

Persecution of the Hindus

In his zeal to propagate Islam in India, Aurangzeb forgot all about political and humanitarian obligations or the duties of a sovereign towards his subjects. Instead, he began to treat the Hindus as the enemies of the Mughal state and thereby struck a fatal blow at the foundations of the Empire itself. The provincial governors, the Muslim military generals and administrators all had to obey the imperial commands whether they liked it or not. The fanatics among them vied with each other in the persecution of Hindus so as to win the favours of the emperor, while most of them carried on the imperial directives just to save themselves from the imperial wrath; none dared to offer a word of wisdom to the self-willed, obstinate and fanatic monarch. In the opinion of Adolf-Waley,

"Aurangzeb possessed neither the genius of Akbar nor the wisdom of Jahangir and Shah Jahan, who had by judicious government made the house of Timur a truly Indian dynasty which Mughal and Hindu alike were proud to serve. His insane lapse into the policy of the early Turki and Pathan conquerors struck at the very heart of the great national edifice which had been called into being with so much circumspection by his predecessors. (*The Pageant*, p. 474).

Thereafter, all the resources of the state were reserved for the propagation of Islam and welfare of its Muslim subjects exclusively. During the last 28 years of his reign, Aurangzeb pursued his religious ideals with unabated zeal and determination to establish himself as an ideal Muslim ruler of an Islamic state, and the persecution of the Hindus was carried out by his government on an unprecedented scale. Aurangzeb's concept of public welfare state was thus 'confined to the happiness and welfare of the orthodox Muslims alone'. He did his utmost to ruin the Hindus politically as well as economically while socially they were treated as outcastes even below the status of their Muslim slaves, most of whom, incidentally happened to be Hindu converts to Islam. Hereafter, Aurangzeb's government did very little for the well-being of the peasants and other village folk as most of them happened to be Hindus. The Hindus were subjected to the payment of Octroi duties and many other taxes besides Jaziya and the Land Revenue, whereas the Muslims were either exempt from their payment or asked to pay at the reduced rates. For instance, previously, the Octroi or the custom duty was charged by the government at the rate of 5% of the value of goods; but since April 1665, this rate had been cut to 2.5 % for the Muslim traders in order to give them an edge over their Hindu counterparts. Two years later, the custom duty in the case of Muslim traders was abolished altogether while the Hindus had to pay it at old rates. Yet another method of putting economic pressure on the Hindus to embrace Islam was the grant of public services, cash awards and other incentives on conversion. Aurangzeb never liked the Hindus to hold high *mansabs* in the civil and military services of the state. Therefore, they were hereafter excluded altogether from the imperial cadre and other high public offices. Under the previous regimes, the Persian-educated Hindus had come to occupy a premier position in the revenue establishment of the Mughal dominions. Long before the imposition of *Jaziya* on them, he had issued a *firman* in 1671 to the effect that all the district rent controllers (*karoris*) in the Crown lands must be Muslims. The provincial governors and *talukadars* were ordered to dismiss the Hindu head-clerks (*peshkars*) and accountants (*diwanian*) and replace them by the Muslims. It created almost a crisis as, due to the paucity of competent Muslim personnel, the revenue establishment came practically to a standstill. Aurangzeb was, therefore, left with no other alternative but to tolerate the presence of the Hindu employees in services; but he modified the ordinance to the extent that their number should not be more than half of the *peshkars* of the revenue establishment and the finance department; and that the other half of the civil servants must be Muslims.

SECTION 4: HINDU REACTION AGAINST AURANGZEB'S RELIGIOUS FANATICISM

The Hindus had, since the times of Akbar, looked upon the Mughal state as a secular nation-state which belonged as much to them as to the Muslims of the country. They enjoyed civil liberties as full-fledged citizens of the state and played a significant role in its expansion and consolidation. The Mughal Empire had thus 'expanded and flourished by the corporate activity of the Hindus and Muslims alike'. Accordingly, they were very slow to realise the gravity of Aurangzeb's anti-Hindu policies, and their protests against his policy of religious intolerance were sporadic, localized and casual in their nature for a long time. It was with the public declaration of *Jihad* against the Hindus and their persecutions which converted their protests into organised opposition and armed resistance against the religious tyranny of Aurangzeb.

1. Rebellion of Jats (1669)

The Jat peasants of Mathura and its neighbourhood were the first to raise their organised voice of pretest against Aurangzeb's policy of religious intolerance. Mathura and Vrindaban, being the holy places of the Hindus, situated so close to the imperial capital of Agra, 'wrankled in the eyes of the new monarch'. He appointed Abdun Nabi, a religious bigot, as the *faujdar* of Mathura. Abdun Nabi held charge of this region for about ten years; he desecrated the Hindu shrines and meted out a very harsh treatment towards its Hindu populace. He heavily taxed the Jat peasants and persecuted them. With the tacit approval of the emperor, he built a *Jama Masjid*, with the material of the ruined Hindu temples, in the heart of the town. The historic railings of the Keshav Rai temple at Mathura were also pulled down by him on the orders of Aurangzeb. In desperation, the Jat peasants of Mathura raised their standard of revolt under the leadership of Gokal, the *zamindar* of Tilpat. They refused to pay the land revenue and turned out the government officials from their villages. Abdun Nabi attempted to suppress them by force but he was killed in the encounter with the Jats in 1669. It necessitated the despatch of an imperial army from Agra to crush their revolt. The Jats were defeated and annihilated; their leader, Gokal Jat, was taken captive with family and brought to Agra. He was tortured to death while his family was forcibly converted to Islam.

The revolt of Jats was crushed for a while but 'the populace of the countryside around Mathura and Agra simmered with discontent' over the religious and political tyranny let loose upon them. It gave birth to a new crop of the public leaders from among them to carry on the resistance against Aurangzeb; they included among others Raja Ram of Sansani and Ramchera of Soghar. Raja Ram died fighting against the Mughal forces in July 1688, but his nephew, Churaman, assumed the leadership of the Jats. He carried on the armed struggle against the Mughals even after the death of Aurangzeb, and laid the foundation of the sovereign Jat state of Bharatpur so close to the centres of the imperial Mughal power at Delhi and Agra.

2. Revolt of Satnamis (1672-73)

The Satnamis were a religious sect of the Hindus. They lived around Narnaul and Mewat in the neighbourhood of Delhi. This sect was founded by a *sanyasi,* named Birbhan, in 1543. The Satnamis were a religious people but they lived as householders and earned their living by cultivation and trade. They shaved their heads and faces, including eye-brows, and were nick-named *Mundiya Sadhus* (clean-shaven saints). They numbered about four or five thousand all told. In 1672, they revolted as a government tax-collector (*shiqdar*) had insulted one of them. On the receipt of information, Aurangzeb despatched an army from Delhi to suppress them. The Satnamis gained some victories in the beginning but were soon crushed and totally annihilated.

3. Aurangzeb and the Sikhs

The execution of Guru Arjan Dev by Jahangir, in May 1606, had compelled the peace-loving religious sect of Guru Nanak's followers to bear arms for their self-defence under the guidance of their sixth Guru Hargobind (1606-45). He adopted a 'New Policy' which gradually transformed the Sikh devotees into *soldier-saints* and earned him the status of 'the spiritual as well as temporal head of the Sikhs'. The youthful Guru suffered imprisonment in the fort of Gwalior for a few years during the reign of Jahangir, but his New Policy brought the Sikhs into armed conflict with the Mughal government under Shah Jahan. The Sikhs fought three battles with the Mughals, and then retreated to the foothills of the Shivaliks for reasons of safety. Guru Hargobind setup his abode at Kiratpur, on the borders of the Kahlur (Bilaspur) state which became one of the holy places of the Sikhs.

The seventh Guru Har Rai (1645-61) was devoted exclusively to the missionary work; and the Sikhs remained at peace with the Mughal government during this period. Nevertheless, Aurangzeb kept the Sikhs under surveillance from the very beginning of his reign. On a complaint received from some Muslims regarding the alleged anti-Islamic contents of the *Adi Granth,* he called for Guru Har Rai to Delhi for explanation. The latter excused his presence but sent his elder son Ram Rai to the Mughal court. Ram Rai, frightened by the Mughal authority, played a subservient role to Aurangzeb, and was granted royal favours. Accordingly, he was deprived of his nomination to the *guruship* by his father. Guru Har Rai expired in 1661 and was succeeded by his second son Har Kishan, then a child of five or six, as the eighth Guru of the Sikhs. Ram Rai's attempts to secure the *gur-gaddi* of Sikhs for himself with the support of the Mughal Crown were turned down by the Sikh community, but the Child Guru, Har Kishan, was called by Aurangzeb to Delhi where he was kept under surveillance to avoid any uprising on the part of the Sikhs till his premature death in 1664.

4. Martyrdom of Guru Tegh Bahadur (1675 A.D.)

The child Guru Har Kishan had died issueless which created a controversy about his next successor. *Guru* Tegh Bahadur, who succeeded him as the ninth *Guru* of the Sikhs, was the grandson of Guru Arjan Dev and the youngest son of Guru Hargobind. Born in 1621, he was above 43 at the time of his accession to the *guruship*. His accession was disputed by a number of impostors with the connivance of corrupt *masands* but Tegh Bahadur, ultimately, received universal acclaim from the Sikh community (*Sangat*) as the rightful successor of Guru Har Kishan 'on grounds of his virtuous character and the ability with which he provided spiritual as well as temporal guidance to them'.

Probably, with the object of allowing 'the dust to settle on the dispute about his succession', Tegh Bahadur left the Punjab with family and a few Sikh devotees on a missionary tour to the Eastern India. His wife, Gujari, who was in the family way, was left by him at Patna under the care of her brother, Kripal Chand, and Nanaki, the aged mother of the Guru. They were looked after by the Sikh *sangat* of Patna. It was here that Gobind Rai (the future Guru Gobind Singh), was born on December 26, 1666; Tegh Bahadur received the news about the birth of his son when he was at Dacca. In Assam, Guru Tegh Bahadur came into contact with Raja Ram Singh, son of Raja Jai Singh, who was then engaged in war with the Ahoms. It is said that the Guru helped in restoring peace between the Mughals and the Ahoms. This incident took place at Dhubri on the bank of the River Brahmaputra. The grateful soldiers' raised a huge mound of earth at that place to commemorate the event in honour of Guru Tegh Bahadur'; it became known as the *Nanak Tila or* 'the Mound of Guru Nanak.'

Guru Tegh Bahadur returned to the Punjab some time in 1671-72 and set his religious centre at Makhowal (modern Anandpur Sahib) in district Hoshiarpur for the propagation of Sikhism. His family was re-united with him soon thereafter. We have the reasons to presume that 'Guru Tegh Bahadur's attachment with Raja Ram Singh was not accidental'; it might have been engineered by Aurangzeb who never wanted an intelligent, sober and man of up righteous character like Tegh Bahadur to provide leadership to the Sikhs—'a martial sect of the Kafirs'. 'Aurangzeb would like to lay his icy hands on their Guru whose predecessors like Ram Dass and Arjan Dev were partially responsible for leading Akbar astray from the orthodox *Sunni* faith. It so appears that immediately after suppressing the revolt of the Satnamis, Aurangzeb had put the Sikhs at the top of the list of those *infidels* who were to be cut to size at the first opportunity'. (*Ibid.*, p. 504).

Before long, Aurangzeb found an excuse to charge the Guru with anti-Muslim and anti-state activities. In 1673-74, *Guru* Tegh Bahadur went on his *udasis* in the Malwa region of the Punjab for the propagation of Sikhism. He encouraged his followers to protest against the anti-Hindu policies of Aurangzeb. According to the Sikh tradition, a deputation of Kashmiri *pundits* met him at Makhowal (Anandpur) in June 1675 and complained against the forced conversions to Islam by Sher Afghan, the governor of Kashmir. The *Guru*, being a man of peace, advised them to go back and tell Sher Afghan that they were the disciples of Guru Tegh Bahadur, and that if the Guru could be persuaded to embrace Islam, all of them would pronounce the *Kalima*. On the receipt of information, Aurangzeb immediately issued orders for the arrest of Guru Tegh Bahadur. According to Khafi Khan, 'Aurangzeb ordered the temples of the Sikhs to be destroyed and the Guru's agents, collecting the tithes and presents of his followers to be expelled from the cities'. Guru Tegh Bahadur and his five disciples were brought in chains to Delhi and given the choice between Islam and death. The *Guru* refused to embrace Islam and was tortured to death on November 11, 1675 at the place where now stands *Gurdwara Sisganj*. After his execution, his associates—Bhai Mati Dass, Gurditta, Uda, Chima and Dayala were all tortured and beheaded. According to Indu Bhushan Bannerji, the insinuations of political disorders and highway robberies, levelled against the Guru and his associates by the later Muslim chroniclers, were set afloat by the Mughal officials 'to cloud the issue by giving it a political colour' (*Evolution of the Khalsa*; 2 vols; Calcutta, 1962, ii, p. 63). The execution of Guru Tegh Bahadur was 'universally regarded by the Hindus as a sacrifice for their faith'.

5. Guru Gobind Singh and the Mughals (1675-1708)

The Sikhs assumed studied silence at the martyrdom of their revered Guru as a political expediency. The child Guru Gobind, son of Guru Tegh Bahadur and tenth Guru of the Sikhs, assumed the leadership of his grief-stricken community at the tender age of nine. He was married to Jito, a seven years old girl of a Khatri family of Lahore, to give him semblance as their rightful and competent religious and temporal leader. Anandpur in the neighbourhood of Makhowal was founded by him on the advice of his maternal uncle Kripal Chand in 1678. The child Guru styled as *Sacha Padshah* and dressed in princely costumes met the *Sangat* (congregation) in a beautifully decorated *Darbar* at Anandpur where he was seated on a raised platform like a prince and surrounded by his armed Sikh volunteers. The devotees were encouraged to bring horses, weapons of war and even elephants as offerings for the Guru. It showed the temper and suppressed emotions of the badly bruised Sikh *Sangat*. Within years, Guru Gobind attained maturity as scholar, spiritual guide, expert horse-rider and warrior who commanded real love and reverence from his devotees. To signal the assumption of his effective religious and temporal leadership of the Sikhs, the Guru celebrated his second marriage at Makhowal on May 15, 1685; his second wife Sundari was the daughter of a Soni Khatri of Bajwara. His two wives gave him four sons in the course of years; Sundari gave birth to his eldest son Ajit on November 16, 1685, while Jito was the mother of his other three sons—Jujhar Singh (b. March 20, 1690), Zorawar Singh (b. January 14, 1697) and Fateh Singh (b. February 22, 1699).

In the winter of 1685-86, Guru Gobind and his followers shifted their headquarters in the interior of the Shivalik hills for reasons of safety. They laid the foundation of Paonta in the thickly forested valley of Sirmur on the bank of the River Yamuna. At Paonta, the Guru engaged himself in useful literary activities and peaceful propagation of his faith. It was at Paonta that 'he organised his armed Sikh volunteers into combat troopers like a military general'.

The rise of a Sikh militant sect in the midst of the Hindu chieftains of the hill states aroused their jealousy and fears as most of them were tributaries of the Mughal crown. Accordingly, the Sikhs had to fight a battle against them at Bhangani on October 3, 1688 to establish their prowess. This victory cowed down the hill chiefs while the youthful Hindus and Sikhs flocked around Guru Gobind in ever greater numbers. Thereafter, the Guru returned from Paonta to Anandpur so as to be nearer to the hearths and homes of majority of his followers. During the next two years, the Sikhs built four forts along the foot-hills in the Anandpur-Kiratpur complex, facing the plains of the Punjab—these were named Anandgarh, Keshgarh, Lohgarh and Fatehgarh respectively. The stage was thus set for a major clash of arms between the Sikhs and the tyrannical regime of Aurangzeb. Now many of the hill chiefs made a common cause with the Sikhs to fight against the Mughals. Alif Khan, a Mughal commander, who was sent to the Shivaliks to chastise them, was defeated at Nadaon in 1690 and repulsed by the hill chiefs with the active support of the Sikhs.

Foundation of the Khalsa (1699 A.D.): Nevertheless, after the battle of Nadaon, the hill chiefs again accepted the Mughal suzerainty and gave up the company of the Sikhs. This display of cowardice and change of loyalties by them disappointed Guru Gobind and he began to prepare long-range plans to transform his Sikhs into self-dependent and courageous warriors for all times to come. His efforts culminated in the foundation of the Khalsa. In 1699, he convened a large assembly of the Sikhs, estimated at about 80,000, at Anandpur at the occasion of Baisakhi. A day before the festival, the Guru held a magnificent *darbar* at Keshgarh and, in a dramatic manner, put to the test the courage of the *sangat* by inviting persons who were ready to sacrifice their lives for the sake of the Guru and their faith. It created quite a stir but, after some hesitation, five persons did come forward, one by one, to offer their heads as a *Bali* (sacrifice) to the Guru. These disciples, named Daya Ram, Dharam Dass, Mohkam Chand, Sahib Chand and Himmat Rai respectively, were made the Khalsa or 'the purified ones' by the administration of *Khande ka Pahul*—viz., 'the baptism of the double-edged sword', instead of the traditional *charan Pahul*. The *Panj Pyare*—'the Five Beloveds', as they were called, received new names by the addition of the epithet Singh to their original names, thus becoming Daya Singh, Dharam Singh, Mohkam Singh, Sahib Singh and Himmat Singh respectively. Thereafter, the Guru himself received *Khande ka Pahul* from the hands of the *panj pyaras* and changed his own name to Gobind Singh. It signified very affectionate, intimate and rather devotional relationship between the Guru and his Khalsa which is usually explained as 'Guru in the Khalsa and Khalsa in the Guru'. The Khalsa were to regard themselves as equal between themselves. As the external marks of distinction, they had to keep five things on their person, each beginning with the latter 'k' - viz., *kesh* (long hair), *kangha* (comb), *kachha* (an underwear), *Kara* (iron bangle) and *kirpan* (sword). A strict code of social conduct was prescribed for the *Khalsa*. The foundation of the Khalsa by Guru Gobind Singh 'had a magical effect on the Sikhs; it did create *lions out of jackals* and *hawks out of sparrows* when the poor, backward and down-trodden men like the scavengers, barbers, carpenters, masons, shepherds and the like emerged as fearless warriors, ready to lay down their lives for the defence of their religion and honour after baptism from Guru Gobind Singh. It made the Sikhs as brave as the Rajputs of those days'. (Advanced Study; ii, p. 511).

War with the Mughals: About that time, Aurangzeb, was involved in a deadly struggle against the Marathas in south India. On receipt of information, he directed the Mughal governors of Lahore and Sirhind to suppress the Sikh insurgency in the north in collaboration with the feudatory hill chiefs. Their first attack on Anandpur, in 1701, was repulsed by the Sikhs with heavy losses. In the second encounter, the Mughal forces, under the command of Wazir Khan, the governor of

Sirhind, laid siege to the fort of Anandpur which was heroically defended by the Sikhs for months. Heavily out-numbered by the foe, the Sikhs were put to great straits and thousands of them sacrificed their lives. In December 1704, Anandpur fell to the Mughals but the Guru escaped with a handful of his followers. At this juncture, the Guru's mother and his two youngest sons, Zorawar Singh and Fateh Singh, aged eight and five respectively, fell into the hands of Wazir Khan. They were asked to embrace Islam, and on their refusal to do so, they were mercilessly bricked alive in a wall; their aged grandmother Nanaki died of grief on the site of their execution. This tragedy took place on December 27, 1704.

Meanwhile, Guru Gobind Singh and his party were overtaken by the Mughal troops on December 22 at Chamkaur, near Ropar. In the battle of Chamkaur that followed the Guru's two elder sons, Ajit Singh and Jujhar Singh, died fighting along with the other Sikhs. After a day-long struggle, when only five of the Sikhs were left alive, they persuaded Guru Gobind Singh to escape in the darkness of night. The Guru made good his escape, perhaps, with only three of his followers. They were pursued in the jungle of Machchiwara, where a number of his disciples, including a group of 'forty Sikhs', who had deserted him earlier at Anandpur, also joined his camp. The fourth and last encounter between Guru Gobind Singh and the Mughals took place at Khidrana (Modern Muktsar) in May 1705. In order to atone for their past sin, 'the forty Sikhs' pounced upon the foe and were cut to a man after taking a heavy tool of the Mughal lives. According to the Sikh belief, they received *mukti* or 'salvation' by the grace of the Guru; it imparted the name of Muktsar, i.e. 'the pool of immortality', to the place where they had died fighting. The Mughal commander was terrified so much by the desperate fight put up by 'the Forty Sikhs' that he hurriedly retreated from Khidrana for fear of further Sikh reprisals.

Guru Gobind Singh's next halt was in the forested area of Talwandi Sabo, now called Damdama Sahib or 'the halting place'; here the Guru and his followers enjoyed respite from the Mughal attacks. He stayed there for about a year and came to the conclusion that 'the mission of his life in spiritual as well as temporal matters had been fulfilled'. As none of the Sikhs in his camp had a copy of the Adi Granth which had been lost at Anandpur; the Guru reproduced the whole of the Granth from memory and gave final touches to it by adding a short composition of his own.

The Death of Guru Gobind Singh: Thereafter, the Guru seems to have left the Punjab probably to take stock of his future course of action. In 1707, after the death of Aurangzeb, we find Guru Gobind Singh having taken his abode at Nander on the bank of the river Godavari along with his followers. The tradition has it that Bahadur Shah, the son and successor of Aurangzeb, had made peace with the Sikhs, and that the Guru had accompanied him to the Deccan. It was here that the Guru was fatally wounded with a dagger by a Pathan, who had approached him, apparently as his disciple. The assassin, perhaps an agent of Wazir Khan, the governor of Sirhind, was struck down by Guru Gobind Singh and hacked to pieces by his followers, but the Guru died of the wounds on October 18, 1708, at the relatively young age of forty-two. Before his death, the Great Guru had taken two major policy decisions for the future guidance of his followers: (1) He informed the Sikhs that the period of their 'living Gurus' was over, and that after him they must abide by the teachings of the *Adi Granth* and treat it as their 'Guru in thought, word and deed'. (2) He had baptized a Hindu *Bairagi* (recluse), with a large following of his devotees, as Gurbax Singh, popularly known as Banda Bahadur, and despatched him to the Punjab with some of his followers, to provide political leadership to the Sikhs.

Guru Gobind Singh was not a political or military leader but a religious man of divine disposition who fulfilled his holy mission as spiritual and temporal head of the Sikhs without any self-interest or personal ambitions. Banda Bahadur emerged as the first political leader of the Sikhs who reorganized them under his military command and wreaked his vengeance upon Wazir Khan and others who had committed atrocities on the Sikhs. Under his leadership, the Sikhs took possession of Sirhind in May 1710 and laid the foundations of the first short-lived but sovereign state of the Sikhs in the Punjab.

6. Aurangzeb and the Rajputs

The annexation of the state of Jodhpur (Marwar), on the death of its chief, Maharaja Jaswant Singh, sent a wave of indignation throughout Rajputana. Unmindful of the consequence, Aurangzeb ordered all the feudatory Rajput chiefs to pay *Jaziya* in lump sum on behalf of their Hindu subjects. It turned the Rajputs en-block into the enemies of the Mughal state almost immediately.

The Heroic Deeds of Durga Dass Rathor: Two of Maharaja Jaswant Singh's widowed queens were in their advanced stage of pregnancy at the time of his death at Jamrud in the northwestern frontier. His lieutenant, Durga Dass Rathor and the Rajput troops, numbering about four or five thousand, escorted them from Jamrud to Jodhpur. On the way home, the ladies gave birth to two sons at Lahore in February 1679. On Aurangzeb's orders, they were brought to Delhi much against the protests of Durga Dass. He lodged the royal family in a mansion in the metropolis which was zealously protected by his soldiers. They were surrounded by the Mughal army and placed in a state of siege. Thus the story of Shivaji's imprisonment along with his Maratha guards, at Agra in 1666 was repeated with the difference that now the royal captives of Aurangzeb, i.e. the two ladies and their infant children needed instant liberation from the clutches of a heartless tyrant 'lest something unpleasant might happen'. It goes to the credit of Durga Dass and his dare-devil Rajput fighters who proved themselves equal to the occasion and upheld the honour of their clan by their heroic operation. Through a strategy, they carried the two ladies and their children, in disguise, out of the imperial formations to safety in the interior of Rajputana beyond the reach of the Mughals. This incident took place when Aurangzeb held his court in the Red Fort of Delhi and was personally directing the operations against the Rajputs. Khafi Khan has left for the posterity a graphic account of this marvellous episode in his invaluable treatise, *Muntakhab-ul-Lubab*, which reads like a romantic story of fictional literature. (Refer to E&D, viii, pp. 297-98).

'The birds had escaped' but Aurangzeb, being an embodiment of cunningness and intrigue, 'procured two children of the menials who were declared to be the sons of Maharaja Jaswant Singh and converted them to Islam with fanfare'. It had little effect on the Rajputs although Aurangzeb 'made his own courtiers and imperial officers to sell the story as far as possible'.

War of liberation in Rajputana: Marwar had been annexed to the Mughal Empire by Aurangzeb in March 1679. As an after-thought, he sold out the throne of Jodhpur to Indra Singh of Nagaur, formerly a tributary of Jodhpur, for a sum Rs.36,00,000 in May 1679. Indra Singh took his residence in the royal palace at Jodhpur as a dummy ruler but the real powers were held in the hands of Tahir Khan, the Mughal governor, who formally acted as his deputy. Indra Singh was promptly declared a traitor by the Rajputs of Jodhpur and he lived there under the protection of the Mughal troops.

The shabby treatment meted out to the royal family of the deceased Maharaja Jaswant Singh set the whole of Marwar ablaze. All the people of Marwar, including men and women, old or young, took to fight against the Mughal forces of occupation. By the time Durga Dass and his men reached Jodhpur with the royal family on July 23, 1679, Tahir Khan, Indra Singh and all of their Mughal troops and supporters had fled from the capital. One of the infant sons of Maharaja Jaswant Singh had expired during their escape from Delhi but Durga Dass placed the other infant, named Ajit Singh, on the throne of Jodhpur amidst great rejoicings of its people.

Aurangzeb Declares War on Marwar: Aurangzeb declared *Jehad* on Marwar and ordered the best of his imperial troops to march upon it from all directions. He once again shifted his court to Ajmer to direct the operations against the Rajputs under his personal supervision. He directed his fourth son, Prince Muhammad Akbar to take charge of the campaign against the Rajputs. After a deadly struggle, the Mughals reoccupied Jodhpur and many other towns of Marwar; they plundered all the towns and destroyed the temples but the Rathors 'who had taken shelter in the hills and deserts, continued harassing them'. After the fall of Jodhpur, Durga Dass took Ajit Singh and the queen Dowager to Udaipur (Mewar). The Sisodia chief, Rana Raj Singh, not only gave shelter to them but also betrothed his niece to Ajit Singh. Raj Singh also refused to pay *Jaziya* to Aurangzeb and took up the cause of Ajit Singh. Before long, the whole of Rajputana, except Amber (Jaipur) was at war with Aurangzeb.

Prince Muhammad Akbar Joins the Rajput Camp: Elated by his victories in Marwar, Aurangzeb ordered an all-out assault on Mewar. Rana Raj Singh suffered defeats in a number of encounters and the premier towns of Chittor and Udaipur were lost to the Mughals early in 1680. Thereafter, the emperor returned to Ajmer, leaving behind Prince Akbar in charge of Chittor. Nevertheless, the Sisodia chief reorganised his troops and inflicted a crushing defeat on Prince Akbar at Bednor in a surprise attack. Aurangzeb blamed the prince for his discomfiture and transferred him to Jodhpur; he assumed personal command of the troops in Mewar and called two of his other sons, Azam and Muazzam also to join the operations. The Rana died in harness in November 1680, but his son and successor Rana Jai Singh continued the guerilla war against the Mughals though on a subdued scale.

Under the directions of Aurangzeb, the Mughal forces carried on destruction and devastation of the villages and towns of Mewar and perpetuated inhuman barbarities on its civilian population. Prince Akbar was disgusted by 'the unjust and cruel war' unleashed by his father against the Rajputs 'which threatened the very foundations of the Mughal Empire'. Realising the futility of Aurangzeb's reactionary policies, he entered into negotiations with the Rajputs and joined their camp. The Prince had a *fatwa* issued under the signatures of four Muslim *ulama*, declaring that Aurangzeb had violated the tenets of Islam in starting this unjust war against his subjects, and, thereby forfeited the throne. On January 11, 1681, Akbar proclaimed himself emperor of India and declared war upon Aurangzeb with the active support of the Rathor and Sisodia Rajputs. Next day, he marched upon Ajmer, accompanied by 70,000 Rajput soldiers as his allies, to fight his father.

The rebellion of Prince Akbar came as a bolt from the blue for Aurangzeb. Nevertheless, the crafty Mughal emperor was too much of a match for his son. He marshalled whatever troops he had under his command and took his position at Doraha, about sixteen kilometres from Ajmer. He resorted to cunning diplomacy to wean Akbar away from his Rajput allies. In the first instance, he had a letter written to Prince Akbar's close friend and associate, Tahavvur Khan by the latter's father-in-law, 'promising him pardon if he returned to the imperial service but threatening to ruin his family, then in the imperial camp, in the event of his refusal to comply'. For the safety of his family, Tahavvur deserted Akbar to reach Aurangzeb's camp one night and was immediately murdered by the emperor's attendants. Initial success in his political manoeuvre encouraged Aurangzeb to take the next major step. He wrote a letter of appreciation to Akbar for having hoodwinked and brought the principal Rajput chiefs within his reach so as to have them crushed between the imperial troops and those of Akbar. The letter was purposely dropped by Aurangzeb's agents within the Rajput camp so that it reached the hands of Durga Dass Rathor. The Rajputs, suspecting foul play on the part of Akbar, plundered his camp and deserted him. The very next day, Aurangzeb's troops overran Akbar's camp, and the much bewildered Mughal Prince fled for his life again to the Rajput camp with only a handful of his followers.

Liberation of Mewar and Marwar

The perfidy of Aurangzeb having been exposed, Prince Akbar and the Rajput leaders were shocked but there was no use of crying over spilt milk. Durga Dass took Prince Akbar under his protection and personally escorted him in safety to the Maratha king Sambhaji, the son and successor of Shivaji. Sambhaji was, perhaps, the only sovereign Indian ruler of standing who could help the fugitive Mughal prince in his fight against Aurangzeb for the throne of Delhi. While continuing his war against Aurangzeb, Durga Dass, as a measure of safety, removed Ajit Singh also from the war-torn Marwar; and the young Rajput prince was lodged and educated, in disguise, in an *Ashram* on the Mount Abu under the care of trustworthy Brahmin teachers for many years.

Aurangzeb dreaded his rebellious son Akbar more than any of his other enemies as he posed a direct threat to his existence as the emperor of India. Therefore, he hurriedly concluded peace with Rana Jai Singh of Mewar on June 24, 1681, and made a dash for the Deccan to reckon with Prince Akbar and the Marathas. The Rana of Mewar utilised this opportunity to secure most of his lost territories, including the historic towns of Udaipur and Chittor, from the Mughal possession, and yet continued to offer support to the people of Marwar, who were at perpetual war with the Mughals.

Durga Dass returned to Marwar from the Maratha camp in 1687 and reactivated the war for liberation from the Mughals. Raja Durjan Sal Hara of Bundi was one of his close allies in this struggle. They expelled the Mughal forces from the countryside, encircled the Mughal camps and confined them to isolated pockets in big forts. They boldly carried on raids in the adjoining Mughal territories as well. In 1698, they routed Inayat Khan, the Mughal governor of Ajmer, although they failed to take possession of the Mughal headquarters. Prince Ajit Singh assumed active command of the Rathor freedom fighters in 1701, and, by 1707, he had become the *de facto* ruler of the major part of Marwar. Aurangzeb died in the south on February 20, 1707; Ajit Singh received the news of his death on March 4, and three days later, he organised the final attack on the Mughal forces in occupation of Jodhpur. In the words of J N Sarkar,

"As Ajit entered Jodhpur, the Mughals fled, leaving their property behind; they were slain or made captive. Many of them fled in the disguise of Hindus, to escape the merciless retribution of the Rajputs, smarting under 26 years of oppression...The fort of Jodhpur was purified with Ganga water and *Tulsi* leaves. Ajit Singh was crowned Maharaja of Marwar. Durga Dass's life task was thus crowned with success. (Aurangzeb; v, p. 292).

Bahadur Shah, the son and successor of Aurangzeb, recognised Ajit Singh as the sovereign ruler of Marwar in 1709 A.D.

SECTION 5: AURANGZEB AND THE DECCAN

Aurangzeb Follows His Rebellious Son to the Deccan

Aurangzeb was badly shaken by the untimely rebellion of his son, Prince Muhammad Akbar. Durga Dass Rathor took the rebellious Mughal prince to the Maratha court at Raigarh in Maharashtra in June 1681. Before Shivaji's death in April 1680, the Maratha kingdom had become the most powerful of all the states in the Deccan. His son and successor Sambhaji did not match the calibre of his father, but he was by far the most formidable sovereign ruler of south India besides being a sworn enemy of Aurangzeb. He usually acted in collaboration with the Shia states of Bijapur and Golconda in their conflict with the Mughals. He welcomed the Rajput chief and his ally, the Mughal prince, and assured them of his whole-hearted support in their fight against Aurangzeb. While negotiations for the settling of the details of the proposed alliance between Sambhaji and Prince Akbar were still going on, Aurangzeb, following close upon the heels of his rebellious son, reached Burhanpur on November 23, 1681. He ordered a vigorous offensive against Sambhaji without any loss of time lest his rebellious son was able to consolidate his friendship with the Marathas or establish his foothold somewhere else in the Deccan.

Aurangzeb's Triumph against Sambhaji and Prince Muhammad

With unlimited resources in men and material at his command, Aurangzeb ordered four Mughal armies to invade Maharashtra from four different directions simultaneously. Sayyad Hussain Ali Khan was sent to north Konkan; Shabuddin Khan to Nasik; Ruhulla Khan and Prince Shah Alam to Ahmadnagar to guard it against a possible Maratha attack; and Prince Azam was sent towards Bijapur to cut off Maratha supplies and prevent the sultan from sending any assistance to them. Though surrounded by the imperial troops from all directions, the Marathas had the innate stamina and methodology of guerilla warfare to sustain them. They lost many towns, including Poona and Nasik besides scores of the impregnable forts to the Mughals, but successfully halted their advance on all fronts. Instead, Sambhaji found enough time to settle his scores against the Portuguese and pretended not to be provoked by the angry Mughal emperor. To the misfortune of Prince Akbar, however, the Maratha court was sharply divided on the issue of making an alliance with the fugitive Mughal prince to avoid head-on collision with Aurangzeb directly. Sambhaji lacked the foresight of his father to strike an alliance with Akbar to the gain of the Marathas, and his favourite Peshwa, Kavi Kalash –'a Kanyakubja Brahmin from northern India' was the object of hatred and despise by most of Maratha courtiers and military generals. Hence it was that Prince Akbar stayed in Maharashtra for about six years but Sambhaji neither extended his helping hand to him nor struck an alliance with the Rajput chief, Durga Dass Rathor, the freedom-fighter from Marwar. The hapless Mughal prince left Maharashtra in February 1687 for Persian and died in exile there.

Aurangzeb's Un-ending Wars in the Deccan

Aurangzeb's emergent visit to the Deccan had a very limited object. The rebellious Prince Muhammad Akbar was not allowed to establish his foothold anywhere in India, and with his flight to Persia, the emperor's mission was apparently fulfilled. But,'the fate had decreed that Aurangzeb will have to spend the last twenty-six years of his life in tents and wear out the Empire's revenues, army, and organised administration as well as his own health in an unending and fruitless struggle. Once he came to head-on collision with the Marathas, there was no way of escape from the gimmick of the knotty guerrilla bands. He prepared elaborate plans for the annihilation of the Marathas through *Jehad, albeit* the obstinate religious fanatic was caught like a sick spider in his own web, and the *mountain rats* swallowed his limbs bit by bit. While going to the south, Aurangzeb could never contemplate that a *nemesis* has set in that would lead not only him to the grave but also sound the death-knell of the mighty Mughal Empire'. (Advanced Study; ii, p. 527).

To begin with, Aurangzeb was successful on all the fronts. The Shia states of Bijapur and Golconda were conquered and annexed to the Mughal Empire. Sambhaji, the unworthy son and successor of Shivaji, fell into the hands of Aurangzeb like a little rabbit in 1689 and was tortured to death. 'Nevertheless, *the poisonous seeds of religious bigotry* and the merciless persecution of those who did not conform to his creed, which had been sown by Aurangzeb in the first half of his royal career, *began to sprout up* in the second half of his reign, and he had to *gather their baneful harvest* in the concluding years of his life' (Ibid.) A brief chronicle of his unjust wars and the fateful events which finally led him to his grave in the Deccan may be given.

Annexation of Bijapur and Golconda States

The sultans of Bijapur and Golconda had always been under pressure from the imperial Mughals since the days of Akbar. During the reign of Shah Jahan, Aurangzeb held the viceroyalty of the Deccan twice and his treatment towards the *Shia* rulers of these states was far from friendly. They acknowledged the suzerainty of the Mughals and paid hefty tributes to Delhi but Aurangzeb was not satisfied. To him, their sultans were 'heretics, worthy of being extirpated'. Obviously, Aurangzeb's policy towards these states was dictated less by imperial considerations and more by his attitude of religious orthodoxy. On the eve of the war of succession, Aurangzeb held the second viceroyalty of the Deccan, but before his departure for the north to take part in the war against his brother, he had made a conciliatory settlement with the sultans of Bijapur and Golconda.

Ali Adil Shah II, the sultan of Bijapur from November 1655 to December 1672, enjoyed freedom from the Mughal aggression during the first few years of Aurangzeb's rule. During this period, Aurangzeb was engaged in his armed conflict with the Marathas. Mirza Raja Jai Singh, then the Mughal viceroy of the Deccan, defeated Shivaji and compelled him to make peace with Aurangzeb in June 1665. Thereafter, Jai Singh was ordered by Aurangzeb to launch an attack on the state of Bijapur. The Mughal forces, led by the Rajput stalwart, pierced through the Bijapur territories to reach within 20 kilometres of its capital but their further advance was halted by the Bijapuri guerrilla fighters. Jai Singh was recalled from the Bijapur front and died at Burhanpur in July 1666. It gave another brief spell of peace to Bijapur until the death of Ali Adil Shah II in December 1672. The courts of Bijapur and Golconda maintained friendly relations with the Marathas, dilly-dallied about the payment of tribute to Delhi and held the Mughals at bay. In September 1679, the Mughals invaded Bijapur once again but their attack was repulsed by the Bijapuris with the help of the Marathas.

Aurangzeb himself made it to the Deccan in 1681 and launched a full-fledged campaign against the Marathas. He calculated, though wrongly, that the annexation of the *Shia* states of Bijapur and Golconda might help him in settling his scores with the Marathas. According to Stanley Lane-Poole, 'Aurangzeb's plan seems to have been, first, to cut off the Marathas' funds by exterminating the kingdoms of Golconda and Bijapur, which paid blackmail to the (Maratha) brigands; and then to ferret the mountain rats out of their holes'. (Medieval India; p. 394). The first part of his plan was not difficult. The decadent Shia kingdoms of the Deccan were not in a position to offer serious resistance to the mighty Mughal forces. These might have been annexed long before but for the broad-mindedness and considerate policy adopted towards them by Shah Jahan. In August 1685, Aurangzeb took the command of the Mughal army of invasion in his personal hands and made a frontal attack on the stronghold of Bijapur direct. He reached within ten kilometres of the town and put it under siege. A close blockade was made, and the repeated assaults on the besieged populace and the fort put the defenders to great straits. After 15 months of heroic resistance, the besieged garrison surrendered on September 22, 1686. The state was annexed to the Mughal Empire and the Adil Shahi dynasty came to an end.

Aurangzeb took his residence in the royal palace of Bijapur which was soon denuded of all the *Shia* symbols, including the pictures, furnishings, inscriptions and architectural designs on the walls of the palace. The Muslim nobles and respectable citizens of Bijapur had to discard all *Shia* practices and conform to the puritanical *Sunni* way of life to secure the imperial favours. The young sultan, Sikander Adil Shah, was granted a pension and *mansab* to begin with but was thrown into the prison soon afterwards. He was held in captivity within the military camp of Aurangzeb till his death in April 1700.

While Aurangzeb was engaged in the siege of Bijapur, Prince Muazzam held the command of the Mughal army of invasion in Golconda. He had put the stronghold of Golconda under siege but, at the initiative of his father, concluded a treaty of peace with Sultan Abul Hasan on very favourable terms. According to the terms of the treaty, the sultan agreed to pay one *crore* and twenty *lakhs* of rupees as war indemnity in addition to the annual tribute as he used to pay to Delhi previously. Besides, he had agreed to dismiss his two Brahmin ministers, Madanna and Akhanna from service. Meanwhile, without the knowledge of the sultan, a few ladies of his *harem* had secured the murder of Madanna and Akhanna, and their heads were sent to Prince Muazzam in his army camp. The Qutubshahi dynasty thus seemed to have secured a lease of life. It proved an allusion, however. After the annexation of Bijapur, Aurangzeb reached Golconda in January 1687. Prince Muazzam was then encamped with his forces outside the fort of Golconda which was still in the possession of Sultan Abul Hasan. Aurangzeb felt insulted to see this clumsy arrangement. Elated by his victory against Bijapur, he resolved to make an end of the Qutubshahi dynasty immediately. Without taking his son into confidence, he at once ordered the imperial troops to renew the siege to the fort again in violation of the terms of the treaty, concluded with the sultan a short while ago. Prince Muazzam felt embarrassed at this breach of faith by his father, and entered into a secret understanding with the ill-fated sultan to save the latter's life. When Aurangzeb came to know of it, he at once placed his son with family under arrest and confiscated his entire property. Thus Prince Muazzam—the future Mughal emperor Bahadur Shah, had to suffer in the jail of his father for eight long years for having shown sympathy to the Qutubshahi ruler.

The fall of Bijapur and the cruel treatment meted out by Aurangzeb towards his own son on the Golconda issue, disheartened Sultan Abul Hasan. But his besieged soldiers fought desperately and held the Mughals at bay for over eight months before capitulation. Meanwhile, Aurangzeb's secret agents had created some traitors within the fort who were ready to betray their master. In the wee hours of September 21, 1687, Abdulla Pani—an Afghan official of Sultan Abul Hasan, treacherously opened the eastern gate of the fort to admit the Mughal troops. Taken aback by this development, Sultan Abul Hasan and his nobles surrendered without a fight; only one of the sultan's dedicated officers, named Abdur Razzak Lari, fought the Mughals at the risk of his life. Khafi Khan correctly observes that 'the fate of the Qutubshahi dynasty was finally sealed not by force of sword and spear but the treachery of its own officials'. (*Muntakhab-ul-Lubab*; E&D, vii, p. 332). Golconda was annexed to the Mughal Empire, and Abul Hasan, the last sultan of the Qutubshahi dynasty, was sent to Daulatabad as prisoner to join his ex-neighbouring chief, Sultan Sikander Adil Shah of Bijapur. All assets of the Golconda dynasty, including seven crores of rupees in cash, besides 'heaps' of jewellery, gold and silver ornaments and other commodities of incalculable value were collected by Aurangzeb. The triumphant Mughal forces spread themselves in every nook and corner of the former states of Bijapur and Golconda and brought all of their territories under their effective control in couple of months.

The conquest and annexation of Bijapur and Golconda was the greatest and the last achievement of Aurangzeb as the imperial ruler of India. It extended the boundaries of the Mughal Empire to the maximum dimensions, which now spread from seacoast to seacoast in the South Indian Peninsula. Jadunath Sarkar concludes this achievement of Aurangzeb in the words that follow:

"Aurangzeb's work in the Deccan seemed to have been completed. The long dream of the Mughal emperors, ever since the days of Akbar, seemed at last to have been fully realised. No rival Muslim power was left in the Deccan, and all India now bowed beneath the scepter of Delhi. True, there was a Hindu king (Sambhaji, the successor of Shivaji) still unsubdued; but he was an upstart of limited means and his soldiers no better than brigands; their suppression so it seemed, was only a question of time, now that the Mughal army was set free and the Marathas had no ally left to them anywhere in India."—(*Aurangzeb*, v, pp. 4-5).

Aurangzeb and the Marathas

Aurangzeb, 'from the heights of his power in 1687, could never contemplate that a small principality, carved into existence by Shivaji, in a fringe of the north-western edge of the Deccan plateau, and held by his not so capable a successor as Sambhaji, would not only defy the Mughal arms but also pose a serious threat to the very existence of the mighty Mughal Empire. The Maratha ulcer ruined Aurangzeb'. (Advanced Study, ii, pp. 532-33). As the Marathas played a formidable role in bringing about the downfall of the Mughal empire, the detailed study of their rise to power has been reserved for the next chapter. Here suffice it say that, with the conquest of Bijapur and Golconda, Aurangzeb considered himself master of the Deccan. Like the civil servants and bureaucracy, a large number of ex-soldiers and military officers of the erstwhile states of Bijapur and Golconda were also prepared to join the Mughal camp and they were readily absorbed in the imperial forces to swell their ranks beyond all proportions. For a while, Aurangzeb seemed to be at the top of the world and his armies seemed to carry all before them. He ordered an all-out offensive against the Marathas, and the latter were 'everywhere driven away to their mountain forts'. To crown their successes, Sambhaji (1680-89), the son and successor of Shivaji, was captured along with about 200 others, including 25 high dignitaries and members of the royal family, by an enterprising Mughal officer at a moment of his careless self-indulgence at Sanghmeshwar in February 1689. They were brought to Aurangzeb's military camp at Bahadurgarh and most of them were put to death in March. Sambhaji had failed to accomplish much for the Marathas and their state during his lifetime but, 'by his heroic death, he raised himself to the status of a martyr'. Khafi Khan writes that the captive Maratha king and his notorious prime minister (*Peshwa*) Kavi Kalash, 'dressed as buffoons in long fools caps, with bells fixed on them, and mounted on camels' were paraded through the Mughal camp 'with drums beating and trumpets pealing'. Aurangzeb offered to spare the life of Sambhaji if he surrendered all his forts, disclosed his hidden treasures, and declared the names of those Mughal officers who had been in league with him. As observed by G.S. Sardesai

"Fretting with bitterness of soul at having been publicly insulted and driven to desperation, Sambhaji spurned the offer of life in abuse of the emperor...giving free vent to his long pent-up sentiments...and scurrilously asked for one of Aurangzeb's daughters as the price of his friendship...For once Sambhaji behaved with a stoic firmness worthy of the great Shivaji, and fully atoned by the manner of death for all the sins he had committed in life."(*Marathas*, i, p. 315).

Aurangzeb's blood boiled to hear of this rhetoric of the captive Maratha king, and he ordered him to be tortured to death. According to Khafi Khan, the tongues of Sambhaji and Kavi Kalash were cut out that very night; next day they were blinded, and, thereafter, their limbs were hacked off, one by one, day after day, and their flesh thrown before the dogs. Sambhaji bore this torture heroically for about three weeks until his head was chopped off on March 21, 1689, at Koregaon on the River Bhima where Aurangzeb was then encamped. (*Muntakhab-ul-Lubab*; E&D, viii, p. 341). Sardesai infers that "the fearless manner in which Sambhaji had met his end, united and steeled the hearts of the Marathas as nothing else would have done, and nerved them to avenge the death of their sovereign'. (*Ibid.*, p, 316).

After the death of Sambhaji, the Maratha capital Raigarh was put under siege by the Mughals but the new Maratha king, Raja Ram, the younger half-brother of Sambhaji, was whisked away in the disguise of a hermit to a place of safety at Vishalgarh. Raigarh was defended by the Marathas for about seven months before its occupation by the Mughals on November 13, 1689, which was made possible by the treachery of a Maratha officer. The entire family of Sambhaji, including his widowed queen Yesu Bai and her son Shahu, fell into the hands of the Mughals, and languished in the captivity of Aurangzeb for many years. Raja Ram died in harness on March 12, 1700 but the Marathas installed his four year old infant son on the throne, styled as Shivaji II, under the regency of his mother Tara Bai, and waged war against the Mughals which assumed the form of a full-fledged people's war for liberation. 'The exasperating struggle' between the Marathas and Aurangzeb 'lasted seventeen years' after the execution of Sambhaji and the fall of their capital Raigarh, but success alluded the Mughal emperor. Lane-Poole gives the following 'explanation of this colossal failure' on the part of the last Great Moghal:

'Aurangzeb had alienated the Rajputs forever, and they would not risk their lives for him in exterminating a people who were after all Hindus....the Marathas cared nothing for luxuries: a cake of millet sufficed them for a meal, with perhaps an onion for *point*. They defended a fort to the last, and then defended another fort. They were pursued from place to place, but were never daunted, and they filled up the intervals of sieges by harassing the Mughal armies, stopping convoys of supplies, and laying the country waste in the path of the enemy. There was no bringing them to a decisive engagement. It was one long series of petty victories followed by larger losses. Nothing was gained that was worth the labour; the Marathas became increasingly objects of dread to the demoralized Moghul army; and the country, exasperated by the sufferings of a prolonged occupation by an alien and licentious soldiery, became more and more devoted to the cause of the intrepid bandits, which they identified as their own'. (Medieval India; pp. 402-3).

Death of Aurangzeb

In spite of his best efforts Aurangzeb failed miserably to crush the Maratha war of independence. Lane-Poole expresses pity for that grand old emperor 'who endured numerous hardships and disappointments during his wearisome campaign, lasting over two decades', in his fight against the Marathas. He writes *inter alia* as follows:

'It was he (Aurangzeb), who planned every campaign, issued all the general orders, selected the points for attack and the lines of entrenchments, and controlled every movement of his various divisions in the Deccan. He conducted many of the sieges in person, and when a mine exploded among the besiegers at Satara in 1699, and general despondency fell on the army, the octogenarian mounted his horse and rode to the scene of disaster *as if in search of death*. He piled the bodies of the dead into a human ravelin, and was with difficulty prevented from leading the assault himself'. (*Ibid.*, p. 403)

Jadunath Sarkar concludes Aurangzeb's campaign against the Marathas with the remarks that 'the rest of his life is a repetition of the same sickening tale; a hill fort captured by him in person after a vast expenditure of time, men and money; the fort recovered by the Marathas from the Mughal garrison after a few months and its siege begun again a year or two later'. In consequence, the soldiers and camp-followers of Aurangzeb 'suffered unspeakable hardships in marching over flooded rivers, muddy roads and broken hill tracts; porters disappeared, transport beasts died of hunger and overwork, scarcity of grain was ever present in the camp and the Maratha and *Berad thieves* (as Aurangzeb officially called them) not far off. The mutual jealousy of generals ruined his cause or delayed his success. The siege of eight forts, Satara, Parli, Panhala, Khelna (Vishalgarh), Kondana (Sinhagarh), Raigarh, Torna and Wagingera, besides five places of lesser note, occupied him for five years and a half (1699-1705), after which the broken down old man of eighty-eight retired to die'. (Aurangzeb, v, p. 475). At last, he gave up the struggle and ordered the return of the imperial camp to north India early in 1706. He was, however, not destined to reach Agra which he had left 26 years ago, apparently, 'on a flying visit to the south to chastise his own rebellious son, Prince Akbar'. 'The retreat of the imperial (Mughal) troops' from Maharashtra, writes Sardesai, 'was like a mourning procession'; the Marathas 'hovered' round them 'like vultures and created havoc' in their ranks. (Marathas, i, p. 359).

The royal standards reached Ahmadnagar on January 31, 1706 and no further. Worn out by age and fatigue, Aurangzeb, was physically incapacitated and remained confined to bed there in his army camp for over a year before his death. Of his three surviving sons, the eldest one, Prince Muazzam, aged sixty-three, was then in Kabul, while the other two, Azam and Kam Bakhsh, were in attendance upon him. 'Aurangzeb trembled in his bones to recollect the bitter memories of his own misdeeds, committed by him in the war of succession in 1657-58, when Prince Azam attempted to murder his younger brother, Kam Bakhsh, in the imperial camp, under his very nose'. The emperor immediately sent both of them away from him in February 1707; Prince Kam Bakhsh was entrusted the governorship of Bijapur while Prince Azam was ordered to go and take charge of Malwa. Within a few days of their departure from Ahmadnagar, Aurangzeb was struck with fever which proved fatal. He died on March 3, 1707, and according to his will, was buried 'in a plain grave' near the tomb of Sheikh Zainuddin at Khuldabad, now called Rauza, situated about seven kilometres from Daulatabad.

❑ ❑

18

RISE OF THE MARATHA POWER

SECTION 1: HOMELAND OF THE MARATHAS

The rise to power of Chhatrapati Shivaji, the son of a petty *jagirdar* and self-made leader of the Marathas, who denounced the religious bigotry of Aurangzeb and challenged the mighty Mughal empire at the zenith of its glory in the last quarter of the seventeenth century, was not 'an isolated phenomenon'. It was as much the result of his inborn qualities of virtuous character, courage and conviction as of the peculiar geophysical features and climatic conditions of the homeland of the 'sturdy Marathas', and the unifying socio-religious influences which were animating the people of the Deccan about that time. Shivaji was, in fact, the product of his age.

The geophysical features and climatic conditions of Maharashtra—the original home of the ancient Ratthas, Maharatthas, or Rashtrikes, played an important role in moulding their character and attitude towards life. The principal Maratha habitat lay between the rivers Narbada and the upper Krishna along the western seacoast of India. It stretched from Daman to Karwar, and included within its fold the mountainous regions of Berar (ancient Vidarbha), Konkan, the Godavari basin, and the valley of the River Krishna. It was separated from northern and central India by the Vindhyachal and Satpura mountain ranges. Having been cut off from the outside world by sea on the west, barren plateau of the east and mountains on the other sides, Maharashtra afforded a natural protection to its inhabitants from external attacks under normal circumstances. The greater part of the region comprised 'a rugged plateau, broken into isolated pockets by the hills and deep valleys, covered with forests', which rendered the widely scattered villages and hamlets of the Marathas 'inaccessible to the huge armies of invasion'. The landscape of Maharashtra was 'uneven, the soil unproductive and routes intricate'. It was rather very difficult, if not impossible, for any invader, however resourceful, to overrun the whole of Maharashtra in a single sweep.

The Marathas comprised a homogeneous and well-knit community of the poor and backward yet freedom-loving Hindus who shared the common cultural traits and poverty in equal proportions among themselves. They were short in stature, well-built and hardy. The physical features and bracing climate made them simple but active, self-reliant, courageous and brave in their habits. They built mud fortresses, called *garhis*, and stone castles on the hilltops for their self-defence and were adept in the guerrilla warfare. They lived by agriculture and did not take much interest in trade and industry. The scanty rainfall and meager agricultural produce made them poor and frugal but industrious people. Simple living, self-reliance, courage and patience were the hall-marks of their character. The Marathas were divided into several clans or families some of which claimed their descent from the ancient Mauryas, Rathors and the Yadavas. But there were very few rich men among them and their feudal chiefs were no better than their poverty-stricken peasants from the point of view of their material possessions. Marathi was their common spoken language which had been derived from one of the Prakrit dialects, called Maharashtri; it welded them linguistically as well as territorially into one solid and homogeneous community. They were devoted to their ancestral Hindu faith and, like the Rajputs, were known for their hospitability to their guests.

Among the Muslim rulers of India, Alauddin Khilji was the first who broke the political isolation of Maharashtra by launching a successful raid on Deogiri (modern Daulatabad) in 1295 during the reign of his uncle, Jalaluddin Khilji. Thereafter, this region was gradually conquered and brought under the sway of the Sultanate of Delhi. As a result, the Marathas were subjected to uninterrupted Muslim rule for over three hundred years 'which made them more cunning than chivalrous'. Muhammad Bin Tughluq established the Muslim domination in Maharashtra by transferring his capital to Daulatabad, though for a short while. In 1347, the imperial government of Delhi was replaced by the Bahmani kingdom in the Deccan which, in turn, gave birth to five regional Muslim states in the beginning of the sixteenth century. Most of the Maratha lands fell within the jurisdiction of Ahmadnagar and Bijapur although they were 'scattered like atoms' in all of the Muslim states of the Deccan. They served in the armies or held subordinate administrative positions under the Sultans though some of them rose to be second or third rate officers as well. Nevertheless, 'the Marathas as a community had received sufficient training in the arts of war and administration under the Muslim rulers of the Deccan'; it proved very helpful to them when they were called upon to fight for their freedom under the leadership of Shivaji.

A strong religious reform movement witnessed Maharashtra, like many other parts of India, during the medieval period. Usually referred to as the Bhakti movement, it produced many religious teachers and socio-cultural reformers among the Hindus, some of whom belonged to the lower castes and rubbed shoulders with the highest in the country. They emphasised the essential equality of all the people, irrespective of their caste and socio-economic standing, and laboured hard to foster a sense of Hindu unity. The Bhakti reformers, including saint Tukaram, Vaman Pandit, Eknath and, above all, Guru Ram Dass, carried on vigorous campaigns in Maharashtra, in the spoken language of the people, against caste-system and other socio-religious evils of the Hindus. They inculcated fellow-feelings and fostered a sense of unity among the Marathas. Guru Ram Dass, particularly, played a significant role in arousing political consciousness among the Marathas against the Muslim domination; and, under the influence of his teachings, the much-needed leadership was provided to them by Shivaji. The teachings of Bhakti reformers, some of which were committed to writing, developed the Marathi language and produced a feeling of oneness and democratic temper among the people. The rise of the Marathas was, thus, not a sudden or an isolated phenomenon; it was the outcome of a long and steady training received by them for over two centuries. Accordingly, Shivaji, a born leader of men and genius as military commander and administrator, was not a shooting star either who made his appearance on the political horizon of India by chance or accident. Instead, he was product of the age and represented 'the flowering of the Maratha awakening'. The dynamic personality of Shivaji, coupled with his political and military achievements, and his intense love and spirit of sacrifice for his people has made him immortal in the annuals of the Maratha history. With the strong organizational set-up and socio-political institutions bequeathed by him to his people, the Marathas emerged as the most powerful political force at the national level after the downfall of the Mughal Empire.

SECTION 2: CAREER AND ACHIEVEMENTS OF SHIVAJI

The Ancestors of Shivaji

Shivaji belonged to the Bhosle or Bhonsle clan of the Marathas. The people of this clan were peasant proprietors of Verul (Ellora) and some other villages in the neighbourhood of Daulatabad (ancient Deogiri). G.S. Sardesai, the renowned historian of the Maratha history, traces their descent from the Sisodia Ranas of Chittor and Udaipur. According to him, probably, 'a branch of their family migrated to the south' after the kingdom of Mewar had been devastated by Alauddin Khilji early in the fourteenth century. Shivaji's father Shahji and grandfather Maloji were both associated with the Nizamshahi kingdom of Ahmadnagar as military officers during the days of Malik Ambar- an Abyssinian minister of the state. Shahji was awarded the *parganas* of Poona and Supa as his personal *jagir* by the Sultan of Ahmadnagar. After the fall of Ahmadnagar, he transferred his services to Bijapur in 1632 and carved out a big estate for himself in Mysore and Karnatak regions also.

Birth and Early Life of Shivaji

Shahji had two wives and numerous children. His first wife Jija Bai, whom he married in 1605, was the daughter of Lukhji Jadhava, the *jagirdar* of Sindkher near Daulatabad; he belonged to the ancient Yadava ruling family of Deogiri. Sardesai refers to Shahji as 'a soldier of fortune, who long exerted himself in upholding the falling fortunes of the Nizamshahi kingdom against the Mughal onslaught'. (*History and Culture of the Indian People*, BVB, vii, p.247). Shivaji was born of his first wife Jijabai in the hill-fortress of Shivner, in the estate of Poona, on April 10, 1627. Shahji is said to have cut off his contacts with his father-in-law when the latter transferred his loyalties to the Mughals. That is why Jijabai was practically neglected by him. She was left at Poona with her infant son Shivaji while Shahji shifted his headquarters to Bangalore with the rest of his family.

Accordingly, Shivaji was brought up, far away from his father, at Poona under the personal care of his mother alone and was devotedly attached to her all through her life. Jijabai was a well-educated and virtuous lady of parts. Deeply religious in her outlook, she would, every night, lull her child Shiva to sleep while listening to the bed-time stories of Lord Ram, Krishan and other epic heroes repeatedly and in exhaustive details. Needless to say, it infused in him the spirit of patriotism and chivalry. Apart from Jijabai, two other persons influenced Shivaji's early career and character very deeply; they were Dadaji Kondadev, the manager of his father's *jagir*, and Guru Ram Dass, his spiritual teacher since his boyhood days. Dadaji, who acted as his tutor and guardian, was a brilliant administrator and man of character, courage and conviction. With intense love for his young ward, he made the best arrangements for his education and gave him practical training in civil and military administration. It is said that he used to take Shivaji along with him during his visits to the countryside when he was hardly ten years old. While transacting the business of the *jagir* or settling the disputes between the village folk, Dadaji would seat the child Shiva on a chair or raised platform in their midst to make him conscious of his ultimate role as their feudal chief. Shivaji was good in academic and literary studies but he grew up to be a fine warrior and excellent administrator. Guru Ram Dass familiarized him with the glories of ancient Indian culture and made him a staunch nationalist in his outlook. Under their collective guidance and influence, Shivaji developed an intense desire to liberate his people, the Marathas, from the Muslim domination.

Shahji Bhonsle was deeply impressed to hear of the tales of chivalry and patriotism about his promising son Shivaji from Dadaji and others and invited him with his mother Jijabai to Bangalore in 1639-40. They stayed there for about two months. Shahji utilised this opportunity to celebrate the marriage of his son amidst great rejoicings with Sai Bai, a girl of the Nimbalkar family to which Shivaji's grandmother belonged. Shahji Bhonsle foresaw a great future for his son, and on the eve of his departure, he assigned him the *jagir* of Poona in perpetuity and placed a select band of about 200 best bureaucrats and warriors of Bangalore under his command to assist him in his establishment as a feudal chief independently. Since then Shivaji started taking active part in the administration of the Poona *jagir* which now belonged exclusively to him. After the death of his guardian Dadaji Kondadev in March 1647, Shivaji became his own master when he was yet in his teens.

Early Conquests

The *jagir* of Poona, entrusted to Shivaji by his father, was situated in the heart of what was then called the 'Maval country'; it included primarily 'the valleys to the west of Poona, roughly extending from

Junnar to Wai'. Its inhabitants, called the Kolis and Mavalis, were good fighters. Shivaji had inherited from Dadaji, a small contingent of local militia, composed of the Mavali and Koli youth for the protection of the lives and properties of his estate. Shivaji made personal friends with them and assembled around him a devoted band of quite a few hundred of the Mavalis and Kolis, and, with their assistance, he embarked upon a career of adventure and conquest when he was still in his teens. Being acquainted with every inch of his parental estate, including its valleys, hills, and the forests, Shivaji zealously protected it from the outsiders with the help of his youthful companions and paid militia in the true spirit of a freedom-loving prince. He did not permit the intruders into the territories of Poona which were dotted with a number of mud-forts and police-posts, setup by him at the hilltops. As mentioned above, the petty Maratha estate of Shahji Bhonsle at Poona could not flourish in a vacuum; originally it belonged to the Sultan of Ahmadnagar, and after Shahji's change of masters, it was deemed to have fallen under the control of Bijapur. The state of Ahmadnagar had since been disintegrated. The prevalent political confusion in the Deccan because of the Mughal invasions, coupled with the internal weaknesses of the states of Bijapur and Golconda, their mutual rivalries and war with the Mughals, provided a good opportunity to Shivaji to consolidate his position at Poona and win the hearts of the rustic Marathas in the countryside as 'their benevolent prince and protector'. According to Rawlinson, 'there seems to be little doubt that his career was inspired by a real desire to free his country from what he considered to be a foreign tyranny, and not by a mere love of plunder'. Jadunath Sarkar writes that 'a career of independence was no doubt risky to Shivaji, but it had undreamt of advantages to compensate for the risk if only he could succeed'.

Conquest of Torna: Shivaji started encroachments on the territories of the neighbouring Muslim states in 1646 when Dadaji Kondadev was still alive. His first acquisition was the hill fort of Torna from its Bijapur commandant. It was a border post of Bijapur, situated at a distance of about 32 kilometres to the southwest of Poona and was manned by not more than 200 poorly armed soldiers. In 1646, the Sultan of Bijapur suffered from a paralytic attack and the defences of his state fell into a state of neglect. Taking advantage of the situation, Shivaji surprised its indolent defenders in a night assault and took forced possession of the fort. There he discovered a hidden treasure of two *lakhs* of *huns*, which he wisely utilised in raising an army and building a new fort on a strategic hilltop, situated about eight kilometres to the east of Torna, which was named Raigarh. It was better located for the protection of Poona against attack from Bijapur.

Conquest of Chakan, Kondana and Purandhar Forts: The forced occupation of Torna by Shivaji went almost unnoticed by the Bijapur court because it was treated as a minor incidence of encroachment at the borders. It encouraged Shivaji to lay his hands on three other border hill forts of Chakan, Kondana and Purandhar, one by one, during the next two years. The Sultan of Bijapur felt alarmed at these rebellious activities by a son of the military general and vassal of his state, but on being reprimanded, Shivaji pleaded that he had done it for the protection of his family estate. It is said that Shivaji had created a lobby of his sympathisers in the Bijapur court to intervene on his behalf which deferred action against him. Nevertheless, in 1648, Shahji Bhonsle was interned by the Sultan 'on the ground that he had connived at the acts of aggression of his son'. But Shivaji proved too clever for him to be cowed down so easily. At his persuasion, Shahji openly declared that he was not responsible for the rebellious activities of his grown-up son who was the master of his own *jagir*, while Shivaji threatened the Sultan to join the Mughal camp against Bijapur if any harm came to his father. He actually established contact with Prince Murad, then the Mughal viceroy of the Deccan, for this purpose. It is doubtful if it had any effect on the Mughal viceroy but the Sultan of Bijapur was so much perturbed to hear of it that he at once liberated Shahji Bhonsle in May 1649. Shivaji also thought it fit to pacify the court of Bijapur by offering to surrender the fort of Kondana. However, he refused to hand over the formidable fort of Purandhar to Bijapur on the ground that he had acquired it from another Maratha chief, Niloji Nilakanth—an erstwhile vassal of Bijapur. Shivaji exercised restraint during the next six years from 1649 to 1655; he utilised this period to raise his armed strength and consolidate his possessions by carrying out intensive reforms in the civil administration.

Conquest of Javli: In January 1656, Shivaji doubled his territorial possessions and resources by the conquest of a hereditary Maratha principality of Javli, situated in the heart of the Maval country in the northwestern corner of Satara district. It was under the control of an ancient Deshmukh Maratha family of the Moray clan. According to Sardesai, 'proud of their allegiance to Bijapur, the Mores (Morays) moved heaven and earth to put down this new Bhonsle upstart, of a low origin in their estimation. So the inevitable clash came as Shivaji could not allow such an inimical rival to remain as his neighbour'. Shivaji's exertions to make them 'to fall in with his plan of national uplift' having borne no fruit, he resorted to strategy. He got Chandra Rao Moray, the chief of Javli, murdered through his henchmen and took forced possession of his territories. It brought the entire Maval country under his unified control to the great satisfaction of the Mavalis and Kolis. He promptly took the militia and bureaucracy of Chandra Rao under his service and pacified the people of Javli by introducing reforms for public welfare and thereby established his identity as their true political and national leader. According to Sardesai,

> 'No Maratha clansman dared hereafter to stand in opposition to Shivaji. A small compact little kingdom came into being, comprising roughly the present districts of Poona and Satara. Written evidence gives 1653 as the time of the completion of this first phase of Shivaji's *Swarajya.* To protect this new conquest of Javli, Shivaji erected a new fort and named it Pratapgarh, which can now be sighted from the present hill station of Mahabalesvar'. (BVB, vii, p. 257).

Conquest of Konkan (1657-58): After consolidating his position in the Maval country, Shivaji prepared an ambitious plan to expand his possessions along the seacoast towards the south and west of Javli in the Konkan region. These territories formed a part of the Bijapur state which derived huge benefits from the seaborne trade; this coastline of the Arabian Sea also served as a highway for the inlet of the Muslim immigrants for permanent settlements in the Deccan. In August 1657, Shivaji made an unsuccessful bid to conquer Janjira from the Siddis. He led his army through the modern districts of Thana and Colaba and took possession of the port-towns of Kalyan and Bhivandi, which were converted by him into naval bases. He also raided the Portuguese settlement at Daman and received tribute from them. Khafi Khan records that

> 'This was the beginning of that system of violence which he (Shivaji) and his descendants have spread over the rest of the Konkan and all the territory of the Dakhin. Whenever he heard of a prosperous town, or of a district inhabited by thriving cultivators, he plundered it and took possession of it. Before the *jagirdars* in those troublous times could appeal to Bijapur, he had sent in his own account of the matter, with presents and

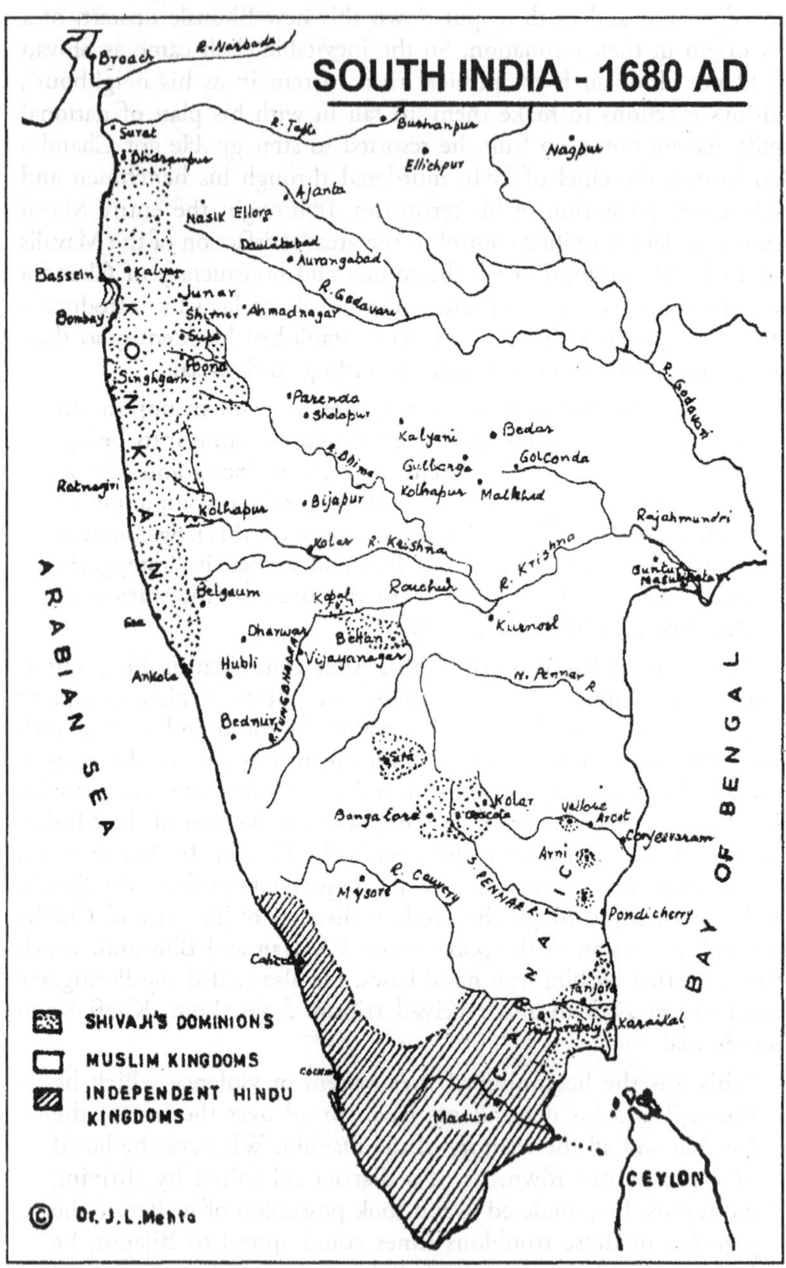
SOUTH INDIA - 1680 AD
R. Narbada
Broach
Surat
R. Tapti
Burhanpur
Nagpur
Ellichpur
Ajanta
Nasik
Ellora
Daulatabad
Aurangabad
Bassein
Kalyan
Junar
R. Godavari
Bombay
Shivner
Ahmadnagar
Poona
Singhgarh
Parenda
Sholapur
Kalyani
Bedar
Golconda
Gulbarga
Ratnagiri
Kolhapur
Malkhed
Bijapur
Rajahmundri
Kolar
R. Krishna
Belgaum
Raichur
Kurnool
Dharwar
Bellari
Vijayanagar
Hubli
Ankola
N. Pennar R.
Bednur
Tungabhadra
Kolar
Vellore
Arcot
Bangalore
Arni
Mysore
R. Cauvery
S. Pennar R.
Pondicherry
Tanjore
Trichinopoly
Karaikal
Madura
CEYLON
ARABIAN SEA
BAY OF BENGAL
SHIVAJI'S DOMINIONS
MUSLIM KINGDOMS
INDEPENDENT HINDU KINGDOMS
© Dr. J. L. Mehta

offerings, charging the *jagirdars* or proprietors with some offence which he had felt called upon to punish, and offering to pay their revenues direct to the government. He communicated these matters to the officials at Bijapur, who, in those disturbed times, took little heed of what anyone did. So when the *jagirdar*'s complaint arrived, he obtained no redress, because no one took any notice of it.

'The country of the Dakhin was never free from commotions and outbreaks, and so the officials, the *raiyats*, and the soldiery, under the influence of surrounding circumstances, were greedy, stupid, and frivolous; thus they applied the axe to their feet with their own hands, and threw their wealth and property to the winds. The greed of the officials increased, especially in those days when the authority of the rulers was interrupted, or their attention diverted. In accordance with the wishes of this disturber (Shivaji), the reins of authority over that country (of Konkan) fell into his hands, and he at length became the most notorious of all the rebels.' (*Muntakhab-ul-Lubab*; E&D, vii, p. 257).

An Anecdote of Shivaji's High Moral Character: When Shivaji led an expedition to Kalyan, a beautiful Muslim lady—the daughter-in-law of the local Bijapuri governor, named Mulla Ahmad Nawayat, fell into the hands of his troops. She was presented by them to Shivaji as 'a trophy of war'. Nevertheless, Shivaji gave a proof of high moral character by comparing her with his own mother. He treated her kindly and sent her with valuable gifts and jewellery to her kinsmen in Bijapur. Shivaji thus proved himself to be 'an ideal prince of his age who held the honour and self-respect of his subjects, irrespective of religious considerations, in the highest esteem'. Unlike Aurangzeb, Shivaji never permitted anyone to ill-treat or show disrespect to the ladies, minors and the unarmed village folk. He never plundered or desecrated the holy shrines and educational and cultural institutions of Muslims and Christians nor injured the religious sentiments of any religious community. That is why he won the gratitude and admiration of his friends as well as foes on this account. Though a staunch Hindu by faith he was truly secular in his outlook and treatment towards his subjects and never discriminated between them on religious grounds in the exercise of his public welfare activities.

War with Bijapur (1659-60)

The court of Bijapur failed to take timely action against Shivaji's encroachments because of its pre-occupations. Sultan Muhammad Adil Shah of Bijapur had died of prolonged illness on November 4, 1656. Aurangzeb, then the Mughal viceroy of the Deccan, had refused to recognise his eighteen-year old successor, Ali Adil Shah II, as his real son and declared war on Bijapur. It afforded an opportunity to Shivaji to strengthen his hold over Konkan. Bijapur lost a big slice of its territories to the Mughals and had to pay a huge war indemnity before Aurangzeb concluded peace with the Sultan and left for the north to take part in the war of succession against his brothers.

Afzal Khan Episode (November 10, 1659): It was only after the departure of Aurangzeb from the Deccan that Bijapur thought of reckoning with Shivaji. Ali Adil Shah, the new Sultan of Bijapur, commissioned Afzal Khan, one of his best military generals, to deal with the rebellious Maratha chief. He is said to have boasted in the Bijapur court that he 'would bring the mountain-rat (Shivaji) in chains to Bijapur without having to dismount from his horse even once.' Afzal Khan left Bijapur with a huge army, consisting of a heavy artillery train and war elephants besides 12,000 well-equipped horsemen and infantry, in September 1659. He adopted a scorched-earth policy to carry out destruction and devastation in the Maval country. He plundered the Maratha towns and villages, massacred the unarmed village-folk, desecrated their temples, and deliberately adopted a stern attitude so as to frighten them into submission. Shivaji, being unable to meet the challenge in the open, retreated into the forested area of Wai in Javli and took his abode in the newly constructed hill-fort of Pratapgarh. 'It was situated on an inaccessible narrow hilltop, surrounded by steep hills and forested ravines, and was totally unsuitable for an open fight'.

On the receipt of intelligence that Shivaji was encamped at Pratapgarh, Afzal Khan setup his military camp at Wai at the mouth of the forested valley, situated about 40 kilometres to the east of Pratapgarh. He chalked out a clever plan 'to allure Shivaji out of his hideout'. He opened negotiations with Shivaji for a settlement. Their agents shuttled between Wai and Pratapgarh with the object of arranging a personal meeting between the two adversaries. Afzal Khan assured Shivaji of a favourable settlement with the court of Bijapur provided the latter professed loyalty to the Sultan and sought forgiveness for his past deeds. After considerable deliberations, Afzal Khan, 'confident of his strength', agreed to meet Shivaji in a specially erected tent with a beautiful canopy on a raised platform at the foothill of

Pratapgarh. The venue of the meeting was thoroughly examined by the representatives of Afzal Khan to their satisfaction.

It was to be a one-to-one meeting between the two stalwarts which took place on the afternoon of November 10, 1659. Shivaji's envoy, Pantaji Gopi Nath, had confided to his master that Afzal Khan intended to arrest him at the interview. Therefore, as it happened, both of them came to the meeting with 'bad intentions'. The Bijapuri general reached the venue of meeting with more than a thousand heavily armed soldiers while Shivaji emerged from the fort with only two personal guards—Jiv Mahala and Shambhuji Kavji, each armed with two swords and a shield. Shivaji's envoy approached the Khan with the request that he should leave his armed men at a safe distance from the meeting place. This was done and Afzal Khan, like Shivaji, also came to the pavilion with only two swordsmen. By comparison, a short-statured and slim Maratha leader, twenty years younger than his adversary, looked like a pigmy before the tall and hefty Khan with a well-built body. Before approaching the dais, their personal attendants were also left below the platform. Afzal Khan ascended the dais first and took his seat. According to one version, as Shivaji entered the pavilion, he bowed in salutation and the Khan rose, apparently to greet him. He took Shivaji in his embrace. As the latter came up to his shoulders, the Khan, in his very first embrace, gripped him tightly in his left arm, and stabbed him with a dagger in his right hand. As Shivaji had worn armour under his coat, it produced little effect. With great presence of mind, however, Shivaji instantaneously ripped open the Khan's bowels with the tiger-claws (*bichhwa*) that he had worn on the fingers of his left hand. The Khan relaxed his grip and cried in agony while Shivaji ran towards his two attendants who were standing below the platform. Meanwhile, Sayyad Banda, a swordsman of Afzal Khan, overtook Shivaji and struck him hard with his sword on the head. His sword broke into two pieces by its violent hit on the steel helmet, worn by Shivaji under his turban while Jiv Mahala cut off the right hand of the Sayyad. Afzal Khan and his attendants lost their lives on the dais and the picked Maratha troops, lying in ambush on both sides of the path leading to the pavilion, as well as those, issuing forth from the fort, pounced upon his accompanying soldiers, taking a heavy toll of their lives. In the grim struggle that followed, Afzal Khan's men picked up his dead body but 'they were quickly disarmed by Shivaji's men, who severed the Khan's head and exhibited it from a high mast of the topmost bastion of the fort'. Next day, the Marathas made a frontal attack on the leaderless army of Bijapur at Wai and routed it with heavy losses.

Shivaji obtained immense booty from the Wai camp, which included heavy artillery, arms and ammunition and rich treasure besides horses, elephants, camels and the entire baggage of the Bijapuri troops. The treasure included, among other valuables, about ten *lakhs* of rupees in cash and large quantities of gold ornaments and jewels. Some of the prominent Bijapuri nobles, including two sons of Afzal Khan, were taken prisoners at the Wai camp, while a large number of their soldiers, including Hindus as well as Muslim, voluntarily laid down their arms and were taken into service by Shivaji. It enhanced the reputation of the Maratha chief throughout the Deccan.

The murder of Afzal Khan in a mutually arranged conference by Shivaji was attributed by Khafi Khan to the latter's treachery and deceit, and Grant Duff in his treatment of the Maratha history, accepted his view. But recent researches in the contemporary records of the English factories absolve Shivaji of this charge. They show that Shivaji had done everything in self-defence; 'instead of allowing him to be killed by Afzal Khan, he killed the latter'. Afzal Khan is believed to have struck the first blow in the scuffle between them. He followed up his victory by dispatching his troops into south Konkan and the Kolhapur districts. Before the end of the year 1659, Shivaji had defeated yet another Bijapuri army under Rustam Zaman and Fazl Khan which enabled him to take possession of Panhala – the last formidable military post of Bijapur, situated in the heart of Maharashtra. Besides Panhala, Shivaji occupied many other Bijapuri forts, including Vasantgarh, Khelna and Pangna, before his return to Raigarh in January 1660 heavily laden with booty It marked a great victory for Shivaji. Khafi Khan pays a rich tribute to 'the rising star of Maharashtra' in the words that follow:

> 'Fortune so favoured this treacherous worthless man (called Shivaji) that his forces increased, and he grew more powerful every day. He erected new forts, and employed himself in setting (consolidating) his own territories, and in plundering those of Bijapur. He attacked the *caravans* which came from distant parts, and appropriated to himself the goods and women (*not to be dishonoured but to be set free*). But he made it a rule that wherever his followers went plundering they should do no harm to the mosques, the Book of God, or the women of anyone. Whenever a copy of the sacred Quran came into his hands, he treated it with respect, and gave it to some of his Mussalman followers. When the women of any Hindu or Muhammadan were taken

prisoners by his men, and they had no friend to protect them, he watched over them until their relations came with a suitable ransom to buy their liberty. Whenever he found out that a woman was a slave-girl, he looked upon her at being the property of her master, and appropriated her to himself.' (*Muntakhab-ul-Lubab*; E&D, vii, pp. 260-61).

War with the Mughals (1660-80)

The Fall of Poona (1660 A.D.): The victories of Shivaji against Bijapur and the tragic end of Afzal Khan at his hands sent its shock-waves in Agra and Delhi. Aurangzeb—a religious fanatic, now firmly established on the imperial throne, had no soft corner for the Shia states of the Deccan but the rise of a powerful Hindu state in their midst was gall and wormwood to him. He immediately sent his maternal uncle, Shaista Khan, as viceroy of the Mughal Deccan, with orders to take on 'the Maratha brigand' before it was too late. Starting from Ahmadnagar, Shaista Khan made a frontal attack on Poona – the nerve-centre of the Maratha homeland, in March 1660 with a well-equipped army. Taken aback by this sudden onslaught, the Marathas failed to offer organised resistance to the invader, and many of their forts which lay on the way to Poona, fell into the hands of the Mughals. A Maratha army fought a pitched battle at Saswad, sixteen kms to the southeast of Poona, for its defence but was routed, and Shaista Khan made a triumphant entry into the Maratha metropolis on May 19, 1660.

About that time, Shivaji himself was engaged against the Bijapuris in their renewed attack on Panhala. The Mughal invasion compelled him to conclude peace with Bijapur by the surrender of Panhala. Shivaji felt concerned by the Mughal aggression but was not disheartened. By this time he had gained sufficient experience in dealing with the external invaders in his own style. His organised resistance to the Mughals was based upon a twofold policy; first, a part of his army, usually under his personal command, fought the invader and attempted to delimit his field of operation; and, secondly, a large number of his guerilla troops, led by his trustworthy companions, were sent to conquer new lands, by way of compensation for the loss of territories, or cut off the supply lines and recover the territories overrun by the invader. This game of hide and seek with Shaista Khan's troops continued for over two years. Besides Poona, the conquest of Chakan and Kalyan by the Mughals were, of course, the major losses suffered by Shivaji.

Night Attack on Shaista Khan (April 15, 1663): After his victory at Chakan in August 1660, Shaista Khan returned to Poona and established his permanent military headquarters there for the operations against Shivaji, while the latter fought the Mughals from his base camp at Raigarh. Shaista Khan took up his residence in the ancestral home of Shivaji, called the Lal Mahal. On April 14, 1663 Shivaji carried out a very daring exploit by organizing a night attack on Shaista Khan in his sleeping chambers at Poona with about 400 Maratha desperadoes. Many popular versions of the episode are available but the one given by Khafi Khan seems to be the most plausible. He writes that 'A regulation had been made that no person, especially no Mahratta, should be allowed to enter the city or the lines of the army without a Pass, whether armed or unarmed, excepting persons in the Imperial service. No Mahratta horseman was taken into the service. Shivaji, beaten and dispirited, had retired into mountains, difficult of access, and was continually changing his position. One day a party of Marhattas, who were serving as foot-soldiers, went to the *kotwal* and applied for a Pass to admit 200 Mahrattas, who were accompanying a marriage party. A boy dressed up as a bridegroom, and escorted by a party of Mahrattas with drums and music, entered the town early in the evening. On the same day, another party (of Maratha foot-soldiers) was allowed to enter the town on the report that a number of the enemy (viz., the Marathas) had been made prisoners at one of the outposts, and that another party was bringing them in, pinioned (in handcuffs or legs tied with ropes) and bare-headed, holding them by ropes, and abusing and reviling them as they went along. They proceeded to the place agreed upon, where the whole party met and put on arms."—(*ibid.*, pp. 269-70).

The Maratha raiders were led by none else but Shivaji himself. In the darkness of night, they tore open 'a small window' of Lal Mahal's sleeping chamber 'which had been closed with bricks and mud' by Shivaji many years ago. Shivaji personally entered the sleeping chambers of the building with 200 men and started massacre of the inmates while the rest of his followers attacked the Mughal guards outside the Lal Mahal. Shaista Khan escaped the bloody carnage that followed but after receiving a serious cut on his hand while a number of Mughal guards, besides one of his sons, six wives and slave-girls, and forty attendants lost their lives and many others were wounded. Before their hues and cries alerted the imperial troops, the raiders had made good their escape. This incidence took place on the night of 15-16 April

1663. Thoroughly humiliated and frightened, Shaista Khan took refuge with his troops outside the town of Poona. The success of this venture 'restored the honour and prestige of Shivaji which had suffered a setback by the loss of Poona to the Mughals'. It made the guerilla bands of the Marathas to hound off the Mughal troops from the outlying posts in the countryside to concentrate themselves within the heavily fortified forts or military camps. 'The incidence', writes Sardesai, 'proved eminently successful for Shivaji's purpose. Without undergoing a large-scale fighting, he struck terror into the heart of his opponents. The mortified Mughal emperor at once transferred Shaista Khan to Bengal and the Mughal hold slackened in the Deccan. Shivaji, now breathing freely, resumed his onward career without check'. (BVB, vii, p. 260).

Sack of Surat (January 1664): G.S. Sardesai writes that 'after the departure of Shaista Khan, Shivaji roamed fearlessly as an invincible conqueror. His spies wandered far and wide, bringing news of treasures and wealth of cities and of the weak links in the Mughal Government. His head spy, Bahirji Naik, reported to Shivaji that of all the rich Mughal possessions Surat was the most undefended and contained enormous wealth. It was the richest port of western India and was highly prized by Aurangzeb as an important port which was used by pilgrims to Mecca'. Accordingly, Shivaji chalked out a dare-devil's plan to make a surprise attack on Surat. He left Nasik with about 400 picked mobile horsemen on January 10, 1664 and proceeded north through the coastal regions. He suddenly appeared at Surat on the 16th by forced marches and encamped in a garden outside the Burhanpur Gate. The Mughal *faujdar*, Inayat Khan, fled the town and took shelter in the fort, leaving the merchants and populace of the town at the mercy of the raiders. Shivaji took many merchants and government officers as captives and put them to ransom. He plundered the town for four days and decamped on January 20, heavily laden with gold, silver, pearls and diamonds, worth more than a crore of rupees. It was taken straight to Raigarh and utilised for the strengthening of his army and fortification of the forts. Shivaji's plea for the sack of Surat was his revenge for the Mughal invasion of his 'homeland' or *Swarajya*.

Jai Singh's Invasion of Maharashtra (1665)

After the recall of Shaista Khan, Aurangzeb had appointed Prince Muazzam as the viceroy of the Deccan while Maharaj Jaswant Singh of Jodhpur held the charge of the Mughal expedition against the Marathas. The prince remained at Aurangabad and Jaswant Singh was stationed at Poona. For over a year, none of them could accomplish anything against the Marathas. Stung by repeated failures, Aurangzeb decided to set all the other valiant Rajputs, under his employ, against the Marathas to bring about their destruction. In December 1664, he ordered a fresh expedition against Shivaji under Mirza Raja Jai Singh of Amber (Jaipur) – the most reputed Rajput general of his empire. The emperor placed a host of brilliant military officers and strategists under the command of Jai Singh and liberally provided him with men, money and material. Dilir Khan, a reputed intelligence officer and close confident of Aurangzeb, accompanied Jai Singh, apparently to assist him but 'probably to spy upon him'. The world-famous Italian traveller, Manucci, then residing at Delhi, was also pressed into service by Aurangzeb to accompany the Mughal army of invasion as an artillery officer. Jai Singh crossed the Narbada on January 12, 1665, and made straight for Maharashtra. He took over charge from Maharaja Jaswant Singh at Poona on March 13. Meanwhile, Shivaji had received intelligence about Jai Singh's arrival in the south in February 1665 when he was engaged in consolidating his southern possessions and was on a visit to Karwar to offer his devotions to the deity of Gokarn. He rushed back to Raigarh to prepare himself for a fresh round of the struggle against the Mughals.

Jai Singh had come prepared with a comprehensive plan of action to launch an all-out offensive against the Marathas. He took up his position in the eastern part of Shivaji's dominions so as to wedge in between the Maratha territory and that of the Bijapur state. He persuaded the Sultan of Bijapur to assist him against Shivaji 'by holding out a prospect of imperial favour and reduction of his tribute'. Similarly, he instigated the Portuguese of Goa and the Siddi of Janjira to attack Shivaji's territories and won over many *zamindars* of Maharashtra and Karnataka by liberal offers. Under the command of Jai Singh, the Mughal army overran the Maratha country like a steam-roller, carrying everything in the sweep. The Maratha villages and towns were plundered and set on fire, their cattle seized and village folk enslaved to be exploited for the advancement of the imperial interests. In his bid to prove his unflinching loyalty to the Mughal throne, Jai Singh adopted a very severe policy to penalize the Marathas for resistance to the Mughal arms. The Maratha forts fell one after another until Shivaji himself was put under siege in fort of Purandhar. To counter the activities of the Maratha guerillas, Jai Singh had already sent flying columns of his army to ravage the Maratha villages in the regions of Raigarh, Sinhagarh and elsewhere so as not to leave any trace of cultivation or habitation. These columns overran the isolated Maratha outposts, and looted and burnt the villages, 'some of which had never before been visited by an enemy'.

Treaty of Purandhar (June 24, 1665)

Meanwhile the siege of Purandhar continued and all the attempts of Shivaji to repulse the Mughal forces failed. After a desperate struggle between the antagonists, that lasted over two months and cost a huge loss of life on both sides, Shivaji sued for peace. He presented himself in person in the army camp of Jai Singh to offer his submission and the war came to an end by the Treaty of Purandhar which was signed on June 24, 1665. It was ratified by Aurangzeb through his *firman* of September 5, 1665, and Shivaji received a copy of this firman along with a robe of honour from the imperial court soon thereafter. According to the terms of this treaty,

(1) Shivaji surrendered 23 forts and the territories appertaining to them to the Mughals which yielded annual revenue of ten *lakhs* of *huns*; they were annexed to the Mughal Empire. Thereafter, Shivaji was left with only 12 forts, including that of Raigarh and their adjoining territories as a vassal of the Mughal emperor. The territorial divisions of his possessions were reckoned in terms of the forts.

(2) Shivaji was granted exemption from personal attendance at the imperial court although his eight-year old son, Sambhaji, who was awarded a *mansab* of 5,000, was to proceed to the imperial court at Agra along with Jai Singh, and attended by a suitable retinue.

(3) Shivaji agreed to fight for the imperial cause in the Deccan.

(4) According to an extra clause, added to the treaty later on, Shivaji received permission to conquer the Bijapuri territories in Konkan and Balaghat, without the imperial aid and on the promise to pay 'forty *lakhs* of *huns* in thirteen annual installments' to the imperial exchequer.

An interesting side-light of the Treaty of Purandhar was that the Mughal commander, Mirza Raja Jai Singh, who had formally received the keys of 23 ceded forts, could not spare enough of his men to garrison them. As a consequence, only the forts of Purandhar; Sinhagarh and

Lohgarh could be supplied with defensive Mughal garrisons with provisions, while the walls and fortifications of some of the ceded forts were demolished. In fact, the imperial Mughal government lacked resources in men and material to take effective military possession of the Maratha territories. It was, however, naïve to expect that the Marathas, like the Rajputs and other docile Hindu chieftains who acknowledged the Mughal suzerainty, would hold their own forts in trust for the imperial government for a long time. In consequence, most of these fortresses, situated particularly in the forested valleys, became the haunts of the Maratha guerrillas who carried on their secret preparations to drive out the Mughals from their land at the first opportunity.

Shivaji in Aurangzeb's Captivity at Agra (1666)

Jai Singh had secured the neutrality of Bijapur in his fight against Shivaji by holding out numerous promises of imperial favours to the Sultan. To the great chagrin of the Rajput general, he was directed by Aurangzeb to invade Bijapur immediately after the treaty of Purandhar with Shivaji. It was to be done without any provocation from the Sultan of Bijapur and in total violation of the solemn promises of imperial favours, made by Jai Singh on behalf of the Mughal emperor. It was too much for a Rajput stalwart to swallow which left him thoroughly dejected and mortified; that explains why he failed to make any headway against Bijapur. Anyway, because of his new assignment, Jai Singh could not find time to take Sambhaji to the imperial court as per the terms of the treaty. He, therefore, persuaded Shivaji to accompany his son to Agra to 'win the favours of the emperor'. The treaty had granted Shivaji 'exemption from personal attendance at the imperial court' but he was on the horns of dilemma as he never wanted his minor son of eight to be sent there like a hostage, obviously, to ensure his loyalty to the Mughal emperor as his vassal. That is why he agreed to pay a personal visit to Agra with Sambhaji when Jai Singh and his son, Raja Ram Singh, *mansabdar* of five thousand, then in attendance upon the emperor, 'pledged their word' for the safety of the lives of Shivaji and his son during this visit. According to Sardesai, another 'weighty consideration' that impelled him to undertake this venture seems to be that it might 'enable him to obtain a firsthand impression about the inherent strength of the Mughal Empire and study men and matters on the spot' with whom he will have to reckon with in the fulfilment of his 'life's mission of a Hindu *Padshahi*'. (BVB; vii, pp. 262-63).

So 'the decision was taken and communicated through Jai Singh to the emperor (Aurangzeb), who paid a *lakh* of rupees for the expenses of Shivaji's journey and assured that Shivaji would be accorded the honours of a *Shahzada* (Prince) during his absence from home'. (*Ibid.*, p. 263). Accordingly, Shivaji nominated his mother Jijabai as the Regent of the state during his period of absence from Maharashtra and put his Peshwa (prime minister), Moro Pant, and other high officers under her orders before he started for the north with Sambhaji and five high officers, accompanied by a small escort of only 350 well-dressed and fully equipped guards of the mobile cavalry. He left Raigarh on March 5, 1666, and proceeded to the north in a procession, like that of an aristocratic marriage party, to the playing of music by the royal Maratha band.

Shivaji reached Agra on May 21, 1666; he was received by Raja Ram Singh and lodged in the Jaipur House—the mansion of the Amber chiefs. Next day, Shivaji and his son were presented to the Mughal emperor in the *Diwan-i-Khas*. There was pin-drop silence in the imperial court. 'Both made their obeisance' and Shivaji presented 1,000 *mohurs* and 2,000 rupees as *Nazr*, besides 5,000 rupees as *Nisar*. Aurangzeb looked at them but said nothing. Thereafter, they were led back and made to stand in the row of the *mansabdars* of five thousand, which was the third line of nobles. Shivaji flew into rage when he noticed that Maharaja Jaswant Singh was standing in front of him in the second line, reserved for the *mansabdars* of seven thousand. He flared up in his mother tongue (Marathi): "Jaswant Singh whose back my soldiers have seen! I have to stand behind him? What does it mean?

Soon thereafter, at the time of presentation of robes of honour, the royal princes, the *wazir* and others, including Jaswant Singh, were honoured with the robes but not Shivaji. 'Noticing this affront', writes Sardesai, 'Shivaji burst out in a sort of open defiance, complaining of the breach of the terms that were agreed upon. The emperor noticed Shivaji's demeanour and sent Ram Singh to pacify him. In the meantime, Shivaji left his place and moved to a corner, vehemently protesting and imprecating, a scene unprecedented in the imperial court. The emperor closed the *durbar* and asked Shivaji to be taken away. It was evident that Shivaji had committed a gross offence by defying the emperor so publicly'. (*Ibid*; p. 263). He was taken to Ram Singh's residence and placed under house-arrest.

Shivaji's Miraculous Escape from Agra

It is presumed that Aurangzeb wanted Shivaji either to be killed or transferred to some state prison like that of the Gwalior fort. He was supported in his designs by a strong lobby of anti-Maratha elements within his *harem* as well as the court. Khafi Khan writes that the wives of Shaista Khan and Aurangzeb's *wazir*, Jaffar Khan, who were related to the imperial family, and Jahanara, a sister of the emperor, 'clamoured for Shivaji's blood'. Similarly, the Rathor party, headed by Maharaja Jaswant Singh, 'desired the disgrace of Jai Singh', and hence pleaded for stern action against the foolhardy Maratha chief. However, all the mechanizations of Aurangzeb for the liquidation of Shivaji and his son were foiled by Raja Ram Singh and his troops as he had stood guarantee for the safety of Shivaji's life. Thus it was that Shivaji and his son were protected and surrounded by their Maratha guards within the house and along the outer walls of the Rajput mansion, while five thousand strong Rajput troops of Ram Singh formed an outer ring of defence for Shivaji; and they were, in turn, encircled in a state of siege by the Mughal army. The metropolis of Agra was thereby converted into a potential battlefield to the great bewilderment and dread of the citizens.

Shivaji thus suffered in the captivity of Aurangzeb for about four months. Meanwhile, left to his own resources, he lost no time in devising a plan to escape from Agra. In the first instance, he advised Ram Singh to withdraw the security bond that he had given to the emperor for the safe custody of himself and his son, as they had been placed under the direct captivity of the Mughal troops. Next, he started sending his Maratha guards in small groups, apparently to their homes in Maharashtra. Actually most of them disappeared in the suburbs of Agra and beyond for establishing contacts with their friends and supporters to devise ways and means for the escape of their leader from imprisonment. Thereafter, Shivaji feigned illness and started sending his attendants to bring Hindu physicians and priests for treatment and commissioned baskets of sweets for distribution among the Brahmins and poor in the local temples. These baskets were searched by the Mughal guards, who were, in turn, frequently obliged by handfuls of sweets by Shivaji's men day after day. Taking advantage of their relaxed watch, Shivaji cleverly escaped with his son Sambhaji in the late afternoon by concealing themselves in the big baskets of sweets on August 29, 1666. Shivaji's half-brother, Hiroji Farzand, who resembled him, was made to lie on his bed, covered with a sheet of cloth but with his right hand outstretched and adorned with Shivaji's gold wristlet to deceive the emperor's agents who visited the mansion at short intervals to ascertain the identity of the detained Maratha chief.

Shivaji and his son had made good their escape in two baskets, each slung from a pole and carried by two men on their shoulders along with some other baskets of sweetmeats. By the fall of darkness, the bearers took them out of the town where Shivaji and his son walked to a village about ten kms from Agra. There Shivaji's lieutenant, Niraji Raoji, was present with horses, and the party, now disguised as *sanyasis* rode to Mathura. Shivaji left his son there under the care of a Maratha Brahmin family, and himself travelled eastwards to Allahabad. From there he adopted a circuitous route through Bundelkhand, Gondwana and Golconda to avoid detection by the imperial scouts and managed to reach Raigarh in the garb of a *sadhu* on September 22, 1666, to the great delight of his mother. Sambhaji was brought to Maharashtra after a couple of months.

At Agra, Shivaji's flight became known in the morning of 30th August, about two hours after Hiroji had quietly walked out of the house, asking the guards not to make noise as Shivaji was fast asleep; the other Maratha attendants, including some women, also slipped away one by one. The royal guard, Faulad Khan, who reported the matter to the emperor, had to say that Shivaji 'vanished all of a sudden from the sight of his men and either flew into the sky or disappeared into the earth by a magical trick'. Taken aback, Aurangzeb refused to believe it and immediately sent his men to keep a watch on all the highways leading to the Deccan on the look-out for the fugitive but to no avail. He suspected Ram Singh and Jai Singh of being privy to Shivaji's escape and disgraced them both. Jai Singh was divested of his imperial charge and recalled from the Deccan; enroute to Agra, he died a broken-hearted man at Burhanpur.

In the words of Sardesai, 'the Agra episode was the most thrilling exploit of all the wonderful deeds of Shivaji which has forever added a super-natural glow to his unique personality. It immediately resounded throughout the country, making Shivaji an all-India figure, divinely endowed with extraordinary powers'. During the absence of Shivaji from Maharashtra, his dominions 'were administered with utmost diligence and loyalty by his officers, high and low'. As observed by J. L. Mehta, Shivaji's discomfiture at the hands of the Mughal emperor 'united the Maratha ranks still further and made them stand as one man against the Mughal rule. On his return to Maharashtra, he received a heroic welcome from his people and acquired a legendary fame as the popular leader of the Marathas and the champion of their civil liberties. After this episode, he never felt any dearth of men and material in his struggle for the independence of Maharashtra from the Muslim rule; he always received unflinching loyalty and devotional service from his officers and associates. On the other hand, Aurangzeb lost his peace of mind and had to suffer much because of Shivaji's escape from his prison; he never forgot this loss till the last moment of his life'. – (Advanced Study; ii, pp. 547-48)

Aftermath of the Agra Episode

The Agra episode exercised a very sobering effect on the adversaries. Shivaji assumed silence on the whole affair and thought it prudent to remain at peace with the Mughals during the next couple of years. The treaty of Purandhar was not formally denounced by him but it was treated as null and void by the Marathas for all intents and purposes. Some of the Maratha forts were still held by the imperial garrisons, but neither the Marathas attempted to dislodge them by force immediately nor the Mughals tried to strengthen their forces of occupation in Maharashtra. There prevailed a condition of *status quo* or stale-mate. It gave much-needed respite to the people and they started coming back to their villages and towns to reclaim their houses and lands for cultivation. Shivaji utilised this time to reorganise the administrative machinery and strengthen the defences of his territories so that they might not be exposed to the Mughal inroads with ease in future.

After the recall of Jai Singh, Aurangzeb had sent his son, Prince Muazzam, as the newt viceroy of the Deccan with Maharaja Jaswant Singh to assist him. Both of them avoided friction and adopted a reconciliatory attitude towards the Maratha chief. On their recommendation, Aurangzeb agreed to confer the title of *Raja* on Shivaji and recognised him the *de facto* ruler of the territories under his possession. Shivaji also came to a peaceful understanding with Bijapur and Golconda, the Sultans of which 'purchased his goodwill by agreeing to pay him the stipulated annual amounts of *chauth*' to save their territories from the traditional Maratha raids. 'Thus Shivaji was accepted as an independent ruler in Maharashtra'.

Nevertheless, 'the peace with the Mughals was a mere truce'. Quietly but firmly Shivaji started recovering his forts, previously ceded by him to the imperialists, which were not adequately manned by the

Mughal troops, on the pretext of restoring law and order in the country around them. Within a year, he had reoccupied most of them without a fight. In the normal course of action, as Shivaji's men made their appearance with intentions to take over the fort, the Mughal officials made their exit without demur. This is what made Aurangzeb to doubt the intentions of his own son, Prince Muazzam, and other Mughal officials who were said to have come to a secret understanding with the Marathas for a compromise to avoid unnecessary bloodshed. Nevertheless, after a brief respite, rupture occurred between the two parties early in 1670 when Shivaji took in service a large number of the mercenary troopers, who had been disbanded by the Mughal viceroy of the Deccan after the treaty of Purandhar because of financial stringencies. Not only this; after the Agra episode, imperial prestige in the Deccan had taken a nosedive. Therefore, there started desertions in the Mughal armies on large scale; and most of these deserters, Hindus as well as Muslims, made a bee-line for enrollment in the Maratha army. It gave Shivaji an upper hand to deal with the Mughals from a position of strength. He signalled his new phase of forward policy by taking over the stronghold of Kondana in a sudden assault in February 1670. This was accomplished by Shivaji's personal friend and guide, Tanaji Malsure, at the cost of his life. In his sweet memory, the fort was renamed as Sinhagarh (Singhgarh) by Shivaji.

The historic fort of Purandhar, associated with Afzal Khan's episode, was attacked next and recovered after a bloody fight with the Mughal garrison. Shivaji followed it up by overrunning the Mughal territories of Kalyan and other places of north Konkan. It spread panic among the Mughal commanders of the various ceded forts; some of them died fighting against the Marathas while the others fled or surrendered the forts without a fight. Some of the Mughal commanders actually changed sides and took up service under Shivaji along with their soldiers. Within a couple of years, Shivaji not only removed all the traces of the former possession of his territories by the Mughals but also began to plunder the Mughal provinces in retaliation. He and his lieutenants carried out extensive raids into the Mughal territories of Ahmadnagar, Berar, Baglan and Khandesh, and collected immense wealth in gold and silver besides horses and enormous quantities of weapons of war and provisions for use by the Maratha armies. Shivaji levied *chauth* on the Mughal territories and made every expedition pay for its own expenses in men and material.

In October 1670, Shivaji sacked Surat for the second time and returned with booty of 66 lakhs of rupees in gold and silver; a Mughal army led by Daud Khan Qureshi, which attempted to intercept him, was routed by Shivaji through a clever manoeuvre. Shivaji continued such devastations upon the Mughal dominions for full three years. In February 1672, he fought a pitched battle with the Mughals at Salher, on the borders of Khandesh and Gujarat. According to Sardesai, in this historic battle, 'ten thousand men were slain on the two sides with countless numbers of horses, elephants and camels. Rivers of blood flowed on the battle ground. The Marathas acquired by way of plunder six thousand horses, as many camels, one hundred and twenty-five elephants, all the camp baggage of the Mughals with treasure and jewellery.' (Marathas, i, pp. 196-97).

Coronation of Shivaji (June 16, 1674)

By this time, Shivaji was well-established as the sovereign ruler of Maharashtra. A stage had been reached when it was deemed necessary to legalise his position to claim a status of equality with the other sovereign monarchs of India. Accordingly, he performed his formal coronation ceremony with great pomp and show at Raigarh on June 16, 1674 and assumed the title of *Maharaja Chhatrapati*, thus proclaiming the establishment of a sovereign Hindu state (*Hindu Padpadshahi*). Learned Brahmins came from Banaras came to perform this ceremony. Shivaji utilised this opportunity to give a shape to the Maratha government and administration. He created eight departments of the central government, each assigned to a minister; the council of ministers, collectively styled the *Ashta Pradhan*, was headed by the prime minister, called *Peshwa* or the *Mukhya Pradhan*. By this time, Shivaji's father, Shahji Bhonsle was no more but the Queen Mother Jijabai was fortunate enough to witness the fulfillment of her son's mission of life; she died with full peace of mind and contentment eleven days after Shivaji's coronation. According to Sardesai, 'the Hindu character of Shivaji's *Swarajya* was clearly marked. He excluded all foreign elements. Instead of Urdu and Persian which were the court languages for centuries past, Shivaji introduced Marathi and coined Sanskrit technical terms for administrative purposes. Thus came into being the famous *Raja-Vyavahara-Kosa*, a dictionary of official terms. This was composed by a panel of experts under the supervision of Raghunath Raghunath Hanumante. The elaborate Sanskrit introduction to this dictionary is worthy of serious study. Similarly, forms of address in official and private correspondence, office regulations, seals for government documents and similar innovations were brought into force so as to complete the scheme of this new kingdom'. (BVB, vii, pp. 268-69)

The Concluding Years of Shivaji's Life

Aurangzeb was shocked to hear of Shivaji's coronation but, because of his war with the Rajputs, could not take the field against him in person. Shivaji, therefore, found sufficient time to consolidate his kingdom and work for the welfare and happiness of his subjects. He humbled the pride of the Sultan of Bijapur and exacted tribute from him. In 1677 he launched a military campaign for the conquest of Karnatak (modern Tamil Nadu) and expanded the boundaries of his kingdom to the eastern seacoast of India from the Tungabhadra to the Kaveri, which included, in its fold, the important forts of Jinji, Vellore and Tanjore. Shivaji created a corridor across the Bijapur and Golconda states, with strong lines of offensive and defensive posts from Panhala to Tanjore.

The last days of Shivaji's life were full of anxiety because of domestic problems. He had two sons, Sambhaji and Raja Ram, from two different wives. The Crown Prince Sambhaji was brought up under the personal care of Shivaji and suffered imprisonment of Aurangzeb along with his father at Agra. He was well-educated and grew up to be a good soldier but became addicted to sensual pleasures on attaining maturity and misbehaved. So to say, as Salim had been to Akbar, so was Sambhaji to his father Shivaji. The Chhatrapati put him under surveillance at Panhala in 1678 but he was induced by Aurangzeb's agents to defect to the Mughal camp at Bahadurgarh with his wife Yesu Bai. He stayed there for about a year. However, when Aurangzeb's agent tried to imprison him, he fled to Bijapur and from there made his way to Panhala to the great relief of Shivaji. The Chhatrapati personally visited Panhala and stayed with his son for many days but Sambhaji failed to mend his ways. Meanwhile Shivaji's health was shattered because of constant struggle and mental strain. Despaired of his successor's bad habits and lack of foresight, he retired to the *ashram* of his spiritual *Guru* Ram Dass at Sajjangarh where he stayed for a month. He returned to Raigarh in February 1680 and performed the sacred thread ceremony of his second son Raja Ram in March. Early in April, Shivaji had an attack of fever which proved fatal. He breathed his last on April 13, 1680 at the age of fifty-three.

The Maratha kingdom, at the time of Shivaji's death, extended from Ramnagar (modern Dharampur near Surat) to Karwar (near Goa) along the western seacoast, and included within its fold the territories of Baglan, Nasik, Poona, Satara and Kolhapur. Besides, he held small pockets of territory in the heart of the Deccan Plateau (Mysore region) and Karnatak along the eastern seacoast from the river Tungabhadra to the Kaveri, which included the districts of Bellary, Chittur and Arcot with their famous forts of Jinji, Vellore and Tanjore. All these territories comprised the *Swarajya*—'the Crown Lands' or 'the Homeland', under the direct supervision and control of Shivaji. For the purpose of civil administration, these were divided into four provinces. Shivaji's conquests in the Kanara region, including the territories of Sunda, Bednur and Dharwar were inconclusive and needed further consolidation, while some parts of the Mughal provinces and the states of Bijapur and Golconda were frequently subjected to raids by Shivaji's troops, from where they collected *Chauth* (one-fourth of the estimated land revenue) and *Sardeshmukhi* (being one-tenth of the standard land revenue). *Sardeshmukhi* was imposed upon the people of Bijapur, Golconda or Mughal territories in token of their recognition of the Maratha king as their *sardeshmukh* or suzerain. The territories of the hostile powers upon which the Marathas levied *Chauth* and *Sardeshmukhi* were usually known as the *Mughlai*. Shivaji's kingdom was defended by strongly built and well-provided 240 forts, of which 111 were said to have been built by him personally. In official records, the estimated annual revenues of his kingdom were given as seven crores of rupees although the actual yield was said to be much less.

SECTION 3: ADMINISTRATION OF THE MARATHA KINGDOM

Maratha Monarchy – A Benevolent Despotism

Shivaji was a popular leader of men and the product of a semi-national upsurge. Ancient Indian polity had preserved the tradition of republicanism and many other democratic practices, but, as luck would have it, the medieval age knew only of the absolute monarchies. And Shivaji could not but conceive of the same system of government and administration for his people. Nevertheless, his was a monarchy with a difference. He was not only a benevolent despot who stood for the happiness and welfare of his subjects but also a leader of the masses who paid due regard to the emergence of other Maratha leaders, with strong public support, as a result of the freedom struggle launched by him. These self-made leaders became his associates and were duly recognised by him as his respectable partners in the fulfilment of their high ideals. It was, therefore, that his ministers and high civil and military officers were men of integrity and proven ability, with a glorious record of selfless services rendered by them to their people. Formally, they received appointments from Shivaji as the monarch and held offices at his pleasure but they were not his creatures or favourites of doubtful merit.

Ashta Pradhan – A Semi Democratic Body of Shivaji's Ministers

Shivaji nominated a council of eight ministers to aid and advice him in the discharge of his duties as king; it was called *Ashta Pradhan*. In theory, he possessed absolute powers of direction and control of the government and his word was law but, in actual practice, he never brushed aside or acted against the advice tendered by his council of eight ministers who ran the administration of the kingdom. The seniomost member of the *Ashta Pradhan* was called *Peshwa* or *Mukhya Pradhan*, viz., the Prime Minister. He was not only the right-hand man of Shivaji but also the second best leader of the Marathas after him. He exercised powers of general supervision over the entire administration, co-ordinated the work of his cabinet colleagues and devised schemes for the well-being of the people. He deputized for the king in his absence and affixed his seal and signatures below those of the king on all royal commands and despatches. The position of the *Peshwa* was thus radically different from that of *Vakil* or prime minister of the Mughal Empire who was nothing better than the chief secretary to the autocratic Mughal emperor. This was the greatest semi-democratic contribution made by Shivaji to the Maratha polity which accorded an element of stability and endurance to it.

Of the other members of the *Ashta Pradhan* mention may be made of *Majumdar* or *Amatya*—'the finance minister' who exercised control over the income and expenditure of the state, devised ways and means for increasing the revenues, and audited the accounts of the provinces as well. The *Mantri* or *Waqia-navis* recorded the proceedings of the court, kept the daily record of the king's activities, and looked after the personal safety of the latter. He scrutinized the lists of all those who came to see the king in the court or in private apartments, and checked the food served to the king. The fourth minister, called *Sachiv* or *Shuru-navis*—'the superintendent', was in charge of the royal orders and official

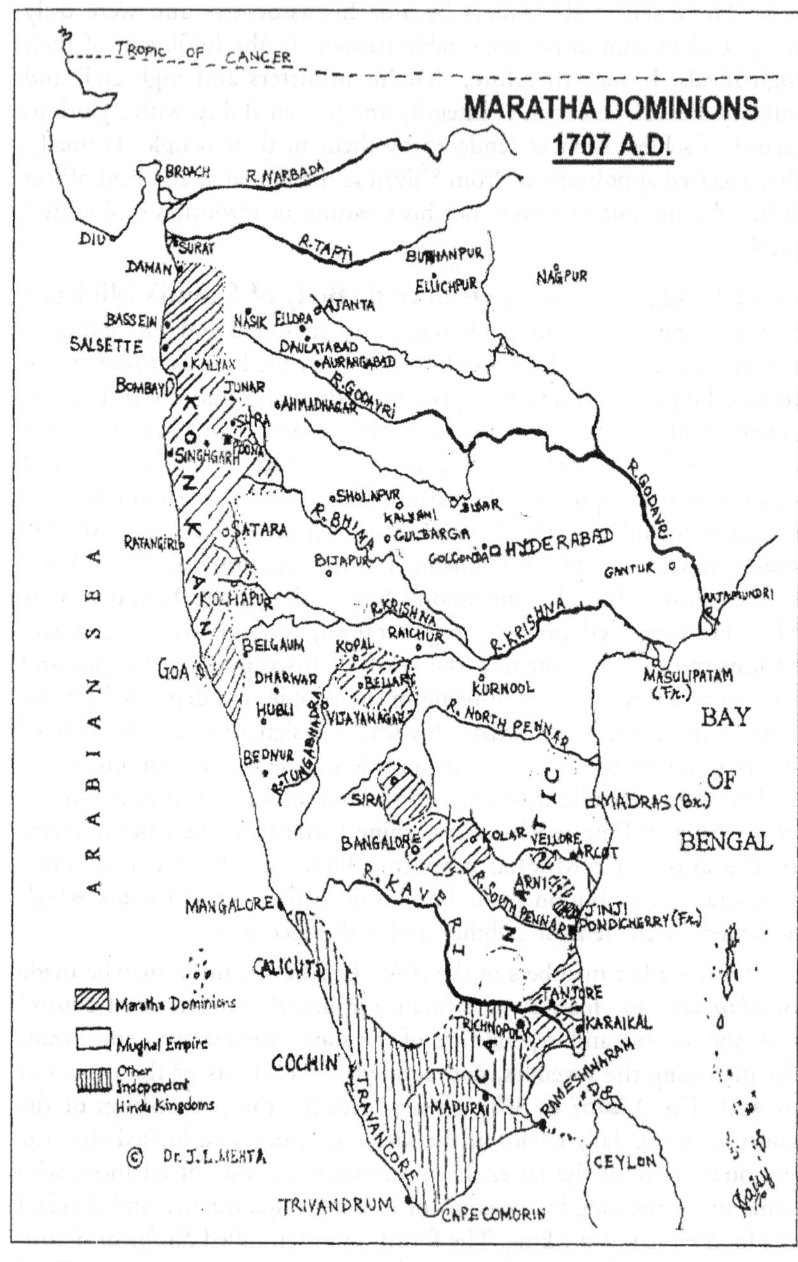
MARATHA DOMINIONS
1707 A.D.
TROPIC OF CANCER
BROACH
R. NARBADA
DIU
SURAT
R. TAPTI
BURHANPUR
NAGPUR
DAMAN
ELLICHPUR
AJANTA
BASSEIN
NASIK
ELLORA
SALSETTE
DAULATABAD
AURANGABAD
KALYAN
BOMBAY
JUNAR
R. GODAVRI
AHMADNAGAR
SINGHGARH
POONA
SHOLAPUR
BIDAR
KALYANI
R. BHIMA
SATARA
RATANGIRI
GULBARGA
HYDERABAD
GOLCONDA
BIJAPUR
GANTUR
R. GODAVRI
KOLHAPUR
R. KRISHNA
RAJAMUNDRI
BELGAUM
KOPAL
RAICHUR
R. KRISHNA
GOA
DHARWAR
BELLARY
KURNOOL
MASULIPATAM (Fr.)
HUBLI
VIJAYANAGAR
R. NORTH PENNAR
BAY OF BENGAL
BEDNUR
R. TUNGABHADRA
ARABIAN SEA
SIRA
MADRAS (Br.)
BANGALORE
KOLAR
VELLORE
ARCOT
R. KAVERI
ARNI
R. SOUTH PENNAR
JINJI
PONDICHERRY (Fr.)
MANGALORE
CALICUT
TANJORE
KARAIKAL
TRICHNOPOLY
COCHIN
RAMESHWARAM
MADURAI
TRAVANCORE
CEYLON
TRIVANDRUM
CAPE COMORIN
Maratha Dominions
Mughal Empire
Other Independent Hindu Kingdoms
© Dr. J. L. MEHTA

communications. The fifth minister was called *Samant* or *Dabir,* i.e. 'the foreign minister'; he advised the king on foreign affairs and problems of war and peace. The *Samant* received the foreign envoys, sent ambassadors to the courts of other powers and kept himself in touch with the political developments which took place beyond the Maratha borders through public as well as confidential means. The *Senapati* or *Sar-i-Naubat*—'the commander-in-chief' was also one of the eight members of the cabinet; in order of seniority, he occupied the sixth position in the council of ministers.

Parallel to the office of the *Sadr* in the Mughal system of administration, Shivaji also appointed a minister in charge of the ecclesiastical establishment of the state; he was called *Pundit Rao* or *Danadhyaksha.* He was the chief religious adviser to the king, fixed dates for religious ceremonies at the court and disbursed royal charities. Like the Mughal *Sadr,* the *Danadhyaksha* granted religious endowments to the temples and distributed financial aid to the saints, scholars and educational institutions. He also decided the religious and caste disputes. And the eighth member of *Ashta Pradhan* was called *Nyayadhish* or the chief justice who constituted the highest court of appeal in civil and criminal cases, next after the king. He held charge of the judicial organisation of the entire state, which was unitary in character. The council of ministers was collectively responsible for the maintenance of law and order and general administration; all the decisions were taken unanimously. Whenever there was a difference of opinion on any policy matter, it was referred to the king who looked into all the points of view before giving his decision. The order of precedence for the ministers was fixed by Shivaji at the time of his coronation; at that occasion, the first four ministers, viz., the *Peshwa, Majumdar, Sachiv* and *Mantri* were seated on the right side of the throne while the next four occupied seats on the left side.

Abolition of *Jagir* System

Shivaji paid cash salaries to the ministers and all the other servants of the state. The salary of the *Peshwa,* besides numerous other privileges and free services permissible to his exalted office, was fixed at 15,000 *huns* a year which works out to be 4,375 rupees per month, as a *hun* was roughly equivalent to 3.5 rupees of silver. The salaries of other ministers were comparatively less but subject to the minimum of 10,000 *huns* per annum. Shivaji did not approve of the *jagirdari* system which was deemed harmful to the interests of the state.

He ruthlessly 'confiscated the landed *watans* (free land grants) of previous regimes, and allowed no middlemen or landlords between the cultivators and the government.' According to Shivaji's *Amatya* Ramchandra Pant,

> 'The king is the supreme owner of all lands. To him the *zamindars* do not render proper loyalty. Nor do they remain contented with what they possess. They are unjust to the cultivators of the soil. They erect independent fortifications, defy the master, grasp what does not belong to them, and commit robberies outside. Once their position is fairly strengthened, they use it as a base for further expansion. If a foreign enemy invades a country, these landholders often openly join him; and secretly convey to him important information. Thus they become fruitful sources of weakness to the State. A *jagirdar* is rarely honest.' (Sardesai in Marathas, i, p. 271).

Provincial and Local Administration

Shivaji's kingdom was parcelled out into four provinces, each under the charge of *Subedar* or *Mamlatdar*. The provinces were further divided into *parganas* and each *pargana* comprised a number of villages. The provincial government, thus, maintained direct contact with each and every pargana or township of importance and eliminated the district or middle-level administration. Most of the *parganas* had their hill forests which usually served as the administrative headquarters of the region. The villages were administered by the *panchayats* which were headed by the *patels*. The *panchayats* enjoyed considerable powers of autonomy in the management of affairs and the bureaucratic establishment of the central government had its minimal existence. As Shivaji had abolished the *zamindari* system, his government maintained direct contact with the peasants and collected land revenue on very rational basis. The cultivable land was measured and graded according to its fertility and the cultivators paid 40 per cent of the produce in cash or kind. Shivaji scrapped the entire revenue establishment of the bygone days to eliminate corruption, and appointed a new set of dedicated revenue collectors who enjoyed the confidence of the local populace. As the rocky land of Maharashtra was not very productive, the state income was supplemented by booty and the collection of taxes like *chauth* and *sardeshmukhi* from the *Mughlai* regions.

Religious Policy of Shivaji

Being a devout Hindu and self-professed champion of *Hindu Swarajya*, Shivaji was very broad-minded and secular in his religious outlook and social conduct towards the people, in general. He, was, accordingly, very liberal and generous in his treatment towards his subjects and never discriminated between them in the matter of implementation of his social welfare schemes. Civil and military services in the Maratha kingdom were open to all of his subjects on merit. While comparing the religious policy of Shivaji with that of Aurangzeb, Adolf Waley makes a significant observation as follows:

> 'Although the new state, Shivaji had founded, was essentially orthodox Hindu, it was particularly in his treatment of all religious institutions that Shivaji differed from Aurangzeb, whose bigoted outlook he never confused with the doctrines of Islam as a faith.
>
> 'Mosques and tombs of Mussalman saints, and colleges of Arabic and Persian learning also received endowment from the Mahratta government; and this broad-minded attitude towards Islam earned for the King the whole-hearted loyalty of his Mohammedan subjects. No blame can attach to Shivaji if, in granting these concessions, wider schemes figured in his mind, all of which had the one great aim of weakening the Emperor's (Aurangzeb's) power and freeing as many of his own coreligionists (Hindus) as possible throughout India. For this purpose, he sought an alliance with the *Shia* Mussalman kingdom of Golconda, knowing full well that Aurangzeb's detestation of the *Shia* equalled, or possibly even exceeded that which he felt for the Hindus. Aurangzeb, though many of his civil and military officials were Persian *Shias*, did not hesitate to level insults at the faith which they professed, and his ambition to overthrow the *Shia* monarchs of Bijapur and Golconda and to annex their kingdoms to his Empire was quite as great as his desire to crush, and, if possible, exterminate the Hindu element." (*The Pageant*, p. 484).

The Maratha Army

Shivaji had raised a well-organised and disciplined force for the defence and expansion of his kingdom, which, at the time of his death, consisted of 45,000 *pagas* and 60,000 *silahdar* cavalry, and above one *lakh* of the Maval infantry; a *paga* or 'horseman' belonged to the state cavalry and *silahadars* were those horsemen or gentlemen troopers who provided for their own horses and armament. He had an elephant corps of 1260 and an equal number of camels, most of which had been acquired as a booty from their foes. Shivaji's naval unit, composed of about 200 war boats, was located at Kolaba.

Shivaji was a born soldier and seasoned military commander who took keen interest in the recruitment and training of each and every one of his soldiers. The cavalry was by far the most important part of the Marathas army. It was of two kinds—*bargirs* or the regular state troopers who received horses and weapons of war from the government, and *silahadars* who provided their own horses and armament and received higher salaries than the *bargirs*. Nevertheless, both types of horsemen served under the same commanders.

Going by the medieval standards, Shivaji's gradation of military commanders and regimentation of the army was most scientific. His army was much better organised than the *Mansabdari* system of the Mughals and was more efficient, mobile and disciplined than its Mughal counterpart. Twenty-five *pagas*—'the horsemen' formed a unit which was placed under the charge of a *havaldar*. There was a *jumladar* over every five *havaldars* and a *hazari* over every ten *jumladars*; thus a *hazari* of Shivaji's cavalry had actually 1250 troopers under his command. The Maratha infantry was likewise graded but on a different scale. The lowest infantry commander, called *nayak*, held charge of ten *paiks* or foot soldiers, including himself. There was a *havaldar* over every five *nayaks* while two or three *havaldars* were placed under the charge of a *jumladar*. There was a *hazari* over every ten *jumladars* as was the case in cavalry. The highest infantry commander was *seven hazari*, while the commander-in-chief of each Maratha army, engaged in a particular field of action, was called *sar-i-naubat*. Shivaji himself was the active supreme commander of the entire Maratha force. Both Hindus and Muslims were recruited in the mixed army units without any distinction. They were paid salaries in cash and had full confidence in their leaders. His soldiers made use of muskets or matchlock guns, besides swords, spears, shields and daggers, but his artillery did not contain many heavy field guns. Those soldiers who showed bravery were amply rewarded.

The forts played a very important part in the military organisation of Shivaji. The hill forts were, in fact, a great asset to the Maratha army, and these were well maintained and abundantly supplied to meet any eventually. The garrisons of the forts were very carefully selected. Every fort was placed under three officers of equal status; they were the *havaldar*, the *sabnis* and the *sar-i-naubat,* and each one of them was under obligation to work in perfect harmony with his other two colleagues. The Maratha army usually spent four months of the rainy season in cantonments. It moved out of the camps and forts immediately after the Dussehra festival and remained busy with foreign expeditions and collection of provisions for the next eight months of the year. Shivaji's army was highly mobile and disciplined force in which every unit was made self-dependent and self-sufficient as regards the baggage and armament, etc. The Maratha soldiers had a simple and frugal living standard and they carried very little baggage on their person. Besides an all-purpose blanket or sheet of cloth and his weapons, a soldier carried a few *seers* of parched gram, *gur*, a water-can and a bit of salt as his fare, to be used in emergency when cooked food was not available. Women and dancing girls were not permitted to accompany the troops, and a severe punishment was given to those who broke the discipline. Shivaji paid cash salaries to the soldiers who were also authorized to retain a part of the specified goods acquired by them as booty.

The Maratha troops were paid salaries in cash but they were not mercenaries; they joined the profession for a career and served the state with a missionary zeal. Shivaji made his army irresistible if not invincible. A small band of ten Maratha guerillas under the charge of a *nayak* or twenty-five horsemen under the command of a *havaldar* were enough to face undauntedly a full-fledged Mughal army and spread fear and consternation among thousands of the enemy's troops.

SECTION 4: AURANGZEB AND THE SUCCESSORS OF SHIVAJI (1680-1707)

Sambhaji (1680-89)

Shivaji died in April 1680 without naming a successor. His eldest son Sambhaji, though a young man of 25, had discredited himself with the Maratha court because of his sedentary habits and unbecoming conduct. Therefore, some of the Maratha leaders espoused the cause of Raja Ram, the second son of Shivaji, then hardly ten years old, to be the *Chhatrapati*. It created an ugly situation. However, Sambhaji asserted his authority and suppressed the rival faction mercilessly. He put to death Soyara Bai, the mother of Raja Ram, and many other Maratha leaders, including ministers, either lost their lives or languished in his captivity for years. It led to a division in the Maratha ranks and weakened their struggle against the Mughals. To his misfortune, Sambhaji failed to work in harmony with his ministers and distrusted his father's old associates and seasoned military generals. Instead, he made friends with a Brahmin scholar from Kanauj, a clever politician but a poet and man of easy virtue. Sambhaji made him his personal counsellor, over and above the head of the Peshwa and the council of ministers, who nicknamed him *Kalusha* or 'the instigator of strife'.

Sambhaji proved to be an incapable ruler and poor diplomat. He failed to realise the gravity of Aurangzeb's hostility towards the Marathas. The fugitive Mughal prince, Akbar, and the Rajput chief, Durga Dass Rathor, stayed in his court for six years but he failed to utilise their association for the benefit of either party. Sambhaji watched the situation with callous indifference when Aurangzeb destroyed and annexed the *Shia* states of Bijapur and Golconda in 1686-87. Thereafter, Aurangzeb stormed the Maratha dominions from all sides. The Mughal forces swept across the Maratha kingdom like a hurricane and Sambhaji himself fell into their hands along with his notorious counsel, Kavi Kalash, and many others in February 1689. As referred to earlier, they were tortured to death by Aurangzeb in March 1689. Sambhaji had done nothing for his people and the state during his period of rule but, 'the fearless manner in which he met his end, united and steeled the hearts of the Marathas as nothing else would have done, and nerved them to avenge the death of their sovereign'. By his heroic death, Sambhaji raised himself to the status of a martyr in the annals of the Maratha history.

Raja Ram (1689-1700)

The unexpected and the most tragic end of Sambhaji united all the Marathas and they stood up like a man to face the Mughal danger. They raised Shivaji's second son Raja Ram to the throne. Sambhaji's widowed queen, Yesu Bai, instead of claiming the throne for her infant son, Shahu, gave her blessings to Raja Ram as the new *Chhatrapati*, and called upon all the Marathas to close their ranks and fight the enemy with determination. Soon after the death of Sambhaji, the Mughal forces laid siege to Raigarh, capital of the Maratha kingdom.

On the advice of Yesu Bai, Raja Ram was whisked out of the fort to a place of safety at Vishalgarh while the capital was heroically defended by her under her personal command. Raigarh was overrun by the Mughals on November 13, 1689 due to the treachery of a Maratha officer and the entire family of Sambhaji along with more than 200 other men and women fell into the hands of the victors and suffered in the captivity of Aurangzeb for many years; they included a real sister of Shahu, two half-brothers and his mother, Yesu Bai, besides his grandmother Sakwar Bai—a widowed queen of Shivaji. Many of them, including Shahu's grandmother died in the Mughal prison while Shahu's sister was forcibly married to a Mughal officer in 1704. Shahu was released from jail in 1708 by Bahadur Shah, after the death of Aurangzeb, and he claimed the Maratha throne.

The Maratha struggle was now transformed into a full-fledged people's war for liberation which consumed all the resources of the Mughal empire. Raja Ram was not a man of his father's caliber but he successfully coordinated the activities of the Maratha leaders under his banner. He shifted his headquarters to Jinji outside Maharashtra while a band of devoted Maratha fighters, including Ramchandra Pant, Prahlad Niraji, Paras Ram Trimbak, Shankarji Narain, Santaji Ghorpade and Dhanaji Jadhav, created havoc in the Mughal camps and frustrated all the plans of Aurangzeb to subjugate Maharashtra. In 1698, Jinji was also conquered by the Mughals after a prolonged siege of eight months but, before its fall, Raja Ram had escaped to Maharashtra, where the Maratha leaders, followed by thousands of selfless freedom fighters, surrounded the Mughal troops and put them on the defensive. Raja Ram fell ill and died a premature death on March 12, 1700.

Tara Bai (1700-1708)

Tara Bai, the widowed queen of Raja Ram assumed the regency of her infant son, aged four, who was installed on the Maratha throne, styled as Shivaji II. According to Khafi Khan 'Tara Bai was a clever and intelligent woman, who had attained reputation during her husband's lifetime for her knowledge of civil and military matters. She proceeded to the hills of difficult approach.' On the receipt of information about the death of Raja Ram, Aurangzeb 'ordered the drums of rejoicings to be beaten' and the Mughal soldiers 'congratulated one another'. They thought their enemy to be 'weak, contemptible and helpless' but Tara

Bai 'showed great powers of command and government, and from day-to-day the war spread and the power of the Marathas increased.'(*Muntakhab-ul-Lubab*; E&D, vii, p. 367). Under her guidance and control, the Marathas re-conquered major part of their territories and carried on successful raids into all the Mughal provinces of central and south India, including Malwa and Gujarat. The Marathas launched night attacks on the imperial Mughal camp and constantly maintained their pressure on it wherever Aurangzeb went. The Mughals conquered the forts and overran the territories only to be lost to the Marathas the very next moment. The Marathas had, in fact, made themselves invincible during the very lifetime of Aurangzeb; the unfortunate Mughal emperor realised it only when he had both of his legs in the grave. Aurangzeb and Shivaji were both devoted to their respective religious faiths; but whereas, Aurangzeb ruined the mighty Mughal empire by his policy of religious intolerance and persecution of his Hindu subjects, Shivaji established a powerful *Hindu Padpadshahi* by winning over the hearts and support of the people of the Deccan, both Hindus as well as Muslims, and accorded them a status of equality as respectable citizens of the Maratha state without any religious discrimination. He proved himself to be a truly secular leader of the masses.

❑ ❑

19

DOWNFALL OF THE MUGHAL EMPIRE

SECTION 1: AURANGZEB'S RESPONSIBILITY

Aurangzeb was the last great ruler of the Mughal dynasty in India. The Mughal empire stretched to its maximum territorial boundaries in 1686-87 when Bijapur and Golconda were conquered and annexed to it by him. It is a matter of conjecture whether thereby he had become the greatest and the most powerful monarch of India but, according to Lane-Poole, it can be said with certainty that 'through the greater part of his long reign, no sovereign was ever more abjectly feared and obeyed'. He pays obituary to the fifty-year long reign of Aurangzeb as follows:

> 'The tedious war in the Deccan exhausted his armies and destroyed his prestige, and no sooner was the dominating mind stilled in death than all the forces that he had sternly controlled, all the warring elements that struggled for emancipation from the grinding yoke, broke out in irrepressible tumult. Even before the end of his reign, Hindustan was in confusion, and the signs of coming dissolution had appeared. As some imperial corpse, preserved for ages in its dread seclusion, crowned and armed and still majestic, yet falls to dust at the mere breath of heaven, so fell the empire of the Moghul when the great name that guarded it was no more. It was as though some splendid palace, reared with infinite skill with all the costliest stones and precious metals of the earth, had attained its perfect beauty only to collapse in undistinguishable ruin when the insidious roots of the creeper (called by H.G. Keene as the *ficus religiosa*) sapped the foundations'. (Medieval India; pp. 410-11)

The vastness of the empire, based on the concentration of powers in the hands of a despotic ruler, bespoke of its short-lived existence, but Aurangzeb added to these factors the most dangerous element of 'religious bigotry' which brought about the fall of the mighty Mughal empire sooner than expected. As a narrow-minded religious fanatic, Aurangzeb was ever eager to assert his authority and exploit all the resources of the state to convert the *Dar-ul-Harb* of Hindustan, i.e. 'the land of the Hindus' into *Dar-ul-Islam.* He lost his patience after the escape of Shivaji from his prison in 1666 and started open discrimination between the people on religious grounds. He encouraged desecration of the temples and destruction of the educational and other cultural institutions of the Hindus as a matter of state policy although the latter formed more than two-thirds of his subjects. Aurangzeb ceased to be a 'just monarch' in November 1675 when he ordered the execution of a saint, Guru Tegh Bahadur, and his innocent companions, on their refusal to embrace Islam. And he lost the mandate to rule Hindustan when, in April 1679, he deprived his Hindu subjects of the civil liberties, declared them as *Zimmis* and imposed *Jaziya* or poll tax on them as the price to be paid by them for the protection of their lives and property in the 'Islamic State'. As described by Khafi Khan,

> 'With the object of curbing the infidels (*Kafirs*), and of distinguishing the land of the faithful (*Dar-ul-Islam*) from an infidel land (*Dar-ul-Harb*), the *Jiziya* was imposed upon the Hindus throughout all the provinces. Upon the publication of this order, the Hindus all round Delhi assembled in vast numbers under the *Jharokha* of the Emperor on the river front of the palace, to represent their inability to pay, and to pray for the recall of the edict. But the Emperor would not listen to their complaints. One day, when he went to public prayer in the great mosque on the *Sabbath*, a vast multitude of Hindus thronged the road from the palace to the mosque, with the object of seeking relief. Money-changers and drapers, all kinds of shopkeepers from the *Urdu Bazaar*, and workmen of all kinds, left off work and business, and pressed into the way. Notwithstanding orders were given to force a way through, it was impossible for the Emperor to reach the mosque. Every moment the crowd increased, and the emperor's equipage was brought to a standstill. At length an order was given to bring out the elephants and direct them against the mob. Many fell trodden to death under the feet of the elephants and horses. For some days the Hindus continued to assemble in great numbers and complain, but at length they submitted to pay the *Jiziya*'. (*Muntakhab-ul-Lubab*, E&D, vii, p. 296).

The public voice was thus silenced by force. It clearly shows that the Hindus did adopt modern methods of peaceful and non-violent public protest against the imposition of *Jaziya* by Aurangzeb. They struck work, observed *hartals*, held protest meetings, and conducted peaceful processions to the accompaniment, probably of black flags and the shouting of slogans. They repeatedly appealed to the emperor with utmost humility for the repeal of the poll-tax but to no avail; the autocratic ruler that Aurangzeb was, he did not care a fig for the public sentiments. In the face of such a rigid attitude adopted by Aurangzeb, the Hindus were left to embrace Islam to seek exemption from the payment of *Jaziya*. Of course, the other alternative open to them was to take up arms and fight to the finish. Some of them adopted the second course of action, thereby giving rise to the armed struggle for freedom against the Mughal rule in various parts of the country. Nevertheless, as late as March 1689, Aurangzeb 'continued to suffer from the greatest delusion of his life to be the invincible and unsurpassed lord of the Indian subcontinent when his imperial camp was converted into a slaughter house for butchering Sambhaji, the Maratha *Chhatrapati*, and his associates on the banks of the river Bhima'.

Aurangzeb had identified the state with himself which he wanted to convert into a true *Dar-ul-Islam* during his very lifetime. This was, however, not to be. The nemesis set in when he was at the pinnacle of his power. The revolts of the Jat peasantry of Mathura (1669-70) and Satnamis (1672-73) against his reactionary religious policies were crushed with iron hands by Aurangzeb but he failed to scuttle the Rajput reaction. His annexation of the Rajput kingdom of Marwar (Jodhpur) on the death of Maharaja Jaswant Singh and the ill-treatment of his royal family by Aurangzeb cost him very heavily. The Rathors of Jodhpur took up arms, under the leadership of Durga Dass, and started a war of independence. They were soon joined in the struggle by the Sisodias of Mewar. Their temporary suppression by the imperial troops, instead of dampening the spirits of the Rajputs, set the whole of Rajputana ablaze. So much so that Prince Akbar, who was sent by Aurangzeb to crush the Rajputs, himself felt disgusted with the anti-national and suicidal policy of his father, and raised a standard of revolt in a bid to put the empire on the right track again. His failure marked the defeat of the forces of nationalism, liberalism and secular state policy at the hands of Muslim diehards who had come to dominate the imperial court under Aurangzeb. The withdrawal of Rajput support to the empire had its immediate repercussions on the turbulent Afghan tribes of the north-west frontier, and the imperial government was hard-pressed to keep either of them under control.

The next major crack in the grand edifice of the Mughal empire occurred in 1689 when Aurangzeb's inhuman and cruel treatment of Sambhaji aroused the deep anger and resentment of the Marathas as a whole and turned them into the sworn enemies of the Mughals. The people's war of liberation that engulfed Maharashtra struck a serious blow to the solidarity and integrity of the Mughal empire. Irfan Habib refers to one of the last 'despairing letters' of Aurangzeb in which he describes the political health of his empire towards the concluding years of his reign as follows: 'There is no province or district where the infidels (Hindus) have not raised a tumult, and since they are not chastised, they have established themselves everywhere. Most of the country has been rendered desolate and if any place is inhabited, the peasants have probably come to terms with the *Ashqiya* (or robbers, an official Mughal name coined for reference to the Marathas).Thus was the Mughal empire destroyed'. (*The Agrarian System of Mughal India*, pp. 350-51). Maharashtra became independent during the very lifetime of Aurangzeb while Rajputana broke away from the Mughal empire immediately after his death.

The Deccan war proved highly expensive and wasteful. Millions of people were uprooted or perished in the war-affected zones. According to Niccolao Manucci, 'the loss of life in the imperial camp in the Deccan alone was about one hundred thousand men and three hundred thousand animals, including horses, elephants and beasts of burden per annum'. (*Storia Mo Mogor; loc. cit.*, iv, p. 96). The peasantry, who formed the backbone of the country, was ruined. 'The village-folk suffered not only from violent capture, forced labour and starvation, but also from epidemics', which frequently broke out. The incessant war emptied the imperial treasury. When the current revenues of the empire failed to meet the recurring expenditure on the war-front, Aurangzeb 'ordered the accumulated treasures of his ancestors from Akbar downwards to be taken out of the vaults of Agra and Delhi forts and sent to him in the Deccan.' Thus the last reserves of the empire were exhausted and once the richest empire of the world actually ran bankrupt by the time of Aurangzeb's death. It left the provincial governments too poor to repair the public buildings, *sarais* and roads, worn out and rendered unusable. The educational institutions, irrigation works and other public utility services broke down for want of funds. J.N. Sarkar writes:

'As money and material stopped reaching the warfront in the Deccan, the salaries of soldiers and civil officers alike fell into arrears for three years. The soldiers starving from lack of pay and the exhaustion of their credit with the local grocers, sometimes created scenes in the emperor's court, sometimes abused and hustled their general's business manager; some, driven to desperation, beat to death the paymaster of their contingent. Hard-pressed, Aurangzeb revived the system of allocation of land or *jagirs* to the imperial officers in lieu of their own services and the salaries of their soldiers. It cut at the very roots of the empire's solidarity in the long run, but Aurangzeb had no other alternative to pacify the unpaid men-in-arms, with the result that 'the entire land in the empire proved insufficient for the total amount of *Jagir* needed to satisfy the dues of all the officers, included in the swollen army lists'. (*Aurangzeb*, v, pp. 448-49).

Above all, Aurangzeb's absence from the imperial capital for quarter of a century (1681-1707) put the state machinery out of gear. The provincial governors became indolent and government servants amassed wealth through corruption and oppression of the public. In many provinces, law and order deteriorated, anti-social elements raised their ugly heads and the life and property of the people was no longer safe. Political unrest and insecurity of roads adversely affected trade and commerce; with the result that 'no relief, either from state or from private sources, was possible to save the lives of the starving populace in the famine-hit areas'. It spread widespread discontentment among the people. 'The honest and capable governors emptied provincial treasuries to meet the imperial demands while the clever and ambitious ones secretly amassed wealth and strengthened their hold over the territories under their control so as to assert their independence at an appropriate occasion'. (*Ibid.*).

SECTION2: LATER MUGHALS—BAHADUR SHAH TO RAFI-UD-DAULAH (1707-1719)

Bahadur Shah (1707-12)

Prince Muazzam, the eldest son and successor of Aurangzeb, ascended the throne with the title of Bahadur Shah at the ripe old age of sixty-four. As there was no fixed law of succession among the Mughals, he had to fight a war of succession with his two younger brothers; and he walked over the dead bodies of the Mughal princes, Aazam, Kam Bakhsh and many other kinsmen, besides ten thousand soldiers, including some of the reputed nobles and seasoned military generals, to claim the throne when he had already passed the age of active enterprise. Everyone cannot be expected to act as Sher Shah Suri did in his advanced age. Bahadur Shah was said to be a 'man of mild and calm temper', 'learned and pious, without any bigotry', but he could not assert his will in any matter. Though styled as 'Bahadur Shah', his bravery had left him and personality badly crippled during the eight years of imprisonment that he had suffered at the hands of his own father. He was, in fact, 'a spent-force and an incapable ruler who failed to stem the rot that had set in during the reign of Aurangzeb'. He was also known as Shah Alam. In history, he has sometimes to be referred as Shah Alam I or Bahadur Shah I because, in the long list of his weak successors, called the Later Mughals, two of them bore the same names or titles, as Shah Alam II and Bahadur Shah II respectively.

Because of his ignorance of state affairs, poor statesmanship and inaction, he was nicknamed *Shah-i-Bekhabar*. During his period of four years' rule, the whole of Rajputana slipped out of the imperial control under the leadership of Ajit Singh, Durga Dass Rathor, Raja Jai Singh Kachhwaha of Ajmer, and Rana Amar Singh of Mewar. The Sikhs, under the leadership of Banda Bahadur, captured Sirhind in May 1710 and setup the first independent Sikh state in the Punjab. Sirhind was recovered by the Mughal troops soon after but the Sikhs were neither reconciled nor crushed. Bahadur Shah failed to bring the governors of the outlying provinces under his effective control. While engaged in his fight against the Sikhs, he died at Lahore on February 27, 1712.

Jahandar Shah (1712-13)

Bahadur Shah's death was followed by a ritual of the self-destructive civil war between his four sons, leading to the success of Jahandar Shah. He was fifty-one at the time of his accession and proved to be a totally weak and degenerate ruler. He buried himself in the enjoyment of sensual pleasures and had no time or intellect to attend to the business of the state. Left to oneself, none of Bahadur Shah's sons qualified to be a capable candidate for the throne like the earlier Mughal princes Salim, Shah Jahan or Aurangzeb, yet the war was fought by the more ambitious among the Mughal nobles on behalf of their royal protégés. Jahandar Shah was placed on the throne as the puppet Mughal ruler by Zulfiqar Khan, son of Asad Khan, the prime minister of

Aurangzeb, who had been retained as his *wazir* by Bahadur Shah. As a reward for his services, Zulfiqar Khan was made his *wazir* by Jahandar Shah while his aged father, Asad Khan, hitherto the *wazir*, relinquished his charge in favour of his son to enjoy a life of peaceful retirement. Zulfiqar Khan played the role of a king-maker because of his close relations with the Mughal ruling house. Taking advantage of the political disorders and personal weaknesses of Jahandar Shah, he concentrated all powers of the state into his own hands and also usurped the royal prerogatives, thus reducing the new emperor to a magnificent cipher.

In fact, the three successive wars of succession, fought in 1657-58, 1707-8 and 1712 respectively, assured the total extermination of the imperial Mughal dynasty, and if a few persons, belonging to the erstwhile royal Mughal blood, continued to have their existence or were sustained, it was because others wanted to exploit them for advancing their own political interests. All the successors of Bahadur Shah, called the Later Mughals, proved to be weaklings. They were incompetent and imbecile rulers, none of whom possessed either the strength of character or resources to stop the dismemberment of the empire which had begun since the days of Aurangzeb. 'The imperial Mughal dynasty had come to an end by 1712 yet the goodwill left by the Great Mughals and their imprint on the minds of the Indians was so great that, even one century and a half after the death of Aurangzeb, they failed to reconcile themselves to the fact that the Mughal rule had come to an end'. (Advanced Study; ii, pp. 571-72)

Farrukh Siyyar (1713-19)

Zulfiqar Khan had set the precedent as kingmaker. His sudden rise to power aroused the jealousy of other ambitious nobles who stepped into his shoes to play the similar roles for gaining power and influence in the court. It gave rise to a new crop of power-brokers and king-makers, among whom the two Sayyad brothers—Hussain Ali and Abdullah Khan, were the first to take the lead. They conspired against the reigning emperor and his *wazir* Zulfiqar Khan on behalf of Farrukh Siyyar, a more ambitious nephew of Jahandar Shah. The latter was got hold of and strangulated to death by the Sayyad brothers after ten months of his rule and Farrukh Siyyar was placed on the throne as the next Mughal emperor on February 13, 1713; Zulfiqar Khan, his *wazir*, had been executed by the henchmen of Farrukh Siyyar two days earlier. As a reward for their services, Sayyad Abdullah Khan became the *Wazir* and his younger brother was conferred the twin offices of *Mir Bakhshi* (paymaster general) and *Sipah Salar* or commander-in-chief of the imperial army.

Farrukh Siyyar was a handsome man of thirty at the time of his accession to the throne. He owed the crown to the Sayyad brothers but being an ambitious man of selfish and vile nature, he was always afraid of the all-powerful kingmakers. Therefore, in his eagerness to get rid of them, he had started hatching conspiracies and intrigues to bring about their fall. Secondly, being a religious fanatic like Aurangzeb, Farrukh Siyyar wanted to adopt stringent measures against the rebellious Hindu forces, including the Rajputs, Marathas and the Sikhs, to restore the credibility of the Mughal regime. To attain his objectives, he mustered all the resources of the state to crush the Sikhs in the Punjab, and, at the same time, appointed Sayyad Abdullah Khan as the viceroy of the Deccan with instructions to carry on uncompromising war against the Marathas. It was a very clever ploy to keep the two Sayyad brothers away from each other and curtail their influence at the imperial court. For a while, he seemed to be playing his cards well for the attainment of his objectives, but he never knew that he was doing it at the cost of his dear life. Two important developments of his reign, which severely undermined the power and prestige of the Mughal empire, and hastened its downfall, were as follows:

1. War against the Sikhs: Execution of Banda Bahadur (June 9, 1716)

When Farrukh Siyyar ascended the throne, the Sikhs were waging a war of attrition against the Mughal rule in the Punjab under the leadership of Banda Bahadur. The exploits of Banda Bahadur had struck terror in the hearts of the imperial soldiery and thoroughly demoralised the Mughal officers of the Punjab. Farrukh Siyyar deputed Abdus Samad Khan, the governor of Kashmir, to intensify operations against the Sikhs in coordination with Amin Khan, the governor of Lahore. Under pressure from the Mughal forces, Banda Bahadur retreated with his followers to the interior of Jammu hills, and, for a while, the Mughal action against the Sikhs came to a standstill. Farrukh Siyyar was not satisfied with this stalemate, and he recalled Amin Khan from Lahore, the governorship of which was now entrusted to Abdus-Samad Khan. Simultaneously, the latter's son, Zakariya Khan, who was himself an ambitious military officer, received appointment as the *faujdar* of Jammu from the Mughal emperor. Abdus-Samad Khan and Zakariya Khan made a frontal attack on the Sikhs with the assistance of some hill chiefs. The Sikhs fought a pitched battle against them near Kalanaur in district Gurdaspur, but were defeated and compelled to retreat to a *haveli* (mansion) of Bhai Duni Chand at Gurdas Nangal, situated at a distance of about seven kilometers to the west of Gurdaspur town. The place was besieged by the Mughals and the siege lasted, amidst bloody battles, until the entire Sikh force of about eight thousand men was annihilated, and Banda Bahadur was captured along with a handful of his companions.

The Sikh captives were taken in chains to Lahore by Abdus-Samad Khan. Banda Bahadur though handcuffed and with chains round his legs, was dreaded so much by the Mughal soldiers that he was put in an iron cage, like a beast, which was locked and heavily guarded; it was mounted on a dirty elephant. His associates, numbering 740 in all, were also mounted on filthy camels and asses; all of them were in chains and tied together, with their hair, in pairs. They were insulted and humiliated by the Mughal soldiery as well as the urchins when they were taken in a procession through the streets of Lahore. Then they were sent to Delhi under the charge of Zakariya Khan. A similar procession of the captives was organised in Delhi also with the addition that it was preceded by two thousand smeared heads of the Sikh warriors, carried on long poles, 'with their hair streaming in the air'. After thus heaping insults on the dead and the dying, they were given the option to save their lives by embracing Islam; the offer was contemptuously turned down by every one of them. The execution of the captives started on March 5, 1716. One hundred Sikh captives were executed on the first day at the spot where Gurudwara Shahidganj is now situated, and their slaughter was carried on in small groups day after day. Banda Bahadur and his infant son of three years were brutally hacked to death on June 19, 1716; they were given a very inhuman treatment by his executioners. The next day, the last batch of twenty-six Sikh prisoners met with a similar fate. Their execution re-enacted the scenes of the execution of Guru Tegh Bahadur and the Maratha *Chhatrapati* Sambhaji during the reign of Aurangzeb.

The Sikhs assumed a low profile after the death of Banda Bahadur. Some of the Sikhs did not approve of Banda Bahadur's war tactics and practices which did not confirm to the tenets of the Khalsa of Guru Gobind Singh. It led to a division in their ranks, leading to the formation of two factions, Bandai Khalsa and the Tat Khalsa. The differences between the two factions were composed by the efforts of Bhai Mani Singh at Amritsar in 1721, and they once again became active. They had lost a battle and their warriors but they were never subdued. They organised a full-fledged war of independence in the Punjab against the tyrannical Mughal rule and did not take rest until the whole of the Punjab was liberated by them from the hands of the Mughal governors as well as Ahmad Shah Abdali in the next few decades.

2. The Affairs of the East India Company

The discovery of a direct sea route to India via the Cape of Good Hope in 1498 by Vasco da Gama, a Portuguese navigator, brought the Europeans to India in a big way. The Portuguese and the Dutch made their presence felt along the seacoasts of India in the sixteenth century, while the English and the French followed suit in due course of time. As a result, long before the death of Aurangzeb, they had established their footholds on the Indian soil. The English East India Company came into being in 1600 when the Mughal empire was at the zenith of its glory. It was constituted by 'the merchants of London' on the basis of a royal charter, granted to them by Queen Elizabeth I of England (1558-1603), who was a contemporary of Akbar the Great (1556-1605). Captain Hawkins, an agent of the Company, landed at Surat (Gujarat) in 1608 and opened the first English trading centre there. Formal permission for the establishment of a permanent factory at Surat was obtained by the Company from the Mughal court sometime in 1612. In 1615, Sir Thomas Roe came to India as an ambassador from King James I of England (1603-25) to the court of Jahangir at Agra, with the object of seeking trade concessions for the English Company. He and his chaplain, Edward Terry, stayed in India for over three years, and won over the favours of the Mughal emperor by their diplomatic skill and highly civilised conduct. The English followed-up their advantages by setting up factories and trading agencies at many places in India. They built-up their permanent settlements at Surat and Bombay on the western coast, and at Masulipatam and Madras along the Coromondal coast. By the year 1680, the Company had extended its trade along the northeastern coast up to Orissa. An English trading centre had been opened on the Hugli in Bengal, and its 'agencies' or supply-lines had been setup in the interior at Patna, Qasim Bazaar, and Raj Mahal, etc.

For a long time, the English East India Company adhered to the 'pacifist' policy of 'peaceful trade' with India, as advocated by Sir Thomas Roe. Its policy underwent a radical change when Sir Joshua Child was elected governor of the Company by its 'directors' in London in 1681. He was 'an arch imperialist' under whose directions the Company developed territorial ambitions. During the reign of Aurangzeb, the English attempted to defy the imperial authority but were suppressed with an iron hand. In February 1690 the Company was granted 'pardon' on payment of a huge war indemnity of Rs. 1,50,000, and permitted to resume trade in various parts of the empire subject to the payment of specified custom duties and other taxes. It was after the conclusion of these hostilities that the East India Company sought permission from the Subedar of Bengal to setup a factory on the sight of modern Calcutta. In 1696, this factory was fortified and, two years later, the Company was accorded permission to acquire on rent three adjoining villages of Sutanati, Kalikata, and Govindpur for the residential accommodation of their servants and agents. The new urban habitat that rapidly grew up on the sight of these villages came to be known as Kalikata or Calcutta. In1700, the fortified factory of Calcutta was renamed as Fort William; it was made the seat of a Presidency, and Sir Charles Eyre was appointed the first 'President and Governor' of Fort William in Bengal.

The imperial Mughal authority started showing signs of weakness after the death of Aurangzeb, but the European traders were not allowed to spread their tentacles or disturb the law and order situation for a long time. Most of the provincial governors, variously styled as *nawabs* or subedars, were strong enough to keep the activities of Europeans under their control. During the first half of the eighteenth century, Bengal was ruled by very strong *nawabs* like Murshid Quli Khan and Ali Vardi Khan. They did not allow the traders and agents of the East India Company to misuse or transgress the trade privileges, granted to them earlier by the imperial Mughal government under the various emperors.

During the reign of Farrukh Siyyar, the East India Company sent two 'factors' from Calcutta to Delhi in July 1715 'to seek redress of their grievances' against Murshid Quli Khan, the *Nawab* of Bengal. They were accompanied by an English surgeon, William Hamilton, and an Armenian merchant of Calcutta, named Khwaja Sarhad, who understood English as well as Persian, and acted as an interpreter. They stayed in Delhi for over two years, spending lavishly on the Mughal courtiers and officials to win their favours. Hamilton won the gratitude of Farrukh Siyyar by 'curing him of a malignant distemper', and, as a reward for it, received from the Mughal emperor 'valuable trade concessions and exemptions from customs duties' for his countrymen 'in perpetuity'. Farrukh Siyyar issued, in January-February 1717, three *firmans*, addressed to the governors of Bengal, Gujarat, and the Deccan respectively. These *firmans* not only reaffirmed the trade privileges, granted to the Company by Aurangzeb earlier, but also extended their scope to other parts of the Mughal empire as well. These concessions included, among others, the freedom to carry on trade and commerce in Bengal (including Bihar and Orissa) without payment of custom duties, subject to the customary payment of three thousand rupees *per annum* to the provincial government. The English merchants were allowed to secure on rent or lease 'additional territory around Calcutta' and 'settle where else they might choose'. Their privilege of trade in the Deccan was recognised for the first time by the Mughal emperor, subject to the condition that the Company would continue to pay tribute or rentals for Madras, as ever before, to the Mughal governor, styled the Nawab of Carnatic. The grant of these trade concessions by Farrukh Siyyar to the East India Company 'legalised its status', and this thing was thoroughly exploited by the English in their ensuing struggle for territorial aggrandizements and the foundation of colonial empire in India. Farrukh Siyyar was done to death by the Sayyad brothers in February 1719 when he fell out with his kingmakers on the issue of making a settlement with the Marathas to avoid a repetition of the political turmoil that had engulfed the Punjab.

Rise of the Marathas as a National Power

The Marathas emerged as the most formidable national force on the ruins of the Mughal empire. As referred to in the preceding chapters of this study, ever since Sambhaji, the son and successor of Shivaji, was captured and tortured to death by Aurangzeb in March 1689, the Marathas had turned into the sworn enemies of the Mughal emperor. The war of liberation started by them caught Aurangzeb in the whirlwind from which he could never extricate himself. Ultimately, he gave up the struggle against the Marathas and decided to retrace his steps towards the north early in 1706. As depicted by Lane-Poole, 'the emperor led the dejected remnant of his once powerful army, in confusion and alarm, pursued by skirmishing bodies of exultant Marathas, back to Ahmadnagar, whence, more than twenty years before, he had set out full of sanguine hope and at the head of a splendid and invincible' army of invasion to take on 'the mountain rats'. He reached Ahmadnagar on January 31, 1706. 'The Maratha generals followed Aurangzeb on his journey to Ahmadnagar, cutting off his supplies and communications, falling upon the stragglers and threatening to attack the emperor's own camp. When the Mughals challenged them in force, they would fall back a little, but like water parted by the oar would close again' as soon as the Mughal defenders returned to their main body. As the emperor reached Ahmadnagar, the Maratha forces besieged his camp in strength, and were repulsed but after a long and severe fighting in May 1706. At this time, they started 'breaking in and invading the adjacent Mughal provinces like Gujarat, Khandesh and even Malwa'. The Marathas 'plundered an imperial envoy which was on its way from Aurangabad to Ahmadnagar' to provide succour to the impoverished Mughal army. In the midst of these troubles, Aurangzeb died on March 3, 1707.

At the time of Aurangzeb's death, his second son, Prince Azam, was present in the imperial camp at Ahmadnagar. While proceeding to the north to fight a war of succession with his brothers, he released Shahu, son of Sambhaji, who had been held in the captivity of Aurangzeb, along with many other members of his royal family, since 1689. He took this step as a matter of political expediency, probably, with a two-fold object, namely (*a*) to befriend the Marathas and seek their cooperation in dealing with the rival claimants to the throne of Delhi; and (*b*) to create dissensions among the Marathas by setting loose the rival claimant to the Maratha monarchy. Shahu was officially recognised as the true successor to his ancestral kingdom, and was also granted the *Chauth* and *Sardeshmukhi* of all the six Mughal *Subas* of the Deccan, besides that of Gujarat, Gondwana, and Tanjore, subject to the provision that three-fourth of his collections were to be remitted by him to the Mughal treasury at Delhi. To ensure his loyalty to the Mughal crown as its vassal, however, Shahu's two wives, mother, and a half-brother among others, were retained as hostages by Prince Azam. In order to attract the attention of Maratha *sardars* as well as the public, in general, Shahu was provided with sufficient funds and the insignia of royalty besides the armed Maratha guards. Prince Azam was killed in the war of succession, but Shahu went to Maharashtra and promptly put forth his claim to the Maratha throne as the rightful successor of his deceased father Sambhaji. As was expected, it created dissensions among the Marathas and led to civil war between the two rival claimants to the Maratha throne; one was led by Shahu and the other by Tara Bai, the widowed queen of Raja Ram, on behalf of her minor son, Sambhaji II, also styled as Shivaji II. Shahu came out successful in this contest with the overwhelming majority of the Maratha nobility, headed by Balaji Vishwanath whom he appointed his Peshwa or the prime minister; he setup his headquarters at Satara.

The Mughal-Maratha Treaty of 1718

Balaji Vishwanath, the *Peshwa*-cum-*Senapati* of Shahu, from 1713 to 1730, consolidated the Maratha power in the Deccan. The rapid decline in the power and prestige of the Mughal emperors and the rise of the Sayyad brothers as kingmakers at Delhi proved very helpful to the Marathas in extending their sphere of influence far and wide. In July 1718, a treaty of friendship was concluded by Sayyad Hussain Ali, in his capacity as the Mughal viceroy of the Deccan, with the Maratha *Chhatrapati* Shahu on behalf of the Mughal emperor, according to which,

1. Shivaji's original dominions, acquired by him (i.e. the Mughal viceroy) from Bijapur and the Mughals (by way of conquest from the Marathas), called the *Swarajya*, were to be restored to Shahu as Shivaji's rightful successor;
2. All the additional territories, conquered recently by the Marathas in Karnataka, Hyderabad, Gondwana, Berar, and Khandesh, were also to be recognised as a part of the Maratha *Swarajya* and formally to be assigned to Shahu;
3. The Maratha *Chhatrapati* was authorised to collect *Chauth* and *Sardeshmukhi* from all the six Mughal provinces of the Deccan;
4. The Maratha hostages, including Shahu's family and friends, were to be set free; and,
5. In return, the Maratha *Chhatrapati* Shahu 'undertook' to (a) 'maintain peace and order' in the six Mughal provinces of the Deccan, (b) depute 'a contingent of fifteen thousand Maratha soldiers for the service of the Mughal emperor'; and (c) 'pay an annual tribute of ten lacs of rupees to the Mughal court'. —(Sardesai, *New History of the Marathas*; ii, pp. 39-41).

In addition, Shahu was given to understand through the agent of Sayyad Hussain Ali that the Mughal emperor would not like the Maratha *Chhatrapati* to do any 'harm' to Sambhaji II of Kolhapur. Sayyad Hussain Ali, on his part, agreed not only to accept the above-mentioned terms of the treaty and implement them in his capacity as the Mughal viceroy of the Deccan but also 'promised to get them formally ratified by the emperor in due course.' Accordingly, on the first of August 1718, Shahu issued orders to his 'local officials' to enforce 'the terms of the above-mentioned treaty and start the collection of *Chauth* and *Sardeshmukhi*' from the territories under their charge.

Sardesai refers to the existence of an official communication from the Peshwa Balaji Vishwanath, bearing the dateline July 30, 1718 and addressed to the *Deshmukhs* and *Deshpandes* of Poona which calls upon them 'to stop the payment of these dues to the Mughal official, Rambhaji Nimbalkar'.(*Ibid.*, p. 41) Instead, Balaji Vishwanath adopted swift measures to take 'possession' of the revenue collection establishment 'from the Mughal officials in the name of Shahu'. He also instantly 'raised a special corps of troops for the service' of the Mughal emperor which, later on, came to be known as the *Hazurat*, i.e., 'the King's Troops'. (*Ibid.*, pp.41-42).

The Mughal-Maratha treaty of 1718, which was formulated by Balaji Vishwanath, 'speaks highly' for the 'diplomatic skill' and statesmanship of the Peshwa. It made 'secure' and consolidated the position of Shahu as the Maratha *Chhatrapati* and the 'lawful ruler' of all the Maratha lands and the people. It enhanced his respect and 'prestige not only in the eyes of the Marathas, but also of the Mughals'. It was this 'legal status' which Shahu 'had all along been trying to acquire since his release and which Balaji's supreme efforts succeeded at last in confirming'. The treaty of 1718 not only enabled the Marathas to become 'masters of their home' but also provided 'fresh facilities' for their 'expansion outside from their base in the Deccan'. (*Ibid.*, p. 42). It proved to be an important milestone towards the spread of the Maratha power in central and northern India and provided a unique opportunity to them to extend their influence at the Mughal court in Delhi. R.D. Nadhkarni characterizes this treaty as 'a very profitable subsidiary alliance, formed by the Marathas long before the times of Lord Wellesley'. (*Rise and Fall of the Maratha Empire*; p. 170). He observes that by entrusting the responsibility 'for the maintenance of peace and order in the Deccan to the Marathas, and by making the Mughal viceroy of the Deccan dependent on them 'for military help', this Mughal-Maratha Treaty of 1718 accorded 'sovereign rights' to the Maratha state to rule over the whole of the Deccan. Such being the case, this treaty was, in no way, less important than the subsequent grant of Diwani of Bengal, Bihar and Orissa to the British East India Company by the fugitive Mughal emperor Shah Alam II in 1765 because it gave *de jure* recognition to the Marathas as the rightful successors of the Imperial Mughals in the Deccan. The credit for this achievement goes to Balaji Vishwanath.

It is sometimes argued that the Mughal-Maratha Treaty of 1718 had reduced the status of the Maratha *Chhatrapati* to that of a 'vassal' of the Mughal Crown, and that he was put under obligation to offer his allegiance and pay annual tribute to the latter. Be that as it may, an equally significant aspect of the treaty was that the so-called 'vassal' had undertaken to protect his suzerain 'with his own troops', and 'when a sovereign seeks protection from a vassal, it means, in actual practice, that the comparative strength of the two contracting parties is reversed. Exactly similar was the position of the British East India Company vis-a-vis the Mughal emperor, Shah Alam II, when the latter granted the Diwani of Bengal, Bihar, and Orissa to the former in 1765 after the battle of Buxar.

The Marathas at Delhi (1718-19)

The Mughal emperor, Farrukh Siyyar, was not pleased to hear of the above treaty of friendship, signed by Sayyad Hussain Ali, the Mughal viceroy of the Deccan, with the Marathas as 'it strengthened the hands of the Sayyad brothers'. He did not approve of the terms of the treaty and wanted it to be scrapped. Instead, he wanted that Hussain Ali should have plunged into a deadly struggle against the Marathas even at the cost of his own life, but the Mughal commander, on the advice of his elder brother, who held the premier position at the Mughal court as *wazir* or prime minister of the state, adopted a conciliatory attitude towards them. It was because, unlike Farrukh Siyyar, the Sayyad brothers were *Shias* by faith and were very broad-minded, far-sighted and rational in their political views. They did not believe in permanently antagonizing their non-Muslim adversaries. They did not approve of the policy of unnecessarily harsh and cruel treatment that was meted out to Banda Bahadur and other vanquished Sikh captives. About that time, the Mughal court was divided into two rival factions. One faction was led by the Turani and Irani nobles of foreign pedigree, and was composed of the foreign immigrants and their immediate descendants primarily; they were predominated by the *Sunnis* and other orthodox Muslims. They looked down upon the other faction of the so-called 'Hindustani Mughals', most of whose members were 'Indian Muslims', born and bred in India; they were either Hindu converts to Islam and their offspring, or remote descendants of the foreign immigrants. The Sayyad brothers belonged to the faction of the 'Hindustani Mughals' who enjoyed the support of many powerful Hindu chieftains, especially the Jats and the Rajputs. Incidentally, Farrukh Siyyar had come to occupy a very dubious position in the game of power-politics between these two rival factions of the court. He had acquired the throne with the help of the so-called Hindustani party but, after having established himself on the throne, shifted his sympathies to their antagonists of the Turani party. Its consequences were bound to be very grave and Farrukh Siyyar had to pay heavily for it.

Nevertheless, Hussain Ali came to Delhi with his army, reinforced by a fifteen thousand strong contingent of the Maratha troops of the *Hazurat* as per the terms of the treaty; they were commanded by Khande Rao Dabhade, a close confident of the Peshwa Balaji Vishwanath. They were paid fifty thousand rupees as 'daily allowance' by the Mughal viceroy 'as long as they stayed with him'. On the persuasion of Hussain Ali, the Peshwa had agreed to accompany them to Delhi to secure the ratification of the treaty from the Mughal emperor in person. (William Irvine, *Later Mughals*: 1707-1739; loc.cit., i, pp.359-60). *Chhatrapati* Shahu readily permitted his Peshwa to accompany the Mughal viceroy to Delhi with the hope of securing the release of his family members from Mughal imprisonment.

Accordingly, Balaji Vishwanath went to Delhi as 'an Imperial Ally' of the Mughal emperor with great pomp and show. He was accompanied by magnificent Maratha band and picked escort of one thousand Maratha guards besides a number of seasoned Maratha generals and strategists. Their primary object in undertaking this sojourn to Delhi was, of course, to gain first-hand knowledge of the Mughal court and its politics, and make their own assessment of the Mughal prowess and the general political condition of northern India. Balaji's entourage also included his own youthful son, Baji Rao, who was still in his teens.

The sudden arrival of Sayyad Hussain Ali with his army and the Maratha allies at Delhi, early in September 1718, un-nerved Farrukh Siyyar and his supporters. Of course, Raja Ajit Singh of Jodhpur (Marwar) and Raja Jai Singh of Jaipur (Amber) also joined Hussain Ali's camp along with their troops; they were introduced to Balaji Vishwanath in an atmosphere of cordiality and friendship. Of them, Raja Ajit Singh, who met Balaji Vishwanath and other Maratha dignitaries 'under the walls of the Red Fort of Delhi', made a lasting friendship with Baji Rao, who was destined to succeed his father as the next Peshwa and rise to the pinnacle of glory on the national horizon before long.

Deposition of Farrukh Siyyar (February 27, 1719): Farrukh Siyyar bluntly refused to ratify the treaty of friendship, made by Sayyad

Hussain Ali with the Marathas on behalf of the Mughal Crown. Instead, he publicly called upon his supporters to take up arms against the Sayyad brothers, who were declared *persona non-grata.* A contingent of the imperial troops surprised the Maratha camp in a treacherous move, and, 'in the bloody scuffle' that took place near the Red Fort of Delhi, about two thousand Maratha soldiers lost their lives. Nevertheless, the Marathas fought like daredevils and took a still heavier toll of the Mughal soldiery. It instantly turned the scales in favour of the Sayyad brothers. As a follow-up action, the Sayyads stormed the Red Fort with the active support of the Maratha and Rajput contingents, and overpowered the supporters of Farrukh Siyyar. The victors made a triumphant entry into the Red Fort and took control of the imperial court as well as the royal palace. Farrukh Siyyar was taken prisoner, blinded, and deposed by the Sayyad brothers, who brought out another Mughal prince, aged 24 and named Rafi-ud-Darajat, and installed him as the emperor on February 28, 1719.

Ratification of the Treaty by the Mughal Emperor

The new Mughal emperor, Rafi-ud-Darajat, ratified the Mughal-Maratha Treaty of July 1718 without any reservations when Balaji Vishwanath and other Maratha veterans were present in the imperial court as guests of honour and *grandees* of the empire at that historic occasion. This treaty is rightly considered to be 'one of the most noteworthy state documents' on the history of modern India. Sir Richard Temple refers to it as the Magna Carta of the Maratha empire in India.

Balaji Vishwanath secured three *firmans* from the Mughal emperor on the basis of the above-mentioned treaty. The first of these, dated March 3, 1719, empowered *Chhatrapati* Shahu to collect *Chauth* from all the six provinces of 'the Mughal Deccan' as also from the tributary states of Tanjore, Trichnapoli and Mysore; while the second one, issued on 15 March, authorised him to collect *Sardeshmukhi* from the Deccan. The third *firman* confirmed *Chhatrapati* Shahu in the possession of the Maratha *Swarajya,* as per the terms of the treaty, being the 'legitimate successor' of Shivaji.

The Release of Shahu's Family (March 1719)

Shahu's mother Yesu Bai, his wife Savitribai, half-brother Madan Singh, and some other members of the Maratha royal family, who had been kept in confinement by Aurangzeb for many years, were still held in detention as hostages by the Mughal emperors since 1707.

All of them were released in March 1719 and allowed to go to Satara in the company of Balaji Vishwanath. Their reunion with Shahu was ' an occasion of immense joy for the Maratha *Chhatrapati* for which he was highly indebted to his Peshwa. The second wife of Shahu, Ambikabai, had already breathed her last in the Mughal captivity. As for Yesu Bai, 'the pious and revered' mother of Shahu, she had suffered Mughal imprisonment for more than 29 years. She was fully 'satisfied' to see her son securely seated on the Maratha throne at Satara. She bore two children, a daughter, named Bhavanibai, and a son, Shahu. Greatly loved by her people, the grand old lady lived for at least twelve years more 'leaving behind a pious memory of a pure and selfless soul'. In the words of Sardesai, 'Shahu and Yesu Bai live in Maratha memory almost as much as Shivaji and his mother Jija Bai do. Shahu ever felt that he owed all his good fortune to the blessings of his mother'. (New History, ii, p. 49).

Sayyad Brothers as Kingmakers and *de facto* Rulers

The Sayyad brothers held the reins of government as *de facto* rulers and kingmakers for about eight years. They dealt with Farrukh Siyyar very harshly but with the full cooperation and support of the liberal party of the 'Hindustani Mughals' who occupied the predominant positions in the imperial court. Deposition of the 'notorious' Mughal emperor received universal applause from the inhabitants of Delhi and the people at large for having committed barbarous atrocities against his political rivals. By one stroke of diplomacy, the Sayyad brothers had succeeded in befriending the Marathas as vassals and useful allies of the Mughal crown. The Marathas left Delhi for the south in March 1719 with full satisfaction and were accorded warm farewell not only by the imperial court but also the overwhelming majority of the citizens of Delhi.

It was after the departure of the Marathas from Delhi that Farrukh Siyyar, then 'held in confinement in a room at the top of the *Tirpauliya*' in the Red Fort of Delhi, was 'strangled to death on the night of 27-28 April 1719. The room, referred to as *Tirpauliya* by Khafi Khan, was the same as that in which Jahandar Shah had been murdered on the orders of Farrukh Siyyar in 1713. Khafi Khan characterizes Farrukh Siyyar to be 'the most incapable ruler of the House of Timur that had so far occupied the throne of Delhi'. Nature wreaks its own vengeance upon the power-hungry tyrants who, blinded by their personal prejudices and self-interests, utterly disregard the humanitarian considerations while dealing with their opponents. The tragic end of Farrukh Siyyar was exactly in keeping with the inhuman treatment that he had meted out to Banda Bahadur and his companions a few years earlier.

As *de facto* rulers of the state, the Sayyad brothers sincerely stood for the reversal of all the reactionary policies of Aurangzeb to restore the credibility of the Mughal empire. It goes to their credit that both of them were not only good soldiers but also capable administrators. While at the helm of affairs, they restored law and order and attempted to tone up the administration according to the limited resources at their command. The Sayyad brothers were committed to the policy of religious toleration, and they never hesitated to utilise the services of the Indians of various religious denominations in running the administration. They revived the earlier policy of consolidating their alliance with the Jats, the Rajputs and the Marathas by winning their confidence and support. Immediately after the deposition of Farrukh Siyyar, *Jaziya* was abolished by them from the Mughal dominions, and the pilgrim tax, payable by the Hindus at some of their holy places was scrapped. They adopted a conciliatory attitude towards the age-old ruling houses of the Rajputs and the Jats, and did their best to win their active service and support to the benefit of the Mughal empire. Raja Ajit Singh of Marwar (Jodhpur) and Sawai Raja Jai Singh of Amber (Jaipur) were restored their high positions in the Mughal court as before. Churaman, the Jat ruler of Bharatpur, was befriended, and all the religious disabilities of the Hindus were removed. Farrukh Siyyar, during his reign, had demanded and received the hand of Raja Ajit Singh's daughter in marriage as the price of his vassalage and loyalty to the Mughal throne. Now that Farrukh Siyyar was no more, Ajit Singh's daughter, who had been converted to Islam, was permitted by the Sayyad brothers as a gesture of goodwill, to revert to her Hindu faith and return to her parental home at Jodhpur. She was also allowed to take all her property and wealth with her. The Sayyads put down all opposition to this step by the orthodox Muslim *ulama* and *qazis* who argued that renunciation of Islam was illegal. Khafi Khan confirms the positive effects of Sayyad brothers' policy of religious toleration upon the Hindus by his oblique remarks that 'from the environs of the capital to the banks of the Narbada, the infidels were engaged in repairing temples and attempting to forbid cow-slaughter'.

After the deposition of Farrukh Siyyar, the Sayyad brothers had raised another Mughal prince, Rafi-ud-Darajat, on the throne but he was 'suffering from consumption' and tuberculosis. No wonder, he became a puppet in the hands of the Sayyads who carried on the administration in his name. Within four months of his accession, his health began to decline fast, and on his own suggestion, the Sayyads raised to the throne his elder brother, named Rafi-ud-Daulah, on June 6, 1719. The new emperor, styled Shah Jahan II, was 'virtually held as a prisoner under the charge of Sayyad Himmat Khan Barha. He was not permitted to attend the Friday prayers, or to go out hunting, nor even to converse with any noble, except in the presence of his custodian'. He was taken ill and died on September 17, 1719. Thereafter, the Sayyad brothers put up Muhammad Shah on the throne.

SECTION 3: MUHAMMAD SHAH *RANGILA* (1719-48)

The original name of Muhammad Shah was Raushan Akhtar. He was one of the sons of Jahan Shah—the youngest son of the emperor Bahadur Shah. Jahan Shah had been killed in the war of succession against Jahandar Shah in 1712. Muhammad Shah wore the insignia of royalty for about 30 years and was lucky enough to die a natural death. Though a 'raw youth of seventeen' at the time of his accession, he had been held in confinement as royal prisoner for seven years in his boyhood, and was not cast in the mould of princely order. He had not received any education or training in the statecraft, and was a debauch that spent most of his time in merry making and thus rightly earned the nickname of *Rangila*.

Fall of the Sayyad Brothers: Muhammad Shah was treated as a puppet by the Sayyad brothers. The latter continued to hold all the strings of government and state policy in their hands as usual and wielded immense powers as the virtual rulers of the Mughal dominions. Nevertheless, the new emperor did not prove so 'docile' as to resign himself to his fate easily. Like Farrukh Siyyar, he also started making attempts to establish secret contacts with the leaders of the rival faction to secure his liberation from the hands of the Sayyads. The ringleaders of the Turani party had assumed considered silence when the Sayyad brothers were at their game, but after the departure of the Marathas and other Hindu chieftains from Delhi and the execution of Farrukh Siyyar in April 1719, they became active and established liaison with Muhammad Shah. The liberal policy and non-sectarian outlook of the Sayyad brothers excited the jalousies of the orthodox elements among the Muslims who made a common cause with the Turani and Irani nobles to bring about their fall. They were led by Nizam-ul-Mulk, who had been divested of the viceroyalty of 'the Mughal Deccan' and asked to take charge of Malwa as its governor. Instead, Sayyad Abdullah Khan, the *wazir*, assigned the viceroyalty of all the six Mughal provinces of the Deccan in the name of Hussain Ali who already held the most powerful twin offices as *mir bakhshi* and *sipah-salar* at the imperial court. It was nothing short of humiliation and demotion for Nizam-ul-Mulk. He left Delhi bag and baggage on March 3, 1719 but retained his nexus with the anti-Sayyad lobby of the court. In the dragnet, laid out by them, the Sayyad brothers were entangled and wiped out, one by one, in quick succession. Hussain Ali was assassinated in his army camp on October 9, 1720 by a henchman of Muhammad Amin Khan, a Turani noble, who held a junior command under him. Abdullah Khan, the *wazir*, who moved out of Delhi to punish the conspirators, was defeated in an action at Bilochpur on November 15, 1720, and taken prisoner, apparently by the emperor Muhammad Shah; he was put to death in royal captivity two years later. Fall of the Sayyad brothers marked the end of the rational and liberal state policy initiated by them for the revival of the fortunes of the Mughal empire. The benefactors of Muhammad Shah were none else but the Turani and Irani nobles of the foreign pedigree who did not allow him to have a sigh of relief over his liberation from the Sayyad brothers.

Domination of the Turani and Irani Nobles at the Court: In appreciation of the valuable service rendered to him by Muhammad Amin Khan in his conflict with the Sayyad brothers, Muhammad Shah made him his *wazir* or prime minister, and conferred the exalted title of Itimad-ud-Daulah on him. However, before the emperor could exercise his powers as the sovereign ruler, he found himself a virtual prisoner in the hands of the ringleaders of the Turani party, Itimad-ud-Daulah being one of them. The political vacuum created by the fall of the Sayyads was readily filled up by the more aggressive and selfish leaders of foreign pedigree, who had least regard for the ruling house of Babar in India. 'As foreign adventurers and fortune-hunters, they looked upon India as the land for conquest and subjugation'. Muhammad Shah's case seemed to corroborate the proverbial saying: *Out of the frying pan into the fire.* Thus it was that the emperor was doomed to play the role of a puppet ruler in the hands of a new class of the Mughal nobles. The hapless emperor resigned himself to his fate and stopped taking any interest in the administrative affairs of the state. Itimad-ud-Daulah died in January 1721, and his office was occupied, after a brief interval, by Nizam-ul-Mulk, the viceroy of Malwa as well as 'the Mughal Deccan'. He belonged to the reputed family of hereditary Turani nobles and held the *wizarat* of Delhi for about two years 'as an additional assignment'.

Dismemberment of the Mughal Empire: Muhammad Shah *Rangila* sat over the total dismemberment of the Mughal empire, which, at the time of his death, was reduced to the town of Delhi and its suburbs only. Thus, Ali Vardi Khan asserted his independence in Bengal, Muhammad Amin, a Persian adventurer, styled as Saadat Khan, in Awadh and Nizam-ul-Mulk in Hyderabad (Deccan). Besides, the governors of Bihar, Orissa, Sindh and Kashmir also defied the Mughal authority while the Jats and Rohillas setup their sovereign states in the heart of the empire. By this time, the Sikhs were in revolt in the Punjab and the Marathas had emerged as a sovereign power in the Deccan. In 1737-38, Afghanistan was overrun by a Persian adventurer, called Nadir Shah, who invaded India and sacked Delhi in 1739 when Muhammad Shah *Rangila* formally held the reins of government as the Mughal emperor.

Nadir Shah's Invasion (1738-39)

Nadir Shah belonged to a poor Turkoman family of Khurasan (Iran). Born in 1688, he passed his early life in abject poverty as a shepherd but soon turned a 'robber' and became the ringleader of highwaymen during the reign of Shah Tahmasp. Taking advantage of the prevalent political disorders in the country, Iran was targeted by the foreign invaders, including the Afghans, Russians and Turks from various directions almost simultaneously. The Shah failed to stem the foreign aggression and the independence and integrity of the country was seriously endangered. It aroused the patriotic sentiments of Nadir Shah and his fellow dacoits who, almost overnight, turned into freedom-fighters. In 1732, Nadir Shah organised the rowing bands of free-booters and gangsters into a volunteer force of daredevil fighters and launched a successful struggle for the liberation of his country from foreign aggression. He thereby earned the gratitude of his countrymen and rose to become the *shahinshah* (emperor) in 1736 by transplanting the ruling dynasty of Iran. Though an illiterate person, he enjoyed popular support and full-cooperation from the Iranian bureaucracy in the discharge of his administrative functions.

Nadir Shah continued his military campaign against the foreign intruders and drove out the Russians and the Turks from the Iranian soil within a year of his accession to the throne. Thereafter, he liberated

Balkh, Herat and Qandahar from the hands of the Ghilzai Afghans and entered Afghanistan in May 1738 in hot chase of the Ghilzai fugitives. The Mughal governor of Kabul (incidentally, he was also named Nadir Khan and was the namesake of the invader), fled from Kabul without a fight towards the Khyber Pass for reasons of safety. Nadir Shah overran Kabul, Ghazni and Jalalabad and, following close upon the heels of the fugitive Mughal governor, crossed the Khyber and destroyed his army near Peshawar in November 1738. The easy victory over Afghanistan wetted the political ambitions of Nadir Shah. The decadent Mughal empire and 'the fabulous wealth' of India tempted him to invade Delhi and revive the memories of Amir Timur's invasion of 1398. Lahore fell in January 1739 when Zakariya Khan, the Mughal governor, offered submission to the invader after a half-hearted fight and saved his skin by declaring his change of loyalties; he paid twenty lacs of rupees as war indemnity and led the invader to Delhi via Sirhind, Ambala and Shahabad Markanda. Nadir Shah defeated the army of Muhammad Shah in a pitched battle near Karnal on February13, 1739 in which about twenty thousand Indian soldiers are said to have died fighting.

Muhammad Shah *Rangila* offered submission to Nadir Shah and welcomed him to the metropolis 'to the great chagrin and humiliation of the Mughal nobility and the populace of Delhi'. Nevertheless, the phantom Mughal emperor was treacherously put under arrest by the conqueror that got the *khutba* read in his name in the mosques of Delhi. Nadir Shah occupied the Red Fort of Delhi, took his residence in the imperial palace, and indulged in merry-making, while his victorious commanders and soldiers fleeced the public. They spread themselves in the countryside `to plunder princes and the people alike'. After a few days, a rumour spread in the capital that Nadir Shah had been assassinated. Thereupon, the people of Delhi killed some of his soldiers. It made Nadir Shah `mad with rage' and he ordered the general massacre (*katal-i-aam*) of the populace. The bloody carnage lasted six or seven hours and claimed more than twenty thousand innocent lives. The city of Delhi was sacked and the unarmed and hapless men, women and children were killed in cold blood by the army of occupation. The massacre was stopped only when Muhammad Shah personally fell at the feet of Nadir Shah and pleaded for mercy. Nadir Shah stayed in Delhi for about two months and returned to Iran just before the beginning of the rainy season, heavily laden with booty, amounting to 70 or 80 *crores*. The famous Peacock Throne (*Takhat-i-Taus*) and the

Koh-e-Noor diamond were also taken away by him along with thousands of horses, camels and elephants. According to Dr. H.R. Gupta, Nadir Shah allowed Muhammad Shah to rule over Delhi, but married his own son, Nasrullah Mirza, to a Mughal princess of Delhi, and annexed 'trans-Indus territories, comprising Afghanistan, Baluchistan, North-West Frontier, Sindh, and the four cis-Indus districts of the Punjab, including Gujarat, Aurangabad, Pasrur, and Sialkot (collectively known as the *Chahar Mahal*) to his Persian empire'. (*Marathas and Panipat*; *loc. cit*; p. 63).

The invasion of Nadir Shah marked the total dismemberment of the Mughal empire and end of the Mughal sovereignty. It cleared the way for the rise of the Marathas as a national power.

SECTION 4: AHMAD SHAH TO ALAMGIR II (1748-59)

Ahmad Shah ((1748-54)

Muhammad Shah *Rangila* died on April 26, 1748. His son Ahmad Shah, aged twenty-one and born of a dancing girl, was placed on the throne of Delhi by a coterie of the Mughal nobles, led by Safdar Jang. He was the nephew and son-in-law of Saadat Khan, the Nawab of Awadh, styled as Burhan-ul-Mulk. He had received investiture as the *Nawab* of Awadh from the hands of Nadir Shah in 1739 on the unnatural death by suicide of Burhan-ul-Mulk. Safdar Jang emerged as one of the ringleaders of the Turani nobles who had come to dominate the Mughal court ever since the fall of the Sayyad brothers. He took over as *wazir* of Ahmad Shah. As he held this office while retaining the governorship of Awadh, he and his successors became known as the Nawab Wazirs of Awadh.

Ahmad Shah was a non-entity as ruler. He was detested and held cheap by his ministers and the government officials. His mother was a woman of loose character who did not give up her 'lecherous ways even after her formal admission to the royal household as Queen Mother', with the high-sounding title of *Malika-i-Zamani*. Being a true replica of his mother, and devoid of any formal education or training in the art of government, Ahmad Shah adopted a dissolute course of life; he spent most of his time in bad company and further tarnished the image of royalty.

Marathas at the Centre-Stage of National Politics

The Marathas had attained sovereignty as the regional rulers during the very lifetime of Aurangzeb. Within a decade of his death, they made their presence felt at the echelons of power at Delhi and, while professing their loyalty to the Mughal crown as vassals, they secured legal and constitutional rights as the guardians and protectors of Aurangzeb's weak and imbecile scions. It was very clearly the case of a servant stepping into the shoes of his master to establish his position as his rightful successor as did the successive dynasties of the Mamluk (slave) Sultans of Delhi in the thirteenth century India. The Maratha *Chhatrapati* Shahu enjoyed a long reign of over forty years. He was a man of average abilities but he won the confidence and support of the people and semi-democratic national Maratha leadership, headed by the *Ashta-Pradhan,* to advance the interests of the sovereign Maratha state. He reposed full confidence in his Peshwa Balaji Vishwanath (1713-20), conferred on him the twin offices of *Peshwa* and *Senapati* in hereditary succession, and voluntarily handed over the royal powers to him. It made the Peshwa *de facto* as well as *de jure* ruler and made the *Chhatrapati* a symbolic or constitutional head of the state. The Peshwa setup his administrative headquarters at Poona while Shahu continued to hold his court at Satara to live a life of virtual retirement. By transferring the powers and functions of the crown to the hereditary family of the Peshwa, the *Chhatrapati* perpetuated the Maratha royal family as well as that of the Peshwas simultaneously.

The case of the Maratha constitutional monarchy was thus radically different from that of the Mughals. In the case of the latter, the weak Mughal princes were being held as puppets by their ambitious and self-seeking nobles much against their will; there was no bond of mutual consent and goodwill between them. There was no sanctity in the rightful hereditary succession of monarchy or any guarantee for the stability or perpetuation of the usurpers or the *de facto* ruling families of the nobles. They were constantly engaged in self-destructive games of power-politics to let down one another to the detriment of the empire. It explains the rise to power of Peshwa Balaji Vishwanath and consolidation of the Maratha kingdom by the collective action of all the Maratha stalwarts.

Baji Rao (1720-40), the son and successor of Balaji Vishwanath, conquered Malwa, including Bundelkhand, and Gujarat with the active participation of numerous other Maratha *sardars*. They were all granted extensive *jagirs* in hereditary succession by the Chhatrapati but as an indispensable part of the Maratha empire. The prominent among them were: (1) Raghoji Bhonsle of Nagpur (Berar); (2) Pillaji Gaekwar of Baroda (Gujarat); (3) Malhar Rao Holkar of Indore (Central India); and (4) Ranoji Sindhia of Ujjain (later Gwalior). They came to comprise 'the Maratha Confederacy' so-called under the leadership of the third Peshwa, Balaji Baji Rao (1740-61), and were akin to the hereditary provincial governors of *the* vast Maratha dominions, the supreme authority of which was exercised by the Peshwa. Such was the peculiar character of the feudal Maratha polity as it finally emerged in the second half of the eighteenth century.

The Marathas became an all-India power under Balaji Baji Rao, who aspired to bring about the unification of the whole country under the sovereign authority of the Maratha state. During the two decades of his rule, all the political rivals of the Marathas, including the Nizam of Hyderabad, Siddis of Janjira, and the Portuguese of Goa were humbled, and Maratha conquests extended from Kanya Kumari and Rameshwaram in the south to the foot of the Himalayas in the north, and the Khyber Pass in the northwest. The Marathas subjected the provinces of Bengal, Bihar and Orissa (Cuttack) to annual raids from 1742 to 1751 until Nawab Alivardi Khan made peace with them by ceding Orissa to the Maratha dominions in perpetuity. Delhi became the hub of Maratha political and military activities with effect from 1752, and they used the Mughal emperor as a mere tool in their hands to wield the imperial powers in his name and under his nominal suzerainty. The Peshwa's agents collected *chauth* in the heartland of northern India, including the Ganga Doab and modern Uttar Pradesh. The Jats and Rajput chiefs were made to acknowledge the suzerainty of the Maratha Chhatrapati, and the provinces of Lahore and Multan, besides the North-West Frontier and the Derajat, were incorporated into the Maratha dominions. The Marathas had become a national power, and Delhi the imperial capital of India, was under their control by the year 1760.

The Rise of Ahmad Shah Abdali

Nadir Shah was assassinated by some of his own disaffected Irani nobles in June 1747. Thereafter, one of his junior Afghan officers, named Ahmad Shah Abdali, who had commanded 'the Abdali Regiment' of Nadir Shah during his invasion of India in 1738-39, asserted his independence at Qandahar and Kabul. He retained Qandahar as his seat of governance. In his capacity as the successor of Nadir Shah, he claimed the overlordship of all the above territories of the Punjab and northwestern India which had earlier been ceded by

Muhammad Shah to his empire. It became the root-cause of his repeated invasions on India subsequently. He led as many as seven invasions on India from 1748 to 1767.

Invasions of Ahmad Shah Abdali: Ahmad Shah Abdali, the newly emerged ruler of Afghanistan since 1747, and the namesake of the phantom Mughal emperor, started his invasions about this time. His first two invasions in 1748 and 1749 were confined to the Punjab. The invader was induced to return to Kabul on the receipt of hefty tribute by Muin-ul-Mulk *alias* Mir Mannu, the Mughal governor of Lahore. The latter sent express appeals to Delhi for help but received no reinforcements. Abdali made his appearance on the Indian borders, in the winter of 1751, for the third time, on the pretext that Mir Mannu had failed to remit the promised tribute for the *Chahar Mahal* to him regularly. None from Delhi came forward for the defence of Lahore. Mannu suffered a defeat under the walls of Lahore on March 6, 1752, and next day offered unconditional surrender and change of loyalties to the invader. He paid a huge war indemnity to Abdali and signed a formal treaty of peace with him ceding the two provinces of Lahore and Multan, up to Sirhind to the Afghan empire. Abdali lost no time in dispatching his troops to take possession of Multan and also sent an envoy to Delhi for the ratification of the treaty by the Mughal emperor. About that time, Safdar Jang, the *wazir* of Ahmad Shah, was engaged in suppressing the revolts of the Bangash Pathans and Rohillas in Awadh. Dreaded by the memories of Nadir Shah's attack on Delhi during the reign of his father, Ahmad Shah, on the advice of his eunuch adviser Javed Khan, immediately affixed his signatures on the treaty, under the royal seal, on April 3, 1752. Thus the Punjab, together with the previously ceded provinces of Baluchistan, Sindh and the northwest frontier, were all cut off from the Mughal empire forever.

The Marathas at Delhi (1752): Safdar Jang returned to Delhi on May 5, accompanied by 50,000 Maratha troops as his allies to challenge Abdali. The Marathas were commanded by Malhar Rao Holkar and Jayappa Sindhia, the lieutenants of Peshwa Balaji Baji Rao, with whom Safdar Jang had concluded an agreement, on behalf of the Mughal emperor, to protect the imperial capital from its internal as well as external foes, including Ahmad Shah Abdali. In return, they were to receive 50 *lakhs* of rupees in cash from the emperor besides 'the grant of *chauth* from provinces of the Punjab and Sindh, and the appointment of the Peshwa as *subedar* of Ajmer and Agra, including the *faujdari* of

Nagpur and Mathura'. He was taken aback to know that the Mughal emperor had already bartered away the major part of his dominions to the invader. Meanwhile, Abdali had decamped from Lahore on April 21, and he returned to Afghanistan via Multan, Sindh and Baluchistan to assert his claim over these Indian territories. Safdar Jang pacified the Marathas by making a part-payment of the promised amount. The Maratha commanders did not deem it fit to take sides in the mutual conflict between the emperor and his *wazir*, and returned on their specified mission to spread their sway in the North as per the instructions of the Peshwa.

Nevertheless, it was too much for the all-powerful *wazir*, Safdar Jang, to tolerate 'the irresponsible and cowardly action of the puppet Mughal emperor. His eunuch adviser Javed Khan was put to death at his bidding; and in the political wrangles that followed between the various power-hungry nobles, Safdar Jang made an exit from Delhi after obtaining confirmation of the viceroyalty of Awadh and Allahabad, and the office of the *wazir* was, ultimately passed on to Imad-ul-Mulk, a grandson of the late Nizam-ul-Mulk of Hyderabad (Deccan). Extremely selfish and power-hungry, like his grandfather, he dismayed Ahmad Shah and members of his family by his highly autocratic and dictatorial attitude. Imad-ul-mulk was very cunning and suspicious by nature and was 'treacherous to the backbone'. On June 2, 1754, he dethroned Ahmad Shah and threw him along with his mother into prison. He brought out another Mughal prince, Azizuddin, from the royal prison and placed him on the throne with the title of Alamgir II. After about a week, the deposed emperor Ahmad Shah and his mother were both blinded and later put to death.

Alamgir II (1754-59)

Azizuddin, styled Alamgir II, was the second son of Jahandar Shah and was about 55 years old at the time of his accession. As he had spent the best part of his life in royal captivity since 1713, and knew nothing about administration or fighting skills, he could not but play in the hands of his *wazir*, Imad-ul-Mulk. Thoroughly humbled by the force of circumstances, he was devoid of any ambition or zest for life. Otherwise, he shunned pleasures and spent his time in prayers or reading books. Of course, he was always kept by his crafty *wazir* and kingmaker under his vigilant eyes, either in his own camp or under the care of his most trusted guards. Thus Alamgir II was 'as good a captive as he had been in jail' before his installation as dummy emperor.

The Fourth Invasion of Abdali (1756-57): During the reign of Alamgir II, Imad-ul-Mulk made an abortive attempt to re-establish the Mughal control over the Punjab. Twice he led the forces under his personal command to the Punjab; once he had to retrace his steps to Delhi from Panipat because of mutiny in his troops; and at the second time, he did not dare to move beyond Ludhiana for fear of direct confrontation with Ahmad Shah Abdali. Nevertheless, it invited the wrath of Abdali, who took it as an intrusion into his territories and launched his fourth invasion in December 1756. He reoccupied Lahore without a fight and from there made straight for Delhi. Abdali faced little opposition and entered the capital in triumph on January 28, 1757. Imad-ul-Mulk surrendered to the Afghan invader with utmost humility and was granted pardon. Abdali stayed in Delhi for about a month. During this period, Alamgir II was held as virtual prisoner by Abdali and all the Mughal nobles, including the *wazir* remained in attendance upon the victor and were mercilessly fleeced. Before his return to Kabul, Abdali annexed the whole of the Punjab, including even the 'Sirhind division' up to the town of Panipat and the River Yamuna. These territories were placed by him under the charge of his son Timur Shah, assisted by a large number of experienced Afghan officers with his headquarters at Lahore. Prince Timur was married to a daughter of Alamgir II to strengthen his claim over the Indian dominions. Ahmad Shah Abdali solemnized his own marriage with two young princesses of the royal Mughal blood; one was a sixteen year old daughter of the late emperor Muhammad Shah Rangila, and the other was the daughter of the ex-emperor Ahmad Shah. In addition, the victor carried with him to Kabul 16 other ladies of the Mughal household and numerous concubines and maid servants' by way of their rehabilitation'. In April 1757, he reached Qandahar richly laden with booty worth crores of rupees and hundreds of horses, elephants, mules and other beasts of burden. At the time of his departure from Delhi, Abdali reinstated Alamgir II as the emperor and Imad-ul-Mulk was allowed to continue as his *wazir* but he made the appointment of his Indian ally, Najib Khan Rohilla, as the *mir bakhshi* of the emperor and conferred the title of Najib-ud-Daulah on him. He was also made the plenipotentiary of Ahmad Shah Abdali in Delhi and entrusted the responsibility of protecting the Mughal emperor.

SECTION 5: MUGHALS, MARATHAS AND ABDALI

The decline of Mughal empire and the resultant invasions of Nadir

Shah and Ahmad Shah Abdali had started a fresh wave of foreign immigrants and adventurers from Afghanistan, Iran and other Muslim countries of central Asia to seek their fortunes in India. They were received with open arms by the Muslim chieftains, provincial governors, military officers and all sections of the Muslim society as they added to their numbers and increased their manpower. They included, among others, the Rohillas and Bangash Pathans- the two tribes of the Afghans, who had migrated to India *en mass* and made settlements in the fertile Ganga valley. They welcomed the expansion of Abdali's influence in India and began to look towards him as their leader and saviour. In support of this contention, it may be mentioned that when Abdali was preparing to return to Afghanistan after the successful conclusion of his fourth invasion, thousands of the Afghan settlers along the river-bed of the Yamuna around Kunjpura, near Panipat, had presented him a purse of 20 lacs of rupees as *nazrana* to mark their presence in India as his faithful allies and supporters.

It aroused Abdali's ambitions and encouraged him to nurture imperial designs towards India. No wonder, he began to dream of transplanting the now defunct Mughal dynasty of Delhi in successive stages. He thereby became a serious rival of the Marathas, who were also nourishing similar designs under the leadership of the Peshwas. The entry of Marathas and Abdali in the imperial politics of India posed a serious threat to the ambitions of some of the powerful Mughal nobles, who were already striving to establish their sovereignty in various parts of the country on the ruins of the Mughal empire. Therefore, after the success of the fourth invasion of Abdali, there started a triple contest for supremacy among the Mughal nobility, the Marathas and the Afghans, with their eyes fixed on the imperial capital of Delhi, with effect from the year 1757, to be very precise. All of these contenders to the imperial authority of the country showed eagerness to acquire control over Delhi and exploit the name of the phantom Mughal emperors to meet their political ends.

Marathas in Control of Agra and Delhi (1757)

All the political arrangements made by Ahmad Shah Abdali at Delhi and Lahore during his fourth invasion crumbled down before long. A vast Maratha army despatched by the third Peshwa, Balaji Baji Rao, under the command of his younger brother Raghunath Rao, reached Agra in May 1757 when Abdali had hardly crossed the Indus on his way back to Qandahar. The Marathas overran the Ganga Doab and made their appearance at Delhi in July. At that time, Abdali's agent, Najib-ud-Daulah, was in control of the Red Fort of Delhi and the puppet Mughal emperor, Alamgir II, was being held by him as a virtual prisoner in his hands while his *wazir*, Imad-ul-Mulk, was kept in surveillance by the Rohilla chief. But for fear of the Marathas, both of them might have been put to death or held in imprisonment to make way for the setup of his personal rule at Delhi either on behalf of Abdali or as his vassal. He would not mind bringing India under the permanent subjugation of the Shah of Afghanistan. Imad-ul-Mulk and the Mughal emperor both were aware of Najib's evil intentions and rightly apprehended persecution at his hands. That is why they became anxious to get rid of Najib at the earliest. The very first thing that Imad-ul-Mulk did, after the departure of Abdali from Delhi in April 1757, was to send his secret envoy, Raja Nagarmal, to contact the Peshwa's diplomatic envoy, Mahadeo Hingane, in the Doab, and seek his help to secure liberation from the clutches of 'the traitor' Najib-ud-Daulah.

Expulsion of Najib from Delhi: On the other hand, Najib also did not sit idle on his oars at Delhi. As a religious fanatic, he was deeply influenced by a strong movement, started by Shah Waliullah, an orthodox Muslim theologian of Delhi, about that time, 'to keep the whole of *Hindustan* under the Muslim rule' by all means. Najib-ud-Daulah dreaded the Marathas and strove to avoid head-on collision with them single-handed. Therefore, he kept a close watch, through his agents, about the activities of the Marathas at Agra and in the Doab. He sent the intelligence about the arrival of the Maratha army in the Doab and its impending march upon Delhi to Abdali at Qandahar. At the same time, he pe-empted the Mughal emperor and his *wazir* by sending his envoy with a letter to Malhar Rao Holkar, in which he sought forgiveness and pleaded for mercy for his dubious role as the agent of the foreign invader. Nevertheless, the Marathas had to fight against Najib to wrest the Red Fort of Delhi from him on September 6, 1757. Najib was taken prisoner but the wily Rohilla chief secured his liberation 'by playing upon the tender sentiments' of Holkar; perhaps, he had bribed the deputy Maratha chief with a hefty amount, including cart-loads of gold and silver ornaments to secure his freedom. Najib-ud-Daulah disappeared in the Ganga valley to muster support from the Muslims, particularly the foreigners, who had migrated to India from Afghanistan and Iran in the recent past, in the cause of Ahmad Shah Abdali.

The Marathas liberated Alamgir II from the hands of Najib-ud-Daulah and re-installed him on the throne as their nominal 'suzerain', and also allowed Imad-ul-Mulk to continue as his *wazir.* During the next two months, they overran the whole of the Upper Doab and Najib fled across the Ganga to Najibabad. Because of the shortsightedness and callousness of Malhar Rao Holkar - the deputy Maratha commander, the Rohilla chief, the agent of Abdali and sworn enemy of 'the Maratha *kafirs*', was allowed to go scot free without molestation.

Conquest of Lahore and Northwest Frontier: As for the Punjab, the Sikh bands plundered the royal entourage of Prince Timur Shah on his way from Delhi to Lahore at the very beginning of his rule as the Afghan viceroy of the province. Jahan Khan, the Afghan commander, was, therefore, compelled to organise punitive expeditions against the Sikhs and sought the support of some Muslim fanatics for their suppression. He defiled and destroyed the holy temple of the Sikhs at Amritsar and filled its tank (*sarover*) with debris. Thousands of the Sikhs fell fighting against the Afghans in this bloody carnage. Adina Beg, the *faujdar* of Jalandhar Doab, raised a standard of revolt against Abdali's rule, however; and made a compromise with two Sikh chiefs, Sodhi Barbhag Singh and Jassa Singh Ahluwalia, with the object of liberating the Punjab from Abdali's control. Their joint forces defeated an Afghan army at Mahalpur (district Hoshiarpur) and the triumphant Sikhs started loot and plunder around Lahore. A fresh contingent of Afghan troops, sent by Jahan Khan against them, was also worsted by the Sikhs on January 6, 1758. Yet another Sikh chief, Jassa Singh Ramgarhia, became active with his armed followers in the Jalandhar Doab and put its Pathan *faujdar* to great straits.

The Marathas, who had by that time become the masters of Delhi and the Ganga Doab, were pleased to know of the above developments in the Punjab. In March-April 1758, they conquered Sirhind and Lahore in collaboration with Adina Beg and the Sikhs. On the approach of the Marathas, Prince Timur and his commander Jahan Khan fled from Lahore without a fight; The Marathas entered Lahore on 20 April and converted it into a base of operations for their further advance. They chased the retreating Afghans up to the Indus without meeting any resistance from any quarter but Prince Timur was successful in taking back his army and treasures intact to Afghanistan. Raghunath Rao left a strong body of Maratha troops on the Indus under the command of Datta Patel to protect the Indian borders against foreign intruders. Besides, Tukoji Holkar, with 10,000 Maratha soldiers, was posted at Peshawar, and Narsoji Pandit took charge of the fort of Attock but with a contingent of 4,000 troops only. Meanwhile Raghunath Rao had despatched Bapuji Trimbak with 6,000 Maratha troops to acquire control of Multan. The local population and officials of Multan readily submitted to the Maratha authority in spite of the fact that they were too small in number to maintain their hold on the province for long. Bapuji is also credited to have led his troops across the Indus to extend the Maratha sway over Dera Ghazi Khan and its neighbourhood. Thus nature provided a golden opportunity to the Marathas to establish their rule over the whole of the Punjab and northwestern India, up to Attock and the Khyber Pass, although the spell of their rule proved very short-lived.

The Maratha Settlement of the Punjab and Delhi: The easy victory of the Marathas over northern and northwestern India, including the vast territories and historic towns like Agra, Delhi, Sirhind, Lahore, Multan, Peshawar and Attock, etc. turned the heads of the Maratha commanders and gave them a totally false perception of their military prowess and capabilities. Within three months of their arrival in the Punjab, Raghunath Rao *alias* Raghoba and Malhar Rao Holkar decided to return to the south with the bulk of their forces, leaving behind only skeletal troops to man the various strategic posts. They entrusted the government of the Punjab 'on lease' to Adina Beg on the promise of remitting 75 lacs of rupees as annual tribute to the Peshwa, before their return. In their hurry to leave the north, the Maratha commanders simply glossed over the fact that they were leaving behind the whole of northwestern India (comprising modern Pakistan and much besides), at the mercy of the same foreign invader in shining armour beyond the Khyber, from whose hands they had liberated it very recently. For want of time, they did not attempt even to establish direct contact with any of the Sikh leaders, and left it to Adina Beg to deal with them as he thought fit.

It is held that Raghunath Rao, the younger brother of the Peshwa, having been brought up in luxury in the cozy atmosphere of the home front, could not bear the strain of camp life in an entirely unfamiliar landscape and its people for long. Perhaps, the Peshwa himself had cut short the stay of the Maratha commanders in the north as their services were needed in the Deccan. Be as it might, the Maratha commanders treated the Sikhs almost as a non-entity in the Punjab affairs and were taken by the expressions of loyalty and friendly overtures of Adina

Beg, the nominee of the dummy Mughal emperor, in whose name they intended to conquer the Punjab. The Marathas thus intended to maintain the fiction of the Mughal sovereignty in the Punjab which was not acceptable to the Sikhs. The Marathas suffered from lack of vision and diplomatic skill as they failed to forge friendly alliances with the more agile and freedom loving Sikhs, Rajputs and Jats, in their national struggle against the foreign invader while Abdali had successfully created pockets of Indian allies and traitors by raising 'a cry of *Jehad* against the infidels' on the eve of the third battle of Panipat.

The Maratha political settlement of Delhi and the Punjab proved even more fragile than the one which had been made earlier by Ahmad Shah Abdali after the success of his fourth invasion. Najib Khan (now styled Najib-ud-Daulah), a powerful Afghan agent of Abdali and a religious fanatic, was left free to consolidate his position in the Ganga valley. He had carved out a big estate, now located by the famous town of Najibabad, near Saharanpur in modern Uttar Pradesh. Ever since his eviction from Delhi by the Marathas in September 1757, he had been pestering Abdali to come again and liberate Delhi from the hands of the 'the infidel Marathas'. He created a strong anti-Maratha front in the heart of northern India by persuading the Rohillas and other Muslim chieftains to take up the cause of the Afghan invader. Najib remained in constant touch with Abdali at Qandahar and passed on the intelligence about all the political developments at Delhi and its neighbourhood to him regularly.

The Maratha Commanders Leave Lahore and Delhi Unprotected: Raghunath Rao and Holkar left Lahore with the bulk of their forces on May 10, 1758. They did not bother even to pay a casual visit to Delhi, the imperial capital of India, to see the efficacy of the arrangements made by them for its security in their absence; they did not wait even for the arrival of their substitute Maratha commanders from the south, to whom they ought to have handed over the charge of their assignments before making their exit. They reached Karnal early in June 1758 and halted there for a few days. Both of the Maratha leaders, accompanied by their women, paid a visit to Thanesar for a holy bath on the *Somavati Amaavas* on 5 June. Thereafter, they decamped from Karnal and marched to the south post-haste, separately and through different routes. It was nothing short of dereliction of their official duties for which not only the Marathas but also the country and its people had to pay very dearly.

Turmoil in the Punjab: As soon as the Marathas turned their back, the Punjab was ablaze. Adina Beg, the agent of the Mughal emperor in the Punjab, did not trust the Sikhs. The Sikhs coveted Lahore but Adina Beg refused to share political power with them. There was no agreement or understanding between the two parties. Therefore, instead of making an amicable settlement with them, Adina Beg denounced the Sikhs as 'outlaws' and launched a fresh campaign of persecution against them. His two expeditions against the Sikhs remained indecisive and he died a premature death on September 15, 1758. The Sikhs were left with no other alternative but to 'assert themselves and wreak their vengeance upon their persecutors'. The junior Maratha commanders in the Punjab, with highly inadequate troops and without any provisions, were isolated and became apprehensive of their personal safety. Khwaja Mirza, who officiated for Adina Beg at Lahore, apparently on behalf of the Peshwa, recalled the Maratha detachments from Attock and Peshawar to safeguard his own position at Lahore. The whole of the Punjab and the northwestern India lay undefended and prostrate before the prospective invader to be trampled under the feet of his soldiers whenever he so pleased.

The Changing Fortunes of Delhi: Breakdown of the Maratha settlement in the Punjab had its parallel repercussion at Delhi also. The phantom Mughal emperor, Alamgir II, and his *wazir*, Imad-ul-Mulk, felt insecure because of the inadequate arrangements made by their new masters – the Marathas, for the defence of the imperial capital. The departure of the Maratha commanders from the north signalled the re-emergence of Najib-ud-Daulah from his hideout which posed an immediate threat to the survival of Alamgir II and Imad-ud-Daulah. The *wazir* sent repeated appeals to the Maratha representatives in the north and the Peshwa but there was no immediate relief in sight. The puppet Mughal emperor, Alamgir II, spent a miserable life as the virtual prisoner of his all-powerful *wazir,* but the revival of a fresh struggle between Imad-ul-Mulk and Najib for the occupation of Delhi made him apprehensive about his own safety. In his desperation, the emperor wrote secretly to Abdali at Qandahar, apprehending danger to his life at the hands of his unscrupulous *wazir*, Imad-ul-Mulk, pleaded for his protection as his vassal and insisted on his early next visit to India to safeguard his imperial interests; and so did Najib and his associates.

The Change of Maratha Guards in the North

Raghunath reached Poona on September 16, 1758 while Malhar Rao

Holkar returned to his permanent headquarters at Indore. The Peshwa was not satisfied to hear of what he and his deputy had done in the north. Holkar was summoned by the Peshwa to see him immediately but the latter delayed his visit to Poona because of his purported illness. He met the Peshwa only in December 1758 to apprise him of the provisional arrangements made by him at Delhi. By that time, Najib-ud-Daulah and other agents of Ahmad Shah Abdali had consolidated their positions and matured their plans to take on the Marathas in league with the foreign invader.

Meanwhile, the Peshwa had nominated the substitutes of Raghunath and Holkar. The supreme command of the northern forces was entrusted to Dattaji Sindhia while Jankoji Sindhia received appointment as his deputy. They proceeded towards the north separately, at different times and through different routes. Their forces made junction at Rewari in November 1758 and reached Delhi early in December. 'The new Maratha guards of the north were neither familiar with the topography and climate of their vast field of operations nor possessed firsthand knowledge about the nature, character and loyalties of the various dramatis personae of the political arena of Delhi and the Punjab. Their armies encamped along the Yamuna, on both of its banks, at sufficient distance from the capital to avoid any inconvenience or hardships to its inhabitants. They sent a contingent of Maratha troops to deal with Najib in the district of Saharanpur while an army under Dattaji reached Machchiwara in the Punjab and encamped on the southern bank of the Satluj in March 1759. As there was no news or rumours of any threat from Abdali, the new Maratha commander did not bother to visit Lahore, and instead, called for Sabaji Patel from Peshawar to his presence at Machchiwara to apprise him of the latest developments in the Punjab. He left Sabaji Patel to take care of the Punjab and northwest frontier with a few other junior commanders and himself returned to Delhi in May 1759 for the suppression of Najib in the Ganga valley. Finding the Maratha post at Peshawar without its commander, the disaffected Afghans of the frontier march on Peshawar in strength and took the citadel with heavy losses to the besieged Maratha garrison. The news about the fall of Peshawar to the Afghans was received with jubilation at Kabul.

The Fifth Invasion of Ahmad Shah Abdali: Ahmad Shah Abdali invaded India for the fifth time in October 1759. He and his commander Jahan Khan left Qandahar with a preconceived two-pronged attack on India. Jahan Khan proceeded, at the head of 20,000 storm troopers, through Kabul and the Khyber Pass while Abdali himself marched through the Bolan Pass with 40,000 horsemen, accompanied by heavy field-guns. On stepping into the Indian territories, the invader was joined by the troops of Nasir Khan, the Baluch chief of Qalat, and so did the two Afghan tribal chiefs, Begu and Khan Zaman of Bannu. His forces continued to swell in India, right up to the third battle of Panipat in January 1761, by the constant inflow of his Rohilla and Afghan supporters and other disgruntled Indian elements, who were irked by the rising power of the Marathas in north India. By the first week of November, the whole of the northwestern frontier and Punjab were overrun by the invader. The Maratha troops under Sabaji and all other junior commanders, posted at various stations, including Multan, Peshawar. Attock and Lahore fled before the invaders and many of them were completely annihilated. Besides, the fleeing Marathas were also put to plunder by the *gawars* or rustic village folk in the Jalandhar Doab while crossing the Satluj. Unlike the Marathas, the Sikhs gave a better account of themselves in obstructing the path of the invader. They did not allow Abdali to take on Lahore without a fight in which more than two thousand Afghan soldiers were killed and their commander Jahan Khan was wounded. As observed by H.R. Gupta,

> 'Some aspects of Indian history present a sad spectacle. All of its decisive battles have been fought far into the interior, nearly 900 kms away from the Khyber Pass. The government which could not guard the country's frontiers, and which allowed the invader to cover such a long distance unimpeded had no right to exist. On this occasion, the Marathas were not taken unawares. They knew that a fresh Durrani invasion was as sure as death. They had about two years and a half to make preparations. Was it not criminal negligence on their part to ignore the defence of their frontiers? (*Marathas and Panipat*; p. 124)

The Fall of Sirhind (November 27, 1759): After making provisional arrangements for the administration of Lahore, Abdali crossed the Beas at the ferry of Goindwal on November 20, 1759, and moved with his main army, at a leisurely pace, along the foothills of Shiwaliks, while Jahan Khan made straight for Sirhind with his advance guard. The historic fort of Sirhind fell to the invader without a fight as it was deserted by the Marathas without a fight on 27 November. Abdali reached there with the main army via Ropar by mid-December.

The Tragic End of Alamgir II (November 29, 1759): Ahmad Shah Abdali's fourth invasion and the fall of Lahore to the Afghan invader, early in November 1759, spread consternation in north India. It had immediate repercussions on the political developments at Delhi. Imad-ul-Mulk had intercepted some secret letters, written by Alamgir II to Abdali at Qandahar and Shuja-ud-Daulah, the Nawab Wazir of Awadh, against him. It enraged the *wazir* who tightened his grip over the puppet emperor and held him as a virtual prisoner under his watchful eyes. The news about the conquest of Sirhind by Abdali reached Delhi on 29 November, and, that very day, Alamgir II was treacherously murdered by the agents of Imad-ul-Mulk at a deserted place in the neighbourhood of Kotla Firoze Shah lest he might fall into the hands of Najib-ud-Daulah or Ahmad Shah Abdali. His badly mutilated and 'stark naked' body was thrown on the bank of the Yamuna from where some citizens of Delhi picked it up and buried it near the tomb of Humayun after a couple of days. Imad-ul-Mulk brought out another Mughal prince from the royal prison, named Muhi-ul-Mulk, a grandson of Kam Bakhsh, who was proclaimed the new Mughal emperor with the title of Shah Jahan III although there were no takers for his fresh gimmick.

Abdali came to know about the ghastly murder of the Mughal protégé on his arrival at Sirhind in December. It infuriated the invader and hastened his march towards Delhi.

The Battle of Taraori (December 24, 1759): Abdali reached Ambala on December 20, 1759. He was kept fully informed about the movements of the Maratha forces by the scouts of Najib. Dattaji Sindhia had crossed over the Yamuna with his army, from the Doab towards Panipat, south of Kunjpura, two days earlier, to block the passage of the invader to Delhi. Meanwhile, Imad-ul-Mulk had also moved out of Delhi with Mughal troops and made a junction with the Maratha army at Karnal. Abdali, therefore, made a dash for Delhi to overtake the Marathas and prevent them from consolidating their hold on the capital. At Taraori, his soldiers were provided with 'scarlet caps by the Afghans of Kunjpura', on the instructions of Najib Khan, 'as a mark of distinction as *mujahids*' or the 'defenders of Islam'. On 24 December, the advance columns of the adversaries collided with each other near Taraori. The Afghans were defeated and fell back, with the Marathas and the Mughals in their hot pursuit. Abdali, who was in close contact with his advance guard, at once sent reinforcements under the command of his renowned general, Shah Pasand Khan. Accordingly, a fresh contingent of 5,000 troops, with scarlet caps on their heads, suddenly intercepted the pursuers. At their sight, the Mughal troops of Imad-ul-Mulk 'disengaged and quietly slipped away'. The treacherous conduct of their Mughal allies exposed the Maratha guards to the sharp 'musket fire' of the Afghan mobile cavalry and took a heavy toll of their lives. Abdali, instead of challenging the main Maratha force, hurriedly withdrew his troops from Taraori, and, in the darkness of night, crossed over the Yamuna into the Ganga Doab.

Abdali had started playing 'hide-and-seek' game with the antagonists, under the guidance of his local agents, headed by Najib, to the great bewilderment of the new Maratha commanders who knew nothing about the surrounding landscape and credentials of their local scouts and guides. According to the proverbial saying: 'coming events cast their shadow before', the minor skirmish of Taraori, accompanied by the incident of 'scarlet caps', set the trend for the future course of events in the armed conflagration between Abdali and the Marathas. The Maratha commanders took note of it with concern but what was going to follow completely nonplussed them.

Death of Dattaji Sindhia at Barari Ghat (January 9, 1760): The sudden change of route by Abdali, with his huge army, made Dattaji apprehensive of Delhi's safety. He decamped from Karnal with his entire force and hastened towards Delhi lest it might fall into the hands of the Afghan invader and his Indian allies. The invader also marched towards Delhi through the Ganga Doab. Najib met him at Saharanpur and placed his entire army at his disposal. He furnished enormous food supplies and other provisions for Abdali's troops. Najib's soldiers moved ahead of the Afghan army and escorted it to Delhi while hundreds of his scouts hovered around the Maratha army on the other side of the Yamuna and posted him with their latest movements. Abdali reached the outskirts of Delhi and pitched his tents at Luni, on the eastern bank of the river, at a distance of hardly 10 kms from the Red Fort.

Dattaji rightly anticipated that the next major encounter with Abdali could not be delayed for long. He also led his troops towards Delhi, and, on January 4, 1760, pitched his tents at the Barari Ghat, in the proximity of the Afghan camp at Luni, with the partially dry bed of the Yamuna separating them. The Maratha soldiers were deputed to keep a vigil at all the fords of the Yamuna in the neighbourhood of Delhi to check the infiltration of the Afghans. On the night of 8-9 January1760, Abdali took the initiative to probe the Maratha defences and sent a column of camels and small elephants, each carrying a pair of light field-guns and the artillerymen. They crossed the water channel of their side and took cover in the wild growth of bushes and shrubs on the raised tableland in the midst of the dry bed of the river. On the winter morning of 9 January, visibility was very poor because of dense fog; but the intruders were sighted when some of them showed up on the sandy bed. A small body of the Maratha guards, led by Sabaji Patel, some on horse backs and others on foot, and armed with only swords and spears, at once crossed the stream of their side to confront the intruders. They were met by a hail of bullets from the invisible musketeers, from behind the reeds and bushes, and were soon overpowered by the Afghans. The unlucky Maratha chief, who had rushed to the spot to take stock of the situation, instead of ordering some one of his juniors to take the field with a contingent, himself jumped into the fray with his personal guards without a second thought. In the barrage of deadly fire from the opposite side, a chance bullet struck Dattaji dead instantly. His deputy Jankoji Sindhia, who rushed to his aid, also received a shot and fell down unconscious. Jotiba, the younger brother of Dattaji and some other Maratha officers, who were in the train of their Commander, also fell fighting in the dry bed of the river.

The Marathas Retreat to Kotputli (Jaipur): The debacle of Barari Ghat was a mere skirmish like that of Taraori. Jankoji was taken back to safety and the Afghan combatants were also withdrawn from the bed of the river by Abdali for a while. Truth of the matter came to light only when Najib's men spread in the dry river bed to collect the trophies of war and assess the enemy's losses. It was Najib's preceptor, Qutubshah Rohilla, who discovered and recognised the dead body of Dattaji Sindhia; he cut off his head and took it to his disciple, who, in turn, carried it to his master, Ahmad Shah Abdali. According to some, Abdali intended to cross the river at Barari Ghat; if so, he must have been ignorant of the exact deployment of the Maratha troops on the opposite side of the Yamuna; otherwise, he might not have attempted to do so in the face of the main Maratha force. No wonder, he jumped on his feet to discover the prized catch and sent the flying columns of his horsemen and others to take on the fleeing Maratha soldiers.

On the other hand, the Maratha army had been arranged in battle array and was fully prepared for the combat; but the sudden fall of their leader non-plussed the junior Maratha leadership. They immediately decamped and fled for their dear lives. Most of them retreated towards Kotputli in Jaipur state, which was their nearest halting station enroute to the Deccan. They carried their wounded deputy commander Jankoji with them and reached their destination on January 15, 1760, without much inconvenience, but those of them who fled towards Delhi were hotly pursued by the Afghans and Rohillas much beyond the imperial capital, and hundreds of them lost their lives. On regaining consciousness, Jankoji took command of the Marathas during their flight to Kotputli. They soon overtook the non-combatants and the Maratha families who had been sent by Dattaji from Delhi for Rewari only a couple of days before his death; they were all safely escorted to Kotputli. All the Marathas, ultimately, assembled at Kotputli, where Malhar Rao Holkar reached with reinforcements soon thereafter to their great relief.

The Marathas retreated but were not defeated or disheartened. Jankoji, being young and inexperienced, voluntarily handed over the command of the entire Maratha camp to Holkar. The latter, after holding consultations with the fugitive officers, despatched the non-combatants with families, under the charge of Govind Pant Bundele, to Poona on 23 January. The very next day, Holkar ordered the Marathas to retrace their steps towards Delhi to engage the Afghan invaders until the arrival of reinforcements and regular incumbent of the supreme command from the south.

Abdali in Control of Delhi

The Afghan troops entered the city of Delhi before the nightfall of January 9, 1760. The city had already been deserted by most of its inhabitants, and the rest of them, belonging to 'the lower strata of the society, had shut themselves behind doors in their homes. Next morning, Najib reported to Abdali at Luni that 'Imad-ul-Mulk and his Mughal bureaucracy and soldiery had fled the metropolis earlier, and that the Red Fort was lying totally unprotected and defenseless. It was in the possession of the new Mughal princeling, styled Shah Jahan II, who had been placed on the throne, after the murder of Alamgir II by his *wazir*. Abdali at once declared him under his protection and instructed his lieutenants not to put the puppet Mughal emperor and his retainers to any embarrassment.' (Advanced Study; iv, p. 270)

Ahmad Shah Abdali stayed at Luni for another two weeks while permitting his soldiers to carry on loot and plunder in and around Delhi. He neither overthrew the Mughal dynasty nor effected any change in its administrative set-up but deputed his officer, Yaqub Ali

Khan, to charge of Delhi as its governor and instructed him to recruit a militia from among the local inhabitants (read Muslims) to restore law and order and arrange for the collection of revenues. He entered the town un-announced as there was none to greet him on behalf of the citizens of the capital. Abdali was fully aware of the fact that, before securing a decisive victory against the Marathas and their Indian allies in the North, he could not assert his claim to be the master of Delhi. Therefore, he deployed the best of his troops to hold Delhi firmly in his hands and left with the bulk of his forces, on 27 January, to subjugate the Ganga valley and prepare for the final round of the contest against his imperial rivals.

From January 9, 1760 to January 14, 1761, when the rival claimants for the imperial power of India fought the Third Battle of Panipat, both the parties had full one year at their disposal to arm themselves and consolidate their position before measuring their swords with each other. During this long period, Ahmad Shah Abdali received no fresh supplies from Kabul or Qandahar, but exerted himself to the full in collecting the material resources and mustering the support of all the anti-Maratha elements and Indian chieftains in his fight against the adversaries.

Abdali's first target of attack was Suraj Mal, the Jat chief of Bharatpur, who had given shelter to Imad-ul-Mulk, the Mughal *wazir.* The Jats put up resistance and refused to offer submission or payment of tribute. Abdali made a forced entry into the Jat territories and laid siege to the stronghold of Dig. Suraj Mal remained at Bharatpur but the besieged Jat garrison stubbornly defended the fort and inflicted heavy losses on the besiegers. Without standing on prestige or making it an issue, Abdali quietly raised the siege and vacated the Jat territories as he did not want to fritter away his energy and resources before settling his scores with the Marathas. A Maratha contingent was confronted and repulsed by the Afghan troops near Sikandrabad on 4 March but they were not pursued beyond Agra. On the advice of Najib-ud-Daulah, however, Abdali overran the *pargana* of Koil (modern Aligarh) that belonged to Suraj Mal, by wresting the fort of Ramgarh from its Jat governor. In this enterprise, Najib, with his army, formed the advance guard of the invader. Najib-ud-Daulah persuaded his master to setup his headquarters at the town of Koil, now renamed as Aligarh, so close to Delhi, and spend his rainy season there, while making preparations for his next encounter with the fresh Maratha armies from the Deccan. (Nuruddin Hussain, *Najib-ud-Daulah*; p. 32).

Accordingly, Ahmad Shah Abdali pitched up his tents at Aligarh, and unlike his previous practice, made up his mind to overstay in India to give a fillip to his imperial designs. The Marathas had some isolated posts in the region, all of which, with the exception of Etawah, were overrun by Najib in collaboration with Abdali's troops.

Shuja-ud-Daulah, the Nawab Wazir of Awadh and Allahabad, had very cordial relations with the Marathas. He was successfully prevailed upon by the diplomatic overtures of Naib-ud-Daulah to join the invader's camp. 'Hereafter, following the example of Najib, Shuja-ud-Daulah also began to play the dubious game of conducting deceitful parleys with the Jats and the Marathas, by feigning friendship with them as before'. (Advanced Study; iv, p. 273).

Arrival of Fresh Maratha Armies in the North

The Peshwa entrusted the command of the Maratha forces in northern India to Sadashiv Rao, popularly known as Bhau Saheb or simply Bhau (brother); he was the son of Chimnaji Appa and a cousin of the Peshwa Balaji Baji Rao. Aged about 29, he had earned reputation as a brilliant military general and financier. Unfortunately, he was not given complete freedom 'to decide matters in his own responsibility' because the seventeen years old son of the Peshwa, named Vishwas Rao, was formerly appointed as the supreme commander of the Maratha forces. According to Sardesai, Bhau left Patdur (near Jalna) on March 14, 1760, 'with 30,000 select and well-armed troops, with the best military equipment and the finest artillery, the best horses and the choicest elephants'. They included 8,000 musketeers and artillerymen, trained in the European fashion, who were equipped with 200 pieces heavy field-guns. The Maratha army was manned by a galaxy of seasoned military officers. Bhau took four months to reach the Jat territories on the Yamuna in July. By that time, the monsoons had set in and the river was in spate. Suraj Mal joined the Maratha camp with 10,000 soldiers and Imad-ul-Mulk also followed suit.

Reoccupation of Delhi by the Marathas (August 1, 1760): The Marathas made straight for Delhi. They reached there on 22 July and took the city by storm the same day. Yaqub Ali, the Afghan governor of Delhi, shut himself into the Red Fort. The Marathas promptly invested the fort. Abdali rushed to Delhi with his crack troops, but in spite of his best efforts, he failed to provide succour to the besieged garrison. Cowed down by the heavy bombardment of the fort by the Marathas, Yaqub Ali sued for mercy. The Maratha commander responded favourably and allowed Yaqub Ali not only to vacate the fort with the remnant of his soldiers, families and valuables, unmolested but also to ferry across the Yamuna, to join his master, Ahmad Shah Abdali, in the Ganga Doab.

The Red Fort was re-occupied by the Marathas on the 1st of August 1760, and Sadashiv Rao made a formal entry into the fort, along with the other dignitaries of the Maratha camp, including Suraj Mal and Imad-ul-Mulk, next day. 'It was a great achievement of the Maratha arms, the credit for which goes exclusively to Sadashiv Rao Bhau; it was he who had contemplated this venture and executed it to the great opposition and unwillingness of his associates, Suraj Mal and Malhar Rao Holkar'. The re-conquest of the imperial capital of India restored the Maratha prestige which had been rudely shaken as a consequence of its occupation by the foreign invader on the death of Dattaji Sindhia'. (Advanced Study; iv, p. 274).

The recovery of Delhi by the Marathas from the hands of Abdali 'caused despair and dismay in the Afghan camp'. Abdali left Koil with his entire army, and 'arriving on the other side of the River Jamuna, encamped near Shahdra. He was burning with rage that the Marathas should have taken possession of ShahJahanabad (Delhi). Though he could see their camp at a distance of barely two *kos* (about five kms), he could not attack them since he was unable to cross the river owing to flood'. (*Najib-ud-Daulah*; pp. 34-35)

Imad-ul-Mulk and Suraj Mal Desert the Marathas: Unfortunately, both of the Indian allies of the Marathas had their own self-interests in joining them. Whereas, Imad-ul-Mulk wanted to be recognised as the *de facto* ruler of Delhi in his capacity as the *wazir* of his puppet Mughal emperor, Shah Jahan II, who lived in the Red Fort, the Jat chief wanted himself to be put in charge of the Red Fort and allowed to administer Delhi in collaboration with Imad-ul-Mulk . Besides, on the very first day of Bhau's entry into the Red Fort, he received a secret envoy, in the person of Raja Devi Datta, from Shuja-ud-Daulah, the Nawab Wazir of Awadh and Allahabad, with some confidential communication. Soon after, Shuja-ud-Daulah himself also arrived and encamped on the other side of the Yamuna, opposite the Red Fort, to negotiate with the Maratha commander directly for a political settlement. Shuja-ud-Daulah reminded Sadashiv Rao that Alamgir II had been murdered by Imad-ul-Mulk but he had left behind his representative in the person of his eldest son, Ali Gauhar, who had escaped alive from Delhi before his father's assassination, and was then living in exile in Bihar, styled as Shah Alam II. The latter had already declared Shuja as his *wazir*. Therefore, Shuja demanded that Shah Alam II and not the protégé of Imad-ul-Mulk should be recognised as the rightful successor of Alamgir II, and that he, being the ex-*wazir* of Alamgir II and now the *wazir* of Shah Alam II, should be handed over the charge of Delhi. Bhau, in fact knew all about Shah Alam II, and he found his minor son, named Jawan Bakht, still being held as captive in the Red Fort. It created a piquant situation, and the Maratha commander took his time to respond to the entreaties of Imad-ul-Mulk and Suraj Mal regarding the settlement of Delhi.

Sadashiv Rao tried to keep Shuja's mission a secret from Suraj Mal and Imad-ul-Mulk but they came to know of it, and became apprehensive about the success of their plans. Finding the Maratha chief adamant about their demands both of them decamped from Delhi secretly and retired to the Jat fortress of Ballabgarh. Bhau was shocked to know of it, and he sent his envoys post-haste to reconcile them but all in vain. Thus it was that the only two princes of northern India, who had made a common cause with the Marathas to fight against the foreign invader, deserted them for reasons of their own.

After the desertion of Imad-ul-Mulk, Sadashiv Rao Bhau deposed his protégé, Shah Jahan III, and proclaimed Shah Alam II to be the rightful Mughal emperor; the latter's minor son, Jawan Bakht, who was already under the protection of the Marathas, was made to act for his father during his absence from Delhi. It fulfilled Shuja's first demand about the recognition of Shah Alam II as the Mughal emperor by the Maratha chief; he, therefore, felt encouraged to assert his second demand that he should be recognised as his *wazir*.

Parleys with Shuja-ud-Daulah and Abdali for a Settlement: It was known to Sadashiv Rao, however, that Shuja-ud-Daulah, like Najib, had changed his loyalties to Abdali, and that he was feigning friendship with the Marathas to deceive them. When confronted with the truth, he accepted his position without regrets or apologies, but, by adopting a very respectful and friendly approach, 'engaged in prolonged and deceitful negotiations for over ten weeks' to gain time while the monsoons lasted. Through him, Abdali was also made a party to the negotiations, and Bhau appointed his own emissary to find out an amicable solution for the political settlement, if possible. Shuja demanded the control of Delhi in his capacity as the *wazir* of Shah Alam II and wanted the Marathas to go back to the Deccan. The Marathas, instead, demanded the Afghan invader to vacate the aggression and give up all pretensions of his sovereignty over the Indian territories, pending the settlement of Delhi with the native princes. Abdali, on the other hand, demanded cession of the Punjab, up to and inclusive of the district of Sirhind to his Afghan empire as the price for his return to Qandahar. Obviously, these demands of the foreign invader and his Indian allies were not acceptable to the Maratha leadership and broke down unceremoniously.

Meanwhile, Ahmad Shah Abdali had concentrated his troops around Delhi, on the Doab side of the river bank, while the soldiers and scouts of his Indian allies had spread themselves all along the Yamuna in search of suitable fords for crossing it. The Marathas had their own plans of action. They attacked Kunjpura, the nearest fortified Afghan post, that was accessible from their side of the Yamuna, and took it by storm on 18 October, a day before the festival of Dussehra. It was situated midway between Delhi and Sirhind, and was used by Abdali as a halting place to facilitate his return march to Afghanistan. To the pleasant surprise of Sadashiv Rao, he found that Abdus Samad Khan, the notorious Mughal governor of Sirhind, 'who had duped and betrayed the Marathas more than once', was also killed at Kunjpura along with its Afghan defenders. Another big catch of the Marathas at Kunjpura was Qutub Shah Rohilla, the precept of Najib-ud-Daulah, who had cut off the head of Dattaji Sindhia at Barari Ghat. He was taken prisoner but was 'tortured to death' by the victors 'to avenge the death of their beloved leader'. The rich booty collected by the Marathas at Kunjpura included 'two hundred thousand *maunds* of wheat and other food stuffs, 3,000 horses, and hundreds of camels and elephants, besides seven *lacs* of rupees in cash'.

Abdali, who was then encamped at Shahdra, opposite Delhi, was apprised of the sudden departure of the main Maratha army from the outskirts of the capital by his secret agents. The rains had abated but the Yamuna was still flowing to the brim. The fall of Kunjpura to the Marathas cut him to the quick. He at once decamped from Shahdra, and 'by a night march' reached Baghpat, about 14 kms from Delhi, where the scouts of Shuja-ud-Daulah had discovered a ford nearby to cross the river. Abdali pushed through that ford the whole of his army with artillery across the river, in spite of the flood, within two days, at the loss of about one thousand men, who were drowned. To the misfortune of the Marathas, 'their bad discipline and the notorious love of plunder, proved their undoing'. While they were engaged in ransacking Kunjpura, and celebrating the Dussehra feast, they failed to keep the enemy, on the other side of the bank, under observation, and prolonged their stay at Kunjpura for about a week. Bhau setup a military post at Kunjpura and returned with the bulk of his troops towards Delhi on 25 October. The next day, at Taraori, he received the information that the Afghans were crossing the river at Baghpat. He at once called for his troops of Kunjpura to join him at Panipat and sent an advance guard of horsemen to probe the whereabouts of the foe. On 29 October, he reached Panipat and was told that the Afghans had already crossed the river and blocked his passage near Sonepat. Thus it was that the die was cast and the Marathas decided to entrench themselves at the historic battlefield of Panipat to reckon with the Afghan invader. Abdali reached there with his forces in battle array and halted at a distance of about ten kms from the hostile formations. By the 1st of November, 1760, the adversaries stood face to face with each other, ready for action. As the Marathas had decided to entrench themselves at Panipat, they did not move forward and the final encounter was delayed by two months and a half.

The Third Battle of Panipat (January 14, 1761)

Our description of this historic event is based primarily on the eye-witness account of Pandit Kashi Raj, a Maratha employee of Malhar Rao Holkar, who was present on the battlefield of Panipat as a non-combatant on that fateful day. His narrative has been used extensively by Sidney J. Owen in his valuable treatise, *India on the Eve of the British Conquest – an Analytical History of India: 1627-1767* (Calcutta, 2nd ed; 1954). Unlike their traditional methods of warfare, the Marathas entrenched themselves at Panipat. It had been done by them on the advice of their artillery commander, Ibrahim Khan Gardi, who intended to make the most effective use of his heavy field-guns. Incidentally, Ibrahim Gardi was the only senior Muslim officer of the Peshwa, who served the Marathas faithfully at this critical juncture; he had started his career under the French officer, M. de Bussy, and received training as an artilleryman on the European model. According to Kashi Raj, the Marathas were encamped on the old *Sher Shah Suri Shahrah* (modern G.T. Road) with the town of Panipat to their right. Their vast camp was spread over 10 kms. in length towards the west in such a way that their right flank was hidden behind the town. Its western flank was partly protected by *Shah Nahar* (the Grand Canal) which ensured sufficient supply of water. The camp was about three to four kms. in depth. On the other hand, Abdali had organised his troops in battle array for fighting a running battle with the foe, to facilitate their swift movements. He was encamped with the town of Sonepat at its back, and his battle line spread in the direction of the Yamuna. The front line of Abdali's camp also extended about 11 kms, so large was his force. The rival camps were separated by about 13 kms.

During the first three weeks of November, the Marathas were on the offensive. Sadashiv Rao hoped to provoke the Afghans to attack the Maratha formations by making intensive raids on their flanks and the lines of communications, but the Afghan chief, being a seasoned warrior and strategist, refused to be drawn into a conflict except on his own terms. Thereafter, it was Abdali's turn to despatch small parties of his light cavalry to hover around the Maratha camp, and cut off their supplies and the lines of communication. The Afghan agents intercepted even the messengers and couriers of the Marathas, carrying confidential letters, with the result that for two months, preceeding the battle, no news reached the Deccan from Panipat, and their army camp was completely isolated from the outside world; the lion had been caught in his den.

Meanwhile, Kunjpura was re-occupied by the Rohillas and made safe for their Afghan master. The Maratha commander, Govind Pant Bundele of Etawah, proceeded with his 10,000 troops to join battle at Panipat but was intercepted by 15,000 strong Rohilla soldiers; Bundele was killed in an action near Meerut on 17 December 1760 and his entire army was annihilated. Bhau had left his lieutenant, Naro Shankar, with 7,000 troops to guard the Red Fort and the city of Delhi. He held his charge intact and no attempt was made by Abdali or his Indian agents to dislodge him until after their victory at Panipat. Through his clever moves, Abdali gradually established his dominance all along the river bank right up to Delhi while the Marathas were stuck up where they were. After the recession of the river waters and with the restoration of his direct contacts with the Ganga Doab, abundant supplies of food stuff, fodder and other provisions became available to the Afghans while the Marathas consumed their limited provisions and were put on the verge of starvation.

This interregnum was also utilized by the antagonists, through the agency of Shuja-ud-Daulah, to arrive at some settlement to avoid confrontation. On the 13th of January 1761, Bhau, after a midnight council, held with his commanders the previous night, sent his last communication to Shuja, 'offering to accept any conditions that might be obtainable', but without waiting for Abdali's reply, the Marathas, at daybreak on 14 January, 'after having eaten their last rations, issued from their lines, with turbans unbound, their faces smeared with turmeric, as devotees of death', and advanced *en bloc* towards the Afghan camp in battle formations. 'The women and non-combatants, who far outnumbered the fighters, were put in the centre. Sadashiv Rao did not keep any reserves behind at his base camp as he intended to make an intensive assault on the enemy, to force a passage through his battle lines, in a bid to make a junction with the left-out Maratha troops at Delhi'. According to Kashi Raj, on 29 October 1760, when Bhau reached Panipat, the Kunjpura regiment of the Marathas had also joined his camp; he was red-faced with rage and intended to make a dash with his whole army to fall upon the foe before he was able to reorganise his forces in battle array, but he was held back by the determined opposition, put up by Malhar Rao Holkar, Ibrahim Gardi and others, who exerted pressure on him through Vishwas Rao, the nominal generalissimo of the Maratha camp, to exercise restraint and cool down. The Marathas had lost their battle on that very day; 'this was the crisis of Sadashiv Rao Bhau's fortune; had he boldly attacked the Shah (Abdali) while the latter was crossing the Jamuna, he would probably have totally defeated him'. (Owen; op, cit., pp. 249). Bhau had not been entrusted the independent command of his army.

As for the details of the bloody carnage that followed at Panipat, we want to skip over for want of space. Suffice it to say that the onslaught began three hours after sunrise, and the battle lasted about six to seven hours. The first round went on until noon in which the Marathas had a clear edge. In the second round, there was 'a close and hard-fought combat'. In the afternoon, Abdali threw in reinforcements of crack troops and reserves in successive waves to frighten and demoralize the disorganized and exhausted Maratha fighters. In the last hour or two, 'the result was plain as a pikestaff and all that remained to be decided was how many of the men and their leaders could escape the certain and inexorable calamity which threatened to engulf everyone'.—H.R. Gupta in *Marathas and Panipat*'; p. 220).

Maratha Casualties: A conservative estimate puts the Maratha casualties at Panipat to be about seventy-five thousand. Abdali himself estimated that forty to fifty thousand Maratha soldiers were killed on the battlefield though the number of the Afghan casualties was much less because of his well-planned and carefully executed military operation. James Grant Duff opines that of the Maratha fighters "one-fourth only are supposed to have escaped, and of the camp-followers about an equal proportion'.(*History of the Mahrattas*, ii, Delhi reprint,

1990, pp. 111-12). Of course, 'there was not a home in Maharashtra that had not to mourn the loss of a member, and several homes their very heads, and the entire generation of leaders was cut off at one stroke'. (Sarkar; *Fall of the Mughal Empire*; ii, p. 257). The biographer of Najib-ud-Daulah has to say that for two days, about nine thousand Marathas, who had sought shelter in the town of Panipat and elsewhere, were tracked down and beheaded. All the Marathas, who fell fighting in the battle or were wounded, were subsequently beheaded by the ferocious Afghans, and their heads were taken away by them as trophies of war to their camp. In consequence, in the camp of Ahmad Shah Abdali, 'except the quarters of himself and his nobles, every tent had a heap of severed heads before it'. They had fought the battle in the true spirit of *Jehadis* and claimed it as a victory of Islam. Besides Vishwas Rao and Sadashiv Rao, many other renowned Maratha stalwarts, including Yashwant Rao Pawar and Tukoji Sindhia, fell fighting by the side of Bhau. Jankoji Sindhia and Ibrahim Gardi were seriously wounded and taken prisoners by the Afghans, but they were put to death with the other Maratha captives. Balaji Janardhan, who subsequently became famous as Nana Farnavis, was on the personal staff of Bhau; then hardly a young lad of sixteen, he remained at the battlefield until Bhau and a handful of his fighters were overwhelmed by the foe. Farnavis and other non-combatants, including some ladies, then fled for their dear lives on the steeds, and bypassed the town of Panipat safely by the sunset on that fateful day. The mother of Farnavis was killed in the flight but his wife fled to safety. Parvatibai, the wife of Sadashiv Rao was also taken to safety by some of her faithful servants, on a mare, to the Jat fortress of Ballabgarh. Antaji Mankeshwar, though wounded, escaped alive in the company of some others, but they were all waylaid and put to death by the Baluchi settlers of Farrukhnagar. Shamsher Bahadur, who had accompanied Bhau in his last assault on the foe, was carried to safety by his followers but he died of the wounds during the flight. Mahadaji Sindhia escaped alive from the battlefield but was pursued by the Afghan soldiers and seriously wounded; he was carried to safety by his followers but lamed for life.

Of all the Maratha leaders, Malhar Rao Holkar alone played the cowardly role and left the battlefield with the whole of his contingent much before the battle came to an end. As he had taken the lead in his flight, he reached the outskirts of Delhi with his train without molestation. Holkar's minister, Gangoba Tatya, paid a flying visit to the Red Fort to inform its commander, Naro Shankar, about the

Maratha debacle at Panipat and induced him to make an exit from Delhi before it was too late. After waiting for some time to ascertain the facts about the ultimate fate of Sadashiv Rao, Naro Shankar also fled from Delhi with his troops, and, by forced marches, joined the fugitives' train of Malhar Rao Holkar. In fact, the Red Fort of Delhi was so well-built and fortified that it was almost impregnable. As it had been provided with ample food stuffs, armour, and all sorts of other provisions, Naro Shankar, with his seven thousand strong Maratha contingent, could have easily held the fort against the foe for a couple of months till the arrival of reinforcements. And if he had been joined by Malhar Rao Holkar, all the other Maratha fugitives, making their way to Delhi, would have not only found the shelter but also immensely added to the strength of its defenders.

Pandit Kashi Raj was well-known to Shuja-ud-Daulah as an envoy of Malhar Rao Holkar. We find him, along with some non-combatant Marathas, in the camp of Shuja-ud-Daulah at Panipat on the day of the battle. Obviously, he had brought the last message of Sadashiv Rao for the *nawab* on the 13th of January. After the battle, he was instantly taken on his personal staff by Shuja while the other Marathas were sent by him in safety to the Jat territories of Raja Suraj Mal. That is how Kashi Raj and another Hindu employee of Shuja-ud-Daulah, named Anupgir Gosain, were sent by him to the battlefield to make an assessment of the Maratha casualties two days after the battle. They found as many as 32 spots of the slain Marathas, lying in concentration, ranging from 500 to 1500 bodies, where 'they had engaged the enemy in close combat'. They were estimated at 28,000. Almost an equal number of the corpses were found in and around the Maratha base camp and its ditches. Kashi Raj writes that the dead body of Vishwas Rao and the headless trunk of Bhau, besides that of another well-known Maratha *sardar* Santaji Vagh, were recovered and cremated according to Hindu rites by Anupgir Gosain, for which Shuja-ud-Daulah had to pay a consideration of three lacs of rupees to Ahmad Shah Abdali. He also claims that the severed head of Sadashiv Rao was recovered by the exertions of the *nawab* from an Afghan trooper, and put to the flames a couple of days later.

The Jat chief had not taken sides in the battle of Panipat, but, unmindful of the consequences, he extended help to the Marathas in distress. He at once offered protection to all the Marathas who made their way to the Jat territories, and warded off their predators by show of force. He and his queen made generous provisions for their food, clothing and medical aid, on which they spent more than ten lacs of rupees. The Maratha annals preserve sweet memories of the most considerate and hospitable treatment accorded to their fugitives from Panipat by the royal family of Bharatpur.

The Peshwa Balaji Baji Rao received vague information about the defeat of the Marathas at Panipat on January 24, 1761 when he was encamped at Bhilsa (Bundelkhand) on his way to Delhi with reinforcements. The Maratha scouts intercepted a *qassid* (courier) with a letter, engaged by a *sahukar* (merchant) of Delhi to carry it to his principals in Aurangabad; scribbled in 'enigmatical expression', it read *inter alia*: 'Two pearls dissolved, 27 gold *mohurs* have been lost, and of the silver and copper, the total cannot be cast up'. It alluded to the death of Vishwas Rao and Sadashiv Rao Bhau along with 27 senior Maratha *sardars* and unaccountable number of junior commanders and soldiers in the battle of Panipat. Thereafter, more disturbing news started reaching his camp, followed quickly by the arrival of Maratha fugitives from the north. The debacle of Panipat shattered the dream of a Maratha empire for the whole of India. Shocked of this disaster, the Peshwa was confined to bed and died a premature death on June 23, 1761, but before his death, Balaji Baji Rao had electrified the entire Maratha establishment and put its leadership on the move again for the revival of the Maratha power in the North.

Ahmad Shah Abdali in Control of Delhi

The victorious Afghan troops ransacked the deserted Maratha camp and then indulged in the massacre of 'the infidels' and loot and plunder to their heart's content for full four days after the battle before they marched to Delhi to take possession of the Red Fort. There was none to offer resistance or accord welcome to them. The main gate of the fort was closed but not locked; and it was guarded by a handful of the smart Maratha livery, dressed in their typical southern costumes, and symbolically armed with swords and spears. At this solemn occasion, Mahadeo Hingane, popularly known as the Raja Bapu or Bapuji, the diplomatic agent of the Peshwa at Delhi, who alone had stuck to his duty, and continued to stay in the Red Fort after the flight of all other Marathas, 'made his sudden appearance, in the attendance of his retainers, to the great bewilderment of the ferocious Afghans. Dressed in gorgeous attire, befitting a Maratha noble of status, Hingane unhesitatingly approached their commandant and introduced himself as the plenipotentiary of the Peshwa at Delhi. He at once sought personal interview with their master, Ahmad Shah Abdali'. His presence in the Red Fort was promptly reported to Abdali's *wazir*, Shah Wali Khan. He was allowed to stay where he was, formally under detention but without any molestation. The fort was taken possession of by the Afghan troops and decorated for the reception of their master.

Ahmad Shah Abdali made a formal entry into the fort on 29 January and held a grand *darbar* in the *Diwan-i-Khas* in the likeness of the Mughal emperors; the *khutba* had already been read in his name and the coins were duly struck to mark his sovereignty over India. All of his Indian allies, including the *amir-ul-umara* Najib-ud-Daulah, Shuja-ud-Daulah and other Rohilla chiefs, were in attendance upon him but there was no Mughal bureaucracy and no Muslim aristocracy of Delhi to receive his favours. Najib-ud-Daulah, for a while, occupied the centre-stage of the court politics; he came out with his here-brain schemes of doing away with the fiction of the Mughal monarchy, and suggested the transplantation of Babar's dynasty in India. He strove his best to induce Abdali for an invasion of the south to crush the Maratha power once and for all times to come. For this purpose, he not only 'took upon himself the responsibility of paying the expenses of the Afghan army' but also assured the invader that he would 'bring the Nizam of Hyderabad to join him on the Narbada'. (Nuruddin Hussain, *Najib-ud-Daulah*, pp. 56-57). Abdali did not oblige him, however. He was advised by his crafty *wazir* and other Afghan counsels that while the fiction of the Mughal sovereignty was deeply engrained in the hearts of the Indians, Hindus as well as Muslims, he stood no chance of establishing his dynasty at Delhi. All the Indian hands, whether those of his friends or foes, pointed to the presence of the shadowy Mughal emperor behind his back in the fort.

The Settlement of Delhi: Before Ahmad Shah Abdali could chalk out a tentative plan of action for the future, he was rudely shaken by a voice of protest against the rhetoric of Najib-ud-Daulah, which was raised by his commanders and soldiers, barely eight days after his arrival in the Red Fort. They were all opposed to the intentions of their master to stay put in Delhi. Abdali's hard-earned victory over the Marathas seemed to have proved equally disastrous for him and his soldiers too. Apart from the immense booty, acquired by his troops, 'he did not derive much material benefit out of it. So much so, the Afghan chief had not been able to pay even the salaries to his troops for more than a year and a half. Notwithstanding the extensive support of his Indian allies, about one-third of his personal army of invasion had been wiped out as a result of the casualties, suffered by it in the prolonged warfare and because of the scorching heat of the Indian summers. Worn out by the unbearable stress and strain of their wanderings in a foreign land, the Afghan soldiers were determined on returning to their homes immediately. They raised a hue and cry and held public demonstrations to convince their commanders of the urgency of their demands. The Shah was warned by his senior military generals of the outbreak of mutiny in the army; some of his commanders, out of desperation, were planning to desert their leader and march back to Afghanistan with their contingents, of their own. The exasperated and much confused Shah looked askance towards Shah Wali Khan, his *wazir*, who politely advised him to accede to their demand. Hence, Abdali hurriedly made a political settlement of his Indian conquests before retracing his steps towards Afghanistan. He approved of the arrangements, as had been made earlier by Sadashiv Rao Bhau, to regulate the administrative affairs of Delhi. He recognised Shah Alam II as the Mughal emperor; his teenage son, Prince Jawan Bakht was accepted as the heir apparent to the throne of Delhi as before, and Najib-ud-Daulah was appointed his *mir bakhshi*. The administration of Delhi was entrusted by Abdali to Najib and Jawan Bakht jointly, but Najib's hands were further strengthened by him by his reaffirmation as the Afghan plenipotentiary in India as before.

Shah Alam II, then living at Allahabad, had already appointed Shuja-ud-Daulah as his *wazir*. The *nawab wazir* of Awadh, therefore, aspired to take charge of Delhi in his capacity as the *wazir* of the puppet Mughal emperor. He was won over to the cause of the Afghan invader by Najib by holding out a promise to this effect, on behalf of his master. As Abdali refused to fulfil his promise and handed over the administration of Delhi to the Rohilla chief, he felt disappointed and abruptly left for Lucknow on March 7, 1761. Abdali made no attempt to placate the *nawab wazir*, and instead, decided to confer the *wizarat* of Delhi on its old incumbent, Imad-ul-Mulk, who was then living at Mathura as an ally of Raja Suraj Mal. The Afghan chief despatched his envoy, Yaqub Ali Khan, the younger brother of his *wazir*, Shah Wali Khan, with the robes of the *wizarat* of Delhi for Imad-ul-Mulk, and asked him to reach the metropolis immediately to take charge of his office. Of course, Ahmad Shah Abdali made his intentions clearly known to all of his Indian princes, friends or foes that he would like to keep northwestern India and the Punjab up to the district of Sirhind under his direct control. No amicable settlement could be made with his Jat and Maratha adversaries to ensure peace but, on the advice of the Maratha plenipotentiary Mahadeo Hingane, Yaqub Ali Khan was assigned another diplomatic function; he carried with him letters from Abdali and his *wazir* in the name of the Peshwa to restrain their activities in the north for their mutual benefit.

Abdali leaves for Afghanistan

After making these arrangements, Ahmad Shah Abdali decamped from Delhi on March 20, 1761 and ordered his troops for the return march to Afghanistan. The victors carried with them immense booty, the contemporary accounts of which are considerably exaggerated. But 'their gains in horses, camels, elephants and the beasts of burden, besides the men and women slaves, were enormous. The real worth of the Afghan booty lay, however, in the collection of weapons of war, including swords, spears and shields, besides thousands of the muskets and the finest pieces of heavy artillery, surely enough to equip an equally huge army that Abdali had himself brought to India'. (Advanced Study; ii, p.298). According to an estimate, the Marathas lost 50,000 horses, 500 elephants and two lacs of oxen which were used by them for their wheeled carts for the carriage of provisions. According to another version, the Afghans carried with them 25,000 horses, 700 elephants and about the same number of camels besides bullock-carts, laden with property 'which fell into their hands as booty'. As regards the incalculable quantities of gold and silver currency, jewellry, and other precious metals, the Marathas had not much to yield but these valuables were looted by them from the state treasuries and populace of the Doab and the Ganga valley. On his way back to Afghanistan, Abdali's army faced considerable harassment at the hands of the Sikhs. As mentioned by H.R. Gupta, 'the roving bands of the Sikh fighters hovered around the retreating columns of the Afghan troops from the moment they crossed the Satluj. They rode close to the Afghan lines on their flanks and the rear, and moved at a distance from them, like casual rustic passersby, with apparent unconcern towards the army'. Nevertheless, 'they pounced upon the swaggerers and carried away their booty and the baggage along with their horses all the same. They usually attacked the Afghan supplies at night, but kept themselves at a safe distance from their mobile cavalry and the camel swivels, and avoided direct confrontation with them'. The Sikhs made a surprise attack on the Afghan camp in strength at the ferry of Goindwal on the Beas and 'secured the liberation of a large number of the Maratha captives, who were being held by the Afghans as enslaved labourers for the carriage of their baggage to Afghanistan; they were subsequently sent to their homes in the south with suitable provisions'. Abdali sent a few expeditions from Lahore to chastise the Sikhs. In consequence, 'numerous Sikh fighters were captured and tortured to death by the Afghans but their activities did not abate. The Sikh desperados did not allow any rest to the retreating Afghan army till the Indus was crossed by it'. (A *History of the Sikhs*; i, Simla, 1952; 2nd revised ed., pp. 154-55).

SECTION 6: REVIVAL OF THE MARATHA POWER IN THE NORTH

The Fallout of Panipat

The third battle of Panipat stands unique in the annals of Indian history. As a one-day contest between the two rival contenders for political ascendancy in the country, accompanied by the tremendous loss of human life, and the magnitude of destruction, the first two historic battles of Panipat simply pale into insignificance before it. This battle had disastrous effects on the fortunes of both the parties. It gave a serious set-back to the power and prestige of the Marathas throughout the country, tarnished their image as the invincible warriors and eclipsed their credibility as the sole inheritors of the Mughal imperial legacy in India. On the other hand, Abdali had won the battle but he did not win the war. His position in his own dominions at Qandahar and Kabul was never beyond challenge. He had started his career as a usurper and his military despotism was repeatedly challenged by his political rivals and rebellious Afghan chiefs, who successfully thwarted the path of his ambitions. According to H. R. Gupta, Abdali's 'victory on the Indian soil in 1759-61 was achieved with the help of his Indo-Muslim allies who contributed all the urgency, most of the money and above all the troops that fought at Panipat. It was Najib's diplomacy that won over Shuja to his side. It was Najib's infantry that virtually decided the day for him'. And it is on record that 'just within a fortnight after the greatest success of his life, his army potential was so undependable and the diplomatic structure so shaky as to oblige him to beat a hasty retreat from Delhi'. (*Marathas and Panipat*; p. 268).

The Peshwa's Predicament

The Peshwa Balaji Baji Rao was extremely angry with Malhar Rao Holkar who 'had played a cowardly, if not treacherous role at Panipat'.

He inflicted severe punishments upon Holkar, Naro Shankar and their associates for the dereliction of their duty. Their estates were confiscated although they were not deprived of their personal troops, with the hope that they might atone for their acts of omission and commission, and redeem their honour by rendering some useful service to the Maratha state. The Peshwa's punitive action against the defaulters created quite a sensation throughout the Maratha dominions, and had a salutary effect on the rest of the officers too. The panic-stricken Maratha *sardars* were on their toes and vied with one another to prove their professional acumen and loyalty to the Peshwa. Malhar Ro Holkar was cut to the quick by the Peshwa's stern action. His apparent inertness and immobility, attributed to his old age, all vanished in thin air, and he regained his agility as a brave warrior once again.

There is no denying the fact that 'the Marathas at Panipat fought in a glorious cause. They were the only power that faced the might and main of the Afghan hordes at all hazards, *pro patria*', (R. R. Sethi in *Marathas and Panipat*; edited by H. R. Gupta, p. 260), while the other Indian powers either stood aloof or joined hands with the foreign invader in betrayal of the country on the instigation of some Muslim religious fanatics. Major Evans Bell rightly observes that the battle of Panipat was 'a triumph for the Marathas in the cause of India for the Indians'. Likewise, H.G.R. Rawlinson 'characterizes the defeat of the Marathas 'as honourable as a victory', with the remarks that 'never in all the annals did the Maratha armies cover themselves with greater glory than when the flower of the chivalry of the Deccan perished on the stricken field of Panipat, fighting against the enemies of their creed and country'. (*An Account of the Last Battle of Panipat*; pp. xii-xiii).

Pricked by his guilty conscience, Malhar Rao Holkar became the first to take the lead in restoring the lost Maratha power and prestige in the North. Though the Peshwa was himself struck down by illness and grief, 'there were men and captains about him', who spread themselves in various directions like a whirlwind and quickly re-established the Maratha rule not only in Malwa and Bundelkhand but also in Rajputana and the Ganga Doab. Ahmad Shah Abdali had scored a victory over the Marathas but he failed to arrive at an amicable settlement with them. It was to the knowledge of the victor that Gwalior had become an important military camp of the Marathas. Ten thousand Maratha fugitives from Panipat and Delhi, who had assembled there earlier, went away to their homes, but a fresh Maratha army made its appearance in Gwalior early in March 1761 on the directions of the

Peshwa. Having come to know of all these developments, Abdali became afraid of the renewal of hostilities with them for which his troops were not prepared at all. To our mind, that inborn fear of the Maratha reprisals was one of the pressing reasons which hastened his exit from Delhi in a hurry.

Raja Madho Singh of Jaipur, a prominent Rajput chief of the day, who had formed a liaison with the invader, and exhibited anti-Maratha stance, was taken to task by none else but Holkar himself. As a consequence, within two months of the battle of Panipat, the political situation underwent a sea change, and the feudal chiefs of northern India, instead of scoffing at the Maratha discomfiture, began to take them seriously.

As referred to earlier, the Peshwa had received the news of the Maratha defeat when he was stationed at Bhilsa in Bundelkhand while proceeding towards Delhi with reinforcements. He did not give up his mission nor returned to Poona all at once, as wrongfully alluded to by some of the writers. Instead, he prolonged his stay at Bhilsa, wherefrom he moved 52 kms. further north to Pachhor to safeguard the imperial interests of the Maratha state, north of Narbada, in the prevalent situation. On the persuasion of his advisers, the Peshwa retraced his steps from Pachhor on 22 March to the south. He died a broken-hearted man at the shrine of the Goddess Parvati in Poona on June 23, 1761 at the age of thirty-one and a half, but, before his death, he was fully satisfied to know that the Marathas were on the move again. The revival of the Maratha power in the north, thus, commenced during the very lifetime of Balaji Baji Rao.

Delhi under Najib

With the retirement of the Afghan invader and the Marathas after the battle of Panipat, 'the way was opened for a revival of local power in Delhi'. Percival Spear prefers to call it the 'kingdom of Delhi' to distinguish it from the pro-Panipat imperial government which had continued to exercise some sort of authority over parts of northern India until 1760. According to his thesis, 'the Delhi kingdom lasted in some sort until the blinding of Shah Alam II in 1788'. (*Twilight of the Mughals*; CUP, 1951, pp. 14-15). In those 27 years, Delhi underwent 'a number of vicissitudes.' The first period is associated with the name of Najib Khan, the Rohilla Afghan immigrant and soldier of fortune. In 1753, he was granted *jagirs* in the upper Doab for aiding Imad-ul-Mulk, the *wazir* and *de facto* ruler of Delhi. In the fashion of the times, he extended his power by seizing many villages in the Saharanpur and Meerut districts. During the fourth invasion of Ahmad Shah Abdali (1756-57), Imad-ud-Mulk fought against the invader but suffered a defeat and sought pardon while Najib Khan changed sides and 'joined his fellow Afghan'. Thereby, Najib earned the status of *amir-ul-umara* with the title of Najib-ud-Daulah from the hands of Abdali. He received the office of *mir bakhshi* and was made the plenipotentiary of the Afghan invader in India with the responsibility of protecting the puppet Mughal emperor. During the fifth invasion of Abdali (1759-61), leading to the third battle of Panipat, Najib stood as the right-hand man of the invader in establishing his sway in the whole of the Ganga valley and made a major contribution in his victory at Panipat. He earned the gratitude of his master by 'covering the Afghan retirement' from Delhi in March 1761 as his most trustworthy and reliable friend and guide. No wonder, Abdali made him the *de facto* ruler of Delhi by entrusting its administration to him at the time of his departure. From 1761 to 1770, he held the reins of government at Delhi for about nine years. In the absence of Shah Alam II, he took charge of the government of Delhi, jointly with the minor prince Jawan Bakht, and setup as virtually independent ruler of Delhi and began to exercise all the powers and prerogatives of the crown as he pleased; Imad-ul-Mulk joined him as *wazir* soon afterwards but he was left high and dry as he had to play the subservient role to the all-powerful *mir bakhshi* and official representative of the Afghan overlord at Delhi.

Najib-ud-Daulah ruled over Delhi for over nine years from 1761 to 1770. He acted like a virtual dictator, created a new crop of the Mughal (read Afghan) bureaucracy and carried on ceaseless warfare with the Jats and the Sikhs, apparently on behalf of his master, but failed to permanently crush either of them. The Jat chief Suraj Mal was killed in the battle against Najib-ud-Daulah on 25 December 1763 and was succeeded by his adopted son Jawahir Singh at Bharatpur. The Jats were thus held back from Delhi but the rising tide of the Sikh war of liberation in the Punjab overflowed to Delhi and the Ganga Doab. In October 1765, about 50,000 Sikh fighters marched through the district of Sirhind and divided themselves into two bodies. The Tarun Dal crossed the Yamuna at Buriya Ghat and entered Saharanpur district, while the Buddha Dal, consisting of 25,000 horse, under the leadership of Jassa Singh Ahluwalia, Tara Singh, Sham Singh and others, attacked Najib's estates 'in the country north of Delhi'. An indecisive battle was fought between the antagonists at Shamli, about 20 kms to the east of Karnal. In December 1765, the Sikhs spread themselves into the Ganga Doab and carried on loot and plunder there all through the year 1766. *Najib-ud-Daulah's* distress call to Ahmad Shah Abdali led to his eighth invasion in December 1766, but the latter was held back in the Punjab by the armed bands of the Sikhs, who surrounded his army and threatened it with total annihilation. He, therefore, could not make it to Delhi. Najib met his master for the last time at his army camp at the Machchiwara Ghat on the Satluj, early in May 1767, and then returned to Delhi to fight a losing battle against his Sikh and Jat adversaries.

By this time, the Marathas had also overtaken the North and Najib realised to his dismay that their supremacy was about to be re-established in Hindustan. The new Maratha leaders were sharply divided about the policy to be adopted by them towards Najib-ud-Daulah. Most of them stood for the complete destruction of the notorious Afghan traitor, but Najib was lucky to placate the Maratha commander, Ram Chandra Ganesh, through his hereditary friend Tukoji Holkar, son of Malhar Rao Holkar. Accordingly, the Maratha commander accepted Najib's offer of cooperation in the re-establishment of their sway in Delhi. Najib-ud-Daulah promptly 'placed the hand of his son, Zabita Khan, into the hands of Tukoji, 'praying to the latter to be as kind to the son as Malhar Rao Holkar had been to the father'. Thereafter, 'he sent the Maratha *sardars* away, escorted by Zabita Khan to Delhi', and, worn out by age and thoroughly exhausted, he retired in broken health to his stronghold of Najibabad in March 1768; he died there on October 31, 1770, leaving his son Zabita Khan to rule over Delhi under the patronage of none else but the Marathas, his sworn enemies of yester years.

The Sikh War of Liberation in the Punjab

The Marathas had failed to win the confidence of the Sikhs and did not bother to secure their cooperation and support in the administration of the Punjab under the Maratha rule. Accordingly, the Sikhs also stood aloof when Abdali wrested the Punjab from the hands of the Marathas. Because of the same reason, the Sikhs did not support the Marathas in their conflict at Panipat. However, they took up arms against the Afghan forces of occupation in the Punjab and drove them out of their homeland by force during the very lifetime of Ahmad

Shah Abdali. The Sikhs had already formed their militant organisation, called the Dal Khalsa, at the Golden Temple, Amritsar, in 1748 under the leadership of Jassa Singh Ahluwalia. It controlled the various *jathas* or 'armed bands' of the Sikh freedom fighters in their renewed struggle for the liberation of their homeland, now from the Afghan domination. Therefore, after his victory at Panipat, Abdali was constrained to organise five more invasions in the years 1762, 1764-65, 1766-67, 1768-69 and 1769-70 respectively, all of which were confined to the Punjab and were undertaken by him with the sole object of crushing the rising power of the Sikhs.

In his sixth invasion, a bloody battle was fought between Abdali and Sikhs at Kup, near Malerkotla, on February 5, 1762, in which about 12,000 Sikhs were killed. On his way back to Lahore in triumph, Abdali sacked Amritsar and desecrated the Golden Temple. Its holy tank was filled up by the Afghans with the debris of the buildings and refuse. The Sikhs retaliated in December 1763, when they inflicted a crushing defeat on Bhikhan Khan, the Nawab of Malerkotla, a local agent of Abdali, and took a heavy toll of the lives of the Afghan settlers in the Punjab. In his seventh invasion of India (1764-65), Abdali marched with his troops as far as Sirhind and raised the cry of *Jehad* against the 'infidels' but the Sikhs defeated the Afghans in a number of skirmishes and established their parity with them. Lahore was first occupied by the Sikhs, though for a short time, in November 1761, but finally liberated by them from the hands of the Afghans in May 1765 when they asserted their sovereignty over the Punjab and struck coins in the name of the Sikh Gurus. In spite of his best efforts, Abdali failed to perpetuate his rule in the Punjab. In December 1769, Abdali crossed the Khyber with a fresh army of invasion, for the tenth time, to suppress the Sikhs. At Peshawar, when his soldiers came to know that 'the cis-Indus territories of Doaba Sindh Sagar, including the historic fort of Rohtas, had also fallen into the hands of the Sikhs, they were frightened to cross the Indus for their onward march to Lahore. 'In despair, the *Baba-i-Afghanistan* looked upon his Eldorado with his ever longing eyes for wealth and fame, but the burly Sikhs had beaten him back with a bloody nose, and turned the fertile plains of the Punjab into a nightmare for his ferocious Afghan soldiers. Overtaken by sorrow and dismay, because of the total failure of his lifelong struggle for the establishment of his imperial sway over India, Abdali retraced his steps from Peshawar to Kabul'. (Advanced Study; iv, p. 305). He died of cancer on April 14, 1772. By that time, the armed bands of the Sikh fighters had started settling down in different parts of the Punjab and northwestern India, and they gave birth to what were known as the Sikh Misls under the *Jathedars* or *Misldars*. After their debacle at Panipat, the Marathas were never destined to re-occupy Lahore and Multan or Peshawar and Attock, but it were the Sikhs whc shattered the dreams of Abdali to establish the Afghan hegemony over India, and the object, with which the Marathas had fought the foreign invader at Panipat but failed, was fulfilled by the Sikhs, within a decade of the battle of Panipat.

We do not regard the invasions of Nadir Shah and Ahmad Shah Abdali, or the intrusion of the Europeans into the Indian politics to be the causes of the downfall of the Mughal Empire; these were rather the after-effects and consequences of the decline and disintegration of the mighty Mughal empire of medieval India, built so laboriously by Akbar the Great.

Shah Alam II in Exile

Shah Alam II, who had been duly recognised as the Mughal emperor by the Marathas as well as Ahmad Shah Abdali, was still living in exile at Allahabad under the protection of Shuja-ud-Daulah, the Nawab Wazir of Awadh. Shuja, being a *Shia* by faith did not see eye to eye with the fanatic Muslims like Najib Khan and the Shah of Afghanistan although he had made a common cause with them in their fight with the Marathas. He had been nominated as his *wazir* by Shah Alam II and he aspired to take control of Delhi in this capacity along with the emperor. However, Abdali did not oblige him after his victory at Panipat, and instead, entrusted the administration of Delhi to his favourite Najib-ud-Daulah. At the same time, before his departure from India, Abdali had disappointed Shah Alam II also by declaring Imad-ul-Mulk to be his *wazir*, who had murdered his father, Alamgir II. Such being the case, Shah Alam II was, obviously, doomed to stay away from the imperial capital so long as Imad-ul-Mulk, Najib-ud-Daulah and their associates were at the helm of affairs there. Unfortunately, Shah Alam was not an ordinary individual; being the scion of the once imperial Mughal dynasty, he carried on his uneasy head the Mughal Crown for forty-seven long years till his death in 1806. He was hunted down like a musk-deer from place to place by the power-hungry Mughal and Afghan nobles and other native powers of India to be used as a pawn in their hands for the achievement of their political ends. To this category of the political hunters were now joined the two foreign imperial powers, the Afghan chief and the European merchants. Accordingly, all through his life, Shah Alam had to play his role as a puppet in the hands of one or the other power.

In 1764, he was obliged to join Shuja-ud-Daulah and Mir Qasim, the ex-*nawab* of Bengal, in a conflict with the English but they were defeated in the battle of Buxar on 23 October. Mir Qasim fled the field while Shuja and Shah Alam II offered their submission. They signed the Treaty of Allahabad on August 12, 1765, according to which, Shuja-ud-Daulah was given back his kingdom of Awadh, with the exception of the districts of Kara and Allahabad, on payment of 50 lacs of rupees to the East India Company. These two districts were handed over to the phantom Mughal emperor by the Company, in return for the grant of *Diwani* of Bengal, Bihar and Orissa by him to the Company; in lieu of this grant, the Company offered to undertake his protection, besides the payment of 26 lacs of rupees per annum as the subsistence allowance. In a way, it made the so-called 'Emperor of India' a pensioner of the British; he remained under their tutelage from 1765 to 1771. It was really humiliating and disgraceful that a Mughal prince, who claimed sovereignty over the whole of India, should end as a pensioner of the foreign adventurers. Shah Alam realised his predicament after having signed the treaty with the English and became restless to liberate himself from their clutches at the earliest opportunity. Incidentally, Najib-ud-Daulah's death in 1770 coincided with a revival of the Maratha power in the North and 'brought matters to a crisis for Shah Alam'. His prolonged absence from Delhi, the seat of his potential power and symbolic status as emperor, did not auger well for him. According to Percival Spear,

> 'If Shah Alam continued in Allahabad, the chances were that Delhi would fall either to the belligerent Sikhs or to the revivified Marathas. There was a large supply of Mughal princes, available in the Fort, whom the Sikhs would not hesitate to exploit, and while the Marathas, with their love of precedent and established tradition, might be more tender (sic.) to existing authority, the net result would be the same. Shah Alam would be condemned to perpetual pensionhood either at Allahabad at the hands of Shuja-ud-Daulah or the Company, or at Delhi at the hands of the Marathas or the Sikhs. He had, therefore, to face the dilemma of moving to Delhi with all the risks involved or of continued

residence in Allahabad with probable extinction as a serious political factor'.—(*Twilight of the Mughals*; p. 18).

Apart from the above, there were two other contributory causes which added to Shah Alam's anxiety to make an exit from Allahabad in his bid to retrace his steps to Delhi. Firstly, he had lowered his dignity and compromised his position as a Mughal prince by accepting a pittance from the foreigners for his livelihood. No wonder, he was hated and despised by the inhabitants of Allahabad who chided him as a 'clown', while he was detested and held cheap by the servants of the East India Company too. None found fault with him so long as he had played the puppet in the hands of the Indian princes. Secondly, several ladies and children of the Mughal dynasty still resided in the Red Fort of Delhi; they included, among others, Zinat Mahal, the widow of Alamgir II and the mother of Shah Alam II, besides his sister, Khair-un-nisa, and minor son Jawan Bakht. Obviously, they were all deemed to be under the protection of Najib-ud-Daulah while he acted as the administrator of Delhi. Of course, the Prince Jawan Bakht was always kept under surveillance by the Rohilla guards, but, Zabita Khan, the son and successor of Najib, 'transgressed his limits as the protector of the royal family, and committed a disgraceful deed when he entered the royal *harem* and dishonoured some of the ladies, including Shah Alam's sister. In deep anguish, therefore, Zinat Mahal wrote repeated letters to her son at Allahabad to come and save the honour of his family'.—*(Advanced Study; iv, p.464).*

Reoccupation of Delhi by the Marathas (1769-72)

The fourth Peshwa Madhava Rao, the son and successor of Balaji Baji Rao, sent two military expeditions to the north for the revival of their power and influence at Delhi. The first expedition, led by Raghunath Rao, the younger brother of Balaji Baji Rao, in 1765-67, ended in a fiasco because of the incompetence of its commander as before, but the second expedition (1769-72), despatched by the Peshwa under the command of Ramchandra Ganesha and Visaji Krishna, produced its desired results. The Maratha armies left Poona for Delhi in March 1769, while Tukoji Holkar and Mahadaji Sindhia had already proceeded with their contingents towards Agra. Raja Madho Singh of Jaipur, who had previously defied the Maratha authority and had to be chastised, had died in December 1767. His son and successor, Raja Pratap Singh, offered his wholehearted cooperation to the Marathas and so did the *Nawab* of Bhopal. The Jat chief Jawahir Singh of Bharatpur, the successor of Raja Suraj Mal, had been assassinated by one of his own disgruntled soldiers in July 1768, but his son and successor Nawal Singh, like his father, was hostile towards the Marathas. Najib-ud-daulah was still at the helm of affairs at Delhi although, because of his old age and ill health, he had entrusted the administration of the imperial capital to his youthful son Zabita Khan, and himself resided at Najibabad. His Afghan patron, Ahmad Shah Abdali, was no more, while the fugitive Mughal emperor Shah Alam II lived at Allahabad, now under the protection of the British.

The Peshwa wanted his commanders to proceed straight to Delhi but the Jat chief Nawal Singh opposed the Maratha advance through his territories. He suffered a defeat in a pitched battle at Govardhan on April 5, 1770 and fled the field. The victorious Marathas took forced possession of Agra and Mathura. This spectacular victory of the Marathas at once changed the political situation in their favour. It showed the Maratha determination to deal sternly with their opponents.

Najib-ud-daulah, therefore, lost no time in dispatching his envoys to the Maratha camp with conciliatory proposals. He was prepared to help them 'in recovering the old Maratha possessions beyond the Jamuna' provided he was allowed to rule at Delhi under the Peshwa's suzerainty. The Maratha commanders were taken in by his offer which was quite tempting indeed! Najib had, in fact, contrived to divert their attention from Delhi and bring about their destruction in league with the Rohilla chief Ahmad Khan Bangash of Farrukhabad. As soon as Ramchandra Ganesh received intelligence about his sinister motives, he cleverly extricated his army from their trap and marched upon Delhi. Meanwhile, Najib-ud-daulah fell ill and died at Hapur on October 31, 1770. His son Zabita Khan was no match for the Marathas, and they reoccupied Delhi without much resistance on February 9, 1771. Zabita Khan was placed in detention but he made good his escape from the Maratha captivity with the connivance of Tukoji Holkar. Delhi fell to the Marathas but Zabita Khan had inherited a flourishing estate of Najibabad from his father, which enabled him to maintain a vast army and leadership of the Rohillas in the Ganga valley.

Installation of Shah Alam II at Delhi

The Maratha commander Ramchandra Ganesh established contacts with the Mughal emperor Shah Alam II at Allahabad soon after his arrival in the North. As per the directions of the Peshwa, the emperor was invited to come back to reoccupy the throne of Delhi with the Maratha assistance. Shah Alam was very glad to hear of it. The temptation for him was so great that he became rather impatient to throw off the British tutelage and make his way to the Maratha camp at the earliest. The Maratha records (Persian Records of Maratha History; i, Delhi Affairs: 1761-88) throw a flood of light on the re-conquest of Delhi and the re-installation of the Mughal emperor on the throne in the Red Fort during this period. A Persian newsletter, written by a Maratha agent to the Peshwa from Delhi on November 3, 1769, informed him that the emperor was still in Allahabad. He sent his envoy 'to summon Shuja-ud-Daulah, the *Wazir ul Mamalik,* and demanding plain answer whether he was ready to accompany the emperor (in his march to Delhi)'. Shuja, who was then at Lucknow, hesitated to accompany the emperor; he, therefore, detained the emperor's envoy on the plea that he will make up his mind after consulting his senior officers. The British did not want the emperor to slip out of their hands. The above-mentioned newsletter mentions *inter alia:* "The Emperor wished to send Saifuddin Muhammad Khan, with *khilats* and jewels to Ramchandra Ganesh and other Maratha *sardars*, but at the report of the coming of Munir-ud-Daulah and the *Firangis*, he has put off this idea". (Delhi Newsletter, 3 November 1769, *Ibid.*, pp. 18-19).

This statement is revealing. It shows, in the first instance that the emperor was so pleased with the Maratha offer that he 'wished to send' robes of honour and costly gifts to their premier commanders. *Secondly*, he had to 'put off this idea' when he heard of the arrival from Calcutta of Munir-ud-daulah, an agent of the British Company, along with some other Englishmen, to meet him. Obviously, he wanted to keep his warm sentiments towards the Marathas a top secret. *Thirdly,* his proposed envoy, Saifuddin Muhammad Khan, was actually sent by him to the Maratha camp after some time as his representative. It was he to whom the Marathas ultimately handed over the administrative charge of the metropolis on behalf of the emperor.

As soon as the emperor heard of Maratha victory over the Jats and occupation of Agra by them, he left Allahabad bag and baggage without the consent of his British patrons or Shuja-ud-Daulah. He had with him 'about ten thousand horse and foot, including his menials'. On his way back to Delhi, Shah Alam remained in constant touch with the Maratha forces, then operative in the Ganga Doab and the neighbourhood of Delhi. He arrived on the Jamuna and encamped on its bank, opposite to the Red Fort, in the last week of November 1771. On January 7, 1772, the emperor, escorted by Visaji Krishna and Mahadaji Sindhia, entered the Red Fort with his family and select bodyguards. His main army remained encamped on the other side of the Jamuna with the consideration that it had to launch military operations against the Rohillas in association with the Maratha forces. The Mughal emperor was thus rehabilitated on the ancestral throne of Delhi by the Marathas after twelve years' wanderings as a fugitive. He felt immensely relieved to have got rid of the British tutelage much against their will. They had thoroughly exploited the emperor's person and regal status to enhance their own imperial interests. G.S. Sardesai correctly observes that "the British always dreaded a combination of northern powers under Maratha hegemony, and had, since the days of Plassey, made it the main object of their policy to oppose such a combination....As the emperor would be the central figure of any hostile combination, the British held him tightly in their grip at Allahabad. None understood these currents and cross-currents of the political situation better than the emperor himself". (New History, ii, p. 513).

The Mughal emperor paid 40 *lacs* of rupees to the Marathas towards the expenses and ceded the districts of Kara and Allahabad, besides Meerut, to the Peshwa out of gratitude. The British were, however, quick to establish their hold over the districts of Kara and Allahabad, with the assistance of Shuja-ud-Daulah, and saved them from falling into the hands of the Marathas. Once the Marathas were at the helm of affairs in Delhi, the vanquished Jat chief, Nawal Singh, made peace with them by acknowledging their overlordship, and agreed to pay a war indemnity of 65 *lacs* in installments. On the intervention of the Marathas, his rebellious younger brother, Ranjit Singh, also gave up his claim to the Jat kingship and accepted a *jagir* worth 20 *lacs* from Nawal Singh and thus peace was restored in the Jat territories. Zabita Khan of Najibabad also sought apologies from the Maratha commander and the Mughal emperor, through the mediation of Tukoji Holkar, and was granted pardon by them. It enabled the Marathas to re-establish their hegemony over the Ganga Doab. Thereafter, the Marathas launched a major offensive against the Rohillas beyond the Ganga in collaboration with the Mughal emperor's troops and defeated them in many pitched battles. Mahadaji Sindhia maintained close contacts with the emperor on behalf of the Peshwa to deal with all the political and administrative problems. The grateful emperor conferred on him the *mansab* of 7,000 *zat* and *swar*, with the title of *Maharaja Patel Saheb* on November 7, 1772. Mahadaji Sindhia also received the districts of Anupshahr and Karnal in personal *jagir* befitting his imperial title. As for the Punjab, it had passed into the hands of the Sikhs and was lost by the Marathas forever.

The Peshwa Madhav Rao died a premature death at Poona on November 18, 1772 when their operations against the Rohillas in the Ganga valley were in full swing. It necessitated the withdrawal of the bulk of the Maratha forces from the north. Leaving behind skeletal Maratha troops at strategic places and their plenipotentiaries to deal with the major Indian chieftains, most of Maratha *sardars* either hastened towards Poona or made their way to their hereditary estates to safeguard their interests in the internal political upheaval that overtook the Peshwa's ruling house. Because of the defective Maratha polity and immaturity of their diplomatic skills, the Maratha influence in the north once again suffered a setback until Mahadaji Sindhia re-established the Maratha power at Delhi.

Mahadaji Sindhia's Contributions to the Spread of Maratha Power and Influence in the North (1769-92)

After the death of Madhav Rao I, the office of the Peshwa itself fell from its early importance like that of the Maratha Chhatrapati. Thereafter, it was Nana Farnavis, the hereditary chief minister of the Peshwa, who came to wield all powers of the central Maratha government at Poona, on behalf of the Peshwa, while Mahadaji Sindhia emerged as the premier Maratha chief at Delhi. He kept the Maratha flag fluttering in the North, particularly from 1772 to 1792. Mahadaji was 'an illegitimate son' of Ranoji Sindhia, an army officer of the first Peshwa, Balaji Vishwanath. As a reward for the valuable services rendered to the Maratha state, Ranoji was granted an estate in northern Malwa. He setup his headquarters at Ujjain and rose into prominence during the reigns of the first two Peshwas. Mahadaji was born in c.1728, and like the other four legitimate sons of Ranoji, started his career as a soldier. He held a junior command at the third battle of Panipat. He escaped alive from the battlefield but was seriously wounded and lamed for life. All the other four sons of Ranoji died in the active service of the state before or after the battle of Panipat, but Mahadaji was lucky enough to outlive his father and inherit his patrimony after the death of Ranoji.

Mahadaji Sindhia was a born soldier and excellent military commander. He raised a very powerful army for the defence of his estate and always carried with him a compact body of 15,000 strong mobile cavalry with which he fought many battles and humbled the pride of Rajput and Rohilla chiefs to establish the Maratha supremacy in central India and the Doab. He joined the Maratha expedition, led by Ramchandra Ganesha, in 1769-72, with a well-equipped regiment of Maratha troops, and was assigned the special duty of receiving the Mughal emperor Shah Alam II on the borders of Awadh and escorting him safely to Delhi. He performed this duty successfully and lodged him in the Red Fort without any untoward incident. The receipt of the exalted *mansab* of seven thousand *zat* and *swar* from the emperor raised his status as *amir-ul-umara* and enhanced his reputation and prestige among the Mughal nobility of Delhi; it enabled him to develop rapport with them in the establishment of law and order there. He utilised this opportunity to spread the Maratha power and influence in the Upper Doab and the Ganga valley. After the death of the fourth Peshwa, Madhav Rao I, he had also to go back to the Deccan with the bulk of his troops but before his departure from Delhi, he had setup a number of Maratha military outposts all through the region, and a contingent of 5,000 Maratha soldiers was posted at Delhi for the assistance of the Mughal emperor. Besides, the Maratha political and military agents were posted at the state headquarters of various Hindu and Muslim rulers of Rajputana and the Doab, who had acknowledged the suzerainty of the Peshwa.

In the first Anglo-Maratha war, Mahadaji Sindhia commanded the imperial Maratha forces in their grim struggle against the British and their treacherous Maratha collaborators, including Raghoba and the Gaekwar of Baroda, and saved the honour and sovereignty of the Maratha state. The war came to a close by the signing of the Treaty of Salbai (1782) between the belligerents, according to which the Poona Government received an assurance from the British not to interfere in the affairs of the Mughal emperor under the Maratha protection at Delhi. It enhanced Mahadaji's prestige and his power grew rapidly thereafter.

The Kingdom of Delhi during Mahadaji's Absence (1772-82): During the long absence of Mahadaji Sindhia from Delhi, the Maratha influence in the north received a temporary setback. The petty Maratha commanders, posted at far-flung places with small contingents of troops, did not command much fear or confidence in the hearts of the landed aristocracy and feudal chiefs of the region, who professed their allegiance to Poona. The self-seeking and incompetent officials of the emperor were unable to collect even the just enough revenues from the metropolis and the crown lands of Delhi to meet the expenses of the royal *harem* and salary of the ill-equipped Mughal soldiery and retainers. During this period, the emperor's only capable and trustworthy officer was Mirza Najaf Khan, a Persian immigrant to India, who commanded the Mughal army and managed the royal affairs with some success. After his death on 6 April 1782, the emperor fell into the hands of his totally worthless and greedy officials who started fighting with one another in their bid to use him as a puppet and establish their control over Delhi. Their cut-throat struggle for power assumed the form of a petty civil war, which was fought in the streets of Delhi, and 'made-up the blood-red history' of the imperial capital during the next two years and a half until the Marathas staged their comeback under the command of Mahadaji Sindhia and restored order there.

The Marathas in Control of Delhi (1783-1803)

As soon as Shah Alam II heard of the arrival of the Maratha forces on the borders of Rajputana by mid-1783, the Mughal emperor established his contacts with Mahadaji Sindhia and eagerly awaited his arrival. Mahadaji first of all recovered his fort of Gwalior from the *Rana* of Gohad in July and established his headquarters there for the further pursuit of his military targets. He demanded the accumulated arrears of *chauth,* due from the *Rana* for the last many years. As the latter evaded the issue, Mahadaji marched upon his capital, which fell to the Marathas after a pitched battle in February 1784. Gohad was not restored to its Rajput chief until the latter had re-affirmed his allegiance to Poona and cleared all the arrears of the tribute.

About this time, Sindhia came into contact with a French adventurer, Benoit de Boigne, who was employed by the Maratha chief to raise two trained battalions of infantry for him. Sindhia was so much pleased with the military acumen of Boigne that he took him under his permanent service and asked him to modernize all of his troops by engaging as many European military officers as he liked. Thereafter, Sindhia discarded the time-tested guerilla methods of Maratha warfare, and, in his enthusiasm, began to entrust his European officers with the actual commands of his forces also, which ruined his successor, Daulat Rao Sindhia, because of their treacherous desertions during the Second Anglo-Maratha War.

In October 1784, Mahadaji Sindhia crossed the Yamuna and entered the territories of the Doab. Meanwhile, Shah Alam II had left Delhi with family for reasons of his personal safety and shifted his residence to Agra. It was because one of his power-hungry Afghan officers, called Muhammad Beg Hamdani, was contriving to get hold of the emperor and compel him to secure appointment for himself as *Vakil-i-Mutlaq* or Regent of the empire much against the will of Shah Alam. After the death of Najaf Khan, Shah Alam had appointed Mirza Shafi Khan as his Regent, but Hamdani murdered him in cold blood in September 1783. Thereafter, the emperor nominated Afrasiyab Khan, a Hindu convert to Islam, as his Regent but Hamdani condemned the emperor's action and became a rebel. He took forced possession of the Mughal army camp, including heavy field guns, and prepared to offer armed resistance to the Maratha allies of the emperor. Afrasiyab was assassinated in his own camp at Khanua, about 9 kms off Fatehpur Sikri, on November 2, 1784. The emperor immediately alerted the Maratha commander to restrain his disaffected noble before proceeding towards Delhi. Thereupon, Mahadaji Sindhia, acting 'promptly but with admirable vigilance, tact and suppleness', ordered his troops to cordon off the army camp of Hamdani on the night of 6 November, and after a bloody encounter, that lasted three days, compelled him to lay down arms. Muhammad Beg and his officers were brought to Sindhia's camp as captives but set free 'on conditions that made him powerless for mischief'. All of his arms and military equipment, including 46 pieces of heavy artillery, were attached and 'his vanquished battalions were deprived of their flintlocks'; his *jagirs* were confiscated, and his family was sent to Ujjain 'to be held in Sindhia's capital as hostages for his fidelity', and, thereafter, his request to serve under the Maratha chief was granted.

The Mughal emperor was immensely pleased to know of all these developments. On November 14, 1784, 'the first day of the sacred month of *Muharram*', Mahadaji met him in the royal camp at Khanua, and after some reluctance, 'undertook his protection'. The very next day, Shah Alam II moved 'into the circuit of the Maratha camp', and, on the 17th, 'held the eagerly awaited secret conference with Sindhia, which was to shape the destiny of the Delhi empire for the next two decades'. (Sarkar, *Fall of the Mughal Empire*; iii, pp. 204-5). The Mughal emperor appointed the Peshwa as his *Vakil-i-Mutlaq* or 'Vice-regent of the Empire', with Mahadaji Sindhia as the Peshwa's deputy in Delhi; this title combined in it the two exalted Mughal offices of *Wazir* and *Mir*

Bakhshi of the empire. Sindhia was entrusted, on behalf of the Peshwa, the supreme command of the imperial Mughal army, and assigned the *Subas* of Delhi and Agra 'as a guarantee for the pay of his troops', including the Mughal and Maratha forces, under his command. By virtue of his imperial titles, Mahadaji Sindhia was now 'officially entitled to occupy all the royal forts, to receive payment of the fixed tributes from the vassal princes, and to take over the revenue collection of the Crown lands. The custodians of the royal treasuries and stores also were bound to him for what they held on behalf of the (Mughal) state'. (*Ibid.*, p. 209). Mahadaji Sindhia thus came to control the major part of northern India from the Ganga Valley to the Satluj, including the imperial cities of Delhi and Agra, and 'made the Marathas the supreme power in *Hindustan*'. These territorial rights and political powers of Mahadaji were over and above all the valuable estates, held by him in Malwa and the Deccan from the Maratha Government at Poona. He possessed a fine army, trained and disciplined by de Boigne and other European officers, and became the most powerful and celebrated warrior-statesman of the times.

Though armed with all the imperial titles and special powers to control the aforementioned territories and exercise his authority, Mahadaji Sindhia, according to J.N. Sarkar, had obtained but 'only two sheets of paper, signed by a titular Sovereign. He did not yet hold a single inch of the imperial domains beyond the ground his camp stood on. His dead predecessor's men occupied the two royal seats of Delhi and Agra. The royal treasuries and even the revenue records were in their possession. If Mahadaji was to be the Emperor's deputy in anything more than the name, he must get possession of the royal forts, the official treasures and the land still subject to the Crown. At first he hoped that the mere order of the Sovereign would transfer these adjuncts of the *Mir Bakhshi's* office to him...but at last the bitter truth dawned on his mind that, in the troubled politics of Delhi, force alone could win for him what was his due by law'. (*Ibid.*, pp. 208-9). This is what Mahadaji accomplished at the cost of huge sacrifices in men and material during the next two years. The cities of Delhi and Agra had to be wrested from the hands of the defiant Mughal officials before the emperor and his family were brought back to Delhi and lodged comfortably in their 'Palace Fort' (viz., the Red Fort). The Marathas recovered the fort of Agra on 31 March 1785 from the disaffected Mughal *Qiladar*, Ismail Beg Hamdani son of Muhammad Beg, who had been brought to book earlier. Ismail escaped to the Ganga

Valley and made common cause with the rebellious Rohilla chief, Ghulam Qadir. As Mahadaji intended to keep the stronghold of Agra under his personal control, the emperor regularized its possession by the Maratha chief by his formal appointment as the deputy of prince Akbar Khan, the second son of Shah Alam, who was the nominal *subedar* of Agra.

Mahadaji Sindhia had to launch a full-fledged military expedition to recover the fort of Aligarh from its rebellious Mughal *Qiladar* Jahangir Khan, a brother of the late *Mir Bakhshi* Afrasiyab; he was conspiring with the *Nawab Wazir* of Awadh and the British agents to forge an alliance against the Marathas. When Mahadaji invested the fort, a British army, commanded by Sir John Cummings, made its appearance at Atrauli, within 25 kms. of the scene of action, 'to watch the Maratha movements'. 'This unexpected and unjustifiable threat of British intervention caused the greatest alarm and perplexity to Sindhia', who vigorously protested to the British Resident, James Anderson, attached to his court. In consequence, Anderson 'secured orders from the Governor General, recalling Cummings to his own station'. With the instant withdrawal of British troops, 'the threatening clouds' of Anglo-Maratha conflagration were blown over; which was a great diplomatic victory of Sindhia. Finding further resistance useless, Jahangir Khan agreed to vacate the fort on the promise of safe exit with family and his followers. The fort of Aligarh was taken possession of by the Marathas on 20 November with its entire fortifications intact; which included 65 pieces of artillery and one mortar for throwing shells, besides huge quantities of ammunitions and provisions. The victory of Maratha arms at Aligarh raised the prestige of Sindhia throughout the Ganga Valley and facilitated his task of further conquests.

Prince Jawan Bakht (Jahandar Shah), the heir apparent of the emperor, had fled from Delhi to Lucknow in 1783 when the capital was engulfed in political anarchy; he had been granted protection by the *Nawab Wazir* of Awadh, and was also welcomed by the British. Warren Hastings actually intended to exploit the physical presence of the Mughal prince in their camp to see 'if Delhi could be brought within the English sphere'. In his eagerness, the Governor General came down from Calcutta to Lucknow and resided there for full six months, from March to August 1784, for this purpose, but the timely arrival of Mahadaji Sindhia with a vast army into the Doab dampened his spirits and foiled his attempts to take the imperial Mughal capital by storm. In desperation, the Governor General asked the Maratha chief to provide for the appanage of the fugitive Mughal prince from the revenues of Delhi, but neither the emperor nor Sindhia accepted his demand and, in the long run, Jawan Bakht got nothing from his royal patrimony and ended his life as a British pensioner at Benaras.

Mahadaji Sindhia was bold enough to demand tribute from the British on behalf of the Mughal emperor or recall the imperial grants, made to them under the Treaty of Allahabad (1765), but Macpherson, the successor of Warren Hastings, curtly refused to oblige the Maratha chief and indirectly denounced the sovereignty of the Mughal emperor. The British felt extremely worried about the revival of Maratha power in *Hindustan* but scrupulously avoided any conflict with Mahadaji Sindhia.

Most of the Rajput chiefs had thrown off the Maratha overlordship during the first Anglo-Maratha war and stopped the payment of *chauth* to Poona nor did they pay any tribute to the Mughal emperor at Delhi. The *Rana* of Gohad was reduced by Mahadaji Sindhia in 1783 before proceeding towards Delhi, but the other Rajput princes remained adamant to his reminders to fall in line. Therefore, immediately after the conquest of Aligarh, Sindhia made up his mind to bring under subjugation all the Rajput and other feudal chiefs of central India, in his new role as the deputy *Vakil-i-Mutlaq* of the Mughal empire. It gave rise to a piquant situation, which implied the re-establishment of the Maratha imperialism, now reinforced by the Mughal sanctions. It aroused the indignation of the freedom-loving Rajputs who joined their hands together to resist Mahadaji's demands. *Sawai Raja* Prithvi Singh Kachhwaha of Jaipur used to be a personal friend and admirer of Sindhia but, on his death in April 1778, his younger brother Pratap Singh succeeded him as the ruler of Jaipur. He was a haughty young man in his teens; he not only refused to pay any tribute to the Marathas or the Mughal emperor but also forged an alliance with *Raja* Bijay Singh of Jodhpur and many other Rajput princes to fight against the Marathas. During his Lalsot campaign in 1787, a hundred thousand strong army of the Rajput confederacy, equipped with 400 cannons, all of a sudden confronted Mahadaji Sindhia; they were also joined by a contingent of Ismail Beg Hamdani. A pitched battle was fought between the antagonists on 28 July 1787 at Tunga, in the vicinity of Lalsot, about 50 kms southeast of Jaipur. The battle raged for three days with heavy loss of lives on both sides before the Maratha chief disengaged his troops. The battle of Tunga (Lalsot) was not a victory for the Rajputs or for Mahadaji. The latter's tactical retreat from the battlefield 'was due, not to the threats of the enemy but to the treachery and dissensions in his own ranks, and the utter failure of provisions'. Most of the Muslim commanders and soldiers of Mahadaji's camp deserted him in the course of the battle and the Marathas were literally 'starved out of Rajputana'. (*Ibid.*, pp. 267-68). Flushed with victory, Bijay Singh marched upon the Maratha stronghold of Ajmer and took it by an assault. However, Mahadaji kept his cool and retired with his army to the Chambal, where he halted for a few months to reorganize his forces and replenish his equipment and provisions. By March 1788, he was able to renew his offensive against his foes.

Ghulam Qadir's Outrages in Delhi (July to October 1788)

Taking advantage of Sindhia's absence from Delhi and his discomfiture in the Lalsot campaign against the Rajputs, the Rohilla chief Ghulam Qadir started depredations in the Doab. He was 'a determined foe' of the Marathas and bore personal grievances against the Mughal emperor, who had ill-treated his father, Zabita Khan, and confiscated his *jagirs.* Ghulam Qadir overran some of the isolated Maratha outposts in the Doab and sneaked into Delhi on 14 July 1788 with 2,000 Rohilla miscreants. As described by Jadunath Sarkar, the imperial army was sent to oppose them, but 'treason had done its work' and the Mughal commander, Badal Beg, went over to the enemy with his entire contingent. Thereupon, Himmat Bahadur, the loyal Hindu general of the emperor, and the Maratha commander Ravloji Sindhia 'withdrew from their positions to avoid being caught in a trap'; that very night, they retreated to Faridabad and 'the capital lay defenseless'. The next day, Ismail Beg Hamdani also reached the metropolis with his troops and, within a couple of days, the combined forces of Ghulam Qadir, Badal Beg and Hamdani 'took full possession of the city'. The chief eunuch of the emperor, named Manzur Ali, who acted as the *Nazir*, viz., the 'superintendent of the royal *harem*', was also won over by the rebels, and it was through his treachery that they gained entry into the Red Fort and took its forced possession by disarming the royal guards.

'Thus began the last Afghan occupation of Delhi, which lasted for two months and a half, from 18 July to 2 October 1788'. Hell was then let loose on the hapless Mughal emperor and his family. He was deposed on 30 July and blinded ten days later. Ghulam Qadir took out Bidar Bakht, son of Ahmad Shah, the ex-emperor, from the royal prison and made him the new puppet emperor with the title of Jahan

Shah; he is said to have received 12 *lacs* of rupees from Malika-i-Zamani, the oldest surviving Mughal lady and widow of Muhammad Shah *Rangila,* to wreak her vengeance against Shah Alam, whose father Alamgir II had secured the throne by deposing and blinding Ahmad Shah, the only son and successor of Muhammad Shah Rangila. So, 'to the personal vendetta of Ghulam Qadir was added the internal rivalry of the Timurid princes which accentuated the agony and shame' of the phantom Mughal emperor and his royal family. All the 19 surviving sons of Shah Alam were tortured and thrown into the prison-cells; his eldest son, Jawan Bakht, who had escaped to Lucknow, was his twentieth son. The plunder of the palace and atrocities on the inmates of the Mughal *harem* had commenced the same evening of 30 July and the vandalism of Rohillas and other Afghan marauders continued till the last day of Ghulam Qadir's stay in Delhi. 'Princes were flogged, princesses were dishonoured, and maidservants and eunuchs were tortured and beaten to death to make them confess where the royal treasures were buried. The Red Fort was denuded of all the valuables, and the entire palace area as well as the mansions of the rich inhabitants of the city were ransacked and ripped up throughout in search for the hidden treasures. 'It was a dance of the demons for nine weeks'. —(Sarkar, Fall of the Mughal Empire; iii, p. 310).

Mahadaji Sindhia Brings the Culprits to Justice

On the receipt of information, Mahadaji Sindhia at once dispatched the Maratha contingents to restore law and order in Delhi and to track down the Rohilla culprits. He himself marched through the Doab with his main army to intercept the Rohilla marauders in flight from the capital. The Maratha forces reached the suburbs of Delhi on 28 September 1788 and liberated the metropolis of Shahjahanabad (Delhi) from Rohillas after a few skirmishes by 2 October. Ghulam Qadir held out at the Red Fort up to 10 October in his desperate bid to evacuate his besieged men with the booty. The Rohillas ferried across the Jamuna into the Doab by means of boats, and carried away with them a few surviving sons of Shah Alam, besides their own royal stooge, Bidar Bakht, as captives. About 20 of the Mughal princes and princesses died of torture or grievous shock of the Rohilla outrages. Before making their exit from Delhi, the Rohillas did not spare even their collaborators, including the *Nazir*, Manzur Ali, and Malika-i-Zamani; they were also shabbily treated and robbed of their entire wealth by the marauders.

The Marathas took possession of the Red Fort on 11 October 1788 and their flag once again fluttered on its walls, 'and was to continue there without a break' for the next 13 years, until the British dislodged them from Delhi. Immediate succour, in the form of cooked food, fresh water, and scavenging services, besides medical aid, were provided to 'the half-dead Shah Alam' and other surviving members of the royalty, some of whom had to be liberated from the dirty prison-cells by breaking open their locks. It took some days before the blinded emperor, wreathing in pain, regained full consciousness and responded to his saviours with a sense of great relief. Thereafter, the Maratha forces launched a vigorous campaign to hunt down Ghulam Qadir and his camp followers. They gave a hot chase to the culprits from place to place till they captured Ghulam Qadir himself on 19 December; he and his accomplices were sent in chains to Sindhia's camp at Mathura. They included the treacherous *Nazir* Manzur Ali also. The other notorious Afghan miscreant, Ismail Beg, son of Muhammad Beg Hamdani, finally surrendered to Perron, the French commander of Mahadaji Sindhia, in April 1792, and died in Maratha imprisonment in the fort of Agra in 1799. Ghulam Qadir was ordered to be tortured to death by Mahadaji in deference to the earnest desire of Shah Alam II.

The emperor, in gratitude to the Maratha chief, granted him the government of Mathura and Vrindaban in personal *jagir* and issued a *firman* 'forbidding cow-slaughter throughout his empire', whatever it implied. Two victories against the Rajputs enabled the Marathas to establish their complete dominance over the whole of Rajputana; the one was at Patttan on 20 June 1790 against Jaipur, and the other was at Merta, against *Raja* Bijay Singh of Jodhpur, on 10 September. The vanquished Rajput rulers acknowledged the suzerainty of the Poona Government and paid huge war indemnities besides tribute. Chittor, which fell within the sphere of influence of the Holkars, was also wrested by Mahadaji Sindhia from the hands of a rebellious scion of the Sisodia dynasty in November 1791, and restored to *Rana* Bhim Singh of Udaipur, who had reaffirmed his loyalty to the Peshwa. 'Thus by the end of 1791', writes Nilakanta Sastri, 'all North from the Narbada to the Satluj', had been brought under the suzerainty of the Maratha Chhatrapati 'by Mahadaji Sindhia, who had reduced the country to some kind of political order'.—(*History of India*; iii, Madras, 1952, p. 136).

Mahadaji Sindhia and Nana Farnavis at Poona

Ever since the Treaty of Salbai (1782), Mahadaji Sindhia had remained engrossed in the Maratha affairs in the North for over ten years before his return to Poona in June 1792. He came 'laden with honours and riches' and his prestige soared very high. His friends and admirers accorded him a rousing reception, although his arrival in Poona created quite 'a sensation', and Nana Farnavis—'the strong man of Poona', particularly felt alarmed. All this time, Mahadaji had maintained contacts with the imperial government at Poona only through correspondence, and had had no chance of a personal meeting or exchange of views with Nana Farnavis. The Nana had always apprehensions about him and the rumours were afloat that Mahadaji Sindhia might attempt to transplant the Maratha Government at Poona as a military dictator. The rise to power of Nana Farnavis at Poona, after the decline of the Peshwa's power, therefore, needs an explanation. After the death of the fourth Peshwa Madho Rao in 1772, his younger brother Narayan Rao, then aged seventeen years, became the fifth Peshwa, but being a minor, his uncle, Raghunath Rao – the younger brother of Balaji Baji Rao, became his Regent. Being an ambitious man of wicked nature, Raghunath Rao or Raghoba got the Peshwa murdered on August 30, 1773, with intentions to usurp the *Peshwaship* for himself. His perfidy having been exposed, the senior ministers of the deceased Peshwa and other prominent Maratha leaders, led by Nana Farnavis, took over the Government at Poona in the name of Ganga Bai, the widow of Narain Rao, who was then in the family way, to prevent Raghoba from usurping the office of the Peshwa. The Nana setup a council of twelve seniormost Maratha leaders, called the *Bara Bhais* (council of elders), to rule the Maratha state. It was a great 'constitutional revolution' at Poona, the full fruits of which could not be reaped towards the modernization of the Maratha political institutions because of the deep-rooted medieval practice of hereditary succession, attached to every office of importance in the Maratha polity. Ganga Bai gave birth to the posthumous child of the deceased Peshwa, on April 18, 1774, who was named Madhav Rao Narayan and promptly declared as the sixth Peshwa by the council of elders; and Nana Farnavis became his Regent during his minority. The original name of the Nana was Balaji Janardhan Bhanu; he held the hereditary charge of the *Hazur Daftar* or the Imperial Secretariat at Poona in his capacity as the Chief Auditor (*Farnavis*) and Secretary to the Peshwa since the days of Madho Rao. It spoiled all chances of Raghoba to make any compromise with the ruling elite at Poona. Thus everything having been set in the medieval mould of hereditary succession, Nana Farnavis held the reins of the imperial Maratha Government at Poona as its *de facto* ruler during the minority of the Peshwa.

Of course, Mahadaji Sindhia had emerged as the most powerful Maratha general of the times but he did not intend to disturb the constitutional setup, however odd, of the Maratha state. By this time, the young Peshwa Madhav Rao Narayan had come of age, and begun 'to express himself in striking administrative acts of his own'. Mahadaji Sindhia had his first formal meeting with the Peshwa in his palace in the presence of Nana Farnavis on June 13, 1772. He took the initiative in his own hands, thereafter, and organized a grand *darbar* for the Peshwa on 21 June. Sindhia presented to the Peshwa, with utmost humility, the royal *firman* and insignia of the imperial office and titles, conferred on him by the Mughal emperor; these included the office of *Vakil-i-Mutlaq* and title of *Maharajadhiraja* for the Peshwa and that of *Maharaja* for Mahadaji Sindhia. The next day, the Peshwa ceremoniously declared the appointment of Mahadaji Sindhia as his *naib* or deputy in the Mughal court at Delhi, in his capacity as the *Vakil-i-Mutlaq* of the Mughal empire. Nana Farnavis was completely upset by these goings-on. He kept mum in public but, after the conclusion of these proceedings, took Mahadaji Sindhia to task for compromising the Maratha sovereignty by giving undue importance to the titles and sanctions of the dummy Mughal emperor. He believed in the absolute sovereignty of the Maratha state, as had been conceived by *Chhatrapati* Shivaji, and always wanted that 'whatever honour the Maratha chiefs won, should be only in the name of the Maratha *Chhatrapati* and the Imperial Government of the Marathas at Poona'. It struck a discordant note between the two Maratha stalwarts in the matter of policy and the line of approach to be adopted in the interests of the Maratha state. Sindhia 'began to interest himself in the administration of the state', but, the Nana resented the move, and complained against him to the Peshwa. He offered 'to resign and betake himself to the life of an ascetic unless his master reposed full confidence in him'. Mahadaji was taken aback to note these developments. His aspirations were all shattered and, after hanging on at Poona for 20 months without achieving any material result, he was struck with fever and breathed his last, after a brief illness, on 12 February 1794. Mahadaji Sindhia was the greatest Maratha general of his times. In the words of Ishwari Prasad, 'he was a born military leader and had shown his great qualities in the battles he had fought. He had a rare organizing capacity and enjoyed, in a large measure, the confidence and devotion of his officers and men. Mahadaji was a man of sense and sagacity, who had a clear perception of the political issues that confronted him during his life. He was never swayed by emotions'. (*History of Modern India*; Allahabad, 1975, pp. 253-54). So long as Mahadaji Sindhia and Nana Farnavis were at the helm of affairs, the Marathas constituted the greatest political power of the country; they had successfully beaten their Mughal and Afghan rivals and aspired to transplant the imperial Mughal authority in India.

The celebrated Sindhia chief had no male issue. Therefore, a few months before his death, he had nominated Daulat Rao, a 14 years old son of his nephew Anand Rao, as his successor. Daulat Rao Sindhia was in attendance upon Mahadaji at the time of his death, and was immediately granted his patrimony by the Peshwa, on the recommendation of Nana Farnavis. Accordingly, he took charge of Mahadaji's army camp with its entire property and the estates intact. Daula Rao Sindhia was naturally beholden to Nana Farnavis and ready to serve his master wholeheartedly. It gave an added strength to the Nana in consolidating his hold over all the other members of the Maratha Confederacy.

Defeat of the Nizam at Kharda (March 1795)

Nana Farnavis immediately cashed on his improved relations with Mahadaji's successor and the presence of his vast army at Poona, and resumed his campaign to extend the Maratha power and prestige in the Deccan. The Marathas had already humbled the pride of Tipu Sultan. The Nana, therefore, directed his attention towards Nizam Ali of Hyderabad, and revived his demand for the recovery of huge arrears of *chauth* overdue from him. The Nizam and his minister, Mushir-ul-Mulk, not only rejected his demand but also repudiated the claims of the Bhonsle chief 'on the revenues of Berar'. In consequence, the combined armies of the Peshwa, Daulat Rao Sindhia, Tukoji Holkar and Raghoji Bhonsle II, invaded the Nizam's dominions early in March 1795. Nizam Ali appealed to the English for help but they shrugged off their shoulders. A decisive engagement between the antagonists took place at Kharda (Kurdla), halfway between Poona and Bidar. Unable to face the Marathas in the open, the Nizam shut himself in the fort of Kharda, which was immediately put under siege by the Marathas. They cut off food and water supply to the fort and installed heavy artillery around its walls for bombardment when the Nizam panicked and sued for peace on 13 March. According to the treaty of peace, concluded by him with the Marathas, he promised to pay five *crores* of rupees as accumulated arrears of *chauth* and war indemnity besides the surrender of about a third of his territorial possessions. The lands thus surrendered by him to the Marathas comprised (i) the stronghold of Daulatabad and all of its dependent territories were ceded to the Peshwa, and (ii) all the erstwhile Maratha lands, including the province of Berar, with its accumulated revenues, were restored to the *Raja* of Nagpur. This was 'the last occasion when all the important Maratha chiefs had acted in concert', under the central authority of the Poona Government; its credit goes exclusively to Nana Farnavis.

The historical towns of Delhi, Agra, Aligarh and Gwalior etc; and the vast territories of northern and central India, including Bundelkhand, Rajputana, the Doab and the Ganga valley were firmly held by the Marathas under their control until they were conquered by Lord Wellesley as a result of the Second Anglo-Maratha War (1803-6) and annexed to the dominions of the East India Company.

SECTION 7: ANGLO-MARATHA STRUGGLE FOR SUPREMACY IN INDIA

By the year 1772, the Marathas had made a spectacular recovery from the debacle of Panipat and become the masters of Delhi once again. In their triple contest for supremacy with the other two contenders for imperial power, viz., the Mughal nobles, and the foreign invader Ahmad Shah Abdali, supported by his Afghan and Rohilla immigrants in India, the Marathas clearly emerged as the predominant political power in the country, and they aspired to transplant the tottering Mughal empire as the imperial rulers of India. Simultaneously, the British traders turned colonialists had acquired their territorial possessions at three strategic places, Bombay, Madras and Calcutta, of the Indian coastline, and they were striving hard to knock out all other European rivals, including the French, in their bid to establish their hegemony on the Indian waters. The decline of the imperial Mughal authority and decadent political condition of the country encouraged them to nurture territorial designs on the mainland also. Murshid Quli Khan, the Mughal viceroy (*nawab*) of Bengal, Bihar and Orissa, had become virtually independent of Delhi since 1719; the newly built town of Murshidabad was his headquarters. His dynasty was transplanted by Alivardi Khan in 1740. During his period of rule (1740-56), Bengal, Bihar and Orissa witnessed repeated Maratha invasions, which compelled Alivardi Khan to purchase peace with them by ceding the province of Orissa to them in lieu of the *chauth*. Alivardi Khan had no male issue; therefore, on his death, one of his maternal grandsons, named Siraj-ud-Daulah, ascended the throne of Bengal in April 1756. His accession did not go unchallenged, however. Mir Jaffar, the commander-in-chief of Siraj-ud-Daulah's forces, conspired against him in connivance with the employees of the English East India Company to bring about his fall. The battle of Plassey (23 June 1757), fought by the English against Siraj-ud-Daulah, made them the 'power behind the throne' of their creature, Mir Jaffar, who secured the throne of Bengal with their help. It enabled Clive, 'the governor of Company's affairs in Bengal' to exploit the rich resources of the province to destroy the French power in the Deccan in the third Karnatak war (1758-63). Mir Jaffar, in turn, exploited the name of the 'defunct' Mughal dynasty, to legitimatize his position as the Nawab of Bengal. He sent his envoy with rich presents to Alamgir II, the puppet Mughal emperor at Delhi, and secured from him the viceroyalty of the provinces of Bengal, Bihar and Orissa for himself and honorific title of *amir-ul-umara* (*Omara*) for Clive. It made Clive a noble (*mansabdar*) of the Mughal empire and also entitled him to the grant of a *jagir*. That is how Clive frequently flaunted this title to style himself as 'the Indian Nawab', and it was on this very ground that he had exhorted from Mir Jaffar the grant of quit-rents of 24 Parganas, to the tune of 30,000 pounds per annum, in his own name. Amusingly, when the Mughal *Shahzada* (Prince) Ali Gauhar (future Shah Alam II), heir-apparent to the same phantom Mughal emperor, entered Bihar in 1759, he was treated as an invader and expelled from Bihar by the combined forces of Mir Jaffar and Clive.

About that very time, the Marathas, in their northward march, had scored successive victories over their Afghan and Mughal rivals. On 6 September 1757, Delhi fell into the hands of the Marathas and they took the phantom Mughal Emperor, Alamgir II, under their protection, apparently as their suzerain. The repeated invasions of Ahmad Shah Abdali, turned the scales in favour of the invader and his Indian protégés, but the Marathas retrieved their position very quickly and their flag fluttered from the ramparts of the Red Fort of Delhi once again on the first of August 1760. In the interregnum, the weak and imbecile Mughal emperors played as mere pawns in the hands of the victors whosoever they were. Alamgir II, who was held as virtual prisoner in the hands of his crafty *Wazir*, Imad-ul-Mulk, was got murdered by the latter on 29 November 1759. Prince Ali Gauhar, the eldest son of the deceased, had, however, escaped from Delhi a year earlier, and sought shelter with Shuja-ud-daulah, the Nawab Wazir of Awadh. On the receipt of information about the assassination of his father, Ali Gauhar installed himself as his rightful successor, styled as Shah Alam II, and the Nawab Wazir of Awadh was declared to be his *wazir* or prime minister. On regaining their control over Delhi in August 1760, the Marathas disclaimed Shah Jahan III, another Mughal princeling, whom Imad-ud-Mulk had installed on the throne in the Red Fort, and, instead, espoused the cause of Shah Alam II. They took out Jawan Bakht, a minor son of Alamgir II (the younger brother of Shah Alam II) from the underground royal prison cells of the Red Fort, and set him up as Regent of his elder brother (Shah Alam II) until his arrival at Delhi. Thus the Marathas and English were both contenders for power; they nurtured imperial designs and started their race for political ascendancy in the country almost simultaneously.

The debacle of Panipat, on 14 January 1761, gave a setback to the Maratha imperial interests in the North though their victors, Abdali and his Indian accomplices, also failed to enjoy the fruits of their hard-earned victory for long. When the Marathas were reeling back to the Deccan after their defeat at Panipat, Shah Alam II, in his third successive bid to recover Bihar with the support of the *Nawab Wazir* of Awadh, suffered a defeat on the river Son at the hands of the British forces, led by Major Carnac on 15 January 1761. The very next day, viz., on 16 January 1761, the French stronghold of Pondicherry, in the Deccan, fell into the British hands. The British colonial star was definitely on the ascent.

The British colonialists were not oblivious of the political upheaval that had engulfed northern India in the wake of the Afghan invasions, penetration of the Marathas into the north and their active intervention in the political developments at Delhi, the imperial capital of India. They knew all about the imperial ambitions of the Marathas and were also fully informed about the huge sacrifices made by them in checkmating the repeated invasions of Abdali on India. The British governors of Bombay and Madras always attempted to maintain friendly relations with the Peshwas and usually desisted from such political ventures as were likely to earn their displeasure. They earned the goodwill of the third Peshwa Balaji Baji Rao by observing neutrality in his armed conflict with the Portuguese. It was the 'myopic vision' of the Peshwa, however, that he failed to see through the colonial designs of the British traders, and felt encouraged even to seek their armed assistance in chastising his disaffected Maratha naval chief, Tulaji Angre, in March 1755. It weakened the Maratha naval power and removed a major hurdle from the path of the British in establishing their predominance in the Arabian Sea. When Tulaji was defeated and taken captive to the Peshwa, the British thoroughly exploited their role as allies of Balaji Baji Rao to completely destroy the century-old and renowned naval base of the Marathas at Vijaydurg, in their apparent bid to wrest it from the hands of the rebellious Angre chief. And all this was done by the British Admiral Watson on behalf of, and in the name of the Peshwa. It gave a fatal blow to the Maratha naval power and proved disastrous for the Maratha state in the long run. The fort of Vijaydurg was taken possession of by the British admiral, complete with its military stores and property, including the unspecified quantity of hoarded treasures of the famous Angre family, on the night of 13-14 February 1756, after heavy bombardment, and was held by them forcibly by preventing entry of the Peshwa's troops therein. Such a development was never visualised by Balaji Baji Rao nor did it form a part of the agreement, signed by him with the British Governor of Bombay. In resorting to such measures, the British, obviously, transgressed the provisions of the agreement, overstepped the stipulated plans, and acted against the desire or approval of the Peshwa. Having inadvertently been asked to give a helping hand to the Peshwa's forces, the British seized the opportunity to push forward their aggressive designs with full force to weaken the Maratha naval power.

Balaji Baji Rao fretted and fumed and demanded the evacuation of Vijaydurg by the British. The fort was not surrendered by them to the Peshwa until the latter agreed to pay a price for it. In return for the recovery of Vijaydurg, Balaji Baji Rao had to sign a treaty with the British agents at Poona on 12 October 1756, according to which, they were granted two small naval fortresses of Bankot and Himatgarh, along with ten adjoining villages. Besides, the Peshwa held out a promise 'to exact no additional inland duties on the English merchandise' and to exclude the Dutch from trade in his territories. Thus, as a result of this mad venture, the Peshwa himself jeopardized the interests of the Maratha state without having made any substantial gain in return. Tulaji Angre, a formidable foe of the British was liquidated, and the British made their inroads into the Maratha lands by legally acquired territorial possessions, however small. 'It was a great success for the British, who had already secured considerable power in Karnatak'. Balaji Baji Rao could not gauge the territorial ambitions of the British at

Madras and Calcutta, and remained indifferent towards their deadly conflict with Siraj-ud-Daulah, the Nawab of Bengal, in 1756-57. In December 1759, when the Peshwa was engrossed in dispatching the Maratha forces to the North to save Delhi, the imperial capital of India, from falling into the hands of the Afghan invader, the British not only built bridges with the Siddis of Janjira but also conspired with the local Siddi officer of the Mughal *subedar* at Surat in Gujarat to take forced possession of the world-famous seaport. Because of his preoccupation with the northern expedition, the Peshwa could not take any action against the British; it is an irony of fate that when the Marathas were deploying their forces at the strongholds of Attock and Peshawar to protect the country from foreign aggression through the Khyber Pass, the British were silently making their entry into Surat 'by the backdoor', and consolidating their position along the seacoasts of India with imperial designs.

Raghunath Rao *alias* Raghoba was the first Maratha chief to establish treaty relationships with the British traders at Bombay in 1761, in his capacity as the Regent of the Maratha Empire on behalf of the minor Peshwa Madhav Rao. Instead of questioning the British aggression on Surat, Raghoba went out of the way to win their friendship through conciliatory measures. The first treaty was signed by Crommelin, the President of Bombay, with Govind Shiv Ram, the agent of Raghoba, on behalf of the Peshwa, on 14 September 1761, which 'assured civility and friendship between the Peshwa and the President of the Bombay Factory' and placed the Siddis of Janjira under British protection at their demand. They utilized the services of the Siddis (Abyssinians) as their junior allies in the ensuing wars against the Marathas in due course of time. Raghoba rushed to the British for the second time in December 1761 with a request for troops and guns from Bombay to fight against the impending attack of Nizam Ali of Hyderabad on Poona. The Bombay Council agreed to furnish him with the required men and material 'provided the island of Salsette and the fort of Bassein were ceded to them'. Raghunath Rao himself turned down their demand as 'most extravagant' as he 'was not yet prepared to jeopardize the Maratha interests' to that extent. (S.N. Sen, *Anglo-Maratha Relations: 1785-96*; Macmillan, 1974, p.5). Nevertheless, soon thereafter, Raghoba threw all interests of the Maratha state to the winds when he 'flirted' with the British agent Brome to seek their help in his fratricidal struggle against Madhav Rao for the attainment of *Peshwaship*.

To his dismay, it were the British who 'politely turned down his request on the pretext of observing non-interference in the internal disputes of the Marathas. In fact, they were not as yet fully prepared or confident of taking on the central Maratha authorities at Poona'. Raghoba was ultimately defeated by Madhav Rao in a pitched battle near Dhodap on 10 June 1768 and put into confinement. To the misfortune of the Marathas, Raghoba was released from captivity by Madhav Rao two days before his death. Not only this; the Peshwa, while lying on his death-bed, entrusted his minor brother, Narayan Rao, to his care 'in the spirit of forget and forgive; and granted him a personal *jagir,* worth five lacs per annum for his comfortable living befitting his regal status'. This un-called for clemency, exercised by Madhav Rao in favour of his most undeserving wily uncle became the major 0f destruction of the Maratha power in the long-run.

Fortune smiled on the British shoulders when they measured their swords with the confederacy of three Mughal princes at the battle of Buxar on 23 October 1764. Clive, the architect of the Treaty of Allahabad (1765), obtained the *Diwani* of Bengal, Bihar and Orissa for the Company from the vanquished Mughal emperor, and thoroughly exploited his name and regal status to legalise the position of the English as imperial servants of the Mughal Crown. They flaunted their Mughal titles and imperial *sanads* to claim their status as ruling elite of the country and make them acceptable to the Indian populace. In return, they provided Shah Alam II with a temporary abode at Allahabad and a tribute of 26 *lacs* of rupees per annum, but all at the cost of his own Mughal *subedars* of Awadh and Bengal respectively Their efforts to keep the emperor under their permanent tutelage failed, however, and Shah Alam II made his way to Delhi under the Maratha protection after 12 years of wanderings. The British looked upon with deep concern the revival of Maratha power at Delhi, and they made hectic efforts to safeguard their territorial possessions from the Maratha encroachments with or without the use of Mughal emperor's name and regal authority. On their own part, they neither openly disavowed the Mughal sovereignty nor remitted any tribute for Bengal to Shah Alam II at Delhi. They, however, took prompt action to prevent the Marathas from taking over the districts of Kara and Allahabad in the name of the Mughal emperor, and strengthened the defences of Awadh, apparently as a buffer state between the Company's possessions and those of the Marathas, to avoid head-on collision with them as far as possible.

First Anglo-Maratha War (1775-82)

In 1773-74, the ruling house of the Peshwa itself fell from grace when Raghunath Rao, the seniormost member of the family, and regent of the minor Peshwa Narayan Rao, got his ward murdered and, thereafter, sought the armed intervention of the East India Company to fight against his own people to acquire the *Peshwaship* for himself. It came as a windfall to the British when Raghoba signed the Treaty of Surat (6 March 1775) with the Company's government at Bombay, according to which he promised to cede the island of Salsette and the seaport of Bassein to them in return for their help. The Company, with the tacit approval of the British Government in London, was now prepared to challenge the Maratha supremacy in India by taking advantage of their mutual dissensions. Their participation in the Maratha War of Succession for the *Peshwaship* as allies of one of the parties to the dispute converted it into the First Anglo-Maratha War (1775-82). It continued for seven long years and was evenly contested by both the parties with determination, in which Nana Farnavis, as the organiser, and Mahadaji Sindhia, as the Commander-in-chief of the Maratha forces, played their roles with competence and perfect harmony with each other to safeguard the interest of the Maratha state. The war came to an end at the British initiative by the Treaty of Salbai on 17 May 1782 with the major provision of returning each other's conquests and restoring *status quo ante* with the exception that the island of Salsette (but not Bassein) had to be ceded to the British as promised by Raghoba to them. In return, the British recognised Madho Rao Narayan as the Peshwa and gave up the cause of Raghunath Rao; the latter was completely deserted by the British, who withdrew from him all financial support and protection or assistance. Raghoba's ally Fateh Singh Gaekwar was recognised as an independent ruler but under the suzerainty of the Peshwa at Poona; according to the terms of the treaty, he had 'to pay to the Peshwa the tribute *as usual previous to the war*, and was to perform such services and to subject himself to such obedience, *as had long been established and customary*'. The British gave an assurance that the East India Company 'would not interfere in the affairs of the Mughal emperor under the Maratha protection at Delhi'. In the words of S. P. Varma, 'all these conditions involved a complete and unconditional surrender on the part of the English of all their recent encroachments on the territories of the Maratha state'. (*A Study in Maratha Diplomacy – Anglo-Maratha Relations: 1772-83*; Agra, 1954, pp. 370-71). It was a great victory of the Marathas. The British had definitely under-estimated the strength of the Poona Government and over-estimated the popularity of the Maratha traitor, Raghoba.

To the misfortune of the Marathas, the unscrupulous Raghunath Rao, nicknamed Raghoba (*Raghoba-bharari* or 'the runaway' – a fugitive) had set the precedent and left a trail of the coming events. 'The day the seniormost member of the Peshwa's ruling house betrayed the interests of the Maratha state and bartered away the honour and self-respect of the country to the foreign adventurers, the sun of the Maratha fortunes set in the western horizon forever. ....It convinced the British that India could be won by the Indians for them; hence their constant search to look out for short-sighted and self-seeking collaborators, if not the outright traitors, among the Indian chiefs to advance their imperial interest in the country'. (*Advanced Study*; iv, pp. 534-40). Percival Spear, therefore, correctly observes that 'from this time onward, the Maratha leaders gradually played more and more for their own individual aggrandizement, and did little for the cause of the Maratha state, thus facilitating the ultimate supremacy of the British in India'. (*Cambridge History of India*; v, 1968, p. 256).

SECTION 8: CONCLUSION

A brief survey of the political developments in India in the eighteenth century brings us to the conclusion that the Marathas had established their sovereignty in the Deccan during the very lifetime of Aurangzeb. The Mughal Empire declined after his death and rapidly disintegrated during the first half of the eighteenth century. The reign of Muhammad Shah Rangila (1719-48) coupled with Nadir Shah's invasion, marked the end of the Mughal sovereignty in the country. It gave rise to the contenders for imperial power who, in the first phase, included the Mughal nobles and the foreign invader, Ahmad Shah Abdali, and his Afghan and Rohilla allies in India, besides the Marathas. By the year 1770, the phantom Mughal emperors and their Mughal bureaucracy, as well as the Afghan and Rohilla chiefs along with their foreign patron from across the Khyber Pass, had all seized to exist as a political factor in the national politics of India, leaving behind the Marathas as the sole contenders for imperial power. But, by that time, the European traders-turned colonialists had become active along the seacoasts of India. Taking advantage of the disintegration of the Mughal Empire, they also jumped into the fray for territorial and political gains, in which the English acquired ascendancy over the French and other

European rivals, in the first instance. The battle of Plassey in 1757 established their foothold in Bengal, and that of Buxar in 1764 enabled them to get hold of the phantom Mughal emperor from whom they secured the *Diwani* of Bengal Bihar and Orissa, to legitimatize their territorial possessions and assert their claim as the local and regional chiefs like the other 'Indian Nawabs'. This set the stage for their entry into the race for imperialism as political rivals of the Marathas. The Anglo-Maratha struggle for supremacy in India continued unabated throughout the eighteenth century and spilled over much beyond the medieval period of Indian history into the nineteenth century. Born and bred on the medieval concepts and values of sovereignty, the Maratha ruling elite confronted the modernized champions of the most highly advanced and industrialized nation-state of Europe on the Indian soil which was still stuck up in the bondage of medieval polity, backward economy and highly conservative socio-cultural order. It goes to the credit of those sons of the soil, like Balaji Baji Rao, Mahadaji Sindhia and Nana Farnavis etc that they surmounted all the hurdles and held their heads high in their highly uneven struggle against their foreign foes from the northwest as well as the high seas for more than a century to save the sovereignty, honour and self-respect of their country and continued their struggle till the bitter end.

When Lord Wellesley (1798-1805), the exponent of 'forward policy' and architect of 'subsidiary alliances' took charge of the Company's dominions in India, 'the Marathas were (still) the strongest Indian power of the times. ...They felt elated on account of their victory over the Nizam.... The Sindhias held their sway at Delhi, and the Mughal emperor Shah Alam II was a mere puppet in their hands. The Maratha conquests in the Ganga valley, *outflanking Awadh and the provinces of Bengal and Bihar*, posed a direct threat to the British fortunes in India. Nevertheless, by that time, the Marathas presented the picture of a house divided against itself. The authority of the Central Government at Poona was considerably weakened for lack of support from its powerful regional chiefs. The so-called Maratha confederacy had lost its old cohesion, and its hereditary warlords, though masters of vast territories and formidable armies were now more disunited and torn asunder by their mutual dissensions than ever before. It was, therefore, not very difficult to infiltrate into their ranks, as allies of some and foes of others, and to make them fight with one another, thus frittering away their energies and resources in their self-destructive activities'. (*Advanced Study*; iv, p. 570). The renewal of the Anglo-Maratha contest for supremacy in India, long after the extinction of the Mughal empire, in the nineteenth century or the modern age so-called, can be understood better in this contest.

It was with the above political background in mind that Lord Wellesley decided to intervene in the Maratha affairs to the advantage of the British. Violent twists in the Maratha politics at Poona had brought forth Baji Rao II, the unworthy son of the notorious traitor Raghoba as the eighth Peshwa; he proved to be the last incumbent of this exalted office who saw through the extinction of the Maratha sovereignty in India during his very lifetime. Like his father, Baji Rao II was also 'ambitious, obstinate, revengeful and treacherous besides being an incapable ruler'; he was hated and despised by the people at large and could not keep the premier Maratha nobles of the confederacy under his control. Nana Farnavis, 'the strong man of Poona', died on 13 March 1800 and 'with him departed all the wisdom and moderation of the Maratha government.' Given the weakening of the Maratha confederacy and hapless condition of the Peshwa, Lord Wellesley was saved the trouble of reckoning with a strong Maratha authority at Poona, which had proved the greatest hurdle in the way of Warren Hastings in the past. Wellesley had his own plans to strangulate the Peshwa to political death by offering his hand of friendship and cooperation to him, apparently, in the spirit of good neighbourliness. After the death of the Nana, two Maratha nobles, Daulat Rao Sindhia and Jaswant Rao Holkar, fell out with each on the issue of establishing their respective domination at Poona with the object of keeping the Peshwa under their thumb. To liberate himself from the tutelage of his over-ambitious chiefs, Baji Rao II fled from Poona and accepted the subsidiary system of the company by the treaty of Bassein which was signed by him on December 31, 1802. On hearing of it, three Maratha chiefs, Jaswant Rao Holkar, Daulat Rao Sindhia and Raghuji Bhonsle II of Nagpur denounced it as a 'national disgrace'. According to them, 'the submission of the Peshwa to a foreign colonial power implied that the whole of the Maratha nation had lost its independence'. Yet they did not take any hostile action against the British, and it was, instead, Lord Wellesley, who declared war on the Maratha confederates, apparently on behalf of the Peshwa. Gaekwar of Baroda detached himself from the central Maratha government at Poona while Holkar held aloof from Sindhia and Bhonsle in the first phase of the war, and had to face the music at a later stage. It is known to history as the Second Anglo-Maratha War which lasted about three years from 1803 to 1806, with a brief interregnum.

There were two theatres of the war, the Deccan and Northern India. The command of the Deccan forces was held by Sir Arthur Wellesley, the younger brother of the Governor General. He engaged Bhonsle in the south, captured Ahmadnagar, and then defeated the Maratha armies at Assaye and Argaon in 1803. At this stage, Bhonsle made peace with the British by the Treaty of Deogaon (17 December 1803), according to which he ceded the province of Cuttack (Orissa), including Balasore to the English and accepted the subsidiary system of Lord Wellesley.

The command of the North Indian forces was entrusted to Lord Lake. He reached Aligarh on 29 August 1803 and found the Maratha troops, under Perron, the French general of Daulat Rao Sindhia, entrenched near Koil; they were composed of mobile cavalry and light artillery. Before the battle warmed up, Perron deserted his charge and fled towards Agra along with other European officers and the bodyguards. Though deserted by their French commander and other foreign officers, Sindhia's soldiers heroically defended the fort of Aligarh for a week before their surrender on 4 September. After leaving a contingent of English army at Aligarh to take effective control of the fort and its dependent territories, Lake left for Delhi on 7 September and fought the next battle against Sindhia's trained soldiers at Patparganj, to the south of the metropolis, on the opposite (left) bank of the Yamuna, on 11 September 1803. Here also the French commander, M. Louis Bourquin, made a false show of resistance and then fled with his personal valuable assets and guards, and left intact not only the whole of Sindhia's artillery and ammunitions in Lake's hands but also the bridge of boats, built across the Yamuna, which was used with advantage by the advancing British forces. Lake crossed over to Delhi by that very bridge of boats on 14 September. In spite of the treacherous desertions by their foreign commanders, Sindhia's soldiers fought desperately all through the day and suffered heavy loss of life before their dispersal on the nightfall. The British forces occupied the Red Fort, and took the phantom Mughal emperor, Shah Alam II, under their protection. By 17 October, the British army had overrun the towns of Mathura and Agra without much resistance. The main army of Daulat Rao Sindhia was defeated by General Lake at Laswari, about 32 kms south of Alwar, on the first of November 1803. According to W.M. James, 'the battle continued till late in the evening, and by the time it was over, the British troops were left with no strength to pursue the vanquished foe'. The British commander conveyed the news of this historic victory to the Governor General as follows:

'All the *sepoys* of the enemy (Sindhia) behaved exceedingly well, and, if they had been commanded by French officers (who had deserted the Maratha chief), the event would have been, I fear, extremely doubtful. I never was in so severe a business in my life, or anything like it, and pray to God I never may be in such a situation again. Their gunners stood to their guns until killed by the bayonet; these fellows fought like devils or rather heroes'. —(*The British Rule in India*, pp. 157-58).

Daulat Rao Sindhia made peace with the British by the Treaty of Surji Anjangaon (30 December 1803), according to which he ceded Broach, Ahmadnagar, the Upper Doab (viz., the territory between the Yamuna and the upper Ganga) together with Delhi and Agra to the British and accepted the subsidiary system. While fighting against Sindhia and Bhonsle, Jaswant Rao Holkar was tactfully spared by the British to wean him away from the rest of 'the Maratha confederates'. Therefore, he observed neutrality in the war and stood aloof while his fellow Maratha chiefs were being thrashed by a foreign imperialist power. However, he was intrigued by the cession of large tracts of the Maratha dominions, particularly in the North, by Sindhia, over which Holkar as well as the Peshwa both had their claims. When he raised objections about the terms of the treaty, signed by the British with Sindhia, Lord Wellesley felt affronted and at once declared war on Holkar. It constituted the second phase of the war and lasted from April 1804 to January 1806. Ranjit Singh, the Jat chief of Bharatpur, also joined hands with Holkar to fight against the British. Holkar inflicted crushing defeats on two English generals, Monson and Murray and marched on Delhi at the head of a huge army, composed of about 60,000 cavalry, 15,000 infantry and a contingent of well-trained artillerymen, equipped with 192 field guns. He was repulsed by Lt. Colonel Ochterlony, but it panicked the British who rushed heavy reinforcements to Delhi under the personal command of General Lake. Holkar put up a joint front against the British in association with the Jat chief of Bharatpur. The fort of Dig fell to the British after a bloody encounter on 13 December 1804, but, in spite of his best efforts, Lake failed to conquer the stronghold of Bharatpur. Meanwhile, Lord Wellesley was recalled to London by the Directors of the Company, and General Lake, on the directions from the home government, concluded the Treaty of Rajpurghat, on the Beas in the Punjab, with Holkar, on 24 December 1805, on very liberal terms. Holkar was restored to all of his lost territories, to the south and east of the River

Chambal. The Company agreed to give him back the most of his possessions in the Deccan. Unlike the Peshwa Baji Rao II, Sindhia and Bhonsle, Holkar bluntly refused to join the subsidiary system but, with the object of isolating him from the other Maratha chiefs, he was asked to renounce all the claims over Poona or the Maratha allies of the British. At the same time, to placate the Sindhia chief, the Company agreed to make some alterations in the Treaty of Surji Anjangaon, according to which the forts of Gwalior and Gohad, with their dependent territories, were restored to him. For the further satisfaction of the Marathas, the new Governor General, Sir George Barlow (1805-1807), in spite of strong protests from General Lake, made public the annexed 'declaratory articles' to the treaties with Sindhia and Holkar, whereby the British protection was withdrawn from the states north of the Chambal 'from Kotah to the Jumna'; it automatically restored the states of Tonk, Rampur and Bundi (but not Bundelkhand) to the suzerainty of Holkar. Likewise, all the subsidiary treaties, made previously by the various Rajput chiefs with the Company were treated as cancelled, thus leaving them to the influence of the Marathas again. Of course, Holkar held out a promise not to entertain any Europeans in his service, and the Company, on its part, undertook not to interfere with his territories south of the Chambal. It was a great triumph of Holkar in extracting such terms from the British who were nurturing the hopes of establishing their undisputed hegemony over the whole of the country. Holkar remained unbeaten and the British struggle against the Marathas for supremacy was a far cry even after half a century of their deadly strife.

The conquest of Delhi, the imperial capital, and the wresting of the territories of the Doab and Ganga valley in the heart of northern India, from the hands of the Marathas was the greatest political and military achievement of the British in 1803-1805, which entitled them to acquire the imperial status in the country in the long run. The puppet Mughal emperor, having been deprived of even the symbolic political or constitutional powers, was reduced to the position of a mere pensioner of the Company. Lord Wellesley 'took care not to enter into any treaty' with him; 'no written engagements of any sort were given, no grants of any kind were requested; anything that was done was done by the authority of the Company's Government at Calcutta'. (*Cambridge History of India;* v, p. 605). Shah Alam II was allowed to reside in the Red Fort of Delhi with family but under the British surveillance, and he lived there as a virtual prisoner till his death in 1806. As the

British wiped out all the vestiges of the Mughal rule in Delhi by introducing civil administration, under the control of the Company's bureaucracy, 'the writ of Shah Alam II was now confined to the interior of the Palace Fort of Delhi' as expressed in the popular saying: *Badashahi Shah Slam, As Dilli ta Palam.* Shah Alam was followed by his son, Akbar II, as the 'head of the royal establishment', who held the formal 'imperial dignity but only by courtesy of the Company'. He lived and died a pensioner of the British in 1838. His son Bahadur Shah II also lived on the British pension and retained the formal imperial dignity. He participated in the 'Great Revolt of 1857' and was deported to Rangoon where he died a few years later.

As for the Marathas, war with them was brought to a close but the British struggle for supremacy with them was as yet incomplete. The Maratha confederates were disunited and humiliated but not completely annihilated. As observed by Grant Duff, 'they sat down exhausted and dismayed, sensible of some of their errors when too late, but with no plan, or even sentiment of union, except hatred to that nation (i.e. the British) by which they had been subdued'. (*History of the Mahrattas*; ii, Delhi reprint, 1990, p. 460). Of these, Jaswant Rao Holkar was by far the most turbulent and 'brilliant', who alone had the acumen to re-unite them for a common cause. Unfortunately, the 'the strain of war with the British, preceded by his long strife against his own people, including Sindhia and the Peshwa', besides the financial stringency and other domestic problems, drove him to insanity. So, he had to be kept under restraint at Indore and died a miserable death on 28 October 1811 at the early age of thirty. It removed the most dangerous potential foe of the British from the scene of action. Nevertheless, the other Maratha chiefs were smarting under the English yoke. None else but the Peshwa Baji Rao II, having been reduced to the position of a mere puppet in the hands of the Company's Resident at Poona, took the disgrace keenly to his heart; and began to conspire with the other Maratha chiefs to throw off the British yoke. Mountstuart Elphinstone, the British Resident at Poona, got a wind of it, and, by carefully calculated moves, the Company forced humiliating treaties upon the Maratha chiefs one by one. On 13 June 1817, Baji Rao II was compelled to sign the Treaty of Poona, by which he was required not only to cede the additional territories of the Konkan to the Company but also renounce his 'leadership of the Maratha confederacy'. It was too much for the Peshwa to bear and he declared war on the British. Daulat Rao Sindhia, Appa Sahib of Nagpur and Malhar Rao Holkar II also followed suit, leading to the outbreak of Third Anglo-Maratha War in 1817-18. Unlike the earlier wars, this was provoked by the Maratha leaders themselves, knowing full well that they were not prepared to face their common foe on equal terms and stood no chance for victory; it was done by them out of desperation to wipe out the humiliation and 'national disgrace', suffered at the hands of a foreign colonial power, and to atone for their acts of omission and commission. In the conflagration that followed, the Peshwa attacked the British Residency at Poona and burnt it to ashes but was defeated by the Company's troops at Kirkee and fled southwards. Appa Sahib was defeated at Sitabaldi while the army of Holkar II was routed at Mahidpur. The Peshwa fought two more losing battles with the British at Koregaon and Ashti before offering his submission. As a result of this war, the whole territory of the Peshwa (comprising the greater part of the modern Maharashtra state) was annexed to the British dominions. The office of the Peshwa was abolished and Baji Rao II was allowed to live as British pensioner at Bithur near Kanpur (modern U.P.), far away from Poona. While annexing the Peshwa's dominions, the small principality of Satara, held by a descendant of Chhatrapati Shivaji, was made a British protectorate. All the other Maratha chiefs were deprived of most of their territorial possessions and powers and reduced to the status of petty feudal chieftains, tied to the Company by the bondage of subsidiary alliances. Thus the mighty Maratha power came to an end and the British claimed their paramountcy over India. James Cunningham Grant Duff (1789-1858), who had joined Company's service at Bombay as a military cadet, and held the captain's rank when he received appointment as the Political Agent to the puppet Maratha Chhatrapati at Satara, in 1818, paid a scholarly tribute to the fallen foe – 'the great Mahrattas, the immediate predecessors of the British rulers of India', by producing *History of the Mahrattas* (3 vols; London, 1826). In the preface to his study, he proudly refers to the Marathas as 'our predecessors in the conquest of India'. The famous Maratha leader and writer Mahadeo Govind Ranade, in his scholarly exposition, *Rise of the Maratha Power* (Publications Division; Ministry of Information and Broadcasting, G.O.I) elaborates this point by highlighting the fact that 'except in Bengal and on the Coromandel Coast, the powers displaced by the English conquest were not Mahommedan *subedars*, but native Hindu rulers who had successfully asserted their independence. Among these native powers, the first place must be assigned to the members of the Maratha Confederacy'.

We would like to conclude this study by paying tribute to the sweet memory of Bahadur Shah (II) Zaffar and the Peshwa Baji Rao II, the last scions of the two imperial ruling dynasties of medieval India, who in spite of their historical placements as mere creatures of the circumstances, trepidations and follies, redeemed themselves by harkening to their voices of reason and national sentiments and made supreme sacrifices which make us proud to think of them even today.

Quia mihi pulchrum in primis
Videtur non pati occidere

❑ ❑

SELECT BIBLIOGRAPHY

Afif, Shams-i-Siraj — *Tarikh-i-Firoze Shahi*; Eng. trs. by R C Jauhri, Sundeep Prakashan, New Delhi, 2001.

Ahluwalia, Manjeet Singh — *Studies in Medieval Rajasthan History*, Aligarh, 1970.

Aiyengar, K. Swami — *Sources of Vijayanagar History;* Madras, 1919.

" " — *South India and her Muhammadan Invaders*, Madras, 1921.

Alberuni, Abu Raihan — *Alberuni's India*: Eng. trs. by Edward C. Sachau; entitled: "An Account of the Religion, Philosophy, Literature, Geography, Astronomy, Customs and Astrology of India about 1030 A.D"; 2 vols., (London & Berlin, 1887-88); Indian reprint, consolidated volume by Rupa & Co, 2002.

Amir, Khwand — *Qanun-i-Humayuni or Humayun Namah*: Eng. trs. by Beni Parshad, Calcutta, 1940.

Ashraf, Muhammad — *Life and Condition of the People of Hindustan*; Reprinted from the J.A.S.B. vol. i, 1935.

Askari, S.H. — *Amir Khusrau as Historian*; Khuda Bakhsh Oriental Public Library, Patna, 1980.

Babar — *Tuzuk-i-Baburi or Babarnama*; Eng. trs. by A. S. Beveridge, (London, 1922, 2 vols.), Indian reprint, New Delhi, 1970.

Banerjee, I.B. — *Evolution of the Khalsa*; 2 vols., Calcutta, 1962-63.

Barani, Ziauddin	*Tarikh-i-Firoze Shahi*; Eng. trs. by Muhammad Habib, Aligarh; Extracts, E&D, iii, pp. 93-262.
Battuta, Ibn	*The Rehla or Travels of Ibn Battuta in Asia and Africa* (1325-35); Eng. trs. by Broadway Travellers, London, 1920.
Bernier, Francois	*Travels in the Moghul Empire*; Eng. trs. by Irving Brock (1826); revised by Archibald Constable (1891), New Print, London, 1914.
Bhandarkar, R.G.	*Early History of the Dekkan, Down to the Mahommedan Conquest*; Calcutta, 1957.
Bhargava, V.S.	*Marwar and the Mughal Emperors:* 1526-1748, Delhi, 1966.
Bhattacharyya, S.N.	*A History of Mughal North-East Frontier Policy*, Calcutta, 1929.
Brown, A. Percy	*Indian Architecture (Islamic Period)*; Bombay, 1944.
,, ,,	*Indian Architecture (Buddhist and Hindu)*; Bombay, 2nd ed., 1949.
Beale; Thomas William	*An Oriental Biographical Dictionary*, New Edition, revised by Henry George Keene, London, 1910.
Beveridge, Henry	*The Life of Hiuen Tsiang by the Shaman Hwui Li*, London, 1911.
Blochmann, Henry	*The Ain-i-Akbari of Abul Fazl Allami*, Calcutta, 1873.
Chandra, Satish	*Parties and Politics at the Mughal Court*; Aligarh, 1959.
,, ,,	*Mughal Religious Politics, Rajputs and Deccan*; New Delhi, 1994.
Chand Bardai	*Prithviraj Raso,* edited by Shyam Sunder Das (in Hindi), Benares.
Chand, Tara	*Influence of Islam on Indian Culture;* Allahabad, 1943.
,, ,,	Society and State in the Mughal Period, Delhi, 1961.
Cunningham, A.	*Reports of the Archaeological Survey of India*: 1902-1914.

Cunningham, Joseph Davy *History of the Sikhs*; edited by Garrett, Oxford, 1918.

De, U.N. *Administrative System of Delhi Sultanate* (1206-1413); Kitab Mahal, 1959.

Dighe, V.G. *Peshwa Baji Rao I & Maratha Expansion*, 1944.

Dughlat, Mirza M.H. *Tarikh-i-Rashidi*; Eng. trs. by N Elias & E Denison Ross, entitled, "A History of the Moghuls of Central Asia"; Indian reprint, Patna, 1973.

Eaton, Richard M. (ed.) *India's Islamic Traditions*: 711-1750; OUP (2003); India paperbacks, 2006.

Edward, S.M. & Garrett, H.L.O. *Mughal Rule in India*, Delhi, 1962.

Elliot & Dowson *History of India as Told by Its Own Historians*; 8 vols., London, Trubner Company, 1867-77.

Elphinstone, Mount Stuart *The History of India*: The Hindu and Muhammadan Periods, with notes and additions by E.B. Cowell, 9th Edition, London, 1911.

Encyclopaedia of Islam *By various authors*, London, 1913-14.

Erskine, William *A History of India under the Two First Sovereigns of the House of Taimur – Babar and Humayun*; 2 vols., (London, 1854), Indian reprint, Delhi, 1973.

Fazl, Abul *Ain-i-Akbari; 2 vols.*, Trs. from Persian by H. Blochmann, Calcutta, 1867-77, second revised edition by D. C. Phillott (1927), Oriental Books reprint, 1977.

" " *Akbarnama*; Eng. trs. by H. Beveridge, Bib. Indica, Calcutta, 1897-1909.

Fergusson, James *History of Indian and Eastern Architecture*; 2 vols., 2nd revised edition by James Burgess & Spiers; London, 1910.

Firishta, Muhammad Qasim Hindu Shah *Gulshan-i-Ibrahimi or Tarikh-i-Firishta*; Eng. trs. by John Briggs under the title, "History of the Rise of the Mahommedan Power in India till the Year 1611"; 4 vols., (London, 1829), Indian reprint, Calcutta, 1966.

Fredunbeg, Mirza Kalichbeg — *The Chachnama*; An Ancient History of Sind, Translated from the Persian, Printed at the Commissioner's Press, 1900.

Gibb, H.A.R. — *Ibn Battuta's Travels in Asia and Africa* (1325-1354); Trs. & edited by; Broadway Travellers, London, 1929.

Gupta, Hari Ram — *History of the Sikhs*; 3 vols., Lahore, 1943-44, Reprint by the P.U. Chandigarh.

" " — *Marathas and Panipat*, P.U. Chandigarh, 1961.

Habib, Muhammad — *The Political Theory of the Delhi Sultanate (Being the Eng. trs. of Fatawa-i-Jahandari of Barani)*; Kitab Mahal, Allahabad.

Habib, M. et el — *A Comprehensive History of India*, vol. 5, People's Publishing House, Delhi, 1970.

Habib, Irfan — *The Agrarian System of Mughal India*; Asia, 1963.

Habibullah, A.B.M. — *Foundation of Muslim Rule in India*; Allahabad, 2nd ed., 1961.

Haig, Sir Wolseley — *Cambridge History of India*, Vol. III, Cambridge, 1928.

Havell, E.B. — *Ancient and Medieval Architecture of India*, London, 1915.

" " — *Indian Architecture* – Its Psychology, Structure & History: From the Muhammedan Invasions to the Present Day: London, 1913.

Hodivala, S.H. — *Studies in Indo-Muslim History;* Bombay, 1939.

Hutchinson, Lester — *European Freebooters in Moghul India;* Asia, London, 1965.

Hunter (ed.) — *The Imperial Gazetteer of India*; Vol. II: The Indian Empire-Historical; New Edition, Oxford, 1908.

Husain, Agha Mahdi — *Rise and fall of Muhammad-bin-Tughluq*; Luzac & Co., London, 1938.

Husain, Yusuf — *Indo-Muslim Polity; (Turko-Afghan Period)*; Simla, 1971.

Irvine, William — *The Army of the Indian Moguls*, London, 1903; New Delhi, 1962.

„ „ *Later Mughals:* 2 vols., Tej Publications, Delhi, 1989.

Jaffar, S.M. *The Mughal Empire from Babar to Aurangzeb*; (1936); Delhi reprint, 1974.

Jahangir *Tuzuk-i-Jahangiri*; Eng. trs. by Alexander Rogers & edited by Henry Beveridge; Oriental Translation Fund, London, 1909.

Keene, H.G. *The Fall of the Moghul Empire*, Reprint, Delhi, 1971.

Keene, Henri George *The Fall of the Mughal Empire* – A Historical Essay (1876), Delhi reprint, 1973.

Khan, Khafi *Muntakhab-ut-Lubab*; E&D. Vol.vii.

Khosla, R.P. *Mughal Kingship and Nobility*; Allahabad. 1934.

Khusrau, Amir *Khazainul Futuh*; Eng. trs. by M. Habib under the title, The Campaigns of Alauddin Khalji; Madras, 1931; Extracts, E&D. iii, pp. 67-92.

Kincaid, C.A. and Parasnis, D.B. *A History of the Maratha People*, 2 vols, Oxford (1918), 1922.

Lal, K. S. *History of the Khaljis* (1290-1320), Allahabad, 1950.

„ „ *Studies in Medieval Indian History*, Delhi, 1966.

„ „ *Twilight of the Sultanate*; APH, 1963.

Lane-Poole, Stanley *Babar, (Oxford, 1899)*; Indian reprint, S Chand, New Delhi.

„ „ *Medieval India under Mohammedan Rule*; London, 9th ed. 1916.

Lee, Rev.Samuel *Travels of Ibn Battuta*, Translation with Notes, London, 1829.

Lee, Major *Tabaqat-i-Nasiri of Minhaj-us-Siraj*-Vols. I and II.

Macauliffe, Max Arthur *The Sikh Religion*, "Its Gurus, Sacred Writings and Authors." 6 vols., Oxford, 1909.

Majumdar, R.C.(ed.) *The History and Culture of the Indian People*; BVB, Bombay, vols. v, vi & vii.

Major, R.H. *India in the 15th Century*. (Hakluyt) London, 1857.

Manucci, Niccolao *Storia Do Mogor or Mughal India:* 1653-1708; trs. By William Irvine, 4 vols., London, 1907.

Mehta, J.L. *Advanced Study in the History of Medieval India*; 3 vols., Sterling Publishers, New Delhi, 1979-83.

Minhaj-us-Siraj *Tabaqat-i-Nasiri*; Eng. trs. by H.G. Raverty (Bib. Indica, 1881); extracts E&D. i, pp. 256-379.

Misra, Yogendra *The Hindu Shahis of Afghanistan and the Punjab*; Patna, 1972.

Moreland, W.H. *India at the Death of Akbar—An Economic Study*; London, 1920.

Mujeeb, M. *The Indian Muslims*, London; Allen & Unwin, 1967.

Nadhkarni, R.V. *Rise and Fall of the Maratha Empire*; Bombay, 1966.

Narang, G.C. *Transformation of Sikhism*; New Delhi, 1960.

Nizami, K.A. *Some Aspects of Religion and Politics in India during the Thirteenth Century*; Asia, 1961.

" " *Studies in Medieval Indian History and Culture*; Allahabad, 1966.

Nizamuddin, Ahmad *Tabakat-i-Akbari*; 3 vols., Trs. & ed. by Brajendranath De and Baini Prasad (1911); Delhi reprint, 1992.

Nuruddin Hussain *Najib-ud Daulah;* Eng. trs. by Abdur Rashid, Cosmopolitan Publishers,Aligarh, 1952.

Ojha, Gauri Shankar *Rajputana ka Itihas*; Vol. iii; Ajmer, 1937.

Owen, Sidney J. *India on the Eve of the British Conquest* – "an Analytical History of India; 1624-1767"; Calcutta, 1954.

Parasnis, D.B. *A History of the Maratha People*; 2 vols., Oxford, 1918.

Prasad, Ishwari *History of Medieval India*; Allahabad, 1940.

Prasad, Ram Chandra *Early English Travellers in India;* Motilal Banarsidas,1965.

Qanungo, K.R. *Sher Shah*; Calcutta, 1921.

Ranade, Mahadeo Govind *Rise of the Maratha Power*; Publication Division, Ministry of I & B; G.O.I., New Delhi.

Ranking George, S.A. and Lowe, W. H. — *Al-Badaoni*: A translation of Badaoni's *Muntakhab-ut-Tawarikh*. 3 vols. Calcutta, 1898.

Raverty, Major H. G. — *Tabaqat-i-Nasiri*: A General History of the Muhammadan Dynasties of Asia including Hindustan. Translated from Original Persian Manuscripts, 2 vols. London, 1881.

Saksena, Banarsi Prasad — *History of Shahjahan of Delhi;* Allahabad, 1958.

,, ,, — *Travels of Peter Mundy,* Hakluyt Society, London, 1908.

Saran, P. — *Studies in Medieval Indian History,* Delhi, 1952.

Sardesai, G. S. — *New History of the Marathas;* 2 vols., Bombay, 1946.

,, ,, — *The Main Currents of Maratha History,* 1926.

,, ,, — *House of Shivaji,* 3rd ed., Calcutta, 1933.

,, ,, — *History of Aurangzeb,* 5 Vols. Calcutta, 1912-25.

,, ,, — *Anecdotes of Aurangzeb,* 2nd ed., Calcutta, 1919.

Sarkar, Jadunath — *Fall of the Mughal Empire* (1738-1803); 4 vols., Calcutta, 1932-50.

,, ,, — *Ahkam-i-Alamgiri or The Anecdotes of Aurangzeb,* Calcutta, 1912.

,, ,, — *English Records of Maratha History,* Vol. I, Mahadaji Sindhia and North Indian Affairs, (1785-1794), Bombay, 1936.

,, ,, — *Mughal Administration;* (1924), 4th edition, Calcutta, 1972.

,, ,, — *History of Aurangzeb;* 5 vols., Calcutta, 1912-25.

,, ,, — *Shivaji and His Times;* 4th edition; Calcutta, 1952.

Sewell, Robert — *A Forgotten Empire (Vijayanagar),* London, 1900; Indian reprint, NBT, 2nd edition; 1970.

Sharma, S. R. — *The Crescent in India – A Study in Medieval History;* 3rd ed., Bombay, 1966.

Sharma, S. R. — *Mughal Empire in India,* revised ed., Agra, 966.

,, ,, — *The Founding of Maratha Freedom;* Orient Longmans (1934), revised edition, 1964.

Sharma, Sri Ram — *The Religious Policy of the Mughal Emperors*, New Delhi: Munshiram Manoharlal, 1988.

Singh, Ganda — *Banda Singh Bahadur*; Amritsar, 1935.

„ „ — *Ahmad Shah Durrani*; Bombay, 1959.

Sinha, N. K. — *Rise of the Sikh Power*; Calcutta, 1969.

Smith, V. A. — *Oxford History of India*; Oxford, 1920.

Spear, Percival — *Twilight of the Mughals*, CUP, 1951.

„ „ — *Cambridge History of India Vol. V*, London, 1968.

Srivastava, A.L. — *The Sultanate of Delhi*; Agra, 1950.

„ „ — *The Mughal Empire*; 4th revised ed., Agra, 1964.

Thomas, Edward — *The Chronicles of the Pathan Kings of Delhi*, with The Revenue Resources of the Mughal Empire in India from 1593 to 1707, (London, 1871), 2nd enlarged ed., Delhi, 1967.

Timur, Amir — *Tuzuk-i-Timuri or Malfuzat-i-Timuri*; Eng. Trs. from Persian by Major Stewart, OTF, 1830; Extracts, E&D, iii, 389-477.

Tod, James — *Annals and Antiquities of Rajasthan*; 2 vols., edited by William Crooke; Indian reprint, (London; 1914).

Tripathi, R. P. — *Rise and Fall of the Mughal Empire*; Allahabad, 1956.

„ „ — *Some Aspects of Muslim Administration*; Allahabad, 2nd ed., 1959.

Utbi — *Tarikh-i-Yamini or Kitab-ul Yamini (Arabic)*; Eng. trs. From Persian by James Reynolds; (OTF, London, 1858).

Vaidya, C. V. — *History of Medieval Hindu India*; 3 vols., Poona, 1926.

„ „ — *Downfall of Hindu India*; Delhi reprint, 1986.

Waley, Adolf — *A Pageant of India (1926);* Delhi reprint, 1925.

❑ ❑

INDEX

C

D

E

F

H

I

J

L

M

O

P

T

U

Z

❑ ❑

Other Books on

EDUCATION

1. History of Medieval India **(New)**
2. Methodology of Educational Research **(New)**
3. Philosophical & Sociological Foundations of Education **(New)**
4. Research Methods in Education **(New)**
5. Psychology of Learning & Human Development **(New)**
6. A New Approach to Teacher & Education in the Emerging Indian Society **(New)**
7. Safety and Disaster Management **(New)**
8. Measurement and Evaluation in Psychology and Education
9. Special Education
10. Principles of Office Management
11. History of Ancient India
12. Select World Constitutions
13. Environmental Education
14. Experimental Psychology
15. Teaching of Home Science
16. Educational Thought and Practice
17. Guidance and Counselling A Manual
18. School Organisation and Administration
19. Developmental Psychology
20. Social Work Theory and Practice
21. Modern Education for New Generation
22. Advanced Educational Technology
23. Comparative Education
24. Introduction to Educational Research
25. Computer Education
26. Teaching of Chemistry
27. Teaching of Physics
28. Handbook of Journalism & Mass Media
29. Advanced Educational Psychology
30. Educational Administration & Origanisation Management
31. Social Psychology
32. Teaching of Commerce
33. Educational Development & Technology
34. Disaster Management
35. Information Technology
36. Human Resource Development
37. Mass Media Communication Theory & Practice
38. Adult Education
39. General Psychology

40. Distance Education in India
41. Teacher Education
42. Educational Philosophy
43. Science Teaching in Schools
44. Indian National Congress
45. Indian Polity **(Revised Edition)**
46. New Comparative Government **(Revised Edition)**

Advanced Study in the History of Modern India

47. (Volume-1: 1707-1813)
48. (Volume-2: 1813-1920)
49. (Volume-3: 1920-1947)
50. Handbook of Nutrition & Dietetics
51. Development of Education in India
52. A Text Book of Environmental Studies
53. Teaching of History
54. Administrative Thinkers
55. Research Methodology
56. Curriculum Development
57. Teaching of Science
58. Teaching of Mathematics
59. Principles of Educational &Vocational Guidance
60. Child Psychology
61. Abnormal Psychology
62. Indian Education in Emerging Society
63. Human Resource Management
64. Higher Education and Global Challenges
65. Teaching of Geography
66. Teaching of Social Studies
67. Teaching of English
68. Education for All The Indian Saga
69. Value Education in Global Perspective
70. Teacher Training
71. Public Administration
72. Public Relations & Integrated Communications
73. Educational Psychology
74. Introduction to Educational Technology
75. Textbook of Food and Nutrition

Unit No. 220, 2nd Floor, 4735/22, Prakash Deep Building,
Ansari Road, Darya Ganj, New Delhi- 110002

• E-mail : lotuspress1984@gmail.com, www.lotuspress.co.in